Writers'
& Artists'
YEARBOOK
2007

Writers' & Artists' YEARBOOK 2007

One Hundredth Edition

A directory for writers, artists, playwrights, writers for film, radio and television, designers, illustrators and photographers

A & C Black · London

© 2006 A & C Black Publishers Ltd
38 Soho Square, London W1D 3HB

The publishers make no representation, express or
implied, with regard to the accuracy of the
information contained in this book and cannot
accept any legal responsibility for any errors or
omissions that may take place.

This book is produced using paper that is made
from wood grown in managed, sustainable forests.
It is natural, renewable and recyclable. The logging
and manufacturing processes conform to the
environmental regulations of the country of origin.

A CIP catalogue record for this book is available
from the British Library.

ISBN 10 0-7136-7712-0
ISBN 13 978-0-7136-7712-6

Typeset by QPM from David Lewis XML
Associates Ltd

Printed in Great Britain by
William Clowes Ltd, Beccles, Suffolk

The *Writers' & Artists' Yearbook* story

This year the *Writers' & Artists' Yearbook* celebrates its 100th anniversary.
Jo Herbert looks back at the *Yearbook's* century of success: 1906–2006.

Over the last century the *Writers' & Artists' Yearbook* has grown into a compendious source of information with over two million sales worldwide, firmly placed as the No 1 bestseller for books of its kind. For 100 years the *Yearbook* has provided a breadth of factual, unbiased information and practical advice, giving an insight into the people and processes involved in the publishing industry. It has continuously attracted correspondence from aspiring, disgruntled and successful writers, and played its part in reminding publishers of the ethics of the trade and their obligation to their contributors. Many writers, artists and others working in the media regard the *Yearbook* as essential to their profession.

The *Yearbook* had a humble beginning in 1906 as a small 80-page booklet containing a mere seven literary agents and 89 publishers, with a cover price of a modest one shilling. It was geared solely towards writers and was endorsed by the press. A review in the *Standard* (1910) declared: 'Professional and amateur dabblers in ink no longer have any excuse for sending the offspring of their brains on the wrong road to public admiration and emolument'.

Lists of markets for the work of illustrators were added to those for writers and, later, for photographers. In 1914 the first articles by the experts of the day were included and within a few decades the *Yearbook* had grown into a 400-page hardback. It continued to be published during the two World Wars (the 1940 edition contained a special war supplement outlining emergency and evacuation details), and 1978 saw the introduction of the present paperback version with the distinctive bright red cover that has become the *Yearbook's* trademark. The content and language of each edition are indications of the changing face of publishing and the media – from silent movies and hot metal presses to e-books and iPods.

The Foreword was a new addition for the 1998 edition, the first of which was written by Michael Ridpath. It has since been penned by some of the *Yearbook's* famous fans – including Doris Lessing, Fay Weldon, J.K. Rowling, Maeve Binchy, Terry Pratchett and, this year, Ian Rankin. There is no shortage of citations from successful authors revealing how the *Yearbook* has played a significant role in their path to fame and fortune. So many say they are 'pleased and honoured' to contribute – what bigger compliment could a book have?

The *Writers' & Artists' Yearbook* has 100 years of success to celebrate. A & C Black is launching the *Yearbook's* own website (www.writersandartists.co.uk), organising a special centenary writing competition (see page viii) and sponsoring many literary events throughout the year. Join us in wishing the *Writers' & Artists' Yearbook* a Happy 100th Birthday and saying a big 'thank you' to 100 years of readers (we wouldn't be here without them!). We hope the *Yearbook* continues to help, inspire and encourage them on their creative journey.

Contents

Writers' & Artists' Yearbook 2007
Novel Writing Competition

Enter the *Writers' & Artists' Yearbook 2007* novel writing competition.

There are 100 critiques by The Literary Consultancy to be won, plus the chance to be one of three overall winners whose work is forwarded to a top literary agent.

For full details visit www.writersandartists.co.uk

Good luck!

'Congratulations on a century of inspiring so many dreams and helping so many of us to be published!' **Bernard Cornwell**

'I first bought the *Writers' & Artists' Yearbook* in the 1950s, when I started getting serious about being a writer. I could always find somebody in there who hadn't already seen and rejected my dog-eared masterpieces. Happy Birthday!' **Andrew Davies**

'Happy Hundredth Birthday! What would we do without you?' **Raymond Briggs**

'Life can be lonely for an author and that little book makes things just that little bit better. Happy Birthday!' **G.P. Taylor**

Foreword

Ian Rankin is the award-winning author of the *Inspector Rebus* series of novels, which have been translated into 27 languages. He has also published short stories, poems and journalism, and has written several full-length plays for radio. He was awarded the OBE for services to literature in 2004.

By the age of 12, I was ready for pop stardom.

I'd invented a group called *The Amoebas*, for whom I wrote lyrics, designed album sleeves, and compiled tour schedules. They might only exist on paper, but they were destined for greatness. At one point, I replied to a dodgy advert in the classified section of one of the music papers – something along the lines of 'Are you a budding songwriter? We will set your lyrics to music.' Though the stanzas I submitted were of the moon-June-spoon variety, their letter back to me was enthusiastic. They couldn't wait for me to send them a wad of cash so they could get started on the tune.

Happily, my parents were reluctant to stump up: an early lesson in the pitfalls of 'vanity publishing'.

By the age of 17, my lyrics had become poems. One of them won second prize in a competition, and I received five pounds. At university, I moved on to short stories, and started winning prizes with them, too. These prizes gave me the confidence to produce something longer – a novel called 'Summer Rites'. I was in my twenties by this stage, and wanted nothing more than to be a published novelist. The first *Writers' & Artists' Yearbook* I picked up was from a second-hand shop. Out-of-date as it was, I read it pretty much from cover to cover, finding it as engrossing as any bestseller.

My girlfriend was working in London (while I was still in Edinburgh). I would travel south as often as possible – usually on the overnight bus, which probably explained the near-hallucinatory daze in which I wandered around the capital. During the day, I would plan itineraries which took me past as many publishing houses as possible. Thanks to the *Writers' & Artists' Yearbook*, I had their addresses. I think my plan was to bump into a famous editor as they left the building. They would instantly recognise my talent and usher me back inside to sign a lucrative five-book deal. It didn't happen. I only ever once plucked up the courage to cross the threshold – into the fairly seedy, Soho-based offices of John Calder. My nerve failed me at the last, and I told the secretary I wanted to buy some books. She was good enough to accept a cheque.

When Christmas came, so did a bang up-to-date copy of the *Yearbook* (courtesy of my girlfriend). I duly sent the manuscript of 'Summer Rites' to a publishing house – one whose exterior I'd thought acceptable on my London walks – bypassing the 'slush pile' by adding the Managing Director's name to the envelope. The rejection letter – my first (of many) – arrived in time for Valentine's Day. Eventually, that first novel was dispatched to the bottom drawer of my cabinet. It rests there still, slumbering and contented.

My next effort was called 'The Flood', and it did gain a publisher. Consequent to which, a literary agent came calling. She did a deal for my next book, this time with a publishing house in Bedford Square. What a thrill! Lots of publishers were berthed in that quiet, leafy region between Tottenham Court Road and the British Museum. The next time I visited, I climbed the steps and pushed open the door as an author. I half-expected to meet Graham Greene and Muriel Spark in the waiting room.

Not that this was the end of my involvement with the *Yearbook*. My agent vanished into thin air one day. I turned again to the *Yearbook*, studied the section on agents, and plumped for one of long standing. I plucked a name from the list of directors and wrote him a letter. We met, got along, and I stayed with that agency for the best part of 20 years.

Getting into print requires nerve, stamina, luck, stubbornness and talent. Even established authors can feel as though they're climbing a mountain. Think of the *Writers' & Artists' Yearbook* as your sherpa.

Happy trails.

Ian Rankin OBE

Newspapers and magazines
Getting started

Of the titles included in the newspapers and magazines section of this *Yearbook*, almost all offer opportunities to the writer. Many publications do not appear in our lists because the market they offer for the freelance writer is either too small or too specialised, or both. To help writers get started, we offer some guidelines to consider before submitting material.

Study the market

● The importance of studying the market cannot be overemphasised. It is an editor's job to know what readers want, and to see that they get it. Thus, freelance contributions must be tailored to fit a specific market; subject, theme, treatment, length, etc must meet the editor's requirements. This is discussed further in *Writing for newspapers* on page 3 and *Writing for magazines* on page 27.

● Magazine editors frequently complain about the unsuitability of many submissions, so before sending an article or feature, always carefully study the editorial requirements of the magazine – not only for the subjects dealt with but for the approach, treatment, style and length. These comments will be obvious to the practised writer but the beginner can be spared much disappointment by buying copies of magazines and studying their target market in depth.

● For additional information on markets, see the UK volume of *Willings Press Guide*, which is usually available at local reference libraries.

Check with the editor first

● Before submitting material to any newspaper or magazine it is advisable to first contact the relevant editor. The listings beginning on page 7 give the names of editors for each section of the national newspapers. A quick telephone call or email to a magazine will establish the name of the relevant commissioning editor.

● Most newspapers and many magazines expect copy to be sent by email.

● Editors who accept postal submissions expect them to be well presented: neatly typed, double spaced, with good margins, on A4 paper is the standard to aim at. Always enclose an sae for the return of unsuitable material.

● It is not advisable to send illustrations 'on spec'; check with the editor first. See *Digital imaging for writers* on page 626; listings of *Picture agencies and libraries* start on page 483. For a list of publications that accept cartoons see page 768.

Explore the overseas market

● The lists of overseas newspapers and magazines in the *Yearbook* contain only a selection of those journals which offer a market for the freelance writer. For fuller listings, refer to *Willings Press Guide* Volume 2 (Europe) and Volume 3 (world). The overseas market for stories and articles is small and editors often prefer their fiction to have a local setting. Some editors require their contributors to be residents of that country.

● Some overseas magazine titles have little space for freelance contributions but many of them will consider outstanding work.

- Proposals or finished articles mailed from the UK overseas (including the Republic of Ireland) should always be accompanied by return postage in the form of International Reply Coupons (IRCs). IRCs can be exchanged in any foreign country for stamps representing the minimum postage payable on a letter sent from one country to another. For further information *tel* (08457) 223344.

- Using an agent to syndicate material written for the overseas market is worth considering. Most agents operate on an international basis and are more aware of current market requirements. Again, return postage should always be included. Listings for *Syndicates, news and press agencies* start on page 117.

Understand how newspapers and syndicates work

- The larger newspapers and magazines buy many of their stories, and the smaller papers buy general articles, through well-known syndicates. Another avenue for writers is to send printed copies of their stories published at home to an agent for syndication overseas.

- For the supply of news, most of the larger UK and overseas newspapers depend on their own staffs and press agencies. The most important overseas newspapers have permanent representatives in Britain who keep them supplied, not only with news of special interest to the country concerned, but also with regular summaries of British news and with articles on events of particular importance. While many overseas newspapers and magazines have a London office, it is usual for manuscripts from freelance contributors to be submitted to the headquarters' editorial office overseas. Listings of *National newspapers UK and Ireland* start on page 7.

Payment

- It has always been our aim to obtain and publish the rates of payment offered for contributions by newspapers and magazines. Many publications, however, are reluctant to state a standard rate, since the value of a contribution may be dependent not upon length but upon the standing of the writer or of the information given. Many other periodicals prefer to state 'by negotiation' or 'by arrangement', rather than giving precise payment information.

- A number of magazines will accept and pay for letters to the editor, brief fillers and gossip paragraphs, as well as puzzles and quizzes. *Magazines by subject area* starting on page 751 provides a rough guide to these markets.

See also...

- *Regional newspapers UK and Ireland*, page 16
- *Newspapers are listed together with magazines for Australia* (page 104), *Canada* (page 109), *New Zealand* (page 112), *South Africa* (page 113) and *USA* (page 115)

Writing for newspapers

Richard Keeble outlines the huge scope for freelance journalists writing for newspapers.

The national mainstream press comprises 10 morning dailies and 10 Sundays. The 'qualities' (*Daily Telegraph, Financial Times, Guardian, Independent, The Times*) sell around 2.8 million copies daily, the mid-market tabloids (*Daily Mail, Daily Express*) 3.26 million, and the red top tabloids (*Daily Star, Daily Mirror, Sun*) 5.5 million. On Sundays, the 'qualities' (*Observer, Independent on Sunday, Sunday Telegraph* and *Sunday Times*) sell 2.76 million copies; the *Mail on Sunday* and *Sunday Express* 3.14 million; while the *News of the World, Sunday Mirror, Sunday People, Daily Star Sunday* and *Sunday Sport* sell 6.63 million. At the local level, 36.7 million regional dailies are sold or given away every week, while over six million local paid-for weeklies and 24.7 million free weeklies are distributed. In addition, there are a vast range of alternative peace-movement, ethnic-minority, religious and leftist newspapers.

Newspapers clearly offer writers an enormous range of opportunities. And freelancing has its definite attractions. As a freelance you can often work from home and so avoid the hassles of office politics and commuting. You can develop a specialist interest. You may have a particular knowledge of wines (built up through attending tasting classes, holidays and reading) and be familiar with some prominent names in the business. Writing reviews and features in this area for the few specialist newspaper sections could well prove financially (and personally) rewarding.

The freelance challenge

Yet launching into a freelance career is not easy. Many freelances are former full-time staffers who have developed a specialism, sent out linage (freelance copy paid by the line) to nationals and then, through either choice or redundancy, taken the plunge and gone solo or started a small agency. With newspapers increasingly laying off experienced full-time staffers, competition amongst freelances has intensified. And while freelances enjoy certain 'freedoms' not permitted to staff writers, they still cannot avoid the constraints and ethical dilemmas that all journalists face. For instance, you may be very critical of the political and ethical stances of the mainstream press. Thus you may decide to launch your own blog or contribute (largely unpaid) to an ethnic-minority, left-wing, religious, peace-movement or environmental newspaper, news magazine or website and gain your money from other employment. One of the greatest journalists of the last century, George Orwell, committed himself to small-scale, left-wing, literary journals and largely ignored the seductive appeal of Fleet Street. It was his deliberate political choice. Or you may be happy to sell your copy to a Rupert Murdoch-owned newspaper (such as *The Times* or *Sunday Times*). But always be fully aware there are political and ethical implications behind your journalistic decisions.

Why contacts are crucial

Very few freelances are generalists. They instead develop a specialism (or a discreet range of linked specialisms) and become valuable to editors because of their specialist knowledge, experience and contacts. Thus your major task in launching into a freelance career is to build up a contacts book containing sources' phone numbers, addresses, fax and pager numbers, email and website details. You may have to go to meetings, conferences and press launches, and/or ring up spokespersons of political parties, companies and campaigning bodies. All this takes a lot of time. But from your sources will come ideas for stories, details of events to attend, quotes, and specialist (and hopefully exclusive) information. Many freelances place contact details on a computer database as a back-up while those investigating sensitive issues (such as national security, spying, the arms and drugs trade, share dealings) tend to keep details of important exclusive sources in their heads. Police have been known to raid the homes and computers of journalists involved in sensitive areas and thus every step has to be taken to preserve the anonymity of such contacts.

The skills of interviewing are crucial to all freelances. You normally have to prepare in advance of the meeting and be confident enough in the subject to maintain a flowing interview – while recording accurately at the same time. It's far from easy. You may be tempted to use a tape recorder. But what if it breaks down at the crucial moment? For all interviews you need to make a written note. You may not have the time to learn a shorthand technique such as Teeline (in which 100 words a minute is the industry standard) but you do need to develop your own reliable rapid writing technique.

Get to know the market for your specialist area of interest. Study the different writing styles, the lengths of the sentences and articles in the differing publications. Try to establish, by examining byline patterns, the amount of freelance work accepted and in which particular areas. Analyse the advertising in the publications to get a feel for the intended target readership. Read recent issues (in either their print or online versions) carefully to get an idea of the stories covered and, more importantly, not covered. See who are the prominent sources used in stories and those who have been missed or marginalised. Get used to creating files of cuttings and printouts of web pages. Well-maintained filing cabinets can be invaluable research tools. And when you read documents, journal articles and books, file the notes from these too. But don't become over-reliant on cuttings and websites. Journalists often report inaccurately so checking is usually necessary. Significantly, in its March 1992 report, the Press Complaints Commission (the watchdog promoting an ethical Code of Practice for print journalists) commented: 'Cuttings are an essential part of newspaper research but too many journalists now seem to act in the belief that to copy from 10 old stories is better than to write a new one with confirmation by proper fresh enquiry.'

The need for imaginative flair

As a freelance you will have to develop a special journalistic imagination. Ideas will be your lifeblood. A new report highlights a national survey showing students are increasingly going without sleep and as a result their academic work and health are suffering. Do a local follow-up: go to the colleges and universities in your area and interview students, counsellors, lecturers, etc about the issues involved. Better still, take the opposite line and do a feature for the women's section of a Sunday newspaper highlighting career women who need only a few hours sleep a day – and yet still thrive. Or take a major international story such as the dispute between the two nuclear-armed neighbours India and Pakistan. Again think local. Many British cities have Indian and Pakistani communities but their views have been largely ignored. So why not interview people from these countries about the issues? Are they afraid? What do they see as the political factors behind the crisis and what are their solutions? Are there any human interest angles to help humanise the reports? In all these cases you have to move quickly while the issues are still newsworthy.

A lot of starting-up freelances imagine a life sitting at home bashing out on the computer words of wisdom on a range of topics to an admiring public. But it is rare for a freelance career to start in this way. Columnists tend to be experienced journalists, novelists, comedians or other media celebrities and their views are seen by editors to carry authority. As Andrew Marr, former editor of the *Independent* and the BBC's political editor, comments in *My Trade: A Short History of British Journalism* (Macmillan 2004), 'A very few top journalists are earning salaries that would be regarded as good in the City. One tabloid columnist is said by colleagues to be on £500,000. There is a broadsheet writer on £300,000.' But there are exceptions to this rule. A local newspaper may want to carry an opinionated column from a reader presenting a particular viewpoint – such as that of a youngster, a football fan or an asylum seeker. In this way the paper is striving to make its mark on the local community, with a column aimed at getting people talking – and possibly provoking letters (for or against).

The rewards of reviewing

Arts reviewing for local papers has its obvious attractions. Most journalists come from humanities backgrounds (resulting in the unfortunate marginalisation of science news in the press) and so there tends to be fierce competition for these posts. Most will be filled by staffers or experienced freelances. But if you have the necessary specialist knowledge, have built up contacts in the area and can write in a lively, original way, you may well find an opening. Reviews serve many functions. They provide basic information: for example, that a play has just opened and can be seen at the theatre indicated. For people who intend to see, read or hear a work (or in the case of broadcasting have already seen or heard it), the review gives an opinion carrying some authority to compare with their own. Yet usually the vast majority of readers will never experience directly the work under review. A concert may have been attended by no more than a hundred people. The review must then exist as a piece of writing in its own right. It must entice the reader through the colour and quality of its prose.

All newspapers have their own house style. This is outlined in a document called the stylebook (occasionally handbook or sheet), though it is increasingly carried onscreen and on the newspaper's website. For instance, you can check out the *Guardian's* stylebook on its website. Stylebooks tend to focus on such elements as spellings (gaol or jail?, Gaddafi or Khadaffi?), punctuation, abbreviations, the use of capitals, titles, Americanisms to avoid, the handling of quotations. Ethical issues, such as the handling of anonymous quotes or how to refer to people with disabilities, can also be covered. Take a close look at your target publications and study their styles. Freelances are not expected to present copy perfectly according to style: sub-editors are on hand to prepare copy for publication. But if your copy shows some awareness of the house style, then the editors will be impressed.

Some basic requirements

As a freelance you will need internet access on your computer. Most copy is now supplied via email and companies are increasingly supplying press releases through email. You will also need an accountant to advise on tax liabilities, and a pension plan. If you become particularly successful you will have to pay VAT. Most freelances keep in regular touch with their local tax inspector. Remember to log for tax purposes all relevant expenses, such as stationery, office equipment, book and travel expenses. Christopher Browne (in his book *The Journalist's Handbook*, A & C Black, 1999) suggested that beginning freelances should negotiate an overdraft facility of at least £3000–£4000 with their bank manager after presenting them with a business plan drawn up by an accountant. Membership of the freelance branch of the National Union of Journalists (NUJ) is worth considering. The NUJ, along with local education centres, runs courses for starting-up freelances which can help develop skills and confidence.

Journalism remains a job carrying enormous personal rewards. It is difficult, challenging (politically, ethically, physically) and fun. It requires a formidable range of knowledge and skills. And journalists need to be curious, persistent, imaginative and daring. In the words of Nicholas Tomalin, the *Sunday Times* foreign correspondent killed on the Golan Hights in 1973, journalists should cultivate 'rat-like cunning, a plausible manner and a little literary ability'. There is a glamorous side to the job, which Hollywood has helped to promote. No wonder the queues for entering the industry are so long.

Richard Keeble is Professor of Journalism at Lincoln University. His publications include *The Newspapers Handbook* (Routledge, 4th edn 2005) and *Ethics for Journalists* (Routledge, 2001). He is also editor of *Ethical Space: The International Journal of Communication Ethics* (www.ethicalspace.org).

Further reading

Adams, Sally, *Interviewing for Journalists*, Routledge, 2001

Bell, Emily and Alden, Chris, *Guardian Media Directory 2006*, Atlantic Books, 2005

Evans, Harold, *Essential English for Journalists, Editors and Writers*, Pimlico, 2000

Franklin, Bob, *Packaging Politics: Political Communications in Britain's Media Democracy*, Arnold, 2nd edn, 2004

Frost, Chris, *Reporting for Journalists*, Routledge, 2002

Greenslade, Roy, *Press Gang*, Macmillan, 2003

Harcup, Tony, *Journalism: Principles and Practice*, Sage, 2004

Hicks, Wynford, *English for Journalists*, Routledge, 2nd edn 1998

Hicks, Wynford, with Harriett Gilbert and Sally Adams, *Writing for Journalists*, Routledge, 1999

Keeble, Richard (ed.), *Print Journalism: A Critical Introduction*, Routledge, 2005

Pilger, John, *Hidden Agendas*, Vintage, 1998

Randall, David, *The Universal Journalist*, Pluto, 2nd edn 2003

Sarikakis, Karen, *British Media in a Global Era*, Arnold, 2004

National newspapers UK and Ireland

The Business

292 Vauxhall Bridge Road, London SW1V 1DE
tel 020-7961 0000 *fax* 020-7961 0101
website www.thebusinessonline.com
Editor Ian Watson
Sun £1

Standalone Sunday newspaper for the business and financial community. All aspects of business news with in-depth features ranging from captains of industry to the entrepreneurial and small business sector. Wide economic coverage, IT news, and personal finance features. Length: from 200-word news stories to 2500-word features. Payment: by arrangement.

Deputy Editor Alistair Heath
Editor-in-Chief Andrew Neil
Political Editor Fraser Nelson

Daily Express

Northern & Shell Building, 10 Lower Thames Street, London EC4R 6EN
tel (0871) 434 1010
website www.express.co.uk
Editor Peter Hill
Daily Mon–Fri 40p, Sat 70p
Supplements **Daily Express Saturday**

Exclusive news; striking photos. Leader page articles (600 words); facts preferred to opinions. Payment: according to value.

City Editor Stephen Kahn
Deputy Editor Hugh Whittlow
Diary Editor Kathryn Spencer
Environment Editor John Ingham
Features Editor Fergus Kelly
Foreign Editor Gabriel Milland
Literary Editor Caroline Jowitt
News Editor Greg Swift
Political Editor Macer Hall
Sports Editor Bill Bradshaw
Women's Editor Tina Mora

Daily Express Saturday
Editor Graham Bailey
Free with paper
Magazine.

Daily Mail

Northcliffe House, 2 Derry Street, London W8 5TT
tel 020-7938 6000 *fax* 020-7937 3251
website www.dailymail.co.uk
Editor Paul Dacre
Daily Mon–Fri 40p, Sat 70p
Supplements **Weekend**

Highest payment for good, exclusive news. Ideas welcomed for leader page articles (500–800 words). Exclusive news photos always wanted. Founded 1896.

City Editor Alex Brummer
Diary Editor Richard Kay
Education Correspondent Laura Clark
Features Editor Jim Gillespie
Foreign Editor Gerry Hunt
Health Editor Justine Hancock
Industrial Editor Becky Barrow
Literary Editor Jane Mays
Money Editor Tony Hazell
News Editor Chris Evans
Picture Editor Paul Silva
Political Editor David Hughes
Showbiz Editor Nicole Lampert
Sports Editor Lee Chaylton
Travel Editor (acting) Verity Smith
Weekend Editor Heather McGlone

Daily Mirror

1 Canada Square, Canary Wharf, London E14 5AP
tel 020-7293 3000 *fax* 020-7293 3409
website www.mirror.co.uk
Editor Richard Wallace
Daily Mon–Fri 38p, Sat 55p
Supplements **The Ticket, We Love Telly!**

Top payment for exclusive news and news pictures. Freelance articles used, and ideas bought: send synopsis only. 'Unusual' pictures and those giving a new angle on the news are welcomed; also cartoons. Founded 1903.

Business Editor Clinton Manning
Features Editor Carole Watson
Health Editor Simone Cave
Letters Editor Henry Sutton
News Editor Anthony Harwood
Picture Editor Greg Bennett
Political Editor Oonagh Blackman
Sports Editor Dean Morse

Daily Record

1 Central Quay, Glasgow G3 8DA
tel 0141-309 3000 *fax* 0141-309 3340
London office 1 Canada Square, Canary Wharf, London E14 5AP
tel 020-7293 3000
website www.record-mail.co.uk/rm
Editor Bruce Waddell
Daily Mon–Fri 35p, Sat 45p
Supplements **Saturday, Living, TV Record, Road Record, Recruitment Record**

Topical articles, from 300–700 words; exclusive stories of Scottish interest and exclusive colour photos.

Executive Editor Bob Caldwell
Features Editor Melanie Harvey
News Editor Tom Hamilton
Sports Editor James Traynor

Saturday
Editor James Savva
Free with paper

Lifestyle magazine and entertainment guide. Reviews, travel features, shopping, personalities. Payment: by arrangement. Illustrations: colour.

Daily Sport

19 Great Ancoats Street, Manchester M60 4BT
tel 0161-236 4466 *fax* 0161-236 4535
website www.dailysport.co.uk
Editor David Beevers, *Editor-in-Chief* Tony Livesey
Daily Mon–Fri 45p

Factual stories and series. Length: up to 1000 words. Illustrations: b&w and colour photos, cartoons. Payment: £30–£5000. Founded 1988.
    Features & News Editor Jane Field
    Sports Editor Mark Smith

Daily Star

Express Newspapers, Northern & Shell Building, 10 Lower Thames Street, London EC3R 6EN
tel (0871) 434 1010 *fax* (0871) 520 7766
website www.dailystar.co.uk
Editor Dawn Neesom
Daily Mon–Fri 35p, Sat 50p
Supplements Star TV

Hard news exclusives, commanding substantial payment. Major interviews with big-star personalities; short features; series based on people rather than things; picture features. Payment: short features £75–£100; full page £250–£300; double page £400–£600, otherwise by negotiation. Illustrations: line, half-tone. Founded 1978.
    Deputy Editor Jim Mansell
    Entertainment Editor Joe Mott
    Features Editor Samm Parker
    News Editor Ian Trueman
    Sports Editor Howard Wheatcroft

Daily Star Sunday

Express Newspapers, The Northern and Shell Building, 10 Lower Thames Street, London EC3R 6EN
tel (0871) 434 1010
website www.dailystarsunday.co.uk
Editor Gareth Morgan
Sun 75p

Opportunities for freelances.

The Daily Telegraph

1 Canada Square, Canary Wharf, London E14 5DT
tel 020-7538 5000 *fax* 020-7538 6242
website www.telegraph.co.uk,
www.sport.telegraph.co.uk,
www.travel.telegraph.co.uk,
www.money.telegraph.co.uk
Editor John Bryant
Daily Mon–Fri 65p, Sat 1.30

Supplements **Arts & Books, Business2 & Jobs, Gardening, Motoring, Property, Sport, Telegraph Magazine, Television & Radio, Travel, Weekend, Your Money**

Articles on a wide range of subjects of topical interest considered. Preliminary letter and synopsis required. Length: 700–1000 words. Payment: by arrangement. Founded 1855.
    Arts Editor Sarah Crompton
    City Editor Damian Reece
    Education Editor John Clare
    Environment Editor Charles Clover
    Fashion Editor Hilary Alexander
    Features Editor Liz Hunt
    Foreign Editor Alan Philps
    Health Features Editor Georgina Cover
    Health News Editor Celia Hall
    Literary Editor Sam Leith
    News Editor Mike Smith
    Picture Editor Bob Bodman
    Political Editor George Jones

Electronic Telegraph

email et@telegraph.co.uk
website www.telegraph.co.uk/
Editor Richard Burton
Daily Free to internet subscribers

Based on *The Daily Telegraph*. Founded 1994.

Juiced

website www.juiced.com
Weekly Free to internet subscribers

Student magazine.

Planet

website www.the-planet.co.uk
Free to internet subscribers

Travel writing from *The Daily Telegraph* and *The Sunday Telegraph*.

Telegraph Magazine

Editor Michelle Lavery
Free with Sat paper

Short profiles (about 1600 words); articles of topical interest. Preliminary study of the magazine essential. Illustrations: all types. Payment: by arrangement. Founded 1964.

Financial Times

1 Southwark Bridge, London SE1 9HL
tel 020-7873 3000 *fax* 020-7873 3076
website www.ft.com
Editor Lionel Barber
Daily Mon–Fri £1, Sat £1.20
Supplements **Business Books, Companies & Markets, FT Digital Business, FTfm, FT Reports, How To Spend It, Weekend FT, Weekend Money**

Articles of financial, commercial, industrial and economic interest. Length: 800–1000 words. Payment: by arrangement. Founded 1888.

Arts Editor Jan Dalley
Banking Editor Peter Thal-Larsen
Deputy Editor Martin Dickson
Travel Editor Rahul Jacob
International Affairs Editor Quentin Peel
Investment Editor Philip Coggan
Lex Editor Tracy Corrigan
Political Editor James Blitz
Reports Editor Andrew Baxter
US Editor Chrystia Freeland
Weekend FT Editor Michael Skapinker
World News Editor James Lamont

The Guardian

119 Farringdon Road, London EC1R 3ER
tel 020-7278 2332 *fax* 020-7837 2114
164 Deansgate, Manchester M60 2RR
tel 0161-832 7200 *fax* 0161-832 5351
website www.guardian.co.uk, commentisfree.com
Editor Alan Rusbridger
Daily Mon–Fri 60p, Sat £1
Supplements **Education, Film & Music, G2, The Guide, Review, Media Guardian, Office Hours, Society, Technology, Weekend**

Few articles are taken from outside contributors except on its feature and specialist pages. Illustrations: news and features photos. Payment: from £255 per 1000 words; from £75 for illustrations. Founded 1821.

Arts Editor Melissa Denes
Business Editor Deborah Hargreaves
commentisfree.com Editor Georgina Henry
Deputy Editor Paul Johnson
Economics Editor Larry Elliott
Education Editor Claire Phipps
Fashion Editor Jess Cartner-Morley
Features Editor Katharine Viner
Film & Music Editor Michael Hann
Foreign Editor Harriet Sherwood
Home Editor Nick Hopkins
Literary Editor Claire Armitstead
Media Editor Matt Wells
Political Editor Patrick Wintour
Religious Editor Stephen Bates
Review Editor Annalena McAfee
Sports Editor Ben Clissitt
Technology Editor Charles Arthur
Travel Editor Andy Pietrasik

Guardian Unlimited
website www.guardian.co.uk
Editor-in-Chief Emily Bell

Weekend
Editor Merope Mills
Free with Sat paper
Features on world affairs, major profiles, food and drink, home life, the arts, travel, leisure, etc. Also good reportage on social and political subjects. Illustrations: b&w photos and line, cartoons. Payment: apply for rates.

The Herald

Newsquest Ltd, 200 Renfield Street, Glasgow G2 3PR
tel 0141-302 7000 *fax* 0141-302 7171
London office 30 Cannon Street, London EC4M 6YJ
tel 020-7618 3421
website www.theherald.co.uk
Editor Charles McGhee
Daily Mon–Fri 70p, Sat 75p

Articles up to 1000 words. Founded 1783.
Arts Editor Keith Bruce
Assistant Editor Melanie Reid
Business Editor Ian McConnell
Deputy Editor Joan McAlpine
Diary Editor Ken Smith
Executive Editor Colin McDiarmid
Features Editor Mark Smith
News Editor Magnus Llewellin
Sports Editor Donald Cowey

The Independent

Independent House, 191 Marsh Wall, London E14 9RS
tel 020-7005 2000 *fax* 020-7005 2999
website www.independent.co.uk
Editor-in-Chief Simon Kelner
Daily Mon–Fri 60p, Sat £1.10
Supplements **Business Review, Education, The Information, Media Weekly, Property Supplement, Review, Save & Spend, Traveller, Weekend Review**

Occasional freelance contributions; preliminary letter advisable. Payment: by arrangement. Founded 1986.
Arts Editor David Lister
Business & City Editor Jeremy Warner
Education Editor Richard Garner
Environment Editor Mike McCarthy
Features Editor Adam Leigh
Foreign Editor Leonard Doyle
Health Editor Jeremy Laurance
Literary Editor Boyd Tonkin
Media Editor tba
News Editor Danny Groom
Picture Editor Lynn Cullen
Political Editor Andrew Grice
Sports Editor Paul Newman

The Independent Magazine
Editor Laurence Earle
Free with Sat paper
Profiles and illustrated articles of topical interest; all material commissioned. Preliminary study of the magazine essential. Length: 500–3000 words. Illustrations: cartoons; commissioned colour and b&w photos. Payment: by arrangement. Founded 1988.

Independent on Sunday

Independent House, 191 Marsh Wall, London E14 9RS
tel 020-7005 2000 *fax* 020-7005 2999
website www.independent.co.uk

Editor Tristan Davies, *Editor-at-Large* Janet Street-Porter
Sun £1.60
Supplements **Business, The Sunday Review, ABC Magazine, Time Off**

News, features and articles. Illustrated, including cartoons. Payment: by negotiation. Founded 1990.
  Arts Editor, ABC Marcus Field
  Assistant Editor David Randall
  Business Editor Jason Nissé
  Comment Executive Editor James Hanning
  Deputy Editor Michael Williams
  Environment Editor Geoffrey Lean
  Features Editor, ABC Ian Irvine
  Foreign Editor Ray Whitaker
  Executive Editor (News) Andy Malone
  Picture Editor Sophie Batterbury
  Political Editor Marie Woolf
  Sports Editor Neil Morton

The Sunday Review
tel 020-7005 2000 *fax* 020-7005 2027
Deputy Editor Bill Tuckey
Free with paper

Original features of general interest with potential for photographic illustration. Material mostly commissioned. Length: 1000–5000 words. Illustrations: transparencies. Payment: £150 per 1000 words.

Ireland on Sunday
Associated Newspapers Ireland Ltd, Embassy House, Ballsbridge, Dublin 4, Republic of Ireland
tel (01) 6375800 *fax* (01) 6375880
email news@irelandonsunday.com
website www.irelandonsunday.com
Editor Paul Drury
Sun €1.80

Mid-market tabloid. Considers unsolicited material. Length: 2500 words (articles/features), 800 words (news). Illustrations: cartoons. Payment: by negotiation. Founded 1997.
  Assistant Editor John Cooper
  Sports Editor Jack White

Irish Daily Star
Independent Star Ltd, Star House, 62ᴀ Terenure Road North, Dublin 6w, Republic of Ireland
tel (01) 4901228 *fax* (01) 4902193
website www.thestar.ie
Editor Gerard Colleran
Daily Mon–Sat €1.30

General articles relating to news and sport, and features. Length: 1000 words. Illustrations: colour photos. Payment: by negotiation. Founded 1988.
  Deputy Editor Danny Smyth
  News Editor Michael O'Kane
  Picture Editor Brian Dowling
  Political Editor John Downing
  Sports Editor Eoin Brannigan

Irish Examiner
1–6 Academy Street, Cork, Republic of Ireland
tel (021) 4272722, 4802101 (newsroom)
fax (021) 4275477
email (department)@irishexaminer.ie
website www.irishexaminer.ie
Editor Tim Vaughan
Daily Mon–Sat €1.60

Features. Material mostly commissioned. Length: 1000 words. Payment: by arrangement. Founded 1841.
  Deputy Editor tbc
  Features Editor Fionnuala Quinlan
  News Editor John O'Mahony
  Picture Editor John O'Donovan
  Sports Editor Tony Leen

Irish Independent
Independent House, 90 Middle Abbey Street, Dublin 1, Republic of Ireland
tel (01) 7055333 *fax* (01) 8720304/8731787
website www.independent.ie
Editor Gerard O'Regan
Daily Mon–Sat €1.30

Special articles on topical or general subjects. Length: 700–1000 words. Payment: editor's estimate of value.
  Business Editor Richard Curran
  Deputy Editor Michael Wolsey
  Diary Editor Angela Phelan
  Features Editor Peter Carvosso
  News Editor Philip Molloy
  Picture Editor Danny Thornton
  Political Editor Gene McKenna
  Sports Editor Patrick J. Cunningham

Irish Times
11–15 D'Olier Street, Dublin 2, Republic of Ireland
tel (01) 6758000 *fax* (01) 6758035
website www.ireland.com
Editor Geraldine Kennedy
Daily Mon–Sat €1.60
Supplements **The Irish Times Magazine (Sat)**

Mainly staff-written. Specialist contributions (800–2000 words) by commission on basis of ideas submitted. Payment: at editor's valuation. Illustrations: photos and line drawings.
  Arts Editor Deirdre Falvey
  Features Editor Sheila Wayman
  Finance Editor John McManus
  Foreign Editor Paddy Smyth
  Literary Editor Caroline Walsh
  News Editor Miriam Donohoe
  Picture Editor Peter Thursfield
  Sports Editor Malachy Logan

The Irish Times on the Web
website www.ireland.com

Mail on Sunday
Northcliffe House, 2 Derry Street, London W8 5TS
tel 020-7938 6000 *fax* 020-7937 3829

website www.mailonsunday.co.uk
Editor Peter Wright
Sun £1.20
Supplements **Financial Mail on Sunday, Night & Day, Property on Sunday, Review, You**

Articles. Payment: by arrangement. Illustrations: line, half-tone; cartoons. Founded 1982.
  City Editor Lisa Buckingham
  Features Editor Sian James
  Literary Editor Marilyn Warnick
  News Editor Sebastian Hamilton
  Picture Editor Liz Cocks
  Political Editor Simon Walters
  Sports Editor Malcolm Vallerius

Financial Mail on Sunday
tel 020-7938 6984
Editor Lisa Buckingham, *Personal Finance Editor* Jeff Prestridge
Free with paper
City, industry, business, and personal finance. News stories up to 1500 words. Payment by arrangement. Full colour illustrations and photography commissioned.

Live Magazine
tel 020-7938 7051 *fax* 020-7937 7488
Editor Gerard Greaves
Free with paper
Interviews, entertainment-related features and TV listings. Length: 1000–3000 words. Illustrations: colour photos. Founded 1993.

Review
Editor Jim Gillespie
Investigative journalism, reportage, features, and film, TV, book and theatre reviews.

You
Editor Sue Peart, *Deputy Editor* Catherine Fenton
Free with paper
Women's interest features. Length: 500–2500 words. Payment: by arrangement. Illustrations: full colour and b&w drawings commissioned; also colour photos.

Morning Star
(formerly Daily Worker)
People's Press Printing Society Ltd, William Rust House, 52 Beachy Road, London E3 2NS
tel 020-8510 0815 *fax* 020-8986 5694
email morsta@geo2.poptel.org.uk
website www.morningstaronline.co.uk
Editor John Haylett
Daily Mon–Sat 60p

Newspaper for the labour movement. Articles of general interest. Illustrations: photos, cartoons, drawings. Founded 1930.
  Arts, Media & Features Editor Katie Gilmore
  Diary Editor Richard Bagley

  Financial Editor Bill Benfield
  Foreign Editor Dave Williams
  Health Editor Louise Nousratpour
  Industrial & News Editor Dan Coysh
  Political Editor Roger Bagley
  Sports Editor Mark Barber

News of the World
1 Virginia Street, London E98 1NW
tel 020-7782 1000 *fax* 020-7583 9504
website www.newsoftheworld.co.uk
Editor Andy Coulson
Sun 85p

Uses freelance material. Payment: by negotiation. Founded 1843.
  Assistant Editor (Features) Jules Stenson
  Assistant Editor (News) Gary Thompson
  Deputy Editor Neil Wallis
  Political Editor Ian Kirby
  PR Manager Hayley Barlow
  Royal Editor Clive Goodman
  Sports Editor Mike Dunn

Sunday Magazine
Phase 2, 5th Floor, 1 Virginia Street, London E1 9BD
tel 020-7782 7900 *fax* 020-7782 7474
Editor Judy McGuire
Free with paper

The Observer
3–7 Herbal Hill, London EC1R 5EJ
tel 020-7278 2332 *fax* 020-7837 7817
website www.observer.co.uk
Editor Roger Alton
Sun £1.60
Supplements **Business, Cash, Escape, Observer Magazine, Observer Sport Monthly, Observer Food Monthly, Observer Music Monthly, Observer Review, The Observer Television, Observer Woman, Sport**

Some articles and illustrations commissioned. Payment: by arrangement. Founded 1791.
  Arts Editor Sarah Donaldson
  Business Editor Richard Wachman
  Cash Editor Jill Insley
  City Editor Richard Wachman
  Comment Editor Barbara Gunnell
  Fashion Editor Jo Adams
  Film & Music Editor Akin Ojomu
  Foreign News Editor Tracy McVeigh
  Health Editor Jo Revill
  Home News Editor Lucy Rock
  Literary Editor Robert McCrum
  Executive Editor, News Kamal Ahmed
  Observer Woman Editor Nicola Jeal
  OFM Editor Nicola Jeal
  OMM Editor Caspar Llewellyn Smith
  OSM Editor Jason Cowley

Picture Editor Greg Whitmore
Political Editor Gaby Hinsliff
Readers' Editor Stephen Pritchard
Review Editor Jane Ferguson
7 Days Editor Rob Yates
Sports Editor Brian Oliver
Travel Editor Joanne O'Connor

Observer Magazine
tel 020-7713 4175 *fax* 020-7239 9837
Editor Allan Jenkins
Free with paper

Commissioned features. Length: 2000–3000 words.
Illustrations: first-class colour and b&w photos.
Payment: NUJ rates; £150 per illustration.

The Observer Online
website www.observer.co.uk

The People
(formerly Sunday People)
1 Canada Square, Canary Wharf, London E14 5AP
tel 020-7293 3000 *fax* 020-7293 3517
website www.people.co.uk
Editor Mark Thomas
Sun 80p
Supplements **The SP, Take it Easy**
  Features Editor Chris Bucktin
  Investigations Editor Roger Insall
  News Editor Ben Proctor
  Picture Editor Paula Derry
  Political Editor Nigel Nelson
  Sports Editor Lee Horton

Exclusive news and news-feature stories needed.
Investigative features, single articles and series
considered. Features should be of deep human
interest, whether the subject is serious or light-
hearted. Very strong sports following. Payment: rates
high, even for tips that lead to published news stories.

Take it Easy
Editor Maria Coole
Free with paper

Scotland on Sunday
108 Holyrood Road, Edinburgh EH8 8AS
tel 0131-620 8620 *fax* 0131-620 8491
website www.scotlandonsunday.co.uk
Acting Editor Tom Nittle
Sun £1.20

Features on all subjects, not necessarily Scottish.
Payment: varies. Founded 1988.
  News Editor Peter Laing
  Political Editor Eddie Barnes

Spectrum Magazine
Editor Clare Trodden
Free with paper

The Scotsman
Barclay House, 108 Holyrood Road, Edinburgh
EH8 8AS
tel 0131-620 8620 *fax* 0131-620 8615
website www.scotsman.com
Editor John McGurk
Daily Mon–Fri 55p, Sat 70p
Supplements **Saturday Magazine, Critique, Property,
Motoring, Recruitment**

Considers articles on political, economic and general
themes which add substantially to current
information. Prepared to commission topical and
controversial series from proved authorities. Length:
800–1000 words. Illustrations: outstanding news
pictures, cartoons. Payment: by arrangement.
Founded 1817.
  Arts Editor Andrew Eaton
  Business Editor Nick Bevens
  Books Editor David Robinson
  Education Correspondent Kevin Schofield
  Features Editor Jacqueline Hunter
  Foreign Editor Rob Corbidge
  News Editor James Hall
  Political Editor (Westminster) James Kirkup
  Assistant Editor (Politics) Hamish Macdonell
  Saturday Magazine Editor Alison Gray
  Sports Editor Donald Walker

Star Sunday
Independent Star Ltd, Star House, 62ᴀ Terenure
Road North, Dublin 6w, Republic of Ireland
tel (01) 4901228 *fax* (01) 4901538
email news.sunday@thestar.ie
Editor Des Gibson
Sun €1.80
  Deputy Editor Paul Mallon
  News Editor Bernard Phelan
  Sports Editor Gavan Becton

The Sun
News Group Newspapers Ltd, 1 Virginia Street,
London E1 9XP
tel 020-7782 4000 *fax* 020-7488 3253
website www.the-sun.co.uk
Editor Rebekah Wade
Daily Mon–Fri 35p, Sat 55p
Supplements **Cashflow, The TV Mag**

Takes freelance material, including cartoons.
Payment: by negotiation. Founded 1969.
  Associate Editor Geoff Webster
  Business Editor Ian King
  Features Editor Ben Jackson
  Health Editor Jacqui Thornton
  Letters Editor Sue Cook
  News Editor Jamie Pyatt
  Picture Editor John Edwards
  Political Editor George Pascoe-Watson
  Showbiz Editor Dominic Mohan

Sports Editor Ted Chadwick
Travel Editor Lisa Minot
Women's Editor Sharon Hendry

The Sunday Business Post

80 Harcourt Street, Dublin 2, Republic of Ireland
tel (01) 6026000 *fax* (01) 6796496/6796498
website www.thepost.ie
Editor Cliff Taylor
Sun €2.10

Features on financial, economic and political topics;
also lifestyle, media and science articles. Illustrations:
colour and b&w photos, graphics, cartoons. Payment:
by negotiation. Founded 1989.
Assistant Editor Kieron Wood
Assistant Editor/Agenda Editor Fiona Ness
Assistant Editor/Political Correspondent Pat Leahy
Assistant Editor/Property Editor Gillian Nelis
Business Editor Eamon Quinn
IT Editor/Deputy News Editor Gavin Daly
Media Editor Catherine O'Mahony
News Editor Simon Carswell
Political Reporter Niamh Connolly

Sunday Express

Northern & Shell Building, 10 Lower Thames Street,
London EC4R 6EN
tel (0871) 434 1010
website www.express.co.uk
Editor Martin Townsend
Sun £1.20
Supplements **'S' Sunday Express**

Exclusive news stories, photos, personality profiles
and features of controversial or lively interest. Length:
800–1000 words. Payment: top rates. Founded 1918.
Business Editor Lawrie Holmes
Features Editor Giulia Rhodes
Literary Editor Graham Ball
News Editor James Murray
Political Editor Julia Harltley-Brewes
Sports Editor Scott Wilson

'S' Sunday Express
tel 020-7922 7297
Editor Louise Robinson
Free with paper

Sunday Herald

200 Renfield Street, Glasgow G2 3QB
tel 0141-302 7800 *fax* 0141-302 7815
website www.sundayherald.com
Editor Richard Walker
Sun £1.10
Supplements **Business, Seven Days, Sport, Sunday
Herald Magazine, Recruitment**

News and stories about Scotland, its characteristics
and people. Opportunities for freelances with quality
contacts. Founded 1999.

Business Editor Ken Symon
Deputy Editor David Milne
Features Editor Susan Flockhart
Magazine Editor Jane Wright
News Editor Charlene Sweeney
Political Editor Paul Hutcheon
Sports Editor Stephen Penman

Sunday Independent

27–32 Talbot Street, Dublin 1, Republic of Ireland
tel (01) 7055333 *fax* (01) 7055779
website www.independent.ie
Editor Aengus Fanning
Sun €2

Special articles. Length: according to subject.
Illustrations: topical or general interest, cartoons.
Payment: at editor's valuation.
Business Editor Shane Ross
Deputy Editors Anne Harris, Willie Kealy
Executive News Editor Jody Corcoran
Sports Editor Adhamhnan O'Sullivan

Sunday Mail

1 Central Quay, Glasgow G3 8DA
tel 0141-309 3000 *fax* 0141-309 3582
London office 1 Canada Square, Canary Wharf,
London E14 5AP
website www.sundaymail.com
Editor Allan Rennie
Sun £1
Supplements **Entertainment, 7-Days, Right at Home**

Exclusive stories and pictures of national and Scottish
interest; also cartoons. Payment: above average.
Deputy Editor Jim Wilson
Health Editor Dr Gareth Smith
News Editor Brendan McGinty
Picture Editor Andrew Hosie
7-Days Editor Liz Cowan
Showbiz Editor Billy Sloan
Sports Editor George Cheyne

Sunday Mirror

1 Canada Square, Canary Wharf, London E14 5AP
tel 020-7293 3000 *fax* 020-7293 3939
website www.sundaymirror.co.uk
Editor Tina Weaver
Sun Mirror 85p
Supplements **Celebs On Sunday**

Concentrates on human interest news features, social
documentaries, dramatic news and feature photos.
Ideas, as well as articles, bought. Payment: high,
especially for exclusives. Founded 1963.
Associate Editor Mike Small
Associate Editor (News) Nick Buckley
FeaturesEditor Nicki Dawson
Picture Editor Mark Sharp
Sport Editor David Walker

Sunday Post

D.C. Thomson & Co. Ltd, 144 Port Dundas Road,
Glasgow G4 0HZ
tel 0141-332 9933 *fax* 0141-331 1595
Albert Square, Dundee DD1 9QJ
tel (01382) 223131 *fax* (01382) 201064
website www.sundaypost.com
Editor David Pollington
Sun 80p

Human interest, topical, domestic and humorous
articles, and exclusive news. Payment: on acceptance.

The Sunday Post Magazine
tel (01382) 223131 *fax* (01382) 201064
Editor Jan Gooderham
Monthly Free with paper
General interest articles. Length: 1000–2000 words.
Illustrations: colour transparencies. Payment: varies.
Founded 1988.

Sunday Telegraph

1 Canada Square, Canary Wharf, London E14 5DT
tel 020-7538 5000 *fax* 020-7513 2504
website www.telegraph.co.uk
Editor Patience Wheatcroft
Sun £1.20
Supplements **Business, City, Home & Living, Money
& Jobs Sport, Travel**

Occasional freelance material accepted.
 Arts Editor Lucy Tuck
 City Editor George Trefgarne
 Comment Editor Robert Cowan
 Deputy Editor Richard Ellis
 Diary Editor Tim Walker
 Foreign Editor David Wastell
 Literary Editor Michael Prodger
 News Editor Tim Woodward
 Picture Editor Nigel Skelsey
 Political Editor Patrick Hennessy
 Seven Editor Suzannah Herbert
 Sports Editor John Ryan
 Travel Editor Maggie O'Sullivan

Stella
tel 020-7538 7590 *fax* 020-7538 7074
email sunmag@telegraph.co.uk
Editor Anna Murphy
Free with paper
All material is commissioned. Founded 1995.

The Sunday Times

1 Virginia Street, London E1 9BD
tel 020-7782 4000 *fax* 020-7583 9504
website www.timesonline.co.uk
Editor John Witherow
Sun £1.80
Supplements **Appointments, Business, Culture,
Funday Times, Home, Money, News Review, Sport,
Style, The Sunday Times Magazine, Travel**

Special articles by authoritative writers on politics,
literature, art, drama, music, finance and science, and

topical matters. Payment: top rate for exclusive
features. Founded 1822.
 Culture Editor Helen Hawkins
 Economics Editor David Smith
 Education Correspondent Judith O'Reilly
 Literary Editor Caroline Gascoigne
 News Editor Charles Hymas
 Sports Editor Alex Butler
 Travel Editor Christine Walker

The Sunday Times Magazine
tel 020-7782 7000
Editor Robin Morgan
Free with paper
Articles and pictures. Illustrations: colour and b&w
photos. Payment: by negotiation.

The Sunday Times Scotland

Times Newspapers Ltd, 124 Portman Street, Kinning
Park, Glasgow G41 1EJ
tel 0141-420 5100 *fax* 0141-420 5262
website www.timesonline.co.uk
Editor Dean Nelson
Sun £1.50
Founded 1988.

The Times

1 Pennington Street, London E98 1TT
tel 020-7782 5000 *fax* 020-7488 3242
website www.timesonline.co.uk
Editor Robert Thomson
Daily Mon–Fri 60p, Sat £1.10
Supplements **Books, Body & Soul, Bricks & Mortar,
Crème, Football Handbook, The Game, The
Knowledge, Money, Times 2, Times Law, The
Times Magazine, Times Sport, Travel**

Outside contributions considered from: experts in
subjects of current interest and writers who can make
first-hand experience or reflection come readably
alive. Phone appropriate section editor. Length: up to
1200 words. Founded 1785.
 Arts and Entertainment Editor Alex O'Connell
 Body & Soul Editor Hilly Janes
 Business/City Editor tba
 Deputy Editor Ben Preston
 Education Editor Tony Halpin
 Features Editor Michael Harvey
 Foreign Editor Bronwen Maddox
 Health Editor Nigel Hawkes
 Home Editor John Wellman
 Industrial Correspondent Christine Buckley
 Literary Editor Erica Wagner
 Media Editor Dan Sabbagh
 Political Editor Philip Webster
 Saturday Times Editor George Brock
 Science Correspondent Mark Henderson
 Sports Editor Tim Hallissey
 Travel Editor Cath Urquhart

The Times Magazine
Editor Gill Morgan
Free with Sat paper
Features. Illustrated.

Wales on Sunday

Thomson House, Havelock Street, Cardiff CF10 1XR
tel 029-2058 3583 *fax* 029-2058 3725
website www.icwales.co.uk
Editor Tim Gordon
Sun 80p

National Sunday newspaper of Wales offering comprehensive news, features and entertainments coverage at the weekend, with a particular focus on events in Wales. Accepts general interest articles, preferably with a Welsh connection. Founded 1989.
Assistant Editor (Sport) Nick Rippington
Deputy Editor Wayne Davies
News Editor Laura Kemp

Regional newspapers UK and Ireland

Regional newspapers are listed in alphabetical order under region. Some will accept and pay for letters to the editor, brief fillers, and gossip paragraphs, as well as puzzles and quizzes. See also *Writing for newspapers* on page 3.

BELFAST

Belfast Telegraph
124–144 Royal Avenue, Belfast BT1 1EB
tel 028-9026 4000 *fax* 028-9033 1332 (also photographic), 9055 4540 (news only), 9055 4517 (features), 9055 4508 (sport)
email editor@belfasttelegraph.co.uk
website www.belfasttelegraph.co.uk
Editor Martin Lindsay
Daily Mon–Fri 55p, Sat 60p
   Features Editor Gail Walker
   News Editor Paul Connolly
   Picture Editor Gerry Fitzgerald
   Sports Editor Steven Beacom

Any material relating to Northern Ireland. Payment: by negotiation. Founded 1870.

Irish News
113–117 Donegall Street, Belfast BT1 2GE
tel 028-9032 2226 *fax* 028-9033 7505
website www.irishnews.com
Editor Noel Doran
Daily Mon–Sat 55p
   Business Editor Gary McDonald
   Features Editor Joanna Braniff
   News Editor Stephen McCaffery
   Picture Editor Ann McManus
   Sports Editor Thomas Hawkins

Articles of historical and topical interest. Payment: by arrangement. Founded 1855.

News Letter
46–56 Boucher Crescent, Boucher Road, Belfast BT12 6QY
tel 028-9068 0000 *fax* 028-9066 4412
website www.newsletter.co.uk
Editor Austin Hunter
Daily Mon–Fri 50p, Sat 60p
   Sports Editor Brian Millar

Pro-Union. Founded 1737.

The People
415 Holywood Road, Belfast BT4 2GU
tel 028-9056 8000 *fax* 028-9056 8053
4th Floor, Park House, North Circular Road, Dublin 7, Republic of Ireland
website www.mirror.co.uk
Editor Stephen Maguire
Sun 35p

Northern Ireland edition of *The People*.

Sunday Life
124 Royal Avenue, Belfast BT1 1EB
tel 028-9026 4300 *fax* 028-9055 4507
email slfeatures@belfasttelegraph.co.uk
website www.sundaylife.co.uk
Editor Jim Flanagan
Sun £1.10
   Features Editor Audrey Watson
   Deputy Editor and News Editor Martin Hill
   Photographic Editor Mark McCormick
   Sports Editor Jim Gracey

Items of interest to Northern Ireland Sunday tabloid readers. Payment: by arrangement. Illustrations: colour and b&w pictures and graphics. Founded 1988.

CHANNEL ISLANDS

Guernsey Press and Star
PO Box 57, Braye Road, Vale, Guernsey GY1 3BW
tel (01481) 240240 *fax* (01481) 240235
website www.guernseypress.com
Editor Richard Digard
Daily Mon–Sat 40p
   Features Editor Suzanne Heneghan
   News Editor James Falla
   Sports Editor Rob Batiste

News and feature articles. Length: 500–700 words. Illustrations: colour and b&w photos. Payment: by negotiation. Founded 1897.

Jersey Evening Post
PO Box 582, Five Oaks, St Saviour, Jersey JE4 8XQ
tel (01534) 611611 *fax* (01534) 611622
email editorial@jerseyeveningpost.com
website www.thisisjersey.com
Editor Chris Bright
Daily Mon–Sat 40p
   Features Editor Elaine Hanning
   News Editor Sue le Ruez
   Picture Editor Peter Mourant
   Sports Editor Ron Felton

News and features with a Channel Islands angle. *Reality* monthly supplement. Length: 1000 words (articles/features), 300 words (news). Illustrations: colour and b&w. Payment: £98 per 1000 words. Founded 1890.

CORK

Evening Echo (Cork)
Evening Echo Publications Ltd, 1–6 Academy Street, Cork, Republic of Ireland
tel (021) 4272722 *fax* (021) 4802135

email firstname.secondname@eecho.ie
website www.eveningecho.ie
Editor Maurice Gubbins
Daily Mon–Sat €1.10
   Deputy Editor Vincent Kelly
   Features Editor John Dolan
   News Editor Emma Connolly
   Picture Editor Brian Lougheed

Articles, features and news for the area. Illustrations: colour prints.

DUBLIN

Evening Herald
90 Middle Abbey Street, Dublin 1, Republic of Ireland
tel (01) 7055333
email eveningherald@unison.independent.ie
website www.unison.ie
Editor Stephen Rae
Daily Mon–Sat €1
   Associate Editor Dave Lawlor
   Assistant Editors Dave Kenny, Mark Evans, Alan Steerson
   Features Editor Dave Diebold
   News Editor Ian Mallon
   Deputy News Editor Mick McCaffrey
   Assistant News Editor Bairbre Power
   Picture Editor Tara McGinn
   Sports Editor Pat Keene

Articles. Payment: by arrangement. Illustrations: line, half-tone, cartoons.

The Sunday Tribune
Tribune Publications plc, 15 Lower Baggot Street, Dublin 2, Republic of Ireland
tel (01) 661 5555 *fax* (01) 661 5302
email editorial@tribune.ie
website www.tribune.ie
Editor Noirin Hegarty
Sun €2
Supplements **People, Review**
   Deputy Editor Diarmuid Doyle
   Assistant Editor Kevin Rafter
   Chief Sub Editor Ger Siggins
   News Editor Olivia Doyle
   Magazine Editor Fionnuala McCarthy
   Sports Editor P.J. Cunningham

Newspaper containing news (inc. foreign), articles, features and photo features. Length: 600–2800 words. Illustrations: colour and b&w photos and cartoons. Payment: £100 per 1000 words; £100 for illustrations. Founded 1980.

EAST ANGLIA

Cambridge Evening News
Winship Road, Milton, Cambs. CB4 6PP
tel (01223) 434437 *fax* (01223) 434415
website www.cambridge-news.co.uk

Editor Murray Morse
Daily Mon–Sat 38p
   News Editor John Deex
   Sports Editor Chris Gill

The voice of Mid-Anglia – news, views and sport. Illustrations: colour prints, b&w and colour graphics. Payment: by negotiation. Founded 1888.

East Anglian Daily Times
30 Lower Brook Street, Ipswich, Suffolk IP4 1AN
tel (01473) 230023 *fax* (01473) 324871
website www.eadt.co.uk
Editor Terry Hunt
Daily Mon–Fri 47p, Sat 60p
   Features Editor Julian Ford
   Head of Photos Andy Abbott
   News Editor Brad Jones
   Sports Editor Nick Garnham

Features of East Anglian interest, preferably with pictures. Length: 500 words. Illustrations: colour, b&w. Payment: negotiable; illustrations NUJ rates. Founded 1874.

Eastern Daily Press
Prospect House, Rouen Road, Norwich NR1 1RE
tel (01603) 628311 *fax* (01603) 612930
London office House of Commons Press Gallery, House of Commons, London SW1A 0AA
tel 020-7219 3384 *fax* 020-7222 3830
website www.edp24.co.uk
Editor Peter Franzen OBE
Daily Mon–Fri 45p, Sat 65p

Limited market for articles of East Anglian interest not exceeding 900 words. Founded 1870.

Evening News
Prospect House, Rouen Road, Norwich NR1 1RE
tel (01603) 628311 *fax* (01603) 219060
website www.eveningnews24.co.uk
Editor David Bourn
Daily Mon–Sat 38p
   Features Editor Derek James
   News Editor Alistair McGregor
   Picture Editor Nolan Lincoln
   Sports Editor David Cuffley

Interested in local news-based features. Length: up to 500 words. Payment: NUJ or agreed rates. Founded 1882.

EAST MIDLANDS

Burton Mail
Burton Daily Mail Ltd, 65–68 High Street, Burton on Trent DE14 1LE
tel (01283) 512345 *fax* (01283) 515351
website www.burtonmail.co.uk
Editor Paul Hazeldine
Daily Mon–Sat 36p

Deputy Editor Andy Parker
Features Editor Louise Warrall
Picture Editor Neil Barker
Sports Editor Rex Page

Features, news and articles of interest to Burton and south Derbyshire readers. Length: 400–500 words. Illustrations: colour and b&w. Payment: by negotiation. Founded 1898.

Chronicle & Echo, Northampton

Northamptonshire Newspapers Ltd, Upper Mounts, Northampton NN1 3HR
tel (01604) 467000 *fax* (01604) 467190
Editor Mark Edwards
Daily Mon–Sat 37p

Articles, features and news – mostly commissioned – of interest to the Northampton area. Length: varies. Payment: by negotiation. Founded 1931.

Derby Evening Telegraph

Northcliffe House, Meadow Road, Derby DE1 2DW
tel (01332) 291111 *fax* (01322) 253027
website www.thisisderbyshire.co.uk
Editor Steve Hall
Daily Mon–Sat 32p
Features Editor Jill Gallone
News Editor Cheryl Hague
Picture Editor Mike Inman
Sports Editor Peter Green

Articles and news of local interest. Payment: by negotiation.

The Leicester Mercury

St George Street, Leicester LE1 9FQ
tel 0116-251 2512 *fax* 0116-253 0645
website www.thisisleicestershire.co.uk
Editor Nick Carter
Daily Mon–Sat 33p

Occasional articles, features and news; submit ideas to editor first. Length/payment: by negotiation. Founded 1874.

Nottingham Evening Post

Castle Wharf House, Nottingham NG1 7EU
tel 0115-948 2000 *fax* 0115-964 4049
email newsdesk@nottinghameveningpost.co.uk
website www.thisisnottingham.co.uk
Editor Graham Glen
Daily Mon–Sat 33p

Material on local issues considered. Founded 1878.

Peterborough Evening Telegraph

Telegraph House, 57 Priestgate, Peterborough PE1 1JW
tel (01733) 555111 *fax* (01733) 313147
website www.peterboroughtoday.co.uk
Editor Rebecca Stephens
Daily Mon–Sat 35p

LONDON

Evening Standard

Northcliffe House, 2 Derry Street, London W8 5EE
tel 020-7938 6000
website www.thisislondon.com
Editor Veronica Wadley
Daily Mon–Fri 40p
Features Editor Guy Eaton
News Editor Ian Walker
Picture Editor David Ofield
Political Editor Joe Murphy
Sports Editor Raoul Simon

Articles of general interest considered, 1500 words or shorter; also news, pictures and ideas. Founded 1827.

ES Magazine
Editor Mimi Spencer
Weekly Free with paper on Fri

Feature ideas, exclusively about London. Payment: by negotiation. Illustrations: all types.

Homes and Property
Editor Janice Morley
Weekly Free with paper on Wed

UK property. Payment: by negotiation.

Metrolife
Editor Mark Booker
Weekly Free with paper on Thurs

Articles, interviews and features on London life. Payment: by negotiation.

NORTH

Evening Chronicle

Newcastle Chronicle and Journal Ltd, Groat Market, Newcastle upon Tyne NE1 1ED
tel 0191-232 7500 *fax* 0191-232 2256
website www.icnewcastle.co.uk
Editor Paul Robertson
Daily Mon–Sat 40p
Features Editor Jennifer Bradbury
News Editor James Marley
Picture Editor Rod Wilson
Sports Editor Paul New

News, photos and features covering almost every subject of interest to readers in Tyne and Wear, Northumberland and Durham. Payment: by prior arrangement.

Evening Gazette

Gazette Media Company Ltd, Borough Road, Middlesbrough TS1 3AZ
tel (01642) 245401 *fax* (01642) 232014
email editor@eveninggazette.co.uk
website www.tees.net
Editor Darren Thwaites

Daily Mon–Sat 35p

News, and topical and lifestyle features. Length: 600–800 words. Illustrations: line, half-tone, colour, graphics, cartoons. Payment: £75 per 1000 words; scale rate or by agreement for illustrations. Founded 1869.

Hartlepool Mail
Northeast Press Ltd, New Clarence House, Wesley Square, Hartlepool TS24 8BX
tel (01429) 239333 *fax* (01429) 869024
email mail.news@northeast-press.co.uk
website www.hartlepooltoday.co.uk,
www.peterleetoday.co.uk
Acting Editor Brian Nuttney
Daily Mon–Sat 35p
   Deputy Editor Brian Nuttney
   News Editor Peter McCusker
   Sports Editor Roy Kelly

Features of local interest. Length: 500 words. Illustrations: colour, b&w photos, line. Payment: by negotiation. Founded 1877.

The Journal
Groat Market, Newcastle upon Tyne NE1 1ED
tel 0191-232 7500 *fax* 0191-261 8869
email jnl.newsdesk@ncjmedia.co.uk
website www.icnewcastle.co.uk
Editor Brian Aitken
Daily Mon–Fri 45p, Sat 50p
   Features Editor Jane Hall
   News Editor Matt McKenzie
   Picture Editor Simon Greener
   Sports Editor Kevin Dinsdale

News, sport items and features of topical interest considered. Payment: by arrangement.

North-West Evening Mail
Newspaper House, Abbey Road, Barrow-in-Furness, Cumbria LA14 5QS
tel (01229) 840150 *fax* (01229) 840164/832141
website www.nwemail.co.uk
Editor Steve Brauner
Daily Mon–Sat 37p
   News Editor Jon Townend
   Sports Editor Frank Cassidy

'The Voice of Furness and West Cumbria.' Articles, features and news. Length: 500 words. Illustrations: b&w photos and occasional artwork. Payment: £30 (minimum); £10 for illustrations. Founded 1898.

The Northern Echo
Priestgate, Darlington, Co. Durham DL1 1NF
tel (01325) 381313 *fax* (01325) 380539
website www.thisisthenortheast.co.uk
Editor Peter Barron
Daily Mon–Sat 35p
   Features Editor Jenny Needham
   News Editor Nigel Burton
   Picture Editor Mike Gibb

Sports Editor Nick Loughlin

Articles of interest to North-East and North Yorkshire; all material commissioned. Preliminary study of newspaper advisable. Length: 800–1000 words. Illustrations: line, half-tone, colour – mostly commissioned. Payment: by negotiation. Founded 1870.

The Sunday Sun
Groat Market, Newcastle upon Tyne NE1 1ED
tel 0191-201 6158 *fax* 0191-201 6180
email scoop.sundaysun@ncjmedia.co.uk
website www.sundaysun.co.uk
Acting Editor Colin Patterson
Sun 75p

Key requirements: immediate topicality and human sidelights on current problems. Particularly welcomed are special features of family appeal and news stories of special interest to the North of England. Length: 200–700 words. Payment: normal lineage rates, or by arrangement. Illustrations: photos. Founded 1919.

Sunderland Echo
Echo House, Pennywell, Sunderland, Tyne & Wear SR4 9ER
tel 0191-501 5800 *fax* 0191-534 5975
website www.sunderlandtoday.co.uk
Editor Rob Lawson
Daily Mon–Sat 38p
   Deputy Editor Richard Ord
   Features Editor Paul Taylor
   Sports Editor Neil Watson

Local news, features and articles. Length: 500 words. Illustrations: colour and b&w photos, line, cartoons. Payment: negotiable. Founded 1875.

NORTH WEST

The Blackpool Gazette
Blackpool Gazette & Herald Ltd, Avroe House, Avroe Crescent, Blackpool Business Park, Squires Gate, Blackpool FY4 2DP
tel (01253) 400888 *fax* (01253) 361870
email editorial@blackpoolgazette.co.uk
website www.blackpooltoday.co.uk
Editor David Helliwell
Daily Mon–Sat 35p

Local news and articles of general interest, with photos if appropriate. Length: varies. Payment: on merit. Founded 1929.

Bolton Evening News
Newspaper House, Churchgate, Bolton, Lancs. BL1 1DE
tel (01204) 522345 *fax* (01204) 365068
email ben_editorial@boltoneveningnews.co.uk
website www.thisisbolton.co.uk

Editor-in-Chief Steve Hughes
Daily Mon–Sat 35p
  News Editor James Higgins
  Sports Editor Peter Mensforth

Founded 1867.

Lancashire & Wigan Evening Post

Unit 4, Fulwood Buiness Park, Caxton Road,
Fulwood, Preston, Lancs. PR2 9NZ
tel (01772) 254841 *fax* (01772) 204941
website www.lep.co.uk
Editor Simon Reynolds
Daily Mon–Sat 37p

Topical articles on all subjects. Area of interest Wigan
to Lake District, Lancs, and coast. Length: 600–900
words. Illustrations: colour and b&w photos,
cartoons. Payment: by arrangement.

Lancashire Evening Telegraph

Newspaper House, High Street, Blackburn, Lancs.
BB1 1HT
tel (01254) 678678
website www.thisislancashire.co.uk
Editor Kevin Young
Daily Mon–Sat 35p
  News Editor Andrew Turner
  Picture Editor Neil Johnson
  Sports Editor Paul Plunkett

Will consider general interest articles, such as
property, motoring, finance, etc. Payment: by
arrangement. Founded 1886.

Liverpool Daily Post

PO Box 48, Old Hall Street, Liverpool L69 3EB
tel 0151-227 2000 *fax* 0151-472 2474
website www.liverpool.com
Editor Jane Wolstenholme
Daily Mon–Sat 45p
Supplements **Box Office, Business Week, Day Six,
Post Match, Retail Therapy**
  Features Editor Louise Douglas
  News Editor Gregg Fray
  Picture Editor Stephen Shakeshaft
  Sports Editor Richard Williamson

Articles of general and topical interest to North West
England. No verse or fiction. Payment: according to
value. News and feature illustrations. Founded 1855.

Liverpool Echo

PO Box 48, Old Hall Street, Liverpool L69 3EB
tel 0151-227 2000 *fax* 0151-236 4682
website www.icliverpool.co.uk
Editor Alastair Macray
Daily Mon–Fri 38p, Sat 45p
  News Editor Alison Gow
  Picture Editor Stephen Shakeshaft
  Sports Editor John Thompson

Articles of up to 600–800 words of local or topical
interest; also cartoons. Payment: according to merit;

special rates for exceptional material. Connected
with, but independent of, the *Liverpool Daily Post*.
Articles not interchangeable.

Manchester Evening News

164 Deansgate, Manchester M60 2RD
tel 0161-832 7200 (editorial) *fax* 0161-834 3814
features fax 0161-839 0968
website www.manchesteronline.co.uk
Editor Paul Horrocks
Daily Mon–Sat 35p
  Features Editor Deanna Delamotta
  News Editor Ian Wood
  Picture Editor John Jeffay
  Sports Editor Peter Spencer

Feature articles of up to 1000 words, topical or
general interest and illustrated where appropriate,
should be addressed to the Features Editor. Payment:
on acceptance.

Oldham Evening Chronicle

PO Box 47, Union Street, Oldham, Lancs. OL1 1EQ
tel 0161-633 2121 *fax* 0161-652 2111
email news@oldham-chronicle.co.uk
website www.oldham-chronicle.co.uk
Editor Jim Williams
Daily Mon–Fri 35p

News and features on current topics and local history.
Length: 1000 words. Illustrations: colour and b&w
photos and line. Payment: £20–£25 per 1000 words;
£16.32–£21.90 for illustrations. Founded 1854.

SCOTLAND

The Courier and Advertiser

D.C. Thomson & Co. Ltd, 80 Kingsway East, Dundee
DD4 8SL
tel (01382) 223131 *fax* (01382) 454590
London office 185 Fleet Street, London EC4A 2HS
tel 020-7400 1030 *fax* 020-7400 1089
website www.thecourier.co.uk
Daily Mon–Sat 38p

Founded 1816 and 1801.

Dundee Evening Telegraph and Post

D.C. Thomson & Co. Ltd, 80 Kingsway East, Dundee
DD4 8SL
tel (01382) 223131 *fax* (01382) 454590
email general@eveningtelegraph.co.uk
London office 185 Fleet Street, London EC4A 2HS
tel 020-7400 1030 *fax* 020-7400 1089
website www.eveningtelegraph.co.uk
Daily Mon–Fri 30p

Evening Express (Aberdeen)

Aberdeen Journals Ltd, PO Box 43, Lang Stracht,
Mastrick, Aberdeen AB15 6DF
tel (01224) 690222 *fax* (01224) 699575

website www.thisisaberdeen.co.uk
Editor Damien Bates
Daily Mon–Sat 36p
  Features Editor Susan Welsh
  News Editor Louise Redvers
  Sports Editor Charlie Allan

Lively evening paper. Illustrations: colour and b&w.
Payment: by arrangement.

Evening News (Edinburgh)
108 Holyrood Road, Edinburgh EH8 8AS
tel 0131-620 8620 *fax* 0131-620 8696
website www.edinburghnews.scotsman.com
Editor John McLellan
Daily Mon–Sat 35p
  Features Editor Gina Davidson
  News Editor Euan McGrory
  Picture Editor Roger Jonathan
  Sports Editor Graham Lindsay

Features on current affairs, preferably in relation to
our circulation area. Women's talking points, local
historical articles; subjects of general interest; health
and beauty, fashion.

Glasgow Evening Times
200 Renfield Street, Glasgow G2 3PR
tel 0141-302 7000 *fax* 0141-302 6600
website www.eveningtimes.co.uk
Editor Donald Martin
Daily Mon–Sat 35p

Founded 1876.

Inverness Courier
New Century House, Stadium Road, Inverness
IV1 1FF
tel (01463) 732222 *fax* (01463) 732273
email editorial@inverness-courier.co.uk
website www.inverness-courier.co.uk
Editor Jim Love
2 p.w. Tue 53p, Fri 63p
  News Editor Robert Taylor
  Sports Editor David Beck

Articles of Highland interest only. Unsolicited
material accepted. Illustrations: colour and b&w
photos. Payment: by arrangement. Founded 1817.

Paisley Daily Express
Scottish and Universal Newspapers Ltd, 14 New
Street, Paisley, Renfrewshire PA1 1YA
tel 0141-887 7911 *fax* 0141-889 7148
website www.insidescotland.co.uk
Editor Gordon Bury
Daily Mon–Sat 40p
  Sports Editor Paul Behan

Articles of Paisley interest only. Considers unsolicited
material.

The Press and Journal
Lang Stracht, Aberdeen AB15 6DF
tel (01224) 690222

email pj.editor@ajl.co.uk
website www.thisisnorthscotland.co.uk
Editor Derek Tucker
Daily Mon–Fri 42p, Sat 45p
  Deputy Editor Richard Neville
  News Editor Andrew Hebden
  Picture Desk Joanna Fraser
  Sports Editor Alex Martin

Contributions of Scottish interest. Payment: by
arrangement. Illustrations: half-tone. Founded 1748.

The Scottish Sun
News International Newspapers, Scotland,
124 Portman Street, Kinning Park, Glasgow G41 1EJ
tel 0141-420 5200 *fax* 0141-420 5248
email thescottish-sun@the-sun.co.uk
Editor David Dinsmore
Daily Mon–Sat 30p
  Features Editor David Reynolds
  News Editor Alan Muir
  Picture Editor Mark Sweeney
  Sports Editor Steve Wolstencroft

Scottish edition of *The Sun*. Illustrations:
transparencies, colour and b&w prints, colour
cartoons. Payment: by arrangement. Founded 1985.

SOUTH EAST

The Argus
Argus House, Crowhurst Road, Hollingbury,
Brighton BN1 8AR
tel (01273) 544544 *fax* (01273) 505703
email news@theargus.co.uk
website www.newsquest.co.uk, www.theargus.co.uk
Editor Michael Beard
Daily Mon–Sat 35p
  Features Editor Jakki Phillips
  News Editor Melanie Dowding

Established 1880.

Echo
Newspaper House, Chester Hall Lane, Basildon, Essex
SS14 3BL
tel (01268) 522792 *fax* (01268) 469281
website www.thisisessex.co.uk/echo
Editor Martin McNeill
Daily Mon–Fri 35p
  Features Editor Sara Taylor
  News Editor Chris Hatton
  Picture Editor Nick Ansell
  Sports Editor Paul Alton

Mostly staff-written. Only interested in local material.
Payment: by arrangement. Founded 1969.

Medway Messenger
Medway House, Ginsbury Close, Sir Thomas Longley
Road, Medway City Estate, Strood, Kent ME2 2DU
tel (01634) 227800 *fax* (01634) 715256

website www.kentonline.co.uk
Mon 40p, Fri 50p
 Senior Editor Bob Dimond
 Community Editor David Jones
 Senior News Editor Sarah Clarke
 Sports Editor Mike Rees
 Business Editor Trevor Sturgess

Paper with emphasis on news and sport from the Medway towns. Illustrations:line, half-tone.

The News, Portsmouth

The News Centre, Hilsea, Portsmouth PO2 9SX
tel 023-9266 4488 *fax* 023-92673363
email newsdesk@thenews.co.uk
website www.thenews.co.uk
Editor Mike Gilson
Daily Mon–Sat 36p
 Features Editor John Millard
 News Editor Colin McNeill
 Picture Editor Dean Kedward
 Sports Editor John Carter

Articles of relevance to southeast Hampshire and West Sussex. Payment by arrangement. Founded 1877.

Oxford Mail

Newspaper House, Osney Mead, Oxford OX2 0EJ
tel (01865) 425262 *fax* (01865) 425554
email nqonews@nqo.com
website www.thisisoxfordshire.co.uk
Editor Simon O'Neill
Daily 33p
 News Editor Jason Collie

Reading Evening Post

8 Tessa Road, Reading, Berks. RG1 8NS
tel 0118-918 3000 *fax* 0118-959 9363
website www.getreading.co.uk
Editor Andy Murrill
Daily Mon–Fri 30p
 Features Editor Jennie Lawrence
 News Editor Lucy Rimmer
 Picture Editor Steve Templeman
 Sports Editor Dave Wright

Topical articles based on current local news. Length: 800–1200 words. Payment: based on lineage rates. Illustrations: half-tone. Founded 1965.

The Southern Daily Echo

Newspaper House, Test Lane, Redbridge, Southampton SO16 9JX
tel 023-8042 4777 *fax* 023-8042 4770
website www.thisishampshire.net
Editor Ian Murray
Daily Mon–Sat 35p
 News Editor Gordon Sutter
 Picture Editor Paul Collins
 Sports Editor Simon Carter
 Supplements Editor Emma Green

News, articles, features, sport. Length: varies. Illustrations: line, half-tone, colour, cartoons. Payment: NUJ rates. Founded 1888.

Swindon Advertiser

100 Victoria Road, Old Town, Swindon SN1 3BE
tel (01793) 528144 *fax* (01793) 542434
email editor@newswilts.co.uk
website www.swindonadvertiser.co.uk
Editor Mark Waldron
Daily Mon–Sat 35p

News and information relating to Swindon and Wiltshire only. Considers unsolicited material. Founded 1854.

SOUTH WEST

The Bath Chronicle

Bath Newspapers, Windsor House, Windsor Bridge, Bath BA2 3AU
tel (01225) 322322 *fax* (01225) 322296
website www.bathchronicle.co.uk
Editor Sam Holliday
Daily Mon–Fri 35p, Sat 40p
 Features Editor Georgette McCready
 News Editor Paul Wiltshire
 Picture Editor Kevin Bates
 Sports Editor Julie Riegal

Welcomes local news and features. Length: 200–500 words. Illustrations: colour photos. Payment: 10p–13p per printed line; £5 per photo. Founded 1760.

Bristol Evening Post

Temple Way, Bristol BS99 7HD
tel 0117-934 3000 *fax* 0117-934 3570
website www.thisisbristol.com
Editor-in-chief Mike Norton
Daily Mon–Sat 35p
 Features Editor David Webb
 News Editor Rob Perkins
 Picture Editor Shaun Thompson
 Sports Editor Chris Spittles

Takes freelance news and articles. Payment: by arrangement. Founded 1932.

The Citizen

1 Clarence Parade, Cheltenham GL50 3NY
tel (01242) 271900 *fax* (01242) 271848
website www.nng.co.uk
Editor Ian Mean
Daily Mon–Fri 35p, Sat 40p

Local news and features for Gloucester and its districts. Length: 1000 words (articles/features), 300 words (news). Illustrations: colour. Payment: negotiable.

Daily Echo

Richmond Hill, Bournemouth BH2 6HH
tel (01202) 554601 *fax* (01202) 292115

The Standen
Literary Agency

The Standen Literary Agency is a dynamic agency based in London, we are looking for new and exciting talent. Therefore, we are particularly interested in submissions from first time writers.

We are interested in adult and children's works of fiction.

For further information see our listing under Agents or visit:
www.standenliteraryagency.com

WY2007/WR31/f

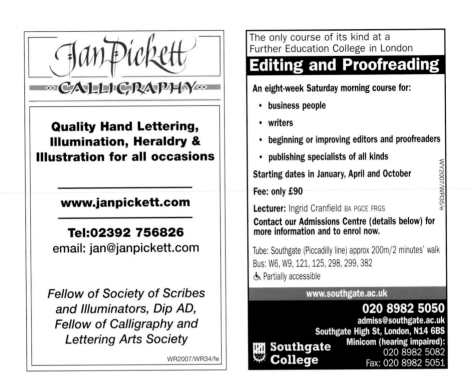

MA Creative Writing

This is one of the most successful MA writing courses in the country. It is also one of the very few to offer individual tutorial support from experienced professional writers right up to completion of a novel, script, poetry or short stories collection.

You can choose from options including • novel • poetry • script • literary editing • short story.

The Masterclass programme offers opportunities to meet writers, publishers and agents.

'I found the MA Writing at Hallam enormously stimulating - both intellectually and creatively. And it helped me to get my first novel published.'

Marina Lewycka, graduate and author of bestseller, *'A Short History of Tractors in Ukranian'*

MA English Studies

You can choose a general or specialist route from options including
  • Children's literature • Romantic literature
  • Renaissance literature • English language
  • Contemporary and modern literature

Arts and Humanities Research Council studentships may be available.

Application forms are available from Postgraduate Office, Sheffield Hallam University, Faculty of Development and Society, Collegiate Campus, Sheffield S1 1WB
Tel: 0114 225 5555.

www.shu.ac.uk/cultural/english/index.html

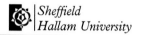 *Sheffield Hallam University*

WY2007/WR40/e

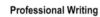

email newsdesk@bournemouthecho.co.uk
website www.thisisbournemouth.co.uk
Editor Neal Butterworth
Daily Mon–Sat 35p
  News Editor Andy Martin
  Features Editor Kevin Nash

Established 1900.

Dorset Echo
Newscom, Fleet House, Hampshire Road,
Weymouth, Dorset DT4 9XD
tel (01305) 830930 *fax* (01305) 830956
email newsdesk@dorsetecho.co.uk
website www.dorsetecho.co.uk
Editor David Murdock
Daily Mon–Fri 32p, Sat 40p
  Features Editor Diarmuid Macdonigh
  News Editor Paul Thomas
  Picture Editor Finnbar Webster
  Sports Editor Paul Baker

News and occasional features (1000–2000 words).
Illustrations: b&w photos. Payment: by negotiation.
Founded 1921.

Evening Herald
17 Brest Road, Derriford Business Park, Plymouth,
Devon PL6 5AA
tel (01752) 765529 *fax* (01752) 765527
email news@eveningherald.co.uk
website www.thisisplymouth.co.uk
Editor Bill Martin
Daily Mon–Sat 34p

Local news, articles and features. Will consider
unsolicited material. Welcomes ideas for articles and
features. Illustrations: colour and b&w prints.

Express & Echo
Express & Echo Publications Ltd, Heron Road,
Sowton, Exeter EX2 7NF
tel (01392) 442211 *fax* (01392) 442294/442287
website www.thisisexeter.co.uk
Editor Marc Astley
Daily Mon–Sat 33p
  Head of Content Sue Kemp
  Picture Editor James Millar
  Sports Editor Richard Davies

Features and news of local interest. Length: 500–800
words (features), up to 400 words (news).
Illustrations: colour. Payment: lineage rates;
illustrations negotiable. Founded 1904.

Gloucestershire Echo
1 Clarence Parade, Cheltenham, Glos. GL50 3NY
tel (01242) 271900 *fax* (01242) 271803
email editor@glosecho.co.uk
website www.thisisgloucestershire.co.uk
Editor Anita Syvret
Daily Mon–Fri 35p, Sat 40p

Specialist articles with Gloucestershire connections;
no fiction. Material mostly commissioned. Length:

350 words. Payment: £30 per article, negotiable.
Founded 1873.

Herald Express
Harmsworth House, Barton Hill Road, Torquay,
Devon TQ2 8JN
tel (01803) 676000
website www.thisissouthdevon.co.uk
Editor Brendan Hanrahan
Daily Mon–Sat 35p

Sunday Independent
The Sunday Independent Newspapers Ltd, Webbs
House, Tindle Suite, Liskeard, Cornwall PU4 6AH
tel (01579) 342174 *fax* (01579) 341851
website www.thisisplymouth.co.uk
Editor John Noble
Sun 80p

News features on West Country topics; features/
articles with a nostalgic theme; short quirky news
briefs (must be original). Length: 600 words
(features/articles), 300 words (news). Illustrations:
colour, b&w. Payment: by arrangement. Founded
1808.

Western Daily Press
Bristol Evening Post and Press Ltd, Temple Way,
Bristol BS99 7HD
tel 0117-934 3000 *fax* 0117-934 3574
website www.westpress.co.uk
Editor Andy Wright
Daily Mon–Fri 40p, Sat 55p

National, international or West Country topics for
features or news items, from established journalists,
with or without illustrations. Payment: by
negotiation. Founded 1858.

The Western Morning News
17 Brest Road, Derriford, Plymouth PL6 5AA
tel (01752) 765500 *fax* (01752) 765535
website www.westernmorningnews.co.uk
Editor-in-chief Alan Qualtrough
Daily Mon–Fri 40p, Sat 60p
  News Editor Steve Grant
  Picture Editor Michael Cranmer
  Sports Editor Mark Stevens

Articles plus illustrations considered on West
Country subjects. Founded 1860.

WALES

South Wales Argus
South Wales Argus, Cardiff Road, Maesglas,
Newport, Gwent NP20 3QN
tel (01633) 777219 *fax* (01633) 777202
Editor Gerry Keighley
Daily Mon–Sat 38p

News and features of relevance to Gwent. Length:
500–600 words (features); 350 words (news).

Illustrations: colour prints and transparencies.
Payment: £30 (features), £20 (news) per item;
£20–£25 (photos). Founded 1892.

South Wales Echo
Thomson House, Havelock Street, Cardiff CF10 1XR
tel 029-2058 3622/20223333 *fax* 029-2058 3624
email echo.newsdesk@wme.co.uk
website www.icwales.co.uk
Editor Richard Williams
Daily Mon–Sat 34p

Evening paper: news, sport, features, showbiz, news
features, personality interviews. Length: up to 700
words. Illustrations: photos, cartoons. Payment: by
negotiation. Founded 1884.

South Wales Evening Post
PO Box 14, Adelaide Street, Swansea SA1 1QT
tel (01792) 51000 *fax* (01792) 514697
email postbox@swwp.co.uk
website www.thisissouthwales.co.uk
Editor-in-Chief Spencer Feeney
Daily 36p
  News Editor Peter Slee
  Sports Editor David Evans

The Western Mail
Thomson House, Havelock Street, Cardiff CF10 1XR
tel 029-2058 3583 *fax* 029-2058 3652
website www.icwales.co.uk
Editor Alan Edmunds
Daily Mon–Fri 40p, Sat 50p

Articles of political, industrial, literary or general and
Welsh interest are considered. Illustrations: topical
general news and feature pictures, cartoons. Payment:
according to value; special fees for exclusive news.
Founded 1869.

WEST MIDLANDS

Birmingham Mail
Weaman Street, Birmingham B4 6AY
tel 0121-236 3366 *fax* 0121-233 0271
London office 1 Canada Square, Canary Wharf,
London E14 5AP
tel 020-7293 3000 *fax* 020-7293 3793
website www.icbirmingham.co.uk
Editor Steve Dyson
Daily Mon–Sat 40p
  Deputy Editor Ray Dunn
  Features Editor (acting) Paul Fulford

Features of topical Midland interest considered.
Length: 400–800 words. Payment: by arrangement.
Founded 1870.

The Birmingham Post
Weaman Street, Birmingham B4 6AT
tel 0121-236 3366 *fax* 0121-625 1105

London office 22nd Floor, 1 Canada Square, Canary
Wharf, London E14 5AP
tel 020-7293 3455 *fax* 020-7293 3400
website www.go2birmingham.co.uk
Editor Mark Reeves
Daily Mon–Sat 60p
  Assistant Editor (Content) Ellen Campbell
  Assistant Editor (Production) Mike Hughes
  News Editor Mo Ilyas
  Picture Editor Simon Hadley
  Head of Sport Barry Kinghorn

Authoritative and well-written articles of industrial,
political or general interest are considered, especially
if they have relevance to the Midlands. Length: up to
1000 words. Payment: by arrangement.

Coventry Evening Telegraph
Corporation Street, Coventry CV1 1FP
tel 024-7663 3633 *fax* 024-7655 0869
website www.go2coventry.co.uk
Editor Alan Kirby
Daily Mon–Sat 38p

Topical, illustrated articles with a Coventry or
Warwickshire interest. Length: up to 600 words.
Payment: by arrangement.

Express & Star
Queen Street, Wolverhampton WV1 1ES
tel (01902) 313131 *fax* (01902) 319721
email editor@expressandstar.co.uk
London office Room 7, Press Gallery, House of
Commons, London SW1A 0AA
website www.expressandstar.com
Editor Adrian Faber
Daily Mon–Sat 35p
  Head of Features Jim Walsh
  Head of News Mark Drew
  Head of Pictures Tony Adams
  Sports Editor Tim Walters
Founded 1874.

The Sentinel
Staffordshire Sentinel Newspapers Ltd, Sentinel
House, Etruria, Stoke-on-Trent ST1 5SS
tel (01782) 602525 *fax* (01782) 602616
email editor@thesentinel.co.uk
website www.thisisthesentinel.co.uk
Editor Michael Sassi
Daily Mon–Sat 30p, Sun 50p
  Features Editor Charlotte Littlejones
  Business Correspondent David Elks
  News Editor Rob Cotterill
  Picture Editor Martin Elliott
  Senior Assistant Editor Paul Dutton
  Sports Editor Keith Wales

Articles and features of topical interest to the north
Staffordshire/south Cheshire area. Illustrations:
colour and b&w. Payment: by arrangement. Founded
1873.

Shropshire Star

Ketley, Telford TF1 5HU
tel (01952) 242424 *fax* (01952) 254605
website www.shropshirestar.com
Editor Sarah Jane Smith
Daily Mon–Sat 35p
  News Editor John Simcock
  Picture Editor Paul Morstatt-Higgs
  Sports Editor Keith Harrison
  Supplements Dept Sharon Walters

Evening paper: news and features. No unsolicited material; write to features editor with outline of ideas. Payment: by arrangement. Founded 1964.

Sunday Mercury

Weaman Street, Birmingham B4 6AT
tel 0121-236 3366 *fax* 0121-233 3958
website www.go2birmingham.co.uk
Editor David Brookes
Sun 80p
  Deptuy Editor Paul Cole
  Assistant Editor Tony Larner
  Picture Editor Adam Fradgley
  Sports Editor Lee Gibson

News specials or features of Midland interest. Illustrations: colour, b&w, cartoons. Payment: special rates for special matter.

Worcester News

Berrows House, Hylton Road, Worcester WR2 5JX
tel (01905) 742244 *fax* (01905) 742277
email sg@thisisworcester.co.uk
website www.thisisworcester.co.uk
Editor Stewart Gilbert
Daily Mon–Sat 30p

Local and national news, sport and features. Will consider unsolicited material. Welcomes ideas for articles and features. Length: 800 words (features), 300 words (news). Payment: £50 (features), £35 (news). Illustrations: colour prints.

YORKSHIRE/HUMBERSIDE

Evening Courier

PO Box 19, King Cross Street, Halifax HX1 2SF
tel (01422) 260200 *fax* (01422) 260341
email editor@halifaxcourier.co.uk
website www.halifaxcourier.co.uk
Editor John Furbisher
Daily Mon–Sat 37p
  News Editor John Kenealy
  Sports Editor Ian Rushworth

Articles of local interest and background to news events. Length: up to 500 words. Illustrations: colour photos. Payment: £25–£40 per article; photos per quality/size used. Founded 1832.

Evening News

17–23 Aberdeen Walk, Scarborough, North Yorkshire YO11 1BB
tel (01723) 363636 *fax* (01723) 383825
website www.scarborougheveningnews.co.uk
Editor Ed Asquith
Mon–Sat 27p
  Deputy Editor Sue Wilkinson
  News Editor Neil Pickford
  Sports Editor Charles Place

Evening Press

York and County Press, PO Box 29, 76–86 Walmgate, York YO1 9YN
tel (01904) 653051 *fax* (01904) 612853
email newsdesk@ycp.co.uk
website www.thisisyork.co.uk
Editor Kevin Booth
Daily Mon–Sat 38p
  Deputy Editor Bill Hearld
  Assistant Editor Francine Clee
  News Editor Scott Armstrong
  Picture Editor Martin Oates
  Sports Editor Martin Jarred

Articles of North and East Yorkshire interest, humour, personal experience of current affairs. Length: 500–1000 words. Payment: by arrangement. Illustrations: line, half-tone. Founded 1882.

Grimsby Telegraph

80 Cleethorpe Road, Grimsby, North East Lincolnshire DN31 3EH
tel (01472) 360360 *fax* (01472) 372257
email newsdesk@grimsbytelegraph.co.uk
website www.thisisgrimsby.co.uk
Editor Michelle Lalor
Daily Mon–Sat 32p
  Business & News Editor David Laister
  Features Editor Barrie Farnsworth
  Sports Editor Geoff Ford

Considers general interest articles. Illustrations: line, half-tone, colour, cartoons. Payment: by arrangement. Founded 1897.

The Huddersfield Daily Examiner

Trinity Mirror Huddersfield Ltd, PO Box A26, Queen Street South, Huddersfield HD1 2TD
tel (01484) 430000 *fax* (01484) 437789
email editor@examiner.co.uk
website www.examiner.co.uk
Editor Roy Wright
Daily Mon–Sat 40p
  Assistant Editor Mike O'Connell
  Features Editor Andrew Flynn
  Head of Content Jenny Parkin
  News Editor Neil Atkinson

No contributions required at present. Founded 1871.

Hull Daily Mail

Blundell's Corner, Beverley Road, Hull HU3 1XS
tel (01482) 327111 *fax* (01482) 315353
website www.thisishullandeastriding.co.uk
Editor John Meehan
Daily Mon–Sat 30p
  Features Editor Paul Johnson

Lincolnshire Echo

Brayford Wharf East, Lincoln LN5 7AT
tel (01522) 820000 *fax* (01522) 804491
website www.thisislincolnshire.co.uk
Editor Jon Grubb
Daily Mon–Sat 32p

Sheffield Star

York Street, Sheffield S1 1PU
tel 0114-276 7676 *fax* 0114-272 5978
website www.sheffieldtoday.net
Editor Alan Powell
Daily Mon–Sat 32p
  Features Editor John Highfield
  News Editor Charles Smith
  Picture Editor Dennis Lound
  Sports Editor Bob Westerdale

Well-written articles of local character. Length: about 500 words. Payment: by negotiation. Illustrations: topical photos, line drawings, graphics, cartoons. Founded 1887.

Telegraph & Argus

Hall Ings, Bradford, West Yorkshire BD1 1JR
tel (01274) 729511 *fax* (01274) 723634
email bradford.editorial@bradford.newsquest.co.uk
website www.thisisbradford.co.uk
Editor Perry Austin-Clarke
Daily Mon–Sat 38p
  Head of News Martin Heminway
  Assistant Editor (sport & pictures) Simon Waites

  Features Editor David Barnett
  Sports Editor Blake Richardson

Evening paper: news, articles and features relevant to or about the people of West Yorkshire. Length: up to 1000 words. Illustrations: line, half-tone, colour. Payment: features from £15; line from £5, b&w and colour photos by negotiation. Founded 1868.

Yorkshire Evening Post

PO Box 168, Wellington Street, Leeds LS1 1RF
tel 0113-2432701 *fax* 0113-2388535
website www.ypn.co.uk
Editor Paul Napier
Daily Mon–Sat 32p
  Features Editor Anne Pickles
  News Editor Gillian Haworth
  Picture Editor Andy Manning
  Sports Editor Phil Rostron

News stories and feature articles. Illustrations: colour and b&w, cartoons. Payment: by negotiation. Founded 1890.

Yorkshire Post

Wellington Street, Leeds LS1 1RF
tel 0113-243 2701 *fax* 0113-238 8537
London office St Martin's House, 16 St Martin's le Grand, London EC1A 4EN
tel 020-7397 8723
website www.yorkshireposttoday.co.uk
Editor Peter Charlton
Daily Mon–Fri 42p, Sat 65p
Supplements **Yorkshire Post Magazine**
  Deputy Editor Duncan Hamilton
  Acting Picture Editor Mike Cowling
  Sports Editor Matt Reeder

Authoritative and well-written articles on topical subjects of general, literary or industrial interests. Length: max. 1200 words. Payment: by arrangement. Founded 1754.

Writing for magazines

Richard Keeble explains the different types of features that magazines run and offers advice to freelance writers on how to approach writing for magazines.

There are well over 8000 mainstream magazines published in Britain – and many hundreds of alternative publications. Research suggests that weekly consumer magazines are read by 39% of adults and monthlies by 48%. Yet while there appears to be an enormous variety of publications, the sector is dominated by just two companies: IPC and EMAP. IPC was sold by Reed Elsevier to Cinven, an investment company, in January 1998 for £860 million and then to AOL Time Warner for £1.3 billion in August 2001. Magazine publishing is clearly big business!

The differing genres

Freelancing for magazines will normally involve writing features. So it's important from the outset to have a clear idea about the different journalistic genres. Each will have its own writing style, research strategy, tone, and place in the publication. Here is a selection of the genres you might expect to find in a representative range of magazines.

Hard news

Hard news has the highest status in newspapers and tends to be on the front pages, while magazines may have an opening section carrying hard news. Hard news features usually open with the most striking details and the information given subsequently is generally of lesser importance. Some background details may be needed to make the news intelligible but description, analysis, comment and the subjective 'I' of the reporter are either excluded or included only briefly.

Soft news

Here the news element is strong and prominent at or near the opening but is treated in a lighter way. Largely based on factual information and quotations, the writing is nonetheless more colourful, with an emphasis on description and comment. The tone, established in the intro (opening) section, may be witty or ironic. The separation of hard and soft news emerged in the second half of the nineteenth century: the first, linked to notions of accuracy, objectivity, neutrality, was used for transmitting information; the second was more an entertainment genre. Magazine opening sections usually adopt this softer approach to news.

News features

A news feature is usually longer than a straight news story. The news angle is prominent, though not necessarily in the opening section, and quotes again are important. It can contain analysis, comment, descriptions, historical background detail, eye-witness reporting and deeper coverage of the issues and the range of sources.

Timeless features

These have no specific news angle; the special interest is provided by the subject or sources. For example, such a feature could explore young people's experiences of dealing with sexually transmitted diseases or coming out in terms of sexual orientation.

Backgrounder/preview/curtain-raiser features

Here the emphasis is not so much on reporting the news as on explaining it, or setting the scene for an event about to happen. For instance, if a major anti-globalisation demonstration is planned for mid-July, that month's magazine (produced well in advance) might carry a feature highlighting the historical background, the arguments of the protestors, the range of voices expected on the march, the hopes of the organisers and the predicted turn-out, and so on. A retrospective is a similar feature looking back on an event.

Colour features

These concentrate on descriptive, eye-witness reporting, quotations and the build-up of factual details. They need not have a strong news angle. You may visit Highgate cemetery and describe (for a travel or tourist magazine) your experience of walking through it and talking to people. What do they think of Karl Marx, who is buried there?

Eye-witness news features

These are based on your observations of a newsy event, incorporating such elements as description, conversations, interviews, analysis and comment. You may accompany a rock star for a week as they tour the country and describe the experience for a rock magazine.

Profiles (sometimes called interviews)

These are portraits in words, usually based on interviews with the subject and sometimes also with their friends, critics, relations, work colleagues, etc.

Reviews

Reviews include descriptions and assessments of works of art, television programmes, exhibitions, books, theatre shows, CDs, rock gigs and so on.

Lifestyle features

Lifestyle features include advice columns (such as on health or education matters, gardening or computer problems).

Comment pieces

If you have an original voice, confidence in your personal writing style and a wide range of interests, then you might well aim to become a columnist. Editorials, on the other hand, reflect the institutional voice of the publication and are rarely written by freelances.

Getting ideas

You must be immersed in your specialist area, regularly reading and building up cuttings files from the relevant publications, websites, press releases, newsletters of pressure groups, etc. You will need to generate a network of contacts at public events, informal social gatherings, conferences, press launches. And ideas will emerge from conversations with friends and family. Remember your best resources are your own experiences. You have a teenage son who is showing no interest in politics; you could then plan a feature looking at the broader picture, talking to teachers, the youngsters themselves, other parents and political commentators. After 20 years in the same rat-race job you (your family, four dogs and three cats) are quitting to live simply in a remote cottage in Northumbria; so why not write about it?

Developing magazine feature ideas from news reports needs a special imaginative flair. A report from a university media monitoring unit criticises the increasing intrusiveness of the paparazzi photographers. A daily or weekly newspaper (working to relatively short deadlines) will follow up the report, interviewing editors and photographers and placing the current controversy in its historical context. A magazine writer, on the other hand, will have the luxury of a slightly longer deadline – and this throws up opportunities. You could spend a week on the back of a paparazzi's motorbike zooming about the streets of London and describe the experience, the feelings of the photographer and the people they shoot. The feature could involve eye-witness descriptions, dialogue, factual details: as you describe your movements around London so your copy is given extra movement and colour.

The ethical/political challenge

Always be aware of the ethical/political dilemmas stories can throw up. You are planning a vox pop (a collection of snappy quotes usually accompanied by photographs) about the work of paparazzi photographers: think about the range of people to be shown, in terms of race, gender, age and authority. If someone will speak to you only 'off the record' what do you do? How important is it for your feature to present a balancing range of views? One of your sources is an outspoken racist or sexist: how do you deal with their quotes? And so on.

The feature package

It's often best to think in terms of producing not just one single article (of say 2500 words) but a package of contrasting features. These will have different lengths and tones and will provide the sub-editor with material for a more interesting layout. Thus the paparazzi package might contain the main eye-witness, participatory feature (1200 words), a background piece outlining the history of the paparazzi and taking in their alleged role in the death of Princess Diana and the ensuing controversy (700 words) and a profile of a prominent photographer who argues strongly for (or against) legislation to restrain intrusive photographers (600 words).

The structure of the feature

The opening section

Most features do not start with the traditional five Ws (who, what, where, when, why) and the H (how) of the hard news opening section. The writing can be more flexible – but there is still an urgency needed in the copy to attract the attention of the reader. One of the most popular devices for helping the reader understand a complex event or issue is to begin by focusing on the experience or views of an individual. You are writing a piece about poverty on a bleak housing estate in Manchester, so you focus on the plight of an elderly woman, shivering in her unheated semi and terrified of the yobs who have raided her home three times over the last year and thrown fireworks through her letterbox.

According to the convention in the UK, most news stories don't begin with direct quotations. But features – and in particular profiles – often do. Quotes are useful because they can be colourful, succinct, and convey a lot about the personality of the person quoted. Thus a feature about 'flexploitation' (as employers are increasingly using flexi-time working arrangements to extend their exploitation of white-collar staff) could begin: 'We all sit in rows now. You log in and log out – even for your 20-minute lunch break. It's more like clocking in at a factory.'

The 'I' of the reporter is only rarely prominent in news intros. But the tone of magazine features (and not just those by regular columnists) can be far more personal, idiosyncratic, even witty. A feature exploring an issue such as fox-hunting, or debt in the developing world, can open with your views; an intro section for a piece about hairdressing can focus on a recent bad experience; and so on. Similarly, while news reports hardly ever begin with a question, features often do. Thus a feature about the boom in ski-ing in the Alps in the New Year could start: 'Have you tried to secure your travel ticket for the Alps yet?'

The body of the text

While colour, description, opinion, analysis, narrative, quotes, dialogue and historical context may be important in features, they are all still built on the cement of factual or emotional accuracy and a clear sense of structure. Just as in news stories the most important information comes first, with the less important details thereafter, so the body of the feature text is usually intended to expand on an opening section. At the same time, the writing styles of magazine features can be far more colourful. Emotional tones (angry, witty, ironic, condemnatory, adulatory) can vary along with textual rhythms. Indeed, before launching into your writing, as well as planning the structure, it is crucial to identify the emotional core of the piece. Try always to be as authentic as possible (within the constraints of the editorial policy of your target publication).

The closing section

A hard news story carries information in the order of its news value. The last paragraph is the least important and can be cut without destroying the overall impact. Features can be different, with the final section carrying its own, crucial significance. One feature may explore a range of views or experiences and conclude by passing a comment on them; another may argue a case and come to a conclusion in the final section. The final paragraph may raise a pointed question, contain a striking direct quote, summarise an argument or look ahead to a possible future.

Pitching ideas

You can choose to write or phone in your idea to a commissioning editor. There is no hard rule here. But even after you have spoken to an editor, they may well want you to spell out the idea by fax, letter or email. Make sure the grammar, spelling, facts, and punctuation in your proposal (as in your copy) are spot on. And don't be tempted to spell out the idea at length. The essential idea should be summarised in one paragraph at most: 'With Martin Scorsese's *Gangs of New York* due to be released in two months, my 1200-word feature will look critically at the way in which Hollywood has represented street gangs in the past.' Don't be vague. Don't say: 'I propose a feature about prostitution in inner cities.' Rather: 'A report published this week has highlighted the rise of prostitution in inner cities. To what extend are students (both male and female) funding their studies through prostitution?'

Dangers

Publications may steal your ideas and give them to someone else to follow up. And the freelance has absolutely no protection in law against this kind of theft. While written work can be copyrighted, ideas can occur to two people at the same time. One solution is to provide only a bare minimum of background details before the idea is accepted. Personal contact with the commissioning editor also helps create mutual trust and confidence. The best solution is to prove your abilities to the publication with a series of stories, sent on spec or to commission, so they will be concerned not to lose your work to other competitors. Make sure you have a copy of all submitted work. If it is rejected you may want to rework it with some new angles/quotes for a different publication. And be persistent: remember that *Gone with the Wind* was rejected 25 times before it was published.

Payment

How much should you expect to be paid? Well, theNational Union of Journalists draws up a regularly updated list of minimum freelance rates which will give you some idea of what to expect. And remember that if you are a self-employed freelance you own the copyright to your work. This does not mean refusing further use of the material: you can license it, giving permission for a specific use for an agreed fee. Whatever freelancing you end up doing, enjoy the ethical, political, writing challenges. It's not easy but the personal rewards can be substantial. Good luck!

Richard Keeble is Professor of Journalism at Lincoln University. He has feelanced for a range of publications including *Tribune*, *Press Gazette*, *Peace News*, the *Journalist* and MediaLens.org

Further reading

Atton, Chris, *Alternative Media*, Sage, 2002

Glover, Stephen (ed.), *The Penguin Book of Journalism*, Penguin, 1999

Hennessy, Brendan, *Writing Feature Articles*, Focal Press, 4th edn 2006

Hicks, Wynford, with Harriett Gilbert and Sally Adams, *Writing for Journalists*, Routledge, 1999

McKay, Jenny, *The Magazines Handbook*, Routledge, 2nd edn 2005

Willings Press Guide, Media Information Ltd, annual

Magazines UK and Ireland

Listings for regional newspapers start on page 16 and listings for national newspapers start on page 7. For quick reference, magazines are listed by subject area starting on page 751.

Accountancy
145 London Road, Kingston-upon-Thames, Surrey KT2 6SR
tel 020-8247 1419 *fax* 020-8247 1424
email accountancynews@cch.co.uk
website www.accountancymagazine.com
Editor Chris Quick
Monthly £71.70 p.a.

Articles on accounting, taxation, financial, legal and other subjects likely to be of professional interest to accountants in practice or industry, and to top management generally. Founded 1889.

Accountancy Age
VNU Business Publications, VNU House, 32–34 Broadwick Street, London W1A 2HG
tel 020-7316 9236 *fax* 020-7316 9250
email accountancy_age@vnu.co.uk
website www.accountancyage.com
Editor Gavin Hinks
Weekly £2 (£100 p.a.)

Articles of accounting, financial and business interest. Illustrations: colour photos; freelance assignments commissioned. Payment: by arrangement. Founded 1969.

Accounting & Business
Association of Chartered Certified Accountants, 10–11 Lincolns Inn Fields, London WC2A 3BP
tel 020-7059 5966 *fax* 020-7059 5982
email john.prosser@accaglobal.com
website www.accaglobal.com
Editor John Rogers Prosser
10 p.a. £85 p.a.

Journal of the Association of Chartered Certified Accountants. Accountancy, finance and business topics of relevance to accountants and finance directors. Length: 1300 words. Payment: £150 per 1000 words. Illustrated. Founded 1998.

Active Life
Zuru Media Ltd, Chapel Farm Business Park, Cwmcarn, Newport NT11 7ZB
tel (01495) 272920
website www.activelifemag.com
Editor Gill Williams
Monthly £1.95

Lifestyle advice for the over 50s, including holidays and health, fashion and food, finance and fiction, hobbies and home, personality profiles. Submit ideas in writing. Length: 600–1200 words. Illustrations:

colour. Payment: £100 per 1000 words; photos by negotiation. Founded 1989.

Acumen
6 The Mount, Higher Furzeham, Brixham, South Devon TQ5 8QY
tel (01803) 851098
email patricia@acumen-poetry.co.uk
website www.acumen-poetry.co.uk
Editor Patricia Oxley
3 p.a. (Jan/May/Sept) £13 p.a.

Poetry, literary and critical articles, reviews, literary memoirs, etc. Send sae with submissions. Payment: small. Founded 1985.

Aeroplane Monthly
IPC Media Ltd, King's Reach Tower, Stamford Street, London SE1 9LS
tel 020-7261 5849 *fax* 020-7261 5269
email aeroplane_monthly@ipcmedia.com
website www.aeroplanemonthly.com
Editor Michael Oakey
Monthly £3.65

Articles and photos relating to historical aviation. Length: up to 3000 words. Illustrations: line, half-tone, colour, cartoons. Payment: £60 per 1000 words, payable on publication; photos £10–£40; colour £80 per page. Founded 1973.

Africa Confidential
Blackwell Publishers Ltd, 73 Farringdon Road, London EC1M 3JQ
tel 020-7831 3511 *fax* 020-7831 6778
website www.africa-confidential.com
Editor Patrick Smith
Fortnightly £96 p.a. students, £422 p.a. institutions

News and analysis of political and economic developments in Africa. Unsolicited contributions welcomed, but must be exclusive and not published elsewhere. Length: 1200-word features, 200-word pointers. Payment: from £200 per 1000 words. No illustrations. Founded 1960.

Africa: St Patrick's Missions
St Patrick's, Kiltegan, Co. Wicklow, Republic of Ireland
tel (059) 6473600 *fax* (059) 6473622
email africa@spms.org
website www.spms.org
Editors Rev. John Carroll, Rev. Martin Smith
9 p.a. £8 p.a. (€10)

Articles of missionary and topical religious interest. Length: up to 1000 words. Illustrations: line, half-tone, colour.

African Business

IC Publications Ltd, 7 Coldbath Square, London
EC1R 4LQ
tel 020-7713 7711 *fax* 020-7713 7898
email icpubs@africasia.com, a.versi@africasia.com
website www.africasia.com
Editor Anver Versi
Monthly £2.50

Articles on business, economic and financial topics of
interest to businessmen, ministers, officials concerned
with African affairs. Length: 400–750 words; shorter
coverage 100–400 words. Illustrations: line, half-tone,
cartoons. Payment: £80 per 1000 words; £1 per
column cm for illustrations. Founded 1978.

Agenda

The Wheelwrights, Fletching Street, Mayfield, East
Sussex TN20 6TL
tel/fax (01435) 873703
email editor@agendapoetry.co.uk
website www.agendapoetry.co.uk
Editor Patricia McCarthy
Quarterly £28 p.a. (£35 p.a. libraries, institutions and
overseas); £22 OAPs/students

Poetry and criticism. Study the journal before
submitting MSS with an sae, or by email. Include
email address and a brief biography. Young poets and
artists aged 16–38 are invited to submit work for
online Broadsheets Workshop; details online.

Air International

Key Publishing Ltd, PO Box 100, Stamford, Lincs.
PE9 1XQ
tel (01780) 755131 *fax* (01780) 757261
email malcolm.english@keypublishing.com
Editor Malcolm English
Monthly £3.60

Technical articles on aircraft; features on topical
aviation subjects – civil and military. Length: up to
3000 words. Illustrations: colour transparencies/
prints, b&w prints/line drawings. Payment: £50 per
1000 words or by negotiation; £20 colour, £10 b&w.
Founded 1971.

All Out Cricket

The Brit Oval, Kennington, London SE11 5SS
tel 020-7820 4190
email matt@alloutcricket.co.uk
website www.alloutcricket.co.uk
Editor Andy Afford
10 p.a. £3.50

Magazine of the Professional Cricketers' Association.
Humour, insight, expert commentary interviews,
photography and lifestyle. Email editor with ideas
first. Payment by negotiation. Founded 2004.

Amateur Gardening

IPC Media Ltd, Westover House, West Quay Road,
Poole, Dorset BH15 1JG
tel (01202) 440840 *fax* (01202) 440860
email amateurgardening@ipcmedia.com
website www.ipcmedia.com
Editor Tim Rumball
Weekly £1.50

Topical, practical or newsy articles up to 1200 words
of interest to keen gardeners. Payment: by
arrangement. Illustrations: colour. Founded 1884.

Amateur Photographer

(incorporating Photo Technique)
IPC Magazines Ltd, King's Reach Tower, Stamford
Street, London SE1 9LS
tel 020-7261 5100 *fax* 020-7261 5404
email amateurphotographer@ipcmedia.com
Editor Garry Coward-Williams
Weekly £2.10

Editorial submissions are not encouraged. Founded
1884.

Amateur Stage

Platform Publications Ltd, Hampden House,
2 Weymouth Street, London W1W 5BT
tel 020-7636 4343 *fax* 020-7636 2323
email cvtheatre@aol.com
website www.amdram.org.uk/amstagel.htm
Editor Charles Vance
Monthly £2.40

Articles on all aspects of the amateur theatre,
preferably practical and factual. Length: 600–2000
words. Illustrations: photos, line drawings. Payment:
none. Founded 1946.

Ambit

17 Priory Gardens, London N6 5QY
tel 020-8340 3566
website ambitmagazine.co.uk
Editor Martin Bax, *Poetry Editors* Henry Graham,
Carol-Ann Duffy, *Prose Editors* J.G. Ballard, Geoff
Nicholson, *Art Editor* Mike Foreman, *Assistant Editor*
Kate Pemberton
Quarterly £6.50 inc. p&p (£25 p.a. UK, £27/€48
Europe, £29/$56 rest of world; £36 p.a., £38/€64 p.a.,
£40/$73 p.a. institutions)

Poetry, short fiction, art, poetry reviews. New and
established writers and artists. Payment: by
arrangement. Illustrations: line, half-tone, colour.
Founded 1959.

AN Magazine

AN: The Artists Information Company, 1st Floor,
7–15 Pink Lane, Newcastle upon Tyne NE1 5DW
tel 0191-241 8000 *fax* 0191-241 8001
email edit@a-n.co.uk
website www.a-n.co.uk
Contact Editorial Team
Monthly £4.45 (£30 p.a. artists, £53 p.a.
organisations)

Articles, news and features for visual and applied
artists and arts professionals. Illustrations:

transparencies and digital images. Payment: £130 per 1000 words. Founded as *Artists Newsletter* in 1980.

Angler's Mail

IPC Media Ltd, King's Reach Tower, Stamford Street, London SE1 9LS
tel 020-7261 5778 *fax* 020-7261 6016
website www.anglersmail.com
Editor Tim Knight, *Features Editor* Richard Howard
Weekly £1.30

News items about coarse and sea fishing. Payment: by agreement.

Angling Times

EMAP Active, Bushfield House, Orton Centre, Peterborough PE2 5UW
tel (01733) 232600 *fax* (01733) 465844
email richard.lee@emap.com
website www.anglingtimes.co.uk
Editor Richard Lee
Weekly £1.40

Articles, pictures, news stories, on all forms of angling. Illustrations: line, half-tone, colour. Payment: by arrangement. Founded 1953.

Antiques & Collectables

Merricks Media Ltd, 3–4 Riverside Court, Lower Bristol Road, Bath BA2 3DZ
tel (01225) 786800 *fax* (01225) 786801
email sarah.seamarks@merricksmedia.co.uk
website www.antiques-collectables.co.uk
Editor Sarah Seamarks
Monthly £2.95

Features on ceramics, furniture, glass, memorabilia, ephemera, etc aimed at the antiques trade and general collectors. Includes price guide and news. Write with idea in the first instance. Length: 1500–2000 (features). Illustrations: transparencies and colour prints. Payment £100–£150. Founded 1998.

Apollo

20 Theobalds Road, London WC1X 8PF
email editorial@apollomag.com
website www.apollo-magazine.com
Editor Michael Hall
Monthly £4.95

Scholarly articles of about 3000 words on art, architecture, ceramics, photography, furniture, armour, glass, sculpture, and any subject connected with art and collecting. Exhibition and book reviews, articles on current developments in museums and art galleries, regular columns and shorter news items on the art market and contemporary art. Payment: by arrangement. Illustrations: colour. Founded 1925.

Aquila

New Leaf Publishing Ltd, PO Box 2518, Eastbourne, East Sussex BN21 2BB
tel (01323) 431313 *fax* (01323) 731136
email info@aquila.co.uk
website www.aquila.co.uk
Editor Jackie Berry
Monthly £35 p.a.

Dedicated to encouraging children aged 8–13 to reason and create, and to develop a caring nature. Short stories and serials of up to 4 parts. Occasional features commissioned from writers with specialist knowledge. Approach in writing with ideas and sample of writing style, with sae. Length: 700–800 words (features), 1000–1100 words (stories or per episode of a serial). Payment: £75 (features); £90 (stories), £80 (per episode). Founded 1993.

The Architects' Journal

EMAP Business Communications, 151 Rosebery Avenue, London EC1R 4GB
tel 020-7505 6700 *fax* 020-7505 6701
website www.ajplus.co.uk
Editor Isabel Allen
Weekly £3.25 (£129 p.a.)

Articles (mainly technical) on architecture, planning and building accepted only with prior agreement of synopsis. Illustrations: photos and drawings. Payment: by arrangement. Founded 1895.

Architectural Design

Academy Editions, The Atrium, Southern Gate, Chichester, West Sussex PO19 8SQ
tel (01243) 779777 *fax* (01243) 770367
Editor Helen Castle
6 double issues p.a., £22.50 single issue, £99 p.a. personal rate (£70 p.a. students)

International architectural publication comprising an extensively illustrated thematic profile and magazine back section, *AD Plus*. Uncommissioned articles not accepted. Illustrations: drawings and photos, line (colour preferred). Payment: by arrangement. Founded 1930.

The Architectural Review

EMAP Construct, 151 Rosebery Avenue, London EC1R 4GB
tel 020-7505 6725 *fax* 020-7505 6701
email paul.finch@emap.com
website www.arplus.com
Editor Paul Finch
Monthly £7.25

Articles on architecture and the allied arts. Writers must be thoroughly qualified. Length: up to 3000 words. Payment: by arrangement. Illustrations: photos, drawings, etc. Founded 1896.

Architecture Today

161 Rosebery Avenue, London EC1R 4QX
tel 020-7837 0143 *fax* 020-7837 0155
Editor Ian Latham
10 p.a. £4 Free to architects

Mostly commissioned articles and features on today's European architecture. Length: 200–800 words.

Illustrations: colour. Payment: by negotiation. Founded 1989.

Arena

EMAP East, Endeavour House, 189 Shaftesbury Avenue, London WC2H 8JG
tel 020-7437 9011
email arenamag@emap.com
Editor William Drew
Monthly £3.50

Profiles, articles on a wide range of subjects intelligently treated; art, architecture, politics, sport, business, music, film, design, media, fashion. Length: up to 3000 words. Illustrations: b&w and colour photos. Payment: £300 per 1000 words; varies for illustrations. Founded 1986.

Art Business Today

The Fine Art Trade Guild, 16–18 Empress Place, London SW6 1TT
tel 020-7381 6616 *fax* 020-7381 2596
email abt@fineart.co.uk
website www.abtonline.co.uk
Editor Mike Sims
5 p.a. £24 p.a.

Distributed to the fine art and framing industry. Covers essential information on new products and technology, market trends and business analysis. Length: 800–1600 words. Illustrations: colour photos, cartoons. Payment: by arrangement. Founded 1905.

Art Monthly

4th Floor, 28 Charing Cross Road, London WC2H 0DB
tel 020-7240 0389 *fax* 020-7497 0726
email info@artmonthly.co.uk
website www.artmonthly.co.uk
Editor Patricia Bickers
10 p.a. £3.75

Features on modern and contemporary visual artists and art history, art theory and art-related issues; exhibition and book reviews. All material commissioned. Length: 750–1500 words. Illustrations: b&w photos. Payment: features £100–£200; none for photos. Founded 1976.

The Art Newspaper

70 South Lambeth Road, London SW8 1RL
tel 020-7735 3331 *fax* 020-7735 3332
email contact@theartnewspaper.com
website www.theartnewspaper.com
Editor Christina Ruiz
11 p.a. £6 (£60 p.a.)

International coverage of visual art, news, politics, law, exhibitions with some feature pages. Length: 200–1000 words. Illustrations: b&w photos. Payment: £120 per 1000 words. Founded 1990.

Art Review

Art Review Ltd, 1 Sekforde Street, London EC1R 0BE
tel 020-7107 2760 *fax* 020-7075 6001

email info@art-review.co.uk
website www.art-review.com
Editor Rebecca Wilson
Monthly £4.90

Modern and contemporary art and style features and reviews. Proposals welcome. Payment: from £400 per 1000 words. Illustrations: colour. Founded 1949.

The Artist

The Artists' Publishing Co. Ltd, Caxton House, 63–65 High Street, Tenterden, Kent TN30 6BD
tel (01580) 763673
Editor Sally Bulgin
Monthly £3.10

Practical, instructional articles on painting for all amateur and professional artists. Payment: by arrangement. Illustrations: line, half-tone, colour. Founded 1931.

Artists and Illustrators

226 City Road, London EC1V 2TT
tel 020-7700 8500 *fax* 020-7700 4985
email aim@quarto.com
website www.aimag.co.uk
Editor John Swinfield
Monthly £2.80

Practical and inspirational articles for amateur and professional artists. Length: 1000–1500 words. Illustrations: colour transparencies, high resolution digital images. Payment: variable. Founded 1986.

Asian Times

Ethnic Media Group, Unit 2, Whitechapel Technology Centre, 65 Whitechapel Road, London E1 1DU
tel 020-7650 2000 *fax* 020-7560 2001
email asiantimes@ethnicmedia.com
Editor Burhan Ahmad
Weekly 50p

News stories, articles and features of interest to Britain's Asian community. Founded 1983.

Astronomy Now

Pole Star Publications, PO Box 175, Tonbridge, Kent TN10 4ZY
tel (01732) 446110 *fax* (01732) 300148
email editorial2006@astronomynow.com
website www.astronomynow.com
Editor Stuart Clark
Monthly £3.25

Specialises in translating exciting astronomy research into articles for the lay reader. Also covers amateur astronomy with equipment reviews and observing notes. Send sae for writers' guidelines. Length: 800–2000 words. Payment: 15p per word; from £10 per photo. Founded 1987.

Athletics Weekly

Descartes Publishing Ltd, 83 Park Road, Peterborough PE1 2TN

tel (01733) 898440 *fax* (01733) 898441
email jason.henderson@athletics-weekly.co.uk
Editor Jason Henderson
Weekly £2.45

News and features on track and field athletics, road running, cross country, fell and race walking. Material mostly commissioned. Length: 300–1500 words. Illustrations: colour and b&w action and head/shoulder photos, line. Payment: varies. Founded 1945.

Attitude

Remnant Media, 4 Seldon Way, City Harbour, London E14 9GL
tel 020-7308 5090 *fax* 020-7308 5384
email attitude@nasnet.co.uk
website www.attitude.co.uk
Editor Adam Mattera
Monthly £3.25

Men's style magazine aimed primarily but not exclusively at gay men. Covers style/fashion, interviews, reviews, celebrities, humour. Illustrations: colour transparencies, b&w prints. Payment: £150 per 1000 words; £100 per full page illustration. Founded 1994.

The Author

84 Drayton Gardens, London SW10 9SB
tel 020-7373 6642
Editor Andrew Taylor
Quarterly £12

Organ of the Society of Authors. Commissioned articles from 1000–2000 words on any subject connected with the legal, commercial or technical side of authorship. Little scope for the freelance writer: preliminary letter advisable. Illustrations: line, occasional cartoons. Payment: by arrangement. Founded 1890.

Auto Express

Dennis Publishing Ltd, 30 Cleveland Street, London W1T 4JD
tel 020-7907 6200 *fax* 020-7907 6234
email editorial@autoexpress.co.uk
website www.autoexpress.co.uk
Editor David Johns
Weekly £1.80

News stories, and general interest features about drivers as well as cars. Illustrations: colour photos. Payment: features £350 per 1000 words; photos, varies. Founded 1988.

Autocar

Haymarket Publishing Ltd, Teddington Studios, Broom Road, Teddington, Middlesex TW11 9BE
tel 020-8267 5630 *fax* 020-8267 5759
email autocar@haynet.com
Editor Rob Aherne
Weekly £2.10

Articles on all aspects of cars, motoring and the motor industry: general, practical, competition and technical. Illustrations: line (litho), colour and electronic (Illustrator). Press day news: Thursday. Payment: varies; mid-month following publication. Founded 1895.

Aviation News

HPC Publishing, Drury Lane, St Leonards-on-Sea, East Sussex TN38 9BJ
tel (01424) 205530 *fax* (01424) 443693/434086
Editor David Baker
Monthly £3.60

Covers all aspects of aviation. Many articles commissioned; will consider competent articles exploring fresh ground or presenting an individual point of view on technical matters. Illustrated, mainly with photos. Payment: by arrangement.

Back Street Heroes

19th Floor, 1 Canada Square, Canary Wharf, London E14 5AP
tel 020-7772 8300 *fax* 020-7772 8585
Editor Stu Garland
Monthly £3.60

Custom motorcycle features plus informed lifestyle pieces. Illustrations: colour, cartoons. Payment: by arrangement. Founded 1983.

Backtrack

Pendragon Publishing, PO Box 3, Easingwold, York YO61 3YS
tel/fax (01347) 824397
email mike.blakemore@virgin.net
Editor Michael Blakemore
Monthly £3.50

British railway history from1820s to 1980s. Welcomes ideas from writers and photographers. Articles must be well researched, authoritative and accompanied by illustrations. Length: 3000–5000 words (main features), 500–3000 words (articles). Illustrations: colour and b&w. Payment: £30 per 1000 words, £17.50 colour, £7.50 b&w. Founded 1986.

Balance

Diabetes UK, 10 Parkway, London NW1 7AA
tel 020-7424 1000 *fax* 020-7424 1081
email balance@diabetes.org.uk
website www.diabetes.org.uk
Editor Martin Cullen
Bi-monthly £3.50

Articles on diabetes and related health and lifestyle issues. Length: 1000–1500 words. Payment: by arrangement. Illustrations: colour. Founded 1935.

The Banker

FT Business, Tabernacle Court, 16–28 Tabernacle Court, London EC2 4DD
tel 020-7382 8000 *fax* 020-7382 8568

email stephen.timewell@ft.com
Editor-in-Chief Stephen Timewell
Monthly £245 p.a.

Articles on investment banking and finance, retail banking, banking technology, banking services and systems; bank analysis and top 1000 listings. Illustrations: half-tones and full colour of people, charts, tables, maps, etc. Founded 1926.

Baptist Times

PO Box 54, 129 Broadway, Didcot, Oxon OX11 8XB
tel (01235) 517670 *fax* (01235) 517678
Editor Mark Woods
Weekly 75p

Religious or social affairs, news, features and reviews. Payment: by arrangement. Founded 1855.

BBC magazines – see Inside the BBC, page 350

The Beano

D.C. Thomson & Co. Ltd, Albert Square, Dundee DD1 9QJ
tel (01382) 223131 *fax* (01382) 322214
185 Fleet Street, London EC4A 2HS
tel 020-7400 1030 *fax* 020-7400 1089
Editor Euan Kerr
Weekly 80p

Comic strips for children aged 6–12. Series, 11–22 pictures. Artwork only. Payment: on acceptance.

Bella

H. Bauer Publishing, Academic House, 24–28 Oval Road, London NW1 7DT
tel 020-7241 8000 *fax* 020-7241 8056
Editor Jayne Marsden
Weekly 70p

General interest magazine for women: practical articles on fashion and beauty, health, cooking, home, travel; real life stories, plus fiction up to 1000 words. Payment: by arrangement. Illustrations: line including cartoons, half-tone, colour. Founded 1987.

Best

ACP–NatMag, 33 Broadwick Street, London W1F 0DQ
tel 020-7339 4500 *fax* 020-7339 4580
Editor Michelle Hather, *Fiction Editor* Pat Richardson, *Features Editor* Charlotte Seligman
Weekly 70p

Short stories. No other uncommissioned work accepted, but always willing to look at ideas/outlines. Length: 1000 words for short stories, variable for other work. Payment: by agreement. Founded 1987.

Best of British

Church Lane Publishing Ltd, Bank Chambers, 27A Market Place, Market Deeping, Lincs. PE6 8EA

tel (01778) 342814, 380906 *fax* (01778) 342814
email mail@british.fsbusiness.co.uk
website www.bestofbritishmag.co.uk
Editor-in-Chief Ian Beacham
Monthly £3.20

Nostalgic features about life in the 1940s, 1950s and 1960s together with stories celebrating interesting aspects of Britain today. Length: max. 1200 words. Illustrations: colour and b&w. Payment: at editor's discretion. Founded 1994.

The Big Issue

1–5 Wandsworth Road, London SW8 2LN
tel 020-7526 3200
website www.bigissue.com
Editor John Bird
Weekly £1.40

Features, current affairs, reviews, interviews – of general interest and on social issues. Length: 1000 words (features). No short stories or poetry. Illustrations: colour and b&w photos and line. Payment: £160 per 1000 words. Founded 1991.

The Big Issue Cymru

55 Charles Street, Cardiff CF10 2GD
tel 029-2025 5670 *fax* 029-2025 5673
email edit@bigissuecymru.fsnet.co.uk
Editor Cathryn Scott
Weekly £1.40

The Welsh edition of the *Big Issue*. Content is relevant to Wales: some articles are taken from the main London edition but some news features, arts and music coverage is locally sourced. Considers unsolicited material. Welcomes ideas for articles and features. No poetry or short stories. Length: 1000–1500 words (articles/features), 200–400 words (news). Illustrations: colour and b&w prints and artwork. Payment: by arrangement. Founded 1994.

The Big Issue in the North

The Big Issue in the North Ltd, 135–141 Oldham Street, Manchester M4 1LL
tel 0161-834 6300 *fax* 0161-819 5000
Editor Ato Erzan-Essien
Weekly £1.40

Articles of general interest and on social issues; arts features and news covering the north of England. No fiction or poetry, except by the homeless. Contact the editorial department to discuss ideas. Length: 1000 words (features/articles), 300–500 (news), 700 (arts features). Payment: £120 per 1000 words/12p per word. Colour transparencies, puzzles and quizzes. Founded 1992.

The Big Issue in Scotland

The Big Issue in Scotland Ltd, 71 Oxford Street, Glasgow G5 9EP
tel 0141-418 7000 *fax* 0141-418 7061
email editorial@bigissuescotland.com

Editor Clare Harris
Weekly £1.20

Features on social issues, human rights, the environment, injustice, Scotland, medical, health and crime plus news and arts coverage. Also international features/news. Length: 1000–2000 words (articles); 300–400 words (news). Illustrations: colour and b&w. Payment: £120 per 1000 words; £60 per photo/illustration. Founded 1993.

The Big Issue South West

5 Brunswick Court, Brunswick Square, Bristol BS2 8PE
tel 0117-916 6593 *fax* 0117-916 6599
email editorial@bigissuesouthwest.co.uk
website www.bigissuesouthwest.co.uk
Editor Cathryn Scott
Weekly £1.40

Social news, general interest features and arts information for the South West. Considers unsolicited material. Length: 1200 words (articles/features), 100–1200 words (news). Payment: negotiable. Illustrations: colour, payment negotiable. Founded 1991.

Bike

EMAP Automotive Ltd, Media House, Lynchwood, Peterborough PE2 6EA
tel (01733) 468000 *fax* (01733) 468196
email bike@emap.com
Editor John Westlake
Monthly £3.70

Motorcycle magazine: interested in articles, features, news. Length: articles/features 1000–3000 words. Illustrations: colour and b&w photos. Payment: £150 per 1000 words; photos per size/position. Founded 1971.

Bird Watching

EMAP Active Ltd, Bretton Court, Bretton, Peterborough PE3 8DZ
tel (01733) 264666 *fax* (01773) 465376
email david.cromack@emap.com
Editor Kevin Wilmott
Monthly £3.50

Broad range of bird-related features and photography, particularly looking at bird behaviour, bird news, reviews and UK birdwatching sites. Limited amount of overseas features. Emphasis on providing accurate information in entertaining ways. Send synopsis first. Length: 1200 words. Illustrations: colour transparencies and photo images on CD, bird identification artwork. Payment: by negotiation. Founded 1986.

Birding World

Sea Lawn, Coast Road, Cley next the Sea, Holt, Norfolk NR25 7RZ
tel (01263) 740913 *fax* (01263) 741014

email steve@birdingworld.co.uk
website www.birdingworld.co.uk
Editor Steve Gantlett
Monthly £45 p.a. (£52 p.a. Europe; £56 p.a. rest of the world, airmail)

Magazine for keen birdwatchers. Articles and news stories about mainly European ornithology, with the emphasis on ground-breaking new material and identification. Length: up to 3000 words (articles); up to 1500 words (news). Illustrations: good quality colour photos of birds. Payment: up to £25 per 500 words; £10–£40 (illustrations). Founded 1987.

Birdwatch

Solo Publishing Ltd, The Chocolate Factory, 5 Clarendon Road, London N22 6XJ
tel 020-8881 0550 *fax* 020-8881 0990
website www.birdwatch.co.uk
Editor Dominic Mitchell
Monthly £3.50

Topical articles on all aspects of birds and birding, including conservation, identification, sites and habitats, equipment, overseas expeditions. Length: 700–1500 words. Illustrations: high-res jpegs (300 dpi at 1500 pixels min. width) of wild British birds considered; submit on CD/DVD. Artwork by negotiation. Payment: from £50 per 1000 words; colour: photos £15–£40, cover £75, line by negotiation; b&w: photos £10, line £10–£40. Founded 1991.

Bizarre

Dennis Publishing, 30 Cleveland Street, London W1T 4JD
tel 020-7907 6000 *fax* 020-7907 6439
email bizarre@dennis.co.uk
website www.bizarremag.com
Editor Alex Godfrey
Monthly £3.30

Features on strange events, adventure, cults, weird people, celebrities, etc. Study the magazine for style before submitting ideas by post or fax. No fiction. Payment: 20p per word. Colour transparencies and prints: £200 per dps, £125 per page. Founded 1997.

Black Beauty & Hair

Hawker Publications, 2nd Floor, Culvert House, Culvert Road, London SW11 5DH
tel 020-7720 2108 *fax* 020-7498 3023
email info@blackbeautyandhair.com
website www.blackbeautyandhair.com
Editor Irene Shelley
Bi-monthly £2.50

Beauty and style articles relating specifically to the black woman; celebrity features. True-life stories and salon features. Length: approx. 1000 words. Illustrations: colour and b&w photos. Payment: £100 per 1000 words; photos £25–£75. Founded 1982.

Bliss

EMAP Consumer Media, Endeavour House, 189 Shaftesbury Avenue, London WC2H 8JG

tel 020-7437 9011 *fax* 020-7208 3591
website www.blissmag.co.uk
Editor Lisa Smosarski
Monthly £2.10

Glamorous young women's glossy magazine. Bright, intimate, American A5 format, with real life reports, celebrities, beauty, fashion, shopping, advice, quizzes. Payment: by arrangement. Founded 1995.

Blueprint

Wilmington Media, 6–14 Underwood Street, London N1 7JQ
tel 020-7324 2392 *fax* 020-7549 2578
email ggibson@wilmington.co.uk
Editor Vicky Richardson
12 p.a. £4.25

The magazine of modern architecture, design and culture. Interested in articles, features and reviews. Length: up to 2500 words. Illustrations: colour and b&w photos and line. Payment: negotiable. Founded 1983.

BMA News

British Medical Association, BMA House, Tavistock Square, London WC1H 9JP
tel 020-7383 6122 *fax* 020-7383 6566
Joint Editors Julia Bell, Caroline Winter-Jones
51 p.a. £82 p.a.

News and features. Length: 700–2000 words (features), 100–300 words (news). Illustrations: transparencies, colour and b&w artwork and cartoons. Payment: by negotiation. Founded 1966.

Boards

Yachting Press Ltd, 196 Eastern Esplanade, Southend-on-Sea, Essex SS1 3AB
tel (01702) 582245 *fax* (01702) 588434
email editorial@boards.co.uk
website www.boards.co.uk
Editor Bill Dawes
Monthly during summer, Bi-monthly during winter £3.75 (10 p.a.)

Articles, photos and reports on all aspects of windsurfing and boardsailing. Payment: by arrangement. Illustrations: line, half-tone, colour, cartoons. Founded 1982.

The Book Collector

(incorporating Bibliographical Notes and Queries)
The Collector Ltd, PO Box 12426, London W11 3GW
tel 020-7792 3492 *fax* 020-7792 3492
email nicolasb@nixnet.clara.co.uk
Editorial Board Nicolas Barker (Editor), A. Edwards, J. Fergusson, T. Hofmann, D. McKitterick, Joan Winterkorn
Quarterly £47 p.a. (£50/€73.50/$83.50 p.a. overseas)

Articles, biographical and bibliographical, on the collection and study of printed books and MSS. Payment: for reviews only. Founded 1952.

Book and Magazine Collector

Diamond Publishing Ltd, Unit 101, 140 Wales Farm Road, London W3 6UG
tel (0870) 732 8080 *fax* (0870) 732 6060
Editor Jonathan Scott
13 p.a. £3.30

Articles about collectable authors/publications/ subjects. Articles must be bibliographical and include a full bibliography and price guide (no purely biographical features). Approach in writing with ideas. Length: 2000–4000 words. Illustrations: colour and b&w artwork. Payment: £35 per 1000 words. Founded 1984.

Books Ireland

11 Newgrove Avenue, Dublin 4, Republic of Ireland
tel (01) 2692185
email booksi@eircom.net
Editor Jeremy Addis, *Features Editor* Shirley Kelly
Monthly (exc. Jan, Jul, Aug) €3.50 (€32 p.a.)

Reviews of Irish-interest and Irish-author books, articles of interest to librarians, booksellers and readers. Length: 800–1400 words. Payment: €80 per 1000 words. Founded 1976.

The Bookseller

VNU Entertainment Media Ltd, 5th Floor, Endeavour House, 189 Shaftesbury Avenue, London WC2H 8TJ
tel 020-7420 6006 *fax* 020-7420 6103
email letters.to.editor@bookseller.co.uk
website www.thebookseller.com
Editor-in-Chief Neill Denny, *Features Editor* Liz Bury
Weekly £179 p.a.

Journal of the UK publishing, bookselling trade and libraries. While outside contributions are welcomed, most of the journal's contents are commissioned. Length: about 1000–1500 words. Payment: by arrangement. Founded 1858.

Bookworld

Christchurch Publishers Ltd, 2 Caversham Street, London SW3 4AH
tel/fax 020-7351 4995
email leonard.holdsworth@btopenworld.com
Editor Leonard Holdsworth
Monthly £2

Special features and reviews of interest serious book collectors and sellers. Articles and ideas for articles welcome. Must be able to provide b&w or colour illustrations. Payment by negotiation. Established 1980.

Bowls International

Key Publishing Ltd, PO Box 100, Stamford, Lincs. PE9 1XQ
tel (01780) 755131 *fax* (01780) 757261
Editor Melvyn Beck
Monthly £2.99

Sport and news items and features; occasional, bowls-oriented short stories. Illustrations: colour transparencies, b&w photos, occasional line, cartoons. Payment: sport/news approx. 25p per line, features approx. £50 per page; colour £25, b&w £10. Founded 1981.

Brass Band World Magazine

Impromptu Publishing Ltd, 4th Floor, 117–119 Portland Street, Manchester M1 6ED
tel 0161-236 9526 *fax* 0161-247 7978
email info@brassbandworld.com
website www.brassbandworld.com
Editor Alan Jenkins
Monthly £3.85

Artlcles, features and news of brass bands internationally. Reviews of concerts and contests, personality profiles, tips, and news from colleges for students, players and audiences. Payment: negotiable. Founded 1981.

British Birds

The Banks, Mountfield, Robertsbridge, East Sussex TN32 5JY
tel (01580) 882039
email editor@britishbirds.co.uk
Editor Dr Roger Riddington
Monthly £46 p.a. UK, £52 p.a. overseas

Publishes major papers on identification, behaviour, conservation, distribution, ecology, movements, status and taxonomy with official reports on: rare breeding birds, scarce migrants and rare birds in Britain. Payment: token. Founded 1907.

British Chess Magazine

44 Baker Street, London W1U 7RT
tel 020-7486 8222 *fax* 020-7486 3355
email bcmchess@compuserve.com
Editor John Saunders
Monthly £3.25

Authoritative reports and commentary on the UK and overseas chess world. Payment: by arrangement. Founded 1881.

The British Journal of Photography

Incisive Photographics Ltd, Incisive Media, Haymarket House, 28–29 Haymarket, London SW1Y 4RX
tel 020-7484 9700 *fax* 020-7484 9989
email bjp.editor@bjphoto.co.uk
website www.bjp-online.com
Editor Simon Bainbridge
Weekly £2

Focus on all aspects of professional photography: articles on fine art, commercial, fashion, social and press, alongside technical reviews of the latest software and equipment. Founded 1854.

British Journalism Review

Sage Publications, 1 Oliver's Yard, 55 City Road, London EC1Y 1SP
tel 020-7324 8500 *fax* 020-7324 8600
email info@sagepub.co.uk
website www.bjr.org.uk
Editor Bill Hagerty
Quarterly £36 p.a. (overseas rates on application)

Comment/criticism/review of matters published by, or of interest to, the media. Length: 1000–3000 words. Illustrations: b&w photos. Payment: by arrangement. Founded 1989.

British Medical Journal

BMA House, Tavistock Square, London WC1H 9JR
tel 020-7387 4499 *fax* 020-7383 6418
email editor@bmj.com
website www.bmj.com
Editor Dr Fiona Godlee
Weekly £5

Medical and related articles. Payment: by arrangement. Founded 1840.

British Philatelic Bulletin

Royal Mail, 148 Old Street, London EC1V 9HQ
fax 020-7250 2389
Editor J.R. Holman
Monthly £1.20

Articles on any aspect of British philately – stamps, postmarks, postal history; also stamp collecting in general. Length: up to 1500 words (articles); 250 words (news). Payment: £65 per 1000 words. Illustrations: colour. Founded 1963.

Broadcast

EMAP Media, 33–39 Bowling Green Lane, London EC1R 0DA
tel 020-7505 8014 *fax* 020-7505 8050
Editor Conor Dignam
Weekly £3.20

News and authoritative articles designed for all concerned with the UK TV and radio industry, and with programmes and advertising on TV, radio, cable, satellite, digital. Illustrations: colour, b&w, line, cartoons.

Buckinghamshire Countryside

Beaumonde Publications Ltd, PO Box 5, Hitchin, Herts. SG5 1GJ
tel (01462) 431237 *fax* (01462) 422015
email martin_small@btconnect.com
Editor Sandra Small
Bi-monthly £1.25

Articles relating to Buckinghamshire. No poetry, puzzles or crosswords. Length: approx. 1000 words. Illustrations: colour transparencies and b&w prints, artwork. Payment: £30 per article. Founded 1995.

Building

Building Magazine, CMP Information Ltd, 8th Floor, 245 Blackfriars Road, London SE1 9UY
tel 020-7560 4000 *fax* 020-7560 4080

email dchevin@cmpinformation.com
Editor Denise Chevin
Weekly £2.60

Covers the entire professional, industrial and manufacturing aspects of the building industry. Articles on architecture and techniques at home and abroad considered, also news and photos. Payment: by arrangement. Founded 1842.

Building Design

CMP Information Ltd, Ludgate House, 245 Blackfriars Road, London SE1 9UY
tel 020-7921 8560 *fax* 020-7921 8244
email bd@cmpinformation.com
Editor Amanda Baillieu
Weekly Controlled circulation

News and features on all aspects of building design. All material commissioned. Length: up to 1500 words. Illustrations: colour and b&w photos, line, cartoons. Payment: £150 per 1000 words; illustrations by negotiation. Founded 1970.

Built Environment

Alexandrine Press, 1 The Farthings, Marcham, Oxon OX13 6QD
tel (01865) 391518 *fax* (01865) 391687
email alexandrine@rudkinassociates.co.uk
Editors Prof. Sir Peter Hall, Prof. David Banister
Quarterly £95 p.a.

Articles about architecture, planning and the environment. Preliminary letter advisable. Length: 1000–5000 words. Payment: by arrangement. Illustrations: photos and line.

The Burlington Magazine

14–16 Duke's Road, London WC1H 9SZ
tel 020-7388 8157 *fax* 020-7388 1230
email editorial@burlington.org.uk
website www.burlington.org.uk
Editor Richard Shone
Monthly £13.90

Deals with the history and criticism of art; book and exhibition reviews; illustrated monthly Calendar section. Potential contributors must have special knowledge of the subjects treated; MSS compiled from works of reference are unacceptable. Length: 500–5000 words. Payment: up to £140. Illustrations: b&w and colour photos. Founded 1903.

Buses

Ian Allan Publishing Ltd, Riverdene Business Park, Molesey Road, Hersham, Surrey KT12 4RG
tel (01932) 266600 *fax* (01932) 266601
email buseseditor@btconnect.com
Editor Alan Millar, PO Box 14644, Leven KY9 1WX
tel (01333) 340637 *fax* (01333) 340608
website www.busesmag.com
Monthly £3.60

Articles of interest to both road passenger transport operators and bus enthusiasts. Preliminary enquiry

essential. Illustrations: colour transparencies, half-tone, line maps. Payment: on application. Founded 1949.

Business Life

Pegasus House, 37–43 Sackville Street, London W1S 3EH
tel 020-7534 2400 *fax* 020-7534 2553
website www.cedarcom.co.uk
Editor Tim Hulse
10 p.a. Free

Inflight magazine for British Airways passengers. Articles and features of interest to the European business traveller. All material commissioned; approach in writing with ideas. Length: 850–2500 words. Illustrations: colour photos and line. Payment: £250 per 1000 words; £100–£400 for illustrations. Founded 1986.

Business Traveller

Perry Publications Ltd, 68–69 St Martin's Lane, London WC2N 4JS
tel 020-7845 6533 *fax* 020-7845 6512
email editorial@businesstraveller.com
website www.businesstraveller.com
Editor Tom Otley
10 p.a. (£42.95 p.a.)

Articles, features and news on consumer travel aimed at individual frequent international business travellers. Submit ideas with recent clippings and a CV. Length: varies. Illustrations: colour for destinations features; send lists to Deborah Miller, Picture Editor. Payment: on application. Founded 1976.

Cambridgeshire Journal

Cambridge Newspapers Ltd, Winship Road, Milton, Cambridge CB4 6PP
email pippa@acornmagazines.co.uk
Editor Debbie Tweedie
Monthly £1.95

Articles, features and news of interest to Cambridgeshire: history, people, events, natural history and other issues. Also regional lifestyle, i.e. gardens, homes and fashion. Specially commissions most material. Welcomes ideas for articles and features. Length: 1500 words (articles/features), 250 words (news). Payment: £125 (articles/features), none (news). Illustrations: colour transparencies and prints. Founded 1994.

Campaign

Haymarket Business Publications Ltd, 174 Hammersmith Road, London W6 7JP
tel 020-8943 5000
website www.brandrepublic.com
Editor Claire Beale
Weekly £3.20

News and articles covering the whole of the mass communications field, particularly advertising in all its forms, marketing and the media. Features should not exceed 2000 words. News items also welcome. Press day, Wednesday. Payment: by arrangement.

Canals & Rivers

PO Box 618, Norwich NR7 0QT
tel (01603) 708930
email chris@themag.fsnet.co.uk
website www.canalsandrivers.co.uk
Editor Chris Cattrall
Monthly £2.95

News, views and articles on UK inland waterways and cruising features, DIY articles and historical features. Length: 1500 words (articles/features), 300 words (news). Payment: £100; £25 (news). Illustrations: colour, plus b&w cartoons. Founded 1978.

Car

EMAP Automotive Ltd, 3rd Floor, Media House, Lynchwood, Peterborough PE2 6EA
tel (01733) 468000 *fax* (01733) 468660
email car@emap.com
Editor Jason Barlow
Monthly £3.90

Top-grade journalistic features on car driving, car people and cars. Length: 1000–2500 words. Payment: minimum £350 per 1000 words. Illustrations: b&w and colour photos to professional standards. Founded 1962.

Car Mechanics

Cudham Tithe Barn, Berrys Hill, Cudham, Kent TN16 3AG
tel (01959) 541444, (01733) 771292 (editorial) *fax* (01959) 541400
email info@kelsey.co.uk
website www.kelsey.co.uk
Editor Peter Simpson
Monthly £3.25

Practical articles on maintaining, repairing and uprating modern cars for DIY plus the motor trade. Always interested in finding new talent for our rather specialised market but please study a recent copy before submitting ideas or features. Preliminary letter or phone call outlining feature recommended. Payment: by arrangement. Illustrations: line drawings, colour prints, transparencies or digital images. Rarely use words only; please supply package of text and pictures.

Caravan Magazine

IPC Focus Network, Leon House, 233 High Street, Croydon CR9 1HZ
tel 020-8726 8245 *fax* 020-8726 8299
website www.caravanmagazine.co.uk
Editor Steve Rowe
Monthly £3.20

Lively articles based on real experience of touring caravanning, especially if well illustrated by photos. Payment: by arrangement. Founded 1933.

Caribbean Times

(incorporating African Times)
Ethnic Media Group, Technology Centre, 65 Whitehchapel Road, London E1 1DU
tel 020-7650 2000 *fax* 020-7650 2001
website www.ethnicmedia.co.uk
Editor Ron Shillingford
Weekly 50p (£42 p.a.)

News stories, articles and features of interest to Britain's African–Caribbean community. Founded 1981.

Caring Business

Martin Mill Walker Lane, Hebden Bridge, West Yorkshire HX7 8SJ
tel (01422) 874078 *fax* (01422) 847017
email vivshep@aol.com
Editor Vivien Shepherd
Monthly £64 p.a.

Specialist contributions relating to the commercial aspects of nursing and residential care, including hospitals. Payment: £50 per 1000 words. Illustrations: line, half-tone. Founded 1985.

Carousel – The Guide to Children's Books

The Saturn Centre, 54–76 Bissell Street, Birmingham B5 7HX
tel 0121-622 7458 *fax* 0121-666 7526
email carousel.guide@virgin.net
website www.carouselguide.co.uk
Editor Jenny Blanch
3 p.a. £10.50 p.a. (£15 p.a. Europe; £18 p.a. rest of world)

Reviews of fiction, non-fiction and poetry books for children, plus in-depth articles; profiles of authors and illustrators. Length: 1200 words (articles); 150 words (reviews). Illustrations: colour and b&w. Payment: by arrangement. Founded 1995.

Cat World

Ashdown Publishing, Ancient Lights, 19 River Road, Arundel, West Sussex BN18 9EY
tel (01903) 884988 *fax* (01903) 885514
email editor@catworld.co.uk
website www.catworld.co.uk
Editor Jess White
Monthly £2.95

Bright, lively articles on any aspect of cat ownership. Articles on breeds of cats and veterinary articles by acknowledged experts only. No unsolicited fiction. All submissions by email or on disk. Illustrations: colour prints, transparencies, TIFFs. Payment: by arrangement. Founded 1981.

Caterer & Hotelkeeper

Reed Business Information Ltd, Quadrant House, The Quadrant, Sutton, Surrey SM2 5AS

tel 020-8652 3221 *fax* 020-8652 8973/8947
Editor Mark Lewis
Weekly £2.35

Articles on all aspects of the hotel and catering industries. Length: up to 1500 words. Illustrations: line, half-tone, colour. Payment: by arrangement. Founded 1893.

The Catholic Herald

Herald House, Lambs Passage, Bunhill Row, London EC1Y 8TQ
tel 020-7448 3603 *fax* 020-7256 9728
email editorial@catholicherald.co.uk
website www.catholicherald.co.uk
Editor Luke Coppen
Weekly £1

Independent newspaper covering national and international affairs from a Catholic/Christian viewpoint as well as church news. Length: articles 600–1200 words. Illustrations: photos of Catholic and Christian interest. Payment: by arrangement.

Catholic Pictorial

Media House, Mann Island, Pier Head, Liverpool L3 1DQ
tel 0151-236 2426 *fax* 0151-236 2216
email newsdesk@catholicpictorial.co.uk
website www.catholicpictorial.co.uk
Editor David Mahon
Monthly £1

News and photo features (maximum 800 words plus illustration) of Merseyside, regional and national Catholic interest only; also cartoons. Has a strongly social editorial and is a trenchant tabloid. Payment: by arrangement. Founded 1961.

Catholic Times

1st Floor, St James's Buildings, Oxford Street, Manchester M1 6FP
tel 0161-236 8856 *fax* 0161-237 5590
Editor Kevin Flaherty
Weekly 90p

News (400 words) and news features (800 words) of Catholic interest. Illustrations: colour and b&w photos. Payment: £30–£80; photos £50. Relaunched 1993.

Chapman

4 Broughton Place, Edinburgh EH1 3RX
tel 0131-557 2207
email chapman-pub@blueyonder.co.uk
website www.chapman-pub.co.uk
Editor Joy Hendry
3 p.a. £20 p.a.

'Scotland's quality literary magazine.' Poetry, short stories, reviews, criticism, articles on Scottish culture. Illustrations: line, half-tone, cartoons. Payment: £8 per page; illustrations by negotiation. Founded 1969.

Chartered Secretary

16 Park Crescent, London W1B 1AH
tel 020-7612 7045 *fax* 020-7612 7034
email chartsec@icsa.co.uk
website www.charteredsecretary.net
Editor Will Booth
Monthly £67 p.a. (free to members)

Official magazine of The Institute of Chartered Secretaries and Administrators. Practical and topical articles (2000+ words) on law, finance and management affecting company secretaries and other senior administrators in business, not-for-profit sector, local and central government and other institutions in Britain and overseas.

Chat

IPC Connect Ltd, King's Reach Tower, Stamford Street, London SE1 9LS
tel 020-7261 6565 *fax* 020-7261 6534
website www.ipcmedia.com
Editor Gilly Sinclair
Weekly 76p

Tabloid weekly for women: 60 word stories, true life features. Payment: by arrangement. Founded 1985.

Child Education

Scholastic Ltd, Villiers House, Clarendon Avenue, Leamington Spa, Warks. CV32 5PR
tel (01926) 887799 *fax* (01926) 883331
website www.scholastic.co.uk
Editor-in-Chief Helen Freeman
Monthly £3.99

For teachers concerned with the education of children aged 4–7. Articles by specialists on practical teaching ideas and methods. Length: 600–1200 words. Payment: by arrangement. Profusely illustrated with photos and artwork; also A1 full colour picture poster. Founded 1924.

Child Education Topics

Scholastic Ltd, Villiers House, Clarendon Avenue, Leamington Spa, Warks. CV32 5PR
tel (01926) 887799 *fax* (01926) 337322
Editor Michael Ward
Bi-monthly £3.99

Practical articles suggesting project activities for teachers of children aged 4–7; material mostly commissioned. Length: 500–1000 words. Illustrations: colour photos and line illustrations, colour posters. Payment: by arrangement. Founded 1978.

Choice

1st Floor, 2 King Street, Peterborough PE1 1LT
tel (01733) 555123 *fax* (01733) 427500
email editorial@choicemag.co.uk
Editor Norman Wright
Monthly £2.70

Pre- and retirement magazine for 50+ readership. Positive attitude to life – experiences, hobbies, holidays, finance, relationships. If suggesting feature material, include selection of cuttings of previously published work. Payment: by agreement, on publication. Founded 1974.

Church of England Newspaper

Central House, 142 Central Street, London EC1V 8AR
tel 020-7417 5800 *fax* 020-7216 6410
website www.churchnewspaper.com
Editor Colin Blakely
Weekly 80p

Anglican news and articles relating the Christian faith to everyday life. Evangelical basis; almost exclusively commissioned articles. Study of paper desirable. Length: up to 1000 words. Illustrations: photos, line drawings, cartoons. Payment: c. £40 per 1000 words; photos £22, line by arrangement. Founded 1828.

Church Times

33 Upper Street, London N1 0PN
tel 020-7359 4570 *fax* 020-7226 3073
email editor@churchtimes.co.uk
website www.churchtimes.co.uk
Editor Paul Handley
Weekly 90p

Articles on religious topics are considered. No verse or fiction. Length: up to 1000 words. Illustrations: news photos, sent promptly. Payment: £100 per 1000 words; Periodical Publishers' Association negotiated rates for illustrations. Founded 1863.

Classic Boat

IPC Media, Leon House, 233 High Street, Croydon CR9 1HZ
tel 020-8726 8000 *fax* 020-8774 0935
email cb@ipcmedia.com
website www.classicboat.co.uk
Editor Dan Houston
Monthly £3.85

Cruising and technical features, restorations, events, new boat reviews, practical, maritime history; news. Study of magazine essential: read 3–4 back issues and send for contributors' guidelines. Length: 500–2000 words. Illustrations: colour and b&w photos; line drawings of hulls. Payment: £75–£100 per published page. Founded 1987.

Classic Cars

EMAP Automotive Ltd, Media House, Lynchwood, Peterborough Business Park, Peterborough PE2 6EA
tel (01733) 468219 *fax* (01733) 468888
email classic.cars@emap.com
website www.classiccarsmagazine.co.uk
Editor Phil Bell
Monthly £3.60

Specialist articles on older cars. Length: from 500–4000 words (subject to prior contract). Illustrations: half-tone, colour, cartoons. Payment: by negotiation.

Classic Stitches

D.C. Thomson & Co. Ltd, 80 Kingsway East, Dundee DD4 8SL
tel (01382) 223131 *fax* (01382) 452491
email editorial@classicstitches.com
website www.classicstitches.com
Editor Mrs Bea Neilson
Bi-monthly £3.95

Creative needlework ideas and projects; needlework-based features on designers, collections, work-in-progress and exhibitions. Submissions also welcome for e-mag on website. Length: 1000–1500 words. Illustrations: colour photos, preferably not 35mm digital. Payment: negotiable. Founded 1994.

Classical Music

Rhinegold Publishing Ltd, 241 Shaftesbury Avenue, London WC2H 8TF
tel 020-7333 1742 *fax* 020-7333 1769
email classical.music@rhinegold.co.uk
website www.rhinegold.co.uk
Editor Keith Clarke
Fortnightly £3.45

News, opinion, features on the classical music business. All material commissioned. Illustrations: colour photos and line; colour covers. Payment: minimum £100 per 1000 words; from £50 for illustrations. Founded 1976.

Classics Monthly

Future Excite, 30 Monmouth Street, Bath BA1 2BW
tel/fax (01225) 442244
Editor Gary Streatham
Monthly £3.85

News photos and stories of classic car interest and illustrated features on classic car history, repairs, maintenance and restoration. Study magazine before submitting material. Features must have high level of subject knowledge and technical accuracy. Length: up to 2000 words (features); 200 words (news). Illustrations: colour and b&w. Payment: £120 per 1000 words plus £100 per set of supporting photos (features); £120 per 1000 words plus photos based on £100 per page (news). Founded 1997.

Climb Magazine

Telford Way Industrial Estate, Kettering, Northants NN16 8UN
tel (01536) 382500 *fax* (01536) 382501
email neilp@climbmagazine.com
website www.climbmagazine.com
Editor Neil Pearsons
12 p.a. £3.50

Climbing magazine covering mainly British rock climbing. Features all aspects of climbing worldwide from bouldering to mountaineering. Contact Editor to discuss requirements. Founded 1987.

Climber

Warners Group Publications plc, West Street, Bourne, Lincs. PE10 9PH
tel (01778) 391117

Editor Bernard Newman
Monthly £3.30

Articles on all aspects of rock climbing/
mountaineering in Great Britain and abroad, and on
related subjects. Study of magazine essential. Length:
1500–2000 words. Illustrations: colour transparencies.
Payment: according to merit. Founded 1962.

Coin News

Token Publishing Ltd, Orchard House, Duchy Road,
Heathpark, Honiton, Devon EX14 1YD
tel (01404) 46972 *fax* (01404) 44788
Editor John W. Mussell
Monthly £3.25

Articles of high standard on coins, tokens, paper
money. Length: up to 2000 words. Payment: by
arrangement. Founded 1964.

Commando

D.C. Thomson & Co. Ltd, Albert Square, Dundee
DD1 9QJ
tel (01382) 223131 *fax* (01382) 322214
8 per month £1.10

Fictional war stories told in pictures. Scripts: about
135 pictures. Synopsis required as an opener. New
writers encouraged; send for details. Payment: on
acceptance.

Commercial Motor

Reed Business Information Ltd, Quadrant House,
The Quadrant, Sutton, Surrey SM2 5AS
tel 020-8652 3251 *fax* 020-8652 8971
Editor-in-Chief Brian Weatherley, *Editor* Andy Salter
Weekly £1.80

Technical and road transport articles only. Length: up
to 1500 words. Payment: varies. Illustrations:
drawings and photos. Founded 1905.

Communicate

BPL Business Media Ltd, Armstrong House, 38
Market Square, Uxbridge, Middlesex UB8 1TG
tel (01895) 454411 *fax* (01895) 454413
website www.commsnow.com
Editor Joanna Perry
Monthly £3.50 Controlled circulation

Covers all aspects of telecommunications
management: analysis pieces (200–700 words),
features (1000–2000 words), case studies (300 words).
Some material commissioned. Illustrations: colour
photos, line, diagrams. Payment: by arrangement.
Founded 1980.

Community Care

Reed Business Information Ltd, Quadrant House,
The Quadrant, Sutton, Surrey SM2 5AS
tel 020-8652 4861 *fax* 020-8652 4739
email comcare.news@rbi.co.uk
website www.communitycare.co.uk
Acting Editor Mark Ivory

Weekly £2.05

Articles, features and news covering the Social
Services sector.

Company

National Magazine House, 72 Broadwick Street,
London W1V 2BP
tel 020-7439 5000 *fax* 020-7439 6886
email company.mail@natmags.co.uk
website www.natmags.co.uk
Editor Victoria White
Monthly £1.99

Articles on a wide variety of subjects, relevant to
young, independent women. Most articles are
commissioned. Payment: usual magazine rate.
Illustrated. Founded 1978.

Computer Weekly

Reed Business Information Ltd, Quadrant House,
The Quadrant, Sutton, Surrey SM2 5AS
tel 020-8652 8642 *fax* 020-8652 8979
website www.computerweekly.com
Editor Hooman Bassirian, *News Editor* Mike Simons
Weekly £2.95

Feature articles on IT-related topics for business/
industry users. Length: 1200 words. Illustrations:
b&w and colour photos, line, cartoons. Payment:
£253 per 1000 words; negotiable for illustrations.
Founded 1966.

Condé Nast Traveller

Vogue House, Hanover Square, London W1S 1JU
tel 020-7499 9080 *fax* 020-7493 3758
email cntraveller@condenast.co.uk
website www.cntraveller.com
Editor Sarah Miller
Monthly £3.50

Lavishly photographed features on all aspects of
travel, from food and wine to beauty and health.
Illustrations: colour. Payment: by arrangement.
Founded 1997.

Contemporary

Suite K101, Tower Bridge Business Complex,
100 Clements Road, London SE16 4DG
tel 020-7740 1704 *fax* 020-7252 3510
email info@contemporary-magazine.com
website www.contemporary-magazine.com
Editors Michele Robecchi
Monthly £5.95

International magazine with extensive coverage of
visual arts, architecture, fashion, film, photography,
books, music, dance and sport. Also includes
interviews, profiles and art news from around the
world. Length: varies. Illustrations: colour
transparencies, hi-res scans. Payment: £100 per 1000
words; none for photos. Founded 1997; relaunched
2002.

Contemporary Review

(incorporating the Fortnightly)
Contemporary Review Co. Ltd, PO Box 1242, Oxford
OX1 4FJ

tel (01865) 201529 *fax* (01865) 201529
email editorial@contemporaryreview.co.uk
Editor Dr Richard Mullen
Quarterly £10.50

Independent review dealing with questions of the day, chiefly politics, international affairs, religion, literature, the arts. Mostly commissioned, but with limited scope for freelance authors with authoritative knowledge. TS returned only if sae enclosed. Intending contributors should study journal first. Length: 2000–3000 words. No illustrations. Payment: £5 per page (500 words), 2 complimentary copies. Founded 1866.

CosmoGIRL!

National Magazine House, 72 Broadwick Street, London W1F 9EP
tel 020-7439 5081 *fax* 020-7439 5400
email cosmogirl.mail@natmags.co.uk
website www.cosmogirl.co.uk
Editor Celia Duncan
Monthly £2.10

Little sister to *Cosmopolitan*. Features 'to inspire teenage girls to be the best they can be'. Specially commissions most material. Welcomes ideas for articles and features. Length: 600 words. All illustrations commissioned. Founded 2001.

Cosmopolitan

National Magazine House, 72 Broadwick Street, London W1F 9EP
tel 020-7439 5000 *fax* 020-7439 5016
Editor-in-Chief Sam Baker
Monthly £2.99

Articles. Commissioned material only. Payment: by arrangement. Illustrated. Founded 1972.

Cotswold Life

Archant Life South, Cumberland House, Oriel Road, Cheltenham, Glos. GL50 1BB
tel (01242) 216050 *fax* (01242) 255116
website www.cotswoldlife.co.uk
Editor Mike Lowe
Monthly £2.95

Articles on the Cotswolds, including places of interest, high-profile personalities, local events, arts, history and food. Unsolicited ideas welcome.

Country

CGA, Chalke House, Station Road, Codford, Warminster BA12 0JX
tel (01985) 850705 *fax* (01985) 850378
website www.ipcmedia.com
Editor Simon Moss
8 p.a. Controlled circulation: members only

Magazine of the Country Gentlemen's Association. News and features covering rural events, countryside, leisure, heritage, homes and gardens. Some outside contributors used. Payment: by arrangement. Founded 1893.

Country Homes and Interiors

IPC Magazines Ltd, King's Reach Tower, Stamford Street, London SE1 9LS
tel 020-7261 6451 *fax* 020-7261 6895
Editor Rhoda Parry
Monthly £3.20

Articles on property, country homes, interior designs. Illustrations: colour. Payment: from £250 per 1000 words. Founded 1986.

Country Life

IPC Media Ltd, King's Reach Tower, Stamford Street, London SE1 9LS
tel 020-7261 6400 *fax* 020-7261 5139
website www.countrylife.co.uk
Editor Mark Hedges, *Features Editor* Rupert Uloth
Weekly £3

Illustrated journal chiefly concerned with British country life, social history, architecture and the fine arts, natural history, agriculture, gardening and sport. Length: about 1000 or 1300 words (articles). Illustrations: mainly colour photos. Payment: according to merit. Founded 1897.

Country Living

National Magazine House, 72 Broadwick Street, London W1F 9EP
tel 020-7439 5000 *fax* 020-7439 5093
website www.countryliving.co.uk
Editor Susy Smith
Monthly £3.20

Up-market home-interest magazine with a country lifestyle theme, covering interiors, gardens, crafts, food, wildlife, rural and green issues. Do not send unsolicited material or valuable transparencies. Illustrations: line, half-tone, colour. Payment: by arrangement. Founded 1985.

Country Quest

7 Aberystwyth Science Park, Aberystwyth, Ceredigion SY23 3AH
tel (01970) 615000 *fax* (01970) 624699
Editor Beverly Davies
Monthly £2

Illustrated articles on matters relating to countryside, history and personalities of Wales and border counties. No fiction. Illustrated work preferred. Length: 1500–2500 words. Payment: by arrangement.

Country Smallholding

Archant Regional Ltd, Fair Oak Close, Exeter Airport Business Park, Clyst Honiton, Exeter EX5 2UL
tel (01392) 888481 *fax* (01392) 888550
email editorial.csh@archant.co.uk
website www.countrysmallholding.com
Editor Diane Cowgill
Monthly £3

The magazine for smallholders. Practical, how-to articles, and seasonal features, on organic gardening, small-scale poultry and livestock keeping, country crafts, cookery and smallholdings. Approach the Editor in writing with ideas. Length: up to 2000 words. Payment: £45 per 1000 words; photos £10, £50 cover. Founded 1975 as *Practical Self-Sufficiency*.

Country Walking

EMAP Active Ltd, Bretton Court, Bretton, Peterborough PE3 8DZ
tel (01733) 282614 *fax* (01733) 282653
Editor Jonathan Manning
Monthly £3.40

Features. Length: 1200 words on average. Illustrations: colour transparencies. Payment: by arrangement. Founded 1987.

The Countryman

Country Publications Ltd, The Water Mill, Broughton Hall, Skipton, North Yorks BD23 3AG
tel (01756) 701381
email editorial@thecountryman.co.uk
Editor Paul Jackson
Monthly £2.50

Every area of rural life. Copy must be trustworthy, well-written, brisk, cogent and light in hand. Articles up to 1200 words. Skilful sketches of life and character from personal knowledge and experience. Dependable natural history based on writer's own observation. Really good matter from old unpublished letters and MSS. Study magazine before submitting material. Illustrations: b&w and colour photos and drawings, but all must be exclusive and out of the ordinary. Payment: approx. £70 per 1000 words. Founded 1927.

Craftsman Magazine

PO Box 5, Driffield, East Yorkshire YO25 8JD
tel (01377) 255213 *fax* (01377) 255730
email info@craftsman-magazine.com
website www.craftsmanonline.co.uk
Editor Angie Boyer
Monthly £3.25

Articles, features and news on craft makers and other areas of the craft industry. Aims to promote quality craftsmanship. Welcomes ideas for articles and features. Length: 1000 words (articles and features). Payment £100 per 1000 words. Illustrations: colour prints, transparencies or digital images on CD. Founded 1983.

Critical Quarterly

Blackwell Publishing Ltd, Sampson House, Woolpit, Bury St Edmunds IP30 9RN
tel (01359) 242375 *fax* (01359) 242880
website www.blackwellpublishing.com
Editor Colin MacCabe
Quarterly £130 p.a.

Fiction, poems, literary criticism. Length: 2000–5000 words. Study magazine before submitting MSS. Payment: by arrangement. Founded 1959.

Cumbria Magazine

Country Publications Ltd, The Water Mill, Broughton Hall, Skipton, North Yorkshire BD23 3AG
tel (01756) 701381 *fax* (01756) 701326
email editorial@dalesman.co.uk
Editor Terry Fletcher
Monthly £1.75

Articles of genuine rural interest concerning the Lake District and surrounding areas. Short length preferred. Illustrations: first-class photos. Payment: according to merit. Founded 1951.

Custom Car

Kelsey Publishing Ltd, Cudham Tithe Barn, Berry's Hill, Cudham, Kent TN16 3AG
tel (01959) 541444 *fax* (01959) 541400
email cc.ed@kelsey.co.uk
website www.customcarmag.co.uk
Editor Grant Wilson
Monthly £3.30

Hot rods, customs and drag racing. Length: by arrangement. Payment: by arrangement. Founded 1970.

Cycle Sport

IPC Media, Leon House, 233 High Street, Croydon CR9 1HZ
tel 020-8726 8000 *fax* 020-8726 8499
email cyclesport@ipcmedia.com
website www.cyclesport.co.uk
Managing Editor Robert Garbutt, *Deputy Editor* Nigel Wynn
Monthly £3.95

Articles and features on European professional racing. Specially commissions most material but will consider unsolicited material. Welcomes ideas for articles and features. Length: 1500–2500 words. Illustrations: transparencies, colour and b&w artwork and cartoons, digital images. Payment: £120 per 1000 words; £50–£150 illustrations. Founded 1991.

Cycling Weekly

IPC Media, Leon House, 233 High Street, Croydon CR9 1HZ
tel 020-8726 8000 *fax* 020-8726 8499
email cycling@ipcmedia.com
website www.cyclingweekly.co.uk
Editor Robert Garbutt
Weekly £2.35

Racing and technical articles. Illustrations: topical photos with a cycling interest considered; cartoons. Length: not exceeding 2000 words. Payment: by arrangement. Founded 1891.

Cyphers

3 Selskar Terrace, Ranelagh, Dublin 6, Republic of Ireland
tel (01) 4978866 *fax* (01) 4978866

€12/$25 for 3 issues

Poems, fiction, reviews, translations. Payment: €15 per page. Founded 1975.

Dairy Farmer

CMP Information Ltd, Unit 4, Caxton Road, Fulwood, Preston PR2 9NZ
tel (01772) 796220 *fax* (01772) 795901
email phollinshead@cmpinformation.com
Editor Peter Hollinshead
14 p.a. £3.75

In-depth, technical articles on all aspects of dairy farm management and milk marketing. Length: normally 800–1400 words with colour photos. Payment: by arrangement.

Dalesman

Country Publications Limited, The Water Mill, Broughton Hall, Skipton, North Yorkshire BD23 3AG
tel (01756) 701381 *fax* (01756) 701326
email editorial@dalesman.co.uk
Editor Terry Fletcher
Monthly £1.95

Articles and stories of genuine rural interest concerning Yorkshire (1000–1500 words). Payment: according to merit. Illustrations: line drawings and first-class photos preferably featuring people. Founded 1939.

Dance Today

The Dancing Times Ltd, 45–47 Clerkenwell Green, London EC1R 0EB
tel 020-7250 3006 *fax* 020-7253 6679
email dancetoday@dancing-times.co.uk
website www.dancing-times.co.uk
Editor Katie Gregory, *Editorial Adviser* Mary Clarke
Monthly £1.50

Ballroom, popular and social dancing from every aspect, ranging from competition reports to dance holiday features, health and fitness articles, and musical reviews. Well-informed freelance articles are used, but only after preliminary arrangements. Payment: by arrangement. Illustrations: action photos preferred, b&w or colour. Founded 1956.

Dancing Times

The Dancing Times Ltd, 45–47 Clerkenwell Green, London EC1R 0EB
tel 020-7250 3006 *fax* 020-7253 6679
email dt@dancing-times.co.uk
website www.dancing-times.co.uk
Editor Mary Clarke, *Editorial Adviser* Ivor Guest
Monthly £2.60

Ballet, contemporary dance and all forms of stage dancing from general, historical, critical and technical angles. Well-informed freelance articles used occasionally, but only after preliminary arrangements. Payment: by arrangement.

Illustrations: occasional line, action photos preferred; colour welcome. Founded 1910.

The Dandy

D.C. Thomson & Co. Ltd, Albert Square, Dundee DD1 9QJ
tel (01382) 223131 *fax* (01382) 322214
185 Fleet Street, London EC4A 2HS
tel 020-7400 1030 *fax* 020-7400 1089
Weekly £1.20

Comic strips for children. Picture stories with 7–10 pictures per page, 1–4pp per story. Promising artists are encouraged. Payment: on acceptance.

Darts World

World Magazines Ltd, 28 Arrol Road, Beckenham, Kent BR3 4PA
tel 020-8650 6580 *fax* 020-8654 4343
Editor Tony Wood
Monthly £2.70

Articles and stories with darts theme. Illustrations: half-tone, cartoons. Payment: £40–£50 per 1000 words; illustrations by arrangement. Founded 1972.

Day by Day

Woolacombe House, 141 Woolacombe Road, London SE3 8QP
tel 020-8856 6249
Editor Patrick Richards
Monthly £1.25

Articles and news on non-violence and social justice. Reviews of art, books, films, plays, musicals and opera; cricket reports. Short poems and very occasional short stories in keeping with editorial viewpoint. Payment: £2 per 1000 words. No illustrations required. Founded 1963.

Decanter

IPC Country & Leisure Media Ltd, 1st Floor, Broadway House, 2–6 Fulham Broadway, London SW6 1AA
tel 020-7610 3929 *fax* 020-7381 5282
email editor@decanter.com
website www.decanter.com
Editor Amy Wislocki
Monthly £3.60

Articles and features on wines, wine travel and food-related topics. Welcomes ideas for articles and features. Length: 1000–1800 words. Illustrations: colour. Payment: £230 per 1000 words. Founded 1975.

Delicious

Seven Publishing, 20 Upper Ground, London SE1 9PD
tel 020-7775 7757 *fax* 020-7928 8157
email readers@deliciousmagazine.co.uk
website www.deliciousmagazine.co.uk
Editor Matthew Drennan

Monthly £2.50

Articles on food, recipes, preparation, trends, chefs, wine and ingredients. Ideas welcome. Founded 2003.

Derbyshire Life and Countryside
Archant Life, 61 Friargate, Derby DE1 1DJ
tel (01332) 227850 *fax* (01332) 227860
website www.derbyshirelife.co.uk
Editor Joy Hales
Monthly £1.95

Articles, preferably illustrated, about Derbyshire life, people and history. Length: up to 800 words. Some short stories set in Derbyshire accepted; no verse. Payment: according to nature and quality of contribution. Illustrations: photos of Derbyshire subjects. Founded 1931.

Descent
Wild Places Publishing, PO Box 100, Abergavenny NP7 9WY
tel (01873) 737707 *fax* (0871) 750 5277
email descent@wildplaces.co.uk
website www.caving.uk.com
Editor Chris Howes
Bi-monthly £3.75

Articles, features and news on all aspects of cave and mine sport exploration. Submissions must match magazine style. Length: up to 2000 words (articles/features), up to 1000 words (news). Illustrations: colour and b&w. Payment: on consideration of material based on area filled. Founded 1969.

Devon Life
Archant Life South, Archant House, Babbage Road, Totnes, Devon TQ9 5JA
tel (01803) 860910 *fax* (01803) 860926
email devonlife@archant.co.uk
website www.devonlife.co.uk
Editor Jan Barwick
Monthly £2.95

Articles on all aspects of Devon, including places of interest, personalities, local events, arts, history and food. Unsolicited ideas welcome. Founded 1963.

The Dickensian
The Dickens Fellowship, Dickens House, 48 Doughty Street, London WC1N 2LX
fax (01227) 827001
email M.Y.Andrews@ukc.ac.uk
Editor Prof. Malcolm Andrews, School of English, Rutherford College, University of Kent, Canterbury, Kent CT2 7NX
3 p.a. £13.50 p.a. (£16 p.a. institutions; overseas rates on application). Reduced rate for Dickens Fellowship members

Welcomes articles on all aspects of Dickens's life, works and character. Payment: none. Send contributions (enclose sae if return required) and editorial correspondence to the Editor.

Digital Video UK
Future Publishing, 2 Balcombe Street, London NW1 6NW
tel 020-7042 4000
website www.futurenet.co.uk
Editor Robert Hull
13 p.a. £5.99

Features on film/video-making techniques, specifically tailored to the amateur enthusiast. Material mostly commissioned. Length: up to 2000 words. Illustrations: colour and b&w; contact Editor for details. Payment: by arrangement. Founded 1988.

Director
123 Pall Mall, London SW1Y 5ED
tel 020-7766 8950 *fax* 020-7766 8840
Editor Joanna Higgins
Monthly £3.50

Authoritative business-related articles. Send synopsis of proposed article and examples of printed work. Length: 500–2000 words. Payment: by arrangement. Illustrations: colour. Founded 1947.

Disability Now
(published by Scope)
6 Market Road, London N7 9PW
tel 020-7619 7323 *minicom* 020-7619 7332
fax 020-7619 7331
email editor@disabilitynow.org.uk
website www.disabilitynow.org.uk
Acting Editor Sarah Hobson
Monthly £18 p.a., free to people on income support; tape version free to people with visual impairment or severe disability

Newspaper for people with different types of disability, carers and professionals, and anyone interested in disability. News and comment on anything of interest in the disability field: benefits, services, equipment, jobs, politics, motoring, holidays, sport, relationships, the arts. All regular contributors have a disability (unless they are a parent of someone with a disability). Preliminary letter or email desirable. Founded 1984.

Diva
Millivres Prowler Ltd, Spectrum House, 32–34 Gordon House Road, London NW5 1LP
tel 020-7424 7400 *fax* 020-7424 7401
email edit@divamag.co.uk
website www.divamag.co.uk
Editor Jane Czyzselska
Monthly £3.15

Lesbian life and culture: articles and features. Length: 800–1500 words. Illustrations: colour and b&w. Payment: £10 per 100 words; £30–£50 per photo; £25–£80 per drawing. Founded 1994.

Diver
55 High Street, Teddington, Middlesex TW11 8HA
tel 020-8943 4288 *fax* 020-8943 4312

email enquiries@divermag.co.uk
website www.divernet.com
Editor-in-Chief Nigel Eaton, *Editor* Steve Weinman
Monthly £3.70

Articles on sub aqua diving and related developments. Length: 1500–4000 words. Illustrations: line, half-tone and colour. Payment: by arrangement. Founded 1953.

DIY Week

Faversham House Group Ltd, 232A Addington Road, South Croydon CR2 8LE
tel 020-8651 7100 *fax* 020-8651 7117
Editor Sarah McCarthy
Fortnightly £97 p.a.

Product and city news, promotions and special features of recent developments in DIY houseware and garden retailing. Payment: by arrangement. Founded 1874.

Dogs Today

Pet Subjects Ltd, Town Mill, Bagshot Road, Chobham, Surrey GU24 8BZ
tel (01276) 858880 *fax* (01276) 858860
email editorial@dogstodaymagazine.co.uk
Editor Beverley Cuddy
Monthly £3.50

Study of magazine essential before submitting ideas. Interested in human interest dog stories, celebrity interviews, holiday features and anything unusual – all must be entertaining and informative and accompanied by illustrations. Length: 800–1200 words. Illustrations: colour, preferably transparencies or digital, colour cartoons. Payment: negotiable. Founded 1990.

The Dolls' House Magazine

Guild of Master Craftsman Publications Ltd, 86 High Street, Lewes, East Sussex BN7 1XN
website www.gmcpubs.com
Monthly £43.80 p.a.

Dorset Life – The Dorset Magazine

7 The Leanne, Sandford Lane, Wareham, Dorset BH20 4DY
tel (01929) 551264 *fax* (01929) 552099
email office@dorsetlife.co.uk
Editor John Newth
Monthly £2.10

Articles (about 1200 words), photos (colour) and line drawings with a specifically Dorset theme. Payment: by arrangement. Founded 1967.

Drapers

EMAP Retail Ltd, 33–39 Bowling Green Lane, London EC1R 0DA
tel 020-7812 3700 *fax* 020-7812 3760
email drapers@emap.com
website www.drapersonline.com

Editor Josephine Collins
Weekly £3.50

Business editorial aimed at fashion retailers, large and small. Payment: by negotiation. Illustrations: colour and b&w photos. Founded 1887.

The Dublin Review

PO Box 7948, Dublin 1, Republic of Ireland
tel/fax (01) 6788627
website www.thedublinreview.com
Editor Brendan Barrington
Quarterly €30 p.a. (€45 overseas)

Essays, criticism, reportage and fiction for the intelligent general reader. Payment: by arrangement. Founded 2000.

Early Music

c/o Faculty of Music, University of Cambridge, 11 West Road, Cambridge CB3 9DP
tel/fax (01223) 335178
email earlymusic@oupjournals.org
website www.em.oupjournals.org
Editor Tess Knighton
Quarterly £10.50 (£46 p.a., institutions £92 p.a.)

Lively, informative and scholarly articles on aspects of medieval, renaissance, baroque and classical music. Payment: £20 per 1000 words. Illustrations: line, half-tone, colour. Founded 1973.

East Lothian Life

1 Beveridge Row, Belhaven, Dunbar, East Lothian EH42 1TP
tel (01368) 863593 *fax* (01368) 863593
email info@east-lothian-life.co.uk
website www.east-lothian-life.co.uk
Editor Pauline Jaffray
Quarterly £2.50

Articles and features with an East Lothian slant. Length: up to 1000 words. Illustrations: b&w photos, line, cartoons. Payment: negotiable. Founded 1989.

Eastern Art Report

Eastern Art Publishing Group, PO Box 13666, London SW14 8WF
tel 020-8392 1122 *fax* 020-8392 1422
email ear@eapgroup.com
Managing Sajid Rizvi, *Send material to* Shirley Rizvi, Executive Editor
Bi-monthly £6 (£30 p.a. individual, £60 p.a. institutions)

Original, well-researched articles on all aspects of the visual arts – Buddhist, Islamic, Judaic, Indian, Chinese and Japanese; reviews. Length of articles: min. 1500 words. Illustrations: colour transparencies, b&w photos; no responsibility accepted for unsolicited material. Payment: by arrangement. Founded 1989.

Eastern Eye

Ethnic Media Group, Unit 2, 65 Whitechapel Road, London E1 1DU

tel 020-7650 2000 *fax* 020-7650 2001
website www.ethnicmedia.co.uk
Editor Hamant Verma
Weekly 70p

Articles, features and news of interest to British Asians. Magazine covers music, fashion, film gossip. Freelance material considered. Illustrations: colour. Founded 1989.

The Ecologist
Unit 18, Chelsea Wharf, 15 Lots Road, London SW10 0QJ
tel 020-7351 3578 *fax* 020-7351 3617
email jon@theecologist.org
Editors Zac Goldsmith
10 p.a. £3.50

Fully referenced articles on economic, social and environmental affairs from an ecological standpoint. Study magazine first for level and approach. Length: 1000–5000 words. Illustrations: line, half-tone. Payment: by arrangement.

Economica
STICERD, London School of Economics, Houghton Street, London WC2A 2AE
tel 020-7955 7855 *fax* 020-7955 6951
Editors Prof.F.A. Cowell, Prof. Alan Manning, Prof. Tore Ellingsen
Quarterly £30 (apply for subscription rates)

Learned journal covering the fields of economics, economic history and statistics. Payment: none. Founded 1921; New Series 1934.

The Economist
25 St James's Street, London SW1A 1HG
tel 020-7830 7000
website www.economist.com
Editor John Micklethwait
Weekly £3.10

Articles staff-written. Founded 1843.

The Edge
65 Guinness Buildings, London W6 8BD
tel (0845) 456 9337
email davec@theedge.abelgratis.co.uk
website www.theedge.abelgratis.co.uk
Editor David Clark
Quarterly £4

Interviews, features, reviews: books, films, music, modern popular culture; imaginative fiction – science fiction, modern urban fiction, horror, etc. Return postage essential. Payment: £30–£300 negotiable.

Edinburgh Review
22ᴀ Buccleugh Place, Edinburgh EH8 9LN
tel 0131-651 1415 *fax* 0131-651 1415
website www.edinburghreview.org.uk
Editor Brian McCabe
3 p.a. £17 p.a. (£34 p.a. institutions)

Fiction, poetry, clearly written articles on Scottish and international cultural and philosophical ideas. Payment: by arrangement. Founded 1969.

Education Journal
Devonia House, 4 Union Terrace, Crediton, Exeter EX17 3DY
tel (01363) 774455 *fax* (01363) 776592
website www.educationpublishing.com
Editor Demitri Coryton
11 p.a. £3.65

Features on policy, management and professional development issues. Major documents and reports gutted down to a brief digest; documents and research listings. Research section combining original reports and updates on research projects. Coverage of parliamentary debates and answers to parliamentary questions, giving statistical data by LEA. Reference section that includes coverage of all circulars, conference reports and opinion column. Length: 1000 words. Illustrations: photos, cartoons. Payment: by arrangement. Founded 1903; relaunched 1996.

Electrical Review
Highbury Business, Media House, Azalea Drive, Swanley, Kent BR8 8HU
tel (01322) 660070 *fax* (01322) 616376
email e.mackay@highburybiz.com
Editor Elinore MacKay
Monthly £3.50

Technical and business articles on electrical and control engineering; outside contributions considered. Electrical news welcomed. Illustrations: photos and drawings, cartoons. Payment: according to merit. Founded 1872.

ELLE (UK)
Hachette Filipacchi UK, 64 North Row, London W1K 7LL
tel 020-7150 7000 *fax* 020-7150 7670
Editor Lorraine Candy
Monthly £3.20

Commissioned material only. Payment: by arrangement. Illustrations: colour. Founded 1985.

Embroidery
The Embroiderers' Guild, PO Box 42ʙ, East Molesey, Surrey KT8 9BB
email jhall@embroiderersguild.com
website www.embroiderersguild.com/embroidery
Editor Joanne Hall
6 p.a. £4.90 (£29.40 p.a.)

Illustrated features on contemporary textile art. Reports on internationally renowned makers. In-depth articles on ethnographic embroidery. Looks inside important collections, and at the history and social history of embroidery. Plus book and exhibition reviews, news and opportunities.

Empire
Mappin House, 4 Winsley Street, London W1W 8HF
tel 020-7182 8781 *fax* 020-7182 8703

website www.empireonline.com
Editor-in-Chief Colin Kennedy
Monthly £3.50

Guide to film and video: articles, features, news. Length: various. Illustrations: colour and b&w photos. Payment: approx. £300 per 1000 words; varies for illustrations. Founded 1989.

The Engineer

Centaur Communications Ltd, St Giles House, 50 Poland Street, London W1F 7AX
tel 020-7970 4000 *fax* 020-7970 4189
email andrew.lee@centaur.co.uk
website www.e4engineering.com
Editor Andrew Lee
Fortnightly. Controlled circulation (£69 p.a.)

Features and news on innovation and technology, including profiles, analysis. Length: up to 800 words (news), 1000 words (features). Illustrations: colour transparencies or prints, artwork, line diagrams, graphs. Payment: by negotiation. Founded 1856.

Engineering

Gillard Welch Ltd, 6ᴀ New Street, Warwick CV34 4RX
tel (01926) 408244 *fax* (01926) 408206
Editor Steve Welch
12 p.a. £9

'For innovators in technology, manufacturing and management': features and news. Contributions considered on all aspects of engineering. Illustrations: colour. Founded 1866.

Engineering in Miniature

TEE Publishing Ltd, The Fosse, Fosse Way, Radford Semele, Leamington Spa, Warks. CV31 1XN
tel (01926) 614101 *fax* (01926) 614293
email info@teepublishing.com
website www.fotec.co.uk/mehs/tee
Editor C.L. Deith
Monthly £2.45

Articles containing descriptions and information on all aspects of model engineering. Articles welcome but technical articles preferred. Payment dependent on pages published. Founded 1979.

The English Garden

Archant Publishing Ltd, Jubilee House, 2 Jubilee Place, London SW3 3TQ
tel 020-7751 4800 *fax* 020-7751 4848
email theenglishgarden@archant.co.uk
Editor Janine Wookey
Monthly £3.20

Features and photography on gardens in the English style, plant genera and garden design. Length: 800 words. Illustrations: colour photos and artwork. Payment: variable. Founded 1997.

Envoi

44 Rudyard Road, Biddulph Moor, Stoke-on-Trent, Staffs. ST8 7JN

tel (01782) 517892
Editor Roger Elkin
3 p.a. £15 p.a.

New poetry, including sequences, collaborative works and translations, reviews, articles on modern poets and poetic style; poetry competitions; adjudicator's reports. Sample copy: £3. Payment: one complimentary copy. Founded 1957.

The Erotic Review

500 Chiswick High Road, London W4 5RG
tel 020-8956 2448
email info@erotic-review.co.uk
website www.erotic-review.co.uk
Editor Eddy Timons
Monthly £4.99

Up-market literary magazine for sensualists and libertines. Length: 1000 words (articles and features), 1000–2000 (short stories). Illustrations: colour and b&w prints, artwork and cartoons. Payment: £50–£75 (articles and features), £50–£75 (short stories); £50 (prints and artwork), £40 (cartoons). Founded 1997.

Esquire

National Magazine House, 72 Broadwick Street, London W1F 9EP
tel 020-7439 5000 *fax* 020-7439 5675
Editor Simon Tiffin
Monthly £3.99

Quality men's general interest magazine – articles, features. No unsolicited material or short stories. Length: various. Illustrations: colour and b&w photos, line. Payment: by arrangement. Founded 1991.

Essential Water Garden

Aceville Publications Ltd, 23 Phoenix Court, Hawkins Road, The Hythe, Colchester, Essex CO2 8JY
tel (01206) 505984 *fax* (01206) 505945
email paul.wagland@aceville.co.uk
website www.essentialwatergarden.co.uk
Editor Paul Wagland
12 p.a. £3.10

Magazine for owners of all styles and sizes of water gardens, including fish-stocked pools. Practical projects and seasonal solutions. Illustrated step-by-step projects considered; also regular readers' garden feature. Illustrations: colour. Length: approx. 1000 words. Payment: by arrangement. Founded 1998.

Essentials

IPC Media, King's Reach Tower, Stamford Street, London SE1 9LS
tel 020-7261 6970
Editor Julie Barton-Breck
Monthly £2.40

Features, plus fashion, health and beauty, cookery. Illustrations: colour. Payment: by negotiation. Founded 1988.

Essex Life & Countryside

PO Box 1099, Colchester CO1 9DE
tel (01772) 722022
Editor Robyn Bechelet
Monthly £2.75

Features with Essex emphasis. Length: up to 1200 words. Illustrations: colour photos. Payment: negotiable. Founded 1952.

Essex Magazine and East Anglian Life

Winship Road, Milton, Cambridge CB4 6PP
tel (01223) 434409 *fax* (01223) 434415
Editor Debbie Tweedie
Monthly £1.95

Magazine for residents of Essex and East Anglia covering history, people, places, environment, events, homes and gardens. Considers unsolicited material; no acknowledgement. Welcomes ideas for articles and features. Length: 1500 words features/articles. Illustrations: colour. Payment: £100 per 1500-word feature/article; £50 for front cover image. Founded 1999.

Eventing

IPC Media, King's Reach Tower, Stamford Street, London SE1 9LS
tel 020-7261 5388 *fax* 020-7261 5429
Editor Ellie Hughes
Monthly £3.30

News, articles, features, event reports and opinion pieces – all with bias towards the sport of horse trials. Mostly commissioned, but all ideas welcome. Length: up to 1500 words. Illustrations: colour and b&w, mostly commissioned. Payment: by arrangement. Founded 1984.

Evergreen

PO Box 52, Cheltenham, Glos. GL50 1YQ
tel (01242) 537900 *fax* (01242) 537901
Editor Roy Faiers
Quarterly £3.75

Articles about Britain's famous people and infamous characters, its natural beauty, towns and villages, history, traditions, odd customs, legends, folklore, etc; regular articles on old films, songs, radio programmes and variety acts. Length 250–2000 words. Also 'meaningful rather than clever' poetry. Illustrations: colour transparencies. Payment: £15 per 1000 words, £4 poems. Founded 1985.

Everyday Practical Electronics

Wimborne Publishing Ltd, 408 Wimborne Road East, Ferndown, Dorset BH22 9ND
tel (01202) 873872 *fax* (01202) 874562
email editorial@epemag.wimborne.co.uk
website www.epemag.wimborne.co.uk
Editor Mike Kenward
Monthly £3.30

Constructional and theoretical articles aimed at the student and hobbyist. Length: 1000–5000 words.

Payment: £55–£90 per 1000 words. Illustrations: line, half-tone. Founded 1971.

Executive PA

Solutions Publishing, Lyon House, 160-166 Borough High Street, London SE1 1JR
tel 020-7173 5100 *fax* 020-7173 5101
website www.executivepa.net
Editor Natalie Ivmey
Quarterly £21 p.a.

Business to business for working senior secretaries. Length: 700–1400 words. Illustrations: colour. Payment: £140 per 1000 words. Founded 1991.

Executive Woman

Saleworld Ltd, 2 Chantry Place, Harrow, Middlesex HA3 6NY
tel 020-8420 1210 *fax* 020-8420 1691/3
email info@execwoman.com
website www.execwoman.com
Editor Angela Giveon
Bi-monthly £2.50

News and features with a holistic approach to the world of successful working women. Strong business features; articles on management, personnel, networking and mentoring. Length: 500–1000 words. Illustrations: colour and b&w. Payment: £50 per single page, £100 DPS. Founded 1987.

Family Circle

IPC Media, King's Reach Tower, Stamford Street, London SE1 9LS
tel (0870) 444 5000 *fax* 020-7261 5929
website www.familycircle.co.uk
Editor Karen Livermore
Monthly £2.20

Women's lifestyle magazine with articles on fashion, beauty, health, home and cookery. Includes some celebrity features and recipes. Payment by negotiation. Founded 1964.

Family History Monthly

Unit 101, 140 Wales Farm Road, London W3 6UG
tel (0870) 730 1655 *fax* (0870) 737 6060
email orla.thomas@metropolis.co.uk
Editor Orla Thomas
Monthly £3.30

Articles on all aspects of genealogy and British history plus listings, news and reviews. Ideas welcome. Particularly interested in articles on social, military and economic history since 1750. Does not publish anything above 3000 words. Submit via email. Contact editor for guidelines. Payment: £60 per published 1000 words, but pay more for particularly good material. Founded 1995.

Family Law

21 St Thomas Street, Bristol BS1 6JS
tel 0117-923 0600 *fax* 0117-925 0486

email editor@familylaw.co.uk
website www.familylaw.co.uk
Editor Elizabeth Walsh
Monthly £190 p.a.

Articles dealing with all aspects of the law as it affects the family, written from a legal or socio-legal point of view. Length: from 1000 words. Payment: by arrangement. No illustrations. Founded 1971.

Family Tree Magazine
61 Great Whyte, Ramsey, Huntingdon, Cambs. PE26 1HJ
tel (01487) 814050
email peter.w@family-tree.co.uk
website www.family-tree.co.uk
Editor Peter Watson
Monthly £3.30, £36.30 p.a.

Articles on any genealogically related topics. Payment: £45 per 1000 words. Founded 1984.

Farmers Weekly
Reed Business Information, Quadrant House, The Quadrant, Sutton, Surrey SM2 5AS
tel 020-8652 3500 *fax* 020-8652 4005
email farmers.weekly@rbi.co.uk
website www.fwi.co.uk
Editor Jane King
Weekly £1.95

Articles on agriculture from freelance contributors will be accepted subject to negotiation. Founded 1934.

The Feminist Review
Palgrave Macmillan Ltd, Houndsmill, Basingstoke, Hants RG21 6XS
tel (01256) 329242 *fax* (01256) 354018
website www.feminist-review.com
Edited by a Collective, supported by a group of corresponding editors
3 p.a. £38

The journal's objective is to unite 'research and theory with political practice and contributing to the development of both' together with the exploration and articulation of the socio-economic realities of women's lives. Welcomes contributions from the spectrum of contemporary feminist debate. Empirical work – both qualitative and quantitative – is particularly welcome. In addition, each issue contains some papers which are themed around a specific debate. Founded 1979.

FHM (For Him Magazine)
EMAP Elan Network, Mappin House, 4 Winsley Street, London W1W 8HF
tel 020-7436 1515 *fax* 020-7343 3000
email amy.lindsay@fhm.com
website www.fhm.com
Editor Ross Brown
Monthly £3.30

Features, fashion, grooming, travel (adventure) and men's interests. Length: 1200–2000 words. Illustrations: colour and b&w photos, line and colour artwork. Payment: by negotiation. Founded 1987.

The Field
IPC Media Ltd, King's Reach Tower, Stamford Street, London SE1 9LS
tel 020-7261 5198 *fax* 020-7261 5358
website www.thefield.co.uk
Editor Jonathan Young
Monthly £3.20

Specific, topical and informed features on the British countryside and country pursuits, including natural history, field sports, gardening and rural conservation. Overseas subjects considered but opportunities for such articles are limited. No fiction or children's material. Articles, length 800–2000 words, by outside contributors considered; also topical 'shorts' of 200–300 words on all countryside matters. Illustrations: colour photos of a high standard. Payment: on merit. Founded 1853.

Film Ireland
Filmbase, Curved Street, Temple Bar, Dublin 2, Republic of Ireland
tel 353 1 6711303 *fax* 353 1 6796717
email editor@filmbase.ie
website www.filmireland.net
Editor Lir Mac Cárthaigh
Bi-monthly €6

Aims to be an open and pluralist forum for the exchange of ideas and news on filmmaking and cinema, both Irish and international. Special reports, interviews and reviews; acts as a unique archival mirror of film activity in Ireland. Founded 1987.

Film Review
Visual Imagination Ltd, 9 Blades Court, Deodar Road, London SW15 2NU
tel 020-8875 1520 *fax* 020-8875 1588
email filmreview@visimag.com
Editor Nikki Baughan
Four weekly £3.99

Features and interviews on mainstream cinema; film and video reviews. No fiction. Length: 1000–3000 words (features), 350 words (reviews). Illustrations: colour and b&w. Payment: £80 per 1000 words; £20 for first image, £10 per additional image. Founded 1950.

Financial Adviser
FT Finance Ltd, Tabernacle Court, 16–28 Tabernacle Street, London EC2A 4DD
tel 020-7382 8000 *fax* 020-7382 8588
Editor Hal Austin
Weekly £90 p.a. Free to financial intermediaries working in financial services

Topical personal finance news and features. Length: variable. Payment: by arrangement. Founded 1987.

Fire

Westgate, 120–130 Station Road, Redhill, Surrey
RH1 1ET
tel (01737) 855000 *fax* (01737) 855418
website www.fire-magazine.com
Editor Andrew Lynch
Monthly £9.10 (£74 p.a.)

Articles on firefighting and fire prevention from
acknowledged experts only. Length: 600 words. No
unsolicited contributions. Illustrations: dramatic
firefighting or fire brigade rescue colour photos. Also
Fire International. Payment: by arrangement.
Founded 1908.

Fishing News

4th Floor, Albert House, 1–4 Singer Street, London
EC2A 4BQ
tel 020-7017 4531 *fax* 020-7017 4536
email tim.oliver@informa.com
Editor Tim Oliver
Weekly £1.25

News and features on all aspects of the commercial
fishing industry. Length: up to 1000 words (features),
up to 500 words (news). Illustrations: colour and
b&w photos. Payment: negotiable. Founded 1913.

The Fix

(formerly Zene)
TTA Press, 5 Martins Lane, Witcham, Ely, Cambs.
CB6 2LB
email ttapress@aol.com
website www.ttapress.com
Editor Andy Cox
Bi-monthly 15 p.a. (subscription only)

Reviews of short fiction, in-depth coverage of the
world's magazines (both large and small) plus
interviews, columns, news and views. Hundreds of
markets for writers in every issue. Submissions
welcome. Payment: negotiable. Founded 1995.

Flight International

Reed Business Information Ltd, Quadrant House,
The Quadrant, Sutton, Surrey SM2 5AS
tel 020-8652 3842 *fax* 020-8652 3840
email flight.international@rbi.co.uk
website www.flightinternational.com
Editor Jim Muttram
Weekly £2.60

Deals with all branches of aerospace: operational and
technical articles, illustrated by photos, engineering
cutaway drawings; also news, paragraphs, reports of
lectures, etc. News press days: Thurs, Fri.
Illustrations: tone, line, colour. Payment: by
agreement. Founded 1909.

Flora International

The Fishing Lodge Studio, 77 Bulbridge Road,
Wilton, Salisbury, Wilts. SP2 0LE
tel (01722) 743207 *fax* (01722) 743207

email floramag@aol.com
Editor Maureen Foster
Bi-monthly £2.99

Magazine for flower arrangers and florists. Also
features flower-related articles, flower arrangers'
gardens and flower-related crafts. Will consider
unsolicited material. Welcomes ideas for articles and
features. Length: approx. 1000 words (articles/
features). Illustrations: transparencies, colour prints
or high-res files on CD. Payment: £60 per 1000
words, £10–£20 illustrations. Founded 1974.

Fly-Fishing & Fly-Tying

Rolling River Publications, Aberfeldy Road,
Kenmore, Perthshire PH15 2HF
tel (01887) 830526 *fax* (01887) 830526
email MarkB.ffft@btinternet.com
website www.flyfishing-and-flytying.co.uk
Editor Mark Bowler
12 p.a. £2.80

Fly-fishing and fly-tying articles, fishery features,
limited short stories, fishing travel. Length: 800–2000
words. Illustrations: colour photos. Payment: by
arrangement. Founded 1990.

Focus

Bristol Magazines, 9th Floor, Tower House, Fairfax
Street, Bristol BS1 3BN
tel 0117-927 9009 *fax* 0117-934 9008
Editor Paul Parsons
Monthly £3.40

Science and technology magazine. Articles and
features with a science-based or technical slant. All
material is commissioned. Length: 1000–3000 words
(features). Illustrations: colour prints, transparencies
and artwork. Payment: £220 per 1000 words; £220
per full-page photo (negotiable). Founded 1992.

Folio

64–65 North Road, St Andrews, Bristol BS6 5AQ
tel 0117-942 8491 *fax* 0117-942 0369
email editor@venue.co.uk
website www.venue.co.uk
Editor Dave Higgitt
Monthly Free

Articles, features, interviews and news on people,
places and events with a local connection (Bristol,
Bath and Cheltenham area). No short stories or
poems. Unsolicited material considered. Length:
600–2000 words (features), variable (news).
Illustrations: colour and b&w. Payment: by
negotiation. Founded 1994.

Football First

20–26 Brunswick Place, London N1 6DZ
tel 020-7417 5802 *fax* 020-7490 7666
email editorial@sportfirst.com
website www.sportfirst.com
Editor Chris Wiltshire

Weekly £1.20

Tabloid Sunday newspaper covering all sports. Length: 800 words (articles), 300–800 words (news). Payment: £150 per 1000 words. Founded 1998.

For Women

Fantasy Publications, PO Box 55723, London E14 1BE
tel 020-7308 5363
Editor Elizabeth Coldwell
6-weekly £3.95

Women's magazine with erotic emphasis. Features on sex and health; erotic fiction and photos. Erotic fiction welcomed on spec. Fiction guidelines on receipt of sae. Length: 2000–3000 words. Illustrations: colour and b&w photos. Payment: £150 per story. Founded 1992.

Fortean Times

Box 2409, London NW5 4NP
tel 020-7907 6235 *fax* 020-7907 6406
email david_sutton@dennis.co.uk
website www.forteantimes.com
Editor David Sutton
Monthly £3.60

Journal of strange phenomena, experiences, related subjects and philosophies. Articles, features, news, reviews. Length: 500–5000 words; longer by arrangement. Illustrations: colour photos, line and tone art, cartoons. Payment: by negotiation. Founded 1973.

Fortnight – An Independent Review of Politics and the Arts

11 University Road, Belfast BT7 1NA
tel 028-9023 2353 *fax* 028-9023 2650
email editor@fortnight.org
website www.fortnight.org
Editor Malachi O'Doherty
Monthly £2.20

Current affairs analysis, reportage, opinion pieces, cultural criticism, book reviews, poems. Illustrations: line, half-tone, cartoons. Payment: by arrangement. Founded 1970.

FourFourTwo

Haymarket Leisure Publications Ltd, 38–42 Hampton Road, Teddington TW11 0JE
tel 020-8267 5337 *fax* 020-8267 5019
Editor Hugh Sleight
Monthly £3.60

Football magazine with 'adult' approach: interviews, in-depth features, issues pieces, odd and witty material. Length: 2000–3000 (features), 100–500 words (news/latest score). Illustrations: colour transparencies and artwork, b&w prints. Payment: £200 per 1000 words. Founded 1994.

France

Archant House, Oriel Road, Cheltenham, Glos. GL50 1BB
tel (01242) 216050 *fax* (01242) 216074
email editorial@francemag.com
website www.francemag.com
Editor Nick Wall
Monthly £3.99

Informed quality features and articles on the real France, ranging from cuisine to customs to architecture to exploring the hidden France. Length: 800–2000 words. Illustrations: colour transparencies (mounted and captioned). Payment: £100 per 1000 words; £50 per page/pro rata for illustrations. Founded 1989.

Freelance Market News

Sevendale House, 7 Dale Street, Manchester M1 1JB
tel 0161-228 2362 ext. 210 *fax* 0161-228 3533
email fmn@writersbureau.com
website www.writersbureau.com/fmn
Editor Angela Cox
11 p.a. £29 p.a.

Information on UK and overseas publications with editorial content, submission requirements and contact details. News of editorial requirements for writers. Features on the craft of writing, competitions, letters page. Founded 1968.

The Friend

173 Euston Road, London NW1 2BJ
tel 020-7663 1010
email editorial@thefriend.org
website www.thefriend.org
Editor Judy Kirby
Weekly £1.40

Material of interest to Quakers and like-minded people; political, social, economic, environmental or devotional, considered from outside contributors. Length: up to 1200 words. Illustrations: b&w or colour prints, b&w line drawings and cartoons. Payment: not usually but will negotiate a small fee with professional writers. Founded 1843.

The Furrow

St Patrick's College, Maynooth, Co. Kildare, Republic of Ireland
tel (01) 7083741 *fax* (01) 7083908
email furrow.office@may.ie
website www.thefurrow.ie
Editor Rev. Ronan Drury
Monthly €2.75

Religious, pastoral, theological, social articles. Length: up to 3000 words. Payment: average €20 per page (450 words). Illustrations: line, half-tone. Founded 1950.

The Garden

4th Floor, Churchgate, New Road, Peterborough PE1 1TT
tel (01733) 775775 *fax* (01733) 775819
email thegarden@rhs.org.uk

Editor Ian Hodgson
Monthly £4.25

Journal of The Royal Horticultural Society. Features of horticultural or botanical interest on a wide range of subjects. Commissioned material only. Length: 1200–2500 words. Illustrations: 35mm or medium format colour transparencies, occasional b&w prints, botanical line drawings; digital images are not accepted for features. Payment: varies. Founded 1866.

Garden Answers

EMAP Active Ltd, Bretton Court, Bretton, Peterborough PE3 8DZ
tel (01733) 264666 *fax* (01733) 282695
Editor Kevin Wilmot
Monthly £3

Commissioned features and articles on all aspects of gardening. Study of magazine essential. Approach by letter with examples of published work. Length: approx. 750 words. Illustrations: colour transparencies and artwork. Payment: by negotiation. Founded 1982.

Garden News

EMAP Active Ltd, Bretton Court, Bretton Centre, Peterborough PE3 8DZ
tel (01733) 264666 *fax* (01733) 465990
email sarah.page@ecm.emap.com
Editor Sarah Page
Weekly £1.50

Up-to-date information on everything to do with plants, growing and gardening. Illustrations: line, colour, cartoons. Payment: by negotiation. Founded 1958.

Gay Times

Spectrum House, 32–34 Gordon House Road, London NW5 1LP
tel 020-7424 7400 *fax* 020-7424 7401
email edit@gaytimes.co.uk
website www.gaytimes.co.uk
Editor Vicky Powell
Monthly £3.25

Feature articles, full news and review coverage of all aspects of gay and lesbian life. Length: up to 2000 words. Illustrations: colour, line and half-tone, cartoons. Payment: by arrangement. Founded 1972.

Geographical

Circle Publishing, 83–84 George Street, Richmond, Surrey TW9 1HE
tel 020-8332 2713 *fax* 020-8332 9307
email magazine@geographical.co.uk
website www.geographical.co.uk
Deputy Editor Geordie Torr
Monthly £3.50

Magazine of the Royal Geographical Society. Covers culture, wildlife, environment, science and travel. Illustrations: top quality transparencies, vintage material. Payment: by negotiation. Founded 1935.

Geographical Journal

Royal Geographical Society (with the Institute of British Geographers), Kensington Gore, London SW7 2AR
tel 020-7591 3026 *fax* 020-7591 3001
email journals@rgs.org
Editor Prof. John Briggs
4 p.a. £124 p.a. (standard)

Papers on all aspects of geography and development of current interest and concern. Large reviews section. Illustrations: photos, maps, diagrams. Founded 1893.

Geological Magazine

Cambridge University Press, The Edinburgh Building, Shaftesbury Road, Cambridge CB2 2RU
tel (01223) 312393
Editors Prof. I.N. McCave, Dr M.B. Allen, Dr D.M. Pyle, Dr G.E. Budd
Bi-monthly £339/$564 p.a. print only, £325/$540 online only, £378/$630 print and online

Original articles on all earth science topics containing the results of independent research by experts. Also reviews and notices of current geological literature, correspondence on geological subjects – illustrated. Length: variable. Payment: none. Founded 1864.

Gibbons Stamp Monthly

Stanley Gibbons Ltd, 7 Parkside, Ringwood, Hants BH24 3SH
tel (01425) 472363 *fax* (01425) 470247
email hjefferies@stanleygibbons.co.uk
Editor Hugh Jefferies
Monthly £3 (£36 p.a.)

Articles on philatelic topics. Contact the Editor first. Length: 500–2500 words. Payment: by arrangement, £45 or more per 1000 words. Illustrations: photos, line, stamps or covers.

Girl About Town Magazine

Independent Magazines, Independent House, 191 Marsh Wall, London E14 9RS
tel 020-7005 5000 *fax* 020-7005 5333
Editor-in-Chief Bill Williamson
Weekly Free

Articles of general interest to women. Length: about 1100–1500 words. Payment: negotiable. Founded 1972.

Glamour

The Condé Nast Publications Ltd, 6–8 Old Bond Street, London W15 4PH
tel 020-7499 9080 *fax* 020-7491 2551
email features@glamourmagazine.co.uk
website www.glamour.com
Editor Jo Elvin, *Features Editor* Jade Beer
Monthly £2

Lifestyle magazine containing fashion, beauty, real life features and celebrity news aimed at women aged

18–34. Feature ideas welcome; approach with brief outline. Length: 500–800 words. Payment: by arrangement. Founded 2001.

Global Adventure

Castle House, 97 High Street, Colchester, Essex CO1 1TH
tel (01206) 505921 *fax* (01206) 505929
website www.globalmagazine.com
Editor Ian Miller
8 p.a. £2.95

Magazine for people who love to travel. Combines inspirational tales and spectacular images with down-to-earth advice for the novice and seasoned travellers alike. See website for Contributor's Guidelines. Length: 3000 (features). Illustrations: colour transparencies. Payment: £300 (with images) Founded 1998.

Go Girl Magazine

Egmont Magazines, 184 Drummond Street, London NW1 3HP
tel 020-7380 6430
website www.egmontmagazines.co.uk
Editor Sarah Delmege
Fortnightly £1.85

Magazine for 7–11-year-old girls including fashion, beauty, celebrity news and gossip. Payment: by arrangement. Founded 2003.

Golf Monthly

IPC Media Ltd, King's Reach Tower, Stamford Street, London SE1 9LS
tel 020-7261 7237 *fax* 020-7261 7240
email golfmonthly@ipcmedia.com
website www.golf-monthly.co.uk
Editor Jane Carter
Monthly £3.60

Original articles on golf considered (not reports), golf clinics, handy hints. Illustrations: half-tone, colour, cartoons. Payment: by arrangement. Founded 1911.

Golf World

EMAP Active Ltd, Bushfield House, Orton Centre, Peterborough PE2 5UW
tel (01733) 237111 *fax* (01733) 288025
Editor Paul Hamblin, *General Manager* Greg Sharp
Monthly £3.60

Expert golf instructional articles, 500–3000 words; general interest articles, personality features 500–3000 words. No fiction. No unsolicited material. Payment: by negotiation. Illustrations: line, half-tone, colour, cartoons. Founded 1962.

The Good Book Guide

29–30 Monument Business Park, Chalgrove, Oxon OX44 7RW
tel (01865) 893434 *fax* (01865) 893430
email enquiries@gbgdirect.com

website www.thegoodbookguide.com
Contact Hilary Foakes
Monthly

Review magazine recommending and selling the best books published in Britain.

Good Housekeeping

National Magazine House, 72 Broadwick Street, London W1F 9EP
tel 020-7439 5000 *fax* 020-7439 5616
website www.natmags.co.uk
Editor-in-Chief Lindsay Nicholson
Monthly £2.90

Articles on topics of interest to intelligent women. No unsolicited features or stories accepted; approach by letter only. Homes, fashion, beauty and food covered by staff writers. Payment: magazine standards. Illustrations: commissioned. Founded 1922.

GQ

Condé Nast Publications, Vogue House, Hanover Square, London W1S 1JU
tel 020-7499 9080 *fax* 020-7495 1679
website www.gq/magazine.co.uk
Editor Dylan Jones
Monthly £3.60

Style, fashion and general interest magazine for men. Illustrations: b&w and colour photos, line drawings, cartoons. Payment: by arrangement. Founded 1988.

Granta

2–3 Hanover Yard, Noel Road, London N1 8BE
tel 020-7704 9776 *fax* 020-7704 0474
website www.granta.com
Editor Ian Jack
Quarterly £9.99 (£26.95 p.a.)

Original literary fiction, non-fiction and journalism. Study magazine before submitting work. No poems, essays or reviews. Length: determined by content. Illustrations: photos. Payment: by arrangement. Founded 1889; new series 1979.

Green Futures

Overseas House, 19–23 Ironmonger Row, London EC1V 3QN
email post@greenfutures.org.uk
website www.greenfutures.org.uk
Editor Roger East, *Send material to* Hannah Bullock, Deputy Editor
Bi-monthly £24 p.a. individuals, £34 p.a. organisations, £57 p.a. businesses (subscription only)

Articles and features on environmental solutions and sustainable futures for people in government, business and higher education. Specially commissions most material. Welcomes ideas for news stories and features. Illustrations: high-res digital photos, prints and transparencies. Founded 1996.

Greetings Today

(formerly Greetings Magazine)
Lema Publishing, 1 Churchgates Wilderness, Berkhamstead, Herts. HP4 2AZ

tel (01442) 289930 *fax* (01442) 289950
website www.greetingstoday.co.uk
Publisher-in-Chief Malcolm Naish, *Editor* Charlotte Cowell
Monthly £45 p.a. (other rates on application)

Articles, features and news related to the greetings card industry; includes Artists Directory for aspiring artists wishing to attract the eye of publishers. Mainly written in-house; some material taken from outside. Length: varies. Illustrations: line, colour and b&w photos. Payment: by arrangement. Founded 1999; first published 1972.

The Grocer

(incorporating CTN – Confectioner, Tobacconist, Newsagent)
William Reed Publishing Ltd, Broadfield Park, Crawley, West Sussex RH11 9RT
tel (01293) 613400 *fax* (01293) 610333
website www.thegrocer.co.uk
Editor Julian Hunt
Weekly £1.60

Trade journal: articles or news or illustrations of general interest to the grocery and provision trades. Payment: by arrangement. Founded 1861.

The Grower

Highbury-Business Ltd, Media House, Azalea Drive, Swanley, Kent BR8 8HU
tel (01322) 660070 *fax* (01322) 616324
email editor.horticulture@nexusmedia.com
Editor Adrian Tatum
Weekly £1.60

News and practical articles on commercial horticulture, covering all sectors including fruit, vegetable, salad crop and ornamentals. Founded 1923.

Guiding magazine

17–19 Buckingham Palace Road, London SW1W 0PT
tel 020-7834 6242 *fax* 020-7828 5791
website www.girlguiding.org.uk
Editor Wendy Kewley
Monthly £2

Official magazine of Girlguiding UK. Articles of interest to women of all ages, with special emphasis on youth work and the Guide Movement. Articles on simple crafts, games and the outdoors especially welcome. Length: up to 600 words. Illustrations: line, half-tone, colour. Payment: £70 per 1000 words.

Guitarist

Future Publishing UK, 30 Monmouth Street, Bath BA1 2BW
tel (01225) 442244 *fax* (01225) 732285
website www.futurenet.co.uk
Editor Michael Leonard
13 p.a. £5.25

Aims to improve readers' knowledge of the instrument, help them make the right buying choices

and assist them in becoming a better player. Ideas for articles welcome. Founded 1984.

H&E Naturist

New Freedom Publications Ltd, Burlington Court, Carlisle Street, Goole, East Yorkshire DN14 5EG
tel (01405) 760298 *fax* (01405) 763815
email editor@henaturist.co.uk
website www.henaturist.co.uk
Editor Sara Backhouse
Monthly £3.75

Articles on naturist travel, clubs, beaches and naturist lifestyle experiences from the UK, Europe and the world. Length: 800–1200 words. Illustrations: line, colour transparencies, prints and digital images featuring naturists in natural settings; also cartoons, humorous fillers and features with naturist themes. Payment: by negotiation but guidelines for contributors and basic payment rates available on request.

Hairflair & Beauty

Haversham Publications Ltd, Freebournes House, Freebournes Road, Witham, Essex CM8 3US
tel (01376) 534527 *fax* (01376) 534546
Editor Ruth Page
Bi-monthly £2.95

Hair, beauty, fashion and related features for the 16–55 age group. Does not accept freelance submissions. Illustrations: colour and b&w photos. Payment: negotiable. Founded 1985.

Hampshire – The County Magazine

74 Bedford Place, Southampton SO15 2DF
tel 023-8022 3591/8033 3457
Editor Philip Wettingsteel
Monthly £2.30

Factual articles concerning all aspects of Hampshire, past and present. Length: 400–1000 words. Payment: by arrangement. Illustrations: mainly colour photos. Founded 1960.

Harper's Bazaar

National Magazine House, 72 Broadwick Street, London W1F 9EP
tel 020-7439 5000 *fax* 020-7439 5506
website www.natmags.co.uk
Editor Lucy Yeomans
Monthly £3.60

Features, fashion, beauty, art, theatre, films, travel, interior decoration – some commissioned. Illustrations: line and wash, full colour and 2- and 3-colour, and photos. Founded 1929.

Health & Fitness Magazine

Future Publishing Ltd, 1 Balcombe Street, London NW1 6NW
tel (01225) 442244 *fax* (01225) 732295
email contacthf@futurenet.co.uk

website www.healthandfitnessonline.co.uk
Editor Mary Comber
Monthly £2.99

Articles on all aspects of health and fitness.
Illustrations: line, half-tone, colour. Payment: by
arrangement. Founded 1984.

Health Club Management

Leisure Media Company Ltd, Portmill House,
Portmill Lane, Hitchin, Herts. SG5 1DJ
tel (01462) 471920 *fax* (01462) 433909
email catherinelarner@leisuremedia.com
website www.health-club.co.uk
Editor Liz Terry
Monthly £48 p.a. with *Leisure Management* magazine

Official publication of the Fitness Industry
Association. Articles on the operation of health clubs,
day spas, fitness and sports centres. Items on
consumer issues and lifestyle trends as they affect
club management are welcomed. Length: up to 1500
words. Illustrations: colour and b&w photos.
Payment: by arrangement. Founded 1995.

Healthy

River Publishing Ltd, Victory House, 14 Leicester
Place, London WC2H 7BZ
tel 020-7306 0304 *fax* 020-7306 0314
website www.therivergroup.co.uk
Editor Heather Beresford
Bi-monthly £1.50

Holland & Barrett magazine. Health and nutrition
information, features, tips, news and recipes, all from
a holistic health angle. Ideas from freelancers
welcome, with a view to commissioning. Email ideas
in first instance. Payment by negotiation. Founded
1996.

Heat

Emap plc, Endeavour House, 189 Shaftesbury
Avenue, London WC2H 8JG
tel 020-7437 9011 *fax* 020-7859 8670
email heat@emap.com
Editor Mark Frith
Weekly £1.55

Features and news on celebrities. Founded 1999.

Hello!

Wellington House, 69–71 Upper Ground, London
SE1 9PQ
tel 020-7667 8700 *fax* 020-7667 8716
Editor Ronnie Whelan
Weekly £1.90

News-based features – showbusiness, celebrity,
royalty; exclusive interviews. Payment: by
arrangement. Illustrated. Founded 1988.

Hertfordshire Countryside

Beaumonde Publications Ltd, PO Box 5, Hitchin,
Herts. SG5 1GJ

tel (01462) 431237 *fax* (01462) 422015
email martin_small@btconnect.com
Editor Sandra Small
Monthly £1.25

Articles of county interest. No poetry, puzzles or
crosswords. Length: approx. 1000 words. Payment:
£30 per 1000 words. Illustrations: line, half-tone.
Founded 1946.

Hi-Fi News

IPC Country & Leisure Media Ltd, Focus House,
Dingwall Avenue, Croydon CR9 2TA
tel 020-8774 0846 *fax* 020-8774 0940
email hi-finews@ipcmedia.com
Editor Steve Fairclough
Monthly £3.50

Articles on all aspects of high-quality sound recording
and reproduction; also extensive record review
section and supporting musical feature articles. Audio
matter is essentially technical, but should be
presented in a manner suitable for music lovers
interested in the nature of sound. Length: 2000–3000
words. Illustrations: line, half-tone. Payment: by
arrangement. Founded 1956.

History Today

20 Old Compton Street, London W1D 4TW
tel 020-7534 8000
email admin@historytoday.com
website www.historytoday.com
Editor Peter Furtado
Monthly £4.20

History in the widest sense – political, economic,
social, biography, relating past to present; world
history as well as British. Length: 3500 words
(articles); 600–1200 words (news/views). Illustrations:
prints and original photos. Do not send original
material until publication is agreed. Accepts freelance
contributions dealing with genuinely new historical
and archaeological research. Payment: by arrangement.
Send sae for return of MS. Founded 1951.

Home and Family

The Mothers' Union, Mary Sumner House,
24 Tufton Street, London SW1P 3RB
tel 020-7222 5533 *fax* 020-7222 1591
email home&family@themothersunion.org
Editor Jill Worth
Quarterly £1.75

Short articles related to Christian family life.
Payment: approx. £70 per 1000 words. Illustrations:
colour photos. Founded 1954.

Home Words

The Church Times, 33 Upper Street, London N1 0PN
tel 020-7359 4570 *fax* 020-7359 8132
Editor Paul Handley
Monthly

Leading national insert for C of E parish magazines.
Articles of interest to parishes; poems. Items should

bear the author's name and address; include return postage or send by email. Length: up to 450 words, accompanied by photos/illustrations. Payment: by arrangement. Founded 1905.

Homes and Gardens

IPC Magazines Ltd, King's Reach Tower, Stamford Street, London SE1 9LS
tel 020-7261 5000 *fax* 020-7261 6247
website www.ipcmedia.com
Editor Deborah Barker
Monthly £3.10

Articles on home interest or design, particularly well-designed British interiors (snapshots should be submitted). Length: articles, 900–1000 words. Illustrations: all types. Payment: generous, but exceptional work required; varies. Founded 1919.

Homestyle

Essential Publishing, The Tower, Phoenix Square, Colchester, Essex CO4 9PE
tel (01206) 796911 *fax* (01206) 796922
website www.essentialpublishing.co.uk
Editor Sarah Gallaher
Monthly £1.95

Ideas and practical features on home and garden improvements. Merchandise reviews. Length: 2–6 page spreads. Illustrations: colour transparencies, digital images. Payment: by negotiation. Founded 1992.

The Horror Express

PO Box 11600, Birmingham B30 2WQ
email horrorexpress@blueyonder.co.uk
website www.horrorexpress.pwp.blueyonder.co.uk
Editor Marc Shemmans
3 p.a. £4

A dark fiction magazine. Interested in horror, thriller, mystery and suspense stories; tales that are creepy, powerful and emotional but that are also chilling and disturbing. Also welcomes science fiction, fantasy, crime, supernatural and psychological tales. Length: 6000 words (stories), 1000 words (articles). Payment: £5 per 1000 words. Founded 2003.

Horse & Hound

IPC Media Ltd, King's Reach Tower, Stamford Street, London SE1 9LS
tel 020-7261 6315 *fax* 020-7261 5429
email jenny_sims@ipcmedia.com
website www.horseandhound.co.uk
Editor Lucy Higginson
Weekly £2

Special articles, news items, photos, on all matters appertaining to equestrian sports. Payment: by negotiation.

Horse and Rider

Headley House, Headley Road, Grayshott, Surrey GU26 6TU

tel (01428) 601020 *fax* (01428) 601030
email alison@djmurphy.co.uk
website www.horseandrideruk.com
Editor Alison Bridge
Monthly £3.25

Sophisticated magazine covering all forms of equestrian activity at home and abroad. Good writing and technical accuracy essential. Length: 1500–2000 words. Illustrations: photos and drawings, the latter usually commissioned. Payment: by arrangement. Founded 1959.

Horticulture Week

Haymarket Magazines Ltd, 174 Hammersmith Road, London W6 7JP
tel 020-8267 4977
Editor Kate Lowe
Weekly £2.20 (£85 p.a.)

News, technical and business journal for the nursery and garden centre trade, landscape industry and public parks and sports ground staff. Outside contributions considered. No fiction. Length: 500–1500 words. Illustrations: line, half-tone, colour. Payment: by arrangement.

Hortus

Bryan's Ground, Stapleton, Nr Presteigne, Herefordshire LD8 2LP
tel (01544) 260001 *fax* (01544) 260015
email all@hortus.co.uk
website www.hortus.co.uk
Editor David Wheeler
Quarterly £36 p.a.

Articles on decorative horticulture: plants, gardens, history, design, literature, people; book reviews. Length: 1500–5000 words, longer by arrangement. Illustrations: line, half-tone and wood-engravings. Payment: by arrangement. Founded 1987.

Hospital Doctor

Elsevier Healthcare Publishing, Quadrant House, The Quadrant, Sutton, Surrey SM2 5AS
tel 020-8652 8745 *fax* 020-8652 8701
email hospital.doctor@rbi.co.uk
Editor Mike Broad
Weekly £3 (£89 p.a.) Free to 40,000 doctors

Commissioned features of interest to all grades and specialities of hospital doctors; demand for news tip-offs. Length: features 800–1500 words. Illustrations: colour photos, transparencies, cartoons and commissioned artwork. Payment: £165 per 1000 words, £16 per 100 words (news). Founded c.1977.

Hot Press

13 Trinity Street, Dublin 2, Republic of Ireland
tel (01) 2411500 *fax* (01) 2411539
email info@hotpress.ie
website www.hotpress.com
Editor Niall Stokes

Fortnightly €3.50

High-quality, investigative stories, or punchily written offbeat pieces, of interest to 16–39 year-olds, including politics, music, sport, sex, religion – whatever's happening on the street. Length: varies. Illustrations: colour with some b&w. Payment: by negotiation. Founded 1977.

Hotdog

Jordan House, 47 Brunswick Place, London N1 6EB
tel 020-7608 6500
website www.hotdog-magazine.co.uk
Editor Xavier Robleda
13 p.a. £3.99

In-depth news and features for film fanatics. Specially commissions most material but will consider unsolicited material. Welcomes ideas for articles and features. Length: 1500–3000 words (features), 200–1000 words (news). Payment: 20p per word. Founded 2000.

House & Garden

Vogue House, Hanover Square, London W1S 1JU
tel 020-7499 9080 *fax* 020-7629 2907
Editor Susan Crewe
Monthly £3.30

Articles (always commissioned), on subjects relating to domestic architecture, interior decorating, furnishing, gardening, household equipment, food and wine.

House Beautiful

National Magazine Co. Ltd, National Magazine House, 72 Broadwick Street, London W1F 9EP
tel 020-7439 5000 *fax* 020-7439 5141
website www.housebeautiful.co.uk
Editor Julia Goodwin
Monthly £2.99

Specialist 'home' features for the homes of today. Preliminary study of magazine advisable. Payment: according to merit. Illustrated. Founded 1989.

Housebuilder

Byron House, 7–9 St James's Street, London SW1A 1DW
tel 020-7960 1630
email allison.heller@house-builder.co.uk
website www.house-builder.co.uk
Editor Allison Heller, *Send material to* Allison Heller
11 p.a. £66 p.a.

Official Journal of the Home Builders Federation published in association with the National House-Building Council. Technical articles on design, construction and equipment of dwellings, estate planning and development, and technical aspects of house-building, aimed at those engaged in house and flat construction and the development of housing estates. Preliminary letter advisable. Length: articles from 500 words, preferably with illustrations.

Payment: by arrangement. Illustrations: photos, plans, construction details, cartoons.

HQ Poetry Magazine

(The Haiku Quarterly)
39 Exmouth Street, Swindon SN1 3PU
tel (01793) 523927
Editor Kevin Bailey
3–4 p.a. £2.80 (4 issues £10 p.a., £13 non-UK)

International in scope, publishes both experimental and traditional work. About one third of the content is devoted to haikuesque and imagistic poetry. Also includes review section and articles. Payment: small. Founded 1990.

ICIS Chemical Business

Reed Business Information, Quadrant House, The Quadrant, Sutton, Surrey SM2 5AS
tel 020-8652 3153 *fax* 020-8652 3375
email icbeditorial@icis.com
Editor John Baker
Weekly £379 p.a. Europe ($669/€557 p.a. overseas)

Articles and features concerning business, markets and investments in the chemical industry. Length: 1000–2000 words; news items up to 400 words. Payment: £150–£200 per 1000 words.

Ideal Home

IPC Media Ltd, King's Reach Tower, Stamford Street, London SE1 9LS
tel 020-7261 5000 *fax* 020-7261 6697
Editor Susan Rose
Monthly £2.99

Lifestyle magazine, articles usually commissioned. Contributors advised to study editorial content before submitting material. Payment: according to material. Illustrations: usually commissioned. Founded 1920.

Improve Your Coarse Fishing

Emap Active, Bushfield House, Orton Centre, Peterborough PE2 5UW
tel (01733) 237111 *fax* (01733) 288047
email kevin.green@emap.com
website www.iycf.co.uk
Editor Kevin Green
Monthly £2.80

Articles on technique and equipment, the best venues, news and features. Ideas welcome by email. Founded 1991.

In Balance Health & Lifestyle Magazine

Pintail Media Ltd, 50 Parkway, Welwyn Garden City, Herts. AL8 6HH
tel (01707) 339007
email vrb@inbalancemagazine.com
website www.inbalancemagazine.com
Editor Val Reynolds Brown
3 p.a. £12 for 6 issues; weekly email update

Health and lifestyle magazine with therapy listings. Features on alternative therapies and related environmental issues. Ideal platform for unpublished fiction writers. Only commissioned work accepted. Founded 1990.

In Style

12th Floor, Kings Reach Tower, Stamford Street, London SE1 9LS
tel 020-7261 4747 *fax* 020-7261 6664
Acting Editor Tammy Perry
Monthly £3.20

Fashion, beauty and celebrity lifestyle magazine for style-conscious women aged 25–44. Rarely accepts unsolicited material. Founded 2001.

Index on Censorship

6–8 Amwell Street, London EC1R 1UQ
tel 020-7278 2313 *fax* 020-7278 1878
email judith@indexoncensorship.org
website www.indexoncensorship.org
Editor-in-Chief Ursula Owen, *Send material to* Natasha Schmidt, Editorial Co-ordinator
Quarterly £9.50 (£39 p.a.)

Articles up to 3000 words dealing with all aspects of free speech and political censorship. Illustrations: b&w, cartoons. Payment: £75 per 1000 words. Founded 1972.

Inside Soap

Hachette Filipacchi (UK) Ltd, 64 North Row, London W1K 7LL
tel 020-7750 7570 *fax* 020-7150 7683
website www.insidesoap.co.uk
Editor Steven Murphy
Weekly £1.25

Gossip and celebrity interviews with soap and popular TV characters on terrestrial and satellite channels. Submit ideas by email in first instance. Payment by negotiation.

Inspire Magazine, CPO

Garcia Estate, Canterbury Road, Worthing, West Sussex BN13 1BW
tel (01903) 264556 *fax* (01903) 821081
email editor@inspiremagazine.org.uk
website www.inspiremagazine.org.uk
Monthly free/donation; available in churches

Magazine with 'good news' stories of Christian faith in action and personal testimonies. Length: 400–700 words (features). Freelance articles used rarely. Payment: up to £80.

Insurance Age

Incisive Media plc, Haymarket House, 28–29 Haymarket, London SW1Y 4RX
tel 020-7484 9700 *fax* 020-7484 9988
website www.insuranceage.com
Editor Michelle Worvell

Monthly £5

News and features on general insurance and the broker market, personal, commercial, health and Lloyd's of London. Illustrations: transparencies. Payment: by negotiation. Founded 1979.

Insurance Brokers' Monthly

7 Stourbridge Road, Lye, Stourbridge, West Midlands DY9 7DG
tel (01384) 895228 *fax* (01384) 893666
email info@brokersmonthly.co.uk
website www.brokersmonthly.co.uk
Editor Andrew Newman
Monthly £110 p.a.

Articles of technical and non-technical interest to insurance brokers and others engaged in the insurance industry. Occasional articles of general interest to the City, on finance, etc. Length: 1000–1500 words. Payment: from £40 per 1000 words on last day of month following publication. Authoritative material written under true name and qualification receives highest payment. Illustrations: line and half-tone. Founded 1950.

InterMedia

International Institute of Communications, 24–25 Nutford Place, London W1H 5YN
tel 020-7323 9622 *fax* 020-7323 9623
Editor Rex Winsbury
Bi-monthly £70 p.a. individuals, £150 p.a. library subscription

International journal concerned with policies, events, trends and research in the field of communications, broadcasting, telecommunications and associated issues, particularly cultural and social. Preliminary letter essential. Illustrations: b&w line. Payment: by arrangement. Founded 1970.

International Affairs

The Royal Institute of International Affairs, Chatham House, 10 St James's Square, London SW1Y 4LE
tel 020-7957 5700
email ktaylor@chathamhouse.org.uk
Editor Caroline Soper
6 p.a. (£59 p.a. individuals, £275 p.a. institutions)

Serious long-term articles on international affairs; approx. 50 books reviewed each issue. Preliminary letter advisable. Article length: average 7000 words. Illustrations: none. Payment: by arrangement. Founded 1922.

Interzone

TTA Press, 5 Martins Lane, Ely, Cambs. CB6 2LB
tel (01353) 777931
website www.ttapress.com/iz
Editor Andy Cox
Bimonthly £3.50 (£20 p.a.)

Science fiction and fantasy short stories, articles, interviews and reviews. Read magazine before submitting. Length: 2000–6000 words. Illustrations: line, half-tone, colour. Payment: by arrangement. Founded 1982.

Investors Chronicle

Tabernacle Court, 16–28 Tabernacle Street, London EC2A 4DD
Editor Matthew Vincent
Weekly £3.35

Journal covering investment and personal finance. Occasional outside contributions for surveys are accepted. Payment: by negotiation.

Ireland of the Welcomes

Fáilte Ireland, Baggot Street Bridge, Dublin 2, Republic of Ireland
tel (01) 6024000 *fax* (01) 6024335
email iow@failteireland.ie
website www.irelandofthewelcomes.com
Editor Letitia Pollard
Bi-monthly €3.50

Articles on cultural, sporting or topographical aspects of Ireland; designed to arouse interest in Irish holidays. Mostly commissioned – preliminary letter advised. No unsolicited MSS. Length: 1200–1800 words. Payment: by arrangement. Illustrations: scenic and topical transparencies, line drawings, some cartoons. Founded 1952.

Ireland's Own

Channing House, Upper Rowe Street, Wexford, Republic of Ireland
tel (053) 91 40140 *fax* (053) 91 40192
email irelands.own@peoplenews.ie
Editors Sean Nolan, Phil Murphy
Weekly €1

Short stories: non-experimental, traditional with an Irish orientation (1800–2000 words); articles of interest to Irish readers at home and abroad (750–900 words); general and literary articles (750–900 words). Monthly special bumper editions, each devoted to a particular seasonal topic. Suggestions for new features considered. Payment: varies according to quality and length. Illustrations: photos, cartoons. Founded 1902.

Irish Farmers Journal

Irish Farm Centre, Bluebell, Dublin 12, Republic of Ireland
tel (01) 4199500 *fax* (01) 4520876
email editdept@ifj.ie
website www.farmersjournal.ie
Editor Matthew Dempsey
Weekly €2.10

Readable, technical articles on any aspect of farming. Length: 700–1000 words. Payment: £100–£150 per article. Illustrated. Founded 1948.

Irish Journal of Medical Science

Royal Academy of Medicine, International House, 20–22 Lower Hatch Street, Dublin 2, Republic of Ireland

tel (01) 6623706 *fax* (01) 6611684
email journal@rami.ie
website www.ijms.ie
Send material to Prof. David Bouchier-Hayes
Quarterly €42 (Ireland and EU €156 p.a., non-EU €192 p.a.)

Official Organ of the Royal Academy of Medicine in Ireland. Original contributions in medicine, surgery, midwifery, public health, etc; reviews of professional books, reports of medical societies, etc. Illustrations: line, half-tone, colour.

Irish Medical Times

24–26 Upper Ormond Quay, Dublin 7, Republic of Ireland
tel (01) 8176300 *fax* (01) 8176345
email editor@imt.ie
website www.imt.ie
Editor Colin Kerr
Weekly €5.10 (€236 p.a.)

Medical articles. Length: 850–1000 words. Payment: £100 per 1000 words.

Irish Pages: A Journal of Contemporary Writing

The Linen Hall Library, 17 Donegall Square North, Belfast BT1 5GB
tel 028-9064 1644
email irishpages@yahoo.co.uk
website www.irishpages.org
Editor Chris Agee
Biannual £10/€14

Poetry, short fiction, essays, creative non-fiction, memoir, essay reviews, nature writing, translated work, literary journalism, and other autobiographical, historical and scientific writing of literary distinction. Publishes in equal measure writing from Ireland and abroad. Payment: only pays for certain commissions and occasional serial rights. Founded 2002.

The Irish Post

Irish Post Media Ltd, Cambridge House, Cambridge Grove, London W6 0LE
tel 020-8741 0649 *fax* 020-8741 3382
email irishpost@irishpost.co.uk
website www.irishpost.co.uk
Editor Frank Murphy
Weekly, Wed 90p

Coverage of all political, social and sporting events relevant to the Irish community in Britain. Contains the best guide to Irish entertainment in Britain.

Irish Printer

Jemma Publications Ltd, 52 Glasthule Road, Sandycove, Co. Dublin, Republic of Ireland
tel (01) 2800000 *fax* (01) 2801818
email f.venturini@jemma.ie
Editor Fabio Venturini
Monthly €60.95 p.a. (€76.18 UK/overseas)

Technical articles and news of interest to the printing industry. Length: 800–1000 words. Illustrations: colour and b&w photos. Payment: €140 per 1000 words; photos £30. Founded 1974.

Irish Tatler
Clanwilliam House, Clanwilliam Place, Harmonia, Dublin 2, Republic of Ireland
tel (01) 2405367 *fax* (01) 6619757
email feeback@ivenus.com
website www.ivenus.com
Editor Jennifer Stevens
Monthly €2.95

General interest women's magazine: beauty, interiors, fashion, cookery, current affairs, reportage and celebrity interviews. Length: 2000–4000 words. In association with ivenus.com. Payment: by arrangement.

Jane's Defence Weekly
Sentinel House, 163 Brighton Road, Coulsdon, Surrey CR5 2YH
tel 020-8700 3700 *fax* 020-8763 1007
website jdw.janes.com
Editor Peter Felstead
Weekly £240 p.a. online £705 p.a. (5-year archive on CD-Rom)

International defence news; military equipment; budget analysis, industry, military technology, business, political, defence market intelligence. Payment: minimum £200 per 1000 words used. Illustrations: colour. Founded 1984.

Jazz Journal International
Jazz Journal Ltd, 3 & 3A Forest Road, Loughton, Essex IG10 1DR
tel 020-8532 0456/0678 *fax* 020-8532 0440
Publisher/Editorial Consultant Eddie Cook
Monthly £3.75

Articles on jazz, record reviews. Telephone or write before submitting material. Payment: by arrangement. Illustrations: photos. Founded 1948.

Jewish Chronicle
25 Furnival Street, London EC4A 1JT
tel 020-7415 1500
website www.thejc.com
Editor David Rowan
Weekly 70p

Authentic and exclusive news stories and articles of Jewish interest from 500–1500 words are considered. Includes a lively arts and leisure section and regular travel pages. Payment: by arrangement. Illustrations: of Jewish interest, either topical or feature. Founded 1841.

The Jewish Quarterly
PO Box 37645, London NW7 1WB
tel 020-8343 4675

email editor@jewquart.freeserve.co.uk
website www.jewishquarterly.org
Editor Matthew Reisz
Quarterly £4.95 (£25 p.a., £35 Europe, £45 overseas)

Articles of Jewish interest, literature, history, music, politics, poetry, book reviews, fiction. Illustrations: half-tone. Founded 1953.

Jewish Telegraph
Telegraph House, 11 Park Hill, Bury Old Road, Prestwich, Manchester M25 0HH
tel 0161-740 9321 *fax* 0161-740 9325
email manchester@jewishtelegraph.com
1 Shaftesbury Avenue, Leeds LS8 1DR
tel 0113-295 6000 *fax* 0113-295 6006
email leeds@jewishtelegraph.com
Harold House, Dunbabin Road, Liverpool L15 6XL
tel 0151-475 6666 *fax* 0151-475 2222
email liverpool@jewishtelegraph.com
May Terrace, Giffnock, Glasgow G46 6LD
tel 0141-621 4422 *fax* 0141-621 4333
email glasgow@jewishtelegraph.com
website www.jewishtelegraph.com
Editor Paul Harris
Weekly Manchester 50p, Leeds 45p, Liverpool 35p, Glasgow 50p

Non-fiction articles of Jewish interest, especially humour. Exclusive Jewish news stories and pictures, international, national and local. Length: 1000–1500 words. Payment: by arrangement. Illustrations: line, half-tone, cartoons. Founded 1950.

Journal of Alternative and Complementary Medicine
Oxford Brooks University, Broom House, 5 Jasmine Lane, St Mary's Park, Burghill, Herefordshire HR4 7QS
tel (01432) 761340 *fax* (01432) 761463
Editor Dr K.A. Jobst
Monthly £200 p.a.

Feature articles on complementary and alternative medicine, paradigm, practise and policy (up to 3000 words) and news stories (up to 500 words). Unsolicited material welcome but not eligible for payment unless commissioned. Illustrations: line, half-tone, colour. Payment: by negotiation. Founded 1983.

Junior
Future Living, 1 Balcombe Street, London NW1
tel 020-7042 4000 *fax* 020-7761 8901
email editorial@juniormagazine.co.uk
website www.juniormagazine.co.uk
Editor Catherine O'Dolan
Monthly £3.50

Glossy up-market parenting magazine aimed at mothers of children aged 0–8 and reflects the shift in today's society towards older mothers and fathers who have established their careers and homes.

Intelligent and insightful features and the best in fashion. Specially commissions most material. Welcomes ideas for articles and features. Payment: £150 per 1000 words (articles/features/short fiction), £300 per feature (colour and b&w photos/artwork). Founded 1998.

Junior Education

Scholastic Ltd, Villiers House, Clarendon Avenue, Leamington Spa, Warks. CV32 5PR
tel (01926) 887799 *fax* (01926) 883331
email juniored@scholastic.co.uk
website www.scholastic.co.uk
Editor Alex Albrighton
Monthly £3.99

For teachers of 7–11 year-olds. Articles by specialists on practical teaching ideas, coverage of primary education news; posters; photocopiable material for the classroom. Length: 800–1000 words. Payment: by arrangement. Illustrated with photos and drawings; includes 2 A2 colour posters. Founded 1977.

Junior Education Topics

Scholastic Ltd, Villiers House, Clarendon Avenue, Leamington Spa, Warks. CV32 5PR
tel (01926) 887799 *fax* (01926) 883331
email jet@scholastic.co.uk
website www.scholastic.co.uk
Editor Alex Albrighton
Monthly £3.99

Aimed at teachers of 7–11 year-olds, each issue is based on a theme, closely linked to the National Curriculum. Includes A1 and A3 full-colour posters, 12 pages of photocopiable material and 16 pages of articles. All material commissioned. Length: 800 words. Illustrations: photos and drawings. Payment: £100 per double-page spread; varies for illustrations. Founded 1982.

Justice of the Peace

LexisNexis Butterworths, 35 Chancery Lane, London WC2A 1EL
tel 020-7400 2828
email jpn@lexisnexis.co.uk
Consulting Editor Adrian Turner, *Send material to* Diana Rose
Weekly £269 p.a.

Professional journal. Articles on magisterial and local government law and associated subjects including family law, criminology, medico-legal matters, penology, police, probation. Information on articles and contributions sent on request. Length: 3000 words. Payment: £200 per feature article or £20 per column (articles). Founded 1837.

Kent Life

25A Pudding Lane, Maidstone, Kent ME14 1PA
tel (01622) 762818 *fax* (01622) 663294
email sarah.sturt@kent-life.co.uk,
michael.palmer@kent-life.co.uk

website www.kent-life.co.uk
Editor Sarah Sturt, *Editorial Assistant* Michael Palmer
Monthly £2.75

Local lifestyle magazine 'celebrating the best of county life'. Features local people, social events and entertainment and promotes local towns and villages, walks and heritage. Will consider unsolicited material. Welcomes ideas for articles and features. Length: 1000 words (articles/features), 200 words (news), 500 words (short fiction). Illustrations: transparencies, colour and b&w prints, colour artwork. Payment: negotiable.

Kerrang!

EMAP Performance 2001, Mappin House, London W1W 8HF
tel 020-7436 1515 *fax* 020-7312 8910
website www.kerrang.com
Editor Paul Brannigan
Weekly £1.99

News, reviews and interviews; music with attitude. All material commissioned. Illustrations: colour. Payment: by arrangement. Founded 1981.

Kids Alive! (The Young Soldier)

The Salvation Army, 101 Newington Causeway, London SE1 6BN
tel 020-7367 4910 *fax* 020-7367 4710
email kidsalive@salvationarmy.org.uk
website www.salvationarmy.org.uk/kidsalive
Editor Justin Reeves
Weekly 50p (£25 p.a. including free membership of the Kids Alive! Club)

Children's magazine: pictures, scripts and artwork for cartoon strips, puzzles, etc; Christian-based with emphasis on education re addictive substances. Payment: by arrangement. Illustrations: half-tone, line and 4-colour line, cartoons. Founded 1881.

Kitchen Garden

Mortons Media Group Ltd, Media Centre, Morton Way, Horncastle, Lincs. LN9 6JR
tel (01507) 529396 *fax* (01507) 529495
website www.kitchengarden.co.uk
Editor Steve Ott
Monthly £3.30

Magazine for people with a passion for growing their own vegetables, fruit and herbs. Includes practical tips and inspirational ideas. Specially commissions most material. Welcomes ideas for articles and features. Length: 700–2000 (articles/features). Illustrations: colour transparencies, prints and artwork; all commissioned. Payment: varies. Founded 1997.

Koi

Origin Publishing, Tower House, Fairfax Street, Bristol BS1 3BN
tel 0117-927 9009 *fax* 0117-934 9008

email hilaryclapham@originpublishing.co.uk
website www.koimag.co.uk
Editor Hilary Clapham
4-weekly £3.50

A practical and informative guide to keeping Koi as a hobby, from pond construction to Koi health care. Also includes features on the hobby in Japan. Length 800–1700 words (articles), 2000–3000 words (features), 150 words (news). Payment: £80–£170 (articles), £200–£300 (features). Illustrations: colour.

The Lady

39–40 Bedford Street, London WC2E 9ER
tel 020-7379 4717 *fax* 020-7836 4620
website www.lady.co.uk
Editor Arline Usden
Weekly £1

British and foreign travel, countryside, human-interest, celebrity interviews, animals, cookery, art and antiques, historic-interest and commemorative articles (preliminary letter advisable for articles dealing with anniversaries). Send proposals for articles by post. Length: 900–1200 words; Viewpoint: 500 words. Annual Short Story Competition with prize of £1000 plus. Winning entries printed in magazine. Payment: by arrangement. Founded 1885.

Lancashire Magazine

Blackpool FC Stadium, Seasiders Way, Blackpool FY1 6JJ
tel (01253) 408332
email info@lancashiremagazine.co.uk
Editor Brian Hargreaves
Bi-monthly £1.60

Articles about people, life and places in all parts of Lancashire. Length: 700–1000 words. Payment: £70–£100. Illustrations: full colour. Founded 1977.

Lancet

32 Jamestown Road, London NW1 7BY
tel 020-7424 4910 *fax* 020-7424 4911
website www.thelancet.com
Editor Dr Richard Horton
Weekly £5

Research papers, review articles, editorials, correspondence and commentaries on international medicine, medical research and policy. Consult the Editor before submitting material. Founded 1823.

The Lawyer

Centaur Communications Group, 50 Poland Street, London W1V 4AX
tel 020-7970 4614 *fax* 020-7970 4640
email lawyer.edit@chiron.co.uk
website www.thelawyer.com
Editor Catrin Griffiths
Weekly £2.65

News, articles, features and views relevant to the legal profession. Length: 600–900 words. Illustrations: as

agreed. Payment: £125–£150 per 1000 words. Founded 1987.

Legal Week

Global Professional Media Ltd, 28–29 Haymarket, London SW1Y 4RX
tel 020-7484 9700 *fax* 020-7004 7547
email john.malpas@legalweek.com
website www.legalweek.com
Editor John Malpas
Weekly £5

News and features aimed at business lawyers. Length: 750–1000 words (features), 300 words (news). Payment: £200 upwards (features), £75–£100 (news). Considers unsolicited material and welcomes ideas for articles and features. Founded 1999.

The Leisure Manager

The Institute of Leisure and Amenity Management, ILAM House, Lower Basildon, Reading, Berks. RG8 9NE
tel (01491) 874800 *fax* (01491) 874801
email leisuremanager@ilam.co.uk
website www.ilam.co.uk
Editor Carolyn Thackrah
Monthly £40 p.a. (£50 p.a. overseas)

Official Journal of The Institute of Leisure and Amenity Management. Articles on amenity, children's play, tourism, leisure, parks, entertainment, recreation and sports management, cultural services. Payment: by arrangement. Illustrations: line, half-tone. Founded 1985.

Leisure Painter

63–65 High Street, Tenterden, Kent TN30 6BD
tel (01580) 763315 *fax* (01580) 765411
Editor Ingrid Lyon
Monthly £3.10

Instructional articles on painting and fine art. Payment: £75 per 1000 words. Illustrations: line, half-tone, colour, original artwork. Founded 1967.

Let's Talk! Norfolk

Archant Norfolk, Prospect House, Rouen Road, Norwich NR1 1RE
tel (01603) 628311 *fax* (01603) 615343
email letstalk@archant.co.uk
Editor Cathy Brown
Monthly £1.25

Magazine for people aged 50+ in Norfolk. Ideas for articles welcome. Payment by negotiation. Founded 2002.

LGC (Local Government Chronicle)

Greater London House, Hampstead Road, London NW1 7EJ
tel 020-7874 0200 *fax* 020-7874 0201
email lognews@emap.com
website www.lgcnet.com

Editor Richard Vize, *Features Editor* Anne Gulland
Weekly £3.45

Aimed at senior managers in local government. Covers politics, management issues, social services, education, regeneration, industrial relations and personnel, plus public sector finance and Scottish and Welsh local government. Length: 1000 words (features). Illustrations: b&w and colour, cartoons. Payment: by arrangement. Founded 1855.

Life & Work: Editorially Independent Magazine of the Church of Scotland

121 George Street, Edinburgh EH2 4YN
tel 0131-225 5722 *fax* 0131-240 2207
email magazine@lifeandwork.org
Editor Lynne McNeil
Monthly £1.60

Articles not exceeding 1200 words and news; occasional stories. Study the magazine and contact the Editor first. Payment: up to £100 per 1000 words, or by arrangement. Illustrations: photos and line drawings, colour illustrations, cartoons.

Lincolnshire Life

PO Box 81, Lincoln LN1 1HD
tel (01522) 527127 *fax* (01522) 560035
email editorial@lincolnshirelife.co.uk
website www.lincolnshirelife.co.uk
Editor Judy Theobald
Monthly £2

Articles and news of county interest. Approach in writing. Length: up to 1500 words. Illustrations: colour photos and line drawings. Payment: varies. Founded 1961.

The Linguist

The Institute of Linguists, Saxon House,
48 Southwark Street, London SE1 1UN
tel 020-7226 2822
email linguist@patricia.treasure.co.uk
website www.linguistonline.co.uk
Editor Pat Treasure
Bi-monthly £7 (£39 p.a.)

Articles of interest to professional linguists in translating, interpreting and teaching fields. Articles usually contributed, but payment by arrangement. All contributors have special knowledge of the subjects with which they deal. Length: 1500–2000 words.

The List

The List Ltd, 14 High Street, Edinburgh EH1 1TE
tel 0131-550 3050 *fax* 0131-557 8500
email editor@list.co.uk
Editor Nick Barley
Fortnightly £2.20

Events guide for Glasgow and Edinburgh covering film, theatre, music, clubs, books, city life, art, and TV and video. Publishes special issues to support

major arts events and festivals. Considers unsolicited material and welcomes ideas. Length: 200 words (articles), 800 words and above (features). Illustrations: transparencies and colour prints. Payment: £20 (articles), from £60 (features); £25–£50. Founded 1985.

The Literary Review

44 Lexington Street, London W1F 0LW
tel 020-7437 9392 *fax* 020-7734 1844
Editor Nancy Sladek
Monthly £3 (£32 p.a.)

Reviews, articles of cultural interest, interviews, profiles, monthly poetry competition. Material mostly commissioned. Length: articles and reviews 800–1500 words. Illustrations: line and b&w photos. Payment: £25 per article; none for illustrations. Founded 1979.

Loaded

IPC Media Ltd, King's Reach Tower, Stamford Street, London SE1 9LS
tel 020-7261 5000 *fax* 020-7261 5557
website www.ipcmedia.com
Editor Martin Daubney
Monthly £2.50

Magazine for men aged 18–30. Music, sport, sex, humour, travel, fashion, hard news and popular culture. Address longer features (2000 words) to Features Editor, and shorter items to Handbook Editor. Payment: by arrangement. Founded 1994.

LOGOS

5 Beechwood Drive, Marlow, Bucks. SL7 2DH
tel (01628) 483371 *fax* (01628) 477577
email charles@nyc.rr.com
Editor Emeritus Gordon Graham
Editor Charles Levine, 71–43 Kessel Street, Forest Hills, NY 11375–5931, USA
Quarterly £48 p.a. (£120 p.a. institutions)

In-depth articles on publishing, librarianship and bookselling with international or interdisciplinary appeal. Length: 3500–7000 words. Payment: 10 offprints/copy of issue. Founded 1990.

The London Magazine: A Review of Literature and the Arts

Editorial 70 Wargrave Avenue, London N15 6UB
tel 020-8400 5882 *fax* 020-8994 1713
email editorial@thelondonmagazine.net
Administration 32 Addison Grove, London W4 1ER
email admin@thelondonmagazine.net
website www.thelondonmagazine.net
Editor Sebastian Barker, *Publisher* Christopher Arkell
Bi-monthly £6.95 (£32 p.a.)

Poems, stories (2000–5000 words), memoirs, critical articles, features on art, photography, theatre, music, architecture, etc. Sae essential (3 IRCs from abroad). Submissions by email are not accepted except when agreed with the Editor. Payment: by arrangement. First published in 1732.

London Review of Books

28 Little Russell Street, London WC1A 2HN
tel 020-7209 1101 *fax* 020-7209 1102
email edit@lrb.co.uk
Editor Mary-Kay Wilmers
Fortnightly. £2.99

Features, essays, poems. Payment: by arrangement. Founded 1979.

Lothian Life

Ballencrieff Cottage, Ballencrieff Toll, Bathgate, West Lothian EH48 4LD
tel (01506) 632728 *fax* (01506) 635444
email editor@lothianlife.co.uk
website www.lothianlife.co.uk
Editor Susan Coon
Online publication only

Articles, profiles etc with a Lothians angle. Length: 500–2000 words. Founded 1995.

MacUser

Dennis Publishing Ltd, 30 Cleveland Street, London W1T 4JD
tel 020-7907 6000 *fax* 020-7907 6369
email mailbox@macuser.co.uk
website www.macuser.co.uk
Editor Nik Rawlinson
Fortnightly £3.95

News, reviews, tutorials and features on Apple Macintosh computer products and topics of interest to their users. Commissioned reviews of products compatible with Mac computers required. Occasional requirement for features relating to Mac-based design and publishing and general computing and internet issues. Ideas welcome. Length: 2000–5000 words (features), approx. 500 words (news), 300–2500 words (reviews). Illustrations: commissioned from Mac-based designers. Payment: £190 per 1000 words; competitive (artwork). Founded 1985.

Macworld

IDG Communications, 99 Gray's Inn Road, London WC1X 8TY
tel 020-7071 3615
email editor@macworld.co.uk
website www.macworld.co.uk
Editor Simon Jary
14 p.a. £4.99

All aspects of Apple Macintosh computing, primarily for professional users: industry news, product testing, tips and how-to features. Specially commissions most material. Welcomes ideas for articles and features. Payment: £210 per 1000 words. Digital pictures only. Founded 1989.

Management Today

174 Hammersmith Road, London W6 7JP
tel 020-8267 4610 *fax* 020-7267 4966

Editor Matthew Gwyther
Monthly £46.80 p.a.

Company profiles and analysis – columns from 1000 words, features up to 3000 words. Payment: £330 per 1000 words. Illustrations: colour transparencies, always commissioned. Founded 1966.

Marie Claire

European Magazines Ltd, 13th Floor, King's Reach Tower, Stamford Street, London SE1 9LS
tel 020-7261 5240 *fax* 020-7261 5277
email marieclaire@ipcmedia.com
Editor Marie O'Riordan
Monthly £2.70

Feature articles of interest to today's woman; plus fashion, beauty, health, food, drink and travel. Commissioned material only. Payment: by negotiation. Illustrated in colour. Founded 1988.

Market Newsletter

Bureau of Freelance Photographers, Focus House, 497 Green Lanes, London N13 4BP
tel 020-8882 3315/6 *fax* 020-8886 5174
email info@thebfp.com
website www.thebfp.com
Editor John Tracy
Monthly £49 p.a. UK (£69 overseas); free to members of BFP

Current information on markets and editorial requirements of interest to writers and photographers. Founded 1965.

Marketing Week

Centaur Communications, 50 Poland Street, London W1F 7AX
tel 020-7970 4262 *fax* 020-7970 4295
website www.marketing-week.co.uk
Editor Stuart Smith
Weekly £2.75

Aimed at marketing management. Accepts occasional features and analysis. Length: 1000–2000 words. Payment: £200 per 1000 words. Founded 1978.

Maxim

Dennis Publishing Ltd, 30 Cleveland Street, London W1T 4JD
tel 020-7907 6410 *fax* 020-7907 6439
email editorial.maxim@dennis.co.uk
website www.maxim-magazine.co.uk
Editor Eoin McSorley
Monthly £3.30

Glossy men's lifestyle magazine with news, features and articles. All material is commissioned. Length: 1500–2500 words (features), 150–500 words (news). Illustrations: transparencies. Payment: by negotiation. Founded 1995.

Mayfair

Paul Raymond Publications, 2 Archer Street, London W1D 7AW

tel 020-7292 8000
email mayfair@pr-org.co.uk
website www.sexclub.co.uk
Editor Steve Sheilds
Monthly £3.20

Classic British adult magazine containing features ranging from those on motorbikes and celebrities to those of a more explicit nature, as well as several photo sets. Short stories. Welcomes ideas for articles and features. Length: 1200–1500 words. Illustrations: colour, cartoons. Payment: negotiable. Founded 1965.

Medal News

Token Publishing Ltd, Orchard House, Duchy Road, Heathpark, Honiton, Devon EX14 1YD
tel (01404) 46972 *fax* (01404) 44788
email info@tokenpublishing.com
website www.tokenpublishing.com
Editor John Mussell
10 p.a. £3.25

Well-researched articles on military history with a bias towards medals. Length: up to 2000 words. Illustrations: b&w preferred. Payment: by arrangement; none for illustrations. Founded 1989.

Media Week

Haymarket Publishing Ltd, 174 Hammersmith Road, London W6 7JP
tel 020-8267 8026
email mweeked@mediaweek.co.uk
Editor Philip Smith
Weekly £2.70

News and analysis of the UK advertising media and marketing industry. Illustrations: full colour and b&w. Founded 1985.

Men Only

Paul Raymond Publications, 2 Archer Street, London W1D 7AW
tel 020-7292 8000 *fax* 020-7734 5030
Editor Nat Saunders
Monthly £3.20

High-quality glamour photography; explicit sex stories (no erotic fiction); male interest features – sport, humour, entertainment, hedonism! Proposals welcome. Payment: by arrangement. Founded 1971.

Men's Health

Natmag Rodale Ltd, 33 Broadwick Street, London W1F 9EP
tel 020-7339 4400
website www.menshealth.co.uk
Editor Morgan Rees
10 p.a. £3.60

Active pursuits, grooming, fitness, fashion, sex, career and general men's interest issues. Length 1000–4000 words. Ideas welcome. No unsolicited MSS. Payment: by arrangement. Founded 1994.

Methodist Recorder

122 Golden Lane, London EC1Y 0TL
tel 020-7251 8414
email editorial@methodistrecorder.co.uk
website www.methodistrecorder.co.uk
Managing Editor Moira Sleight
Weekly 90p

Methodist newspaper; ecumenically involved. Limited opportunities for freelance contributors. Preliminary letter advised. Founded 1861.

Military Modelling

Encanta Media, Berwick House, 8–10 Knoll Rise, Orpington, Kent BR8 0PS
tel (01689) 899200 *fax* (01689) 899266
Editor Ken Jones
Monthly £3.60

Articles on military modelling. Length: up to 2000 words. Payment: by arrangement. Illustrations: line, half-tone, colour.

Minor Monthly

Poundbury Publishing Ltd, Middle Farm, Middle Farm Way, Poundbury, Dorchester DT1 3RS
tel (01305) 266360 *fax* (01305) 262760
website www.minormonthly.com
Editor Brian J. Elliott
Monthly £2.40

Magazine for the Morris Minor owner and enthusiast: news, features, profiles and workshops. Specially commissions most material but will consider unsolicited material. Length: 1000 words (articles/features). Illustrations: colour prints. Payment: negotiable. Founded 1995.

Mixmag

Development Hell Ltd, 90–92 Pentonville Road, London N1 9HS
tel 020-7520 8625 *fax* 020-7520-9900
email mixmag@mixmag.net
website www.mixmag.net
Editor Andrew Harrison
Monthly £3.85

Dance music and clubbing magazine. Considers unsolicited material. Length: 300–1000 words (articles), 2500–3000 (features). Payment: £200 per 1000 words. Illustrations: colour and b&w. Founded 1984.

Mizz

Panini UK, Panini House, Coach & Horses Passage, The Pantiles, Tunbridge Wells, Kent TN2 5UJ
tel (01892) 500100 *fax* (01892) 545666
email mizz@ipcmedia.com
website www.ipcmedia.com
Editor Leslie Sinoway
Fortnightly £1.60

Articles on any subject of interest to girls aged 10–14. Approach in writing. Payment: by arrangement. Illustrated. Founded 1985.

Model Boats

Encanta Media, Berwick House, 8–10 Knoll Rise, Orpington, Kent BR6 0EL
tel (01689) 899200 *fax* (01689) 899266
website www.modelboats.co.uk
Editor John Curdell
Monthly £3.30

Articles, drawings, plans, sketches of model boats. Payment: £25 per page; plans £100. Illustrations: line, half-tone. Founded 1964.

Model Engineer

Encanta Media, Berwick House, 8–10 Knoll Rise, Orpington, Kent BR6 0PS
tel (01689) 887200 *fax* (01689) 886666
Editor David Carpenter
Fortnightly £2.50

Detailed description of the construction of models, small workshop equipment, machine tools and small electrical and mechanical devices; articles on small power engineering, mechanics, electricity, workshop methods, clocks and experiments. Payment: up to £40 per page. Illustrations: line, half-tone, colour. Founded 1898.

Modern Language Review

Modern Humanities Research Association, c/o Maney Publishing, Hudson Road, Leeds LS9 7DL
Quarterly Price on application

Articles and reviews of a scholarly or specialist character on English, Romance, Germanic and Slavonic languages and literatures. Payment: none, but offprints are given. Founded 1905.

Modern Painters

3rd Floor, 52 Bermondsey Street, London SE1 3UD
tel 020-7407 9247 *fax* 020-7407 9242
email info@modernpainters.co.uk
website www.modernpainters.co.uk
Editor Karen Wright
Monthly £5.99

Journal of modern and contemporary fine arts and architecture – commissioned articles and features; also interviews. Length: 1000–2500 words. Illustrated. Founded 1986.

Modern Woman Nationwide

Meath Chronicle Ltd, Market Square, Navan, Co. Meath, Republic of Ireland
tel (046) 79600 *fax* (046) 23565
Editor Margot Davis
Monthly €63 cents

Articles and features on a wide range of subjects of interest to women over the age of 18 (e.g. politics, religion, health, social, personal, sexuality and sex). Length: 200–1000 words. Illustrations: colour photos, line drawings and cartoons. Payment: NUJ rates. Founded 1984.

Mojo

EMAP Metro, Mappin House, 4 Winsley Street, London W1W 8HF
tel 020-7436 1515 *fax* 020-7312 8296
email mojo@emap.com
website www.mojo4music.com
Editor Phil Alexander
Monthly £3.95

Serious rock music magazine: interviews, news and reviews of books, live shows and albums. Length: up to 10,000 words. Illustrations: colour and b&w photos, colour caricatures. Payment: £250 per 1000 words; £200–£400 illustrations. Founded 1993.

Moneywise

69 Old Broad Street, London EC2M 1QS
tel 020-7382 4300 *fax* 020-7374 4520
website www.moneywise.co.uk
Editor Emma-Lou Montgomery, *Send material to* Rachel Williams, Deputy Editor
Monthly £3.95

Financial and consumer interest features, articles and news stories. No unsolicited MSS. Length: 1500–2000 words. Illustrations: willing to see designers, illustrators and photographers for fresh new ideas. Payment: by arrangement. Founded 1990.

More

EMAP Élan, Endeavour House, 189 Shaftesbury Avenue, London WC2H 8JG
tel 020-7208 3165 *fax* 020-7208 3595
website www.moremagazine.co.uk
Editor Donna Armstrong
Fortnightly £1.70

Celebrities, fun, gossip and sexy features, how-to articles aimed at young women. Study of magazine essential. Length: 900–1100 words. Illustrated. Founded 1988.

Mother & Baby

EMAP Esprit, Greater London House, Hampstead Road, London NW1 7EJ
tel 020-7347 1869
website www.motherandbabymagazine.com
Editor Elena Dalrymple
Monthly £2.30

Features and practical information including pregnancy and birth and babycare advice. Expert attribution plus real-life stories. Length: 1000–1500 words (commissioned work only). Payment: by negotiation. Illustrated. Founded 1956.

Motor Boat and Yachting

IPC Media Ltd, Room 2309, King's Reach Tower, Stamford Street, London SE1 9LS
tel 020-7261 5333 *fax* 020-7261 5030
email mby@ipcmedia.com
website www.mby.com
Editor Hugo Andreae

Monthly £3.80

General interest as well as specialist motor boating material welcomed. Features up to 2000 words considered on all sea-going aspects. Payment: varies. Illustrations: photos (mostly colour and transparencies preferred). Founded 1904.

Motor Boats Monthly

IPC Magazines Ltd, King's Reach Tower, Stamford Street, London SE1 9LS
tel 020-7261 5308 *fax* 020-7261 7900
email mbm@ipcmedia.com
website www.mbmclub.com
Editor Simon Collis
Monthly £3.70

News on motorboating in the UK and Europe, cruising features practical guides and anecdotal stories. Mostly commissioned – send synopsis to the Editor. Length: news up to 200 words, features up to 4000 words. Illustrations: colour transparencies. Payment: by arrangement. Founded 1987.

Motor Caravan Magazine

IPC Focus Network, Leon House, 233 High Street, Croydon CR9 1HZ
tel 020-8726 8248 *fax* 020-8726 8299
email helen_avery@ipcmedia.com
website www.motorcaravanmagazine.co.uk
Editor Helen Avery
Monthly £2.99

Touring, Your Travels, products, motorhome tests, practical features. Length: up to 2000 words. Payment: £60 per page. Founded 1985.

Motor Cycle News

EMAP Active Ltd, Media House, Peterborough Business Park, Lynchwood, Peterborough PE2 6EA
tel (01733) 468000 *fax* (01733) 468028
email mcn@emap.com
website www.emapbikes.com
Editor Marc Potter
Weekly £1.70

Features (up to 1000 words), photos and news stories of interest to motorcyclists. Founded 1955.

Motorcaravan Motorhome Monthly (MMM)

Warners Publications, The Maltings, West Street, Bourne, Lincs. PE10 9PH
tel (01778) 391027 *fax* (01778) 425437
website www.mmmonline.co.uk
Editor Mike Jago
Monthly £3.10

Articles including motorcaravan travel, owner reports and DIY. Length: up to 2500 words. Payment: by arrangement. Illustrations: line, half-tone, colour prints and transparencies. Founded 1966 as *Motor Caravan and Camping.*

Mslexia

PO Box 656, Newcastle upon Tyne NE99 1PZ
tel 0191-261 6656 *fax* 0191-261 6636
email elizabet@mslexia.demon.co.uk
website www.mslexia.co.uk
Editor Daneet Stephans
4 p.a. £18.75 p.a.

Magazine for women writers which combines features and advice about writing, with new fiction and poetry by women. Considers unsolicited material. Length: up to 3000 words (short stories), articles/features by negotiation, up to 4 poems of no more than 40 lines each in any style which must relate to current themes (or adhere to poetry competition rules). Illustrations: mono art, photos, colour transparencies. Payment: by negotiation. Founded 1998.

Muscle & Fitness

Weider Publishing, 10 Windsor Court, Clarence Drive, Harrogate, North Yorkshire HG1 2PE
tel (01423) 504516 *fax* (01423) 561494
website www.muscle-fitness-europe.com
Editor Geoff Evans
Monthly £3.40

A guide to muscle development and general health and fitness. Founded 1988.

Music Teacher

Rhinegold Publishing Ltd, 241 Shaftesbury Avenue, London WC2H 8TF
tel 020-7333 1747 *fax* 020-7333 1769
email music.teacher@rhinegold.co.uk
website www.rhinegold.co.uk
Editor Clare Stevens
Monthly £3.75

Information and articles for both school and private instrumental teachers, including reviews of books, music, CD-Roms and other music–education resources. Articles and illustrations must both have a teacher, as well as a musical, interest. Length: articles 1000–2000 words. Payment: £120 per 1000 words. Founded 1908.

Music Week

CMPi, 1st Floor, Ludgate House, 245 Blackfriars Road, London SE1 9UR
tel 020-7921 8348
email martin@musicweek.com
Editor Martin Talbot
Weekly £4.25 (£199 p.a.)

News and features on all aspects of producing, manufacturing, marketing and retailing music. Payment: by negotiation. Founded 1959.

Musical Opinion

2 Princes Road, St Leonards-on-Sea, East Sussex TN37 6EL
tel (01424) 715167 *fax* (01424) 712214

email musicalopinion2@aol.com
website www.musicalopinion.com
Editor Denby Richards
Bi-monthly £5 (£28 p.a.)

Suggestions for contributions of musical interest, scholastic, educational, anniversaries and ethnic. Dance, DVD, CD, opera, festival, book, music reviews. All editorial matter must be commissioned. Payment: on publication. Illustrations: colour photos. Founded 1877.

Musical Times
7 Brunswick Mews, Hove, East Sussex BN3 1HD
Editor Antony Bye
4 p.a. £4.95 (£36 p.a.)

Musical articles, reviews, 500–6000 words. All material commissioned; no unsolicited material. Illustrations: music. Founded 1844.

My Weekly
D.C. Thomson & Co. Ltd, 80 Kingsway East, Dundee DD4 8SL
tel (01382) 223131 *fax* (01382) 452491
email myweekly@dcthomson.co.uk
185 Fleet Street, London EC4A 2HS
tel 020-7400 1030 *fax* 020-7400 1089
Send material to The Editor
Weekly 68p

Short complete stories of 1000–2500 words with humorous, romantic or strong emotional themes. Articles on all subjects of women's interest. Contributions should appeal to women everywhere. Send material to The Editor. Payment: on acceptance. Illustrations: colour and b&w. Founded 1910.

My Weekly Story Collection
D.C. Thomson & Co. Ltd, Albert Square, Dundee DD1 9QJ
tel (01382) 223131 *fax* (01382) 322214
email tsteel@dcthomson.co.uk
185 Fleet Street, London EC4A 2HS
tel 020-7400 1030 *fax* 020-7400 1089
Editor Tracey Steel
4 p.m. £1.20

25,000–30,000-word romantic stories aimed at the adult market. Payment: on acceptance; competitive for the market. No illustrations.

The National Trust Magazine
The National Trust, Heclis, Kemble Drive, Swindon SN2 2NA
website www.nationaltrust.org.uk
Editor Sue Herdman
3 p.a. Free to members

News and features on the conservation of historic houses, coasts and countryside in the UK. No unsolicited articles. Length: 1000 words (features), 200 words (news). Illustrations: colour transparencies and artwork. Payment: by arrangement; picture library rates. Founded 1969.

Natural World
EMAP Active Ltd, Bretton Court, Bretton, Peterborough PE3 8DZ
tel (01733) 264666 *fax* (01733) 282654
Editor Rupert Paul
3 p.a. Free to members

National magazine of the Wildlife Trusts. Short articles on the work of the UK's 47 wildlife trusts. Unsolicited MSS not accepted. Length: up to 1200 words. Payment: by arrangement. Illustrations: line, colour. Founded 1981.

Naturalist
The University, Bradford BD7 1DP
tel (01274) 234212 *fax* (01274) 234231
email m.r.d.seaward@bradford.ac.uk
Editor Prof M.R.D. Seaward MSc, PhD, DSc
Quarterly £20 p.a.

Original papers on all kinds of British natural history subjects, including various aspects of geology, archaeology and environmental science. Length: immaterial. Illustrations: photos and line drawings. Payment: none. Founded 1875.

Nature
Macmillan Magazines Ltd, The Macmillan Building, 4 Crinan Street, London N1 9XW
tel 020-7833 4000 *fax* 020-7843 4596
email nature@nature.com
website www.nature.com/nature
Editor Philip Campbell
Weekly £10 (£130 p.a.)

Devoted to scientific matters and to their bearing upon public affairs. All contributors of articles have specialised knowledge of the subjects with which they deal. Illustrations: line, half-tone. Founded 1869.

Nautical Magazine
Brown, Son & Ferguson Ltd, 4–10 Darnley Street, Glasgow G41 2SD
tel 0141-429 1234 *fax* 0141-420 1694
email info@skipper.co.uk
website www.skipper.co.uk
Editor L. Ingram-Brown
Monthly £32.40 p.a. (£36.60 p.a. overseas)

Articles relating to nautical and shipping profession, from 1500–2000 words; also translations. Payment: by arrangement. No illustrations. Founded 1832.

NB Magazine
RNIB, 105 Judd Street, London WC1H 9NE
email nbmagazine@rnib.org.uk
Editor Ann Lee
Monthly £3, (£28.80 p.a.)

Articles on eye health and sight loss for professionals. Published in clear print, braille, disk, tape editions and email. Length: from 500 words. Payment: by arrangement. Illustrations: high-res jpg files on disk only. Founded 1930; as *Beacon* 1917, then *New Beacon*.

.net The Internet Magazine

Future Publishing Ltd, Beaufort Court, 30 Monmouth Street, Bath BA1 2BW
tel (01225) 442244 *fax* (01225) 732291
email netmag@futurenet.co.uk
website www.netmag.co.uk
Editor Lisa Jones
Monthly CD edition £4.99

Articles, features and news on the internet. Length: 1000–3000 words. Payment: negotiable. Illustrations: colour. Founded 1994.

New Humanist

1 Gower Street, London WC1E 6HD
tel 020-7436 1151
email editor@newhumanist.org.uk
website www.newhumanist.org.uk
Editor Casper Melville
Bimonthly £2.50

Articles on current affairs, philosophy, science, literature and humanism. Length: 500–1500 words. Illustrations: b&w photos. Payment: nominal. Founded 1885.

New Internationalist

55 Rectory Road, Oxford OX4 1BW
tel (01865) 811400 *fax* (01865) 793152
email ni@newint.org
website www.newint.org
Editors Vanessa Baird, Katharine Ainger, David Ransom
Monthly £3.25 (£32.85 p.a.)

World issues, ranging from food to feminism to peace – examines one subject each month. Length: up to 2000 words. Illustrations: line, half-tone, colour, cartoons. Payment: £80 per 1000 words. Founded 1973.

New Law Journal

Lexis Nexis Butterworths, Halsbury House, 35 Chancery Lane, London WC2A 1EL
tel 020-7400 2500 *fax* 020-7400 2583
email newlaw.journal@lexisnexis.co.uk
website www.new-law-journal.co.uk
Editor Sarah Grainger, *Deputy Editor* Jan Miller
48 p.a. £5.75

Articles and news on all aspects of the legal profession. Length: up to 2000 words. Payment: by arrangement.

New Musical Express (NME)

(incorporating Melody Maker)
IPC Magazines Ltd, 25th Floor, King's Reach Tower, Stamford Street, London SE1 9LS
tel 020-7261 5000 *fax* 020-7261 6022
Editor Conor McNicholas, *Deputy Editor* Alex Needham

Weekly £1.50

Authoritative articles and news stories on the world's rock and movie personalities. Length: by arrangement. Preliminary letter or phone call desirable. Payment: by arrangement. Illustrations: action photos with strong news angle of recording personalities, cartoons.

New Scientist

Lacon House, 84 Theobalds Road, London WC1X 8NS
tel 020-7611 1200 *fax* 020-7611 1250
email enquiries@newscientist.com
website www.NewScientist.com
Editor Jeremy Webb
Weekly £2.60

Authoritative articles of topical importance on all aspects of science and technology. Intending contributors should study recent copies of the magazine and initially send only a 200-word synopsis of their idea. NB: Does not publish non-peer reviewed theories, poems or crosswords. Payment: varies but average £300 per 1000 words. Illustrations: all styles, cartoons; contact art dept.

New Statesman

(formerly New Statesman & Society)
3rd Floor, 52 Grosvenor Gardens, London SW1W 0AU
tel 020-7730 3444 *fax* 020-7259 0181
email info@newstatesman.co.uk
Editor John Kampfner
Weekly £2.75

Interested in news, reportage and analysis of current political and social issues at home and overseas, plus book reviews, general articles and coverage of the arts, environment and science seen from the perspective of the British Left but written in a stylish, witty and unpredictable way. Length: strictly according to the value of the piece. Illustrations: commissioned for specific articles, though artists' samples considered for future reference; occasional cartoons. Payment: by agreement. Founded 1913.

New Theatre Quarterly

Oldstairs, Kingsdown, Deal, Kent CT14 8ES
email simontrussler@btinternet.com
Editors Simon Trussler, Maria Shevtsova
Quarterly £24 (£33 p.a.)

Articles, interviews, documentation, reference material covering all aspects of live theatre. An informed, factual and serious approach essential. Preliminary discussion and synopsis desirable. Payment: by arrangement. Illustrations: line, half-tone. Founded 1985; as *Theatre Quarterly* 1971.

New Welsh Review

PO Box 170, Aberystwyth, Ceredigion SY23 1WZ
tel (01970) 628410

email editor@newwelshreview.com
website www.newwelshreview.com
Editor Francesca Rhydderch
Quarterly £5.40 (£20 p.a.)

Literary – critical articles, short stories, poems, book reviews, interviews and profiles. Especially, but not exclusively, concerned with Welsh writing in English. Length: up to 3000 words (articles). Illustrations: colour. Payment: £50 per 1000 words (articles); £25 per poem, £75 per short story, £40 per review, £60 per illustration. Founded 1988.

Send a hard copy to the editor with an S.A.E. with sufficient postage for the return of material. Email submissions only with the permission of the editor. Decisions within 3 months of submission.

New Woman

EMAP Élan, Endeavour House, 189 Shaftesbury Avenue, London WC2H 8JG
tel 020-7437 9011 *fax* 020-7208 3585
email kirsten.brearley@emap.com
website www.newwoman.co.uk
Editor Helen Johnston
Monthly £2.60

Features up to 2000 words. Occasionally accepts unsolicited articles; enclose sae for return. No fiction. Payment: at or above NUJ rates. Illustrated. Founded 1988.

The New Writer

PO Box 60, Cranbrook, Kent TN17 2ZR
tel (01580) 212626 *fax* (01580) 212041
email admin@thenewwriter.com
website www.thenewwriter.com
Editor Suzanne Ruthven *Publisher* Merric Davidson
6 p.a. £4.50 plus monthly e-news bulletin

Features, short stories from guest writers and from subscribers, poems, news and reviews. Seeks forward-looking articles on all aspects of the written word that demonstrate the writer's grasp of contemporary writing and current editorial/publishing policies. Length: approx. 1000 words (articles), longer pieces considered; 1000–2000 words (features). Payment: £20 per 1000 words (articles), £10 (stories), £3 (poems). Founded 1996.

newbooks magazine

4 Froxfield Close, Winchester SO22 0NN
tel (01962) 620320
email guy@newbooksmag.com
website www.newbooksmag.com
Publisher Guy Pringle

Bi-monthly £16.20 p.a.

The magazine for readers and reading groups. Includes extracts from new books, articles and features about and by authors, how the book trade works and how books reach publication and find a readership. Check out our website or email for a free introductory copy.

The Newspaper

Young Media Holdings Ltd, PO Box 8215, Sawbridgeworth, Herts. CM21 9WW
tel/fax (0870) 240 5845
email editor@thenewspaper.org.uk
website www.thenewspaper.org.uk
Editors Buffy Whiting, Tracey Comber
6 p.a. Free; subscription only

Newspaper aimed at 8–14-year-old schoolchildren for use as part of the National Curriculum. Contains similar columns as in any national daily newspaper. Length: 800–1000 words for features and short stories (non-fiction). No payment for contributions. Illustrations: colour. Founded 1999.

Now

IPC Media Ltd, King's Reach Tower, Stamford Street, London SE1 9LS
tel 020-7261 7366 *fax* 020-7261 6789
Editor Jane Ennis
Weekly £1

Showbiz magazine of celebrity gossip, news, fashion, health and cookery. Most articles are commissioned or are written by in-house writers. Founded 1996.

Nursery Education

Scholastic Ltd, Villiers House, Clarendon Avenue, Leamington Spa, Warks. CV32 5PR
tel (01926) 887799 *fax* (01926) 883331
email earlyyears@scholastic.co.uk
website www.scholastic.co.uk
Editor Sarah Sodhi
Monthly £3.99

News, features, professional development and practical theme-based activities for professionals working with 0–5 year-olds. Activity ideas based on the Early Learning Goals. Material mostly commissioned. Length: 500–1000 words. Illustrations: colour and b&w; colour posters. Payment: by arrangement. Founded 1997.

Nursery World

Admiral House, 66–68 East Smithfield, London E1W 1BX
tel 020-7782 3120
website www.nurseryworld.co.uk
Editor Liz Roberts
Weekly £1.30

For all grades of primary school, nursery and child care staff, nannies, foster parents and all concerned with the care of expectant mothers, babies and young children. Authoritative and informative articles, 800 or 1300 words, and photos, on all aspects of child welfare and early education, from 0–8 years, in the UK. Practical ideas, policy news and career advice. No short stories. Payment: by arrangement. Illustrations: line, half-tone, colour.

Nursing Times

EMAP Healthcare, Greater London House, Hampstead Road, London NW1 7EJ

tel 020-7874 0500 *fax* 020-7874 0505
Editor Rachel Downey
Weekly £1.20

Articles of clinical interest, nursing education and nursing policy. Illustrated articles not longer than 2000 words. Press day: Friday. Illustrations: photos, line. Payment: NUJ rates; by arrangement for illustrations. Founded 1906.

Official UK Playstation2 Magazine

Future Publishing UK, 30 Monmouth Street, Bath BA1 2BW
tel (01225) 442244 *fax* (01225) 732285
website www.futurenet.co.uk
Editor Stephen Pierce
13 p.a. £5.99

Non-technical magazine for the Playstation owner. Payment: by arrangement. Founded 1995.

OK

Northern & Shell plc, Lower Thames Street, London EC3R 6EN
tel (0871) 520 7066 *fax* (0871) 434 7305
Editor Lisa Byrne
Weekly £2

Exclusive celebrity interviews and photographs. Submit ideas in writing. Length: 1000 words. Illustrations: colour. Payment: £150–£250,000 per feature. Founded 1993.

Old Tractor

Kelsey Publishing Ltd, Cudham Tithe Barn, Berry's Hill, Cudham, Kent TN16 3AG
tel (01959) 541444 *fax* (01959) 541400
website www.kelsey.co.uk
Editor Stuart Gibbard
Monthly £32.45 p.a.

Articles and features on tractors and agricultural engineering for the enthusiast, the collector and the serious historian. Ideas welcome but an in-depth knowledge of the subject is essential. Payment by negotiation. Founded 2003.

The Oldie

65 Newman Street, London W1T 3EG
tel 020-7436 8801 *fax* 020-7436 8804
email theoldie@theoldie.co.uk
website www.theoldie.co.uk
Editor Richard Ingrams
Monthly £2.95

General interest magazine reflecting attitudes of older people but aimed at a wider audience. Welcomes features (800–2000 words) on all subjects. Enclose sae for reply/return of MSS. No poetry. Illustrations: welcomes b&w and colour cartoons. Payment: approx. £80–£100 per 1000 words; minimum £50 for cartoons. Founded 1992.

Opera

36 Black Lion Lane, London W6 9BE
tel 020-8563 8893 *fax* 020-8563 8635

email editor@opera.co.uk
website www.opera.co.uk
Editor John Allison
13 p.a. £4.20

Articles on general subjects appertaining to opera; reviews; criticisms. Length: up to 2000 words. Payment: by arrangement. Illustrations: photos.

Opera Now

241 Shaftesbury Avenue, London WC2H 8TF
tel 020-7333 1740 *fax* 020-7333 1769
email opera.now@rhinegold.co.uk
website www.rhinegold.co.uk
Editor Ashutosh Khandekar
Bi-monthly £5.25

Articles, news, reviews on opera. All material commissioned only. Length: 150–1500 words. Illustrations: colour and b&w photos, line, cartoons. Payment: £120 per 1000 words. Founded 1989.

Orbis

17 Greenhow Avenue, West Kirby, Wirral CH48 5EL
tel 0151-625 1446
email carolebaldock@hotmail.com
Editor Carole Baldock
Quarterly £4 (£15 p.a.); £5/€10/$11 (£20/€30/$36 p.a.) overseas

Poetry, prose (1000 words), news, reviews, views, letters. Up to 4 poems by post; via email, overseas only, up to 2 in body (no attachments). Enclose sae/2 IRCs with all correspondence. Payment: £50 for featured writer. £50 Readers' Award: for piece(s) receiving the most votes (4 winners submitted to Forward Poetry Prize, Single Poem Category); £50 split between 4 (or more) runners-up. Founded 1968.

Organic Gardening

Sandvoe, North Roe, Shetland ZE2 9RY
tel (01806) 533319
email organic.gardening@virgin.net
Editor Gaby Bartai Bevan
Monthly £2.95

Articles on all aspects of gardening by experienced organic gardeners. Unsolicited material welcome. Length: 600–2000 words. Illustrations: digital images, transparencies, line drawings, cartoons. Payment: by arrangement. Founded 1988.

OS Magazine

Peebles Media Group, Bergins House, Clifton Street, Glasgow G3 7LA
tel 0141-567 6000 *fax* 0141-331 1365
email info@peeblesmedia.com
website www.peeblesmedia.com
Editor Cath Jones
Bi-monthly £31 p.a.

Serious features on anything of interest to senior secretaries and executive PAs. No unsolicited MSS; ideas only. Illustrations: colour transparencies and prints. Payment: by negotiation. Founded 1986.

Other Poetry

29 Western Hill, Durham DH1 4RL
website www.otherpoetry.com
Editors Michael Standen (Managing), Crista Ermiya,
Peter Bennet, J.R. Burns, Peter Armstrong
(consulting)
3 p.a. £4.50 (£13/$30 p.a.)

Poetry. Submit up to 4 poems with sae. Payment: £10
per poem. Founded in 1979.

Our Dogs

5 Oxford Road, Station Approach, Manchester
M60 1SX
tel 0870 731 6500 *fax* 0870 731 6501
Editor Anne Williams
Weekly £2

Articles and news on the breeding and showing of
pedigree dogs. Illustrations: b&w photos. Payment:
by negotiation; £10 per photo. Founded 1895.

Outposts Poetry Quarterly

22 Whitewell Road, Frome, Somerset BA11 4EL
tel (01373) 466653 *fax* (01373) 466653
email rjhippopress@aol.com
Editor Roland John, *Founder* Howard Sergeant MBE,
Send material to M. Pargitter
Quarterly £4 (£14 p.a.)

Poems, essays and critical articles on poets and their
work. Payment: by arrangement. Founded 1943.

Oxford Poetry

Magdalen College, Oxford OX1 4AU
email editors@oxfordpoetry.co.uk
website www.oxfordpoetry.co.uk
Editors Kelly Grovier, Carmen Bogan, Sarah Hesketh
(business & subscriptions)
3 p.a. £3 (£9 p.a.)

Previously unpublished poems and translations, both
unsolicited and commissioned; interviews, articles
and reviews. Payment: none. Founded 1910;
refounded 1983.

Park Home & Holiday Caravan

(formerly Mobile & Holiday Homes)
IPC Media Ltd, Leon House, 233 High Street,
Croydon CR9 1HZ
tel 020-8726 8252 *fax* 020-8726 8299
email phhc@ipcmedia.com
Editor Emma Bartlett
Every 4th Friday (13 p.a.) £2.60

Informative articles on residential mobile homes
(park homes) and holiday static caravans – personal
experience articles, site features, news items. No
preliminary letter. Payment: by arrangement.
Illustrations: line, half-tone, colour transparencies,
digital images, cartoons. Founded 1960.

PC Advisor

IDG Communications Ltd, 99 Gray's Inn Road,
London WC1X 8UT

tel 020-7071 3615 *fax* 020-7405 0262
email pcadvisor_letters@idg.com
website www.pcadvisor.co.uk
Editor Andrew Charlesworth
Monthly CD edition £3.50, DVD edition £4.99

Aimed at PC-proficient individuals who are looking
for IT solutions that will enhance their productivity
at work and at home. Includes information on the
latest hardware and software and advice on how to
use PCs to maximum effect. Features are
commissioned; unsolicited material may be
considered. Length: 1500–3000 words (features).
Illustrations: colour artwork. Payment: £200 per 1000
words; artwork £200 (A5), £300 (A4). Founded 1995.

PC Answers

Future Publishing Ltd, 30 Monmouth Street, Bath
BA1 2BW
tel (01225) 442244 *fax* (01225) 732295
email pcanswers@futurenet.co.uk
website www.pcanswers.co.uk
Editor Simon Pickstock
13 p.a. £5.99

Reviews, news and practical/how-to features for
home PC users, excluding games. Length: 2500 words
(features). Illustrations: colour. Payment: by
negotiation. Founded 1991.

Peace News

5 Caledonian Road, London N1 9DY
tel 020-7278 3344 *fax* 020-7278 0444
email editorial@peacenews.info
website www.peacenews.info
Submit material to The Editor
10 p.a. £10 p.a.

Political articles based on nonviolence in every aspect
of human life. Illustrations: line, half-tone. No
payment. Founded 1936.

Pensions World

LexisNexis Butterworths, Tolley House,
2 Addiscombe Road, Croydon CR9 5AF
tel 020-8686 9141 *fax* 020-8212 1970
email stephanie.hawthorne@lexisnexis.co.uk
website www.pensionsworld.co.uk
Editor Stephanie Hawthorne
Monthly £93 p.a.

Specialist articles on pensions, investment and law.
No unsolicited articles; all material is commissioned.
Length: 1500 words. Payment: by negotiation.
Founded 1972.

People Management

Personnel Publications Ltd, 17 Britton Street, London
EC1M 5TP
tel 020-7296 4200 *fax* 020-7296 4215
email editorial@peoplemanagement.co.uk
website www.peoplemanagement.co.uk
Editor Steve Crabb

Fortnightly £5 (£95 p.a.)

Journal of the Chartered Institute of Personnel and Development. News items and feature articles on recruitment and selection, training and development; pay and performance management; industrial psychology; employee relations; employment law; working practices and new practical ideas in personnel management in industry and commerce. Length: up to 2500 words. Payment: by arrangement. Illustrations: contact art editor.

People's Friend

D.C. Thomson & Co. Ltd, 80 Kingsway East, Dundee DD4 8SL
tel (01382) 223131 *fax* (01382) 452491
185 Fleet Street, London EC4A 2HS
tel 020-7400 1030 *fax* 020-7400 1089
Send material to The Editor
Weekly 68p

Fiction magazine for women of all ages. Serials (60,000–70,000 words) and complete stories (1500–3000 words) of strong romantic and emotional appeal. Considers stories for children. Includes knitting and cookery. No preliminary letter required. Illustrations: colour and b&w. Payment: on acceptance. Founded 1869.

People's Friend Story Collection

D.C. Thomson & Co. Ltd, 80 Kingsway East, Dundee DD4 8SL
tel (01382) 223131 *fax* (01382) 452491
email sblair@dcthomson.co.uk
185 Fleet Street, London EC4A 2HS
tel 020-7400 1030 *fax* 020-7400 1089
Editor Shirley Blair
2 p.m. £1.50

50,000–55,000-word family and romantic stories aimed at 30+ age group. Payment: by arrangement. No illustrations.

Period Living

Centaur Special Interest Magazines, 50 Poland Street, London W1F 7AX
tel 020-7970 4433 *fax* 020-7970 4438
email period.living@centaur.co.uk
Editor Liz Walker
Monthly £3.25

Articles and features on decoration, furnishings, renovation of period homes; gardens, crafts, decorating in a period style. Illustrated. Payment: varies, according to work required. Founded 1990.

Personal Computer World

VNU House, 32–34 Broadwick Street, London W1A 2HG
tel 020-7316 9000 *fax* 020-7316 9313
website www.pcw.co.uk
Editor-in-Chief Dylan Armbrust
Monthly £3.25

Articles about computers, reviews, features and how-to advice. Length: 800–5000 words. Payment: from £150 per 1000 words. Illustrations: line, half-tone, colour. Founded 1978.

The Photographer

The British Institute of Professional Photography, Fox Talbot House, 2 Amwell End, Ware, Herts. SG12 9HN
tel (01920) 487268 *fax* (01920) 487056
website www.bipp.com
Editor Steve Bavister
Monthly £4.25

Journal of the BIPP covering conventional and digital imaging and images. Authoritative reviews, news, views and high-quality photographs.

Picture Postcard Monthly

15 Debdale Lane, Keyworth, Nottingham NG12 5HT
tel 0115-937 4079 *fax* 0115-937 6197
email reflections@postcardcollecting.co.uk
website www.postcardcollecting.co.uk
Editor Brian Lund
Monthly £2.40 (£29 p.a.)

Articles, news and features for collectors of old or modern picture postcards. Length: 500–2000 words. Illustrations: colour and b&w. Payment: £27 per 1000 words; 50p per print. Founded 1978.

Pilot

The Mill, Bearwalden Business Park, Wendens Ambo, Essex CB11 4GB
tel 01799 544200 *fax* 01799 544201
email nick.bloom@archant.co.uk
website www.pilotweb.aero
Editor Nick Bloom
Monthly £3.60

Feature articles on general aviation, private and business flying. Photographs, Illustrations and cartoons. Payment: £125–£1000 per article on acceptance; £25 per photo. Founded 1966.

The Pink Paper

Millivres Prowler Group, Spectrum House, 32–34 Gordon House Road, London NW5 1LP
tel 020-7424 7400 *fax* 020 7424 7401
email editorial @pinkpaper.com
website www.pinkpaper.com
Editor Tris Reid-Smith
Weekly Free

National news magazine for lesbians and gay men. Features (500–1000 words) and news (100–500 words) plus lifestyle section (features 350–1000 words) on any gay-related subject. Illustrations: b&w photos and line plus colour 'scene' photos. Payment: £40–£90 for words; £30–£60 for illustrations. Founded 1987.

Planet

PO Box 44, Aberystwyth, Ceredigion SY23 3ZZ
tel (01970) 611255 *fax* (01970) 611197

email planet.enquiries@planetmagazine.org.uk
website www.planetmagazine.org.uk
Editor John Barnie
6 p.a. £3.75 (£16 p.a.)

Short stories, poems, topical articles on Welsh
current affairs, politics, the environment and society.
New literature in English. Length of articles:
2000–3500 words. Payment: £50 per 1000 words for
prose; £30 minimum per poem. Illustrations: line,
half-tone, cartoons. Founded 1970–9; relaunched
1985.

PN Review

(formerly Poetry Nation)
Carcanet Press Ltd, 4th Floor, Alliance House,
30 Cross Street, Manchester M2 7AQ
tel 0161-834 8730 *fax* 0161-832 0084
email info@carcanet.co.uk
website www.carcanet.co.uk
Editor Michael Schmidt
6 p.a. £6.99 (£29.50 p.a.)

Poems, essays, reviews, translations. Submissions by
post only. Payment: by arrangement. Founded 1973.

Poetry Ireland Review/Éigse Éireann

2 Prouds Lane, off St Stephens Green, Dublin 2,
Republic of Ireland
tel (01) 478 9974 *fax* (01) 478 0205
email poetry@iol.ie
Editor Peter Sirr
Director Joseph Woods
Quarterly €7.99 (€30.50/$52 p.a.)

Poetry. Features and articles by arrangement.
Payment: €32 per contribution or one year's
subscription; €51 reviews. Founded 1981.

Poetry London

1ᴀ Jewel Road, London E17 4QU
tel 020-8521 0776 *fax* 020-8521 0776
email editors@poetrylondon.co.uk
website www.poetrylondon.co.uk
Editors Maurice Riordan, Scott Verner, Martha Kapos
3 p.a. £13 p.a.

Poems of the highest standard, articles/reviews on
any aspect of modern poetry. Comprehensive listings
of poetry events and resources. Contributors must be
knowledgeable about contemporary poetry. Payment:
£20 minimum. Founded 1988.

Poetry Nottingham

11 Orkney Close, Stenson Fields, Derby DE24 3LW
Editor Adrian Buckner
4 p.a. £3.50 (£12/£18 p.a. UK/overseas)

Poems; reviews; articles. Payment: complimentary
copy. Founded 1946.

Poetry Review

22 Betterton Street, London WC2H 9BX
tel 020-7420 9883 *fax* 020-7240 4818

email poetryreview@poetrysociety.org.uk
website www.poetrysociety.org.uk
Editors Fiona Sampson
Quarterly £30 p.a. (£40 p.a. institutions, schools and
libraries)

Poems, features and reviews; also cartoons. Send no
more than 6 poems with sae. Preliminary study of
magazine essential. Payment: £50 per poem.

Poetry Wales

38–40 Nolton Street, Bridgend CF31 3BN
tel (01656) 663018 *fax* (01656) 649226
email poetrywales@seren-books.com
website www.seren-books.com,
www.poetrywales.co.uk
Editor/Reviews Editor Robert Minhinnick
Quarterly £4 (£16 p.a.)

Poetry, criticism and commentary from Wales and
around the world. Payment: by arrangement.
Founded 1965.

Police Journal

Vathek Publishing, Bridge House, Dalby, Isle of Man
IM5 3BP
tel (01624) 844056 *fax* (01624) 845043
email mlw@vathek.com
website www.vathek.com
Editor John Jones
Quarterly £93 p.a.

Articles of technical or professional interest to the
Police Service throughout the world. Payment: none.
Illustrations: line drawings. Founded 1928.

Police Review

180 Wardour Street, London W1F 8FY
tel 020-8276 4701 *fax* 020-7287 4765
Editor Catriona Marchant
Weekly £1.75

News and features of interest to the police and legal
professions. Length: 200–1500 words. Illustrations:
colour photos, line, cartoons. Payment: NUJ rates.
Founded 1893.

The Political Quarterly

Blackwell Publishing, 9600 Garsington Road, Oxford
OX4 2DQ
tel (01865) 791100
website www.blackwellpublishing.com
Editors Tony Wright ᴍᴘ, Prof. Andrew Gamble,
Literary Editor Prof. Donald Sassoon
4 p.a. (£135 p.a. institutions, £23 p.a. individuals)

Topical aspects of national and international politics
and public administration; takes a progressive, but
not a party, point of view. Send articles to Assistant
Editor. Length: average 5000 words. Payment: about
£100 per article. Founded 1930.

Pond & Gardener

25 Phoenix Court, Hawkins Road, Colchester
CO2 8JY

tel (01206) 505984 *fax* (01206) 505905
website www.essentialwatergarden.co.uk
Editor Paul Wagland
Monthly £3.10

Magazine for water gardeners of all levels of expertise. Covers ponds and water features of all sizes; also fish and wildlife. Will consider unsolicited material. Welcomes ideas for articles and features. Length: 1000 words (articles), 1500 words (features) 200 words (news). Illustrations: transparencies and colour prints. Payment: varies.

Pony Magazine
Headley House, Headley Road, Grayshott, Surrey GU26 6TU
tel (01428) 601020 *fax* (01428) 601030
Editor Janet Rising
Monthly £2.30

Lively articles and short stories with a horsy theme aimed at readers aged 8–16 . Technical accuracy and young, fresh writing essential. Length: up to 800 words. Payment: by arrangement. Illustrations: drawings (commissioned), photos, cartoons. Founded 1949.

Post Magazine & Insurance Week
Incisive Media plc, Haymarket House, 28–29 Haymarket, London SW1Y 4RX
tel 020-7484 9700 *fax* 020-7484 9990
email postmag@incisivemedia.com
website www.postmagazine.co.uk
Editor Anthony Gould
Weekly £4.20 (£210 p.a.)

Commissioned specialist articles on topics of interest to insurance professionals; news, especially from overseas stringers. Illustrations: colour photos and illustrations, colour and b&w cartoons and line drawings. Payment: £200 per 1000 words; photos £30–£120, cartoons/line by negotiation. Founded 1840.

Poultry World
Reed Business, Quadrant House, The Quadrant, Sutton, Surrey SM2 5AS
tel 020-8652 4020 *fax* 020-8652 4042
email poultry.world@rbi.co.uk
Editor Graham Cruikshank
Monthly £2.70

Articles on poultry breeding, production, marketing and packaging. News of international poultry interest. Payment: by arrangement. Illustrations: photos, line.

PR Week
Haymarket Marketing Publications, 174 Hammersmith Road, London W6 7JP
tel 020-8267 4520 *fax* 020-8267 4509
Editor Daniel Rogers
Weekly £3

News and features on public relations. Length: approx. 800–3000 words. Payment: £185 per 1000 words. Illustrations: colour and b&w. Founded 1984.

Practical Boat Owner
Westover House, West Quay Road, Poole, Dorset BH15 1JG
tel (01202) 440820
email pbo@ipcmedia.com
website www.pbo.co.uk
Editor Sarah Norbury
Monthly £3.50

Sailing magazine that also covers motorboats. Hints, tips and practical articles for cruising skippers – power and sail. Send synopsis first. Payment: by negotiation. Illustrations: photos or drawings. Founded 1967.

Practical Caravan
Haymarket Magazines, Teddington Studios, Teddington Lock, Broom Road, Teddington TW11 9BE
tel 020-8267 5629 *fax* 020-8267 5725
email practical.caravan@haynet.com
website www.practicalcaravan.com
Editor David Motton
Monthly £3.40

Caravan-related travelogues, caravan site reviews; travel writing for existing regular series; technical and DIY matters. Illustrations: colour. Payment negotiable. Founded 1967.

Practical Fishkeeping
EMAP Active Ltd, Bretton Court, Bretton, Peterborough PE3 8DZ
tel (01733) 264666
website www.practicalfishkeeping.co.uk
Editor Karen Youngs
13 p.a. £3.25

Practical fishkeeping in tropical and coldwater aquaria and ponds. Heavy emphasis on inspiration and involvement. Good colour photography always needed, and used. No verse or humour, no personal biographical accounts of fishkeeping unless practical. Payment: by worth. Founded 1966.

Practical Parenting
IPC Media Ltd, King's Reach Tower, Stamford Street, London SE1 9LS
tel 020-7261 5058 *fax* 020-7261 6542
Editor Mara Lee
Monthly £2.45

Articles on parenting, baby and childcare, health, psychology, education, children's activities, personal birth/parenting experiences. Send synopsis with sae. Illustrations: colour photos, line; commissioned only. Payment: by agreement. Founded 1987.

Practical Photography
EMAP Active Ltd, Bretton Court, Bretton, Peterborough PE3 8DZ
tel (01733) 264666 *fax* (01733) 465246
email practical.photography@emap.com

website www.practicalphotography.co.uk
Editor Andrew James, *Features Editor* Ben Hawkins
Monthly £3.70

Aimed at anyone who seeks to take excellent quality pictures. Excellent potential for freelance pictures: must be first rate – technically and pictorially – and have some relevance to photographic technique. Freelance ideas for words welcome (the more unusual ideas stand the greatest chance of success). Send synopsis of feature ideas in the first instance. Payment: negotiable but typically £80 per page and £120 per 1000 words. Founded 1959.

Practical Wireless

PW Publishing Ltd, Arrowsmith Court, Station Approach, Broadstone, Dorset BH18 8PW
tel (0870) 2247810 *fax* (0870) 2247850
email rob@pwpublishing.ltd.uk
Editor Rob Mannion G3XFD
Monthly £3

Articles on the practical and theoretical aspects of amateur radio and communications. Constructional projects. Write or email for advice and author's guide. Illustrations: in b&w and colour; photos, line drawings and wash half-tone for offset litho. Payment: by arrangement. Founded 1932.

Practical Woodworking

Encanta Media Ltd, Berwick House, 8–10 Knoll Rise, Orpington, Kent BR6 0EL
tel (01689) 899200 *fax* (01689) 899266
email mark.chisholm@encanta.co.uk
Editor Mark Chisholm
Monthly £3.30

Articles of a practical nature covering any aspect of woodworking, including woodworking projects, tools, joints or timber technology. Payment: £75 per published page. Illustrated.

The Practising Midwife

Elsevier Ltd, 32 Jamestown Road, London NW1 7BY
tel 020-7424 4352
email prac.mid@ntlworld.com
Managing Editor Vivienne Riddoch
Monthly £45 p.a.

Disseminates research-based material to a wide professional audience. Research and review papers, viewpoints and news items pertaining to midwifery, maternity care, women's health and neonatal health with both a national and an international perspective. All articles submitted are anonymously reviewed by at least 2 external acknowledged experts. Length: 1000–2000 words (articles); 150–400 words (news); up to 1000 words (viewpoints). Illustrations: colour transparencies and artwork. Payment: by arrangement. Founded 1991.

The Practitioner

CMP Information Ltd, City Reach, 5 Greenwich View Place, Millharbour, London E14 9NN

tel 020-7861 6478 *fax* 020-7861 6544
email gmatkin@cmpinformation.com
Editor Gavin Atkin
Monthly £13 (£85 p.a. UK, $200 p.a. overseas)

Articles of interest to GPs and vocational registrars, and others in the medical profession. Payment: approx. £200 per 1500 words. Founded 1868.

Prediction

IPC Country & Leisure, Leon House, 233 High Street, Croydon CR9 1HZ
tel 020-8726 8000 *fax* 020-8726 8299
email prediction@ipcmedia.com
website www.predictionmagazine.co.uk
Editor Marion Williamson
Monthly £2.95

Articles on astrology and all esoteric subjects. Length: up to 3000 words. Payment: by arrangement. Illustrations: large-format colour transparencies or photos. Founded 1936.

Pregnancy, Baby & You

Future Publishing, 2 Balcombe Street, London NW1 6NW
tel 020-7042 4000
email pregnancy@futurenet.co.uk
Editor Claire Roberts
13 p.a. £2.99

Articles, features and news on health, lifestyle and labour for expectant parents. Payment £150 per 1000 words. Illustrations: b&w and colour. Founded 1997.

Press Gazette

Press Gazette Ltd, 10 Old Bailey, London EC4M 7NG
tel 020-7038 1055 *fax* 020-7038 1155
email ianr@pressgazette.co.uk
website www.pressgazette.co.uk
Editor Ian Reeves
Weekly £2.60

News and features of interest to journalists and others working in the media. Length: 1200 words (features), 300 words (news). Payment: approx. £230 (features), news stories negotiable. Founded 1965.

Pride

Hamilton House, 55 Battersea Bridge Road, London SW11 3AX
tel 020-7228 3110 *fax* 020-7228 3130
Managing Editor Sherry Dixon
Monthly £2.80

Lifestyle magazine incorporating fashion and beauty, travel, food and entertaining articles for the woman of colour. Length: 1000–3000 words. Illustrations: colour photos and drawings. Payment: £100 per 1000 words. Founded 1993; relaunched 1997, 1998.

Prima

National Magazine Company, 72 Broadwick Street, London W1F 9EP

tel 020-7439 5000 *fax* 020-7312 4100
Editor Maire Fahey
Monthly £2.30

Articles on fashion, home, crafts, health and beauty, cookery; features. Founded 1986.

Prima Baby

National Magazine Co Ltd, 72 Broadwick Street, London W1F 9EP
tel 020-7312 3852 *fax* 020-7312 3744
email prima.baby@natmags.co.uk
Editor Elaine Griffiths
Monthly £2.40

Magazine for women covering all aspects of pregnancy and childbirth and life with children aged up to 3 years; plus health, fashion. Length: up to 1500 words. Illustrations: colour transparencies. Payment: by arrangement. Founded 1994.

Printing World

Haymarket Publishing, 174 Hammersmith Road, London W6 7JP
tel 020-8267 5000 *fax* 020-8267 4455
email printing.world@cmpinformation.com
website www.dotprint.com
Editor Barney Cox
Weekly £2.75 (£94.50 p.a., overseas £142 p.a.)

Commercial, technical, financial and labour news covering all aspects of the printing industry in the UK and abroad. Outside contributions. Payment: by arrangement. Illustrations: line, half-tone, colour, cartoons. Founded 1878.

Private Eye

6 Carlisle Street, London W1D 3BN
tel 020-7437 4017 *fax* 020-7437 0705
email strobes@private-eye.co.uk
website www.private-eye.co.uk
Editor Ian Hislop
Fortnightly £1.40

Satire. Payment: by arrangement. Illustrations: b&w, line, cartoons. Founded 1961.

Professional Nurse

EMAP Healthcare Ltd, Greater London House, Hampstead Road, London NW1 7EJ
tel 020-7874 0384 *fax* 020-7874 0386
email pn@emap.com
website www.professionalnurse.net
Editor Carolyn Scott
Monthly £39 p.a.

Articles of interest to the senior nurse. Length: articles: 1500–2000 words; letters: 250–500 words. Payment: by arrangement. Illustrations: commissioned. Founded 1985.

Professional Photographer

Archant Specialist Ltd, The Mill, Bearwalden Business Park, Wendens Ambo, Saffron Walden, Essex CB11 4GB

tel (01799) 544246 *fax* (01799) 544201
Editor Terry Hope
Monthly £3.60

Articles on professional photography, including technical articles, photographer profiles and coverage of issues affecting the industry. Length: 1000–2000 words. Illustrations: colour and b&w prints and transparencies, or digital files; diagrams if appropriate. Payment: from £200. Founded 1961.

Prospect

Prospect Publishing Ltd, 2 Bloomsbury Place, London WC1A 2QA
tel 020-7255 1281 *fax* 020-7255 1279
email editorial@prospect-magazine.co.uk
website www.prospect-magazine.co.uk
Editor David Goodhart
Monthly £4.50

Political and cultural monthly magazine. Essays, features, special reports, reviews, short stories, opinions/analysis. Length: 3000–6000 words (essays, special reports, short stories), 1000 words (opinions). Illustrations: colour and b&w. Payment: by negotiation. Founded 1995.

Publishing News

7 John Street, London WC1N 2ES
tel (0870) 870 2345 *fax* (0870) 870 0385
website www.publishingnews.co.uk
Editor Liz Thomson, *Children's Editor* Graham Marks
Weekly by subscription only

Articles and news items on the book publishing and bookselling industry. Articles by agreement only. Founded 1979.

Pulse

CMP Information Ltd, Ludgate House, 245 Blackfriars Road, London SE1 9UY
tel 020-7921 8102 *fax* 020-7921 8132
email pulse@cmpinformation.com
website www.pulse-i.co.uk
Editor Phil Johnson
Weekly £160 p.a.

Articles and photos of direct interest to GPs. Purely clinical material can only be accepted from medically qualified authors. Length: 600–1200 words. Payment: £150 average. Illustrations: b&w and colour photos. Founded 1959.

Q Magazine

EMAP Performance, Mappin House, 4 Winsley Street, London W1W 8HF
tel 020-7182 8000 *fax* 020-7182 8547
email q@ecm.emap.com
website www.q4music.com
Editor Paul Rees
Monthly £3.80

Glossy music guide. All material commissioned. Length: 1200–2500 words. Illustrations: colour and b&w photos. Payment: £350 per 1000 words; illustrations by arrangement. Founded 1986.

QWF

PO Box 1768, Rugby CV21 4ZA
tel (01788) 334302
email jo@qwfmagazine.co.uk
website www.qwfmagazine.co.uk
Editor Jo Good, *Send material to* Sally Zigmond, Assistant Editor, 18 Warwick Crescent, Harrogate, North Yorkshire HG2 8JA
4 p.a. £16 p.a.

Thought-provoking short stories by female writers (no traditional romances, domestic crises or mainstream fiction) and articles of general interest. Study magazine first. Length: up to 4000 words. Payment: £5 (articles), £10 (short stories). Annual short story competition (up to 5000 words) in any style or genre, on any theme; first prize: £200. Founded 1994.

RA Magazine

Royal Academy of Arts, Burlington House, Piccadilly, London W1J 0BD
tel 020-7300 5820 *fax* 020-7300 5882
email ramagazine@royalacademy.org.uk
website www.royalacademy.org.uk
Editor Sarah Greenberg
Quarterly £4.95

Visual arts and culture articles relating to the Royal Academy of Arts and the wider British and international arts scene. Length:150–1800 words. Illustrations: consult the Editor. Payment: average £250 per 1000 words; illustrations by negotiation. Founded 1983.

Racing Post

Trinity Mirror, Floor 23, 1 Canada Square, Canary Wharf, London E14 5AP
tel 020-7293 3291 *fax* 020-7293 3758
email editor@racingpost.co.uk
website www.racingpost.co.uk
Editor Chris Smith
Mon–Fri £1.40, Sat £1.50, Sun £1.40

News on horseracing, greyhound racing and sports betting. Founded 1986.

Radio Control Models and Electronics

Encanta Media, Berwick House, 8–10 Knoll Rise, Orpington, Kent BR6 0EL
tel (01689) 899200 *fax* (01689) 899266
Editor Graham Ashby
Monthly £3.50

Well-illustrated articles on topics related to radio control. Payment: £45 per published page. Illustrations: line, half-tone. Founded 1960.

Radio Times

BBC Worldwide Ltd, 80 Wood Lane, London W12 0TT
tel 020-8433 3400 *fax* 020-8433 3160
email radio.times@bbc.co.uk
website www.radiotimes.com
Editor Gill Hudson
Weekly 95p

Articles that preview the week's programmes on British TV and radio. All articles are specially commissioned – ideas and synopses are welcomed but not unsolicited MSS. Length: 600–2500 words. Payment: by arrangement. Illustrations: mostly in colour; photos, graphic designs or drawings.

Rail

EMAP Active Publications, Bretton Court, Bretton, Peterborough PE3 8DZ
tel (01733) 264666 *fax* (01733) 282720
email rail@emap.com
Managing Editor Nigel Harris
Fortnightly £3

News and in-depth features on current UK railway operations. Length: 2000–3000 words (features), 250–400 words (news). Illustrations: colour and b&w photos and artwork. Payment: £75 per 1000 words; £20 per photo except cover (£70). Founded 1981.

Railway Gazette International

Reed Business Information, Quadrant House, The Quadrant, Sutton, Surrey SM2 5AS
tel 020-8652 8608 *fax* 020-8652 3738
website www.railwaygazette.com
Editor Chris Jackson
Monthly £77 p.a.

Deals with management, engineering, operation and finance of railways worldwide. Articles of practical interest on these subjects are considered and paid for if accepted. Illustrated articles, of 1000–2000 words, are preferred. A preliminary letter is required.

Railway Magazine

IPC Media Ltd, King's Reach Tower, Stamford Street, London SE1 9LS
tel 020-7261 5821 *fax* 020-7261 5269
Editor Nick Pigott
Monthly £3.35

Illustrated magazine dealing with all railway subjects; no fiction or verse. Articles from 1500–2000 words accompanied by photos. Preliminary letter desirable. Payment: by arrangement. Illustrations: colour transparencies, half-tone and line. Founded 1897.

Reader's Digest

The Reader's Digest Association Ltd, 11 Westferry Circus, Canary Wharf, London E14 4HE
tel 020-7715 8000
email excerpts@readersdigest.co.uk
website www.readersdigest.co.uk
Editor-in-Chief Katherine Walker
Monthly £2.95

Original anecdotes – £100 for up to 150 words – are required for humorous features.

Real

Essential Publishing, The Tower, Phoenix Square,
Colchester, Essex CO4 9HU
tel (01206) 851117 *fax* (01206) 849079
Editor Sally Narroway
Fortnightly £1

Fashion, beauty, health issues and lifestyle features for
women aged 25–40 and real life celebrity profiles.
Will consider unsolicited material. Approach
Commissioning Editor with ideas and outlines.
Payment: by arrangement. Founded 2001.

Reality

Redemptorist Publications, 75 Orwell Road, Rathgar,
Dublin 6, Republic of Ireland
tel (01) 4922488 *fax* (01) 4922654
email info@redemptoristpublications.com
website www.redemptoristpublications.com
Editor Rev. Gerry Moloney CSSR
Monthly €1.25

Illustrated magazine for Christian living. Illustrated
articles on all aspects of modern life, including family,
youth, religion, leisure. Length: 1000–1500 words.
Payment: by arrangement; average £50 per 1000
words. Founded 1936.

Record Collector

Unit 101, Wales Farm Road, London W3 6UG
tel (0870) 732 8080 *fax* (0870) 732 6060
email alan.lewis@metropolis.co.uk
website www.recordcollectormag.com
Editor-in-Chief Alan Lewis
(alan.lewis@metropolis.co.uk), *Production Editor*
Jason Draper (jason.draper@metropolis.co.uk),
Reviews Editor Jake Kennedy
(jake.kennedy@metropolis.co.uk), *News Editor* Tim
Jones (tim.jones@metropolis.co.uk)
Monthly £3.50

Covers all areas of music, with the focus on
collectable releases and the reissues market. Specially
commissions most material but will consider
unsolicited material. Welcomes ideas for articles and
features. Length: 2000 (articles/features), 200 (news).
Illustrations: transparencies, colour and b&w prints,
scans of rare records; all commissioned. Payment:
negotiable. Founded 1980.

Red

Hachette Filipacchi UK Ltd, 64 North Row, London
W1K 7LL
tel 020-7150 7000 *fax* 020-7150 7685
website www.redmagazine.co.uk
Editor Trish Halpin, *Send material to* Harriet Cooper,
Features Editor
Monthly £3

High-quality articles on topics of interest to women
aged 28–40: humour, memoirs, interviews and well-
researched investigative features. Approach with ideas
in writing in the first instance. Length: 1500 words

upwards. Illustrations: transparencies. Payment: NUJ
rates. Founded 1998.

Red Pepper

Socialist Newspaper (Publications) Ltd, 1B Waterlow
Road, London N19 5NJ
email redpepper@redpepper.org.uk
website www.redpepper.org.uk
Editor Hilary Wainwright
Monthly £2.50

Independent radical magazine: news and features on
politics, culture and everyday life of interest to the left
and greens. Material mostly commissioned. Length:
news/news features 200–800 words, other features
800–2000 words. Illustrations: b&w photos, cartoons,
graphics. Payment: for investigations, otherwise only
exceptionally. Founded 1994.

Reform

(published by United Reformed Church)
86 Tavistock Place, London WC1H 9RT
tel 020-7916 8630 *fax* 020-7916 2021 (FAO 'Reform')
email reform@urc.org.uk
Contact The Editor
Monthly £1.60 (£13.25 p.a.)

Articles of religious or social comment. Length: 700
or 1400 words. Illustrations: line, half-tone, colour,
cartoons. Payment: by arrangement. Founded 1972.

Report

ATL, 7 Northumberland Street, London WC2N 5RD
tel 020-7930 6441 *fax* 020-7930 1359
email report@atl.org.uk
website www.atl.org.uk
Editors Guy Goodwin, Victoria Poskitt
10 p.a. £2.50 (£15 p.a. UK; £27 p.a. overseas)

The magazine from the Association of Teachers and
Lecturers (ATL). Features, articles, comment, news
about nursery, primary, secondary and further
education. Payment: minimum £120 per 1000 words.

Restaurant Magazine

6th Floor, 103 Regent Street, London W1B 4HL
tel 020-7434 9180 *fax* 020-7434 4517
email info@restaurantmagazine.co.uk
website www.restaurantmagazine.co.uk
Editor Joe Warwick
Bi-weekly £2.50

Articles, features and news on the restaurant trade.
Specially commissions most material. Welcomes ideas
for articles and features. Illustrations: colour
transparencies, prints and artwork. Payment: variable.
Founded 2001.

Retail Week

EMAP Retail, 33–39 Bowling Green Lane, London
EC1R 0DA
tel 020-7505 8000
website www.retail-week.com

Editor Tim Danaher
Weekly £160 p.a.

Features and news stories on all aspects of retail management. Length: up to 1400 words. Illustrations: colour photos. Payment: by arrangement. Founded 1988.

The Rialto

PO Box 309, Aylsham, Norwich NR11 6LN
website www.therialto.co.uk
Editor Michael Mackmin
3 p.a. £5 (£15 p.a., £11 p.a. low income)

For poets and poetry. Submit up to 6 poems; sae essential. Payment: by arrangement. Founded 1984.

Right Start

McMillan-Scott plc, 9 Savoy Street, London WC2E 7HR
tel 020-7878 2338 *fax* 020-7379 6261
Editor Lynette Lowthian
Bi-monthly £2.25

Features on all aspects of preschool and infant education, child health and behaviour. No unsolicited MSS. Length: 800–1500 words. Illustrations: colour photos, line. Payment: varies. Founded 1989.

Royal National Institute of the Blind

PO Box 173, Peterborough, Cambs. PE2 6WS
tel (0845) 7023153 *fax* (01733) 375001
textphone (0845) 7585691
helpline (0845) 7669999
email cservices@rnib.org.uk
website www.rnib.org.uk

Published by the Royal National Institute of the Blind, the following titles are available via email, on floppy disk and in braille, unless otherwise stated. *3FM* (email and braille), *Access IT*, *After Hours* (11–14-year-olds; braille), *Aphra*, *Big Print newspaper* (large print only), *Blast Off!* (children's magazine; disk and braille), *Braille at Bedtime* (7–11-year-olds; braille), *Broadcast Times* (email and disk), *Channels of Blessing* (disk and braille), *Chess Magazine* (braille), *Christmas Radio Guide* (email and braille), *Christmas Television Guide* (email and braille), *Compute IT*, *Contention*, *Conundrum* (disk and braille), *Cricket Fixtures*, *Daily Bread* (disk and braille), *Daisy TV Listings* (Daisy format), *E-Access Bulletin* (email only), *Football Fixtures* (email and braille), *Good Vibrations*, *Insight* (clear print, audio CD, disk, braille, email), *The Max* (boys aged 16–19), *Missy* (girls aged 12–15)*Money Matters*, *Music Magazine* (disk and braille), *NB* (print, email, disk, cassette tape, braille), *New Literature on Sight Problems* (print and email), *New Product Guide* (braille, email, tape, disk), *Journal of Physiotherapy*, *Physiotherapy* (disk, cassette tape, braille), *Physiotherapy Frontline* (cassette tape), *Piano Tuners' Quarterly* (email, disk, cassette tape, braille), *Progress*, *Proms Guide*, *Pure* (girls aged 16–19), *Radio Guide* (email and braille), *Ready, Steady, Read* (for new readers of braille in braille only), *Rhetoric*, *Scientific Enquiry* (disk and braille), *Shaping Up*, *Shop Window*, *Shop Window Christmas Guide*, *Short Stories*, *Soundings* (cassette tape and web), *SP* (disk and braille), *Television Guide* (email and braille), *Theological Times* (disk, cassette tape, braille), *Upbeat*, *Vibe* (boys aged 12–15), *You & Your Child*, *Vision* (clear print, email, disk, cassette tape, braille, Daisy format).

Rugby World

IPC Media Ltd, Kings Reach Tower, Stamford Street, London SE1 9LS
tel 020-7261 6830 *fax* 020-7261 5419
email Paul_Morgan@ipcmedia.com
Editor Paul Morgan
Monthly £3.60

Features and exclusive news stories on rugby. Length: approx. 1200 words. Illustrations: colour photos, cartoons. Payment: £120. Founded 1960.

Runner's World

Natmag Rodale Ltd, 72 Broadwick Street, London W1F 9EP
tel 020-7339 4400 *fax* 020-7339 4420
email rwedit@natmag-rodale.co.uk
website www.runnersworld.co.uk
Editor Steven Seaton
Monthly £3.80

Articles on jogging, running, health and fitness. Payment: by arrangement. Illustrations: line, half-tone, colour. Founded 1979.

Running Fitness

Kelsey Publishing Ltd, Arcade Chambers, Westgate Arcade, Peterborough PE1 1PY
tel (01733) 347559 *fax* (01733) 352749
email paul.larkins@kelsey.co.uk
Editor Paul Larkins
Monthly £3.30

Practical articles on all aspects of running lifestyle, especially road running training and events, and advice on health, fitness and injury. Illustrations: colour photos, cartoons. Payment: by negotiation. Founded 1985.

RUSI Journal

Whitehall, London SW1A 2ET
tel 020-7930 5854 *fax* 020-7321 0943
email journal@rusi.org
website www.rusi.org
Editor Dr Terence McNamee
Bi-monthly £12 p.a.

Journal of the Royal United Services Institute for Defence Studies. Articles on international security, the military sciences, defence technology and procurement, and military history; also book reviews and correspondence. Length: 3000–3500 words. Illustrations: b&w photos, colour transparencies, maps and diagrams. Payment: £12.50 per printed page upon publication.

Safety Education

Royal Society for the Prevention of Accidents, Edgbaston Park, 353 Bristol Road, Birmingham B5 7ST
tel 0121-248 2000 *fax* 0121-248 2001
website www.rospa.org.uk
Editor Janice Cave
3 p.a. £12.50 p.a. for members of Safety Education Department (£15 p.a. non-members)

Articles on every aspect of good practice in safety education including safety of teachers and pupils in school, and the teaching of road, home, water, leisure and personal safety by means of established subjects on the school curriculum. All ages. Founded as *Child Safety* 1937; became *Safety Training* 1940; 1966.

Saga Magazine

Saga Publishing Ltd, The Saga Building, Middelburg Square, Folkestone, Kent CT20 1AZ
tel (01303) 771523 *fax* (01303) 776699
Editor Emma Soames
Monthly £17.95 p.a. Subscription only,
tel 0800 056 1057

General interest magazine aimed at the intelligent, literate 50+ reader. Wide range of articles from human interest, 'real life' stories, intriguing overseas interest (not travel), some natural history, celebrity interviews, photographic book extracts – all relevant to 50+ audience. Articles mostly commissioned or written in-house, but genuine exclusives welcome. Illustrations: colour, digital media; mainly commissioned but top-quality photo feature suggestions sometimes accepted. Payment: competitive rate, by negotiation. Founded 1984.

Sainsbury's Magazine

Seven Publishing Group Ltd, 20 Upper Ground, London SE1 9PD
tel 020-7633 0266 *fax* 020-7401 9423
website www.sainsburysmagazine.co.uk
Editor Sue Robinson
Monthly £1.20

Features: general, food and drink, health, beauty, homes; all material commissioned. Length: from 1500 words. Illustrations: colour and b&w photos and line illustrations. Payment: varies; £400 per full page for illustrations. Founded 1993.

The School Librarian

The School Library Association, Unit 2, Lotmead Business Village, Lotmead Farm, Wanborough, Swindon SN4 0UY
tel (0870) 777 0979 *fax* (0870) 777 0987
email info@sla.org.uk
website www.sla.org.uk
Editor Nancy Chambers, Lockwood, Station Road, South Woodchester, Stroud, Glos. GL5 5EQ

Quarterly Free to members (£55 p.a.)

Official journal of the School Library Association. Articles on school library management, use and skills, and on authors and illustrators, literacy, publishing. Reviews of books, CD-Roms, websites and other library resources from preschool to adult. Length: 1800–3000 words (articles). Payment: by arrangement. Founded 1937.

Scientific Computing World

Europa Science Ltd, 275 Newmarket Road, Cambridge CB5 8JE
tel (01223) 477411 *fax* (01223) 327356
website www.scientific-computing.com
Editor Warren Clark
6 p.a. Free to qualifying subscribers

Features on hardware and software developments for the scientific community, plus news articles and reviews. Length: 800–2000 words. Illustrations: colour transparencies, photos, electronic graphics. Payment: by negotiation. Founded 1994.

The Scots Magazine

D.C. Thomson & Co. Ltd, 2 Albert Square, Dundee DD1 9QJ
tel (01382) 223131 *fax* (01382) 322214
email mail@scotsmagazine.com
website www.scotsmagazine.com
Monthly £1.55

Articles on all subjects of Scottish interest and poetry, but must also be Scottish. Illustrations: colour and b&w photos. Articles paid on acceptance: unsolicited material considered. Founded 1739.

The Scottish Farmer

Newsquest, 200 Renfield Street, Glasgow G2 3PR
tel 0141-302 7700 *fax* 0141-302 7799
email farmer.sales@thescottishfarmer.co.uk
Editor Alasdair Fletcher
Weekly £1.80

Articles on agricultural subjects. Length: 1000–1500 words. Payment: £80 per 1000 words. Illustrations: line, half-tone, colour. Founded 1893.

Scottish Field

Special Publications, Craigcrook Castle, Craigcrook Road, Edinburgh EH4 3PE
tel 0131-312 4550 *fax* 0131-312 4551
email editor@scottishfield.co.uk
Editor Claire Grant
Monthly £3.30

Lifestyle magazine: interiors, food, travel, wildlife, heritage, general lifestyle. Founded 1903.

Scottish Home and Country

42 Heriot Row, Edinburgh EH3 6ES
tel 0131-225 1724 *fax* 0131-225 8129
email magazine@swri.demon.co.uk
website www.swri.org.uk

Editor Liz Ferguson
Monthly £1

Articles on crafts, cookery, travel, personal experience, rural interest, women's interest, health, books. Length: up to 1000 words, preferably illustrated. Illustrations: colour prints/transparencies, b&w, hi-res jpg files, cartoons. Payment: by arrangement. Founded 1924.

Scottish Memories

Lang Syne Publishers Ltd, Strathclyde Business Centre, 120 Carstairs Street, Glasgow G40 4JD
tel 0141-554 9944 *fax* 0141-554 9955
email info@scottish-memories.co.uk
website www.scottish-memories.co.uk
Editor George Forbes
Monthly £2.80

Features on any aspect of Scottish nostalgia or history, from primeval times to the 1990s. Contact the Editor with an outline in the first instance. Length: 1000 words. Illustrations: colour and b&w. Payment: £70 per 1000 words; £20 per photo. Founded 1993.

Screen International

EMAP Media, 33–39 Bowling Green Lane, London EC1R 0DA
tel 020-7505 8000 *fax* 020-7505 8117
email screeninternational@hotmail.com
website www.screendaily.com
Editor Michael Gubbins
Weekly £3.20 (£140 p.a.)

International news and features on the international film business. No unsolicited material. Length: variable. Payment: by arrangement.

Sea Angler

EMAP Active Ltd, Bushfield House, Orton Centre, Peterborough PE2 5UW
tel (01733) 237111 *fax* (01733) 465658
Editor Mel Russ
Monthly £2.80

Topical articles on all aspects of sea-fishing around the British Isles. Payment: by arrangement. Illustrations: colour. Founded 1973.

Sea Breezes

Media House, Tromode, Douglas, Isle of Man IM4 4SB
tel (01624) 626018 *fax* (01624) 696573
Editor A.C. Douglas
Monthly £3

Factual articles on ships and the sea past and present, preferably illustrated. Length: up to 4000 words. Illustrations: line, half-tone, colour. Payment: by arrangement. Founded 1919.

SelfBuild & Design

151 Station Street, Burton on Trent, Staffs. DE14 1BG
tel (01283) 742950 *fax* (01283) 742957

email ross.stokes@sbonline.co.uk
website www.selfbuildanddesign.com
Editor Ross Stokes
Monthly £3.80

Articles on house construction for individual builders. Welcomes ideas for articles. Payment: £100–£200 per 1000 words. Illustrations: colour prints, transparencies and digital.

Sewing World

Traplet Publications Ltd, Traplet House, Pendragon Close, Malvern WR14 1GA
tel (01684) 588500 *fax* (01684) 594888
email sw@traplet.co.uk
Editor Wendy Gardiner
Monthly £3.50

'Sewing magazine for sewing machine enthusiasts.' Articles and step-by-step projects. Length: 1000–1500 words (articles). Illustrations: colour. Payment: £100 per article including illustrations. Founded 1995.

She

National Magazine House, 72 Broadwick Street, London W1F 9EP
tel 020-7439 5000 *fax* 020-7312 3940
email marie.campbell@natmags.co.uk
Deputy Features Editor Siân Rees, *Send material to* Marie Campbell, PA to Editor (*tel* 020-7312 3757)
Monthly £3

No unsolicited MSS. Ideas with synopses welcome on subjects ranging from health and relationships to child care. Payment: NUJ freelance rates. Illustrations: photos. Founded 1955.

SHERLOCK

(formerly Sherlock Holmes – The Detective Magazine)
Overdale, 69 Greenhead Road, Huddersfield HD1 4ER
tel (01484) 426957 *fax* (01484) 426957
email overdale@btinternet.com
Editor David Stuart Davies
6 p.a. £3.95

Articles relating to Sherlock Holmes, crime fiction and writers. Also short stories. Contact the Editor with ideas/synopsis in the first instance. Length: 1800 words (articles), 6000–7000 words (short stories). Payment: by negotiation. Founded 1991.

Ships Monthly

IPC Country & Leisure (Marine), 222 Branston Road, Burton-on-Trent, Staffs. DE14 3BT
tel (01283) 542721 *fax* (01283) 546436
Editor Iain Wakefield
Monthly £3.25

Illustrated articles of shipping interest – both mercantile and naval, preferably of 20th and 21st century ships. Well-researched, factual material only. No short stories or poetry. 'Notes for Contributors' available. Mainly commissioned material; preliminary letter essential, with sae. Payment: by arrangement. Illustrations: half-tone and line, colour transparencies, prints and digital images on CD with thumbprint contact sheet. Founded 1966.

Shoot Monthly

IPC Magazines Ltd, King's Reach Tower, Stamford Street, London SE1 9LS
tel 020-7261 6287 *fax* 020-7261 6019
Editor Colin Mitchell
Monthly £3

Football magazine for fans of all ages. Features, profiles of big names in football. Length: 500–2000 words (features). Illustrations: colour transparencies. Payment: negotiable. Freelance opportunities very limited. Founded 1969.

Shooting Times and Country Magazine

IPC Media Ltd, King's Reach Tower, Stamford Street, London SE1 9LS
tel 020-7261 6180 *fax* 020-7261 7179
email steditorial@ipcmedia.com
website www.shootingtimes.co.uk
Editor Camilla Clark
Weekly £1.90

Articles on fieldsports, especially shooting, and on related natural history and countryside topics. Unsolicited MSS not encouraged. Length: up to 2000 words. Payment: by arrangement. Illustrations: photos, drawings, colour transparencies. Founded 1882.

The Shop: A Magazine of Poetry

Skeagh, Schull, Co. Cork, Republic of Ireland
email wakeman@iolfree.ie (not for submissions)
website www.theshop-poetry-magazine.ie
Editors John Wakeman, Hilary Wakeman
3 p.a. £7/€8.50

Poems on any subject in any form and occasional essays on poetry, especially Irish poetry. No submissions by email. No illustrations required. Length: 2000–3000 words (essays); any (poems). Payment: by arrangement. Founded 1999.

The Short Wave Magazine

Arrowsmith Court, Arena Business Centre, 9 Nimrod Way, Wimborne, Dorset BH21 7SH
tel (01202) 862760 *fax* (01202) 862301
email kevin.nice@pwpublishing.ltd.uk
website www.pwpublishing.ltd.uk
Editor Kevin Nice
Monthly £3.60 (£39.90 p.a.)

Technical and semi-technical articles, 500–5000 words, on design, construction and operation of radio receiving equipment. Radio-related photo features welcome. Payment: £55 per page. Illustrations: line, half-tone, colour. Founded 1937.

Shout

D.C. Thomson & Co. Ltd, Albert Square, Dundee DD1 9QJ

tel (01382) 223131 *fax* (01382) 200880
email shout@dcthomson.co.uk
185 Fleet Street, London EC4A 2HS
tel 020-7400 1030 *fax* 020-7400 1089
Editor-in-Chief Jackie Brown
Fortnightly £2

Colour gravure magazine for 11–14 year-old girls. Pop, film and 'soap' features and pin-ups; general features of teen interest; emotional features, fashion and beauty advice. Illustrations: colour transparencies. Payment: on acceptance. Founded 1993.

The Shropshire Magazine

Shropshire Newspapers, Ketley, Telford TF1 5HU
tel (01952) 242424 *fax* (01952) 222451
Editor Henry Carpenter
Monthly £2.50

Articles on topics related to Shropshire, including countryside, history, characters, legends, education, food; also home and garden features. Length: up to 1500 words. Illustrations: colour. Founded 1950.

Sight and Sound

British Film Institute, 21 Stephen Street, London W1T 1LN
tel 020-7255 1444 *fax* 020-7436 2327
website www.bfi.org.uk/sightandsound
Editor Nick James
Monthly £3.95

Topical and critical articles on the cinema of any country; reviews of every film theatrically released in the UK; book reviews; reviews of every video released; regular columns from around the world. Length: 1000–5000 words. Payment: by arrangement. Illustrations: relevant photos, cartoons. Founded 1932.

The Sign

The Church Times, 33 Upper Street, London N1 0PN
tel 020-7359 4570 *fax* 020-7359 8132
Editor Paul Handley
Monthly

Leading national insert for C of E parish magazines. Articles of interest to parishes; poems. Items should bear the author's name and address; return postage essential or send by email. Length: up to 450 words, accompanied by photos/illustrations. Payment: by arrangement. Founded 1905.

Signmatters

British Deaf Association, 10th Floor, Coventry Point, Marhat Way, Coventry CV1 1EA
tel (02476) 550936 (text) *fax* (02476) 221541
email midlands@bda.org.uk
website www.signcommunity.org.uk
Editor Yvonne Carolan
Monthly £2.50, £20 p.a. non-members (£15 p.a. BDA members)

Interviews, features, reviews, articles, news items, letters dealing with deafness. Payment: by arrangement. Illustrations: line, half-tone. Founded 1872.

Ski and Board

The Ski Club of Great Britain, The White House, 57–63 Church Road, London SW19 5SB
tel (0845) 4580780 *fax* (0845) 4580781
email editor@skiclub.co.uk
website www.skiclub.co.uk
Editor Arnie Wilson
Monthly (Oct–Jan) £3.60

Articles, features, news, true life stories, ski tips, equipment reviews, resort reports – all in connection with skiing and snowboarding. Welcomes ideas for articles and features. Length: 600–2000 words. Illustrations: colour and b&w digital, artwork and cartoons. Payment: up to £250 per 1000 words; £50–£200 per photo/illustration. Founded as *Ski Survey* 1972.

The Skier and The Snowboarder Magazine

Mountain Marketing Ltd, PO Box 386, Sevenoaks, Kent TN13 1AQ
tel (0845) 3108303 *fax* (01732) 779266
email skierandsnowboarder@hotmail.com
Editor Frank Baldwin
5 p.a. (July–May) £2.95

Ski features, based around a good story. Length: 800–1000 words. Illustrations: colour action ski photos. Payment: by negotiation. Founded 1984.

Slimmer, Healthier, Fitter

Aceville Publications Ltd, 25 Phoenix Court, Hawkins Road, Colchester CO2 8JY
tel (01206) 505972 *fax* (01206) 505945
email rachel@aceville.co.uk
Editor Rachel Callen
10 p.a. £2.40

Features on health, nutrition, slimming. Personal weight loss stories. Length: 600 or 1200 words. No unsolicited MSS at this time. Send feature summary by email in first instance. Payment: by arrangement. Founded 1972.

Smallholder

Hook House, Wimblington March, Cambs.
PE15 0QL
tel (01326) 213333 *fax* (01326) 318749
email liz.wright1@btconnect.com
website www.smallholder.co.uk
Editor Liz Wright
Monthly £3

Articles of relevance to small farmers about livestock and crops, organics, conservation, poultry, equipment. Items relating to the countryside considered. Send for specimen copy. Length: single-

page article 700 words; DPS 1200–1400 words with pictures. Payment: 4p per word; more for commissions and technical livestock articles. Founded 1985.

Snooker Scene

Hayley Green Court, 130 Hagley Road, Halesowen, West Midlands B63 1DY
tel 0121-585 9188 *fax* 0121-585 7117
email clive.everton@talk21.com
website www.snookerscene.com
Editor Clive Everton
Monthly £2.50 (£25 p.a.)

News and articles about the snooker and billiards scene for readers with more than a casual interest in the games. Payment: by arrangement. Illustrations: photos. Founded 1971.

Solicitors Journal

Wilmington Business Information Ltd, Paulton House, 8 Shepherdess Walk, London N1 7LB
tel 020-7490 0049 *fax* 020-7324 2366
email editorial@solicitorsjournal.co.uk
Editor Jean-Yves Gilg
Weekly £209 for 48 issues

Articles, by practising lawyers or specialist journalists, on subjects of practical interest to solicitors. Articles on spec should be sent on disk or by email. Length: up to 1800 words. Payment: by negotiation. Founded 1856.

The Songwriter

International Songwriters Association, PO Box 46, Limerick City, Republic of Ireland
tel (061) 228837
Editor James D. Liddane
Monthly

Articles on songwriting and interviews with music publishers and recording company executives. Length: 400–5000 words. Payment: by arrangement. Illustrations: photos. Founded 1967.

Songwriting and Composing

Sovereign House, 12 Trewartha Road, Praa Sands, Penzance, Cornwall TR20 9ST
tel (01736) 762826 *fax* (01736) 763328
email songmag@aol.com
website www.songwriters-guild.co.uk
General Secretary Carole Jones
Quarterly Free to members

Magazine of the Guild of International Songwriters and Composers. Short stories, articles, letters relating to songwriting, publishing, recording and the music industry. Payment: negotiable upon content £25–£60. Illustrations: line, half-tone. Founded 1986.

The Spark Magazine

Blue Sax Publishing Ltd, 86 Colston Street, Bristol BS1 5BB

tel 0117-914 3434 *fax* 0117-914 3444
email john@thespark.co.uk
website www.thespark.co.uk
Editor John Dawson
Quarterly Free

'A free... thinking magazine about positive change for the West Country.' Features on health, fitness, the environment, social and community issues. Welcomes ideas for features and articles. Send A4 envelope for writers' guidelines or see website. Length: varies. Illustrations: colour cover. Payment: £10 per 100 words. Founded 1993.

The Spectator

56 Doughty Street, London WC1N 2LL
tel 020-7405 1706 *fax* 020-7242-0603
website www.thespectator.co.uk
Editor Matthew d'Ancona, *Publisher* Kimberly Quinn
Weekly £2.95

Articles on current affairs, politics, the arts; book reviews. Illustrations: colour and b&w, cartoons. Payment: on merit. Founded 1828.

Spirit & Destiny

H. Bauer Publishing, Academic House, 24–28 Oval Road, London NW1 7DT
tel 020-7241 8000 *fax* 020-7241 8056
Editor Elayne DeLaurian
Monthly £2.90

'For women who want the best possible future.' Entertaining and informative women's interest magazine with additional features on astrology and psychic matters, holistic therapies and alternative lifestyles. Founded 2002.

The Sportsman

Sports Betting Media Ltd, 3rd Floor, 1 Riverside, Manbre Road, London W6 9WA
tel 020-8846 3000 *fax* 020-8846 3014
email info@thesportsman.com
website www.thesportsman.com
Editor Charlie Bain
Daily £1
    Associate Editor (Racing) Richard Evans
    Racing Editor Simon Rowlands
    Sports Editor James Eastham
    Features Editor Dan Townend

National daily sports betting and racing newspaper. Welcomes ideas/stories from freelances with a specific betting angle. Launched 2006.

Springboard

Corrimbla, Ballina, County Mayo, Republic of Ireland
email sboard@eircom.net
Editor Robert Groom
Quarterly £15/€20

A non-profit making magazine with short stories, poetry, articles and competition news. Aims to bring together writers from all countries and has 4 competitions that are free to subscribers: short story, poetry, article and children's short story. The winner and runner up in each category is published in the following issue and receives a certificate and cash prize. No unsolicited material. Founded 1990.

The Squash Player

460 Bath Road, Longford, Middlesex UB7 0EB
tel (01753) 775511 *fax* (01753) 775512
email editor@squashplayer.co.uk
Editor Ian McKenzie
6 p.a. £24 p.a.

Covers all aspects of playing squash. All features are commissioned – discuss ideas with the Editor. Length: 1000–1500 words. Illustrations: unusual photos (e.g. celebrities), cartoons. Payment: £75 per 1000 words; £25–£40 for illustrations. Founded 1971.

Staffordshire Life Magazine

Staffordshire Newspapers Ltd, The Publishing Centre, Derby Street, Stafford ST16 2DT
tel (01785) 257700 *fax* (01785) 253287
email editor@staffordshirelife.co.uk
website www.staffordshirelife.co.uk
Editor Philip Thurlow-Craig
11 p.a. £1.90

County magazine for Staffordshire. Historical articles; features on county personalities. No short stories. Contact the Editor in the first instance. Length: 500–800 words. Illustrations: colour transparencies and prints. Founded 1948; relaunched 1980.

The Stage

(incorporating Television Today)
Stage House, 47 Bermondsey Street, London SE1 3XT
tel 020-7403 1818 *fax* 020-7357 9287
email editor@thestage.co.uk
website www.thestage.co.uk
Editor Brian Attwood
Weekly £1.20

Original and interesting articles on professional stage and broadcasting topics may be sent for the Editor's consideration. Length: 500–900 words. Payment: £100 per 1000 words. Founded 1880.

Stamp Lover

National Philatelic Society, British Philatelic Centre, 107 Charterhouse Street, London EC1M 6PT
tel 020-7490 9610
email nps@philately.org.uk
Editor David Alford
6 p.a. £2.50

Articles on stamps and postal history. Illustrations: line, half-tone. Payment: by arrangement. Founded 1908.

Stamp Magazine

IPC Media Ltd, Leon House, 233 High Street, Croydon CR9 1HZ

tel 020-8726 8241 *fax* 020-8726 8299
Editor Guy Thomas
Monthly £3

Informative articles and exclusive news items on stamp collecting and postal history. No preliminary letter. Payment: by arrangement. Illustrations: line, half-tone, colour. Founded 1934.

Stand Magazine

School of English, University of Leeds, Leeds LS2 9JT
tel 0113-233 4794 *fax* 0113-233 4791
email stand@leeds.ac.uk
website www.standmagazine.org
Managing Editor Jon Glover
Quarterly £6.50 plus p&p (£25 p.a.)

Poetry, short stories, translations, literary criticism. Send sae/IRCs for return. Payment: £20 per 1000 words (prose); £20 per poem. Founded 1952.

Staple

74 Rangeley Road, Walkley, Sheffield S6 5DW
Editors Elizabeth Barrett, Ann Atkinson
3 issues p.a. £5. (£15 p.a. £20 p.a. overseas)

Poetry, short fiction, articles and reviews. Payment: £5 per poem, £10 fiction/articles. Founded 1982.

Star Trek Monthly

Titan Magazines, Titan House, 144 Southwark Street, London SE1 0UP
tel 020-7620 0200 *fax* 020-7803 1803
Editor Nick Jones
13 p.a. £3.50

Up-to-date news about every aspect of *Star Trek*, including all TV series and films, cast interviews, behind-the-scenes features and product reviews. Payment: by arrangement. Founded 1995.

Starburst

Visual Imagination Ltd, 9 Blades Court, Deodar Road, London SW15 2NU
tel 020-8875 1520 *fax* 020-8875 1588
email starburst@vismag.com
website www.visimag.com
Editor Stephen Payne
13 p.a. £3.99

Features and interviews on all aspects of science fiction. Length: 2000 words. Illustrations: colour and b&w photos. Payment: £80 per 1000 words; £10–£20 per image. Founded 1977.

The Strad

Orpheus Publications, Newsquest Magazines, 2nd Floor, 30 Cannon Street, London EC4M 6YJ
tel 020-7618 3456 *fax* 020-7618 3483
email thestrad@orpheuspublications.com
website www.thestrad.com
Editor Naomi Sadler
12 p.a. £3.95

Features, news and reviews for string instrument players, teachers, makers and enthusiasts – both professional and amateur. Specially commissions most material but will consider unsolicited material. Welcomes ideas for articles and features. Length: 1000–2000 (articles/features), 100–150 (news). Payment: £150–£300 (articles/features), varies for news. Illustrations: transparencies, colour and b&w prints and artwork, colour cartoons; some commissioned. Founded 1890.

Studies, An Irish quarterly review

35 Lower Leeson Street, Dublin 2, Republic of Ireland
tel (01) 6766785 *fax* (01) 6762984
email studies@jesuit.ie
website www.studiesirishreview.com
Editor Rev. Fergus O'Donoghue SJ
Quarterly €9.00

General review of social comment, literature, history, the arts. Published by the Irish Jesuits. Articles written by specialists for the general reader. Critical book reviews. Preliminary letter. Length: 4000 words. Founded 1912.

Stuff

Haymarket Ltd, 38–42 Hampton Road, Teddington, Middlesex TW11 0JE
tel 020-8267 5000 *fax* 020-8267 5815
website www.haymarketgroup.co.uk
Editor Michael Brook
Monthly £3.80

Articles on gadgets, gear, technology, lifestyle, news and reviews. Payment by negotiation. Founded 1996.

Suffolk Norfolk Life

Today Magazines Ltd, The Publishing House, Station Road, Framlingham, Suffolk IP13 9EE
tel (01728) 622030 *fax* (01728) 622031
email todaymagazines@btopenworld.com
website www.suffolknorfolklife.com
Editor William Locks
Monthly £1.90

Articles relevant to Suffolk and Norfolk – current topics plus historical items, art, leisure, etc. Considers unsolicited material and welcomes ideas for articles and features. Length: 900–1500 words. Illustrations: transparencies, colour and b&w prints, b&w artwork and cartoons. Payment: £30–£60 per article. Founded 1989.

Sugar

Hachette Filipacchi, 64 North Row, London W1K 7LL
tel 020-7150 7000 *fax* 020-7150 7001
Editor Annabel Brog
Monthly £2.10

Magazine for young women aged 13–19. Fashion, beauty, entertainment, features. Send synopsis first. Will consider unsolicited material. Interested in real-life stories (1200 words), quizzes. Payment: negotiable. Founded 1994.

Surrey Life

Holmesdale House, 46 Croydon Road, Reigate,
Surrey RH2 0NH
tel (01737) 248802 fax (01737) 246596
website www.surreylife.co.uk
Editor Katherine Simmons
Monthly £2.75

Articles on Surrey, including places of interest, high-profile personalities, local events, arts, history and food. Unsolicited ideas welcome. Founded 1970.

Swimming Magazine

(formerly Swimming Times)
Swimming Times Ltd, 41 Granby Street,
Loughborough, Leics. LE11 3DU
tel (01509) 632230 fax (01509) 632233
Editor Peter Hassall
Monthly £2.80 (post free) (£22 p.a.)

Official journal of the Amateur Swimming Association and the Institute of Swimming Teachers and Coaches. Reports of major events and championships; news and features on all aspects of swimming including synchronised swimming, diving and water polo, etc; accompanying photos where appropriate; short fiction with a swimming theme. Unsolicited material welcome. Length: 800–1500 words. Payment: by arrangement. Founded 1923.

The Tablet

1 King Street Cloisters, Clifton Walk, London
W6 0QZ
tel 020-8748 8484 fax 020-8748 1550
email thetablet@thetablet.co.uk
website www.thetablet.co.uk
Editor Catherine Pepinster
Weekly £1.95

Catholic weekly: religion, philosophy, politics, society, books and arts. International coverage. Freelance work commissioned: do not send unsolicited material. Length: various. Illustrations: cartoons. Payment: by arrangement. Founded 1840.

Take a Break

H. Bauer Publishing Ltd, Academic House,
24–28 Oval Road, London NW1 7DT
tel 020-7241 8000 fax 020-7241 8056
website www.bauer.com
Editor John Dale
Weekly 76p

Lively, tabloid women's weekly. True life features, celebrities, health and beauty, family, travel; short stories (up to 1500 words); lots of puzzles. Payment: by arrangement. Illustrated. Founded 1990.

Take a Break's Take a Puzzle

H. Bauer Publishing, Academic House, 24–28 Oval
Road, London NW1 7DT
tel 020-7241 8000 fax 020-7241 8056
email take.puzzle@bauer.co.uk
website www.bauer.com
Editor Guy Haslam
Monthly £1.75

Puzzles. Fresh ideas always welcome. Illustrations: colour transparencies and b&w prints and artwork. Work supplied on Mac-compatible disk preferred. Payment: from £25 per puzzle, £30–£90 for picture puzzles and for illustrations not an integral part of a puzzle. Founded 1991.

TATE ETC

20 John Islip Street, London SW1P 4RG
tel 020-7887 8724 fax 020-7887 8729
email tateetc@tate.org.uk
website www.tate.org.uk/tateetc
Editor Simon Grant
3 p.a. £5

Independent visual arts magazine: features, interviews, previews and opinion pieces. Length: up to 3000 words but always commissioned. Illustrations: colour and b&w photos. Payment: negotiable.

Tatler

Vogue House, Hanover Square, London W1S 1JU
tel 020-7499 9080 fax 020-7409 0451
website www.tatler.co.uk
Editor Geordie Greig
Monthly £3.50

Smart society magazine favouring sharp articles, profiles, fashion and the arts. Illustrations: colour, b&w, but all commissioned. Founded 1707.

Taxation

2 Addiscombe Road, Croydon CR9 5AF
tel 020-8686 9141 fax 020-8212 1988
email taxation@lexisnexis.co.uk
website www.taxation.co.uk
Editor Mike Truman
Weekly £4.98

Updating and advice concerning UK tax law and practice for accountants and tax experts. All articles written by professionals. Length: 2000 words (articles). Payment £100 per 800 words. Founded 1927.

The Teacher

National Union of Teachers, Hamilton House, Mabledon Place, London WC1H 9BD
tel 020-7380 4708 fax 020-7383 7230
Editor Mitch Howard
8 p.a. Free to NUT members

Articles, features and news of interest to all those involved in the teaching profession. Length: 750 words. Payment: NUJ rates to NUJ members. Founded 1872.

Technology Ireland

Enterprise Ireland, Merrion Hall, Strand Road,
Dublin 4, Republic of Ireland

tel (01) 206 6337 *fax* (01) 206 6342
email tecnology.ireland@enterprise-ireland.com
website www.technologyireland.ie
Editor Kathy Burke
6 p.a. €79 p.a.

Articles, features, reviews, news on current business, innovation and technology. Length: 1500–2000 words. Illustrations: line, half-tone, colour. Payment: varies. Founded 1969.

Television
Media House, Azalea Drive, Swanley, Kent BR8 8HH
tel (01322) 660070 *fax* (01322) 616376
Editor Boris Sedacca
Monthly £3.75

Articles on the technical aspects of domestic TV and video equipment, especially servicing, long-distance TV, constructional projects, satellite TV, video recording, teletext and viewdata, test equipment, monitors. Payment: by arrangement. Illustrations: photos and line drawings for litho. Founded 1950.

Tempo
Cambridge University Press, The Edinburgh Building, Shaftesbury Road, Cambridge CB2 2RU
Editorial address PO Box 171, Herne Bay, Kent CT6 6WD
email macval@compuserve.com
Editor Calum MacDonald
Quarterly £22/$35 p.a. print only, (£52/$86 p.a. print and online, institutions; £46/$76 online only

Authoritative articles on contemporary music. Length: 2000–4000 words. Payment: by arrangement. Illustrations: music type, occasional photographic or musical supplements.

TES Cymru
Sophia House, 28 Cathedral Road, Cardiff CF11 9LJ
tel 029-2066 0201 *fax* 029-2066 0207
email cymru@tes.co.uk
website www.tes.co.uk/cymru
Editor Karen Thornton
Weekly £1.30

Education newspaper. Articles on education, teachers, teaching and learning, and education policy in Wales. Length: up to 800 words (articles). Illustrations: line, half-tone. Payment: by arrangement. Founded 2004.

TGO (The Great Outdoors) Magazine
Newsquest, 200 Renfield Street, Glasgow G2 3QB
tel 0141-302 7700 *fax* 0141-302 7799
email cameron.mcneish@magazines.newsquest.co.uk
website www.tgomagazine.co.uk
Editor Cameron McNeish
Monthly £3.20

Articles on walking or lightweight camping in specific areas, mainly in the UK, preferably illustrated. Length: 700–2000 words. Payment: by arrangement. Illustrations: colour. Please apply for guidelines. Founded 1978.

that's life!
H. Bauer Publishing Ltd, Academic House, 24–28 Oval Road, London NW1 7DT
tel 020-7241 8000 *fax* 020-7241 8008
Editor Jo Checkley
Weekly 68p

Dramatic true life stories about women. Length: average 1000 words. Illustrations: colour photos and cartoons. Payment: £750. Founded 1995.

Therapy Weekly
EMAP Healthcare Ltd, Greater London House, Hampstead Road, London NW1 7EJ
tel 020-7874 0360 *fax* 020-7874 0368
Editor Nina Lovelace
Weekly Free to NHS and local authority therapists (£38.50 p.a. personal rate)

Articles of interest to chartered physiotherapists, occupational therapists and speech and language therapists. Guidelines to contributors available. Send proposals only initially. Length: up to 1000 words. Payment: by arrangement. Founded 1974 as *Therapy*.

The Third Alternative
TTA Press, 5 Martins Lane, Witcham, Ely, Cambs. CB6 2LB
email ttapress@aol.com
website www.ttapress.com
Editor Andy Cox
Bi-monthly £4.50 (£21 for 6 issues)

Extraordinary new fiction: science fiction, fantasy, horror, slipstream. Also interviews with, and profiles of, authors and film-makers. Send sae with all submissions. Considers unsolicited material and welcomes ideas for articles and features. Length: 3000–4000 words (articles and features), short stories unrestricted. Illustrations: send samples and portfolios. Payment: £30 per 1000 words on acceptance. Founded 1994.

Third Way
St Peter's, Sumner Road, Harrow, Middlesex HA1 4BX
tel 020-8423 8494 *fax* 020-8423 5367
email editor@thirdway.org.uk
Editor Simon Jones
10 p.a. £3.50

Aims to present biblical perspectives on the political, social and cultural issues of the day. Payment: by arrangement on publication. Email submissions preferred. Founded 1977.

This England
PO Box 52, Cheltenham, Glos. GL50 1YQ
Editor Roy Faiers
Quarterly £4.25

Articles on towns, villages, traditions, customs of England, stories of people, poetry. Send sae for guidelines. Length: 250–2000 words. Illustrations: half-tone, colour. Founded 1968.

Time Out

Time Out Group Ltd, Universal House,
251 Tottenham Court Road, London W1T 7AB
tel 020-7813 3000 *fax* 020-7813 6001
website www.timeout.com
Editor Gordon Thomson
Weekly £2.50

Listings magazine for London covering all areas of the arts, plus articles of consumer and news interest. Illustrations: colour and b&w. Payment by negotiation. Founded 1968.

The Times Educational Supplement

Admiral House, 66–68 East Smithfield, London
E1W 1BX
tel 020-7782 3000 *fax* 020-7782 3202 (news),
020-7782 3199(features)
email friday@tes.co.uk (feature outlines),
teacher@tes.co.uk (curriculum-related outlines)
website www.tes.co.uk
Editor Judith Judd
Weekly £1.20

Education newspaper. Articles on education written with special knowledge or experience; news items; books, arts and equipment reviews. Check with the news or picture editor before submitting material. Outlines of feature ideas should be faxed or emailed. Illustrations: suitable photos and drawings of educational interest, cartoons. Payment: standard rates, or by arrangement.

Times Educational Supplement Scotland

Scott House, 10 South St Andrew Street, Edinburgh
EH2 2AZ
tel 0131-557 1133 *fax* 0131-558 1155
Editor Neil Munro
Weekly £1.30

Education newspaper. Articles on education, preferably 800–1000 words, written with special knowledge or experience. News items about Scottish educational affairs. Illustrations: line, half-tone. Payment: by arrangement. Founded 1965.

Times Higher Education Supplement

Admiral House, 66–68 East Smithfield, London
E1W 1BX
tel 020-7782 3000 *fax* 020-7782 3300
Editor John O'Leary
Weekly £1.40

Articles on higher education written with special knowledge or experience, or articles dealing with academic topics. Also news items. Illustrations: suitable photos and drawings of educational interest. Payment: by arrangement. Founded 1971.

The Times Literary Supplement

Times House, 1 Pennington Street, London E98 1BS
tel 020-7782 5000 *fax* 020-7782 4966

Editor Peter Stothard
Weekly £2.40

Will consider poems for publication, literary discoveries and articles on literary and cultural affairs. Payment: by arrangement.

Today's Golfer

EMAP Active Ltd, Bushfield House, Orton Centre, Peterborough PE2 5UW
tel (01733) 237111 *fax* (01733) 288014
Editor Andy Calton
Monthly £3.60

Specialist features and articles on golf instruction, equipment and courses. Founded 1988.

Today's Pilot

Key Publishing Ltd, PO Box 100, Stamford, Lincs.
PE9 1XQ
tel (01780) 755131 *fax* (01780) 757261
email dave.unwin@keypublishing.com
website www.todayspilot.co.uk
Editor Dave Unwin
Monthly £3.50

General aviation magazine providing information and inspiration for the recreational aviator. Considers unsolicited material. Submit suggestions or an outline in the first instance. Length: 3000 words (articles/ features), 1000 words (news). Illustrations: colour. Payment: negotiable (words); £20 per image. Founded 2000.

Top Santé Health & Beauty

EMAP Elán, Endeavour House, 189 Shaftesbury Avenue, London WC2H 8JG
tel 020-7437 9011 *fax* 020-7208 3514
Editor Lauren Libbert
Monthly £2.20

Articles, features and news on all aspects of health and beauty. Ideas welcome. No unsolicited features. Illustrations: colour photos and drawings. Payment: £350 per 1300 words; illustrations by arrangement. Founded 1993.

Total Film

Future Publishing, 2 Balcombe Street, London
NW1 6NW
tel 020-7042 4000 *fax* 020-7317 0275
email totalfilm@futurenet.co.uk
website www.futurenet.com
Editor Mark Dinning
Monthly £3.50

Movie magazine covering all aspects of film. Email ideas before submitting material. Not seeking interviews or reviews. Length: 400 words (news items); 1000 words (funny features). Payment: £150 per 1000 words; up to £1500 per picture. Founded 1996.

Total Off Road

151 Station Street, Burton on Trent, Staffs. DE14 1BG
tel (01283) 742950 *fax* (01283) 742957

email editorial@toronline.co.uk
Editor Alan Kidd
Monthly £3.75

Features on off-roading: competitions, modified vehicles, overseas events. Length 1200–3000 words. Payment: £100 per 1000 words. Illustrations: colour and b&w prints, transparencies and digital images. keen to hear from photographers attending UK/overseas off-road events. Preliminary email strongly advised.

Traditional Woodworking

151 Station Street, Burton-on-Trent, Staffs. DE14 1BG
tel (01283) 742950 *fax* (01283) 742957
email enquiries@twonline.co.uk
Editor Carmen Konopka
Monthly £3.20

Articles and features for woodworking hobbyists. Includes projects, news and timber-related articles. Length: 2500 words. Payment: by arrangement.

Trail

(formerly Trail Walker)
EMAP Active Ltd, Bretton Court, Bretton, Peterborough PE3 8DZ
tel (01733) 264666 *fax* (01733) 282653
email trail@emap.com
Editor Guy Procter
Monthly £3.40

Outdoor activity magazine focusing mainly on high level walking with some scrambling, moutain biking and climbing. Very limited opportunities for freelances.

Traveller

Wexas Ltd, 45 Brompton Road, London SW3 1DE
tel 020-7589 0500 *fax* 020-7581 1357
email traveller@wexas.com
website www.traveller.org.uk
Editor Amy Sohanpaul
Quarterly Free to Wexas members; back issues £4.95, payable to Wexas

Adventurous and authentic travel writing. Narrative features describe personal journeys to remarkable places. Unsolicited material considered if prose and pictures are excellent. See website for guidelines. Length: 1000 words. Illustrations: transparencies, b&w prints. Payment: £200 per 1000 words; colour £50 (£150 cover). Founded 1970.

Tribune

9 Arkwright Road, London NW3 6AN
tel 020-7433 6410
email george@tribpub.demon.co.uk, tribuneweb@btconnect.com
Editor Chris McLaughlin, *Books Editor* Amanda Day, *Arts Editor* George Osgerby
Weekly £2

Political, literary, with Socialist outlook. Informative articles (about 900 words), news stories (250–300 words). No unsolicited reviews or fiction. Payment: by arrangement. Illustrations: cartoons, photos.

Trout and Salmon

EMAP Active Ltd, Bushfield House, Orton Centre, Peterborough PE2 5UW
tel (01733) 237111 *fax* (01733) 465820
email andrew.flitcroft@emap.com
Editor Andrew Flitcroft
Monthly £2.90

Articles of good quality with strong trout or salmon angling interest. Length: 400–2000 words, accompanied if possible by colour transparencies or good quality colour prints. Payment: by arrangement. Illustrations: line, colour transparencies and prints, cartoons. Founded 1955.

Truck & Driver

Reed Business Information, Quadrant House, The Quadrant, Sutton, Surrey SM2 5AS
tel 020-7652 3682 *fax* 020-7652 8988
Editor Dave Young
Monthly £2.40

News, articles on trucks, personalities and features of interest to truck drivers. Words (on disk or electronically) and picture packages preferred. Length: approx. 2000 words. Illustrations: colour transparencies, digital and artwork, cartoons. Payment: negotiable. Founded 1984.

Trucking

Future Publishing Ltd, 30 Monmouth Street, Bath BA1 2BW
tel (01225) 442244
Editor Ivor Carroll
Monthly £2.50

For truck drivers, owner–drivers and operators: news, articles, features and technical advice. Length: 750–2500 words. Illustrations: mostly 35mm digital. Payment: by negotiation. Founded 1983.

The Trumpet

44ᴀ Selby Road, London E11 3LT
tel 020-8522 6600 *fax* 020-8522 6699
email info@the-trumpet.com
Editor-in-Chief Femi Okutubo
Fortnightly

Newspaper for the UK's African population. Founded 1995.

TV Quick

H. Bauer Publishing Ltd, Academic House, 24–28 Oval Road, London NW1 7DT
tel 020-7241 8000 *fax* 020-7241 8066
website www.bauer.co.uk
Editor-in-Chief Jon Peake
Weekly 70p

TV listings magazine featuring TV-related material. Payment: by arrangement. Founded 1991.

TV Choice
Editor-in-Chief Jon Peake
Weekly 33p
Founded 1999.

The Total TV Guide
Editor-in-Chief Jon Peake
Weekly 95p
Founded 2003.

TVTimes Magazine
IPC Media Ltd, 10th Floor, King's Reach Tower, Stamford Street, London SE1 9LS
tel 020-7261 7000 *fax* 020-7261 7888
Editor Ian Abbott
Weekly 90p

Features with an affinity to ITV, BBC1, BBC2, Channels 4 and 5, satellite and radio personalities and TV generally. Length: by arrangement. Photographs: commissioned only. Payment: by arrangement.

U magazine
Harmonia, 2 Clanwilliam Court, Lower Mount Street, Dublin 2, Republic of Ireland
tel (01) 240 5300 *fax* (01) 661 9757
email letters@umagazine.ie
Editor Fionnuala McCarthy
Monthly €41.16 p.a.

Fashion and beauty magazine for 18–25 year-old Irish women, with celebrity interviews, talent profiles, real-life stories, sex and relationship features, plus regular pages on the club scene, movies, music and film. Also travel, interiors, health, food, horoscopes. Material mostly commissioned. Payment: varies. Founded 1978.

Ulster Business
Greer Publications, 5ᴮ Edgewater Business Park, Edgewater Road, Belfast Harbour Estate, Belfast BT3 9JQ
tel 028-9078 3223 *fax* 028-9078 3210
email russellcampbell@greenpublications.com
website www.ulsterbusiness.com
Editor Russell Campbell
Monthly £27.50 p.a.

Feature-based magazine with general business-related editorial for management level and above. Specially commissions most material but will consider unsolicited material. Welcomes ideas for articles and features. Length: 800 words (articles), 1500 words (features). Payment: £60–£80 (articles), £120 (features). No illustrations required. Founded 1987.

Ulster Grocer
Greer Publications, 5ᴮ Edgewater Business Park, Belfast Harbour Estate, Belfast BT3 9JQ
tel 028-9078 3200 *fax* 028-9078 3210

email kathyj@writenow.prestel.co.uk
Editor Kathy Jensen
Monthly Controlled circulation

Topical features (1000–1500 words) on food/grocery retailing and exhibitions; news (200 words) with a Northern Ireland basis. All features commissioned; no speculative articles accepted. Illustrations: colour photos. Payment: features £275, product news £160. Founded 1972.

Under 5
Pre-school Learning Alliance, The Fitzpatrick Building, 158 York Way, London N7 9AD
tel 020-7697 2500 *fax* 020-7697 8607
email editor.u5@pre-school.org.uk
Contact Anna Roberts
10 p.a. £30 p.a.

Articles on the role of adults – especially parents/preschool workers – in young children's learning and development, including children from all cultures and those with special needs. Length: 750 words. Payment: £60 per article. Founded 1962.

The Universe
1st Floor, St James's Buildings, Oxford Street, Manchester M1 6FP
tel 0161-236 8856 *fax* 0161-236 8530
Editor Joe Kelly
Weekly £1

Catholic Sunday newspaper. News stories, features and photos on all aspects of Catholic life required; also cartoons. Send sae with MSS. Payment: by arrangement. Founded 1860.

Vanity Fair
The Condé Nast Publications Ltd, Vogue House, Hanover Square, London W1S 1JU
tel 020-7499 9080 *fax* 020-7493 1962
website www.vanityfair.co.uk
London Editor Graydon Carter *tel* 020-7221 6228 *fax* 020-7221 6269
Monthly £3.60

Media, glamour and politics for grown-up readers. No unsolicited material. Payment: by arrangement. Illustrated.

The Vegan
The Vegan Society, Donald Watson House, 7 Battle Road, St Leonards-on-Sea, East Sussex TN37 7AA
tel (01424) 448829 *fax* (01424) 717064
email editor@vegansociety.com
website www.vegansociety.com
Editor Catriona Toms
Quarterly £2.50

Articles on health, nutrition, cookery, vegan lifestyle, land use, animal rights. Length: approx. 1000 words. Payment: by arrangement. Illustrations: photos, cartoons, line drawings – foods, animals, livestock systems, crops, people, events; colour for cover. Founded 1944.

Venue

Venue Publishing, 64–65 North Road, Bristol
BS6 5AQ
tel 0117-942 8491 *fax* 0117-942 0369
email editor@venue.co.uk
website www.venue.co.uk
Editor Rebecca Dean
Weekly £1.30

Listings magazine for Bristol and Bath combining
comprehensive entertainment information with local
features, profiles and interviews. Length: by
agreement. Illustrations: colour. Payment: £8.75 per
100 words. Founded 1982.

Veterinary Review

John C. Alborough Ltd, Lion Lane, Needham Market,
Suffolk IP6 8NT
tel (01449) 723800 *fax* (01449) 723801
email enquiries@jca.uk.com
Editor David Ritchie
Monthly £60 p.a.

News, articles – both topical and technical – for
veterinarians. Payment: negotiable.

Animal Health News

Editor Chris Ritchie
Monthly £30 p.a.
News, articles and product listings for the agricultural
supply trade.

La Vie Outre-Manche

Concorde French Language Publications, 8 Skye
Close, Maidstone, Kent ME15 9SJ
tel (01622) 749167 *fax* (01622) 744508
email ken.murray1@concordefrench.com
website www.concordefrench.com
Editor Kenneth Murray
6 p.a. £24 p.a.

Articles on France and French life, in French with
translation of more difficult words and phrases.
Aimed at adult improvers in the UK. Also contains
news items, features and short stories. Length:
500–1000 words (articles/features), up to 500 words
(news), 1000–3000 words (short fiction), written in
English or good French. Payment: £150 per 1000
words; £30 per photo/illustration, £100 cover.
Founded 1990.

Viz

Dennis Publishing, 30 Cleveland Street, London
W1T 4JD
tel 020-7687 7000 *fax* 020-7687 7099
email viz@viz.co.uk
website www.viz.co.uk
Editor Simon Donald
10 p.a. £2.50

Cartoons, spoof tabloid articles, spoof
advertisements. Illustrations: half-tone, line, cartoons.
Payment: £300 per page (cartoons). Founded 1979.

Vogue

Vogue House, Hanover Square, London W1S 1JU
tel 020-7499 9080 *fax* 020-7408 0559
website www.vogue.co.uk
Editor Alexandra Shulman
Monthly £3.60

Fashion, beauty, health, decorating, art, theatre, films,
literature, music, travel, food and wine. Length:
articles from 1000 words. Illustrated.

The Voice

Blue Star House, 8th Floor, 234–244 Stockwell Road,
London SW9 9UG
tel 020-7737 7377 *fax* 020-7274 8894
email newsdesk@the-voice.co.uk
website www.voice-online.co.uk
Editor-in-Chief Deidre Forbes, *Head of News* Andrew
Clunis, *Deputy Editor* Vic Motune, *Arts &
Entertainment Editor* Russell Myrie, *Sports Editor*
Rodney Hinds
Weekly 85p

Weekly newspaper for black Britons. Includes news,
features, arts, sport and a comprehensive jobs and
business section. Illustrations: colour and b&w
photos. Open to ideas for news and features on
sports, business, community events and the arts.
Founded 1982.

Young Voices

website www.young-voices.co.uk
Editor Emelia Kenlock
Monthly, 2nd Tues of each month £1.95
News, features, reviews, showbiz highlights and
current affairs for 11–19 year-olds. Founded 2003.

walk

The Ramblers' Association, 2nd Floor, Camelford
House, 87–90 Albert Embankment, London
SE1 7TW
tel 020-7339 8500 *fax* 020-7339 8501
email ramblers@ramblers.org.uk
website www.ramblers.org.uk
Editor Christopher Sparrow
Quarterly Free to members

Magazine of the Ramblers' Association. Articles on
walking, access to countryside and related issues.
Material mostly commissioned. Length: up to 1200
words. Illustrations: colour photos. Payment: by
agreement. Founded 1935.

Wallpaper

IPC Media, Brettenham House, Lancaster Place,
London WC2E 7TL
tel 020-7322 1177 *fax* 020-7322 1171
email contact@wallpaper.com
website www.wallpaper.com
Editor-in-Chief Jeremy Langmead
10 p.a. £3.90

Interiors, architecture, fashion, entertainment and
travel. Payment: by arrangement. Founded 1996.

Wanderlust

PO Box 1832, Windsor SL4 1YT
tel (01753) 620426
website www.wanderlust.co.uk
Editor Dan Linstead, *Publisher* Lyn Hughes
8 p.a. £3.80

Features on independent, adventure and special-interest travel. Send sae or visit website for 'Guidelines for contributors'. Length: up to 2500 words. Illustrations: high-quality colour slides (send stocklist first). Payment: by arrangement. Founded 1993.

The War Cry

The Salvation Army, 101 Newington Causeway, London SE1 6BN
tel 020-7367 4900 *fax* 020-7367 4710
email warcry@salvationarmy.org.uk
website www.salvationarmy.org/warcry
Editor Major Nigel Bovey
Weekly 20p (£26 p.a.)

Voluntary contributions: Christian comment on contemporary issues, human interest stories of personal Christian faith; puzzles. Illustrations: line and photos, cartoons. Founded 1879.

Waterways World

Waterways World Ltd, 151 Station Street, Burton-on-Trent DE14 1BG
tel (01283) 742952 *fax* (01283) 742957
email richard.fairhurst@wwonline.co.uk
Editor Richard Fairhurst
Monthly £3.25

Feature articles on all aspects of inland waterways in Britain and abroad, including historical material; factual and technical articles preferred. No short stories or poetry. Send sae or email for 'Notes for WW Contributors'. Payment: £42 per 1000 words. Illustrations: digital, colour transparencies or prints, line. Founded 1972.

Wedding

IPC Magazines Ltd, King's Reach Tower, Stamford Street, London SE1 9LS
tel 020-7261 7471 *fax* 020-7261 7459
email weddingandhome@ipcmedia.com
Acting Editor Margie Collingson
Bi-monthly £4.50

Ideas and inspiration for modern brides. Fashion and beauty, information for grooms, real life weddings, planning advice, gift list ideas and honeymoon features. Unsolicited features not accepted. Founded 1985.

The Weekly News

D.C. Thomson & Co. Ltd, Albert Square, Dundee DD1 9QJ
tel (01382) 223131
137 Chapel Street, Manchester M3 6AA
tel 0161-834 5122
144 Port Dundas Road, Glasgow G4 0HZ
tel 0141-332 9933
185 Fleet Street, London EC4A 2HS
tel 020-7400 1030
Send material to Rod Cameron, Deputy Editor
Weekly 60p

Real-life dramas of around 1000 words told in the first person. Non-fiction articles with lively themes or about interesting people. Keynote throughout is strong human interest. General interest fiction. Illustrations: cartoons. Payment: on acceptance.

Weight Watchers Magazine

River Publishing Ltd, Victory House, Leicester Place, Leicester Square, London WC2H 7BZ
tel 020-7306 0304 *fax* 020-7306 0314
email info@weightwatchers.co.uk
Editor Mary Frances
8 p.a. £2.50

Features: health, beauty, news, astrology; food-orientated articles; success stories. All material commissioned. Length: up to 3 pages. Illustrations: colour photos and cartoons. Payment: by arrangement.

What Digital Camcorder

Future Publishing Ltd, 2 Balcombe Street, London NW1 6NW
tel 020-7042 4000 *fax* 020-7317 0275
Editor Alistair Upham
Monthly £3.99

Technique articles aimed at the beginner on how to use camcorders and equipment tests of camcorders and accessories. Material mostly commissioned. Length: 1000–1800 words. Illustrations: colour photos, diagrams. Payment: £95 per 1000 words; £70 per page for illustrations. Founded 2000.

What Car?

Haymarket Motoring Magazines Ltd, Teddington Studios, Broom Road, Teddington, Middlesex TW11 9BE
tel 020-8267 5000 *fax* 020-8267 5688
website www.whatcar.com
Editor Ian Reid
Monthly £3.90

Road tests, buying guide, consumer stories and used car features. No unsolicited material. Illustrations: colour and b&w photos, line drawings. Payment: by negotiation. Founded 1973.

What Laptop

Future Publishing Ltd, 2 Balcombe Street, London NW1 6NW
tel 020-7042 4000 *fax* 020-7317 0275
email letters@whatlaptop.co.uk
website www.whatlaptop.co.uk
Editor Michael Browne

Monthly £3.99

News, reviews and help for anyone who wants to buy or has bought a laptop or handheld computer. Discuss ideas for features with the Editor in the first instance; welcomes ideas for features. Length: up to 1600 words. Payment: by arrangement. Founded 1999.

What's on TV

IPC Media Ltd, 9th Floor, King's Reach Tower, Stamford Street, London SE1 9LS
tel 020-7261 7767 *fax* 020-7261 7739
Editor Colin Tough
Weekly 40p

Features on TV programmes and personalities. All material commissioned. Length: up to 500 words. Illustrations: colour and b&w photos. Payment: by agreement. Founded 1991.

WI Home and Country

104 New King's Road, London SW6 4LY
tel 020-7731 5777 *fax* 020-7736 4061
Editor Joanna Gray
Monthly £1.30

Journal of the National Federation of Women's Institutes for England and Wales. Publishes material related to the Federation's and members' activities; also considers articles of general interest to women, particularly country women, e.g. craft, environment, humour, health, rural life stories, of 800–1200 words. Illustrations: colour and b&w photos and drawings, cartoons. Payment: by arrangement. Founded 1919.

Wine

Quest Magazines Ltd, Wilmington Publishing, 6–8 Underwood Street, London N1 7JQ
tel 020-7549 2571 *fax* 020-7549 8622
email wine@wineint.com
website www.wineint.com
Editor Catharine Lowe
12 p.a. £3.30

Articles, features and news on new developments in wine and spirits; travelogues, tastings and profiles. Illustrations: colour. Payment: £220 per 1000 words. Founded 1983.

The Wisden Cricketer

1–4 Shepherds Building, Charecroft Way, London W14 0EE
tel 020-7471 6900 *fax* 020-7471 6901
Editor John Stern
Monthly £3.75

Cricket articles of exceptional interest (unsolicited pieces seldom used). Length: up to 3000 words. Payment: by arrangement. Illustrations: half-tone, colour.

Woman

IPC Media, King's Reach Tower, Stamford Street, London SE1 9LS
tel 020-7261 5000 *fax* 020-7261 5997
Editor Jackie Hatton
Weekly 85p

Human interest stories and practical articles of varying length on all subjects of interest to women. Payment: by arrangement. Illustrations: colour transparencies and photos. Founded 1937.

Woman Alive

(formerly Christian Woman)
Christian Publishing and Outreach, Garcia Estate, Canterbury Road, Worthing, West Sussex BN13 1BW
tel (01903) 264556 *fax* (01903) 821081
email womanalive@cpo.org.uk
Editor Jackie Stead
Monthly £2.20

Aimed at women aged 25 upwards. Celebrity interviews, topical features, Christian issues, profiles of women in interesting occupations, Christian testimonies and real life stories, fashion, beauty, travel, health, crafts. Unsolicited material should include colour slides or photos. Length: 750–1600 words. Payment: £65–£120. Founded 1982.

Woman and Home

IPC Magazines Ltd, King's Reach Tower, Stamford Street, London SE1 9LS
tel 020-7261 5000 *fax* 020-7261 7346
Editor Sandra Curzon
Monthly £3

Centres on the personal and home interests of the lively minded mature, modern woman. Articles dealing with fashion, beauty, leisure pursuits, gardening, home style; features on topical issues, people and places. Fiction: complete stories from 3000–4500 words in length. Illustrations: commissioned colour photos and sketches. Please note: non-commissioned work is not accepted and regrettably cannot be returned. Founded 1926.

The Woman Writer

31 Eaton Court, Eaton Gardens, Hove, East Sussex BN3 3PL
email swwjnews@morrisdancer.fsnet.co.uk
website www.swwj.co.uk
Editor Jean Morris
6 p.a. Free to members

Periodical of the Society of Women Writers and Journalists. See under Societies section for further information. Founded 1894.

Woman's Own

IPC Connect Ltd, King's Reach Tower, Stamford Street, London SE1 9LS
tel 020-7261 5000
Editor Elsa McAlonan
Weekly 78p

Modern women's magazine aimed at the 20–35 age group. No unsolicited features or fiction.

Illustrations: colour and b&w: interior decorating and furnishing, fashion. Address work to relevant department editor. Payment: by arrangement.

Woman's Way

Harmonia Ltd, Clanwilliam House, Clanwilliam Place, Dublin 2, Republic of Ireland
tel (01) 240 5300 *fax* (01) 662 2979
email skenny@harmonia.ie
Editor Simone Kenny
Weekly €1.30

Human interest, personality interviews, features on fashion, beauty, celebrities and investigations. Founded 1963.

Woman's Weekly

IPC Media Ltd, King's Reach Tower, Stamford Street, London SE1 9LS
tel (0870) 4445000 *fax* 020-7261 6322
Editor Sheena Harvey
Weekly 74p

Lively, family-interest magazine. One fiction serial, averaging 4000 words each instalment, of general emotional interest, and several short stories of 1000–2500 words of general emotional interest. Stories up to 6000 considered for fiction specials. Celebrity and strong human interest features, health, finance and consumer features, plus beauty, diet and travel; also inspirational and entertaining personal stories. Payment: by arrangement. Illustrations: full colour fiction illustrations, small sketches and photos. Founded 1911.

Woman's Weekly Fiction Special

IPC Media Ltd, King's Reach, Stamford Street, London SE1 9LS
tel (0870) 4445000 *fax* 020-7261 6322
Editor Olwen Rice
Bi-monthly £1.60

At least 24 stories each issue of 1000–5,000 words of varied emotional interest, including romance, humour and mystery. Payment: by arrangement. Illustrations: full colour. Founded 1998.

The Woodworker

Encanta Media Ltd, Berwick House, 8–10 Knoll Rise, Orpington, Kent BR6 0EL
tel (01689) 899256
Editor Mark Ramuz
Monthly £3.40

For the craft and professional woodworker. Practical illustrated articles on cabinet work, carpentry, wood polishing, wood turning, wood carving, rural crafts, craft history, antique and period furniture; also wooden toys and models, musical instruments; timber procurement, conditioning, seasoning; tool, machinery and equipment reviews. Payment: by arrangement. Illustrations: line drawings and photos.

The Word

Divine Word Missionaries, Maynooth, Co. Kildare, Republic of Ireland
tel (01) 5054467 *fax* (01) 6289184
email wordeditor@eircom.net
website www.theword.ie
Editor-in-Chief Vincent Twomey svd, *Editor* Sarah MacDonald
Monthly €1.50 (€25 p.a.)

General interest magazine with a religious emphasis. Illustrated articles up to 1200 words and good picture features. Payment: by arrangement. Illustrations: photos and large colour transparencies. Founded 1953.

The Word

Development Hell Ltd, 90–92 Pentonville Road, London N1 9HS
tel 020-7520 8625 *fax* 020-7833 9900
email mail@wordmagazine.co.uk
website www.wordmagazine.co.uk
Editor Mark Ellen
Monthly £4.20

Music magazine focusing on music legends and their lives. Founded 2003.

Workbox Magazine

Ebony Media Ltd, PO Box 25, Liskeard, Cornwall PL14 6XX
tel (01579) 340100 *fax* (01579) 340400
email workbox@ebony.co.uk
website www.ebony.co.uk/workbox
Editor Victor Briggs
Bi-monthly £2.75

Features, of any length, on all aspects of needlecrafts. No 'how-to' articles. Send sae with enquiries and submissions. Illustrations: good colour transparencies. Payment: by agreement. Founded 1984.

World Fishing

Nexus Media Communications Ltd, Media House, Azalea Drive, Swanley, Kent BR8 8HU
tel (01322) 660070 *fax* (01322) 616324
email pilar.santamaria@nexusmedia.com
website www.worldfishing.net
Editor Pilar Santamaria
Monthly £95 p.a.

International journal of commercial fishing. Technical and management emphasis on catching, processing and marketing of fish and related products; fishery operations and vessels covered worldwide. Length: 500–1500 words. Payment: by arrangement. Illustrations: photos and diagrams for litho reproduction. Founded 1952.

The World of Interiors

The Condé Nast Publications Ltd, Vogue House, Hanover Square, London W1S 1JU
tel 020-7499 9080 *fax* 020-7493 4013
email interiors@condenast.co.uk
website www.worldofinteriors.co.uk

Editor Rupert Thomas
Monthly £4

All material commissioned: send synopsis/visual reference for article ideas. Length: 1000–1500 words. Illustrations: colour photos. Payment: £500 per 1000 words; photos £125 per page. Founded 1981.

World Soccer

IPC Media Ltd, King's Reach Tower, Stamford Street, London SE1 9LS
tel 020-7261 5737 *fax* 020-7261 7474
Editor Gavin Hamilton
Monthly £3.10

Articles, features, news concerning football, its personalities and worldwide development. Length: 600–2000 words. Payment: by arrangement. Founded 1960.

The World Today

Chatham House, 10 St James's Square, London SW1Y 4LE
tel 020-7957 5712 *fax* 020-7957 5710
email wt@chathamhouse.org.uk
website www.theworldtoday.org
Editor Graham Walker
Monthly £2.50

Analysis of international issues and current events by journalists, diplomats, politicians and academics. Length: 1600–2300 words. Payment: nominal. Founded 1945.

Writers' Forum

(incorporating World Wide Writers)
Writers' International Ltd, PO Box 3229, Bournemouth BH1 1ZS
website www.writers-forum.com
Publisher John Jenkins
12 p.a. £3.50 (£33 p.a. UK, £46 p.a. worldwide)

Welcomes articles on any aspect of the craft and business of writing. Length: 800–2000 words. Payment: by arrangement. Poetry and short story competitions in each issue. Founded 1993.

Writers' News

1st Floor, Victoria House, 143–145 The Headrow, Leeds LS1 5RL
tel 0113-200 2929 *fax* 0113-200 2928
website www.writersnews.co.uk
Publishing Editor Derek Hudson
Monthly £44.90 p.a. (£39.90 p.a. CC/DD), inc. subscription to *Writing Magazine*

News, competitions, markets. Length: up to 350 words. Illustrations: colour, line, half-tone. Payment: by arrangement. Founded 1989.

Writing Magazine

1st Floor, Victoria House, 143–145 The Headrow, Leeds LS1 5RL
tel 0113-200 2929 *fax* 0113-200 2928
website www.writersnews.co.uk
Publishing Editor Derek Hudson
Monthly £3.40 (£25 p.a., free to *Writers' News* subscribers)

Articles on all aspects of writing. Length: 400–1500 words. Illustrations: full colour, line, half-tone. Payment: by arrangement. Founded 1992.

Yachting Monthly

IPC Media Ltd, Room 2215, King's Reach Tower, Stamford Street, London SE1 9LS
tel 020-7261 6040 *fax* 020-7261 7555
Editor Paul Gelder
Monthly £3.60

Articles on all aspects of seamanship, navigation, the handling of sailing craft, and their design, construction and equipment. Well-written narrative accounts of cruises in yachts. Length: up to 1800 words (articles), up to 1800 words (narratives). Illustrations: colour transparencies and prints, cartoons. Payment: quoted on acceptance. Founded 1906.

Yachting World

IPC Media Ltd, Room 2332, King's Reach Tower, Stamford Street, London SE1 9LS
tel 020-7261 6800 *fax* 020-7261 6818
email yachting_world@ipc.media.com
website www.yachtingworld.com
Editor Andrew Bray
Monthly £3.80

Practical articles of an original nature, dealing with sailing and boats. Length: 1500–2000 words. Payment: varies. Illustrations: digital files, colour transparencies, drawings, cartoons. Founded 1894.

Yachts and Yachting

196 Eastern Esplanade, Southend-on-Sea, Essex SS1 3AB
tel (01702) 582245 *fax* (01702) 588434
email editorial@yachtsandyachting.com
website www.yachtsandyachting.com
Editor Gael Pawson
Fortnightly £3.75

Technical sailing and related lifestyle articles. Payment: by arrangement. Illustrations: line, halftone, colour. Founded 1947.

Yoga & Health

PO Box 16969, London E1W 1FY
tel 020-7480 5456 *fax* 020-7480 5456
website www.yogaandhealthmag.com
Editor Jane Sill
Monthly £2.50

Payment: by arrangement. Founded 1983.

Yorkshire Life

3 Tustin Court, Port Way, Preston, Lancs. PR2 2YQ
tel (01772) 722022 *fax* (01772) 736496

website www.yorkshirelife.co.uk
Editor Sarah Todd
Monthly £2.50

Articles on Yorkshire, including places of interest, high-profile personalities, local events, arts, history and food. Unsolicited ideas welcome. Founded 1946.

Yorkshire Ridings Magazine

33 Beverley Road, Driffield, Yorkshire YO25 6SD
tel (01377) 253232 *fax* (01377) 253232
Editor Winston Halstead
Bi-monthly £1.40

Articles exclusively about people, life and character of the 3 Ridings of Yorkshire. Length: up to 1000 words. Payment: approx. £40 per published page. Illustrations: colour, b&w photos; prints preferred. Founded 1964.

You & Your Wedding

NatMag Specialist Media (AIM) Ltd, National Magazine House, 72 Broadwick Street, London W1F 9EP
tel 020-7439 5000 *fax* 020-7439 2985
email debbie.codd@natmags.co.uk
website www.youandyourwedding.co.uk
Editor Carole Hamilton, *Send material to* Debbie Codd, Associate Editor
Bi-monthly £4.50

Articles, features and news covering all aspects of planning a wedding. Submit ideas in writing only. Illustrations: colour. Payment: £300 per 1000 words.

Young People Now

Haymarket Publishing Ltd, 174 Hammersmith Road, London W6 7JP
tel 020-8267 4793 *fax* 020-8267 4728
email ypn.editorial@haynet.com
website www.ypnmagazine.com
Editor Steve Barrett
Weekly £1.80

Informative articles, highlighting issues of concern to all those who work with young people, including youth workers, youth justice workers, the voluntary youth sector, probation and social services, Connexions, teachers and volunteers. Founded 1989.

Young Writer

Glebe House, Webley, Herefordshire HR4 8SD
tel (01544) 318901 *fax* (01544) 318901
email editor@youngwriter.org
website www.youngwriter.org
Editor Kate Jones
3 p.a. £3.75 (£10 for 3 issues)

Specialist magazine for young writers under 18 years old: ideas for them and writing by them. Includes interviews by children with famous writers, fiction and non-fiction pieces, poetry; also explores words and grammar, issues related to writing (e.g. dyslexia), plus competitions with prizes. Length: 750 or 1500

words (features), up to 400 words (news), 750 words (short stories – unless specified otherwise in a competition), poetry of any length. Illustrations: colour – drawings by children, snapshots to accompany features. Payment: most children's material is published without payment; £25–£100 (features); £15 (cover cartoon). Free inspection copy. Founded 1995.

Your Cat Magazine

BPG (Stamford) Ltd, Roebuck House, 33 Broad Street, Stamford, Lincs. PE9 1RB
tel (01780) 766199 *fax* (01780) 766416
email s.parslow@bournepublishinggroup.co.uk
Editor Sue Parslow
Monthly £2.85

Practical advice on the care of cats and kittens, general interest items and news on cats, and true life tales and fiction. Length: 800–1500 words (articles), 200–300 (news), up to 1000 (short stories). Illustrations: colour transparencies and prints. Payment: £80 per 1000 words. Founded 1994.

Your Dog Magazine

BPG (Stamford) Ltd, Roebuck House, 33 Broad Street, Stamford, Lincs. PE9 1RB
tel (01780) 766199 *fax* (01780) 766416
email s.wright@bournepublishinggroup.co.uk
Editor Sarah Wright
Monthly £3.10

Articles and information of interest to dog lovers; features on all aspects of pet dogs. Length: approx. 1500 words. Illustrations: colour transparencies, prints and line drawings. Payment: £80 per 1000 words. Founded 1994.

Your Horse

Emap Active, Bretton Court, Bretton, Peterborough PE3 8DZ
tel (01733) 264666 *fax* (01733) 465200
email natasha.simmonds@emap.com
Editor Natasha Simmonds
Every 4 weeks £3.30

Practical horse care and riding advice for the leisure rider and horse owner. Send feature ideas with examples of previous published writing. Specially commissions most material. Welcomes ideas for articles and features. Length: 1500 words. Payment: £120 per 1000 words. Founded 1983.

Yours

EMAP Esprit Ltd, Bretton Court, Peterborough PE3 8DZ
tel (01733) 264666 *fax* (01733) 465266
Editor Valery McConnell
Monthly £1.50

Features and news about and/or of interest to the over-50s age group, including nostalgia and short stories. Study of magazine essential; approach in writing in the first instance. Length: articles up to 1000 words, short stories up to 1500 words. Illustrations: preferably colour transparencies/prints but will consider good b&w prints/line drawings, cartoons. Payment: at the Editor's discretion or by agreement. Founded 1973.

Zest

National Magazine House, 72 Broadwick Street, London W1F 9EP
tel 020-7439 5000 *fax* 020-7312 3750
email zest.mail@natmags.co.uk
Editor Alison Pylkkanen, *Send material to* Susie Whalley, Features Editor
Monthly £2.99

Health and beauty magazine. Commissioned material only: health, fitness and beauty, features, news and shorts. Length: 50–2000 words. Illustrations: colour and b&w photos and line. Payment: by arrangement. Founded 1994.

Zoo

Mappin House, 4 Winsley Street, London W1W 8HF
tel 020-7182 8355
email info@zooweekly.co.uk
website www.zooweekly.co.uk
Editor Anthony Noguera
Weekly £1.30

Entertainment magazine for young men with news, sport, photos, stories, jokes, listings and reviews. Founded 2004.

Newspapers and magazines overseas

Listings are given for newspapers and magazines in Australia (below), Canada (page 109), New Zealand (page 112) and South Africa (page 113). For information on submitting material to the USA see page 115. Newspapers are listed under the towns in which they are published.

AUSTRALIA

(Adelaide) Advertiser
121 King William Street, Adelaide, SA 5000
tel (08) 8206 2000 *fax* (08) 8206 3669
London office PO Box 481, 1 Virginia Street, London E1 9BD
tel 020-7702 1355 *fax* 020-7702 1384
Editor Mel Mansell
Daily Mon–Fri 90c, Sat $1.30

Descriptive and news background material, 400–800 words, preferably with pictures; also cartoons. Founded 1858.

(Adelaide) Sunday Mail
31 Waymouth Street, Adelaide, SA 5000
postal address GPO Box 339, Adelaide, SA 5001
tel (08) 8206 2000 *fax* (08) 8206 3646
website www.sundaymail.com.au
Editor Phillip Gardner
Sun $1.60

Founded 1912.

AQ – Australian Quarterly
Australian Institute of Political Science, PO Box 145, Balmain, NSW 2041
tel (02) 9810 5642 *fax* (02) 9810 2406
website www.aips.net.au
6 p.a. $66 p.a. individuals/schools, $110 p.a. organisations ($125 Asia/Oceania; $140 elsewhere)

Peer-reviewed articles for the informed non-specialist on politics, law, economics, social issues, etc. Length: 3500 words preferred. Payment: none. Founded 1929.

Art and Australia
Art and Australia Pty Ltd, 11 Cecil Street, Paddington NSW 2021
email info@artandaustralia.com.au
website www.artandaustralia.com.au
Editor Claire Armstrong
Quarterly $20 ($75 p.a.)

Articles with a contemporary perspective on Australia's traditional and current art, and on international art of Australian relevance, plus exhibition and book reviews. Length: 2000–3000 words (articles), 600–1200 words (reviews). Payment: $500 per 1000 words. Illustrations: colour transparencies or tiff files. Founded 1916 as *Art in Australia*.

Art Monthly Australia
PO Box 8321, ANU Acton, ACT 2601
tel (02) 6125 3988 *fax* (02) 6125 9794
email art.monthly@anu.edu.au
website www.artmonthly.org.au
Editor Deborah Clark
10 p.a. March–Dec $6.00

Contemporary visual arts: reviews, commentary, news and book reviews. Specially commissions most material but will consider unsolicited material. Welcomes ideas for articles and features. Length: negotiable. Payment: $200 per 1000 words. Founded 1987.

Artlink
363 Esplanade, Henley Beach, South Australia 5022
tel (61) 8356 8511 *fax* (61) 8825 1280
email info@artlink.com.au
website www.artlink.com.au, www.artlink.com.au
Quarterly

Thematic art magazine linking art and society. Relevant articles and ideas welcome. Payment: $250 per 1000 words. Email CV and examples of work.

The Australian Financial Review
Level 25, 201 Sussex Street, Sydney, NSW 2000
tel (02) 9282 1959 *fax* (02) 9267 2094
Editor Glenn Burge
London office 1 Bath Street, London EC1V 9LB
tel 020-7688 2777 *fax* 020-7688 3499
Daily Mon–Fri $2.50

Investment business and economic news and reviews; government and politics, production, banking, commercial, and Stock Exchange statistics; company analysis. General features in Friday *Weekend Review* supplement.

Australian Flying
Yaffa Publishing Group, 17–21 Bellevue Street, Surry Hills, NSW 2010
tel (02) 9281 2333 *fax* (02) 9281 2750
email shelleyross@yaffa.com.au
Editor Shelley Ross
6 p.a. $6.50

Covers the Australian light aircraft industry. Payment: by arrangement.

Australian Geographic
PO Box 321, Terrey Hills, NSW 2084
tel (02) 9473 6700 *fax* (02) 9473 6701
website www.australiangeographic.com.au
Editorial Director Dee Nolan
Quarterly $49.95 p.a.

Articles and features about Australia, particularly life, technology and wildlife in remote parts of the country. Material mostly commissioned. Length: articles, 300–800 words, features, 2000–3000 words. Illustrations: all commissioned. Payment: from $500 per 1000 words; illustrations by negotiation. Founded 1986.

Australian Heritage

Hallmark Editions, PO Box 84, Hampton, Victoria 3188
email editor@halledit.com.au
website www.heritageaustralia.com.au
Editor Rosalind Stirling
Quarterly $7.50 ($60 p.a. outside Australia)

Non-fiction articles on Australia's history and cultural and natural heritage. Length: 1500–3000 words. Payment: $500–$1500 by arrangement. Illustrations: photos, artwork. Founded 2005.

Australian Home Beautiful

Private Bag 9700, North Sydney, NSW 2059
tel (02) 9464 3218 *fax* (02) 9464 3263
email homebeaut@pacpubs.com.au
Editor Andrea Jones
Monthly $6.50

Interior decoration, furnishing, gardening, cookery, etc. Unsolicited MSS not accepted. Founded 1925.

Australian House and Garden

54 Park Street, Sydney, NSW 1028
postal address GPO Box 4088, Sydney, NSW 1028
tel (02) 9282 8456 *fax* (02) 9267 4912
email h@ampcaacp.com.au
website www.acp.com.au
Editorial Director Anny Friis
Monthly $6.75

Factual articles dealing with interior decorating, home design, gardening, wine, food. Preliminary letter essential. Payment: by arrangement. Illustrations: line, half-tone, colour. Founded 1948.

Australian Journal of Politics and History

School of Political Science and International Studies and the Department of History, University of Queensland, St Lucia, Queensland 4067
tel (07) 3365 3163 *fax* (07) 3365 1388
email i.ward@mailbox.uq.edu.au
Editor Ian Ward and Andrew Bonnell
4 p.a. $66/£38 p.a. individuals; $144/£110 institutions

Australian, European, Asian, Pacific and international articles. Special feature: regular surveys of Australian Foreign Policy and State and Commonwealth politics. Length: 8000 words max. Illustrations: line, only when necessary. Payment: none.

Australian Photography

Yaffa Publishing Group, 17–21 Bellevue Street, Surry Hills, NSW 2010
tel (02) 9281 2333 *fax* (02) 9281 2750

email robertkeeley@yaffa.com.au
Editor Robert Keeley
London office 2 Milford Road, London W13 9HZ
tel 020-8579 4836
Contact Robert Logan
Monthly $6.25

Illustrated articles: picture-taking techniques, technical. Length: 1200–2500 words with colour and/or b&w prints or slides. Payment: $80 per page. Founded 1950.

Australian Powerboat

Yaffa Publishing Group, GPO Box 606, Sydney, NSW 2001
tel (02) 9281 2333 *fax* (02) 9281 2750
Editor Vanessa Dudley
London office 2 Milford Road, London W13 9HZ
tel 020-8579 4836
Contact Robert Logan
Bi-monthly $6.25

Articles and news on boats and boating, racing, water skiing and products. Length: 1500 words (articles), 200 words (news). Illustrations: colour (transparencies preferred). Payment: $100 per 1000 words; from $30. Founded 1976.

The Australian Women's Weekly

ACP Magazines Ltd, 54 Park Street, Sydney, NSW 2000
tel (02) 9282 8000 *fax* (02) 9267 4459
email womensweekly@acpmagazines.com.au
postal address GPO Box 4178, Sydney, NSW 2000
Editorial Director Deborah Thomas
Monthly $6.20

Fiction and features. Length: fiction 1000–5000 words; features 1000–4000 words plus colour or b&w photos. Payment: according to length and merit. Fiction illustrations: sketches by own artists and freelances.

Aviation Business

GPO Box 606, Sydney 2001
tel (02) 9213 8267 *fax* (02) 9281 2750
email dougnancarrow@yaffa.com.au
website www.yaffa.com.au
Editor Doug Nancarrow
11 p.a.

Aviation business magazine for industry professionals focusing on Asia Pacific. Welcomes ideas for features. Length: 800–2000 words (features). Payment: on application. Illustrations: digital images only. Founded 1918.

The Big Issue Australia

GPO Box 4911VV, Melbourne, Victoria 3001
tel (03) 9663 4522
email bigissue@bigissue.org.au
Editor Martin Hughes
Fortnightly $4

Profiles and features of general interest and on social issues and entertainment, arts reviews. No fiction. Length: 1000–2500 words (features), up to 900 words (news), 200 words (reviews). Payment: 15c per word (features), $30 (reviews). Founded 1996.

Bookseller & Publisher

Thorpe-Bowker, Building C3, 85 Turner Street, Port Melbourne, Victoria 3207
tel (03) 8645 0300 *fax* (03) 8645 0368
email bookseller.publisher@thorpe.com.au
website www.thorpe.com.au
Editor Tim Coronel
9 p.a. $120 p.a. ($160 NZ/Asia; $180 elsewhere)

Founded 1921.

(Brisbane) The Courier-Mail

Queensland Newspapers Pty Ltd, Campbell Street, Bowen Hills, Brisbane, Queensland 4006
tel (07) 3666 8000 *fax* (07) 3666 6696
email cmletters@qnp.newsltd.com.au
website www.news.com.au
Editor David Fagan
Daily $1

(Brisbane) The Sunday Mail

Queensland Newspapers Pty Ltd, PO Box 130, Campbell Street, Bowen Hills, Brisbane, Queensland 4006
tel 300 304 020 *fax* (07) 3666 6787
email smletters@qnp.newsltd.com.au
Editor Michael Prain
Sun $1.60 GST inc.

Anything of general interest. Length: up to 1500 words. Illustrations: line, photos, b&w and colour, cartoons. Rejected MSS returned if postage enclosed.

The Bulletin

GPO Box 3957, Sydney, NSW 1028
tel (02) 9282 8227 *fax* (02) 9267 4359
email bulletin@acp.com.au
website http://bulletin.ninemsn.com.au
Editor Garry Linnezi
Weekly $5.50

'Australia's most quoted news magazine'. News, features and comment on current issues. Length: 1000–2000 words (articles), 1000–2000 words (features), 500–2000 (news). Payment: by negotiation. Founded 1880.

Camera

Horwitz Publications Pty Ltd, 55 Chandos Street, St Leonards, NSW 2065
tel (02) 9901 6100 *fax* (02) 9901 6198
email paulb@horwitz.com.au
Editor Paul Burrows
Bi-monthly $6.50

Magazine for amateur photographers and digital imaging enthusiasts covering techniques, test reports, new products. Considers unsolicited material. Welcomes ideas for articles and features. Length: 750–1500 words (features/articles). Illustrations: colour prints and transparencies. Payment: $300–$500. Founded 1979.

Cordite Poetry Review

PO BOx 14022, City Mail Processing Centre, Melbourne 8000
email cordite@cordite.org.au
website www.cordite.org.au
Editor David Prater
2 p.a. Free

Publishes on the internet poetry by new and emerging Australian authors, alongside feature articles, reviews, news and gossip items, audio poetry and special competitions. Welcomes material from overseas writers (no payment). Length: 100–3000 words (articles and features). Payment: $50–$100; $50 per poem. Illustrations: colour and b&w. Founded 1997.

Dance Australia

Yaffa Publishing Group, Box 606, GPO Sydney, NSW 2001
tel (02) 9281 2333 *fax* (02) 9281 2750
email dance@yaffa.com.au
Editor Karen van Ulzen
London office 2 Milford Road, London W13 9HZ
tel 020-8579 4836
Contact Robert Logan
Bi-monthly $5.50

Articles and features on all aspects of dance in Australia. Material mostly commissioned, but will consider unsolicited contributions. Illustrations: b&w photos, line drawings, cartoons. Payment: $200 per 1000 words; illustrations by negotiation. Founded 1980.

Dolly

54–58 Park Street, Sydney, NSW 2000
tel (02) 9282 8437 *fax* (02) 9267 4911
website www.ninemsn.com.au/dolly
Editor Bronwyn McCahon
Monthly $5.20

Features on teen fashion, health and beauty, personalities, music, social issues and how to cope with growing up, etc. Length: not less than 1000 words. Illustrations: colour, b&w, line, cartoons. Payment: by arrangement. Founded 1970.

Harper's Bazaar

ACP Publishing Pty Ltd, 54 Park Street, Sydney, NSW 2000
tel (02) 9282 8703 *fax* (02) 9267 4456
email bazaar@acp.com.au
Editor Alison Veness-McGourty
10 p.a. $7.50

Fashion, health and beauty, celebrity news, plus features. Length: 3000 words. Illustrations: colour and b&w photos. Founded 1998.

Island

PO Box 210, Sandy Bay, Tasmania 7006
website www.islandmag.com, www.islandmag.com
Editor Gina Mercer

Short stories, poetry, extracts from novels and articles and essays on social, environmental and cultural significance. Payment: $60 per poem, $100 for short stories, $100 per 1000 words for articles.

(Launceston) Examiner

Box 99, PO Launceston, Tasmania 7250
tel (03) 633 67111 *fax* (03) 633 47328
website www.examiner.com.au
Editor Dean Southwell
Daily $1.10

Accepts freelance material. Payment: by arrangement.

Meanjin

Meanjin Company Ltd, 131 Barry Street, Carlton, Victoria 3054
tel (03) 8344 6950 *fax* (03) 9347 2550
email meanjin@unimelb.edu.au
website www.meanjin.unimelb.edu.au
Editor Dr Ian Britain
Quarterly $22.95

Cultural commentary, fiction, poetry, essays and discussion of contemporary issues, e.g. biography, drugs, travel. See website for submission guidelines. Payment: $50 per poetry item, min. $100 prose. Founded 1941.

(Melbourne) Age

The Age Company Ltd, 250 Spencer Street, Melbourne, Victoria 3000
tel (03) 9600 4211 *fax* (03) 9601 2412
London office 1 Bath Street, London EC1V 9LB
tel 020-7688 2777 *fax* 020-7688 3499
Editor-in-Chief Andrew Jaspan, *Senior Deputy Editor* Paul Ramadge, *Deputy Editor* Gay Alcorn
Daily Mon–Fri $1.10, Sat $1.90, Sun $1.50

Independent liberal morning daily; room occasionally for outside matter. *Good Weekend* and *Sunday Life* (illustrated weekend magazines); *Insight*; *A2* (includes literary reviews). Accepts occasional freelance material.

(Melbourne) Herald Sun

HWT Tower, 40 City Road, Southbank, Victoria 3006
tel (03) 9292 1145 *fax* (03) 9292 2112
Editor Peter Blunden
Send material to Peter Helme, Syndications Manager
Daily Mon–Fri $1, Sat $1.40, Sun $1.60

Accepts freelance articles, preferably with illustrations. Length: up to 750 words. Illustrations: half-tone, line, cartoons. Payment: on merit.

(Melbourne) Sunday Herald Sun

HWT Tower, 40 City Road, Southbank, Victoria 3006
tel (03) 9292 2000 *fax* (03) 9292 2080

Editor Simon Pristel
Weekly $1.50

Accepts freelance articles, preferably with illustrations. Length: up to 2000 words. Illustrations: colour. Payment: on merit.

New Vegetarian and Natural Health

PO Box 56, Surry Hills, NSW 2010
email avs@veg-soc.org
website www.naturalhealth.org.au, www.veg-soc.org
Editors Roger French, Mark Berriman

Magazine of the Natural Health Society of Australia and the Australian Vegetarian Society. Welcomes contributions. Length: 700–2500 words.

New Woman

Level 6, 187 Thomas Street, Haymarket, NSW 2000
tel (02) 9581 9400 *fax* (02) 9211 9540
Editor Frances Sheen
Monthly $6.95

Irreverent and humorous style of magazine for the single, professional woman aged 25–35. Includes celebrity gossip, fashion, beauty, sex and relationships, and entertainment reviews. Founded 1989.

NW Magazine

54 Park Street, Sydney, NSW 2000
tel (02) 9282 8285 *fax* (02) 9264 6005
Editor Louisa Hatfield
Weekly $3.50

News and features on celebrities, food, new products, fashion and astrology. Illustrated. Payment: by negotiation. Founded 1993.

Overland

PO Box 14428, Melbourne, Victoria 8001
tel (03) 9919 4163 *fax* (03) 9687 7614
email overland@vu.edu.au
website www.overlandexpress.org
Editor Nathan Hollier
Quarterly $45 p.a. ($80 overseas)

Literary and cultural. Australian material preferred. Payment: by arrangement. Illustrations: line, half-tone, cartoons.

People Magazine

Stocklard House, 175–183 Castlereagh Street, Sydney, NSW 2000
tel (02) 9288 9648 *fax* (02) 9283 6179
Editor Martin Vine
Weekly $3.95

National weekly news-pictorial. Mainly celebrity stories. Photos depicting exciting happenings, glamour, show business, unusual occupations, rites, customs. Payment: $300 per page, text and photos.

(Perth) The Sunday Times

34–40 Stirling Street, Perth, Western Australia 6000
tel (08) 9326 8476 *fax* (08) 9326 8330

Editor Brett McCarthy
Sun $1.80

Topical articles to 800 words. Payment: on acceptance. Founded 1897.

(Perth) The West Australian

50 Hasler Road, Osborne Park, Western Australia 6017
tel (08) 9482 3111 *fax* (08) 9482 3177
website www.thewest.com.au
Editor Paul Armstrong
Daily Mon–Fri $1.10, Sat $2.20

Articles and sketches about people and events in Australia and abroad. Length: 300–700 words. Payment: Award rates or better. Illustrations: line, half-tone. Founded 1833.

Positive Words

466 Old Melbourne Road, Traralgon 3844, Victoria
Editor Lynn Evans

Creative writing. Length: short stories up to 1000 words; poetry (one page). Payment: complementary copy.

Quadrant

437 Darling Street, Balmain, NSW 2041
postal address PO Box 82, Balmain, NSW 2041
tel (02) 9818 1155 *fax* (02) 9818 1422
email quadrnt@ozemail.com.au
Editor P.P. McGuinness
Literary Editor Les Murray
Monthly $6.50

Articles, short stories, verse, etc. Prose length: 2000–5000 words. Payment: min. $90 articles/stories, $60 reviews, $40 poems; illustrations by arrangement.

Reader's Digest (Australia)

30–32 Waterloo Street, Surry Hills, NSW 2010
tel (02) 9690 6111 *fax* (02) 9690 6390
Editor-in-Chief Thomas Moore
Monthly $5.79 (inc. GST)

Articles on Australian subjects by commission only. No unsolicited MSS accepted. Length: 2500–5000 words. Payment: up to $6000 per article; brief filler paragraphs, $50–$250. Illustrations: half-tone, colour.

Rock

Wild Publications Pty Ltd, PO Box 415, Prahran, Victoria 3181
tel (03) 9826 8482 *fax* (03) 9826 3787
email management@wild.com.au
website www.rock.com.au
Editor Megan Holbeck
Quarterly $8.99

Australian rockclimbing and mountaineering articles, features and news. See website for guidelines to contibutions. Length: 2000 words (articles/features), 200 words (news). Illustrations: colour

transparencies. Payment: $85 per page (words and pictures). Founded 1978.

Scuba Diver

Yaffa Publishing Group, 17–21 Bellevue Street, Surry Hills, NSW 2010
tel (02) 9281 2333 *fax* (02) 9281 2750
email yaffa@flex.com.au
Editor Sue Crowe
London office 2 Milford Road, London W13 9HZ
tel 020-8579 4836
Contact Robert Logan
Bi-monthly $6.50

News, features, articles and short stories on scuba diving. Length: 1500 words (articles/features), 300–800 words (news), 800–1000 (short stories). Illustrations: colour. Payment: $70 per page, negotiable (words and pictures).

The Sun-Herald

GPO Box 506, Sydney, NSW 2001
tel (02) 9282 2822 *fax* (02) 9282 2151
London office John Fairfax (UK) Ltd, 1 Bath Street, London EC1V 9LB
tel 020-7688 2777 *fax* 020-7688 3499
Editor Philip McLean
Weekly $1.50

Topical articles to 1000 words; news plus sections on current affairs, entertainment, finance, sport and travel. Payment: by arrangement.

(Sydney) The Daily Telegraph

News Ltd, 2 Holt Street, Surry Hills, NSW 2010
tel (02) 9288 3000 *fax* (02) 9288 2608
Editor David Penberthy
Daily Mon–Fri $1, Sat $1.50

Modern feature articles and series of Australian or world interest. Length: 1000–2000 words. Payment: according to merit/length.

The Sydney Morning Herald

201 Sussex Street, Sydney, NSW 2000
tel (02) 9282 2822 *fax* (02) 9282 3253
London office 1 Bath Street, London EC1V 9LB
tel 020-7688 2777 *fax* 020-7688 3499
Editor Suzy Baldwin
Daily $1.20

Saturday edition has pages of literary criticism and also magazine articles, plus glossy colour magazine. Topical articles 600–4000 words. Payment: varies, but minimum $100 per 1000 words. Illustrations: all types. Founded 1831.

(Sydney) The Sunday Telegraph

News Ltd, 2 Holt Street, Surry Hills, Sydney, NSW 2010
tel (02) 9288 3000 *fax* (02) 9288 3311
Editor Neil Breen
Weekly $1.60

News and features. Illustrations: transparencies. Payment: varies. Founded 1935.

Traveltalk Australia

PO Box 329, North Beach, Western Australia 6920
tel 618 9240 3888 *fax* 618 9240 2796
email jane@traveltalk.biz
website www.traveltalk.biz
Editor Jane Hammond Foster
Quarterly $3.95

Travel news and features focusing on popular travel destinations, in Australia and international. Prefers to receive a list of ideas and sample of material initially. Length: 600 words (articles), 1200–1800 words (features), 150–450 words (news). Payment: 40 cents per printed word. Founded 2002.

Vive

125–127 Little Eveleigh Street, Redfern, NSW 2016
tel (02) 9318 0500 *fax* (02) 9318 1140
email vive@pol.net.au
Editor Louise Upton
Bi-monthly $8.50

A business/lifestyle publication aimed at successful executive women. Content includes business profiles, career-related features, travel, food, beauty, working mothers. Specially commissions most material. Welcomes ideas for articles and features via email. Do not send unsolicited material. Length: 1500–2000 words (articles/features). Payment: 65c per word. Illustrations: transparencies, colour and b&w prints and artwork; all commissioned. Founded 1996.

Vogue Australia

180 Bourke Road, Alexandria, NSW 2015
postal address Locked Bag 5030, Alexandria NSW 2015
tel (02) 9353 6666 *fax* (02) 9353 6600
Editor-in-Chief Kirstie Clements
Monthly $7.95

Articles and features on fashion, beauty, health, business, people and the arts of interest to the modern woman of style and high spending power. Ideas welcome. Length: from 1000 words. Illustrations: colour and b&w. Founded 1959.

Wild

Wild Publications Pty Ltd, PO Box 415, Prahran, Victoria 3181
tel (03) 9826 8482 *fax* (03) 9826 3787
email management@wild.com.au
website www.wild.com.au
Editor Megan Holbeck
4 p.a. $7.99

'Australia's wilderness adventure magazine.' Illustrated articles of first-hand experiences of the Australian wilderness, plus book and track reviews, product tests. See website for guidelines for contributors. Length: 2500 words (articles), 200

words (news). Colour transparencies. Payment: $125 per published page. Founded 1981.

Woman's Day

54–58 Park Street, Sydney, NSW 2000
tel (02) 9282 8000 *fax* (02) 9267 4360
Editor Alana House
Weekly $3.80

National women's magazine; news, show business, fiction, fashion, general articles, cookery, home economy, health, beauty.

CANADA

The Beaver: Canada's History Magazine

Canada's National History Society, Suite 478, 167 Lombard Avenue, Winnipeg, Manitoba R3B 0T6
tel 204-988-9300 *fax* 204-988-9309
email editors@historysociety.ca
website www.thebeaver.ca
Editor Doug Whiteway
Bi-monthly $29.95 p.a. ($37.95 USA, $44.95 p.a. elsewhere)

Articles on Canadian history. Length: 1500–3000 words, with illustrations. Payment: on acceptance. Illustrations: b&w and colour archival photos or drawings. Founded 1920.

C Magazine

PO Box 5, Station B, Toronto, Ontario M5T 2T2
tel 416-539-9495 *fax* 416-539-9903
email general@cmagazine.com
Quarterly US$8.25

Arts and artists' projects, features, reviews. Accepts submissions. Length: features (varies), reviews (500 words). Illustrations: transparencies, photos. Payment: $250–$500 features, $100 reviews. Founded 1972.

Canadian Literature

University of British Columbia, Buchanan E158, 1866 Main Mall, Vancouver, BC V6T 1Z1
tel 604-882-2780 *fax* 604-822-5504
Editor Laurie Ricou
4 p.a. $50 p.a. ($79 p.a. institutions; outside Canada add $20 postage)

Articles on Canadian writers and writing in English and French. No fiction. Length: up to 6500 words. Payment: none. Founded 1959.

Canadian Theatre Review (CTR)

Drama Program, University of Guelph, Guelph, Ontario N1G 2W1
Contact Editorial Committee
Quarterly $10.50 ($35 p.a.)

Feature and review articles on Canadian theatre aimed at theatre professionals, academics and general audience; book and play reviews. Send MSS

accompanied by PC compatible disk. Length:
2000–3000 words. Illustrations: b&w. Payment:
$200–$275 (features/articles), $75 (book/play
reviews). Founded 1974.

Canadian Writer's Journal

PO Box 1178, New Liskeard, Ontario P0J 1P0
tel 705-647-5424 *fax* 705-647-8366
email cwj@cwj.ca
website www.cwj.ca
Editor Deborah Ranchuk
Bi-monthly $35 p.a.

News on markets and articles on writers' aspirations
for dedicated apprentice and professional Canadian
writers. Considers unsolicited material. Founded
1984.

Chatelaine

One Mount Pleasant Road, Toronto, Ontario
M4Y 2Y5
tel 416-764-1888
Editor Kim Pittaway
Monthly $4.50

Women's interest articles; Canadian angle preferred.
Payment: on acceptance; from $1000.

The Dalhousie Review

Dalhousie University, Halifax, Nova Scotia B3H 4R2
tel 902-494-2541 *fax* 902-494-3561
email Dalhousie.Review@dal.ca
website www.dal.ca/~dalrev/
Editor Robert Martin
3 p.a. ($35.50 p.a., $44/$110 outside Canada)

Articles on history, literature, political science,
philosophy, sociology, popular culture, fine arts;
short fiction; verse; book reviews. Usually not more
than 3 stories and 10–12 poems in any one issue.
Length: prose, up to 5000 words; verse, less than 40
words. Contributors receive 2 copies of issue and 10
offprints of their work.

Descant

PO Box 314, Station P, Toronto, Ontario M5S 2S8
tel 416-593-2557 *fax* 416-593-9362
email info@descant.on.ca
website www.descant.on.ca
Editor Karen Mulhallen
Quarterly $15

Literary magazine: short fiction, poetry and essays,
previously unpublished. Payment: $100 (articles and
fiction) on publication. Illustrations: b&w. Founded
1970.

The Fiddlehead

Campus House, 11 Garland Court,
UNB PO Box 4400, Frederiction, NB E3B 5A3
tel 506-453-3501
email fiddlehd@unb.ca
website www.lib.unb.ca/texts/fiddlehead

Editor Ross Leckie
Quarterly US$10 (US$25 p.a.)

Reviews, poetry, short stories. Payment: approx. $20
per printed page. Founded 1945.

(Hamilton) The Spectator

44 Frid Street, Hamilton, Ontario L8N 3G3
tel 905-526-3333
website www.hamiltonspectator.com
Publisher Mr Patrick J. Collins
Daily Mon–Fri $1, Sat $1.75

Articles of general interest, political analysis and
background; interviews, stories of Canadians abroad.
Length: 800 words maximum. Payment: rate varies.
Founded 1846.

Inuit Art Quarterly

2081 Merivale Road, Ottawa, Ontario K2G 1G9
tel 613-224-8189 *fax* 613-224-2907
email iaq@inuitart.org
website www.inuitart.org
Editor Marybelle Mitchell
Quarterly $7.95

Features, original research, artists' perspectives, news.
Freelance contributors are expected to have a
thorough knowledge of the arts. Length: varies.
Illustrations: colour and b&w photos and line.
Payment: by arrangement. Founded 1985.

Journal of Canadian Studies

Trent University, Peterborough, Ontario K9J 7B8
tel 705-748-1279 *fax* 705-748-1110
email jcs_rec@trentu.ca
Editors Stephen Bocking, Jill Smith
Quarterly US$50 p.a. (US$60 p.a. institutions)

Major academic review of Canadian studies. Articles
of general as well as scholarly interest on history,
politics, literature, society, arts. Length: 7000–10,000
words.

The Malahat Review

University of Victoria, PO Box 1700 STN CSC,
Victoria, BC V8W 2Y2
tel 250-721-8524 *fax* 250-472-5051
email malahat@uvic.ca (queries only)
website www.malahatreview.ca
Editor John Barton
Quarterly $35 p.a. ($40 p.a. US, $45 p.a. elsewhere)

Short stories, poetry, short plays, reviews. Payment:
$30 per magazine page. Founded 1967.

Neo-opsis Science Fiction Magazine

4129 Carey Road, Victoria, BC V8Z 4G5
tel 250-881-8893
email neoopsis@shaw.ca
website www.neo-opsis.ca
Editor Karl Johanson
Quarterly $6.95 (£4.98 UK, $7.59 US)

Science fiction short stories, articles, opinion columns
and reviews. Considers unsolicited material. Length:

up to 4000 words (articles), up to 6000 words (short stories). Illustrations: b&w cartoons. Payment: 2.5 cents per word with max. of $125 for short stories; $30 per illustration. Founded 2003.

Outdoor Canada

25 Sheppard Avenue West, Suite 100, Toronto, Ontario M2N 6S7
tel 416-733-7600 *fax* 416-227-8296
email editorial@outdoorcanada.ca
website www.outdoorcanada.ca,
www.outdoorcanada.ca
Editor Patrick Walsh

Articles on Canada's best fishing and hunting adventures and destinations, conservation issues related to angling and hunting, plus news on gear and techniques. Send idea first. Length: 2000–4000 words for articles, 100–600 words for shorter features. Average payment .50 cent per word.

Photo Life

185 Rue St Paul, Quebec, QC G1K 3W2
tel 418-692-2110 *fax* 418-692-3392
email editor@photolife.com
website www.photolife.com
Editor Guy Poirier
6 p.a. $35 p.a.

Covers all aspects of photography of interest to amateur and professional photographers. Length: 800–1500 words. Illustrations: colour and b&w photos. Payment: by arrangement. Founded 1976.

Queen's Quarterly

Queen's University, Kingston, Ontario K7L 3N6
tel 613-533-2667 *fax* 613-533-6822
email qquarter@post.queensu.ca
website http://info.queensu.ca/quarterly
Editor Dr Boris Castel
Quarterly $6.50 ($20 p.a.; $40 p.a. institutions)

A multidisciplinary scholarly journal aimed at the general educated reader – articles, short stories and poems. Length: 2500–3500 words (articles), 2000 (stories). Payment: by negotiation. Founded 1893.

Quill & Quire

111 Queen Street East, Toronto, Ontario M5C 1S2
tel 416-364-3333 *fax* 416-595-5415
email info@quillandquire.com
Editor Derek Weiler
12 p.a. $59.95 p.a. (outside Canada $95 p.a.)

Articles of interest about the Canadian book trade. Payment: from $100. Illustrations: line, half-tone. Subscription includes Canadian Publishers Directory (2 p.a.). Founded 1935.

Reader's Digest (Canada)

1125 Stanley Street, Montreal, QC H3B 5H5
tel 514-940-0751 *fax* 514-940-3637
website www.readersdigest.ca

Editor Murray Lewis
Monthly $38 p.a.

Original articles on all subjects of broad general appeal, thoroughly researched and professionally written. Outline or query only. Length: 3000 words approx. Payment: from $2700. Also previously published material. Illustrations: line, half-tone, colour.

(Toronto) The Globe and Mail

444 Front Street West, Toronto, Ontario M5V 2S9
Publisher Phillip Crawley, *Editor-in-Chief* Edward Greenspon
Daily 60c

Unsolicited material considered. Payment: by arrangement. Founded 1844.

Toronto Life

111 Queen Street East, Suite 320, Toronto, Ontario M5C 1S2
tel 416-364-3333 *fax* 416-861-1169
website www.torontolife.com
Editor John Macfarlane
Monthly $4.95

Articles, profiles on Toronto and Torontonians. Illustrations: line, half-tone, colour. Founded 1966.

Toronto Star

1 Yonge Street, Toronto, Ontario M5E 1E6
tel 416-869-4000 *fax* 416-869-4328
London office Level 4A, PO Box 495, Virginia Street, London E1 9XY
tel 020-7833 0791
website www.thestar.com
Editor Eddie Lee
Daily Mon–Fri 30c, Sat $1, Sun 75c ($123 p.a.)

Features, life, world/national politics. Payment: by arrangement. Founded 1892.

(Vancouver) The Province

200 Granville Street, Suite 1, Vancouver, BC V6C 3N3
tel 604-605-2030 *fax* 604-605-2378
Editor-in-Chief Wayne Moriarty
Daily Mon–Fri 70c, Sun $1.40

Founded 1898.

Vancouver Sun

200 Granville Street, Vancouver, BC V6C 3N3
tel 604-605-2000 *fax* 604-605-2308
email intouch@png.canwest.com
London office Canwest News, 8 Heath Mansions, Hampstead Grove, London NW3 6SL
tel 020-7435 5103
website www.vancouversun.com
Editor Nick Palmer
Daily Mon–Thu 75c; Fri, Sat $1.40 ($205 p.a.)

Mix arts magazine. Travel, Op-Ed pieces considered. Payment: by arrangement.

Winnipeg Free Press

1355 Mountain Avenue, Winnipeg, MB R2X 3B6
tel 204-697-7000 *fax* 204-697-7412
website www.winnipegfreepress.com
Editor Bob Cox
Daily Sun–Thurs 75c, Fri $1, Sat $1.50

Some freelance articles. Founded 1872.

NEW ZEALAND

(Auckland) New Zealand Herald

PO Box 32, Auckland
tel (09) 379 5050 *fax* (09) 373 6421
email editor@herald.co.nz
website www.nzherald.co.nz
Editor Tim Murphy
Daily Mon–Fri $1.20, weekend $2.50

Topical and informative articles 800–1100 words.
Payment: minimum $150–$300. Illustrations: colour
negatives or prints. Founded 1863.

(Auckland) Sunday News

PO Box 1327, Auckland
tel (09) 302 1300 *fax* (09) 358 3003
email editor@sunday-news.co.nz
Editor Chris Baldock
Sun $1.50

News, sport and showbiz, especially with NZ interest.
Illustrations: colour and b&w photos. Founded 1963.

(Christchurch) The Press

Private Bag 4722, Christchurch
tel (03) 379 0940 *fax* (03) 364 8238
email editorial@press.co.nz
Editor Paul Thompson
Daily Mon–Fri $1, Sat $1.80

Articles of general interest not more than 800 words.
Illustrations: photos and line drawings, cartoons.
Payment: by arrangement.

(Dunedin) Otago Daily Times

PO Box 181, Dunedin
tel (03) 477 4760 *fax* (03) 474 7422
email odt.editor@alliedpress.co.nz
website www.odt.co.nz
Editor R.L. Charteris
Daily 90c, Sat/Sun $1.30

Any articles of general interest up to 1000 words, but
preference is given to NZ writers. Topical illustrations
and personalities. Payment: current NZ rates.
Founded 1861.

Freelance

328 College Street, Palmerston North 5301
website www.nzfreelancewriters.org.nz
Editor Alyson B. Cresswell
Quarterly

Magazine of the NZ Freelance Writers' Association.
Welcomes ideas for articles on all genres of writing.
Payment: $10 (490–900 words). Payment on
acceptance.

Hawke's Bay Today

PO Box 180, Karamu Road North, Hastings
tel (06) 878 5155 *fax* (06) 876 0655
Editor L. Pierard
Daily $1

Limited requirements. Payment: $30 upwards for
articles, $30 upwards for photos.

(Invercargill) The Southland Times

PO Box 805, Invercargill
tel (03) 211 1130 *fax* (03) 214 9905
email news@stl.co.nz
website www.stuff.co.nz
Editor F.L. Tulett
Daily Mon–Fri 80c, Sat $1.20

Articles of up to 800 words on topics of Southland
and Otago interest. Payment: by arrangement.
Illustrations: colour, cartoons. Founded 1862.

Management Magazine

Profile Publishing, PO Box 5544, Auckland
tel (09) 630 8940 *fax* (09) 630 1046
email editor@management.co.nz
Editor Reg Birchfield
Monthly $6.95

Articles on the practice of management skills and
techniques, individual and company profiles,
coverage of organisational leadership and
management trends and topics. A NZ/Australian
angle or application preferred. Length: 2000 words.
Payment: by arrangement; minimum 30c per word.
Illustrations: photos, line drawings.

The Nelson Mail

PO Box 244, 15 Bridge Street, Nelson
tel (03) 548 7079 *fax* (03) 546 2802
email nml@nelsonmail.co.nz
Editor Bill Moore
Daily 70c

Features, articles on NZ subjects. Length: 500–1000
words. Payment: up to $100 per 1000 words.
Illustrations: half-tone, colour.

(New Plymouth) The Daily News

Level 3, 40 Boulcott Street, PO Box 2595, Wellington
tel (644) 496 9800 *fax* (644) 496 9841
website www.tnl.co.nz
Editor Lance G. Butcher
Daily 90c

Articles preferably with a Taranaki connection.
Payment: by negotiation. Illustrations: half-tone,
cartoons. Founded 1857.

(New Zealand) Sunday Star-Times

PO Box 1409, Auckland
tel (09) 302 1300 *fax* (09) 309 0258

email editor@star-times.co.nz
Editor Cate Brett
Sun $2

New Zealand Woman's Day
Private Bag 92512, Wellesley Street, Auckland
tel (09) 308 2718 *fax* (09) 357 0978
Editor Megan McChesney
Weekly $3.50

Celebrity interviews, exclusive news stories, short stories, gossip. Length: 1000 words. Illustrations: colour transparencies; payment according to use. Payment: by arrangement. Founded 1989.

NZ House & Garden
PO Box 6341, Wellesley Street, Auckland
tel (09) 353 1010 *fax* (09) 353 1020
Editor Michal McKay
Monthly $8.95

Glossy magazine that celebrates New Zealand's most interesting houses and beautiful gardens. Inspiration for food and entertaining, and a resource for decor and travel. Considers unsolicited material. Welcomes ideas for articles and features. Length: 500–1000 words. Payment: $400–$600. Illustrations: colour transparencies. Founded 1994.

She
Private Bag 92512, Wellesley Street, Auckland 1036
tel (09) 308 2700 *fax* (09) 302 0667
Editor Hannah Dickinson
Monthly $6.20

Lifestyle magazine for women aged 25–40. Length: 1000–2000 words (features and profiles). Illustrations: colour. Payment: negotiable. Founded 1996.

Takahe
Takahe Collective Trust, PO Box 13335, Christchurch 8001
tel (03) 359 8133
3 p.a. $25 p.a. ($35 international)

Quality short fiction and poetry by both new and established writers. Payment: approx. $30 per issue. Founded 1989.

The Timaru Herald
PO Box 46, Bank Street, Timaru
tel (03) 684 4129 *fax* (03) 688 1042
email editor@timaruherald.co.nz
website www.timaruherald.co.uk
Editor Dave Wood
Daily 65c

Topical articles. Payment: by arrangement. Illustrations: colour or b&w prints.

(Wellington) The Dominion Post
PO Box 3740, 40 Boulcott Street, Wellington
tel (04) 474 0000 *fax* (04) 474 0350, (04) 474 0185 (editor)

email editor@dompost.co.nz
website www.stuff.co.nz
Editor Tim Pankhurst
Daily Mon–Fri $1.10, Sat $2

General topical articles, 600 words. Payment: NZ current rates or by arrangement. News illustrations, cartoons. Founded 2002 with the merger of *The Dominion* and *The Evening Post*.

Your Home and Garden
Australian Consolidated Press (New Zealand) Ltd, Private Bag 92512, Wellesley Street, Auckland
tel (09) 308 2700 *fax* (09) 377 6725
Editor Brenda Ward
Monthly $6.80

Advice, ideas and projects for homeowners – interiors and gardens. Length: 1000 words. Illustrations: digital images. Payment: 35c per word/ $75 per transparency. Founded 1991.

SOUTH AFRICA

Bona
Caxton Magazines, PO Box 32083, Mobeni 4060, KwaZulu-Natal
tel (031) 910-5745
website bona@dbn.caxton.co.za
Monthly R6.95

Articles on human drama, sport, music, health, social and consumer issues of interest to black people. Length: up to 1000 words. Payment: on publication. Illustrations: colour jpegs or prints.

(Cape Town) Cape Times
Newspaper House, 4th Floor, 122 St George's Mall, Cape Town 8001
postal address PO Box 11, Cape Town 8000
tel (021) 488-4911 *fax* (021) 488 4744
website www.iol.co.za
Editor Chris Whitfield
Daily R4.30

Contributions must be suitable for a daily newspaper and must not exceed 800 words. Illustrations: photos of outstanding South African interest. Founded 1876.

Car
PO Box 180, Howard Place 7450
tel (021) 530-3156 *fax* (021) 532-2698
email johnb@rsp.co.za
website www.cartoday.com
Editor John Bentley
Monthly R23.95

New car announcements with photos and full colour features of motoring interest. Payment: by arrangement. Illustrations: colour, cartoons. Founded 1957.

Daily Dispatch
Dispatch Media (Pty) Ltd, 35 Caxton Street, East London 5201

tel (043) 702-2000 *fax* (043) 743 5155
email eledit@iafrica.com
postal address PO Box 131, East London 5200
website www.dispatch.co.za
Editor Gavin Stewart
Daily Mon–Sat R2.70

Newspaper for the Eastern Cape region. Features of general interest, especially successful development projects in developing countries. Contributions welcome. Illustrations: colour and b&w photographs, artwork, cartoons; provides research facility for a fee to authors and publications. Length: approx. 1000 words (features). Payment: R500; R100 photographs. Founded 1872.

(Durban) The Mercury

Independent Newspapers KwaZulu-Natal Ltd,
PO Box 47549, Durban 4000
tel (031) 308-2306 *fax* (031) 308-2258
Editor D. Canning
Daily Mon–Fri R3.60

Serious background news and inside details of world events. Length: 700–900 words. Illustrations: photos of general interest. Founded 1852.

Fairlady

PO Box 1802, Cape Town 8000
tel (021) 406-2121 *fax* (021) 406-2930
email flmag@fairlady.com
website www.fairlady.com
Editor Ann Donald
Bi-weekly R18.50

Magazine for women in their 30s covering beauty, fashion, food and interior design. Includes 8 features per issue for which it seeks topical stories written to style. Considers unsolicited material. Length: about 1800 words. Illustrations: colour and b&w prints, colour artwork. Payment: R1.50 per word; R250 per photo, approx. R500 per illustration. Founded 1965.

Farmer's Weekly

Caxton Magazines, PO Box 1797, Pinegowie 2123, Johannesburg
tel (021) 889-0862
email farmersweekly@caxton.co.za
Editor Chris Burgess
Weekly R9.95

Articles, generally illustrated, up to 1000 words, on all aspects of practical farming and research with particular reference to conditions in Southern Africa. Includes women's section which accepts suitable, illustrated articles. Illustrations: line, half-tone, colour, cartoons. Payment: according to merit. Founded 1911.

Femina Magazine

Associated Magazines, Box 3647, Cape Town 8000
tel (021) 464-6200 *fax* (021) 461-2501
email femina@assocmags.co.za

Editor Robynne Kahn
Monthly R19.95

For busy young professionals, often with families. Humour, personalities, real-life drama, medical breakthroughs, popular science, news-breaking stories and human interest. Payment: by arrangement.

Garden and Home

Caxton Magazines, PO Box 32083, Mobeni 4060
tel (031) 910-5713
Editor Les Abercrombie
Monthly R19.95

Well-illustrated articles on gardening suitable for southern hemisphere. Articles for home section on furnishings, decor ideas, food. Payment: by arrangement. Illustrations: half-tone, colour, cartoons.

Independent Newspapers Gauteng

PO Box 1014, Johannesburg 2000
tel (011) 633-9111 *fax* (011) 836-8398
website www.iol.co.za
  Johannesburg **The Star** Daily R3.50
  Saturday Star R3.97
  Sunday Independent R11
  Pretoria **Pretoria News** Daily R3.50

Accepts articles of general and South African interest; also cartoons. Payment: in accordance with an editor's assessment.

Independent Newspapers Kwa-Zulu Natal Ltd

18 Osborne Street, Greyville, Durban 4023
tel (031) 308-2400 *fax* (031) 308-2427
website www.iol.co.za
  Durban **Daily News** R62.60 p.m.
  The Mercury Daily R16.60 p.m.
  The Post Bi-weekly R16.60 p.m.
  Independent on Saturday R15.25 p.m.

Accepts articles of general and South African interest; also cartoons. Payment: in accordance with an editor's assessment.

Independent Newspapers (South Africa) Ltd

PO Box 56, Cape Town 8000
tel (021) 488-4911 *fax* (021) 488-4762
website www.iol.co.za
  Cape Town **Argus** Daily R3.52
  Saturday Argus R7.13
  Sunday Argus R7.13
  Cape Times Daily R3.99

Accepts articles of general and South African interest; also cartoons. Payment: in accordance with an editor's assessment.

(Johannesburg) Sunday Times

PO Box 1742, Saxonwold 2132
tel (011) 280-3000 *fax* (011) 280-5151

email suntimes@sundaytimes.co.za
Editor M.Makhavya
Sun R8.50

Illustrated articles of political or human interest, from a South African angle if possible. Maximum 1000 words long and 2–3 photos. Shorter essays, stories and articles of a light nature from 500–750 words. Payment: average rate £100 a column. Illustrations: colour and b&w photos, line drawings.

Living and Loving

CTP Caxton Magazines, 4th Floor, Caxton House, 368 Jan Smuts Avenue, Craighall Park, Johannesburg
tel (011) 889 0621 *fax* (011) 889 0668
postal address PO Box 218 Parklands 2121
website www.living-loving.co.za
Editor Kerese Thom
Monthly R13.95

Parenting magazine: from pregnancy to preschool. Articles about behaviour and development in the first 5 years of life. First-person parenting experiences – pregnancy and the growing child. Medical news/breakthroughs of interest to parents worldwide. Payment: by merit, on acceptance and publication. Founded 1970.

Sailing

(incorporating SA Yachting)
PO Box 1849, Westville 3630
tel (031) 709 6087 *fax* (031) 709 6143
email sailing@iafrica.com
website www. sailing.co.za
Editor Richard Crockett
Monthly

Articles and features for the safety of dinghy, cruising, keelboat and racing sailors. Welcomes ideas for articles and features. Will consider unsolicited material. Illustrations: colour.

Southern Cross

PO Box 2372, Cape Town 8000
tel (021) 465-5007 *fax* (021) 465-3850
email scross@global.co.za
website www.thesoutherncross.co.za
Editor Gunther Simmermacher
Weekly R285 p.a.

National English-language Catholic weekly. Catholic news reports, world and South African. Length: 550-word articles. Illustrations: photos of Catholic interest from freelance contributors. Payment: 14c per word; illustrations R28

The Witness

Box 362, Pietermaritzburg, KwaZulu-Natal 3200
tel (033) 355-1111 *fax* (033) 355-1122
email features@witness.co.za
Editor J.H. Conyngham
Daily R3.40

Accepts topical articles. All material should be submitted direct to the Editor in Pietermaritzburg.

Length: 500–1000 words. Payment: average of R500 per 1000 words. Founded 1846.

Woman's Value

Media 24, PO Box 1802, Cape Town 8000
tel (021) 406-2205 *fax* (021) 406-2929
email wvditedit@womansvalue.com
website www.womansvalue.com
Editor Karen Geldenhuys
Monthly R16.45

Features on beauty, food, finance, knitting, needlecraft, crafts, home and garden, health and parenting; short stories. Length: up to 1400 words (features/stories). Payment: R1.50 per word. Colour transparencies. Founded 1980.

World Airnews

PO Box 35082, Northway, Durban 4065
tel (31) 564-1319 *fax* (31) 563-7115
email tom@airnews.co.za
Editor Tom Chalmers
Monthly £36 p.a.

Aviation news and features with an African angle. Payment: by negotiation.

Your Family

PO Box 473016, Parklands 2121, Gauteng
tel (011) 889-0600
Editor Patti Garlick
Monthly R14.95

Cookery, knitting, crochet and homecrafts. Family drama, happy ending. Payment: by arrangement. Illustrations: continuous tone, colour and line, cartoons.

USA

The *Yearbook* does not contain a detailed list of US magazines and journals. Volume 3 of *Willings Press Guide* is the most useful general reference guide to US publications, available in most reference libraries. For readers with a particular interest in the US market, the publications listed here will be helpful (payments to the US should be made in US funds).

In many cases it is best to send a preliminary enquiry by email giving a rough outline of your article or story. Most magazines will supply guidelines to authors. Make it clear what rights are being offered for sale as some editors like to purchase material outright, thus securing world copyright, i.e. the traditional British market as well as the US market. Send the material direct to the US office of the journal and not to any London office.

If you submit material to US journals by post, include a covering letter, together with return postage in the form of International Reply Coupons (IRCs). IRCs can be exchanged in any foreign country for stamps representing the minimum postage payable on a letter sent from one country to another.

American Markets Newsletter

175 Westland Drive, Glasgow G14 9JQ
email sheila.oconnor@juno.com
Editor Shelia O'Connor
6 p.a. £34 p.a. (£63 for 2 years)

Editorial guidelines for US, Canadian and other overseas markets, plus information on press trips, non-fiction/fiction markets and writers' tips. Free syndication for all subscribers. Sample issue £5.95 (payable to S. O'Connor).

Willings Press Guide

Romeike Ltd, Chess House, 34 Germain Street, Chesham, Bucks. HP5 1SJ
tel 08707 360010 (UK), (1494) 797225
(int.) *fax* 08707 360011 (UK), (1494) 797224
email willings@romeike.com
website www.willingspress.com
£375 3-volume set; £325 2 volumes; £225 1 volume

Three volumes contain details of over 50,000 newspapers, broadcasters, periodicals and special interest titles in the UK and internationally. Usually available at local reference libraries or direct from the publisher. Also available as an online product.

The Writer

Kalmbach Publishing Co., 21027 Crossroads Circle, PO Box 1612, Waukesha, WI 53187
tel 262-796-8776 *fax* 262-798-6468
email queries@writermag.com
website www.writermag.com
Monthly $22.95 p.a. (or introductory rate of $24.95)

Contains articles of instruction on all writing fields, lists of markets for MSS and special features of interest to fiction writers and freelance writers everywhere.

Writer's Digest

Writer's Digest, 4700 E. Galbraith Road, Cincinnati, OH 45236
tel 513-531-2690 *fax* 513-531-2902
email writersdig@fwpubs.com
website www.writersdigest.com
Monthly $27 p.a.

Monthly magazine for writers who want to write better and sell more; aims to inform, instruct and inspire the freelance and fiction writer.

Writer's Digest Books

4700 E. Galbraith Road, Cincinnannti, OH 45236
tel 513-531-2690 *fax* 513-531-2902
website www.writersdigest.com

Publishes annually *Novel & Short Story Writer's Market, Children's Writer's & Illustrator's Market, Poet's Market, Photographer's Market, Artist's & Graphic Designer's Market, Guide to Literary Agents* and many other books on creating and selling writing and illustrations. Also *Writer's Digest* magazine (see above).

Writer's Market

Writer's Digest Books, Kalmbach Publishing Co., 21027 Crossroads Circle, PO Box 1612, Waukesha, WI 53187–1612
website www.writersmarket.com
$29.99

An annual guidebook giving editorial requirements and other details of over 4000 US markets for freelance writing. Also available on website.

Syndicates, news and press agencies

Before submitting material, you are strongly advised to make preliminary enquiries and to ascertain terms of work. Strictly speaking, syndication is the selling and reselling of previously published work although some news and press agencies handle original material.

Academic File Information Services

Eastern Art Publishing Group, PO Box 13666, London SW14 8WF
tel 020-8392 1122 *fax* 020-8392 1422
email afis@eapgroup.com
website www.eapgroup.com
Managing Editor Sajid Rizvi, *Executive Editor* Shirley Rizvi

Feature and photo syndication with special reference to the developing world and immigrant communities in the West. Founded 1985.

Advance Features

Stubbs Wood Cottage, Hammerwood, East Grinstead, West Sussex RH19 3QE
tel (01342) 850480
email advancefeatures@aol.com
website www.advancefeatures.uk.com
Managing Editor Peter Norman

Crosswords: daily, weekly and theme; general puzzles. Daily and weekly cartoons for the regional, national and overseas press (not single cartoons).

AFX News Ltd

Finsbury Tower, 103–105 Bunhill Row, London EC1Y 8TN
tel 020-7422 4800 *fax* 020-7422 4994
email info@afxnews.com
website www.afxnews.com
Managing Director Stefan Ploghaus

Provides real-time financial news to the international banking and investor community. Has 13 bureaux in major European financial centres. News services available in English, French, German, Dutch, Italian and Spanish covering local and international markets. Wholly owned subsidiary of Agence France Presse (AFP). Founded 1990.

Agencia Efe

299 Oxford Street, London W1C 2DZ
tel 020-7493 7313 *fax* 020-7493 7314
email efelondon@btclick.com
website www.efe.es
Director Joaquin Rabago

Spain's international news agency specialising in news writing about Spain and Latin America.

The Associated Press Ltd

(News Department), The Associated Press House, 12 Norwich Street, London EC4A 1BP
tel 020-7353 1515 *fax* 020-7353 8118
website www.ap.org

Supplies international news to the UK media and collects UK material for the USA.

Australian Associated Press

12 Norwich Street, London EC4A 1QJ
tel 020-7353 0153 *fax* 020-7583 3563
website www.aap.com.au

News service to the Australian, New Zealand and Pacific Island press, radio and TV. Founded 1935.

Neil Bradley Puzzles

Linden House, 73 Upper Marehay, Ripley, Derbyshire DE5 8JF
tel (01773) 741500 *fax* (01773) 741555
email bradcart@aol.com
Director Neil Bradley

Supplies visual puzzles to national and regional press; emphasis placed on variety and topicality with work based on current media listings. Daily single frame and strip cartoons. Founded 1981.

Brainwarp

PO Box 51, Newton-le-Willows, Merseyside WA3 3NZ
tel (01942) 271817
email trixie@brainwarp.com
website www.brainwarp.com
Partners Trixie Roberts, Tony Roberts

Writes and supplies original crosswords, brainteasers, wordsearches, quizzes and word games to editors for the printed page. Does not accept work from external sources. Standard fees for syndicated puzzles. Customised work negotiable. Founded 1987.

Bulls Presstjänst AB

Tulegatan 39, Box 6519, S-11883 Stockholm, Sweden
tel (08) 55520600 *fax* (08) 55520665
website www.bullspress.com
Bulls Pressedienst GmbH
Eysseneckstrasse 50, D-60322 Frankfurt am Main, Germany
tel (069) 959 270 *fax* (069) 959 27111
email sales@bullspress.de
Bulls Pressetjeneste A/S
Hammersborg torg 3, N-0179 Oslo, Norway
tel 22 98 26 60 *fax* 22 20 49 78
email info@bulls.se
Bulls Pressetjeneste
Ostbanegade 9, DK–2100 Copenhagen, Denmark

tel 35 38 90 99 *fax* 35 38 25 16
email kjartan@bulls.dk
Oy Fennopress Ab – a Bulls Company
Arabianranta 6, FIN–00560, Helsinki, Finland
tel (09) 612 96 50 *fax* (09) 656 092
email info@bullspress.fi
Bulls Press SP. z o.o.
17 Rejtana str. 24, 02–516 Warsaw, Poland
tel (22) 845 90 10 *fax* (22) 845 90 11
email office@bulls.com.pl
Bulls Press
Narva mnt. 7 D, EE–10117 Tallinn, Estonia
tel (372) 66 96 737 *fax* (372) 660 13 13
email pilt@bulls.ee

Market newspapers, magazines, weeklies and
advertising agencies in Sweden, Denmark, Norway,
Finland, Iceland, Poland, The Baltic States, Germany,
Austria and German-speaking Switzerland.
  Syndicates human interest picture stories; topical
and well-illustrated background articles and series;
photographic features dealing with science, people,
personalities, glamour; genre pictures for advertising;
condensations and serialisations of best-selling fiction
and non-fiction; cartoons, comic strips, film and TV
rights, merchandising and newspaper graphics online.

Celebritext
223 Broomwood Road, London SW11 6JX
tel 020-7350 2555
email info@celebritext.com
website www.celebritext.com
Contact Lee Howard

Specialises in music, film and TV celebrity interviews.
Commission: 50%. Founded 2000.

Children's Express UK
Exmouth House, 3–11 Pine Street, London
EC1R 0JH
tel 020-7833 2577 *fax* 020-7278 7722
website www.childrens-express.org
Director Fiona Wyton

Offers young people aged 8–18 the opportunity to
write on issues of importance to them, for
newspapers, radio and TV. It operates after school
and at weekends. Founded 1995.

Copyline Scotland
70 Tomnahunch Street, Inverness IV3 5DJ
tel (01463) 710695 *fax* (01463) 713695
email copylinescotland@aol.com
Directors David Love, Maureen Love, Alistair Munro,
Steve Mackenzie

Copywriting, writing press releases, covering news
events for national and local media. Founded 1988.

J.W. Crabtree and Son
135 Main Street, Burley-in-Wharfdale LS29 7GN
tel (01274) 732937 (office), (01535) 655288
(home) *fax* (01274) 732937

News and sport. Founded 1919.

Daily & Sunday Telegraph Syndication
The Telegraph Group Ltd, 1 Canada Square, Canary
Wharf, London E14 5DT
tel 020-7538 7505 *fax* 020-7538 7319
email syndicat@telegraph.co.uk
website http://syndication.telegraph.co.uk

News, features, photography; worldwide distribution
and representation.

Environmental & Occupational Health Research Foundation
Penrose House, 56 Birtles Road, Whirley, Cheshire
SK10 3JQ
tel (01625) 615323 *fax* (01625) 615323
email eorhfl@aol.com
Managing Editor Peggy Bentham

Undertakes individual commissions and syndicates
articles to diverse science and technology journals
and general consumer media. Peer reviewed and
accredited contributors from academia and
professional institutions.

Europa-Press
Sveavägen 47, 2nd Floor, Box 6410, S-113 82,
Stockholm
tel 8-34 94 35 *fax* 8-34 80 79
email anna@europapress.se
Managing Director Anna Holmström

Market: newspapers, magazines, weeklies and
websites in Sweden, Denmark, Norway, Finland, and
the Baltic states. Syndicates high-quality features of
international appeal such as topical articles, photo
features – b&w and colour, women's features, short
stories, serial novels, non-fiction stories and serials
with strong human interest, comic strips.

Europress Features (UK)
18 St Chads Road, Didsbury, Nr Manchester
M20 9WH
tel 0161-445 2945
email lauenbergandpartners@yahoo.com

Representation of newspapers and magazines in
Europe, Australia, United States. Syndication of top-
flight features with exclusive illustrations – human
interest stories – showbusiness personalities. 30–35%
commission on sales of material successfully
accepted; 40% on exclusive illustrations.

FAMOUS*
13 Harwood Road, London SW6 4QP
tel 020-7731 9333 *fax* 020-7731 9330
email info@famous.uk.com
website www.famous.uk.com

Celebrity picture and feature agency. Supplies
showbiz content to newspapers, magazines, websites,
TV stations, mobile phone companies, books and
advertisers worldwide. Represents celebrity journalists
and photographers from LA, New York, Europe and

Australia, syndicating their copy around the globe. Open to new material. Terms: 50%. Founded 1990.

Graphic Syndication
4 Reyntiens View, Odiham, Hants RG29 1AF
tel (01256) 703004
email flantoons@btinternet.com
Manager M. Flanagan

Cartoon strips and single frames supplied to newspapers and magazines in Britain and overseas. Terms: 50%. Founded 1981.

Guardian/Observer Syndication
119 Farringdon Road, London EC1R 3ER
tel 020-7886 9290
Contact Eve Thompson

International syndication services of news and features from *The Guardian* and *The Observer*.

Hayters Teamwork
Image House, Station Road, London N17 9LR
tel 020-8808 3300 *fax* 020-8808 1122
email sport@haytersteamwork.com
website www.hayters.com
Managing Director Nick Callow, *Chief Executive* Gerry Cox

Sports news, features and data supplied to all branches of the media. Commission: negotiable according to merit. Founded 1955.

India-International News Service
Head office Jute House, 12 India Exchange Place, Kolkata 700001, India
tel 22209563
Proprietor Eur Ing Dr H. Kothari Bsc, DWP(Lond), PhD(hc)(USA), FIMechE, FIE, FVI, FInstD(Lond), FRAS, FRSA, FRSH

'Calcutta Letters' and Air Mail news service from Calcutta. Specialists in industrial and technical news.

INS (International News Service) and Irish News Service
UK office 7 King's Avenue, Minnis Bay, Birchington-on-Sea, East Kent CT7 9QL
tel (01843) 845022
Editor & Managing Director Barry J. Hardy PC, *Photo Editor* Jan Vanek, *Secretary* K.T. Byrne

News, sport, book and magazine reviews (please forward copies), TV, radio, photographic department; also equipment for TV films, etc.

International Fashion Press Agency
Penrose House, Birtles Road, Whirley, Cheshire SK10 3JQ
tel (01625) 615323 *fax* (01625) 615323
email ifpressagy@aol.com
Directors P. Bentham (managing), P. Dyson, L.C. Mottershead, L.B. Fell

Monitors and photographs international fashion collections and developments in textile and fashion industry. Specialist writers on health, fitness, beauty and personalities. Undertakes individual commissioned features. Supplies syndicated columns/pages to press, radio and TV (NUJ staff writers and photographers).

International Press Agency (Pty) Ltd
Sunrise House, 56 Morningside, Ndabeni 7405, South Africa
tel (021) 531 1926 *fax* (021) 531 8789
email inpra@iafrica.com
UK office 12 Marion Court, 134–142 Tooting High Street, London SW17 0RU
tel 020-8767 4828
Manager Mrs T. Temple
Managing Editor Mrs U.A. Barnett PhD

South African agents for many leading British, American and continental press firms for the syndication of jokes, feature articles, short stories, serials, press photos for the South African market. Founded 1934.

Joker Feature Service (JFS)
PO Box 253, 6040 AG, Roermond, The Netherlands
tel (0475) 337338 *fax* (0475) 315663
email info@jfs.nl
Managing Director Ruud Kerstens

Feature articles, serial rights, tests, cartoons, comic strips and illustrations, puzzles. Handles TV features, books, internet sites; also production for merchandising.

Knight Features
20 Crescent Grove, London SW4 7AH
tel 020-7622 1467 *fax* 020-7622 1522
website www.knightfeatures.co.uk
Director Peter Knight, *Associates* Gaby Martin, Andrew Knight, Samantha Ferris

Worldwide selling of strip cartoons and major features and serialisations. Exclusive agent in UK and Republic of Ireland for United Feature Syndicate and Newspaper Enterprise Association of New York. Founded 1985.

London at Large
Zenith House, 155 Curtain Road, London EC2A 3QY
tel 020-7613 2299 *fax* 020-7613 4492
email newsbreaks@londonatlarge.com
website www.londonatlarge.com
Directors Chris Parkinson, Sharon Aneja

Forward planner serving the media: lists press contacts for parties, celebrities, launches, premieres, music, film, video and book releases. Founded 1985.

Maharaja Features Pvt. Ltd (1969)
5–226 Sion Road East, Bombay 400022, India
tel 22-4097951 *fax* 22-4097801
email mahafeat@bom2.vsnl.net.in
website www.welcomeindia.com/maharaja

Editor Mrs R. Ravi, *Managing Editor* K.R.N. Swamy

Syndicates feature and pictorial material, of interest to Asian readers, to newspapers and magazines in India, UK and abroad. Specialists in well-researched articles on India by eminent authorities for publication in prestige journals throughout the world. Also topical features 1000–1500 words. Illustrations: b&w prints and colour transparencies.

National Association of Press Agencies (NAPA)

41 Lansdowne Crescent, Leamington Spa, Warks. CV32 4PR
tel (0870) 609 1935, (01926) 420 566 *fax* (01926) 424760
website www.napa.org.uk
Directors Denis Cassidy, Chris Johnson, Barrie Tracey
Membership £250 p.a.

A network of independent, established and experienced press agencies serving newspapers, magazines, TV and radio networks. Founded 1983.

National Sports Reporting

10 Elmete Grange, Menston, Ilkley, West Yorkshire LS29 6LA
tel (01943) 884228
email 100654.463@compuserve.com
Managing Editor Christopher Harte, *Managers* Michael Latham (Northern Region), David Fox (South West Region), Diana Harding (South East Region), Dave Hammond (Scotland), Hilary Barlow (office manager), Robin Isherwood (accounts manager)

News and reporting service for sporting events. Research facilities for radio and TV, particularly sports documentaries. Commission: NUJ rates. Founded 1994.

New Blitz Literary & TV Agency

Via di Panico 67, 00186 Rome, Italy
postal address CP 30047–00193, Rome 47, Italy
tel (06) 686 4859 *fax* (06) 686 4859
email blitzgacs@inwind.it
Manager Giovanni A.S. Congiu

Syndicates worldwide: cartoons, comic strips, humorous books with drawings, feature and pictorial material, topical, environment, travel. Average rates of commission 60/40%, monthly report of sales, payment 60 days after the date of monthly report.

Newsflash Scotland Press & Picture Agency

3 Grosvenor Street, Edinburgh EH12 5ED
tel 0131-226 5858 *fax* 0131-225 9009
email news@nflash.co.uk
website www.newsflashcotland.com
Director Frank Gilbride

News, features and picture agency. Also accepts PR commissions and any other related work. Founded 1993.

PA Puzzles

BEP Building, Temple Way, Bristol BS99 7HD
tel 0117-934 3600 *fax* 0117-934 3642
email info@pa-entertainment.co.uk
website www.pa-entertainment.co.uk

Supplies features, cartoons, crosswords, horoscopes and graphics strips to newspapers, magazines and other publications (including internet sites) in 50 countries. Included in over 100 daily and weekly services are columns of international interest on health and beauty, medicine, employment, sports, house and home, motoring, computers, film and video, children's features, gardening, celebrity profiles, food and drink, finance and law. Also runs a parliamentary service as well as supplying editorial material for advertising features.

Chandra S. Perera

Cinetra Worldwide Createch (PVT) Ltd,
437 Pethiyagoda, Kelaniya–11600, Sri Lanka
tel 94-11-2911885 *fax* 94-11-2911885/2394629
ATTN Chandra Perera
email cinetraww@sltnet.lk
website www.geocities.com/cinetramovie_01/

Press and TV news, news films on Sri Lanka and Maldives, colour and b&w photo news and features, photographic and film coverage, screenplays and scripts for TV and films, press clippings. Broadcasting, TV and newspapers; journalistic features, news, broadcasting and TV interviews. Film production location shooting facilities and services provided and arranged in Sri Lanka.

Photoshot

(formerly Universal Pictorial Press & Agency)
29–31 Saffron Hill, London EC1N 8SW
tel 020-7421 6000 *fax* 020-7421 6006
email ctaylor@uppa.co.uk
website www.photoshot.com
Managing Director Charles Taylor

Photographic news agency and picture library: the UK's leading archive for British and international personalities from 1944 to present. Digital archive from 1994. Founded 1929.

Pixfeatures

5 Latimer Road, Barnet, Herts. EN5 5NU
tel 020-8449 9946 *fax* 020-8449 9946
Spanish office tel (00349) 6647 6379 *mobile* (00346) 52806222
Contacts Peter Wickman, Roy Wickman

News agency and picture library. Specialises in selling Spanish pictures and features to British and European press.

The Press Association

292 Vauxhall Bridge Road, London SW1V 1AE
tel 020-7963 7000 *fax* 020-7963 7192
website www.pressassociation.co.uk

Chief Executive/Editor-in-Chief Paul Potts, *Managing Director* Steven Brown

PA News Fast and accurate news, photography and information to print, broadcast and electronic media in the UK and Ireland.

PA Sport In-depth coverage of national and regional sports, transmitting a huge range of stories, results, pictures and updates every day.

PA Listings Page- and screen-ready information from daily guides to 7-day supplements on sports results, TV and radio listings, arts and entertainment, financial and weather listings tailored to suit requirements.

PA Digital Top quality content including news and sport for a wide range of multimedia customers.

PA WeatherCentre Continuously updated information on present and future weather conditions; consultancy services for media and industry. Founded 1868.

The Puzzle House

Ivy Cottage, Battlesea Green, Stradbroke, Suffolk IP21 5NE
tel (01379) 384656 *fax* (01379) 384656
email puzzlehouse@btinternet.com
Partners Roy Preston and Sue Preston

Supply original crosswords, quizzes and puzzles of all types. Commissions taken on any topic, with all age ranges catered for. Wide range of puzzles available for one-off usage. Founded 1988.

Rann Communication

Level 1, 18–20 Grenfell Street, Adelaide, SA 5000, Australia
postal address GPO Box 958, Adelaide, SA 5000, Australia
tel (08) 8211 7771 *fax* (08) 8212 2272
email chrisrann@rann.com.au
website www.rann.com.au
Managing Director Chris Rann

Full range of professional PR, press releases, special newsletters, commercial and political intelligence, media monitoring. Welcomes approaches from organisations requiring PR representation or press release distribution. Founded 1982.

Reuters Group plc

The Reuters Building, South Colonade, Canary Wharf, London E14 5EP
tel 020-7250 1122
email editor@reuters.com
website ww.reuters.com

Global provider of news and financial information. One of the world's biggest agencies. Founded 1851.

Sirius Media Services

100 Bridge Street, Stowmarket, Suffolk IP14 1BS
tel (01449) 674218
email mail@siriusmedia.co.uk
website www.siriusmedia.co.uk

Crosswords, puzzles and quizzes, plus horoscopes and TV features.

Solo Syndication Ltd

17–18 Haywards Place, London EC1R 0EQ
tel 020-7566 0360 *fax* 020-7566 0388
Contact Nick York

Worldwide syndication of newspaper features, photos, cartoons, strips and book serialisations. Agency represents the international syndication of Associated Newspapers (*Daily Mail*, *Mail on Sunday*, *Evening Standard*).

Southern News Service

Exchange House, Hindhead, Surrey GU26 6AA
tel (01428) 607330 *fax* (01428) 606351
email denis@cassidyandleigh.com
Partners Denis Cassidy and Donald Leigh

News stories, features and court coverage. Full picture service, digital and ISDN. Public relations words and pictures. Founded 1960.

United Press UK Ltd

Empire House, Empire Way, Middlesex HA9 0EW
tel 020-8970 2607 *fax* 020-8970 2613
website www.upi.com

Visual Humour

5 Greymouth Close, Stockton-on-Tees TS18 5LF
tel (01642) 581847
email peterdodsworth@btclick.com
website enquiries@businesscartoons.co.uk
Contact Peter Dodsworth

Daily and weekly humorous cartoon strips; also single panel cartoon features (not gag cartoons) for possible syndication in the UK and abroad. Picture puzzles also considered. Submit photocopy samples only initially, with sae. Founded 1984.

Books
Getting started

To help authors get started with writing we offer some guidelines to consider before submitting material to a publisher. Notes from successful authors in fiction (Joanna Trollope), fantasy (Terry Pratchett), crime (Mark Billingham), historical fiction (Bernard Cornwall), travel (William Dalrymple), non-fiction (Simon Winchester), children's writing (J.K. Rowling) and self-publishing (G.P. Taylor) start on page 229. For notes from a successful television screenwriter (Andrew Davies), see page 329.

There is more competition to get published than ever before. Hundreds of manuscripts (also referred to as typescripts) of would-be books land on the desks of publishers and literary agents every day. Both publishers and literary agents acknowledge that potential authors have to be really dedicated (or perhaps very lucky) in order to get their work published. So how can you give yourself the best chance of success? The following seven pointers will give you a head start to get your material noticed by a publisher.

1. Agent or publisher?
● First decide whether to approach an agent or to go it alone and submit your material direct to a publisher. Many publishers, particularly of fiction, will only consider material submitted through a literary agent. See *The role of the literary agent* on page 403, *How to get an agent* on page 407, *'I think I need an agent'* on page 410 and *Publishing agreements* on page 297 for some of the pros and cons of each approach.
● Whether you choose to approach an agent or a publisher, your work will be subjected to rigorous commercial assessment.

2. Choose the right publisher or agent
● Study the entries in this *Yearbook*, examine publishers' lists and their websites, and look in the relevant sections in libraries and bookshops for the names of publishers which might be interested in seeing your material.
● A list of literary agents starts on page 416.
● Listings of publishers' names and addresses start on page 131.
● A list of *Publishers of fiction*, by fiction genre, is on page 759.
● The market for children's books is considered in *Writing and the children's book market* on page 247. The list of *Children's book publishers and packagers* on page 763 includes publishers of poetry for children and teenage fiction. A list of *Literary agents for children's books* is on page 767.
● Publishers which consider poetry for adults are listed on page 766. See also *Getting poetry published* on page 311 and *Poetry organisations* on page 321.
● The electronic book market is in its infancy and has no set standards or provision but holds potential for some authors. See *E-publishing* on page 597 and *A brief introduction to electronic rights* on page 602.
● Authors are strongly advised not to pay for the publication of their work. A reputable publishing house will undertake publication at its own expense, except possibly for works of an academic nature. See *Doing it on your own* on page 264 and *Notes from a successful*

self-publisher on page 244 for an introduction to self publishing and *Vanity publishing* on page 294.

3. Prepare your material well

- Presentation is important. For example, no editor will read a handwritten manuscript. If your material is submitted in the most appropriate format a publisher will be more inclined to give attention to it. See *Dos and don'ts of approaching a publisher* on page 126.
- Many publishers' websites give guidance for new writers.
- It is understandable that writers, in their eagerness to show their work to others in the hope of getting it published as soon as possible, will send their manuscript in a raw state. Do not send your manuscript to a publisher until it is *ready* to be seen as it could ruin your chances. Be confident that your work is as good as it can be.

4. Approach the publisher or literary agent in the way they prefer

- Submit your work to the right person within the publishing company or literary agency. Ring or email first to find out who is the best person to receive your work. If the listing in this *Yearbook* does not specify, also ask whether they want a synopsis and sample chapters or the complete manuscript. Many publishers' and literary agents' and websites give guidance on how to submit material.
- Never send your only copy of the manuscript. Whilst every reasonable care will be taken of material in a publisher's possession, responsibility cannot be accepted if material is lost or damaged.
- Always include an sae with enough postage for the return of your material. (Send International Reply Coupons if you are writing from outside the country or if you are submitting material from the UK to the Republic of Ireland; for further information *tel* (08457) 223344.)

5. Write a convincing letter

- Compose your preliminary letter with care. Writers have been known to send out such letters in duplicated form, an approach unlikely to stimulate a publisher's interest. See *Dos and don'ts on approaching a publisher* on page 126.
- When submitting a manuscript to a publisher, it is a good idea to let them know that you know (and admire!) what they already publish. You can then make your case about where your submission will fit in their list. Let them know that you mean business and have researched the marketplace. See *Understanding the publishing process* on page 224.

Publishers' contracts

Following a publishing company's firm interest in a MS, a publisher's contract is drawn up between the author and the publisher (see *Publishing agreements* on page 297). If the author is not entirely happy with the contract presented to them or wishes to take advice, he/she could ask their literary agent, the Society of Authors or the Writers' Guild of Great Britain to check the contract on their behalf – providing the author has an agent and/or is a member of those organisations. Otherwise, the author can either check it for himself (for guidance, see *An Author's Guide to Publishing* and *Understanding Publishers' Contracts*, both books by Michael Legat; see page 297), or seek advice from a solicitor. Before consulting a solicitor, make sure that they are familiar with publishing agreements and can give informed advice. Many local firms have little or no experience of such work and their opinion can often be of limited value and the cost may outweigh any possible gains. See *Editorial, literary and production services* on page 658 for practitioners who undertake these legal services.

- What is the unique selling point of the material you are submitting for publication? You may have an original authorial 'voice', or you may have come up with an amazingly brilliant idea for a series. If, after checking out the marketplace, you think you have something truly original to offer, then believe in yourself and be convincing when you offer it around.

6. Get out and network

- Writing can be a lonely business – don't work in a vacuum. Talk to others of your discipline at literature festivals, conferences and book groups; find out if there are any writer groups in your area. Consider doing a course – see *Creative writing courses* on page 649.
- Go to a festival and be inspired! There are many literature festivals held throughout the year (see *Literature festivals* on page 588) which new and well-known authors appear at. You may be able to hear an author you admire speak, and even meet them afterwards.

7. Don't give up!

- Editors receive hundreds of manuscripts every day. For a publisher, there are many factors that have to be taken into consideration when evaluating these submissions, the most important of which is 'Will it sell?'
- Be prepared to wait for a decision on your work. Editors and agents are both very busy people so be patient when waiting for a response. Don't pester them too soon.
- Publishing is a big business and it is ever more competitive. Even after an editor has read your work, there are many other people involved before a manuscript is acquired for publication. People from the sales, marketing, publicity, rights and other departments all have to be convinced that the book is right for their list and will sell.
- The harsh reality of submitting a manuscript to a publisher or literary agent is that you have to be prepared for rejection. But all successful authors have received such rejections from a publisher at some time so you are in good company.
- Have patience, persevere. Good luck!

See also ...

Dos and don'ts of approaching a publisher

You want the book you've written to be published. So how do you set about it? Where will you send the typescript? Probably to a publisher, but to which one? Michael Legat offers guidelines on how to proceed.

Finding a publisher

Do your market research in public libraries and bookshops, and especially in *Writers' & Artists' Yearbook*, to find out which publishers bring out the kind of book you have written. While looking at the *Yearbook* entries, note which publishers are willing to consider books submitted to them directly, rather than through an agent, and which require a letter of enquiry first. Incidentally, if you are hoping to interest an agent, they almost all want an enquiry letter first.

Enquiry letters

An enquiry letter should be businesslike. Don't grovel ('it would be an honour to be published by so distinguished a firm'), don't make jokes ('my Mum says it's smashing, but maybe you'll think she's prejudiced'), don't be aggressive ('I have

> 10 Any Street, Any Town,
> Any County
>
> Messrs Dickens and Thackray,
> 83 Demy Street,
> London WC45 9BM   12th March
>
> Dear Sirs,
>
> May I please send for your consideration the novel I have written.
>
> Yours sincerely,
>
> L. Hopeful

This letter is far too brief. It gives no information about the kind of novel the author wishes to submit, nor of its length, it doesn't include a sae, and it doesn't even reveal the writer's sex. And since the writer doesn't use a question mark and has misspelt 'Thackeray', it's a good bet that the book will need meticulous and time-consuming copy-editing.

chosen you to publish my book, kindly send me your terms by return'). It is a good idea to write to whichever editor in the publishing house is responsible for books of the kind you have written (a phone call will provide this information – but take care to get the right title and spelling of the editor's name). Enclose a stamped addressed envelope. Look at the examples of the two poor enquiry letters followed by a good one on page 129.

You may have noticed that none of the letters refers to sending a disk or email. Such submissions may well become standard in a few years' time, but that stage has not yet been reached. However, once a book has been accepted, the publisher will certainly want a copy of the book on disk if it is available.

Presentation

Assuming that a publishing firm agrees to look at your book, the editor will expect to see a well-presented typescript (sometimes called a manuscript, abbreviated to MS). Here are some dos and don'ts about its appearance.

Use a typewriter or a word processor, or get a secretarial service to translate your handwriting on to a disk. Don't expect a publisher to read a handwritten script, even if you have a fine Italian hand.

Choose a good quality white A4 paper (preferably not continuous listing paper, or if you must use it, at least separate the pages and remove the perforated edges). Whatever paper you use don't type on both sides, and don't use single spacing (which publishers abhor, and usually refuse to read) – one side of the paper only and double spacing is the rule. And do leave a good margin, at least 3cm, all around the text, using the same margins throughout, so as to have the same number of lines on each page (except at the beginning and end of chapters). Double spacing and good margins allow space for your last-minute corrections to the typescript, for any copy-editor's amendments, and for instructions to the printer. And, not least in importance, a typescript in that style is much easier to read.

Always begin chapters on a new page. Justify on the left hand side only. Don't use blank lines between paragraphs (in the style of most typed letters nowadays), but indent the first line of each paragraph a few spaces. Blank lines should be used only to indicate a change of subject, or time, or scene, or viewpoint.

Be consistent in your choice of variant spellings, capitalisation, use of subheadings, etc. Make up your mind whether you are going to use -ise or -ize suffixes, for example, and whether, if 'village hall' appears in your text, you will type 'village hall' or Village Hall'.

For plays, use capitals for character names and underline stage directions or print them in italics. Use single spacing for dialogue, but leave a blank line between one character's speech and that of the next character to speak.

Poetry should be typed in exactly the way that the poem would appear in a printed version, using single or double spacing and various indentations as the poet wishes.

Organising the pages

Number the pages (or 'folios', as publishers like to call them) straight through from beginning to end. Don't start each chapter at folio 1. If you need to include an extra folio after, say, folio 27, call it folio 27a and write at the foot of folio 27: 'Folio 27a follows'. Then write at the foot of 27a: 'Folio 28 follows'. Obviously, if you want to insert more than one page, you would use '27a', '27b', '27c', and so on. Some writers like to use part of the book's title as well as the folio number: 'Harry 27', for example, but this is not essential.

Create a title page for the book, showing the title and your name or pseudonym. Add your name and address in the bottom right hand corner, and also type it on the last folio of the typescript, in case the first folio becomes detached. You can also add a word count, if you wish (if using the word-counting facility on your word processor, round the figure up or down to the nearest thousand or five thousand). If you want to include a list of your previously published books, a dedication, a quotation, a list of contents or of illustrations, an assertion of your moral rights, or any similar material, use a separate page for each item. Leave these pages unnumbered or use small roman figures – i, ii, iii, etc – so that the first folio to have an Arabic number will be the first page of your text.

When fastening the typescript together, don't use pins (which scratch), paperclips (which pick up other papers from a busy editor's desk), or staples (which make it difficult to read). Don't ever fasten the pages together in one solid lump, and it's best to avoid ring binders too. Don't use plastic folders – they are slippery and can very easily cascade off a pile on the editor's desk (which won't please the editor). Almost all publishers prefer to handle each folio separately, so put the typescript into a wallet-type folder, or more than one if necessary. Put the title of the book and your name and address on the outside of the folder.

If illustrations form a large part of your book and you expect to provide them yourself they should be included with the typescript, and equally a selection should accompany a synopsis and specimen chapters. Send copies rather than originals. If your book is for children don't complete all the illustrations until the publisher has decided on the size of the book and the number of illustrations. If you have a friend who wants to supply illustrations for your book, do make sure that they will be up to publishing standard before you accept the offer. You may put off a children's publisher by suggesting an illustrator – they like to choose.

Waiting for a decision

Many publishers take what seems to be an unconscionable time to give a verdict on typescripts submitted to them. However, a decision whether or not to publish may not be easy, and several readings and consultations with other departments in the publishing house often have to take place before the editor can be sure of the answer. If you have heard nothing after two months, send a polite letter of enquiry; if you get no response, ask for your typescript back, and try another publisher.

Don't expect to be given reasons for rejection. Publishers do not have time to spend on books and authors which they are not going to publish. However, if the rejection letter

---

12 Any Street, Any Town,
Any County

Messrs Dickens and Thackeray,
83 Demy Street,
London WC45 9BM   14th March

Dear Sirs,

May I please send you the novel I have written, which I want to get published? It's called Wendy Chiltern. That's the name of the heroine. I am a 76-year-old grandmother, but all my friends say that I am very young for my age and I can certainly claim to be 'with it'. I belong to the Townswomen's Guild, and I do a lot of work at the local Church, and I play Bridge regularly, so you can tell my mind's still as sharp as ever.

I have been writing ever since I was a little girl, without trying to get anything published, but my friends have persuaded me to try my luck with this book. One of them said it was better than anything by Jackie Collins. Any publisher would jump at it, she said. They are all so enthusiastic, that I just had to 'have a go'…

The book is 57 pages long. It is properly typed, and all the spelling mistakes have been corrected. I should tell you that I am aware that the novel has some faults. It is just a little slow to get started, but once you're into it I am sure you won't be able to put it down.

If your reply is favourable, I shall bring the typescript to your office and perhaps you could spare me a few minutes to talk about it.

Yours sincerely,

Louise Hopeless (Mrs)

This letter is far too long, and includes masses of irrelevant information about the author. The fact that the lady's friends said they liked the book is no recommendation – what else are they going to say to their friend? And no editor is going to be tempted by a slow beginning, however honest it may be for the author to point it out. The book is almost certainly typed in single spacing with minuscule margins, and even so will be a long way short of book-length. And publishers do not spend time interviewing would-be authors – the lady should leave the typescript at reception, and let it speak for itself.

contains any compliments on your work, you can take them at face value – publishers tend not to encourage authors unless they mean it.

Copyright material

Copyright exists as soon as you (or anyone else) records anything original to you on paper or film or disk. If you want to quote or otherwise use any material which is someone else's copyright, even if it is a short extract, you will have to get permission to do so, and possibly pay a fee. This applies not only to the text of a book, but also to letters and photographs, the copyright of which belongs to the letter-writer and photographer respectively. You must always give full acknowledgement to the source of the material. Use copyright material without such clearance and acknowledgement, and you are guilty of plagiarism – and another name for plagiarism is stealing. There are some circumstances in which you may use small amounts of text under a rule called 'Fair Dealing'. If your book has been accepted for publication, the publisher will be able to give you advice on the matter. (See also articles on copyright starting on page 685.)

Proofs

When your book is accepted by a publisher you may be asked to do further work on it, and a copy-editor may check the typescript line by line and word by word. As the author you should see the final copy before it goes to the printer, and this is almost your last chance to make any changes, whether they are simply the correction of literals or are more

---

14 Any Street, Any Town,
Any County

Ms Ann Clarke,
Messrs Dickens and Thackeray,
83 Demy Street,
London WC45 9BM

16th March

Dear Ms Clarke,

May I please send you my novel, My Son, my Son, for your kind consideration? It is approximately 87,000 words in length and is a contemporary story, telling of the devastating effect on the marriage of the central characters when their 17-year-old son announces that he is gay. It is aimed at the same market as that of Joanna Trollope, although my characters might be described as a little further down the class scale.

I have written a number of articles which have been published not only in my local newspaper, but in a couple of cases in 'The Lady', and once in 'The Observer'. This is my first work of fiction, but I have two other novels with similar backgrounds in mind.

I enclose a sae and look forward to hearing from you. Perhaps you will let me know whether you would prefer to see a synopsis and specimen chapters, or the entire book.

Yours sincerely,

Lucilla Possible

A good enquiry letter. The writer has (we can presume) found out to whom to address the letter, and how the lady spells her name. The letter is brief, but gives a clear picture of what the novel is about, and suggests its possible market, telling the publisher all that is necessary at this stage. It makes the two points that the writer has had some success with her work (do always include such details, provided that they are for professional publications), and that she intends to write other books. It also asks about the possibility of sending a synopsis and specimen chapters rather than the complete book, and that is in fact the way in which most publishers nowadays like to see new material (especially for non-fiction books, but also for novels). Of course, no enquiry letter, however satisfactory, can guarantee a favourable response, but at least with this one no editorial hackles should rise.

extensive than that. You should be aware that many publishers nowadays do not use copy-editors and rely on the author to provide an error-free typescript.

At a later stage you will be sent proofs from the printer, which you will have to read with great care. Any errors which the printer has made are corrected without charge, but if you alter anything else, the publisher will have to pay for the changes and will be entitled to pass on to you any costs which exceed 10–15% of the cost of composition (i.e. the setting of the book in type). That sounds as though it gives you a lot of leeway, but alterations at proof stage are hugely expensive, so avoid them if you possibly can.

Michael Legat became a full-time writer after a long and successful publishing career. He is the author of a number of highly regarded books on publishing and writing.

See also...

Book publishers UK and Ireland
*Member of the Publishers Association or Scottish Publishers Association
†Member of the Irish Book Publishers' Association

AA Publishing
Automobile Association and Business Services,
Fanum House, Basingstoke, Hants. RG21 4EA
tel (01256) 491573 *fax* (01256) 322575
website www.theAA.com
Directors Simon Davies (managing), David Watchus
(editorial), Robert Firth (production), Jon Bygate
(cartography), Terry Lee (sales & marketing)

Travel, atlases, maps, leisure interests, including
Essential Guides, Spiral Guides, City Packs and
Explorer Travel Guides. Founded 1979.

Abacus – see Little, Brown Book Group

ABC-Clio
(formerly Clio Press Ltd)
7277 The Quorum, Oxford Business Park North
OX4 2JZ
tel (01865) 481403 *fax* (01865) 481482
email salesuk@abc-clio.com
website www.abc-clio.com
Senior Acquisitions Editor Deborah Harman

General and academic reference: print and electronic
encyclopedias in history, mythology, literature, ethnic
studies; bibliography. Publishes *The Clio Montessori
Series*, and CD-Rom and web versions of abstracting
services in American studies and history. Branch of
ABC-CLIO Inc. Founded 1971.

Absolute Classics – see Oberon Books

Absolute Press
Scarborough House, 29 James Street West, Bath
BA1 2BT
tel (01225) 316013 *fax* (01225) 445836
email sales@absolutepress.co.uk
website www.absolutepress.co.uk
Publisher Jon Croft, *Directors* Meg Avent (editorial),
Matt Inwood (art)

General list: cookery, food-related topics, wine,
lifestyle, travel. No unsolicited MSS. Founded 1979.

Academic Press – see Elsevier Ltd

Academy Editions – acquired by Wiley
Europe Ltd

Academy of Light Ltd
Unit Ic, Delta Centre, Mount Pleasant, Wembley,
Middlesex HA0 1UX
tel 020-8795 2695 *fax* 020-8903 3748
email yubraj@academyoflight.co.uk

website www.academyoflight.co.uk
Managing Director & Chief Editor Dr Yubraj Sharma,
Marketing & Financial Director Mrs Mita Shah

Spirituality and alternative medicine; children's.
Founded 2000.

Access Press – see HarperCollins Publishers

Acorn Editions – see James Clarke & Co. Ltd

Addison-Wesley – see Pearson Education

Adlard Coles Nautical – see A & C Black Publishers Ltd

Age Concern Books
Age Concern England, 1268 London Road, London
SW16 4ER
tel 020-8765 7397 *fax* 020-8765 7211
email books@ace.org.uk
Commissioning Editor Becky Senior

Age Concern works with and for older people. Books
on health and care, advice, finance, gerontology,
leisure, policy, retirement, housing, computing,
training, rights. Founded 1973.

Airlife Publishing – see The Crowood Press

Ian Allan Publishing Ltd
Riverdene Business Park, Molesey Road, Hersham,
Surrey KT12 4RG
tel (01932) 266600 *fax* (01932) 266601
email info@ianallanpublishing.co.uk
website www.ianallanpublishing.com
Publishing Manager Peter Waller

Transport: railways, aircraft, shipping, road; naval
and military history; reference books and magazines;
sport and cycling guides; no fiction.

Classic Publications (imprint)
Transport, aviation.

Midland Publishing (imprint)
Transport: aviation; naval and military history.

Oxford Publishing Company (imprint)
Transport: railways, road.

J.A. Allen
Clerkenwell House, 45–47 Clerkenwell Green,
London EC1R 0HT
tel 020-7251 2661 *fax* 020-7490 4958
email allen@halebooks.com

Publisher Cassandra Campbell

Horse and equestrianism including bloodstock breeding, racing, polo, dressage, horse care, carriage driving, breeds, veterinary and farriery. Books usually commissioned but willing to consider any serious, specialist TSS on the horse and related subjects. Imprint of **Robert Hale Ltd**. Founded 1926.

George Allen & Unwin
Publishers – acquired by HarperCollins Publishers

Allen Lane – see Penguin Group (UK)

W.H. Allen – acquired by Virgin Books Ltd

Allison & Busby Ltd
13 Charlotte Mews, London W1T 4EJ
tel 020-7580 1080 *fax* 020-7580 1180
email susie@allisonandbusby.com
website www.allisonandbusby.com
Publishing Director Susie Dunlop, *Publicity Manager* Chiara Priorelli

Fiction, crime fiction, popular culture, true crime. No unsolicited MSS accepted.

Allyn & Bacon – see Pearson Education

The Alpha Press – see Sussex Academic Press

Alphabet & Image Ltd
77 High Street, The Narrows, Totnes, Devon TQ9 5PB
tel (01803) 868861/866946
Publisher/Director Miranda Spicer

Illustrated books on ceramics, horticulture, architecture, bee-keeping, craft and 'one-offs'. Imprints include Marston House. Founded 1972.

Amber Lane Press Ltd
Church Street, Charlbury, Oxon OX7 3PR
tel (01608) 810024 *fax* (01608) 810024
email info@amberlanepress.co.uk
website www.amberlanepress.co.uk
Chairman Brian Clark, *Director/Managing Editor* Judith Scott

Plays, theatre, music. Founded 1978.

AN The Artists Information Company
1st Floor, 7–15 Pink Lane, Newcastle upon Tyne NE1 5DW
tel 0191-241 8000 *fax* 0191-241 8001
email edit@a-n.co.uk
website www.a-n.co.uk
AN Editor Gillian Nicol

Provides information, advice and critical debate on contemporary visual arts practice through *AN* magazine (monthly), its website, and a programme of artists' training and professional development for Northern England. Founded 1980.

Andersen Press Ltd
20 Vauxhall Bridge Road, London SW1V 2SA
tel 020-7840 8703 (editorial) *fax* 020-7233 6263
email andersenpress@randomhouse.co.uk
website www.andersenpress.co.uk
Managing Director/Publisher Klaus Flugge, *Directors* Philip Durrance, Joëlle Flugge (company secretary), Rona Selby (editorial)

Children's books: picture books, junior and teenage fiction (send synopsis and first 3 chapters with sae); no short stories or poetry. International co-productions. Founded 1976.

Andromeda Children's Books – see Pinwheel Ltd

The Angels' Share – see Neil Wilson Publishing Ltd

Anness Publishing
88–89 Blackfriars Road, London SE1 8HA
tel 020-7401 2077 *fax* 020-7633 9499
email info@anness.com
website www.annesspublishing.com
Managing Director Paul Anness, *Publisher* Joanna Lorenz

Practical illustrated books on lifestyle, cookery, crafts, gardening, Mind, Body & Spirit, health and children's non-fiction. Founded 1989.

Aquamarine (hardback imprint)
website www.aquamarinebooks.com
Lifestyle, cookery, crafts and gardening.

Hermes House (imprint)
Illustrated promotional books on practical subjects.

Lorenz Books (hardback imprint)
website www.lorenzbooks.com
Lifestyle, cookery, crafts, gardening, Mind, Body & Spirit, health and children's non-fiction.

Southwater (paperback imprint)
website www.southwaterbooks.com
Lifestyle, cookery, crafts, gardening, Mind, Body & Spirit, health and children's non-fiction.

Practical Pictures (image licensing)
Lifestyle, cookery, crafts, gardening, Mind, Body & Spirit, health and children's non-fiction.

Anova Books
151 Freston Road, London W10 6TH
tel 020-7314 1400 *fax* 020-7314 1594
website www.chrysalisbooks.co.uk
Ceo Robin Wood, *Publishing Director* Polly Powell, *Executive Director* Roger Huggins, *Operations & Production Director* David Proffit

Founded 2005; formerly Chrysalis Books Group.

B.T. Batsford (imprint)
Associate Publisher Tina Persaud

Chess and bridge, art techniques, film, fashion and costume, practical craft, gardening, embroidery, lace, woodwork.

Conway (inc. Brasseys Military, Putnam Aeronautical)
Associate Publisher John Lee

Highly illustrated reference books on naval and maritime, aviation and military subjects.

Collins & Brown (imprint)
Associate Publisher Katie Cowen

Lifestyle and interiors, gardening, photography, practical arts, health and beauty, hobbies and crafts, natural history, history, ancient civilisation and general interest.

National Trust (imprint)
Heritage, gardens, cookery.

Paper Tiger (imprint)
Commissioning Editor Chris Stone

Science fiction and fantasy art.

Pavilion (imprint)
Associate Publisher Kate Oldfield

Cookery, gardening, travel, humour, sport, photography, art.

PRC/Salamander (imprint)
Publishing Director Jo Messham

Cookery, crafts, military, natural history, music, gardening, hobbies, transport, sports.

Robson Books (imprint)
Publisher Jeremy Robson

General non-fiction, biography, music, humour, sport.

Anova Children's Books (imprint)
Publisher Ben Cameron

Children's books: from baby and picture books to illustrated classics and educational books. Founded 2003 as Chrysalis Children's Books.

Antique Collectors' Club Ltd
Sandy Lane, Old Martlesham, Woodbridge, Suffolk IP12 4SD
tel (01394) 389950 *fax* (01394) 389999
email sales@antique-acc.com
website www.antique-acc.com
Managing Director Diana Steel

Fine art, antiques, gardening and garden history, architecture. Founded 1966.

Anvil Books/The Children's Press†
45 Palmerston Road, Dublin 6, Republic of Ireland
tel (01) 4973628
Directors Rena Dardis (managing), Margaret Dardis (editorial)

Anvil: Irish history and biography. Only considers MSS by Irish-based authors and of Irish interest. Send synopsis with IRCs (no UK stamps); unsolicited MSS not returned. Children's Press: adventure, fiction, ages 9–14. Founded 1964.

Anvil Press Poetry
Neptune House, 70 Royal Hill, London SE10 8RF
tel 020-8469 3033 *fax* 020-8469 3363
email anvil@anvilpresspoetry.com
website www.anvilpresspoetry.com
Director Peter Jay

Poetry. Submissions only with sae. Founded 1968.

Appletree Press Ltd
14 Howard Street South, Belfast BT7 1AP
tel 028-9024 3074 *fax* 028-9024 6756
email reception@appletree.ie
website www.appletree.ie
Director John Murphy

Gift books, biography, cookery, guidebooks, history, Irish interest, literary criticism, music, photographic, social studies, sport, travel. Founded 1974.

Aquamarine – see Anness Publishing

Arc Publications
Nanholme Mill, Shaw Wood Road, Todmorden, Lancs. OL14 6DA
tel (01706) 812338 *fax* (01706) 818948
email info@arcpublications.co.uk
website www.arcpublications.co.uk
Directors Tony Ward (managing), Angela Jarman, *Associate Editors* John Kinsella (international), Jean Boase-Beier (translation), Jo Shapcott (UK & Ireland), Angela Jarman (music)

Specialises in contemporary poetry, international English, bi-lingual translation editions and new or neglected work from the UK. No unsolicited MSS.

Arcadia Books Ltd
15–16 Nassau Street, London W1W 7AB
tel 020-7436 9898 *fax* 020-7436 9898
email info@arcadiabooks.co.uk
website www.arcadiabooks.co.uk
Managing Director Gary Pulsifer, *Publishing Director* Daniela de Groote

Original paperback fiction, fiction in translation, autobiography, biography, travel, gender studies, gay books. Submissions via literary agents only. *Sunday Times* Small Publisher of the Year 2002/3. Imprints include BlackAmber, Bliss Books and EuroCrime. Founded 1996.

BlackAmber (imprint)
website www.blackamber.com
Commissioning Editor Rosemarie Hudson
Black and Asian writing.

Bliss Books (imprint)
Popular fiction and non-fiction.

Architectural Press – see Elsevier Ltd

Arcturus – see W. Foulsham & Co. Ltd

Arena Books
6 Southgate Green, Bury St Edmunds, Suffolk
IP33 2BL
tel (01284) 754123
email arenabooks@tiscali.co.uk
Directors James Farrell, Robert Corfe

Political science and specialised academic. Founded 2000.

Arris Publishing Ltd
12 Main Street, Adlestrop, Moreton-in-Marsh, Glos.
GL56 0YN
tel (01608) 658758 fax (01608) 659345
email victoriama.huxley@btinternet.com
website www.arrisbooks.com
Managing Director Geoffrey Smith, Publishing Director Victoria Huxley

History, military history, politics, translated fiction, The Traveller's History series, ancient mysteries. Imprint: Chastleton Travel. Founded 2003.

Arrow Books Ltd – see Random House Group Ltd

Ashgate Publishing Ltd
Gower House, Croft Road, Aldershot, Hants
GU11 3HR
tel (01252) 331551 fax (01252) 344405
email info@ashgatepub.co.uk
website www.ashgate.com
Chairman Nigel Farrow, Managing Director and Humanities Publishing Director Rachel Lynch, Social Sciences Publishing Director Dymphna Evans, President Ashgate US Barbara Church
Humanities Ann Donahue (Literary Studies, 19th–20th centuries), Erika Gaffney (Literary Studies to 18th century; Women & Gender Studies), Heidi May (Music), Paul Coulam (Philosophy), Sarah Lloyd (Theology & Religious Studies), Thomas Gray (History), John Smedley (Publishing Director, Variorum imprint; History)
Social Sciences Alison Kirk (Law), Brendan George (Academic Business; Economics; Development Studies), Caroline Wintersgill and Mary Savigar (Sociology; Social Policy; Social Work), Guy Loft (Aviation), Kirstin Howgate (International Relations; Politics), Val Rose (Human Geography; Planning & Design), John Irwin (Library Reference Publishing)

Publishes a wide range of academic research in the social sciences and humanities, professional practice publications in the management of business and public services, and illustrated books on art, architecture and design. Founded 1967.

Gower (imprint)
website www.gowerpub.com
Publishing Director & Commissioning Editor Jonathan Norman
Business, management and training.

Lund Humphries (imprint)
website www.lundhumphries.com
Managing Director Lucy Myers
Art and architectural history.

Variorum (imprint)
Publishing Director John Smedley
History.

Ashmolean Museum Publications
Beaumont Street, Oxford OX1 2PH
tel (01865) 288070 fax (01865) 278106
website www.ashmol.ox.ac.uk
Contact Declan McCarthy

Fine and applied art of Europe and Asia, archaeology, history, numismatics. No unsolicited MSS. Photographic archive. Museum founded 1683.

Aslib (The Association for Information Management)
Holywell Centre, 1 Phipp Street, London EC2A 4PS
tel 020-7613 3031 fax 020-7613 5080
email aslib@aslib.com
website www.aslib.com

For books contact Taylor & Francis (01235) 828600; for journals contact Emerald (01206) 796351; for Managing Information magazine contact Graham Coult (editor), www.managinginformation.com

Atlantic Books
Ormond House, 26–27 Boswell Street, London WC1N 3JZ
tel 020-7269 1610 fax 020-7430 0916
email enquiries@groveatlantic.co.uk
Managing Director/Publisher Toby Mundy

Literary fiction, history, current affairs, biography, politics, reference, autobiography; The Guardian and The Observer books. No unsolicited submissions. Subsidiary of Grove/Atlantic Inc., New York. Founded 2000.

Atlantic Europe Publishing Co. Ltd
Greys Court Farm, Greys Court, Henley-on-Thames, Oxon RG9 4PG
tel (01491) 628188 fax (01491) 628189
email enquiries@atlanticeurope.com
website www.atlanticeurope.com, www.curriculumvisions.com
Director Dr B.J. Knapp

Children's colour illustrated information books, co-editions and primary school class books: science, geography, technology, mathematics, history, religious education. No MSS accepted by post; submit by email only with no attachments. Founded 1990.

Atom – see Little, Brown Book Group

Attic Press and Atrium – see Cork University Press

Aureus Publishing Ltd

Castle Court, Castle-upon-Alun, St Bride's Major,
Vale of Glamorgan CF32 0TN
tel (01656) 880033 *fax* (01656) 880033
email info@aureus.co.uk
website www.aureus.co.uk
Director Meuryn Hughes

Rock and pop, autobiography, biography, sport,
aviation; also music. Founded 1993.

Aurum Press Ltd

25 Bedford Avenue, London WC1B 3AT
tel 020-7637 3225 *fax* 020-7580 2469
email firstname.surname@aurumpress.co.uk
website www.aurumpress.co.uk
Directors Bill McCreadie (managing), Piers Burnett
(editorial), Laurence Orbach (non-executive), Mick
Mousley (non-executive)

General, illustrated and non-illustrated adult non-
fiction: biography and memoirs, military, visual arts,
film, sport, travel, fashion, home interest. Imprints:
Argentum (photography), Jacqui Small (lifestyle).
Founded 1977.

Authentic Media

9 Holdom Avenue, Bletchley, Milton Keynes
MK1 1QR
tel (01908) 364204 *fax* (01908) 277169
email charlotte.hubback@stl.org
Publisher Mark Finnie

Biblical studies, Christian theology, ethics, history,
mission, commentaries. Imprints: Paternoster,
Authentic, Spring Harvest, Keswick, Youthwork,
Evangelical Alliance, Regnum, Rutherford House,
Paternoster Periodicals.

Award Publications Ltd

The Old Riding School, The Welbeck Estate,
Worksop, Notts. S80 3LR
tel (01909) 478170 *fax* (01909) 484632
email info@awardpublications.co.uk

Children's books: full colour picture story books;
early learning, information and activity books. No
unsolicited material. Founded 1954.

Bernard Babani (publishing) Ltd

The Grampians, Shepherds Bush Road, London
W6 7NF
tel 020-7603 2581/7296 *fax* 020-7603 8203
Director M.H. Babani

Practical handbooks on radio, electronics and
computing.

Duncan Baird Publishers

6th Floor, Castle House, 75–76 Wells Street, London
W1T 3QH
tel 020-7323 2229 *fax* 020-7580 5692
website www.dbponline.co.uk

Directors Duncan Baird (managing), Bob Saxton
(editorial), Roger Walton (art), Alex Mitchell
(international sales), Ryan Tring (financial), Adela
Cory (production)

Non-fiction, illustrated reference. Founded 1992.

Balliere Tindall – see Elsevier Ltd (Health Sciences)

Bantam – see Transworld Publishers

Bantam Press – see Transworld Publishers

Barefoot Books Ltd

124 Walcot Street, Bath BA1 5BG
tel (01225) 322400 *fax* (01225) 322499
email info@barefootbooks.co.uk
website www.barefootbooks.co.uk
Editor-in-Chief Tessa Strickland, *Group Project
Manager* Jo Collins

Children's picture books and audiobooks: myth,
legend, fairytale, cross-cultural stories. Picture book
MSS only with return p&p. Founded 1993.

B.T. Batsford – see Anova Books

BBC Audiobooks Ltd*

St James House, The Square, Lower Bristol Road,
Bath BA2 3BH
tel (01225) 878000 *fax* (01225) 310771
website www.bbcaudiobooks.com
Directors Paul Dempsey (managing), Jan Paterson
(publishing)

Large print books and complete and unabridged
audiobooks: general fiction, crime, romance, mystery/
thrillers, westerns, non-fiction. Does not publish
original books. Imprints: Chivers Large Print, Chivers
Audio Books, Black Dagger Crime, Windsor Large
Print, Galaxy Children's Large Print. Formed in 2002
from the amalgamation of Chivers Press, Cover To
Cover and BBC Radio Collection.

BBC Children's Books – see Penguin Group (UK)

BBC Worldwide Ltd – see page 350

Belair – see Folens Publishers

Bell & Hyman Ltd – acquired by HarperCollins Publishers

Berg Publishers

1st Floor, Angel Court, 81 St Clements Street, Oxford
OX4 1AW
tel (01865) 245104 *fax* (01865) 791165
email enquiry@bergpublishers.com
Managing Director Kathryn Earle

Social anthropology, cultural studies, sport, dress and
fashion studies, European studies, politics, history.
Founded 1983.

Berlin Verlag – see Bloomsbury Publishing Plc

Berlitz Publishing – see Insight Guides/Berlitz Publishing

BFI Publishing
British Film Institute, 21 Stephen Street, London
W1P 2LN
tel 020-7255 1444 *fax* 020-7636 2516
website www.bfi.org.uk
Head of Publishing Rebecca Barden

Film, TV and media studies; general, academic and
educational resources on moving image culture.
Founded 1982.

Clive Bingley Ltd – see Facet Publishing

BIOS Scientific Publishers – see Taylor and Francis Books Ltd

Birlinn Ltd*
West Newington House, 10 Newington Road,
Edinburgh EH9 1QS
tel 0131-668 4371 *fax* 0131-668 4466
email info@birlinn.co.uk
website www.birlinn.co.uk
Directors Hugh Andrew, Neville Moir, Ronnie Shanks

Scottish history, local interest/history, Scottish
humour, guides, military, adventure, history,
archaeology, vernacular architecture, sport, general
non-fiction. Imprints: John Donald, Polygon.
Founded 1992.

Polygon (imprint)
New international and Scottish fiction, poetry, short
stories, popular Scottish and international general
interest. No unsolicited poetry accepted.

Birnbaum – see HarperCollins Publishers

A & C Black Publishers Ltd*
38 Soho Square, London W1D 3HB
tel 020-7758 0200 *fax* 020-7758 0222
email enquiries@acblack.com
website www.acblack.com
Chairman Nigel Newton, *Managing Director* Jill
Coleman, *Deputy Managing Director* Jonathan
Glasspool, *Directors* Colin Adams, Oscar Heini
(production), Janet Murphy (Adlard Coles Nautical),
Kathy Rooney, David Wightman (sales)

Children's and educational books (including music)
for 3–15 year-olds (preliminary enquiry appreciated –
fiction guidelines available on request); ceramics, art
and craft, drama, ornithology, reference (*Who's Who,
Whitaker's Almanack*), sport, theatre, books for
writers, dictionaries. Subsidiary of Bloomsbury
Publishing plc. Founded 1807.

Adlard Coles Nautical (imprint)
Nautical.

Andrew Brodie (imprint)
Children's, educational.

Christopher Helm (imprint)
Ornithology.

The Herbert Press (imprint)
Visual arts.

Methuen Drama (imprint)
Drama.

Pica Press (imprint)
Ornithology.

T & AD Poyser (imprint)
Ornithology, natural history.

Thomas Reed (imprint)
Nautical.

Reed Nautical Almanac (imprint)
Navigation and port information.

Black Ace Books
PO Box 7547, Perth PH2 1AU
tel (01821) 642822 *fax* (01821) 642101
website www.blackacebooks.com
Publisher Hunter Steele, *Art, Publicity & Sales Director*
Boo Wood

Fiction, Scottish and general; new editions of
outstanding recent fiction. Some biography, history,
psychology and philosophy. No submissions without
first visiting website for latest list details and
requirements. Imprints: Black Ace Books, Black Ace
Paperbacks. Founded 1991.

Black & White Publishing Ltd*
99 Giles Street, Edinburgh EH6 6BZ
tel 0131-625 4500 *fax* 0131-625 4501
email mail@blackandwhitepublishing.com
website www.blackandwhitepublishing.com
Directors Campbell Brown (managing), Alison
McBride

Non-fiction: humour, biography, crime, sport,
cookery, general. Fiction: classic Scottish,
contemporary, crime. Founded 1990.

Black Lace – see Virgin Books Ltd

Black Swan – see Transworld Publishers

BlackAmber – see Arcadia Books Ltd

Blackstaff Press Ltd†
4c Heron Wharf, Sydenham Business Park, Belfast
BT3 9LE
tel 028-9045 5006 *fax* 028-9046 6237
email info@blackstaffpress.com
website www.blackstaffpress.com
Managing Editor Patsy Horton

Adult fiction, poetry, biography, history, sport, politics, cookery, natural history, humour and travel. Founded 1971.

Blackstone Press Ltd – acquired by Oxford University Press

Blackwater Press – see Folens Publishers

Blackwell Publishing Ltd*
9600 Garsington Road, Oxford OX4 2DQ
tel (01865) 776868 *fax* (01865) 714591
website www.blackwellpublishing.com
Chairman Nigel Blackwell, *President* Robert Campbell, *Chief Executive* René Olivieri

Books and journals in medicine, veterinary medicine, dentistry, nursing and allied health, science (particularly biology, chemistry and geology), social sciences, business and humanities. Journals are delivered online through Blackwell Synergy. Formed by merging Blackwell Science (founded 1939) and Blackwell Publishers (founded 1922).

BMJ Books (imprint)
Medicine, self-help, alternative medicine.

John Blake Publishing Ltd
(incorporating Metro Books and Smith Gryphon Ltd)
3 Bramber Court, 2 Bramber Road, London W14 9PB
tel 020-7381 0666 *fax* 020-7381 6868
email words@blake.co.uk

Popular non-fiction, including biographies, true crime, food and drink, health. No unsolicited fiction. Founded 1991.

Bliss Books – see Arcadia Books Ltd

Bloodaxe Books Ltd
Highgreen, Tarset, Northumberland NE48 1RP
tel (01434) 240500 *fax* (01434) 240505
email editor@bloodaxebooks.com
website www.bloodaxebooks.com
Directors Neil Astley, Simon Thirsk

Poetry, literary criticism. No submissions from new authors this year. Founded 1978.

Bloomsbury Publishing Plc*
36 Soho Square, London W1D 3QY
tel 020-7494 2111 *fax* 020-7434 0151
website www.bloomsbury.com
Chairman & Chief Executive Nigel Newton, *Directors* Liz Calder (publishing), Alexandra Pringle (publishing), Michael Fishwick (publishing), Kathleen Farrar (international), Karen Rinaldi (Bloomsbury USA), David Ward (sales), Minna Fry (marketing), Katie Bond (publicity), Ruth Logan (rights), Penny Edwards (production), Arzu Tahsin (paperbacks), Sarah Odedina (children's), Colin

Adams (finance), Will Webb (design), Jill Coleman (A & C Black), Kathy Rooney (Berlin Verlag), Elisabeth Ruge (Berlin Verlag), Stephanie Duncan (Dot.com) Charles Black (non-executive), Paul Scherer (non-executive), Mike Mayer (non-executive), Jeremy Wilson (non-executive), *Company Secretary* Richard Cordeschi

Fiction, biography, illustrated, travel, children's, trade paperbacks and mass market paperbacks. Founded 1986.

Berlin Verlag (imprint)
Joint Managing Directors Kathy Rooney and Elisabeth Ruge, *Editorial Director* Dorothee Grisebach
Hardback fiction and non-fiction.

BMJ Books – see Blackwell Publishing Ltd

Boatswain Press Ltd – now Nautical Data Ltd

Bodley Head Children's Books – see Random House Group Ltd

Booth-Clibborn Editions
12 Percy Street, London W1T 1DW
tel 020-7565 0688
email info@booth-clibborn.com
website www.booth-clibborn.com

Illustrated books on art, popular culture, graphic design, photography. Founded 1974.

Bounty – see Octopus Publishing Group

Bowker
3rd Floor, Farringdon House, Wood Street, East Grinstead, West Sussex RH19 1UZ
tel (01342) 310450 *fax* (01342) 310486
email vales@bowker.co.uk
website www.bowker.co.uk
Managing Director Doug McMillan

Print and electronic publishers of bibliographies and serials databases, trade and reference directories and library and information titles. Part of the Cambridge Information Group.

Boxtree – see Macmillan Publishers Ltd

Marion Boyars Publishers Ltd
24 Lacy Road, London SW15 1NL
tel 020-8788 9522 *fax* 020-8789 8122
email catheryn@marionboyars.com
website www.marionboyars.co.uk
Directors Catheryn Kilgarriff, Rebecca Gillieron (editorial)

Literary fiction, film, memoirs, travel, cultural studies, jazz, music. Will only consider fiction submitted through an agent. Founded 1975.

Boydell & Brewer Ltd
PO Box 9, Woodbridge, Suffolk IP12 3DF
tel (01394) 610600 *fax* (01394) 610316

website www.boydellandbrewer.com

Medieval studies, history, maritime history, literature, archaeology, art history, music. No unsolicited MSS. See website for submissions guidelines. Founded 1969.

Bradt Travel Guides Ltd

23 High Street, Chalfont St Peter, Bucks. SL9 9QE
tel (01753) 893444 *fax* (01753) 892333
email info@bradtguides.com
website www.bradtguides.com
Managing Director Hilary Bradt

Guides for the adventurous traveller who seeks off-beat places and 'the dreamer who would like to travel there but never will'.

Brandon/Mount Eagle Publications†

(incorporating Brandon Book Publishers Ltd, 1982)
Cooleen, Dingle, Co. Kerry, Republic of Ireland
tel (353) 66 9151463 *fax* (353) 66 9151234
Publisher Steve MacDonogh

Fiction, biography and current affairs. No unsolicited MSS.

Brasseys Military – see Anova Books

Nicholas Brealey Publishing

3–5 Spafield Street, London EC1R 4QB
tel 020-7239 0360 *fax* 020-7239 0370
email rights@nbrealey-books.com
website www.nbrealey-books.com
Managing Director Nicholas Brealey

Business and finance, intelligent self-help, popular psychology, cross-cultural studies, travel writing. Founded 1992.

Breedon Books Publishing Co. Ltd

Breedon House, 3 The Parker Centre, Mansfield Road, Derby DE21 4SZ
tel (01332) 384235 *fax* (01332) 292755
email submissions@breedonpublishing.co.uk
website www.breedonbooks.co.uk
Directors Steve Caron (managing), Jane Caron (finance), *Commissioning Editor* Susan Last

Football, sport, local history, archive photography, heritage. No fiction. Unsolicited MSS welcome. Preliminary letter essential. Founded 1981.

Breese Books Ltd

19A Hanover Crescent, Brighton BN2 9SB
tel (01273) 687555
email martin@HanoverCrescent.com
Publisher Martin Breese

Conjuring books and *Breese's Guide to Modern First Editions*. All work is commissioned and unsolicited submissions are not required. Founded 1980.

Brilliant Publications*

1 Church View, Sparrow Hall Farm, Edlesborough, Dunstable LU6 2ES
tel (01525) 229720 *fax* (01525) 229725
email editorial@brilliantpublications.co.uk
website www.brilliantpublications.co.uk
Managing Director Priscilla Hannaford

Resource books for teachers and others concerned with the education of 0–13 year-olds. All areas of the curriculum published. Series for reluctant readers, aimed at 7–11 year-olds. Does not publish children's picture books. Study catalogue or visit website before sending proposal. Founded 1993.

The British Library (Publications)*

Publishing Office, The British Library, 96 Euston Road, London NW1 2DB
tel 020-7412 7469 *fax* 020-7412 7768
email blpublications@bl.uk
website www.bl.uk
Managers David Way (publishing), Lara Speicher (managing editor), Catherine Britton (sales & marketing)

Book arts, bibliography, music, maps, oriental, manuscript studies, history, literature, facsimiles, audiovisual, and multimedia CD-Rom. Founded 1979.

British Museum Company Ltd*

38 Russell Square, London WC1B 3QQ
tel 020-7323 1234 *fax* 020-7436 7315
website www.britishmuseum.co.uk
Managing Director Andrew Thatcher, *Publications Director* Rosemary Bradley

General and specialised adult and children's books on art history, archaeology, numismatics, history, oriental art and archaeology, horology, ethnography. Division of The British Museum Company Ltd. Founded 1973.

Brockhampton Press – see Caxton Publishing Group

Andrew Brodie – see A & C Black Publishers Ltd

Brown, Son & Ferguson, Ltd*

4–10 Darnley Street, Glasgow G41 2SD
tel 0141-429 1234 (24 hours) *fax* 0141-420 1694
email info@skipper.co.uk
website www.skipper.co.uk
Editorial Director L. Ingram-Brown

Nautical books, plays. Founded 1860.

Bryntirion Press

(formerly Evangelical Press of Wales)
Bryntirion, Bridgend CF31 4DX
tel (01656) 655886 *fax* (01656) 665919
email office@emw.org.uk
website www.emw.org.uk
Press Manager Huw Kinsey

Theology and religion (in English and Welsh). Founded 1955.

Burns & Oates – see The Continuum International Publishing Group Ltd

Buster Books – see Michael O'Mara Books Ltd

Butterworth-Heinemann – see Elsevier Ltd

Butterworths – see LexisNexis Butterworths

Cadogan Guides
2nd Floor, 233 High Holborn, London WC1V 7DN
tel 020-7611 4660 *fax* 020-7611 4665
email info@cadoganguides.co.uk
website www.cadoganguides.com
Managing Director Jenny Calcutt, *Managing Editor* Natalie Pomier

Travel guides and travel literature. Founded 1982.

Calder Publications UK Ltd
51 The Cut, London SE1 8LF
tel 020-7633 0599 *fax* 020-7928 5930
email info@calderpublications.com
website www.calderpublications.com
Directors John Calder, Toby Fenton

European, international and British fiction and plays, art, literary, music and social criticism, biography and autobiography, essays, humanities and social sciences, European classics. No unsolicited MSS. Inquiry letters must include an sae. Series include: *English National Opera Guides, Scottish Library, New Writing and Writers, Opera Library, Historical Perspectives, Thought Bites.*

Calmann & King Ltd – see Laurence King Publishing Ltd

Cambridge University Press*
The Edinburgh Building, Shaftesbury Road, Cambridge CB2 2RU
tel (01223) 325892 *fax* (01223) 325891
email information@cambridge.org
website www.cambridge.org
Chief Executive of the Press Stephen R.R. Bourne, *Managing Director, Europe, Middle East & Africa* Michael Holdsworth, *Managing Director, Academic Publishing* Andrew Brown, *Publishing Director, Humanities & Social Sciences* Richard Fisher, *Publishing Director, Science, Technology & Medicine* Richard Barling, *Managing Director, Cambridge Learning* Andrew Gilfillan, *Chief Executive, Cambridge-Hitachi* John Tuttle, *Editorial Director, Journals* Geoffrey Nuttall

Anthropology and archaeology, astronomy, biological sciences, classical studies, computer science, dictionaries, earth sciences, economics, educational (primary, secondary, tertiary), e-learning products, engineering, English language teaching, history, language and literature, law, mathematics, medical sciences, music, philosophy, physical sciences, politics, psychology, reference, technology, social sciences, theology, religion. Journals (humanities, social sciences, STM). The Bible and Prayer Book. Founded 1534.

Cameron & Hollis
PO Box 1, Moffat, Dumfriesshire DG10 9SU
tel (01683) 220808 *fax* (01683) 220012
email editorial@cameronbooks.co.uk
website www.cameronbooks.co.uk
Directors Ian A. Cameron, Jill Hollis

Modern art, decorative art, collecting and film (serious critical works only). Founded 1976.

Campbell Books – see Macmillan Publishers Ltd

Canongate Books Ltd*
14 High Street, Edinburgh EH1 1TE
tel 0131-557 5111 *fax* 0131-557 5211
email info@canongate.co.uk
website www.canongate.net
Publisher Jamie Byng, *Directors* David Graham (managing), Kathleen Anderson (financial), Caroline Graham (production), Jenny Todd (sales & marketing), Polly Collingridge (rights)

Adult general non-fiction and fiction: literary fiction, translated fiction, music, travel, pop culture, history and biography. No unsolicited MSS. Founded 1973.

Canongate Classics (imprint)
Senior Editor Rory Watson
Reprint series of key works of Scottish literature ranging from fiction to poetry, to biography, philosophy and travel.

Canopus Publishing Ltd
27 Queen Square, Bristol BS1 4ND
tel 0117-922 6660
email robin@canopusbooks.com
website www.canopusbooks.com
Director Robin Rees

Popular science and astronomy. Founded 1999.

Canterbury Press – see SCM Canterbury Press Ltd

Jonathan Cape – see Random House Group Ltd

Jonathan Cape Children's Books – see Random House Group Ltd

Carcanet Press Ltd
4th Floor, Alliance House, 28–34 Cross Street, Manchester M2 7AQ
tel 0161-834 8730 *fax* 0161-832 0084
email info@carcanet.co.uk
website www.carcanet.co.uk
Director Michael Schmidt

Poetry, *Fyfield* series, Oxford Poets, translations. Founded 1969.

Carlton Publishing Group

20 Mortimer Street, London W1T 3JW
tel 020-7612 0400 *fax* 020-7612 0401
email enquiries@carltonbooks.co.uk
Managing Director Jonathan Goodman, *Editorial Director* Piers Murray Hill

No unsolicited MSS; synopses and ideas welcome, but no fiction, poetry or children's books. Imprints: Carlton Books, André Deutsch, Prion Books. Founded 1992.

Carlton Books (division)

Mass market illustrated leisure and entertainment books: history, sport, TV tie-ins, health and wellbeing, popular science, design, music, puzzles.

André Deutsch (division)

Autobiography, biography, history, current affairs, humour, drink, the arts.

Prion Books (division)

Humour, nostalgia, drink.

Frank Cass – see Taylor and Francis Books Ltd

Cassell Illustrated – see Octopus Publishing Group

Cassell Reference – see Weidenfeld & Nicolson

Kyle Cathie Ltd

122 Arlington Road, London NW1 7HP
tel 020-7692 7215 *fax* 020-7692 7260
email general.enquiries@kyle-cathie.com
website www.kylecathie.com
Publisher & Managing Director Kyle Cathie

Health, beauty, food and drink, gardening, reference, style, design, Mind, Body & Spirit. Founded 1990.

Catholic Truth Society

40–46 Harleyford Road, London SE11 5AY
tel 020-7640 0042 *fax* 020-7640 0046
email editorial@cts-online.org.uk
website www.cts-online.org.uk
Chairman Most Rev. Peter Smith DCL, LLB, *General Secretary* Fergal Martin LLB, LLM

General books of Roman Catholic and Christian interest, bibles, prayer books, RE, and booklets of doctrinal, historical, devotional or social interest. MSS of 11,000–15,000 words with up to 6 illustrations considered for publication as pamphlets. Founded 1868.

Cavendish Publishing Ltd*

The Glass House, Wharton Street, London WC1X 9PX
tel 020-7278 8000 *fax* 020-7278 8080
email info@cavendishpublishing.com
website www.cavendishpublishing.com
Executive Chairman Sonny Leong

A wide range of legal and medico–legal books and journals. Imprints: Birkbeck Law Press, Glass House Press, UCL Press. Founded 1990.

Caxton Publishing Group

20 Bloomsbury Street, London WC1B 3QA
tel 020-7636 7171 *fax* 020-7636 1922
website www.caxtonbooks.com
Managing Director John Maxwell

Reprints, promotional books, remainders. Imprints: Caxton Editions, Brockhampton Press, Knight Paperbacks.

CBD Research Ltd

15 Wickham Road, Beckenham, Kent BR3 5JS
tel 020-8650 7745 *fax* 020-8650 0768
email cbd@cbdresearch.com
website www.cbdresearch.com
Directors S.P.A. Henderson, A.J.W. Henderson

Directories, reference books, bibliographies, guides to business and statistical information. Founded 1961.

Chancery House Press (imprint)

Unusual non-fiction/reference works. Preliminary letter and synopsis with return postage essential.

Centaur Press – acquired by Open Gate Press

Century – see Random House Group Ltd

Chambers Harrap Publishers Ltd*

7 Hopetoun Crescent, Edinburgh EH7 4AY
tel 0131-556 5929 *fax* 0131-556 5313
email admin@chambersharrap.co.uk
website www.chambersharrap.co.uk
Managing Director Wendy Rimmington, *Publishing Manager* Patrick White

English language and bilingual dictionaries, reference, word games, writing guides, puzzles. Book proposals should include synopsis, sample pages and a CV.

Chancery House Press – see CBD Research Ltd

Channel 4 Books – see Transworld Publishers

Chapman Publishing

4 Broughton Place, Edinburgh EH1 3RX
tel 0131-557 2207
email chapman-pub@blueyonder.co.uk
website www.chapman-pub.co.uk
Editor Joy Hendry

Poetry and drama: *Chapman New Writing Series*. Also the *Chapman Wild Women Series*. Founded 1970.

Paul Chapman Publishing – see SAGE Publications Ltd

Chartered Institute of Personnel and Development
CIPD Publishing, 151 The Broadway, London SW19 1JQ
tel 020-8612 6200 *fax* 020-8612 6201
email publish@cipd.co.uk
website www.cipd.co.uk/bookstore
Publishing Manager Sarah Brown

Personnel management, training and development.

Chatto & Windus – see Random House Group Ltd

Cherrytree Books – see Zero to Ten Ltd

The Chicken House
2 Palmer Street, Frome, Somerset BA11 1DS
tel (01373) 454488 *fax* (01373) 454499
email chickenhouse@doublecluck.com
website www.doublecluck.com
Managing Director & Publisher Barry Cunningham,
Deputy Managing Director Rachel Hickman

Fiction and non-fiction for age 7+, picture books. Acquired by Scholastic Inc.

Child's Play (International) Ltd
Ashworth Road, Bridgemead, Swindon, Wilts. SN5 7YD
tel (01793) 616286 *fax* (01793) 512795
email allday@childs-play.com
website www.childs-play.com
Chairman Adriana Twinn, *Publisher* Neil Burden

Children's educational books: board, picture, activity and play books; fiction and non-fiction. Founded 1972.

Chivers Press – see BBC Audiobooks Ltd

Christian Education*
(incorporating RE Today Services and International Bible Reading Association)
1020 Bristol Road, Selly Oak, Birmingham B29 6LB
tel 0121-472 4242 *fax* 0121-472 7575
email enquiries@christianeducation.org.uk
website www.christianeducation.org.uk

Publications and services for teachers of RE including *RE today* magazine, curriculum booklets, training material for children and youth workers in the Church. Worship resources for use in primary schools. Christian drama and musicals, Activity Club material and Bible reading resources.

Chrysalis Books Group – see Anova Books

Churchill Livingstone – see Elsevier Ltd
(Health Sciences)

Churchwarden Publications Ltd
PO Box 420, Warminster, Wilts. BA12 9XB
tel (01985) 840189 *fax* (01985) 840243
email churchwardens@btinternet.com
Directors J.N.G. Stidolph, S.A. Stidolph

Church administration. Ideas and MSS welcome.

Cicerone Press
2 Police Square, Milnthorpe, Cumbria LA7 7PY
tel (01539) 562069 *fax* (01539) 563417
email info@cicerone.co.uk
website www.cicerone.co.uk
Managing Director Jonathan Williams

Guidebooks: walking, trekking, mountaineering, climbing, cycling, etc in Britain, Europe, and worldwide.

Cico Books
20–21 Jockey's Fields, London WC1R 4BW
tel 020-7025 2280 *fax* 020-7025 2281
email mail@cicobooks.co.uk
Directors Mark Collins (managing), Lucinda Richards (publishing)

Lifestyle and interiors, crafts and Mind, Body & Spirit. Imprint of Ryland Peters and Small. Founded 1999.

Cima Books – now Cico Books

Cisco Press – see Pearson Education

T&T Clark International – see The Continuum International Publishing Group Ltd

James Clarke & Co. Ltd*
PO Box 60, Cambridge CB1 2NT
tel (01223) 350865 *fax* (01223) 366951
email publishing@lutterworth.com
website www.lutterworth.com
Managing Director Adrian Brink

Theology, academic, reference books. Imprints: Acorn Editions, Patrick Hardy Books. Founded 1859.

Lutterworth Press (subsidiary)
The arts, biography, educational, environmental, general, history, leisure, philosophy, science, sociology, theology and religion.

Classic Publications – see Ian Allan Publishing Ltd

Cló Iar-Chonnachta Teo.†
Indreabhán, Conamara, Co. Galway, Republic of Ireland
tel (091) 593307 *fax* (091) 593362
email cic@iol.ie
website www.cic.ie
Director Micheál Ó Conghaile, *General Manager* Deirdre O'Toole

Irish-language – novels, short stories, plays, poetry, songs, history; CDs (writers reading from their works in Irish and English). Promotes the translation of contemporary Irish fiction and poetry into other languages. Founded 1985.

Co & Bear Productions

565 Fulham Road, London SW6 1ES
tel 020-7385 0888 *fax* 020-7385 0101
email info@cobear.co.uk
website www.scriptumeditions.co.uk
Publisher Beatrice Vincenzini

High-quality illustrated books on lifestyle, photography, art. Imprints: Scriptum Editions, Cartago. Founded 1996.

Collins & Brown – see Anova Books

Collins – see HarperCollins Publishers

Collins Dictionaries/COBUILD – see HarperCollins Publishers

Collins Gem – see HarperCollins Publishers

Collins Maps and Road Atlases – see HarperCollins Publishers

Colourpoint Books

Colourpoint House, Jubilee Business Park, 21 Jubilee Road, Newtownards, Co. Down, Northern Ireland BT23 4YH
tel (028) 9182 0505 *fax* (028) 9182 1900
email info@colourpoint.co.uk
website www.colourpoint.co.uk
Directors Wesley Johnston, Malcolm Johnston, Norman Johnston (transport editor), Sheila Johnston (commissioning editor), *Administrator* Michelle Chambers

Educational textbooks; transport – buses, road and railways; Irish and general interest. Initial approach in writing please, with full details of proposal and sample chapters. Include return postage. Founded 1993.

The Columba Press

55A Spruce Avenue, Stillorgan Industrial Park, Blackrock, Co. Dublin, Republic of Ireland
tel (1) 2942556 *fax* (1) 2942564
email info@columba.ie
website www.columba.ie
Publisher & Managing Director Seán O'Boyle

Religion (Roman Catholic and Anglican) including pastoral handbooks, spirituality, theology, liturgy and prayer; counselling and self-help. Founded 1985.

Currach Press (imprint)
General non-fiction.

Connections Book Publishing Ltd

St Chad's House, 148 King's Cross Road, London WC1X 9DH
tel 020-7837 1968 *fax* 020-7837 2025
email reception@eddisonsadd.co.uk
website www.connections-publishing.com
Directors Nick Eddison, Ian Jackson, David Owen

Illustrated books and gift titles: Mind, Body & Spirit (particularly tarot), health and relationships, marshall arts. Founded 1993.

Conran Octopus – see Octopus Publishing Group

Constable & Robinson Ltd*

3 The Lanchesters, 162 Fulham Palace Road, London W6 9ER
tel 020-8741 3663 *fax* 020-8748 7562
email enquiries@constablerobinson.com
website www.constablerobinson.com
Chairman & Publisher Nick Robinson, *Joint Managing Directors* Jan Chamier and Nova Jayne Heath, *Finance Director* Adrian Andrews

Unsolicited sample chapters, synopses and ideas welcome with return postage. Do not send MSS; no email submissions. Founded 1890 (Constable); 1983 (Robinson).

Constable (imprint)
Biography, fiction, general and military history, travel and endurance, climbing, landscape photography, psychology, current affairs.

Magpie (imprint)
Promotional books. Unsolicited MSS not accepted.

Robinson (imprint: paperbacks)
Crime fiction, *The Daily Telegraph* health books, the Mammoth series, psychology, true crime, military history.

Consumers' Association – see Which? Ltd

The Continuum International Publishing Group Ltd

The Tower Building, 11 York Road, London SE1 7NX
tel 020-7922 0880 *fax* 020-7922 0881
email info@continuumbooks.com
website www.continuumbooks.com
Chairman & Ceo Philip Sturrock, *Directors* Robin Baird-Smith (general trade and Continuum religion: publishes under Continuum, Burns & Oates, Morehouse), Anthony Haynes (academic humanities: publishes education, social sciences, literature, film and music, philosophy (including Thoemmes imprint), linguistics, biblical studies and theology printed under T&T Clark), Frank Roney (finance), Ed Suthon (sales & marketing), Benn Linfield (publishing services)

Serious non-fiction, academic and professional, including scholarly monographs and educational texts and reference works in history, politics and social thought; literature, criticism, performing arts;

religion and spirituality; education, psychology, women's studies, business. Imprints: Burns & Oates, Continuum, Hambledon, Morehouse, T&T Clark International, Thoemmes Press.

Conway – see Anova Books

Thomas Cook Publishing
Unit 15-16, Coningsby Road, Peterborough PE3 8SB
tel (01733) 416477 *fax* (01733) 416688
email publishing-sales@thomascook.com
website www.thomascookpublishing.com
Managing Director John Sadler

Travel guides, rail maps and timetables. Founded 1875.

Corgi – see Transworld Publishers

Corgi Children's Books – see Random House Group Ltd

Cork University Press†
Youngline Industrial Estate, Pouladuff Road, Togher, Cork, Republic of Ireland
tel (021) 4902980 *fax* (021) 4315329
website www.corkuniversitypress.com
Publications Director Mike Collins

Irish literature, history, cultural studies, medieval studies, English literature, musicology, poetry, translations. Founded 1925.

Attic Press and Atrium (imprints)
email corkuniversitypress@ucc.ie
Books by and about women in the areas of social and political comment, women's studies, reference guides and handbooks.

Corvo Books Ltd
64 Duncan Terrace, London N1 8AG
tel 020-7288 0651
email editor@corvobooks.com
website www.corvobooks.com
Publisher Scott McDonald, *Editor* Julia Rochester

Specialises in personal histories with an international flavour: memoir, history, travel, philosophy. Welcomes submissions of previously unpublished, full-length works of non-fiction which use a strong personal voice (or voices) to document historical or contemporary events in any part of the world. Submit the first 3 chapters (or approx. 30pp) and include a sae for its return. Founded 2002.

Council for British Archaeology
St Mary's House, 66 Bootham, York YO30 7BZ
tel (01904) 671417 *fax* (01904) 671384
email info@britarch.ac.uk
website www.britarch.ac.uk
Director Mike Heyworth, *Publications Officer* Jane Thorniley-Walker

British archaeology – academic; practical handbooks; general interest archaeology. *British Archaeology* magazine. Founded 1944.

Countryside Books
2 Highfield Avenue, Newbury, Berks. RG14 5DS
tel (01635) 43816 *fax* (01635) 551004
website www.countrysidebooks.co.uk
Partners Nicholas Battle, Suzanne Battle

Books of local or regional interest, usually on a county basis: walking, outdoor activities, local history; also genealogy, aviation. Founded 1976.

Cover to Cover – see BBC Audiobooks Ltd

CRC Press – see Taylor and Francis Books Ltd

Crescent Books – see The Mercat Press

Crescent Moon Publishing
PO Box 393, Maidstone, Kent ME14 5XU
tel (01622) 729593
email cresmopub@yahoo.co.uk
website www.crescentmoon.org.uk
Director Jeremy Robinson, *Editors* C. Hughes, B.D. Barnacle

Literature, poetry, arts, cultural studies, media, cinema, feminism. Submit sample chapters or 6 poems plus sae, not complete MSS. Founded 1988.

Cressrelles Publishing Co. Ltd
10 Station Road Industrial Estate, Colwall, Malvern, Herefordshire WR13 6RN
tel (01684) 540154 *fax* (01684) 540154
email simonsmith@cressrelles4drama.fsbusiness.co.uk
Directors Leslie Smith, Simon Smith

General publishing. Founded 1973.

J. Garnet Miller (imprint)
Plays and theatre textbooks.

Kenyon-Deane (imprint)
Plays and drama textbooks for amateur dramatic societies. Plays for women.

Crown House Publishing Ltd
Crown Buildings, Bancyfelin, Carmarthen SA33 5ND
tel (01267) 211345 *fax* (01267) 211882
email books@crownhouse.co.uk
website www.crownhouse.co.uk
Chairman Martin Roberts, *Directors* David Bowman (managing director), Glenys Roberts, David Bowman, Karen Bowman, Caroline Lenton

Publishes titles in the areas of psychotherapy, education, business training and development, Mind, Body & Spirit. Aim to demystify the latest psychological advances, particularly in the fields of Accelerated Learning, Neuro-Linguistic Programming (NLP) and Hypnosis. Crown House provide professional therapists, consultants and trainers with books detailing the latest cutting edge developments in their fields. Founded 1998.

The Crowood Press
The Stable Block, Ramsbury, Marlborough, Wilts. SN8 2HR

tel (01672) 520320 *fax* (01672) 520280
email enquiries@crowood.com
website www.crowood.com
Directors John Dennis (chairman), Ken Hathaway (managing)

Sport, motoring, aviation, military, martial arts, walking, fishing, country sports, farming, natural history, gardening, DIY, crafts, dogs, equestrian, theatre. Founded 1982.

Airlife Publishing (imprint)
Aviation, technical and general, military, military history.

Benjamin Cummings – see Pearson Education

Currach Press – see The Columba Press

Current Science Group
34–42 Cleveland Street, London W1T 4LB
tel 020-7323 0323 *fax* 020-7580 1938
email csg@cursci.co.uk
website www.current-science-group.com
Chairman Vitek Tracz

Biological sciences, medicine, pharmaceutical science, internet communities, electronic publishing.

James Currey Ltd
73 Botley Road, Oxford OX2 0BS
tel (01865) 244111 *fax* (01865) 246454
website www.jamescurrey.co.uk
Directors James Currey, Prof Wendy James FBA, Dr Douglas H. Johnson, Keith Sambrook

Academic studies of Africa and Third World: history, anthropology, archaeology, economics, agriculture, politics, literary criticism, sociology. Founded 1985.

Curzon Press Ltd – now RoutledgeCurzon – see Taylor and Francis Books Ltd

Terence Dalton Ltd
Water Street, Lavenham, Sudbury, Suffolk CO10 9RN
tel (01787) 249289 *fax* (01787) 248267
Directors T.A.J. Dalton, E.H. Whitehair

Non-fiction.

Darton, Longman & Todd Ltd*
1 Spencer Court, 140–142 Wandsworth High Street, London SW18 4JJ
tel 020-8875 0155 *fax* 020-8875 0133
email editorial@darton-longman-todd.co.uk
website www.darton-longman-todd.co.uk
Editorial Director Brendan Walsh

Religious books and bibles, including the following themes: bible study, spirituality, prayer and meditation, anthologies, daily readings, healing, counselling and pastoral care, bereavement, personal growth, mission, political, environmental and social issues, biography/autobiography, theological and historical studies. Founded 1959.

David & Charles Ltd
Brunel House, Newton Abbot, Devon TQ12 4PU
tel (01626) 323200 *fax* (01626) 323319
Managing Director & Publisher Sara Domville

High-quality illustrated non-fiction specialising in military history, crafts, hobbies, art techniques, gardening, natural history, equestrian, DIY, photography. Founded 1960.

Christopher Davies Publishers Ltd
PO Box 403, Swansea SA1 4YF
tel (01792) 648825 *fax* (01792) 648825
email editor@cdaviesbookswales.com
website www.cdaviesbookswales.com
Directors Christopher Talfan Davies (editorial), D.M. Davies

History, leisure, sport and general books of Welsh interest only, *Triskele Books*. Founded 1949.

Giles de la Mare Publishers Ltd
PO Box 25351, London NW5 1ZT
tel 020-7485 2533 *fax* 020-7485 2534
email gilesdelamare@dial.pipex.com
website www.gilesdelamare.co.uk
Chairman Giles de la Mare

Non-fiction: art, architecture, biography, history, music, travel. Telephone before submitting MSS. Founded 1995.

Dean – see Egmont Books

Dedalus Ltd
24 St Judith's Lane, Sawtry, Cambs. PE28 5XE
tel (01487) 832382
email info@dedalusbooks.com
website www.dedalusbooks.com
Chairman Juri Gabriel, *Directors* Eric Lane (managing), Robert Irwin (editorial), Lindsay Thomas (marketing), Mike Mitchell (translations)

Original fiction in English and in translation; Dedalus European Classics, Dedalus concept books. Founded 1983.

Dekker Publishing – see Taylor and Francis Books Ltd

Richard Dennis Publications
The Old Chapel, Shepton Beauchamp, Ilminster, Somerset TA19 0LE
tel (01460) 240044 *fax* (01460) 242009
email books@richarddennispublications.com
website www.richarddennispublications.com

Books for collectors specialising in ceramics, glass, illustration, sculpture and facsimile editions of early catalogues.

André Deutsch – see Carlton Publishing Group

diehard
91–93 Main Street, Callander FK17 8BQ
tel (01877) 339449
website www.poetryscotland.co.uk
Directors Ian William King (managing), Sally Evans (marketing)

Scottish poetry. Founded 1993.

Digital Press – see Elsevier Ltd

Discovery Walking Guides Ltd
10 Tennyson Close, Dallington, Northampton NN5 7HJ
tel (01604) 244869 *fax* (01604) 752576
website www.walking.demon.co.uk
Chairman Rosamund C. Brawn

'Walk!' and '34/35 Walks' walking guide books to UK and European destinations. 'Tour & Trail Super-Durable' large-scale maps for outdoor adventures. 'Drive' touring maps. GPS The Easy Way. Digital 'Personal Navigator Files' for GPS users. Welcomes project proposals from technologically proficient walking writers. Founded 1994.

Dorling Kindersley – see Penguin Group (UK)

Doubleday Children's Books – see Random House Group Ltd

Doubleday (UK) – see Transworld Publishers

The Dovecote Press Ltd
Stanbridge, Wimborne Minster, Dorset BH21 4JD
tel (01258) 840549 *fax* (01258) 840958
email online@dovecotepress.com
website www.dovecotepress.com
Editorial Director David Burnett

Books of local interest: *County in Colour* series, natural history, architecture, history. Founded 1974.

Dref Wen
28 Church Road, Whitchurch, Cardiff CF14 2EA
tel 029-2061 7860 *fax* 029-2061 0507
Directors Roger Boore, Anne Boore, Gwilym Boore, Alun Boore

Welsh language publisher. Original Welsh language novels for children and adult learners. Original, adaptations and translations of foreign and English language full-colour picture story books for children. Educational material for primary/secondary schoolchildren in Wales and England. Founded 1970.

Dublar Scripts
204 Mercer Way, Romsey, Hants SO51 7QJ
tel (01794) 501377 *fax* (01794) 502538
email scripts@dublar.freeserve.co.uk
website www.dublar.co.uk

Managing Director Robert Heather
Pantomimes. Imprint: Sleepy Hollow Pantomimes. Founded 1994.

University College Dublin Press[†]
Newman House, 86 St Stephen's Green, Dublin 2, Republic of Ireland
tel (01) 716 7397 *fax* (01) 716 7211
email ucdpress@ucd.ie
website www.ucdpress.ie
Executive Editor Barbara Mennell

Irish studies, history and politics, literary studies. Founded 1995.

Gerald Duckworth & Co. Ltd
First Floor, 90–93 Cowcross Street, London EC1M 6BF
tel 020-7490 7300 *fax* 020-7490 0080
email info@duckworth-publishers.co.uk
website www.ducknet.co.uk
Directors Peter Mayer (publisher), Dan Hind (editorial), Deborah Blake (editorial), Ray Davies (production)

General trade publishers with a strong academic division. Imprints: Bristol Classical Press. Founded 1898.

Dunedin Academic Press[*]
Hudson House, 8 Albany Street, Edinburgh EH1 3QB
tel 0131-473 2397 *fax* (01250) 870920
email mail@dunedinacademicpress.co.uk
website www.dunedinacademicpress.co.uk
Director Anthony Kinahan

Earth science, social sciences, music, humanities. Founded 2000.

Martin Dunitz – see Taylor and Francis Books Ltd

Earthscan
8–12 Camden High Street, London NW1 0JH
tel 020-7387 8558 *fax* 020-7387 8998
email earthinfo@earthscan.co.uk
website www.earthscan.co.uk
Publishing Director Jonathan Sinclair Wilson

Academic and professional: sustainable development, climate and energy, natural resource management, cities and built environment, business and economics, heritage conservation. Imprint of James & James (Science Publishers) Ltd.

Ebury Press – see Random House Group Ltd

Eden – see Transworld Publishers

Edinburgh University Press[*]
22 George Square, Edinburgh EH8 9LF
tel 0131-650 4218 *fax* 0131-662 0053
website www.eup.ed.ac.uk

Chairman Tim Rix, *Chief Executive* Timothy Wright, *Deputy Chief Executive* Ms Jackie Jones

Academic publishers of scholarly books and journals: African studies, media and cultural studies, Islamic studies, geography, history, law, linguistics, literary studies, philosophy, politics, Scottish studies, American studies, religious studies, sociology, classical and ancient history.Trade: Scottish language, literature and culture, Scottish history and politics.

Éditions Aubrey Walter

99A Wallis Road, London E9 5LN
fax 020-8533 5821
email aubrey@gmppubs.co.uk
website www.gmppubs.co.uk
Publisher Aubrey Walter

Visual work by gay artists and photographers, usually in the form of a monograph showcasing one artist's work. Work may be submitted on disk, email, transparency, photocopy or photograph.

The Educational Company of Ireland†

Ballymount Road, Walkinstown, Dublin 12, Republic of Ireland
tel (01) 4500611 *fax* (01) 4500993
email info@edco.ie
website www.edco.ie
Executive Directors Frank Maguire (chief executive), R. McLoughlin, *Financial Controller* A. Harrold, *Sales & Marketing Manager* M. Harford-Hughes, *Publisher* Frank Fahy

Educational MSS on all subjects in English or Irish language. Trading unit of Smurfit Kappa Group – Ireland. Founded 1910.

Educational Explorers (Publishers)

Unit 5, Feidr Castell Business Park, Fishguard SA65 9BB
tel/fax (08456) 123912
email explorers@cuisenaire.co.uk
website www.cuisenaire.co.uk
Directors M.J. Hollyfield, D.M. Gattegno

Educational. Mathematics: *Numbers in colour with Cuisenaire Rods*; languages: *The Silent Way*; literacy, reading: *Words in Colour*; educational films. No unsolicited material. Founded 1962.

Egmont Books*

239 Kensington High Street, London W8 6SA
tel 020-7761 3500 *fax* 020-7761 3510
email firstname.surname@ecb.egmont.com
website www.egmont.co.uk
Managing Director Robert McMenemy, *Publishing Director* David Riley

Children's books: picture books, fiction (ages 4–16), illustrated non-fiction, licensed character list. Publishes under Egmont and Dean. Founded 1878.

Element – see HarperCollins Publishers

11:9 – see Neil Wilson Publishing Ltd

Edward Elgar Publishing Ltd

Glensanda House, Montpellier Parade, Cheltenham, Glos. GL50 1UA
tel (01242) 226934 *fax* (01242) 262111
email info@e-elgar.co.uk
website www.e-elgar.com
Managing Director Edward Elgar

Economics, business, law, public and social policy. Founded 1986.

Elliot Right Way Books

Kingswood Buildings, Brighton Road, Lower Kingswood, Tadworth, Surrey KT20 6TD
tel (01737) 832202 *fax* (01737) 830311
email info@right-way.co.uk
website www.right-way.co.uk
Managing Directors Clive Elliot, Malcolm Elliot

Independent publishers of practical non-fiction 'how to' paperbacks. The low-price *Right Way* and *Right Way Plus* series include games, pastimes, horses, pets, motoring, sport, health, business, public speaking and jokes, financial and legal, cookery and etiquette. Similar subjects are covered in the *Clarion* series of large-format paperbacks, sold in supermarkets and bargain bookshops. No freelance proofreaders or editors required. Founded 1946.

Elliott & Thompson

27 John Street, London WC1N 2BX
tel 020-7831 5013 *fax* 020-7831 5011
email gmo73@dial.pipex.com
website www.elliottthompson.com
Directors David Elliott, Brad Thompson

Fiction, belles-lettres, biography, history, media, travel. Founded 2001.

Aidan Ellis Publishing

Whinfield, Herbert Road, Salcombe, Devon TQ8 8HN
tel (01548) 842755
email mail@aidanellispublishing.co.uk
website www.aepub.demon.co.uk
Publisher Aidan Ellis

Non-fiction: gardening, maritime, biography, general. Founded 1971.

ELM Publications and Training

Seaton House, Kings Ripton, Huntingdon, Cambs. PE28 2NJ
tel (01487) 773254
email elm@elm-training.co.uk
website www.elm-training.co.uk
Managing Director Sheila Ritchie

Business and management development books, packs and resources; training materials and training courses; some e-learning materials. Actively seeking good tested management development materials, telephone in the first instance please, no MSS. Founded 1977.

Elsevier Ltd*
(incorporating Pergamon Press and Harcourt Publishers International)
The Boulevard, Langford Lane, Kidlington, Oxford OX5 1GB
tel (01865) 843000 *fax* (01865) 843010
website www.elsevier.com
Coo Ops Gavin Howe, *Ceo Health Sciences Division (Books & Journals)* Brian Nairn

Academic and professional reference books; scientific, technical and medical books, journals, CD-Roms and magazines. No unsolicited MSS, but synopses and project proposals welcome. Imprints: Academic Press, Architectural Press, Bailliere Tindall, Butterworth-Heinemann, Churchill Livingstone, Digital Press, Elsevier, Elsevier Advanced Technology, Focal Press, Gulf Professional Press, JAI, Made Simple Books, Morgan Kauffman, Mosby, Newnes, North-Holland, Pergamon, Saunders. Division of Reed Elsevier, Amsterdam.

Elsevier Ltd (Butterworth Heinemann)*
Linacre House, Jordan Hill, Oxford OX2 8DP
tel (01865) 310366 *fax* (01865) 314541
website www.bh.com
Managing Director Philip Shaw (Science & Technology Books)

Books and electronic products across business, technical, for students and professionals.

Elsevier Ltd (Health Sciences)*
32 Jamestown Road, London NW1 7BY
tel 020-7424 4200 *fax* 020-7424 4431
website www.elsevier.com, www.elsevierhealth.com
Managing Director, Health Sciences Europe Mary Ging

Medical books and journals. No unsolicited MSS but synopses and project proposals welcome. Imprints: Bailliere Tindall, Churchill Livingstone, Elsevier, Mosby, Pergamon, Saunders.

Encyclopaedia Britannica (UK) Ltd
2nd Floor, Unity Wharf, 13 Mill Street, London SE1 2BH
tel 020-7500 7800 *fax* 020-7500 7878
email enquiries@britannica.co.uk
website www.britannica.co.uk
Managing Director Leah Mansoor, *VP of Operations* Jane Helps

Enitharmon Press
26B Caversham Road, London NW5 2DU
tel 020-7482 5967 *fax* 020-7284 1787
email books@enitharmon.co.uk
website www.enitharmon.co.uk
Director Stephen Stuart-Smith

Poetry, literary criticism, fiction, translations, artists' books. No unsolicited MSS. No freelance editors or proofreaders required. Founded 1967.

Euromonitor International plc
60–61 Britton Street, London EC1M 5UX
tel 020-7251 8024 *fax* 020-7608 3149
email info@euromonitor.com
website www.euromonitor.com
Directors T.J. Fenwick (managing), R.N. Senior (chairman)

Business and commercial reference, marketing information, European and International Surveys, directories. Founded 1972.

Europa Publications Ltd – see Taylor and Francis Books Ltd

Evangelical Press of Wales – see Bryntirion Press

Evans Brothers Ltd*
2A Portman Mansions, Chiltern Street, London W1U 6NR
tel 020-7487 0920 *fax* 020-7487 0921
email sales@evansbooks.co.uk
website www.evansbooks.co.uk
Directors Stephen Pawley (managing), Brian D. Jones (international publishing), A.O. Ojora (Nigeria), *UK Publisher* Su Swallow

Educational books, particularly preschool, school library and teachers' books for the UK, primary and secondary for Africa, the Caribbean. Part of the Evans Publishing Group. Founded 1908.

Everyman – see The Orion Publishing Group Ltd

Everyman's Library
Northburgh House, 10 Northburgh Street, London EC1V 0AT
tel 020-7566 6350 *fax* 020-7490 3708
Publisher David Campbell

Everyman's Library (clothbound reprints of the classics); *Everyman's Library Children's Classics*; *Everyman's Library Pocket Poets*; *Everyman Guides*; *Everyman City Map Guides*. No unsolicited submissions. An imprint of **Alfred A. Knopf**.

The Exeter Press
Reed Hall, Streatham Drive, Exeter, Devon EX4 4QR
tel (01392) 263066 *fax* (01392) 263064
email uep@exeterpress.co.uk
website www.exeterpress.co.uk
Publishers/Directors Simon Baker, Anna Henderson

Academic and scholarly books on history, local history (Exeter and the South West), archaeology, classical studies, English literature, film history, performance studies, medieval studies, maritime studies. Founded 1958.

Exley Publications Ltd
16 Chalk Hill, Watford, Herts. WD19 4BG
tel (01923) 250505 *fax* (01923) 818733/249795
website www.helenexleygiftbooks.com
Directors Dalton Exley, Helen Exley (editorial),
Lincoln Exley, Richard Exley

Popular colour giftbooks for an international market.
No unsolicited MSS. Founded 1976.

Expert Books – see Transworld Publishers

Faber and Faber Ltd*
3 Queen Square, London WC1N 3AU
tel 020-7465 0045 *fax* 020-7465 0034
website www.faber.co.uk
Chief Executive & Publisher Stephen Page,
Commercial Director David Tebbutt, *Editorial
Directors* Lee Brackstone, Walter Donohue, Julian
Loose, Belinda Matthews, *Sales Director* Will
Atkinson, *Publicity Director & Associate Publisher*,
Original Arts Rachel Alexander, *Marketing Director*
Noel Murphy, *Production Director* Nigel Marsh,
Rights & Contracts Director Camilla Smallwood,
Children's Director Suzy Jenvey

High-quality general fiction and non-fiction,
children's fiction and non-fiction, drama, film, music,
poetry. Unsolicited submissions accepted for poetry
only. For information on poetry submission
procedure ring 020-7465 0189, or consult website. No
unsolicited MSS.

Fabian Society
11 Dartmouth Street, London SW1H 9BN
tel 020-7227 4900 *fax* 020-7976 7153
email info@fabian-society.org.uk
website www.fabian-society.org.uk
General Secretary Sunder Katwala

Current affairs, political thought, economics,
education, environment, foreign affairs, social policy.
Also controls NCLC Publishing Society Ltd. Founded
1884.

Facet Publishing*
7 Ridgmount Street, London WC1E 7AE
tel 020-7255 0590 *fax* 020-7255 0591
email info@facetpublishing.co.uk
website www.facetpublishing.co.uk
Managing Director CILIP Enterprises John Woolley

Library and information science, information
technology, reference works, directories,
bibliographies.

Clive Bingley Ltd (imprint)
Library and information science, reference works.

Library Association Publishing (imprint)
Library and information science, information
technology, reference works, directories,
bibliographies.

CJ Fallon
Ground Floor, Block B, Liffey Valley Office Campus,
Dublin 22, Republic of Ireland
tel (01) 6166400 *fax* (01) 6166499
email editorial@cjfallon.ie
website www.cjfallon.ie
Executive Directors H.J. McNicholas (managing),
P. Tolan (financial), N. White (editorial)

Educational textbooks. Founded 1927.

Falmer Press – now RoutledgeFalmer, see
Taylor and Francis Books Ltd

Fernhurst Books
Duke's Path, High Street, Arundel, West Sussex
BN18 9AJ
tel (01903) 882277 *fax* (01903) 882715
email sales@fernhurstbooks.co.uk
website www.fernhurstbooks.co.uk
Publisher Tim Davison

Sailing, watersports. Founded 1979.

David Fickling Books – see Random House
Group Ltd

First and Best in Education Ltd
Earlstrees Court, Earlstrees Road, Corby, Northants.
NN17 4HH
tel (01536) 399004 *fax* (01536) 399012
email info@firstandbest.co.uk
website www.firstandbest.co.uk
Contact Anne Cockburn (editor)

Education-related books (no fiction). Currently
actively recruiting new writers for schools; ideas
welcome. Sae must accompany submissions.
Founded 1992.

Fitzroy-Dearborn – see Taylor and Francis
Books Ltd

Five Star – see Serpent's Tail

Flambard Press
Stable Cottage, East Fourstones, Hexham,
Northumberland NE47 5DX
tel (01434) 674360 *fax* (01434) 674178
email flambardpress@btinternet.com
website www.flambardpress.co.uk
Managing Editor Peter Lewis, *Deputy Editors*
Margaret Lewis, Will Mackie

Poetry and literary fiction. Only hard-copy
submissions with sae considered. Preliminary letter
required. No phone calls. See website for further
information. Founded 1990.

Flame Tree Publishing
Crabtree Hall, Crabtree Lane, London SW6 6TY
tel 020-7386 4700 *fax* 020-7386 4701
email info@flametreepublishing.com

website www.flametreepublishing.com
Managing Director Frances Bodiam, *Publisher/ Creative Director* Nick Wells

Music, reference, art, cookery, education. Part of The Foundry Creative Media Company Ltd. Founded 1992.

Floris Books*
15 Harrison Gardens, Edinburgh EH11 1SH
tel 0131-337 2372 *fax* 0131-347 9919
email floris@florisbooks.co.uk
website www.florisbooks.co.uk
Editors Christopher Moore, Gale Winskill, *Children's Editor* Gale Winskill

Religion, science, Celtic studies, craft; children's books: picture and board books, activity books. Founded 1978.

Flyleaf Press†
4 Spencer Villas, Glenageary, Co. Dublin, Republic of Ireland
tel (1) 2845906
email books@flyleaf.ie
website www.flyleaf.ie
Managing Editor James Ryan

Irish family history. Founded 1988.

Focal Press – see Elsevier Ltd

Folens Publishers*
Apex Business Centre, Boscombe Road, Dunstable LU5 4RL
tel (0870) 609 1237 *fax* (0870) 609 1236
email folens@folens.com
website www.folens.com
Managing Director Malcolm Watson, *Director of Publishing* Peter Burton, *Primary Publisher* Zoe Nichols

Primary and secondary educational books, learn-at-home books. Imprints: Folens, Belair. Founded 1987.

Folens Publishers
Hibernian Industrial Estate, Greenhills Road, Tallaght, Dublin 24, Republic of Ireland
tel (01) 4137200 *fax* (01) 4137282
website www.folens.ie
Chairman Dirk Folens, *Managing Director* John O'Connor

Educational (primary, secondary, comprehensive, technical, in English and Irish). Founded 1956.

Blackwater Press (imprint)
General non-fiction, Irish interest, children's fiction. Founded 1993.

Footprint Handbooks
6 Riverside Court, Lower Bristol Road, Bath BA2 3DZ
tel (01225) 469141 *fax* (01225) 469461

website www.footprintbooks.com
Directors Patrick Dawson (managing), Andy Fiddle (marketing & sales), *Managing Editor* Sophie Blacksell

Travel guides.

W. Foulsham & Co. Ltd
The Publishing House, Bennetts Close, Slough, Berks. SL1 5AP
tel (01753) 526769 *fax* (01753) 535003
Managing Director B.A.R. Belasco, *Editorial Director* W. Hobson

Life issues. General know-how, cookery, health and alternative therapies, hobbies and games, gardening, sport, travel guides, DIY, collectibles, popular new age. Imprints: Arcturus, Foulsham, Quantum. Founded 1819.

Arcturus (imprint)
Units 26–27, Bickels Yard, 151–153 Bermondsey Street, London SE1 3HA
Military, art and drawing, popular psychology.

Quantum (imprint)
Mind, Body & Spirit, popular philosophy and practical psychology.

Foundery Press – see Methodist Publishing House

Four Courts Press†
7 Malpas Street, Dublin 8, Republic of Ireland
tel (01) 4534668 *fax* (01) 4534672
email info@four-courts-press.ie
website www.four-courts-press.ie
Managing Director Michael Adams

Academic books in the humanities, especially history, Celtic and medieval studies, art, theology. Founded 1970.

Fourth Estate – see HarperCollins Publishers

Free Association Books
PO Box 37664, London NW7 2XU
tel 020-8906 0396 *fax* 020-8906 0006
email info@fabooks.com
website www.fabooks.com
Publisher & Managing Director T.E. Brown

Social sciences, psychoanalysis, psychotherapy, counselling, cultural studies, social welfare, addiction studies, child and adolescent studies. No poetry, science fiction or fantasy. Founded 1984.

Free Press – see Simon & Schuster UK Ltd

W.H. Freeman
Palgrave Publishers Ltd, Houndmills, Basingstoke, Hants RG21 6XS
tel (01256) 332807 *fax* (01256) 330688
Science, medicine, economics, psychology, sociology.

Samuel French Ltd*

52 Fitzroy Street, London W1T 5JR
tel 020-7387 9373 *fax* 020-7387 2161
email theatre@samuelfrench-london.co.uk
website www.samuelfrench-london.co.uk
Directors Charles R. Van Nostrand (chairman, USA),
Vivien Goodwin (managing), Amanda Smith, Paul
Taylor

Publishers of plays and agents for the collection of
royalties. Founded 1830.

The Friday Project

83 Victoria Street, London SW1H 0HW
email clare@thefridayproject.co.uk
website www.thefridayproject.co.uk
Publishing Director Clare Christian, *Editor-in-Chief*
Paul Carr

Books developed from popular websites. Imprint:
Friday Books. Founded 2005.

FT Prentice Hall – see Pearson Education

David Fulton Publishers Ltd*

Chiswick Centre, 414 Chiswick High Road, London
W4 5TF
tel 020-8996 3610 *fax* 020-8996 3622
email mail@fultonpublishers.co.uk
website www.fultonpublishers.co.uk
Publishing Director Tracey Alcock

Initial teacher training and continuing professional
development (early years, primary and secondary),
special educational needs, early years education,
school and nursery management. Unsolicited MSS
returned if accompanied by sae. Division of Granada
Learning, part of ITV plc. Founded 1987.

Gaia Books Ltd – see Octopus Publishing Group

The Gallery Press

Loughcrew, Oldcastle, Co. Meath, Republic of Ireland
tel (049) 8541779 *fax* (049) 8541779
email gallery@indigo.ie
website www.gallerypress.com
Editor/Publisher Peter Fallon

Poetry, drama, occasionally fiction, by Irish authors
only at this time. Founded 1970.

Garland Science – see Taylor and Francis Books Ltd

J. Garnet Miller – see Cressrelles Publishing Co. Ltd

Garnet Publishing Ltd

8 Southern Court, South Street, Reading RG1 4QS
tel (01189) 597847 *fax* (01189) 597356
email enquiries@garnetpublishing.co.uk
Editorial Manager Emma G. Hawker

Art, architecture, photography, fiction, religious
studies, travel and general, mainly on Middle and Far
East, and Islam. Founded 1991.

Ithaca Press (imprint)
Post-graduate academic works, especially on the
Middle East.

South Street Press (imprint)
Non-fiction, including *Behind the Headlines* series.

Geddes & Grosset*

David Dale House, New Lanark ML11 9DJ
tel (01555) 665000 *fax* (01555) 665694
email info@gandg.sol.co.uk
Publishers Ron Grosset, Mike Miller

Popular reference, children's non-fiction and activity
books. Founded 1988.

Gibson Square

47 Lonsdale Square, London N1 1EW
tel 020-7096 1100 *fax* 020-7993 2214
email info@gibsonsquare.com
website www.gibsonsquare.com
Publisher Martin Rynja

Non-fiction: biography, current affairs, philosophy,
politics, cultural criticism, psychology, history, travel,
art history. Submissions must have a high publicity
potential; include sae.

Gill & Macmillan Ltd†

Hume Avenue, Park West, Dublin 12, Republic of
Ireland
tel (01) 500 9500 *fax* (01) 500 9599
website www.gillmacmillan.ie

Biography or memoirs, educational (secondary,
university), history, literature, cookery, current
affairs, guidebooks. Founded 1968.

Ginn & Co. – see Harcourt Education Ltd

Godsfield Press – see Octopus Publishing Group

The Goldsmith Press

Newbridge, Co. Kildare, Republic of Ireland
tel (045) 433613 *fax* (045) 434648
email viv1@iol.ie
website www.gerardmanleyhopkins.org
Directors V. Abbott, D. Egan, *Secretary* B. Ennis

Literature, art, Irish interest, poetry. Unsolicited MSS
not returned. Founded 1972.

Gollancz – see The Orion Publishing Group Ltd

Gomer Press

Llandysul, Ceredigion SA44 4JL
tel (01559) 363090 *fax* (01559) 363758
email gwasg@gomer.co.uk

website www.gomer.co.uk
Managing Director Jonathan Lewis, *Publishing Director* Mairwen Prys Jones, *Editors* Bethan Mair, Bryan James (Adult, Welsh), Ceri Wyn Jones (Adult, English), Sioned Lleinau, Helen Evans, Rhiannon Davies (Children's, Welsh), Viv Sayer (Children's, English)

Picture books, novels, stories, poetry and teaching resources all relevant to Welsh culture. No unsolicited MSS; prelimary enquiry essential. English books for children are printed under the imprint Pont Books. Founded 1892.

Government Supplies Agency[†]
Publications Division, Office of Public Works, 51 St Stephen's Green, Dublin 2, Republic of Ireland
tel (01) 6476000 *fax* (01) 6476843

Irish government publications.

Gower – see Ashgate Publishing Ltd

Granta Publications
2–3 Hanover Yard, Noel Road, London N1 8BE
tel 020-7704 9776 *fax* 020-7354 3469
website www.granta.com
Editorial Director George Miller, *Senior Editor* Sara Holloway, *Magazine Editor* Ian Jack

Literary fiction, memoir, political non-fiction, travel, history, etc. Founded 1982.

Green Books
Foxhole, Dartington, Totnes, Devon TQ9 6EB
tel (01803) 863260 *fax* (01803) 863843
email edit@greenbooks.co.uk
website www.greenbooks.co.uk
Publisher John Elford

Environment (practical and philosophical). No fiction or children's books. No MSS; submit synopsis with covering letter, preferably by email. Founded 1987.

Alison Green Books – see Scholastic Ltd

Green Print – see Merlin Press Ltd

Greenhill Books/Lionel Leventhal Ltd
Park House, 1 Russell Gardens, London NW11 9NN
tel 020-8458 6314 *fax* 020-8905 5245
email info@greenhillbooks.com
website www.greenhillbooks.com
Managing Director Lionel Leventhal, *Deputy Managing Director* Mark Wray

Military history. Founded 1984.

Gresham Books Ltd
46 Victoria Road, Oxford OX2 7QD
tel (01865) 513582 *fax* (01865) 512718
email info@gresham-books.co.uk
website www.gresham-books.co.uk

Chief Executive Paul Lewis

Hymn books, Prayer books, Service books, school histories.

Grub Street Publishing
4 Rainham Close, London SW11 6SS
tel 020-7924 3966/738 1008 *fax* 020-7738 1009
email post@grubstreet.co.uk
website www.grubstreet.co.uk
Principals John B. Davies, Anne Dolamore

Adult non-fiction: military, aviation history, cookery, wine. Founded 1992.

Guild of Master Craftsman Publications Ltd
166 High Street, Lewes, East Sussex BN7 1XU
tel (01273) 477374 *fax* (01273) 478606
Joint Managing Directors Jennifer Phillips, Jonathan Phillips

Practical, illustrated crafts, including photography, needlecrafts, dolls' houses, woodworking and other leisure and hobby subjects. Founded 1979.

Guinness World Records
338 Euston Road, London NW1 3BD
tel 020-7891 4567 *fax* 020-7891 4501
website www.guinnessworldrecords.com

Guinness World Records, British Hit Singles, Guinness World Records TV shows. A HIT Entertainment company. Founded 1954.

Gulf Professional Press – see Elsevier Ltd

Gullane Children's Books – see Pinwheel Ltd

Hachette Children's Books*
338 Euston Road, London NW1 3BH
tel 020-7873 6000 *fax* 020-7873 6024
Managing Director Marlene Johnson

Children's non-fiction, reference, information, gift, fiction, picture, novelty and audio books. Unsolicited material is not considered other than by referral or recommendation. Formed by combining Watts Publishing with Hodder Children's Books in 2005.

Hodder Children's Books (imprint)
Publishing Director Anne McNeil
Fiction, picture books, novelty, general non-fiction and audiobooks.

Orchard Books (imprint)
Publishing Director Ann-Janine Murtagh
Fiction, picture and novelty books.

Franklin Watts (imprint)
Publishing Director Rachel Cooke
Non-fiction and information books.

Wayland (imprint)
Publishing Director Joyce Bentley
Non-fiction and information books.

Halban Publishers
22 Golden Square, London W1F 9JW
tel 020-7437 9300 *fax* 020-7437 9512
email books@halbanpublishers.com
website www.halbanpublishers.com
Directors Martine Halban, Peter Halban

General fiction and non-fiction; history and biography; Jewish subjects and Middle East. No unsolicited MSS considered; preliminary letter essential. Founded 1986.

Haldane Mason Ltd
PO Box 34196, London NW10 3YB
tel 020-8459 2131 *fax* 020-8728 1216
email info@haldanemason.com
Directors Sydney Francis, Ron Samuel

Illustrated non-fiction books and box sets, mainly for children. Imprint: Red Kite Books (children's). Founded 1995.

Robert Hale Ltd
Clerkenwell House, 45–47 Clerkenwell Green, London EC1R 0HT
tel 020-7251 2661 *fax* 020-7490 4958
email enquire@halebooks.com
website www.halebooks.com
Directors John Hale (managing & editorial), Robert Kynaston (financial)

Adult general non-fiction and fiction. Founded 1936.

Hambledon and London – see The Continuum International Publishing Group Ltd

Hamish Hamilton – see Penguin Group (UK)

Hamlyn – see Octopus Publishing Group

Harcourt Education Ltd*
Halley Court, Jordan Hill, Oxford OX2 8EJ
tel (01865) 310533 *fax* (01865) 314641
email uk.schools@harcourteducation.co.uk
website www.harcourteducation.co.uk
Chief Executive Chris Jones

Division of Reed Elsevier (UK) Ltd.

Ginn & Co. (imprint)
fax (01865) 314189
Textbook/other educational resources for primary schools.

Heinemann Educational (imprint)
website www.heinemann.co.uk
Textbooks, literature and other educational resources for all levels.

Rigby Heinemann (imprint)
fax (01865) 314189
website www.myprimary.co.u
Textbook/other educational resources for primary schools.

Patrick Hardy Books – see James Clarke & Co. Ltd

Harlequin Mills & Boon Ltd*
Eton House, 18–24 Paradise Road, Richmond, Surrey TW9 1SR
tel 020-8288 2800 *fax* 020-8388 2899
website www.millsandboon.co.uk
Directors Guy Hallowes (managing), Stuart Barber (financial & IS), Angela Meredith (production & operations), Ian Roberts (retail sales), Alison Byrne (retail marketing), Karin Stoecker (editorial), Brent Lewis (direct marketing), Jackie McGee (human resources),

Founded 1908.

Historical™ (imprint)
Senior Editor L. Fildew
Romance fiction.

Medical™ (imprint)
Senior Editor S. Hodgson
Romance fiction.

Mira Books® (imprint)
Editorial Manager Sarah Ritherdon
Women's fiction.

Modern Romance™ (imprint)
Executive Editor Tessa Shapcott
Contemporary romance fiction in paperback and hardback.

Red Dress Ink™ (imprint)
Editorial Manager Sarah Ritherdon
Contemporary women's fiction with energy and attitude.

Silhouette® (imprint)
Editorial Manager Sarah Ritherdon
Popular romantic women's fiction.

Tender Romance™ (imprint)
Associate Senior Editor Bryony Green
Contemporary romance fiction in paperback and hardback.

HarperCollins Entertainment – see HarperCollins Publishers

HarperCollins Publishers*
77–85 Fulham Palace Road, London W6 8JB
tel 020-8741 7070 *fax* 020-8307 4440
also at Westerhill Road, Bishopbriggs, Glasgow G64 2QT
tel 0141-772 3200 *fax* 0141-306 3119
website www.harpercollins.co.uk
Ceo/Publisher Victoria Barnsley

All fiction and trade non-fiction must be submitted through an agent. Unsolicited submissions should be made in the form of a typewritten synopsis. Owned by News Corporation. Founded 1819.

General Books Division
Managing Director Amanda Ridout

Harper Fiction
Publisher Lynne Drew
General, historical fiction, crime and thrillers, women's fiction.

HarperCollins (imprint)
Publishing Directors Susan Watt, Julia Wisdom

Voyager (imprint)
Publishing Director Jane Johnson
Fantasy/science fiction.

HarperEntertainment
Managing Director/Publisher Trevor Dolby

HarperCollins (imprint)
Publishing Director Ben Dunn, *Publishing Director* David Brawn (Agatha Christie, J.R.R. Tolkien, C.S. Lewis)
Media-related books from film companions to celebrity autobiographies and TV tie-ins.

HarperSport (imprint)
Publishing Director Michael Doggart
Sporting biographies, guides and histories.

HarperCollins Audio (imprint)
*Publishing Director*tba
See under *Audio publishers*.

Harper Thorsons/Element (division and imprint)
Managing Director Belinda Budge, *Publishing Directors* Wanda Whiteley (health), Carole Tonkinson (Mind, Body & Spirit), Sally Potter (media tie-ins)

HarperCollins Children's Books
website www.harpercollinschildrensbooks.co.uk
Managing Director Sally Gritten, *Publishing Directors* Gillie Russell (fiction), Sue Buswell (picture books)
Quality picture books for under 7s; fiction for age 6 up to young adult; graphic novels; TV and film tie-ins; properties.

Press Books Division
Managing Director John Bond

Fourth Estate (imprint)
Publishing Director/Publisher Nick Pearson
Fiction, literary fiction, current affairs, popular science, biography, humour, travel.

HarperPress (imprint)
Publishing Directors Arabella Pike (non-fiction), Clare Smith (fiction)

Harper Perennial (imprint)
Publishing Director Paul Baggaley
Paperback fiction and non-fiction.

Collins Division
Managing Director Thomas Webster

Collins Reference
Publishing Directors Denise Bates (illustrated reference), Martin Toseland (text reference), Sheena Barclay (world atlases), *Associate Publisher* Myles Archibald (natural history)
Guides and handbooks, Times World Atlases, phrase books and manuals on popular reference, art instruction, illustrated, cookery and wine, crafts, DIY, gardening, military, natural history, pet care, pastimes. Imprints: Collins, Collins Gem, Jane's, Times Books.

Collins Dictionaries/COBUILD (division and imprint)
Managing Director Lorna Knight, *Publishing Directors* Helen Newstead (digital development), Michela Clari (editorial), Elaine Higgleton (editorial)
Bilingual and English dictionaries, English dictionaries for foreign learners.

Collins Education (division)
Managing Director Jim Green, *Publishing Director* Paul Cherry
Books, CD-Roms and online material for UK primary and secondary schools and colleges.

Collins Maps and Road Atlases (division and imprint)
General Manager & Publisher Mike Cottingham, *Publishing Director* Helen Gordon
Maps, atlases, street plans and leisure guides.

Harrap – see Chambers Harrap Publishers Ltd

Harvill Secker Press – see Random House Group Ltd

Haus Publishing Ltd
26 Cadogan Court, Draycott Avenue, London SW3 3BX
tel 020-7584 6738 *fax* 020-7584 9501
email haus@hauspublishing.com
website www.hauspublishing.co.uk
Publisher Barbara Schwepcke, *Editorial Director* Robert Pritchard

The *Life & Times* series of illustrated biographies. Imprints: Armchair Traveller (literary travel writing), HausBooks (biography, general non-fiction). Founded 2002.

Hay House Publishers
292B Kensal Road, London W1D 5BE
tel 020-8962 1230 *fax* 020-8962 1239
email info@hayhouse.co.uk
website www.hayhouse.co.uk, www.hayhouseradio.com
Managing Director Megan Slyfield, *Publisher* Michelle Pilley

Mind, Body & Spirit, self-help, health. Head office in San Diego, California. Founded 1984; in UK 2003.

Haynes Publishing

Sparkford, Yeovil, Somerset BA22 7JJ
tel (01963) 440635 *fax* (01963) 440001
website www.haynes.co.uk
Directors J.H. Haynes (chairman), J. Haynes
(managing), D.J. Hermelin, M. Minter, M.J. Hughes,
G.R. Cook, J. Bunkum, M. Webb

Car and motorcycle service and repair manuals, car
handbooks/servicing guides; DIY books for the home;
car, motorcycle, motorsport and leisure activities.

Haynes Book Division (imprint)
email mhughes@haynes.co.uk
Editorial Director Mark Hughes

Cars, motorcycles and motorsport (including related
biographies), plus other transport; practical books on
home DIY and computing.

Haynes Motor Trade Division (imprint)
email mminter@haynes.co.uk
Editorial Director Matthew Minter

Car and motorcycle service and repair manuals and
technical data books.

Headland Publications

Editorial office Ty Coch, Galltegfa, Llanfwrog, Ruthin,
Denbighshire LL15 2AR
and 38 York Avenue, West Kirby, Wirral CH48 3JF
Director & Editor Gladys Mary Coles

Poetry, anthologies of poetry and prose. No
unsolicited MSS. Founded 1970.

Headline – see Hodder Headline Ltd

Headline Review – see Hodder Headline Ltd

Headway – see Hodder Headline Ltd

William Heinemann – see Random House Group Ltd

Heinemann Educational – see Harcourt Education Ltd

Heinemann English Language Teaching – now Macmillan Heinemann English Language Teaching

Christopher Helm – see A & C Black Publishers Ltd

The Herbert Press – see A & C Black Publishers Ltd

Hermes House – see Anness Publishing

Nick Hern Books Ltd

The Glasshouse, 49A Goldhawk Road, London
W12 8QP
tel 020-8749 4953 *fax* 020-8735 0250
email info@nickhernbooks.demon.co.uk
website www.nickhernbooks.co.uk
Publisher Nick Hern

Theatre, professionally produced plays, screenplays.
Initial letter required. Founded 1988.

Hesperus Press Ltd

4 Rickett Street, London SW6 1RU
tel 020-7610 3331 020-7610 3217
email info@hesperuspress.com
website www.hesperuspress.com

Fiction and poetry by Classical authors in English and
in translation. Founded 2001.

Hilmarton Manor Press

Calne, Wilts. SN11 8SB
tel (01249) 760208 *fax* (01249) 760379
email mailorder@hilmartonpress.co.uk
website www.hilmartonpress.co.uk
Editorial Director Charles Baile de Laperriere

Fine art, antiques, visual arts, wine, *Who's Who in
Art*. Founded 1964.

Hippo Books – see Scholastic Ltd

Hippopotamus Press

22 Whitewell Road, Frome, Somerset BA11 4EL
tel (01373) 466653 *fax* (01373) 466653
email rjhippopress@aol.com
Editors Roland John, Anna Martin

Poetry, essays, criticism. Publishes *Outposts Poetry
Quarterly*. Poetry submissions from new writers
welcome. Founded 1974.

Historical™ – see Harlequin Mills & Boon Ltd

Hobsons Publishing plc

Challenger House, 42 Adler Street, London E1 1EE
tel 020-7958 5000 *fax* 020-7958 5001
website www.hobsons.com
Managing Director Chris Letcher

Database publisher of educational and careers
information under licence to CRAC (Careers
Research and Advisory Centre). Founded 1974.

Hodder & Stoughton – see Hodder Headline Ltd

Hodder & Stoughton Educational – see Hodder Headline Ltd

Hodder Children's Books – see Hachette Children's Books

Hodder Gibson*

2A Christie Street, Paisley PA1 1NB
tel 0141-848 1609 *fax* 0141-889 6315
email hoddergibson@hodder.co.uk

website www.hoddergibson.co.uk,
www.hoddereducation.co.uk,
www.madaboutbooks.com
Managing Director John Mitchell

Educational books specifically for Scotland. No
unsolicited MSS. Formed by an amalgamation of
Robert Gibson & Sons (Glasgow) and the Scottish
branch of Hodder & Stoughton Educational. Part of
the Hodder Headline Group.

Hodder Headline Ltd*

338 Euston Road, London NW1 3BH
tel 020-7873 6000 *fax* 020-7873 6024
website www.hodderheadline.co.uk
Group Chief Executive Tim Hely Hutchinson,
Directors Martin Neild (managing, Hodder
Headline), Jamie Hodder-Williams (managing,
Hodder & Stoughton General), Malcolm Edwards
(managing, Australia & New Zealand), Philip Walters
(managing, Hodder Education), Pierre de Cacqueray
(finance), Graham Money (managing, Bookpoint),
Mary Tapissier (group personnel/training/admin)

Owned by Hachette Livre. Founded 1986.

Headline Book Publishing Ltd (division)

Managing Director Martin Neild, *Deputy Managing
Directors* Jane Morpeth (editorial fiction & non-
fiction), Kerr Macrae (sales & marketing)

Commercial and literary fiction (hardback and
paperback), and popular non-fiction including
autobiography, biography, food and wine, gardening,
history, popular science, sport, TV tie-ins. Publishes
under Headline and Headline Review.

Hodder Education (division)

Directors Philip Walters (managing), Elisabeth Tribe
(schools publishing), Katie Roden (consumer
education), Joanna Koster (health sciences), Peter
McKay (journals & reference books), Alyssum Ross
(production & design), Catherine Newman (sales &
marketing)

Textbooks for the primary, secondary, tertiary and
further education sectors and for self-improvement.
Academic and professional books and journals.
Publishes under Hodder & Stoughton Educational,
Teach Yourself, Headway.

Hodder & Stoughton General (division)

Managing Director Jamie Hodder-Williams, *Deputy
Managing Director* Lisa Highton, *Publisher* Nick
Sayers, *Non-fiction* Rowena Webb, *Sceptre* Carole
Welch, *Fiction* Carolyn Mays, *Audio* Rupert Lancaster

Commercial and literary fiction; biography,
autobiography, history, self-help, humour, Mind,
Body & Spirit, travel and other general interest non-
fiction; audio. No unsolicited MSS or synopses.
Publishes under Hodder & Stoughton, Sceptre, Lir,
Mobius.

Hodder & Stoughton Religious (division)

Managing Director Martin Mullin, *Publishing Director*
Judith Longman

Bibles, Christian books, biography/memoir, self-help,
gift, health. Publishes under New International
Version (NIV) of the Bible, Today's New
International Version (TNIV) of the Bible, New
International Reader's Version (NIrV) of the Bible,
Hodder, Hodder & Soughton.

Hodder Wayland – see Hodder Headline Ltd

Hollis Publishing Ltd

Harlequin House, 7 High Street, Teddington,
Middlesex TW11 8EL
tel 020-8977 7711 *fax* 020-8977 1133
email gary@hollis-pr.co.uk
website www.hollis-pr.co.uk
Managing Director Gary Zabel

Publications include *Hollis PR Annual*, *Hollis
Sponsorship Yearbook*, *Advertisers Annual*, *Marketing
Handbook*, Hollis Europe, *A.S.K. Hollis* (Directory of
Associations) and *SHOWCASE* (International Music
Business Guide), Hollis *Media Guide*.

Honno Ltd (Welsh Women's Press)

Honno Editorial Office, c/o Canolfan Merched y
Wawr, Vulcan Street, Aberystwyth, Ceredigion
SY23 1JB
tel (01970) 623150 *fax* (01970) 623150
email post@honno.co.uk
website www.honno.co.uk
Editor Caroline Oakley

Literature written by women in Wales or with a
Welsh connection. All subjects considered – fiction,
non-fiction, autobiographies. Honno is a community
co-operative. Founded 1986.

Hopscotch Educational Publishing Ltd

Unit 2, 56 Pickwick Road, Corsham, Wilts. SN13 9BX
tel (01249) 701701 *fax* (01249) 701987
email sales@hopscotchbooks.com
website www.hopscotchbooks.com
Editorial Director Margot O'Keeffe, *Creative Director*
Frances Mackay

National Curriculum teaching resources for primary
schools. Founded 1997.

House of Lochar*

Isle of Colonsay, Argyll PA61 7YR
tel (01951) 200232 *fax* (01951) 200232
email lochar@colonsay.org.uk
website www.houseoflochar.com
Managing Director Georgina Hobhouse, *Editorial
Director* Kevin Byrne

Scottish history, transport, Scottish literature.
Founded 1995.

How To Books Ltd

3 Newtec Place, Magdalen Road, Oxford OX4 1RE
tel (01865) 793806 *fax* (01865) 248780
email info@howtobooks.co.uk

website www.howtobooks.co.uk
Publisher & Managing Director Giles Lewis, *Editorial Director* Nikki Read

Self-help reference. Practical books that inspire. Subjects covered include small business and self-employment, business and management, career development, living and working abroad, property, lifestyle, personal transformation, study skills and student guides, creative writing. Book proposals welcome. Founded 1991.

Hugo's Language Books – see Penguin Group (UK)

John Hunt Publishing Ltd
(incorporating O-Books)
The Bothy, Deershot Lodge, Park Lane, Ropley, Hants SO24 0BE
email john.hunt@o-books.net
Director John Hunt

Children's and adult religious full-colour books for the international market. MSS welcome; send sae. Founded 1989.

O-Books (imprint)
Global spirituality and Mind, Body & Spirit.

C. Hurst & Co. (Publishers) Ltd
41 Great Russell Street, London WC1B 3PL
tel 020-7255 2201 *fax* 020-7255 2204
email hurst@atlas.co.uk
website www.hurstpub.co.uk
Directors Christopher Hurst, Michael Dwyer

Scholarly 'area studies' covering contemporary history, politics, sociology and religion of East and Southeast Europe, Middle East, Asia and Africa. Founded 1967.

Hutchinson – see Random House Group Ltd

Icon Books Ltd
The Old Dairy, Brook Road, Thriplow, Cambridge SG8 7RG
tel (01763) 208008 *fax* (01763) 208080
email info@iconbooks.co.uk
website www.iconbooks.co.uk
Directors Peter Pugh (managing), Simon Flynn (publishing)

Popular, intelligent non-fiction: *Introducing* series, literature, history, philosophy, politics, psychology, sociology, cultural studies, religion, science, current affairs, computers, women, anthropology, humour, music, cinema, linguistics, economics. Imprint: Wizard Books (children's, *Fighting Fantasy* gamebook series). Founded 1991.

ICSA Publishing Ltd
16 Park Crescent, London W1B 1AH
tel 020-7612 7020 *fax* 020-7612 7034

email icsa.pub@icsa.co.uk
website www.icsapublishing.co.uk
Joint Managing Directors Clare Grist Taylor, Susan Richards

Publishing company of the Institute of Chartered Secretaries and Administrators, specialising in information solutions for legal and regulatory compliance. Founded 1981.

The Ilex Press Ltd
The Old Candlemakers, West Street, Lewes, East Sussex BN7 2NZ
tel (01273) 487440 *fax* (01273) 487441
website www.ilex-press.com

Highly illustrated technical books on digital photography, digital art and imaging, video and audio, web design, 3D art and design. See website before submitting MS.

Imprint Academic
PO Box 200, Exeter EX5 5YX
tel (01392) 851550 *fax* (01392) 851178
email keith@imprint.co.uk
website www.imprint-academic.com
Publisher Keith Sutherland, *Managing Editor* Anthony Freeman

Books and journals in politics, philosophy and psychology for both academic and general readers. Book series include *St Andrews Studies in Philosophy and Public Affairs*. Unsolicited MSS, synopses and ideas welcome with return postage only. Founded 1980.

In Pinn – see Neil Wilson Publishing Ltd

Independent Music Press/IMP Fiction
PO Box 69, Church Stretton, Shrops. SY6 6WZ
tel/fax (01694) 720049
email info@impbooks.com
website www.impbooks.com
Music Editor Martin Roach, *Fiction Editor* Kaye Roach

Music: biography, youth culture/street style/subcultures. Fiction: general (no sci-fi, horror, chick lit or crime). No unsoliticed MSS; submissions via literary agents only. Founded 1992 (Music), 1998 (Fiction).

Infinite Ideas
36 St Giles, Oxford OX1 3LD
tel (01865) 514888 *fax* (01865) 514777
email info@infideas.com
website www.infideas.com, www.infideas.com
Joint Managing Directors David Grant, Richard Burton

Lifestyle, *52 Brilliant Ideas* series (health, fitness, relationships; leisure and lifestyle; sports, hobbies and games; careers, finance and personal development). Founded 2004.

Insight Guides/Berlitz Publishing
58 Borough High Street, London SE1 1XF
tel 020-7403 0284 *fax* 020-7403 0290
website www.insightguides.com,
www.berlitzpublishing.com
Managing Director Jeremy Westwood

Travel, language and related multimedia. Founded 1970.

Institute of Public Administration†
Vergemount Hall, Clonskeagh, Dublin 6, Republic of Ireland
tel (01) 2403600 *fax* (01) 2698644
email dmcdonagh@ipa.ie
website www.ipa.ie
Publisher Declan McDonagh

Government, economics, politics, law, public management, health, education, social policy and administrative history. Founded 1957.

Inter-Varsity Press
Norton Street, Nottingham NG7 3HR
tel 0115-978 1054 *fax* 0115-942 2694
email ivp@ivpbooks.com
website www.ivpbooks.com
Senior Project Editor E. Trotter

Theology and religion.

Irish Academic Press Ltd†
44 Northumberland Road, Ballsbridge, Dublin 4, Republic of Ireland
tel (01) 6688244 *fax* (01) 6601610
email info@iap.ie
website www.iap.ie

Scholarly books especially in 19th and 20th century history, literature, heritage and culture. Imprints: Irish University Press, Irish Academic Press. Founded 1974.

IRS/Eclipse – see LexisNexis Butterworths

The Islamic Foundation*
Markfield Conference Centre, Ratby Lane, Markfield, Leics. LE67 9SY
tel (01530) 244944 *fax* (01530) 244946
email publications@islamic-foundation.org.uk
website www.islamic-foundation.org.uk
Director General Dr Manazir Ahsan, *Executive Director* Irshad Baqui

Books on Islam for adults and children. Founded 1973.

Ithaca Press – see Garnet Publishing Ltd

JAI – see Elsevier Ltd

Jane's – see HarperCollins Publishers

Jane's Information Group
163 Brighton Road, Coulsdon, Surrey CR5 2YH
tel 020-8700 3700 *fax* 020-8763 1005
website www.janes.com
Managing Director Alfred Rolington

Professional business-to-business publishers in hardcopy and electronic multimedia of military, aviation, naval, defence, reference, police, geo-political. Consumer books in association with **HarperCollins Publishers**.

Jarrold Publishing
(incorporating Pitkin and Unichrome brands)
Whitefriars, Norwich NR3 1JR
tel (01603) 763300 *fax* (01603) 662748
Directors Margot Russell-King (managing), Ben Carter (finance), Steve Plackett (supply chain gift & stationery)

UK tourism and heritage guidebooks and souvenirs, calendars, diaries and gift stationery. Unsolicited MSS, synopses and ideas welcome but approach in writing before submitting to Marketing Department.

Jordan Publishing Ltd
21 St Thomas Street, Bristol BS1 6JS
tel 0117-923 0600 *fax* 0117-925 0486
website www.jordanpublishing.co.uk
Director of Publishing Caroline Vandridge-Ames

Law and business administration. Also specialist Family Law imprint (including the *Family Law Journal*). Books, looseleaf services, serials, CD-Roms and online.

Michael Joseph – see Penguin Group (UK)

Karnak House
157 Dudden Hill Lane, London NW10 1AU
tel 020-8830 8301
email karnakhouse@aol.com
website www.karnakhouse.co.uk
Directors Amon Saba Saakana (managing), Seheri Sujai (art)

Specialists in African/Caribbean studies worldwide: anthropology, education, Egyptology, fiction, history, language, linguistics, literary criticism, music, philosophy, prehistory. Founded 1979.

Kenilworth Press – see Quiller Publishing Ltd

Kenyon-Deane – see Cressrelles Publishing Co. Ltd

Laurence King Publishing Ltd*
(formerly Calmann & King Ltd)
71 Great Russell Street, London WC1B 3BP
tel 020-7430 8850 *fax* 020-7430 8880
email enquiries@laurenceking.co.uk
website www.laurenceking.co.uk
Directors Laurence King (managing), Nicholas Perren (chairman), Lee Ripley (publishing), Philip Cooper (editorial), Judy Rasmussen (production), John Stoddart (financial)

Illustrated books on graphic design, contemporary architecture, art, interiors and fashion for the professional, student and general market. Founded 1976.

Kingfisher Publications plc

(formerly Larousse plc)
New Penderel House, 283–288 High Holborn, London WC1V 7HZ
tel 020-7903 9999 *fax* 020-7242 4979
email sales@kingfisherpub.co.uk
website www.kingfisherpub.com
Directors Nancy Grant (managing), John Richards (deputy managing), Géraud de Durand (finance), Catherine Potter (UK sales)

Kingfisher (imprint)

Non-fiction Publishing Director Melissa Fairley, *Fiction Publishing Director* Anne Marie Ryan

Children's books. Non-fiction: activity books, encyclopedias, general history, religion, language, mathematics, nature, science and technology. Also fiction, poetry and humour, picture books, board books. No unsolicited MSS or synopses considered.

Kingscourt – see McGraw-Hill Education

Jessica Kingsley Publishers*

116 Pentonville Road, London N1 9JB
tel 020-7833 2307 *fax* 020-7837 2917
email post@jkp.com
website www.jkp.com
Managing Director Jessica Kingsley

Psychology, psychiatry, arts therapies, social work, special needs (especially autism and Asperger Syndrome), education, law, practical theology and a small children's list focusing on books for children with special needs. Founded 1987.

Klutz – see Scholastic Ltd

Kluwer Law International

Prospero House, 241 Borough High Street, London SE1 1GA
tel 020-7357 0923
website www.kluwerlaw.com
Publisher Sasha Radoja

International law.

Charles Knight – see LexisNexis Butterworths

Knight Paperbacks – see Caxton Publishing Group

Kogan Page Ltd

120 Pentonville Road, London N1 9JN
tel 020-7278 0433 *fax* 020-7837 6348
website www.kogan-page.co.uk
Managing Director Philip Kogan, *Directors* Helen Kogan (deputy MD), Pauline Goodwin (editorial),

Louise Cameron (publishing services), Gordon Watts (financial), Andrew Luck (sales)

Education, training, business and management, human resource management, transport and distribution, marketing, sales, advertising and PR, finance and accounting, directories, small business, careers and vocational, personal finance, international business. Founded 1967.

Ladybird – see Penguin Group (UK)

Lawrence & Wishart Ltd

99A Wallis Road, London E9 5LN
tel 020-8533 2506 *fax* 020-8533 7369
email lw@lwbooks.co.uk
website www.lwbooks.co.uk
Directors Sally Davison (editorial), J. Rutherford, A. Greenaway, G. Andrews

Cultural studies, current affairs, history, socialism and Marxism, political philosophy, politics, popular culture.

Letts Educational*

Chiswick Centre, 414 Chiswick High Road, London W4 5TF
tel 020-8996 3333 *fax* 020-8742 8390
email mail@lettsed.co.uk
website www.lettsed.co.uk
Directors Nigel Ward (managing), Andrew Thraves (publishing, education group), Helen Jacobs (publishing), Lee Warren (finance)

Accountancy and taxation; children's; computer science; economics; educational and textbooks; industry, business and management; mathematics and statistics; vocational training and careers; homework and revision books. Associate and subsidiary companies: Granada Learning, nferNelson, Black Cat, Granada Media, Semerc. Founded 1979.

Lewis Masonic

Riverdene Business Park, Molesey Road, Hersham, Surrey KT12 4RG
tel (01932) 266600 *fax* (01932) 266601

Masonic books; *Masonic Square Magazine*. Founded 1870.

LexisNexis Butterworths

(formerly LexisNexis UK)
Halsbury House, 35 Chancery Lane, London WC2A 1EL
tel 020-7400 2500 *fax* 020-7400 2842
email customer.services@lexisnexis.co.uk
website www.lexisnexis.co.uk

Division of Reed Elsevier (UK) Ltd. Founded 1974.

Butterworths (imprint)

Legal and tax and accountancy books, journals, looseleaf and electronic services.

Charles Knight (imprint)

Looseleaf legal works and periodicals on local government law, construction law and technical subjects.

IRS/Eclipse (imprint)
Company and employment law.

Tolley (imprint)
Law, taxation, accountancy, business.

Library Association Publishing – see Facet
Publishing

Libris Ltd
26 Lady Margaret Road, London NW5 2XL
tel 020-7482 2390
email libris@onetel.com
website www.librislondon.co.uk
Directors Nicholas Jacobs, S.A. Kitzinger

Literature, literary biography, German studies,
bilingual poetry. Founded 1986.

The Lilliput Press Ltd†
62–63 Sitric Road, Dublin 7, Republic of Ireland
tel (01) 6711647 *fax* (01) 6711233
email info@lilliputpress.ie
website www.lilliputpress.ie
Managing Director Antony T. Farrell

General and Irish literature: essays, memoir,
biography/autobiography, fiction, criticism; Irish
history; philosophy; Joyceana contemporary culture;
nature and environment. Founded 1984.

Frances Lincoln Ltd
4 Torriano Mews, Torriano Avenue, London
NW5 2RZ
tel 020-7284 4009 *fax* 020-7485 0490
email reception@frances-lincoln.com
website www.frances-lincoln.com
Directors John Nicoll (managing), Anne Fraser
(editorial, adult books), Janetta Otter-Barry
(editorial, children's books), Jon Rippon (finance),
Martin Oestreicher (sales), Andrew Dunn (rights),
Tim Rix, David Kewley, Sarah Roberts (non-
executive)

Illustrated, international co-editions: gardening,
architecture, environment, interiors, art, walking and
climbing, gift, children's books. Founded 1977.

Lion Hudson plc*
Mayfield House, 256 Banbury Road, Oxford
OX2 7DH
tel (01865) 302750 *fax* (01865) 302757
email enquiries@lionhudson.com
website www.lionhudson.com
Directors Paul Clifford (managing & editorial), Denis
Cole, Tony Wales, John O'Nions, Roy McCloughry,
Nick Jones, Stephen Price, Rodney Shepherd

Reference, paperbacks, illustrated children's books,
educational, gift books, religion and theology; all
reflecting a Christian position. Send preliminary
letter before submitting MSS. Founded 1971.

Monarch Books
email tonyc@lionhudson.com
Editorial Director Tony Collins

Christian books: biography, issues of faith and
society, humour, church resources. Submit synopsis
and 2 chapters with return postage.

Lir – see Hodder Headline Ltd

Little, Brown Book Group*
Brettenham House, Lancaster Place, London
WC2E 7EN
tel 020-7911 8000 *fax* 020-7911 8100
email uk@littlebrown.co.uk
website www.littlebrown.co.uk
Ceo & Publisher Ursula Mackenzie, *Coo* Nigel Batt,
Directors Richard Beswick (editorial), Antonia
Hodgson (editorial), Peter Cotton (design), David
Kent (group sales), Melanee Winder (export sales),
Robert Manser (deputy group sales), Roger Cazalet
(marketing), Karen Blewett (commercial), Rosalie
MacFarlane (publicity), Diane Spivey (rights)

Hardback and paperback fiction and general non-
fiction. No unsolicited MSS. Acquired by Hachette
Livre Group of Companies in 2006. Founded 1988.

Abacus (division)
Publishing Director Richard Beswick
Trade paperbacks.

Atom (division)
website www.atombooks.co.uk
Editorial Director Tim Holman, *Senior Editor* Darren
Nash
Teen fiction with a fantastical edge.

Orbit (division)
website www.orbitbooks.com
Publishing Director Tim Holman, *Senior Editor*
Darren Nash
Science fiction and fantasy.

Little, Brown (division)
Publishing Director Richard Beswick
General books: politics, biography, crime fiction,
general fiction.

Sphere (division)
website www.twbookjuice.co.uk
Publishing Director Antonia Hodgson, *Editorial
Directors* Hilary Hale, Joanne Dickinson, David
Shelley
Hardbacks and paperbacks: original fiction and non-
fiction.

Hachette Audio (division)
Editor Sarah Shrubb
CDs and cassettes.

Virago (division)
website www.virago.co.uk
Publisher Lennie Goodings
Fiction and non-fiction, including *Modern Classics*
series, biography, autobiography and general non-
fiction which highlight all aspects of women's lives.

160 Books

Little Hippo – see Scholastic Ltd

Little Tiger Press – see Magi Publications

Liverpool University Press
4 Cambridge Street, Liverpool L69 7ZU
tel 0151-794 2233 *fax* 0151-794 2235
email robblo@liv.ac.uk
website www.liverpool-unipress.co.uk
Publisher Robin Bloxsidge

Academic and scholarly books in a range of disciplines. Special interests: art history, European and American literature, science fiction criticism, all fields of history, sociology. New series established include *Liverpool Latin American Studies* and *Studies in Social and Political Thought*. Founded 1899.

Livewire – see The Women's Press

Marion Lloyd Books – see Scholastic Ltd

Logaston Press
Little Logaston, Logaston, Woonton, Almeley, Herefordshire HR3 6QH
tel (01544) 327344
email logastonp@aol.com
website www.logastonpress.co.uk
Proprietor Andy Johnson

History, social history, archaeology and guides to rural west Midlands and central and south Wales. Welcomes submission of ideas: send synopsis first. Founded 1985.

Lonely Planet Publications
72–82 Rosebery Avenue, London EC1R 4RW
tel 020-7841 9000 *fax* 020-7841 9001
email go@lonelyplanet.co.uk
website www.lonelyplanet.com
Directors Tony Wheeler, Maureen Wheeler

Country and regional guidebooks, city guides, *Best Of* citybreak guides, city maps, phrasebooks, walking guides, diving and snorkelling guides, pictorial books, healthy travel guides, food guides, cycling guides, wildlife guides, travel photography. Also a commercial slide library (Lonely Planet Images) and a TV company. London office established 1991.

Longman – see Pearson Education

Lorenz Books – see Anness Publishing

Lund Humphries – see Ashgate Publishing Ltd

Lutterworth Press – see James Clarke & Co. Ltd

McGraw-Hill Education*
McGraw-Hill House, Shoppenhangers Road, Maidenhead, Berks. SL6 2QL

tel (01628) 502500
email emea_queries@mcgraw-hill.com
website www.mcgraw-hill.co.uk
Managing Director, EMEA Paul Maraviglia, *Operations* Alan Martin, *Vice President, Market Development/Director Professional Division* Derek Stordahl, *General Manager, Higher Education* Shona Mullen

Higher education: business, economics, computing, maths, humanities, social sciences, world languages. Professional: business, medical, computing, science, technical, medical, general reference.

Kingscourt (imprint)
website www.kingscourt.co.uk
Primary and secondary education.

Open University Press (imprint)
email enquiries@openup.co.uk
website www.openup.co.uk
Social sciences.

Osborne (imprint)
Science, engineering, maths, computer science.

Macmillan Children's Books Ltd – see Macmillan Publishers Ltd

Macmillan Education Ltd – see Macmillan Publishers Ltd

Macmillan Heinemann English Language Teaching – see Macmillan Publishers Ltd

Macmillan Publishers Ltd*
The Macmillan Building, 4 Crinan Street, London N1 9XW
tel 020-7833 4000 *fax* 020-7843 4640
website www.macmillan.com
Chief Executive Richard Charkin, *Chief Operating Officer* Julian Drinkall, *Directors* G.R.U. Todd, M. Barnard, C.J. Paterson, D.J.G. Knight, D. North, Dr A. Thomas, D. Macmillan, N. Byam Shaw, G. Elliot, J. Gutbrod (Germany), S. von Holtzbrinck (Germany), R. Gibb (Australia)

Pan Macmillan (division)
20 New Wharf Road, London N1 9RR
tel 020-7014 6000 *fax* 020-7014 6001
website www.panmacmillan.com
Managing Director David North, *Publishers* Andrew Kidd (Macmillan fiction & Picador), Richard Milner (Macmillan non-fiction, Sidgwick & Jackson, Boxtree), *Publishing Manager* Alison Muirden (Macmillan Audio)

Novels, literary, crime, thrillers, romance, science fiction, fantasy and horror. Autobiography, biography, business, gift books, health and beauty, history, humour, natural history, travel, philosophy, politics, world affairs, theatre, film, gardening, cookery, popular reference. Publishes under Macmillan, Tor, Pan, Picador, Sidgwick & Jackson, Boxtree, Macmillan Audio, Macmillan New Writing. No unsolicited MSS except through Macmillan New Writing. Founded 1843.

Macmillan (imprint)
Fiction Publisher Andrew Kidd, *Non-Fiction Publisher* Richard Milner, *Publishing Directors* Maria Rejt, Jeremy Trevathan, *Editorial Directors* Imogen Taylor, Georgina Morley

Hardback commercial fiction including genre fiction, romantic, crime and thrillers. Hardback serious and general non-fiction including autobiography, biography, economics, history, military history, philosophy, politics and world affairs, popular reference titles.

Tor (imprint)
Editorial Director Peter Lavery

Science fiction, fantasy and thrillers published in hardback and paperback.

Pan (imprint)
Paperback imprint for Macmillan and Sidgwick & Jackson imprints. Founded 1947.

Picador (imprint)
Publisher Andrew Kidd, *Publishing Director* Maria Rejt, *Senior Editorial Director* Ursula Doyle

Literary international fiction, non-fiction and poetry published in hardback and paperback. Founded 1972.

Sidgwick & Jackson (imprint)
Publisher Richard Milner, *Editorial Director* Ingrid Connell

Hardback popular non-fiction including celebrity and show business to music and sport. Founded 1908.

Boxtree (imprint)
Publisher Richard Milner

Brand and media tie-in titles, including TV, film, music and internet, plus entertainment licences, pop culture, humour in hardback and paperback.

Macmillan Audio (imprint)
Publishing Manager Alison Muirden

Audio imprint for the entire Pan Macmillan list.

Macmillan New Writing (imprint)
email newwriting@macmillan.co.uk
website www.macmillannewwriting.com
Publisher Mike Barnard

Imprint designed to give an opportunity to new fiction authors to achieve publication. Send the complete novel by email as an attachment. Do not send previously published work. Only open to unpublished authors. Do not send ideas, children's or non-fiction books. Founded 2005.

Macmillan Children's Books (division)
20 New Wharf Road, London N1 9RR
tel 020-7014 6000 *fax* 020-7014 6001

website www.panmacmillan.com
Managing Director & Publisher Emma Hopkin, *Publishing Director* Sarah Davies, *Editorial Directors* Sarah Dudman (fiction), Gaby Morgan (non-fiction & poetry), Suzanne Carnell (picture books)

Fiction, non-fiction, poetry, picture books, early learning, pop-up, novelty, board books for 0–16 year-olds. Publishes under Macmillan Children's Books, Campbell Books, Young Picador.

Campbell Books (imprint)
Editorial Director Sarah Fabiny

Early learning, pop-up, novelty, board books for the preschool market.

Young Picador (imprint)
Editorial Director Sarah Dudman

Literary fiction in paperback and hardback for the young adult market.

Palgrave Macmillan (division)
Brunel Road, Houndmills, Basingstoke, Hants RG21 6XS
tel (01256) 329242 *fax* (01256) 479476
website www.palgrave.com
Managing Director Dominic Knight, *Publishing Directors* Frances Arnold (college), Sam Burridge (scholarly & reference), David Bull (journals)

Textbooks, monographs and journals in academic and professional subjects. Publishes in both hard copy and electronic formats.

Macmillan Education Ltd (division)
Macmillan Oxford, 4 Between Towns Road, Oxford OX4 3PP
tel (01865) 405700 *fax* (01865) 405701
email info@macmillan.com
website www.macmillaneducation.com
Executive Chairman Christopher Paterson, *Managing Director* Christopher Harrison, *Publishing Directors* Alison Hubert (Africa, Central & Eastern Europe, Middle East), Ian Johnstone (internet), *Publishers* David Riley (ELT), Gwyneth Fox (dictionaries), David Williamson (Asia), Kate Melliss (Iberia), Susan Jones (Latin America), Fiona McKenzie (internet)

ELT titles and school and college textbooks and materials in all subjects for the international education market in both book and electronic formats.

Made Simple Books – see Elsevier Ltd

Magi Publications
1 The Coda Centre, 189 Munster Road, London SW6 6AW
tel 020-7385 6333 *fax* 020-7385 7333
website www.littletigerpress.com
Publisher Monty Bhatia, *Editors* Jude Evans, Ellena Mann

Little Tiger Press (imprint)
email info@littletiger.co.uk
Children's picture books, novelty books, board books, pop-up books and activity books for preschool

age to 10 year-olds. Will consider new material from authors and illustrators; see website for guidelines. Founded 1987.

Magpie – see Constable & Robinson Ltd

The Maia Press Ltd
82 Forest Road, London E8 3BH
tel 020-7683 8141
website www.maiapress.com
Directors Maggie Hamand (editorial), Jane Havell (design)

Original fiction by new and established authors. No unsolicited MSS. Founded 2003.

Mainstream Publishing Co. (Edinburgh) Ltd*
7 Albany Street, Edinburgh EH1 3UG
tel 0131-557 2959 *fax* 0131-556 8720
email enquiries@mainstreampublishing.com
website www.mainstreampublishing.com
Directors Bill Campbell, Peter MacKenzie, Fiona Brownlee (marketing & rights), Sharon Atherton (publicity), Neil Graham (production), Ailsa Bathgate (editorial)

Biography, autobiography, art, sport, health, guidebooks, humour, current affairs, history, politics, true crime. Founded 1978.

Mainstream Sport (imprint)
Sport.

Management Books 2000 Ltd
Forge House, Limes Road, Kemble, Cirencester, Glos. GL7 6AD
tel (01285) 771441 *fax* (01285) 771055
email info@mb2000.com
website www.mb2000.com
Directors N. Dale-Harris, R. Hartman, *Publisher* James Alexander

Practical books for working managers and business professionals: management, business and lifeskills, and sponsored titles. Unsolicited MSS, synopses and ideas for books welcome.

Manchester University Press
Oxford Road, Manchester M13 9NR
tel 0161-275 2310 *fax* 0161-274 3346
email mup@manchester.ac.uk
website www.manchesteruniversitypress.co.uk
Chief Executive David Rodgers, *Head of Sales & Marketing* Ben Stebbing, *Head of Editorial* Matthew Frost

Works of academic scholarship: literary criticism, cultural studies, media studies, art history, design, architecture, history, politics, economics, international law, modern language texts. Textbooks and monographs. Founded 1904.

Mandrake of Oxford
PO Box 250, Oxford OX1 1AP
tel (01865) 243671

email mandrake@mandrake.uk.net
website www.mandrake.uk.net
Directors Mogg Morgan, Kim Morgan

Art, biography, classic crime studies, fiction, Indology, magic, witchcraft, philosophy, religion. Query letters only. Founded 1986.

Manson Publishing Ltd*
73 Corringham Road, London NW11 7DL
tel 020-8905 5150 *fax* 020-8201 9233
email manson@mansonpublishing.com
website www.mansonpublishing.com
Managing Director Michael Manson

Medical, scientific, veterinary. Founded 1992.

Mantra Lingua
Global House, 303 Ballards Lane, London N12 8NP
tel 020-8445 5123 *fax* 020-8446 7745
email sales@mantralingua.com
website www.mantralingua.com
Managing Director M. Chatterji

Children's multicultural picture books; multilingual friezes/posters; dual language books/cassettes; South Asian literature/teenage fiction; CD-Roms and videos. Founded 1984.

Marino Books – see The Mercier Press

Marshall Cavendish Partworks Ltd*
119 Wardour Street, London W1F 0UW
tel 020-7565 6000 *fax* 020-7734 6221
email editorial@marshallcavendish.co.uk
website www.marshallcavendish.co.uk
Managing Editor Clive Gregory

Cookery, crafts, gardening, do-it-yourself, history, children's fiction and children's interests, football and sport, general illustrated non-fiction, English language teaching. Founded 1969.

Martin Books – see Simon & Schuster UK Ltd

Kenneth Mason Publications Ltd
The Book Barn, Westbourne, Hants PO10 8RS
tel (01243) 377977 *fax* (01243) 379136
Directors Kenneth Mason (chairman), Piers Mason (managing), Michael Mason, Anthea Mason

Nautical, slimming, health, fitness; technical journals. Founded 1958.

Kevin Mayhew Ltd
Buxhall, Stowmarket, Suffolk IP14 3BW
tel (01449) 737978 *fax* (01449) 737834
email info@kevinmayhew.com
website www.kevinmayhew.com
Directors Kevin Mayhew (chairman), Kevin Whomes (production)

Christianity: prayer and spirituality, pastoral care, preaching, liturgy worship, children's, youth work, drama, instant art. Music: hymns, organ and choral, contemporary worship, piano and instrumental. Contact Manuscript Submissions Dept before sending MSS/synopses. Founded 1976.

Meadowside Children's Books

185 Fleet Street, London EC4A 2HS
tel 020-7400 1061 *fax* 020-7400 1037
email info@meadowsidebooks.com
website www.meadowsidebooks.com
Publisher Simon Rosenheim

Picture books and children's fiction. Founded 2003.

Medical™ – see Harlequin Mills & Boon Ltd

Mentor Books†

43 Furze Road, Sandyford Industrial Estate, Dublin 18, Republic of Ireland
tel (353) 1 295 2112 *fax* (353) 1 295 2114
email all@mentorbooks.ie
website www.mentorbooks.ie
Managing Director Daniel McCarthy, *Managing Editor* Claire Haugh

General: fiction, non-fiction, children's, guidebooks, biographies, history. Educational (secondary): languages, history, geography, business, maths, science. No unsolicited MSS. Founded 1980.

The Mercat Press*

10 Coates Crescent, Edinburgh EH3 7AL
tel 0131-225 5324 *fax* 0131-226 6632
email enquiries@mercatpress.com
website www.mercatpress.com
Managing Editors Seán Costello, Tom Johnstone

Mainly Scottish books of general interest. No new poetry. Founded 1970.

Crescent Books (imprint)
Fiction.

The Mercier Press†

Douglas Village, Cork, Republic of Ireland
tel (021) 4899858 *fax* (021) 4899887
email pr@mercierpress.ie
website www.mercierpress.ie
Directors J.F. Spillane (chairman), C. Feehan (managing), M.P. Feehan

Irish literature, folklore, history, politics, humour, academic, current affairs, health, mind and spirit, general non-fiction, children's. Imprint: Marino Books. Founded 1944.

Merlin Press Ltd

99ᴮ Wallis Road, London E9 5LN
tel 020-8533 5800
email info@merlinpress.co.uk
website www.merlinpress.co.uk
Managing Director Anthony Zurbrugg

Radical history and social studies. Letters/synopses only.

Green Print (imprint)
Green politics and the environment.

Merrell Publishers Ltd

81 Southwark Street, London SE1 0HX
tel 020-7928 8880 *fax* 020-7928 1199
email mail@merrellpublishers.com
website www.merrellpublishers.com
Publisher Hugh Merrell, *Editorial Director* Julian Honer, *Sales & Marketing Manager* Kim Cope

High-quality illustrated books on all aspects of visual culture, including art, architecture, photography and design, cars and motorcycles. Unsolicited proposals welcomed but must be accompanied by return postage.

Methodist Publishing House

4 John Wesley Road, Werrington, Peterborough PE4 6ZP
tel (01733) 325002 *fax* (01733) 384180
email sales@mph.org.uk
Chief Executive Martin Stone, *Commissioning Editor* Natalie K. Watson

Hymn and service books, general religious titles, church supplies. Imprints: Epworth, Inspire, Methodist Publishing House. Founded 1773.

Foundery Press (imprint)
Ecumenical titles.

Methuen Publishing Ltd

11–12 Buckingham Gate, London SW1E 6LB
tel 020-7798 1600 *fax* 020-7828 2098
website www.methuen.co.uk
Managing Director Peter Tummons, *Publishing Director* Max Eilenberg, *Sales Manager* James Stephens, *Publicity Manager* Catherine Bailey

Literary fiction and non-fiction: biography, autobiography, travel, history, sport, humour, film, performing arts, plays. No unsolicited MSS.

Politico's Publishing (imprint)
Publishing consultant Alan Gordon Walker
Politics, current affairs, political biography and autobiography.

Metro Books – see John Blake Publishing Ltd

Michelin Travel Publications

Hannay House, 39 Clarendon Road, Watford, Herts. WD17 1JA
tel (01923) 205240 *fax* (01923) 205241
website www.michelin.co.uk/travel
Commercial Director J. Lewis

Tourist guides, maps and atlases, hotel and restaurant guides.

Midland Publishing – see Ian Allan Publishing Ltd

Milestone Publications

62 Murray Road, Horndean, Waterlooville PO8 9JL
tel (023) 9259 7440 fax (023) 9259 1975
email info@gosschinaclub.co.uk
website www.gosschinaclub.co.uk
Managing Director Lynda J. Pine

Goss & Crested heraldic china, antique porcelain.
Publishing and bookselling division of Goss &
Crested China Club. Founded 1967.

Miller's – see Octopus Publishing Group

Mills & Boon® – see Harlequin Mills & Boon Ltd

Milo Books Ltd

The Old Weighbridge, Station Road, Wrea Green,
Preston PR4 2PH
tel (01772) 672900 fax (01772) 687727
email info@milobooks.com
Publisher Peter Walsh

True crime, sport, autobiography/biography, current
affairs. Founded 1997.

Mira Books® – see Harlequin Mills & Boon Ltd

Mitchell Beazley – see Octopus Publishing Group

Mobius – see Hodder Headline Ltd

Modern Romance™ – see Harlequin Mills & Boon Ltd

Monarch Books – see Lion Hudson plc

Morehouse – see The Continuum International Publishing Group Ltd

Morgan Kauffman – see Elsevier Ltd

Morrigan Book Company

Killala, Co. Mayo, Republic of Ireland
tel (096) 32555
email morriganbooks@gmail.com
Publisher Gerry Kennedy, Administrator Hilary
Kennedy, Irish Language Editor Judy-Meg Ní
Chinneide

Non-fiction: general Irish interest, biography, history,
local history, folklore and mythology. Publishers to
State and public bodies including Foras na Gaeilge,
Údarás na Gaeltachta and the Dublin Cemeteries
Committee. Founded 1979.

Mosby – see Elsevier Ltd (Health Sciences)

Mount Eagle Publications Ltd – see Brandon/Mount Eagle Publications

MQ Publications Ltd

12 The Ivories, 6–8 Northampton Street, London
N1 2HY
tel 020-7359 2244 fax 020-7359 1616
email mail@mqpublications.com
website www.mqpublications.com
Ceo Zaro Weil

Lifestyle, Mind, Body & Spirit, inspirational,
photography, cookery, popular culture, biography,
gift books. Founded 1993.

Murdoch Books UK Ltd

Erico House, 6th Floor North, 93–99 Upper
Richmond Road, London SW15 2TG
tel 020-8785 5995 fax 020-8785 5985
Managing Director Tim Whale, Publisher Kay Scarlett

Non-fiction: homes and interiors, gardening,
cookery, craft, DIY, narrative non-fiction. Owned by
Murdoch Books Pty Ltd.

John Murray (Publishers) Ltd*

338 Euston Road, London NW1 3BH
tel 020-7873 6000 fax 020-7873 6446
Managing Director Roland Philipps, Non-fiction
Eleanor Birne, Fiction Anya Serota, Kate Parkin

General: biography and autobiography, letters and
diaries, travel, exploration, general history, fiction.
No unsolicited MSS without preliminary letter.
Founded 1768; acquired by Hodder Headline Ltd
2002.

Myriad Editions

6–7 Old Steine, Brighton BN1 1EJ
tel (01273) 606700 fax (01273) 606708
email info@myriadeditions.com
website www.MyriadEditions.com
Directors Candida Lacey (managing), Bob Benewick,
Judith Mackay

State of the World atlases, literary fiction and non-
fiction. Founded 1993.

National Trust – see Anova Books

National Trust Books

c/o Anova Books, 151 Freston Road, London W10
6TH
tel 020-7314 1400 fax 020-7314 1594
email sales@anovabooks.com
website www.anovabooks.com
Publisher Tim Persaud

History, cookery, architecture, gardening and
heritage. No unsolicited MSS. Founded 1895.

Natural History Museum Publishing

Cromwell Road, London SW7 5BD
tel 020-7942 5336 fax 020-7942 5010
email publishing@nhm.ac.uk
website www.nhm.ac.uk/publishing

Natural sciences, entomology, botany, geology,
mineralogy, palaeontology, zoology, history of
natural history. Founded 1881.

Nautical Data Ltd
The Book Barn, Westbourne, Hants PO10 8RS
tel (01243) 389352 *fax* (01243) 379136
Directors Piers Mason, Michael Benson-Colpi

Yachting titles.

NCVO Publications
(incorporating Bedford Square Press)
Regent's Wharf, 8 All Saints Street, London N1 9RL
tel 020-7713 6161 *fax* 020-7713 6300
email ncvo@ncvo-vol.org.uk
website www.ncvo-vol.org.uk
Head of Publications Bo Priestly

Imprint of the National Council for Voluntary
Organisations. Practical guides, reference books,
directories and policy studies on voluntary sector
concerns including management, employment,
trustee development and finance. No unsolicited MSS
accepted.

Neate Publishing
33 Downside Road, Winchester SO22 5LT
tel (01962) 841479 *fax* (01962) 841743
email sales@neatepublishing.co.uk
website www.neatepublishing.co.uk
Directors Bobbie Neate (managing), Ann Langran,
Maggie Threadingham

Non-fiction books, educational packs, CDs and
posters for primary schoolchildren. Founded 1999.

Thomas Nelson Ltd – see Nelson Thornes Ltd

Nelson Thornes Ltd*
Delta Place, 27 Bath Road, Cheltenham, Glos.
GL53 7TH
tel (01242) 267100 *fax* (01242) 221914
email name@nelsonthornes.com
website www.nelsonthornes.com
Managing Director Mary O'Connor

Print and electronic publishers for the educational
market: primary, secondary, further education,
professional. Part of the Wolters Kluwer Group of
Companies.

New Beacon Books
76 Stroud Green Road, London N4 3EN
tel 020-7272 4889 *fax* 020-7281 4662
email newbeaconbooks@btconnect.com
Directors Sarah White, Michael La Rose, Janice
Durham

Small specialist publishers: general non-fiction,
fiction, poetry, critical writings, concerning the
Caribbean, Africa, African–America and Black
Britain. No unsolicited MSS. Founded 1966.

New Cavendish Books
3 Denbigh Road, London W11 2SJ
tel 020-7229 6765 *fax* 020-7792 0027

email sales@newcavendishbooks.co.uk
website www.newcavendishbooks.co.uk
Specialist books for the collector; art reference, Thai
guidebooks. Founded 1973.

River Books (associate imprint)
The art and architecture of Southeast Asia.

New Holland Publishers (UK) Ltd
Garfield House, 86–88 Edgware Road, London
W2 2EA
tel 020-7724 7773 *fax* 020-7258 1293
email postmaster@nhpub.co.uk
website www.newhollandpublishers.com
Managing Director John Beaufoy

Illustrated non-fiction books on natural history,
sports and hobbies, animals and pets, travel pictorial,
travel maps and guides, reference, gardening, health
and fitness, practical art, DIY, food and drink,
outdoor pursuits, craft, humour, gift books. New
proposals accepted (send CV and synopsis and
sample chapters in first instance; sae essential).

New Island Books[†]
2 Brookside, Dundrum Road, Dundrum, Dublin 14,
Republic of Ireland
tel (01) 2986867/2989937 *fax* (01) 2982783
email thomas.cooney@newisland.ie
Directors Edwin Higel (managing), Fergal Stanley

Fiction, poetry, drama, humour, biography, current
affairs. Founded 1992.

New Playwrights' Network
10 Station Road Industrial Estate, Colwall,
Nr Malvern, Herefordshire WR13 6RN
tel (01684) 540154 *fax* (01684) 540154
email simonsmith@cressrelles4drama.fsbusiness.co.uk
Publishing Director Leslie Smith

General plays for the amateur, one-act and full
length.

New Rider – see Pearson Education

New Theatre Publications/The Playwrights' Co-operative
2 Hereford Close, Woolston, Warrington, Cheshire
WA1 4HR
tel (0845) 331 3513
email info@plays4theatre.com
website www.plays4theatre.com
Directors Ian Hornby, Alison Warburton

Plays for the professional and amateur stage.
Submissions encouraged. Founded 1987.

Newnes – see Elsevier Ltd

Nexus – see Virgin Books Ltd

nferNelson Publishing Co. Ltd*
The Chiswick Centre, 414 Chiswick High Road,
London W4 5TF

tel (0845) 602 1937 *fax* 020-8996 3660
email information@nfer-nelson.co.uk
website www.nfer-nelson.co.uk
Managing Director Nigel Ward

Testing and assessment services for education and health care, including literacy, numeracy, thinking skills, ability, learning support and online testing. Founded 1981.

Nia – see The X Press

Nielsen BookData*
Editorial office 89–95 Queensway, Stevenage, Herts. SG1 1EA
tel (0845) 450 0016 *fax* (01438) 745578
website www.nielsenbookdata.co.uk
Editorial Director Michael Healy

Jointly publishes the *Directory of UK & Irish Book Publishers* with the Booksellers Association. See also page 658.

Nightingale Press
6 The Old Dairy, Melcombe Road, Bath BA2 3LR
tel (01225) 478444 *fax* (01225) 478440
email sales@manning-partnership.co.uk
website www.manning-partnership.co.uk
Directors Garry Manning (managing), Roger Hibbert (sales)

Humour, gift, health, language and learning, lifestyle and relationships. Owned by the Manning Partnership Ltd. Founded 1997.

James Nisbet & Co. Ltd
Pirton Court, Hitchin, Herts. SG5 3QA
tel (01462) 713444 *fax* (01462) 713444
Directors Miss E.M. Mackenzie-Wood, Mrs A.A.C. Bierrum

Business management. Founded 1810.

North-Holland – see Elsevier Ltd

Northcote House Publishers Ltd
Horndon House, Horndon, Tavistock, Devon PL19 9NQ
tel (01822) 810066 *fax* (01822) 810034
email northcote.house@virgin.net
website www.northcotehouse.co.uk
Directors B.R.W. Hulme, A.V. Hulme (secretary)

Education and education management, educational dance and drama, literary criticism (*Writers and their Work*). Founded 1985.

W.W. Norton & Company
Castle House, 75–76 Wells Street, London W1T 3QT
tel 020-7323 1579 *fax* 020-7436 4553
website www.wwnorton.com
Managing Director Alan Cameron

English and American literature, economics, music, psychology, science. Founded 1980.

NWP – see Neil Wilson Publishing Ltd

O-Books – see John Hunt Publishing Ltd

Oak Tree Press†
19 Rutland Street, Cork, Republic of Ireland
tel (021) 431 3855 *fax* (021) 431 3496
email info@oaktreepress.com
website www.oaktreepress.com
Directors Brian O'Kane, Rita O'Kane

Business management, enterprise, accountancy and finance, law. Special emphasis on titles for small business owner/managers. Founded 1991.

Oberon Books
521 Caledonian Road, London N7 9RH
tel 020-7607 3637 *fax* 020-7607 3629
email info@oberonbooks.com
website www.oberonbooks.com
Managing Director Charles Glanville, *Publisher* James Hogan, *Editor* Dan Steward

New and classic play texts, programme texts and general theatre and performing arts books. Founded 1986.

The O'Brien Press Ltd†
20 Victoria Road, Rathgar, Dublin 6, Republic of Ireland
tel (01) 492 3333 *fax* (01) 492 2777
email books@obrien.ie
website www.obrien.ie
Directors Michael O'Brien, Ide ní Laoghaire, Ivan O'Brien

Adult: biography, politics, local history, true crime, sport, humour, reference. Children's: fiction for all ages; illustrated fiction series – *Solos* (age 3+), *Pandas* (age 5+), *Flyers* (age 6+) and *Red Flag* (8+); substantial novels (10+) – contemporary, historical, fantasy. No poetry, adult fiction or academic. Unsolicited MSS (sample chapters only), synopses and ideas for books welcome – submissions will not be returned. Founded 1974.

The Octagon Press Ltd
78 York Street, London W1H 1DP
tel/fax 020-7168 5308
email admin@octagonpress.com
website www.octagonpress.com
Managing Director George R. Schrager

Travel, biography, literature, folklore, psychology, philosophy, with the focus on East–West studies. Welcomes single page book proposals via email. Unsolicited MSS not accepted. Founded 1960.

Octopus Publishing Group
2–4 Heron Quays, London E14 4JP
tel 020-7531 8400 *fax* 020-7531 8650
email firstname.lastname@octopus-publishing.co.uk
website www.octopus-publishing.co.uk

Chief Executive Alison Goff, *Executive Director* Henri Masurel

Bounty (imprint)
tel 020-7531 8601 *fax* 020-7531 8607
email bountybooksinfo-bp@bountybooks.co.uk
Publishing & International Sales Director Polly Manguel

Promotional publishing, adult books.

Cassell Illustrated (imprint)
tel 020-7531 8400 *fax* 020-7531 8650
email info-ci@cassell-illustrated.co.uk
website www.cassell-illustrated.co.uk
Publisher Iain MacGregor

Illustrated books for the international market specialising in gardening, history and heritage, health and humour.

Conran Octopus (imprint)
tel 020-7531 8628 *fax* 020-7531 8627
email info-co@conran-octopus.co.uk
website www.conran-octopus.co.uk
Publishing Director Lorraine Dickey

Quality illustrated books, particularly lifestyle, cookery, gardening.

Gaia Books (imprint)
email enquiries@gaiabooks.com
website www.gaiabooks.com
Publisher Jane Birch

Illustrated reference books on ecology, natural living, health and the mind.

Godsfield Press (imprint)
email enquiries@godsfieldpress.com
website www.godsfieldpress.com
Publisher Jane Birch

Highly illustrated books for adults in the area of Mind, Body & Spirit with an emphasis on practical application and personal spiritual awareness.

Hamlyn (imprint)
tel 020-7531 8573 *fax* 020-7537 0514
email info-ho@hamlyn.co.uk
website www.hamlyn.co.uk
Publisher Jane Birch

Popular illustrated non-fiction, particularly cookery, health and parenting, home and garden, sport and reference.

Miller's (imprint)
The Cellars, High Street, Tenterden, Kent TN30 6BN
tel (01580) 766411 *fax* (01580) 766100
email firstname.lastname@millers.uk.com
Publisher David Lamb

Quality illustrated books on antiques and collectables.

Mitchell Beazley (imprint)
tel 020-7531 8400 *fax* 020-7531 8650
email info-mb@mitchell-beazley.co.uk

website www.mitchell-beazley.co.uk
Publisher David Lamb

Quality illustrated books, particularly antiques, gardening, craft and interiors, wine.

Philip's (imprint)
tel 020-7531 8459 *fax* 020-7531 8460
email george.philip@philips-maps.co.uk
website www.philips-maps.co.uk
Publisher/Managing Director John Gaisford

Atlases, maps, astronomy, encyclopedias, globes.

Oldcastle Books Ltd
PO Box 394, Harpenden, Herts. AL5 1XJ
tel (01582) 761264 *fax* (01582) 761264
website www.noexit.co.uk, www.pocketessentials.com, www.highstakes.com
Director Ion Mills

Imprints: No Exit Press (crime fiction), High Stakes (gambling), Pocket Essentials (reference guides). Founded 1985.

The Oleander Press
16 Orchard Street, Cambridge CB1 1JT
tel (01223) 357768
website www.oleanderpress.com
Managing Director Dr Jane Doyle

Travel, language, literature, Libya, Arabia and Middle East, Cambridgeshire, history, humour, reference, classics. MSS welcome with sae for reply. Founded 1960.

Michael O'Mara Books Ltd
9 Lion Yard, Tremadoc Road, London SW4 7NQ
tel 020-7720 8643 *fax* 020-7627 8953
website www.mombooks.com
Chairman Michael O'Mara, *Managing Director* Lesley O'Mara, *Commissioning Editorial Director* Lindsay Davies, *Editorial Director* Toby Buchan

General non-fiction: biography, humour, history. Imprint: Buster Books (novelty and picture books for young children). Founded 1985.

Omnibus Press/Music Sales Ltd
8–9 Frith Street, London W1D 3JB
tel 020-7434 0066 *fax* 020-7734 9718
email music@musicsales.co.uk
Chief Editor Chris Charlesworth

Rock music biographies, books about music. Founded 1976.

On Stream Publications Ltd
Currabaha, Cloghroe, Blarney, Co. Cork, Republic of Ireland
tel (353) 214385
email info@onstream.ie
website www.onstream.ie
Owner Rosalind Crowley

Cookery, wine, travel, human interest non-fiction, local history, academic and practical books. Founded 1986.

Oneworld Publications

185 Banbury Road, Oxford OX2 7AR
tel (01865) 310597 *fax* (01865) 310598
email info@oneworld-publications.com
website www.oneworld-publications.com
Directors Juliet Mabey (publisher), Novin Doostdar
(publisher)

Religion, world religions, inter-religious dialogue,
Islamic studies, philosophy, history, psychology, self-
help, popular science. Founded 1986.

Onlywomen Press Ltd

40 St Lawrence Terrace, London W10 5ST
tel 020-8354 0796 *fax* 020-8960 2817
email onlywomenpress@btconnect.com
website www.onlywomenpress.com
Managing Director Lilian Mohin

Lesbian feminist: theory, fiction, poetry, crime fiction
and cultural criticism. Founded 1974.

Open Gate Press*

(incorporating Centaur Press, founded 1954)
51 Achilles Road, London NW6 1DZ
tel 020-7431 4391 *fax* 020-7431 5129
email books@opengatepress.co.uk
website www.opengatepress.co.uk
Directors Jeannie Cohen, Elisabeth Petersdorff,
Sandra Lovell

Psychoanalysis, philosophy, social sciences, religion,
animal welfare, the environment. Founded 1988.

Open University Press – see McGraw-Hill
Education

Orbit – see Little, Brown Book Group

Orchard Books – see Hachette Children's
Books

The Orion Publishing Group Ltd*

Orion House, 5 Upper St Martin's Lane, London
WC2H 9EA
tel 020-7240 3444 *fax* 020-7240 4822
website www.orionbooks.co.uk
Directors Arnaud Nourry (chairman), Peter Roche
(chief executive), Malcolm Edwards (deputy chief
executive)

No unsolicited MSS; approach in writing in first
instance. Founded 1992.

Orion Paperbacks (division)
Managing Director Susan Lamb
Mass market fiction and non-fiction under
Everyman, **Orion** and **Phoenix** imprints.

Orion Trade (division)
Directors Malcolm Edwards (managing), John Wood
(publishing)
Hardcover fiction (popular fiction in all categories),
non-fiction and audio.

Gollancz (imprint)
Contact Simon Spanton, Jo Fletcher
Science fiction and fantasy.

Orion Children's Books (division)
Publisher Fiona Kennedy
Fiction for younger and older readers, picture books.

Weidenfeld & Nicolson
See page 186.

Osborne – see McGraw-Hill Education

Osprey Publishing Ltd

Midland House, West Way, Botley, Oxford OX2 0PH
tel (01865) 727022 *fax* (01865) 727017
email info@ospreypublishing.com
website www.ospreypublishing.com
Directors William Shepherd (managing), Sarah Lough
(finance), Rebecca Smart (operations), Joanna
Sharland (sales), Richard Sullivan (marketing), Doug
France (US sales & marketing)

Illustrated history of war and warfare, and military
aviation. Founded 1969.

Peter Owen Publishers

73 Kenway Road, London SW5 0RE
tel 020-7373 5628/370 6093 *fax* 020-7373 6760
email admin@peterowen.com
website www.peterowen.com
Directors Peter L. Owen (managing), Antonia Owen
(editorial)

Art, belles lettres, biography and memoir, literary
fiction, general non-fiction, history, theatre and
entertainment. No highly illustrated books. Do not
send fiction without first speaking to the Editorial
Dept unless it is by an established novelist. No mass-
market genre fiction, short stories or poetry; first
novels only rarely published.

Oxford Publishing Company – see Ian
Allan Publishing Ltd

Oxford University Press*

Great Clarendon Street, Oxford OX2 6DP
tel (01865) 556767 *fax* (01865) 556646
email enquiry@oup.com
website www.oup.com
Ceo Henry Reece, *Group Finance Director* Roger
Boning, *Academic Division Managing Director* Tim
Barton, *UK Children's & Educational Division
Managing Director* Kate Harris, *ELT Division
Managing Director* Peter Marshall, *Publishing Director
Journals* Martin Richardson, *UK Human Resources
Director* John Williams, *Sales Directors* Phil Garratt,
Alastair Lewis

Anthropology, archaeology, architecture, art, belles-
lettres, bibles, bibliography, children's books (fiction,
non-fiction, picture), commerce, current affairs,
dictionaries, drama, economics, educational (infants,

primary, secondary, technical, university),
encyclopedias, English language teaching, electronic
publishing, essays, foreign language learning, general
history, hymn and service books, journals, law, maps
and atlases, medical, music, oriental, philosophy,
political economy, prayer books, reference, science,
sociology, theology and religion; educational
software; *Grove Dictionaries of Music & Art*. Trade
paperbacks published under the imprint of Oxford
Paperbacks. Founded 1478.

Palgrave Macmillan – see Macmillan Publishers Ltd

Pan – see Macmillan Publishers Ltd

Pan Macmillan – see Macmillan Publishers Ltd

Pandora Press – see Rivers Oram Press

Paper Tiger – see Anova Books

Parthenon Press – see Taylor and Francis Books Ltd

Pavilion – see Anova Books

Pavilion Publishing (Brighton) Ltd
Richmond House, Richmond Road, Brighton BN2
3RL
tel (01273) 623222 *fax* (01273) 625526
email info@pavpub.com
website www.pavpub.com
Directors Chris Parker, Julie Gibson, Loretta Harrison

Health and social care training resources in a variety
of fields including learning disability, mental health,
community care management, older people, looked-
after young people, community justice, drugs,
supported housing. Founded 1987.

Peachpit Press – see Pearson Education

Pearson Education*
Edinburgh Gate, Harlow, Essex CM20 2JE
tel (01279) 623623 *fax* (01279) 414130
email firstname.lastname@pearsoned-ema.com
website www.pearsoned.co.uk
President, Pearson Education Ltd Rod Bristow

Materials for school pupils, students and practitioners
globally.

Addison-Wesley (imprint)
Technical.

Allyn & Bacon (imprint)
Higher education, humanities, social sciences.

Cisco Press (imprint)
Cisco-systems authorised publisher. Material for
networking students and professionals.

Benjamin Cummings (imprint)
Higher education, science.

FT Prentice Hall (imprint)
Business for higher education and professional.

Longman (imprint)
Education for higher education, schools, ELT.

New Rider (imprint)
Graphics and design.

Peachpit Press (imprint)
Internet and general computing.

Penguin Longman (imprint)
English language teaching.

QUE Publishing (imprint)
Computing.

SAMS Publishing (imprint)
Professional computing.

York Notes (imprint)
Literature guides for students.

Pen & Sword Books Ltd
47 Church Street, Barnsley, South Yorkshire S70 2AS
tel (01226) 734222 *fax* (01226) 734438
email enquiries@pen-and-sword.co.uk
website www.pen-and-sword.co.uk
Managing Director Charles Hewitt, *Publishing
Manager* Henry Wilson, *Commissioning Editors* Peter
Coles, Rupert Harding

Military history, aviation history, naval and maritime,
general history, local history. Imprints: Leo Cooper,
Pen & Sword Military Classics, Pen & Sword
Aviation, Pen & Sword Naval & Maritime.

Wharncliffe* (imprint)
Local history.

Penguin Group (UK)*
80 Strand, London WC2R 0RL
tel 020-7010 3000 *fax* 020-7010 6060
website www.penguin.co.uk
Ceo John Makinson, *Managing Directors* Helen Fraser
(Penguin), Gary June (Dorling Kindersley)

Owned by Pearson plc.

Penguin General Books (division)
Managing Directors Tom Weldon (Penguin General
Division), Louise Moore (Michael Joseph), *Publishing
Directors* Tony Lacey (Penguin), Juliet Annan (Fig
Tree/Penguin), Simon Prosser (Hamish Hamilton/
Penguin), Venetia Butterfield (Viking/Penguin),
Rowland White (Michael Joseph/Penguin)
No unsolicited MSS or synopses.

Hamish Hamilton (imprint)
Fiction, belles-lettres, biography and memoirs,
current affairs, history, literature, politics, travel. No
unsolicited MSS or synopses.

Michael Joseph (imprint)
Biography and memoirs, current affairs, fiction, history, humour, travel, health, spirituality and relationships, sports, general leisure, illustrated books. No unsolicited MSS or synopses.

Penguin (imprint)
Adult paperback books – wide range of fiction, non-fiction, TV and film tie-ins. No unsolicited MSS or synopses.

Viking (imprint)
Fiction and general non-fiction for adults. Founded 1925.

Penguin Ireland (imprint)
25 St Stephen's Green, Dublin 2, Republic of Ireland
tel (01) 661 7695 *fax* (01) 661 7696
email www.penguin.ie
website info@penguin.ie
Managing Director Michael McLoughlin, *Senior Editor* Patricia Deevy, *Editor* Brendan Barrington
Fiction and non-fiction, mainly of Irish origin, but published to travel beyond the Irish market. No unsolicited MSS.

Penguin Press (division)
Managing Director Stefan McGrath, *Publishing Directors* Stuart Proffitt (Allen Lane), Simon Winder (Allen Lane), Adam Freudenheim (Penguin Classics)
Serious adult non-fiction, reference, specialist and classics. Imprint: Allen Lane. Series: Penguin Classics, Penguin Modern Classics. No unsolicited MSS or synopses.

Puffin (division)
Managing Director Francesca Dow, *Publishing Directors* Rebecca McNally (fiction), Mandy Suhr (picture books)
Children's paperback and hardback books: wide range of picture books, board books and novelties; fiction; non-fiction and popular culture. No unsolicited MSS or synopses.

Warne (division)
website www.funwithspot.com,
www.flowerfairies.com, www.peterrabbit.com
Managing Director Sally Floyer, *Publishing Director* Stephanie Barton
Specialises in preschool illustrated developmental books for 0–6, non-fiction 0–8; licensed brands; children's classic publishing and merchandising properties. No unsolicited MSS.

Ladybird (division)
website www.ladybird.co.uk
Managing Director Sally Floyer

Dorling Kindersley (division)
Managing Director Gary Dune, *Publisher* Christopher Davis, *Adult Publisher* John Roberts, *Children's Publisher* Miriam Farbey

Illustrated non-fiction for adults and children: gardening, medical, travel, food and drink, Mind, Body & Spirit, history, reference, pregnancy and childcare, antiques. Age groups: preschool, 5–8, 8+.

Hugo's Language Books (imprint)
Hugo's language books and courses.

Penguin Travel (division)
Managing Director John Duhigg

Rough Guides (imprint)
email mail@roughguides.com
website www.roughguides.com
Managing Director Kevin Fitzgerald, *Publishing Director* Martin Dunford, *Publishing Development Officer* Mark Ellingham
Trade paperbacks, travel guides, phrasebooks, music reference, music CDs and internet reference. Founded 1982.

DK Travel
Publishing Director Douglas Amrine

BBC Children's Books (division)
Managing Director Sally Floyer, *Editorial Director* Catherine Johnson

Penguin Longman – see Pearson Education

Pergamon – see Elsevier Ltd

Persephone Books
59 Lamb's Conduit Street, London WC1N 3NB
tel 020-7242 9292 *fax* 020 7242 9272
email sales@persephonebooks.co.uk
website www.persephonebooks.co.uk
Managing Director Nicola Beauman

Reprints of forgotten classics by 20th century women writers with prefaces by contemporary writers. Founded 1999.

Peterloo Poets
The Old Chapel, Sand Lane, Calstock, Cornwall PL18 9QX
tel (01822) 833473 *fax* (01822) 833989
email info@peterloopoets.com
website www.peterloopoets.com
Publishing Director Harry Chambers, *Trustees* Brian Perman, Hannah Elliott, Rose Taw, *Honorary President* Michael Longley

Poetry. Founded 1976.

Phaidon Press Ltd
Regent's Wharf, All Saints Street, London N1 9PA
tel 020-7843 1000 *fax* 020-7843 1010
email enquiries@phaidon.cometro
website www.phaidon.com
Publisher Richard Schlagman, *Chairman* Andrew Price, *Directors* Christopher North (managing), Amanda Renshaw (deputy publisher), Frances Johnson, James Booth-Clibborn, Karen Stein

Quality books on the visual arts, including fine art and art history, architecture, design, decorative arts, photography, music, fashion, film.

Philip's – see Octopus Publishing Group

Phillimore & Co. Ltd

(incorporating Darwen Finlayson Ltd)
Shopwyke Manor Barn, Chichester, West Sussex
PO20 2BG
tel (01243) 787636 *fax* (01243) 787639
email bookshop@phillimore.co.uk
website www.phillimore.co.uk
Directors Noel Osborne (managing), Hilary Clifford Brown (marketing), Nicola Willmot (production)

Local and family history; architectural history, archaeology, genealogy and heraldry; also *Darwen County History* and *History from the Sources* series. Founded 1897.

Phoenix – see The Orion Publishing Group Ltd

Piatkus Books

5 Windmill Street, London W1T 2JA
tel 020-7631 0710 *fax* 020-7436 7137
email info@piatkus.co.uk
website www.piatkus.co.uk
Directors Judy Piatkus (managing, Philip Cotterell (deputy managing), Gill Bailey (non-fiction editorial), Gillian Green (fiction editorial), Simon Colverson (production), Diane Hill (UK sales), Preeya Modessa (financial)

Portrait (imprint)

Biography, history, memoirs, sport, popular culture, music, humour.

Piatkus (imprint)

Fiction, self-help, health, Mind, Body & Spirit, pop psychology, business, parenting and childcare.

Pica Press – see A & C Black Publishers Ltd

Picador – see Macmillan Publishers Ltd

Piccadilly Press

5 Castle Road, London NW1 8PR
tel 020-7267 4492 *fax* 020-7267 4493
email books@piccadillypress.co.uk
website www.piccadillypress.co.uk
Managing Director & Publisher Brenda Gardner

Early picture books, parental advice trade paperbacks, trade paperback teenage non-fiction and humorous teenage fiction. Founded 1983.

Pimlico – see Random House Group Ltd

Pinwheel Ltd

Winchester House, 259–269 Old Marylebone Road, London NW1 5XJ
tel 020-7616 7200 *fax* 020-7616 7201
email sales@pinwheel.co.uk
website www.pinwheel.co.uk
Managing Director Andrew Flatt

Children's non-fiction, picture books and novelty titles. Unsolicited MSS will not be returned.

Andromeda Children's Books (imprint)

Publishing/Creative Director Linda Cole
Illustrated non-fiction for children aged 3–12 years.

Gullane Children's Books (imprint)

Creative Director Paula Burgess
Picture books for children aged 0–8 years.

Pinwheel Children's Books (imprint)

Publishing/Creative Director Linda Cole
Cloth and novelty books for children aged 0–5 years.

Pipers' Ash Ltd

Pipers' Ash, Church Road, Christian Malford, Chippenham, Wilts. SN15 4BW
tel (01249) 720563 *fax* (0870) 0568916
email pipersash@supamasu.com
website www.supamasu.com
Editorial Director Alfred Tyson

Poetry, contemporary short stories, science fiction stories; short novels, biographies, plays, philosophy, translations, children's, general non-fiction. New authors with talent and potential encouraged. Founded 1976.

The Playwrights Publishing Company

70 Nottingham Road, Burton Joyce, Notts.
NG14 5AL
tel 0115-931 3356
email playwrightspublishingco@yahoo.com
website www.geocities.com/playwrightspublishingco
Proprietor Liz Breeze, *Consultant* Tony Breeze

One-act and full-length drama published first on the internet and if popular, later in hard copy: serious work and comedies, for mixed cast, all women or schools. Reading fee unless professionally produced; sae required. Founded 1990.

Plexus Publishing Ltd

25 Mallinson Road, London SW11 1BW
tel 020-7924 4662 *fax* 020-7924 5096
email plexus@plexusuk.demon.co.uk
website www.plexusbooks.com
Directors Terence Porter (managing), Sandra Wake (editorial)

Film, music, biography, popular culture, fashion. Imprint: Eel Pie. Founded 1973.

Pluto Press

345 Archway Road, London N6 5AA
tel 020-8348 2724 *fax* 020-8348 9133
email pluto@plutobooks.com
website www.plutobooks.com

Chairman Roger van Zwanenberg, *Managing Director* Anne Beech, *Sales Director* Simon Liebesny, *Head of Marketing* Melanie Patrick

Politics, anthropology, development, media, cultural, economics, history, Irish studies, Black studies, Islamic studies, Middle East, international relations.

Pocket Books – see Simon & Schuster UK Ltd

Point – see Scholastic Ltd

The Policy Press
University of Bristol, 4th Floor, Beacon House, Queen's Road, Bristol BS8 1QU
tel 0117-331 4054 *fax* 0117-331 4093
email tpp-info@bristol.ac.uk
website www.policypress.org.uk
Director Alison Shaw, *Assistant Director* Julia Mortimer

Social science publisher, specialising in social and public policy, social work and social welfare. Founded 1996.

Policy Studies Institute (PSI)
50 Hanson Street, London W1W 6UP
tel 020-7468 0468 *fax* 020-7388 0914
email website@psi.org.uk

Economic, cultural, social and environmental policy, political institutions, social sciences.

Politico's Publishing – see Methuen Publishing Ltd

Polity Press
65 Bridge Street, Cambridge CB2 1UR
tel (01223) 324315 *fax* (01223) 461385
website www.polity.co.uk
Directors Anthony Giddens, David Held, John Thompson

Social and political theory, politics, sociology, history, media and cultural studies, philosophy, literary theory, feminism, human geography, anthropology. Founded 1983.

Polygon – see Birlinn Ltd

Poolbeg Press Ltd
123 Grange Hill, Baldoyle, Dublin 13, Republic of Ireland
tel (01) 8321477 *fax* (01) 8321430
email poolbeg@poolbeg.com
website www.poolbeg.com
Directors Kieran Devlin (managing), Paula Campbell (publisher)

Popular fiction, non-fiction, current affairs. Imprint: Poolbeg. Founded 1976.

Portland Press Ltd
3rd Floor, Eagle House, 16 Procter Street, London WC1V 6NX
tel 020-7280 4100 *fax* 020-7280 4170
email editorial@portlandpress.com
website www.portlandpress.com
Directors Rhonda C. Oliver (managing), Chris J. Finch (finance), John Day (IT), Adam Marshall (marketing)

Biochemistry and molecular life science books for graduate, postgraduate and research students. Illustrated science books for children: *Making Sense of Science* series. Founded 1990.

Portobello Books Ltd
Eardley House, 4 Uxbridge St, London W8 7SY
tel 020-7908 9890 *fax* 020-7908 9899
email mail@portobellobooks.com
website www.portobellobooks.com
Managing Director David Graham, *Publisher* Philip Gwyn Jones

'Encouraging voices, supporting writers, challenging readers.' Internationalist literature; activist non-fiction. Founded 2005.

Portrait – see Piatkus Books

T & AD Poyser – see A & C Black Publishers Ltd

PRC/Salamander – see Anova Books

Mathew Price Ltd
The Old Glove Factory, Bristol Road, Sherborne, Dorset DT9 4HP
tel (01935) 816010 *fax* (01935) 816310
email mathewp@mathewprice.com
Chairman Mathew Price

Illustrated fiction and non-fiction children's books for all ages for the UK and international market. Specialist in flap, pop-up, paper-engineered titles as well as conventional books. Founded 1983.

Princeton University Press – Europe
3 Market Place, Woodstock, Oxon OX20 1SY
tel (01993) 814500 *fax* (01993) 814504
email admin@pupress.co.uk
website http://pup.princeton.edu
Publishing Director – Europe Richard Baggaley

Economics, finance, philosophy and political theory. Part of **Princeton University Press**, USA. European office founded 1999.

Prion Books – see Carlton Publishing Group

Profile Books Ltd
3A Exmouth House, Pine Street, London EC1R 0JH
tel 020-7841 6300 *fax* 020-7833 3969
email info@profilebooks.co.uk
website www.profilebooks.co.uk
Publisher & Managing Director Andrew Franklin, *Editorial Director* Stephen Brough

General non-fiction: current affairs, politics, social sciences, history, psychology, business, management. Also publishes in association with *The Economist* and the *London Review of Books*. No unsolicited MSS; phone or send preliminary letter. Founded 1996.

Psychology Press*
27 Church Road, Hove, East Sussex BN3 2FA
tel (01273) 207411 *fax* (01273) 205612
email info@psypress.co.uk
website www.psypress.co.uk

Psychology textbooks and monographs. Imprint of **Taylor and Francis**.

Routledge (imprint)
website www.routledgementalhealth.co.uk
Clinical psychology and psychiatry.

Puffin – see Penguin Group (UK)

Pushkin Press
12 Chester Terrace, London NW1 4ND
tel (01362) 861089
email christopher@pushkinpress.com
Publisher Melissa Ulfane

Continental European literature in translation. Founded 1997.

Putnam Aeronautical – see Anova Books

Quadrille Publishing
5th Floor, Alhambra House, 27–31 Charing Cross Road, London WC2H 0LS
tel 020-7839 7117 *fax* 020-7839 7118
email enquiries@quadrille.co.uk
website www.quadrille.co.uk
Directors Alison Cathie (managing), Jane O'Shea (editorial), Helen Lewis (art), Vincent Smith (production)

Illustrated non-fiction: cookery, food and drink, gift and humour, craft, health and beauty, gardening, interiors, Mind, Body & Spirit. Founded 1994.

Quantum – see W. Foulsham & Co. Ltd

Quartet Books Ltd
27 Goodge Street, London W1T 2LD
tel 020-7636 3992 *fax* 020-7637 1866
email quartetbooks@easynet.co.uk
Chairman N.I. Attallah

General fiction and non-fiction, foreign literature in translation, classical music, jazz, contemporary music, biography. Member of the Namara Group. Founded 1972.

QUE Publishing – see Pearson Education

Quiller Publishing Ltd
Wykey House, Wykey, Shrewsbury, Shrops. SY4 1JA
tel (01939) 261616 *fax* (01939) 261606

email info@quillerbooks.com
website www.countrybooksdirect.com
Managing Director Andrew Johnston

Kenilworth Press (imprint)
Specialist equestrian publisher. Covers riding, training, dressage, eventing, show jumping, driving and polo. Publisher of BHS official publications.

Quiller Press (imprint)
Specialises in sponsored books and publications sold through non-book trade channels as well as bookshops: architecture, biography, business and industry, collecting, cookery, DIY, gardening, guidebooks, humour, reference, sports, travel, wines and spirits.

The Sportsman's Press (imprint)
All country subjects and general sports including fishing, fencing, shooting, equestrian and gunmaking; wildlife art.

Swan Hill Press (imprint)
Country and field sports activities, including fishing, cookery, shooting, falconry, equestrian, gundog training, natural history, humour.

Radcliffe Publishing Ltd
18 Marcham Road, Abingdon, Oxon OX14 1AA
tel (01235) 528820 *fax* (01235) 528830
email contact.us@radcliffemed.com
website www.radcliffe-oxford.com
Directors Andrew Bax (managing), Gill Nineham (editorial), Margaret McKeown (financial), Gregory Moxon (marketing)

Primary care, child health, palliative care, nursing, pharmacy, dentistry, counselling, healthcare organisation and management. Founded 1987.

Ragged Bears Publishing Ltd
Unit 14A, Bennett's Field Trading Estate, Southgate Road, Wincanton, Somerset BA9 9DT
tel (01963) 824184 *fax* (01963) 31147
email info@raggedbears.co.uk
website www.raggedbears.co.uk
Managing Director Henrietta Stickland, *Submissions Editor* Barbara Lamb

Preschool and primary age picture and novelty books. Takes very few unsolicited ideas as the list is small. Send sae for return of MSS; do not send original artwork. Imprint: Ragged Bears. Founded 1994.

Random House Audio Books – see Random House Group Ltd and page 215

Random House Children's Books – see Random House Group Ltd

Random House Group Ltd*
20 Vauxhall Bridge Road, London SW1V 2SA
tel 020-7840 8400 *fax* 020-7233 8791
website www.randomhouse.co.uk
Chairman/Ceo Gail Rebuck, *Deputy Ceo* Ian Hudson, *Directors* Larry Finlay (managing, Transworld), Mark Gardiner (finance), Brian Davies (managing director, overseas operations), Peter Bowron (group managing), Clare Harington (group communications), Philippa Dickinson (managing, children's), Richard Cable (managing, Random House Division), Mark Booth (publishing), Dan Franklin (publisher, CCV)
Subsidiary of Bertelsmann AG.

Arrow Books Ltd (imprint)
tel 020-7840 8557 *fax* 020-7840 6127
Publishing Director Kate Elton
Fiction, non-fiction, romance, humour, film tie-ins.

Jonathan Cape (imprint)
tel 020-7840 8576 *fax* 020-7233 6117
Directors Dan Franklin (publisher), Christian Lewis (publicity)
Biography and memoirs, current affairs, drama, fiction, history, poetry, travel, politics.

Yellow Jersey Press (imprint)
tel 020-7840 8637
Editorial Director Tristan Jones
Sport.

Century (imprint)
tel 020-7840 8554 *fax* 020-7233 6127
Directors Susan Sandon (publisher CHA), Mark Booth (publishing), Oliver Johnson (editorial), Charlotte Bush (publicity)
Fiction, biography, autobiography, general non-fiction.

Chatto & Windus (imprint)
tel 020-7840 8522 *fax* 020-7233 6117
Directors Alison Samuel (publishing), Penny Hoare (deputy publishing)
Art, belles-lettres, biography and memoirs, current affairs, drama, essays, fiction, history, poetry, politics, philosophy, translations, travel, hardbacks and paperbacks. No unsolicited MSS.

C.W. Daniel (imprint of Ebury Division)
Homeopathy, mysticism, metaphysical, astrology. Incorporates Health Science Press, L.N. Fowler & Co Ltd and Neville Spearman Publishers.

Ebury Press (imprint of Ebury Division)
tel 020-7840 8400 *fax* 020-7840 8406
Directors Fiona MacIntyre (publisher), Jake Lingwood (deputy publisher), Hannah MacDonald (publishing, non-illustrated), Carey Smith (publishing, illustrated)
General non-fiction, autobiography, popular history, sport, travel writing, popular science, humour, film

and TV tie-ins, music, travel guides, reference, cookery, lifestyle, health and beauty.

Vermilion (imprint of Ebury Division)
tel 020-7840 8400 *fax* 020-7840 8406
Directors Fiona MacIntyre (publisher), Clare Hulton (editorial)
Personal development, health, diet, relationships, parenting.

Rider (imprint of Ebury Division)
tel 020-7840 8400 *fax* 020-7840 8406
Directors Fiona MacIntyre (publisher), Judith Kendra (editorial)
Psychology, philosophy, spirituality and personal development, travel, history, inspirational memoir, paranormal, divination.

BBC Books (imprint of Ebury Division)
tel 020-7840 8400 *fax* 020-7840 8406
Director Fiona MacIntyre (publisher)

Fodor's (imprint of Ebury Division)
tel 020-7840 8400 *fax* 020-7840 8406
Worldwide annual travel guides.

Harvill Secker Press (imprint)
Publisher Geoff Mulligan
English-language and world literature in translation (literary fiction, non-fiction and some narrative thrillers); monographs in the fields of ethnography, art, horticulture, natural history. Unsolicited MSS only accepted with sae.

Hutchinson (imprint)
tel 020-7840 8564 *fax* 020-7233 7870
Directors Sue Freestone (publishing), Anthony Whittome, Paul Sidey (editorial), Charlotte Bush (publicity)
Fiction and non-fiction: biography, memoirs, thrillers, crime, general history, politics, travel, adventure, current affairs.

Pimlico (imprint)
tel 020-7840 8630 *fax* 020-7233 6117
Publishing Director Will Sulkin
History, biography, literature.

Vintage (imprint)
tel 020-7840 8400 *fax* 020-7233 6117
Publisher Rachel Cugnoni, *Associate Publishing Director* Will Sulkin, *Editorial Director* Jason Arthur
Quality fiction and non-fiction.

William Heinemann (imprint)
tel 020-7840 8400 *fax* 020-7233 6127
Publicity Director Cassie Chadderton
Fiction and general non-fiction: crime, thrillers, women's fiction, literary fiction, translations, history, biography, science. No unsolicited MSS and synopses considered.

Random House Audio Books
tel 020-7840 8419 *fax* 020-7233 6127
Editor Zoe Howes

Random House Books
(incorporating Random House Business Books)
tel 020-7840 8550 *fax* 020-7840 6127
Publisher Nigel Wilcockson

Business strategy and management, personal and career development, business narrative, general finance.

Time Out (joint venture within Ebury Division)
tel 020-7840 8798 *fax* 020-7840 8406
Brand Manager Luthfa Begum

Travel guides published in a unique partnership with *Time Out*.

Random House Children's Books (division)
61–63 Uxbridge Road, London W5 5SA
tel 020-8579 2652 *fax* 020-8579 5479
Managing Director Philippa Dickinson, *Publishing Director – Fiction* Annie Eaton, *Publisher – Doubleday Picture Books* Penny Walker, *Senior Commissioning Editor – Fiction* Alex Antscherl, *Senior Commissioning Editor* Natascha Biebow, *Senior Commissioning Editor – Jonathan Cape Picture Books* Helen Mackenzie-Smith, *Editorial Director (Fiction)* Charlie Sheppard, *Publishing Director (Custom Publishing)* Fiona Macmillan, *Publicity Director* Clare Hall-Craggs

Publishes picture books, fiction, poetry, non-fiction and audio cassettes under Bodley Head Children's Books, Jonathan Cape Children's Books, Corgi Children's Books, Doubleday Children's Books, Hutchinson Children's Books, Red Fox Children's Books, David Fickling Books.

David Fickling Books (imprint)
31 Beaumont Street, Oxford OX1 2NP
tel (01865) 339000 *fax* (01865) 339009
email dfickling@randomhouse.co.uk
website davidficklingbooks.co.uk
Publisher David Fickling, *Editor* Bella Pearson

Quality children's fiction and picture books.

Transworld Publishers (division)
See page 184.

Ransom Publishing Ltd

Rose Cottage, Howe Hill, Watlington, Oxon OX49 5HB
tel (01491) 613711 *fax* (01491) 613733
email ransom@ransom.co.uk
website www.ransom.co.uk
Directors Jenny Ertle (managing), Steve Rickard (creative)

Books for preschool to teens, including fiction, non-fiction and special needs (high interest age, low reading age). Range of digital content from preschool to secondary for literacy, numeracy, science and geography. Founded 1995.

RBI Search

(formerly Reed Business Information)
Windsor Court, East Grinstead House, Wood Street, East Grinstead, West Sussex RH19 1XA
tel (01342) 326972 *fax* (01342) 335612
email information@reedinfo.co.uk
website www.reedbusiness.com
Managing Director Jerry Gosney

Online information specialists including leading search engines such as kellysearch.com and bankersalmanac.com covering industrial, financial, travel and media sectors, including gazetteers.com, hotelsearch and Kemps. Part of Reed Elsevier plc. Founded 1983.

The Reader's Digest Association Ltd
11 Westferry Circus, Canary Wharf, London E14 4HE
tel 020-7715 8000 *fax* 020-7715 8600
Managing Director A.T. Lynam-Smith, *Editorial Directors* Katherine Walker (magazine), Julian Browne (books)

Monthly magazine, condensed and series books; also DIY, computers, puzzles, gardening, medical, handicrafts, law, touring guides, encyclopedias, dictionaries, nature, folklore, atlases, cookery, music; videos.

Reaktion Books
33 Great Sutton Street, London EC1V 0DX
tel 020-7253 1071 *fax* 020-7253 1208
email info@reaktionbooks.co.uk
website www.reaktionbooks.co.uk
Editorial Director Michael R. Leaman

Art history, design, architecture, history, cultural studies, film studies, Asian studies, travel writing, photography. Founded 1985.

Red Dress Ink™ – see Harlequin Mills & Boon Ltd

Red Fox Children's Books – see Random House Group Ltd

Thomas Reed – see A & C Black Publishers Ltd

Reed Books – now Octopus Publishing Group

William Reed Directories
Broadfield Park, Crawley, West Sussex RH11 9RT
tel (01293) 610488 *fax* (01293) 610310
email directories@william-reed.co.uk
website www.william-reed.co.uk
Director Mark de Lange, *Content Manager* Daniel Verrells, *Sales Manager* Helen Chater

Publishers of leading business-to-business directories and reports, including *The Retail and Shopping Centre Directory* and *The Grocer Directory of Manufacturers and Suppliers*.

Reed Educational and Professional Publishing Ltd – see Harcourt Education Ltd

Reed Nautical Almanac – see A & C Black Publishers Ltd

Religious and Moral Education Press (RMEP)*

St Mary's Works, St Mary's Plain, Norwich NR3 3BH
tel (01603) 612914 fax (01603) 624483
email admin@scm-canterburypress.co.uk
website www.rmep.co.uk
Chief Executive Andrew Moore, Editorial Director
Mary Mears

Books for primary and secondary school pupils, college students, and teachers on religious, moral, personal and social education. Division of SCM–Canterbury Press Ltd, a subsidiary of Hymns Ancient & Modern Ltd. Founded 1980.

Reynolds & Hearn Ltd

61A Priory Road, Kew, Richmond, Surrey TW9 3DH
tel 020-8940 5198 fax 020-8940 7679
email enquiries@rhbooks.com
website www.rhbooks.com
Directors Richard Reynolds (managing), Marcus Hearn (editorial), David O'Leary, Geoffrey Wolfson

Rider – see Random House Group Ltd

Rigby Heinemann – see Harcourt Education Ltd

River Books – see New Cavendish Books

Rivers Oram Press

144 Hemingford Road, London N1 1DE
tel 020-7607 0823 fax 020-7609 2776
email ro@riversoram.com
website www.riversoram.co.uk,
www.pandorapress.co.uk
Directors Elizabeth Rivers Fidlon (managing), Anthony Harris

Non-ficton: social and political science, current affairs, social history, gender studies, sexual politics, cultural studies. Founded 1991.

Pandora Press (imprint)

Feminist press. General non-fiction: biography, arts, media, health, current affairs, reference and sexual politics.

Robinson – see Constable & Robinson Ltd

Robson Books – see Anova Books

Rodale Books International

7–10 Chandos Street, London W1G 9AD
tel 020-7291 6000 fax 020-7291 6020
email rights@rodale.co.uk
website www.rodale.co.uk
Managing Director Louise Rice, Managing Editor Anne Lawrance

Health and fitness, wellbeing, self-help, gardening. Subsidiary of Rodale Inc. Founded 2003.

George Ronald

3 Rosecroft Lane, Oaklands, Welwyn, Herts.
AL6 0UB
tel (01438) 716062 fax (0870) 762 6242
email sales@grbooks.com
website www.grbooks.com
Managers E. Leith, M. Hofman

Religion, specialising in the Bahá'í Faith. Founded 1939.

Barry Rose Law Publishers Ltd

Little London, Chichester, West Sussex PO19 1PG
tel (01243) 783637 fax (01243) 779278
email books@barry-rose-law.co.uk

Law, local government, police, legal history. Founded 1972.

Rough Guides – see Penguin Group (UK)

Roundhouse Publishing Ltd

Millstone, Limers Lane, Northam, North Devon EX39 2RG
tel (01237) 474474 fax (01237) 474774
email roundhouse.group@ukgateway.net
website www.roundhouse.net
Publisher Alan T. Goodworth

Film, cinema, and performing arts; reference books. No unsolicited MSS. Founded 1991.

Route

PO Box 167, Pontefract, West Yorkshire WF8 4WW
tel (01977) 797695
email info@route-online.com
website www.route-online.com,
www.id-publishing.com
Contact Ian Daley, Isabel Galan

Contemporary fiction (novels and short stories) and performance poetry, with a commitment to new writing. Unsolicited MSS discouraged. See website for current guidelines. Ring or write for a free catalogue. Imprint of ID Publishing.

Routledge – see Taylor and Francis Books Ltd

RoutledgeCurzon – see Taylor and Francis Books Ltd

RoutledgeFalmer – see Taylor and Francis Books Ltd

Royal Collection Publications

York House, St James's Palace, London SW1A 1BQ
tel 020-7024 5584 fax 020-7839 8168
website www.royalcollection.org.uk
Publisher Jacky Colliss Harvey, Editor Marie Leahy

Subjects from within the Royal Collection. Founded 1993.

Royal National Institute of the Blind

PO Box 173, Peterborough, Cambs. PE2 6WS
tel (0845) 7023153 *fax* (01733) 371555
email cservices@rnib.org.uk
website www.rnib.org.uk
textphone (0845) 7585691

Magazines, catalogues and books for blind and partially sighted people, to support daily living, leisure, learning and employment reading needs. Produced in braille, audio, large/legible print, disk and email. For complete list of magazines see page 85. Founded 1868.

Ryland Peters & Small

20–21 Jockey's Fields, London WC1R 4BW
tel 020-7025 2200 *fax* 020-7025 2201
email info@rps.co.uk
website www.rylandpeters.com
Directors David Peters (managing), Alison Starling (publishing), Joanna Everard (rights), Meryl Silbert (production), Anne-Marie Bulat (art), Helen Thewlis (UK & export sales)

High-quality illustrated books on food and drink, home and garden, wellbeing, gift books. Founded 1995.

SAGE Publications Ltd*

1 Oliver's Yard, 55 City Road, London EC1Y 1SP
tel 020-7324 8500 *fax* 020-7324 8600
email info@sagepub.co.uk
website www.sagepub.co.uk
Directors Stephen Barr (managing), Katharine Jackson, Ziyad Marar, Richard Fidczuk, Phil Denvir, Clive Parry, Jane Quick, Blaise Simqu (USA), Sara Miller McCune (USA), Paul R. Chapman

Social sciences, behavioural sciences, humanities, STM, software. Founded 1971.

Paul Chapman Publishing (imprint)

website www.paulchapmanpublishing.co.uk
Publisher Marianne Lagrange

Education: academic and professional books for students, practitioners and school leaders.

St Pauls

St Pauls Publishing, 187 Battersea Bridge Road, London SW11 3AS
tel 020-7978 4300 *fax* 020-7978 4370
email editions@stpauls.org.uk
website www.stpauls.ie

Theology, ethics, spirituality, biography, education, general books of Roman Catholic and Christian interest. Founded 1948.

Salariya Book Company Ltd

Book House, 25 Marlborough Place, Brighton BN1 1UB
tel (01273) 603306 *fax* (01273) 693857
email salariya@salariya.com

website www.salariya.com
Director David Salariya

Children's non-fiction. Imprint: Book House. Founded 1989.

SAMS Publishing – see Pearson Education

Saunders – see Elsevier Ltd (Health Sciences)

Alastair Sawday Publishing Ltd

The Old Farmyard, Yauley Lane, Long Ashton, Bristol BS41 9LR
tel (01275) 395430 *fax* (01275) 393388
email info@sawdays.co.uk, info@fragile-earth.com
website www.sawdays.co.uk,
www.specialplacestostay.co.uk,
www.fragile-earth.com

Special Places to Stay series of guidebooks and *Fragile Earth Books* on global green issues. Founded 1996.

S.B. Publications

14 Bishopstone Road, Seaford, East Sussex BN25 2UB
tel (01323) 893498 *fax* (01323) 893860
email sbpublications@tiscali.co.uk
website www.sbpublications.co.uk
Proprietor Lindsay Woods

Local history, local themes (e.g. walking books, guides), specific themes. Founded 1987.

Scala Publishers

Northburgh House, Northburgh Street, London EC1V 0AT
tel 020-7490 9900 *fax* 020-7336 6870
email jmckinley@scalapublishers.com
website www.scalapublishers.com
Chairman David Campbell, *Directors* Henry Channon, Jan Baily, Antony White, *Director of Museum Publications US* Jennifer Wright, *Commissioning Editor UK* Jenny McKinley

Art, architecture, guides to museums and art galleries, antiques. Founded 1992.

Sceptre – see Hodder Headline Ltd

Schofield & Sims Ltd

Dogley Mill, Fenay Bridge, Huddersfield HD8 0NQ
tel (01484) 607080 *fax* (01484) 606815
email sales@schofieldandsims.co.uk
website www.schofieldandsims.co.uk
Chairman C.N. Platts

Educational: nursery, infants, primary; posters. Founded 1901.

Scholastic Ltd*

Villiers House, Clarendon Avenue, Leamington Spa CV32 5PR
tel (01926) 887799 *fax* (01926) 883881
website www.scholastic.co.uk
Chairman M.R. Robinson, *Group Managing Director* Kate Wilson

Children's fiction and non-fiction and education for primary schools. Owned by Scholastic Inc. Founded 1964.

Scholastic Children's Books (division)
Euston House, 24 Eversholt Street, London NW1 1DB
tel 020-7756 7756 *fax* 020-7756 7795
email publicity@scholastic.co.uk
Managing Director Elaine McQuaide, *Editorial Director, Non-fiction* Lisa Edwards, *Editorial Director, Fiction* Kristen Skidmore, *Senior Commissioning Editor, Preschool* Paulina Malinen, *International Trade Director* Gavin Lang, *Rights Director* Antonia Pelari, *Sales & Marketing Director* Hilary Murray Hill

Activity books, novelty books, picture books, fiction for 5–12 year-olds, teenage fiction, series fiction and film/TV tie-ins. Imprints include Young Hippo, Scholastic Press, Alison Green Books, Marion Lloyd Books, Klutz, Hippo Books, Little Hippo, Point. Will consider unsolicited submissions: send synopsis and sample chapter only.

The Chicken House
See page 141.

Scholastic Educational Publishing (division)
Villiers House, Clarendon Avenue, Leamington Spa CV32 5PR
tel (01926) 887799 *fax* (01926) 883881
Managing Director Denise Cripps

Professional books and classroom materials for primary teachers and magazines (*Child Education, Junior Education, Junior Focus, Child Education Topics, Nursery Education, Litreracy Time*).

Scholastic Book Clubs (division)
See page 309.

Scholastic Book Fairs (division)
See page 309.

Science Museum
Exhibition Road, London SW7 2DD
tel 020-7942 4361 *fax* 020-7942 4362
email publicat@nmsi.ac.uk
website www.nmsi.ac.uk/publications
Publications Manager Ela Ginalska

History of science and technology, museum guides.

SCM Canterbury Press Ltd*
9–17 St Albans Place, London N1 0NX
tel 020-7359 8033 *fax* 020-7359 0049
email admin@scm-canterburypress.co.uk
website www.scm-canterburypress.co.uk
Publishing Director Christine Smith

Theological books with special emphasis on text and reference books and contemporary theology for both students and clergy. Founded 1929.

Canterbury Press (imprint)
St Mary's Works, St Mary's Plain, Norwich NR3 3BH
tel (01603) 612914 *fax* (01603) 624483

Religious books for the general market, church resources and liturgy.

SCP Childrens Ltd
(trading as Scottish Children's Press)
Unit 6, Newbattle Abbey Business Park, Newbattle Road, Dalkeith EH22 3LJ
tel 0131-660 4757 *fax* 0131-660 4666
email info@scottishbooks.com
website www.scottishbooks.com
Directors Brian Pugh, Avril Gray

Scottish fiction, Scottish non-fiction and Scots language, children's writing. Unsolicited MSS not accepted; send letter, telephone or email before sending material. Founded 1992.
No unsolicited MSS; send letter, phone or email before sending material. Founded 1992.

Scottish Cultural Press
tel 0131-660 6366 *fax* 0131-660 4666
'Scottish books for anyone interested in Scotland.' Literature, poetry, history, archaeology, biography and environmental history.

Scribner – see Simon & Schuster UK Ltd

Scripture Union
207–209 Queensway, Bletchley, Milton Keynes, Bucks. MK2 2EB
tel (01908) 856000 *fax* (01908) 856111
email postmaster@scriptureunion.org.uk
website www.scriptureunion.org.uk
Head of Resource Development Terry Clutterham

Christian books and Bible reading materials for people of all ages; educational and worship resources for churches; children's fiction and non-fiction; adult non-fiction. Founded 1867.

Seafarer Books
102 Redwald Road, Rendlesham, Woodbridge, Suffolk IP12 2TE
tel (01394) 420789
email info@seafarerbooks.com
website www.seafarerbooks.com
Commissioning Editor Patricia Eve

Books on traditional sailing, mainly narrative.

Search Press Ltd
Wellwood, North Farm Road, Tunbridge Wells, Kent TN2 3DR
tel (01892) 510850 *fax* (01892) 515903
email searchpress@searchpress.com
website www.searchpress.com
Directors Martin de la Bédoyère (managing), Caroline de la Bédoyère (rights), Rosalind Dace (editorial)

Arts, crafts, leisure, gardening. Founded 1970.

Seren
57 Nolton Street, Bridgend CF31 3AE
tel (01656) 663018 *fax* (01656) 649226

email general@seren-books.com
Publisher Mick Felton

Poetry, fiction, drama, history, film, literary criticism, biography, art – mostly with relevance to Wales. Founded 1981.

Serpent's Tail
4 Blackstock Mews, London N4 2BT
tel 020-7354 1949 *fax* 020-7704 6467
email info@serpentstail.com
website www.serpentstail.com
Director Peter Ayrton

Fiction and non-fiction in paperback; literary and non-mainstream work, and work in translation. No unsolicited MSS. Imprint: Five Star. Founded 1986.

Severn House Publishers
9–15 High Street, Sutton, Surrey SM1 1DF
tel 020-8770 3930 *fax* 020-8770 3850
email editorial@severnhouse.com
website www.severnhouse.com
Chairman Edwin Buckhalter, *Publishing Director* Amanda Stewart

Hardcover and paperback adult fiction for the library market: romances, crime, thrillers, detective, adventure, war, science fiction, some large print. No unsolicited MSS.

Sheldon Press – see Society for Promoting Christian Knowledge

Sheldrake Press
188 Cavendish Road, London SW12 0DA
tel 020-8675 1767 *fax* 020-8675 7736
email enquiries@sheldrakepress.co.uk
website www.sheldrakepress.co.uk
Publisher J.S. Rigge

History, travel, architecture, cookery, music; stationery. Founded 1979.

Shepheard-Walwyn (Publishers) Ltd
Suite 604, 50 Westminster Bridge Road, London SE1 7QY
tel 020-7721 7666 *fax* 020-7721 7667
email books@shepheard-walwyn.co.uk
website www.shepheard-walwyn.co.uk
Directors A.R.A. Werner, M.M. Werner

History, biography, political economy, perennial philosophy; illustrated gift books; Scottish interest. Founded 1971.

Shire Publications Ltd
Cromwell House, Church Street, Princes Risborough, Bucks. HP27 9AA
tel (01844) 344301 *fax* (01844) 347080
email shire@shirebooks.co.uk
website www.shirebooks.co.uk
Director J.W. Rotheroe

Discovering paperbacks, Shire Albums, Shire Archaeology, Shire Natural History, Shire Ethnography, Shire Egyptology, Shire Garden History. Founded 1962.

Short Books Ltd
3A Exmouth House, Pine Street, London EC1R 0JH
tel 020-7833 9429 *fax* 020-7833 9500
email emily@shortbooks.biz
website www.shortbooks.co.uk
Editorial Directors Rebecca Nicolson, Aurea Carpenter

Non-fiction, mainly biography and journalism. Also biographies of famous people from the past for children. No unsolicited MSS. Founded 2000.

Sidgwick & Jackson – see Macmillan Publishers Ltd

Sigma Press
5 Alton Road, Wilmslow, Cheshire SK9 5DY
tel (01625) 531035 *fax* (01625) 531035
email info@sigmapress.co.uk
website www.sigmapress.co.uk
Partners Graham Beech, Diana Beech

Leisure: country walking, cycling, regional heritage, ecology, sport, folklore; biographies. Founded 1979.

Silhouette® – see Harlequin Mills & Boon Ltd

Simon & Schuster UK Ltd*
Africa House, 64–78 Kingsway, London WC2B 6AH
tel 020-7316 1900 *fax* 020-7316 0331/2
website www.simonsays.co.uk
Directors Ian Chapman (managing), Suzanne Baboneau (publishing), Charlotte Robertson (sales), Jonathan Atkins (international publishing & sales), Ingrid Selberg (children's publishing)

Commercial and literary fiction; general and serious non-fiction; children's. No unsolicited MSS. Founded 1986.

Free Press (imprint)
Publisher Andrew Gordon
Serious adult non-fiction: history, biography, current affairs, science.

Simon & Schuster Martin Books (imprint)
Director Janet Copleston
Illustrated non-fiction and bespoke publishing.

Pocket Books (imprint)
Publisher Julie Wright
Mass-market fiction and non-fiction paperbacks.

Scribner (imprint)
Literary fiction and non-fiction.

Simon & Schuster Audioworks
Fiction, non-fiction and business.

Simon & Schuster Children's Publishing
Picture books, pop-up, novelty, fiction and non-fiction.

Smith Gryphon Ltd – see John Blake Publishing Ltd

Colin Smythe Ltd*
PO Box 6, Gerrards Cross, Bucks. SL9 8XA
tel (01753) 886000 *fax* (01753) 886469
website www.colinsmythe.co.uk
Directors Colin Smythe (managing & editorial), Leslie Hayward, Ann Saddlemyer

Biography, phaleristics, heraldry, Irish literature and literary criticism, history. Founded 1966.

Society for Promoting Christian Knowledge*
36 Causton Street, London SW1P 4ST
tel 020-7592 3900 *fax* 020-7592 3939
email publishing@spck.org.uk
website www.spck.org.uk
Director of Publishing Simon Kingston, *Editorial Director* Joanna Moriarty

Founded 1698.

Sheldon Press (imprint)
Popular medicine, health, self-help, psychology.

SPCK (imprint)
Theology and academic, liturgy, prayer, spirituality, biblical studies, educational resources, mission, gospel and culture.

Society of Genealogists Enterprises Ltd
14 Charterhouse Buildings, Goswell Road, London EC1M 7BA
tel 020-7251 8799 *fax* 020-7250 1800
email sales@sog.org.uk
website www.sog.org.uk
Chief Executive June Perrin

Local and family history books, fiche, disks, CDs, software and magazines plus extensive library facilities.

South Street Press – see Garnet Publishing Ltd

Southwater – see Anness Publishing

Souvenir Press Ltd
43 Great Russell Street, London WC1B 3PD
tel 020-7580 9307/8
email sp.trade@ukonline.co.uk
Managing Director Ernest Hecht

Archaeology, biography and memoirs, educational (secondary, technical), general, humour, practical handbooks, psychiatry, psychology, sociology, sports, games and hobbies, travel, supernatural, parapsychology, illustrated books. No unsolicited fiction or children's books; initial enquiry by letter essential for non-fiction.

SPCK – see Society for Promoting Christian Knowledge

Spellmount Ltd – see Tempus Publishing Group Ltd

Spindlewood – see Ragged Bears Publishing Ltd

Spon Press – see Taylor and Francis Books Ltd

Sportsbooks Ltd
PO Box 422, Cheltenham, Glos. GL50 2YN
tel (01242) 256755 *fax* (0870) 0750 888
email randall@sportsbooks.ltd.uk
website www.sportsbooks.ltd.uk
Directors Randall Northam, Veronica Northam

Sport.

The Sportsman's Press – see Quiller Publishing Ltd

Springer-Verlag London Ltd
Ashbourne House, The Guildway, Old Portsmouth Road, Guildford GU3 1LP
tel (01483) 734433 *fax* (01483) 734411
website www.springer.com
General Manager Beverly Ford

Medicine, computing, engineering, astronomy, mathematics, chemistry, biosciences. Founded 1972.

Stacey International
128 Kensington Church Street, London W8 4BH
tel 020-7221 7166 *fax* 020-7792 9288
email enquiries@stacey-international.co.uk
website www.stacey-international.co.uk
Chairman Tom Stacey, *Managing Director* Max Scott

Illustrated non-fiction, encyclopedic books on regions and countries, Islamic and Arab subjects, world affairs, children's books, art, travel, belles-lettres. Founded 1973.

Stainer & Bell Ltd
PO Box 110, Victoria House, 23 Gruneisen Road, London N3 1DZ
tel 020-8343 3303 *fax* 020-8343 3024
email post@stainer.co.uk
website www.stainer.co.uk
Directors Keith Wakefield (joint managing), Carol Wakefield (joint managing & secretary), Peter Braley, Antony Kearns, Andrew Pratt, Nicholas Williams

Books on music, religious communication. Founded 1907.

Stenlake Publishing Ltd
54–58 Mill Square, Catrine Ayrshire KA5 6RD
tel (01290) 552233
email sales@stenlake.co.uk
website www.stenlake.co.uk
Managing Director Richard Stenlake

Local history, railways, transport, aviation, canals and mining covering Wales, Scotland, England, Northern

Ireland, Isle of Man and Republic of Ireland. Founded 1997.

Patrick Stephens Ltd – see Sutton Publishing Ltd

Stride Publications
11 Sylvan Road, Exeter, Devon EX4 6EW
email editor@stridebooks.co.uk
website www.stridebooks.co.uk
Managing Editor Rupert M. Loydell

Poetry, prose poetry, contemporary music and visual arts, interviews. No submissions are currently being sought. Founded 1980.

Summersdale Publishers Ltd
46 West Street, Chichester, West Sussex PO19 1RP
tel (01243) 771107 *fax* (01243) 786300
email submissions@summersdale.com
website www.summersdale.com
Directors Alastair Williams, Stewart Ferris,
Commissioning Editor Jennifer Barclay

Commercial non-fiction, particularly travel, martial arts, self help, history and gift books. No poetry or children's literature. Founded 1990.

Sunflower Books
12 Kendrick Mews, London SW7 3HG
tel 020-7589 1862 *fax* 020-7589 1862
email mail@sunflowerbooks.co.uk
website www.sunflowerbooks.co.uk
Directors P.A. Underwood (editorial),
J.G. Underwood, S.J. Seccombe

Travel guidebooks.

Sussex Academic Press
PO Box 139, Eastbourne, East Sussex BN24 9BP
tel (01323) 479220 *fax* (01323) 478185
email edit@sussex-academic.co.uk
website www.sussex-academic.co.uk
Editorial Director Anthony Grahame

Theology and religion, British history and Middle East studies. Founded 1994.

The Alpha Press (imprint)
Religion, history, sport.

Sutton Publishing Ltd
Phoenix Mill, Thrupp, Stroud, Glos. GL5 2BU
tel (01453) 731114 *fax* (01453) 731117
email publishing@sutton-publishing.co.uk
website www.suttonpublishing.co.uk
Managing Director Jeremy Yates-Round, *Editorial*
Jaqueline Mitchell (biography), Christopher Feeney (general history), Jonathan Falconer (military), Simon Fletcher (local history)

General academic and specialist publishers of high-quality illustrated books: history, military, biography, archaeology, heritage. Owned by Haynes Publishing. Founded 1978.

Patrick Stephens Ltd (imprint)
Aviation, maritime and military. New titles and new editions now published under Sutton imprint.

Swan Hill Press – see Quiller Publishing Ltd

The Swedenborg Society
20–21 Bloomsbury Way, London WC1A 2TH
tel 020-7405 7986 *fax* 020-7831 5848
email swed.soc@netmatters.co.uk
website www.swedenborg.org.uk

The works of Swedenborg, biographies and studies of Swedenborg and his influence.

Sweet & Maxwell*
100 Avenue Road, London NW3 3PF
tel 020-7393 7000 *fax* 020-7393 7010
Directors Peter Lake (managing), John Galvin (finance), Milan Taylor (regulatory business), Hilary Lambert (legal business), Alina Lourie (legal online business), Mark Seaman (editorial & production), Kim Massana (sales), Louise Gillard (marketing)

Law. Part of Thomson Legal & Regulatory (Europe) Ltd. Founded 1799; incorporated 1889.

Tamarind Ltd
PO Box 52, Northwood, Middlesex HA6 1UN
tel 020-8866 8808 *fax* 020-8866 5627
email info@tamarindbooks.co.uk
website www.tamarindbooks.co.uk
Managing Director Verna Wilkins

Multicultural children's picture books and posters. All books give a high positive profile to black children. Unsolicited material welcome with return postage. Founded 1987.

Tango Books
PO Box 32595, London W4 5YD
tel 020-8996 9970 *fax* 020-8996 9977
email sales@tangobooks.co.uk
website www.tangobooks.co.uk
Directors Sheri Safran, David Fielder

Children's novelty books, including pop-up, touch-and-feel and cloth books.

Tarquin Publications
99 Hatfield Road, St Albans AL1 4ET
tel (0870) 1432568 *fax* (0845) 4566385
email editorial@tarquinbooks.com
website www.tarquinbooks.com
Director Andrew Griffin

Mathematics and mathematical models; paper cutting, paper engineering and pop-up books for intelligent children. No unsolicited MSS; send suggestion or synopsis in first instance. Founded 1970.

Taschen UK Ltd
5th Floor, 1 Heathcock Court, 415 Strand, London WC2R 0NS

tel 020-7845 8580 *fax* 020-7836 3696
email contact-uk@taschen.com
website www.taschen.com

Art, architecture, design, film, lifestyle, photography, popular culture, sex. Founded in 1980.

Tate Publishing

The Lodge, Millbank, London SW1P 4RG
tel 020-7887 8869/70 *fax* 020-7887 8878
email tgpl@tate.org.uk
website www.tate.org.uk
Chief Executive Celia Clear, *Publishing Director* Roger Thorp, *Operations Director* Tahir Hussain, *Production Manager* Sophie Lawrence, *Head of Licensing* Jo Matthews, *Head of Product* Rosey Blackmore

Publishers for Tate in London, Liverpool and St Ives. Exhibition catalogues, art books (contemporary, modern and from 1500 if British) and diaries, posters, etc. Also product development, picture library and licensing. Division of Tate Enterprises Ltd. Founded 1995.

I.B.Tauris & Co. Ltd

6 Salem Road, London W2 4BU
tel 020-7243 1225 *fax* 020-7243 1226
email mail@ibtauris.com
website www.ibtauris.com
Chairman/Publisher Iradj Bagherzade, *Managing Director* Jonathan McDonnell

History, biography, politics, international relations, current affairs, Middle East, religion, cultural and media studies, film, art, archaeology, travel guides. Founded 1983.

Tauris Academic Studies (imprint)

Academic monographs on history, political science and social sciences.

Tauris Parke Books (imprint)

Illustrated books on architecture, design, photography, cultural history and travel.

Tauris Parke Paperbacks (imprint)

Non-fiction trade paperbacks: biography, history, travel, cinema, art, cultural history.

Taylor and Francis Books Ltd*

4 Park Road, Milton Park, Abingdon, Oxon OX14 4RN
tel (01235) 828600 *fax* (01235) 828000
email info@tandf.co.uk
website www.tandf.co.uk, www.tfinforma.com
Managing Director, Taylor & Francis Books Ltd Roger Horton

Taylor and Francis Group plc merged with Informa Group plc in May 2004 to form T&F Informa plc.

BIOS Scientific Publishers (imprint)

website www.bios.co.uk
Bioscience textbooks.

Frank Cass (imprint)

email info@frankcass.com
website www.frankcass.com
History, economic and social history, military and strategic studies, politics, international affairs, development studies, African studies, Middle East studies, sports studies, law, business management and academic journals in all of these fields.

CRC Press (imprint)

website www.crcpress.com
Engineering and science books.

Dekker Publishing (imprint)

Engineering, science and medical.

Martin Dunitz (imprint)

Medical books.

Europa Publications Ltd (imprint)

Haines House, 21 John Street, London WC1N 2BP
tel 020-7583 9855 *fax* 020-7842 2249
Directories, international relations, reference, yearbooks.

Fitzroy-Dearborn (imprint)

Reference and academic encyclopedias and handbooks.

Garland Science (imprint)

website www.garlandscience.com
Science textbooks and scholarly works.

Parthenon Press (imprint)

Medical books.

Psychology Press Ltd

See page 173.

Routledge (imprint)

website www.routledge.com
Addiction, anthropology, archaeology, Asian studies, business, classical studies, counselling, criminology, development and environment, dictionaries, economics, education, geography, health, history, Japanese studies, library science, language, linguistics, literary criticism, media and culture, nursing, performance studies, philosophy, politics, psychiatry, psychology, reference, social administration, social studies/sociology, women's studies.

RoutledgeCurzon (imprint)

website www.routledgecurzon.com
Academic/scholarly books in the social sciences, particularly Asian studies.

RoutledgeFalmer (imprint)

website www.routledgefalmer.com
Education books.

Spon Press (imprint)

website www.sponpress.com
Architecture, civil engineering, construction, leisure and recreation management, sports science.

Taylor & Francis (imprint)
website www.tandf.co.uk/books
Educational (university), science: physics, mathematics, chemistry, electronics, natural history, pharmacology and drug metabolism, toxicology, technology, history of science, ergonomics, production engineering, remote sensing, geographic information systems.

Teach Yourself – see Hodder Headline Ltd

Telegraph Books
Telegraph Group Ltd, 1 Canada Square, Canary Wharf, London E14 5DT
tel 020-7538 6826 *fax* 020-7538 6064
website www.books.telegraph.co.uk
Publisher Morven Knowles

Personal finance, crosswords, sport, humour, cookery, health, general, gardening, history – usually by *Telegraph* journalists and contributors, and co-published with major publishing houses. Founded 1920.

Tempus Publishing Group Ltd
The Mill, Brimscombe Port, Stroud, Glos. GL5 2QG
tel (01453) 883300 *fax* (01453) 883233
website www.tempus-publishing.com
Directors Alan Sutton (chief executive), William Andrewes (finance), Martin Palmer (sales), Peter Kemmis Betty (publishing), Stephane Mallegol, Jamie Wilson

The Chalford Press (imprint)
History and historiography of pornography, erotica and scatology.

Nonsuch Publishing Ltd (imprint)
Local and national history, travel, exploration, military, biography, letters and diaries, literature. Founded 2003.

Spellmount Ltd (imprint)
Military history. Founded 1993.

Stadia (imprint)
Sport and sport history.

Tempus Publishing Ltd (imprint)
Local and national history throughout the British Isles; modern; medieval; archaeology; industrial and transport history. Founded 1993.

Torque (imprint)
Historical fiction.

Tender Romance™ – see Harlequin Mills & Boon Ltd

Thames & Hudson Ltd*
181A High Holborn, London WC1V 7QX
tel 020-7845 5000 *fax* 020-7845 5050

email sales@thameshudson.co.uk
website www.thamesandhudson.com
Directors T. Neurath (chair), C. Kaine (deputy chair), J. Camplin (managing), E. Bates, L. Dietrich, T. Evans, C. Ferguson, C. Frederking, P. Hughes, P. Meades, B. Meek, T. Naylor, J. Neurath, N. Palfreyman

Illustrated non-fiction for an international audience, especially art, architecture, graphic design, garden and landscape design, archaeology, cultural history, historical reference, fashion, photography, ethnic arts, mythology, religion.

Think Books
Think Publishing Ltd, The Pall Mall Deposit, 124–128 Barlby Road, London W10 6BL
tel 020-8962 3020 *fax* 020-8962 8689
email watchdog@thinkpublishing.co.uk
website www.thinkpublishing.co.uk
Publishing Director Ian McAuliffe, *Managing Director* Tilly Boulter, *Publisher* John Innes, *Head of Editorial* Emma Jones

Specialises in books on the outdoors, gardening and wildlife. Publishes with the Wildlife Trust, the Royal Horticulture Society and the Campaign to Protect Rural England, and others. Founded 2005.

Thoemmes Press – see The Continuum International Publishing Group Ltd

D.C. Thomson & Co. Ltd – Publications
2 Albert Square, Dundee DD1 9QJ
London office 185 Fleet Street, London EC4A 2HS

Publishers of newspapers and periodicals. Children's books (annuals), based on weekly magazine characters; fiction. For fiction guidelines, send a large sae to Central Fiction Dept.

Thomson Round Hall
43 Fitzwilliam Place, Dublin 2, Republic of Ireland
tel (01) 6625301 *fax* (01) 6625302
email info@roundhall.ie
website www.roundhall.ie
Director & General Manager Julie Clarke

Law. Part of Thomson Legal & Regulatory (Europe) Ltd.

Stanley Thornes (Publishers) Ltd – see Nelson Thornes Ltd

Time Out – see Random House Group Ltd

Time Warner – see Little, Brown Book Group

Times Books – see HarperCollins Publishers

Titan Books
144 Southwark Street, London SE1 0UP
tel 020-7620 0200 *fax* 020-7620 0032

email editorial@titanemail.com
website www.titanbooks.com
Publisher & Managing Director Nick Landau, *Editorial Director* Katy Wild

Graphic novels, including *Simpsons* and *Batman*, featuring comic strip material; film and TV tie-ins and cinema reference books. No fiction or children's proposals, no email submissions and no unsolicited material without preliminary letter; email or send large sae for current author guidelines. Division of Titan Publishing Group Ltd. Founded 1981.

Tolley – see LexisNexis Butterworths

Top That! Publishing plc
Marine House, Tide Mill Way, Woodbridge, Suffolk IP12 1AP
tel (01394) 386651 *fax* (01394) 386011
email info@topthatpublishing.com
website www.topthatpublishing.com
Directors Barrie Henderson (managing), Simon Couchman (creative), Dave Greggor (sales)

Top That! Kids (imprint)
Children's information and novelty books. Founded 1998.

Kudos Books (imprint)
Adult books, humour and gift sets. Founded 1999.

Tor – see Macmillan Publishers Ltd

TownHouse, Dublin†
Trinity House, Mountpleasant Business Centre, Mountpleasant Avenue, Rathmines, Dublin 6, Republic of Ireland
tel (01) 4972399 *fax* (01) 4970927
email books@townhouse.ie
website www.townhouse.ie
Directors Treasa Coady, Jim Coady

General illustrated non-fiction, art, archaeology and biography. Imprints: TownHouse, Simon and Schuster/TownHouse. Founded 1981.

Transworld Publishers*
61–63 Uxbridge Road, London W5 5SA
tel 020-8579 2652 *fax* 020-8579 5479
email info@transworld-publishers.co.uk
website www.booksattransworld.co.uk
Managing Director Larry Finlay, *Publisher* Bill Scott-Kerr, *Senior Publishing Director* Francesca Liversidge

Division of **Random House Group Ltd**; subsidiary of Bertelsmann AG. No unsolicited MSS accepted.

Bantam (imprint)
Senior Publishing Director Francesca Liversidge
Paperback general fiction and non-fiction, Mind, Body & Spirit, self-help, travel.

Bantam Press (imprint)
Publishing Director Sally Gaminara
Fiction, general, cookery, business, crime, health and diet, history, humour, military, music, paranormal,

self-help, science, travel and adventure, biography and autobiography.

Black Swan (imprint)
Publisher Bill Scott-Kerr
Paperback quality fiction.

Channel 4 Books (imprint)
Publishing Director Doug Young
TV tie-ins.

Corgi (imprint)
Publisher Bill Scott-Kerr
Paperback general fiction and non-fiction.

Doubleday (UK) (imprint)
Publishing Director Marianne Velmans
Literary fiction and non-fiction.

Eden (imprint)
Publishing Director Susanna Wadeson
Environmental: the Eden Project.

Expert Books (imprint)
Co-ordinator Gareth Pottle
Gardening and DIY.

Treehouse Children's Books
2nd Floor Offices, Old Brewhouse, Lower Charlton Trading Estate, Shepton Mallet, Somerset BA4 5QE
tel (01749) 330529 *fax* (01749) 330544
email treehouse-books@btconnect.com
Editorial Director Richard Powell

Preschool children's books and novelty books. Imprint of Emma Treehouse Ltd. Founded 1989.

Trentham Books Ltd
Westview House, 734 London Road, Oakhill, Stoke-on-Trent, Staffs. ST4 5NP
tel (01782) 745567 *fax* (01782) 745553
email tb@trentham.books.co.uk
Editorial office 28 Hillside Gardens, London N6 5ST
tel 020-8348 2174
website www.trentham-books.co.uk
Directors Dr Gillian Klein (editorial), Barbara Wiggins (executive)

Education (including specialist fields – multi-ethnic issues, equal opportunities, bullying, design and technology, early years), social policy, sociology of education, European education, women's studies. Does not publish books for use by parents or children, or fiction, biography, reminiscences and poetry. Founded 1978.

Trotman & Company Ltd
2 The Green, Richmond, Surrey TW9 1PL
tel 020-8486 1150 *fax* 020-8486 1161
website www.trotman.co.uk
Publishing Director Mina Patria, *Commissioning Editor* Rachel Lockhart

Independent advice and guidance on careers and higher education. Founded 1970.

TSO (The Stationery Office)*

Head office St Crispins, Duke Street, Norwich
NR3 1PD
tel (0870) 6005522 *fax* (0870) 6005533
website www.tso.co.uk
Chief Executive Tim Hailstone, *Sales & Marketing
Director* J. Hook

Publishing and information management services:
business, current affairs, directories, general,
pharmaceutical, professional, reference, *Learning to
Drive.*

Ulric Publishing

PO Box 55, Church Stretton, Shrops. SY6 6WR
tel (01694) 781354 *fax* (01694) 781372
email books@ulricpublishing.com
website www.ulricpublishing.com
Directors Ulric Woodhams, Elizabeth Oakes

Military history and motoring. No unsolicited MSS.
Founded 1992.

Ulverscroft Group

The Green, Bradgate Road, Anstey, Leicester LE7 7FU
tel 0116-236 4325 *fax* 0116-234 0205
website www.ulverscroft.com

Large print books: fiction and non-fiction, Classics.

Merlin Unwin Books

Palmers House, 7 Corve Street, Ludlow, Shrops.
SY8 1DB
tel (01584) 877456 *fax* (01584) 877457
email books@merlinunwin.co.uk
website www.merlinunwin.co.uk
Proprietor Merlin Unwin

Countryside, country cooking and fieldsports books.
Founded 1990.

Usborne Publishing Ltd

Usborne House, 83–85 Saffron Hill, London
EC1N 8RT
tel 020-7430 2800 *fax* 020-8636 3758
email mail@usborne.co.uk
website www.usborne.com
Directors Peter Usborne, Jenny Tyler (editorial),
Robert Jones, Keith Ball, David Harte, Lorna Hunt

Children's books: reference, practical, computers,
craft, natural history, science, languages, history,
geography, preschool, fiction. Founded 1973.

V&A Publications

V&A Museum, South Kensington, London SW7 2RL
tel 020-7942 2966 *fax* 020-7942 2967
email vapubs.info@vam.ac.uk
website www.vandashop.co.uk/books
Head of Publications Mary Butler

Popular and scholarly books on fine and decorative
arts, architecture, contemporary design, fashion and
photography. Founded 1980.

Vallentine Mitchell

Suite 314, Premier House, 112–114 Station Road,
Edgware, Middlesex HA8 7BJ
tel 020-8952 9526 *fax* 020-8952 9242
email info@vmbooks.com
website www.vmbooks.com
Directors Frank Cass (managing), Stewart Cass,
A.E. Cass, H.J. Osen, Hon. C.V. Callman

Jewish history, Judaism, Holocaust studies, general
history, politics and biography.

Variorum – see Ashgate Publishing Ltd

Veritas Publications†

Veritas House, 7–8 Lower Abbey Street, Dublin 1,
Republic of Ireland
tel (01) 8788177 *fax* (01) 8786507
email publications@veritas.ie
website www.veritas.ie

Liturgical and Church resources, religious school
books for primary and post-primary levels,
biographies, academic studies, and general books on
religious, moral and social issues.

Vermilion – see Random House Group Ltd

Verso Ltd

6 Meard Street, London W1F 0EG
tel 020-7437 3546 *fax* 020-7734 0059
email verso@verso.co.uk
Directors Giles O'Bryen (Managing Director), Rowan
Wilson (sales & marketing), Robin Blackburn, Tariq
Ali, Perry Anderson

Politics, sociology, economics, history, philosophy,
cultural studies. Founded 1970.

Viking – see Penguin Group (UK)

Vintage – see Random House Group Ltd

Virago – see Little, Brown Book Group

Virgin Books Ltd

Thames Wharf Studios, Rainville Road, London
W6 9HA
tel 020-7386 3300 *fax* 020-7386 3360
website www.virgin.com/books
Directors K.T. Forster (managing), Natalie Jerome
(editorial), Carolyn Thorne (editorial, illustrated),
Jamie Moore (marketing), Stina Smemo (publicity),
Ray Mudie (sales)

Black Lace (imprint)
Erotic fiction by women for women.

Nexus (imprint)
Editor Adam Nevill
Erotic fiction.

Virgin (imprint)
Editorial Carolyn Thorne (general), Stuart Slater
(music), Kirstie Addis (general)

Health and popular culture: entertainment, showbiz, arts, film and TV, music, humour, biography and autobiography, popular reference, true crime, sport, travel.

Virtue Books Ltd
Edward House, Tenter Street, Rotherham S60 1LB
tel (01709) 365005 *fax* (01709) 829982
email info@virtue.co.uk
website www.virtue.co.uk
Directors Peter E. Russum, Margaret H. Russum

Books for the professional chef: catering and drink.

The Vital Spark – see Neil Wilson Publishing Ltd

Voyager – see HarperCollins Publishers

University of Wales Press
10 Columbus Walk, Brigantine Place, Cardiff CF10 4UP
tel 029-2049 6899 *fax* 029-2049 6108
email press@press.wales.ac.uk
website www.wales.ac.uk/press
Director Ashley Drake

Academic and educational (Welsh and English). Publishers of *Welsh History Review, Studia Celtica, Llên Cymru, Efrydiau Athronyddol, Contemporary Wales, Welsh Journal of Education, Journal of Celtic Linguistics,* ALT-J *(Association for Learning Technology Journal), Kantian Review, Mercator Media Forum, Welsh Writing in English.* Founded 1922.

Walker Books Ltd
87 Vauxhall Walk, London SE11 5HJ
tel 020-7793 0909 *fax* 020-7587 1123
website www.walkerbooks.co.uk
Directors David Heatherwick, David Lloyd, Karen Lotz, Roger Alexander (non-executive), Michel Blake, Sarah Foster, Harold G. Gould OBE (non-executive), Mike McGrath, Henryk Wesolowski, Jane Winterbotham, *Company Secretary* Barley Moss

Children's: picture books, non-fiction and novelty titles; junior and teenage fiction. Founded 1980.

Wallflower Press
6A Middleton Place, Langham Street, London W1W 7TE
tel 020-7436 9494
email info@wallflowerpress.co.uk
website www.wallflowerpress.co.uk
Editorial Director Yoram Allon

Cinema and the moving image, including TV, animation, documentary and artists' film and video – both academic and popular. Founded 1999.

Warburg Institute
University of London, Woburn Square, London WC1H 0AB
tel 020-7862 8949 *fax* 020-7862 8955
email warburg@sas.ac.uk
website www.sas.ac.uk/warburg/

Cultural and intellectual history, with special reference to the history of the classical tradition.

Ward Lock Educational Co. Ltd
BIC Ling Kee House, 1 Christopher Road, East Grinstead, West Sussex RH19 3BT
tel (01342) 318980 *fax* (01342) 410980
email wle@lingkee.com
website www.wardlockeducational.com
Directors Au Bak Ling (chairman, Hong Kong), Au King Kwok (Hong Kong), Au Wai Kwok (Hong Kong), Albert Kw Au (Hong Kong), *Company Secretary* Eileen Parsons

Primary and secondary pupil materials, Kent Mathematics Project: *KMP BASIC* and *KMP Main* series covering Reception to GCSE, *Reading Workshops, Take Part* series and *Take Part* starters, teachers' books, music books, *Target* series for the National Curriculum: *Target Science* and *Target Geography,* religious education. Founded 1952.

Warne – see Penguin Group (UK)

Warner/Chappell Plays Ltd – see Josef Weinberger Plays Ltd

Franklin Watts – see Hachette Children's Books

The Watts Publishing Group Ltd – see Hachette Children's Books

Wayland – see Hachette Children's Books

Websters International Publishers Ltd
2nd Floor, Axe & Bottle Court, 70 Newcomen Street, London SE1 1YT
tel 020-7940 4700 *fax* 020-7940 4701
website www.websters.co.uk, www.ozclarke.com
Chairman & Publisher Adrian Webster, *Managing Director* Jean-Luc Barbanneau, *Publishing Director* Susannah Webster

Wine, food, travel, health. Founded 1983.

Weidenfeld & Nicolson
(part of the Orion Publishing Group Ltd)
Orion House, 5 Upper St Martin's Lane, London WC2H 9EA
tel 020-7240 3444 *fax* 020-7240 4823
Managing Director Malcolm Edwards, *Publisher* Alan Samson, *Publishing Director* Ian Drury, *Publishing Director, Fiction* Helen Garnons-Williams

Biography and autobiography, current affairs, history, travel, fiction, literary fiction, military history and militaria

Weidenfeld & Nicolson Illustrated
Editor-in-Chief Michael Dover

Quality illustrated non-fiction: gardening, cookery, wine, art and design, health and lifestyle, history, popular culture, archaeology, British heritage, literature, fashion, architecture, natural history, sport and adventure.

Cassell Reference (imprint)

Language and general interest reference, including Mrs Beeton, the *Brewer's* series and Jonothan Green's *Dictionary of Slang* and in association with Peter Crawley: *Master Bridge Series*.

Josef Weinberger Plays Ltd

12–14 Mortimer Street, London W1T 3JJ
tel 020-7580 2827 *fax* 020-7436 9016
email general.info@jwmail.co.uk
website www.josef-weinberger.com

Stage plays only, in both acting and trade editions. Preliminary letter essential.

Welsh Academic Press

PO Box 733, Cardiff CF14 7ZY
tel/fax 029-2069 1282
email post@welsh-academic-press.com
website www.welsh-academic-press.com

History, politics, biography, Celtic studies. Founded 1994.

Wharncliffe – see Pen & Sword Books Ltd

Which? Ltd

2 Marylebone Road, London NW1 4DF
tel 020-7770 7000 *fax* 020-7770 7660
email books@which.co.uk
Head of Which? Books Angela Newton

Part of Consumers' Association. Founded 1957.

Which? Books (imprint)

Restaurant guide (*The Good Food Guide*), law and personal finance.

J. Whitaker & Sons Ltd – see Nielsen BookNet

Whittet Books Ltd

Hill Farm, Stonham Road, Cotton, Stowmarket, Suffolk IP14 4RQ
tel (01449) 781877 *fax* (01449) 781898
email annabel@whittet.dircon.co.uk
website www.whittetbooks.com
Directors Annabel Whittet, John Whittet

Natural history, countryside, horticulture, poultry, livestock, pets, horses. Founded 1976.

Whurr Publishers Ltd – see Wiley Europe Ltd

Wiley Europe Ltd*

(incorporating Interscience Publishers)
The Atrium, Southern Gate, Chichester, West Sussex PO19 8SQ
tel (01243) 779777 *fax* (01243) 775878

email europe@wiley.co.uk
website www.wiley.com
Managing Director/Senior Vice President J.H. Jarvis, *Vice President/Director, STM Publishing* M. Davis, *Senior Vice President, P&T Publishing* S. Smith

Physics, chemistry, mathematics, statistics, engineering, architecture, computer science, biology, medicine, earth science, psychology, business, economics, finance. Imprints: Audel, Betty Crocker, Bible, Capstone, CliffsNotes, Ernst & Sohn, ExpressExec, For Dummies, Frommer's, Howell Book House, Interscience, Jossey–Bass, J.K. Lasser, Pillsbury, Pfeiffer, Red Hat Press, Scripta Technica, Sybex, The Unofficial Guide, Visual, Webster's New World, Wiley Academy, Wiley–InterScience, Wiley–Liss, WILEY–VCH, VNR, Wrox.

Whurr Publishers Ltd

Disorders of human communication, medicine, psychology, psychiatry, psychotherapy, occupational therapy, physiotherapy, nursing, for professional markets only. Founded 1987.

Philip Wilson Publishers Ltd

109 The Timber Yard, Drysdale Street, London N1 6ND
tel 020-7033 9900 *fax* 020-7033 9922
email pwilson@philip-wilson.co.uk
website www.philip-wilson.co.uk
Chairman P. Wilson, *Director* S. Prohaska, *Managing Editor* C. Venables, *Production Manager* N. Turpin

Fine and applied art, collecting, museums. Founded 1975.

Neil Wilson Publishing Ltd*

303 The Pentagon Centre, 36 Washington Street, Glasgow G3 8AZ
tel 0141-221 1117 *fax* 0141-221 5363
email info@nwp.co.uk
website www.nwp.co.uk
Managing Director Neil Wilson

The Angels' Share (imprint)
website www.angelshare.co.uk

Whisky-related matters (leisure, reference, history, memoir); other food and drink categories.

11:9 (imprint)
website www.11-9.co.uk

Scottish Arts Council/National Lottery-funded project to bring new Scottish fiction writing to the marketplace. Not commissioning at present.

In Pinn (imprint)
website www.theinpinn.co.uk

The outdoors: travel, hillwalking, climbing.

NWP (imprint)

Scottish interest subjects including history, biography, culture and reference.

The Vital Spark (imprint)
website www.vitalspark.co.uk
Scottish humour.

Wizard – see Icon Books Ltd

Wolters Kluwer (UK) Ltd
(fomerly Croner.CCH Group Ltd)
145 London Road, Kingston-upon-Thames, Surrey
KT2 6SR
tel (0870) 2415719 *fax* 020-8247 1184
email info@croner.cch.co.uk
website www.croner.cch.co.uk, www.cch.co.uk

Law, taxation, finance, insurance, looseleaf and
online information services. Founded 1948.

The Women's Press
Top Floor, 27 Goodge Street, London W1P 2LD
tel 020-7580 7806 *fax* 020-7637 1866
website www.the-womens-press.com
Acting Managing Director Stella Kane

Books by women in the areas of literary and crime
fiction, biography and autobiography, health, culture,
politics, handbooks, literary criticism, psychology and
self-help, the arts. Founded 1978.

Livewire (imprint)
Books for teenagers and young women.

Wooden Books
13 High Street, Butleigh, Glastonbury BA6 8SU
website www.woodenbooks.com
Directors John Martineau (managing), Anthony
Brandt (secretary), Michael Glickman (overseas)

Magic, mathematics, ancient sciences, esoteric.
Quality b&w illustrators may submit samples.
Founded 1996.

Woodhead Publishing Ltd
Abington Hall, Abington, Cambridge CB1 6AH
tel (01223) 891358 *fax* (01223) 893694
email wp@woodheadpublishing.com
website www.woodheadpublishing.com
Managing Director Martin Woodhead

Engineering, materials, welding, textiles,
commodities, food science and technology,
environmental science. Founded 1989.

Wordsworth Editions Ltd
8ʙ East Street, Ware, Herts. SG12 9HJ
tel (01920) 465167 *fax* (01920) 462267
email enquiries@wordsworth-editions.com
website www.wordsworth.editions.com
Directors Helen Trayler (managing), Dennis Hart
(sales)

Reprints of classic books: literary, children's; poetry;
reference; Special Editions; mystery and supernatural.
Founded 1987.

The X Press
PO Box 25694, London N17 6FP
tel 020-8801 2100 *fax* 020-8885 1322

email vibes@xpress.co.uk
website www.xpress.co.uk
Editorial Director Dotun Adebayo, *Marketing Director*
Steve Pope

Black interest popular novels, particularly reflecting
contemporary ethnic experiences. *Black Classics*
series: reprints of classic novels by black writers.
Founded 1992.

Nia (imprint)
Literary black fiction.

Y Lolfa Cyf.
Talybont, Ceredigion SY24 5AP
tel (01970) 832304 *fax* (01970) 832782
email ylolfa@ylolfa.com
website www.ylolfa.com
Director Garmon Gruffudd, *Editor* Lefi Gruffudd

Welsh-language popular fiction and non-fiction,
music, children's books; Welsh-language tutors;
Welsh politics in English and a range of Welsh-
interest books for the tourist market. Founded 1967.

Yale University Press London*
47 Bedford Square, London WC1B 3DP
tel 020-7079 4900 *fax* 020-7079 4901
email firstname.lastname@yaleup.co.uk
website www.yalebooks.co.uk
Managing Director Robert Baldock, *Marketing
Director* Kate Pocock, *Publishers* Gillian Malpass (art
history), Sally Salvesen (Buildings of England),
Heather McCallum (trade books)

Art, architecture, history, economics, political science,
religion, philosophy, history of science, biography,
current affairs and music. Founded 1961.

Yellow Jersey Press – see Random House
Group Ltd

York Notes – see Pearson Education

Young Hippo – see Scholastic Ltd

Young Picador – see Macmillan Publishers Ltd

Zed Books Ltd
7 Cynthia Street, London N1 9JF
tel 020-7837 4014 (general) *fax* 020-7833 3960
email zed@zedbooks.net
website www.zedbooks.co.uk
Editors Ellen McKinlay, Anna Hardman

Social sciences on international issues; women's
studies, politics, development and environmental
studies; area studies (Africa, Asia, Caribbean, Latin
America, Middle East and the Pacific). Founded
1976.

Zero to Ten Ltd*
2ᴀ Portman Mansions, Chiltern Street, London
W1U 6NR

tel 020-7487 0920 *fax* 020-7487 0921
email sales@evansbrothers.co.uk
Publishing Director Su Swallow

Non-fiction for children aged 0–10: board books, toddler books, first story books, etc. Part of the Evans Publishing Group. Founded 1997.

Cherrytree Books (imprint)
UK Publisher Su Swallow
Children's non-fiction illustrated books mainly for schools and libraries.

Zoë Books

15 Worthy Lane, Winchester, Hants SO23 7AB
tel (01962) 851318
email enquiries@zoebooks.co.uk
website www.zoebooks.co.uk
Managing/Publishing Director Imogen Dawson

Children's information books for the school and library markets in the UK; specialists in co-editions for world markets. No unsolicited MSS. No opportunities for freelances. Founded 1990.

Book publishers overseas

Listings are given for book publishers in Australia (below), Canada (page 193), New Zealand (page 197), South Africa (page 199) and the USA (page 201).

AUSTRALIA

*Member of the Australian Publishers Association

Access Press

54 Railway Parade, Bassendean, Western Australia 6054
postal address PO Box 446, Bassendean, Western Australia 6054
fax (08) 9379 3188
website (08) 9379 3199
Managing Editor Helen Weller

Australiana, biography, non-fiction. Commissioned works and privately financed books published and distributed. Founded 1974.

Allen & Unwin Pty Ltd*

83 Alexander Street, Crows Nest, NSW 2065
postal address PO Box 8500, St Leonards, NSW 1590
tel (02) 8425 0100 *fax* (02) 9906 2218
email info@allenandunwin.com
website www.allenandunwin.com
Directors Patrick Gallagher (publishing), Paul Donovan (managing), Peter Eichhorn (finance), Sue Hines (trade publishing)

General trade, including fiction and children's books, academic, especially social science and history. Founded 1990.

Michelle Anderson Publishing Pty Ltd*

PO Box 6032, Chapel Street North, South Yarra 3141
tel (03) 9826 9028 *fax* (03) 9826 8552
email mapubl@bigpond.net.au
website www.michelleandersonpublishing.com
Director Michelle Anderson

General health and mind/body, children's, babies and motherhood. Founded 1965.

The Australian Council *for* Educational Research

19 Prospect Hill Road, Private Bag 55, Camberwell, Victoria 3124
tel (03) 9277 5555 *fax* (03) 9277 5500
email info@acer.edu.au
website www.acer.edu.au
Ceo Prof. Geoff Masters

Range of books and kits: for teachers, trainee teachers, parents, psychologists, counsellors, students of education, researchers.

Blackwell Publishing Asia Pty Ltd

550 Swanston Street, Carlton, Victoria 3053
tel (03) 8359 1100 *fax* (03) 8359 1120

email info@asia.blackwellpublishing.com
website www.blackwellpublishing.com
President Mark Robertson

Medical, healthcare, life, earth sciences, professional.

Books & Writers Network Pty Ltd

(incorporating Wild & Woolley and Fast Books)
PO Box W76, Watsons Bay, NSW 2030
tel (02) 9337 6844
website www.wildandwoolley.com.au
Director Pat Woolley

Offers short and long run printing, design, editing, layout, promotion, and a new on-line bookshop for self published books. Founded 1974.

Cambridge University Press Australian Branch*

477 Williamstown Road, Private Bag 31, Port Melbourne, Victoria 3207
tel (03) 8671 1411 *fax* (03) 9676 9955
email info@cambridge.edu.au
website www.cambridge.edu.au
Director Kim Harris

Academic, educational, reference, English as a second language.

Dominie Pty Ltd

Drama (Plays & Musicals), 8 Cross Street, Brookvale, NSW 2100
tel (02) 9938 8600 *fax* (02) 9938 8695
email drama@dominie.com.au
website www.dominie.com.au

Australian representatives of publishers of plays and agents for the collection of royalties for Samuel French Ltd, Hanbury Plays, Samuel French Inc., The Society of Authors, Bakers Plays of Boston, Nick Hern Books, Pioneer Drama and Dramatic Publishing, Dominie Musicals.

EA Books

Engineers Media, PO Box 588, 2 Ernest Street, Level 4, Crows Nest, NSW 2065
tel (02) 9438 1533 *fax* (02) 9438 5934
website www.engaust.com.au
Managing Editor Dietrich George

Publishing company of the Institution of Engineers Australia.

Elsevier Australia*

30–52 Smidmore Street, Marrickville, NSW 2204
tel (02) 9517 8999 *fax* (02) 9550 6007

email customerserviceau@elsevier.com
Managing Director W. Fergus Hall

Science, medical and technical books. Imprints: Academic Press, Architectural Press, Butterworth-Heinemann, Cell Press, Churchill Livingstone, Elsevier Science, Engineering Information, Excerpta Medica, The Lancet, MD Consult, MDL, Mosby, North-Holland, Pergamon, Science Direct, Saunders. Established 1972.

Hachette Livre Australia Pty Ltd*
Level 17, 207 Kent Street, Sydney, NSW 2000
tel (02) 8248 0800 *fax* (02) 2848 0810
email auspub@hachette.com.au
website www.hachette.com.au
Directors Malcolm Edwards (managing), Mary Drum, Chris Raine, David Cocking, Louise Sherwin-Stark, Matt Richell, Sandy Weir, Fiona Hazard

General, children's. No unsolicited MSS.

HarperCollins Publishers (Australia) Pty Ltd Group*
postal address PO Box 321, 25 Ryde Road, Pymble, NSW 2073
tel (02) 9952 5000 *fax* (02) 9952 5555
Managing Director Robert Gorman, *Publishing Director* Shona Martyn, *Publishers* Linda Funnell (fiction), Amruta Slee (non-fiction), Alison Urquhart (non-fiction), Lisa Berryman (children's)

Literary fiction and non-fiction, popular fiction, children's, reference, biography, autobiography, current affairs, sport, lifestyle, health/self-help, humour, true crime, travel, Australiana, history, business, gift, religion.

Kangaroo Press – see Simon & Schuster (Australia) Pty Ltd

Lantern – see Penguin Group (Australia)

Lawbook Co.
Level 5, 100 Harris Street, Pyrmont, NSW 2009
tel (02) 8587 7000 *fax* (02) 8587 7100
email service@thomson.com.au
website www.thomson.com.au
Ceo Tony Kinnear

Law. Part of Thomson Legal.

LexisNexis Butterworths Australia
Tower 2, 475–495 Victoria Avenue, Chatswood, NSW 2067
tel (02) 9422 2189 *fax* (02) 9422 2406
postal address Level 9, Locked Bag 2222, Chatswood Delivery Centre, Chatswood, NSW 2067
website www.butterworths.com.au
Publishing Director James Broadfoot

Accounting, business, legal, tax and commercial.

Lonely Planet Publications*
90 Maribyrnong Street, Footscray 3011, Victoria
tel (03) 8379 8000 *fax* (03) 8379 8111
email talk2us@lonelyplanet.com.au
website www.lonelyplanet.com
Directors Tony Wheeler, Maureen Wheeler

Country and regional guidebooks, city guides, *Best Of* citybreak guides, city maps, phrasebooks, walking guides, diving and snorkelling guides, pictorial books, healthy travel guides, food guides, cycling guides, wildlife guides, travel photography. Also a commercial slide library (Lonely Planet Images) and a TV company. Offices in London and Oakland, USA. Founded 1973.

Lothian Books*
132 Albert Road, South Melbourne, Victoria 3205
tel 613-9694-4900 *fax* 613-9645-0705
email books@lothian.com.au
website www.lothian.com.au
Ceo Peter Lothian, *Sales & Marketing Manager* Bruce Hilliard, *Children's Publisher* Helen Chamberlain

Juvenile, health, gardening, reference, Australian history, business, sport, biography, New Age, humour, Buddhism. Imprint of Time Warner Book Group.

McGraw-Hill Education*
Level 2, The Everglade Building, 82 Waterloo Road, North Ryde NSW 2113
Private Bag 2233, Business Centre, North Ryde, NSW 1670
tel (02) 9900 1905, 9900 1800
email eiko_bron@mcgraw-hill.com
website www.macgraw-hill.com.au
Publishing Manager Michael Tully, *Schools Acquisitions Editor* Eiko Bron

Educational publisher: higher education, primary and secondary education (grades K–12) and professional (including medical, general and reference). Division of the McGraw-Hill Companies. Founded 1964.

Macmillan Education Australia Pty Ltd*
Melbourne office Level 4, 627 Chapel Street, South Yarra, Victoria 3141
tel (03) 9825 1025 *fax* (03) 9825 1010
email mea@macmillan.com.au
Sydney office Level 2, St Martin's Tower, 31 Market Street, Sydney, NSW 2000
tel (02) 9285 9200 *fax* (02) 9285 9290
Directors Shane Armstrong (managing), Peter Huntley (sales), Sandra Iversen (primary publishing), Rex Parry (secondary publishing), George Smith (production), *Company Secretary/Financial Controller* Terry White, *Children's Publisher* Sandra Iverson

Educational books.

Melbourne University Publishing*
187 Grattan Street, Carlton, Victoria 3053
tel (03) 9342 0300 *fax* (03) 9342 0399
email mup-info@unimelb.edu.au
website www.mup.unimelb.edu.au

Ceo/Publisher Louise Adler

Academic, scholastic and cultural; educational textbooks and books of reference. Imprint: Miegunyah Press. Founded 1922.

National Archives of Australia*

PO Box 7425, Canberra Business Centre, ACT 2610
tel (02) 6212-3603 *fax* (02) 6213-3914
email angelam@naa.gov.au
website www.naa.gov.au
Assistant Director-General, Access & Communication Anne Lyons, *Director, Publications & Websites* Margaret Chalker, *Publications Manager* Angela McAdam

Australia history (post Federation), genealogy, reference. Founded 1944; publishing books since 1989.

NCELTR Publishing*

(National Centre for English Language Teaching & Research)
Macquarie University, NSW 2109
tel (02) 9850-7966 *fax* (02) 9850 6055
email louise.melou@mq.edu.au
website www.nceltr.mq.edu.au/publications
Publishing Manager Louise Melov, *Executive Director* DeniseMurray

English language materials for teaching and learning and for the adult migrant English area. Founded 1988.

Pan Macmillan Australia Pty Ltd*

Level 25, 1 Market Street, Sydney, NSW 2000
tel (02) 9285 9100 *fax* (02) 9285 9190
email pansyd@macmillan.com.au
website www.macmillan.com.au
Directors Ross Gibb (chairman), James Fraser (publishing), Roxarne Burns (publishing), Siv Toigo (finance), Peter Phillips (sales), Jeannine Fowler (publicity & marketing)

Commercial and literary fiction; children's fiction, non-fiction and character products; non-fiction; sport.

Penguin Group (Australia)*

250 Camberwell Road, Camberwell, Victoria 3124
tel (03) 9811 2400 *fax* (03) 9811 2620
postal address PO Box 701, Hawthorn, Victoria 3122
website www.penguin.com.au
Managing Director Gabrielle Coyne, *Publishing Director* Robert Sessions

Fiction, general non-fiction, current affairs, sociology, economics, environmental, travel guides, anthropology, politics, children's, health, cookery, gardening, pictorial and general books relating to Australia. Imprints: Penguin Books, Lantern, Viking. Founded 1946.

University of Queensland Press*

PO Box 6042, St Lucia, Queensland 4067
tel (07) 3365 2127 *fax* (07) 3365 7579

email uqp@uqp.uq.edu.au
website www.uqp.uq.edu.au
General Manager Greg Bain

Scholarly works, tertiary texts, indigenous Australian writing, Australian fiction, young adult fiction, poetry, history, general interest. Founded 1948.

Random House Australia Pty Ltd*

20 Alfred Street, Milsons Point, NSW 2061
tel (02) 9954 9966 *fax* (02) 9954 4562
email random@randomhouse.com.au
website www.randomhouse.com.au
Managing Director Margaret Seale, *Head of Publishing, Random House* Jane Palfreyman, *Head of Publishing, Bantam Doubleday* Fiona Henderson, *Children's Publisher* Lindsay Knight, *Illustrated Publisher* Jude McGee, *Sales & Marketing Director* Carol Davidson, *Publicity Director* Karen Reid

General fiction and non-fiction; children's, illustrated. MSS submissions – for Random House and Transworld Publishing, unsolicited non-fiction accepted, unbound in hard copy addressed to Submissions Editor. Fiction submissions are only accepted from previously published authors, or authors represented by an agent or accompanied by a report from an accredited assessment service. Imprints: Arrow, Avon, Ballantine, Bantam, Black Swan, Broadway, Century, Chatto & Windus, Corgi, Crown, Dell, Doubleday, Ebury, Fodor, Heinemann, Hutchinson, Jonathan Cape, Knopf, Mammoth UK, Minerva, Pantheon, Pavilion, Pimlico, Random House, Red Fox, Rider, Vermilion, Vintage, Virgin. Subsidiary of Bertelsmann AG.

Scholastic Australia Pty Ltd*

PO Box 579, Gosford, NSW 2250
tel (02) 4328 3555 *fax* (02) 4323 3827
website www.scholastic.com.au
Managing Director Ken Jolly, *Publisher* Andrew Berkhut

Children's fiction and non-fiction. Founded 1968.

Simon & Schuster (Australia) Pty Ltd*

PO Box 507, East Roseville, NSW 2069
tel (02) 9415 9900 *fax* (02) 9417 3188
postal address PO Box 33, Pymble NSW 2073
website www.simonand schuster.com.au
Managing Director/Publisher Jon Attenborough

General non-fiction including anthropology, child care, hobbies, house and home, how-to, craft, biography, motivation, management, outdoor recreation, sport, travel. Imprints: Simon & Schuster Australia, Kangaroo Press. Founded 1987.

Spinifex Press

504 Queensberry Street, North Melbourne, Victoria 3051
tel (03) 9329 6088 *fax* (03) 9329 9238
website www.spinifexpress.com.au

Managing Director Susan Hawthorne

Feminism and women's studies, art, astronomy, occult, education, gay and lesbian, health and nutrition, technology, travel. No unsolicited MSS. Founded 1991.

Thomson Learning Australia*
Level 7, 80 Dorcas Street, South Melbourne, Victoria 3205
tel (03) 9685 4111 *fax* (03) 9685 4199
email customerservice@thomsonlearning.com.au
website www.thomsonlearning.com.au

Educational books.

Transworld Publishers (Aust) Pty Ltd – merged with Random House Australia Pty Ltd

UNSW Press*
University of New South Wales, UNSW Sydney NSW 2052
tel (02) 9664 0900 *fax* (02) 9664 5420
email info.press@unsw.edu.au
website www.unswpress.com.au
Managing Director Dr Robin Derricourt, *Publishing Manager* John Elliot

Environmental studies, ecology, botany, education, sociology, cultural studies, politics, history; general reference; tertiary textbooks. Founded 1962.

Viking – see Penguin Group (Australia)

University of Western Australia Press*
UWA, 35 Stirling Hwy, Crawley 6009, Western Australia
tel (618) 6488 3670 *fax* (618) 6488 1027
email admin@uwapress.uwa.edu.au
website www.uwapress.uwa.edu.au
Acting Director Terri-Ann White

Natural history, history, maritime history, critical studies, women's studies, general non-fiction, contemporary issues, children's picture books, young fiction. Imprints: Cygnet Books, Staples, UWA Press. Founded 1935.

John Wiley & Sons Australia, Ltd
42 McDougall Street, Milton, Queensland 4064
tel (07) 3859 9755 *fax* (07) 3859 9715
email brisbane@johnwiley.com.au
website www.johnwiley.com.au
Managing Director P. Donoughue

Educational, technical, atlases, professional, reference, trade. Imprints: John Wiley & Sons, Jacaranda, Wrightbooks. Founded 1954.

CANADA

*Member of the Canadian Publishers' Council
†Member of the Association of Canadian Publishers

Annick Press Ltd†
15 Patricia Avenue, Toronto, Ontario M2M 1H9
tel 416-221-4802 *fax* 416-221-8400
email annickpress@annickpress.com
website www.annickpress.com
Co-editors Rick Wilks, Colleen MacMillan, *Creative Director* Sheryl Shapiro

Preschool to young adult fiction and non-fiction. Founded 1975.

Arabesque – see Harlequin Enterprises Ltd

Boardwalk Books – see Dundurn Press

Butterworths Canada Ltd – see LexisNexis Canada Inc.

Castle Street Mysteries – see Dundurn Press

The Charlton Press
PO Box 820, Station Willowdale B, North York, Ontario M2K 2R1
tel 416-488-1418 *fax* 416-488-4656
email chpress@charltonpress.com
website www.charltonpress.com
President W.K. Cross

Collectibles, Numismatics, Sportscard price catalogues. Founded 1952.

Doubleday Canada
1 Toronto Street, Suite 300, Toronto, Ontario M5C 2V6
tel 416-364-4449 *fax* 416-957-1587
website www.randomhouse.ca
Chairman John Neale, *Publisher* Maya Mavjee

General trade non-fiction; fiction; young adults. Division of **Random House of Canada Ltd**. Founded 1942.

Douglas & McIntyre Ltd
2323 Quebec Street, Suite 201, Vancouver, BC V5T 4S7
tel 604-254-7191 *fax* 604-254-9099
email dm@douglas-mcintyre.com

General list, including Greystone Books imprint: Canadian biography, art and architecture, natural history, history, native studies, Canadian fiction. No unsolicited MSS. Founded 1964.

Dundurn Press†
3 Church Street, Suite 500, Toronto, Ontario M5E 1MZ
tel 416-214-5544 *fax* 416-214-5556
email info@dundurn.com

website www.dundurn.com
Directors J. Kirk Howard (President), Beth Bruder (Vic-President, sales & marketing), Tony Hawke (editorial)

Popular non-fiction, fiction, scholarship, history, biography, young adult, art. Part of the Dundurn Group. Founded 1973.

Boardwalk Books (imprint); Sandcastle Books (imprint)
Young adult fiction.

Castle Street Mysteries (imprint)
Mystery fiction.

Hounslow Press (imprint)
Popular non-fiction.

Simon & Pierre Publishing (imprint)
Theatre, drama, fiction, translations.

ECW Press Ltd†
2120 Queen Street E, Suite 200, Toronto, Ontario M4E 1E2
tel 416-694-3348 *fax* 416-698-9906
email info@ecwpress.com
website www.ecwpress.com
Publisher Jack David

Popular culture, TV and film, sports, humour, general trade books, biographies, guidebooks. Founded 1979.

Fitzhenry & Whiteside Ltd†
195 Allstate Parkway, Markham, Ontario L3R 4T8
tel 800-387-9776 *fax* 800-260-9777
email godwit@fitzhenry.ca
website www.fitzhenry.ca
Director Sharon Fitzhenry, *Children's Publisher* Gail Winskill

Trade, educational, children's books. Founded 1966.

Gold Eagle Books – see Harlequin Enterprises Ltd

Harcourt Canada Ltd
55 Horner Avenue, Toronto, Ontario M8Z 4X6
tel 800-268-2222 *fax* 800-430-4445
website www.nelson.com

Educational materials from K–Grade 12, testing and assessment. Imprints: Harcourt Religion (formerly Brown-ROA), Harcourt Brace & Company, Holt, Rinehart and Winston, MeadowBrook Press, The Psychological Corporation, Therapy Skill Builders/ Communications Skill Builders. Distributed by Thomson Nelson. Founded 1922.

Harlequin Enterprises Ltd*
225 Duncan Mill Road, Don Mills, Ontario M3B 3K9
tel 416-445-5860 *fax* 416-445-8655
website www.eharlequin.com
Publisher/Ceo Donna Hayes, *Executive Vice President, Global Publishing & Strategy* Loriana Sacilotto

Fiction for women, romance, inspirational fiction, African–American fiction, action adventure, mystery. Founded 1949.

Harlequin Books (imprint)
Contemporary and historical romance fiction in series.

Silhouette Books (imprint)
Contemporary romance fiction in series.

Steeple Hill (imprint)
Director, Global Single Titles Editorial Dianne Moggy
Contemporary inspirational romantic fiction in series.

Luna Books (imprint)
Romantic fantasy.

HQN Books (imprint)
Romantic single title fiction, contemporary and historical.

Mira Books (imprint)
Fiction for women, contemporary and historical dramas, family sagas, romantic suspense and relationship novels.

Red Dress Ink (imprint)
Women's fiction for the 20-somethings.

Gold Eagle Books (imprint)
Series action adventure fiction.

Worldwide Mystery (imprint)
General Manager, Kimani Press Linda Gill
Contemporary mystery fiction. Reprints only.

Kimani Romance (imprint)
Contemporary romance fiction in series.

Arabesque (imprint)
Contemporary romance fiction for African Americans.

Sepia (imprint)
Contemporary fiction for African Americans.

New Spirit (imprint)
Inspirational fiction and non-fiction for African Americans.

HarperCollins Publishers Ltd*
2 Bloor Street East, 20th Floor, Toronto, Ontario M4W 1A8
tel 416-975-9334 *fax* 416-975-9884
website www.harpercollins.ca
President David Kent

Publishers of literary fiction and non-fiction, history, politics, biography, spiritual and children's books. Founded 1989.

Hounslow Press – see Dundurn Press

HQN Books – see Harlequin Enterprises Ltd

Key Porter Books Ltd[†]
6 Adelaide Street East, 10th Floor, Toronto, Ontario
M5C 1H6
tel 416-862-7777 *fax* 416-862-2304
email info@keyporter.com
website www.keyporter.com
Publisher Jordan Fenn

Fiction, nature, history, Canadian politics,
conservation, humour, biography, autobiography,
health, children's books. Founded 1981.

Kids Can Press Ltd[†]
29 Birch Avenue, Toronto, Ontario M4V 1E2
tel 416-925-5437 *fax* 416-960-5437
email info@kidscan.com
website www.kidscanpress.com
Publisher Valerie Hussey, Karen Boersma

Juvenile/young adult books. Founded 1973.

Kimani Romance – see Harlequin Enterprises Ltd

Knopf Canada – see Random House of Canada Ltd

LexisNexis Canada Inc.*
123 Commerce Valley Drive East, Suite 700,
Markham, Ontario L3T 7W8
tel 905-479-2665 *fax* 905-479-2826
email info@lexisnexis.ca

Law and accountancy. Division of Reed Elsevier plc.

Lone Pine Publishing
10145–81 Avenue, Edmonton, Alberta T6E 1W9
tel 780-433-9333 *fax* 780-433-9646
email info@lonepinepublishing.com
website www.lonepinepublishing.com
Chairman Grant Kennedy, *Manager* Shane Kennedy

Natural history, outdoor recreation and wildlife
guidebooks, self-help, gardening, popular history.
Founded 1980.

Luna Books – see Harlequin Enterprises Ltd

McClelland & Stewart Ltd[†]
75 Sherbourne Street, 5th Floor, Toronto, Ontario
M5A 2P9
tel 416-598-1114 *fax* 416-598-7764
website www.mcclelland.com
President & Publisher Douglas Pepper

General. Founded 1906.

McGill-Queen's University Press[†]
3430 McTavish Street, Montreal, Quebec H3A 1X9
tel 514-398-3750 *fax* 514-398-4333
email mqup@mqup.ca

Queen's University, Kingston, Ontario K7L 3N6
tel 613-533-2155 *fax* 613-533-6822
email mqup@qucdn.queensu.ca
website www.mqup.ca

Academic, non-fiction, poetry. Founded 1969.

McGraw-Hill Ryerson Ltd*
300 Water Street, Whitby, Ontario L1N 9B6
tel 905-430-5000 *fax* 905-430-5020
website www.mcgrawhill.ca
Executive Vice-President Robert Bahash

Educational and trade books.

Mira Books – see Harlequin Enterprises Ltd

Napoleon Publishing/Rendez Vous Press[†]
178 Willowdale Avenue, Suite 201, Toronto, Ontario
M2N 4Y8
tel 416-730-9052 *fax* 416-730-8096
email napoleon.publishing@transmedia95.com
website www.napoleonpublishing.com
Publisher Sylvia McConnell, *Editor* Allister Thompson

Children's books and adult fiction. Founded 1990.

New Spirit – see Harlequin Enterprises Ltd

NeWest Press[†]
201–8540–109 Street, Edmonton, AB T6G 1E6
tel 780-432-9427 *fax* 780-433-3179
email info@newestpress.com
website www.newestpress.com
Directors Doug Barbour (President), Don Kerr (Vice-
President), Ross Jopling (Secretary), Donna Weis
(Treasurer)

Fiction, drama and poetry, and regional non-fiction
with a western Canadian focus. Founded 1977.

Oberon Press
205–145 Spruce Street, Ottawa, Ontario K1R 6P1
tel 613-238-3275 *fax* 613-238-3275
website www.oberonpress.ca

General.

Oxford University Press, Canada*
70 Wynford Drive, Don Mills, Ontario M3C 1J9
tel 416-441-2941 *fax* 416-444-0427
website www.oup.com/ca
President David Stover

Educational and academic.

Pearson Education Canada*
(formerly Prentice Hall Canada and Addison-Wesley
Canada)
26 Prince Andrew Place, Toronto, Ontario M3C 2T8
tel 416-447-5101 *fax* 416-443-0948
website www.pearsoned.ca
President Allan Reynolds

Academic, technical, educational, children's and adult, trade.

Penguin Group (Canada)*
90 Eglinton Avenue East, Suite 700, Toronto, Ontario M4P 2Y3
tel 416-925-2249 *fax* 416-925-0068
email info@penguin.ca
website www.penguin.ca

Literary fiction, memoir, non-fiction (history, business, current events). No unsolicited MSS; submissions via an agent only. Imprints: Penguin Canada, Viking Canada, Puffin Canada. Founded 1974.

Pippin Publishing Corporation
PO Box 242, Don Mills, Ontario M3C 2S2
tel 416-510-2918 *fax* 416-510-3359
email cynthia@pippinpub.com
website www.pippinpub.com
President/Editorial Director Jonathan Lovat Dickson

ESL/EFL, teacher reference, adult basic education, school texts (all subjects), general trade (non-fiction).

Random House of Canada Ltd*
1 Toronto Street, Suite 300, Toronto, Ontario M5C 2V6
tel 416-364 4449 *fax* 416-364-6863
website www.randomhouse.ca
Chairman John Neale

Imprints: Canada, Doubleday Canada, Knopf Canada, Random House Canada, Seal Books, Vintage Canada. Subsidiary of Bertelsmann AG. Founded 1944.

Red Dress Ink – see Harlequin Enterprises Ltd

Ronsdale Press†
3350 West 21st Avenue, Vancouver, BC V6S 1G7
tel 604-738-4688 *fax* 604-731-4548
email ronsdale@shaw.ca
website www.rondalepress.com
Director Ronald B. Hatch

Canadian literature: fiction, poetry, biography, books of ideas. Founded 1988.

Sandcastle Books – see Dundurn Press

Sepia – see Harlequin Enterprises Ltd

Silhouette Books – see Harlequin Enterprises Ltd

Simon & Pierre Publishing – see Dundurn Press

Steeple Hill – see Harlequin Enterprises Ltd

Thompson Educational Publishing*
6 Ripley Avenue, Suite 200, Toronto, Ontario M6S 3N9
tel 416-766-2763 *fax* 416-766-0398
email publisher@thompsonbooks.com
website www.thompsonbooks.com
President Keith Thompson, *Vice-President* Faye Thompson

Social sciences. Founded 1989.

Thomson Nelson*
1120 Birchmount Road, Scarborough, Ontario M1K 5G4
tel 416-752-9100 *fax* 416-752-9646
email inquire@nelson.com
website www.nelson.com
President George W. Bergquist, *Vice President, Market Development* Chris Besse, *Senior Vice President, School* Greg Pilon, *Senior Vice President, Media Services* Susan Cline, *Senior Vice President, Higher Education* Lesley Gouldie

Educational publishing: school (K–12), college and university, career education, measurement and guidance, professional and reference, ESL titles. Division of Thomson Canada Ltd. Founded 1914.

University of Toronto Press Inc.†
10 St Mary Street, Suite 700, Toronto, Ontario M4Y 2W8
tel 416-978-2239 *fax* 416-978-4738
email publishing@utpress.utoronto.ca
website www.utpress.utoronto.ca
President/Publisher John Yates

Founded 1901.

Tundra Books Inc.†
75 Sherbourne Street, 5th Floor, Toronto, Ontario M5A 2P9
tel 416-598-4786 *fax* 416-598-0247
website www.tundrabooks.com
Children's Publisher Kathy Lowinger

High-quality children's picture books.

Women's Press†
180 Bloor Street West, Suite 801, Toronto, Ontario M5S 2V6
tel 416-929-2774 *fax* 416-929-1926
email info@cspi.org
website www.womenspress.ca
President & Publisher Dr Jack Wayne, *General Manager* C. Dick Yu, *Editorial Director* Megan Mueller

The ideas and experiences of women: fiction, creative non-fiction, children's books, plays, biography, autobiography, memoirs, poetry. Owned by Canadian Scholars' Press. Founded 1987.

Worldwide Mystery – see Harlequin Enterprises Ltd

NEW ZEALAND

**Member of the New Zealand Book Publishers'
Association*

Auckland University Press*
University of Auckland, Private Bag 92019, Auckland
tel (09) 373-7528 *fax* (09) 373-7465
email aup@auckland.ac.nz
website www.auckland.ac.nz/aup
Director Elizabeth Caffin

NZ history, NZ poetry, Maori and Pacific studies,
politics, sociology, literary criticism, art history,
biography, media studies, women's studies. Founded
1966.

David Bateman Ltd*
30 Tarndale Grove, Albany, Auckland
tel (09) 415-7664 *fax* (09) 415-8892
email bateman@bateman.co.nz
postal address PO Box 100242, North Shore Mail
Centre, Auckland 1330
website www.bateman.co.nz
Chairman/Publisher David L. Bateman, *Directors*
Janet Bateman, Paul Bateman (joint managing), Paul
Parkinson (joint managing)

Natural history, gardening, encyclopedias, sport, art,
cookery, historical, juvenile, travel, motoring,
maritime history, business, art, lifestyle. Founded
1979.

Bush Press Communications Ltd
4 Bayview Road, Hauraki Corner, Takapuna
tel/fax (09) 486-2667
email bush.press@clear.net.nz
postal address PO Box 33–029, Takapuna,
Auckland 1309
Governing Director/Publisher Gordon Ell ONZM

NZ non-fiction, particularly outdoor, nature, travel,
architecture, crafts, Maori, popular history; children's
non-fiction. Founded 1979.

The Caxton Press
113 Victoria Street, Christchurch
tel (03) 366-8516 *fax* (03) 365-7840
postal address PO Box 25–088, Christchurch
Director E.B. Bascand

Local history, tourist pictorial, Celtic spirituality,
parent guide, book designers and printers. Founded
1935.

Dunmore Press Ltd*
PO Box 2580, Wellington
tel (04) 472-2705 *fax* (04) 471-0604
email books@dunmore.co.nz
website www.dunmore.co.nz
Directors Murray Gatenby, Sharmian Firth

Education, history, sociology, business studies,
general non-fiction. Founded 1970.

Godwit Publishing Ltd – acquired by
Random House New Zealand Ltd

Hachette Livre NZ Ltd*
PO Box 100–749, North Shore Mail Centre,
Auckland 1333
tel (09) 478-1000 *fax* (09) 478-1010
email admin@hachette.co.nz
Managing Director Kevin Chapman, *Editorial Director*
Warren Adler

Sport, cooking, travel, general.

Halcyon Publishing Ltd
PO Box 360, Auckland 1015
tel (09) 489 5337 *fax* (09) 489 5218
email info@halcyonpublishing.co.nz
Managing Director/Publisher Graham Gurr, *Editorial
Consultant* Antony Entwistle

Hunting, shooting, fishing, outdoor interests.
Founded 1982.

HarperCollins Publishers (New
Zealand) Ltd*
PO Box 1, Auckland
tel (09) 443-9400 *fax* (09) 443-9403
Postal address PO Box 1, Auckland
website www.harpercollins.co.nz
Managing Director Tony Fisk, *Commissioning Editor*
Lorain Day

General literature, non-fiction, reference, children's.

Learning Media Ltd*
Level 4, Willeston House, 22–28 Willeston Street,
PO Box 3293, Wellington 6001
tel (4) 472-5522 *fax* (4) 472 6444
email info@learningmedia.co.nz
website www.learningmedia.com,
www.learningmedia.co.nz

Educational books, websites and CD-Roms for New
Zealand and international markets. Texts in English,
Maori and 6 Pacific languages. Founded 1993.

LexisNexis NZ Ltd*
205–207 Victoria Street, Wellington 1
tel (04) 385-1479 *fax* (04) 385-1598
email Russell.Gray@lexisnexis.co.nz
postal address PO Box 472, Wellington 1
website www.lexisnexis.co.nz
Managing Director Russell Gray

Law, business, academic.

McGraw-Hill Book Company New
Zealand Ltd*
56–60 Cawley Street, Level 8, Ellerslie, Auckland
Private Bag 11904, Ellerslie, Auckland 1005
tel (09) 526 6200 *fax* (09) 526 6216
website www.mcgrawhill.com.au

Educational publisher: higher education, primary and
secondary education (grades K–12) and professional

(including medical, general and reference). Division of the McGraw-Hill Companies. Founded 1974.

Mallinson Rendel Publishers Ltd*
Level 5, 15 Courtenay Place, PO Box 9409, Wellington
tel (04) 802-5012 *fax* (04) 802-5013
email publisher@mallinsonrendel.co.nz
Director Ann Mallinson

Children's books. Founded 1980.

Nelson Price Milburn Ltd
1 Te Puni Street, Petone
tel (04) 568-7179 *fax* (04) 568-2115
email jacqui.rivera@thomson.com
postal address PO Box 38–945, Wellington Mail Centre, Wellington

Children's fiction, primary school texts, especially school readers and maths, secondary educational.

New Zealand Council for Educational Research
Box 3237, Education House, 178–182 Willis Street, Wellington 1
tel (04) 384-7939 *fax* (04) 384-7933
email info@nzcer.org.nz
website www.nzcer.org.nz
Director Robyn Baker, *Publisher* Bev Webber

Education, including educational policy and institutions, early childhood education, educational achievement tests, Maori education, curriculum and assessment, etc. Founded 1934.

University of Otago Press*
University of Otago, PO Box 56, Dunedin
tel (03) 479-8807 *fax* (03) 479-8385
email university.press@otago.ac.nz
website www.otago.ac.nz
Managing Editor Wendy Harrex

Student texts and scholarly works in many disciplines and general books, including Maori and women's studies, natural history and environmental studies, health and fiction. Also publishes journals including *Landfall* and the *Women's Studies Journal*. Founded 1958.

Pearson Education New Zealand Ltd*
Private Bag 102908, North Shore Mail Centre, Glenfield, Auckland 10
tel (09) 414-9980 *fax* (09) 414-9981
email firstname.lastname@pearsoned.co.nz
Managing Director Rosemary Stagg

New Zealand educational books.

Penguin Books NZ Ltd
Corner Rosedale & Airborne Roads, Albany, Private Bag 102902, NSMC, Auckland
tel (09) 415 4700 *fax* (09) 415 4701

website www.penguin.co.nz
Managing Director Tony Harkins, *Publishing Director* Geoff Walker

Adult and children's fiction and non-fiction. Imprints: Penguin, Viking, Puffin Books. Founded 1973.

Random House New Zealand Ltd*
Private Bag 102950, North Shore Mail Centre, Auckland 10
tel (09) 444-7197 *fax* (09) 444-7524
Managing Director M. Moynahan

Fiction, general non-fiction, gardening, cooking, art, business, health. Subsidiary of Bertelsmann AG. Founded 1977.

Reed Publishing (New Zealand) Ltd*
(incorporating Reed Books and Heinemann Education)
39 Rawene Road, PO Box 34901, Birkenhead, Auckland 10
tel (09) 441 2960 *fax* (09) 480-4999
Chairman Chris Jones, *Managing Director* David O'Brien, *Publishing Manager* Peter Dowling

NZ specialist and general titles, primary and secondary textbooks, children's titles.

RSVP Publishing Company*
PO Box 47166, Ponsonby, Auckland
tel (09) 372-3480 *fax* (09) 372 8480
email rsvppub@iconz.co.nz
website www.rsvp-publishing.co.nz
Managing Director/Publisher Stephen Picard

Fiction, metaphysical, children's. Founded 1990.

Scholastic New Zealand Ltd*
21 Lady Ruby Drive, East Tamaki, Auckland
tel (09) 274-8112 *fax* (09) 274-8114
email publishing@scholastic.co.nz
postal address Private Bag 94407, Greenmount, Auckland
website www.scholastic.co.nz
Manager Neil Welham, *Publishing Manager* Christine Dale

Children's books. Founded 1962.

Shortland Publications*
PO Box 11–904, Auckland 5
tel (09) 687-0128 *fax* (09) 6203-0143
website www.mcgraw-hill.com.au
Managing Director Avelyn Davidson

International primary reading market: potential authors should familiarise themselves with Shortland products. Currently seeking submissions for emergent/early and fluency reading material (8–24pp) and short fiction (ages 9–12) – MSS up to 1500 words long. All submissions should cater for an international market; include sae. Acquired by

McGraw-Hill Australia & New Zealand. Founded 1984.

Tandem Press
PO Box 34272, Birkenhead, Auckland
tel (09) 480-1452 *fax* (09) 480-1455
email customers@tandempress.co.nz
website www.tandempress.co.nz
Joint Managing Directors Robert M. Ross
(publishing), Helen E. Benton (sales & marketing)

Self-help, health, business, food and wine, New Zealand interest, fiction. Founded 1990.

Victoria University Press*
Victoria University of Wellington, PO Box 600, Wellington
tel (04) 463-6580 *fax* (04) 463-6581
email victoria-press@vuw.ac.nz
website www.vuw.ac.nz
Publisher Fergus Barrowman

Academic, scholarly books on NZ history, sociology, law; Maori language; fiction, plays, poetry. Founded 1974.

Viking Sevenseas NZ Ltd
201A Rosetta Road, Raumati
tel (04) 902-8240 *fax* (04) 902-8240
email vikings@paradise.net.nz
Managing Director M.B. Riley

Natural history books on New Zealand only.

SOUTH AFRICA

*Member of the Publishers' Association of South Africa

Ad Donker (Pty) Ltd – see Jonathan Ball Publishers (Pty) Ltd

Jonathan Ball Publishers (Pty) Ltd*
10–14 Watkins Street, Denver Ext. 4, Johannesburg
tel (011) 622-2900 *fax* (011) 622-7610
postal address Box 33977, Jeppestown 2043
Publishing Director Francine Blum

Founded 1977.

Ad Donker (imprint)
Africana, literature, history, academic.

Jonathan Ball (imprint)
General publications, reference books, South African business, history, politics.

Delta Books (imprint)
General South African trade non-fiction.

Cambridge University Press*
(African Branch)
Lower Ground Floor, Nautica Building, The Water Club, Beach Road, Granger Bay, Cape Town 8005

tel (021) 412-7800 *fax* (021) 419-0594
email capetown@cambridge.org
website www.cambridge.org
Director Hanri Pieterse

African Branch of CUP, responsible for sub-Saharan Africa and English-speaking Caribbean. Publishes distance learning materials and textbooks for various African countries, as well as primary reading materials in 28 local African languages.

Clever Books Pty Ltd*
PO Box 13816, Hatfield, Pretoria 0028
tel (012) 342-3263 *fax* (012) 430-2376
email cillierss@cleverbooks.co.za
Managing Director Steven Cilliers
Educational titles for the RSA market. Founded 1981.

Delta Books – see Jonathan Ball Publishers (Pty) Ltd

Fernwood Press (Pty) Ltd
PO Box 481, Simon's Town, 7995 Cape
tel (21) 786 2460 *fax* (21) 786 2478
email ferpress@iafrica.com
website www.fernwoodpress.co.za
Members Pieter Struik, Pam Struik

Illustrated non-fiction reference works on southern Africa's cultural and natural history. Founded 1991.

Galago Publishing (Pty) Ltd
PO Box 1645, Alberton 1450
tel (11) 907-2029 *fax* (11) 869-0890
email lemur@mweb.co.za
website www.galago.co.za
Managing Director Fran Stiff, *Publisher* Peter Stiff
Southern African interest: military, political, hunting. Founded 1981.

Jacklin Enterprises (Pty) Ltd
PO Box 521, Parklands 2121
tel (011) 265-4200 *fax* (011) 314-2984
email mjacklin@jacklin.co.za
Managing Director M.A.C. Jacklin

Children's fiction and non-fiction; Afrikaans large print books. Subjects include aviation, natural history, romance, general science, technology and transportation. Imprints: Mike Jacklin, Kennis Onbeperk, Daan Retief.

Juta & Company Ltd*
PO Box 14373, Landsdown 7779, Cape Town
tel (021) 797-5101 *fax* (021) 797-5569
email books@juta.co.za
website www.juta.co.za
Ceo Rory Wilson

School, academic, professional, law and electronic. Founded 1853.

University of KwaZulu-Natal Press*
Private Bag X01, Scottsville, 3209 KwaZulu-Natal
tel (033) 260-5226 *fax* (033) 260-5801

email books@ukzn.ac.za
website www.ukznpress.co.za
Publisher Glenn Cowley

Southern African social, political, economic and military history, gender, natural sciences, African poetry and literature, genealogy, education, biography. Founded 1948.

Maskew Miller Longman (Pty) Ltd*

PO Box 396, Howard Drive, Pinelands 7405, Cape Town 8000
tel (021) 531-7750 *fax* (021) 531-4877
email firstname@mml.co.za
website www.mml.co.za
Publishing Director Japie Pienaar

Educational and general publishers.

NB Publishers (Pty) Ltd*

PO Box 879, Cape Town 8000
tel (021) 406-3033 *fax* (021) 406-3812
email nb@nb.co.za
website www.nb.co.za
Managing Director Eloise Wessels

General: Afrikaans fiction, politics, children's and youth literature in all the country's languages, non-fiction. Imprints include Tafelberg, Human & Rousseau, Pharos and Kwela. Founded 1950.

New Africa Books (Pty) Ltd

99 Garfield Road, Claremont, Cape Town 7700
tel (21) 674-4136 *fax* (21) 674-3358
website www.newafricabooks.co.za
Managing Director Brian Wafawarowa

General books, textbooks, literary works, contemporary issues, children and young adult. Formed as a result of the merger of David Philip Publishers (founded 1971), Spearhead Press (founded 2000) and New Africa Educational Publishing.

David Philip (imprint)

Academic, history, social sciences, politics, biography, reference, education.

Spearhead (imprint)

Current affairs, also business, self-improvement, health, natural history, travel.

Oxford University Press Southern Africa*

Vasco Boulevard, N1 City, Goodwood, Cape Town 7460
tel (021) 596-2300 *fax* (021) 596-1234
email oxford.za@oup.com.za
postal address PO Box 12119, N1 City, Cape Town 7463
website www.oup.com.za
Managing Director E. Kotze, *Publishing Director* M.R. Griffin

Ravan Press

PO Box 32484, Braamfontein, Johannesburg 2125
tel (011) 484 0916 *fax* (011) 484 2631

General Manager Monica Seeber

South African studies: history, politics, social studies; fiction, literature, biography. Founded 1972.

Shuter and Shooter Publishers (Pty) Ltd*

21c Cascades Crescent, Cascades, Pietermaritzburg 3201, KwaZulu-Natal
tel (033) 3427-6130 *fax* (033) 347-6100
email dryder@shuter.co.za
postal address PO Box 13016, Cascades 3202, KwaZulu-Natal
website www.shuters.com
Publishing Director D.F. Ryder

Core curriculum-based textbooks for use at Foundation, Intermediate, Senior and Further Education phases. Supplementary readers in various languages; dictionaries; reading development kits, charts. Literature titles in English, isiXhosa, Sesotho, Sepedi, Setswana, Tshivenda, Xitsonga, Ndebele and Siswati. Shuters is a SABS ISO 9001–2000 certified company. Founded 1925.

Struik Publishers

Cornelius Struik House, 80 McKenzie Street, Cape Town 8001
tel (021) 462-4360 *fax* (021) 462-4379
email books@struik.co.za
website www.struik.co.za
Managing Director Steve Connolly

General illustrated non-fiction. Division of New Holland Publishing (South Africa) (Pty) (Ltd). Founded 1962.

Unisa Press

PO Box 392, Pretoria 0003
tel (012) 429-3316 *fax* (012) 429-3221
email unisa-press@unisa.ac.za
website www.unisa.ac.za/press/
Head Elizabeth le Roux

Theology and all academic disciplines. Publishers of University of South Africa. Imprint: UNISA. Founded 1957.

Van Schaik Publishers*

PO Box 12681, Hatfield, Pretoria 0028
tel (012) 342-2765 *fax* (012) 430-3563
email vanschaik@vanschaiknet.com
website www.vanschaiknet.com

Texts for tertiary, FET and ABET markets in South Africa. Founded 1915.

Wits University Press*

PO Wits, Johannesburg 2050
tel (011) 484-5906/07/10 *fax* (011) 484-5971
email witspress@wup.wits.ac.za
website http://witspress.wits.ac.za

Zebra Press

80 McKenzie Street Gardens, Cape Town 8001
tel (021) 462-4360 *fax* (021) 462-4379

email moniquev@zebrapress.co.za
postal address PO Box 1144, Cape Town 8000
website www.zebrapress.co.za

Business, contemporary, humour. Imprint of Struik Publishers. Division of New Holland Publishing (South Africa) (Pty) Ltd, a member of Johnnic Publishing Ltd.

USA

*Member of the Association of American Publishers Inc.

Abbeville Press
137 Varick Street, 5th floor, New York, NY 10013
tel 212-366-5585 *fax* 212-366-6966
email abbeville@abeville.com
website www.abbeville.com
Publisher/President Robert Abrams

Art and illustrated books. Founded 1977.

Abingdon Press
201 Eighth Avenue, PO Box 801, Nashville, TN 37202–0801
tel 615-749-6290 *fax* 615-749-6372
website www.abingdonpress.com
President Neil Alexander, *Senior Vice President, Publishing* Harriett Jane Olson

General interest, professional, academic and reference – primarily directed to the religious market; children's non-fiction.

Harry N. Abrams Inc.
115 West 18th Street, New York, NY 10011
tel 212-206-7715 *fax* 212-519-1210
website www.hnabooks.com
Ceo/President Michael Jacobs

Art and architecture, photography, natural sciences, performing arts, children's books. No fiction. Founded 1949.

The University of Alabama Press
Box 870380, Tuscaloosa, AL 35487
tel 205-348-5180 *fax* 205-348-9201
Director Daniel J.J. Ross, *Managing Editor* Suzette Griffith

American and Southern history, African–American studies, religion, rhetoric and communication, Judaic studies, literary criticism, anthropology and archaeology. Founded 1945.

Applause Theatre and Cinema Book Publishers
19 West 21st Street, Suite 201, New York, NY 10010
tel 212-575-9265 *fax* 212-575-9270
website www.applausepub.com
Publisher Michael Messina

Performing arts. Founded 1980.

Arcade Publishing
141 Fifth Avenue, New York, NY 10010
tel 212-475-2633 *fax* 212-353-8148

email arcadeinfo@arcadepub.com
website www.arcadepub.com
President/Editor-in-Chief Richard Seaver, *Publisher* Jeannette Seaver

General trade, including adult hard cover and paperbacks. No unsolicited MSS. Founded 1988.

The University of Arkansas Press
The University of Arkansas, McIlroy House, 201 Ozark Avenue, Fayetteville, AR 72701
tel 479-575-3246 *fax* 479-575-6044
email uapress@uark.edu
website www.uapress.com
Director Lawrence J. Malley

History, humanities, literary criticism, Middle East studies, African–American studies, poetry. Founded 1980.

Atlantic Monthly Press – see Grove/Atlantic Inc.

Avery – see The Putnam Publishing Group

Avon – see HarperCollins Publishers

Walter H. Baker Company
PO Box 699222, Quincy, MA 02269–9222
tel 617-745-0805 *fax* 617-745-9891
website www.bakersplays.com
President Charles Van Nostrand, *General Manager* Kurt Gombar, *UK Agent* Samuel French Ltd

Plays and books on the theatre. Also agents for plays. Founded 1845.

Ballantine Books – see Random House Inc.

Barron's Educational Series Inc.
250 Wireless Boulevard, Hauppage, NY 11788
800-645-3476 *fax* 631-434-3723
website www.barronseduc.com
Chairman/Ceo Manuel H. Barron, *President/Publisher* Ellen Sibley

Test preparation, juvenile, cookbooks, Mind, Body & Spirit, crafts, business, pets, gardening, family and health, art, study guides, school guides. Founded 1941.

Beacon Press
25 Beacon Street, Boston, MA 02108
tel 617-742-2110 *fax* 617-723-3097
website www.beacon.org
Director Helene Atwan

General non-fiction in fields of religion, ethics, philosophy, current affairs, gender studies, environmental concerns, African–American studies, anthropology and women's studies, nature.

Bella Books Inc.
PO Box 10543, Tallahessee, FL 32302
tel 800-729-4992 *fax* 850-576-3498

website www.bellabooks.com
Coo Linda Hill

Lesbian fiction: mystery, romance, science fiction. Founded 1973.

Berkley Books – see Berkley Publishing Group

Berkley Publishing Group
375 Hudson Street, New York, NY 10014
tel 212-366-2000 *fax* 212-366-2666
email online@penguinputnam.com
website www.penguinputnam.com
President, Mass Market Paperbacks Leslie Gelbman

Fiction and general non-fiction. Imprints: Ace Books, Berkley Books, Boulevard, Diamond Books, HP Books, Jam, Jove, Perigee, Prime Crime, Riverhead Books (trade paperback). No unsolicited MSS. Division of **Penguin Putnam Inc.** Founded 1954.

Berkley Books (imprint)
President & Publisher Leslie Gelbman

Fiction and general non-fiction for adults. Imprints: Ace Books, Berkley Books, Boulevard Books, Diamond Books, Jam, Jove, Prime Crime. Founded 1954.

HP Books (imprint)
Editorial Director, Automotive Michael Lutfy

Non-fiction trade paperbacks. Founded 1964.

Perigee Books (imprint)
Vice President/Publisher John Duff

Non-fiction paperbacks: psychology, spirituality, reference, etc. Founded 1980.

Riverhead Books (Trade Paperback)
Editor Christopher Knutsen

Fiction and general non-fiction for adults. Founded 1995.

Bloomsbury USA
Suite 315, 175 Fifth Avenue, New York, NY 10010
tel 212-674-5151 *fax* 212-982-2837
website www.bloomsburyusa.com
Publisher & Editorial Director Peter Ginna, *Publisher & Editorial Director, Adult Books* Karen Rinaldi, *Deputy Editorial Director, Adult Books* Colin Dickerman, *Executive Editor* Gillian Blake, *Editorial Director, Children's Books* Victoria Wells Arms, *Director of Marketing & Publicity (Children's)* Kate Kubert

Literary fiction, general non-fiction and children's. Branch of **Bloomsbury UK**. Founded 1998.

BlueHen – see The Putnam Publishing Group

R.R. Bowker
630 Central Avenue, New Providence, NJ 07974
tel 908-286-1090 *fax* 908-219-0098
email info@bowker.com

website www.bowker.com
President Michael Cairns, *Managing Editor* Lisa Heft

Bibliographies and reference tools for the book trade and literary and library worlds, available in hardcopy, on microfiche, online and CD-Rom. Reference books for music, art, business, computer industry, cable industry and information industry. Division of Cambridge Information Group.

Boyds Mills Press
815 Church Street, Honesdale, PA 18431
tel 570-253-1164 *fax* 570-253-0179
email contact@boydsmillspress.com
website www.boydsmillspress.com
President Clay Winters, *Publisher* Kent L. Brown Jr, *Associate Publisher* Stephen Roxburgh, *Editorial Director* Larry Rosler, *Art Director* Tim Gillner

Fiction, non-fiction, and poetry trade books for children and young adults. Founded 1991.

Burford Books
32 Morris Avenue, Short Hills, NJ 07078
tel 973-258-0960 *fax* 973-258-0113
email info@burfordbooks.com
website www.burfordbooks.com
President Peter Burford

Outdoor activities: golf, sports, fitness, nature, travel. Founded 1997.

Cambridge University Press*
40 West 20th Street, New York, NY 10011
tel 212-924-3900 *fax* 212-691-3239
website www.cambridge.org
President Richard L. Ziemacki

Candlewick Press
2067 Massachusetts Avenue, Cambridge, MA 02140
tel 617-661-3330 *fax* 617-661-0565
email bigbear@candlewick.com
website www.candlewick.com
President/Publisher Karen Lotz, *Editorial Director/Associate Publisher* Liz Bicknell, *Executive Editor* Mary Lee Donovan, *Editor-at-Large, Non-fiction Picture Books* Joan Powers

Books for 6 months–18 year-olds: board books, picture books, novels, non-fiction, novelty books. Submit material through a literary agent. Subsidiary of **Walker Books Ltd**, UK. Founded 1991.

Carroll & Graf Publishers Inc.
245 West 17th Street, 11th Floor, New York, NY 10011
tel 212-981-9919 *fax* 646-375-2571
website www.carrollandgraf.com
Vice President & Publisher Will Balliett

History, biography, literary fiction, popular culture, mystery and crime. Imprint of Avalon Publishing Group Inc. Founded 1983.

University of Chicago Press*
1427 East 60th Street, Chicago, IL 60637
tel 773-702-7700 *fax* 773-702-2705

website www.press.uchicago.edu
Director Paula Barker Duffy

Scholarly books and monographs (humanities, social sciences and sciences) general trade books, reference books, and 43 scholarly journals.

Chronicle Books
85 Second Street, 6th Floor, San Francisco, CA 94105
tel 415-537-4200 *fax* 415-537-4460
email frontdesk@chroniclebooks.com
website www.chroniclebooks.com,
www.chroniclekids.com
Chairman & Ceo Nion McEvoy, *President & Publisher* Jay Schaefer, *Associate Publishers* Debra Lande, Victoria Rock, Alan Rapp

Cooking, art, fiction, general, children's, gift, new media, gardening, regional, nature. Founded 1967.

Coffee House Press
27 N 4th Street, Suite 400, Minneapolis, MN 55401
tel 612-338-0125 *fax* 612-338-4004
website www.coffeehousepress.com
Publisher Allan Kornblum

Literary fiction and poetry; collectors' editions. Founded 1984.

Columbia University Press*
61 West 62nd Street, New York, NY 10023
tel 212-459-0600 *fax* 212-459-3678
UK office 1 Oldlands Way, Bognor Regis, West Sussex PO22 9SA
tel (01243) 842165 *fax* (01243) 842167
website www.columbia.edu/cu/cup
Editorial Director Jennifer Crewe

General reference works in print and electronic formats, translations and serious non-fiction of more general interest.

Concordia Publishing House
3558 South Jefferson Avenue, St Louis, MO 63118
tel 314-268-1000 *fax* 314-268-1329
website www.cph.org
President Paul T. McCain, *Commissioning Editor* Peggy Kuethe

Religious books, Lutheran perspective. Few freelance MSS accepted; query first. Founded 1869.

Contemporary Books
130 East Randolph Street, Suite 900, Chicago, IL 60601
tel 312-233-6520 *fax* 312-233-7570
Vice President Philip Ruppel

Non-fiction. Imprints: Contemporary Books, Lowell House, Passport Books, VGM Career Books. Division of the McGraw-Hill Companies.

The Continuum International Publishing Group Inc.
80 Maiden Lane, Suite 704, New York, NY 10038
tel 212-953-5858 *fax* 212-953-5944

email info@continuum-books.com
website www.continuum-books.com
Chairman/Publisher Philip Sturrock

General non-fiction, education, literature, psychology, politics, sociology, history, literary criticism, religious studies. Founded 1999.

Cornell University Press*
(including ILR Press and Comstock Publishing Associates)
Sage House, 512 East State Street, Ithaca, NY 14850
tel 607-277-2338 *fax* 607-277-2374
email cupressinfo@cornell.edu
website www.cornellpress.cornell.edu
Director John G. Ackerman

Scholarly books. Founded 1869.

Council Oak Books
1615 S. Baltimore Avenue, Suite 3, Tulsa, OK 74119
tel 918-587-6454 *fax* 918-583-4995
email jclark@counciloakbooks.com
website www.counciloakbooks.com
Publishing Director Melissa Lilly, *Editor-in-Chief* Paulette Millichap

Non-fiction: native American, multicultural, life skills, life accounts, Earth awareness, meditation. Founded 1984.

The Countryman Press
PO Box 748, Woodstock, VT 05091
tel 802-457-4826 *fax* 802-457-1678
email countrymanpress@wwnorton.com
website www.countrymanpress.com
Editorial Director Kermit Hummel

Outdoor recreation guides for anglers, hikers, cyclists, canoeists and kayakers, US travel guides, New England non-fiction, how-to books, country living books, books on nature and the environment, classic reprints and general non-fiction. No unsolicited MSS. Division of **W.W. Norton & Co. Inc.** Founded 1973.

DAW Books Inc.
375 Hudson Street, 3rd Floor, New York, NY 10014
tel 212-366-2096 *fax* 212-366-2090
email daw@penguinputnam.com
website www.dawbooks.com
Publishers Elizabeth R. Wollheim, Sheila E. Gilbert

Science fiction, fantasy, horror, mainstream thrillers: originals and reprints. Imprints: DAW/Fantasy, DAW/Fiction, DAW/Science Fiction. Affiliate of **Penguin Putnam Inc.** Founded 1971.

Dial Books for Young Readers – see
Penguin Putnam Books for Young Readers

Dover Publications Inc.
31 East 2nd Street, Mineola, NY 11501
tel 516-294-7000 *fax* 516-742-5049
website www.doverpublications.com

President, Dover Publications Paul Negri, *Editor-in-Chief* Mary Carolyn Waldrep

Art, architecture, antiques, crafts, juvenile, food, history, folklore, literary classics, mystery, language, music, math and science, nature, design and ready-to-use art. Founded 1941.

Dutton
(formerly Dutton/Signet)
375 Hudson Street, New York, NY 10014
tel 212-366-2000 *fax* 212-366-2666
email online@penguinputnam.com
website www.penguinputnam.com

Fiction and general non-fiction for adults. Imprint: Dutton. Division of **Penguin Putman Inc.**

Dutton Children's Books – see Penguin Putnam Books for Young Readers

Faber & Faber, Inc.
19 Union Square West, New York, NY 10003
tel 212-741-6900 *fax* 212-633-9385
website www.fsgbooks.com
Senior Editor Denise Oswald

Drama, film, poetry, music and cultural criticism. No unsolicited MSS.

Facts On File Inc.
132 West 31st Street, 17th Floor, New York, NY 10001–2006
tel 800-322-8755 *fax* 800-678-3633
website www.factsonfile.com
President Mark McDonnell, *Editorial Director* Laurie E. Likoff

General reference books and services for colleges, libraries, schools and general public. Founded 1940.

Family Tree – see Writer's Digest Books

Farrar, Straus and Giroux, Inc.
19 Union Square West, New York, NY 10003
tel 212-741-6900 *fax* 212-633-9385
website www.fsgbooks.com, www.fsgkidsbooks.com
President/Publisher Jonathan Galassi

General publishers: literary fiction, non-fiction, poetry, children's. Founded 1946.

North Point Press
– see Farrar, Straus and Giroux, Inc.

Fodor's Travel Publications – see Random House Inc.

Four Walls Eight Windows – see Thunder's Mouth Press

Samuel French Inc.
45 West 25th Street, New York, NY 10010
tel 212-206-8990 *fax* 212-206-1429

email samuelfrench@earthlink.net

Play publishers and authors' representatives (dramatic).

Getty Publications
1200 Getty Center Drive, Suite 500, Los Angeles, CA 90049–1682
tel 310-440-7365 *fax* 310-440-7758
email pubsinfo@getty.edu
website www.getty.edu/bookstore
Publisher Christopher Hudson, *General Manager* Kara Kirk, *Editor-in-Chief* Mark Greenberg

Art, art history, architecture, classical art and archaeology, conservation. Founded 1958.

David R. Godine, Publisher Inc.
9 Hamilton Place, Boston, MA 02108
tel 617-451-9600 *fax* 617-350-0250
email info@godine.com
website www.godine.com
President David R. Godine

Fiction, photography, poetry, art, biography, children's, essays, history, typography, architecture, nature and gardening, music, cooking, words and writing, and mysteries. No unsolicited MSS. Founded 1970.

Grosset & Dunlap – see Penguin Putnam Books for Young Readers

Grove/Atlantic Inc.*
841 Broadway, New York, NY 10003–4793
tel 212-614-7850 *fax* 212-614-7886
website www.groveatlantic.com
Publisher Morgan Entrekin

MSS of permanent interest, fiction, biography, autobiography, history, current affairs, social science, belles-lettres, natural history. No unsolicited MSS. Imprints: Atlantic Monthly Press, Cannongate US, Grove Press. Founded 1952.

Harcourt Trade Publishers*
525 B Street, Suite 1900, San Diego, CA 92101
tel 619-231-6616 *fax* 619-699-6320
website www.harcourt.com
President/Publisher, Adult Books Dan Farley, *Vice President/Publisher, Children's Books* Louise Pelan

Fiction and non-fiction (history, biography, etc) for readers of all ages. Imprints: Harcourt (hardcover books), Harvest Books (paperbacks), Harcourt Children's Books. Division of Harcourt Inc.

HarperCollins Publishers*
10 East 53rd Street, New York, NY 10022
tel 212-207-7000 *fax* 212-207-7145
HarperCollins SanFrancisco 1160 Battery Street, San Francisco, CA 94111
tel 415-477-4400 *fax* 415-477-4444
website www.harpercollins.com

President/Ceo Jane Friedman

Fiction, history, biography, poetry, science, travel, cookbooks, juvenile, educational, business, technical and religious. No unsolicited material; all submissions must come through a literary agent. Founded 1817.

HarperCollins General Books Group (division)
President/Publisher Cathy Hemming

HarperInformation (division)
Imprints: Access, HarperBusiness, HarperResource, William Morrow Cookbooks.

HarperSanFrancisco (division)
Imprint: HarperSanFrancisco.

HarperTrade (division)
Imprints: Amistad, Cliff Street Books, Ecco, Fourth Estate, HarperAudio, HarperCollins, Large Print Editions, Perennial, PerfectBound (e-books), Quill, Rayo, ReganBooks.

Morrow/Avon (division)
Imprints: Avon, Eos, HarperEntertainment, HarperTorch, William Morrow.

HarperCollins Children's Books Group
1350 6th Avenue, New York, NY 10019
tel 212-261-6500
website www.harperchildrens.com
President/Publisher Susan Katz
Imprints: Avon, Joanna Cotler Books, Laura Geringer Books, Greenwillow Books, HarperCollins Children's Books, HarperFestival, HarperTempest, HarperTrophy.

Harvard University Press*
79 Garden Street, Cambridge, MA 02138–1499
tel 617-495 2600 *fax* 617-495-5898
website www.hup.harvard.edu
Director William P. Sisler, *Editor-in-Chief* Michael G. Fisher

History, philosophy, literary criticism, politics, economics, sociology, music, science, classics, social sciences, behavioural sciences, law.

Hastings House/Daytrips Publishers
PO Box 908, Winter Park, FL 32790-0908
tel 407-339-3600 *fax* 407-339–5900
email hastings_daytrips@earthlink.net
website www.hastingshousebooks.com
Publisher Peter Leers

Travel.

Hill and Wang
19 Union Square West, New York, NY 10003
tel 212-741-6900 *fax* 212-633-9385
website www.fsgbooks.com
Publishers Thomas Lebien, Elisabeth Sifton

General non-fiction, history, public affairs. Division of **Farrar, Straus and Giroux**. Founded 1956.

Hippocrene Books Inc.
171 Madison Avenue, New York, NY 10016
tel 212-685-4371 *fax* 212-779-9338
email orders@hippocrenebooks.com
website www.hippocrenebooks.com
President/Editorial Director George Blagowidow

International cookbooks, foreign language dictionaries, travel, military history, Polonia, general trade. Founded 1971.

Holiday House
425 Madison Avenue, New York, NY 10017
tel 212-421-6134
website www.holidayhouse.com
Vice-President/Editor-in-Chief Regina Griffin

General children's books. Send query letter before submitting MSS. Always include sae. No multiple submissions. Founded 1935.

Henry Holt and Company LLC*
175 Fifth Avenue, New York, NY 10010
tel 646-307-5095 *fax* 646-307-5285
website www.henryholt.com
President/Publisher John Sterling

History, biography, nature, science, novels, mysteries; books for young readers; trade paperback line. Imprints: Henry Holt, Metropolitan Books, Times Books, Owl Books. Founded 1866.

The Johns Hopkins University Press*
2715 North Charles Street, Baltimore, MD 21218–4319
tel 410-516-6900 *fax* 410-516-6968
Director Kathleen Keane

History, literary criticism, classics, politics, environmental studies, biology, medical genetics, consumer health, religion, physics, astronomy, mathematics, education. Founded 1878.

Houghton Mifflin Company*
222 Berkeley Street, Boston, MA 02116
tel 617-351-5000
website www.houghtonmifflinbooks.com

Fiction and non-fiction – cookbooks, history, political science, biography, nature (Peterson Guides), and gardening guides; reference, both adult and juvenile. No unsolicited MSS. Imprints: Mariner (original and reprint paperbacks); Houghton Mifflin Children's Books; American Heritage® Dictionaries. Founded 1832.

HP Books – see Berkley Publishing Group

Hyperion*
77 West 66 Street, New York, NY 10023–6298
tel 212-456-0100 *fax* 212-456-0157

website www.hyperionbooks.com
President Robert Miller, *Vice-President/Publisher* Ellen Archer, *Vice-President/Publisher (Hyperion Books for Children)* Lisa Holton

General fiction and non-fiction, children's books. Division of Buena Vista Publishing, formerly Disney Book Publishing Inc. Founded 1990.

University of Illinois Press*
1325 South Oak Street, Champaign, IL 61820
tel 217-333-0950 *fax* 217-244-8082
Director Willis G. Regier

American studies (history, music, literature, religion), working-class and ethnic studies, communications, regional studies, architecture, philosophy, women's studies, film, Classics. Founded 1918.

Indiana University Press
601 North Morton Street, Bloomington, IN 47404–3797
tel 812-855-8817 *fax* 812-855-8507
email iupress@indiana.edu
website www.indiana.edu/~iupress
Director Janet Rabinowitch

African studies, Russian and East European studies, music, history, women's studies, Asian studies, Jewish studies, African–American studies, film, philosophy, medical ethics, anthropology, paleontology. Reference and high level trade books. Founded 1950.

International Marine Publishing
PO Box 220, Camden, Maine 04843
tel 207-236-4837 *fax* 207-236-6314
email nancy_dowling@mcgraw-hill.com
website www.internationalmarine.com
www.raggedmountainpress.com
Editorial Director Jonathan F. Eaton

Imprints: International Marine (boats, boating and sailing); Ragged Mountain Press (sport, adventure/travel, natural history). Division of McGraw-Hill Trade.

University Press of Kansas
2502 Westbrooke Circle, Lawrence, KS 66045–4444
tel 785-864-4154 *fax* 785-864-4586
email upress@ku.edu
website www.kansaspress.ku.edu
Director Fred Woodward, *Editor-in-Chief* Michael Briggs, *Senior Production Editor* Susan McRory, *Assistant Director/Marketing Manager* Susan K. Schott

American history (political, social, cultural, environmental), military history, American political thought, American presidency studies, law and constitutional history, political science. Founded 1946.

Krause Publications
700 East State Street, Iola, WI 54990–0001
tel 715-445-2214 *fax* 715-445-4087

email info@Krause.com
website www.Krause.com
Acquisitions Editors Julie Stephani (sewing/crafts), Steve Smith (firearms/outdoors), Paul Kennedy (antiques/collectibles), Brian Earnest (transportation)

Antiques and collectibles: coins, stamps, automobiles, toys, trains, firearms, comics, records; sewing, ceramics, outdoors, hunting.

Little, Brown & Company
1271 Avenue of the Americas, New York, NY 10020
tel 212-522-8700 *fax* 212-522-7997
website www.hachettebookgroupusa.com
Publisher Megan Tingley

General literature, fiction, non-fiction, biography, history, trade paperbacks, children's.

Llewellyn Worldwide
2143 Wooddale Drive, Woodbury, MN 55125
tel 800-843-666
email info@llewellyn.com
website www.llewellyn.com
President & Publisher Carl L. Weschcke

New Age: alternative health and healing, astrology, earth-based religions, shamanism, Gnostic Christianity and Kabbalah; mystery novels. Founded 1901.

The Lyons Press
246 Goose Lane, Guilford, CT 06437
tel 203-458-4500
Associate Publisher Gene Brissie

Fishing, hunting, sports, health and fitness, outdoor skills, animals/pets, horses, games, history/current affairs, military history, nature, games, reference and non-fiction. Founded 1978.

McGraw-Hill*
2 Penn Plaza, New York, NY 10121
tel 212-512-2000
website www.books.mcgraw-hill.com
Group Vice-President Theodore Nardin

Professional and reference: engineering, scientific, business, architecture, encyclopedias; college textbooks; high school and vocational textbooks: business, secretarial, career; trade books; training materials for industry. Division of The McGraw-Hill Companies.

McPherson & Company
PO Box 1126, Kingston, NY 12402
tel 845-331-5807 *fax* 845-331-5807
email bmcpher@verizon.net
website www.mcphersonco.com
Publisher Bruce R. McPherson

Literary fiction; non-fiction: art criticism, writings by artists, film-making, etc; occasional general titles (e.g. anthropology). No poetry. No unsolicited MSS; query first. Distributed in UK by Central Books, London. Founded 1974.

The University of Massachusetts Press

PO Box 429, Amherst, MA 01004–0429
tel 413-545-2217 *fax* 413-545-1226
website www.umass.edu/umpress
Director Bruce G. Wilcox

Scholarly books and works of general interest: American studies and history, black and ethnic studies, women's studies, cultural criticism, architecture and environmental design, literary criticism, poetry, fiction, philosophy, political science, sociology, books of regional interest. Founded 1964.

Merrell Publishers

49 West 24th Street, 8th Floor, New York, NY 10010
tel 212-929-8344 *fax* 212-929-8346
email info@merrellpublishersusa.com
website www.merrellpublishers.com
US Director Joan Brookbank

Illustrated books on all aspects of visual culture, including art, architecture, photography and design, including exhibition catalogues and other museum co-editions.

The University of Michigan Press

839 Greene Street, Ann Arbor, MI 48104–3209
tel 734-764-4388 *fax* 734-615-1540
email um.press@umich.edu
website www.press.umich.edu/
Director Philip Pochoda, *Assistant Director* Mary Erwin, *Executive Editor* Jim Reische, *Managing Editor* Christina Milton

Scholarly and general interest works in literary and cultural theory, classics, history, theatre, women's studies, political science, law, American history, American studies, anthropology, economics, jazz; textbooks in English as a second language; regional trade titles. Founded 1930.

Microsoft Press*

One Microsoft Way, Redmond, WA 98052–6399
tel 425-882-8080 *fax* 425-936-7329
website www.microsoft.com
Publisher Don Falley, *Editorial Director* Kim Fields

Computer books. Division of Microsoft Corp. Founded 1983.

Milkweed Editions

1011 Washington Avenue South, Suite 300, Minneapolis, MN 55415
tel 612-332-3192 *fax* 612-215-2550
email editor@milkweed.org
website www.milkweed.org
Editor Daniel Slager

Fiction, poetry, essays, the natural world, children's novels (ages 8–14). Founded 1979.

University of Missouri Press

2910 LeMone Boulevard, Columbia, MO 65201
tel 573-882-7641 *fax* 573-884-4498
website www.system.missouri.edu/upress
Director/Editor-in-Chief Beverly Jarrett, *Acquisitions Editors* Clair Willcox, Gary Kass

American and European history, African American studies, American, British and Latin American literary criticism, journalism, political philosophy, regional studies; short fiction. Founded 1958.

The MIT Press*

5 Cambridge Center, Cambridge, MA 02142–1493
tel 617-253-5646 *fax* 617-258-6779
website mitpress.mit.edu
Director Ellen Faran, *Managing Editor* Michael Sims

Architecture, art and design, cognitive sciences, neuroscience, linguistics, computer science and artificial intelligence, economics and finance, philosophy, environment and ecology, natural history. Founded 1961.

Morehouse Publishing Co.

PO Box 1321, Harrisburg, PA 17105
tel 717-541-8130 *fax* 717-541-8136
email morehouse@morehousegroup.com
website www.morehousepublishing.org
Vice President & Publisher Ken Arnold

Religious books, spirituality, children's.

William Morrow – see HarperCollins Publishers

NAL

375 Hudson Street, New York, NY 10014
tel 212-366-2000 *fax* 212-366-2666
email online@penguinputnam.com
website www.penguinputnam.com
Vice President/Publisher Kara Welch

Fiction and general non-fiction. Imprints: Mentor, Meridian, New American Library, Onyx, Roc, Signet, Signet Classics, Topaz. Division of **Penguin Putnam Inc.** Founded 1948

Thomas Nelson Publisher

501 Nelson Place, Nashville, TN 37214–1000
tel 800-251-4000 *fax* 615-391-5225
email publicity@thomasnelson.com
website www.thomasnelson.com
Executive Vice President, Thomas Nelson Publishing Group Lee Gessner

Bibles, religious, non-fiction and fiction general trade books for adults and children. Founded 1798.

University of New Mexico Press

1601 Randolph Road SE, Albuquerque, NM 87106
tel 505-277-2346 *fax* 505-277-9270
email unmpress@unm.edu
website www.unmpress.com
Director Luther Wilson

Western history, anthropology and archaeology, Latin American studies, photography, multicultural literature, poetry. Founded 1929.

The University of North Carolina Press

116 South Boundary Street, Chapel Hill, NC 27514
tel 919-966-3561 *fax* 919-966-3829
website www.uncpress.unc.ed
Director Kate Douglas Torrey

American history, American studies, Southern
studies, European history, women's studies, Latin
American studies, political science, anthropology and
folklore, classics, regional trade. Founded 1922.

North Light Books – see Writer's Digest Books

North Point Press – see Farrar, Straus and Giroux, Inc.

W.W. Norton & Company Inc.

500 Fifth Avenue, New York, NY 10110
tel 212-354-5500 *fax* 212-869-0856
website www.wwnorton.com
Editor-in-Chief Robert Weil

General fiction and non-fiction, music, boating,
psychiatry, economics, family therapy, social work,
reprints, college texts, science.

University of Oklahoma Press

2800 Venture Drive, Norman, OK 73069–8216
tel 405-325-2000 *fax* 405-325-4000
Director John N. Drayton

American West, American Indians, Mesoamerica,
classics, natural history, political science. Founded
1928.

The Overlook Press*

141 Wooster Street, New York, New York 10012
tel 212-673-2210 *fax* 212-673-2296
website www.overlookpress.com
President & Publisher Peter Mayer

Non-fiction, fiction, children's books (*Freddy the Pig*
series). Founded 1971.

Oxford University Press Inc.*

198 Madison Avenue, New York, NY 10016
tel 212-726-6000 *fax* 212-726-6455
website www.oup.com/us
President Laura Brown

Scholarly, professional, reference, bibles, college
textbooks, religion, medical, music.

Paragon House Publishers

1925 Oakcrest Avenue, Suite 7, St Paul,
MN 55113–2619
tel (212) 629 9773 *fax* (212) 629 9751
email rby@paragonhouse.com
website www.paragonhouse.com
Executive Director Gordon L. Anderson

Textbooks in philosophy and religion; general non-
fiction. Member of the **Continuum International
Publishing Group Inc.**

Peachtree Publishers

1700 Chattahoochee Avenue, Atlanta,
GA 30318–2112
tel 404-876-8761 *fax* 404-875-2578
email hello@peachtree-online.com
website www.peachtree-online.com
President & Publisher Margaret Quinlin, *Editorial
Director* Kathy Landwehr, *Art Director* Loraine Joyner

Children's picture books, novels and non-fiction.
Adult non-fiction subjects include self-help,
parenting, education, health, regional guides. No
adult fiction.

Pelican Publishing Company*

1000 Burmaster Street, Gretna, LA 70053
tel 504-368-1175 *fax* 504-368-1195
email editorial@pelicanpub.com
website www.pelicanpub.com, www.epelican.com
Publisher/President Milburn Calhoun

Art and architecture, cookbooks, travel, history,
business, children's, motivational. Founded 1926.

Penguin AudioBooks – see Viking Penguin

Penguin Books – see Viking Penguin

Penguin Putnam Books for Young Readers*

345 Hudson Street, New York, NY 10014
tel 212-366-2000 *fax* 212-366-2666
email online@penguinputnam.com
website www.penguinputnam.com
President & Publisher Douglas Whiteman

Children's picture books, board and novelty books,
young adult novels, mass merchandise products.
Imprints: Dial Books for Young Readers, Dutton
Children's Books, Dutton Interactive, Phyllis
Fogelman Books, Grosset & Dunlap, PaperStar,
Philomel, Planet Dexter, Platt & Munk, Playskool,
Price Stern Sloan, PSS, Puffin Books, G.P. Putnam's
Sons, Viking Children's Books, Frederick Warne.
Division of **Penguin Putnam Inc.** Founded 1997.

Dial Books for Young Readers (imprint)

fax 212-414-3394
President/Publisher Nancy Paulsen, *Editorial Director*
Laura Hornik, *Vice President/Publisher, Phyllis
Fogelman Books* Phyllis Fogelman, *Acquisitions Editor*
Nancy Mercado, *Senior Editor* Cecile Goyette, *Art
Director* Lily Malcom

Children's fiction and non-fiction, picture books,
board books, interactive books, novels.

Dutton Children's Books (imprint)

tel 212-366 2792 *fax* 212-243-6002
President/Publisher Stephanie Lurie, *Editorial Director,
Dutton Children's Trade* Donna Brooks, *Art Director*
Sara Reynolds

Picture books, young adult novels, non-fiction
photographic books. Founded 1852.

Grosset & Dunlap (imprint)
President/Publisher, Grosset & Dunlap Debra Dorfman
Children's picture books, activity books, fiction and non-fiction.

Price Stern Sloan (imprint)
President/Publisher Debra Dorfman
Children's novelty/lift-flap books, picture books, activity books, middle-grade fiction, middle-grade and young adult non-fiction, graphic readers, books plus. Founded 1963.

Puffin Books (imprint)
President & Publisher Tracy Tang
Children's paperbacks. Founded 1935.

G.P. Putnam's Sons (imprint)
tel 212-414-3610
President/Publisher Nancy Paulsen, *Executive Editor* Kathy Dawson, *Art Director* Cecilia Yung
Children's hardcover and paperback books.

Viking Children's Books (imprint)
tel 212-414-3600
President Regina Hayes
Fiction, non-fiction and picture books for preschool–young adult.

Frederick Warne (imprint)
Original publisher of Beatrix Potter's *Tales of Peter Rabbit*. Founded 1865.

Penguin Putnam Inc.*
(formerly Penguin USA and Putnam Berkley)
375 Hudson Street, New York, NY10014
tel 212-366-2000 *fax* 212-366-2666
email online@penguinputnam.com
website www.penguinputnam.com
President, The Penguin Group David Wan, *Chairman* John McKinson, *Ceo* David Shanks

Consumer books in both hardcover and paperback for adults and children; also maps, calendars, audiobooks and mass merchandise products. Adult imprints: Ace, Ace/Putnam, Allen Lane The Penguin Press, Avery, Berkley Books, BlueHen, Boulevard, DAW, Dutton, Grosset/Putnam, HP Books, Jove, Mentor, Meridian, Onyx, Penguin, Penguin Classics, Penguin Compass, Perigee, Plume, Prime Crime, Price Stern Sloan Inc., Putnam, G.P. Putnam's Sons, Riverhead Books, Roc, Signet, Signet Classics, Jeremy P. Tarcher, Topaz, Viking, Viking Compass, Viking Studio, Marian Wood Books. Children's imprints: Dial Books for Young Readers, Dutton Children's Books, Grosset & Dunlap, PaperStar, Philomel Books, Planet Dexter, Price Stern Sloan Inc., Puffin, G.P. Putnam's Sons, Viking Children's Books, Wee Sing, Frederick Warne. Divisions: **Berkley Publishing Group**, **Dutton**, **Plume**, **NAL**, **Penguin Putnam Books for Young Readers**, **The Putnam Publishing Group**, **Viking Penguin** (see separate entries).

Penguin Putnam Books for Young Readers
345 Hudson Street, New York, NY 10014
tel 212-366-2000 *fax* 212-366-2666
email online@penguinputnam.com
website www.penguinputnam.com
President & Publisher Douglas Whiteman
Children's picture books, board and novelty books, young adult novels, mass merchandise products. Imprints: Dial Books for Young Readers, Dutton Children's Books, Dutton Interactive, Phyllis Fogelman Books, Grosset & Dunlap, PaperStar, Philomel, Planet Dexter, Platt & Munk, Playskool, Price Stern Sloan, PSS, Puffin Books, G.P. Putnam's Sons, Viking Children's Books, Frederick Warne. Division of **Penguin Putnam Inc**. Founded 1997.

Dial Books for Young Readers (imprint)
fax 212-414-3394
President/Publisher Nancy Paulsen, *Editorial Director* Laura Hornik, *Vice President/Publisher, Phyllis Fogelman Books* Phyllis Fogelman, *Acquisitions Editor* Nancy Mercado, *Senior Editor* Cecile Goyette, *Art Director* Lily Malcom
Children's fiction and non-fiction, picture books, board books, interactive books, novels.

Dutton Children's Books (imprint)
tel 212-366 2792 *fax* 212-243-6002
President/Publisher Stephanie Lurie, *Editorial Director, Dutton Children's Trade* Donna Brooks, *Art Director* Sara Reynolds
Picture books, young adult novels, non-fiction photographic books. Founded 1852.

Grosset & Dunlap (imprint)
President/Publisher, Grosset & Dunlap Debra Dorfman
Children's picture books, activity books, fiction and non-fiction.

Price Stern Sloan (imprint)
President/Publisher Debra Dorfman
Children's novelty/lift-flap books, picture books, activity books, middle-grade fiction, middle-grade and young adult non-fiction, graphic readers, books plus. Founded 1963.

Puffin Books (imprint)
President & Publisher Tracy Tang
Children's paperbacks. Founded 1935.

G.P. Putnam's Sons (imprint)
tel 212-414-3610
President/Publisher Nancy Paulsen, *Executive Editor* Kathy Dawson, *Art Director* Cecilia Yung
Children's hardcover and paperback books.

Viking Children's Books (imprint)
tel 212-414-3600
President Regina Hayes
Fiction, non-fiction and picture books for preschool–young adult.

Frederick Warne (imprint)
Original publisher of Beatrix Potter's *Tales of Peter Rabbit*. Founded 1865.

Penn State University Press*
820 North University Drive, USB1, Suite C,
University Park, PA 16802
tel 814-865-1327 *fax* 814-863-1408
website www.psupress.org
Editor-in-Chief tba

Art history, literary criticism, religious studies, philosophy, political science, sociology, history, Russian and East European studies, Latin American studies and medieval studies. Founded 1956.

University of Pennsylvania Press
3905 Spruce Street, Philadelphia, PA 19104–4112
tel 215-898-6261 *fax* 215-898-0404
website www.upenn.edu/pennpress
Director Eric Halpern

American and European history, anthropology, art, architecture, cultural studies, ancient studies, human rights, literature, health, Pennsylvania regional studies. Founded 1890.

Perigee Books – see Berkley Publishing Group

The Permanent Press and Second Chance Press
4170 Noyac Road, Sag Harbor, NY 11963
tel 631-725-1101 *fax* 631-725-8215
website www.thepermanentpress.com
Directors Martin Shepard, Judith Shepard

Quality fiction. Founded 1978.

Plume
375 Hudson Street, New York, NY 10014
tel 212-366-2000 *fax* 212-366-2666
email online@penguinputnam.com
website www.penguinputnam.com
Publisher Kathryn Court, *President* Clare Ferraro, *Editor-in-Chief* Trena Keating

Fiction and general non-fiction for adults. Division of **Penguin Putnam Inc.**

Popular Woodworking – see Writer's Digest Books

Price Stern Sloan – see Penguin Putnam Books for Young Readers

Princeton University Press*
Princeton, NJ 08540
tel 609-258-4900 *fax* 609-258-6305
postal address 41 William Street, Princeton, NJ 08540
website www.pup.princeton.edu
Director Peter J. Dougherty, *Editor-in-Chief* Sam Elworthy

Scholarly and scientific books on all subjects. Founded 1905.

Puffin Books – see Penguin Putnam Books for Young Readers

The Putnam Publishing Group*
375 Hudson Street, New York, NY 10014
tel 212-366-2000 *fax* 212-366-2643
email online@penguinputnam.com
website www.penguinputnam.com

General trade books for adults; books on cassette. Imprints: Avery, BlueHen, G.P. Putnam's Sons, Riverhead Books, Jeremy P. Tarcher, Tarcher/Penguin, Putnam Berkley Audio, Marian Wood Books. Division of **Penguin Putnam Inc.**

G.P. Putnam's Sons (children's) – see Penguin Putnam Books for Young Readers

G.P. Putnam's Sons (adult) – see The Putnam Publishing Group

Rand McNally
PO Box 7600, Chicago, IL 60680
tel 847-329-2178
website www.randmcnally.com
Chairman John Macomber, *President/Ceo* Norman E. Wells, Jr

Maps, guides, atlases, educational publications, globes and children's geographical titles and atlases in print and electronic formats.

Random House Inc.*
1745 Broadway, 10th Floor, New York, NY 10019
tel 212-782-9000 *fax* 212-302-7985
website www.randomhouse.com
Chairman/Ceo Peter Olson, *President/Coo* Erik Engstrom

General fiction and non-fiction, children's books. Subsidiary of Bertelsmann AG.

Bantam Dell Publishing Group (division)
General fiction and non-fiction. Imprints: Bantam Dell, Crimeline, Delacorte, Dell, Delta, Dial Press, Domain, DTP, Fanfare, Island, Spectra.

Crown Publishing Group (division)
General fiction, non-fiction, illustrated books. Imprints: Bell Tower, Clarkson Potter, Crown Business, Crown Publishers, Inc., Harmony Books, Prima Health, Shaye Areheart Books, Three Rivers Press.

Doubleday Broadway (division)
General fiction and non-fiction. Imprints: Broadway Books, Currency, Doubleday, Doubleday Image, Doubleday Religious Publishing, Harlem Moon, Main Steet Books, Morgan Road Books, Nan A. Talese.

Knopf Publishing Group (division)
Chairman Sonny Mehta, *Vice-President & Senior Editor* Judith Jones

Literature, fiction, poetry, cooking, biography, history, nature, travel. Imprints: Alfred A. Knopf, Anchor Books, Everyman's Library (including *Pocket Poets* and *Children's Classics* series), Pantheon Books, Schocken Books, Vintage.

Random House Publishing Group (division)

General fiction and non-fiction. Imprints: Ballantine Books, Ballantine Reader's Circle, Del Rey, Fawcett, Ivy, Modern Library, One World, Presidio Press, Random House, Random House Trade Paperbacks, Villard.

Random House Audio Publishing Group (division)

President Jenny Frost

BDD Audio Publishing, Random House Audio Publishing.

Random House Children's Media Group (division)

President & Publisher Craig W. Virden

Children's imprints: Bantam Books for Young Readers, Crown Books for Young Readers, Delacorte Press Books for Young Readers, Disney Books for Young Readers, Doubleday Books for Young Readers, Dragonfly Books, David Fickling Books, Golden Books for Young Readers, Alfred A. Knopf Books for Young Readers, Wendy Lamb Books, Laurel-Leaf Books, Lucas Books, Random House Books for Young Readers, Yearling Books.

Random House Diversified Publishing Group (division)

President Jenny Frost

Random House Large Print Publishing; Random House Value Publishing (Children's Classics, Crescent Books, Derrydale, Gramercy Books, Testament Books, Wings Books).

The Random House Information Group (division)

President Bonnie Ammer

Imprints: Fodor's Travel Publications, Living Language, Princeton Review, Random House Reference, Random House Puzzles and Games.

Riverhead Books (Trade Paperback) – see Berkley Publishing Group

Rizzoli International Publications Inc.

300 Park Avenue South, New York, NY 10010
tel 212-387-3400 *fax* 212-387-3535
website www.rizzoliusa.com
Publisher Marta Hallett

Art, architecture, photography, fashion, gardening, design, gift books, cookbooks. Founded 1976.

Rodale Book Group

400 South 10th Street, Emmaus, PA 18098
tel 610-967-5171 *fax* 610-967-8961
Ceo Steve Murphy, *Executive Editor, Rodale General Books* Stephanie Tade, *Editor-in-Chief, Women's Health Books* Tami Booth, *Executive Editor, Home Arts* Ellen Phillips, *Executive Editor, Lifestyle Books*

Margot Schupf, *Executive Editor, Men's Health/Sports & Fitness Books* Jeremy Katz, *Senior Editor, Parenting Books* Lou Cinquino

General health, women's health, men's health, senior health, alternative health, fitness, healthy cooking, gardening, pets, spirituality/inspiration, trade health, biography, memoir, current affairs, science, parenting, organics, lifestyle, self-help, how-to, home arts. Founded 1932.

Rough Guides – see Viking Penguin

Routledge

270 Madison Avenue, New York, NY 10016
tel 212-216-7800 *fax* 212-563-7854
website www.routledge-ny.com
Vice President of Marketing Mary MacInnes

Music, history, psychology and psychiatry, politics, women's studies, education, sociology, urban studies, religion, lesbian and gay studies, film, media, literary and cultural studies, reference. Editorial office in the UK. Subsidiary of Taylor & Francis Books Inc.

Running Press Book Publishers

125 South 22 Street, Philadelphia, PA 19103–4399
tel 215-567-5080 *fax* 215-568 2919
website www.runningpress.com
Publisher Jon Anderson, *Directors* Bill Jones (design), Greg Jones (editorial), Joanne Cassetti (production), Craig Herman (marketing)

Art, craft/how-to, general non-fiction, children's books. Imprints: Courage Books, Running Press Miniature Editions, Running Press Kids. Founded 1972.

Rutgers University Press

100 Joyce Kilmer Avenue, Piscataway, NJ 08854–8099
tel 732-445-7762 *fax* 732-445-7039
website www.rutgerspress.rutgers.edu
Directors Marlie Wasserman, *Editor-in-Chief* Leslie Mitchner

Women's studies, anthropology, film and media studies, sociology, public health, popular science, cultural studies, literature, religion, history of medicine, Asian–American studies, African–American studies, American history, American studies, art history, regional titles. Founded 1936.

St Martin's Press Inc.*

175 Fifth Avenue, New York, NY 10010
tel 212-674-5151 *fax* 212-420-9314
website www.stmartins.com
President John Sargent

Trade, reference, college. No unsolicited MSS. Founded 1952.

Scholastic Inc.*

557 Broadway, New York, NY 10012
tel 212-343-6100 *fax* 212-343-6930

website www.scholastic.com
Chairman/President/Ceo Richard Robinson, Editorial
Director Elizabeth Szabla

Innovative textbooks, magazines, technology and
teacher materials for use in both school and the
home. Scholastic is a global children's publishing and
media company with a corporate mission to instill
the love of reading and learning for lifelong pleasure
in all children. Founded 1920.

Orchard Books (imprint)
555 Broadway, New York, NY 10012
tel 212-343-6782 fax 212-343-4890
website www.scholastic.com
Editorial Director Ken Geist, Art Director David Saylor

Picture books and fiction for children and young
adults. Founded 1987.

Sheridan House Inc.*

145 Palisade Street, Dobbs Ferry, NY 10522
tel 914-693-2410 fax 914-693-0776
email info@sheridanhouse.com
website www.sheridanhouse.com
President Lothar Simon

Sailing, nautical, travel. Founded 1940.

Simon & Schuster Adult Publishing Group*

1230 Avenue of the Americas, New York, NY 10020
tel 212-698-7000 fax 212-698-7007
website www.simonsays.com
President Carolyn K. Reidy

General fiction and non-fiction. No unsolicited MSS.
Imprints: Atria, Downtown Press, Fireside, Free
Press, MTV®, Pocket Books, Scribner, Scribner
Paperback Fiction, S&S Libros en Espanol, Simon &
Schuster, Star Trek®, Strebor Books, Threshold
Editions, Touchstone, Washington Square Press,
Washington Square Press VHI®. Division of Simon
& Schuster Inc. Founded 1924.

Simon & Schuster Children's Publishing Division*

1230 Avenue of the Americas, New York, NY 10020
tel 212-698-7200 fax 212-698-2793
website www.simonsayskids.com
President Rick Richter

Preschool to young adult, fiction and non-fiction,
trade, library and mass market. Imprints: Aladdin
Paperbacks, Atheneum Books for Young Readers,
Libros para ninos, Little Simon, Little Simon
Inspirations, Margaret K. McElderry Books, Simon &
Schuster Books for Young Readers, Simon Scribbles,
Simon Pulse, Simon Spotlight. Division of Simon &
Schuster, Inc. Founded 1924.

Soho Press Inc.

853 Broadway, New York, NY 10003
tel 212-260-1900 fax 212-260-1902

email soho@sohopress.com
website www.sohopress.com
Publisher Laura Hruska

Literary fiction, commercial fiction, mystery, thrillers,
travel, memoir, general non-fiction. Founded 1986.

Stackpole Books

5067 Ritter Road, Mechanicsburg, PA 17055–6921
tel 717-796-0411 fax 717-796-0412
email sales@stackpolebooks.com
website www.stackpolebooks.com
Directors David Detweiler (chairman), David Ritter
(president), Publisher Judith Schnell

Nature, outdoor sports, Pennsylvania, crafts and
hobbies, history, military history. Founded 1930.

Stanford University Press*

Palo Alto, CA 94304–1124
tel 650-723-9434 fax 650-725-3457
website www.sup.org
Director Geoffrey Burn

Scholarly non-fiction, college text, professional.

Strawberry Hill Press

21 Isis Street, Apt 102, San Francisco, CA 94103–4365
President Jean-Louis Brindamour PHD, Executive Vice-
President/Art Director Ku Fu-Sheng, Treasurer
Edward E. Serres

Health, self-help, cookbooks, philosophy, religion,
history, drama, science and technology, biography,
mystery, Third World. No unsolicited MSS;
preliminary letter and return postage essential.
Founded 1973.

Ten Speed Press

PO Box 7123, Berkeley, CA 94707
tel 510-559-1600 fax 510-524-1052
email order@tenspeed.com
website www.tenspeed.com
President Philip Wood, Publisher Lorena Jones

Career/business, cooking, practical non-fiction,
health, women's interest, self-help, children's.
Founded 1971.

University of Tennessee Press*

110 Conference Center Building, Knoxville,
TN 37996–4108
tel 865-974-3321 fax 865-974-3724
email danforth@utk.edu
website www.utpress.org
Director Jennifer Siler

American studies: African–American studies,
Appalachian studies, history, religion, literature,
historical archaeology, folklore, vernacular
architecture, material culture. Founded 1940.

University of Texas Press*

PO Box 7819, Austin, TX 78713–7819
tel 512-471-7233 fax 512-232-7178

email utpress@uts.cc.utexas.edu
website www.utexaspress.com
Director Joanna Hitchcock, *Assistant Director &
Editor-in-Chief* Theresa May, *Assistant Director &
Financial Officer* Joyce Lewandowski, *Assistant
Director & Design/Production Manager* David Cavazos

Scholarly non-fiction: anthropology, classics and the
Ancient World, conservation and the environment,
film and media studies, geography, Latin American
and Latino studies, Middle Eastern studies, natural
history, ornithology, Texas and Western studies.
Founded 1950.

Theatre Arts Books

270 Madison Avenue, New York, NY 10016
tel 212-216-7877
Publisher Talia Rodgers

Theatre, performance, dance and allied books –
acting techniques, voice, movement, costume,
textbooks. Imprint of **Routledge**.

Thunder's Mouth Press

(formerly Four Walls Eight Windows)
245 West 17th Street, 11th Floor, New York, NY
10011–5300
tel 212-646/375-2570 *fax* 212-646/375-2571
email edit@4w8w.com
website www.4w8w.com
Publisher John Oakes

Art, autobiography, biography, business, cookery,
fiction, health, history, language and literature,
nature, philosophy, poetry, politics, science-fiction
sport, women's studies. No unsolicited MSS.
Acquired by Avalon Publishing Group. Founded
1987.

Tor Books

175 Fifth Avenue, 14th Floor, New York, NY 10010
tel 212-388-0100 *fax* 212-388-0191
website www.tor.com

Fiction: general, historical, western, suspense,
mystery, horror, science fiction, fantasy, humour,
juvenile, classics (English language); non-fiction:
adult and juvenile. Affiliate of Holtzbrinck
Publishers. Founded 1980.

Tuttle Publishing/Periplus Editions

364 Innovation Drive, North Clarendon, VT 05759
tel 802-773-8930 *fax* 802-747-0423
Periplus Editions, 130 Joo Seng Road #6–01/03,
Olivine Building, Singapore 368357
tel 65-6280-3320 *fax* 65-6280-6290
website www.tuttlepublishing.com
Ceo Eric Oey, *Publishing Director* Ed Walters

Asian art, culture, cooking, gardening, Eastern
philosophy, martial arts, health. Founded 1948.

Van Nostrand Reinhold – acquired by John
Wiley & Sons Inc.

Viking – see Viking Penguin

Viking Children's Books – see Penguin
Putnam Books for Young Readers

Viking Penguin

375 Hudson Street, New York, NY 10014
tel 212-366-2000 *fax* 212-366-2666
email online@penguinputnam.com
website www.penguinputnam.com
Chairman Susan Petersen Kennedy, *President* Clare
Ferraro

Fiction and general non-fiction for adults. Imprints:
Stephen Greene Press, Pelham, Penguin Books,
Penguin Classics, Penguin Compass, Rough Guides,
Viking, Viking Compass, Penguin AudioBooks, Allen
Lane The Penguin Press. Division of **Penguin
Putnam Inc.** Founded 1975.

Penguin AudioBooks (imprint)

Senior Editor David Highfill

Imprints: Penguin AudioBooks, Penguin HighBridge
Audio. Founded 1990.

Penguin Books (imprint)

President/Publisher Kathryn Court

Fiction and general non-fiction for adults. Imprints:
Penguin, Penguin Classics, Penguin Compass,
Penguin 20th Century Classics. Founded 1935.

Rough Guides (imprint)

email mail@roughguides.com
website www.roughguides.com
Managing Director Kevin Fitzgerald, *Publishing
Director* Martin Dunford, *Publishing Development
Officer* Mark Ellingham

Trade paperbacks, travel guides, phrasebooks, music
reference, music CDs and internet reference.
Founded 1982.

Viking (imprint)

Fiction and general non-fiction for adults. Founded
1925.

Walker & Co.

104 Fifth Avenue, New York, NY 10011
tel 212-727-8300 *fax* 212-727-0984
website www.walkerbooks.com,
www.walkeryoungreaders.com
Publisher Emily Easton

General publishers, biography, popular science,
health, business, mystery, history, juveniles. Founded
1960.

Warner Books Inc.

1271 Avenue of the Americas, New York, NY 10020
tel 212-522-7200 *fax* 212-522-7991
website www.twbookmark.com
Ceo Laurence K. Kirshbaum, *President/Coo/Publisher*
Maureen Mahon Egen

Paperback originals and reprints, fiction and non-fiction, trade paperbacks and hardcover books, audio books, gift books. Subsidiary of AOL Time Warner Book Group. Founded 1961.

University of Washington Press

PO Box 50096, Seattle, WA 98145–5096
tel 206-543-4050 *fax* 206-543-3932
website www.washington.edu/uwpress
Director Patrick Soden

Anthropology, Asian–American studies, Asian studies, art and art history, aviation history, environmental studies, forest history, Jewish studies, literary criticism, marine sciences, Middle East studies, music, regional studies, including history and culture of the Pacific Northwest and Alaska, Native American studies, resource management and public policy, Russian and East European studies, Scandinavian studies. Founded 1909.

WaterBrook Press

12265 Oracle Blvd, Suite 200, Colorado Springs, CO 80921
tel 719-590-4999 *fax* 719-590-8977
email info@waterbrookpress.com
website www.waterbrookpress.com
President Stephen Cobb

Broad range of Christian fiction and non-fiction. Imprint: Shaw Books. Division of **Random House Inc.**

Watson-Guptill Publications

770 Broadway, New York, NY 10003
tel 646-654-5000 *fax* 646-654-5487
email info@watsonguptill.com
website www.watsonguptill.com
Senior Acquisitions Editors Candace Raney, Bob Nirkind, Victoria Craven, Joy Aquilino, Julie Mazur

Art, crafts, how-to, comic/cartooning, photography, performing arts, architecture and interior design, graphic design, music, entertainment, writing, reference, children's. Imprints: Amphoto Books, Back Stage Books, Billboard Books, Watson-Guptill, Whitney Library of Design. Founded 1937.

Franklin Watts

90 Sherman Turnpike, Danbury, CT 06816
tel 203-797-3500 *fax* 203-797-6986

School and library books for grades K–12.

Westminster John Knox Press

100 Witherspoon Street, Louisville, KY 40202–1396
tel 502-569-5052 *fax* 502-569-8308
email wjk@presbypub.com
website www.wjkbooks.com
President & Publisher Davis Perkins

Religious, academic, reference, general.

John Wiley & Sons Inc.*

111 River Street, Hoboken, NJ 07030
tel 201-748-6000 *fax* 201-748-6088
email info@wiley.com
website www.wiley.com
President/Ceo William J. Pesce

Specialises in scientific and technical books and journals, textbooks and educational materials for colleges and universities, as well as professional and consumer books and subscription services. Subjects include business, computer science, electronics, engineering, environmental studies, reference books, science, social sciences, multimedia, and trade paperbacks. Founded 1807.

Workman Publishing Company

708 Broadway, New York, NY 10003–9555
tel 212-254-5900 *fax* 212-254-8098
email info@workman.com
website www.workman.com

Adult and juvenile books: art and architecture, biography and memoirs, BRAIN QUEST®, business, children's, cooking, food and wine, crafts, fiction, gardening, gift books, health, history, home reference/how-to, humour, film and TV, music, parenting and families, pets and animals, poetry, science, sport, travel. Founded 1968.

Writer's Digest Books

4700 East Galbraith Road, Cincinnati, OH 45236
tel 513-531-2690 *fax* 513-891-7185
website www.writersdigest.com
Executive Editor Jane Friedman

Market directories, books for writers, photographers and songwriters.

Popular Woodworking (imprint)

How-to in home building, remodelling, woodworking, home organisation.

Family Tree (imprint)

Genealogy.

North Light Books (imprint)

Fine art, decorative art, crafts, graphic arts instruction books.

Yale University Press*

302 Temple Street, New Haven, CT 06511
tel 203-432-0960 *fax* 203-432-0948/2394
email firstname.lastname@yale.edu
postal address PO Box 209040, New Haven, CT 06520
website www.yale.edu/yup
Editorial Director Jonathan Brent

Scholarly books and art books.

Audio publishers

Many of the audio publishers listed below are also publishers of books.

Abbey Home Entertainment plc

435–437 Edgware Road, London W2 1TH
tel 020-7563 3910 *fax* 020-7563 3911
Contact Anne Miles

Specialises in the acquisition, production and distribution of quality audio/visual entertainment for children. Bestselling children's spoken word and music titles are available on CD and cassette in the Tempo range including *Postman Pat*, *Watership Down*, *Michael Rosen*, *Baby Bright*, *Wide Eye*, *SuperTed* and *Golden Nursery Rhymes*.

Barefoot Books Ltd

124 Walcot Street, Bath BA1 5BG
tel (01225) 322400 *fax* (01225) 322499
email info@barefootbooks.co.uk
website www.barefootbooks.co.uk
Publisher Tessa Stickland, *Group Project Manager* Emma Parkin

Narrative unabridged audiobooks, spoken and sung. Established 1993.

Barrington Stoke

18 Walker Street, Edinburgh EH3 7LP
tel 0131-225 4113 *fax* 0131-225 4140
email info@barringtonstoke.co.uk
website www.barringtonstoke.co.uk
Chairman David Croom, *Managing Director* Sonia Raphael, *Editorial Manager* Kate Paice

Cassette tapes accompanied by 2 books: *Virtual Friends* and *Virtual Friends Again* by Mary Hoffman, *Problems with a Python* and *Living with Vampires* by Jeremy Strong, *Tod in Biker City* and *Bicycle Blues* by Anthony Masters, *Hat Trick* and *Ghost for Sale* by Terry Deary. Limited output. Founded 1998.

BBC Audiobooks Ltd

St James House, The Square, Lower Bristol Road, Bath BA2 3BH
tel (01225) 335336 *fax* (01225) 310771
email bbcaudiobooks@bbc.co.uk
website www.bbcaudiobooks.com
Managing Director Paul Dempsey, *Publishing Director* Jan Paterson

Spoken word entertainment that can be enjoyed at convenience. Imprints include BBC Radio Collection, Cover to Cover Classics, BBC Cover to Cover, BBC Word for Word, Chivers Audiobooks, Chivers Children's Audiobooks. Formed in 2003 from the amalgamation of Chivers Press, Cover To Cover and BBC Radio Collection.

Bloomsbury Publishing Plc

36 Soho Square, London W1D 3QY
tel 020-7494 2111 *fax* 020-7734 8656
website www.bloomsbury.com
Contact Alexandra Pringle

A broad selection of literary fiction and non-fiction.

Bolinda Publishing Ltd

2 Ivanhoe Road, London SE5 8DH
tel 020-7733 1088
email marisa@bolinda.com
website www.bolinda.com
UK Publisher Marisa McGreevy

CDs and cassettes of children's, teenage and adult fiction titles. Based in Melbourne, Australia; established in the UK in 2003.

Chrome Dreams

12 Seaforth Avenue, New Malden, Surrey KT3 6JP
tel 020-8715 9781 *fax* 020-8241 1426
website www.chromedreams.co.uk
Owner Rob Johnstone

Cló Iar-Chonnachta Teo.

Indreabhán, Conamara, Co. Galway, Republic of Ireland
tel (091) 593307 *fax* (091) 593362
email cic@iol.ie
website www.cic.ie
Ceo Micheál Ó Conghaile, *General Manager* Deirdre O'Toole

Irish-language – novels, short stories, plays, poetry, songs; CDs (writers reading from their works), bilingual books. Promotes the translation of contemporary Irish poetry and fiction into other languages. Founded 1985.

CSA Word

6A Archway Mews, London SW15 2PE
tel 020-8871 0220 *fax* 020-8877 0712
email info@csaword.co.uk
website www.csaword.co.uk
Managing Director Clive Stanhope, *Audio Director* Victoria Williams

CDs and cassettes of classic literature such as Jane Austen, Charles Dickens, D.H. Lawrence and P.G. Wodehouse; also current literary authors. Publishes 25 titles a year and has 150 titles available, including many short stories. Founded 1991.

57 Productions

57 Effingham Road, London SE12 8NT
tel/fax 020-8463 0866
email paul@57productions.com
website www.57productions.com
Director Paul Beasley

An agency and production company specialising in the spoken word, especially poetry in a contemporary and multicultural context. Represents and publishes a wide range of writers and performers, including Jean 'Binta' Breeze, Lemn Sissay, John Cooper Clarke, Adrian Mitchell and Benjamin Zephaniah. Established 1992.

Hachette Audio

Brettenham House, Lancaster Place, London WC2E 7EN
tel 020-7911 8044 *fax* 020-7911 8109 (editorial)
email sarah.shrub@twbg.co.uk
tel 020-7911 8057 *fax* 020-7911 8102 (publicity)
email cecilia.duraes@twbg.co.uk
Editor Sarah Shrubb

The AudioBooks list includes abridged titles from Time Warner Books' bestselling authors Alexander McCall Smith, Mitch Albom and David Sedaris. In 2004 the audio list was set to publish around 20 titles, including new fiction from Anita Shreve and Peter Mayle, further tales from Alexander McCall Smith, and Mark Billingham's detective series featuring D.I. Tom Thorne. Readings are by talented and recognisable actors including Tim Pigott-Smith and Andjoa Andoh. Launched 2003.

Harper Thorsons/Harper Element

77–85 Fulham Palace Road, London W6 8JB
tel 020-8307 4706 *fax* 020-8307-4788 (editorial)
email carole.tonkinson@harpercollins.co.uk (editorial)
Publishing Director Carole Tonkinson

The eclectic lifestyle list at HarperCollins (see *Book publishers UK and Ireland*). The list includes *Ghost Hunting* with Derek Acorah, John Gray's *Men Are from Mars, Women Are from Venus* and Paulo Coelho's *The Alchemist*.

HarperCollins Audio

77–85 Fulham Palace Road, London W6 8JB
tel 020-8741 7070 *fax* 020-8307 4517
website www.harpercollins.co.uk
Editorial Nicola Townsend

Publishers of a wide range of genres including fiction, non-fiction, poetry, Classics, Shakespeare, comedy, personal development and children's. All works are read by famous actors. Established 1990.

Hodder Headline Audiobooks

338 Euston Road, London NW1 3BH
tel 020-7873 6000 *fax* 020-7873 6024

Publishes outstanding authors from within the Hodder Headline group and from elsewhere. The list is made up of quality non-fiction; fiction, from John le Carré to Louis de Bernieres to Ardal O'Hanlon; WHSmith's Classic Collection; self-help titles from authors such as Susan Jeffers and Richard Carlson; religious titles; children's (i.e. the highly acclaimed

dramatised *Winnie the Pooh*); sporting autobiographies including Alex Ferguson, Brian Moore and Dickie Bird; comedy titles such as *Wallace & Gromit* and the *Magic Roundabout Adventures*, bestselling collaborations with Classic FM; Derek Jacobi's acclaimed readings of the *Brother Cadfael* mysteries, and C.S. Forester's *Hornblower* novels read by Ioan Gruffudd. Founded 1994.

Isis/Soundings

Isis Publishing Ltd, 7 Centremead, Osney Mead, Oxford OX2 0ES
tel (01865) 250333 *fax* (01865) 790358
website www.isis-publishing.co.uk
Chief Executive Robert Thirlby

Complete and unabridged audiobooks: fiction, non-fiction, autobiography, biography, crime, thrillers, family sagas, mysteries, health, poetry, humour; large print books.

Macmillan Audio Books

20 New Wharf Road, London N1 9RR
tel 020-7014 6040 *fax* 020-7014 6023
email a.muirden@macmillan.co.uk
website www.panmacmillan.com
Audio Publisher Alison Muirden

Adult fiction, non-fiction and autobiography, and children's. Established 1995.

Naxos AudioBooks

18 High Street, Welwyn, Herts. AL6 9EQ
tel (01438) 717808 *fax* (01438) 717809
email naxos_audiobooks@compuserve.com
website www.naxosaudiobooks.com
Managing Director Nicolas Soames

Classic literature, modern fiction, non-fiction, drama and poetry on CD. Also junior classics and classical music. Founded 1994.

The Orion Publishing Group Ltd

5 Upper St Martin's Lane, London WC2H 9EA
tel 020-7520 4425 *fax* 020-7379 6158
email pandora.white@orionbooks.co.uk
Audio Manager Pandora White

Adult and children's fiction and non-fiction. Established 1998.

Penguin Audiobooks

Penguin Books Ltd, 80 Strand, London WC2R 0RL
tel 020-7010 3000
email audio@penguin.co.uk
website www.penguin.co.uk/audio
Audio Publisher Jeremy Ettinghausen

The audiobooks list reflects the diversity of the Penguin book range, including classic and contemporary fiction and non-fiction, autobiography, poetry, drama and, in Puffin Audiobooks, the best of contemporary and classic literature for younger listeners. Authors include Nick

Hornby, Sue Townsend, Seamus Heaney, Roald Dahl and Eoin Colfer. Readings are by talented and recognisable actors. Over 500 titles are now available. Founded 1993.

Random House Audio Books
The Random House Group Ltd, 20 Vauxhall Bridge Road, London SW1V 2SA
tel 020-7840 8400 *fax* 020-7233 6127
email zhowes@randomhouse.co.uk
website www.randomhouse.co.uk
Commissioning Editor Zoe Howes

Fiction, non-fiction, self-help. Authors include John Grisham, Kathy Reichs, Andy McNab, Chris Ryan, Robert Harris, Mark Haddon, Ruth Rendell, Karin Slaughter, Peter Ackroyd. Established 1991.

Red Audio
7–14 Green Park, Sutton on the Forest, York YO61 1ET
tel (01347) 810055 *fax* (01347) 812705
email pam.reed@theredgroup.co.uk
website www.redaudio.biz
Ceo & Editor Steve Parks, *Head of Production* Pam Reed

CDs and cassettes of business topics such as marketing, start-ups, management and motivation. Publishes approx. 3 titles a year and has 13 titles available. Part of Red Studios UK Ltd. Founded 2001.

Simon & Schuster Audioworks
Simon & Schuster, Africa House, 64–78 Kingsway, London WC2B 6AH
tel 020-7316 1900 *fax* 020-7316 0331/2
email editorial.enquiries@simonandschuster.co.uk
website www.simonsays.co.uk
Publisher Jonathan Atkins, *Audio Manager* Rumana Haider

Fiction and non-fiction audiobooks. Fiction authors include Jackie Collins, Alan Titchmarsh and Lynda La Plante. Non-fiction authors include Stephen Covey, Anthony Robbins, Robin Cook and Stephen Ambrose. Established 1997.

SmartPass Ltd
15 Park Road, Rottingdean, Brighton BN2 7HL
tel (01273) 300742
email info@smartpass.co.uk
website www.smartpass.co.uk,
www.spaudiobooks.com
Managing Director Phil Viner, *Creative Director* Jools Viner

Dramatised English literature texts and discussion for individual study and classroom use. Full-cast unabridged novels.

Walker Books Ltd
87 Vauxhall Walk, London SE11 5HJ
tel 020-7793 0909 *fax* 020-7587 1123
Publisher Lorraine Taylor

Audiobooks include bestselling fiction titles such as the *Alex Rider* series, *Judy Moody* and *Confessions of a Teenage Drama Queen*. For younger children, the *Listen and Join In* audio range comprises entertaining story-based activities based on favourite picture books, including *We're Going on a Bear Hunt*, *Guess How Much I Love You* and *Can't You Sleep Little Bear?*

Book packagers

Many modern illustrated books are created by book packagers, whose particular skills are in the areas of book design and graphic content. In-house desk editors and art editors match up the expertise of specialist writers, artists and photographers who usually work on a freelance basis.

act-two ltd – now John Brown Junior

Aladdin Books Ltd
2–3 Fitzroy Mews, London W1T 6DF
tel 020-7383 2084 *fax* 020-7388 6391
email firstname.surname@aladdinbooks.co.uk
website www.aladdinbooks.co.uk
Directors Charles Nicholas, Bibby Whittaker

Full design and book packaging facility specialising in children's non-fiction and reference. Founded 1980.

The Albion Press Ltd
Spring Hill, Idbury, Oxon OX7 6RU
tel (01993) 831094 *fax* (01993) 831982
Directors Emma Bradford (managing), Neil Philip (editorial)

Produces quality integrated illustrated titles from the initial idea to the printed copy. Specialises in children's books. Publishers' commissions undertaken. No unsolicited MSS. Founded 1984.

Amber Books Ltd
Bradley's Close, 74–77 White Lion Street, London N1 9PF
tel 020-7520 7600 *fax* 020-7520 7606/7607
email enquiries@amberbooks.co.uk
website www.amberbooks.co.uk
Managing Director Stasz Gnych, *Deputy Managing Director* Sara Ballard, *Publishing Manager* Charles Catton, *Head of Production* Peter Thompson, *Design Manager* Mark Batley, *Picture Manager* Terry Forshaw

Illustrated non-fiction. Subject areas include history, military technology, aviation, transport, sport, crime, music, natural history, encyclopedias and children's books. Opportunities for freelances. Imprints: Brown Books Ltd. Founded 1989.

Nicola Baxter
PO Box 215, Framingham Earl, Yelverton, Norwich NR14 7UR
tel (01508) 491111
email nb@nicolabaxter.co.uk
website www.nicolabaxter.co.uk
Proprietor, Commissioning Editor & Author Nicola Baxter, *Design Manager* Amy Barton, *Submissions* Sally Delaney

Full packaging service for children's books, from concept to film or any part of the process in between. Produces both fiction and non-fiction titles in a wide range of formats, from board books to encyclopedias. Experienced in novelty books and licensed publishing. Opportunities for freelances. Founded 1990.

BCS Publishing Ltd
2nd Floor, Temple Court, 109 Oxford Road, Cowley, Oxford OX4 2ER
tel (01865) 770099 *fax* (01865) 770050
email bcs-publishing@dsl.pipex.com
Managing & Art Director Steve McCurdy

Specialises in the preparation of illustrated non-fiction; provides a full creative, design, editorial and production service. Opportunities for freelances. Commissioned work undertaken.

Bender Richardson White
PO Box 266, Uxbridge, Middlesex UB9 5NX
tel (01895) 832444 *fax* (01895) 835213
email brw@brw.co.uk
website www.brw.co.uk
Directors Lionel Bender (editorial), Kim Richardson (sales & production), Ben White (design)

Specialises in children's natural history, science and family information. Opportunities for freelances. Founded 1990.

BLA Publishing Ltd
BIC Ling Kee House, 1 Christopher Road, East Grinstead, West Sussex RH19 3BT
tel (01342) 318980 *fax* (01342) 410980
Directors Au Bak Ling (chairman, Hong Kong), Albert Kw Au (Hong Kong)

High-quality illustrated reference books, particularly science dictionaries and encyclopedias, for the international market. Founded 1981.

The Book Guild Ltd
Temple House, 25 High Street, Lewes, East Sussex BN7 2LU
tel (01273) 472534 *fax* (01273) 476472
email info@bookguild.co.uk
website www.bookguild.co.uk
Directors G.M. Nissen CBE (chairman), Carol Biss (managing), Anthony Nissen, Paul White (financial), Janet Wrench (production)

Offers a range of publishing options: a comprehensive package for authors incorporating editorial, design, production, marketing, publicity and distribution; editorial and production only for authors requiring private editions; or a complete service for companies and organisations requiring books for internal or promotional purposes – from brief to finished book. Founded 1982.

Breslich & Foss Ltd
2A Union Court, 20–22 Union Road, London SW4 6JP
tel 020-7819 3990 *fax* 020-7819 3998
Directors Paula G. Breslich, K.B. Dunning

Books produced from MS to bound copy stage from in-house ideas. Specialising in crafts, interiors, health and beauty, children's non-fiction. Founded 1978.

The Bridgewater Book Company Ltd
The Old Candlemakers, West Street, Lewes, East Sussex BN7 2NZ
tel (01273) 403120 *fax* (01273) 487441
email (surname)@bridgewaterbooks.co.uk
website www.bridgewaterbooks.co.uk
Directors Peter Bridgewater, Stephen Paul

Provides full editorial, design (and where required, production) service to develop ideas owned by its publishing clients. Specialises in building entire lists of illustrated books in all subject areas; developing individual titles; designing jackets/covers; producing sales material; rebranding. Opportunities for freelancers. Part of the Ivy Publishing Group.

John Brown Junior
The New Boathouse, 136–142 Bramley Road, London W10 6SR
tel 020-7565 3000 *fax* 020-7565 3060
email info@jbjunior.com
website www.jbjunior.com
Directors Andrew Jarvis (operations), Sara Lynn (creative)

Creative development and packaging of children's products including books, magazines, partworks, CD-Roms and websites.

The Brown Reference Group Plc
8 Chapel Place, Rivington Street, London EC2A 3DQ
tel 020-7920 7500 *fax* 020-7920 7501
email info@brownreference.com
website www.brownreference.com
Managing Director Sharon Hutton, *Children's Publisher* Anne O'Daly

Book, partwork and continuity set packaging services for trade, promotional and international publishers. Opportunities for freelances. Founded 1989.

Brown Wells & Jacobs Ltd
Foresters Hall, 25–27 Westow Street, London SE19 3RY
tel 020-8771 5115 *fax* 020-8771 9994
email graham@bwj-ltd.com
website www.bwj.org
Director Graham Brown

Design, editorial, illustration and production of high-quality non-fiction illustrated children's books.

Specialities include pop-up and novelty books. Opportunities for freelances. Founded 1979.

Cambridge Language Services Ltd
Greystones, Allendale, Northumberland NE47 9PX
tel (01434) 683200 *fax* (01434) 683200
email paul.oakleaf@homecall.co.uk
Managing Director Paul Procter

Suppliers to publishers, societies and other organisations of customised database management systems, with advanced retrieval mechanisms, and electronic publishing systems for the preparation of dictionaries, reference books, encyclopedias, catalogues, journals, archives. PC (windows) based. Founded 1982.

Cambridge Publishing Management Ltd
Unit 2, Burr Elm Court, Main Street, Caldecote, Cambs. CB3 7NU
tel (01954) 214000 *fax* (01954) 214001
email initial.surname@cambridgepm.co.uk
website www.cambridgepm.co.uk
Managing Director Jackie Dobbyne, *Managing Editor* Karen Beaulah

Creative and highly skilled editorial and book production company specialising in complete project management of business, education, ELT, travel and illustrated non-fiction titles, from MS to delivery of final files on disk. Opportunities for freelances; send CV to Managing Editor. Founded 1999.

Cameron & Hollis
PO Box 1, Moffat, Dumfriesshire DG10 9SU
tel (01683) 220808 *fax* (01683) 220012
email editorial@cameronbooks.co.uk
website www.cameronbooks.co.uk
Directors Ian A. Cameron, Jill Hollis

Illustrated non-fiction: fine arts (including environmental and land art), film, the decorative arts, crafts, architecture, design, antiques, collecting. Founded 1976.

Edition
Design, editing, typesetting, production work from concept to finished book for galleries, museums, institutions and other publishers. Founded 1976.

Canopus Publishing Ltd
27 Queen Square, Bristol BS1 4ND
tel 0117-922 6660 *fax* 0117-922 6660
email robin@canopusbooks.com
website www.canopusbooks.com
Director Robin Rees

Highly illustrated popular science and astronomy titles for international markets. Founded 1999.

Carroll & Brown Ltd
20 Lonsdale Road, London NW6 6RD
tel 020-7372 0900 *fax* 020-7372 0460

email mail@carrollandbrown.co.uk
website www.carrollandbrown.co.uk
Directors Amy Carroll (managing), Denise Brown
(publishing)

Publishers and packagers of health, craft, Mind, Body
& Spirit, and lifestyle titles. Opportunities for
freelances. Founded 1989.

Cowley Robinson Publishing Ltd
(incorporating David Hawcock Books)
8 Belmont, Bath BA1 5DZ
tel (01225) 339999 *fax* (01225) 339995
website www.cowleyrobinson.com
Directors Stewart Cowley (publishing), Rob Kendrew
(production), David Hawcock

Specialises in children's novelty and paper-engineered
formats for international co-editions. Licence and
character publishing developments. Information and
early learning. Imprint: Whizz Kids. Founded 1998.

Design Eye Ltd
226 City Road, London EC1V 2TT
tel 020-7700 9000 *fax* 020-7812 8601
email sueg@quarto.com, geoffs@quarto.com
Publisher Sue Grabham, *Art Director* Geoff Sida

Co-edition publisher of innovative Books-Plus for
children and adults. Children's: highly illustrated
paper-engineered, novelty and component-based
titles for all ages, but primarily children's preschool
(3+), 5–8 and 8+ years. Mainly non-fiction, early
concepts and curriculum-based topics for the trade in
all international markets. Adults: highly illustrated
component-based kits and books for arts, crafts,
lifestyle and hobbies. Opportunities for freelance
paper engineers, artists, authors, editors and
designers. Founded 1988.

Diagram Visual Information Ltd
195 Kentish Town Road, London NW5 2JU
tel 020-7482 3633 *fax* 020-7482 4932
email carole.office@diagramgroup.com
Director Bruce Robertson

Research, writing, design and illustration of reference
books, supplied as film or disk. Opportunities for
freelances. Founded 1967.

Eddison Sadd Editions Ltd
St Chad's House, 148 King's Cross Road, London
WC1X 9DH
tel 020-7837 1968 *fax* 020-7837 2025
email reception@eddisonsadd.co.uk
website www.eddisonsadd.co.uk
Directors Nick Eddison, Ian Jackson, David Owen,
Elaine Partington, Susan Cole

Illustrated non-fiction books, kits and gift titles for
the international co-edition market. Broad, popular
list with emphasis on Mind, Body & Spirit
(particularly tarot), health and relationships and
marshall arts. Founded 1982.

Elm Grove Books Ltd
Elm Grove, Henstridge, Somerset BA8 0TQ
tel (01963) 362498
email hugh@elmgrovebooks.com,
susie@elmgrovebooks.com
Directors Hugh Elwes, Susie Elwes

Packager of children's books. Opportunities for
freelances. Founded 1993.

Focus Publishing
Focus Publishing (Sevenoaks) Ltd, 11ᴀ St Botolph's
Road, Sevenoaks, Kent TN13 3AJ
tel (01732) 742456 *fax* (01732) 743381
email info@focus-publishing.co.uk
website www.focus-publishing.co.uk
Directors Guy Croton, Caroline Watson

Illustrated non-fiction: gardening, wine and food,
sport, aviation, DIY and crafts, transport.
Opportunities for freelances. Founded 1997.

Graham-Cameron Publishing & Illustration
The Studio, 23 Holt Road, Sheringham, Norfolk
NR26 8NB
tel (01263) 821333 *fax* (01263) 821334
email enquiry@graham-cameron-illustration.com
and Duncan Graham-Cameron, 59 Redvers Road,
Brighton BN2 4BF
tel (01273) 385890
website www.graham-cameron-illustration.com
Partners Mike Graham-Cameron, Helen Graham-
Cameron, Duncan Graham-Cameron

Educational and children's books; information
publications; sponsored publications. Illustration
agency with 37 artists. Do not send unsolicited MSS.
Founded 1985.

Hart McLeod Ltd
14 Greenside, Waterbeach, Cambridge CB5 9HP
tel (01223) 861495 *fax* (01223) 862902
email inhouse@hartmcleod.co.uk
website www.hartmcleod.co.uk
Directors Graham Hart, Chris McLeod, Joanne Barker

Primarily educational and general non-fiction with
particular expertise in revision books, school texts,
ELT and electronic content. Opportunities for
freelances and work experience. Founded 1985.

HL Studios Ltd
17 Fenlock Court, Blenheim Office Park, Long
Hanborough, Oxford OX29 8LN
tel (01993) 881010 *fax* (01993) 882713
email info@hlstudios.eu.com
website www.hlstudios.eu.com
Managing Director Robin Hickey

Primary, secondary academic education (geography,
science, modern languages) and co-editions (travel
guides, gardening, cookery). Multimedia (CD-Rom

programming and animations). Opportunities for freelances. Founded 1985.

The Ivy Press Ltd

The Old Candlemakers, West Street, Lewes, East Sussex BN7 2NZ
tel (01273) 487440 *fax* (01273) 487441
email surname@ivypress.co.uk
Directors Peter Bridgewater, Stephen Paul

Packagers of illustrated trade books on art, lifestyle, popular culture, design, health and Mind, Body & Spirit. Opportunities for authors and freelances. Founded 1996.

Lexus Ltd

60 Brook Street, Glasgow G40 2AB
tel 0141-556 0440 *fax* 0141-556 2202
email peterterrell@lexusforlanguages.co.uk
website www.lexusforlanguages.co.uk
Director P.M. Terrell

Reference book publishing (especially bilingual dictionaries) as contractor, packager, consultant; translation. *Lexus Travelmates* series. Founded 1980.

Lion Hudson International Co-Editions

Mayfield House, 256 Banbury Road, Oxford OX2 7DH
tel (01865) 302750 *fax* (01865) 302757
website www.lionhudson.com
Managing Director Paul Clifford

Books for children and adults. Subject areas include Christian Spirituality, reference, biography, history, contemporary issues and inspiration. Also specialises in children's Bibles and prayer collections, as well as fiction, picture stories and illustrated non-fiction. Founded 1971 as Angus Hudson; merged with Lion Publishing in 2004.

Little People Books

The Home of BookBod, Knighton, Radnorshire LD7 1UP
tel (01547) 520925
email littlepeoplebooks@thehobb.tv
website www.thehobb.tv/postings/000182.php
Directors Grant Jessé (production & managing), Helen Wallis (rights & finance)

Packager of audio, children's educational and textbooks, digital publications. Parent company: Grant Jessé UK.

Market House Books Ltd

2 Market House, Market Square, Aylesbury, Bucks. HP20 1TN
tel (01296) 484911 *fax* (01296) 437073
email books@mhbref.com
website www.mhbref.com
Directors Dr John Daintith, P.C. Sapsed

Compilation of dictionaries, encyclopedias, and reference books. Founded 1970.

Marshall Editions Ltd

The Old Brewery, 6 Blundell Street, London N7 9BH
tel 020-7700 6764 *fax* 020-7700 4191
email info@marshalleditions.com
Publisher Richard Green

Highly illustrated non-fiction for adults and children, including history, health, gardening, home design, pets, natural history, popular science.

Monkey Puzzle Media Ltd

Gissing's Farm, Fressingfield, Eye, Suffolk IP21 5SH
tel (01379) 588044 *fax* (01379) 588055
email info@monkeypuzzlemedia.com
Director Roger Goddard-Coote

High-quality illustrated children's and adult non-fiction for trade, institutional and mass markets worldwide. Publishers' commissions undertaken. Founded 1998.

Orpheus Books Ltd

6 Church Green, Witney, Oxon OX28 4AW
tel (01993) 774949 *fax* (01993) 700330
email info@orpheusbooks.com
website www.orpheusbooks.com
Executive Director Nicholas Harris (editorial, design & marketing)

Children's illustrated non-fiction/reference. Opportunities for freelance artists. Founded 1993.

Paragon Publishing

4 North Street, Rothersthorpe, Northants NN7 3JB
tel (01604) 832149
email mark.webb@tesco.net
website www.intoprint.net
Proprietor Mark Webb

Packagers of non-fiction books: architecture and design, educational and textbooks, electronic (academic and professional), languages and linguistics, sports and games. All editorial and design services to complete PDFs.

Playne Books Ltd

Park Court Barn, Trefin, Haverfordwest, Pembrokeshire SA62 5AU
tel (01348) 837073 *fax* (01348) 837063
email playne.books@virgin.net
Design & Production Director David Playne, *Editor* Gill Davies

Specialises in highly illustrated adult non-fiction and books for very young children. All stages of production undertaken from initial concept (editorial, design and manufacture) to delivery of completed books. Include sae for return of work. Founded 1987.

Tony Potter Publishing Ltd

1 Stairbridge Court, Bolney Grange Business Park, Stairbridge Lane, Bolney, West Sussex RH17 5PA

tel (01444) 232889 fax (01444) 232142
email sheilamortimer@zoo.co.uk
website www.tonypotter.com
Directors Tony Potter (managing), Christine Potter,
Sheila Mortimer

Creates custom children's book and own brand
innovative paper-based products for children and
adults. Also creates high-quality children's titles as a
packager and occasionally publishes under its own
imprint: Over the Moon. Opportunities for freelance
designers and illustrators. Founded 1997.

Quantum Publishing
6 Blundell Street, London N7 8BH
tel 020-7700 6700 fax 020-7700 4191
email quantum@quarto.com
website www.quarto.com
Publisher Isabel Leao

Packager of a wide range of non-fiction titles. Part of
the Quarto Group. Founded 1995.

Quarto Children's Books Ltd
226 City Road, London EC1V 2TT
tel 020-7700 9000 fax 020-7812 8601
email sueg@quarto.com, jonathang@quarto.com
Publisher Sue Grabham, Art Director Jonathan Gilbert

Co-edition publisher of innovative Books-Plus for
children. Highly illustrated paper-engineered, novelty
and component-based titles for all ages, but primarily
preschool (3+), 5–8 and 8+ years. Mainly non-
fiction, early concepts and curriculum-based topics
for the trade in all international markets.
Opportunities for freelance paper engineers, artists,
authors, editors and designers.

Quarto Publishing plc/Quintet Publishing Ltd
The Old Brewery, 6 Blundell Street, London N7 9BH
tel 020-7700 6700 fax 020-7700 4191
website www.quarto.com
Publisher (Quarto) Paul Carslake, Publisher (Quintet)
Judith More, Director of Co-edition Publishing Piers
Spence, Directors L.F. Orbach, R.J. Morley,
M.J. Mousley

International co-editions. Highly illustrated non-
fiction books for international markets, with
particular emphasis on art, crafts, interior design,
gardening, health and well-being, cookery and
illustrated reference. Founded 1976/1984.

Savitri Books Ltd
25 Lisle Lane, Ely, Cambridgeshire CB7 4AS
tel (01353) 654327 fax (01353) 654327
email munni@savitribooks.demon.co.uk
Director Mrinalini S. Srivastava

Packaging, publishing, design, production. Founded
1983.

Studio Cactus Ltd
13 Southgate Street, Winchester, Hants SO23 9DZ
tel (01962) 878600

email mail@studiocactus.co.uk
website www.studiocactus.co.uk
Editorial Director Damien Moore, Art Director
Amanda Lunn, Managing Editor Mic Cady, Senior
Designer Sharon Moore

High-quality illustrated non-fiction books for the
international market. Undertakes book packaging/
production service, from initial concept to delivery of
final electronic files. Opportunities for freelances.
Founded 1998.

Tangerine Designs Ltd
2 High Street, Freshford, Bath BA2 7WE
tel/fax (01225) 720001
email tangerinedesigns@btinternet.com
Managing Director Christine Swift

Packagers and co-edition publishers of children's
books including novelty books and licensed titles.
Submissions only accepted if sae is enclosed. Founded
2000.

The Templar Company plc
Pippbrook Mill, London Road, Dorking, Surrey
RH4 1JE
tel (01306) 876361 fax (01306) 889097
email info@templarco.co.uk
website www.templarco.co.uk
Directors Amanda Wood, Ruth Huddleston, Elaine
Hunt

High-quality children's gift, novelty, picture and
illustrated information books; most titles aimed at
international co-edition market. Established links
with major co-publishers in USA, Australia and
throughout Europe. Imprints: Templar Publishing,
Amazing Baby.

Toucan Books Ltd
3rd Floor, 89 Charterhouse Street, London
EC1M 6HR
tel 020-7250 3388 fax 020-7250 3123
website www.toucanbooks.co.uk
Directors Robert Sackville West, Ellen Dupont

International co-editions; editorial, design and
production services. Founded 1985.

Emma Treehouse Ltd
Little Orchard House, Mill Lane, Beckington,
Somerset BA11 6SN
tel (01373) 831215 fax (01373) 831216
email sales@emmatreehouse.com
website www.emmatreehouse.com
Directors David Bailey, Richard Powell (creative &
editorial)

Specialist creator of novelty books for children aged
0–7: bath books, books with a sound concept, cloth
books, novelty books, flap books, touch-and-feel
books. Packager and co-edition publisher with
international recognition for its innovative and often
unique concepts. The company has produced over 30

million books, translated into 33 different languages. Opportunities for freelance artists. Founded 1992

Tucker Slingsby Ltd
5th Floor, Regal House, 70 London Road, Twickenham TW1 3QS
tel 020-8744 1007 *fax* 020-8744 0041
email firstname@tuckerslingsby.co.uk
Directors Janet Slingsby, Del Tucker

Packager specialising in highly illustrated books and magazines. Creation, editorial and design to disk, digital files or finished copy of children's books, magazines and general interest adult titles. Commissioned work undertaken. Opportunities for freelances and picture book artists. Founded 1992.

Working Partners Ltd
1 Albion Place, London W6 0QT
tel 020-8748 7477 *fax* 020-8748 7450
email enquiries@workingpartnersltd.co.uk

website www.workingpartnersltd.co.uk
Chairman Ben Baglio, *Managing Director* Chris Snowdon, *Creative Director* Rod Ritchie

Children's and young adult fiction series. Genres include: animal fiction, fantasy, horror, historical fiction, detective, magical, adventure. Unable to accept any MS or illustration submissions. Pays advance and royalty. Selects writers from unpaid writing samples based on specific brief provided. Always looking to add writers to database (contact writers@workingpartnersltd.co.uk to register details). Founded 1995.

Working Partners Two (division)
Managing Director Charles Nettleton

Adult fiction. Aims to create novels across most adult genres for publication in the UK, US and international houses. See above for submission guidelines. Founded 2006.

Understanding the publishing process

To someone who has never worked in publishing the way in which a manuscript is turned into a book can seem like magic but in reality, the process is fairly straightforward. However, no two publishing houses (big or small) do things quite alike and the real magic comes in the way that the different departments work together to give every book the best possible chance of success. Bill Swainson explains the process.

For the purposes of this article I have assumed a medium-sized publishing house, big enough to have a fairly clear division of roles – in smaller houses these roles frequently overlap – and I talk mainly about original (rather than paperback reprint) publishing.

To begin at the beginning. Communication is everything in publishing and while more and more business is done by email, publishers still receive the majority of their submissions by post. So, the post-room staff, the computer wizards, the office management team, the receptionist who answers the telephone or welcomes visitors, all play a vital part in the process of making books. But it is the managing director who is the 'fat controller' of a company, and who draws all the threads together and gives the company its direction and drive.

Editorial

Every editorial department has a similar staff structure: commissioning editors (sometimes called acquiring editors) who take on a book and become its champion in the company, copy-editors (sometimes called desk editors) who do the close work on the manuscript, and editorial assistants who support them.

Every publishing company acquires their books from similar sources: literary agents and scouts, other publishers throughout the world, a direct commission from editor to author and, very occasionally, by unsolicited proposal (known unceremoniously in the business as the 'slush pile'). The in-house process goes something like this: the commissioning editor will make a case for a book's acceptance at an 'acquisitions meeting' which is attended by all the other departments directly involved in publishing the book, including sales, marketing, publicity and rights. Lively discussions follow and final decisions are determined from a mixture of commercial good sense (estimated sales figures, likely production costs and an author's track record) and taste – and every company's and every editor's taste is different.

Shortly after acquisition, an 'advance information' sheet is drafted by the commissioning editor. This is the earliest attempt to harness the excitement that led to the book being signed, and it contains all the basic information needed by the rest of the company, including the title, ISBN, format, extent (length), price, rights holder, sales points, short blurb and biographical note. It is the first of many pieces of 'copy' that will be written about the book, and will be used as the template for all others, such as a catalogue entry, jacket blurb or press release.

It is now that the journey of the book really begins, with the finishing line some 10–12 months away. As soon as it arrives in the editorial department the manuscript will receive a 'structural edit'. This involves looking at the book as a whole, i.e. everything from its structure and narrative pacing to characterisation and general style, and in the case of non-fiction, looking at illustrations, appendices, bibliography, notes and index. The actual copy-editing usually only takes place when all of the main structural editorial decisions have been made. While commissioning editors may see certain titles through from beginning to end, it is more likely that they'll pass them to their editorial team to manage, while still keeping a watching brief on every aspect of publication. It is at this stage that the more detailed work begins.

The copy-edit is another filtering process done with a very fine mesh net, designed to catch all the errors and inconsistencies in the text, from spelling and punctuation to facts, figures and tics of style. In some publishing houses this work is done onscreen, but surprisingly many editors prefer to work direct on the typescript because it is easier to spot changes and see where decisions have been made along the way. Once the copy-edit has been completed, the author will be asked to answer any queries that may have arisen. When the commissioning editor, copy-editor and author are happy that the marked-up typescript is in the best possible shape, it is sent to the production department for design and typesetting.

From now on the book will shuttle between the editorial and production departments in the form of proofs, usually in three separate stages. First proofs are read by the author and a proofreader. This is the author's last chance to make any cuts or additions as amendments after this stage become tricky and expensive to implement. Both sets of amendments are then collated and sent to the production department to be made into second proofs. (An index, if needed, will be compiled at this stage.) Second proofs, or 'revises', are checked against the collated first proofs and any last-minute queries are attended to. They are then returned to the production department to be made into 'final' proofs. Final proofs are, in a perfect publishing world, what the name implies. They are checked against the second proofs, the index (if there is one) is proofread, the prelim pages double-checked and when all is present and correct – the text is ready for press.

Design

The design department's work on a new book begins usually 10 months in advance of the publication date. Hardback jackets and the paperback covers are publishing's main selling tool. People say you can't judge a book by its cover, but because most (if not all) buying decisions are made by the trade's buyers before the book is printed – up until that time the cover *is* the book. It's what makes the buyer believe in a book enough to order it, and it's one of the most important things that makes a browsing customer pick up a book in the bookshop and pay for it at the till.

Design also produces all other sales material that the marketing department decides it needs to make a good job of the 'sell in', including catalogues, order forms, 'blads' (illustrated sales material), 'samplers' (booklets containing tantalising extracts), posters, book proofs (bound reading proofs) and advertisements.

Most companies try to develop a distinctive look for their books and it's the design department that creates it.

Production

The production department handles all aspects of book production including text design, although some of the very big companies have a separate department for this. The production department style (or format) the copy-edited typescript by drafting a brief known as a 'type specification' or 'spec'. The spec may be designed specifically for a unique book, or if the book is part of a series, the series spec will be used to give the books the same look and feel. The typescript is then usually despatched to an out-of-house typesetter, although some companies do typesetting in-house, to be made to page proofs. Meanwhile, the production manager (working with the commissioning editor) will choose the binding materials and any embellishments, such as headband, coloured or printed endpapers, or marker ribbon. The print run is also decided (based on advance sales and track record) and an order is placed with the printer.

Most publishing companies use only a few printers, negotiating the best possible rate per book depending on the volume of work they agree to place with the printer. A key role of the production department is to buy print at a rate that allows each tightly budgeted book to make money, and equally important (especially when a book takes off) to manage the supply of reprints so that the publisher's warehouse is never short of stock.

Sales

'Selling in' in the home market (Britain and Ireland) is done increasingly by key account managers working with the chain buyers, as well as by a team of sales representatives. The reps visit bookshops in their designated area and try to achieve the set sales targets for each book. The number of copies sold pre-publication is known as the subscription sale, or 'sub'.

Selling books effectively to bookshops, both chains and independents and nowadays to supermarkets and other retailers, takes time and careful planning. The British and Irish book trade has developed in such a way that the sales cycle has extended to cover the best part of a year. Even though the actual business of selling may not begin in earnest until eight or nine months prior to publication, the work of preparing sales material begins up to a year ahead. It can, however, be achieved in a shorter time frame and this allows a degree of flexibility for the publisher in case of a crisis or to take advantage of prime opportunities, such as issuing instant books on a burning topic of the day.

Many sales are also made in-house by phone, email and fax and, nowadays, the internet. Most publishers have their own websites and provide customers with the opportunity to buy their books either directly or by a link to another bookselling website. Book clubs still remain an important market for publishers, but they are having a tough time of it in the face of stiff competition from the internet and the supermarkets.

Export sales are achieved using teams of international agents and reps run from in-house by the export sales department. While the bigger companies tend to have their own teams and the smaller companies use freelance agencies and reps, all face a different range of challenges to the home sales team. Here format, discount, royalty rates, shipping, and exchange rates are the key components. The margins are much tighter and it requires a lot of skill and *chutzpah* to generate significant sales and then to maintain a successful international prescence.

Marketing

It could be said that the marketing department is the engine room of the sales department. It's responsible for preparing all the sales material (catalogues, blads, samplers, etc) used by the sales team to persuade others in the book trade to buy the company's books. Marketing also works alongside the sales department in dealing directly with the big book-shops on special promotions ('Book of the Month', '3 for 2', etc) that are now such a common feature of the larger chains.

This department also prepares the advertising for the trade, such as the post-publication press advertising that, along with reviews and other publicity, persuades customers into the shops to buy a particular book. It also organises the company sales conferences where the new season's publishing is for the first time presented to the sales reps and overseas agents. The run-up to the sales conference and the event itself is an exciting time and stimulates many of the best ideas on how to sell the new books.

Publicity

As the marketing department works to sell books with the emphasis on the 'sell in', the publicity department works with the author and the media on 'free' publicity with the emphasis on the 'sell through'. This covers reviews, features, author interviews, bookshop readings and signings, festival appearances, book tours and radio and television interviews and so on.

For each author and their book, the publicity department devises a campaign that will play to the book's or the author's strengths. For instance, best use will be made of written features or radio interviews for authors who are shy in public, just as full advantage will be made of public appearances for those authors who thrive on the thrill of showmanship. In short, the publicist's careful work (which like much of publishing is a mixture of inspiration and enthusiasm on the one hand and efficient planning and flexibility on the other) is designed to get the best results for each individual author and book.

Rights

It is the aim of the rights department to make the best use of all the rights that were acquired when the contract was first negotiated between publisher and author or the author's agent.

While literary agents are understandably keen to handle foreign and serial rights, many publishing houses have well-developed rights departments with good contacts and are also well placed to sell the rights of a book. Selling rights is very varied and includes anything from requests for film or television rights, translation rights to other countries, or serial rights to a newspaper, to smaller permission requests to reprint a poem or an extract. All are opportunities to promote the book and earn additional income for author and publisher, and at the time of first publication the rights, sales, marketing and publicity departments all work closely together.

Book fairs are key venues for the sale of foreign rights. At the Frankfurt Book Fair in October and at the London Book Fair in March, publishers and agents from all participating countries meet to form a rights 'bazaar'. Here, editors have the opportunity to hear about and buy new books from publishing houses all over the world. Occasionally rights are sold on the spot, but more commonly the acquisition process is completed later.

Paperbacks

Paperbacks are published approximately a year after the original publication. Paperback publishing is a key part of publishing today but is a quite different skill to hardback publishing, and is in many respects all about marketing. Efforts are made to identify and broaden the likely market (readership) for a book, making sure that the cover and presentation will appeal to a wide audience, and being ingenious about positioning an author's books in the marketplace where they can be best seen, bought and read. The means used vary from in-store promotions and advertising campaigns to author-led publicity and renewed press coverage in the paperback round-ups. But the energy that drives this inspired and careful work of reinvention comes from the paperback publisher's vision and passion for the book, author and the list as a whole.

Accounts

Finally, every successful business needs a good finance department. Most publishing houses split the work into two areas – purchase ledger and royalties. Purchase ledger deals with all incoming invoices associated with the company's business. The royalties department deals exclusively with author advances (payable on acquisition, and on delivery or publication of a book) and with keeping account of the different royalty percentages payable on book sales, serial deals, film rights, permissions, etc. This is done so that both author and agent can see that an accurate record has been kept against the day when the book earns back its advance (the point at which the royalties earned equal the advance paid) and the author starts earning additional income.

A special business

This has been a potted breakdown of the inner workings of a medium-sized company. Publishing is a business, and commercial considerations will be apparent in every department, but it is a very special kind of business, one which frequently breaks many of the accepted business rules and often seems to make no sense at all – just think of the hundreds of different lines, formats, price points and discounts. At times it shouldn't work – but somehow, miraculously, it does.

Bill Swainson has worked for small, medium and large publishers since 1976 and is currently a Senior Commissioning Editor at Bloomsbury Publishing Plc. He is the editor of *The Encarta Book of Quotations* (Bloomsbury 2000).

See also...

Notes from a successful fiction author

Joanna Trollope shares her experiences of writing success.

I once said to a journalist – rather crossly – that it had only taken me 20 years to be an overnight success. This was in 1993, with my first number one (the paperback of *The Rector's Wife*) and the accompanying media assumption that I had come from nowhere to somewhere at meteoric speed.

People do, of course. Rare, rare people do, but most of us are trudging for years across the creative plateau, honing our skills and cajoling our sinking hearts and *hoping*. I wrote my first published book when my younger daughter was three. When *The Rector's Wife* appeared, she was almost 23, and there'd been 10 books in the interim. Hardly *Bridget Jones*. Scarcely *White Teeth*.

But, on reflection, the long haul suited me. I learned about structure and dialogue and pace and characterisation at my own pace. I might have started with a readership so small it was almost invisible to the naked eye, but it grew, and it grew steadily in a manner that made it feel reliable, as is the case with long-term friendships. It also meant that when success came, it was absolutely lovely, no doubt about that, but there was no question of it turning my middle-aged head.

When I wrote my first published book – a historical novel called *Eliza Stanhope* set around the battle of Waterloo – the publishing climate was very different to how it is now. Many of the great publishing individuals were still alive, agents were a scarcer breed and writing was not seen as a way to becoming instantly, absurdly rich (and, in my view, never should be). I sent my manuscript – poorly typed on thin paper – off to Hamish Hamilton in a brown paper parcel. It was politely returned. I sent it – heart definitely in sink – to Hutchinson. They wrote back – a letter I still have – and invited me, like a job interview, to 'come and discuss my future'.

Even if the rest is history, it is not easy or simple history. There weren't any great dramas, to be sure, no cupboards stuffed with rejection slips, no pulped copies (that came later), but what there was instead was a simply enormous amount of perseverance. I don't want to sound too austere, but I find I rather believe in perseverance when it comes to writing. As V.S. Pritchett once said, most people write better if they *practise*.

And I have to say that I am still practising. I think it very unlikely that I will ever feel I have got it right, and I would be uneasy if that feeling went away. After all, only a very few geniuses – Sophocles, Shakespeare – could claim to be prophets or inventors. Most writers are translators or interpreters of the human condition, but no more. A hefty dose of humility in writing seems to me both seemly and healthy.

Readers, after all, are no fools. Readers may not have a writer's gift of the arrangement of events and people and language, but they know about life and humanity all right. They may even know much more about both than the writer. So not only must they never be forgotten, but they must never be underestimated or patronised either.

Which is one of the reasons, in my case, why I research my novels. For the readers' sake, as well as my own, I have to be as accurate as possible about, say, being the child of a broken home, or the widow of a suicide, or a mistress or an adopted man in his thirties. So, once I've decided upon the theme of a novel (and those can have brewed in my brain for years or be triggered by a chance remark overheard on a bus) I go and talk to people who are in the situation that I am exploring. And I have to say that in all the years of working this way, no one has ever turned me down, and everyone has exceeded my expectations.

This habit has had an unlooked-for advantage. During all the years I've been writing, the business of promotion has grown and grown, and fiction is notoriously difficult to talk about in any medium. But the research gives me – and journalists – subject matter which is, to my relief, honourably relevant but, at the same time, miles away from the inexplicable private, frequently uncomfortable place where writing actually goes on. 'Tell me,' people say, not actually understanding what they are asking, 'Tell me how you write'. Pass.

Joanna Trollope is the author of 12 contemporary novels, as well as a number of historical novels published under the name of Caroline Harvey, and a study of women in the British Empire called *Britannia's Daughters*. She divides her time between London and the Cotswolds.

Notes from a successful fantasy author

Terry Pratchett gives pointers on how to write successfully in the fantasy genre.

Since a lot of fiction is in some way fantasy, can we narrow it down to 'fiction that transcends the rules of the known world'? And it might help to add 'and includes elements commonly classed as magical'. There are said to be about five fantasy sub-genres, from contemporary to mythic, but they mix and merge and if the result is good, who cares?

If you want to write it, you've probably read a lot of it – in which case, stop (see below). If you haven't read any, go and read lots. Genres are harsh on those who don't know the history, don't know the *rules*. Once you know them, you'll know where they can be broken.

Genres are also – fantasy perhaps most of all – a big bulging pantry of plots, conceits, races, character types, myths, devices and directions, most of them hallowed by history. You're allowed to borrow, as many will have done before you; if this were not the case there would only ever have been one book about a time machine. To stay with the cookery metaphor, they're all just ingredients. What matters is how you bake the cake: every decent author should have their own recipe and the best find new things to add to the mix.

Word building is an integral part of a lot of fantasy, and this applies even in a world that is superficially our own – apart, say, from the fact that Nelson's fleet at Trafalgar consisted of hydrogen-filled airships. It is said that, during the fantasy boom in the late Eighties, publishers would maybe get a box containing two or three three-runic alphabets, four maps of the major areas covered by the sweep of the narrative, a pronunciation guide to the names of the main characters and, at the bottom of the box, the manuscript. Please … there is no need to go that far.

There is a term that readers have been known to apply to fantasy that is sometimes an unquestioning echo of better work gone before, with a static society, conveniently ugly 'bad' races, magic that works like electricity and horses that work like cars. It's EFP, or Extruded Fantasy Product. It can be recognised by the fact that you can't tell it apart from all the other EFP.

Do not write it, and try not to read it. Read widely outside the genre. Read about the Old West (a fantasy in itself) or Georgian London or how Nelson's navy was victualled or the history of alchemy or clock-making or the mail coach system. Read with the mindset of a carpenter looking at trees.

Apply logic in places where it wasn't intended to exist. If assured that the Queen of the Fairies has a necklace made of broken promises, ask yourself what it looks like. If there is magic, where does it come from? Why isn't everyone using it? What rules will you have to give it to allow some tension in your story? How does society operate? Where does the food come from? You need to know how your world *works*.

I can't stress that last point enough. Fantasy works best when you take it seriously (it can also become a lot funnier, but that's another story). Taking it seriously means that there must be rules. If *anything* can happen, then there is no real suspense. You are allowed to make pigs fly, but you must take into account the depredations on the local bird life and the need for people in heavily over-flown areas to carry stout umbrellas at all times. Joking aside, that sort of thinking is the motor that has kept the *Discworld* series moving for 22 years.

Somehow, we're trained in childhood not to ask questions of fantasy, like: how come only one foot *in an entire kingdom* fits the glass slipper? But look at the world with a questioning eye and inspiration will come. A vampire is repulsed by a crucifix? Then surely it can't dare open its eyes because everywhere it looks, in a world full of chairs, window frames, railings and fences, it will see something holy. If werewolves as Hollywood presents them were real, how would they make certain that when they turned back into human shape they had a pair of pants to wear? And in *Elidor*, Alan Garner, a master at running a fantasy world alongside and entwined with our own, memorably asked the right questions and reminded us that a unicorn, whatever else it may be, is also a big and very dangerous horse. From simple questions, innocently asked, new characters arise and new twists are put on an old tale.

G.K. Chesterton summed up fantasy as the art of taking that which is humdrum and everyday (and therefore unseen) and picking it up and showing it to us from an unfamiliar direction, so that we see it anew, with fresh eyes. The eyes could be the eyes of a tiny race of humans, to whom a flight of stairs is the Himalayas, or creatures so slow that they don't see fast-moving humanity at all. The eyes could even be the nose of our werewolf, building up an inner picture of a room by an acute sense of smell, seeing not just who is there now but who was there yesterday.

What else? Oh yes. Steer clear of 'thee' and 'thou' and 'waxing wroth' unless you are a genius, and use adjectives as if they cost you a toenail. For some reason adjectives cluster around some works of fantasy. Be ruthless.

And finally: the fact that it is a fantasy does not absolve you from all the basic responsibilities. It doesn't mean that characters needn't be rounded, the dialogue believable, the background properly established and the plots properly tuned. The genre offers all the palettes of the other genres, and new colours besides. They should be used with care. It only takes a tweak to make the whole world new.

Terry Pratchett OBE has written 34 novels in the *Discworld* series, the most recent of which is *Thud!* (HarperCollins 2005). The last 30 novels in this series have all reached the No 1 position in the bestseller lists. He has written or been co-author of over 50 books. His latest young adult *Discworld* novel, *Wintersmith*, is due to be published in October 2006.

Notes from a successful crime author

Mark Billingham shares his experiences of writing success.

I am a writer because I'm a reader. That I'm a *crime* writer, however, is probably down to a desire to get free books... I'd always written stuff of one sort or another: silly stories at school, terrible poetry at university, so-so plays for community theatre companies. I'd drifted into a career in stand-up and writing comedy for television but my passion as a reader was for crime fiction, primarily of the darker and more disturbing kind.

Devouring the work of my favourite writers from both sides of the Atlantic was firing my imagination, feeding my head and heart, but as I had also developed an obsession for collecting the first editions of these authors, it was doing very little for my bank balance. My wife made the choice quite a simple one: get the books for free or get a divorce.

I'm still amazed at how easy it was – how little time and effort was involved. A couple of phone calls to the publicity departments of several big publishers, a bit of blather about how I was reviewing for my local paper, and suddenly the books came tumbling through the letterbox: package after package carried manfully to the door by my less-than-delighted postman. I did indeed start to review for my local paper and soon I was writing longer pieces, then articles for national magazines, and it wasn't very long before I was asked if I'd like to interview a couple of crime writers – this was major!

I can vividly remember the enormous and terrifying thrill of interviewing such crime-writing giants as Michael Connelly and Ian Rankin, and I still get a secret buzz from the fact that I can now count them among my friends. (This, for me, remains one of the greatest pleasures in becoming a published writer; that if you're lucky, those whose work you've admired for many years can end up propping up bars with you in exotic countries at ungodly hours...) So, I was a reader who adored crime fiction, who was lucky enough to be writing *about* it and who, occasionally, talked to those who actually *wrote* it.

Writing it myself, however, at the time seemed completely out of the question. Talking now to unpublished writers, I discover that such terror at the thought of sitting down and writing a novel is hugely common. Some of them are like housebricks for heaven's sake! Now, I tell those as daunted as I was then, that if you write 1000 words a day for a month, you're more or less a third of the way through a novel. It all sounds terribly straightforward of course, but it certainly didn't feel like that as I began trying to write my own crime novel.

One of the most common pieces of advice given to aspiring writers is to read, and it was at the point of starting what would become my first book, that I saw just how important this was. I was writing in an already overcrowded genre, and having read a great deal within it (or should that be *around* it?) I had a pretty good idea what not to write – that is, I knew those areas to which claims had already been successfully staked by others. Having decided therefore that my detective would not be a deerstalker-wearing cocaine fiend, or an Edinburgh-based Rolling Stones fan, I tried quite simply to write the sort of crime novel I enjoyed reading. I always imagine that such a stunningly basic notion would be obvious to all those who want to write. However, I'm constantly amazed to meet those claiming to have studied the industry carefully and to have spotted a sizeable gap on the bookshelves. Those who announce confidently that the world is finally ready for the crime-fighting antique-dealer/amateur veterinarian who, while not cooking and listening to opera, cracks tough cases with the help of a cat, in the mid-18th century Somerset countryside. If this is really what you're driven to write, then all power to you, but if you simply try and fill what you perceive to be a gap in the market, you're on a hiding to nothing.

I fully believed myself to be on a hiding to somewhat less than this, when I picked half a dozen agents from the *Writers' & Artists' Yearbook* and sent off the first 30,000 words of my novel. From this point on in the career path of almost any published writer, luck will play a part, and I must confess that I had more than my fair share of the very good sort.

Being taken on by an agent is wonderful, and if you're very fortunate, you will be taken on by a good one. Getting published is one thing but it helps if that publisher has enough faith in the book to spend a decent amount on marketing it – an amount so much more important than your advance. My still incomplete manuscript landed on all the right desks, and it was while in the incredible position of having to choose between agents, that I received the single best piece of advice I was given, or am able to pass on. Don't imagine that things are going well. Imagine that they are going badly. Imagine that *nobody* wants to publish your book, that the rejection letters come back in such numbers that the Royal Mail lays on special deliveries. When that happens, who will be the agent who will give you up as a bad lot, and who will be the one willing to fight? Which one will say 'well, if *they* don't want it I'm going to try X'? This is the agent to choose. In the course of any writer's life, a good agent, not to mention a good editor, will probably need to show more than once that they aren't afraid of a good scrap.

As far as further advice goes – beyond the encouragement to read and to write something every day – it is important to remember that lies (white or whoppers) and luck (of both kinds) may play a disproportionately large part in the way things turn out. Oh, and if you could avoid writing crime novels about a north London copper with a weakness for Tottenham Hotspur and Hank Williams, I'd be very grateful.

However, one small drawback to getting published and finding yourself trying to produce a book a year, is that you suddenly have far less time to read. This is hugely upsetting, and in my case doubly ironic considering that, with requests for reviews and endorsements, I now get more free books than ever. In fact, the only person unhappy about the way things turned out is my postman.

Mark Billingham is the author of an award-winning series of novels featuring London-based Detective Inspector Tom Thorne, the latest of which is *Buried* (Little, Brown 2006). He has also worked for many years as a stand-up comedian but now prefers to concentrate on crime writing, as those that read the books are not usually drunk and can't throw things at him.

Notes from a successful historical novelist

Bernard Cornwall shares his experience of writing successful historical novels.

You are going to get things wrong. None of us mean to, but we do. There were no rabbits in King Arthur's Britain, which I knew, but a helpful reader (there's always a helpful reader) wrote to tell me there were no snowdrops either. Got that wrong.

So, how to write an historical novel? The real question is how to write a successful novel and I know only one answer. Story, story, story. You are *not* an historian, your job is to be a storyteller. If you set out to educate folk then you will probably bore them. Your job is to entertain them, and the way to do that is by telling a story. If your ambition is to inform readers of the intricacies of the Elizabethan religious settlement then be honest about that ambition and write a non-fiction history. But if you want a bestseller then devise a story with Jesuits in the shrubbery, secret chambers behind the linenfold panelling and the flames of Tyburn waiting for the tale's climax. Then, having written that book, write another with the same main characters. Write a series.

Why a series? Because the sales of the tenth book, or the twentieth, will encourage the sales of the first and the second and the rest. Series do not go out of print like standalone novels. I began to write because I had fallen in love with an American woman who could not come to live in Britain, which meant I had to emigrate to the United States. The fly in that romantic ointment was that the American government refused me a work permit, so I airily told my bride-to-be that I would make a living by writing novels. That was 27 years ago and we're still married and I'm still writing, so it was not so desperate an idea as it seemed at the time. Yet it was desperate and, before emigrating, I sought advice. Peter Wolfe, a friend and the owner of his own publishing company, took me to lunch and told me never, never, to attempt fiction. He would not publish fiction. 'The market's too crowded,' he told me. So what do I do?, I asked him. You write a book, he said, called *My Friend the Cocker Spaniel*, a book full of good advice on how to raise, feed and exercise a Cocker Spaniel, and wherever puppies are sold and wherever dog food is sold and, indeed, wherever books are sold, *My Friend the Cocker Spaniel* will be on sale. He saw an objection coming and raised a hand to stop it. Once you've written *My Friend the Cocker Spaniel*, he continued, you go through the manuscript and you cross out the words Cocker and Spaniel and replace them with Dachshund. You have now written a second book called *My Friend the Dachshund*. Then you cross out Dachshund and put in Scottish Terrier. You get the idea. You write a series. I took that piece of Peter's advice even if I ignored his well meant injunction to avoid fiction.

I wrote historical fiction because I wanted to, because I liked it and because I was not capable of writing non-fiction. But I still needed help, so I did something which, in retrospect, seems obvious, but which very few aspiring writers actually do. I set out to learn how successful historical novelists wrote their books. I used three books: two of them were *Hornblower* novels by C.S. Forester and the third was *Imperial Governor* by George Shipway (an excellent and undervalued writer). I then disassembled those books. If you wanted the world to beat a path to your door by making a better mousetrap then the first thing you would do is discover how existing mousetraps work. You would take them apart, discover their secrets, and set out to do better. I am not saying I did better, but I did take those three books apart. I made huge charts which showed, paragraph by paragraph, where there was dialogue, where there was action, where there was flashback, where there was romance and so on. The charts revealed a structure. I did not slavishly copy the structure – indeed one reason to make the charts was a determination to use less of the things I disliked (flashback) and more of the things I liked, but when I found myself in difficulties with my first two or three books the charts were there to show me how successful writers had tackled the same problems. The answers to a lot of aspiring writers' problems are as close as the bookshelf. Use it.

Kurt Vonnegut once offered a splendid piece of advice. Every book starts with a question – a question the reader probably didn't know they wanted answered but the search for that answer is what will pull the reader through the book. That's the story. But too many historical novels begin by establishing a world. I have just finished the third in my series of novels around Alfred the Great and his successors, and once the book was done I discovered I could tear 9000 words out of a 10,000-word first chapter. Those words were delivering information I thought the reader needed but they slowed the story to a crawl, so they had to go. I don't know if pacing a story can be taught, or whether it is an intuitive thing, but I do know that pacing needs work and, even after 43 novels, I still have to do that work.

Can writing be taught? I have a thoroughly old-fashioned view of this, which is probably founded on prejudice rather than on informed opinion, but I do know writing is a solitary vice and believe that it is best practised in solitude. Writing can be encouraged, perhaps, but taught? To teach something implies there is something to be taught and that suggests that the activity can be reduced to, if not rules, maxims. But there are no rules except to tell a story. I have met dozens of folk who belong to writers' groups or pay for writing courses but the chief activity of both seems to be criticism and I am not sure criticism helps aspiring writers whose confidence is frail. Only three opinions matter. The first is your own. You write for yourself. You write the books you want to read. The second opinion which matters is that of the professional gatekeeper, whether agent or publisher, and their views on writing differ hugely from the folk who teach it. The third vital opinion is the reader, and on that your success depends. I accept that I probably do not understand creative writing courses. None was available when I was an aspiring author so I managed without. Writers I admire tell me such courses can be helpful, so I shall merely say that the majority of successful writers never submit to them. Draw your own conclusion.

The most frequent questions I get are about research: how do I do it? How much time do I spend on it? The questions are virtually unanswerable. I assume no one writes historical fiction unless they first love history, and so virtually all your reading is research. I still read more history for pleasure than any other kind of book. Of course research has to be focused, but the real danger is doing too much research. If you are writing a novel about Jesuits in the Elizabethan shrubbery then you need to know a lot about the religious settlement, about social life and probably clothes, but do you need to know about Tudor farming practices? Maybe you do, but you will discover that need as you write the book – and a great deal of research is done while the book is being written. To believe that you must equip yourself with an encyclopaedic knowledge of the Tudor world before you begin writing is to guarantee you won't begin. Get on with it! Tell the story! The gaps in your knowledge will show up soon enough and there will be time to fill them. On the other hand, doing too little research has obvious dangers and can also deprive you of good story ideas. I'm currently writing a new *Sharpe* novel which is set in Cadiz in 1811 and I discovered, in an extremely dry and academic history of the diplomatic relations between Britain and Spain, a reference to the fire-rafts with which the French had hoped to burn the British fleet in Cadiz Harbour. That single unexpected reference has already supplied 10,000 words of the new book. The whole plot for *Gallow's Thief* came from a single footnote in an academic history of crime and punishment. In the end you will have to decide how much research to do, but beware the danger of doing too much and so never starting the novel.

Then, having done the research, you must reject a great deal of it. There is a terrible impulse to put in everything, just to prove how much you know, but nothing kills an historical novel like long passages written straight from your notebooks. And sometimes you must reject the true history to make the story work. When I wrote *Sharpe's Company*, which was about the ghastly siege of Badajoz in 1812, I knew that no British soldiers had succeeded in penetrating any of the three breaches on the night of the assault. The feint attack worked instead and the major attacks were all failures. But the drama of the story was in those three breaches and, if Sharpe was involved, Sharpe would get through, so I changed the history. You have to confess such inventions in a note at the book's end because many readers rely on an historical novelist to teach them something about history. It is always a pleasure, of course, when history serves up a plot and a timeline that does not need changing, but history is rarely so generous.

Above all, have fun. You write because you want to, not because you're forced to. If you enjoy the story then your excitement and enjoyment will show in the novel. You are an entertainer, not an historian, so entertain. And remember the one immutable rule in a business without any rules – tell a story!

Bernard Cornwell is the author of more than 40 novels, most of them historical, of which the best known are the Sharpe books. He lives in Cape Cod, Massachusetts, with his wife.

Notes from a successful travel author

Bestselling travel writer William Dalrymple explains the rise of the travel genre and gives guidance on how to write a travel book.

In the summer of 1973 a minor American novelist named Paul Theroux asked his publishers if they would be interested in a book about trains.

Trains mean travel – a travel book: it was a novel idea (at least in 1973) and the publishers liked it. In fact they liked it so much they gave Theroux an advance, his first, of £250. *The Great Railway Bazaar*, an account of a journey from London Victoria to Tokyo Central, was published in 1975. None of Theroux's novels had ever sold in any quantity. But the *Great Railway Bazaar* swiftly sold over 1.5 million copies in 20 different languages.

The book did more than revive Theroux's flagging literary career: it kick-started what was to be the most important publishing phenomenon of the 1980s. The success of *The Great Railway Bazaar* inspired Bruce Chatwin to give up his job on *The Sunday Times Magazine* and to head off to South America. The result – *In Patagonia* – was published in 1977, the same year Patrick Leigh Fermor produced his great masterpiece, *A Time of Gifts*. By the early 1980s Eland Books were busy reprinting the great 19th century travellers and Thomas Cook had announced its Travel Writing Award. Soon the travel sections in bookshops were expanding from a single shelf at the rear of the shop to a wall at the shop front, flanking fiction.

Two decades later, however, after several hundred sub-Therouxs have penned rambling accounts of every conceivable rail, road or river journey between Kamchatka and Patagonia, the climate has changed from enthusiasm to one of undisguised boredom. Travel writers have found, to their alarm, that Theroux's feelings have increasingly been shared by the critics. The reaction has yet to filter down from the book pages to the bookshops: the likes of Bill Bryson, Tony Hawks and Dave Gorman continue to dominate the bestseller lists. But what is certain is that travel writing has lost some of its chic.

This backlash is not the end of the line. But now that everyone travels, writing travel books is a much more difficult business than it used to be, and while it's still fairly easy to write a travel book, to write a *good* travel book now takes real ingenuity. However fluent or witty your prose, it is simply no longer enough just to jump on a train: writers have had to dress up their journeys in some pretty fancy packaging if they want to be taken seriously. Certainly your proposal must be that much more spectacular than it used to have to be.

The travel book is potentially a vessel into which a wonderfully varied cocktail of ingredients can be poured: politics, archaeology, history, philosophy, art, magic –whatever. You can cross-fertilise the genre with other literary forms: biography, or anthropological writing; or, perhaps more interesting still, following in Bruce Chatwin's footsteps and muddying the boundaries of fiction and non-fiction by crossing the travel book with some of the wilder forms of the novel. The result of this tendency has been a crop of one or two rather wonderful books by younger writers: Katie Hickman's travels with a Mexican circus (wonderful idea), William Fiennes's quest for the snow goose or Jeremy Seal searching Turkey for the anthropology of the fez. Perhaps the best hybrid travel book is John Berendt's immensely successful *Midnight in the Garden of Good and Evil* – the book is half travel writing and half murder mystery, but wholly enjoyable. Below are some hints on how you can get into print.

The concept

These days you need some pretty fancy packaging – it's simply not enough to go off and write a book about travelling through France or Russia or Bolivia; it's certainly not the time to start putting in proposals about taking a dustbin cart to Borneo or a pogo stick to the Antarctic: the killing off of the Gimmicks School of Travel Writing is one of the more happy results of the recession (although Tony Hawks's hilarious parody of that sort of book, *Round Ireland with a Fridge,* is of course one of the bestselling travel books of the last few years).

To write about a country in a very general and unfocused way you have to be very good: Thubron can do it. But you have to be very good indeed to write a getting-into- the-soul-of-a-country travel book. An easier, less ambitious and more commercial option is the Relocation Book – about setting off from London or New York and building a new life for yourself in Tuscany, Spain or Provence. Peter Mayle's *A Year in Provence* kicked off a fashion for travel books of this sort and was followed by ex-Genesis drummer Chris Stewart's Andalucian memoir, *Driving Over Lemons* (and its sequel *A Parrot in the Pepper Tree*) and Frances Mayes's *Under the Tuscan Sun,* all of which got little critical attention but nevertheless turned into major bestsellers.

There is also a more serious strand of travel writing that aims to delve into the soul of a city: my own book on Delhi, *City of Djinns,* was written in the tradition of studies of remarkable cities such as Jan Morris's classic, *The World of Venice* and Geoffrey Moorhouse's wonderfully apocalyptic *Calcutta.*

If falling in love with a small fragment of the globe is as good a starting point for a travel book as any, then other passions can also provide a good take-off point. I think it's fair to say that to be a really interesting travel writer you've got to have some small obsession: Ryszard Kapuscinski loves revolutions and watching dictators fall; Redmond O'Hanlon likes birds, beasts and exotic diseases; Bruce Chatwin was on the lookout for ideas and for nomads. I don't think it really matters what your interest is – stamp collecting, trainspotting or whatever – as long as it's genuine and you can convey your enthusiasm for it, you've probably got the seed of a travel book in there.

The research

If your book is to have any sort of authority, a card index is a very useful tool for keeping track of your research. For my last two travel books, I kept two card indexes: one with anecdotes and references listed under places and one listed under themes. So for *From the Holy Mountain* one index contained a list of places I expected to pass through on and around my projected route (Istanbul, Aleppo, Damascus, etc)

> ### Travel book shortlist
>
> There is no better way to learn how to write travel books than simply to read other travel books. My own personal shortlist of the great travel books would include:
>
> *The Road to Oxiana* by Robert Byron
>
> *Behind the Wall* by Colin Thubron
>
> *Into the Heart of Borneo* by Redmond O'Hanlon
>
> *Midnight in the Garden of Good and Evil* by John Berendt
>
> *In Patagonia* by Bruce Chatwin

and the other a list of potential themes, which grew as I read (magic, monks, ghost stories, miracle stories, etc). So, when I came to write about a place or a theme, I had to hand a long list of the best stories I knew associated with each place.

The journey

Everyone goes about writing a travel book in a different way. I can only speak for myself when I talk of technique: for me the biggest mistake was to try to keep a logbook when I was exhausted at the end of the day. I think it is absolutely vital to have a notebook in your hands, always, and to scribble constantly: not so much full sentences, so much as lists of significant detail: the colour of a hillside, the shape of a tulip, the way a particular tree haunts a skyline. Creating fine prose comes later – back at home in front of the computer. On the road – even in a rickety bus or a bumpy jeep – the key is to get the raw material down before it is lost to memory.

Noting down dialogue is especially important —it's the key to any half-decent travel book and you simply can't remember the exact words even half an hour later, never mind at the end of an exhausting day. The travel writers I really admire all keep exceptionally detailed notes: Theroux, Thubron, Chatwin. So the first golden rule is: get it down. If you can't write down dialogue immediately, or openly, find some stratagem to get around the problem. I know one travel writer who, when in customs posts and police stations, pretends to have a bad stomach in order to keep disappearing to the lavatory to note dialogue, as doing it openly would be inadvisable.

Dialogue is the heart and soul of modern travel writing, for if 19th century travel writing was principally about place – about filling in the blanks of the map and describing remote places that few people had seen – 21st century travel writing is all about people: exploring the extraordinary diversity that still exists in the world beneath the veneer of globalisation. As Jonathan Raban once remarked: 'Old travellers grumpily complain that travel is now dead and that the world is a suburb. They are quite wrong. Lulled by familiar resemblances between all the unimportant things, they meet the brute differences in everything of importance.'

The second golden rule is to be open to the unexpected. Often one can set oneself a task – perhaps to go and search out some aspect of a particular place – and not notice good material if it's not what one is looking for at that moment. For example, in 1990 I went to Simla to interview two 'Stayers On' who had lived in Delhi in the 1930s and would, I hoped, be able to recreate the lost world of the Raj for me. In the event, however, I arrived 10 years too late: both the ladies had gone badly senile and now imagined that they were being persecuted by prostitutes who popped up from beneath the floorboards and put dope in their food. I failed to get anything at all usable about 1930's Delhi, and left the old ladies feeling disappointed that I had wasted an afternoon. It was only later when I told my wife Olivia about the meeting that she pointed out that the bizarre afternoon would in fact make an excellent sequence in itself. It duly became one of the very best – and much the strangest – sections in *City of Djinns*. If the art of travel writing is at least partly about spotting the significant moment and discarding the irrelevant, then you have to be constantly alert.

In the same way, you often come across the best stories when you least expect them: when you've ticked off your interviews and visits for the day and settle down to have a drink in a bar or eat dinner. So often its exactly when you close your notebook and settle down to relax that you stumble across the most intriguing characters and funniest anecdotes.

A final rule: when you are taking notes, make sure you try to capture all the senses. When you write about a place, don't just give a physical description of somewhere: try to capture significant sounds and smells and the physical feel of a place. Also how your body responds to a particular location: in a hot climate, the roll of perspiration down the forehead, the grit of sand in your shoes, the grind of cicadas or the smell of frying chillies can recreate a sense of place much more immediately than a long physical description.

The same is true of building up a character: the way someone smells, or the timbre of their voice can help visualise a person much better than a lengthy physical description. Most important of all is dialogue: a well-chosen snatch of conversation can bring a person to life in a single sentence.

> ## Evocative travel writing
> - Here are some of my favourite examples of exceptionally good evocations of place or people:
> - For a short and perfect evocation of a city look at Bruce Chatwin's description of Buenos Aires at the beginning of *In Patagonia* (p7)
> - For a totally different approach – as wonderfully purple as Chatwin is sparse – see Patrick Leigh Fermor's description of walking through a German winter in *A Time of Gifts* (pp117–8)
> - For bringing a character to life in a single page, take a look at John Berendt's description of the Lady Chablis in *Midnight in the Garden of Good and Evil* (pp96–8), or two passages by Bruce Chatwin in *In Patagonia*: the hippy miner (p54) and the Scottish farmer (pp66–7)
> - See also Eric Newby's famous description of the explorer Wilfred Thesiger on pp246–8 of *A Short Walk in the Hindu Kush*.

The writing

Everyone has their own rhythm. When I'm steaming away actually writing a book – a process that takes me anything between six months and a year – I tend to be unusually disciplined: getting up early, finishing email and chores by 8.30am and at my desk writing by no later than 9.30am. I break for lunch, go for a walk and then come back and go through a printout of the morning's work at teatime, and continue correcting and planning the next day until 7ish. My wife Olivia is incredibly good at telling me when what I have written is boring. If your partner is no good at this, find a friend who is. Going over and over and over a piece of prose until it is as perfect as you can make it is as important as anything else in the formation of a book.

The selling

Find an agent for this: never try to do it for yourself. If you know any writers, however distantly, ask them for an introduction to their agent. Otherwise, look in the literary agents section (page 416) of this *Yearbook*. Send the agent a well-written covering letter asking whether they would like to look at the finished manuscript, plus a four- or five-page synopsis of the plot together with a short biographical paragraph about yourself. During the 1980s it was possible to get book contracts and advance payments before you had actually written your travel book but these days that is less and less likely to happen, and the writing of a book is by its nature a big financial gamble. Only go ahead with the project if you are really passionate about it. But if you have something to say, don't despair and don't let early rebuffs from agents or publishers put you off: if you can make it work, travel writing is one of the most enjoyable and stimulating ways of life imaginable – especially when you're young and single and able to leave home for great chunks of the year. Go for it!

William Dalrymple was born in Scotland and brought up on the shores of the Firth of Forth. He has written many award-winning and bestselling books including *In Xanadu*, *City of Djinns* and *The Age of Kali*. He has also written and presented documentary series for television and radio. In 2002 William was awarded the Mungo Park Medal by the Royal Scottish Geographical Society for his 'outstanding contribution to travel literature'.

Notes from a successful non-fiction author

Simon Winchester shares his experiences of writing success.

The research is all done, the reading is complete. Files have been pored over, archives have been plundered. Those Who Know have been consulted. That Which Was Unknown has been explained and one fondly prays, made clear. I am, in consequence, or so I hope, now fully steeped in facts and awash with understanding. The book I have been planning for so very long is at last all in the forefront of my mind – structure, content, tone, pace and rhythm are all there. What now remains is simply – would that it were *simply* – to write it: 100,000 words, says the contract, due in just 100 days.

I live on a farm in the Berkshire Hills of western Massachusetts, and I have a small and ancient wooden barn, 100 yards or so from the main house. I have furnished it with books and a long desk on which are a variety of computers and two typewriters, one manual, the other electric. The farm is where I live. The barn is where I work. Each morning, well before the sun is up, I leave the comforts of the farm and enter this spartan, bookish little universe, and shut the allurements of domesticity behind me for the day. For a 100 days, in fact: for a 100 identical days of a solitary, writerly routine that, for me at least, is the only way I know to get a book properly and fully written.

Inside the barn I tend to follow an unvarying routine. First, as the dawn breaks, I spend two hours looking back over what I wrote the day before: I examine it with what I hope is a sharp and critical eye, checking it for infelicities of language, impropriety of grammar, expanding the inexact, refining the imprecise, making as certain as I can the minutiae of fact and detail. Only when I feel satisfied (never smug) that what I have on the screen represents as good a first draft as I can offer do I press the *print* button on the keyboard, and a few pages of A4 slither into the out-tray. Once that task is done I leave the barn and walk through the early sunlight back to the house for breakfast. I read the papers, drink enough coffee to kick-start both mind and body, and, at nine exactly, I head back again, this time to write for real.

I have a word counter at the top left of my computer screen. Purists may object, but my newspaper days have left me with deadline commitment, and this is the way that I like to work. Whenever I begin a book I set the counter with the start date, the number of words I have to write, the contract date and a very simple calculation – the number of words needed each day to meet the deadline. One hundred days, 100,000 words: 1000 words each day is the initial goal. But things change: the writing life is imperfect, however noble the intentions. Some days are good and maybe I'll write 1500 words, while others are much less satisfactory and, for a variety of reasons, I may write virtually nothing. So the following day's necessary word total will rise and fall depending on the achievement of the day before. It is that figure my system obliges me to set the night before that I'll see on my screen when I arrive in the cold dark before dawn: 1245 words needed today, with 68 more days before the deadline? So be it.

I sit down, arrange my thoughts and hammer away without stopping for the next six hours – each day from nine in the morning until three in the afternoon. This is the solitary pleasure of writing – total concentration, pure lexical heaven. I write on, oblivious to everything around me. Except that I do know when I have done my six hours – because by the time the mid-afternoon is upon me, the sun will have shifted to the window in front of my desk, and in wintertime I have to suffer an uncomfortable hour or so of the sunset's glare. This gives me a perfect excuse to end this second stage of the day and to go off to do something quite different: a run along my country road, usually, followed by tea. By then it is six or so, the sun has fully set and the glare has been replaced by twilight glow. Then I return, for the day's third and final phase: planning for the next day.

I go back to my desk and arrange the papers, books and thoughts that I think I need for the next day's writing. Then I close down the computers – having been sure, of course, to have made the necessary calculations and set the counter to tell me how many words are due on the morrow – and walk back to the house. For a while I try to forget about the book (though I never can). I have dinner, go to a movie, have friends round – and am in bed, invariably, by midnight.

The next day it begins all over again. As before, I spend the first two hours of the morning looking back over what I have written in those six sunlit hours of the day before. As soon as I have tinkered and tweaked, I press *print*. I stack the A4 sheets neatly on the pile from the preceding day. Millimetre by millimetre, day by day, the pile grows taller and thicker, looking ever more substantial. In the first week it has the look and feel of a newspaper essay; after 10 days or so, a magazine article; by a month, it's an outline, then chapter, a monograph, a dissertation – until finally, on one heaven-sent morning, I pick up the pile of paper and it has heft, weight and substance. And then it all changes.

The dream has been made solid. The former featherweight piece of ephemera has been transformed by time into a work-in-progress, a book-in-the-making. After a precisely calculated number of sunrises and sunsets, after yet more walks between barn and farmhouse, after setting and resetting the counter a score of times, and after hours spent reviewing and re-doing and printing and piling and collating and collecting – there, suddenly, is a finished product.

The pile of printed paper and digital confection of finished text will now be placed in the hands of the publishers, who by mysterious dint of designing, printing, binding and jacketing, will in due course turn it into a full-fledged book. *My* new book. After 100 days it is ready to be offered to the world. As for its fate – well, there lies ahead of it what will seem a lifetime of hoping – hoping that it will be lucky, do well and be loved by all. The wish and the prayer of any new parent, who has taken time and care to bring a newborn into the world. But that, of course, is another story. This is just the writing. What follows next is the reading, and that is much less exact of a science.

Simon Winchester, who worked as a foreign correspondent for the *Guardian* and the *Sunday Times* for thirty years before turning to full-time writing, is the author of some twenty books including *The Surgeon of Crowthorne*, *The Map that Changed the World*, *Krakatoa* and *A Crack in the Edge of the World*. He divides his time between his small farm in the Berkshire Hills of western Massachusetts and a flat in Chelsea, New York, where he is working on a new book about Joseph Needham and the understanding of China. He was made OBE in 2006.

Notes from a successful self-publisher

G.P. Taylor shares his experiences of writing and self-publishing success.

Lying in bed and hearing that horrendous thud on the doormat is the unpublished author's worst nightmare. It is the thud of a returned manuscript – the tell-tale sound of rejection. Nevertheless, you get out of bed and grimly hold on to *faux* hope that this time the letter will read differently and that you've been accepted and will be published. But no, nothing is further from the truth. Instead, you're faced with a note, hastily typed by a spotty faced 16 year-old who says she enjoyed your manuscript but it doesn't 'fit in' with the list and the niche in the market for romantic-fantasy-gothic literature isn't as big as it once was.

The trouble is, there are just too many people writing these days. Since a certain young lady put pen to paper, fiction (especially children's fiction) has become a *perceived* means of gathering fame and fortune. Even the prestigious Faber and Faber have now closed its doors to the unsolicited manuscript. So why bother? Only a few titles get produced each year from new authors but I don't feel all is lost. The writer has now, thanks to the advent of the internet and email, a publishing house at their fingertips.

Once self-publishing was known as the 'vanity press' – for those failed authors who didn't feel their pride would allow them to die without first seeing a book in print. For a monumental fee, you would receive five copies of your book along with the promise that your book would appear in their magazine for the entire world to see and that copies would be sent to reviewers so that they could herald your arrival to a greater world. Sadly, editors and reviewers knew the names of all the vanity press imprints and, once spotted, would be heaped at the back of the office and sent to the local charity shop once a year.

It was when I found out this information that I decided to avoid the usual route to publication and go it *alone*. In a nutshell, Mount Publishing Ltd was born – established via Companies House and a credit card. I became the director, editor and tea boy of the newest and most prestigious name in publishing! However, I knew nothing and it showed. A PDF what? Typeset? Margins? All these were very new concepts, but thankfully there is help out there.

The first problem I faced was the printing. Very quickly I realised that the prices varied immensely. One company wanted to charge me £6 per paperback, which would have meant pricing my book at £12 – who would buy it at that price? This is the area where you have to be very careful. If you are self-publishing you have to keep the costs of your book down and there are many hidden overheads to look out for (don't forget postage!).

So, once again, reach out for help that's available. My blessing came in the shape of Mr David Sowter, who I found courtesy of the Society of Authors. David was the UK rep for W.S. Bookwell of Finland and quickly became the fount of all knowledge and good advice at the end of a phone. He knew what I wanted and where I should go, and was a guiding hand through the difficulties of file preparation and submission.

Within two weeks of sending off the manuscript to the printer I was greeted with 2000 copies of my first book *Shadowmancer*. They filled my house – they were under the bed, in the toilet, I couldn't even enter my small office. All these books with nowhere to go. Now I faced my biggest problem so far: how to sell them.

Thankfully for us self-publishers, there is a ready supply of independent bookshops all too willing to help the new author on a 'sale or return' basis. The Whitby Bookshop quickly set me off on the right foot. A book signing and press call were all arranged for a rainy October morning, and as my wife tramped through the wet streets with a pram full of books, she turned to me and said 'I bet J.K. Rowling didn't have to do this'. Too true – but the excitement and hope I was feeling at this point more than made up for it.

Very quickly I came across another hurdle – the national bookshop chains (known to self-publishers as the Mafia). No one would deal with me, no one would talk to me. 'Graham who?' Was all they asked. 'Self-publisher? No thank you.' The kindly manager of my local Waterstone's suggested I contact a book distributor but when I did they turned me down flat. I then went to Bertram Books, another wholesaler which supplies Waterstone's, and thankfully they opted to give me a chance. Bingo! I was now selling my book to the shops.

Luck was well and truly on my side. Somewhere around this time, the story of *Shadowmancer* was spreading by word of mouth. From nowhere, people from all over the country were ringing my home wanting copies of the book. I couldn't believe it! Suddenly, hundreds of people wanted to read *Shadowmancer* and my house started to empty of books. I knew I was doing well when copies were selling on Ebay for large sums of money – I was out-bidding J.K. Rowling!

Within a matter of weeks of the start of my self-publishing venture, I was signed to Faber and Faber. It was good timing because everyday was a constant stream of wrapping and posting books, an operation so large that my local Post Office could no longer accommodate me and I was forced to find alternative arrangements. Self-publishing is definitely not for the faint hearted!

From then on, the path to notoriety has been a fast one. *Shadowmancer* spent many weeks at the number one spot on the bestseller lists in both the USA and UK. The film rights were quickly bought by Universal Pictures and a multi-book deal was in the bag. I had sold out and gone the way of the establishment!

Would I recommend others to self-publish? Definitely. In fact, I receive several emails a day asking me what to do and how to do it. Ultimately, my advice is simple – research the area and check prices, get quotes and be as wary as a fox. Be prepared for disappointment as self-publishing is certainly not a get-rich-quick scheme. It cost me all I had in time, money and resources – and more! Finally, it is always best to set up a limited company just in case all goes wrong, oh and *never* remortgage your house – sell your vintage motorbike instead.

G.P. Taylor self-published his debut novel *Shadowmancer* in 2002. He was soon signed to Faber and Faber and G.P. Putnam & Son in the USA. The book became an international bestseller, translated into 42 languages. His subsequent book *Wormwood* has also been an international bestseller and both books are to be turned into film and video games. Until recently, he was an Anglican Vicar, but now writes full-time and guests on television and radio programmes.

Notes from a successful children's author

J.K. Rowling shares her experiences of writing success.

I can remember writing *Harry Potter and the Philosopher's Stone* in a café in Oporto. I was employed as a teacher at the language institute three doors along the road at the time, and this café was a kind of unofficial staffroom. My friend and colleague joined me at my table. When I realised I was no longer alone I hastily shuffled worksheets over my notebook, but not before Paul had seen exactly what I was doing. 'Writing a novel, eh?' he asked wearily, as though he had seen this sort of behaviour in foolish young teachers only too often before. '*Writers' & Artists' Yearbook*, that's what you need,' he said. 'Lists all the publishers and … stuff' he advised before ordering a lager and starting to talk about the previous night's episode of *The Simpsons*.

I had almost no knowledge of the practical aspects of getting published; I knew nobody in the publishing world, I didn't even know anybody who knew anybody. It had never occurred to me that assistance might be available in book form.

Nearly three years later and a long way from Oporto, I had almost finished *Harry Potter and the Philosopher's Stone*. I felt oddly as though I was setting out on a blind date as I took a copy of the *Writers' & Artists' Yearbook* from the shelf in Edinburgh's Central Library. Paul had been right and the *Yearbook* answered my every question, and after I had read and re-read the invaluable advice on preparing a manuscript, and noted the time-lapse between sending said manuscript and trying to get information back from the publisher, I made two lists: one of publishers, the other of agents.

The first agent on my list sent my sample three chapters and synopsis back by return of post. The first two publishers took slightly longer to return them, but the 'no' was just as firm. Oddly, these rejections didn't upset me much. I was braced to be turned down by the entire list, and in any case, these were real rejection letters – even real writers had got them. And then the second agent, who was high on the list purely because I like his name, wrote back with the most magical words I have ever read: 'We would be pleased to read the balance of your manuscript on an exclusive basis…'

J.K. Rowling is the best-selling author of the *Harry Potter* series (Bloomsbury). The first in the series, *Harry Potter and the Philosopher's Stone*, was the winner of the 1997 Nestlé Smarties Gold Prize and *Harry Potter and the Goblet of Fire* (2000) broke all records for the number of books sold on the first day of publication. The sixth book in the series, *Harry Potter and the Half-Blood Prince*, was published in 2005. All four of the published *Harry Potter* novels were voted into the BBC Big Read's top 100 in April 2003.

Writing and the children's book market

Around 10,000 new children's titles are published in the UK every year. Chris Kloet suggests how a potential author can best ensure that their work is published.

The profile of children's books has never been higher, yet it can be difficult for the first-time writer to get published. It is a diverse, overcrowded market, with many thousands of titles currently in print, available both in the UK and from elsewhere via the internet. Children's publishers tend to fill their lists with commissioned books by writers they publish regularly, so they may have little space for the untried writer, even though they seek exceptional new talent. This is a selective, highly competitive, market-led business. Since every new book is expected to meet its projected sales target, your writing must demonstrate solid sales potential, as well as strength and originality, if it is to stand a chance of being published.

Is your work right for today's market? Literary tastes and fashions change. Publishers cater to children whose reading is now almost certainly different from that of your own childhood. In the present electronic media-driven age, few want cosy tales about fairies and bunnies, jolly talking cars or magic teapots. Nor anything remotely imitative. Editors choose *original*, lively material – something witty, innovative and pacey. They look for polished writing with a fresh, contemporary voice that speaks directly and engages today's critical, media-savvy young readers, who are often easily bored.

Develop a sense of the market so that you can judge the potential for your work. Read widely and critically across the children's book spectrum for an overview, especially noting recent titles. Talk to children's librarians, who are expert in current tastes, and visit children's bookshops and dedicated children's books websites, such as Achuka. As you read, pay attention to the different categories, series, genres and publishers' imprints. This will help you to pinpoint likely publishers. Before submitting your typescript, ensure that your targeted publisher currently publishes in your particular form or genre. Request catalogues from their marketing department; check out their website. Consult the publisher's entry under *Book publishers UK and Ireland* (see page 131). Many publishing houses now stipulate 'No unsolicited MSS or synopses'. Don't spend your time and postage sending work to them; choose instead a publisher who accepts unsolicited work.

You might consider approaching a literary agent who knows market trends, publishers' lists and the faces behind them. Most editors regard agents as filters and may prefer submissions from them, knowing that a preliminary critical eye has been cast over them.

Picture books

Books for babies and toddlers are often board books and novelties. Unless you are also a professional illustrator (see *Illustrating for children's books*, page 251) they present few opportunities for a writer. Picture books are aimed at children aged between two and five or six, and are usually 32 pages long, giving 12–14 double-page spreads, and illustrated in colour.

Although a story written for this format should be simple, it must be structured, with a compelling beginning, middle and end. The theme should interest and be appropriate

Publisher	Series name	Length	Age group	Comments
Andersen Press	Tiger Cubs	1000–3000 words; 64 pages	5–8	B&w illustrations throughout
	Tigers	3000–5000 words; 64 pages	6–9	B&w illustrations throughout
A & C Black	Chameleons	1200 words; 48 pages	5–7	Colour illustrations throughout
	Black Cats	9000–14,000 words; 80–128 pages	7–10	B&w illustrations throughout
	Flashbacks	12,000–14,000 words; 96 pages	8+	Historical fiction
Egmont Books	Green Bananas	500 words; 48 pages	4+	Colour illustrations
	Blue Bananas	1000 words; 48 pages	5+	Colour illustrations
	Red Bananas	2000 words; 48 pages	6+	Colour illustrations
Franklin Watts	Tadpoles	70 words; 24 pages	4–6	Colour illustrations throughout
	Leapfrog	180 words; 32 pages	4–6	Colour illustrations throughout
	Hopscotch	350–400 words; 32 pages	5–7	Colour illustrations throughout
Hodder Children's Books	Bite	35,000+ words	12+	Contemporary fiction
Kingfisher	I Am Reading	1200 words; 48 pages	5–7	Colour illustrations throughout
Orchard Books	Crunchies	1000–1500 words	5–7	B&w line illustrations
	Colour Crunchies	1000–1500 words	5–7	Colour illustrations
	Super Crunchies	5000 words	7–9	B&w line illustrations
	Red Apples	20,000–25,000 words	9–12	
	Black Apples	30,000–40,000 words	12+	
Penguin Group	Colour Young Puffin	2500 words; 64 pages	5–7	Colour illustrations
Walker Books	Walker Stories	1800 words; 64 pages	5+	B&w illustrations throughout
	Racing Reads	8000 words; 80–96 pages	7–9	B&w illustrations throughout

for the age and experience of its audience. As the text is likely to be reread, it should possess a satisfying rhythm (but beware of rhymes). Ideally, it should be fewer than 1000 words (and could be much shorter), must offer scope for illustration and, finally, it needs strong international appeal. Reproducing full-colour artwork is costly and the originating publisher must be confident of achieving co-productions with publishers overseas, to keep unit costs down. It has to be said: it is a tough field.

Submit a picture book text typed either on single-sided A4 sheets, showing page breaks, or as a series of numbered pages, each with its own text. Do not go into details about illustrations, but simply note anything that is not obvious from the text that needs to be included in the pictures.

Younger fiction

This area of publishing may present opportunities for the new writer. It covers stories written for the post-picture book stage, when children are reading their first whole novels. Texts vary in length and complexity, depending on the age and fluency of the reader, but tend to be between 1000 and 6000 words long.

Some publishers continue to bring out titles under the umbrella of various series, each targeted at a particular level of reading experience and competency, although these are now often replaced by individual author series. Categories are: beginning or first readers, developing or newly confident, confident, and fluent readers. Note that these are not the same as reading schemes published for the schools market and do not require such a restricted vocabulary. Stories for the bottom end of the age range are usually short, straight-through narratives illustrated throughout in colour, whereas those for older children are broken down into chapters and may be illustrated in black and white. The table on page 248 lists publishers' requirements for some currently published series. Check that your material is correct in terms of length and interest level when approaching a publisher with a sub-mission for a series.

General fiction

Many novels for children aged 9–12+ are published, not in series, but as 'standalone' titles, each judged on its own merits. The scope for different types of stories is wide – adventure stories, fantasies, historical novels (increasingly popular), science fiction, ghost and horror stories, humour, and stories of everyday life. Generally, their length is 20,000– 40,000 words. This is a rough guide and is by no means fixed. For example, J.K. Rowling's recent *Harry Potter* novels weigh in at between 600–750+ closely printed pages, and publishers now seem more willing to publish longer texts, particularly fantasies, although the market is presently overloaded with hefty trilogies.

Perhaps more than in other areas of juvenile fiction, the individual editor's tastes will play a significant part in the publishing decision, i.e they want authors' work which *they* like. They, and their sales and marketing departments, also need to feel confident of a new writer's ability to go on to write further books for their lists – nobody is keen to invest in an author who is just a one-book wonder.

When submitting your work it is probably best to send the entire typescript (see *Dos and don'ts of approaching a publisher*, page 126). Although some people advise sending in a synopsis with the first three chapters, a prospective publisher will need to see whether you can sustain a reader's interest to the end of the book.

Teenage fiction

Some of the published output for teenaged readers is published in series but increasingly, publishers are targeting this area of the market with edgy, hard-hitting novels about contemporary teenagers, which they publish as standalone titles. There is also a current vogue for 'young adult' novels that have a crossover appeal to an adult readership. Indeed, recent award-winning titles such as Philip Pullman's *His Dark Materials* sequence and Mark Haddon's *The Curious Incident of the Dog at Night-time* and J.K. Rowling's *Harry Potter* books, have all been published in both juvenile and adult editions.

Non-fiction

The last few years have seen fundamental and striking changes in the type of information books published for the young. Hitherto the province, by and large, of specialist publishers catering for the educational market, the field has now broadened to encompass an astonishing range of presentations and formats which are attractive to the young reader. Increasingly, children who use the internet to furnish their information needs are wooed into learning about many topics via entertaining and accessible paperback series such as the *Horrible Histories* published by Scholastic, and similar series from other publishers. In writing for this market, it goes without saying that you must research your subject thoroughly and be able to put it across clearly, with an engaging style. Familiarise yourself with the relevant parts of the National Curriculum. Check out the various series and ask the publishers for any guidelines. You will be well advised to check that there is a market for your book before you actually write it, as researching a subject can be both time consuming and costly. Submit a proposal to your targeted publisher, outlining the subject matter and the level of treatment, and your ideas about the audience for your book.

Chris Kloet worked as Children's Publisher at Victor Gollancz Ltd, and is now Editor-at-Large at Walker Books. She has written and reviewed children's books and has lectured widely on the subject.

Further reading

Children's Writers' & Artists' Yearbook 2007, A & C Black, 2006

See also...

- *Notes from a successful children's author*, page 246
- *Illustrating for children's books*, page 251

Illustrating for children's books

The world of children's publishing is big business. The huge range of books published each year all carry artwork – lots of it. Maggie Mundy offers guidance for people who are at the start of their career in illustrating for children's books.

The portfolio

Your portfolio should reflect the best of you and your work, and should speak for itself. Keep its content simple – if too many styles are included, for instance, your work will not leave a lasting impression.

Include some artwork other than those carried out for college projects, e.g. an illustration from a timeless classic to show your abilities, and something modern which reflects your own taste and the area in which you wish to work.

If your strength is for black and white illustration, include pieces with and without tone and with or without a wash. Some publishers want line and tone and some want only line. As cross hatching and stippling can add a lot of extra time to an illustration deadline, it might be advisable to leave out these samples. If you can, include a selection of humour as it can be used effectively in educational books and elsewhere. It is best not to sign and date your work: some artworks can stand the test of time and still look good after a year or two, but if it looks dated … so is the illustrator!

An A3 portfolio is probably the ideal size. Place your best piece of artwork on the opening page and your next best piece on the last page. See *Freelancing for beginners* on page 449 for further information on portfolio presentation.

Looking at the market

Start by looking thoroughly at what is being published today for children. Take your studies to branches of big retail chains, some independent bookshops, as well as your local library (a helpful librarian should be able to tell you which are the most borrowed books). Absorb the picture books, explore the novelty books, look at the variety of colour covers, and note the range of black line illustrations inside books for children and teenagers. Make a list of the publishers you think may be able to use your particular style.

By making these investigations you will gain an insight into not only the current trends and styles but also the much favoured, oft-published classic children's literature. Most importantly, it will help you identify your market.

In books for a young age range every picture must tell the story – some books have no text and the illustrations say it all. Artwork should be uncluttered, shapes clear, and colour bright. If this does not appeal to you, go up a year or two and note the extra details that are added to the artwork (which still tells the story). Children now need to see more than just clear shapes: they need extra details added to the scene – e.g. a quirky spider hanging around, or a mouse under the bed.

Children are your most critical audience: never think that you can get away with 'any old thing'. Indeed, at the Bologna Book Fair it is a panel of children which judges what they consider to be the best picture book.

Current trends

Innovative publishers are always on the lookout for something new in illustration styles: something completely different from the tried and tested. More and more they are turning to European and overseas illustrators, often sourced from the Bologna Book Fair exhibitions and illustrators catalogue.

Always strive to improve on your work. Don't be afraid to try out something different and to work it up into acceptable examples. Above all, don't get left behind.

Making approaches for work

With your portfolio arranged and your target audience in mind, compile a list of publishing houses, packagers and magazines which you think may be suitable for your work.

An agent should know exactly where to place your work, and this may be the easier option (see below). However, you may wish to market yourself by making and going to appointments until you crack your first job.

Alternatively, you could make up a simple broadsheet comprising a black and white and two or three colour illustrations, together with your contact details, and have it colour photocopied or printed. Another inexpensive option is to have your own CDs made up and to send them instead. Send a copy to either the Art Director, the Creative Director or the Senior Commissioning Editor (for picture books) of each potential client on your list. Try to find out the name of the person you would like to see your work. Wait at least a week and then follow up your mailing with a phone call to ask if someone would like to see your portfolio.

Also consider investing in your own website which you can easily update yourself.

Know your capabilities

Know your strengths, but be even more aware of your weaknesses. You will gain far more respect if you admit to not being able to draw something particularly well than by going ahead and producing an embarrassing piece of artwork and having it rejected. You will be remembered for your professional honesty and that client may well try to give you a job where you can use your expertise.

Publishers need to know that you can turn out imaginative, creative artwork while closely following a text or brief, and be able to meet their deadline. It may take an illustrator three weeks to prepare roughs for 32 pages, three weeks to finish the artwork, plus a week to make any corrections. In addition, time has to be allowed for the roughs to be returned. On this basis, how many books can an illustrator realistically take on? Scheduling is of paramount importance (see below).

You will need to become familiar with 'publishing speak' – terms such as gutters, full bleed, holding line, overlays, vignettes, tps, etc. If you don't know the meaning of a term, ask – after all, if you have only recently left college you will not be expected to know all the jargon.

In the course of your work you will have to deal with such issues as contracts, copyright, royalties, public lending rights, rejection fees, etc. The Association of Illustrators, which exists to give help to illustrators in all areas, is well worth joining.

Organising your workload

When you have reached the stage when you have jobs coming through on a fairly regular basis, organise a comprehensive schedule for yourself so you do not overburden yourself with work. Include on it when roughs have to be submitted, how much work you can fit in while waiting for their approval, the deadline for the artwork, and so on. A wall chart can be helpful for this but another system may work better for you. It is totally unacceptable to deliver artwork late. If you think that you might run over time with your work, let your client know in advance as it may be possible to reach a new agreement for delivery.

Payment

There are two ways in which an illustrator may be paid for a commission for a book: a flat fee on receipt and acceptance of the artwork, or by an advance against a royalty of future sales. The advance offered could be less than a flat fee but it may result in higher earnings overall. If the book sells well, the illustrator will receive royalty payments twice a year for as long the book is in print.

You need to know from the outset how you are going to be paid. If it is by a flat fee, you may be given an artwork order with a number to be quoted when you invoice. Always read through orders to make sure you understand the terms and conditions. If you haven't been paid within 30 days, send a statement to remind the client, or make a quick phone call to ask when you can expect to receive payment.

With a royalty offer, a contract will be drawn up and this must be checked carefully. One of the clauses will state the breakdown of how and when you will be paid.

Once you have illustrated your first book you should register with the Public Lending Right Office (see page 304) so that you can receive a yearly payment on all UK library borrowings. You will need to cooperate with the author regarding percentages before submitting your own form. The PLR office will give you a reference number, and you then submit details to them of each book you illustrate. It mounts up and is a nice little earner!

Agents

The role of the agent is to represent the illustrator to the best of their ability and to the illustrator's best advantage. A good agent knows the marketplace and will promote illustrators' work where it will count. An agent may ask you to do one or two sample pieces to strengthen your portfolio, giving them a better chance of securing work for you.

Generally speaking, agents will look after you, your work schedules, payments, contracts, royalties, copyright issues, and try to ensure you have a regular flow of work which you not only enjoy but will stretch your talents to taking on bigger and better jobs. Without exposing your weaknesses, check that you have adequate time in which to do a job and that you are paid a fair rate for the work.

Some illustrators manage well without an agent, and having one is not necessarily a pathway to fame and fortune. Choose carefully: you need to both like and trust the agent and vice versa.

Agents' charges range from 25% to 30%. Find out from the outset how much a prospective agent will charge.

Finally

Do not be downhearted if progress is at first slow. Everyone starts by serving an apprenticeship, and it is a great opportunity to learn, absorb and soak up as much of the business as possible. Ask questions, get all the advice you can, and use what you learn to improve your craft and thereby your chances of landing a job. Publishers are always on the lookout for fresh talent and new ideas, and one day your talent will be the one they want.

Maggie Mundy has been representing illustrators for children's books since 1983. Her agency represents 25 European and British illustrators for children's books.

Further reading

Children's Writers' & Artists' Yearbook 2007, A & C Black, 2006

See also...

- *Children's book publishers and packagers*, page 763
- *Art agents and commercial art studios*, page 456

Is there a book in you?

Alison Baverstock examines what resources a writer needs to be a successfully published author.

One of the most disappointing things about finally getting a book published is the reaction of other people. You might have imagined they would be dead impressed by your achievement. Think again. The reality is that most will use your success as a spur to their own aspirations, and rather than even *pausing* to admire what you have done, they will most likely come straight out with one of the following comments:

- 'That's something I have always planned to do';
- 'I've always felt there was a book in me too'; or even more frustratingly,
- 'Lucky you to have the time.'

The desire to have a book with one's name on the front cover is seemingly universal: so many people daydream that one day, somehow, this will appear. For some, the desire is for the object with their name on it; others anticipate that this will be the springboard to greater things: fame, riches and a celebrity lifestyle. And there really are lots of people wanting this. The competition organised by the Channel 4 *Richard & Judy* daytime television show at the end of 2004 attracted over 45,000 entries, or 20 Royal Mail van loads.

Quite why it is such a common ambition is not hard to fathom. A book with your name on the cover is a solid achievement; it makes you feel both valid and validated (because others are investing in your talent). It offers significance and permanence amidst the 'changes and chances of this fleeting world'.

But given the vast disparity in numbers between those who want to try to get into print, and those who actually make it, how can you influence the process? Is it really true, as many suspect, that it is only the famous and well connected who get publishing deals, or will writing talent always win through?

Given that I have been a publisher, still work freelance within the industry (mainly running training courses on how to market books) and am also a writer (with 14 books and lots of articles to my name), I decided to try to theorise about *why* some people get into print and others do not; to define what are the resources would-be writers need. Some necessary talents are obvious (can you write?) and some less so, but it's not necessarily true that having all the obvious qualifications for writing will guarantee you a publication deal. Those running creative writing courses often say that it's not necessarily the best writers who get published; more likely it's those with the most self-belief or determination – or those who make pragmatic choices about the publishing house most likely to take them on.

I have always liked lists, so here is my list of 10 resources needed by would-be writers:

1. Real determination

If you lack this core attribute, you are missing the one key requirement for getting published. Writing for publication demands an intense determination because so many things are stacked against you. There is huge competition – publishers and agents have vast numbers of would-be writers to choose between; writing is hard and takes a long time; most writers earn little; there are bands of others helpfully telling you not to bother trying, as well as endless trying circumstances that present themselves, from manuscripts lost in the post to the editor who was about to commission your work changing job and moving to a house that has no interest in the kind of book you want to write. Those who make it into print will be sustained by the knowledge that nothing matters to them more, and just keep going.

2. An ability to write what other people want to read

Canny observers might start by asking whether would-be writers can write sufficiently well for publication. I am risking annoyance by dealing with this issue from the other side of the fence: placing emphasis on the consumer's judgement rather than just a quota of literary merit.

In any case, there is *no* particular style of writing or mastery of literary structure that will guarantee an audience; writing that one person finds banal or staid may find a wider audience amongst those who relate to the story told or the characters described. So rather than displaying your ease with syntax to your potential publisher and feeling aggrieved that those who are less 'literary' than you get published, concentrate your energies on trying to prove that other people want to read what you are able to write.

Assemble proof. Find parallels. If your work compares in subject matter or style to a popular writer, name them. Many books these days are announced as having parents ('Jilly Cooper and Joanna Trollope'). If your area of writing relates to a popular television programme or magazine, state how many people subscribe/watch and when. Tell the publisher how others respond to your work. For example, if you are writing for children, give readings in a local school and obtain feedback. If you are writing popular fiction, find out if your local paper would like to reproduce an extract and monitor the response. If you have just finished a novel, get friends to give you honest feedback on what they think, and if it is positive, pass it on with your manuscript to the publisher or agent you choose to approach.

3. Creativity

It is simply not possible for all writers to have imaginations that rival Shakespeare, but creativity is vital for the would-be writer, whatever the field you choose to publish in.

Whatever you are writing about, in whatever format, your decision on how you decide to present your ideas is a creative one; there are many possibilities and part of the writer's job is to choose the style and format that you consider both most appropriate and interesting. Even if you are writing academic papers, the logic of presentation and the examples chosen to illustrate the points you want to make will come across best if they are selected with a creative sense of what will help to develop the reader's understanding, rather than just being the first 10 that occur to you.

4. Support mechanisms for your writing

Some writers work best at times of personal turmoil; they find the spirit of 'this will show 'em' helps them produce their best work. Others need tea, toast and sympathy at regular intervals. The most valuable support mechanism is money; writing is, most usually, badly paid and someone needs to be able to pay the rent/mortgage and provide enough money for food whilst you are busy crafting your masterpiece. The second most valuable support mechanism is appreciation: being shown that you are taken seriously is immensely helpful to a writer.

5. A writing habit

It is surprising how many people long to write but can never quite get down to it. Getting published demands self-discipline and self-knowledge; an understanding of when are your best times for writing and a determination to stick to the schedules you establish. Having a 'writing habit' means you prioritise your writing, where you do it, what time you get started, how long you stick at it, under what circumstances you can be disturbed – and, of course, how everyone else in your life is conditioned to respond to these things. If you are not willing to alter your priorities and put the writing first – not all the time, but when you have promised yourself you will – it will be very difficult to get published.

6. Something to write about

Few books arrive in the writer's imagination fully formed. Writers I talk to often mention the importance of the random in sparking ideas: an overheard conversation, a curious coincidence, an unexpected gift, and there was general agreement on the importance of novels developing best when characters you believe in start to shape events – rather than relying on plot alone for narrative development. Find someone who interests you and write about them, rather than dreaming up an exciting series of events and then deciding to whom they should happen. In your search of interesting ideas, try to lead an interesting life. Keep fit and healthy, eat well, listen to as wide a variety of people as possible, whether in print or socially. It's surprising how often the spark occurs when you least expect it!

7. An ability to present yourself as a writer

Years ago someone commented to me that 'other people take you at your own estimation'. It is true, but it's an area of real difficulty for many writers: we want our writing to be taken seriously, yet, exposing our hopes of publication for general inspection feels as if we are tempting fate; will it compromise our ability to achieve anything? The ability to 'play the writer' on occasion demands self-confidence and the suspension of self-doubt – but will probably be well received by publishers and agents who are looking for not only someone who can write what others want to read, but who interviews well (for publicising the books) and is 'promotable'. Don't forget that a publisher who decides to back your book is making an *investment* decision, on the grounds that you will, in the long or short term, make a profit for the house that sponsored you!

8. The ability to deal positively with rejection

All writers get rejected – whether it is their initial ideas ('we can see no market for that'), their initial outline ('this does not fit our list at the present time') or their final draft ('editorial policy has changed and your book no longer fits our list as we are seeking to develop it. Please feel free to approach another house'). Even once accepted, having your precious manuscript edited can feel close to rejection – especially if it comes back covered with red ink and 'suggestions for change/development'.

What matters here is how you *deal* with rejection. A publisher's rejection is not a rejection of you or your ability to write, or indeed you as a person – although it may feel like all those things. Rather, it is a specific reader's response to what you sent at that particular time. Absorb all the advice you get given and try to do nothing in a hurry (certainly not a rude email back) but if you want to get published, don't let rejections grind you down! The publishing industry abounds with stories of the much-turned-down manuscript that went on to make a fortune (*Harry Potter*, *Day of the Jackal*, *Mary Wesley*, etc).

9. A wide knowledge of other people's books

Good writers are almost invariably well read: because why would you seek to contribute to the canon of published writers if you do not respect the output of those who are already part of it? Some writers find that whilst writing a particular type of book, they read other things (maybe works in translation or non-fiction if they're writing fiction); others withdraw from reading while they're writing as it puts them off – then they are further motivated to get writing so they can get back to reading once they've finished their manuscript. Others have favourite writers who inspire them – one described reading Jane Austen as 'like having a blood transfusion'. And don't think that writing a particular type of book (children's titles or romantic fiction are commonly cited here) excludes you from being well read; such a view reveals a very patronising attitude towards just how hard it is to write any kind of book. Whatever you want to write, you do best if you understand how *other* writers develop ideas. Trying to write without the inspiration of reading yourself is like leaving the house without breakfast, the car without petrol, the hand-held console without batteries (you quickly run out of juice).

10. An understanding of how publishing works

Publishing is not a charity. Publishers and agents are not in business to help you achieve personal satisfaction by writing a book; rather they exist to make products available to the reading public who will pay for access to them. Different houses commission different kinds of books according to their experience of the market, their customer base and their future plans. The more you know about this market the more specific you can make your pitch – and the more you are likely to be successful!

Conclusion

Most would-be writers are pessimistic optimists. They are doubtful whether their writing will find its true appreciative audience – but they keep going just the same. Each of you can probably point to a published writer whose work got into print without the resources I have outlined: the celebrity whose book was written by someone else; the chicklit novel that for some reason caught popular imagination and having got loads of press coverage achieved huge sales – even though you personally thought it was rubbish.

It's true, chance is a great thing, but please don't assume that all celebrity books are instant hits or that press coverage is routinely unplanned. And so many of today's bestselling writers spent years of hard graft before they achieved the celebrity status that we now assume came overnight. For the vast majority of would-be writers, it is the persistence of their slog, their self-belief and their determination that ultimately keeps them going and achieves the publishing deal. Faint heart never won fair lady. Good luck!

Alison Baverstock is a former publisher who has written 14 books. The most recent, *Is There a Book in You?* (A & C Black 2006) outlines resources needed by writers, and offers advice on how to achieve their ultimate goal of publication. She teaches marketing – to authors and others – at Kingston University. Her website is www.alisonbaverstock.com

Ghostwriting

It is possible for an unknown writer to make a living as a full-time ghostwriter. Andrew Crofts shares some of his secrets on how to do it.

Why do it?

The greatest problem facing any professional writer is finding a steady supply of ideas and subjects so dazzlingly certain to appeal to the book-buying public that publishers are eager to buy. Not only are saleable ideas in short supply, it also takes an inordinate amount of time to research a new subject deeply enough to be able to sell it successfully. You might spend months researching a subject from a number of different sources and still be unable to find a buyer.

One answer is to collaborate with other people who lack writing skills and experience but have good stories to tell, either as fiction or non-fiction, or possess all the necessary information to create a book.

These people can be found in a number of places. They might be celebrities, who would impress publishers because of their notoriety, or ordinary people who have undergone extraordinary experiences. Alternatively, they might be experts in subjects that the public want to know more about.

It's much easier for publishers to market books by celebrities or established experts than those by unknown writers. Apart from a handful of literary stars, few people buy books because of the authors' names, and the media have a limited amount of space in which to write about them. But if you write the autobiography of a soap star, controversial politician or sporting hero, the resulting book will be widely written and talked about in the media. While the author is spending several weeks being whistled around all day from breakfast television to late night television, the ghost can stay comfortably at home and get on with their next project.

The speed with which you can gather the information for a ghosted book means that you can produce far more publishable material in the course of a year than if you were researching each book in order to write them under your own name. Publishers are also willing to pay higher advances because they can see how they will market the book once it is written. Ghosting makes it quite possible for an unknown writer to make a good full-time living as an author. It also provides you with broad writing experience and helps you to build contacts in the publishing industry to whom you can then sell other projects of your own.

Of all the advantages that ghosting offers, however, the greatest must be the opportunities that ghosts get to meet people of interest. It's a licence to ask the sort of impertinent questions that you truly want to know the answers to, and to be allowed inside some of the most extraordinary stories.

Ghosting a book for someone is like being paid to be educated by the best teachers in the world. Imagine, for instance, being asked to ghost *The Origin of the Species* for Darwin, or *The Decline and Fall of the Roman Empire* for Gibbon; being paid to learn everything that is in their heads and then turning their thoughts, words and notes into book form. Could there be a better form of education?

How to start

The first step could be to approach people you would like to ghost for and offer your services. That might mean your favourite celebrities, who you could write to care of their agents or television companies. It might be people you have read about in the press and who you think have stories that could be developed into books. It's usually possible to find some way of getting a letter or email to them.

A more practical first step, however, might be to approach people who you come across in everyday life and who have an expertise that you think would be popular with a wider audience. If you've been on a course, for instance, find out if the trainer has thought of turning their message into book form. Would a garage mechanic who's good at explaining why your car isn't working be able to supply the material for a book on car maintenance? What about your doctor doing a book on healthcare for a specialist sector of the market? The options are endless.

Anyone who has access to a captive marketplace, like training companies or public speakers, has a ready-made market for books. There are companies who might want to produce books by their chief executives for distribution to employees as well as to the outside world and public relations departments who would relish the idea of getting their clients' messages to wider audiences.

If you're already a writer in another field, approach your existing contacts. A show business journalist, for instance, has access to actors and singers. A sports writer can approach sportspeople they've interviewed in the past. People will nearly always prefer to work with a ghost they already know and trust and feel they have a rapport with, than with a stranger.

At the same time as approaching potential authors, you should also be letting the publishing world know that you're available to work as a ghost. Write to the literary agents and publishers listed in this *Yearbook* to let them know what your experience is and how they can contact you. They will often have clients who they know are not capable of doing their own writing.

How to sell projects

It's unusual for any publisher to buy a book idea without seeing a synopsis and some sample material. Once you're experienced you will sometimes be able to charge for writing synopses, but at the beginning it's probably wise to offer to do it for free in order to get projects off the ground.

A synopsis must be a hard-selling document that gives the publisher all the reasons why they should commission the book. It might be worth preparing a one- or two-page version first in order to catch their attention and then a longer document (between 5000 and 10,000 words usually suffices) in order to get the message across. It must give the publishers confidence that the book will be written to a high standard and delivered on time. It must be something that their sales teams can immediately see how to sell. Give a brief biography of the author and demonstrate how promotable they will be.

Involve a literary agent, firstly because most publishers don't like dealing directly with authors and secondly because the agent can handle all the money side of the relationship, removing potential conflicts between the author and ghost.

Whenever possible, have one good agent representing both parties in the arrangement. The agent's prime interest will then be in getting the book well published, not in encouraging the ghost and the author to fight one another for larger shares of the resulting royalties. The agent can also act as a conciliatory go-between should the relationship between author and ghost break down.

Who pays the ghost?

How the ghost gets paid will depend largely on how speculative the project is and on the wishes of the author. It might be that the author is sufficiently confident of the book's success to suggest paying the ghost a fee. How much that fee will be depends on what the author can afford, what they are willing to pay and what the ghost is willing to do the job for. In other words, it's open for negotiation.

If the project already has a publisher and there is no speculative work involved, then it may be that the publisher will suggest a fee. Then there will be little or no room for negotiation. Any writer starting out should accept any book that is offered, even if the money is low, simply in order to build up a track record.

Where there is no publisher involved at the outset, and the author has no money, then suggest splitting all the proceeds 50/50, which includes advances, royalties and foreign rights sales, serialisation fees and payments for film and television rights.

If the author is a celebrity and it's obvious the book will make a large amount of money the ghost might have to accept a lower percentage, or a percentage that will become lower once he or she has received a pre-agreed amount; e.g. the proceeds might be split 50/50 until the ghost has received £50,000, at which stage his or her share might then drop to 40%, and might then drop again at £100,000.

It would be unwise to write an entire book unless some money has been forthcoming, either from a publisher or from the author, but there are cases where even this risk is worth taking. With fiction it is nearly always necessary to write the whole book before any publisher will make an offer, making it a highly risky business. Go into it with your eyes open, knowing that it is closer to buying a lottery ticket than earning a living.

What skills does a ghost need?

Ghosts must suppress their own egos completely when working on an autobiography – a good discipline for any writer. You're fulfilling a similar function to a barrister in court, using your skills to plead the case of your client. Authors need ghosts who will not challenge them, but will simply listen to what they have to say and understand why they did what they did. If the ghost wishes to be critical of the subject then they must step back and create an objective biography, not an autobiography.

It is essential for the ghost to make the subject feel completely comfortable in his or her company. If they think the ghost is going to criticise them, judge them or argue with them they will not relax, open up or talk honestly. It's not the ghost's job to try to make them change their opinions about anything or anyone, but rather to encourage them to tell their story in the most interesting and coherent way possible. The ghost must be able to coax them off their hobbyhorses and persuade them to answer all the questions that the eventual readers are likely to ask. The author must not sound bitter. Part of the ghost's job is to ensure that the author remains attractive and interesting to the reader.

Once the voice is on tape the ghost then has to create what amounts to an 80,000-word monologue, just as a playwright might do, staying completely in the author's character at all times, using the sort of vocabulary the author would use and expressing the same views, ideas and prejudices.

It's important that a ghost is interested in the subject; otherwise the project will become unbearable. Imagine spending that much time talking to someone who bores you, and then having to go away and write it out all over again.

A ghost must also be able to see the structure of a book from early on in the process. He or she then needs to be able to guide the subject into providing the right material, keeping them on track and clearing up any inconsistencies in the telling of the tale.

The ghosting process

Sometimes the author has already produced some written material that can provide the bulk of the background. More often the ghost will have a clean slate to work from.

How many hours of taping will be required depends on how succinct the author can be persuaded to be and how quickly the ghost can master the subject. I find that 10–20 hours of useful taping is generally enough to produce a strong first draft. For autobiographies it's important to get them to tell you the story chronologically, so that you know what they have and have not experienced at each stage of the tale. The sequence can always be changed for dramatic effect once the actual writing commences.

It is usually preferable to interview them on their own home ground, where they will be at their most relaxed and least guarded. You will also get a better idea of what their lives are like.

The first draft should be shown to no one until the author has okayed it. They have final veto on what should and shouldn't be in the final draft. Only if they're confident that they have the final say will they be completely open and honest with you. The ghost can advise and warn, but the author has the last word. (Once given the power to make changes they nearly always decide they can't actually think of a better way of putting things and leave the manuscript virtually untouched). If there is arguing to be done, let it be done by the agent and the publisher.

A ghost must expect no glory. Enjoy the experience of the researching and the writing and of being paid to do pleasant work. Sometimes your name will get mentioned on the cover of a book and sometimes it will appear only on the flyleaf. Sometimes you will get a mention in the acknowledgements and sometimes you will not appear at all. You may get billed as 'co-author', but it is more likely to say 'By Big Shot with Joe Bloggs' or 'as told to Joe Bloggs'. It's always useful to have your name there but it can never be allowed to become a problem if it disappears.

Why publishers use ghosts

Publishers like to use ghostwriters because they know they will be able to rely on them as professionals. They want to know that the book will arrive on time in a publishable form, conforming as nearly as possible to the synopsis or the brief.

Frequently the authors of the books are busy people and hard to get hold of. Sometimes they are temperamental. The publishers consequently rely on the ghosts to act as go-betweens and to make the process of publication as smooth as possible.

The ghost is also the subject's best friend in the publishing business. During the long months when the agent is trying to sell the project and the phone doesn't ring, he or she will assure them that this is perfectly normal and doesn't mean they will never find a publisher. When the publisher wants to change the title or favours a cover in the subject's least favourite colour, the ghost will again have to be there to assure them that it will all be okay on the night. Then, when the book comes out and the subject can't find it on the front table in any of their local book shops, the ghost will have to explain the economics of the business to them and try to dissuade them from ringing the publisher and ranting and raving.

Ghosting is an endlessly varied, interesting and rewarding job – relish every opportunity you are given to practice it.

Andrew Crofts was described in the *Independent* as 'the king of modern ghosts'. He has published over 40 ghosted books and has written a novel, *Maisie's Amazing Maids* (Stratus Books 2001) with a ghostwriter as the central character. He is also the author of *The Freelance Writer's Handbook – How to make money and enjoy life* (Piatkus 2002) and *Ghostwriting* (A & C Black 2004). His website is www.andrewcrofts.com

Doing it on your own

Reasons for self-publishing are varied. Many highly respected comtemporary and past authors have published their own works. Peter Finch introduces the concept and outlines the implications of such an undertaking.

Why bother?

You've tried all the usual channels and been turned down; your work is uncommercial, specialised, technical, out of fashion; you are concerned with art while everyone else is obsessed with cash; you need a book out quickly; you want to take up small publishing as a hobby; you've heard that publishers make a lot of money out of their authors and you'd like a slice – all reason enough. But be sure you understand what you are doing before you begin.

But isn't this cheating? It can't be real publishing – where is the critical judgement? Publishing is a respectable activity carried out by firms of specialists. Writers of any ability never get involved.

But they do. Start self-publishing and you'll be in good historical company: Horace Walpole, Balzac, Walt Whitman, Virginia Woolf, Gertrude Stein, John Galsworthy, Rudyard Kipling, Beatrix Potter, Lord Byron, Thomas Paine, Mark Twain, Upton Sinclair, W.H. Davies, Zane Grey, Ezra Pound, D.H. Lawrence, William Carlos Williams, Alexander Pope, Robbie Burns, James Joyce, Anaïs Nin and Lawrence Stern. All these at some time in their careers dabbled in doing it themselves. William Blake did nothing else. He even made his own ink, handprinted his pages and got Mrs Blake to sew on the covers.

But today it's different?

Not necessarily. This is not vanity publishing we're talking about although if all you want to do is produce a pamphlet of poems to give away to friends then self-publishing will be the cheapest way. Doing it yourself today can be a valid form of business enterprise. Being twice shortlisted for major literary prizes sharpened Timothy Mo's acumen. Turning his back on mass-market paperbacks, he published *Brownout on Breadfruit Boulevard* on his own. Billy Hopkin's Headline bestseller of Lancashire life, *High Hopes*, began as a self-published title. Susan Hill self-produced her short stories, *Listening to the Orchestra*, and as an example to us all Jill Paton Walsh's self-published *Knowledge of Angels* was shortlisted for the Booker Prize.

Can anyone do it?

Certainly. If you are a writer then a fair number of the required qualities will already be in hand. The more able and practical you are then the cheaper the process will be. The utterly inept will need to pay others to help them, but it will still be self-publishing in the end.

Where do I start?

With research. Read up on the subject. Make sure you know what the parts of a book are. You will not need to become an expert but you will need a certain familiarity. Don't rush. Learn.

What about ISBN numbers?

International Standard Book Numbers – a standard bibliographic code, individual to each book published, are used by booksellers and librarians alike. They are issued by the Standard Book Numbering Agency at a cost of £75 plus VAT for 10. Self-publishers may balk at this apparently inordinate expense but the ISBN is the device used by the trade to track titles and if you are serious about your book should be regarded as essential. The Agency issues a free information pack; see *FAQs about ISBNs* on page 302.

Next?

Put your book together – be it the printed-out pages of your novel, your selected poems or your story of how it was sailing round the world – and see how large a volume it will make. If you have no real idea of what your book should look like, go to your local bookshop and hunt out a few contemporary examples of volumes produced in a style you would like to emulate. Take your typescript and your examples round to a number of local printers and ask for a quote.

How much?

It depends. How long is a piece of string? Unit cost is important: the larger the number of copies you have printed the less each will cost. Print too many and the total bill will be enormous. Printing has gone through a revolution in recent years. The arrival of POD (Printing on Demand) and other digital technologies have reduced costs and made short runs much more economic. But books are still not cheap.

Can I make it cost less?

Yes. Do some of the work yourself. If you want to publish poems and you are prepared to use a text set by a word processor, you will make a considerable saving. Many word processing programs have publishing facilities which will enhance the look of your text. Could you accept home production, run the pages off on an office photocopier, then staple the sheets? Editions made this way can be very presentable.

For longer texts savings can be made by supplying the work as a digital file directly to a printer. But be prepared to shop around.

Who decides how it looks?

You do. No one should ever ask a printer simply to produce a book. You should plan the design of your publication with as much care as you would a house extension. Spend as much time and money as you can on the cover. It is the part of the book your buyer will see first. If you're stuck, employ a book designer.

How many copies should I produce?

Poetry books can sell about 200 copies, new novels sometimes manage 1000, literary paperbacks 10,000, mass-market blockbusters half a million. But that is generally where there is a sales team and whole distribution organisation behind the book. Do not, on the one hand, end up with a prohibitively high unit cost by ordering too few copies. Fifty of anything is usually a waste of time. On the other hand can you really sell 3000? Will shops buy in dozens? They will probably only want twos and threes. Take care. Research your market first.

How do I sell it?

With all your might. This is perhaps the hardest part of publishing. It is certainly as time consuming as both the writing of the work and the printing of it put together. To succeed here you need a certain flair and you should definitely not be of a retiring nature. If you intend selling through the trade your costing must be correct and worked out in advance. Shops will want at least 35% (with national chains asking for even more) of the selling price as discount. You'll need about the same again to cover your distribution, promotion and other overheads, leaving the final third to cover production costs and any profit you may wish to make. Multiply your unit production cost by at least four. Commerical publishers often multiply by as much as nine.

Do not expect the trade to pay your carriage costs. Your terms should be at least 35% post free on everything bar single copy orders. Penalise these by reducing your discount to 25%. Some shops will suggest that you sell copies to them on sale or return. This means that they only pay you for what they sell and then only after they've sold it. This is a common practice with certain categories of publications and often the only way to get independent books into certain shops; but from the self-publisher's point of view it should be avoided if at all possible. Cash in hand is best but expect to have your invoices paid by cheque at a later date. Phone the shops you have decided should take your book or turn up in person and ask to see the buyer. Letters and sample copies sent by post will get ignored. Get a freelance distributor to handle all of this for you if you can. But expect to be disappointed. Independent book representatives willing to take on a one-off title are as rare as hen's teeth. Expect to have to go it alone.

What about promotion?
A vital aspect often overlooked by beginners. Send out as many review copies as you can, all accompanied by slips quoting selling price and name and address of the publisher. Never admit to being that person yourself. Invent a name: it will give your operation a professional feel. Ring up newspapers and local radio stations ostensibly to check that your copy has arrived but really to see if they are prepared to give your book space. Buying advertising space rarely pays for itself but good local promotion with 100% effort will generate dividends.

What about depositing copies at the British Library?
Under the Copyright Acts the British Library, the Bodleian Library, Oxford, the University Library, Cambridge, the National Library of Scotland, the Library of Trinity College Dublin and the National Library of Wales are all entitled to a free copy of your book which must be sent to them within one month of publication. One copy should go direct to the Legal Deposit Office at the British Library, Boston Spa, Wetherby, West Yorkshire LS23 7BY. The other libraries use the Agency for the Copyright Libraries, 100 Euston Street, London NW1 2HQ (*email* cma@cla.ac.uk). Contact her directly to find out how many copies she requires.

And what if it goes wrong?
Put all the unsolds under the bed or give them away. It has happened to lots of us. Even the big companies who are experienced at these things have their regular flops. It was an adventure and you did get your book published. On the other hand you may be so successful that you'll be at the London Book Fair selling the film rights and wondering if you've reprinted enough.

Can the internet help?
The web has yet to take the place of traditional print but things are changing fast. A good number of authors are setting up their own home pages. From these they advertise them-

selves and their works, and offer downloadable samples and, in some cases, their complete books. No one has yet made a fortune here and the number of 'hits' some sites claim to get are questionable. Nonetheless, this method of self-promotion comes highly recommended. Self-publishers, if they are not already familiar with the internet, should get on board now. *The Internet: A Writer's Guide* (see further reading) is a good place to start; see also *Setting up a website* on page 606.

Currently, the internet is thick with operators offering to promote or publish work electronically. These range from companies which post sample chapters and then charge readers a fee for the complete work to professional e-book developers who offer books fully formatted for use on hand-held PDAs (Personal Digital Assistants) and other devices (see *E-publishing*, page 597). The jury is still out on where this flux of technological change is going, but if you'd like to test the waters, visit Jane Dorner's site at www.internetwriter.co.uk or consult *Electronic Publishing: The Definitive Guide* by Karen Wiesner.

Peter Finch runs Academi, the Welsh National Literature Promotion Agency and Society of Writers. He is a poet, former bookseller and small publisher and author of the *How to Publish Yourself*. His website contains further advice for self-publishers (www.peterfinch.co.uk).

Further reading

Baverstock, Alison, *Marketing Your Book: An Author's Guide*, A & C Black, 2nd edn, 2006

Coleman, Vernon, *How to Publish Your Own Book*, Blue Books, 1999

Dawes, John (ed.), *The Best of Write to Publish!*, John Dawes Publications, 2002

Domanski, Peter and Irvine, Philip, *A Practical Guide to Publishing Books Using Your PC*, Domanski-Irvine Books, 1997

Dorner, Jane, *The Internet: A Writer's Guide*, A & C Black, 2nd edn, 2001

Finch, Peter, *How to Publish Yourself*, Allison & Busby, 4th edn, 2000

Judd, Karen, *Copyediting*, Robert Hale, 2002

Poynter, Dan, *The Self-Publishing Manual: How to Write, Print and Sell Your Own Book*, Para Publishing, 2003

Ross, Tom and Marilyn, *The Complete Guide to Self-Publishing*, Writer's Digest Books, 4th edn, 2002

Spiers, Hugh, *Introduction to Digital Printing*, Pira, 2005

Wiesner, Karen, *Electronic Publishing: The Definitive Guide*, Hard Shell Word Factory, 2003

Woll, Thomas, *Publishing for Profit*, Kogan Page, 2002

Marketing, publicising and selling books

Publishers have their own staff to market, publicise and sell their books but authors can also contribute to this process. Katie Bond outlines how to be a publisher's 'dream author'.

Newspapers are full of discouraging stories about how publishers only want to take on novels by glamorous young things or misery memoirs or celebrity autobiographies. Let's quash that immediately: publishers want to publish the best books they can find in a wide variety of genres and sell the socks off them. In the selling process, a 'promotable author' can make a major difference and my aim here is to take you through the run-up to your publication and suggest how even the most 'normal' author can give their book a push.

Word-of-mouth sales

When a publisher signs up an author, it is said that every book must be sold three times: by the editor to the rest of the company, by the sales/marketing/publicity departments to the bookseller and by the bookseller to the consumer. The most powerful sales tool in publishing is word-of-mouth and this begins in-house. A commissioning editor can entice everyone in the company to read a book so that a hundred people are talking about it – every mention is a potential sale. A recent example is *The Kite Runner* by Khaled Hosseini. This was one of those slow-burn books that took two years to become an international bestseller and reading group favourite. Such was the passion of its editor, Arzu Tahsin, for this novel that everyone at Bloomsbury read it and was 100% behind the book. Everyone played a part in its success by recommending the book to friends – personal recommendation being the number one factor in influencing a purchase according to all book-buying surveys. If an author is aware of this, every person you meet – at your publishing house (whether they're in the accounts department, on reception or the Sales Director), in bookshops and libraries, or indeed anywhere in your professional capacity as 'an author' – becomes a VIP. I will never forget William Boyd – the first author I spoke to in my first job as a publicity assistant – asking and remembering my name and chatting to me when he called to speak to my boss. Having read and loved his books at university, I would have walked over hot coals to make sure that *The Blue Afternoon* was a success and any request of his was instantly top of my list. Geographical distance from your publisher may mean that you don't get the chance to visit them often but do try to meet as many people in different departments as possible, go to book launches and readings, keep an eye on your publisher's website so you're up to date with what they're doing, and find out if your local sales rep would like to meet up for coffee when they're next on your patch. The only caveat here is that publishers can become flustered by over-keen authors – one used to lurk outside our offices with with 'surprise' cappucinos!

Marketing and publicity

Marketing is an umbrella term that includes all the work a publisher does to promote or sell a book. Traditionally 'marketing' is categorised as anything paid for (catalogues, advertising, posters and bookshop promotions) and 'publicity' (media coverage, bookshop events and festivals) is free. There will be a person in both marketing and publicity departments assigned to your book and creating good relationships with both of them – particularly the publicist (although obviously I'm biased here) is crucial. Ask your editor to let you know who they are and contact them as early as possible to meet up and decide on a marketing and publicity plan.

The sell-in

The sales process begins 6–9 months prior to publication when the sales team use the marketing and publicity plans to begin selling books to the head offices of the major book chains – from Waterstones to Tesco, Amazon and the wholesalers who supply independent bookshops. Closer to publication local sales reps also sell books to individual bookshops in their areas although the front-of-store promotions (3 for 2, Read of the Week, Book of the Month) will be decided at head office level. The 'sell-in' is this process of persuading the bookshops to stock a particular book. The marketing department produces sell-in materials including six-monthly catalogues promoting the publisher's spring and autumn lists, and AIs (advance information sheets), bound proofs and glossy brochures on individual books. The initial print run for a book is based on the sell-in figures of advance orders placed for it. The speed at which a book can be reprinted (except highly illustrated and special format books) minimises the clash between publisher caution and author optimism and prevents lost sales if the initial print run sells out quickly.

The sell-out

This is the magic moment when a customer decides to buy a book. Marketing and publicity are geared towards boosting the sell-out in a myriad of ways from advertising and media coverage to book jacket design and bookseller recommendation. A recent survey reported in *The Bookseller* revealed that 'The consumer needs at least five positive mentions of a product as well as easy availability before he will buy'. With over 120,000 new titles being published in the UK every year, it's a crowded marketplace and clear signposting is essential to enable the book to reach its target readership.

The book jacket and author photograph

'Never judge a book by its cover' is an outdated maxim. This is the most important marketing tool of all and can make or break a publication. Even if your novel was inspired by an old family portrait, don't insist on having it on the cover if it isn't an eye-catching image. Conversely, do ransack old photograph albums, magazines and art galleries for images that you love and that you think are right for your book. Candida Crewe's recent memoir *Eating Myself* has an utterly arresting black and white close-up photograph of her doleful childhood face on the jacket – the photograph was provided by her and taken by her mother. For the author photograph, definitely allow yourself a little vanity– a really good black and white portrait is a must for publicity purposes and you want to look your absolute best.

Publicity

Book publicity is incredibly varied and widespread from reviews to features, discussions to news stories, public appearances at bookshops, libraries and literary festivals to local stock signings and books for competition prizes. As a rough guide, a publicist starts work on book tours and magazine advertising as much as six months ahead of publication. Finished copies of a book are printed approximately 6–8 weeks prior to publication and this period is the key time for confirming the media coverage to run on publication. The publication date is the peg for the media, so coverage becomes increasingly unlikely months or even weeks after the publication date unless the book has taken off in a major way and its success becomes the story.

How authors can help

There is a limited amount that an author can do to help sales and marketing directly beyond being very nice to booksellers and librarians, providing details of any specialist sales outlets prior to publication and (gently, not forcefully) offering to sign copies of your book in bookshops after publication (having first checked anonymously that the bookshop does have copies in stock). If a bookshop doesn't have your book in stock, let your publisher know rather than complaining to the bookshop directly. Also avoid the temptation – however tantalising – of moving your book to a more prominent position on the shelves. One author was repeatedly caught doing this until WHSmith's head office threatened to send all copies of the book back to the publisher and refuse to stock it anymore.

Authors can best focus their energies on publicity where their input is vital. A publicist will be working on anything from 2–10 books in any one month so their time is limited. You need to give your publicist as much information as possible on your book, yourself and any potential publicity angles (see below). Together you can then agree the timescale of the publicity campaign, achievable and optimistic goals, how publicity will best sell your book and discuss any potential pitfalls. Be honest with your publicist and tell them the full story even if you decide not to talk about it to the media. Your publicist can advise you on how much of your private life to mine for publicity and how to maximise your control over the coverage. First-time novelist Clare Allan chose to write newspaper articles about how her 10 years as a patient in mental hospitals had informed her novel *Poppy Shakespeare,* rather than be interviewed. Trust your instincts and don't let journalists pressurise you. Jon McGregor was longlisted for the Man Booker Prize for his first novel *If Nobody Speaks of Remarkable Things*. A *Guardian* journalist and photographer went to interview him in Nottingham and on discovering that he'd washed up dishes in a local restaurant to support himself whilst writing the book, tried to persuade him to be photographed at the kitchen sink. Jon declined. It was a wise decision as otherwise this picture would have haunted him for years.

Pre-publication checklist for the 'dream author'

Your publicist is your primary contact for sales/marketing/publicity so the information below should be given to them to help plan the campaign.

● Make contact with the marketer, publicist and local sales rep at your publisher.

● Fill in the publisher's author questionnaire and write a 500–1000-word piece about how you came to write your book and what's new and different about it (for examples look at the 'I am the author of' section on Amazon.co.uk).

● Make contact with your local bookshop, library, writers' groups, reading groups and literary festival and let them know that your book is being published.

● Research specialist sales outlets (e.g. wool shops for a book about knitting or football club fanzines or maritime museums for a novel about Nelson).

● Give the sales team any relevant information to drive sales regionally (e.g. if you're Welsh/Scottish/Irish or you lived in Cornwall for 20 years and have a huge network of family and friends there though you've recently moved to Derby).

- Make a list of any possible media angles relating either to yourself or the book.
- Make a list of any media contacts, both local and national.
- Research any anniversaries, exhibitions, television series or films that tie in with your book or the themes of your book and could create media hooks.
- If you're writing non-fiction, list what's new and newsworthy in your book (e.g. new source material or new angle). Differentiate your book from others on the same subject and list the other books in the same field.
- As you know your book best, suggest 1000–3000-word extracts that might work as standalone newspaper pieces.
- Write a description of your book in approximately 100–300 words (think book jacket copy style).
- If you think you could write newspaper articles, write paragraph pitches of ideas with potential word lengths. (Think of specific newspapers when you're doing this and be ruthless. Ask yourself if the feature is *really* right for the *Daily Mail's* Femail pages/*The Times'* Comment pages/*The Observer's* Food Monthly.)
- Write a list of the contemporary authors you admire and particularly any authors whose work is similar to yours as their readers might enjoy your book.
- Look at your publisher's website and see if there is additional material you can provide – on your book or a review of another book or article/feature.
- If the idea of standing up in front of people and talking about your book makes you feel queasy, ask your publisher for media and presentation training (budget permitting of course). Alternatively, go to other author events to see what works and what doesn't. (Remember that shorter is *always* better and enlist the help of an honest friend for feedback.)
- Plan, prepare and practice your author event (from choosing the right passage for a reading from the book – one that is dramatic, self-contained, character-introducing, with the all-important want-to-read-on factor – to interacting with the audience). If you are nervous, write out your talk and say it aloud again and again in front of the mirror at home.
- Listen or watch every television or radio programme before you go on it and always know the presenter's name!

Above all, charm, good manners and hard-working professionalism are the staple of the 'dream author' and will open promotional doors time and time again. Joanna Trollope, *doyenne* of the book tour, says: 'I think the advice I'd give to a first time author is that *all* publicity (with some reservations, obviously, about the tabloids…!), however seemingly small, is worth doing because the whole process is really joining up the dots in a dot-to-dot picture (which *might* even turn out to be a little golden goose…) and that whatever you do, do it with the best grace possible because no-one in your professional life will ever forget that you were a treat to deal with.' Finally, when your close friends and family tell you how much they love your book, do ask them for a small favour: a rave review on Amazon never goes amiss.

Katie Bond has been Publicity Director at Bloomsbury since 1999 and has handled PR for many bestsellers including Sheila Hancock's *The Two of Us*, Margaret Atwood's *The Blind Assassin*, Donna Tartt's *The Little Friend* and J.K. Rowling's *Harry Potter* books, as well as winning the first British Book Award's Publicity Nibbie in 2005 for Susanna Clarke's *Jonathan Strange and Mr Norrell*.

Helping to market your book

Alison Baverstock offers guidance on how authors can help to enhance their publisher's efforts to sell their book. The information in this article is also relevant to self-publishers.

Having a book accepted for publication is immensely satisfying – all the more so if in the process you have amassed a thick pile of rejection letters spanning several years. At this stage, some authors decide that, having committed themselves to work with a professional publishing house, this is the end of their involvement in the process. They will move on thankfully to the writing of their next book.

Once you have delivered your manuscript, and it has been accepted for publication, a publisher should handle all aspects of your book's subsequent development, from copy-editing and production to promotion and distribution. But there is a sound pragmatism in remaining vigilant. When it comes to the marketing of your book, there is a huge amount that you can do to help it sell.

The challenging marketplace

Each year in Britain alone, over 130,000 books get published or come out in new editions. All compete for the attention of the same review editors, the same stock buyers in bookshops, and the largely static number of regular book-buying members of the general public. It follows that anything an author can do to help 'position' the book, to make it sound different, or just more interesting than those it competes with, will be a huge advantage.

The marketing of books is not usually an area of high spending and there are many reasons why. Books are cheap (a novel costs about the same as a cinema ticket, and much less than a round of drinks), the publishers' profit margins are low, booksellers claim a percentage of the purchase price as discount (35–50%), and books sell in relatively small quantities (a mass market novel selling 15,000 copies may be considered a 'bestseller' – compare that with the sales figures for CDs or computer games). Your publisher will probably try to make maximum use of (free) publicity to stimulate demand using low-cost marketing techniques. They are far more likely to arrange for the insertion of a simple leaflet as a loose insert in a relevant publication, or organise a specific mailing to members of a relevant society, than book television or billboard advertising. Your assistance in helping them reach the market could be most important.

Examine your resources

Think in detail about what resources you have at your disposal that would help make your book sell, and tell your publisher. Most houses send out an Authors' Publicity Form about six months before publication, asking you for details of your book and how you feel it can best be marketed. Whilst the house will probably not be able to fulfil all your ambitions (mass market advertising is not possible for every book), they will be particularly interested in your contacts. For example, were you at school with someone who is now a features writer on *The Times*? Even if you have not spoken since, they may still remember your name. Do your children attend the same school as a contact on your local paper? Do you belong to a society or professional organisation that produces a newsletter for members, organises a conference or regular dining club? All these communication channels provide opportunities for publishers to send information on your book to potential purchasers.

Even greater things may be achieved if you set up the arrangements yourself. Can you arrange for an editorial mention of your book in a society journal (which will carry more weight than an advertisement) or organise for your publisher to take advertising space at a reduced rate? Remember that the less it costs your publishing house to reach each potential customer, the more of the market they will be able to cover out of their planned budgetary spend.

Offer a peg to your publisher

In trying to stimulate demand for a book, publishers try to achieve publicity (or coverage in the media) at the time of publication. The most usual way of getting this is for the in-house publicist to write a press release about you and your book and send this out to journalists in the hope that they will be interested enough to write about you, or even better decide to interview you.

Your publishing house will need 'pegs' on which to hang stories about you and your book, and it is helpful if you volunteer these rather than waiting to be asked. So, think back over your career and life in general. What is interesting about you? Are there any stories that arise out of the research for the book; incidents that give a flavour of the book and you as a writer?

Try to look at your life as others might see it; events or capabilities you take for granted might greatly interest other people. For example, novelist Catherine Jones is married to a former soldier, and moved house 15 times in 20 years. In that time she has produced three children and has had appointments with over 40 different classroom teachers. She speaks about her life in a very matter of fact way, but when she wrote her first novel, *Army Wives* (Piatkus), the media were quite fascinated by a world they clearly knew nothing about. They found military jargon particularly compelling, and this proved a wonderful (and headline-producing) peg on which to promote her book.

Make yourself available

For a mass market title, any publicity that can be achieved will need to be orchestrated at the time of publication. By this time the publisher will hopefully have persuaded booksellers to take stock and the books will be in the shops. If the publicity is successful, but peaks before the books are available to buy, you have entirely missed the boat. If there is no publicity on publication, and no consequent demand, the bookseller has the right to return the books to the publisher and receive a credit note. And in these circumstances it will be *extremely* difficult to persuade them to restock the title having been let down once.

Timing is therefore absolutely crucial, so make yourself available at the time of publication (this is not the time to take your well-earned break). Remember too that, unless you are a very big star, each different newspaper or programme approached will consider its own requirements exclusively, and will not be interested in your own personal scheduling. Not all journalists work every day, and even if they do they like to decide on their own priorities. If you ask for an interview to be rescheduled, it may be dropped completely.

Don't assume that only coverage in the national media is worth having and turn your nose up at local radio and newspapers; they can reach a very wide audience and be particularly effective in prompting sales. You may be able to extend the amount of time and space you get by suggesting a competition or reader/listener offer. Local journalists usually have a much friendlier approach than those who work on the nationals, so if you are a novice to the publicity process this can be a much easier start, and an opportunity to build your confidence.

Contributing text for marketing

At several stages in the production process your publisher may request your input. You may be asked to provide text for the book jacket or for an author profile, to check information that will be included in the publisher's annual catalogue, or to provide biographical information for their website.

Think in detail about the words you have been asked for, who will read them and in what circumstances, and then craft what you write accordingly. For example, the text on a fiction book jacket (or 'blurb') should not retell the story or give away the plot; rather it should send signals that convey atmosphere, whet the appetite of the reader and show what kind of book they can expect. The potential customer is likely to be reading the blurb in a hurry, perhaps whilst standing in a bookshop being jostled by other shoppers, so it is best to keep it brief.

A non-fiction blurb should establish what the book will do for the reader and what your qualifications are for writing it. Again, keep the details short. The key factor is relevance – what have you done, and what are you qualified to do, that is relevant to the publication in hand?

For both categories of book a third party recommendation will help enormously as this provides objective proof of what a book is like and how useful it is. When books have come out as hardbacks, then extracts from review coverage can be useful on the paperback edition. (Every author should keep a rigorous record of their review coverage, copies of which your publisher should send you. Things do sometimes go missing or get lost, and you are far more likely to remember the good ones given that you are looking after a much smaller number of books than your publisher.) For previously unpublished authors, a relevant quotation is very helpful instead. Do you know anyone established in the appropriate field who could provide an endorsement for what you have written? Can you contact them and ask them to help? The endorsement does not have to be from someone famous, just someone relevant. For example, a children's book endorsed as a gripping read by a 10-year-old child, or an educational text endorsed by a student who had just passed her exams could both be effective.

You may be asked to check your details in a publisher's catalogue. Bear in mind that your entry will sit alongside everything else they publish, so it must be factual and clear, and not 'knock' other titles on their list.

If you are asked to write website copy, be sure to look at the relevant site before you draft something. Think about the context in which your material will be seen and read (by whom, how often and for how long) and use this information as the basis for writing.

Marketing after publication

Although most of the effort in marketing your book will inevitably occur at the time of publication (because next month's schedule will bring forward further titles that need the marketing department's attention), there is a great deal of opportunity to carry on selling your book afterwards.

So, if you are asked to speak at a conference or run a training course, ask if your book can be included in the package available to delegates, either as part of the overall price or at a reduced rate. Ask the publishing house for simple flyers (leaflets) on your book which you can hand out on suitable occasions. Then ask the organisers to put a copy inside the delegate pack, on every seat, or in a pile at the back of the hall (or preferably all three!).

Give your publishing house the details of speaking engagements or conferences at which they could usefully mount a display of all their titles (your own included). Even though they published your book, you cannot reasonably expect them to be specialists in every specific field you know intimately, so give them *all* the details they need. For a conference this would include the full title (not just the initials you refer to it by), the organiser's address and contact numbers (not the chairperson's address to which you should send associated papers), the precise dates and times, and any associated deadlines (e.g. stand bookings placed before a certain date may be cheaper). Finally, try to plan ahead rather than passing on key details at the last minute (this is one of publishers' most common complaints about authors!).

When authors get together they will moan about their publishers. But if that energy is channelled into helping promote the books, everyone benefits!

After 10 years in publishing **Alison Baverstock** set up her own marketing consultancy, specialising in running campaigns for the book trade and training publishers and authors to market more effectively. She is a well-established speaker on the book business and has written widely on how to market books. She is the author of *Marketing Your Book: An Author's Guide* (A & C Black 2001) and *How to Market Books* (Kogan Page 2000). Her most recent book, *Is There a Book in You?* (A & C Black 2006), offers would-be writers a check list of resources they must have if they want to get published. Her website is www.alisonbaverstock.com

How to publicise your book

There are numerous ways that authors can help to promote their books. Isabel Losada created her own interactive website to be in touch with her readers and the book world in general. Here she talks about her website and shares other ideas for author self publicity.

There is a very annoying thing about publishing houses. They are publishing houses. Authors don't like this at all. We want them to be PR houses, promotional entrepreneurs and marketing experts. In an ideal world we would like entire publicity departments dedicated to promoting our books. Alas, this is not how it is.

Publicity departments

In one of my foreign publishing companies, my editor publishes 85 books a year. For every one published she looks at 10–15 books a week and reads at least five of them. The other two editors in this company each publish 75 and 60 books. This company has ONE publicity person who has responsibility for the promotion of 220 titles a year. So how many calls do you reckon he can make to try and sell an interview to the press? And imagine that your book is not about sport or sex… well it's a bleak picture ain't it?

Now, you may be lucky and your book may be published by one of the major UK publishing houses, there may be two people who work in the publicity department. And maybe even a work experience assistant too. But then they will have more books as well. Are you beginning to grasp the reality here?

The person most committed to getting your book out there is you. So don't moan about your publishing company, as many authors do – they have published your book after all. Get proactive and have fun with publicising your book. It's the only way to learn.

Be nice at all times to everyone as people who work in PR, publishing and marketing are under pressure and work very hard. What you need is cooperation – so, when you have a meeting with those who are working to promote your book, try to find out exactly what they are doing so that you can cover what they won't have time to do. Get as much information as you can, so you can help. For example, if you are going to visit a town as part of a promotional tour, it is relatively easy to fix up local radio interviews which can be done either in the town or 'down the line' from wherever you work or even from your home. Your publicity person won't have time to phone local newspapers but if you contact them with information about your event they will often be delighted. The best way to get people along to an event is to have someone you know who lives in the town rally their friends and for you to deal with local press and radio. It's hard work.

And that's the truth – you have to commit yourself to self promotion both with time and with money. I know one author who spends five years writing a book but will not give 10 minutes to promoting it. Where is the logic in that? Your tax allows for expenses in the column 'Advertising and Promotion', so surely it's worth producing postcards, for example, that show the front cover of your book, at your own expense. You can give them to those people at parties who insist on asking 'What do you write?' – sometimes they'll ask you to sign the card and then go out and buy the book. And you can find 100 other uses for the postcards too. So decide whether to spend your money on promotional tools or to give it to the tax man.

Never walk past a bookshop without going in to sign copies of your books. Be very friendly to the booksellers. I once asked a bookseller where my books were and he said they had 75 copies in the basement. I asked if he'd like them signed and he looked at me wearily – he evidently didn't want to go down to the basement and find them. It was a hot day. 'Are you open to bribery?' I asked… 'If you will go and get them I will go out and buy you an ice-cream.' 'Magnum please,' he replied and went off to get the books. While I signed books – he ate his ice-cream. Having fun helps.

Websites

Then there is your website. Gotta have a website. And what is worse is that it's no good getting someone else to do it for you so that you aren't able to use it. You must be able to maintain it yourself and not have to ring someone (who's bound to be on holiday when you want them) every time you want to change or update something. Study other authors' websites. Some of them are truly dull – dead sites that just contain lots of downloadable pictures of the author and are evidently not designed for readers of the books. At the other end of the scale is www.neilgaiman.com, the genius of which few of us can even aspire to. Neil Gaiman's website obviously takes up a lot of his time every day but for his fans the contact must be a continual source of pleasure and satisfaction. My own website (www.isabellosada.com) is basically an amateur site that I built with a couple of flashy touches (such as the message board) which I was given help with. But it gives me huge pleasure and I reply to every email, and accept all invitations to attend reading groups (as long as they pay my fares.) Friendly emails from readers about how much a reader has enjoyed a book is a great way to start or end the day. So you gotta have a website.

The Amazon websites (www.amazon.com and www.amazon.co.uk) are important too. Thousands of people look at them and read the reader reviews. If a reader sends you a glowing email (to your website of course) about your book it's perfectly acceptable to ask them if they would mind repeating their accolade in the form of a reader review on Amazon. It's funny when authors write their own reviews because regular users at Amazon can tell the difference immediately. A review that says it's by 'a reader' and doesn't give the name is usually an author that hasn't done their homework and is writing their own reviews. And why do it? Genuine reviews from fans are much more interesting. But be warned – watching the rating on Amazon can drive authors crazy. One minute your book is at number 12 and the next it's at 5756 and you think – how did that happen? It's obviously a deliberate plan to baffle us.

Publicity events

Keep all your press cuttings and put together your own list of reviews that are complimentary of your work. (Comments from any bad reviews can also be helpful – see 'Rejection letters' on my website!) This 'press pack' can then be sent to people when you want to introduce yourself and your work, for instance for interviews or literary festivals. Keep the details of all the people that you speak to and the conversations that you have with them. Who interviewed you and when? Don't assume that others will remember – they won't. I recently did a radio interview with a regional radio station with a presenter and I only realised at the last minute that he'd interviewed me twice before and I had no notes on this. I remembered just in time before inadvertently insulting him and humiliating myself. So keep notes.

When you do events, plan and prepare them like a professional entertainer would. Reading from your work is a skill that you may or may not have naturally. If you hate reading, don't do it. You'll be far more interesting and the audience will have a better time if you are happy. Have someone interview you about the book and your work instead. Check out the relevance to your audience. Ask them why they have come along. They may all secretly want to hear about your book before last. If you are promoting a book that is not your first – check that bookshops have copies of your backlist titles in stock too as there will always be people in the audience who will want those.

Go to other authors' events. My local Ottakars in Clapham has a fantastic range of author events – and they give free wine too. By turning up for some of these free evenings out you'll soon have a feel of what makes a good evening and you may find other ways to support your fellow authors when you meet them.

Bookshops

Check the stock levels of your books (in the most gentle, kind and supportive way of course). I recently checked in a bookshop and found that orders for six copies of a title had been placed seven months previously. Somewhere between the chain, distributor and warehouse the order had been lost – but a couple of phone calls soon corrected this.

If you have written a book about horses and there isn't a copy in a riding shop you visit – don't be surprised. Small shops don't necessarily have accounts with all the publishing companies. If your book on Buddhism isn't in the Buddhist monastery bookshop that you'd expect to find it in, you could offer the bookshop manager a copy, explain why you think his customers would enjoy the book and ask if he or she would consider it. Sometimes just asking gently works wonders.

Do not turn books that are spine side out face side out in shops. It will simply annoy the booksellers who will turn it back when you are gone. And do not move your books around the shop without first speaking to the manager of the shop. If you think your book is shelved in the wrong place this is a serious problem but needs to be dealt with from the top, i.e. by your publishing company. Getting cross with bookshops won't help as books are shelved according to the category printed on the back cover. So don't annoy booksellers, find out what supports them – they are your friends.

Self-promotion

Be prepared to support other authors. You can use your website for this, for example by linking to other authors' pages if you are recommending their work. I have persuaded people to write articles about books I admire and even once persuaded a charity to promote a book to their 16,000 members. Look out for opportunities to support the work of authors that you admire. If you can benefit charities or causes that you support at the same time you are really making sense.

Always, always have a copy of your latest book about your person that you are happy to sell if someone asks. Sorry – but sometimes people (especially at parties) are thrilled that they can have a signed copy direct from the author. I know you are cringing – but it can be done gracefully and with a smile.

You may like to consider offering to visit book clubs that are reading your books. On my site I offer to go and talk at any club that will pay my fares, and the last offer that came in was from Switzerland. I also sign books and will post them to anyone who asks me to (in return for a cheque, of course) and I often give away foreign edition copies from my website. (What else can I do with six copies in Greek?) So basically be reader friendly. And bookshop friendly. And publishing company friendly and editor and agent friendly.

Lastly, you have to believe passionately in your work and genuinely want everyone to read it. Don't write just because you have been asked to – wait until you have something to say. Enough trees have been destroyed for our trade as it is. If you are passionate about what you write and your work makes a genuine and positive contribution your readers will sell your books for you. And it's true – with a lot of help from you – that ultimately it's still word of mouth that will sell your books.

Isabel Losada is the author of *New Habits: Why Today's Women Become Nuns*, *The Battersea Park Road to Enlightenment* (which has been translated into 12 languages) and *A Beginner's Guide to Changing the World: For Tibet, With Love*. She is also an actress and broadcaster and can be contacted through her website www.isabellosada.com

Book distribution

Despite the large number of bookshops in the UK, a published book is not guaranteed a place in one of them. Mike Petty charts the journey a book may take from publisher to bookshop and offers reasons why so many books don't reach the high street.

'Why aren't my books in the shops?' The *cri de coeur* is a familiar one (not just from authors, I might add – their editors are prone to similar gripes). There has been an explosion in bookshop numbers in the last decade or so: as of December 2004 there were over 133 Ottakar's branches as opposed to nine in 1992, 65 Borders/Books Etc as against 10 Books Etc, and 189 Waterstone's branches as against 178 Waterstone's/Dillon's. Over the same period WHSmith began to take their claim to be Britain's largest booksellers reasonably seriously. I doubt, however, whether the majority of writers would feel that their lot has improved accordingly; according to a KPMG report in 1998, a mere 3% of titles accounted for 50% of the volume of retail sales.

The mechanics of book distribution are, in outline, simple enough. Anywhere between six and three months before publication all books are subscribed either by sales management or reps to customers, whether individual shops, the head office teams of the chains, or wholesalers. ('Customers' in publisher-speak are people who sell books, not people who buy them from bookshops.) The salespeople will have been primed by their editorial and marketing colleagues as to the qualities and saleability (in theory) of each title, and will be wielding at the very least a jacket and an information sheet bearing the salient details. The customer, if sufficiently impressed by the presentation and the author's sales history, if any, will order a quantity ranging from one to many thousands, plus associated paraphernalia such as dumpbins, posters, etc and these will be delivered in time for publication.

(A publication date, by the way, has very little significance these days, except of course for the author, especially if there is a party or a dinner in the offing. Otherwise it is largely a matter of administrative convenience for publishers and booksellers since, unless specifically asked not to for some reason to do with newsworthiness, bookshops will place stock on sale as soon as they receive it. Books hanging around in stockrooms do not earn money.)

Distribution centres

A modern book distribution centre is a vast, echoing place, its offices full of the clatter of computer operators, its warehouse area crammed with racks carrying pallets of books stacked up to a hundred feet high, while the air is filled with the sound of forklift trucks and transistor radios. Littlehampton Book Services (LBS), a typical large distribution centre, handles Canongate, Serpent's Tail, Aurum, Kyle Cathie and Atlantic among others, as well as owners Orion, whose imprints include Weidenfeld and Nicolson, Gollancz and several paperback lists.

The figures are astounding. According to Bridget Radnedge, Publishing Services Director at LBS, the warehouse contains about 20,000 different titles at any one time (out of a database of around 178,000 titles), which translates to somewhere between 28 and 30 million books. Seven to eight thousand separate orders are received per week and are turned round in an average of 3–4 days. In 2005, 39.4 million books were despatched, an average of 758,000 a week. 'Goods In' sees anything up to 400 pallets a day (including 4.3

million returns in 2004), delivered by 20 or so trucks. LBS operates 24 hours a day, though the small hours are reserved for housekeeping chores such as replenishing the forward picking racks, where new and fast-moving titles are stored for easy despatch. These figures will be duplicated at the other half a dozen or so vast distribution centres round the country – and LBS are currently operating at 85% of capacity.

But the mechanics of book distribution do not always work as smoothly as they should. In spite of the best efforts of publishers, warehouses, transport firms, wholesalers and booksellers, the process is best thought of as an obstacle race. The winners will appear in the shops in decent quantities – and, in an ideal world reappear there – while the losers will fall at one of quite a few hurdles along the way.

Small- and medium-size publishers, unable to afford the serious expense of their own warehouses, sign up with one or other of the big boys. In its three warehouses The Book Service (TBS, formerly known as Tiptree Book Services) handles all the Random House and Transworld imprints and dozens of others besides, including Time Warner, Virgin, Lonely Planet, Piatkus and the AA. A more recent recruit is Faber and Faber, who once had their own warehouse. If these larger businesses get into trouble, the knock-on effects for their clients can be serious. The changeover to a new computer system is a frequent and apparently inevitable cause for complaint (as Penguin authors will testify), as is a tendency to overstretch resources in the pursuit of margin. LBS celebrated winning the British Book Award for Distributor of the Year back in January 1998 by expanding their client list. By Christmas of that year their systems were seriously overloaded, they were operating from four sites, and there was talk of books left out in the rain because there was no space under cover. The year ended in a welter of recriminations and threatened lawsuits. Martin Evans, an experienced logistics troubleshooter, was brought in to sort things out, which he did most effectively. But the after-effects, in the shape of compensation claims, lingered for Orion and their French owners Hachette for some time.

Centralised ordering and promotions

The increasing centralisation of ordering is another obstacle. In rare cases as much as 90% of a book's UK subscription can go to perhaps a dozen key accounts, leaving the balance to be fought over by the on-the-road sales force which traditionally has been the main means of communication with individual bookshops. While in most cases the percentage will be lower than this, there is no doubt that in recent years – and in particular since the collapse of the Net Book Agreement – the balance has shifted significantly towards centralised buying. By 'key accounts' is meant wholesalers (the biggest are THE, Gardners and Bertrams); specialised wholesalers such as Aspen who supply supermarkets, motorways and airports; WHSmith; supermarkets who are not otherwise supplied; and – increasingly – the online booksellers. Many of these, such as Blackwell's, Foyles and WHSmith, have their terrestrial counterparts, while others, most notably Amazon, do not. Between centralisation of ordering on the one hand, and increased penetration of the independents by wholesalers on the other, the future for reps is not rosy.

Chains such as Waterstone's are also centralising promotions, leading to the homogenisation of high street bookselling. The range of stock that used to be one of the glories of Waterstone's in particular has inevitably suffered. Promotions such as '3 for 2' or BOGOF (Buy One Get One Free), which are such a common feature in all the chains, arguably get more copies of fewer titles into the hands of more people, but at some cost, one suspects, to the publishers' margins and the authors' royalty accounts. Supermarkets take the process a stage further; if you are one of the few (largely high-profile) authors stocked by the likes of Tesco and Asda you can take pleasure in the expansion – at least in theory – of your readership, but you are entitled to ask whether even your publisher is making any money, let alone you yourself. The demise of Thomas Cork, one of the leading supermarket suppliers, has led to calls for a re-examination of supermarkets' role in the bookselling business.

Publishers

Of course not all the obstacles to literary success lie along the supply chain; some can be laid at the door of the publishers themselves. It is self-evident that booksellers will be disinclined to give a book much shelf space if they feel that the publishers aren't putting any promotion behind it. The higher the advance, the more will be spent on promotion, and the more customers – retailers, wholesalers, library suppliers, etc – will be disposed to give that book adequate display.

Decisions are taken as a book makes its stately way through the publication process – at acquisition meetings, marketing meetings, sales meetings – which can affect its ultimate profile in the marketplace. The author can achieve sudden fame – or notoriety – in another field, for instance, or someone powerful and influential will read a proof and pronounce favourably on it. This sort of thing can provide a boost to the morale of the people whose job it is to sell and market books, and this 'buzz' is passed on to the customers and ultimately to the public. As an editor I would often reflect ruefully on the fact that my enthusiastic advocacy in-house seemed to carry less weight than three lines in the *Bookseller* from paperback pundit Sarah Broadhurst, happy though I was to find her agreeing with me.

On the other hand, it can happen that, for no reason that anybody can put their finger on, a book seems to wither on the vine in the months between acquisition and publication. (Failure to come up with a jacket that anybody likes can be a reason.) 'Surely we didn't really think we were going to sell that many,' someone will say, the print run will be cut (to the accompaniment of outraged bleats from its editor), and the book's chances of making any kind of showing in the marketplace cut accordingly.

And, of course, there are returns, which like the poor are always with us. As the old joke has it: publishers don't sell books, they merely lend them to booksellers. One of the insoluble paradoxes that afflict the book trade is that if a publisher *does* put some energy into selling a book into the trade, an avalanche of returns can be its only reward. "The fact has always remained that an unsaleable book is an unsaleable book no matter how it is dressed up; and it is better not to have it in the supply chain at all, getting in the way of books that do have a market," said Peter Kilborn of Book Industry Communication, an organisation set up by the Publishers Association, Booksellers Association and Library Association (now called CILIP, the Chartered Institute of Library and Information Professionals) and the British Library, and charged *inter alia* with finding a solution to the returns problem. Kilborn's rather Darwinian view is not the whole truth, of course – an unsaleable book is not necessarily a bad book, as any author will tell you. In fact you could make a case for saying that if a book is good enough it will sooner or later be remaindered. But until the problem is solved, a decent showing in a bookshop is only a temporary phenomenon; if the books do not sell quickly enough they will be on their way back to the warehouse in months if not weeks.

Too many books?

So what can the poor author do? While it is certainly the responsibility of publishers to make sure that their products are to be found in bookshops (and far too many books are not so much published as simply made available should anybody happen to want them), it has at least become more possible for authors to make a difference. Online booksellers, while no more immune to cock-ups than their terrestrial counterparts, have made a huge difference to the sheer *availability* of books; the access they offer to writers and their public is absolutely unprecedented. The fact that selling books has been in the forefront of the internet revolution suggests that there is a close correlation between internet users and bookbuyers, and they are out there to be blandished and cajoled. Any author who has a website should make a point of linking to Amazon, or one of the other online booksellers, at the very least. The upcoming print-on-demand revolution means (in theory, at least) that no book need ever go out of print.

"Why isn't my book in the shops?" Everybody seems to agree that too many books are published, though nobody seems disposed to do anything about it, least of all publishers and writers. (Writers may not be incurable optimists, but publishers are.) If your book isn't in the shops, it may simply be that either you or your publisher has failed to differentiate it sufficiently from all the other books in its field, whatever that might be. The odds are not, sadly, on your side. Then again, it's a book trade fact of life that everybody complains; authors complain about publishers and agents, booksellers complain about publishers, publishers complain about absolutely everybody. Yet year after year new discoveries are made, reputations are made, even fortunes are made occasionally. Nothing seems to put writers off writing, including, I trust, the foregoing!

Mike Petty was formerly Editorial Director at Picador, Chatto & Windus, Abacus, Bloomsbury and Victor Gollancz. He now runs the publication programme for the Eden Project. An earlier version of this article appeared in *The Author*, the magazine of the Society of Authors.

Year-in-view of the publishing industry

Joel Rickett reviews changes in the publishing industry during the past 12 months.

A 'perfect storm' has hit the British book trade. It has been buffeted by a high street spending downturn, torn apart by government competition investigations, and rocked by multi-million pound celebrity book deals. There's also a tornado on the horizon in the form of digital content.

The fiercest front has been generated by bookselling chain Ottakar's, which has 140 shops in market towns and cities. Back in August 2005, its charismatic founder James Heneage had grown tired of the vagaries of the stock market, and realised that he needed heavy private investment in stock systems to take the chain to the next level. So he put together a management buyout plan, little knowing that the move would provoke a protracted and bitter ownership battle. Waterstone's, the largest UK bookseller, decided to mount an aggressive takeover. After a series of bids and counter-bids, Waterstone's parent HMV offered an unbeatable £96 million to create a 333-strong chain, nicknamed 'Wottakar's'.

Yet nobody had reckoned on the wrath the deal would provoke among Ottakar's customers, authors and publishers. They lobbied the Office of Fair Trading (OFT), arguing that the deal would restrict choice and diversity in books, with fewer opportunities to break new writers and ever-increasing pressure on royalties. The big shock was that the OFT agreed that consumers valued the fruits of competition between the two chains and referred the bid through to the Competition Commission (CC) for a detailed investigation. Cheers from publishers and authors were short-lived. After 17 weeks of hearings, research and trips to the high street, the CC's finest legal minds were unswayed by the 'anecdotal and impressionistic' arguments against the merger. They said the threat from supermarkets would prevent Waterstone's raising prices, while forces such as Borders and Amazon would stop it cutting back range. A new book that fails to make a '3-for-2' promotion can still get exposure through rival shops, the media and public events; if it starts selling well elsewhere, Waterstone's will quickly notice and start to stock it. Even in a 'Wottakar's' world, there are many routes to readers.

Despite much speculation that WHSmith would enter the fray, at the time of writing Waterstone's looks likely to prevail at the knock-down price of £63 million. That's because both chains had a woeful 2005 Christmas trading period, and their sales stayed in freefall in the first half of 2006. Nobody predicts that HMV will run Ottakar's as a separate set of shops – it wants a greater brand clout for Waterstone's – but it has promised to take on board the 'spirit' of its rival. It can also learn from the way Ottakar's motivates staff, creates alluring children's books sections, and tailors its stock to local tastes.

Supermarket sweep

Despite the torrid state of the high street chains, the overall UK book market continues to grow. Actual till sales of books were up by 3.7% in 2005 compared to the previous year; for the first half of 2006, sales were consistently 5% ahead (Nielsen BookScan). There's no sign of a slump in the appetite for reading.

The discrepancy is explained by the stellar growth of newer areas of book retail, particularly the supermarkets and internet booksellers. Price and convenience are drawing customers away from the high street. In the run-up to the publication of J.K. Rowling's *Harry Potter and the Half-Blood Prince* in summer 2005, Tesco ran a simple but chillingly effective advertising campaign: 'Books. Once upon a time they seemed pricey. So we decided to sell them cheaply. Er – the end'. First day sales of the book were an astonishing 1.9 million copies, and 33% of those were taken by Tesco and Asda – both selling at below half price. It helped Tesco's 2005 book sales leap by 52%. That is not just from obvious bestsellers: some of the larger Tesco Extra stores now stock 3000 paperbacks – including challenging literary fiction and classics – all under £4.

The supermarkets are now shaping the bestseller lists, and influencing where publishers choose to invest their cash. 'Misery memoirs', the life stories of triumph over adversity, show no sign of ceasing – whether from psychologists (Torey Hayden), celebrities (Jenny Tomlin) or even judges (Constance Briscoe). Two tastefully named tomes are due from HarperCollins in late 2006: *Please, Daddy, No* by Stewart Howarth and *Don't Tell Mummy* by Toni Maguire. Britain's celebrity obsession is also spilling into publishing. Bloomsbury bought Gary Barlow's book for an advance of £1 million and Century spent £400,000 on the autobiography of Chantelle from 'Celebrity Big Brother'. Yet even these sums pale into insignificance compared to the £5 million that HarperCollins paid footballer Wayne Rooney, and the $4 million that Random House has gambled on Eric Clapton. The risks are high but the potential rewards are even higher, as shown by Sharon Osbourne's million-selling autobiography *Extreme*. Publishers are frantically repackaging classics to reach these new readers. The commercial Headline list decided to give Jane Austen a makeover, much to the chagrin of the literati. Her novels were given sparkling, wistful covers, subtitled as 'classic romances', and academic introductions were ditched in favour of 'reading group questions'. Even Penguin produced some lower-priced classics with multi-coloured spines, advertising them as the 'best heroes ever written' and the 'best minxes ever written'.

Between the blockbusters and the backlist, the big squeeze has continued. As editors cut back, literary agents are struggling to find homes for well-established authors with loyal readerships. So they are turning to smaller companies or self-publishing to reach a market. The number of books released in the UK in 2005 topped 200,000 – ahead of even the US – and many came from the self-publishing revolution. If authors reach enough readers online or through direct selling, large publishing houses quickly take an interest. And new literary authors can earn astronomical sums, if they have that magic 'accessibility' (e.g. the potential to be picked by Richard & Judy's book club). John Murray paid £450,000 for Oxford academic Michael Cox's Victorian ghost story *The Meaning of Night*, while Orion shelled out an astonishing £800,000 to buy Diana Setterfield's gothic debut *The Thirteenth Tale*.

Get big fast

Spiralling advances are one factor behind publishing consolidation. The new number one UK group is French – Hachette Livre. It bought up Little, Brown in early 2005, adding it to a war chest including Hodder Headline, John Murray, Orion, Octopus, and Chambers Harrap. Hachette now controls about 16% of the UK consumer book market, compared with Random House Group's 14%. But it is unlikely to merge any of the houses: in Paris its myriad publishers compete vigorously, and have even been known to sue each other.

Random will fight back, perhaps with a joint venture deal with BBC Books. The corporate publishing game has become all about scale, as they seek to claw back some precious margin from retailers.

The other imperative for the Little, Brown deal was to give Hachette a foothold into the US market, so it can compete for world rights to books. This is shaping into one of the main challenges for UK publishers, who fear that globalisation and the internet are eroding their hold on international markets. Cheaper US editions are already creeping into the UK via Amazon's Marketplace service, which enables any trader to import and sell via the site.

While the conglomerates wrestle with turf wars and terms structures, their independent cousins focus on the next book. No longer able to guarantee any support from retailers for their titles, they have to whip up media attention, find readers online, and hope for literary awards wins. Proving that this formula can pay dividends is radical Serpent's Tail, with a treble of prizes: the John Llewellyn Rhys Prize for Jonathan Trigell's *Boy A*, the Orange Prize for Lionel Shriver's *We Need to Talk About Kevin*, and the Nobel Prize for *Elfriede Jelinek*. That's why publishers breathed a sigh of relief when sponsorship of the Whitbread Book Awards was picked up by Costa Coffee, while financial group Man re-affirmed its commitment to the Booker Prize.

Another independent success story is a resurgent (and profitable) Faber, which has joined with a handful of fellow indies to build a formidable 'sales alliance'. These include feisty Profile Books, which had three titles in the Christmas 2005 Top 10: quirky science book *Does Anything Eat Wasps?*, Alan Bennett's magisterial *Untold Stories*, and Lynne Truss's polite polemic *Talk to the Hand*. There's also no shortage of new entrepreneurs, such as Bitter Lemon Press, Arris Publishing, Portobello, Cyan, Snowbooks and Reverb. Two start-ups have the backing of Orion founder Anthony Cheetham: web-to-books imprint the Friday Project, and the energetic Quercus, which is balancing contract publishing with accessible non-fiction, crime and women's fiction lists.

There's a growing alliance between these houses and their bookselling counterparts. Independent bookshops have had a bad press, and it is true that many have been forced to shut. But there are plenty of fantastic shops left serving their local communities with verve. Think of London's Daunt Books, catering to affluent buyers, a revived Foyles, or the delightfully idiosyncratic Silverdell of Kirkham, which sells ice-cream alongside books and hosts barnstorming author signings. There's even a potent campaign 'Love Your Local Bookshop' campaign, instigated by Hertfordshire indie Books@Hoddesdon.

And as giant publishers become ever more focused on sales and marketing, editors who want to work more closely with authors are becoming literary agents. Big names making the leap recently include Caroline Michel, who left HarperCollins to run the William Morris agency, Patrick Janson-Smith, who left Transworld to join J. K. Rowling's agent Christopher Little, and Orion co-founder Rosie de Courcy, who has became Editorial Director of young agency Mulcahy & Viney. To fill the gaps, publishers recruited staff from retailers.

The digital divide

Digital developments continue apace. Amazon.co.uk has gone finally live with its Search Inside the Book service, opening the text of 125,000 titles for search. Amazon insists it helps sell more books, but many trade publishers remain unconvinced. HarperCollins, Orion, Pearson, Time Warner and Simon & Schuster are all signed up, but there is no sign of Penguin, Macmillan, or Random House joining them. Unsurprisingly Bloomsbury is not on board – its chief, Nigel Newton, has warned against opening a 'Pandora's box' of free online content. His main target was Google, whose ambitious plan to digitise millions of books held by libraries hit some serious hurdles. In the US and around Europe, groups of authors and publishers have filed lawsuits against the search giant, charging it with theft of intellectual property.

The sensible thing would be for publishers to scan and digitise their own books and then make excerpts available online while controlling access and copyright. Macmillan is developing a searchable online repository of digital book content, while HarperCollins and Random House are investing millions of pounds in digitising their backlists. While no e-book device has yet caught on – people still don't want to read novels on their Blackberrys – it is surely only a matter of time.

Learn to 'Love Libraries'

Another part of the book world affected by digitisation is libraries; swathes of their reference collections have gone online, while local library branches have been neglected or shut by councils. Publishers have tried to ride to the rescue: under the banner of Reading Partners' 30 projects were trialed, including library promotions based on what other borrowers are reading. Of most value has been access to library-based reading groups, helping to stimulate word-of-mouth as well as get feedback on covers, editing and promotion. They also backed the 'Love Libraries' campaign, a bid to visualise a '21st-century reading service'. The project began with a daytime television-style makeover of three libraries in Newquay, Gravesend and Richmond: their interiors were remodelled, opening hours reviewed, and book stocks overhauled.

Any summary of the publishing year cannot close without mention of the *Da Vinci Code* plagiarism trial, which held the bestselling novel of modern times to the full glare of the High Court and the world's media. The extraordinary contention of historians Michael Baigent and Richard Leigh was that Dan Brown stole the 'architecture' of their 1982 tome *The Holy Blood and the Holy Grail*, which itself was 'speculative history'. Unsurprisingly the judge threw the case out, but included his very own cryptic code in his verdict.

Joel Rickett is Deputy Editor of the *Bookseller*. He writes a weekly column on the publishing industry for the *Guardian*, and a monthly column for the film magazine *Screen International*. He sat on the judging panels for the Booktrust Teenage Prize 2006 and the *Observer's* 2006 Publishing Power List.

Who owns whom in publishing

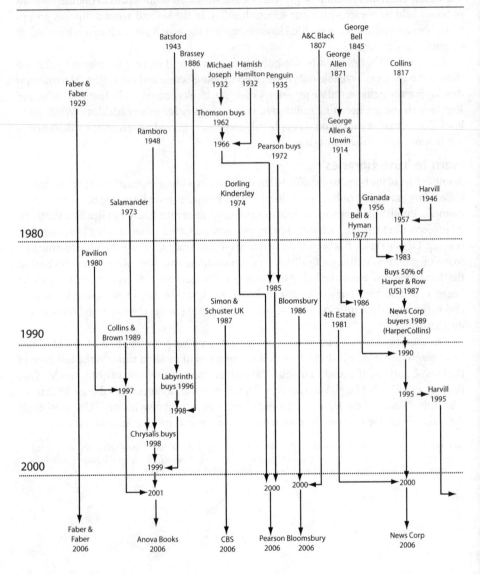

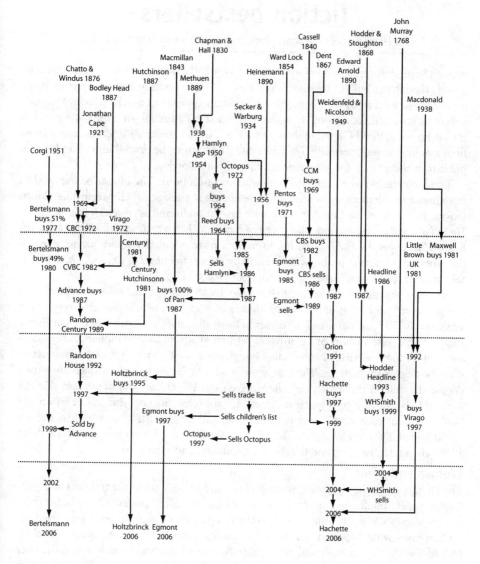

© Christopher Gasson

One hundred years of fiction bestsellers

Alex Hamilton pulls out some plums from 20th century fiction bestsellers.

Among bestsellers published before the Great War half a dozen authors' names still echo faintly, though the bulk of their work is little read. Gene Stratton Porter's *Freckles*, based on her life in a cabin by a swamp, sold two million copies, but is valued today only as a collectors' first edition. Among them also was Winston Churchill – not the statesman, but the author of *Richard Carvel*, the story of a naval officer under Paul Jones, selling more than a million copies, and with *The Crisis* and *The Crossing* he proved himself to be what publishers always look for – a career novelist with a following.

Frank Norris likewise promised well, when his fifth book, *The Pit*, scaled the heights, but almost simultaneously he died of appendicitis at the age of 32. Meanwhile Conan Doyle, the stayer of this bunch, peaked with his most admired Sherlock Holmes tale, *The Hound of the Baskervilles*, and when tired of him launched a second serial character, Professor Challenger, in *The Lost World*. Even their huge popularity could not quite match the exotica of Elinor Glyn who, with five million sales of her novel of passion, *Three Weeks*, set a marker for all candidates for the Number One spot.

If unable to write a book selling five million, try writing five that sell one million. This was more or less a habit of prolific producers of Westerns, whose pioneers were Owen Wister with *The Virginians*, and the daddy of them all, Zane Grey, with *Riders of the Purple Range*. These were authors of a genre that celebrated adventure and individual heroics in a way of life that was virtually obsolete. Though not a Western writer, Jack London in this sense belongs with them: his *The Call of the Wild*, whose heroics were actually those of a dog, sold a million and a half, and *The Sea Wolf* and *White Fang* almost as many. He was reputed to be the best-paid writer in America. Zane Grey, the Englishman J.T. Edson and Louis L'Amour each wrote more than 100 titles and for the latter the publishers claim a world sale of 270 million copies. The Western went great guns, so to speak, until about 1970, when relentless film and television exploitation had exhausted it.

Women and crime

The circumstances of long wars, when authors and readers are in the trenches and publishers' paper supplies are cut back, are a drag on bestselling books. All the same, there were women's names to conjure with in the Great War: Eleanor Porter, who passed the million mark with *Pollyanna*, the girl whose policy it was to be glad regardless; Ethel M. Dell of *The Way of an Eagle* and *Bars of Iron*, whose villains were hardly worse than her sadistic heroes; Mary Roberts Rinehart, first bestselling woman writer of detective fiction and, with *The Circular Staircase* and *K*, setting a rough-and-ready example for a later generation.

Their 'Golden Age' came in the Thirties and Forties. With a 350 million sales total Agatha Christie was top cat, marketed as 'A Christie for Christmas'. For some 50 years she always offered a puzzle, with her Belgian detective Hercule Poirot on hand to solve it until, like Conan Doyle, she took against her odd hero and switched to a second series character,

Miss Marple – with 66 detective stories published altogether. Most in demand were *The Murder of Roger Ackroyd* and *Murder on the Orient Express.* Belgium was not so much proud of Poirot as of the hundreds of brilliant atmospheric crime stories featuring Inspector Maigret by their author Georges Simenon, whose wife was rightly a martinet to scores of foreign translators (recording a thousand translations).

Other women crime writers climbing the ladder behind Christie included Margery Allingham and the New Zealander Ngaio Marsh; Dorothy L. Sayers, who fanned out the subdivisions of the genre editing her jumbo mystery anthologies, intrigued fans with *The Unpleasantness at the Bellona Club* and *Nine Tailors*, with their mandarin style and affected hero, Lord Peter Wimsey. All these and their equally popular male contemporaries, such as Erle Stanley Gardner (not far behind Christie), John Dickson Carr, S.S. Van Dine and Ellery Queen (who named his detective after himself), produced a relatively mild climate of crime compared with later developments, when the ethos (as with the Western in its declining years) turned nasty. Because of its capacity for change, the dexterity of its authors and the sheer bloody-mindedness of its personnel, the crime story has been the dominant genre of the century, even ahead of the romance in its many guises.

Between the wars

Between the wars the entertainers whom today we'd call 'brand names' were: P.G. Wodehouse, creator of *Jeeves* and frothy social comedies whose bubbles have not yet burst; E. Phillips Oppenheim, who lived luxury and deployed it in his high-life fiction, writing 100 books, mostly with a relay of mistresses on his yacht on the Riviera known as 'the floating double bed'; Rafael Sabatini, boisterous historical romantic, best known for *Captain Blood* and *The Sea Hawk*; Jeffrey Farnol, fey and sentimental, as in *The Chronicles of the Imp*; and Sapper, pseudonym for an ex-army officer who was the progenitor of a crude racist type of spy story, with *Bulldog Drummond* selling six million copies. The series was continued nine times after Sapper's death by another ex-army officer (much as Kingsley Amis and John Gardner kept James Bond going after the death of his creator, Ian Fleming). And who could resist the publisher's banner that declared, 'It is impossible not to be thrilled by Edgar Wallace'? He was a journalist able to turn his Dictaphone to any form in his 'factory of fiction', piling up 170 novels in three decades: African adventure with *Sanders of the River*, much melodrama – some, like *The Crimson Circle*, with a brilliant premise – and umpteen thrillers. On his death in 1931, when a packet of cigarettes cost 3d, a trade paperback 2s and a cottage £100, his royalties were running at £75,000 a year.

Beside the genre favourites, there were some *sui generis* storytellers with powerful appeal. Edna Ferber won a Pulitzer Prize in 1925 with *So Big*, followed it with *Show Boat*, and 25 years later when approaching 70, she came up with *Giant*. Pearl S. Buck also won a Pulitzer Prize (in 1932) with *The Good Earth*, which later won the Nobel Prize and led to five million sales. The Southern writer Erskine Caldwell won a $1000 prize from the *Yale Review* for a short story, but his real money-spinners were *God's Little Acre* with eight million sales, and *Tobacco Road* with four million sales plus, as a play, the then longest stage run in American theatre history.

Two other big books, physically and commercially, were historical romances. At several hundred thousand words they seemed to be trying to reinstate the Victorian three-decker in one volume. Margaret Mitchell's *Gone with the Wind* sold eight million copies before the war, took her 10 years to write and was her only book. Hervey Allen's *Anthony Adverse*, the baby-on-the-doorstep who grows up an adventurer, took him five years to write, but he was tougher than Mitchell and produced more hefty novels, even a trilogy, though never with the same *éclat*. By contrast James Hilton took only four days over *Goodbye Mr Chips*, a slight book to add to his other slight book, *Lost Horizon*, about a remote mountain paradise called Shangri-La, but both were commercial heavyweights.

The Second World War and after

The rising flow of big sellers was partly stalled by shortages in the Second World War. The force in fiction lay increasingly with Americans: John Steinbeck's *The Grapes of Wrath*, Ernest Hemingway's *For Whom the Bell Tolls* and the Lutheran minister Lloyd C. Douglas's novel deriving from the Crucifixion, *The Robe*, which accumulated four million sales. Near the end Kathleen Winsor added a saucy three million seller set in the time of Charles II, *Forever Amber*. The two British authors with similar results were Daphne du Maurier, whose *Rebecca* was brilliantly served by the Hitchcock movie (and *Frenchman's Creek* less well) and Somerset Maugham, a lifelong bestseller since 1915, with *The Razor's Edge*. Every one of the last dozen books mentioned was filmed, which of course prompted a second wave of sales.

In the immediate aftermath of the war there was no sudden eruption of blockbusters, despite the launch of new publishing houses and a growth in the number of titles that seems to have continued exponentially to the present day. However, two books carrying blatant messages had the rare distinction among bestsellers of being politically motivated: George Orwell's *Animal Farm*, followed by *1984*, which in 20 years each sold eight million copies. Between them appeared Norman Mailer's emotional response to the war, *The Naked and the Dead*, with a relatively modest three million sales.

The Fifties

In the Fifties the trade geared itself to a clutch of uncouth authors. The notable example is Mickey Spillane, who at one time had seven of his brutal thrillers in the Top 10, led by *I, the Jury*, all selling more than five million copies. Harold Robbins first showed at this time with *Never Love a Stranger* and *The Dream Merchants*, opening shots in a bombardment that for his total *oeuvre* eventually topped 150 million. Charts of two decades were overwhelmed by the glamour and snobbery of Ian Fleming's James Bond stories, starting with *Casino Royale*, and selling unbridled millions (40 plus) to this day. The archetypal blockbusters of the period were novels such as *Airport* and *Wheels* by Arthur Hailey, exploring the works of large organisations; *Peyton Place* by Grace Metalious, in tandem with its long-running television series, and slightly more serious, the vast doorstoppers by James Michener, *South Pacific* and *Hawaii*.

More lasting successes include *To Kill a Mockingbird* by Harper Lee, a classic of racist conflict in the American South, helped on beyond 10 million sales by its prescription for educational courses (William Golding's *Lord of the Flies* benefits in the same way); Joseph Heller's satire on military bureaucracy *Catch-22*, and the reclusive J.D. Salinger's *Catcher in the Rye*, a percentage of whose six million copies are said to have been urged by teenage girls on their boyfriends. Vladimir Nabokov's story of a middle-aged man's obsession with and seduction by a sub-teen girl, *Lolita*, seems to presage the imminent conflicts over censorship in the Sixties. The major test was the trial of Penguin Books in 1960, which ironically made a six million seller of perhaps the least of D.H. Lawrence's novels, *Lady Chatterley's Lover*, banned on its first publication 32 years earlier.

The Sixties

In the Sixties several books were boosted into orbit not so much by their actual sexual content as by the fuss that was made over it: *Candy* by Terry Southern, *Tropic of Cancer* by Henry Miller, *The Exhibitionist* by Henry Sutton, *Couples* by John Updike, *Portnoy's Complaint* by Philip Roth and *Myra Breckinridge* by Gore Vidal. Apart from Vidal, these writers' sales rarely returned to the highest level, despite their range and brilliance. The newcomers who appeared in the Top 10 and retained their position, as it were by right, were Irving Stone with his biographical novels, such as *The Agony and the Ecstasy* (about Michelangelo), Jacqueline Susann with the showbiz misery of *Valley of the Dolls* (10 million sales over 20 years), Mario Puzo with *The Godfather* (12 million), and two who changed the character of the thriller with their grasp of the intricacies of the Cold War: John le Carré opened with *The Spy Who Came in from the Cold*, while Len Deighton challenged Ian Fleming's picture of espionage with his first, *The Ipcress File*. For nearly 40 years there was always a new Deighton book high on the charts, until he called a halt on himself.

The Seventies and after

Other tireless British regulars over the last quarter of a century included the gothic romances of Victoria Holt, the adventures set in Africa by Wilbur Smith and the northern sagas of Catherine Cookson, whose paperback sales at her death had reached 55 million. Beginning with *The Day of the Jackal,* there was usually a million-selling thriller by Frederick Forsyth, and an automatic sale to half a million fans ready for the annual racecourse mystery from Dick Francis. Ahead of them all were the novels that Jeffrey Archer contrived from the extraordinary 'snakes and ladders' pattern of his own life, starting with *Not a Penny More, Not a Penny Less.* Across the eighties some would rack up close on five million copies, though slightly shaded by the actual top seller of the decade, the humorous *Secret Diary of Adrian Mole Aged 13¾* by Sue Townsend.

Almost as many American as British authors figured every year in the 100 fastsellers from British publishers between 1980 and 2000. One phenomenon was Stephen King, the most read horror writer after William Blatty's 10 million for *The Exorcist*, always among the leaders with massive frighteners such as *IT* and *Pet Sematary*. The other who never missed was Danielle Steel, who would prefer that her novels were not called romances, and who, like King and Cookson, sometimes had two or three titles in the same list. In the nineties John Grisham virtually took over the Number One spot with his thrillers about corporation lawyers and their illegal habits. As the millennium approached, however, he had to give way to J.K. Rowling. She with her *Harry Potter* series, and Dan Brown with his conspiracy thrillers, set an undreamt of pace for the 21st century.

Inevitably many unputdownable titles and storytellers are omitted from this fiction survey. Everyone will have a favourite that's been missed. Apologies from **Alex Hamilton**, who kept the *Guardian* Fastseller Chart for the last 25 years.

Vanity publishing

Mainstream publishers invest their own money in the entire publishing process. In contrast, vanity publishers require an up-front payment to produce a book. Johnathon Clifford highlights the perils of vanity publishing.

My research into vanity publishing began in 1990 when a 12-year-old girl wrote to me in my position as founder and Senior Trustee of the National Poetry Foundation, saying she had found a publisher willing to publish her work. I telephoned the 'publisher' under the guise of an aspiring author, and this call was all it took for them to agree to publish my work. Their offer was 100 copies of a 38-page book for a fee of £1900, with no need for them to see my poetry first.

> ### Definition of vanity publishing
>
> 'Vanity publishing, also self-styled (often inaccurately) as 'subsidy', 'joint-venture', 'shared-responsibility' or even 'self' publishing, is a service whereby authors are charged to have their work published. Vanity publishers generally offer to publish a book for a specific fee, or offer to include short stories, poems or other literary or artistic material in an anthology, which the authors are then invited to buy.'
>
> – Advertising Standards Authority definition of vanity publishing, 1997

Since then, I have written *Vanity Press & The Proper Poetry Publishers*, a book based on my extensive feedback from vanity companies, assisted the Advertising Standards Authority and collaborated in the making of television and radio programmes. In 1999, I was invited to the House of Lords to talk about the problem of vanity publishing and the need for a change in the law to stop 'rogue traders' in the publishing world. Despite receiving letters of support from 58 MPs, a change to the existing law has yet to be implemented. As a consequence, I set up an 'awareness campaign' consisting of a website and a free advice pack in an effort to protect aspiring authors. The pack, apart from highlighting the business practices of vanity publishers, gives advice on finding a mainstream publisher, internet publishing, the market for short stories and self-publishing. To date, well over 27,000 copies have been requested.

The perils of vanity publishing

'Vanity publisher' is a phrase I coined in the early 1960s when two American companies were advertising widely in the British press offering to publish poems for £9 and £12 per poem, respectively. Since then the term has also come to mean 'any company that charges a client to publish a book'.

Mainstream publishers invest in the promotion of a book and make their profit from the sale of copies of the book. Vanity publishers, on the other hand, make money from up-front charges. One of the main drawbacks of being published by a vanity publisher is its lack of credibility within the industry. The majority of booksellers and library suppliers are loath to handle vanity books and few reviewers are willing to consider a book published in this way. The Business Unit Director of one of the UK's biggest booksellers wrote: 'We do not buy from vanity publishers except in exceptional circumstances. Their books are, with one or two exceptions, badly produced, over-priced, have poor, uncompetitive jackets and usually have no marketing support.'

I have amassed an extensive collection of documentation from authors who have approached some of the 100-plus vanity publishers operating in the UK. It consists of vanity publishers' initial promotional letters, subsequent written promises, the contracts and letters of complaint from the author, and the vanity publishers' response to those complaints. In recent years, court judgements have found that some vanity publishers are guilty of 'gross misrepresentation of the services they offer' and, as a result, some have been successfully sued and some forced into 'voluntary' liquidation – often only to swiftly reappear under different names.

How vanity publishers operate

Mainstream publishers never advertise for authors and almost never charge a client, whether known or unknown. Vanity publishers place advertisements wherever they possibly can inviting authors to submit manuscripts. Almost without exception, when authors submit work the vanity publisher will reply that they would like to publish the book but that, as an unknown, the author will have to pay towards the cost. Vanity publishers may tell the author they are very selective in the authors they accept and praise the work, but this is false flattery. I have not been able to find one person during the last 14 years, anywhere in the world, who has been turned down by a vanity publisher – however poorly written their book is. The vanity publisher may state that this is the way many famous authors in the past set out. This is untrue: not one of the quoted 'famous authors' started their writing career by paying a vanity publisher. The BBC programme *Southern Eye* reported that many authors had been sent exactly the same 'glowing report', whatever the subject or quality of their book.

Vanity publishers have charged aspiring authors anything from £1800 up to (in one recorded instance) £20,000 for publishing their book. Many authors have borrowed thousands of pounds on the strength of promised 'returning royalties', as authors are often led to believe that the vanity publisher's marketing department will sell their book for them and that they will recoup their outlay via this service. In December 1997, *Private Eye* ran an article about three authors, one of whom had paid £2400 and the other two £1800 each to a vanity publisher, on the basis that their books would command a 'high level of royalties'. These royalties amounted to £16.35, £21.28 and £47.30 respectively. When the authors complained they each received a threatening letter from the vanity publisher's solicitor. The same company's business practices were featured on the BBC programme *Watchdog* in November 2002.

Some vanity publishers ask their clients to pay a 'subvention'. The standard dictionary definition of the word subvention is 'a grant, aid or subsidy paid by a government to an educational institution', so the term is meaningless when used in the context of vanity publishing. The bottom line, however the request for payment is worded, is that the author will bear the full cost of publishing the book. Not a share of, or a subsidy towards, but all the costs and a profit margin on top.

Few vanity publishers quote for a fixed number of copies, leaving the author with little idea what they have paid for. Vanity publishers may simply keep manuscripts 'on file' and only print-on-demand, making it difficult to deliver copies quickly enough to the outlets who *do* order them. There are also companies who propose that once book sales have reached a certain 'target' figure, the client's outlay will be refunded. The number of copies required to be sold is always well in excess of a realistic target.

Some companies claim that part of the service they offer is to send copies of your book to Whitakers, the Copyright Receipt Office and the British Library. In fact, this is a legal requirement for all UK publishers. Other companies claim a 'special' relationship which enables them to supply information on your book to particular outlets on the internet. But Amazon.co.uk, the biggest internet bookseller, does not support this and writes: 'Books are listed on Amazon.co.uk's website in a number of ways – we take feeds from BookData and Whitakers (who automatically update these details on our website) as well as from several wholesalers'.

Authors choosing to vanity publish should be aware that as soon as their last instalment has been paid, the vanity publisher has made maximum profit and does not need to sell a single copy of the author's book.

Self-publishing

Another way for an author to see their book in print is to self-publish (see my website and free Advice Pack). However, since self-publishing has become more acceptable some vanity publishers have tried to pass themselves off as self-publishers. For a book to be genuinely self-published, a name designated by the author as his or her publishing house must appear on the copyright page of the book as 'publisher' and the book's ISBN number must be registered by the ISBN Agency to that author as publisher.

All the copies of a self-published book are the property of the author. If an author does not wish to be involved with the sale and distribution of their book, this can be indicated in the 'Distributor (if different from Publisher)' section on the form sent to the ISBN Agency before publication.

On the title page of every book there is a paragraph which, in essence, states that 'All rights are reserved. No part of this book can be stored on a retrieval system or transmitted in any form or by whatever means without the prior permission in writing from the publisher'. I repeat, without the prior permission of the *publisher*. Not 'the author' who is supposed to have '*self*-published'.

Any company which publishes books under its own name or imprint cannot, by definition, claim to help authors to self-publish. True self-publishing gives authors much greater control over the production and dissemination of their books.

Finally...

Aspiring authors should be careful not to be taken in by the promises of some vanity publishers which have so often proved false. The legal phrase 'Caveat Emptor' (Buyer Beware) here becomes 'Caveat Scriptor' – 'Author Beware!'

Johnathon Clifford may be contacted on *tel* (01329) 822218 or via his website: www.vanitypublishing.info

Publishing agreements

Publisher's agreements are not a standard form and authors must take nothing for granted.
Michael Legat navigates the reader through this complex document.

Any author, presented with so complex a document as a publisher's agreement, should read it carefully before signing, making sure that every clause is understood, and not taking anything for granted. Bear in mind that there is no such thing as a standard form. A given publisher's 'standard' contract may not only differ substantially from those of other publishers, but will often vary from author to author and from book to book. Don't be fooled into believing that it is a standard form because it appears to have been printed – most agreements are individually produced on a word processor to give exactly that effect.

A fair and reasonable agreement

You should be able to rely on your agent, if you have one, to check the agreement for you, or – if you are a member – you can get it vetted by the Society of Authors or theWriters' Guild of Great Britain. But if you are on your own, you must either go to one of the solicitors who specialise in publishing business (probably expensive) or Do It Yourself. In the latter case it will help to compare the contract you have been offered, clause by clause, with a typical Minimum Terms Agreement such as those printed in my own books, *An Author's Guide to Publishing* and *Understanding Publishers' Contracts*.

Minimum Terms Agreement

The Minimum Terms Agreement (MTA), developed jointly by the Society of Authors and the Writers' Guild, is signed by a publisher on the one hand and the Society and the Guild on the other. It is not an agreement between a publisher and an individual author. It commits the publisher to offering his or her authors terms which are at least as good as those in the MTA. The intention is that only members of the Society and the Guild should be eligible for this special treatment, but in practice publishers who sign the agreement tend to offer its terms to all their authors. There is no standard MTA, and most signatory publishers have insisted on certain variations in the agreement; nevertheless, the more important basic principles have always been accepted. It must be pointed out that the MTA does not usually apply to:

- books in which illustrations take up 40% or more of the space;
- specialist works on the visual arts in which illustrations fill 25% or more of the space;
- books involving three or more participants in royalties; or
- technical books, manuals and reference books.

Since its origins in 1980, comparatively few publishers have signed a Minimum Terms Agreement, although the signatories include several major publishing houses. Some publishers have refused, claiming to treat their authors quite well enough already, while others say that each author and each book is so different that standard terms cannot be laid down. Nonetheless, the MTA has been a resounding success. Almost all non-signatory publishers have adopted some or all of its provisions, and even in the case of the excluded books mentioned above, the terms have tended to improve. All authors can now argue, from a position of some strength, that their own agreements should meet the MTA's standards.

The provisions of the MTA

The MTA is a royalty agreement (usually the most satisfactory form for an author), and it lays down the minimum acceptable royalties on sales, and the levels at which the rate should rise. These royalties are expressed as percentages of the book's retail price but can easily be adjusted to apply to royalties based on price received, a system to which a number of publishers are changing, increasing the percentages so that the author's earnings are not adversely affected. The MTA also covers the size of the advance (calculated in accordance with the expected initial print quantity and retail price), and recommended splits between publisher and author of moneys from the sale of subsidiary rights (including US and translation rights).

However, the MTA is not by any means concerned solely with money, but with fairness to the author in all clauses of a publishing agreement, special attention being paid to provisions designed to make the author/publisher relationship more of a partnership than it has often been in the past. While recognising the publisher's right to take final decisions on such matters as print quantity, publication date, retail price, jacket or cover design, wording of the blurb, promotion and publicity, and remaindering, the MTA insists that the author has a right to consultation (which should not be an empty formality but should mean that serious consideration is given to his or her views), in all such cases. Also the author's approval must be sought for the sale of any subsidiary rights.

Some essential clauses

Any publisher's agreement you sign should contain, in addition to acceptable financial terms, clauses covering:

- **Rights licensed.** A clear definition of whichrights you are licensing to the publisher. The publisher will normally require volume rights but the agreement must specify whether such rights will apply in all languages (or perhaps only in English) and throughout the world (or only in an agreed list of territories). The duration of the publisher's licence should be spelt out; commonly this is for the period of copyright (currently the author's lifetime plus 70 years), although some publishers now accept a shorter term. A list of those subsidiary rights of which control is granted to the publisher must be included (make sure that the splits of moneys earned from these rights are in accordance with, or approximate reasonably to, those in the MTA, especially in the currently growing area of merchandising).
- **Publication date.** Commitment by the publisher to publication of the book by a specific date (usually within a year or 18 months from the delivery of the typescript). Avoid signing an agreement which is vague on this point, saying, for instance, only that the book will be published 'within a reasonable period'.
- **Copyright.** Confirmation that in all copies of the book the publisher will print a copyright notice in the author's name and a statement that the author has asserted his or her 'Right of Paternity' (the right to be identified as the author in future exploitation of the material in any form), and that a similar commitment will be required from any subsidiary licensee.
- **Fees and permissions.** Clarification, if the book is to include a professionally prepared index or material the copyright of which does not belong to the author, of whether the author or the publisher will be responsible for the fees (or if costs are to be shared, in what proportions) and the clearance of permissions.
- **Acceptable accounting procedures.** Most publishers divide the year into two six-month periods, accounting to the author, and paying any sums due, three months after the end

of each period. Look askance at any less frequent accounting or longer delay after the royalty period. The publisher should also agree to pay the author the due share of any subsidiary moneys promptly on receipt, provided that the advance on the book has been earned.

- **Termination**. A clear definition of the various conditions under which the agreement shall be terminated, with reversion of rights to the author.

Clauses to question

You can question anything in a publisher's agreement before you sign it. Provided that you do so politely and are not just being difficult, the publisher should be prepared to answer every query, to explain, and where possible to meet your objections. Most publishing contracts are not designed to exploit the author unfairly, but you should watch out for:

- **Rights assigned elsewhere**. It is unwise to accept a clause which allows the publisher to assign the rights in your book to another firm or person without your approval.
- **Non-publication.** The contract for a commissioned book often includes wording which alludes to the publisher's acceptance of the work, implying that there is no obligation to publish it if he or she deems it unacceptable. It may be understandable that the publisher wants an escape route in case the author turns in an inferior work, but he or she should be obliged to justify the rejection, and to give the author an opportunity to revise the work to bring it up to standard. If, having accepted the book, the publisher then wishes to cancel the contract prior to publication, the author can usually expect to receive financial compensation, which should be non-returnable even if the book is subsequently placed with another publisher. However, this point is not normally covered in a publishing agreement.
- **Sole publisher**. Some agreements prohibit the author from writing similar material for any other publisher. This may clearly affect the author's earning ability.
- **Editing consultation**. Don't agree to the publisher's right to edit your work without any requirement for him or her to obtain your approval of any changes made.
- **Royalty rate**. While it is normal practice for an agreement to allow the publisher to pay a lower royalty on books which are sold at high trade discounts, such sales are more frequently made nowadays than in the past, and it is essential to make sure the royalty rate on high discount sales is not unfairly low.
- **Future books**. The Society of Authors and the Writers' Guild are both generally opposed to clauses giving the publisher the right to publish the author's next work, feeling that this privilege should be earned by the publisher's handling of the earlier book. If you accept an option clause, at least make sure that it leaves all terms for a future book to be agreed.

Electronic and other multimedia rights

The importance of electronic, digital and other multimedia rights, which already require a carefully worded clause in a contract, is likely to increase in years to come, when the only form of publication for a book may be on the internet or whatever may replace it as technology develops. In the meantime publishers, on the one hand, and literary agents and authors' organisations on the other, are in dispute about these rights, including other rights as yet unknown.

The two main issues are concerned with control of the rights and with royalties. Should these rights remain in the direct control of the author (possibly negotiating through an agent) or, as publishers maintain, be regarded as a part of volume rights, and therefore licensed to the publisher? If the publisher controls the rights, should the author receive a royalty of 15% or thereabouts on the publisher's receipts from sales of these rights, or at least 50% of the income, as the Society of Authors and the Association of Authors' Agents insist is fair? Until some agreement has been reached on these and other matters, it is advisable for authors to seek advice on suitable wording of the relevant clause from a literary agent or the Society of Authors or any other established body representing writers.

Joint and multiple authorship

In the case of joint authorship (a work so written that the individual contributions of the authors cannot be readily separated), the first written agreement should be between the authors themselves, setting out the proportions in which any moneys earned by the book will be split, specifying how the authors' responsibilities are to be shared, and especially laying down the procedure to be adopted should the authors ever find themselves in dispute. The terms of any publishing agreement which they sign (each author having an identical copy) should reflect their joint understanding. The total earnings should not be less than would be paid were the book by a single author, and the authors should have normal rights of consultation.

In the case of multiple authorship (when the work of each contributor can be clearly separated), each author is likely to have an individual contract, and may not be aware of what terms are offered to the others involved. Because of the possibility of disagreement between the authors, the publisher will probably offer little in the way of consultation. All the individual author can do is to ensure that the agreement appears to be fair in relation to the amount of work contributed, and that the author's responsibilities indicated by the contract refer only to his or her work.

Outright sale

As a general rule no author should agree to surrender his or her copyright to the publisher, although this may be unavoidable in the case of a book with many contributors, such as an encyclopedia. Even then, give up your copyright with great reluctance and only after an adequate explanation from the publisher of why you should (and probably a substantial financial inducement, including, if possible, provision for the payment of a further fee each time the book is reprinted). The agreement itself will probably be no more than a brief and unequivocal letter.

Subsidies and vanity publishing

Few commercial publishers will be interested in publishing your book on a subsidy basis (i.e. with a contribution from you towards costs), unless perhaps it is of a serious, highly specialised nature, such as an academic monograph, when a publisher who is well established within that particular field will certainly behave with probity and offer a fair contract. Vanity publishers, on the other hand, will accept your book with enthusiasm, ask for 'a small contribution to production costs' (which turns out to be a very substantial sum, not a penny of which you are likely to see again), and will fail to achieve any sales for your book apart from the copies which you yourself buy. If you want to put your own money into the publication of your book, try self-publishing (see page 264) – you will be far better off than going to a vanity house. How do you tell which are the vanity publishers? That's easy – they're the ones who put advertisements in the papers saying things like, 'Authors Wanted!'. Regular publishers don't need to do that.

Michael Legat became a full-time writer after a long and successful publishing career. He is the author of a number of highly regarded books on publishing and writing.

Further reading

Clark, Charles (ed.), *Publishing Agreements: A Book of Precedents*, Tottel Publishing, 6th edn, 2002
Flint, Michael F., *A User's Guide to Copyright*, Tottel Publishing, 6th edn, 2006
Legat, Michael, *An Author's Guide to Publishing*, Robert Hale, 3rd edn revised, 1998
Legat, Michael, *Understanding Publishers' Contracts*, Robert Hale, 2nd edn revised, 2002
Unwin, Sir Stanley, *The Truth About Publishing*, HarperCollins, 8th edn, 1976, o.p.

FAQs about ISBNs

The ISBN Agency receives a large number of enquiries about the ISBN system. The most frequently asked questions are answered here.

What is an ISBN?

An ISBN (International Standard Book Number) is a product identifier used by publishers, booksellers and libraries for ordering, listing and stock control purposes. It enables them to identify a specific edition of a specific title in a specific format from a particular publisher. The digits are always divided into four parts, separated by spaces or hyphens. The four parts can be of varying length and are as follows:

Contact details

UK ISBN Agency
3rd Floor, Midas House, 62 Goldsworth Road, Woking GU21 6LQ
tel (0870) 777 8712 *fax* (0870) 777 8714
email isbn@nielsenbookdata.co.uk
website www.isbn.nielsenbookdata.co.uk

● Group Identifier – Identifies a national, geographic or language grouping of publishers. It tells you which of these groupings the publisher belongs to (not the language of the book).

● Publisher Identifier – Identifies a specific publisher or imprint.

● Title Number – Identifies a specific edition of a specific title in a specific format.

● Check Digit – This is always and only the final digit which mathematically validates the rest of the number.

Prior to 2007 ISBNs were always 10 digits long, but all publications from 1 January 2007 onwards will be assigned a 13-digit ISBN. The change is necessary to cope with the dramatically increasing rate of publications.

Do all books need to have an ISBN?

There is no legal requirement for an ISBN and it conveys no form of legal or copyright protection. It is a product identifier.

What can be gained from using an ISBN?

If you wish to sell your publication through major bookselling chains, or internet booksellers, they will require you to have an ISBN to assist their internal processing and ordering systems. The ISBN also provides access to Bibliographic Databases such as BookData's BookFind–Online, which are organised using ISBNs as references. These databases are used by the book trade: publishers, booksellers and libraries for internal purposes, to provide information for customers and to source and order titles. The ISBN therefore provides access to additional marketing opportunities which assist the sales of books and other published media.

Where can we get an ISBN?

ISBN prefixes are assigned to publishers in the country in which the publisher is based by the national agency for that country. The UK and Republic of Ireland Agency is run by Neilsen BookData. The Agency introduces new publishers to the system, assigns prefixes to new and existing publishers and deals with any queries or problems in using the system. The UK ISBN Agency was the first ISBN agency in the world and has been instrumental in the set up and maintenance of the ISBN. Publishers based elsewhere will not be able to get numbers from the UK Agency but may contact them for details of the relevant agency in their market.

Who is eligible for ISBNs?

Any organisation or individual who is publishing a qualifying product for general sale or distribution to the market is eligible (see 'Which products do not qualify for ISBNs?').

What is a publisher?

It is sometimes difficult to decide who the publisher is and who their agent may be, but the publisher is generally the person or body which takes the financial risk in making a product available. For example, if a product went on sale and sold no copies at all, the publisher is usually the person or body which loses money. If you get paid anyway, you are likely to be a designer, printer, author or consultant of some kind.

How long does it take to get an ISBN?

In the UK the 'Standard' service time is 10 working days. There is also a 'Fast Track' service, which is a three-working day processing period.

How much does it cost to get an ISBN?

In the UK there is a registration fee which is payable by all new publishers. The fees during 2006 are £94 including VAT for the Standard service and £148.05 including VAT for the Fast Track service. A publisher prefix unique to you will be provided and allows for 10 ISBNs. Larger allocations are available where appropriate.

ISBNs are only available in blocks. The smallest block is 10 numbers. It is not possible to obtain a single ISBN.

Which products do not qualify for ISBNs?

Calendars and diaries (unless they contain additional text or images such that they are not purely for time-management purposes); greetings cards, videos for entertainment; documentaries on video/CD-Rom; computer games; computer application programs; items which are available to a restricted group of people, e.g. a history of a golf club which is only for sale to members, or an educational course book only available to those registered as students on the course.

Can I turn my ISBN into a barcode?

Up until 2007, ISBNs will remain only 10 digits long, whereas the appropriate barcode is 13 digits long and is derived from the ISBN by adding a prefix and recalculating the check digit. From 1 January 2007, the appropriate barcode number will be the same as the 13-digit ISBN. Further information about barcoding for books is available on the Book Industry Communication website (www.bic.org.uk).

What is an ISSN?

An International Standard Serial Number is the numbering system for journals, magazines, periodicals, newspapers and newsletters. It is administered by the British Library (*tel* (01937) 546959).

Public Lending Right

Under the PLR system, payment is made from public funds to authors (writers, translators, illustrators and some editors/compilers) whose books are lent out from public libraries. Payment is made once a year, and the amount authors receive is proportionate to the number of times that their books were borrowed during the previous year (July to June).

The legislation

Public Lending Right (PLR) was created, and its principles established, by the Public Lending Right Act 1979 (HMSO, 30p). The Act required the rules for the administration of PLR to be laid down by a scheme. That was done in the Public Lending Right Scheme 1982 (HMSO, £2.95), which includes details of transfer (assignment), transmission after death, renunciation, trusteeship, bankruptcy, etc. Amending orders made in 1983, 1984, 1988, 1989 and 1990 were consolidated in December 1990 (SI 2360, £3.90). Some further amendments affecting author eligibility came into effect in December 1991 (SI 2618, £1), July 1997 (SI 1576, £1.10), December 1999 (SI 420, £1), July 2000 (SI 933, £1.50), June 2004 (SI 1258 £3) and July 2005 (SI 1519, £3).

Further information

Public Lending Right
PLR Office, Richard House, Sorbonne Close, Stockton-on-Tees TS17 6DA
tel (01642) 604699 *fax* (01642) 615641
website www.plr.uk.com,
www.plrinternational.com
Contact The Registrar

Application forms, information, publications and a copy of its *Annual Report* are all obtainable from the PLR Office. See website for further information on eligibility for PLR, loans statistics and forthcoming developments.

PLR Advisory Committee
Advises the Secretary of State for Culture, Media and Sport and the Registrar on the operation of the PLR scheme.

How the system works

From the applications he receives, the Registrar of PLR compiles a register of authors and books which is held on computer. A representative sample of book issues is recorded, consisting of all loans from selected public libraries. This is then multiplied in proportion to total library lending to produce, for each book, an estimate of its total annual loans throughout the country. Each year the computer compares the register with the estimated loans to discover how many loans are credited to each registered book for the calculation of PLR payments. The computer does this using code numbers – in most cases the ISBN printed in the book.

Parliament allocates a sum each year (£7,419,000 for 2005–6) for PLR. This Fund pays the administrative costs of PLR and reimburses local authorities for recording loans in the sample libraries. The remaining money is then divided by the total registered loan figure in order to work out how much can be paid for each estimated loan of a registered book.

Limits on payments

Bottom limit. If all the registered interests in an author's books score so few loans that they would earn less than £5 in a year, no payment is due. This will be reduced to £1 for the February 2007 payments.

Top limit. If the books of one registered author score so high that the author's PLR earnings for the year would exceed £6000, then only £6000 is paid. No author can earn more than

£6000 in PLR in any one year. This will increase to £6600 for the February 2007 payments.

Money that is not paid out because of these limits belongs to the Fund and increases the amounts paid that year to other authors.

The sample

The basic sample represents only public libraries (no academic, school, private or commercial libraries are included) and only loans made over the counter (not consultations of books on library premises). It follows that only those books which are loaned from public libraries can earn PLR and make an application worthwhile.

The sample consists of the entire loans records for a year from libraries in more than 30 public library authorities spread through England, Scotland, Wales and Northern Ireland. Sample loans represent around 20% of the national total. Several computerised sampling points in an authority contribute loans data ('multi-site' sampling). This change has been introduced gradually, and began in July 1991. The aim has been to increase the sample without any significant increase in costs. In order to counteract sampling error, libraries in the sample change every two to three years. Loans are totalled every 12 months for the period 1 July to 30 June.

An author's entitlement to PLR depends, under the 1979 Act, on the loans accrued by his or her books in the sample. This figure is averaged up to produce first regional and then finally national estimated loans.

ISBNs

PLR depends on the use of code numbers to identify books lent and to correlate loans with entries on the register so that payment can be made. The system uses the International Standard Book Number (ISBN), which is required for all new registrations. Different editions (e.g. 1st, 2nd, hardcover, paperback, large print) of the same book have different ISBNs.

Summary of the 23rd year's results

Registration: authors. When registration closed for the 23rd year (30 June 2005) the number of shares in books registered was 402,835 for 35,822 authors and assignees.

Eligible loans. Of the 341 million estimated loans from UK libraries, 148 million belong to books on the PLR register. The loans credited to registered books – 43% of all library borrowings – qualify for payment. The remaining 57% of loans relate to books that are ineligible for various reasons, to books written by dead or foreign authors, and to books that have simply not been applied for.

Money and payments. PLR's administrative costs are deducted from the fund allocated to the Registrar annually by Parliament. Operating the Scheme this year cost £822,000, representing some 11% of the PLR fund. The Rate per Loan for 2005–6 increased to 5.57 pence and was calculated to distribute all the £6,540,000 available. The total of PLR distribution and costs is therefore the full £7.419 million which the Government provided in 2005–6.

The numbers of authors in various payment categories are as follows:

*349	payments at	£5000–6000
390	payments between	£2500–4999.99
782	payments between	£1000–2499.99
959	payments between	£500–999.99
3725	payments between	£100–499.99
12,379	payments between	£5–99.99
18,584	TOTAL	

* includes 281 authors where the maximum threshold applied.

Authorship

In the PLR system the author of a book is the writer, illustrator, translator, compiler, editor or reviser. Authors must be named on the book's title page, or be able to prove authorship by some other means (e.g. receipt of royalties). The ownership of copyright has no bearing on PLR eligibility.

Co-authorship/illustrators. In the PLR system the authors of a book are those writers, translators, editors, compilers andillustrators as defined above. Authors must apply for registration before their books can earn PLR. This can now be done online through the PLR website. There is no restriction on the number of authors who can register shares in any one book as long as they satisfy the eligibility criteria.

Writers and/or illustrators. At least one must be eligible and they must jointly agree what share of PLR each will take. This agreement is necessary even if one or two are ineligible or do not wish to register for PLR. Share sizes should be based on contribution. The eligible authors will receive the share(s) specified in the application. PLR can be any whole percentage. Detailed advice is available from the PLR office.

Translators. Translators may apply, without reference to other authors, for a 30% fixed share (to be divided equally between joint translators).

Editors and compilers. An editor or compiler may apply, either with others or without reference to them, to register a 20% share. Unless in receipt of royalties an editor must have written at least 10% of the book's content or more than 10 pages of text in addition to normal editorial work. The share of joint editors/compilers is 20% in total to be divided

Most borrowed authors

Children's authors		Authors of adult fiction	
1.	Jacqueline Wilson	1.	Josephine Cox
2.	Mick Inkpen	2.	Danielle Steel
3.	Janet & Allan Ahlberg	3.	James Patterson
4.	Roald Dahl	4.	John Grisham
5.	Lucy Daniels	5.	Ian Rankin
6.	Enid Blyton	6.	Bernard Cornwell
7.	Nick Butterworth	7.	Catherine Cookson
8.	Eric Hill	8.	Agatha Christie
9.	Lucy Cousins	9.	Audrey Howard
10.	Rose Impey	10.	Nora Roberts
11.	Dick King-Smith	11.	Jack Higgins
12.	R.L. Stine	12.	Lynda M. Andrews
13.	Terry Deary	13.	Ruth Rendell
14.	Martin Waddell	14.	Mary Higgins Clark
15.	Ian Whybrow	15.	Michael Connelly
16.	Francesca Simon	16.	Katie Flynn
17.	Colin & Jacqui Hawkins	17.	Joan Jonker
18.	Debi Gliori	18.	Terry Pratchett
19.	Shirley Hughes	19.	Jeffery Deaver
20.	David McKee	20.	Meg Hutchinson

These two lists are of the most borrowed authors in UK public libraries. They are based on PLR sample loans in the period July 2004–June 2005. They include all writers, both registered and unregistered, but not illustrators where the book has a separate writer. Writing names are used; pseudonyms have not been combined.

equally. An application from an editor or compiler to register a greater percentage share must be accompanied by supporting documentary evidence of actual contribution.

Dead or missing co-authors. Where it is impossible to agree shares with a co-author because that person is dead or untraceable, then the surviving co-author or co-authors may submit an application without the dead or missing co-author but must name the co-author and provide supporting evidence as to why that co-author has not agreed shares. The living co-author(s) will then be able to register a share in the book which will be 20% for the illustrator (or illustrators) and the residual percentage for the writer (or writers). If this percentage is to be divided between more than one writer or illustrator, then this will be in equal shares unless some other apportionment is requested and agreed by the Registrar.

The PLR Office keeps a file of missing authors (mostly illustrators) to help locate co-authors. Help is also available from publishers, the writers' organisations, and the Association of Illustrators.

Life and death. Authors can only be registered for PLR during their lifetime. However, for authors so registered, books can later be registered if first published within one year before their death or 10 years afterwards. New versions of titles registered by the author can be registered posthumously.

Residential qualifications. With effect from 1 July 2000, PLR is open to authors living in the European Economic Area (i.e. EU member states plus Norway, Liechtenstein and Iceland). A resident in these countries (for PLR purposes) has his or her only or principal home there.

Eligible books

In the PLR system each separate edition of a book is registered and treated as a separate book. A book is eligible for PLR registration provided that:

- it has an eligible author (or co-author);
- it is printed and bound (paperbacks counting as bound);
- copies of it have been put on sale (i.e. it is not a free handout and it has already been published);
- it is not a newspaper, magazine, journal or periodical;
- the authorship is personal (i.e. not a company or association) and the book is not crown copyright;
- it is not wholly or mainly a musical score;
- it has an ISBN.

Notification and payment

Every registered author receives from the Registrar an annual statement of estimated loans for each book and the PLR due.

Sampling arrangements

To help minimise the unfairnesses that arise inevitably from a sampling system, the Scheme specifies the eight regions within which authorities and sampling points have to be designated and includes libraries of varying size. Part of the sample drops out by rotation each year to allow fresh libraries to be included. The following library authorities have been designated for the year beginning 1 July 2006 (all are multi-site authorities):

- London – Harrow, Redbridge/Havering/Wandsworth, Tower Hamlets, Corporation of London;

- Metropolitan Boroughs – Bolton, North Tyneside, Coventry, Newcastle upon Tyne, St Helens;
- Counties: Northern – Nottinghamshire/Nottingham, Derbyshire/Derby, Lincolnshire, Northumberland, Darlington;
- Counties: South West – Hampshire, Worcestershire, Gloucestershire, Stoke on Trent;
- Counties: South East – Oxfordshire, Kent, West Sussex, Windsor and Maidenhead, Essex/Southend/Thurrock;
- Scotland – Orkney, Argyll & Bute, Edinburgh, East Lothian;
- Northern Ireland – all five Education and Library Boards;
- Wales – Conwy, Swansea, Neath Port Talbot.

Participating local authorities are reimbursed on an actual cost basis for additional expenditure incurred in providing loans data to the PLR Office. The extra PLR work mostly consists of modifications to computer programs to accumulate loans data in the local authority computer and to transmit the data to the PLR Office at Stockton-on-Tees.

Reciprocal arrangements

Reciprocal PLR arrangements now exist with the German, Dutch and Austrian PLR schemes. Authors can apply for German, Dutch and Austrian PLR through the Authors' Licensing and Collecting Society. (Further information on PLR schemes internationally and recent developments within the EC towards wider recognition of PLR is available from the PLR Office or on the international PLR website.)

Book clubs

Artists' Choice
Artists' Choice Ltd, PO Box 3, Huntingdon, Cambs.
PE28 0QX
tel (01832) 710201 *fax* (01832) 710488
website www.artists-choice.co.uk, www.acaward.com
Quarterly.

Baker Books
Manfield Park, Cranleigh, Surrey GU6 8NU
tel (01483) 267888 *fax* (01483) 267409
email bakerbooks@dial.pipex.com
website www.bakerbooks.co.uk

School book club for children aged 3–13. Operates in
the UK and reaches English medium schools
overseas.

BCA
Greater London House, Hampstead Road, London
NW1 7TZ
tel 020-7760 6500 *fax* 020-7760 6501
website www.bol.com, www.booksdirect.co.uk

Ancient & Medieval History Book Club, Arts Guild,
Book Club of Ireland, Books for Children, Computer
Book Club, English Book Club, Escape (The Fiction
Club), Fantasy & SF Book Club, The History Guild,
Home Software World, Just Good Books, Mango,
Military and Aviation Book Society, Mind, Body &
Spirit, The Mystery & Thriller Club, QPD (Quality
Paperbacks Direct), The Railway Book Club, The
Softback Preview, Taste (A Fresh Approach to Food),
World Books.

Bibliophile
5 Thomas Road, London E14 7BN
tel 020-7515 9222 *fax* 020-7538 4115
email orders@bibliophilebooks.com
website www.bibliophilebooks.com
Secretary Annie Quigley

To promote value-for-money reading. Upmarket
literature and classical music on CD available from
mail order catalogue (10 p.a.). Over 3000 titles
covering art and fiction to travel, history and
children's books. Founded 1978.

The Book People Ltd
Catteshall Manor, Catteshall Lane, Godalming,
Surrey GU7 1UU
tel (01483) 861144 *fax* (01483) 861256
website www.thebookpeople.co.uk

Popular general fiction and non-fiction, including
children's and travel. Monthly.

Cygnus Book Club
PO Box 15, Llandeilo, Carmarthenshire SA19 6YX
tel (01550) 777701, (0845) 456 1577 *fax* (01550)
777569

email enquiries@cygnus-books.co.uk
website www.cygnus-books.co.uk

Includes psychology and self-help, diet, health and
exercise, world religions, new economics and
education, green issues, mythology, spirituality.
Monthly.

The Folio Society
44 Eagle Street, London WC1R 4FS
tel 020-7400 4222 *fax* 020-7400 4242
website www.foliosociety.com

Fine editions of classic literature.

Letterbox Library
71–73 Allen Road, London N16 8RY
tel 020-7503 4801 *fax* 020-7503 4800
email info@letterboxlibrary.com
website www.letterboxlibrary.com

Specialises in children's books that celebrate equality
and diversity.

The Poetry Book Society
4th Floor, 2 Tavistock Place, London WC1H 9RA
tel 020-8870 8403 *fax* 020-8870 0865
email info@poetrybooks.co.uk
website www.poetrybooks.co.uk,
www.poetrybookshoponline.com,
www.childrenspoetrybookshelf.co.uk

Runs the Children's Poetry Bookshelf, a 3 times
yearly book club offering children's poetry to
teachers, parents and grandparents. See also page 321.

Readers' Union Ltd
Brunel House, Forde Close, Newton Abbot, Devon
TQ12 4PU
tel (01626) 323200 *fax* (01626) 323318

Includes The Craft Club, Needlecrafts with Cross
Stitch, Gardeners' Book Society, Photographers' Book
Club, Equestrian Book Society, Country Sports Book
Club, Anglers' Book Club, Painting for Pleasure,
Craftsman's Book Club.

Red House
PO Box 142, Bangor LL57 4ZP
email arrabella.hall@redhouse.co.uk
website www.redhouse.co.uk

Helps parents to select the right books for their
children at affordable prices. A free monthly
magazine featuers the best of the latest titles on offer,
young reader reviews and fascinating insight into the
minds of popular children's writers. Sponsors the Red
House Children's Book Award (page 579). Founded
1979.

Scholastic Book Clubs

Windrush Park, Range Road, Witney, Oxon OX29
0YZ
tel (01993) 893456 *fax* (01993) 776813
website www.scholastic.co.uk
Managing Director Miles Stevens-Hoare

Leading schools book club. Offers 5 age-specific
clubs.

Scholastic Book Fairs

Dolomite Avenue, Coventry Business Park, Coventry
CV5 6UE
tel 0800 212281 (freephone)

website www.scholastic.co.uk/bookfairs
Managing Director Miles Stevens-Hoare

Sells directly to children, parents and teachers in
schools through 25,000 week-long events held in
schools throughout the UK.

Writers' Bookshelf

Writers' News, 1st Floor, Victoria House, 143–145
The Headrow, Leeds LS1 5RL
tel 0113-200 2929 *fax* 0113-200 2928
email janet.davison@writersnews.co.uk

Books and magazines for writers.

Poetry
Getting poetry published

Michael Schmidt examines the challenges for poets who wish to see their work published.

Start with this axiom: you have not come here to make money.

I write as a publisher who has spent over 30 years not making money out of poetry, and as a quondam poet whose rewards were never material, either. Money may be a consequence, but only in a few cases, usually obtained in the form of grants and bursaries, when a career is well beyond the point at which an article such as this is of interest.

In the old days, right up through the 1950s, there was a popular tradition of verse writing: people kept commonplace books for friends to write lines in when visiting. Or folk composed ballads, Christmas poems, dialect eclogues, limericks. Verse was part of social engagement. It took itself seriously in formal terms but made no pretence of being 'art'. There was a level of competence in making conventional verses, sometimes beyond English, in Latin or Greek, and most people could tell a good piece of verse from a bad one. Jane Austen's family was given to playful versing. In second-hand bookshops you find tomes with verse inscriptions. Like weekend painters, verse writers expressed themselves clearly and skilfully, bringing direct, strictly occasional pleasure to another person or a group. The ambition to Get Published At All Costs had not set in. Now it has; it has been endemic for three decades. The social space for verse has almost vanished, and with it the popular versifying skills. Such a loss has consequences. Dr Johnson in *The Life of Savage* reflects that 'negligence and irregularity, long continued, will make knowledge useless, wit ridiculous, and genius contemptible'. The creative writing culture of reception nowadays seems to be defined less as readership or audience, more as 'market'. Is this change regrettable? Yes. Has it brought any benefits? To the art of poetry, to poetry readership, very few.

Even today, weekend painters know their work will never hang in the Tate; amateur musicians (singers, instrumentalists, composers) content themselves with making music as an end in itself. But the occasional versifier is a dying breed, like the red squirrel, replaced by the interloping grey who, a year into writing, submits work to a dozen editors at once, declaring it to be original, relevant, topical. In the twinkling of an eye these strident creatures absorb, without troubling to learn names, the art of Chaucer, Spenser, Milton, Cowper, Dickinson, Walcott, Rich. Their opinion of modern poetry is low. But then they do not base their opinion on a very large sample. They will have heard of the market leaders and remember some of the poetry read at school.

As an editor at a small publishing house I receive over 2000 full manuscripts a year (and many more submissions for *PN Review*). Telephone calls, letters and emails ask what kind of poetry we publish, whether we publish poetry at all, or how much it will cost to have poems printed. Few poets submitting are aware of the editorial contents of a poetry publisher's list, despite websites and other resources offering this information. Many have read, perhaps in this volume, which publishers have a poetry list and try, without doing a smidgen of research. Without reading. Few seem aware of how large a shoal of wannabe poets surrounds the little flotilla of publishers, editors and other validators. Poetry becomes a means to an end, not an end in itself: to be a poet, go for prizes, give readings and all the peripheral rewards which in the end poison and parch the individual spring, assuming it has more than illusory water in it.

Publishing in book form

An article of this kind usually proffers advice: how to present a manuscript, how to address an editor, what to expect from a contract, etc. I'd rather try to give writers who believe they have a body of publishable work a realistic sense of the chance of publication, and a realistic preparation for its aftermath, assuming the first goal is achieved. Better to counsel realism than foster illusion.

First, the chances of book publication. More than 1000 new books of verse are published each year, but few are marketed or sold and fewer still reviewed. A list like the one I edit, with 40 poetry titles a year, accommodates at most two or three first collections. Other substantial poetry publishers go for a year or five without adding new names to their lists. Few first collections sell over 1000 copies. Indeed, some may sell fewer than 300. The book trade has become resistant to all but the market leaders in poetry; few independent presses get their poets even into some of the leading chains.

The ecology of poetry publishing, as distinct from that of standard trade publishing, is based more and more narrowly on events. A poet can publish his or her own work, paying a printer to do the job and selling at readings. But then, who is going to invite a self-published poet to read? A poet can go to one of the vanity presses and pay a more substantial sum for the promise of exposure. Again, such publication capitalises on illusion and, as the title proclaims, vanity (see *Vanity publishing*, page 294).

There *are* new opportunities which can be valuable. Any poet is free to post work on the web, in both text and voice form, inviting response. It's quite cheap to do so and response is almost immediate. There are electronic magazines as well. In a sense, the withering away of the poetry book trade is a harbinger of the wider impact of the web. Unfortunately, the web is not discriminating and it is hard to know how a critical take on work self-published on the web will develop. At every stage, it seems to me, poets are tempted to succumb, in their eagerness for publication, to acts of desperation. Publish and be damned! Luck would be a fine thing. There is not even a sufficient audience to damn new work on the web. The question must be, how to publish and be sufficiently visible to *be* damned, or welcomed, as the case may be. But we are getting ahead of ourselves: the first question must be the quality of the work and the motive of the writer.

Before looking for a publisher, writers of verse (as of anything else) should interrogate themselves. *Why* do I want to be published in book form? Is it mere whim or is my work genuinely original? The only way you can answer these questions is by wide reading, not only of contemporaries but also of poets from the past. To be able to judge your art, you must understand it, as you would any other. What makes my work original? In a few instances subject matter in itself can be sufficiently interesting to justify a book, but this is rare: it has more to do with the accidents of birth and upbringing than with any choices a poet might make. Originality is expressed in diction, prosody and form. It need not be dazzling. Edward Thomas recognised Robert Frost's originality, reviewing *North of Boston* in 1914: 'This is one of the most revolutionary books of modern times, but one of the quietest and least aggressive. It speaks, and it is poetry.'

A poet who sets out to get published without understanding in depth the art practised, and the nature of the work intended for publication, is on a hiding to very little. Chances are that such a poet will make decisions that ensure the poetry remains unread.

Ask, before you solicit editorial judgment, to whom your poetry is likely to appeal: To friends and family? The local community (is it in dialect, locally relevant in some way)? To a religious group? Is your work sufficiently distinctive to appeal beyond those groups from which your identity is derived?

Seeking critical appraisal

If a spouse, relation, teacher or friend, commends your verse, it will be gratifying, but how informed are they, and is their response to you as writer or to the writing? Is it courtesy or real validation? Kind Sir John Betjeman used to write a note to anyone who sent him poems saying 'you show potential' or 'talent'. Thousands of poets thus commended would take his endorsement and include it for the next 20 years with each magazine and volume submission. The commendation of a kind writer is, alas, not worth the paper it is written on. If an established writer believes in your work, he or she will make it a mission to send your work to an editor.

It is important to get a critical purchase on your work, not to overestimate it. Some poets accept that their level is, say, among small magazines; they are content to exist there in a community of similarly committed writers. They do not try for the 'better' magazines, knowing they haven't a chance of getting in. They may blame those magazines as elitist and cliquish and no doubt some of them are, but elites and cliques that are permeable to quality. Finding one's level is an early stage in establishing peace of mind: always to aim too high and so to invite rebuff finally undermines self-respect.

Never ask an editor for comments and criticisms unless you are willing to take them. I am often been asked for 'a serious appraisal'. When work seems genuinely interesting I offer detailed advice, and often receive back angry letters or defences of work I have risked commenting upon. A poem works or fails to work; no amount of argufying can convert an experienced reader. I may come to understand more clearly what the intention of a poem *was*, and therefore better to understand how far short it has fallen.

Magazines, the internet and broadcasting

Most editors advise new writers to seek publication in magazines first. This is mixed advice. It assumes the poet writes 'filler' poems, the fast food that can be served up in a weekly journal. If you are published in magazines the editor does not respect, it may diminish his or her respect for your work. It is crucial, especially if you are not prolific, to try for publication in places where (a) the work will be widely read and (b) publication will increase your visibility. The *Times Literary Supplement* and *London Review of Books* have a curious and unpredictable taste; several specialised journals are worth trying, *Poetry Review*, *London Magazine*, *Stand*, *Poetry London*, *The North* and *PN Review* among them. It is crucial to subscribe to journals you find congenial, read them regularly and get a sense of the wider world of contemporary publication. Among foreign magazines worth close attention are *Parnassus*, *Raritan* and *Salt*.

Publication in web magazines can be satisfying; it can also be dangerous for your and copyright (the work slips out of your control), and few editors of my acquaintance credit the web as a place to look for poems. Remember that a poem first published on the web is unlikely to be published in a reputable magazine.

Broadcasting is as unpredictable a medium of dissemination as the web. There are slots for various kinds of poetry on radio: dramatic, lyric, etc. Look at the broadcasting schedules, familiarise yourself with the poetry programmes and producers, locally and nationally. On many networks a broadcast poem is heard by quite a large, if not a discriminating or informed, audience. Editors have been known to track down poems heard in broadcast, especially in the poet's own voice if that poet is a good performer.

The importance of market research

You can do your market research for a book publisher in your personal library of modern poetry books (you ought to have one, with books by favourite authors from a variety of imprints). Most have editorial priorities which are more or less coherent, expressed in anthologies or in the general choice offered. The chief imprints are Faber, Picador, Penguin, Cape and Chatto among larger players, and Arc, Anvil, Bloodaxe, Carcanet, Enitharmon and Seren among the independents. Many other valuable outlets exist. The Poetry Book Society makes a convenient selection and has useful catalogues, but trusting a book club's choices is no safer for the poetry than for the fiction lover. Always read *beyond*.

In approaching journal editors or publishers it is important to indicate that you know who they are, and why you have chosen them over others. A brief letter is sufficient. If you practise multiple submissions, warn the editors to whom you write. Some editors follow a geological time-scale in replying. If you have not had a reply in six weeks, feel free to send your work elsewhere, but should the first editor accept it in the end, you must immediately withdraw it from other editors.

Success is slow: a hundred rejections may precede an acceptance. Or acceptance may never quite come. If it doesn't, how do you deal with failure? Many wannabe poets who cannot get visibly published develop a strategy of blame. It is not, they insist, the quality of the work that deprives them of readership, it is the cabals that control the avenues of transmission. Jonathan Swift knew this:

> If on Parnassus' top you sit,
> You rarely bite, are always bit:
> Each poet of inferior size
> On you shall rail and criticise ...

Poetry magazines

The North
The Poetry Business, The Studio, Byram Arcade, Westgate, Huddersfield HD1 1ND

Parnassus: Poetry in Review
205 West 89th Street, No 8F, New York, NY 10024, USA
tel 212-362-3492 *fax* 212-875-0148
email parnew@aol.com
No submissions are accepted by email.

Raritan Literary Magazine
Rutgers – The State University of New Jersey, 31 Mine Street, New Brunswick, NJ 08903, USA
tel 732-932-7887 *fax* 732-932-7855

Salt Literary Magazine
PO Box 202, Applecross, Western Australia 6153
email jvk20@hermes.cam.ac.uk
Editor John Kinsella

Details for the other magazines mentioned in the article may be found in either *Magazines UK and Ireland* starting on page 32 or *Poetry organisations*, which follows this article.

Other poets study 'the market' and try to follow the latest fashion. Runt-Raines, runt-Muldoons and Motions, have given way to runt-Duffys and Armitages. Aping success can seem to work: in my late 'teens, when the *New Statesman* had rejected me several times, I wrote a poem in what I took to be the style of Ted Walker, a poet popular with the magazine's poetry editor. Sure enough, my verse was accepted. I had the same experience with *Poetry Now* on radio. The editor loved what he called 'the macabre' and I delivered precisely that. Such poems, cynically composed, had a short half-life. Imitation is part of any serious apprenticeship, but publishing unacknowledged imitations, especially if they are written not to develop skills but to achieve publication, is a form of failure.

Dealing with success

Assuming the Muses of publication smile, how do you deal with success? Success can be failure postponed. A book is edited, designed, published, and then falls into a black hole of neglect. A book is published and receives negative reviews. A book is published, receives good reviews, but fails to sell. A book is published, receives good reviews, sells, but the next book does less well and there is a future of diminishing returns. The judge at the pearly gates will declare, 'It is the sort of verse which was modern in its time'.

Real success is rare and has little to do with the strategies outlined here. No poet living in the UK at this time makes a living solely from writing poems. Most write and teach, or write and perform, or have a day job, or write in other genres (novels, radio and television plays, journalism) as well as poetry. Assuming the poetry is good and/or well received, there will be invitations to perform. Fees vary from about £100 to £1000, depending on the occasion and the venue. A poet who is a good performer will read once or twice a week for a period of time and sell more books than a poet who cannot perform convincingly, even if the latter's poems are better. Indeed some apparently substantial reputations are based on performance skills rather than on the quality of the poetry.

Real success is judged less by the marketplace, more by a culture of reception which gradually grows alert to new work and explores it. It may be, if the work you are writing is original and challenging, that you will have to develop your own means of transmission on paper (a magazine, a pamphlet or book publishing house) or on the web. As long as the vehicles you create exist to serve not only your own work, but poetry more widely, whether the writing of fellow radicals or neglected texts from the past that helped shape your perspectives and formal approaches. The creation of such vehicles means that you retain control of production and dissemination; eventually the endeavour, particular and general, is acknowledged, the work read. You are in dialogue with readers.

The endorsement of an Establishment consisting of the larger publishers, specialist lists, journals and the academy, is not a guarantee of quality. What is a guarantee is a readership which will go out of its way to get hold of your work – a poem in a magazine, a pamphlet, an e-poem, a book – and will invest time and creative energy in reading you and taking bearings from what you propose.

It would be churlish of me not to mention that many poets spend their time and resources on entering competitions, and competitions are a way (the three or four major ones) of making yourself briefly visible. A competition-winning poem is not 'news that stays news', as Pound said poetry ought to be, but mere news. Mere news with money attached: not to be sneezed at. There is also the matter of fees and advances. For a 24-line poem published in a journal, payment will vary from £30 to £500, depending on the outlet.

The advance for a book of poems, especially a first collection, will vary from £300 to £3000, with the occasional mad exception.

In negotiating a publishing contract, it is worth remembering that the greatest value your poems will have in the long term for you, as for your publisher, is unlikely to be the book sales. What will matter in the end, assuming your work becomes established, is the subsidiary rights: anthology, quotation, broadcasting, electronic, translation. Several poetic estates live handsomely on subsidiary rights income. For three decades I have been publishing William Carlos Williams' poetry.

> So much depends
> upon
>
> a red wheel
> barrow...

Eight simple lines have earned Williams' estate, and his publisher, between £27 and £35 per week over that period.

Michael Schmidt is editor of *PN Review* and director of Carcanet Press.

Approaching a poetry publisher

Roddy Lumsden outlines the route to getting a volume of poetry published and advises poets on when and how to approach a publisher.

If you follow the perils and pleasures of British poetry via the newspapers, you are excused for thinking things are in a bad way. The media rarely misses a chance to tell us how little we are selling. Since any article on getting published contains bitter pills, let's start with some optimism. Poetry is, whatever you hear, doing very well these days, thank you. Every tale of woe I've encountered in recent years – from press pieces to official reports – has mistakenly used certain sales figures for poetry which are actually gathered only from high street chains such as WHSmith which carry little poetry other than popular anthologies and big (often deceased) names.

Large bookshops are stocking less poetry, alas, but many poets said to be selling only a few hundred copies per year are shifting several times that amount, thanks to smaller chains, specialist outlets, academic, overseas and online sales, and sales through poetry readings and courses. Although few can make a living from royalties and readings alone, there are certainly a few hundred British poets who make a comfortable, if far from lavish, living from poetry – universities, schoolwork, reviewing, residencies, editing, etc – or who combine this with other part-time employment.

Yet poetry publishing is a tricky business. Time was when a young chap had his mother type up his sheaf of poems – 20 or so would do – and sent them to the publisher, along with his note of recommendation from a mutual acquaintance at Cambridge and a list of a hundred friends and relatives who had vowed to purchase the slim volume. Things have changed. Until recent decades, few working-class or women writers would have considered attempting to publish.

The postwar decades saw shifts in the ethos of British poets but changes affecting them in the century's latter decades were about 'infrastructure' – the rise of independent publishers, the creation of a circuit of poetry venues and literary festivals, government-backed subsidy and promotions, the stiffening of poetic factionalism, the confidence (and sheer numbers) of small magazines, the liberty/tyranny of the internet (with its bookselling and blogging, communities and catfights), the demise of 'broadsheet' interest, the desire for voices from outside the white middle class, the spread of residencies, commissions, fellowships and teaching opportunities.

In his recent controversial T.S. Eliot lecture, Picador editor Don Paterson commented on the abundance of writers who, wanting a slice of these opportunities, push for publication before they are ready. Many writers, with hindsight, feel their first books lack cohesion. Another editor told me that many small press poets would have had a strong chance with bigger publishers had they been less impatient.

How much unpublished poetry is there? Let's look at some rough numbers. A late 1990s survey suggested 8% of the UK adult population had recently written a poem of some sort (of which two-thirds were women). Discounting the many who scribble in a diary or pen a quick verse in a card, we're still left with over a million writers who harbour some hope of publication. A few hundred poetry collections by individual writers are published most years. Most – admirable though they may be – are small-scale, from local presses, in pamphlet form, in small print runs. The better-known independent poetry presses (Anvil, Bloodaxe, Carcanet, Seren and others) publish over a hundred books between them, while the few commercial presses (Cape, Chatto, Picador, etc) venture around half that. However, these mainly comprise books by established poets from here or abroad (and new editions of work by deceased writers).

First books are few and far between, especially from bigger publishers. If I started naming poets who deserve a debut collection, you'd probably stop me after a minute or two and say, OK enough now. And yet, having spoken to most poetry editors, and having done freelance editorial work too, I sympathise with publishers. Space for a debut sometimes comes at the expense of an older poet not selling well. It is difficult to promote a new poet – bookshops want anthologies, promoters want 'names'; despite all the opportunities listed above, poets have to work hard even after publication to make themselves known. Most first-timers are disappointed to find their collection is not met with a raft of reviews, shortlists and reading invitations.

What publishers are looking for

So how do poets get published these days? Well, rarely from what is perceived to be the standard approach of simply submitting a manuscript to a publisher. My advice (and all editors and established poets will concur) is this: you *must* go through the hoops and tasks of learning your craft and proving yourself before considering an approach to a publisher. And no, you're not the exception, even if you are a brilliant young thing, or a late starter expecting short cuts. A first collection will contain 40–70 poems, and most poets will have written a few discarded efforts for each one that makes the cut.

Publishers will expect you to tell them where you have been published in magazine form. Broadly, your work should have appeared in several places. This should include well-established publications: vital though the little magazines are, you are frankly unlikely to be published in book form if the better-known periodicals are consistently turning down your poems. All this is misunderstood – the primary reason is that a track record of magazine publications shows commitment to a developing manuscript and an effort to develop a readership for your work.

A few years ago, I went through several boxes of manuscripts for an independent press. These scripts had already been deemed worth a third look: most submissions are returned quickly since editors become adept at identifying substandard work. They don't often make mistakes, and would make fewer if the process wasn't clogged by those who send too soon. The work I read was generally impressive, carefully assembled by capable writers and much of it as good as work I'd recently seen in book form. But this publisher only has room for one or two debuts each year. My task was to look for exceptional, original manuscripts and after a while, I found myself growing impatient with poems which were well written but overfamiliar in style and subject matter.

If you do feel you are ready to approach a publisher, you must find out their current submissions policy (see the listings in this *Yearbook* and look at publishers' websites). Some of the bigger lists go through periods where they will not look at any unsolicited work. Some prefer sample submissions of a dozen poems only. Don't make common mistakes: email submissions are rarely allowed; full return postage must be supplied; never ask for an email response, or a detailed critique; keep your covering letter short and pertinent; never drop the name of someone who has praised your work unless you have the express permission to do so.

For younger poets, the Eric Gregory Awards (see page 570) have been an important step up for decades now, though far from a guarantee of publication. The annual awards, run by the Society of Authors, offer grants to the most promising poets (published or not) under 30. Competition success can be another way to attract notice to your work, especially the Arvon Foundation (see page 561) and National Poetry (page 576) competitions. Every poet with serious ambitions should seek opportunities to recite their work and should make the effort to learn to read well, which does not require performance skills, just confidence and conviction.

How poets get published

Many people will whisper that it's 'who you know' that really counts. Well, certainly. This is not about nepotism and 'couch casting', rather, if you are keen to progress, you will seek out peers and mentors where you can. Find a writing group run by a worthy tutor. You may not live in an area where good writing classes or writers-in-residence are available, but residential courses such as those run by the excellent Arvon Foundation (see page 649) have been a step towards many a successful publication (and grants are available for those with more promise than funds). Above all else, read lots of poetry which is contemporary and engaging, for that's what you will have to be – there is no market for the retro or pastiche. And read widely – many feel, with some validity, that larger British poetry presses can favour the anodyne.

For myself, a few years of feverish reading, writing and showing work to university writers-in-residence and to other young poets lead to an Eric Gregory Award which was followed by interest from a major publisher (Faber, whose editor had been on the award panel). I spent five years carefully building up a manuscript. Faber then featured my work in an anthology of eight promising poets but turned down the manuscript. I worked hard to improve it and sent a pamphlet (which I cheaply self-published) to a few other publishers. I was quickly approached by Bloodaxe, who were familiar with my work via the Award and publication in magazines. Here are some examples of how other poets got published:

Poet 'A' was a late starter and wrote in various ways. At a group, he found that poems in a certain style (which he had felt came too easy) were well received. He gladly went with this direction, and put effort into reading his poems aloud when he had the opportunity. A poetry editor saw him reading and asked to see his work.

Poet 'B' had a reputation as a performance poet but had begun writing more formally. He read widely and joined a weekly group with a tutor whose poetry he admired and worked hard on developing a new style of writing. He then did an Arvon Foundation course with a tutor he had encountered before, who was so impressed with his new work, she recommended him to a publisher she was working with.

Poet 'C' had placed poems in several magazines and had some commendations and prizes in a few competitions. She sent a dozen poems to a well-known publisher who asked to see more. She sent more for consideration, took some time off work to develop her manuscript and, in time, the book was accepted.

Most poets would prefer to be published by the bigger publishers with their distribution capabilities and the kudos which leads to their books being more widely read and reviewed. But regional presses can offer opportunities too: a poet I know is one of the 'best-known' poets in her region, does well from teaching and readings and sells up to a thousand copies of her small press books, considerably more than some nationally known poets. And just as certain publishers have a geographical bent, some tend towards poetry in certain genres. A few small presses go for work with a 'performance' edge, while others (among them the productive Cambridge-based Salt, see page 314) make available the work of innovative and experimental poets.

One step at a time

To summarise, until you are ready to publish – in fact, until those whose judgement you trust recommend you try – you should concentrate on magazines and journals (and, if you wish, entering competitions). Joining the Poetry Society and the Poetry Book Society (see page 547) are helpful steps. Find out which journals you appreciate and subscribe to them. Magazines constantly change (e.g. *Poetry London* was a low-level newsletter 10 years ago and is now an impressive journal full of internationally known poets); they appear and disappear overnight; they often have strong styles – you know not to send your quatrains on otters to a hard-boiled 'zine, yet this sort of thing happens frequently.

So take your time, find a mentor, or someone who'll be honest and astute about your poetry, build up a manuscript slowly, with lots of revision, read and read more, find opportunities for reading in public, go to a writing group if you can, do an Arvon Foundation course. And keep in mind that there is far more pleasure in writing than in seeing your name on the spine of a book.

Roddy Lumsden has published four books of poetry, most recently *Mischief Night: New & Selected Poems* (Bloodaxe 2004). He has been shortlisted for several major poetry prizes and edited *The Message*, a book on poetry and popular music, and *Anvil New Poets 3*. He is an experienced teacher and editor and also a writer of puzzles and popular reference. His poems can be seen at www.vitamin-p.co.uk

See also...

- *Publishers of poetry*, page 766
- *Getting poetry published*, page 311
- *Poetry organisations, page 321*

Poetry organisations

Poetry is one of the easiest writing art forms to begin with, though the hardest to excel at or earn any money from. Carl Dhiman, Membership Manager at the Poetry Society, lists below the organisations which can help poets take their poetry further.

WHERE TO GET INVOLVED

Academi

Mount Stuart House, Mount Stuart Square, Cardiff Bay, Cardiff CF10 5FQ
tel 029-204 72266
email post@academi.org
website www.academi.org
Coordinator Peter Finch

The Welsh National Literature Promotion Agency which has a huge resource available for poets and poetry. It organises events and tours, promotes poets and poetry, offers poetry advice, locates poetry publishers, offers financial help to poets and to organisers wishing to book poets, and much more. To take advantage of their services you have to live or be in Wales, which has the largest number of poets per 1000 population anywhere in the Western World.

Brightside

33 Churchill Street, Leicester LE2 1FH
website www.brightside.mcmail.com

Opened in April 1996 as a poetry cabaret event in Leicester, the Brightside is now a performance poetry organisation made up of professional performance poets who have backgrounds in teaching, youth work, theatre, mental health and stand-up comedy.

The British Haiku Society

Lenacre Ford, Woolhope, Hereford HR1 4RF
tel (01432) 860328
email davidawalker@btinternet.com
website www.britishhaikusociety.org
Secretary David Walker

The Society runs the prestigious annual James W. Hackett International Haiku Award, the Nobuyuki Yuasa Annual International Award for Haibun and the bienniel Sasakawa Prize worth £2500 for original contributions in the field of haikai. It is active in promoting the teaching of haiku in schools and colleges, and is able to provide readers, course/workshop leaders and speakers for poetry groups, etc. It has created a haiku teaching/learning kit for schools. Write for membership details. Founded 1990.

Commonword

6 Mount Street, Manchester M2 5NS
tel 0161-832 3777
email cathy@commonword.org.uk
website www.commonword.org.uk
Contact Cathy Bolton

Commonword is a valuable resource for poets and writers in the North West. It provides support, training and publishing opportunities for new writers. It has helped to launch the careers of many of the region's leading poets and strives to seek out new talent in unexpected places.

Creative Arts East

Griffin Court, Market Street, Wymondham, Norfolk NR18 0GU
tel (01603) 774789
email lisa.d'onofrio@cae.norfolk.gov.uk
website www.creativearteast.co.uk
Coodinator Lisa D'Onofrio

Creative Arts East is a fast-growing arts development agency which provides practical support to the arts community in Norfolk; directly promotes tours, exhibitions, and one-off performances and readings by professional artists and companies; and develops community-based arts projects which address social issues around isolation and disadvantage.

The agency was formally launched in 2002, and was set up to combine the collective expertise and energy of 4 smaller arts organisations: Rural Arts East, Norfolk Arts Marketing, Norfolk Literature Development and Create! Members receive the Norfolk Literature Network newsletter containing information, news, events listings and competitions.

Mini Mushaira

c/o 11 Donnington Road, Sheffield S2 2RF
tel (01743) 245004, 0114-272390
email simon@shrews1.fsnet.co.uk
Coordinators Simon Fletcher, Debjani Chatterjee

Mushaira is the Arabic word for 'a gathering of poets' and the Mini Mushaira writers (Debjani Chatterjee in Sheffield, Simon Fletcher in Shrewsbury, Basir Sultan Kazmi in Manchester and Brian G. D'Arcy in Sheffield) are a group of multicultural poets and storytellers who seek to build cultural 'bridges' through their work with both children and adults. Mini Mushaira have given excellent multilingual poetry performances and run poetry workshops throughout the country. While each is a well-published poet, they also have a Mini Mushaira anthology: *A Little Bridge* published by Pennine Pens.

The Poetry Book Society

4th Floor, 2 Tavistock Place, London WC1H 9RA
tel 020-7833 9247 *fax* 020-7833 5990

email info@poetrybooks.co.uk
website www.poetrybooks.co.uk,
www.poetrybookshoponline.com,
www.childrenspoetrybookshelf.co.uk
Chair Daisy Goodwin, *Director* Chris Holifield

This unique book club for readers of poetry was founded in 1953 by T.S. Eliot, and is funded by Arts Council England. Every quarter, selectors choose one outstanding publication (the PBS Choice), and recommend 4 other titles, which are sent to members, who are also offered substantial discounts on other poetry books. The PBS also administers the T.S. Eliot Prize (see page 567), produces the quarterly membership magazine, the *Bulletin*, and provides teaching materials for primary and secondary schools. In addition, the PBS runs the Children's Poetry Bookshelf, offering children's poetry for 7–11 year-olds, with parent, school and library memberships and a new child-friendly website. Write for details.

The Poetry Business

Byram Arcade, Huddersfield HD1 1ND
email edit@poetrybusiness.co.uk
Contact Peter Sansom

Dedicated to helping writers reach their full potential by running supportive workshops.

The Poetry Can

Unit 11, 20–22 Hepburn Road, Bristol BS2 8UD
tel 0117-943 6976
email colin@poetrycan.demon.co.uk
website www.poetrycan.com
Coordinator Colin Brown

The Poetry Can is one of the few literature organisations in the UK specialising in poetry. It organises events such as the Bristol Poetry Festival; runs a lifelong learning programme; offers information and advice in all aspects of poetry.

Poetry Ireland

120 St Stephen's Green, Dublin 2, Republic of Ireland
tel (01) 478 9974 *fax* (0) 478 0205
email poetry@iol.ie
website www.poetryireland.ie

Poetry Ireland is the national organisation dedicated to developing, supporting and promoting poetry throughout Ireland. It is a resource and information point for any member of the public with an interest in poetry and works towards creating opportunities for poets working or living in Ireland. It is grant-aided by both the Northern and Southern Arts Councils of Ireland and is a resource centre with the Austin Clarke Library of over 10,000 titles. It publishes the quarterly magazine *Poetry Ireland Review* and the bi-monthly newsletter *Poetry Ireland News*. Poetry Ireland organises readings in Dublin and nationally, and runs a Writers-in-Schools Scheme.

Poetry on Loan

Unit 116, The Custard Factory, Gibb Street, Birmingham B9 4AA
tel 0121-246 2770
email jonathan@bookcommunications.co.uk
Coordinator Jonathan Davidson

Poetry on Loan is a scheme to promote contemporary poetry through libraries in the West Midlands. There are 30 participating libraries and the scheme supports events, displays, stock collections and commissions. It also runs poetry projects for young people.

The Poetry Society

22 Betterton Street, London WC2H 9BX
tel 020-7420 9880 *fax* 020-7240 4818
email info@poetrysociety.org.uk
website www.poetrysociety.org.uk
Membership From £15 p.a.

The Poetry Society was set up to help poetry and poets thrive in Britain and is a registered charity funded by the Arts Council England. The Society offers advice and information to all, with a more comprehensive level of information available to members. Membership is open to anyone interested in poetry and members receive copies of the UK's most prominent poetry magazine, *Poetry Review*, and the Society's newsletter, *Poetry News*, each quarter. The Society's website provides excellent information, news, poetry links and a useful FAQ page, as well as an interactive regional guide to poetry organisations, venues, publishers, magazines and bookshops around the UK through its Poetry Landmarks of Britain section.

The Society also publishes education resources (see later); promotes National Poetry Day; runs Poetry Prescription, a critical appraisal service available to members and non-members (£50 for 100 lines – 20% discount to members); provides an education advisory and training service, school membership, youth membership and a thriving website. A diverse range of events and readings frequently take place at the Poetry Café and the Poetry Studio at the Society's headquarters in London. The Society also programmes events and readings in other regions of the UK.

Competitions run by the Society include the annual National Poetry Competition, which is one of the largest open poetry competitions in the UK with a first prize of £5000, the biannual Corneliu M. Popescu Prize for European Poetry in Translation and the Foyle Young Poets of the Year Award. Founded 1909.

The Seamus Heaney Centre for Poetry

46–48 University Road, Belfast BT7 1NN
tel 028-9097 1070
email shc@qub.ac.uk
website www.qub.ac.uk/heanycentre

The new Seamus Heaney Centre for Poetry (SHC) is designed to celebrate and promote poetry and artistic endeavour by poets from Northern Ireland. The

Centre houses an extensive library of contemporary poetry volumes. It hosts regular creative writing workshops, a poetry reading group, and an ongoing series of readings and lectures by visiting poets and critics from all over the world. The SHC is chaired by the eminent poet, Ciaran Carson, and other resident poets include Medbh McGuckian.

Stop All The Clocks

The Marlborough Theatre, Prince's Street, Brighton BN2 1RD
tel (01273) 207562
email simon@stopalltheclocks.co.uk
website www.stopalltheclocks.co.uk
Coordinator Simon Clayton

Stop All The Clocks was formed from an amalgamation of the 3 best poetry promotion stables in Brighton – Don't Feed The Poets, Holy! Holy! Holy! Holy! and Wanderlust Wonderlust. It is by far the most active of Brighton's many poetry organisations and runs year-round genuinely grassroots events and organises the fringe literature festival every May.

Survivors Poetry

Diorama Arts Centre, 34 Osnaburgh Street, London NW1 3ND
tel 020-7916 5317 *fax* 020-7916 0830
email survivor@survivorspoetry.org.uk

Survivors Poetry provides poetry workshops, performances, readings, publishing, networking and training for survivors of mental distress in London and the UK. Survivors Poetry is funded by the Arts Council England and was founded in 1991 by 4 poets who have had first-hand experience of the mental health system. It works in partnership with local and national arts, mental health, community, statutory and disability organisations. Its outreach project has established a network of 30 writers' groups in the UK.

WHERE TO GET INFORMATION

The first place to start is your local library. They usually have information about the local poetry scene. Many libraries are actively involved in promoting poetry as well as having modern poetry available for loan. Local librarians promote writing activities with, for example, projects like Poetry on Loan and Poetry Places information points in West Midlands Libraries.

Arts Council England
website www.artscouncil.org.uk

Arts Council England has 9 regional offices and local literature officers can provide information on local poetry groups, workshops and societies (see page 519). Some give grant aid to local publishers and magazines and help fund festivals, literature projects and readings, and some run critical services.

The Northern Poetry Library

County Library, The Willows, Morpeth, Northumberland NE61 1TA
tel (01670) 534514 (poetry enquiries) *tel* (01670) 534524 (poetry dept)
Membership Free to anyone living in the areas of Tyne and Wear, Durham, Northumberland, Cumbria and Cleveland

The Northern Poetry Library has over 14,000 titles and magazines covering poetry published since 1945. For information about epic through to classic poetry, a full text database is available of all poetry from 600–1900. A postal lending service is available to members, who pay for return postage. Founded 1968.

The Poetry Library

Level 5, Royal Festival Hall, London SE1 8XX
tel 020-7921 0943/0664 *fax* 020-7921 0939
email poetrylibrary@rfh.org.uk
website www.poetrylibrary.org.uk
Membership Free with proof of identity and current address

The principal roles of the Poetry Library are to collect and preserve all poetry published in the UK since about 1912 and to act as a public lending library. It also keeps a wide range of international poetry. It has 2 copies of each title available and a collection of about 40,000 titles in English and English translation. The Library also provides an education service (see under 'Help for young poets and teachers', below).

The Library runs an active information service, which includes a unique noticeboard for lost quotations, and tracing authors and publishers from extracts of poems. Current awareness lists are available for magazines, publishers, competitions, bookshops, groups and workshops, evening classes and festivals on receipt of a large sae. The Library also stocks a full range of British poetry magazines as well as a selection from abroad. When visiting the Library, look out for the Voice Box, a performance space for literature; a programme is available from 020-7921 0906. Open 11am–8pm Tuesday to Sunday. Founded in 1953 by the Arts Council.

The Scottish Poetry Library

5 Crichton's Close, Canongate, Edinburgh EH8 8DT
tel 0131-558 2876
email admin@spl.org.uk
website www.spl.org.uk

The Scottish Poetry Library is the place for poetry in Scotland for the regular reader, the serious student or the casual browser. It has a remarkable collection of written works, as well as tapes and videos. The emphasis is on contemporary poetry written in Scotland, in Scots, Gaelic and English, but historic Scottish poetry – and contemporary works from almost every part of the world – feature too. They also have collections for the visually impaired. All resources, advice and information are readily accessible, free of charge. It holds regular poetry events, details of which are available on the library website. Founded 1984.

ONLINE RESOURCES

You can obtain a wealth of information at the click of a mouse these days. In addition to those listed above, good starting points are:

The Poetry Archive
website www.poetryarchive.org

The Poetry Kit
website www.poetrykit.org

The Poetry Society of America
website www.poetrysociety.org

WHERE TO GET POETRY BOOKS

See the Poetry Book Society, above. The Poetry Library provides a list of bookshops which stock poetry. For second-hand mail order poetry books try:

Baggins Books
19 High Street, Rochester, Kent ME1 1PY
tel (01634) 811651 *fax* (01634) 840591
email godfreygeorge@btconnect.com

Secondhand bookshop with over half a million books in stock.

The Poetry Bookshop
The Ice House, Brook Street, Hay-on-Wye HR3 5BQ
tel (01497) 821812

Peter Riley
27 Sturton Street, Cambridge CB1 2QG
tel (01223) 576422
email priley@dircon.co.uk

WHERE TO CELEBRATE POETRY

Festival information should be available from Arts Council England offices (see page 520). See also *Literature festivals* on page 588.

The British Council
Information Officer, Literature Dept, The British Council, 11 Portland Place, London W1N 4EJ
tel 020-7930 8466 *fax* 020-7389 3199
website www.britishcouncil.org/arts/literature

Send a large sae or visit the website for a list of forthcoming festivals.

WHERE TO PERFORM

In London, Express Excess, Short Fuse and Aromapoetry are 3 of the liveliest venues for poetry performances and they regularly feature the best performers. Poetry Unplugged at the Poetry Café is famous for its open mic nights (Tuesdays 7.30pm). Poetry evenings are held all over the UK and those listed below are worth checking out. Others can be found by visiting your local library or your Arts Council office, or by visiting the Landmarks of Britain section of the Poetry Society website (www.poetrysociety.org.uk/landmarks.htm).

Apples and Snakes Performance Poetry
Battersea Arts Centre, Lavender Hill, London SW11
tel 020-7223 2223
website www.applesandsnakes.org

Aromapoetry
Charterhouse Bar, Charterhouse Street, London EC1M 6JH
website www.x-bout.com/aroma

Big Word Performance Poetry
Edinburgh Comedy Room, The Tron Bar, 9 Hunter Square, Royal Mile, Edinburgh EH1 1QW
tel 0131-226 0931
email jemrolls@bigword.fsnet.co.uk
website www.geocities.com/poemsandpints/misc/bigword.htm#ed

Coffee House Poetry
Troubadour Coffee House, 265 Old Brompton Road, London SW5
tel 020-7370 1434

Dead Good Poets Society
96 Bould Street, Liverpool L1 4HY
tel 0151-709 5221
email dgps@blueyonder.co.uk
Contact Cath Nichols

Express Excess
The Enterprise, 2 Haverstock Hill, London NW3
tel 020-7485 2659

Poetry Café
22 Betterton Street, London WC2 9BX
tel 020-7420 9888

Shortfuse
The Camden Head, Camden Walk, Islington, London N1
website www.20six.co.uk/shortfuse

Spiel
20 Coxwell Street, Cirencester, Glos. GL7 2BH
tel (01285) 640470
email spiel@scarum.freeserve.co.uk, spiel@arbury.freeserve.co.uk
website www.author.co.uk/spiel/index.htm

Voice Box
Level 5, Royal Festival Hall, London SE1
tel 020-7960 4242

COMPETITIONS

There are now hundreds of competitions to enter and as the prizes increase, the highest being £5000 (first prize in the National Poetry Competition and the Arvon Foundation International Poetry Competition), so does the prestige associated with winning such competitions.

To decide which competitions are worth entering, make sure you know who the judges are and think twice before paying large sums for an anthology of 'winning' poems which will only be read by entrants wanting to see their own work in print. The Poetry Library publishes a list of competitions each month (available free on receipt of a large sae). See also *Getting poetry published* on page 311 and *Prizes and awards* on page 561.

Literary prizes are given annually to published poets and as such are non-competitive. An A–Z guide to literary prizes can be found on the Booktrust website (www.booktrust.org.uk).

WHERE TO WRITE POETRY

The Arvon Foundation
Lumb Bank – The Ted Hughes Arvon Centre, Hebden Bridge, West Yorkshire HX7 6DF
tel (01422) 843714 *fax* (01422) 843714
The Arvon Foundation at Totleigh Barton, Sheepwash, Beaworthy, Devon EX21 5NS
tel (01409) 231338 *fax* (01409) 231144
The Arvon Foundation at Moniack Mhor, Teavarren, Kiltarlity, Beauly, Inverness-shire IV4 7HT
tel (01463) 741675 *fax* (01463) 741733
The Hurst – The John Osborne Arvon Centre, Clunton, Craven Arms, Shrops. SY7 0JA
tel (01588) 640658 *fax* (01588) 640509
email hurst@arvonfoundation.org
website www.arvonfoundation.org

The Arvon Foundation's 4 centres run 5-day residential courses throughout the year to anyone over the age of 16, providing the opportunity to live and work with professional writers. Writing genres explored include poetry, narrative, drama, writing for children, song writing and the performing arts. Bursaries are available to those receiving benefits. Founded in 1968.

The Poetry School
1A Jewel Road, London E17 4QU
tel (0845) 223 5274 *fax* 020-822 30439
email programme@poetryschool.com
website www.poetryschool.com

Using London venues and regional centres in Manchester, York and Exeter, the Poetry School offers a core programme of tuition in reading and writing poetry. It provides a forum to share experience, develop skills and extend appreciation of both traditional and innovative aspects of poetry.

The Poet's House/Teach na hÉigse
Clonbarra, Falcarragh, County Donegal, Republic of Ireland
tel (074) 65470 *fax* (074) 65471
email phouse@iol.ie

The Poet's House runs 3 10-day poetry courses in July and August. An MA degree in creative writing is validated by Lancaster University, and the Irish Language Faculty includes Cathal O'Searcaigh. The poetry faculty comprises 30 writers, including Paul Durcan and John Montagu.

Ty Newydd
Taliesin Trust, Ty Newydd, Llanystumdwy, Criccieth, Gwynedd LL52 0LW
tel (01766) 522811 *fax* (01766) 523095
email post@tynewydd.org
website www.tynewydd.org

Ty Newydd runs week-long writing courses encompassing a wide variety of genres, including poetry, and caters for all levels, from beginners to published poets. All the courses are tutored by published writers. Writing retreats are also available.

GROUPS ON THE INTERNET

It is worth searching for discussion groups and chat rooms on the internet. There are plenty of them; John Kinsella's is highly recommended, which is junk mail-resistant and highly informative:

John Kinsella's
email poetryetc@jiscmail.ac.uk

The Poetry Kit
website www.poetrykit.org/wkshops2.htm

Local groups
Local groups vary enormously so it is worth shopping around to find one that suits your poetry. Up-to-date information can be obtained from Arts Council England regional offices (see page 520).

The Poetry Library publishes a list of groups for the Greater London area which will be sent out on receipt of a large sae.

HELP FOR YOUNG POETS AND TEACHERS

National Association of Writers in Education (NAWE)
PO Box 1, Sheriff Hutton, York YO60 7YU
tel/fax (01653) 618429
email paul@nawe.co.uk
website www.nawe.co.uk

NAWE is a national organisation, which aims to widen the scope of writing in education, and coordinate activities between writers, teachers and funding bodies. It publishes the magazine *Writing in Education* and is author of a writers' database which can identify writers who fit the given criteria (e.g. speaks several languages, works well with special needs, etc) for schools, colleges and the community. Publishes *Reading the Applause: Reflections on Performance Poetry by Various Artists*. Write for membership details.

The Poetry Library

Children's Section, Royal Festival Hall, London
SE1 8XX
tel 020-7921 0664
website www.poetrylibrary.org.uk

For young poets, the Poetry Library has about 4000 books incorporating the SIGNAL Collection of Children's Poetry. It also has a multimedia children's section, from which cassettes and videos are available to engage children's interest in poetry.

The Poetry Library has an education service for teachers and writing groups. Its information file covers all aspects of poetry in education. There is a separate collection of books and materials for teachers and poets who work with children in schools, and teachers may join a special membership scheme to borrow books for the classroom.

Poetry Society Education

The Poetry Society, 22 Betterton Street, London
WC2H 9BX
tel 020-7420 9894 *fax* 020-7240 4818
email education@poetrysociety.org.uk
website www.poetrysociety.org.uk
Membership £50 secondary schools, £30 primary schools

The Poetry Society has an outstanding reputation for its exciting and innovative education work. For over 30 years it has been introducing poets into classrooms, providing comprehensive teachers' resources and producing colourful, accessible publications for pupils.

Poetry Society Education develops projects and schemes to keep poetry flourishing in schools, libraries and workplaces. Schemes like Poets in Schools, Poet in the City and Poetry Places (a 2-year programme of residencies and placements, funded by the Arts Council's 'Arts for Everyone' lottery budget) have enabled the Poetry Society to give work to hundreds of poets and allowed thousands of children and adults to experience poetry for themselves.

Through projects such as the Respect Slam and The Foyle Young Poets of the Year Award the Poetry Society gives valuable encouragement and exposure to young writers and performers.

Schools membership offers publications, training opportunities for teachers and poets, a free subscription to *Poems on the Underground* and a consultancy service giving advice on working with poets in the classroom. *Poetryclass*, an INSET training project funded by the DfES, employs poets to train teachers at primary and secondary level. Youth membership is available to 11–18 year-olds and provides advice on developing writing skills, access to publication on the Poetry Society website, quarterly issues of *Poetry News*, and poetry books and posters.

Poetry Society publications for schools include *The Poetry Book for Primary Schools* and *Jumpstart – Poetry in the Secondary School*, a young poet's pack and posters for Key Stage 1 to GCSE requirements. Information on resources, membership, the Foyle Young Poets of the Year Award and educational residencies is available from the Education department.

YOUNG POETRY COMPETITIONS

Children's competitions are included in the competition list provided by the Poetry Library (free on receipt of a large sae).

Foyle Young Poets of the Year Award

The Poetry Society, 22 Betterton Street, London
WC2H 9BX
tel 020-7420 9894 *fax* 020-7240 4818
email education@poetrysociety.org.uk
website www.poetrysociety.org.uk

Free entry for 11–17 year-olds with unique prizes.

Christopher Tower Poetry Prize

Tower Poetry, Christ Church, Oxford OX1 1DP
tel/fax (01865) 286591
email info@towerpoetry.org.uk
website www.towerpoetry.org.uk/prize/index.html

An annual poetry competition from Christ Church, Oxford, open to 16–18 year-olds in UK schools and colleges. The poems should be no longer than 48 lines, on a different chosen theme each year. Prizes: £1500 (1st), prize £750 (2nd), £500 (3rd). Every winner also receives a prize for their school. Highly commended entries each receive £200.

Further reading

Baldwin, Michael, *The Way to Write Poetry*, Hamish Hamilton, 1982, o.p.

Chisholm, Alison, *The Craft of Writing Poetry*, Allison & Busby, 1997, repr. 2001

Chisholm, Alison, *A Practical Poetry Course*, Allison & Busby, 1997

Corti, Doris, *Writing Poetry*, Writers News Library of Writing/Thomas & Lochar, 1994

Fairfax, John, and John Moat, *The Way to Write*, Elm Tree Books, 2nd edn revised, 1998

Finch, Peter, *How to Publish Your Poetry*, Allison & Busby, 2nd edn, 1998

Forbes, Peter, *Scanning the Century*, Penguin Books, 2000

Hamilton, Ian, *The Oxford Companion to Twentieth Century Poetry in English*, OUP, 1996

Hyland, Paul, *Getting into Poetry*, Bloodaxe, 2nd edn, 1997

Livingstone, Dinah, *Poetry Handbook for Readers and Writers*, Macmillan, 1992

O'Brien, Sean, *The Firebox*, Picador, 1998

Reading the Applause: Reflections on Performance Poetry by Various Artists, NAWE, 1999

Riggs, Thomas (ed.), *Contemporary Poets*, St James Press, 7th edn, 2000

Roberts, Philip Davies, *How Poetry Works*, Penguin Books, 2nd edn, 2000

Sansom, Peter, *Writing Poems*, Bloodaxe, 1994, reprinted 1997

Sweeney Matthew, and John Williams, *Teach Yourself Writing Poetry*, Hodder and Stoughton, 2003

Whitworth, John, *Writing Poetry*, A & C Black, 2001

USA

Breen, Nancy, *Poet's Market*, Writer's Digest Books, USA, 2004

Fulton, Len, *Directory of Poetry Publishers 2004–2005*, Dustbooks, USA, 20th edn, 2004

Fulton, Len, *The International Directory of Little Magazines and Small Presses*, Dustbooks, USA, 40th edn, 2004–2005

Preminger, Alex, *New Princeton Encyclopedia of Poetry and Poetics*, Princeton University Press, 3rd edn, 1993

See also...

- *Publishers of poetry*, page 766
- *Getting poetry published*, page 311
- *Approaching a poetry publisher, page 317*

Television, film and radio
Notes from a successful television screenwriter

Andrew Davies tells how he became a 'proper' writer.

I didn't begin as a screenwriter. I began as a poet. There was no television in the house I grew up in, and there was hardly any such thing as television drama. This was the early Fifties. There was a girl in our village called Jane Grant-Hughes, with a well-off dad, and they had a television. It was as big as a wardrobe with a tiny screen in the middle of it. I remember a bunch of us being invited round to Jane's house to watch a production of *The Merry Wives of Windsor*, and it was very grey and fuzzy and actually excruciatingly boring. The idea of anybody deliberately writing television drama seemed ludicrous to me.

I wanted to be a writer but my father, a teacher, sensibly pointed out that most writers didn't make anywhere near enough money to live on and I should have a job that paid the bills and write in my spare time. Like him, I became a teacher – I was attracted by the short hours and long holidays (time to write) but found that I enjoyed teaching and was quite good at it. I got home at 4.30pm and there were a couple of hours before my wife got home and I wrote in that time: short stories and radio plays mostly. There was a market for short stories in those days, not that I sold any, and there was a market for radio plays by new writers, and there still is (hint hint). I was also writing poetry and articles for *Punch*, sketches and jokes for sketch shows, and a novel, everything, really. Hardly any of it sold, but I was enjoying myself. I always tried to make sure there was at least one thing *out there* with my hopes riding on it. (That's another thing I would recommend to the struggling writer.) When I did sell something, I spent the money immediately, on something specific. I remember I sold a couple of sketches to a radio programme called *Monday Night at Home* and bought a rather fine corduroy jacket with the proceeds.

The late Fifties and early Sixties were a good time for radio plays. There were a lot of poetic and experimental ones on the 'Third Programme' as Radio Three used to be called. Dylan Thomas and Louis MacNeice wrote radio plays; so did Pinter and Stoppard. And my first substantial sale was a radio play. It was based on an extraordinary time I'd spent on teaching practice in a benighted school deep in the Welsh valleys. Hilarious, touching, more than a little obscene, more than a little libellous as it turned out. (I guess another tip is: recognise when you've had a unique experience, and get all the juice you can out of it, but try to avoid getting sued.) The play was later successfully produced after I'd changed the names, physical characteristics and, in some cases, the sex of some of the teachers in the story; but it was a close-run thing, almost the end of my career before I'd even properly got started. That was in 1960.

I continued to write radio plays throughout the Sixties, acquiring an agent in the process. He came to me, not the other way round, and I graciously acceded to his plan to 'exploit me in all media' as he put it. It was the first time I had heard the word 'exploit' used in anything other than a pejorative sense. By 1965 we had a house and a puppy and a baby, and it seemed time to get a television as well. These were the days of the *Wednesday Play*, Dennis Potter, *Cathy Come Home*, and all that. I was entranced. I bought a book of television playscripts – I remember it included a wry little comedy by a guy I'd never heard of called Peter Nichols – and studied the layout and the length of scenes – the whole grammar of television drama. There weren't any creative writing courses or books on how to do it then. But study the best and steal from them has always been a good way to learn.

Early television success

I'm sure there must have been a couple of false starts, but the way I remember it is I sat down and wrote a play about a girl in a knicker factory and sent it off to the *Wednesday Play*, like doing the pools, really, and it was accepted – and produced. And it did very well. I really did think then that I was a made man… but it was FIVE YEARS before I sold another television play. I was still getting the radio plays done, and I could always kid myself I was a teacher really and just a hobby writer, but it was a tough time. And so the next bit of advice is that you have to like writing enough to keep going (that's the most important thing) and have faith in your own ability (also important) and dream the impossible dream (that's complete b******* , actually) and things may eventually get better.

For me they got better when a script editor called Louis Marks took a fancy to a half-hour script I'd written called 'Is That Your Body Boy?' and accepted it for a strand called Thirty-Minute (I keep nagging the BBC to revive the original half-hour play or film, so far with no success.) Anyway, that was done and got great reviews, and Louis Marks became a producer, and for some time his career and mine hung by the same slender thread as he continued to commission me to write single plays, often in 'anthology' series on a common theme. He also recommended me to other producers as fast, clever and cheap. (I am still reasonably fast and clever, I hope, but no longer cheap.) It's still a wonderful and important thing to find a producer who loves your work and will stick his (or nowadays more usually her) neck out for it, but these days producers have very little clout: all depends on the whim (or judgement as they prefer to think of it) of the commissioners.

By the mid-Seventies I was able to think of myself as an established writer, and this was consolidated when I was given the chance to adapt a sprawling Delderfield novel called *To Serve Them All My Days*, about a chap who gets invalided out of World War I and spends what seems like the next hundred years teaching in a West Country boarding school. This established me as a writer who was capable of the long haul, and led to the commissioning of *A Very Peculiar Practice*, an original serial set in a campus university, which went out in the mid-Eighties, and is probably the television work of which I am most proud.

Becoming a 'proper' writer

It was at this time, 1986 to be precise, that I resigned from the day job at Warwick University and became a 'proper' writer. I celebrated this by suffering my first ever writer's block. Now I *had* to keep my family by writing, the thing seemed quite impossible. But fortunately I didn't have to suffer alone for too long: there were too many people who couldn't start their work until I had done mine, and I was coaxed out of my creative paralysis with the traditional application of bullying and whisky. Writer's block is all about performance anxiety, fear of failure, and there's a bit of it in every project – especially in the early stages. Experience and past successes don't help as much as you would think. In fact I am stuck on a script at the moment, which is why I am writing this article way before its deadline.

And unless inspiration descends like a thunderbolt, I am going to have to take the traditional route: if you can't think of anything good, write something bad and rewrite it later.

Enough of such gloomy thoughts. What are the nice things about being a successful television writer? Money, obviously. Lunch at the Ivy is very nice. Fame can be a bit of a nuisance, though I guess most people would like to try it for a bit to see how it goes. Mostly, for me, the joy comes from working in a collaborative medium, which means that you are being stimulated by the bright ideas of producers and script editors; surprised by the creative flair of directors who do things you wouldn't have thought of with your work, but things that seem utterly right; actors who make your lines sound better than they really are. Just about my favourite part of the process is the 'readthrough'. It's the first time the actors come together, and it's the first time you get a feel for what the final thing will be like. And sometimes, if one of the actors can't make it, I get a chance to 'read in' – and when you're playing a scene with Gillian Anderson, say, life doesn't get much better, even if you're sitting in a draughty church hall, which is where these things always seem to take place.

But if you write for performance, that experience – seeing and hearing your words come alive off the page – is something all dramatists can experience, even if the production is by your local amateur group and never gets any further than that draughty church hall. In fact, that's the last bit of advice I'd give: if you write for performance, try to get it done somehow, even if it's just an informal reading with your friends. It's the best way to learn.

Andrew Davies has been writing for the screen since 1965. His television originals include *A Very Peculiar Practice, Getting Hurt, A Few Short Journeys of the Heart, Filipina Dreamgirls, Boudica (The Warrior Queen), The Chatterley Affair,* and the sitcom *Game On* (with Bernadette Davis.) He has adapted *Middlemarch, Pride and Prejudice, Moll Flanders, Emma, Mother Love, House of Cards* (for which he won an Emmy award) *Vanity Fair, Wives and Daughters* and *Take a Girl Like You* for television. Also *Othello, The Way We Live Now* (for which he won a BAFTA) *Daniel Deronda, Dr Zhivago, Tipping The Velvet, He Knew He Was Right, Bleak House* and *The Line of Beauty.* In production or preparation are *Northanger Abbey, Fanny Hill* and *Sense and Sensibility.* He has big-screen credits for *Circle of Friends, Bridget Jones's Diary, The Tailor of Panama,* and *Bridget Jones: The Edge of Reason.* Andrew was awarded a BAFTA Fellowship in 2002.

Adaptations from books

Although every writer wants to create their own work and find their own voice, adaptation is a good way both to generate income and to learn about how to write for other formats. It can also be a chance for a writer to raise their profile, with a successful adaptation sometimes leading to an original commission. Kate Sinclair explains.

Although every writer wants to create their own work and find their own voice, adaptation is a good way both to generate income and to learn about the disciplines of different media: how to write for other formats.

Writers may be approached to adapt their own work from one medium to another during their career. For example, John Mortimer originally wrote *A Voyage Round My Father* for the radio and later adapted it for stage, film and finally, for television. There are also opportunities for both writers and directors to adapt someone else's work from one performance medium to another or from a novel to any of the above.

Every year classic novels are made into adaptations for all media. These may be for the theatre, such as Helen Edmundson's version of *War and Peace* (Shared Experience/RNT), or for radio such as *Rob Roy* (the Classic Serial, Radio 4). Television carries dramatisations like *The Forsyte Saga* (ITV) or *Daniel Deronda* (BBC), and film features screenplays such as Terence Davies' version of Edith Wharton's *The House of Mirth*. Although these are usually costly to produce, involving large casts and – particularly in the visual media – the considerable expense of recreating the period in which they were written, they command loyal audiences and seem to be in steady demand. These classic projects also generate significant income both from DVD/video sales and from sales to overseas companies and networks. Some adapters are as well known as writers who concentrate on their own work. For example, Andrew Davies has become almost a household name for his television dramatisations of *Pride and Prejudice*, *The Way of the World* and, more recently, *Dr Zhivago*.

Producers in radio, television and film are also in regular contact with publishers and literary agents to keep abreast of contemporary novels which may work well in another format. I currently work as the Books Executive for Film Four to find books, both fiction and non-fiction, which may become television dramas or feature films. The BBC also employs someone in this capacity to identify suitable material for their Serials and Film Departments. Both radio producers and film companies are also sent potential books by the publicity departments of publishing houses. Writers may also make direct approaches to producers and commissioners with material that they feel they can successfully transcribe for that particular medium.

There is clearly, then, a market for adaptations of all types, with the added stimulus to the adapter of exploring technically how another writer writes – their use of language, the way they structure a narrative, their characterisation. There is the opportunity to learn from the skill and subtlety of great writers and there is the challenge of finding ways to transport a story from one form to another, with all the creative possibilities that this presents.

What to adapt, and why?

Just because a narrative works in one format doesn't guarantee that it will in another. Form and story are often inextricably bound together. Something works as a radio play precisely because it appeals to a listening audience and is able to exploit the possibilities of sound. A novel may have a reflective subject, or concentrate on a character's inner thoughts, and not on external action. While this may be fine for reading quietly alone, it could leave a theatre, television or film audience bored and longing for something to happen.

There are some stories, however, which seem to work in almost any media and which have almost become universal (though different treatments bring out diverse aspects of the original). For example, Henry James's *The Turn of the Screw* was written as a novella. It subsequently became a much-performed opera, with a libretto by Myfanwy Piper and music by Benjamin Britten; an acclaimed film, re-titled *The Innocents* with the screenplay by John Mortimer; and a recent television adaptation for ITV by Nick Dear. What makes a narrative like this transmute so successfully?

At the most simplistic level it must be dramatic. Radio, television and film, like the theatre, need drama to hold their audiences. Aristotle's premise that 'all drama is action', and should have protagonists whom we identify with, antagonists who oppose them, and the reversals, climaxes and resolutions which typify a dramatic structure. This is not necessarily the case for a novel; it is easy to be seduced by a tale that has personal resonance or beautiful language and forget the basic template which has, after all, worked for thousands of years. Reminding yourself of this when considering the suitability of any material for adaptation could spare you a rejection or a great deal of later reworking.

Knowing the media

The other important consideration is a detailed knowledge of the final medium. The adapter needs to understand why that particular story is specifically suited to it and ideally have experience of writing for that form, as well as an awareness of the current market for the project. It is vital to know precisely what is currently being produced and by whom. Staff and policies change very quickly, so the more up-to-date your research is, the better your chance of creating a successful adaptation and being able to get it accepted.

If you are adapting for the theatre, how often do you go and when was the last time you saw a production that wasn't originally written for the stage? As well as observing how successful it was, both artistically and in box office terms, would you know whether that company or theatre regularly programmes adaptations, and if so, what sort? Do they, like Shared Experience, have a reputation primarily for classics, or do they, like the Loft at the Royal National Theatre, or The Royal Exchange, Manchester, produce versions of contemporary novels? Are you sufficiently aware of the tastes of the current artistic director and the identity of the theatre to know whether to send your project to the Royal Shakespeare Company, the West Yorkshire Playhouse or Southwark Playhouse? This is not necessarily just a question of scale or level, but more a reflection of contemporary trends and the specific policy of each of these institutions. Whilst the overall remit of a theatre or company may remain the same – if they are funded to produce only new plays, it is unlikely that this will alter – individual personnel and fashions will change regularly and it is important to keep in touch.

Television and radio

The same holds true for all the other media and, if anything, is even more important in radio and television. All of the broadcast media are now subject to the rigorous demands of ratings, which in turn make for extremely precise scheduling. Programmes have strong identities, and conversations with producers and commissioners will inevitably involve a discussion of which slot a project is suited to and what has recently been shown or broadcast. Up-to-the-minute knowledge of the work being produced by a company or broadcaster is therefore essential.

For example, BBC Radio 3's *Wire* is specifically for new work by contemporary writers and therefore isn't suitable for a classic adaptation of a novel. Radio 4 produces the Classic Serial on Sunday afternoons and *Women's Hour* has a regular serialisation slot that can be contemporary or classic and is often an adapted novel. Biographies or autobiographies are also frequently abridged and read on Radio 4 at 9.45am on weekdays. For a detailed knowledge of this output there can be no substitute for studying the *Radio Times*, seeing what is programmed, and listening to what gets produced in which slots. Being able to envisage the eventual destination for a chosen adaptation helps you to choose the right project and place it successfully.

In television this process of research is more complex. As well as strong competition between the BBC and the larger independent broadcasters (ITV, Channel 4, Carlton, Granada, etc) to secure an audience, there is also considerable rivalry between the hundreds of independent production companies to receive commissions. The ratings war means that scheduling is paramount and big dramatic adaptations are often programmed at exactly the same time on BBC 2 and ITV. Familiarity with the output of each channel is crucial

Successful collaborations

Here is an entirely subjective list of my personal favourites among successful collaborations, by way of example.

Film

Motorcycle Diaries (Ché Guevara, screenplay Joe Rivera)

Enduring Love (Ian McEwan, screenplay Joe Penhall)

Trainspotting (Irvine Welsh, screenplay John Hodges)

Lord of the Rings (J.R.R. Tolkien, screenplay Fran Walsh)

The House of Mirth (Edith Wharton, screenplay Terence Davis)

Jude (George Eliott, screenplay Hossein Amini)

Persuasion (Jane Austen, screenplay Nick Dear)

Television

Bleak House (Charles Dickens, adaptation Andrew Davies)

The Way of the World (Anthony Trollope, adaptation Andrew Davies)

The Forsyte Saga (John Galsworthy, adaptation Stephen Mallatratt)

Brideshead Revisited (Evelyn Waugh, adaptation John Mortimer)

The Buddha of Suburbia (Hanif Kureshi, adaptation Roger Michell and Hanif Kureshi)

Longitude (Dava Sobel, adaptation Charles Sturridge)

Theatre

The Mill on the Floss (George Eliot, adaptation Helen Edmundson)

Nana (Emile Zola, adaptation Pam Gems)

The Magic Toyshop (Angela Carter, adaptation Bryony Lavery)

Radio

The Old Curiosity Shop (Charles Dickens, adaptation Mike Walker)

when suggesting projects for adaptation, either to a commissioner or a production company. Again, watching dramatisations and noting what format they are in, who is producing them, and when they are being broadcast, is all part of the job.

As a general rule it is helpful to know that both adaptations and writing commissioned directly for television, tend to be divided into several basic categories (not including soaps). Single dramas are usually high profile, broadcast at peak times and are about two hours long. Series consist of a number of weekly parts shown over several weeks (3, 4, 6, 8 and 10 are all common), each part lasting anywhere between 30 and 60 minutes; there has also recently been a trend for fewer 90-minute-long episodes. Finally there are two-part dramas or event pieces which take place on consecutive nights with each part between one and two hours long. The percentage of adaptations will generally be lower than newly commissioned drama, although this is entirely dependent upon the type of slot and the broadcaster. For example, the BBC has approximately double the budget per hour for drama that Channel 4 has, and produces many more dramatisations of classic novels. Likewise, ITV has currently been producing regular serialisations of classics and single adaptations in association with HSBC. Channel 4, when it commissions adaptations, tends to focus on cutting-edge contemporary novels, such as *White Teeth* by Zadie Smith, adapted by Simon Burke. And there are of course always exceptions to all these trends, which is why it is necessary to be an aware and regular viewer.

If you want to adapt for film, the nature of what will work and when, seems to be more open-ended, though it is of course important to go regularly to the cinema and know what has been produced recently. This may be to do with the nature of distribution – the fact that most films are on in a number of cinemas for several weeks – and the time it takes to make a film – often years between the initial idea and eventual screening. However, you still need to keep up-to-date with who is producing what and when. It is worth noting though that there is a strong relationship between books and film. At the current time approximately half of the projects in development at Film Four are based on book adaptations.

The rights

Once you have selected your material and medium, it is vital to establish who has the rights to the original and whether these are available for negotiation. Sometimes this involves a bit of detective work. If the writer is dead, it is necessary to find out whether there is an estate and if the work is still subject to copyright.

Copyright law is extremely complex. In the UK it has altered from 50 to 70 years, so some texts that were out of copyright have gone back in again (for further information see *UK copyright law*, page 688). This varies, however, around the world so it is essential therefore that you seek expert advice concerning the current rules of copyright for any potential project, depending on the country of origin.

It is usually possible to begin the search for the copyright holder and source of rights from the imprint page of the novel, play, film script, etc. If this information is not given, try the publisher, the Society of Authors or the Writers' Guild.

In the case of a living writer, you will need to establish who their literary agent is – if they have one – and contact them to see if adaptation is possible and how much it will cost. The scale of costs will depend upon the medium. Rights for a stage adaptation are often separate from film or television options. If a book or play has already been optioned, this means that it is probably not available for a period of at least 12–18 months. Should the purchaser of the option choose not to renew, or fail to produce the adaptation within the required timescale, rights may become available again. Many agreements include an extension clause for a further fixed time period, however, and this is particularly common in film as the end-product is rarely produced within 18 months.

Large film companies, particularly in Hollywood, will often buy the rights to a book or script outright, sometimes for a substantial sum. The proposed version may never get made but legally the original will not be available for adaptation by anyone else. If the writer or material is famous enough, or if they have a good agent, a time limit will be part of the original agreement. Complete buy-outs are less common in the UK.

The cost of acquiring rights varies significantly with the scale of the project, the profile of the writer and the intended medium. Usually an initial payment will be needed to secure the rights for a fixed period, followed by the same amount again, should an extension be necessary. In addition, there is nearly always some form of royalty for the original writer or estate in the form of a percentage of the overall profits of the final production, film, or broadcast. This will normally have a 'bottom ceiling' – a minimum amount or reserve – which must be paid whether or not the final work is financially successful. With television, film or radio, there may be a further payment for repeats and in the theatre the rate may well alter if the production transfers. Sometimes, with a low-budget production such as a fringe show or short film, a writer or estate will waive any initial rights fee and only expect a royalty.

Legalities aside, time spent forming a relationship with the writer of the original, or whoever manages their estate, has other another much more important function, a creative one, that of getting closer to the source material.

How to adapt

I don't believe it is possible to lay down a set of rules for adapting, any more than one could invent a meaningful template for creative writing. The only observation I can offer, therefore, is personal and a reflection of my own taste.

When I recommend or commission an adaptation, either to direct in the theatre, or for television and film, my first requirement is that something in the original story has hooked me and I want to see the original given another life and another audience. I have to be able to imagine that it has the potential to work dramatically in a different format and can often already see or hear fragments of it.

At this stage I ask myself a lot of questions about the material. Why should it be done in another medium? How is it possible to achieve this particular part of the narrative, this character, this tone, this sequence of action, in a way that is different but still truthful, a sort of creative equivalent, like a metaphor. For me, it is all about thinking laterally and being enthused about the new possibilities another form will generate from the original, or vice versa.

This process generally leads me back to the source, be it book, film or play, in order to dig over everything about it and its writer. As well as looking at other adaptations to see what parts of the original have been enhanced or cut, I like to meet and talk to the writer. If they are no longer alive I try to find out about them from books and/or people who knew them. I want to know what interested them; what were they thinking when they were writing; even what they looked at every day. If possible, I like to go and visit the places they have written about or the place in which they wrote. This process of total immersion helps me to get under the skin of the original.

While this is entirely personal, it raises an interesting question which I believe any adapter needs to answer for themselves. How closely do you wish to replicate the original material and how much do you intend to depart from it? Choosing not to stick closely to the source may be the most creative decision you make but you must understand why you are doing it and what the effect will be. After all, two different trains of thought, styles and imaginations need to be fused together for this transformation to be complete and it is important that the balance between them works. I once spoke to a writer who was commissioned to adapt a well-known myth for Hollywood. Several drafts later, when he had been asked to alter all the key elements of the story to the point where it was unrecognisable, he decided to quit. It was the right decision and the film was a flop.

While respect for the writer and the source material is fundamental, there are of course lots of examples where enormous lateral and creative changes have been made to make a story work to optimum effect in its new medium. What matters ultimately is the integrity of the final product. At its best, it is like a marriage of two minds, celebrating the talents of both writer and adapter in an equally creative partnership.

Kate Sinclair is the Literary Consultant for the UK Film Council. She has also worked as a director in theatre and radio, and is currently producing and directing films.

Writing for television

Writing for television can be extremely rewarding. Anji Loman Field says that any writer with the right aptitude and attitude can succeed, and here she gives advice for screenwriters.

The markets

There are various openings for new writers in television, but apart from competitions and special projects these are hardly ever advertised. The BBC's latest information on opportunities for new writers can be found at www.bbc.co.uk/writersroom. The openings fall into four categories:

Single drama

There are fewer slots nowadays for the single play – a 30- or even 60-minute one-off drama is highly unlikely to find a market. Occasionally broadcasters will gather single plays together under a collective banner but it's best to think of individual projects as either standalone television films, two-parters or even four-parters. It's always worth asking television companies for their guidelines on single drama and film. is currently commissioning 30-minute dramas from new writers via its Independent Film & Video department.

Series and serials

Although it has been known for a new writer to sell an original series or serial, it is a relatively rare occurrence. Writers with a track record of writing for existing strands are far more likely to be taken seriously. Long-running soaps like *EastEnders*, *Doctors* and *Emmerdale* are sometimes in the market for new writers, but check first. If the door is open, a good 'calling card script' is usually the way in. Submit an original piece of work in a similar genre that is at least an hour long and shows your ability to create believable characters, write sparkling dialogue and tell a compelling story. You may be invited to try out for one of these long-running shows.

Dramatisations/adaptations

A new writer is extremely unlikely to be commissioned to adapt or dramatise someone else's work for television. However, if there's something you really want to adapt and you can afford to take out an 'option' on the rights (or already own them, if it is your own novel or play) then write the script on spec. If you have a good script and can show that you own the rights, you could succeed.

Situation comedy

This is the one area where production companies and broadcasters are desperate for new talent to write for existing shows, and there are often competitions open to new writers. If you are a good comedy writer and market your work well, you will undoubtedly succeed (see 'Writing situation comedy' below).

Children's drama/comedy

This is an important market for broadcasters and audiences, and long-running shows always need talented writers.

Aptitude and attitude

The first prerequisite in writing for television is that you enjoy the medium, and actually watch the kinds of shows that you would be interested in writing for. A cynical approach will always show through. And before sitting down to write that first television script, arm yourself with the appropriate skills by examining the medium as a whole.

- **Tape the kind of show you'd like to write for and analyse it**. How many scenes are there? What length are they? How much of the story happens 'off camera'? Knowing the answers to these questions will help you to understand the grammar of screen, and enable you to write a more professional script.
- **Study the structure of story telling**. There are plenty of books on the subject, and although it is never a good idea to follow structural paradigms to the letter, absorb as much information as possible so that the essential 'rules' on character, motivation and plot filter through into your writing.
- **Read scripts**. Some are published in book form, but a huge variety of scripts are also available from specialist bookshops such as Offstage (*tel* 020-7240 3883), the Screenwriter's Store (*tel* 020-7261 1908) and the internet (e.g. www.bbc.co.uk/writersroom/scriptarchive).
- **If you want to write sitcom, see as many live recordings of shows as possible**. This enables you to understand the techniques involved in television production, and particularly the physical constraints imposed by the studio. Free tickets for sitcom recordings are usually available – phone the broadcasters for information.
- **Be realistic**. Don't make your first project too ambitious in terms of screen time, locations or special effects. If you can 'contain the action' and make your first script affordable to shoot, it is far more likely to be taken seriously.

Learning the craft

Even the most successful and experienced screenwriters say they never stop learning. Some have been lucky enough to learn the skill of writing for the screen in a subliminal way. For example, Lynda La Plante (*Prime Suspect*) was an actress with plenty of opportunity for studying scripts and production techniques before she turned her hand to writing; John Sullivan (*Only Fools and Horses*) worked in the props department at the BBC on countless sitcoms, and used to take the scripts home to study. But there are other ways to learn. Script workshops are particularly useful.

There are many courses and workshops available. These range from small self-help groups, where writers give each other feedback on their work, to full- and part-time Screenwriting MA courses at universities (e.g. in London, Sheffield, Leicester, Bournemouth, Manchester and Leeds). Evening classes are springing up in local colleges, and there are even script workshops on the internet. Workshops can help in the following ways:

- **Discipline**. The hardest thing most writers ever have to do is sit down and face that blank screen or page. Joining a script workshop – where you *have* to deliver an outline or a treatment, or the next 20 pages of your script by a certain date – provides the push that so many writers need.
- **Feedback**. Reading and giving feedback on other people's work helps you to focus on getting your own script right. It is also good to get used to the idea of showing your own work to others and getting their feedback. Television writing is generally a collaborative process and writers need to be pleasant to work with, and receptive to ideas. Knowing when to argue a point and when to concede are crucial skills which can be developed in good writing workshops.
- **Rewriting**. Learn to Love the Rewrite. It is such a major achievement to get to the end of a first draft that it is all too easy to rush to the post box and send it off to several

production companies at once. *Four Weddings and a Funeral*, a Channel 4-funded project, went through 17 rewrites before finally reaching the screen. So before you post your masterpiece:

● Leave it to 'settle' for a few days and do something completely different – allow your head to clear completely. Then re-read the script from beginning to end – from as objective a viewpoint as possible – and make necessary changes.

● Get feedback so that you're sure your script is ready to send. Be warned: knowing how to read and analyse a script properly is a particular skill. Unless they are equipped in this area, *never* ask your friends or relations to read your script. Their comments could either lull you into a false sense of security or destroy your confidence for ever. Feedback from other writers in your workshop group is best. There are some organisations (including the Screenwriters' Workshop) which offer a professional script feedback service for a moderate fee.

Writing situation comedy

Situation comedy writing is the most lucrative area of television, and deservedly so. Have you ever tried making an audience laugh several times a minute for 25 minutes for at least six weeks running, and maybe (in the case of *Last of the Summer Wine*) for 20 long years?

Despite its name, sitcom is less about situation and much more about character. It is better to start with funny and engaging characters in mind and then (if it isn't part and parcel of the character) find the perfect situation in which to place them than it is to begin with the premise 'nobody's ever set a sitcom in a nuclear power station before'. It is not the setting that makes the audience laugh, it is the characters.

A good exercise in seeing if you can write funny material is to write an episode of an existing sitcom. If *Fawlty Towers* is your all-time favourite, study a few episodes and then try your own. It will never get made, but you'll learn a lot in the process – and sample scripts like this are often useful as calling card scripts.

Some of the broadcast companies issue guidelines on writing situation comedy – phone their comedy departments for information.

Competitions

Broadcasters occasionally run writing competitions or 'new writing initiatives' (www.bbc.co.uk/writersroom/opportunity). Check their websites – and general screenwriters' websites – for up-to-date information. Also, watch out for annual awards run by organisations such as PAWS (People's Awareness of Science, *tel* 020-7483 4545) and BBC Talent (www.bbc.co.uk/newtalent). Details can be found in the trade press and via relevant websites and screenwriting organisations. See also *Prizes and awards* on page 561.

Breaking in

Do you need an agent?

Many new writers are keen to get an agent before they attempt to sell anything, but this can be an arduous process and there are few agents prepared to take on a completely untried writer.

The best way to get an agent is to first get an offer of a deal on a project. Most *bona fide* production companies and broadcasters will happily recommend a selection of agents to writers they want to do business with. If you can phone an agent and say 'so-and-so wants to option/commission my project and has recommended you as an agent' he or she is far more likely to be interested. And at that point you can pick and choose the agent who is right for you, rather than going with the first one to say 'yes'.

Selling yourself

Once you are sure you have a good script, where do you send it? If you've done your homework, you will already know which channel is the most likely to be interested. But sometimes it is better to send to an independent production company rather than directly to a broadcaster, so do a bit more research. Check out the companies that are making the kind of show you've written and approach them first.

A preliminary letter or phone call can save you time and money because some smaller companies simply don't have the resources to read unsolicited material. If you feel that a certain production company is absolutely right for your project, write a letter giving a brief synopsis of the project and asking if they will read the script. If they agree, your script will join the 'solicited' pile. And if it fits the bill, they may even pick it up and develop it. But

Useful information

Euroscript
tel (0780) 336 9414
email enquiries@euroscript.co.uk
website www.euroscript.co.uk

An independent, UK based, script development organisation for film and TV which offers analysis of screenplays from a team of screenwriters, producers and experienced teachers in the field. It also offers day-long training workshops focusing on different aspects of screenwriting and development.

Film London
Suite 6.10, The Tea Building, 56 Shoreditch High Street, London E1 6JJ
tel 020-7613 7676 *fax* 020-7613 7677
email info@filmlondon.org.uk
website www.filmlondon.org.uk

Aims to support film and media production, exhibition, education, economic and industrial development across London, and to enhance the city's status as a world class film location. It also aims to enable London's film and media culture to develop so that it reflects the diversity of the city and creates access and opportunities for people from all communities to engage with moving image technologies profitably and creatively.

UK Film Council
10 Little Portland Street, London W1W 7JG
tel 020-7861 7861 *fax* 020-7861 7862
email info@ukfilmcouncil.org.uk

Offers funding for short films and features and training for writers.

PACT (Producers Alliance for Cinema and Television)
The Eye, 2nd Floor, 1 Procter Street, London WC1V 6DW
tel 020-7067 4367 *fax* 020-7067 4377
website www.pact.co.uk

Serves the feature film and independent TV production sector. Its fully searchable, password-protected *Directory* is now online. (See also page 546.)

Arts Council England regional offices
Many regional offices offer grants that enable writers, producers and directors to make their projects (see page 520).

The Spotlight
7 Leicester Place, London WC2H 7RJ
tel 020-7437 7631
email info@splotlight.com
website www.splotlight.com

Publishes an annaul handbook called *Contacts*, which contains useful information and contact addresses.

The Writers' Guild of Great Britain
15 Britannia Street, London WC1X 9JN
tel 020-7833 0777 *fax* 020-7833 4777
email admin@writersguild.org.uk
website www.writersguild.org.uk

Trade union-affiliated organisation for professional writers. Negotiates rates for TV drama with the BBC and the ITV Network Centre. (See also page 516.)

don't expect overnight results. It can sometimes take many months before scripts are even read by small and/or busy companies.

Sending your script directly to a broadcaster can lead to a commission, but unless you target a particular producer whose work you admire you will probably have less control over who you work with. However, BBC writersroom remains a dedicated home for all unsolicited drama and comedy submissions (www.bbc.co.uk/writersroom).

Being 'discovered'

If you can get your work 'rehearse-read' by actors in front of an audience it will help your writing, and may even lead to discovery. Many script readings are attended by development executives from television and production companies and there are many stories of individuals being picked up from such projects. TAPS (Training and Performance Showcase; see page 583), Player–Playwrights (see page 547) and the New Producers Alliance (see page 545) all organise rehearsed readings.

Development hell

This is the place between finding someone who wants to produce your script and waiting for the 'suits' at the television companies to give the final go-ahead for the project. In the meantime you will have been paid, perhaps just an option fee, or maybe a commission fee for a script or two. Either way, *never put all your eggs in one development basket*. Aim eventually to have several projects bubbling under for every one that comes to the boil.

A realistic optimism is required for this game. Don't believe anything wonderful will happen until you actually have that signed contract in front of you. In the meantime keep writing, keep marketing and, if you possibly can, keep making contacts in the industry. If you're good at schmoozing, go to as many industry events as possible and make new contacts. If you can send a script to a producer with a covering letter saying 'I heard your talk the other day…' you will immediately arouse interest.

Coping with rejection

The standard rejection letter is the worst part of this business. When it is accompanied by your returned script – looking decidedly un-read – it is very easy to become disillusioned. The trick is this: change your mental attitude to the point where if you don't receive at least one rejection letter in the post every day, you feel rejected! So long as you are absolutely sure that your work is good, keep sending it out. Sooner or later you'll get a nicer, more personalised rejection letter, and then eventually perhaps even a cup of tea with the producer…

Selling ideas

Completely new writers do occasionally sell ideas but are much more likely to sell the idea alone, i.e. the 'format rights', and will probably end up not writing the script. If you have a great calling card script or two, or have had a few episodes of something produced, your ideas will be taken much more seriously. At this stage you might well sell a project on the basis of a short outline or synopsis, and be paid to write the script(s).

All scripts must be typed and properly formatted if they are to be taken seriously. If you dread the practical aspects of getting your script onto the page it might be worth investing in a software program for your computer. They take the pain out of screenwriting by auto-formatting and numbering the pages and scenes, thus enabling you to move scenes around and restructure your script with ease. Such facilities allow writers to concentrate wholly on the creative process and can therefore be quite liberating, even for those who type well. Contact the Screenwriters' Store for details and advice.

Summary

Writing for television is not generally something that can be taken up as a hobby. It may look easy but huge amounts of work and commitment are required in order to succeed. If that doesn't put you off, and it is what you really want to do, then go for it. And good luck!

Anji Loman Field worked as a television producer for several years before turning to writing. She has since written drama, comedy drama and animation for film, television and radio, and has taught writing at the Screenwriters' Workshop, the Royal College of Art and the London Institute.

Further reading

Friedmann, Julian, *How to Make Money Scriptwriting*, Intellect Books, 2000

Kelsey, Gerald, *Writing for Television*, A & C Black, 3rd edn, 1999

Seger, Linda, *Making a Good Script Great*, Samuel French Inc. (pbk), 1994

Vogler, Christopher, *The Writer's Journey*, Pan, 2nd revised edn (pbk), 1999

Wolfe, Ronald, *Writing Comedy*, Robert Hale, 2003

Writing drama for radio

Writing drama for radio allows a freedom which none of the other performing arts can give. Lee Hall guides the radio drama writer to submit a script which will be well received.

With upwards of 300 hours of radio drama commissioned each year, radio is an insatiable medium and, therefore, one which is constantly seeking new blood. It is no surprise to find that many of our most eminent dramatists, such as Pinter and Stoppard, did important radio work early in their careers.

Although the centrality of radio has been eclipsed somewhat by television and fringe theatre, it continues to launch new writers, and its products often find popular recognition in other media (for example, the film version of Anthony Mingella's *Truly Madly Deeply*). Because radio is often cited as the discoverer and springboard of so many talents, this should not obscure the fact that many writers make a living primarily out of their radio writing and the work itself is massively popular, with plays regularly getting audiences of over 500,000 people.

For the dramatist, the medium offers a variety of work which is difficult to find anywhere else: serials, dramatisations, new commissions of various lengths (from a couple of minutes to several hours), musicals, soap operas, adaptations of the classics, as well as a real enthusiasm to examine new forms.

Because it is no more expensive to be in the Hindu Kush than to be in a laundrette in Deptford, the scope of the world is only limited by the imagination of the writer. However, though radio drama in the Fifties and Sixties was an important conduit for absurdism, there is a perceived notion that radio drama on the BBC is domestic, Home Counties and endlessly trotting out psychological trauma in a rather naturalistic fashion. This is not a fair assessment of the true range of work presented. The BBC itself is anxious to challenge this idea and as the face of broadcasting changes, there is a conscious move to attract new audiences with new kinds of work.

Get to know the form

Listen to as many plays as possible, read plays that are in print, and try to analyse what works, what doesn't and why. This may seem obvious, but it is easy to fall back on your preconceived notions of what radio plays are. The more you hear other people's successes and failures, the more tools you will have to discriminate when it comes to your own work.

Plays on radio tend to fit into specific time slots: 30, 60, 75, 90 minutes, and each slot will have a different feel – an afternoon play will be targeted at a different audience from one at 10.30pm.

A radio play will be chosen on artistic grounds but nevertheless a writer should be familiar with the market. This should not be seen as an invitation merely to copy forms or to try to make your play 'fit', but an opportunity to gain some sense of what the producers are dealing with. Producers are looking for new and fresh voices, ones which are unique, open new areas or challenge certain preconceptions. This is not to suggest you should be wilfully idiosyncratic but to be aware that it is the individuality of your 'voice' that people will notice.

Write what you feel strongly about, in the way that most attracts you. It should be bold, personal, entertaining, challenging and stimulating. Radio has the scope to explore drama that wouldn't get produced in theatres or on television, so treat it as the most radical forum for new writing. How many times have you listened to the radio with the sense that you've heard it all before? Never feel limited by what exists but be aware how your voice can enrich the possibilities of the future.

Who to approach

Opportunities for writing for radio in the UK are dominated by the BBC. Whilst there are increasing opportunities with independent stations, BBC Radio Drama overwhelms the field. Its output is huge. The variety of the work – from soaps to the classics – makes it the true national repertory for drama in its broadest sense. However, the BBC is increasingly commissioning productions from independent producers, so you can:

- Send your unsolicited script to the BBC writersroom (formerly the New Writing Initiative; see page 350) where it will be assessed by a reader. If they find it of interest they will put you in contact with a suitable producer.
- Approach a producer directly. This may be a producer at the BBC or at an independent company (see page 369). Both will give a personal response based on their own taste, rather than an institutional one.

Producers have a broad role: they find new writers, develop projects, edit the script, cast the actors, record and edit the play, and even write up the blurb for the *Radio Times*. Because of this intense involvement, the producer needs to have a strong personal interest in the writer or writing when they take on a project.

The system of commissioning programmes at the BBC is such that staff producers or independent production companies offer projects to commissioning editors to decide upon. Thus, a writer must be linked to a producer in the first instance to either get their play produced or get a commission for a new piece of work. Therefore, going direct to a producer can be a convenient short cut, but it requires more preparation.

Approaching a producer

Discovering and developing the work of new writers is only a small part of a producer's responsibilities, so be selective. Do your homework – there is little point in sending your sci-fi series to a producer who exclusively produces one-off period comedies.

To help decide which producer will be the most receptive to your work, become familiar with the work of each producer you are intersted in and the type of writers they work with. Use the *Radio Times* to help with your research and listen to as many of their plays as possible. It is well worth the effort in order to be sure to send your play to the right person. If you can quote the reasons why you've chosen them in particular, it can only help to get a congenial reception. It will also give you confidence in their response, as the comments – good or bad – will be from someone you respect.

Submitting your work

Don't stuff your manuscript into an envelope as soon as you've written 'The End'. You owe it to yourself to get the script into the best possible state before anyone sees it. First impressions matter and time spent refining will pay dividends in attracting attention.

Ask a person you trust to give you some feedback. Try to edit the work yourself, cutting things that don't work and spending time revising and reinventing anything which you think could be better. Make sure that what you send is the best you can possibly do.

Producers have mountains of scripts to read. The more bulky your tome the less enthusiastically it will be received. (It's better to send a sparkling 10-page sample than your whole

300-page masterpiece.) Try to make the first scene excellent. The more you can surprise, engage or delight in the first few pages, the more chance the rest will be carefully read. The adage that a reader can tell whether a play is any good after the first three pages might be wholly inaccurate but it reflects a cynicism versed by the practice of script reading. The reader will probably approach your script with the expectation that it is unsuitable, and part of getting noticed is jolting them out of their complacency.

Have your script presentably typed. Make sure your letter of introduction is well informed and shows that you haven't just picked a name at random. Do not send it to more than one producer at a time, as this is considered bad etiquette. And don't expect an instantaneous response – it may take a couple of months before you receive a reply. Don't be afraid of calling up if they keep you waiting for an unreasonable length of time, but don't badger people as this will inevitably be counterproductive.

Finally

Don't be discouraged by rejection and *don't* assume that because one person has rejected your script that it is no good. It is all a question of taste. Use the criticism positively to help your work, not as a personal attack.

Lee Hall has written several plays for BBC Radio, including the award-winning *Spoonface Steinberg*, which he has since adapted for TV and theatre. His translations of theatre plays include Brecht's *Mr Puntilla and His Man Matti* and *Mother Courage*, and Goldoni's *The Servant with Two Masters*. His play *Cooking with Elvis* was nominated for an Olivier Award for Best New Comedy, and his screenplay for *Billy Elliot* was Oscar nominated.

Digital broadcasting

Digital broadcasting is expanding rapidly. David Teather introduces this new media and looks at the implications for writers.

Digital broadcasting offers choice from hundreds of channels and the chance to offer interactive services to viewers. As many as 10 digital services are able to occupy the frequency previously occupied by one analogue service. Picture quality is far sharper using digital transmission.

Interactive services are so far only being used for e-commerce – for instance, Sky's television shopping and banking service Open. But a number of broadcasters are beginning to explore different ways of using the services for entertainment. In its coverage of Wimbledon, for instance, the BBC used the Sky Digital service to allow viewers to choose which court they wanted to watch. Ultimately, viewers will be able to link straight from a programme to associated websites, merchandising or online discussion points covering issues raised in a show. Digital transmission costs are also much lower which makes it more commercially viable for niche channels to exist.

The technical explanation

The BBC offers this definition: 'Digital Broadcasting is transmission by converting sound and picture into binary digits – a series of ones and noughts. Digital signals are more robust than analogue signals and can occupy parts of the spectrum unavailable to analogue. A process of compression also allows many digital services within the space taken by one analogue service.'

The story so far

The first company to launch digital services was Sky which now has more than 7 million digital subscribers. Its customer numbers for pay-TV stations had plateaued, but are now rising again as a result of digital broadcasting.

Of the cable companies, Telewest began its digital services at the end of 1999 and NTL (which now owns Cable & Wireless) started in mid 2000. The plug was pulled on ITV Digital, a joint venture between Carlton Communications and Granada which enabled digital services to be sent via traditional roof-top aerials, in April 2002. It has been replaced by Freeview, a joint venture between the BBC, BSkyB and Crown Castle, which offers around 30 channels. The service is free as the name suggests and is being received by around 3 million homes. Former ITV Digital subscribers can receive it through their existing set top boxes, while new viewers simply need to buy a box or own a digital television set.

The uptake of digital services was given a huge boost when the fierce competition for subscribers led Sky to scrap the £200 charge for the set-top boxes needed to unscramble the digital signal.

The government is aiming to switch off analogue and would like to do so before 2010. By that time, digital set-top boxes should have been replaced by television sets able to receive digital signals – but sales so far have been slow. The switch-off date for analogue is highly political because it will cause an inevitable outcry when old sets become useless.

Free-to-air channels

There are a number of free-to-air channels. The BBC has controversially set up a number of new channels: BBC3, aimed at the youth market; BBC4, an arts-based channel; and BBC

News 24 which – as the name suggests – screens news 24 hours a day. Rival companies such as Sky have argued that the licence fee should not be used to prop up stations like News 24 in a commercial marketplace. During the day, BBC3 and BBC4 run two children's channels, Cbeebies, for a preschool audience and CBBC for older children. The BBC has committed around £300 million to digital services: BBC3 has the biggest budget of £53 million, BBC4 has a budget of £32 million and the children's channels have a combined budget of £20 million. UK History, a documentary-based channel is also available on Freeview. Each of the channels is a mixture of repeats from other mainstream channels and new commissions.

ITV Network's ITV2 also shows catch-up episodes of programmes like *Coronation Street*, as well trumpeting a large number of US imports. All of the existing five free-to-air channels are also available in digital format. Other channels on Freeview include Sky News, QVC and Full On Entertainment.

Video-on-demand

The next step in the digital revolution is video-on-demand. A number of companies are offering services, including the cable companies and Kingston Communications, which runs a joint venture over telephone wires with BSkyB in Hull. Users are able to download films or television programmes at will, and fast forward, pause and rewind them. Programme-makers like the BBC have already sold packages to some of the video-on-demand firms and writers need to consider the implications for the potential sell-on of copyright.

Video-on-demand could become widespread with the advent of a technology called ADSL (Asymmetrical Digital Subscriber Line), which upgrades existing copper telephone wires for high bandwidth use such as pay-TV without the need to dig up roads. ADSL is becoming more widely available on BT's networks. A ban on broadcasting being carried over BT's lines has now been lifted but costs are still prohibitively high.

Digital technology in the next few years will enable video-quality film to be sent over smobile phone networks. The mobile phone industry has the networks in place and is beginning to sell the necessary handsets after many delays.

New channels, new opportunities?

The explosion of new channels may suggest that there will be an equally huge demand for new writing talent to help fill the extra airtime. Through a joint venture with Flextech Television, the BBC has six pay-TV channels, including UK Gold, UK Play and UK Drama. The evidence so far, however, is that money is being spent largely on three things: sports rights, movies and US imports. Most original programming on pay-TV channels is very low budget and is far more likely to be a cookery or pop music show than original drama.

Unfortunately, rather than playing to their own strengths, the BBC and ITV appear to be drawn into competing with the entertainment channels at their level. 'Once upon a time the BBC set the standards of quality and everyone else had to try and compete,' says one writer. 'That doesn't happen any more. Now the BBC competes with the others for crap.'

The level of competition among broadcasters now also means that where original drama is being commissioned it is often low budget. In fact, many writers believe that in the short term digital technology has not opened opportunities at all and see the future as pretty bleak. Management gurus, though, maintain that 'content is king' and that those broadcasters who triumph will be the ones who produce the most compelling programming.

Copyrights

The Writers' Guild notes a recent case where a writer saw a 30 year-old show he had penned being repeated again and again on a pay-TV channel and demanded to know why he wasn't being paid. It turned out that he had signed his rights away in 1972.

If the explosion of channels made possible by digital technology isn't leading to a wave of new commissioning then writers could at least hope for healthier repeat fees. The culture of broadcasters forcing writers to sign away their rights for a lump sum so that they can show a programme whenever they like is becoming increasingly prevalent. The usual royalty is 5.6% of the sale price, which gives the owner the right to show the programme a set number of times over a given period.

Broadcasters blame the need to sell to the US market programmes which are unencumbered by copyright issues. When selling work, writers should remember how many more times, potentially, a programme will appear on air because of the growth in distribution platforms, and therefore at least try to protect their rights. The rapid changes in technology has also led writers' unions to recommend that contracts over the shortest space of time possible are agreed.

Original programming

There are at last some encouraging signs, however, led by Channel 4 and followed by Sky. Channel 4 has long supported new writing talent through its backing of British film and has found its own pay-TV distribution outlet with FilmFour.

Sky One has a total budget of around £90 million but its efforts in original programming have met with mixed results – probably the most successful has been the football drama *Dream Team*. However, Sky's original programming has largely been forced upon it as the cost of acquiring top US content has soared due to increased competition – the reason why it lost the rights to show *Friends* and *ER*, two of Sky One's biggest ratings pullers, to Channel 4. Channel 4 is commissioning original programming for its digital entertainment channel, E4.

Sky attempted to launch its own film business, Sky Pictures, but abandoned the project after its first few films met with tepid reviews and box office sales. NTL, Britain's largest cable company, has dipped its toe into original programming but like its rival, Telewest, is in a precarious financial position and more in cost-cutting than commissioning mode.

Digital radio

The attributes of digital radio are similar to those of television. It was supposed to be the next revolution, but it has yet to catch on. The growth of stations is still in its infancy. In London, for instance, there will be three so-called 'multiplexes' of eight stations awarded to various consortia of existing radio groups. Interactive services will be on offer with the most obvious for radio including up-to-date traffic or weather reports displayed on a digital monitor on request. Digital radio could also lead to music or programming on demand similar to that of digital television programming.

A number of stations are now being broadcast in both digital and analogue as well as a growing number in digital alone. The BBC has launched five new radio stations, including one devoted to the spoken word, BBC7. So far, though, the industry has been held back by the prohibitive cost of hardware – the radios currently cost around £300.

David Teather is at the *Guardian*.

Inside the BBC

Helen Weinstein has compiled an introduction for writers who want to break into the BBC. For more information visit the BBC website: www.bbc.co.uk

The BBC structure

The BBC has 5 programming divisions:
• Radio & Music
• Drama, Entertainment & Children's
• Factual & Learning
• Sport
• News

To find out about the commissioning process visit www.bbc.co.uk/commissioning

A New Media & Technology division is developing the BBC's output on the internet and interactive TV and radio online activities, as well as on new platforms such as mobile and broadband. The BBC has a very helpful website with advice about applying for BBC jobs and BBC training schemes at www.bbc.co.uk/jobs/gettingintobbc

In addition, there are work experience placements available in just about every area of the BBC across the UK. All placements are unpaid and can last for a few days to four weeks. For information go to www.bbc.co.uk/jobs/workexperience

If you wish to submit an unsolicited idea to the BBC you need to team up with a BBC Production department who will help you develop that idea into a fully formulated proposal which would be ready for the BBC to consider. If it is an idea of local interest then contact your Regional BBC network. If it is your first submission then take a look at the BBC Talent website: www.bbc.co.uk/talent

Writers who want to pitch an idea for radio or TV can contact an independent production company who can take the idea through the same commissioning route as an in-house producer. The best way of getting in touch with an independent production company is to do some research about the companies who produce the type of programmes you have an idea for. Many of these companies are members of PACT (Producers Alliance for Cinema and Television, see page 546), which represents the independent sector and its website gives detailed information on independents: www.pact.co.uk

To submit a programme idea directly to the BBC programme division, send it to the head of department or editor. You will either be put in contact with the Development Producer in that department or your idea will be submitted to a relevant producer for review.

Alternatively, to find in-house BBC producers to contact with a specific programme idea a good route is to select a programme that is of a similar genre to your idea, and then to contact the producer directly by finding their name through the listings in the *Radio Times*.

website www.bbc.co.uk
Director-General Mark Thompson
Deputy Director-General Mark Byford
Director, Television Jana Bennett
Director, Sport Roger Mosey
Director of New Media & Technology Ashley Highfield
Controller, BBC One Peter Fincham
Controller, BBC Two Roly Keating
Controller, BBC Three Julian Bellamy
Controller, BBC Four Janice Hadlow
Controller, Children's Richard Deverell

Radio & Music

BBC Broadcasting House, Portland Place, London W1A 1AA
tel 020-7580 4468

Radio & Music is the division of the BBC responsible for the 5 national analogue networks (Radio 1, Radio 2, Radio 3, Radio 4 and Radio Five Live) and the 5 digital stations (1Xtra, 6Music, BBC7, Five Live Sports Extra and the Asian Network). It provides most of the music production for the BBC on national and World Service Radio, and the Television Classical Music Unit is responsible for dance, performance and classical music on TV. Radio & Music Factual producers also provide speech programming covering a wide range of arts, science, features and readings for domestic radio and the World Service. Other programmes are provided by Factual & Learning (Religion and the Natural History Unit), Sport, Drama and Light Entertainment. All BBC national radio stations are available on DAB digital radio, digital TV and via the internet.
Director, BBC Radio & Music Jenny Abramsky
Controller, Radio One & 1Xtra Andy Parfitt
Controller, Radio Two & 6Music Lesley Douglas
Controller, Radio Three Roger Wright
Controller, Radio Four & BBC7 Mark Damazer
Controller, Radio Five Live, Five Live, Sports Extra & the BBC Asian Network Bob Shennan
Head of Programmes, 6Music Ric Blaxill
Head of Programmes, BBC7 Mary Kalemkerian
Head of BBC Asian Network Vijay Sharma

Radio Drama

Head of Radio Drama Alison Hindell
Editor, Birmingham Drama & The Archers Vanessa Whitburn

Radio Entertainment

Editor, Radio Light Entertainment Paul Schlesinger

Radio & Music Factual

Controller, Radio & Music Factual Graham Ellis
Editor, R&M Factual Bristol Clare McGinn

Editor, R&M Factual Birmingham Andrew Thorman
Editor, R&M Factual Manchester Ian Bent

Radio News
Head of Radio News Steve Mitchell
Head of Radio Current Affairs Gwyneth Williams
Director, World Service & Global News Division
Richard Sambrook

Radio Sport
Head of Radio Sport Gordon Turnbull
Editor Gill Pulsford

Drama, Entertainment & Children's
Director Alan Yentob
Deputy Director Susan Spindler

Drama
BBC Television Centre, Centre House, Wood Lane,
London W12 7SB
tel 020-8743 8000

Drama has departments in London, Birmingham and
Manchester and produces a broad range of plays,
serials, series and readings for TV, film, BBC Radio 3,
BBC Radio 4 and BBC World Service.

The Manchester team also operates radio drama
workshops, primarily for writers in the North of
England. For further information, send an sae
requesting their guidelines.

The Birmingham radio team reads the unsolicited
scripts for writers in the Midlands, East Anglia, and
South West, but does not have a formal new writing
department.

Note that drama proposals must be in the form of
a fully written script. Drama scripts for single plays
and comedy scripts should be sent to the BBC
writersroom (see below).

Drama Development in the North
BBC New Broadcasting House, Oxford Road,
Manchester M60 ISJ
tel 0161-200 2020

TV Drama Village
Archibald House, 1059 Bristol Road, Selly Oak,
Birmingham B29 6LT
tel 0121-567 6767

Radio Drama
The Mailbox, Royal Mail Street, Birmingham B1 1RF
tel 0121-567 6767
Controller, Drama Commissioning Jane Tranter
*Controller, Continuing Drama Series & Head of
Independent Drama* John Yorke
Acting Head of Drama Serials & Series Sally
Woodward
Joint Head Independent Drama Lucy Richer
Executive Producer Manchester Drama tbc
Executive Producer Birmingham Drama Will Trotter
Head of Casting, Drama Series Julia Crampsie

Head of Radio Drama, Bush House Alison Hindell
Executive Producer, Radio Drama, Birmingham
Vanessa Whitburn
Executive Producer, Radio Drama, Manchester Sue
Roberts
Head of Films & Single Drama David Thompson
Head of Development Films Tracey Scoffield
Head of Development TV Series & Serials Sarah Brown
Head of Interactive Drama & Entertainment Sophie
Walpole

BBC Films
Grafton House, 379 Euston Road, London NW1 3AU
tel 020-7765 0261
website www.bbc.co.uk/bbcfilms
Head of Films & Single Drama David Thompson

Entertainment
BBC Television Centre, Wood Lane, London
W12 7RJ
tel 020-8743 8000
website www.bbc.co.uk/entertainment

The BBC provides a wide range of entertainment
programming and has dedicated teams who will
review unsolicited ideas from the public.
Entertainment formats such as quiz and game shows
should be pitched to:

Format Entertainment Development Team and
Factual Entertainment Development, Room 4010 at
the Wood Lane address above.

Comedy and sitcom scripts should be sent with an
A4 sae to:

BBC writersroom, Grafton House, 379–381 Euston
Road, London NW1 3AU
Acting Head of Entertainment Group Mark Cooper
Head of Comedy Jon Plowman
Head of Radio Entertainment Paul Schlesinger
Creative Head, Talent & Comedy Kenton Allen
Editor, New Comedy Mob Darr
Editor, Comedy Development Michael Jacob
Creative Head, Entertainment Events Bea Ballard
Editor, Entertainment Events Kevin Bishop
Editor, Comedy Entertainment Jo Sargent
Creative Head, Format Entertainment Karen Smith
Editor, Format Entertainment Martin Scott
Creative Heads, Factual Entertainment Alan Brown,
Ricky Kelehar
Creative Head, Music Entertainment Mark Cooper

Entertainment, Manchester
BBC New Broadcasting House, PO Box 27, Oxford
Road, Manchester M60 1SJ
tel 0161-200 2020

A network TV department responsible for a wide
range of factual, entertainment and music
programming. The department is also committed to
spotting new comedy talent in the North West.
Managing Editor Helen Bullough
Executive Producers Caroline Roberts, Kieron Roberts,
Ricky Kelehar, Sumi Connock, Mario Dubois

BBC Children's

BBC Television Centre, Wood Lane, London
W12 7RJ
tel 020-8743 8000

The BBC Children's department (which includes
CBBC and CBeebies) is always on the lookout for
new writing and screen presenting talent across its
entire output. For background information on CBBC
and CBeebies and the latest contact details, visit
www.bbc.co.uk/commissioning
Controller, BBC Children's Richard Deverell
Creative Director, CBBC Anne Gilchrist
Creative Director, CBeebies Michael Carrington
Head of Drama Jon East
Head of Entertainment Joe Godwin
Head of News, Factual & Learning Reem Nouss
Head of Interactive & On-Demand Rebecca Shallcross
Head of Presentation Alistair Hughes

BBC writersroom

Grafton House, 379–381 Euston Road, London NW1
3AU
tel 020-7765 2703
website www.bbc.co.uk/writersroom

BBC writersroom identifies and champions new
writing talent and diversity across BBC Drama,
Entertainment and Children's programmes. It
considers unsolicited scripts for TV drama, narrative
comedy and children's drama/comedy, films, radio
drama and comedy, and is also happy to read stage
plays. Writers are strongly advised to read the
submission guidelines and FAQs on the website
before submitting scripts. BBC writersroom can only
consider complete scripts of at least 10pp in hard
copy (emailed scripts are not accepted). Post to the
Development Manager, one at a time. In addition to
submission guidelines, the comprehensive website
provides advice on scriptwriting, contacts, interviews
with prominent writers and BBC executives,
formatting templates, free downloadable scripts from
BBC productions, details of current opportunities
and events, and useful links. Writers can sign up for
the monthly newsletter on the homepage. From time
to time national and regional open competitions for
writers are held. All writers submitting scripts are
considered for targeted professional writing schemes
and workshops.
Creative Director, New Writing Kate Rowland
Development Manager Paul Ashton

Factual & Learning

BBC White City, 201 Wood Lane, London W12 7TS
tel 020-8752 5252

BBC Factual & Learning makes factual programmes
and content for TV, Radio and Interactive, and
learning content and campaigns such as DoNation
and GCSE Bitesize, aiming to harness new technology
and drive the take-up of digital.
   As well as Interactive and Learning departments,
Factual & Learning comprises 9 multi-platform

studios creating some of the BBC's most distinctive
output: Science & History; Documentaries &
Specialist Features; Arts; Features & Formats; Events;
Natural History; Features & Documentaries, Bristol;
Features & Documentaries, Birmingham; and
Religion & Ethics, Manchester.
Divisional Director John Willis
Controller Factual Production Keith Scholey
Controller Learning & Interactive Liz Cleaver
Head of Development Rachel Innes-Lumsden
Studio Head, Science & History John Lynch
Studio Head, Docs & Specialist Features Sarah
Hargreaves
Studio Head, Features & Formats Bridget Boseley
Studio Head, Events Nick Vaughan-Barratt
Studio Head, Arts Mark Harrison
Head of Formal Learning Frank Flynn
Head of Campaigns Clare Laycock
Group Managing Editor Ann Cattini

Features & Documentaries, Birmingham

BBC, The Mailbox, Royal Mail Street, Birmingham
B1 1LX
tel 0121-567 6767
Studio Head, Features & Documentaries Tessa Finch

Features & Documentaries, Bristol

BBC Broadcasting House, White Ladies Road, Bristol
BS8 2LR
tel 0117-973 2211
Studio Head, Features & Documentaries Tom Archer

Natural History Unit

BBC Broadcasting House, White Ladies Road, Bristol
BS8 2LR
tel 0117-973 2211
Studio Head, Natural History Unit Neil Nightingale

Religion & Ethics

BBC New Broadcasting House, PO Box 27, Oxford
Road, Manchester M60 1SJ
tel 0161-200 2020
Studio Head, Religion & Ethics Alan Bookbinder

Sport

BBC Television Centre, Wood Lane, London
W12 7RJ
tel 020-8743 8000

Multimedia coverage of a wide range of sports in the
UK and worldwide.
Director, Sport Roger Mosey
Head of Grandstand, Programmes & Planning Philip
Bernie
Head of General Sports Barbara Slater
Head of Major Events Dave Gordon
Head of Football & Boxing, Development Niall Sloane
Director, Sports Rights & Finance Dominic Coles
Head of Radio Sport Gordon Turnbull
Sports Editor, TV News James Porter

Editor, Sport Interactive Ben Gallop

BBC News Division

BBC Television Centre, Wood Lane, London
W12 7RJ
tel 020-8743 8000
website www.bbc.co.uk/news

BBC News is the biggest news organisation in the
world with over 2500 journalists, 45 bureaus
worldwide and 15 networks and services across TV,
radio and new media.
Director, News Helen Boaden
Deputy Director, News Adrian Van Klaveren
Head of TV News Peter Horrocks
Deputy Head of TV News Rachel Attwell
Head of Radio News Steve Mitchell
Head of Radio Current Affairs Gwyneth Williams
Head of News Production Facilities Peter Coles
Head of Newsgathering Fran Unsworth
Head of Political Programmes, Analysis& Research Sue
Inglish
Head of Current Affairs & Business George Entwistle
Finance Director, News Richard Thomas
Head of News Interactive Peter Clifton
Head of Strategy News Alix Pryde
Head of Communications Janie Ironside Wood

TV programmes

Editor, One o'clock & Six o'clock News Amanda
Farnsworth
Editor, Ten o'clock News Craig Oliver
Editor, Newsnight Peter Barron
Editor, Breakfast David Kermode
Editor, This World Karen O'Connor
Managing Editor, World Service News Programmes
Alan le Breton

Radio programmes

Editor, Today Ceri Thomas
Editor, The Word at One/World This Weekend Colin
Hancock
Editor, PM/Broadcasting House Peter Rippon
Head of News Five Live Matt Morris
Editor, The World Tonight Alistair Burnett

Ceefax

Room 7540, BBC Television Centre, Wood Lane,
London W12 7RJ
tel 020-8576 1801
Editor, Ceefax Paul Brannan

World Service

Bush House, PO Box 76, The Strand, London
WC2B 4PH
tel 020-7557 2941 *fax* 020-7557 1912
email worldservice.press@bbc.co.uk
website www.bbc.co.uk/worldservice

BBC World Service provides radio services in English
and 32 other languages, via short wave and in an
increasing number of cities around the world on FM

and MW. The English service is available 24 hours a
day in real audio on the internet. Classic and
contemporary drama are a feature of its English
service, plus a wide range of news and information
programmes covering arts, business, documentaries,
entertainment, education, features, music, religious
affairs, science, sports and writing. In addition, BBC
World Service provides on-the-spot-coverage of
world news, bringing a global perspective on
international events.
Director Nigel Chapman
Director, English Networks & News Phil Harding

BBC Worldwide

Woodlands, 80 Wood Lane, London W12 0TT
tel 020-8433 2000 *fax* 020-8749 0538
website www.bbcworldwide.com

BBC Worldwide Ltd is the commercial consumer
arm, and a wholly owned subsidiary of the BBC. The
company was formed in 1994 to develop a
coordinated approach to the BBC's commercial
activities. It has 7 businesses: TV channels; TV Sales;
Content & Production; Digital Media; Home
Entertainment; Children's; and Magazines. BBC
Worldwide exists to entertain the world, and bring
value to the BBC.
Chief Executive John Smith

Audio tapes, CDs and books

BBC Audiobooks, St James House, The Square,
Lower Bristol Road, Bath BA2 3SB
tel (01225) 335336 *fax* (01225) 31077
website www.bbcaudiobooks.com

BBC Audiobooks Ltd was established in 2003 with
the integration of BBC Radio Collection, Cover to
Cover and Chivers Audio Books. Since then, it has
become a leading trade and library publisher in the
UK and publishes a wide range of entertainment on a
variety of formats including CD, cassette and
MP3–CD. Ideas should be pitched with a short
synopsis to:
Managing Director Paul Dempsey
Publishing Director Jan Paterson
Sales Director Samantha Newman

Magazines

Freelance contributions are regularly used by BBC
Worldwide magazines, but the use of unsolicited
material is rare as the editorial links closely to BBC
programme content. Ideas for articles that clearly fit
the remit of a magazine should be pitched via a short
written summary to the Editor.
Radio Times Gill Hudson
BBC Gardeners' World Adam Pasco
BBC Easy Gardening Ceri Thomas
Gardens Illustrated Juliet Roberts. Published by BBC
Magazines, Bristol
BBC Good Food Gillian Carter
BBC Easy Food Sara Buenfeld

BBC Good Homes Lisa Allen
BBC History David Musgrove. Published by BBC Magazines, Bristol
BBC Homes & Antiques Gail Dixon. Published by BBC Magazines, Bristol
BBC Music Oliver Conde. Published by BBC Magazines, Bristol
Olive Christine Hayes
BBC Top Gear Michael Harvey
What to Wear Sara Manning
BBC Wildlife Sophie Stafford. Published by BBC Magazines, Bristol, 14th Floor, Tower House, Fairfax Street, Bristol BS1 3BN

All ideas for BBC children's and teenage magazines should be send to:
Editorial Director Corinne Shaffer

Nations and Regions

BBC Media Centre, 201 Wood Lane, London W12 7TQ
tel 020-8743 8000

BBC Nations and Regions is responsible for around three-quarters of all the BBC's domestic output – a total of about 7000 hours of TV and over 250,000 hours of radio programming a year. BBC Northern Ireland, BBC Scotland and BBC Wales produce a growing number of programmes for the national networks, as well as providing comprehensive services for viewers and listeners in their own nations. The BBC's English Regions are responsible for 12 TV regional news and current affairs services across England; for 40 BBC local radio stations and 43 local *Where I Live* websites with their emphasis on news and information for their local communities.
Director, Nations & Regions Pat Loughrey

BBC Northern Ireland

BBC Broadcasting House, Ormeau Avenue, Belfast BT2 8HQ
tel 028-9033 8000
website www.bbc.co.uk/ni

BBC Northern Ireland produces a broad spectrum of radio and TV programmes, both for the BBC's national networks and for the home audience. Output includes news and current affairs, documentaries, education, entertainment, sport, music, religion and ethics and programmes in, and relating to, Irish and Ulster Scots. It also has a thriving drama department which produces material for network radio and TV, including serials, single dramas and readings.

In addition to making network radio programmes for Radios 1, 2, 3, 4, 5 Live, BBC7 and BBC World Service, BBC Northern Ireland also makes programmes for local audiences on BBC Radio Ulster and BBC Radio Foyle.
Controller, BBC Northern Ireland Anna Carragher
Head of Broadcasting Peter Johnston
Head of Programme Production Mike Edgar

Head of News & Current Affairs Andrew Colman
Head of Creative Development Bruce Batten
Head of Drama Patrick Spence
Head of Interactive Services & Learning Kieran Hegarty
Head of Programme Operations Stephen Beckett
Head of Finance Crawford MacClean
Managing Editor, TV Peter McCann
Managing Editor, Radio Susan Lovell
Managing Editor, Radio Foyle Ana Leddy

BBC Radio Ulster

BBC Broadcasting House, Ormeau Avenue, Belfast BT2 8HQ
tel 028-9033 8000

BBC Radio Foyle

8 Northland Road, Londonderry BT48 7JD
tel 028-7126 2244

BBC Scotland

BBC Broadcasting House, Queen Margaret Drive, Glasgow G12 8DG
tel 0141-339 8844
website www.bbc.co.uk/scotland

BBC Scotland is one of the most varied production centres outside London, providing BBC TV and radio networks with drama, comedy, entertainment, children's, leisure, documentaries, religion, education, arts, music, news, current affairs and political coverage, as well as a wide range of online content.

BBC Scotland's drama department produces distinctive work for the BBC's TV and radio networks and Scotland's only soap opera, *River City*. It collaborates with Scottish Screen (see page 553) and other partners to support a range of schemes nurturing Scottish writing and directing talent for film and TV. These range from *Tartan Smalls* and *Tartan Shorts* to Cineworks and the low-budget film scheme, *Fast Forward Features*, which enables filmmakers to move from short film-making into mainstream movies.

In addition to network contributions, BBC Scotland transmits around 900 hours of TV programming a year for Scottish audiences on BBC One and Two Scotland, including year-round arts coverage and a range of projects focusing on aspects of reading, writing and language. BBC Scotland provides the nation's two speech radio networks, Radio Scotland and Radio nan Gaidheal. There are local services for Orkney and Shetland and daily bulletins for listeners in the Highlands, Grampian, Borders, and the South West. Production work takes place at centres across the nation, from Dumfries to Lerwick.
Controller, BBC Scotland Ken MacQuarrie
Head of Programmes Maggie Cunningham & Donalda MacKinnon
Head of News & Current Affairs Blair Jenkins

Head of Drama Anne Mensah
Commissioning Editor, Scotland Ewan Angus
Head of Radio Scotland Jeff Zycinski
Head of Radio Drama Patrick Rayner
Head of Entertainment Alan Tyler
Head of Children's Simon Parsons
Head of Features Andrea Miller
Head of Gaelic Margaret Mary Murray
Head of Radio Drama Patrick Rayner
Editor, Radio nan Gaidheal Marion MacKinnon

BBC Radio Scotland
BBC Broadcasting House, Queen Margaret Drive,
Glasgow G12 8DG
tel 0141-339 8844

BBC Radio nan Gaidheal
Rosebank, Church Street, Stornoway, Isle of Lewis
HS1 2LS
tel (01851) 705000

BBC Inverness
7 Culduthel Road, Inverness IV2A 4AD
tel (01463) 720720

BBC Radio Orkney
Castle Street, Kirkwall, Orkney KW15 1DF
tel (0141) 339884

BBC Radio Shetland
Pitt Lane, Lerwick, Shetland ZE1 0DW
tel (01595) 694747

BBC Radio Selkirk
Unit 1, Ettrick Riverside, Dunsdale Road, Selkirk
TD7 5EB
tel (01750) 724567

BBC Radio Dumfries
Elmbank, Lovers Walk, Dumfries DG1 1NZ
tel (01387) 268008

BBC Cymru/Wales
BBC Broadcasting House, Llandaff, Cardiff CF5 2YQ
tel 029-2032 2000
website www.bbc.co.uk/wales

BBC Wales provides a wide range of services in
Welsh and in English, on radio, TV and online. This
includes more than 20 hours a week of programmes
on BBC 1 Wales and BBC 2 Wales, and the digital
service BBC 2W. Regular output includes the flagship
news programme *Wales Today*, the current affairs
strand *Week In Week Out*, drama such as *Belonging*,
valleys comedy *High Hopes* and sport, including live
rugby on *Scrum V*. Ten hours a week of Welsh-
language programmes are shown on S4C, including
the news programme *Newyddion*, the nightly soap
opera *Pobol y Cwm* and educational programmes.
BBC Radio Wales, in English, and BBC Radio Cymru,
in Welsh, each provide 20 hours a day of news,
entertainment, music and sports output. Political
coverage on all services has expanded following the
creation of the National Assembly for Wales. BBC
Wales also produces a wide range of programmes for
the BBC's network TV channels, and Radios 1, 2, 3
and 4. These include popular drama-documentaries,
education and music programmes for audiences
throughout the UK, including the biennial *BBC
Singer of the World* competition in Cardiff,
accompanied by the BBC National Orchestra of
Wales.

Controller, BBC Wales Menna Richards
Head of Programmes (English) Clare Hudson
Head of Programmes (Welsh) Keith Jones
Head of Marketing & Communications Rhodri Talfan
Davies
Head of News & Current Affairs Mark O'Callaghan
Head of Broadcast Development Cathryn Allen
Head of Drama Julie Gardner
Head of Sport Nigel Walker
Head of Factual Adrian Davies
Head of Music David Jackson
Music Director, BBC National Orchestra of Wales
David Murray
Editor, Radio Cymru Aled Glynne Davies
Editor, Radio Wales Sali Collins
Editor, New Media Mandy Rose
Commissioning Editor Martyn Ingram

BBC Radio Cymru (Welsh Language)
BBC Broadcasting House, Llandaff, Cardiff CF5 2YQ
tel 029-2032 2000

BBC Radio Wales (English Language)
BBC Broadcasting House, Llandaff, Cardiff CF5 2YQ
tel 029-2032 2000

Helen Weinstein has been a documentary maker for more than 10 years. She works as a producer and
presenter in BBC radio and TV, specialising in history programmes, and in 2002 won the Sony Gold Radio
News Programme Award for Radio 4's *Document – The Day They Made it Rain*. She is Professor of History at
the University of York and founding Director of the Institute for the Public Understanding of the Past.

BBC regional television and local radio

The BBC's English Regions are responsible for 12 television regional news and current affairs services across England, as well as for 40 BBC local radio stations providing news and information for their local communities.

BBC English Regions (TV and radio)
BBC Birmingham, The Mailbox, Royal Mail Street, Birmingham B1 1RF
tel 0121-567 6767
Controller, English Regions Andy Griffee
Chief Assistant Laura Ellis
Head of Programming, TV Craig Henderson
Head of New Services John Allen
Head of Sport Charles Runcie
Head of Radio Development Chris Van Schaick

BBC East
The Forum, Millennium Place, Norwich NR2 1BH
tel (01603) 618331
Head of Regional & Local Programmes Tim Bishop

BBC Radio Cambridgeshire
PO Box 96, 104 Hills Road, Cambridge CB2 1LD
tel (01223) 259696
email cambs@bbc.co.uk

BBC Essex
PO Box 765, 198 New London Road, Chelmsford CM2 9XB
tel (01245) 616000
email essex@bbc.co.uk

BBC Radio Norfolk
The Forum, Millennium Place, Norwich NR2 1BH
tel (01603) 617411
email radionorfolk@bbc.co.uk

BBC Radio Northampton
Broadcasting House, Abington Street, Northampton NN1 2BH
tel (01604) 239100
email radionorthampton@bbc.co.uk

BBC Radio Suffolk
Broadcasting House, St Matthew's Street, Ipswich IP1 3EP
tel (01473) 250000
email radiosuffolk@bbc.co.uk

BBC Three Counties Radio
PO Box 3cr, Hastings Street, Luton LU1 5XL
tel (01582) 637400
email 3cr@bbc.co.uk

BBC East Midlands
London Road, Nottingham NG2 4UU
tel 0115-955 0500
Head of Regional & Local Programmes Aziz Rashid

BBC Radio Derby
PO Box 104.5, Derby DE1 3HL
tel (01332) 361111
email radio.derby@bbc.co.uk

BBC Radio Leicester
9 St Nicholas Place, Leicester LE1 5LB
tel 0116-251 6688
email radioleicester@bbc.co.uk

BBC Radio Nottingham
London Road, Nottingham NG2 4UU
tel 0115-955 0500
email radio.nottingham@bbc.co.uk

BBC Radio Humberside
Queens Court, Queens Gardens, Hull HU1 3NP
tel (01482) 323232
email radio.humberside@bbc.co.uk

BBC Yorks & Lincs.
Queens Court, Queens Gardens, Hull HU1 3NP
tel (01482) 323232
Head of Regional & Local Programmes Helen Thomas

BBC Radio Lincolnshire
Radio Buildings, PO Box 219, Newport, Lincoln LN1 3XY
tel (01522) 511411
email radio.lincolnshire@bbc.co.uk

BBC London
35c Marylebone High Street, London W1A 6FL
tel 020-7224 2424
Executive Editor Michael MacFarlane

BBC London 94.9
PO Box 94.9, Marylebone High Street, London W1A 6FL
tel 020-7224 2424
email yourlondon@bbc.co.uk

BBC North East and Cumbria
Broadcasting Centre, Barrack Road, Newcastle upon Tyne NE99 2NE

tel 0191-232 1313
Head of Regional & Local Programmes Wendy Pilmer

BBC Radio Cleveland
Broadcasting House, PO Box 95FM, Newport Road,
Middlesbrough TS1 5DG
tel (01642) 225211
email radio.cleveland@bbc.co.uk

BBC Radio Cumbria
Annetwell Street, Carlisle CA3 8BB
tel (01228) 592444
email radio.cumbria@bbc.co.uk

BBC Radio Newcastle
Broadcasting Centre, Barrack Road, Newcastle upon
Tyne NE99 1RN
tel 0191-232 4141
email radio.newcastle@bbc.co.uk

BBC North West
New Broadcasting House, Oxford Road, Manchester
M60 1SJ
tel 0161-200 2000
Head of Regional & Local Programmes Leo Devine

BBC Manchester
PO Box 27, Oxford Road, Manchester M60 1SJ
tel 0161-200 2000
email manchester.online@bbc.co.uk

BBC Radio Lancashire
26 Darwen Street, Blackburn, Lancs. BB2 2EA
tel (01254) 262411
email radio.lancashire@bbc.co.uk

BBC Radio Merseyside
PO Box 95.8, Liverpool L69 1XJ
tel 0151-708 5500
email radio.merseyside@bbc.co.uk

BBC South
Broadcasting House, Havelock Road, Southampton
SO14 7PU
tel 023-8022 6201
Head of Regional & Local Programmes Eve Turner

BBC Radio Berkshire
Caversham Lodge, Peppard Road, Caversham,
Reading RG4 8TZ
tel 0118-946 4200
email radio.berkshire.news@bbc.co.uk

BBC Radio Oxford
269 Banbury Road, Oxford OX2 7DW
tel (08459) 311444
email radio.oxford@bbc.co.uk

BBC Radio Solent
Broadcasting House, Havelock Road, Southampton
SO14 7PW

tel 023-8063 1311
email radio.solent@bbc.co.uk

BBC South East
The Great Hall, Mount Pleasant Road, Tunbridge
Wells, Kent TN1 1QQ
tel (01892) 670000
Head of Regional & Local Programmes Mike Hapgood

BBC Radio Kent
The Great Hall, Mount Pleasant Road, Tunbridge
Wells, Kent TN1 1QQ
tel (01892) 670000
email radio.kent@bbc.co.uk

BBC Southern Counties Radio
Broadcasting Centre, Guildford GU2 7AP
tel (01483) 306306
email southern.counties.radio@bbc.co.uk

BBC South West
Broadcasting House, Seymour Road, Mannamead,
Plymouth PL3 5BD
tel (01752) 229201
Head of Regional & Local Programmes John Lilley

BBC Radio Cornwall
Phoenix Wharf, Truro, Cornwall TR1 1UA
tel (01872) 275421
email radio.cornwall@bbc.co.uk

BBC Radio Devon
Broadcasting House, Seymour Road, Mannamead,
Plymouth PL3 5YQ
tel (01752) 260323
email radio.devon@bbc.co.uk

BBC Radio Guernsey
Bulwer Avenue, St Sampsons, Guernsey GY2 4LA
tel (01481) 200600
email radio.guernsey@bbc.co.uk

BBC Radio Jersey
18 Parade Road, St Helier, Jersey JE2 3PL
tel (01534) 870000
email jersey@bbc.co.uk

BBC West
Broadcasting House, Whiteladies Road, Bristol
BS8 2LR
tel 0117-973 2211
Head of Regional & Local Programmes Andrew
Wilson

BBC Radio Bristol
PO Box 194, Bristol BS99 7QT
tel 0117-974 1111
email radio.bristol@bbc.co.uk

BBC Radio Gloucestershire
London Road, Gloucester GL1 1SW
tel (01452) 308585

email radio.gloucestershire@bbc.co.uk

BBC Radio Somerset Sound
Broadcasting House, Park Street, Taunton, Somerset
TA1 4DA
tel (01823) 323956
email somerset@bbc.co.uk

BBC Radio Swindon/BBC Radio Wiltshire
Broadcasting House, 56–58 Prospect Place, Swindon
SN1 3RW
tel (01793) 513626
email wiltshire@bbc.co.uk, radio.swindon@bbc.co.uk

BBC West Midlands
The Mailbox, Royal Mail Street, Birmingham B1 1RF
tel 0121-567 6767
Head of Regional & Local Programmes David
Holdsworth

BBC Hereford & Worcester
Hylton Road, Worcester WR2 5WW
tel (01905) 748485
email bbchw@bbc.co.uk

BBC Radio Shropshire
2–4 Boscobel Drive, Shrewsbury SY1 3TT
tel (01743) 248484
email radio.shropshire@bbc.co.uk

BBC Radio Stoke
Cheapside, Hanley, Stoke-on-Trent ST1 1JJ
tel (01782) 208080

email radio.stoke@bbc.co.uk

BBC WM
The Mailbox, Birmingham B1 1RF
tel 0121-567 6000
email bbcwm@bbc.co.uk

BBC Coventry & Warwickshire
Priory Place, Coventry CV1 2WR
tel (02476) 860086
email coventry@bbc.co.uk, warwickshire@bbc.co.uk

BBC Yorkshire
2 St Peter's Square, Leeds LS9 8AH
tel 0113-244 1188
Head of Regional & Local Programmes Tamsin
O'Brien

BBC Radio Leeds
2 St Peter's Square, Leeds LS9 8AH
tel 0113-244 2131
email radio.leeds@bbc.co.uk

BBC Radio Sheffield/BBC South Yorkshire
54 Shoreham Street, Sheffield S1 4RS
tel 0114-273 1177
email radio.sheffield@bbc.co.uk,
southyorkshire@bbc.co.uk

BBC Radio York/BBC North Yorkshire
20 Bootham Row, York YO3 7BR
tel (01904) 641351
email northyorkshire.radio@bbc.co.uk

BBC broadcasting rights and terms

Contributors are advised to check latest details of fees with the BBC.

Rights and terms – television

Specially written material

Fees for submitted material are paid on acceptance. For commissioned material, half the fee is paid on commissioning and half on acceptance as being suitable for television. All fees are subject to negotiation above the minima.

● In November 2002 a new TV script agreement was introduced. It replaced the old BBC/ Guild script agreement for dramatic scripts of 15 minutes and over. The terms were agreed with the PMA and the Writers' Guild. The most significant changes are:

On First Day of Principal Photography an advance payment of either 15% or 115% of script fee will be made against:

(a) repeats/commercial exploitation: 100% of script fee plus/or

(b) 5-year licence of Public Service use (excluding BBC1 and BBC2): 15%

(a) only applies to scripts commissioned for BBC1 or BBC2 (but excludes long-running series; (b) applies to BBC1 and BBC2 commissions and also scripts for BBC3 and BBC4 and long-running series on BBC1 and BBC2.

● Rates for one performance of a 60-minute original television play are a minimum of £7504 for a play written by a beginner and a 'going rate' of £9379 for an established writer, or *pro rata* for shorter or longer timings.

● Fees for a 50-minute episode in a series during the same period are a minimum of £5650 for a beginner and a 'going rate' of £7062 for an established writer.

● Fees for a 50-minute dramatisation are a minimum of £4060 for a beginner and a 'going rate' of £5075 for an established writer.

● Fees for a 50-minute adaptation of an existing stage play or other dramatic work are a minimum of £2472 for a beginner and a 'going rate' of £3090 for an established writer.

Specially written light entertainment sketch material

The BBC Sketch Agreement is currently being reviewed and the minimum rates are expected to go up in the next 12 months.

● The rates for sketch material range from £60 per minute for beginners with a 'going rate' of £75 for established writers.

● The fee for a quickie or news item is half the amount of the writer's per minute rate.

● Fees for submitted material are payable on acceptance and for commissioned material half on signature and half on acceptance.

Published material

● Prose works: £26.62 per minute.
● Poems: £31.95 per half minute.

Stage plays and source material for television

● Fees for stage plays and source novels are negotiable.

Rights and terms – radio

Specially written material

Fees are assessed on the basis of the type of material, its length, the author's status and experience in writing for radio. Fees for submitted material are paid on acceptance. For commissioned material, half the fee is paid on commissioning and half on acceptance as being suitable for broadcasting.

● Rates for specially written radio dramas in English (other than educational programmes) are £51.20 a minute for beginners and a 'going rate' of £77.96 a minute for established writers. This rate covers two broadcasts.

Specially written short stories
● Fees range from £157 for 15 minutes.

Published material
Domestic radio
● Dramatic works: £15.46 per minute.
● Prose works: £15.46 per minute.
● Prose works required for dramatisation: £12.05 per minute.
● Poems: £15.46 per half minute.

World Service Radio (English)
● Dramatic works: £7.73 per minute for broadcasts within a seven-day period.
● Prose works: £7.73 per minute for broadcasts within a seven-day period.
● Prose works required for dramatisation: £6.02 per minute for broadcasts within a seven-day period.
● Poems: £7.73 per half minute for broadcasts within a seven-day period.
● Foreign Language Services are approximately one-fifth of the rate for English Language Services.

Television and radio
Repeats in BBC programmes
● Further proportionate fees are payable for repeats.

Use abroad of recordings of BBC programmes
If the BBC sends abroad recordings of its programmes for use by overseas broadcasting organisations on their own networks or stations, further payments accrue to the author, usually in the form of additional percentages of the basic fee paid for the initial performance or a royalty based on the percentage of the distributors' receipts. This can apply to both sound and television programmes.

Value Added Tax
There is a self-billing system for VAT which covers radio, World Service and television for programmes made in London.

Talks for television
Contributors to talks will be offered the standard television talks contract which provides the BBC certain rights to broadcast the material in a complete, abridged and/or translated manner, and which provides for the payment of further fees for additional usage of the material whether by television, domestic radio or external broadcasting. The contract also covers the assignment of material and limited publication rights. Alternatively, a contract taking in all standard rights may be negotiated. Fees are arranged by the contract authorities in London and the Regions.

Talks for radio

Contributors to talks for domestic radio and World Service broadcasting may be offered either:

● the standard talks contract which takes rights and provides for residual payments, as does the television standard contract; or

● an STC (Short Talks Contract) which takes all rights except print publication rights where the airtime of the contribution does not exceed five minutes and which has set fees or disturbance money payable; or

● an NFC (No Fee Contract) where no payment is made which provides an acknowledgement that a contribution may be used by the BBC.

Independent national television

Channel 4 Television Corporation

124 Horseferry Road, London SW1P 2TX
tel 020-7396 4444, 020-7306 8333 (viewer enquiries),
020-7396 4444 (E4 and FilmFour
information) *fax* 020-7306 8347
website www.channel4.com
Director of Television Kevin Lygo

Commissions and purchases programmes for
broadcast during the whole week throughout the UK
(except Wales). Also broadcasts subscription film
channel FilmFour and digital entertainment channel
E4.

Five Broadcasting Ltd

22 Long Acre, London WC2E 9LY
tel 020-7550 5555, (08457) 050505
(comments) *fax* 020-7550 5554
website www.five.tv
Director of Programmes Dan Chambers

The fifth and last national 'free-to-air' terrestrial
24-hour TV channel. Commissions a wide range of
programmes to suit all tastes. Established 1997.

GMTV

London Television Centre, Upper Ground, London
SE1 9TT
tel 020-7827 7000 *fax* 020-7827 7001
email talk2us@gm.tv.
website www.gm.tv
Director of Programmes Peter McHugh

GMTV1 is ITV's national breakfast TV service,
6–9.25am, 7 days a week. GMTV2 is GMTV's digital,
satellite and cable channel shown on ITV2 daily
6–9.25am.

ITN (Independent Television News Ltd)

200 Gray's Inn Road, London WC1X 8XZ
tel 020-7833 3000 *fax* 020-7430 4868
email editor@itn.co.uk, viewer.liaison@itn.co.uk
(comments)
website www.itn.co.uk
Chief Executive Mark Wood, *Finance Director* Andy
Whitaker, *TV News Editor-in-Chief* David Mannion,
Channel 4 News Editor Jim Gray, *Managing Director,
ITN Multimedia* Nicholas Wheeler, *Managing
Director, ITN Archive* Sue Thexton

Provides news programming for ITV1, London
Tonight, Channel 4, More4 and Independent Radio
News (IRN). ITN is also expanding in the fast-
growing new business areas of ITN Archive,
containing some of the world's most iconic imagery;
and ITN Multimedia, streaming news and

entertainment content to 3G phones; and through
producing factual documentaries and programming.
Owned by ITV Plc, Daily Mail & General Trust,
Reuters and United Business Media.

ITV Network Ltd/ITV Association

200 Gray's Inn Road, London WC1X 8HF
tel 020-7843 8000 *fax* 020-7843 8158
email info@itv.com
website www.itv.co.uk
Managing Director (Granada) Mick Desmond,
Managing Director (Carlton) Clive Jones, *Director of
Programmes* Nigel Pickard

Comprises 16 independent regional TV licensees,
broadcasting across 15 regions of the UK.
Commissions and schedules its own programmes and
from independent production companies, shown
across the ITV network. The ITV terrestrial channel is
ITV1.

The Office of Communications (Ofcom) – see page 679

Radio Telefís Éireann (RTÉ)

Donnybrook, Dublin 4, Republic of Ireland
tel (01) 208 3111 *fax* (01) 208 3080
email info@rte.ie
website www.rte.ie

The Irish national broadcasting service operating
radio and TV.

Television Ongoing production of an urban drama
serial, *Fair City*. Currently of interest: drama series
for mainstream audiences, serials (preferably
contemporary) and situation comedies (preferably set
in Ireland or of strong Irish interest), with preferred
length of commercial half hour or one hour.
Proposals for serials and series suitable for a young
adult RTÉ 2 audience, either cutting edge or
humorous, which could exploit a low-cost DV
production model are of particular interest. Full
scripts will not be considered – treatments and series/
serial outlines only, except in cases where projects are
already part funded. Before submitting material to
the Drama or Entertainment departments, authors
are advised to write to the department in question to
establish initial interest, timing of commissioning
rounds, etc.

Radio The RTÉ Radio 1 arts, features and drama
department regularly produces documentaries, short
stories and radio plays. Email ideas or proposals for
future radio documentaries (documentaries@rte.ie).
RTÉ Radio 1 holds annual competitions for short
stories and radio plays; see the RTÉ Radio 1 website
(www.rte.ie/radio1) for details. For further
information on submissions email radio1@rte.ie

S4C

Parc Ty Glas, Llanishen, Cardiff CF14 5DU
tel 029-20747444 *fax* 029-20754444
email s4c@s4c.co.uk
website www.s4c.co.uk
Chief Executive Iona Jones, *Director of Commissioning*
Rhian Gibson

The Welsh Fourth Channel. S4C's analogue service broadcasts 32 hours per week in Welsh: 22 hours are commissioned from independent producers and 10 hours are produced by the BBC. Most of Channel 4's output is rescheduled to complete this service. S4C's digital service broadcasts 12 hours per day in Welsh.

Independent regional television

It is advisable to check before submitting any ideas/material – in all cases, scripts are preferred to synopses. Programmes should be planned with natural breaks for the insertion of advertisements. These companies also provide some programmes for Channel 4.

Channel Television Ltd

Television Centre, La Pouquelaye, St Helier, Jersey JE1 3ZD
tel (01534) 816816 *fax* (01534) 816817
email broadcast@channeltv.co.uk
Television House, Bulwer Avenue, St Sampson's, Guernsey GY2 4LA
tel (01481) 241888 *fax* (01481) 241889
email broadcastgsy@channeltv.co.uk
website www.channeltv.co.uk
Director of Programmes Karen Rankine

Channel Television, the smallest ITV broadcaster, produces 5.5 hours of local programmes each week relating to Channel Islands news, events and current affairs. Launched 1962.

ITV Anglia

Anglia Television, Rose Lane, Anglia House, Norwich NR1 3JG
tel (01603) 615151 *fax* (01603) 631032
website www.itvregions.com/anglia

Provides news programmes for the East of England and is a major producer of network programmes for the UK and USA.

ITV Border

ITV Border Television, The Television Centre, Carlisle CA1 3NT
tel (01228) 525101 *fax* (01228) 541384
website www.itvregions.com/border

Provides programmes for Cumbria, the Borders and the Isle of Man.

ITV Central

Gas Street, Birmingham B1 2JT
website www.itv.com/central

Provides programmes for the East, West and South Midlands.

ITV Granada

ITV1 Granada, Quay Street, Manchester M60 9EA
tel 0161-832 7211 *fax* 0161-953 0283
website www.itv.com

Provides programmes for the North West of England.

ITV London

London Television Centre, London SE1 9LT
tel 020-7261 8163
website www.itvregions.com/london

Provides programmes for Greater London and much of the South East.

ITV Meridian

Forum One, Solent Business Park, Whiteley, Hants PO15 7PA
tel (01489) 442000
website www.itvregions.com/meridian

Provides programmes for the South and South East.

ITV Tyne Tees

Television House, The Watermark, Gateshead, Tyne & Wear NE11 9SZ
tel 0191-404 8700 *fax* 0191-404 8780
website www.tynetees.tv

Provides programmes for North East England and North Yorkshire.

ITV Wales

The Television Centre, Culverhouse Cross, Cardiff CF5 6XJ
tel 029-2059 0590 *fax* 029-2059 7183
website www.itvregions.com/wales

Provides programmes for Wales.

ITV West

The Television Centre, Bristol BS4 3HG
tel 0117-972 2722 *fax* 0117-972 2400
email firstname.surname@itv.com
website www.itv1west.com

Provides programmes for the West of England during the whole week.

ITV Westcountry

Langage Science Park, Western Wood Way, Plymouth PL7 5BQ
tel (01752) 333333 *fax* (01752) 333444
website www.itv.com/westcountry

Provides programmes for South West England.

ITV Yorkshire

The Television Centre, Leeds LS3 1JS
tel 0113-243 8283 *fax* 0113-244 5107
website www.itvregions.com/yorkshire

Provides programmes for the Yorkshire area.

Scottish Television Ltd

200 Renfield Street, Glasgow G2 3PR
tel 0141-300 3000 *fax* 0141-300 3580
website www.scottishtv.co.uk
Managing Director Bobby Hain

Wholly owned subsidiary of Scottish Media Group, making drama and other programmes for the ITV network. Scottish Television Ltd also includes Ginger Television.

• Material (STV): ideas and formats for long-form series with or without a Scottish flavour. Approach Controller of Drama, Eric Coulter.

• Material (Ginger): produces compelling programmes for groups of all ages. Contact: Elizabeth Partyka.

STV

Television Centre, Craigshaw Business Park, West Tullos, Aberdeen AB12 3QH

tel (01224) 848848
website www.grampiantv.com
Head of Programmes Derrick Thomson

Provides programmes for North Scotland during the whole week. Launched 1961.

UTV

Orneau Road, Belfast BT7 1EB
tel 028-9032 8122 *fax* 028-9024 6695
website www.u.tv

Provides programmes for Northern Ireland.

Digital, satellite and cable television

Digital broadcasting has dramatically increased the number and reception quality of television channels. Approximately 50% of UK homes now have digital television. The UK's main digital suppliers are listed below. Details of multichannel television can be obtained from Ofcom (www.ofcom.org.uk), and a selection is listed below. Teletext is written pages of information (news, weather, holidays, sport, television, entertainment). The two main teletext services are Ceefax on the BBC and Teletext on ITV, Channel 4 and Channel 5. There are teletext services available via the digital format but they are not listed here.

DIGITAL, SATELLITE AND CABLE TELEVISION PROVIDERS

Freeview
DTV Services Ltd, Broadcast Centre (BC3 D5), 201 Wood Lane, London W12 7TP
tel (0870) 8809980
website www.freeview.co.uk

Free digital service run by 5 shareholders: the BBC, National Grid Wireless, BskyB, Channel 4 and ITV.

NTL Group
NTL House, Bartley Wood Business Park, Hook, Hants RG27 9UP
tel (01256) 752000 *fax* (01256) 752100
website www.ntl.com

The UK's top cable TV provider.

Sky Digital
BskyB, Grant Way, Isleworth, Middlesex TW7 5QD
tel (0870) 240 3000
website www.sky.com

The UK's number one digital satellite provider, with over 5 million subscribers. Sky premium channels include: Sky Cinema, Sky Moviemax, Sky News, Sky One, Sky Premier, Sky Sports 1–3, Sky Sports extra, Sky Sports News, Sky Travel.

Telewest Communications Networks Ltd
Export House, Cawsey Way, Woking, Surrey GU21 6QX
tel (01483) 750900
website www.telewest.co.uk

The UK's second largest cable provider.

Video Networks Ltd
205 Holland Park Avenue, London W11 4XB
tel 020-7348 4000
website www.homechoice.co.uk, www.videonetworks.com
Contact Nick Southhall

Currently only available in London and certain areas of Herefordshire.

MULTICHANNEL TELEVISION

BBC Four
Television Centre, Wood Lane, London W12 7RJ
tel (0870) 010 0222
website www.bbc.co.uk/bbcfour

Entertainment and documentary.

BBC News 24
Television Centre, Wood Lane, London W12 7RJ
tel 020-8743 8000
website www.bbc.co.uk/bbcnews24

News and weather.

BBC Three
Television Centre, Wood Lane, London W12 7RJ
tel 020-8743 8000
website www.bbc.co.uk/bbcthree

Entertainment.

BBC World
Television Centre, Wood Lane, London W12 7RJ
tel 020-8443 8000
email bbcworld@bbc.co.uk
website www.bbcworld.com

News and information.

Challenge
Flextech Television, 160 Great Portland Street, London W1W 5QA
tel 020-7299 5000
website www.challenge.co.uk

Game and quizz shows.

CNBC Europe
10 Fleet Place, London EC4M 7QS
tel 020-7653 9300
website www.cnbceurope.com

Europe's main business and financial news channel delivering the latest market information, breaking news, in-depth analysis and interviews with business leaders from around the world.

CNN

Turner Broadcasting System Europe Ltd, Turner House, 16 Great Marlborough Street, London W1F 7HS
tel 020-7693 0942
website www.edition.cnn.com

News.

Discovery Channel

Discovery House, Chiswick Park, 566 Chiswick High Road, London W4 5YB
tel 020-8811 3000
website www.discoverychannel.co.uk

Documentaries.

E4

124 Horseferry Road, London SW1P 2TX
tel 020-7396 4444
website www.channel4.com/e4

Entertainment.

Eurosport

55 Drury Lane, London WC2B 5SQ
tel 020-7468 7777 *fax* 020-7468 0023
email enquiries@eurosport.com
website www.eurosport.co.uk

Sports.

FilmFour

124 Horseferry Road, London SW1P 2TX
tel 020-7396 4444
website www.filmfour.com

Feature films.

God TV

Angel House, Borough Road, Sunderland SR1 1HW
tel 0191-568 0800
website www.god.tv

Religion.

The History Channel

Grant Way, Isleworth, Middlesex TW7 5QD
tel 020-7371 5399
website www.thehistorychannel.co.uk

Historical documentaries.

ITN News

200 Grays Inn Road, London WC1X 8XZ
tel 020-7833 3000
website www.itv.com/news

News.

ITV2

200 Grays Inn Road, London WC1X 8HF
tel 020-7843 8000
website www.itv.com/itv2

Entertainment.

Living

160 Great Portland Street, London W1W 5QA
tel 020-7299 5000
website www.livingtv.co.uk

Daytime magazine.

MTV Network UK & Ireland

17–29 Hawley Crescent, London NW1 8TT
tel 020-7284 7777
email pressinfo@mtvne.com
website www.mtv.co.uk

Music video channels.

MTV2

17–29 Hawley Crescent, London NW1 8TT
tel 020-7284 7777
website www.mtv2europe.co.uk

Music videos.

Paramount Comedy

UK House, 180 Oxford Street London W1D 1DS
tel 020-7478 5300
website www.paramountcomedy.co.uk

American sitcoms.

QVC

Marco Polo House, 346 Queenstown Road, Chelsea Bridge, London SW8 4NQ
tel 020-7705 5600
website www.qvcuk.com

Shopping.

Sci-Fi

Universal Studios Networks Ltd, Oxford House, 76 Oxford Street, London W1D 1BS
tel 020-7307 6600
website www.ukscifi.com

Sky Movies Premier (x5)

Grant Way, Isleworth, Middlesex TW7 5QD
tel 020-7705 3000
website www.skymovies.com

Films.

Sky News

Grant Way, Isleworth, Middlesex TW7 5QD
tel 020-7705 3000
email news@sky.com
website www.skynews.co.uk

News.

Sky One

Grant Way, Isleworth, Middlesex TW7 5QD
tel 020-7705 3000
website www.skyone.co.uk

Entertainment.

Sky Sports 1,2,3, Extra
Grant Way, Isleworth, Middlesex TW7 5QD
tel 020-7705 3000
website www.skysports.com

Sports.

TMF The Music Factory
17–29 Hawley Crescent, London NW1 8TT
tel 020-7284 7777

Music videos.

Travel Channel
64 Newman Street, London W1T 3EF
tel 020-7636 5401 *fax* 020-7636 6424
email petra@travelchannel.co.uk
website www.travelchannel.co.uk

Travel information.

Trouble
160 Great Portland Street, London W1W 5QA
tel 020-7299 5000
website www.trouble.co.uk

Teenage entertainment.

UKTV Food
160 Great Portland Street, London W1W 5QA
tel 020-7299 6200
website www.uktvfood.co.uk

Food programmes.

UKTV Gold
160 Great Portland Street, London W1W 5QA
tel 020-7299 6200
website www.uktv.co.uk/uktvgold

Classic British programmes.

UKTV Style
160 Great Portland Street, London W1W 5QA
tel 020-7299 6200
website www.uktvstyle.co.uk

Lifestyle.

VH1
17–29 Hawley Crescent, London NW1 8TT
tel 020-7284 7777
website www.vh1.co.uk

Current music videos.

VH1 Classic
19–29 Hawley Crescent, London NW1 8TT
website www.vh1.co.uk

Classic music videos.

TELETEXT

Ceefax
Room 7540, BBC Television Centre, Wood Lane,
London W12 7RJ
tel 020-8576 1801
email ceefax@bbc.co.uk
Editor Paul Brannan

Provides service on BBC

Data Broadcasting International
Allen House, Station Road, Egham, Surrey
TW20 9NT
tel (01784) 471515
website www.databroadcasting.co.uk
Managing Director Peter Mason

SimpleActive
Allen House, Station Road, Egham, Surrey
TW20 9NT
tel (01784) 477711
website www.databroadcasting.co.uk

Teletext Ltd
Building 10, Chiswick Park, 566 Chiswick High Road,
London W4 5TS
tel (0870) 731 3000
email listings@teletext.co.uk
website www.teletext.co.uk
Editorial Director John Sage

Provides an information service on ITV1, Channel 4,
S4C and Channel 5 on analogue as well as on digital
TV (Sky and Freeview), the internet and mobile
phones.

Television and film producers

Jean McConnell advises on submitting a screenplay for consideration.

The recommended approach for placing material is through a recognised literary agent (see page 416). Most film companies have a story department to which material can be sent for consideration by its editors. If you choose to submit material direct, first check with the company to make sure it is worth your while. Many of the feature films these days are based on already bestselling books. However, there are some companies, particularly those with a television outlet, which will sometimes accept unsolicited material if it seems to be exceptionally original.

When a writer submits material direct to a company, some of the larger ones – usually those based in the United States – may request that a Release Form be signed before they are prepared to read it. This document is ostensibly designed to absolve the company from any charge of plagiarism if they should be working on a similar idea and also to limit their liability in the event of any legal action. Writers must make up their own minds whether they wish to sign this but, in principle, it is not recommended.

There are a number of independent companies making films specifically for television presentation and some of these are included in the list below.

Jean McConnell is a founder member of the Writers' Guild of Great Britain. She has written screenplays, radio and stage plays, and books. She is a member of the Crime Writers' Association and the Society of Women Writers and Journalists.

Aardman Animations
Gas Ferry Road, Bristol BS1 6UN
tel 0117-984 8485 *fax* 0117-984 8486
email mail@aardman.com
website www.aardman.com
Head of Script Development Mike Cooper

Specialists in model animation. No unsolicited treatments. Founded 1972.

Absolutely Productions
Unit 19, 77 Beak Street, London W1F 9BD
tel 020-7644 5575
website www.absolutely.biz
Contact Miles Bullough

Drama and comedy screenplays for cinema and TV, and TV entertainment programmes. Unsolicited scripts are not accepted. Founded 1989.

Acacia Productions Ltd
80 Weston Park, London N8 9TB
tel 020-8341 9392 *fax* 020-8341 4879
website www.acaciaproductions.co.uk
Managing Director J. Edward Milner

News, documentaries, current affairs programmes for TV and video. Specialises in environmental issues, human rights, Third World development issues and current affairs. No unsolicited MSS.

All3Media
87–91 Newman Street, London W1T 3EY
tel 020-7907 0177 *fax* 020-7907 0199
website www.all3media.com
Chief Executive Steve Morrison, *Coo* Jules Burns,
Finance Director John Pfeil

Comprised of a group of production companies from across the UK, The Netherlands, New Zealand and the USA. Formed following the acquisition of Chrysalis Group's TV division in 2003.

Angel Eye Film and Television
9 Rudolf Place, Miles Street, London SW8 1RP
tel (0845) 230 0062 *fax* (0845) 230 9562
website www.angeleye.co.uk
Contact Susan Turnbull

Unsolicited scripts and ideas for TV and film accepted. See website for 'Procedure for the receipt of creative material'.

Anglo-Fortunato Films Ltd
170 Popes Lane, London W5 4NJ
tel 020-8932 7676 *fax* 020-8932 7491
Contact Luciano Celentino (Managing Director)

Action comedy and psychological thriller screenplays for cinema and TV. Will only accept material if submitted through an agent. Founded 1972.

At It Productions Ltd

68 Salusbury Road, London NW6 6NU
tel 020-8964 2122 fax 020-8964 2133
website www.atitproductions.com
Contact Paul Day

Popular entertainment, music, documentary for TV and film. Founded 1997.

Baby Cow Productions Ltd

77 Oxford Street, London W1D 2ES
tel 020-7399 1267 fax 020-7399 1262
website www.babycow.co.uk

Popular TV entertainment, specialising in cutting edge comedy. Does not invite unsolicited scripts. Send synopsis only. Also Baby Cow Films, Baby Cow Animation and Baby Cow Radio.

Big Heart Media

Unit 22–23, 63 Clerkenwell Road,
London EC1M 5NP
tel 020-7490 2499 fax 020-7490 2556
website www.bigheartmedia.com
Contact Colin Izod

Creates TV drama and documentaries for young people. Founded in 1998.

Big Umbrella Media

The Oracle Building, Blythe Valley Park, West Midlands B90 8AD
email production@bigumbrellamedia.co.uk
website www.bigumbrellamedia.co.uk
Contact Martin Head

Works with other production companies and individuals to co-develop and umbrella proposals to broadcasters. Interested in ideas for single documentaries, entertainment formats or new long-running series. Ideas welcome via email or post.

Brook Lapping Productions Ltd

6 Anglers Lane, London NW5 3DG
tel 020-7428 3100 fax 020-7284 0626
website www.brooklapping.com
Directors Anne Lapping, Brian Lapping, Norma Percy, Phil Craig, Nitil Patel, Tony Allen

TV documentaries, current affairs and radio.

Cactus TV

373 Kennington Road, London SE11 4PS
tel 020-7091 4900 fax 020-7091 4901
email touch.us@cactustv.co.uk
website www.cactustv.co.uk
Joint Managing Directors Amanda Ross, Simon Ross, Head of Entertainment Sinaed Oldnall

Broad-based entertainment, features and chat shows, including Richard & Judy and Saturday Kitchen. Founded 1994.

Carnival (Films and Theatre) Ltd

12 Raddington Road, London W10 5TG
tel 020-8968 0968 fax 020-8968 0177
website www.carnival-films.co.uk
Contact Nicola Gunning

TV, film and theatre drama productions.

Celador Productions Ltd

39 Long Acre, London WC2E 9LG
tel 020-7240 8101 fax 020-7845 9541
website www.celador.co.uk
Joint Managing Directors Christian Colson (films), Danielle Lux (TV)

Develops and produces high-quality, commercially viable feature films across all genres.Film credits include: Dirty, Pretty Things; Separate Lies; The Descent; and Dog Soldiers. All projects are commissioned and developed in-house. Christian Colson is responsible for the commissioning, development and production of all projects presented to the company. Unsolicited scripts are not accepted.

Celtic Films

31 Sackville Street, London W1S 4DZ
tel 020-7734 4434 fax 020-7734 4744
email info@celticfilms.co.uk
website www.celticfilms.co.uk
Contact Steven Russell

Feature films and high-end contemporary drama for TV. Welcomes new scripts; see website for details.

Chatsworth Television Ltd

4 Great Chapel Street, London W1F 8FD
tel 020-7734 4302 fax 020-7437 3301
email info@chatsworth-tv.co.uk
website www.chatsworth-tv.co.uk
Managing Director Malcolm Heyworth

Entertainment, factual and drama. Sister companies in TV distribution and licensing. Founded 1980.

Children's Film and Television Foundation Ltd

3 Liberia Road, London N5 1JP
tel (07887) 53479
email annahome@cftf.org.uk
Chief Executive Anna Home

Involved in the development and co-production of films for children and the family, both for the theatric market and for TV. Will consider screenplays for cinema. Founded 1951.

Collingwood O'Hare Entertainment

10–14 Crown Street, London W3 8SB
tel 020-8993 3666 fax 020-8993 9595
email info@crownstreet.co.uk
website www.collingwoodohare.com
Contact Helen Stroud, Head of Development

Children's animation series for TV for ages 0–12. Will only consider material submitted via an agent. Founded 1988.

The Comedy Unit

Glasgow TV & Film Studios, The Media Park, Craigmont Street, Glasgow G20 9BT

tel 0141-305 6666 *fax* 0141-305 6600
email general@comedyunit.co.uk
website www.comedyunit.co.uk
Contact Niall Clark, Script Editor

Develops and produces a wide range of high-quality scripted and broken comedy series, as well as entertainment and factual entertainment programmes. New comedy writing is encouraged, as are entertainment and factual entertainment programme ideas or formats. Submit material by post or email. Response time approx. one month. Founded 1996.

Company Pictures

Suffolk House, 1–8 Whitfield Place, London W1T 5JU
tel 020-7380 3900 *fax* 020-7380 1166
email enquiries@companypictures.co.uk
website www.companypictures.co.uk
Contact George Faber, Charles Pattinson

Screenplays for TV drama and feature films. All material should be submitted through an agent. Founded 1997.

Convergence Productions

10–14 Crown Street, London W3 8SB
tel 020-8993 3666 *fax* 020-8993 9595
email info@crownstreet.co.uk
Contact Christopher O'Hare, Producer/Managing Director

Documentary series and drama films and series. Limited development capacity – generates own ideas/projects. Prefers material to be submitted through an agent. Founded 1988.

Cosgrove Hall Films Ltd

8 Albany Road, Chorlton-Cum-Hardy, Manchester M21 0AW
tel 0161-882 2500 *fax* 0161-882 2555
email animation@chf.co.uk
website www.chf.co.uk
Managing Director Anthony Utley

Screenplays for cinema and TV for animation (drawn, model or CGI) or a 'live action'/animation mix. Series material especially welcome, preschool to adult. Founded 1976.

Crosshands Ltd/ACP Television

Crosshands, Coreley, Ludlow, Shrops. SY8 3AR
tel (01584) 890893 *fax* (01584) 890893
email mail@acptv.com
Contact Richard Uridge

Radio and TV documentaries.

Cutting Edge Productions

27 Erpingham Road, London SW15 1BE
tel 020-8780 1476 *fax* 020-8780 0102
email juliannorridge@btconnect.com

Documentaries, current affairs. No unsolicited material.

The Walt Disney Company Ltd

3 Queen Caroline Street, London W6 9PE
tel 020-8222 1000 *fax* 020-8222 2795

Screenplays not accepted by London office. Must be submitted by an agent to The Walt Disney Studios in Burbank, California.

Diverse Production Ltd

Gorleston Street, London W14 8XS
tel 020-7603 4567 *fax* 020-7603 2148
website www.diverse.tv

Documentaries, science, history, travel, the arts, music, entertainment, drama.

Eagle and Eagle Ltd

15 Marlborough Road, London W4 4EU
tel 020-8995 1884 *fax* 020-8995 5648
website www.eagletv.co.uk
Contact Robert Eagle

Documentaries, drama and educational programmes for TV.

Ecosse Films Ltd

Brigade House, 8 Parsons Green, London SW6 4TN
tel 020-7371 0290 *fax* 020-7736 3436
website www.ecossefilms.com

High-quality films and dramas for cinema and TV. Material is considered only if it is submitted through an agent. Founded 1988.

The Elstree Production Company

Shepperton Studios, Building 20, Studios Road, Shepperton TW17 0QD
tel (01932) 592680 *fax* (01932) 592682
website www.elsprod.com
Contact Greg Smith

Drama, entertainment and documentaries for TV.

Endemol UK

Shepherd's Building Central, Charechrost Way, London W14 0EE
tel (0870) 333 1700 *fax* (0870) 333 1800
email info@endemoluk.com
website www.endemoluk.com

Entertainment, documentary, children's, arts, factual entertainment, reality, comedy, live events.

Feelgood Fiction Ltd

49 Goldhawk Road, London W12 8QP
tel 020-8746 2535 *fax* 020-8740 6177
email feelgood@feelgoodfiction.co.uk
Managing Director Philip Clarke, *Drama Producer* Laurence Bowen

Film and TV drama.

The First Film Company Ltd

3 Bourlet Close, London W1W 7BQ
tel 020-7436 9490 *fax* 020-7637 1290

email info@firstfilmcompany.com
Producers Roger Randall-Cutler, Robert Cheek

Screenplays for cinema and TV. All material should be submitted through an agent. Founded 1984.

Focus Films Ltd
The Rotunda Studios, rear of 116–118 Finchley Road, London NW3 5HT
tel 020-7435 9004 *fax* 020-7431 3562
email focus@focusfilms.co.uk
Contact Malcolm Kohll

Screenplays for cinema. Will only consider material submitted through an agent. Founded 1982.

Mark Forstater Productions Ltd
27 Lonsdale Road, London NW6 6RA
tel 020-7624 1123 *fax* 020-7624 1124

Film and TV production. No unsolicited scripts.

Free@last TV
2nd Floor, 47 Farringdon Road, London EC1M 3JB
tel 020-7242 4333
website www.freeatlasttv.co.uk
Executive Producer Barry Ryan

Music documentaries and performance, entertainment and factual entertainment.

Gaia Communictions
Sanctuary House, 35 Harding Avenue, Eastbourne, East Sussex BN22 8PL
tel (01323) 727183 *fax* (01323) 734809
email production@gaiacommunications.co.uk
website www.gaiacommunications.co.uk
Directors Robert Armstrong, Loni von Grüner

Specialises in Southeast regional documentary programmes, particularly historical and tourist. Founded 1987.

Noel Gay Television
Shepperton Studios, Studios Road, Shepperton, Middlesex TW17 0QD
tel (01932) 592569 *fax* (01932) 592172
Contact Lesley McKirdy

Treatments only (no scripts) for TV; entertainment, comedy and drama. Founded 1987.

Ginger Television
1st Floor, 3 Waterhouse Square, 138–142 Holborn, London EC1N 2NY
tel 020-7882 1020 *fax* 020-7882 1040
email stephen.joel@ginger.com
website www.ginger.com
Executive Producers Stephen Joel, Ed Stobart

Entertainment, factual entertainment and drama. Part of SMG TV Productions.

The Good Film Company
The Studio, 5–6 Eton Garages, Lambolle Place, London NW3 4PE

tel 020-7794 6222 *fax* 020-7794 4651
website www.goodfilms.co.uk

Commercials. No unsolicited material.

Greenwich Village Productions
14 Greenwich Church Street, London SE10 9BJ
tel 020-8853 5100 *fax* 020-8293 3001
email greenwichvillage@fictionfactory.co.uk
website www.fictionfactory.co.uk
Creative Director John Taylor

Drama, short films, arts documentaries and features. Unsolicited scripts only via agents.

Gruber Films
2 Sheraton Street, London W1F 8BH
tel (0870) 366 9313
email office@gruberfilms.com
website www.gruberfilms.com
Contact Richard Holmes, Ron Fogelman

Feature films.

Hat Trick Productions Ltd
10 Livonia Street, London W1F 8AF
tel 020-7434 2451 *fax* 020-7287 9791
website www.hattrick.com
Managing Director Denise O'Donoghue

Situation and drama comedy series and light entertainment shows. Founded 1986.

Icon Films
10 Redland Terrace, Bristol BS6 6TD
tel 0117-970 6882 *fax* 0117-974 4971
website www.iconfilms.co.uk

TV documentaries. Welcomes new documentary proposals.

Ignition Films Ltd
1 Wickham Court, Bristol BS16 1DQ
tel 0117-958 3087 *fax* 0117-965 7674
email ignition@blueyonder.co.uk
website www.ignitionfilms.org
Contact Alison Sterling

Screenplays for cinema and TV. Material only accepted through agents. Founded 1999.

Illuminations
19–20 Rheidol Mews, Rheidol Terrace, London N1 8NU
tel 020-7288 8400 *fax* 020-7359 1151
email linda@illumin.co.uk
website www.illumin.co.uk
Managing Director Keith Griffiths

Cultural documentaries, arts and entertainment for broadcast TV. Founded 1982.

ITN Factual
16 Mortimer Street, London W1T 3JL
tel 020-7430 4511 *fax* 020-7430 4506

website www.itn.co.uk/factual
Head of Factual Philip Dampier, *Head of Production*
Zoe Loizou

ITN's award-winning documentary-making division.

IWC Media Ltd
Head office St George's Studios, 93–7 St George's
Road, Glasgow G3 6JA
tel 0141-353 3222
and 3–6 Kenrick Place, London W1U 6HD
tel 020-7317 2230
website www.iwcmedia.co.uk
Managing Director Sue Oriel, *Director of Drama*
Eileen Quinn

Drama, features/factual entertainment, contemporary
and specialist factual.

Leopard Films Ltd
1–3 St Peter's Street, London N1 8JD
tel (0870) 420 4232 *fax* (0870) 443 6099
email firstnamelastname@leopardfilms.com
website www.leopardfilms.com
Managing Director Susie Field

Broad range of TV programmes. Sister companies are
Leopard Films USA and Leopardrama, which
specialises in drama productions.

Libra Television Ltd
4th Floor, 22 Lever Street, The Northern Quarter,
Manchester M1 1EA
tel 0161-236 5599 *fax* 0161-236 6877
email hq@libratelevision.com
website www.libratelevision.com
Contact Louise Lynch

Children's and education TV programmes.

Lion Television
Lion House, 26 Paddenswick Road, London W6 0UB
tel 020-8846 2000 *fax* 020-8846 2001
website www.liontv.co.uk

Light entertainment, documentaries, drama,
children's, the arts, news/current affairs, religion.

Little Bird Company Ltd
9 Grafton Mews, London W1P 5LG
tel 020-7380 3980 *fax* 020-7380 3981
email firstname@littlebird.co.uk
website www.littlebird.ie
Contact N. Mirza

Screenplays for cinema and TV. No unsolicited
material. Founded 1982.

Little Dancer Ltd
61 Benthal Road, London N16 7AR
tel 020-8806 7504
email littledancerfilm@aol.com
Producer Robert Smith

Screenplays for cinema and TV; drama. Founded
1992.

LWT and United Productions
London Television Centre, Upper Ground, London
SE1 9LT
tel 020-7620 1620 *fax* 020-7261 3041
Controller of Drama Michele Buck

Producers of TV and film. Founded 1996.

Malone Gill Productions Ltd
27 Campden Hill Road, London W8 7DX
tel 020-7937 0557 *fax* 020-7376 1727
email malonegill@aol.com
Contact Georgina Denison

TV programmes. Founded 1978.

Maya Vision International Ltd
6 Kinghorn Street, London EC1A 7HW
tel 020-7796 4842 *fax* 020-7796 5480
email info@mayavisionint.com
website www.mayavisionint.com
Producer/Director Rebecca Dobbs

Features, TV dramas and documentaries. No
unsolicited scripts. Founded 1983.

Mentorn
43 Whitfield Street, London W1P 6TG
tel 020-7258 6800
website www.mentorn.co.uk

Entertainment, documentaries, current affairs.

Mint Productions
205 Lower Rathmines Road, Dublin 6, Republic
of Ireland
tel 353 1 491 3333 *fax* 353 1 491 3334
13 Fitzwilliam Street, Belfast BT9 6AW
tel (28) 90 240555
website www.mint.ie

Documentaries with an emphasis on historical and
observational films.

Nexus Productions Ltd
113–114 Shoreditch High Street, London E1 6JN
tel 020-7749 7500 *fax* 020-7749 7501
website www.nexusproductions.com

Animation for TV, commercials, music videos and
film. Founded 1997.

Oxford Scientific Films (OSF)
Network House, Station Yard, Thame OX9 3UH
tel (01844) 262370 *fax* (01844) 262380
website www.osf.co.uk

Natural history and science documentaries.
Welcomes new material.

Pathé Pictures
14–17 Kenthouse, Market Place, London W1W 8AR
tel 020-7323 5151 *fax* 020-7631 3568
website www.pathe.co.uk

Feature film production company. Will consider
proposals submitted via an agent or production
company.

Picture Palace Films Ltd

13 Egbert Street, London NW1 8LJ
tel 020-7586 8763 *fax* 020-7586 9048
email info@picturepalace.com
website www.picturepalace.com
Contact Malcolm Craddock

Screenplays for cinema and TV; low budget films; TV drama series. Material only considered if submitted through an agent. Founded 1971.

Portobello Pictures Ltd

Eardley House, 4 Uxbridge Street, London W8 7SY
tel 020-7908 9890 *fax* 020-7908 9899
Contact Sophie Garland

Film, TV and theatre production company. Founded 1987.

Pozzitive Television Ltd

5th Floor, Paramount House, 162–170 Wardour Street, London W1V 4AB
tel 020-7734 3258 *fax* 020-7437 3130
email pozzitive@pozzitive.demon.co.uk
Contact David Tyler

Comedy and entertainment for TV and radio. Hard copy submissions only. Scripts not returned without sae.

Praxis Films Ltd

Unit 3N, Leroy House, 436 Essex Road, London N1 3QP
tel 020-7682 1865
email info@praxisfilms.co.uk
website www.praxisfilms.co.uk
Contact Tony Cook, Head of Development & Training

Documentaries, current affairs, educational, schools programming for TV. New Media, communications consultancy, media training. Founded 1985.

Princess Productions

Whiteley's Centre, 151 Queensway, London W2 4SB
tel 020-7985 1985 *fax* 020-7985 1986
website www.princesstv.com

Popular entertainment.

Prospect Pictures

13 Wandsworth Plain, London SW18 1ET
tel 020-7636 1234
website www.prospect-uk.com

Documentaries, light entertainment.

RDF Television

The Gloucester Building, Kensington Village, Avonmore Road, London W14 8RF
tel 020-7013 4000 *fax* 020-7013 4001
website www.rdfmedia.com

Light entertainment, documentary, drama, arts, news, current affairs, religion.

September Films Ltd

Glen House, 22 Glenthorne Road, London W6 0NG
tel 020-8563 9393 *fax* 020-8741 7214
email september@septemberfilms.com
website www.septemberfilms.com
Director of Production Elaine Day

Factual entertainment and documentary specialists expanding further into TV drama and film. Founded 1993.

So Television

18 Hatfields, London SE1 8GN
tel 020-7960 2000 *fax* 020-7960 2095
website www.sotelevision.co.uk
Contact Graham Stuart

Entertainment. No unsolicited MSS.

Specific Films

25 Rathbone Street, London W1T 1NQ
tel 020-7580 7476 *fax* 020-7494 2676
email info@specificfilms.com
website www.specificfilms.com
Managing Director Michael Hamlyn

Feature-length films.

Spice Factory UK Ltd

14 Regent Hill, Brighton BN1 3ED
tel (01273) 739182 *fax* (01273) 749122
email shirine@spicefactory.co.uk
website www.spicefactory.co.uk
Contact Lucy Shuttleworth (Head of Development), Shirine Best (Development)

Feature film production company. No unsolicited submissions. Founded 1995.

Spire Films

7 High Street, Kidlington, Oxford OX5 2DH
tel (01865) 371979
email mail@spirefilms.co.uk
website www.spirefilms.co.uk

Factual, lifestyle and arts.

Straight forward film and television productions

Building 2, Lesley Office Park, 393 Holyrood Road, Belfast BT4 2LS
tel 04890 651010 *fax* 04830 651012
email enquiries@straightforwardltd.co.uk
Producer Ian Kennedy

Current affairs, news, documentary, lifestyle.

Sunset & Vine

30 Sackville Street, London W1S 3DY
tel 020-7478 7300 *fax* 020-7478 7407
email reception@sunsetvine.co.uk
website www.sunsetvine.co.uk

Documentaries, sports, entertainment.

Talent Television
Lion House, 72–75 Red Lion Square,
London WC1R 4NA
tel 020-7421 7800 *fax* 020-7421 7811
website www.talenttv.com
Head of Production Adam Hayes

Current affairs, entertainment, children's.

Talisman Films Ltd
7 Alan Road, London SW19 7PT
tel 020-8947 4414 *fax* 020-8947 0446
email email@talismanfilms.com
Contact Richard Jackson

Screenplays for cinema and TV. Material only
considered if submitted through an agent. Single page
treatments accepted. Founded 1991.

TalkBackThames
20–21 Newman Street, London W1T 1PG
tel 020-7861 8000 *fax* 020-7861 8001
website www.talkback.co.uk

TV situation comedies and comedy dramas, features,
straight drama. Send material through an agent to
Lorraine Heggessey. Founded 1981.

Television Junction
46 Gas Street, Birmingham B1 2JT
tel 0121-248 4466 *fax* 0121-248 4477
email info@televisionjunction.co.uk
website www.televisionjunction.co.uk

Education programmes for TV.

Thrilanfere
Apartment 12, 5 Bewley Street, London SW19 1XF
tel 020-8543 0284 *fax* 020-8542 9798
email elaine@thrilanfere.com
Contact Elaine Taylor

TV drama.

Tiger Aspect Productions
7 Soho Street, London W1D 3DQ
tel 020-7434 6700 *fax* 020-7434 1798
email general@tigeraspect.co.uk
website www.tigeraspect.co.uk
Managing Director Andrew Zein, *Head of Comedy*
Clive Tulloh, *Head of Factual Group* Paul Sommers,
Executive Producer, Entertainment Anastasia Mouzas,
Head of Production, Animation & Children's
Catherine Elliot

Programme genres include comedy, drama,
entertainment, factual, animation, wildlife (Tigress)
and feature films (Pictures). Children's programmes
include *Star* and *Charlie and Lola*. All material should
be submitted through an agent. Founded 1993.

Twentieth Century Fox Productions Ltd
Twentieth Century House, 31–32 Soho Square,
London W1D 3AP
tel 020-7437 7766 *fax* 020-7434 2170
Will not consider unsolicited material.

Twenty Twenty Television
20 Kentish Town Road, London NW1 9NX
tel 020-7284 2020 *fax* 020-7284 1810
email mail@twentytwenty.tv
Executive Producer Claudia Milne

Current affairs, documentaries, science and
educational programmes, drama. Founded 1982.

TWI UK Ltd
McCormack House, Burlington Lane, London W4
2TH
tel 020-8233 5300 *fax* 020-8233 5301
website www.imgworld.com

Major sporting events including: Wimbledon, Rugby
World Cup, The Olympics, 15th Asian Games Doha
2006, Melbourne 2006 Commonwealth Games, The
PGA European Tour.
Original sports programming: Sport Matters,
UKTV Sport, FIFA Futbol Mundial, World's
Strongest Man, Trans World Sport.
Factual and entertainment programming: award-
winning *Colour of War* documentary series, *All*Star
Cup*, *I'd Do Anything*, the Oscars 2005 and 2006.

Twofour Productions Ltd
Twofour Studios, Estover, Plymouth PL6 7RG
tel (01752) 727400 *fax* (01752) 727450
email enq@twofour.co.uk
website www.twofour.co.uk
Contact Melanie Leach, Development Dept

Factual, factual entertainment, leisure and lifestyle,
and children's TV programmes. Founded 1987.

Upfront Television Ltd
39–41 New Oxford Street, London WC1A 1BN
tel 020-7836 7702/3 *fax* 020-7836 7701
email info@upfronttv.com
website www.celebritiesworldwide.com
Contact Richard Brecker, Joint Managing Director

Books celebrities for high-profile shows and events
around the world. Founded 1991.

Waddell Media Ltd
Strand Studios, 5–7 Shore Road, Holywood, County
Down BT18 9HX
tel 028-9042 7646 *fax* 028-9042 7922
email info@waddellmedia.com
website www.waddellmedia.com

TV documentaries; factual entertainment.

Wall to Wall Television
8–9 Spring Place, London NW5 3ER
tel 020-7485 7424
website www.walltowall.co.uk

Documentaries, drama, the arts.

Warner Bros. Productions Ltd

Warner House, 98 Theobald's Road, London
WC1X 8WB
tel 020-7984 5000

Screenplays for cinema. Will only consider material submitted through an agent.

Working Title Films

Films 76 Oxford Street, London W1D 1BS
tel 020-7307 3000 *fax* 020-7307 3003
website www.workingtitlefilms.com
Chairmen Tim Bevan and Eric Fellner,
Head of Development Debra Hayward (films)
TV 140 Wardour Street, London W1F 82T
tel 020-7534 9740
Head of Television Simon Wright
WT2 76 Oxford Street, London W1D 1BS
Head of Development Natascha Wharton

Screenplays for films; TV drama and comedy; low budget films (WT2).

World Productions Ltd

Eagle House, 50 Marshall Street, London W1F 9BQ
tel 020-7734 3536 *fax* 020-7758 7000
email firstname@world-productions.com
website www.world-productions.com
Contact Office Manager

Screenplays for TV; TV drama series and serials; feature films.

Zenith Entertainment Ltd

43–45 Dorset Street, London W1U 7NA
tel 020-7224 2440 *fax* 020-7224 3194
email general@zenith-entertainment.co.uk
website www.zenith-entertainment.co.uk

Screenplays for TV drama. No unsolicited scripts.

Independent national radio

UK domestic radio services are broadcast across three wavebands: FM (or VHF), medium wave and long wave. For radio stations broadcast in both analogue and digital see page 378.

Classic FM

30 Leicester Square, London WC2H 7LA
tel 020-7343 9000 *fax* 020-7344 2703
email enquiries@classicfm.com
website www.classicfm.com
Station Manager Darren Henley

The UK's only 100% classical music radio station; national and international news. Launched 1992.

Commercial Radio Companies Association (CRCA)

77 Shaftesbury Avenue, London W1D 5DU
tel 020-7306 2603 *fax* 020-7470 0062
email info@crca.co.uk
website www.crca.co.uk

The trade body for UK commercial radio representing commercial radio to Government, Parliament, Ofcom, copyright societies and other organisations concerned with radio. CRCA is the primary source for up-to-date information and advice on all aspects of commercial radio.

CRCA administers the Radio Advertising Clearance Centre (RACC). It jointly owns Radio Joint Audience Research Ltd (RAJAR) with the BBC and JICRIT Ltd (an electronic means of buying, selling and accounting for radio advertisements) with the IPA. It is a founder member of the Association of European Radios (AER), which lobbies European institutions on behalf of commercial radio.

Digital One Ltd

Digital One Ltd, 30 Leicester Square, London WC2H 7LA
tel 020-7288 4600
email info@digitalone.co.uk
website www.ukdigitalradio.com

National commercial digital radio multiplex operator. Founded 1999.

IRN (Independent Radio News)

6th Floor, 200 Gray's Inn Road, London WC1X 8XZ
tel 020-7430 4090 *fax* 020-7430 4092
email news@irn.co.uk
website www.irn.co.uk

National news provider to all UK commercial radio stations, including live news bulletins, sport and financial news, and coverage of the House of Commons.

Oneword Radio

50 Lisson Street, London NW1 5DF
tel 020-7453 1510 *fax* 020-7723 6132
email info@oneword.co.uk
website www.oneword.co.uk
Managing Director Simon Blackmore, *Programme Manager* Paul Kent

The first commercial national radio station to be exclusively dedicated to the transmission of books, plays, comedy and discussion. Broadcasts 7 days a week on Sky (channel 0127), Freeview (channel 717), NTL (channel 893), DAB digital radio and streams live on the internet. Founded 2000.

The Radio Authority – now The Office of Communications (Ofcom) – see page 679

TalkSPORT

18 Hatfields, London SE1 8DJ
tel 020-7959 7800 *fax* 020-7959 7874
website www.talksport.net
Managing Director Michael Franklyn, *Programme Director* Bill Ridley

Sports commentary, comments and coverage. Launched 1995.

TEAMtalk252/Atlantic 252

(formerly called Atlantic 252)
78 Wellington Street, Leeds LS1 2EQ
tel (0870) 128 3333
website www.teamtalk.com

Broadcast from Southern Ireland but with two-thirds of its audience in the UK. Formerly called Atlantic 252. Founded 1989.

Virgin Radio

1 Golden Square, London W1F 9DJ
tel 020-7434 1215 *fax* 020-7434 1197
email reception@virginradio.co.uk
website www.virginradio.co.uk
Chief Executive John Pearson, *Programme Director* Paul Jackson

Rock and contemporary music. Available on digital, analogue and the internet. Launched in 1993.

Digital audio broadcasting

Digital transmission technology has a broadcasting capacity many times bigger than analogue, having many more radio stations. Readers are advised to check with the multiplex operator for accurate listings.

NATIONAL MULTIPLEXES

BBC Radio

Broadcasting House, Portland Place, London W1A 1AA
tel 020-7580 4468
website www.bbc.co.uk/radio

Broadcasts network services to the UK, Isle of Man and the Channel Islands. There are also national services in Wales, Scotland and Northern Ireland and 40 local radio stations in England and the Channel Islands. Launched 1995.

Digital One

Digital One Ltd, 30 Leicester Square, London WC2H 7LA
tel 020-7288 4600
website www.ukdigitalradio.com
Operations Director Glyn Jones, *Operations Manager* Dawn Banks

Digital radio network with more than 85% UK population coverage. Broadcasts Classic FM, Virgin Radio and talkSPORT plus other channels unique to digital radio – Planet Rock, Core, Life, Oneword. Launched 1999.

LOCAL MULTIPLEXES

Aberdeen and Central Scotland

Switchdigital (Scotland) Ltd, 18 Hatfields, London SE1 8DJ
tel 020-7959 7800 *fax* 020-7959 9009
email info@switchdigital.com

Broadcasts 24 hours a day:

Aberdeen: Kiss, Smash Hits!, Waves Radio, NECR, Northsound One and Two, BBC Radio Scotland, BBC Radio nan Gaidheal

Central Scotland: Galaxy, Jazz FM, Beat 106, Real Radio, The Arrow, Heart, Smash Hits!, BBC Radio nan Gaidheal

Ayr, Dundee & Perth, Edinburgh, Glasgow, Inverness, Northern Ireland

Score Digital, 3 South Avenue, Clydebank Business Park, Glasgow G81 2RX
tel 0141-565 2347 *fax* 0141-565 2318
website www.scoredigital.co.uk

Broadcasts 24 hours a day:

Ayr: West FM, West Sound, 3C, UCA, The Storm, Smash Hits!, BBC radio Scotland, BBC Radio nan Gaidheal

Dundee & Perth: Tay FM, Tay Am, 3C, The Access Channel, The Storm, Smash Hits!, BBC Radio Scotland, BBC nan Gaidheal

Edinburgh: 3C, Kiss, Forth One, Forth 2, Xfm, Sunrise Radio, Saga, BBC Radio Scotland

Glasgow: Clyde 1 and 2, 3C, Sunrise Radio, 96.3 QFM, Xfm, Kiss, Saga Radio, BBC Scotland

Inverness: MFR, 3C, MFR 1107, BBC Radio Scotland, BBC nan Gaidheal

Northern Ireland: Downtown, Cool FM, City Beat 96.7, Q102.9, Classic FM, PrimeTime, 3C, Kiss, BBC Radio Ulster

Birmingham, Greater London I, Manchester

CE Digital, 30 Leicester Square, London WC2H 7LA
tel 020-7766 6000 *fax* 020-7766 6100

Broadcasts 24 hours a day:

Birmingham: BRMB, Capital Gold, Xfm, Radio XL, Magic, Kiss, Sunrise, BBC Radio WM

Greater London I: Capital FM, Capital Gold, Century, Kiss, Magic, LBC 1152 and 97.3, Xfm, Sunrise Radio, Smash Hits!, Capital Disney

Manchester: Key 103, Magic 1152, Kiss, Capital Gold, Xfm, Asian Sound, BBC GMR

Bournemouth, Bristol/Bath, Coventry, Exeter and Torbay, Norwich, Peterborough, Southend & Chelmsford, Swindon/West Midlands, Wolverhampton, Shrewsbury, Telford

Now Digital, PO Box 2000, 1 Passage Street, Bristol BS99 7SN
tel 020-7959 7800 *fax* 020-7911 7302
website www.now-digital.com

Broadcasts 24 hours a day:

Bournemouth: 2CR FM, Classic Gold, Kiss, Wave 105, Saga, Passion for the Planet, The Storm, SBN, BBC Radio Solent

Bristol/Bath: GWR FM, Classic Gold, The Storm, Xfm, Kiss, Saga, Passion for the Planet, now.data, SBN, BBC Radio Bristol

Coventry: Mercia FM, Classic Gold, Kix 96, The Storm, Sunrise, SBN, Kiss, YAAR, BBC Radio Coventry & Warwickshire

Exeter & Torbay: Gemini FM, Classic Gold, Kiss, The Storm, Passion for the Planet, SBN, BBC Radio Devon

Norwich: Broadband 102, Vibe, 106.4 The Beach, The Storm, Passion for the Planet, 3C, SBN, AbracaDABra, Smash Hits!

Peterborough: Hereward FM, Classic Gold, Vibe, 3C, Passion for the Planet, SBN, Smash Hits!, BBC Radio Cambridgeshire

Southend & Chelmsford: Essex FM, Breeze, Saga, The Storm, Passion for the Planet, TBC, Kiss, SBN, BBC Radio Essex

Swindon/West Midlands: Swindon only – GWR FM Wilts, Saga, Swindon FM, BBC Radio Swindon
    West Wiltshire only – GWR FM Bath, BBC Radio Wiltshire
    Both – Kiss, Capital Disney, The Storm, Passion for the Planet, SBN

Wolverhampton, Shrewsbury, Telford: Beacon FM, Classic Gold, The Storm, Xfm, Sunrise Radio, YAAR, Kiss, SBN, BBC Radio WM, BBC Radio Shropshire (WST)

Bradford & Huddersfield, Stoke-on-Trent, Swansea

TWG – Emap Digital, 18 Hatfields, London SE1 8DJ
tel 020-7959 7800 *fax* 020-7959 9009
email info@switchdigital.com

Provides 8 programme services.

Bradford & Huddersfield: The Pulse, Classic Gold, Sunrise Radio, Smash Hits!, Kiss

Stoke-on-Trent: Signal 1 and 2, Kiss, Smash Hits!, The Storm, BBC Radio Stoke

Swansea: The Wave, Swansea Sound, Kiss, Smash Hits!, TBC, BBC Radio Cyrmu, BBC Radio Wales

Cardiff & Newport, Kent, South Hampshire, Sussex Coast

Capital Radio Digital, 30 Leicester Square London WC2H 7LA
tel 020-7766 6000 *fax* 020-7766 6100

Contemporary hit radio. Broadcasts 24 hours a day:

Cardiff & Newport: Red Dragon FM, Capital Gold, Century, Xfm, BBC Radio Wales, BBC Radio Cymru

Kent: Invicta FM, Capital Gold, Kent Digital Extra, Saga Radio, Xfm, Kiss, Swale Sound, Totally Radio, BBC Radio Kent

South Hampshire: Ocean FM, 103.2 Power FM, Capital Gold, Wave 105.2, Saga, Passion for the Planet, Xfm, SouthCity FM, Southampton Hospital Radio, BBC Radio Solent

Sussex Coast: Southern FM, Capital Gold, Juice 107.2, Xfm, Saga, Kiss, Gaydar Radio, Spirit FM, Totally Radio, BBC Southern Counties

Central Lancashire, Humberside, Leeds, Liverpool, South Yorkshire, Teesside, Tyne & Wear

Emap Digital Radio Ltd, Mappin House, 4 Winsley Street, London W1W 8HF
tel 020-7436 1515
website www.emapdigitalradio.com

Broadcasts 24 hours a day:

Central Lancashire: 97.4 Rock FM, Kiss, Magic 999, Classic Gold, Xfm, 3C, Smash Hits!, BBC Radio Lancashire

Humberside: 96.9 Viking FM, Magic 1161, Lincs FM, Classic Gold, Xfm, Smash Hits!, Kiss, BBC Radio Humberside

Leeds: 96.3 Aire FM, Classic Gold, Kiss, Magic 828, Ridings FM, Xfm, Smash Hits!, BBC Radio Leeds

Liverpool: Radio City 96.7, Magic 1548, Kiss, Classic Gold, Xfm, 3C, Smash Hits!, BBC Radio Merseyside

South Yorkshire: Hallam FM, Magic, Kiss, Trax FM, Classic Gold, Xfm, Smash Hits!, BBC Radio Sheffield

Teesside: Classic Gold, Kiss, Magic 1170, 96.6 TFM, Xfm, 3C, Smash Hits!, BBC Radio Cleveland

Tyne & Wear: Metro FM, Magic 1152, Kiss, 3C, Classic Gold, Xfm, Smash Hits!, BBC Radio Newcastle

Leicester, Nottingham

Now Digital (East Midland) Ltd, PO Box 2000, 1 Passage Street, Bristol BS99 7SN
tel 020-7911 7300 *fax* 020-7911 7302
website www.now-digital.com

Leicester: Leicester Sound, Classic Gold GEM, Galaxy, Capital Disney, Sabras Sound, A Plus, Century 106, BBC Radio Leicester

Nottingham: 106 Trent FM, Classic Gold GEM, 106 Century FM, Saga, Galaxy, Capital Disney, The Storm, A Plus, BBC Radio Nottingham

Greater London II

Switchdgital Ltd, 18 Hatfields, London SE1 8DR
tel 020-7959 7800 *fax* 020-7401 9009
email info@switchdigital.com

Broadcasts 24 hours a day: Hits, Galaxy, YAAR, The Groove, Travel Now, Hart 106.2 FM, Jazz FM, Saga Radio, Spectrum Radio 558AM, BBC London Live.

Greater London III

The Digital Radio Group (London) Ltd, 7 Swallow Place, London W1R 7AA
tel 020-7911 7300 *fax* 020-7911 7302
website www.thedigitalradiogroup.com

Broadcasts 24 hours a day: The Arrow, AbracaDABra, Choice, Liquid, Passion for the Planet, Gaydar Radio, Mean Country, The Storm, Breeze, SBN.

North East England, North West England, South Wales/Severn Estuary, West Midlands, Yorkshire

MXR, The Chrysalis Building, 13 Bramley Road, London W10 6SP
tel 020-7221 2213 *fax* 020-7314 1062
website www.getdadigitalradio.com

Broadcasts 24 hours a day:

North East England: Urban Choice, Heart, The Arrow, Smooth, Digital News Network, Galaxy, Jazz FM, Century FM, Capital Disney

North West England: Urban Choice, Heart, The Arrow, Smooth, Digital News Network, Galaxy, Jazz FM, Century FM, Capital Disney

South Wales/Severn Estuary: Urban Choice, Heart, The Arrow, Smooth, Digital News Network, Vibe 101, Jazz FM, Real radio, Capital Disney

West Midlands: Galaxy, Heart, Saga Radio, Capital Disney, Jazz FM, The Arrow, Smooth, Digital News Network

Yorkshire: Capital Disney, Urban Choice, Heart, Jazz FM, The Arrow, Smooth, Digital News Network, Galaxy, Real Radio

Independent radio producers

Many writers approach independent production companies direct and, increasingly, BBC Radio is commissioning independent producers to make programmes.

Above the Title Productions

Level 2, 10–11 St George's Mews, London NW1 8XE
tel 020-7916 1984 *fax* 020-7722 5706
email mail@abovethetitle.com
website www.abovethetitle.com
Managing Director Helen Chattwell

Comedy, factual, drama, documentary, discussion, music and arts. Ideas welcome via email.

All Out Productions

50 Copperas Street, Manchester M4 1HS
tel 0161-834 9955 *fax* 0161-834 6978
email mail@allout.co.uk
website www.allout.co.uk
Contact David Cook

Documentaries and feature programmes. Founded 1994.

Athena Media

Digital Depot, Digital Hub, Thomas Street, Dublin 8, Republic of Ireland
tel 353 1488 5850 *mobile* 353 8767 54375
email helen@athenamedia.ie
website www.athenamedia.ie
Managing Director Helen Shaw

Factual programmes, documentaries. Also a specialist consultancy for film, broadcasting and digital media sectors.

Baby Cow Productions Ltd

77 Oxford Street, London W1D 2ES
tel 020-7399 1267 *fax* 020-7399 1262
website www.babycow.co.uk

Popular TV entertainment, specialising in cutting edge comedy. No unsolicited scripts. Send synopsis only. Also Baby Cow Films and Baby Cow Animation.

Big Heart Media

Unit 22–23, 63 Clerkenwell Road, London EC1M 5NP
tel 020-7490 2499 *fax* 020-7490 2556
website www.bigheartmedia.com
Contact Colin Izod

Dramas and documentaries. Keen to develop relationships with writers for radio. Interested to receive unsolicited drama scripts or treatments.

Bona Broadcasting

3rd Floor, 21 Albert Square, Dundee DD1 1DJ
tel (01382) 225403 *fax* (01382) 225408

website www.bonabroadcasting.com
Contact Turan Ali

Features, drama, comedy, documentaries, live magazine programmes. No unsolicited MSS. Send a one paragraph summary by email only.

Campbell Davison Media

110 Gloucester Avenue, London NW1 8JA
tel 020-7209 3740 *fax* 020-7209 3743
website www.campbelldavison.com
Contact Clare Davidson

Daily news programmes, features, live sport, documentaries and entertainment.

Classic Arts Productions Ltd

The Old Rectory, Hampton Lovett, Droitwich, Worcs. WR9 0LY
tel (01299) 851563
email wendy@classicarts.co.uk
website www.classicarts.co.uk
Contact Wendy Thompson

Classical music and arts-related programmes. Ideas welcome.

Crosshands Ltd/ACP Television

Crosshands, Coreley, Ludlow, Shrops. SY8 3AR
tel (01584) 890893 *fax* (01584) 890893
email mail@acptv.com
Contact Richard Uridge

Radio and TV documentaries.

CSA Word

6ᴀ Archway Mews, London SW15 2PE
tel 020-8871 0220 *fax* 020-8877 0712
email info@csaword.co.uk
website www.csaword.co.uk
Audio Manager Victoria Williams

Produces readings, plays and features/documentaries. Allow approx. 2 months for response to submissions. Founded 1992.

Electric Airwaves

Essel House 29 Foley Street London W1W 7JW
tel 020-7323 2770 *fax* 020-7079 2080
email andrew@electricairwaves.com
website www.electricairwaves.com
Director Andrew Caesar-Gordon

Drama, documentary, music and readings. Ideas welcome via email.

Ruth Evans Productions

4 Offlands Cottages, Moulsford, Oxon OX10 9HP
tel (01491) 651331

email ruth@ruthevans.com
Contact Ruth Evans

Documentaries and feature programmes for BBC World Service and Radio 4. Founded 2002.

Festival Productions Ltd
PO Box 70, Brighton BN1 1YJ
tel (01273) 669595 *fax* (01273) 669596
email info@festivalradio.com
website www.festivalradio.com
Managing Director Steve Stark

Plays, docs, features and programmes. Founded 1989.

The Fiction Factory
14 Greenwich Church Street, London SE10 9BJ
tel 020-8853 5100 *fax* 020-8293 3001
email radio@fictionfactory.co.uk
website www.fictionfactory.co.uk
Creative Director John Taylor

Plays, dramatisations, readings, documentaries and features mainly for BBC network radio and the World Service. Original radio drama scripts considered if targeted at existing BBC slots. Submissions only from established writers or literary agents. Email before submitting MSS. Founded 1993.

First Writes Theatre Co Ltd
1 Stables Yard, Waterbeach, Cambridge CB5 9FN
Director Ellen Dryden

Drama for BBC Radio 3 and 4: original plays and adaptations. No unsolicited material. Founded 1991.

Flannel
21 Berwick Street, London W1F 0PZ
tel 020-7287 9277 *fax* 020-7287 7785
Contact Kate Haldane

Drama, comedy and features for BBC Radio. Considers comedy narrative, sketch show and panel game ideas. Will only consider material if submitted via an agent. Founded 2002.

Heavy Entertainment Ltd
Canalot Studios, 222 Kensal Road, London W10 5BN
tel 020-8960 9001/2 *fax* 020-8960 9003
Company Directors David Roper, Davy Nougarède

Audiobooks, radio documentaries and commercials. Showreels and promotional audio and video. Two studios available for hire. Founded 1992.

Loftus Productions Ltd
2ᴀ Aldine Street, London W12 8AN
tel 020-8740 4666
email ask@loftusproductions.co.uk
website www.loftusproductions.co.uk
Contact Nigel Acheson

Produces features, documentaries and readings and drama for BBC Radio. Founded 1996.

Jane Marshall Productions
The Coach House, Westhill Road, Blackdown, Leamington Spa, Warks. CV32 6RA

tel (01926) 831680
email jane@jmproductions.freeserve.co.uk

Single voice readings for BBC Radio – abridged published fiction and non-fiction. Founded 1994.

Neon
Studio Two, 19 Marine Crescent, Glasgow G51 1HD
tel 0141-429 6366 *fax* 0141-429 6377
website www.go2neon.com

Arts and music, documentary/factual, drama.

Pacificus Productions
47 Addison Avenue, London W11 4QU
tel 020-7603 6991 *fax* 020-7603 6593
Contact Clive Brill

Dramas for Radio 4. Ideas welcome via email.

Pennine Productions LLP
Kilmagadwood Cottage, Scotlandwell, Kinross KY13 9HY
tel (05600) 472247
email mike@pennine.biz
website www.pennine.biz
Contact Mike Hally

Wide range of features for BBC Radio 3, 4 and World Service, including book readings and short stories. No unsolicited material – phone, email or write first. Founded 2000.

Pier Productions
Lower Ground Floor, 1 Marlborough Place, Brighton BN1 1TU
tel (01273) 691401 *fax* (01273) 693658
email pier@admin@mistral.co.uk
Contact Peter Hoare

Features, drama and readings for Radio 4.

Promenade Enterprises
6 Russell Grove, London SW9 6HS
tel 020-7582 9354 *fax* 020-7564 3026
email info@promenadeproductions.com
website www.promenadeproductions.com
Contact Nicholas Newton

Drama. Will only consider plays if submitted via an agent. Founded 1998.

SH Radio
Green Dene Cottage, Honeysuckle Bottom, East Horsley, Surrey KT24 5TD
tel (01483) 283223 *fax* (01483) 281792
Contact Robert Symes

Broadcast and non-broadcast commercial material (English and German). Founded 1988.

Smooth Operations
South office PO Box 286, Cambridge CB1 7XW
tel (01223) 244544 *fax* (01223) 244384
email nick@smoothoperations.com

Contact Nick Barraclough
North office 6 Millgate, Delph, Oldham OL3 5JG
tel (01457) 873752 *fax* (01457) 878500
email john@smoothoperations.com
website www.smoothoperations.com
Contact John Leonard

Music-based docs and series and online content provision for BBC radio. Founded 1992.

Lou Stein Associates Ltd
email info@loustein.co.uk
Contact Lou Stein

Plays for BBC Radio. Founded 2000.

Sweet Talk Productions Ltd
22 Montpelier Street, Brighton BN1 3DJ
tel (01273) 772 913 *fax* (01273) 722 824
email karenrose@btclick.com
Contact Karen Rose

Dramas, comedy, features and readings for radio.

Testbed Productions
5th Floor, 14–16 Great Portland Street, London W1W 8QW
tel 020-7436 0555 *fax* 020-7436 2800
email mail@testbed.co.uk
website www.testbed.co.uk
Directors Viv Black, Nick Baker

Documentaries, phone-ins and debates for BBC Radio. Welcomes ideas for radio quizzes and comedies but not drama scripts. Founded 1992.

Tintinna Ltd
Summerfield, Bristol Road,Chew Stoke BS40 8UB
tel (01275) 333128 *fax* (01275) 332316
email tintinna@aol.com
Contact Sandy Bell, Ian Bell

Copywriting, radio production and all types of creative consultancy.

Torpedo Ltd
Llantrisant House, Llantrisant, Cardiff CF72 8BS
tel (01443) 231989
email info@torpedoltd.co.uk
website www.torpedoltd.co.uk
Contact Ceri Wyn Richards

Documentaries for radio and TV.

UBC Media Group plc
50 Lisson Street, London NW1 5DF
tel 020-7453 1600 *fax* 020-7723 6132
email info1@ubcmedia.com
website www.ubcmedia.com

Documentaries, entertainment news, comedy, drama, sport, current affairs, music for BBC and digital radio worldwide.

Whistledown Productions Ltd
66 Southwark Bridge Road, London SE1 0AS
tel 020-7922 1120 *fax* 020-7261 0493
website www.whistledown.net
Contact David Prest, Managing Director

Social, historical and popular culture documentaries as well as authored narratives, biographical features, readings and magazine programmes for BBC network radio. Also syndicated tapes and other work for commercial companies. Founded 1998.

Wise Buddah Radio
Wise Budda Creative Ltd, 74 Great Titchfield Street, London W1P 7AF
tel 020-7307 1600 *fax* 020-7307 1600
website www.wisebuddah.com
Executive Producer Simon Barnett

Music programmes and documentaries for BBC and commercial radio.

Theatre
Writing for the theatre

Writing for the theatre is a competitive market but thoroughly researching this market will improve the chances of your work being accepted. Christopher William Hill offers guidance.

If anybody ever attempts to convince you that writing for the theatre is a soft career option, ignore them and walk away. It is a competitive market and it would be wrong to suggest otherwise. There are many more playwrights than producing theatres. Although the odds are stacked against you, it is still sometimes possible to scrape a living as a playwright. Of course, there are a number of ways in which you can improve the chances of your work being accepted.

Research your market

It is important to try to understand why a theatre company may produce one play and reject another (due to size of theatre, casting limitations, preferences of the artistic management, etc). Go to the theatre as regularly as possible and read as many plays, contemporary and classic, as you can. In addition, theatre reviews in national and regional newspapers can be extremely useful. *Theatre Record* (fortnightly; *tel* 020-8960 0740, *email* editor@theatrerecord.com *website* www.theatrerecord.org, *Editor and Publisher* Ian Shuttleworth) provides comprehensive press cuttings for West End and regional plays. *The Stage* (weekly), gives informed background to current and forthcoming theatre productions.

The Royal National Theatre and the Theatre Museum in Covent Garden both hold video-taped recordings of many recent London theatre productions. It is only possible to view these recordings on site (subject to appointment) but, again, it is a helpful way of expanding your knowledge of contemporary British theatre.

On a more practical level, many theatres offer writing classes. This is an important way of making contact with a theatre and fellow dramatists. Contrary to popular myth, most writers benefit from time away from their draughty garrets.

A number of 'self-help' books on play writing are available, offering advice on every aspect of writing for the theatre. Each author will have a different approach to his or her work, and it is worth spending time finding a book which is suitable for you. As well as providing practical tips on constructing a script, many books also offer reassurance that all the emotions experienced by a playwright (elation, writer's block, despair, etc) are shared by even the most experienced dramatists.

Constructing your script

When writing your play it is worth bearing in mind a number of practical considerations. First and foremost, write the play that you want to write and trust in your own view of the world. Be wary of trying to surf dramatic trends. If you are conscious of a trend developing you have almost certainly missed it.

Be conscious of the cost of mounting a production. It usually follows that the more characters you write into a play, the more actors you need to play them. A script requiring more than six actors may seem prohibitive to a theatre company. From time to time writers will submit plays with casts of 18 plus, and whilst an extremely well-established writer may (occasionally, but rarely) get away with this, an unknown playwright stands little or no chance of having his or her script accepted. Character doubling (with actors playing multiple roles) can be a pragmatic way of negotiating the casting hurdle. This is often a matter for discussion between writer, director and producer, prior to production.

Beware the famous theatrical adage 'you gotta have a gimmick'. Never let anybody convince you that innovation is a bad thing but try not to innovate just for the sake of it. The best way to get noticed is by writing a good play. Be careful of using cynical marketing ploys in order to sell your work. Plays with a strong regional voice are eagerly received by many theatre companies, but do not attempt to 'regionalise' a play that you have already written in order to pitch it at a specific theatre.

It is easy to forget that the primary objective in the theatre is to entertain. Try to grab the audience's attention as quickly as possible. Many scripts suffer from elaborate 'set-up' before the drama of the play can actually begin. A laborious introduction to character and situation is a guaranteed way of losing your audience (metaphorically and physically).

No matter how tightly plotted a play is, it will always be undermined by poor dialogue. Strangely, many writers are apt to forget that dialogue is written to be spoken. It is often useful to read your work aloud, especially if you are new to play writing. If a line is difficult to read, re-write it. Try not to produce 'interchangeable' dialogue. Each character should have their own distinctive voice, tone, rhythm and thought processes (spoken and unspoken). Check back through the play. How easy is it to distinguish between characters?

Do not overload the script with stage directions. Detailed notes about set design and lighting requirements will often be ignored. Ultimately, it is the job of the director to realise your work on stage and, whilst your input will undoubtedly be canvassed, it is not your responsibility to produce the play. It is the director's job to direct and the designer's job to design. Similarly, actors object to detailed notes in the script, indicating how their lines should be delivered.

Reviewing your work

Resist the temptation to start editing your play the moment you have finished writing. Apart from missing glaring errors in the script, you can easily lose sight of the essential qualities of the play, and edit simply for the sake of editing. Allow it to sit for a few weeks before doing anything more. It is very easy to find yourself swept along on a tide of euphoria as you finish writing, but this can be delusional.

Viewing your own work with a truly objective eye is always difficult, but it is an ability that can be cultivated with time. It may be easier to accept constructive criticism from someone whose opinion you value, before entrusting your script to the tender mercies of a theatre's literary department. Make any alterations to your script that you consider appropriate. There will rarely be an opportunity to re-submit a rejected script.

Approaching theatre companies

Once you are satisfied that your script is ready to send out, stop and take stock. Remember, it is not necessary to have an agent in order to send your work to a theatre. Although an agent's relationship with a director or literary manager may result in a faster response to a script, lack of representation should not count against you. Theatre companies are always on the lookout for new talent. However, it is important to bear in mind that a number of opinions about your work will have been formed before the script is even opened.

Many of the initial obstacles you need to overcome are not related to the script itself. Even envelopes and cover letters present problems for the unwary. Never forget that literary managers are sensitive creatures. A script addressed 'dear sir or madam' is an indication that the play is being sent out as a circular, with no specific focus. A bit of research helps avoid this embarrassment. Do not email your script unless a theatre expressly requests that you do this. Even in this technological age, it is still preferable to send a script by post.

Avoid unnecessary script embellishments. A simple cover letter, brief outline of previous work and a clean (white) A4 play text is all that is expected. Fancy binding, photographs, CDs, projected set designs, casting suggestions, etc, will have a strangely dispiriting effect on the script reader. Allow the play to speak for itself. It should go without saying (but unfortunately does not) that all text must be printed in black ink. The use of multi-coloured inks to distinguish between characters will undoubtedly show you up as a novice. Colour blind literary managers will be disinclined to sympathise with you.

You do not need to invest in costly script-formatting software as there is no professionally approved standard for the layout of play texts. A number of software programmes offer script templates; these are also downloadable from the internet. A cursory glance through a handful of contemporary play scripts will reveal the myriad of different page layouts employed by playwrights and publishers. Find the layout that is right for you. Allow wide margins, with space at the head and foot of each page. Secure the script in such a way that pages can be turned easily and make sure that each page is numbered.

Waiting for a response

Once your script has been delivered into the hands of a theatre company, do be prepared to wait. Many theatres will write to acknowledge receipt of the script. Some theatres will also give an indication of how long it will take them to offer a response. If you have heard nothing after six months it might be worth dropping the theatre a line (if only to retrieve your script), but do take into account the sheer volume of scripts they receive.

When the theatre company finally responds, you are unlikely to be offered in-depth analysis of your work, unless they show an interest in producing the play. Again, this is due to the vast quantity of unsolicited material they receive. In certain cases, brief comments may be offered. Companies which focus exclusively on new writing may provide more detailed script reports.

Some theatres offer a script-reading service, providing a comprehensive response to the play for a small fee. This can be one of the most effective ways of gaining objective professional advice about your work. Although charging for this feedback may seem mercenary, it is important to remember that script readers are paid very little for their services. Many readers have considerable knowledge of the theatre and their advice can be invaluable to a new writer.

Even if a script is unsuitable, an artistic director or literary manager may still want to meet with the writer. Although this will not necessarily lead to future production, it is an indication that they see you as a writer of promise. This is a good opportunity to forge a relationship with a theatre, and may result in a speedier response to any work you submit in the future. Unless the theatre requests a rewrite, a play that is rewritten as a result of feedback from the literary department will almost certainly be returned unread.

There is nothing more depressing than the thud of returned play scripts dropping through the letterbox. Choosing a play for production is a subjective process, reflecting the tastes of the literary department and the predilections of the theatre company. Even good plays are rejected. Try not to be disheartened by your first rejection letter. Chances are you will have to endure many more.

Although your play may have been read more than once and discussed at a readers panel meeting, the literary manager's decision is final. There are stories (sadly not apocryphal) of playwrights attempting to employ strong-arm tactics in order to gain production of their work. This is a risky gambit. There is a subtle distinction between single-minded dedication to your work and psychosis. Be careful not to cross this line. Allow a day of mourning for your rejected script, then move on.

In production

On the other hand, what if a theatre is interested in producing your play? Do not feel pressured into making an immediate decision. It is easy, especially if you have never had your work produced, to succumb to flattery. Bide your time. It is worth considering that many theatres enjoy the kudos of premiering new work, but once your play has had its first production (unless it is a runaway success) other theatres may be reluctant to produce it.

If a theatre expresses an interest in commissioning you or optioning an existing play (offering a fixed term within which to produce your play), it is advisable to seek the professional advice of an agent. However, this can take time, so do not lose heart if an agent is not immediately forthcoming. Most theatres will offer an agreed standard contract, which provides a degree of security for the writer and the theatre. If in doubt, consider taking independent legal advice or contact the Writers' Guild.

Do not despair if you are rejected by an agent. Many agencies are simply too busy with existing clients to take on new writers. An agent may enjoy your work but not feel enthusiastic enough to represent you. It is a question of personal taste. Persevere until you find an agent who is as enthusiastic about your work as you are.

Once a theatre has optioned your work, things can move quickly. Even the largest of theatre companies may discover holes in their programming which need to be filled. Conversely, you may have to wait a considerable period of time before your work can be staged. Either way, in principle you should have the right to agree on a director and designer for your play. In practice this may never happen. Many theatres rely on staff directors, or a pool of tried and tested practitioners. Financial considerations can also be restrictive.

The relationship between the writer and director is, of course, vital to the success of a production. Try not to be precious about your work. Be as objective as possible. Cuts or re-writes will often be suggested, before or during the rehearsal process. This is not an attempt to undermine the writer, but an opportunity to consolidate the script. Of course, if you have any reservations about a script alteration, talk to the director or literary manager about it. Changes to the script cannot be made without your express approval, but do not pull rank just for the sake of it.

Insist on access to the publicity material a theatre produces for your play. It is a contractual obligation and the theatre should honour this. In many cases the marketing department will approach you for blurb (for flyers and press releases). This is the first contact most audience members will have with your play, and you will want to make sure that your work is accurately represented.

Again, if you are unhappy about any aspect of the production, speak to the director. Most problems can be easily rectified if nipped in the bud.

Selling your script

Although you would be hard pressed to find a playwright who took up the profession for financial gain, money is still a consideration. In the case of a non-commissioned play, the majority of the fee will be paid on signature of the contract, with a final sum payable on acceptance of the play. This gives the producing theatre the opportunity to request any revisions to the script before agreeing to production. A proportion of the fee will be a non-returnable advance against royalties. In most cases the royalty will be 8% of the net box office receipts.

If a theatre commissions a play from scratch, the fee should be paid in the following way: roughly half of the total fee on signature of the contract; a further quarter of the fee on completion of the first draft; the final quarter on acceptance of the script for production. Again, a proportion of the fee will be a non-returnable advance against royalties. As with a non-commissioned play, the royalty will normally be 8% of net box office receipts.

The most difficult thing to predict is when the final sum of the commission fee will arrive. When is a play ready for production? How long is a piece of string? You may well find that you spend anywhere between six and 18 months, even longer, restructuring your play so that it is suitable for production. Only in exceptional cases will the first draft of a script be accepted. Some theatres may never produce the resulting play, although the 'policy' of over-commissioning is perhaps not such a prevalent evil as writers are often led to believe. Of greater concern is the tendency to option a play, then leave the playwright waiting indefinitely for the work to be produced.

A commission does not guarantee production. Once a script has been rejected, all rights revert to the writer, who will then be entitled to offer the script to another company.

Financially, it is important to pace yourself. The commission fee may have to last you a considerable period of time. Tempting though it may be, resist the urge to cash your first cheque and embark on a shopping spree.

Many established writers choose not to write to commission, preferring instead to write a play as and when the muse takes them. For a young or relatively inexperienced writer this may not be the most practical way of keeping body and soul together.

Playing the field

Even if you have managed to secure the services of an agent, this is no guarantee of work. It is in a playwright's best interests to seek employment as actively as possible.

Nowadays, it would be extremely unusual for a writer's first play to be offered a West End run. A play which proves itself in the regions may be offered a transfer, but this would be the exception, not the rule. However, there are a number of fringe venues in London that may provide an opportunity to see your work staged. This will not necessarily result in overnight success, but it can often bring your work to the attention of reviewers and other theatre companies.

There is also a vibrant theatrical community at work outside London. Regional theatres are keen to foster links with local writers, and this can be a very good way of establishing yourself as a playwright. Many subsidised touring companies may also consider commissioning work, although this will usually be tailored to specific considerations, such as the number of performers in the company, suitability for touring, etc.

Although persistence will not always be rewarded, it is certainly an approach worth trying. If all else fails, turn impresario and produce your own work. Many playwrights have established themselves in this way, forming their own companies and producing plays on the fringe circuit. Without a production a play is little more than a blueprint.

Christopher William Hill is a recent recipient of an Arts Council Theatre Writing Bursary and has been writer-in-residence at Plymouth Theatre Royal (Pearson Playwrights' Scheme Bursary). He has worked as a degree lecturer, reader and script editor. His stage plays include *Lam, Blood Red,, Saffron Yellow, Song of the Western Men, Multiplex, The Jonah Lie, Death to Mr Moody* and *Icons*.

Theatre producers

This list is divided into London theatres (below), provincial theatres (page 394) and touring companies (page 399). See also *Writing for the theatre* on page 385 and *Literary agents for television, film, radio and theatre* on page 767.

There are various types of theatre companies and it is helpful to know what they include. Metropolitan new writing theatre companies are largely London-based theatres which specialise in new writing (Hampstead Theatre, Royal Court, Bush Theatre, Soho Theatre, etc). Regional repertory theatre companies are theatres based in towns and cities across the country which may do new plays as part of their repertoire. Commercial producing managements are unsubsidised profit-making theatre producers who may occasionally be interested in new plays to take on tour or to present in the West End. Small and/or middle-scale touring companies are companies (mostly touring) which may exist to explore or promote specific themes or are geared towards specific kinds of audiences.

Individuals also have a role. Independent theatre practitioners include, for example, actors who may be looking for interesting plays in which to appear, and independent theatre producers such as young directors or producers who are looking for plays to produce at the onset of their career. There are also drama schools and amateur dramatics companies.

LONDON

Bush Theatre
Shepherd's Bush Green, London W12 8QD
tel 020-7602 3703 *fax* 020-7602 7614
email info@bushtheatre.co.uk
website www.bushtheatre.co.uk
Literary Manager Abigail Gonda

Welcomes unsolicited full-length stage scripts (plus one small and one large sae). Commissions writers, including those at an early stage in their career. Produces 9 premieres a year.

Michael Codron Plays Ltd
Aldwych Theatre Offices, Aldwych, London WC2B 4DF
tel 020-7240 8291 *fax* 020-7240 8467

Finborough Theatre
118 Finborough Road, London SW10 9ED
tel 020-7244 7439 *fax* 020-7835 1853
email admin@finboroughtheatre.co.uk
website www.finboroughtheatre.co.uk
Artistic Director Neil McPherson

A new writing venue. Also presents revivals of neglected plays from 1850 onwards, music theatre and UK premieres of foreign work, particularly from Ireland, the USA and Canada. The theatre is also available for hire and the fee is sometimes negotiable to encourage interesting work. Unsolicited scripts can no longer be accepted. Founded 1980.

Robert Fox Ltd
6 Beauchamp Place, London SW3 1NG
tel 020-7584 6855 *fax* 020-7225 1638
email info@robertfoxltd.com

Independent theatre and film production company. Stages productions mainly in the West End and on Broadway. Welcomes scripts from new writers. Founded 1980.

Hampstead Theatre
Eton Avenue, London NW3 3EU
tel 020-7449 4200 *fax* 020-7449 4201
email literary@hampsteadtheatre.com
website www.hampsteadtheatre.com
Contact Literary Manager

The newly opened theatre has been designed with writers in mind. It allows for bold and flexible staging within an intimate auditorium. The artistic policy is the production of the best British and international new plays. All plays are read and discussed, with feedback given to all writers with potential. It usually takes 4 months to respond. Include postage with submissions. No plays accepted by email. For further details of submission process and new writing initiatives, see website.

Bill Kenwright Ltd
BKL House, 106 Harrow Road, London W2 1RR
tel 020-7446 6200 *fax* 020-7446 6222
email info@kenwright.com
website www.kenwright.com

Managing Director Bill Kenwright *Key contacts* Tom Siracusa, David Bingham

Commercial producing management presenting revivals and new works for the West End and for touring theatres. Recent (or current) productions include: in the West End – *Blood Brothers, Hay Fever, Whistle Down the Wind, The Crucible,* and *A Man for All Seasons*; on tour – *Blood Brothers, Festen, Joseph & The Amazing Technicolor Dreamcoat, The Hollow,* and *This Is Elvis.*

King's Head Theatre
115 Upper Street, London N1 1QN
tel 020-7226 8561 *fax* 020-7226 8507
website www.kingsheadtheatre.org
Contact Dan Crawford, Artistic Director

Off-West End theatre producing revivals and new works. No unsolicited submissions.

Lyric Hammersmith
Lyric Square, King Street, London W6 0QL
tel 020-7494 5840 *fax* 020-8741 5965
email enquiries@lyric.co.uk
website www.lyric.co.uk
Directors Jessica Hepburn, David Farr

A producing theatre as well as a receiving venue for work by theatre companies, translators, performers and composers. Unsolicited scripts for in-house productions not accepted.

Moral Support
Studio 2, Greville House, 35 Greville Street, London EC1N 8TB
tel (07958) 418515
website www.moralsupport.org
Contact Zoe Klinger

The company brings together writers, musicians and other freelance practitioners to create new work with the emphasis on producing new writing and performance styles, to be performed in a variety of locations. Its performance technique has been described as 'an utterly original theatrical language'. Available for commissions of new plays, performance and dance. Established 1997.

Neal Street Productions Ltd
1st Floor, 26–28 Neal Street, London WC2H 9QQ
tel 020-7240 8890 *fax* 020-7240 7099
email post@nealstreetproductions.com
Contact Milly Leigh

Independent theatre producer of new work and revivals. No unsolicited scripts. Founded 2003.

Off West End Theatres Ltd
27 New End, London NW3 1JD
tel 020-7472 5800 *fax* 020-7794 4044
email briandaniels@newendtheatre.co.uk
website www.offwestendtheatres.co.uk
Chief Executive/Artistic Director Brian Daniels

Commercial producing management and independent theatre producer of issue-led drama, comedy, musicals, revue, new writing, revivals and cabaret. Stages 25–30 productions a year across several theatres including the New End Theatre, Hampstead, the Shaw Theatre, and is associate producer of the King's Head Theatre, Islington. Occasionally considers scripts from new writers. Founded 2003.

The Old Red Lion Theatre
418 St John Street, London EC1V 4NJ
tel 020-7833 3053
website www.oldredliontheatre.co.uk
Artistic Director Helen Devine

Interested in contemporary pieces, especially from unproduced writers. No funding: incoming production company pays to rent the theatre. Sae essential with enquiries. Founded 1977.

Orange Tree Theatre
1 Clarence Street, Richmond, Surrey TW9 2SA
tel 020-8940 0141 *fax* 020-8332 0369
email admin@orange-tree.demon.co.uk
website www.orangetreetheatre.co.uk

Producing venue. New works presented generally come from agents or through writers' groups. The theatre asks that writers contact the theatre first by letter and do not send unsolicited scripts.

Polka Theatre for Children
240 The Broadway, London SW19 1SB
tel 020-8545 8320 *fax* 020-8545 8365
email info@polkatheatre.com
website www.polkatheatre.com
Artistic Director Annie Wood

Exclusively for children between 18 months and 16 years of age, the Main Theatre seats 300 and the Adventure Theatre seats 80. It is programmed for 18 months–2 years in advance. Theatre of new writing, with targeted commissions. Founded 1967.

The Questors Theatre
Mattock Lane, London W5 5BQ
tel 020-8567 0011 *fax* 020-8567 8736
email susie@questors.org.uk
website www.questors.org
Executive Director Susie Hickson

Largest community theatre in Europe producing around 20 shows a year, specialising in modern and classical world drama. No unsolicited scripts.

Really Useful Theatres
22 Tower Street, London WC2H 9TW
tel 020-7240 0880 *fax* 020-7240 1204
email info@rutheatres.com
website www.rutheatres.com
Chief Executive André Ptazynski

Owns 7 West End theatres: Adelphi, Cambridge, Her Majesty's, London Palladium, New London, Palace, Theatre Royal Drury Lane. Founded 1978.

Royal Court Theatre
(English Stage Company Ltd)
Sloane Square, London SW1W 8AS
tel 020-7565 5050 *fax* 020-7565 5002
website www.royalcourttheatre.com
Literary Manager Graham Whybrow

New plays.

Royal National Theatre
South Bank, London SE1 9PX
tel 020-7452 3323 *fax* 020-7452 3350
Literary Manager Jack Bradley

Limited opportunity for the production of
unsolicited material, but submissions considered. No
synopses, treatments or email submissions. Send to
Literary Manager, together with an sae with return
postage for the script.

Royal Shakespeare Company
1 Earlham Street, London WC2H 9LL
tel 020-7845 0515 *fax* 020-7845 0505
website www.rsc.org.uk
Artistic Director Michael Boyd, *Literary Manager*
Jeanie O'Hare

The RSC is a classical theatre company based in
Stratford-upon-Avon. As well as Shakespeare, it
produces English classics, foreign classics in
translation and new plays, many of which transfer to
a variety of West End venues. New plays are an
important counterpoint to the RSC's repertory. The
literary department seeks out the plays and
playwrights it wishes to commission and will read
contemporary works only where the original writer is
known. The RSC is unable to read unsolicited work
from less established writers but does monitor the
work or emerging playwrights in production
nationally and internationally.

In Stratford-upon-Avon the interior of the Royal
Shakespeare Theatre is being remodelled to create a
thrust stage within a 'one room' theatre, substantially
reducing the distance between the audience and
actors. In 2006 an ambitious year-round Complete
Works of Shakespeare Festival will be held
(page 590).

Soho Theatre and Writers' Centre
21 Dean Street, London W1D 3NE
tel 020-7478 0117 *fax* 020-7287 5061
email erin@sohotheatre.com
website www.sohotheatre.com
Acting Artistic Director Jonathan Lloyd, *Writers'
Centre Director* Nina Steiger

Aims to discover and develop new playwrights,
produce a year-round programme of new plays and
attract new audiences. Producing venue (144-seat
theatre) of new plays and comedy. The Writers'
Centre offers an extensive unsolicited script-reading
service and provides a range of development schemes
including the Writers' Attachment Programme,
Launch Pad Workshops, the Verity Bargate Award
(page 563), the Westminster Prize, a thriving Young
Writers' Programme, commissions and seed bursaries
and more. Three writers' rooms are available free of
charge (Mon–Fri, 10am–6pm). There is also a large
self-contained studio space with 85-seat capacity plus
theatre bar, restaurant, offices, rehearsal, writing and
meeting rooms. Founded 1972.

Tabard Theatre
2 Bath Road, London W4 1LW
tel 020-8994 5985 *fax* 020-8994 5985
website www.tabardtheatre.co.uk

TEG Productions
11–15 Betterton Street, London WC2H 9BP
tel 020-7379 1066
email info@tegproductions.com
Contact Jeremy Meadow

Produces 2–4 new plays with commercial potential
and revivals per year, all with 'star' casting. Send
synopses only; no unsolicited MSS. Founded 1997.

Theatre of Comedy Company
Shaftesbury Theatre, 210 Shaftesbury Avenue,
London WC2H 8DP
tel 020-7379 3345 *fax* 020-7836 8181
Contact Executive Producer

Commercial producing management creating a broad
range of plays. Founded 1983.

Theatre Royal, Stratford East
Gerry Raffles Square, London E15 1BN
tel 020-8534 7374 *fax* 020-8534 8381
website www.stratfordeast.com
Artistic Director Kerry Michael, *Executive Director*
Tim Highman

Middle-scale producing theatre. Specialises in new
writing: currently developing contemporary British
musicals. Welcomes new plays that are unproduced,
full in length, and which relate to its diverse
multicultural, Black and Asian audience.

The Tricycle Theatre Company
Tricycle Theatre, 269 Kilburn High Road, London
NW6 7JR
tel 020-7372 6611 *fax* 020-7328 0795
Contact Nicolas Kent

Metropolitan new writing theatre company with
particular focus on Black, Asian, Jewish and Irish
writing. Script-reading service but fee charged for
unsolicited scripts.

Triumph Proscenium Productions Ltd
Suite 3, Waldorf Chambers, 11 Aldwych, London
WC2B 4DG
tel 020-7836 0186 *fax* 020-7379 4860
email dcwtpp@aol.com

Unicorn Theatre for Children
147 Tooley Street, London SE1 2HZ
tel 020-7645 0500 *fax* 020-7645 0550

email stage.door@unicorntheatre.com
website www.unicorntheatre.com
Executive Director Christopher Moxon, *Artistic Director* Tony Graham, *Associate Director* Rebecca Gatward, *Associate Director & Literary Manager* Carl Miller, *Associate Artist (Literary)* Charles Way

At the end of 2005 Unicorn moved into its new theatre near Tower Bridge, where it produces a year-round programme of theatre for children aged 4–12, their families and schools. In-house productions of full-length plays with professional casts are staged across 2 auditoriums, alongside visiting companies and education work. Unicorn rarely commissions plays from writers who are new to it, but it is keen to hear from writers who are interested to work with Unicorn in the future. Do not send unsolicited MSS. Send a short statement describing why you would like to write for Unicorn and a CV or a summary of your relevant experience.

Warehouse Theatre
Dingwall Road, Croydon CR0 2NF
tel 020-8681 1257 *fax* 020-8688 6699
email info@warehousetheatre.co.uk
website www.warehousetheatre.co.uk
Artistic Director Ted Craig

South London's new writing theatre. Seats 100. Produces 2–3 in-house plays a year and co-produces with companies which share the commitment to new work. The theatre continues to build upon its tradition of discovering and nurturing new writers: activities include a monthly writers' workshop and the annual International Playwriting Festival (see page 591). Unsolicited scripts are accepted but it is more advisable to submit plays via the Festival. Also hosts a youth theatre workshop, Saturday morning children's theatre and a community outreach programme.

Michael White
13 Duke Street, London SW1Y 6DB
tel 020-7734 7707 *fax* 020-7734 7727

White Bear Theatre Club
138 Kennington Park Road, London SE11 4DJ
tel 020-7793 9193 *fax* 020-7793 9193
email itopiaking2002@yahoo.co.uk
Contact Julia Parr

Metropolitan new writing theatre company. Welcomes scripts from new writers. Founded 1988.

Young Vic Theatre Company
66 The Cut, London SE1 8LZ
email info@youngvic.org
website www.youngvic.org
General Manager Mark Feakins

Metropolitan producing theatre producing great plays of the world repertoire. Founded 1969.

PROVINCIAL

Abbey Theatre
26 Lower Abbey Street, Dublin 1, Republic of Ireland
tel (01) 8872000, 878722 (box office) *fax* (01) 8729177
email info@abbeytheatre.ie
website www.abbeytheatre.ie
Director Fiach MacConghail

Produces new writing and classic drama from Irish and international authors.

Actual Theatre
25 Hamilton Drive, Glasgow G12 8DN
tel 0141-339 0654 *fax* 0141-339 0654
Artistic Director Susan C. Triesman

Produces 'difficult and taboo subjects' as well as experimental theatre. Founded 1980.

Yvonne Arnaud Theatre Management Ltd
Millbrook, Guildford, Surrey GU1 3UX
tel (01483) 440077 *fax* (01483) 564071
email yat@yvonne-arnaud.co.uk
website www.yvonne-arnaud.co.uk
Contact James Barber

Producing theatre which also receives productions.

The Belgrade Theatre
Belgrade Square, Coventry CV1 1GS
tel 024-7625 6431 *fax* 024-7655 0680
email admin@belgrade.co.uk
website www.belgrade.co.uk
Contact Denise Duncombe

Repertory theatre producing drama, comedy and musicals.

Birmingham Repertory Theatre Ltd
Broad Street, Birmingham B1 2EP
tel 0121-245 2000 *fax* 0121-245 2100
email info@birmingham-rep.co.uk
website www.birmingham-rep.co.uk
Artistic Director Rachel Kavanaugh, *Executive Director* Stuart Rogers, *Associate Director (Literary)* Ben Payne

Aims to provide a platform for the best work from new writers from both within and beyond the West Midlands region. The development, commissioning and production of new writing takes place across the full range of the theatre's programme including: the Main House (capacity 830); the Door (capacity 190 max.), a space dedicated to new work; and its annual Community tours. Unsolicited submissions are welcome principally from the point of view of beginning a relationship with a writer. Priority in such development work is given to writers from the region.

The Bootleg Theatre Company
23 Burgess Green, Bishopdown, Salisbury, Wilts.
SP1 3EL
tel (01722) 421476
email colin28@btinternet.com
Contact Colin Burden

Metropolitan new writing theatre company and
independent theatre practitioner. Stages 2
productions per year. Welcomes scripts from new
writers. Founded 1985.

Bristol Old Vic
Main House and Studio, King Street, Bristol BS1 4ED
tel 0117-949 3993 *fax* 0117-949 3996
website www.bristol-old-vic.co.uk
Artistic Director Simon Reade, *Administrative Director*
Rebecca Morland

Dedicated to producing a repertoire of Classics,
family shows and specially commissioned new work.
Productions are characterised by innovation and a
high visual content. The Main House is a Georgian
auditorium (650 seats) and the Studio theatre is a
flexible space with a capacity of 145 maximum.
Bristol Old Vic does not process unsolicited scripts
other than from local writers.

The Byre Theatre of St Andrews
Abbey Street, St Andrews KY16 9LA
tel (01334) 476288 *fax* (01334) 475370
email enquiries@byretheatre.com
website www.byretheatre.com
Artistic Director Stephen Wrentmore

Offers an exciting year-round programme of
contemporary and classic drama, dance, concerts,
comedy and innovative education and community
events. Operates a blend of in-house and touring
productions. Maintains a policy of producing new
and established work. Education programme caters
for all ages with Youth workshops and Haydays (for
50+). Offers support for new writing through the
Byre Writers, a well-established and successful
playwrights group.

Chester Gateway Theatre Trust Ltd
Hamilton Place, Chester CH1 2BH
tel (01244) 354951 *fax* (01244) 354953
website www.chestergateway.co.uk
Chief Executive Jasmine Hendry

Mid-scale theatre with 2 in-house productions per
year. Also presents a diverse programme of theatre,
dance, comedy and music. The Learning and
Outreach Department undertakes schools drama
tours and workshops.

Chichester Festival Theatre
Chichester Festival Theatre, Oaklands Park,
Chichester, West Sussex PO19 6AP
tel (01243) 784437 *fax* (01243) 787288
email admin@cft.org.uk

website www.cft.org.uk
Artistic Director Jonathan Church

Summer Festival Season April–Sept in Festival and
Minerva Theatres together with a year-round
education programme, autumn festival of music and
youth theatre Christmas show.

Clwyd Theatr Cymru
Mold, Flintshire CH7 1YA
tel (01352) 756331 *fax* (01352) 701558
email william.james@clwyd-theatr-cymru.co.uk
website www.clwyd-theatr-cymru.co.uk
Director Terry Hands, *Literary Manager* William
James

Produces a season of plays each year performed by a
core ensemble, along with tours throughout Wales
(in English and Welsh). Plays are a mix of classics,
revivals, contemporary drama and new writing.
Considers plays by Welsh writers or with Welsh
themes.

Colchester Mercury Theatre Ltd
Balkerne Gate, Colchester, Essex CO1 1PT
tel (01206) 577006 *fax* (01206) 769607
email info@mercurytheatre.co.uk
website www.mercurytheatre.co.uk
Contact (Playwrights' Group) Adrian Stokes

Regional repertory theatre presenting works to a wide
audience. Produces some new work, mainly
commissioned. Runs local Playwrights' Group for
adults with a serious commitment to writing plays.

The Coliseum Theatre
Fairbottom Street, Oldham OL1 3SW
tel 0161-624 1731 *fax* 0161-624 5318
Chief Executive Kevin Shaw

Interested in new work, particularly plays set in the
North. The Coliseum employs a reader to read all
submitted scripts, which should be clearly typed and
include a page of casting requirements and a brief
symopsis.

Contact Theatre Company
Oxford Road, Manchester M15 6JA
tel 0161-274 3434 *fax* 0161-274 0640
email info@contact-theatre.org.uk
Artistic Director John E. McGrath

Interested in working with and for young people aged
13–30. Send sae for writers' guidelines.

Derby Playhouse Ltd
Theatre Walk, Eagle Centre, Derby DE1 2NF
tel (01332) 363271 *fax* (01332) 547200
email admin@derbyplayhouse.co.uk
website www.derbyplayhouse.co.uk
Chief Executive Karen Hebden, *Creative Producer*
Stephen Edwards

Regional repertory company. Unsolicited scripts:
send a letter with synopsis, a résumé of your writing

experience and any 10 pages of your script. A review of this material will determine whether a complete copy of the script is required.

Druid Theatre Company

Druid Theatre, Chapel Lane, Galway, Republic of Ireland
tel (091) 568660 *fax* (091) 563109
email info@druidtheatre.com
website www.druidtheatre.com, www.druidsynge.com
Artistic Director Garry Hynes, *Managing Director* Fergal McGrath

Producing company presenting a wide range of national and international plays. Emphasis on new Irish writing.

The Dukes

Moor Lane, Lancaster LA1 1QE
tel (01524) 598505 *fax* (01524) 598519
email info@dukes-lancaster.org
website www.dukes-lancaster.org
Artistic Director Ian Hastings

Dundee Repertory Theatre

Tay Square, Dundee DD1 1PB
tel (01382) 227684
website www.dundeereptheatre.co.uk
Artistic Directors James Brining, Dominic Hill

Regional repertory theatre company with resident ensemble. Mix of classics, musicals and new commissions.

Everyman Theatre

Regent Street, Cheltenham, Glos. GL50 1HQ
tel (01242) 512515 *fax* (01242) 224305
email admin@everymantheatre.org.uk
website www.everymantheatre.org.uk
Chief Executive Geoffrey Rowe, *Artistic Director* Sue Colverd

Regional presenting and producing theatre promoting a wide range of plays. Small-scale experimental, youth and educational work encouraged in The Other Space studio theatre. Contact the Artistic Director before submitting material.

Focus Theatre Company (Scotland)

c/o The Ramshorn Theatre, 98 Ingram Street, Glasgow G1 1ES
tel 0141-552 3489 *fax* 0141-553 2036
email susan.triesman@strath.ac.uk
Artistic Director Susan C. Triesman

Produces women's plays and feminist work. Also holds workshops. Welcomes scripts from new writers. Founded 1982.

Grand Theatre

Singleton Street, Swansea SA1 3QJ
tel (01792) 475242 *fax* (01792) 475379

email gary.iles@swansea.gov.uk
website www.swanseagrand.co.uk
General Manager Gary Iles

Regional receiving theatre.

Harrogate Theatre

Oxford Street, Harrogate, North Yorkshire HG1 1QF
tel (01423) 502710 *fax* (01423) 563205
website www.harrogatetheatre.co.uk
Associate Director Steve Ansell

Regional repertory theatre and touring company producing both classic and contemporary plays. Scripts welcome from writers within the Yorkshire region; 10-page excerpts from writers outside the Yorkshire region.

Haymarket Theatre Company

The Haymarket Theatre, Wote Street, Basingstoke, Hants RG21 7NW
tel (0870) 770 1029 *fax* (01256) 357130
email info@haymarket.org.uk
website www.haymarket.org.uk

Produces up to 8 main house shows a year for Basingstoke, national and regional touring and the West End. New writing is central to the programming policy.

Leicester Haymarket Theatre

Belgrave Gate, Leicester LE1 3YQ
tel 0116-253 0021, (0870) 330 3131 (tickets)
fax 0116-251 3310
email enquiry@lhtheatre.co.uk
website www.lhtheatre.co.uk

Regional producing theatre company.

Library Theatre Company

St Peter's Square, Manchester M2 5PD
tel 0161-234 1913 *fax* 0161-228 6481
email ltc@libraries.manchester.gov.uk
website www.librarytheatre.com
Contact Artistic Director

Contemporary drama, classics, plays for children. Aims to produce drama which illuminates the contemporary world. Will consider scripts from new writers. Allow 4 months for response. Founded 1952.

Live Theatre

27 Broad Chare, Quayside, Newcastle upon Tyne NE1 3DF
tel 0191-232 1232
email info@live.org.uk
website www.live.org.uk
Enquiries Wendy Barnfather, *Script Submissions* Jeremy Herrin

New writing theatre company and venue. Stages 3–4 productions per year of new writing, comedy, musical comedy, etc.

Liverpool Everyman and Playhouse

Liverpool and Merseyside Theatres Trust Ltd, 13 Hope Street, Liverpool L1 9BH

tel 0151-708 3700 *fax* 0151-708 3701
email info@everymanplayhouse.com
website www.everymanplayhouse.com
Executive Director Deborah Aydon, *Artistic Director* Gemma Bodinetz, *General Manager* Alison Jones

Produces and presents theatre.

LLT, Liverpool's New Writing Theatre
Unity Theatre, 1 Hope Place, Liverpool L1 9BG
tel 0151-709 4332 *fax* 0151-709 7182
Contact Nicki Green, Administrator

New writing producing company. Scripts developed to production standard, and links created with other new writing theatres and organisations. Send sae for return of script. Founded 1983.

The New Theatre: Dublin
The New Theatre, Temple Bar, 43 East Essex Street, Dublin 2, Republic of Ireland
tel (1) 6703361 *fax* (1) 6711943
email info@thenewtheatre.com
website www.thenewtheatre.com
Joint Artistic Directors Anthony Fox, Ronan Wilmot

Innovative theatre producing plays by classic as well as Irish writers whose work deals with issues pertaining to contemporary Irish society. Welcomes scripts from new writers. Founded 1997.

New Vic Theatre
Etruria Road, Newcastle under Lyme ST5 0JG
tel (01782) 717954 *fax* (01782) 712885
email admin@newvictheatre.org.uk
Artistic Director Gwenda Hughes, *General Manager* Nick Jones

Europe's first purpose built theatre-in-the-round, presenting classics, music theatre, contemporary plays, new plays.

The New Wolsey Theatre
Civic Drive, Ipswich, Suffolk IP1 2AS
tel (01473) 295911 *fax* (01473) 295910
Chief Executive Sarah Holmes, *Artistic Director* Peter Rowe

Mixed economy theatre. New writing and co-productions always considered.

Northcott Theatre
Stocker Road, Exeter, Devon EX4 4QB
tel (01392) 223997
website www.northcote-theatre.co.uk
Artistic Director Ben Crocker

Regional producing theatre company.

Northern Stage (Theatrical Productions) Ltd
Barras Bridge, Newcastle upon Tyne NE1 7RH
tel (0871) 7000124 *fax* 0191-261 8093
email info@northernstage.co.uk

website www.northernstage.co.uk
Chief Executive Erica Whyman

The Newcastle Playhouse is currently closed and will reopen as Northern Stage in Summer 2006 as a European centre for performing arts.

Nottingham Playhouse
Nottingham Theatre Trust Ltd, Wellington Circus, Nottingham NG1 5AF
tel 0115-947 4361 *fax* 0115-947 5759
website www.nottinghamplayhouse.co.uk/playhouse
Chief Executive Stephanie Sirr, *Artistic Director* Giles Croft

Works closely with communities of Nottingham and Nottinghamshire. Takes 6 months to read unsolicited MSS.

Nuffield Theatre
University Road, Southampton SO17 1TR
tel 023-8031 5500 *fax* 023-8031 5511
Script Executive John Burgess

Repertory theatre producing straight plays and musicals, and some small-scale fringe work. Interested in new plays.

Octagon Theatre
Howell Croft South, Bolton BL1 1SB
tel (01204) 529407 *fax* (01204) 556502
email info@octagonbolton.co.uk
website www.octagonbolton.co.uk
Executive Director John Blackmore, *Artistic Director* Mark Babych, *Head of Administration* Lesley Etherington, *Head of Production* Paul Sheard

Fully flexible professional theatre. Year round programme of own productions and visiting companies.

Peacock Theatre
The Abbey Theatre, 26 Lower Abbey Street, Dublin 1, Republic of Ireland
tel (01) 8872200 *fax* (01) 8729177
Director Fiach MacConghail

Part of the Abbey Theatre; presents new writing and contemporary classic drama.

Perth Theatre Ltd
185 High Street, Perth PH1 5UW
tel (01738) 472700 *fax* (01738) 624576
email info@horsecross.co.uk
website www.horsecross.co.uk
Head of Planning & Resources Paul Hackett

Combination of 3- and 4-weekly repertoire of plays and musicals, incoming tours, one-night variety events and studio productions.

Queen's Theatre, Hornchurch
(Havering Theatre Trust Ltd)
Billet Lane, Hornchurch, Essex RM11 1QT

tel (01708) 462362 *fax* (01708) 462363
email info@queens-theatre.co.uk
website www.queens-theatre.co.uk
Artistic Director Bob Carlton

500-seat producing theatre serving outer East London with permanent company of actors/musicians presenting 8 mainhouse and 4 TIE productions each year. Treatments welcome; unsolicited scripts may be returned unread. Also offers writer's groups at various levels.

The Ramshorn Theatre

University of Strathclyde Drama Centre, 98 Ingram Street, Glasgow G1 1ES
tel 0141-552 3489 *fax* 0141-553 2036
email ramshorn.theatre@strath.ac.uk
Contact Susan C. Triesman (Director of Drama, University of Strathclyde)

Develops new writing (including experimental) through Ramshorn New Playwrights Initiative. Founded 1992.

Royal Exchange Theatre Company Ltd

St Ann's Square, Manchester M2 7DH
tel 0161-833 9333 *fax* 0161-832 0881
website www.royalexchange.co.uk
Executive Director Patricia Weller

Varied programme of major classics, new plays, musicals, contemporary British and European drama; also explores the creative work of diverse cultures.

Royal Lyceum Theatre Company

Royal Lyceum Theatre, Grindlay Street, Edinburgh EH3 9AX
tel 0131-248 4800 *fax* 0131-228 3955
email info@lyceum.org.uk
website www.lyceum.org.uk
Artistic Director Mark Thomson

Edinburgh's busiest repertory company, producing an all-year-round programme of classic, contemporary and new drama. Interested in work of Scottish writers.

Salisbury Playhouse

Malthouse Lane, Salisbury, Wilts. SP2 7RA
tel (01722) 320117 *fax* (01722) 421991
email info@salisburyplayhouse.com
website www.salisburyplayhouse.com
Artistic Director Joanna Read

Regional repertory theatre producing a broad programme of classical and modern plays and new writing.

Scarborough Theatre Trust Ltd

Stephen Joseph Theatre, Westborough, Scarborough, North Yorkshire YO11 1JW
tel (01723) 370540 *fax* (01723) 360506
email enquiries@sjt.uk.com
website www.sjt.uk.com

Regional repertory theatre company which produces about 10 plays a year, many of which are premieres. The theatre has an excellent reputation for comedy. Plays should have a strong narrative and a desire to entertain, though nothing too lightweight will be considered. Enclose a sae with all submissions. Send treatments rather than MSS in first instance.

Sheffield Theatres

(Crucible, Crucible Studio & Lyceum)
55 Norfolk Street, Sheffield S1 1DA
tel 0114-249 5999 *fax* 0114-249 6003
Chief Executive Grahame Morris

Large-scale producing house with distinctive thrust stage; smallish studio; Victorian proscenium arch theatre used mainly for touring productions.

The Sherman Theatre

Senghennydd Road, Cardiff CF24 4YE
tel 029-2064 6901 *fax* 029-2064 6902
email admin@shermantheatre.demon.co.uk
website www.shermantheatre.co.uk
Artistic Director Phil Clark, *General Manager* Margaret Jones, *Programme Coordinator* Kate Perridge

Plays mainly for 15–25 age range, plus under 7's Christmas show. Founded 1974.

Show of Strength Theatre Company Ltd

74 Chessel Street, Bedminster, Bristol BS3 3DN
tel 0117-902 0235
website www.showofstrength.org.uk
Creative Producer Sheila Hannon, *Associate Producer* Gill Loats

Small-scale company committed to producing new and unperformed work. Founded 1986.

Theatre Royal

Windsor, Berks. SL4 1PS
tel (01753) 863444 *fax* (01753) 831673
Executive Producer Bill Kenwright, *Executive Director* Mark Piper

Regional producing theatre presenting a wide range of productions from classics to new plays.

Theatre Royal & Drum Theatre Plymouth

Royal Parade, Plymouth PL1 2TR
tel (01752) 230340 *fax* (01752) 230499
website www.theatreroyal.com
Chief Executive Adrian Vinken, *Artistic Director* Simon Stokes

Stages small, middle and large-scale drama and music theatre. Commissions and produces new plays. The theatre no longer accepts unsolicited playscripts but will consider plays that come through known channels – theatre practitioners, regional and national scriptwriters groups, and agents. Predominantly a receiving house, but produces some shows (especially musicals) which transfer to the West End.

Theatre Royal, Bath

Sawclose, Bath BA1 1ET
tel (01225) 448844 (box office)
website www.theatreroyal.org.uk

The main house presents a wide range of productions from classics to new plays. It is the base for the Peter Hall Company's middle-scale productions. The 140-seat Ustinov Theatre stages an eclectic range of drama, dance and classical music, and is the home of Britain's largest annual international festival of adult puppetry. A new children's theatre, the Egg, opened in 2005.

Traverse Theatre

10 Cambridge Street, Edinburgh EH1 2ED
tel 0131-228 3223 *fax* 0131-229 8443
email dave@traverse.co.uk
website www.traverse.co.uk
Literary Manager Katherine Mendelsohn, *Literary Assistant* Dave Overend

Scotland's new writing theatre with a special interest in Scottish writers and writers based in Scotland. Will read unsolicited scripts but an sae must be included for return of script.

Watford Palace Theatre

Clarendon Road, Watford, Herts. WD17 1JZ
tel (01923) 235455 *fax* (01923) 819664
email enquiries@watfordtheatre.co.uk
website www.watfordtheatre.co.uk
Contact Joyce Branagh, Literary Director

Regional theatre. Produces 8 plays each year, both classic and contemporary drama, with an emphasis on new writing. Welcomes synopses of new plays before submitting scripts.

The West Yorkshire Playhouse

Playhouse Square, Quarry Hill, Leeds LS2 7UP
tel 0113-213 7800 *fax* 0113-213 7250
email mail@wyp.org.uk
Artistic Director Ian Brown, *Literary Manager* Alex Chisholm

Twin auditoria complex; community theatre. Has a policy of encouraging new writing from Yorkshire and Humberside region. Send script with an sae for its return to the Literary Manager.

York Citizens' Theatre Trust Ltd

Theatre Royal, St Leonard's Place, York YO1 7HD
tel (01904) 658162 *fax* (01904) 550164
Chief Executive Daniel Bates, *Artistic Director* Damian Cruden

Repertory productions, tours.

TOURING COMPANIES

Actors Touring Company

Malvern House, 15–16 Nassau Street, London W1W 7AB
tel 020-7580 7723 *fax* 020-7580 7724
email atc@atc-online.com
website www.atc-online.com
Executive Producer Emma Dunton

Small to medium-scale company producing innovative contemporary work.

Compass Theatre Company

Carver Street Institute, 24 Rockingham Lane, Sheffield S1 4FW
tel 0114-275 5328 *fax* 0114-278 6931
email info@compasstheatrecompany.com
website www.compasstheatrecompany.com
Artistic Director Neil Sissons, *General Manager* Craig Dronfield

Touring classical theatre nationwide. Does not produce new plays.

Eastern Angles

Sir John Mills Theatre, Gatacre Road, Ipswich IP1 2LQ
tel (01473) 218202 *fax* (01473) 384999
email admin@easternangles.co.uk
website www.easternangles.co.uk
Contact Ivan Cutting

Touring company producing new work with a regional theme. Stages 3–4 productions per year. Welcomes scripts from new writers in the East of England region. Founded 1982.

Graeae Theatre Company

LVS Resource Centre, 356 Holloway Road, London N7 6PA
tel 020-7700 2455 *minicom* 020-7700 8184
fax 020-7609 7324
email info@graeae.org
website www.graeae.org
Ceo/Artistic Director Jenny Sealey, *Executive Director* Judith Kilvington, *General Manager* Kevin Walsh

Small-scale touring company. Welcomes scripts from disabled writers. Founded 1980.

The Hiss & Boo Company Ltd

1 Nyes Hill, Wineham Lane, Bolney, West Sussex RH17 5SD
tel (01444) 881707 *fax* (01444) 882057
email ian@hissboo.co.uk

Not much scope for new plays, but will consider comedy thrillers/chillers and plays/musicals for children. Produces pantomimes. No unsolicited scripts – telephone first. Plays/synopses will be returned only if accompanied by an sae.

Hull Truck Theatre Co. Ltd

Hull Truck Theatre, Spring Street, Hull HU2 8RW
tel (01482) 224800 *fax* (01482) 581182

email admin@hulltruck.co.uk
website www.hulltruck.co.uk
Executive Director Joanne Gower, *Artistic Director*
John Godber, *Associate Director* Gareth Tudor Price

World-renowned small-cast touring company
presenting popular and accessible theatre.
Commissions up to six new plays each year. Produces
plays in-house at Hull Truck Theatre as well as
touring throughout the year to mid, large and small
scale venues. The venue also hosts Sunday Comedy
Nights and Jazz nights and local amateur and student
companies. Also presents the world premieres of the
plays of John Godber, the company's Artistic
Director.

The London Bubble
(Bubble Theatre Company)
3–5 Elephant Lane, London SE16 4JD
tel 020-7237 4434 *fax* 020-7231 2366
email admin@londonbubble.org.uk
website www.londonbubble.org.uk

M6 Theatre Company (Studio Theatre)
Hamer C.P. School, Albert Royds Street, Rochdale,
Lancs. OL16 2SU
tel (01706) 355898 *fax* (01706) 712601
email info@m6theatre.co.uk
website www.m6theatre.co.uk
Contact Dorothy Wood

Theatre-in-education company providing high-
quality theatre for children, young people and
community audiences.

New Perspectives Theatre Company
The Old Library, Leeming Street, Mansfield, Notts.
NG18 1NG
tel (01623) 635225 *fax* (01623) 635240
email info@newperspectives.co.uk
website www.newperspectives.co.uk
Artistic Director Daniel Buckroyd

A new writing company which commisssions 3–4
writers each year and performs small-scale theatre
productions to community and arts venues
nationally.

NITRO
(formerly Black Theatre Co-operative Ltd)
6 Brewery Road, London N7 9NH
tel 020-7609 1331 *fax* 020-7609 1221
email info@nitro.co.uk
website www.nitro.co.uk
Artistic Director Felix Cross, *Project Manager* Sophia
Tarr

Commissions and produces new and innovative
musical theatre writing by black writers, that
expresses the contemporary aspirations, cultures and
issues that concern black people.

Northumberland Theatre Company
The Playhouse, Bondgate, Without, Alnwick,
Northumberland NE66 1PQ

tel (01665) 602586 *fax* (01665) 605837
email admin@ntc-touringtheatre.co.uk
website www.ntc-touringtheatre.co.uk
Artistic Director Gillian Hambleton

Performs a wide cross-section of work: new plays,
extant scripts, classic and modern. Particularly
interested in non-naturalism, physical theatre and
plays with direct relevance to rural audiences.

Out of Joint
7 Thane Works, Thane Villas, London N7 7NU
tel 020-7609 0207 *fax* 020-7609 0203
email ojo@outofjoint.co.uk
website www.outofjoint.co.uk
Contact Max Stafford-Clark

Touring company producing new plays and some
revivals. Welcomes scripts from writers. Founded
1993.

Oxford Stage Company
12 Mercer Street, London WC2H 9QD
tel 020-7438 9940 *fax* 020-7438 9941
email info@oxfordstage.co.uk
website www.oxfordstage.co.uk
Artistic Director Rupert Goold

A middle-scale touring company presenting 3–4
productions per year: revivals of established
masterpieces, modern classics, and new work.

Paines Plough
4th Floor, 43 Aldwych, London WC2B 4DN
tel 020-7240 4533 *fax* 020-7240 4534
email office@painesplough.com
website www.painesplough.com
Artistic Director Roxana Silbert, *General Manager*
Ushi Bagga, *Literary Manager* Pippa Ellis

Tours new plays by British writers nationwide. The
company believes that the playwright's voice should
be at the centre of contemporary theatre and works
with new and experienced writers. A programme of
workshops and readings develops new work. Provides
support for commissioned writers to push
themselves, with the aim to produce the most
ambitious and challenging of new theatre writing.
Considers all unsolicited scripts from UK writers –
send sae for return of script.

Proteus Theatre Company
Queen Mary's College, Cliddesden Road,
Basingstoke, Hants RG21 3HF
tel (01256) 354541 *fax* (01256) 356186
email info@proteustheatre.com
website www.proteustheatre.com
Artistic Director Mary Swan, *Associate Director*
Deborah Wilding, *General Manager* Nicola Oakley

Small-scale touring company particularly committed
to new writing and new work, education and
community collaborations. Produces 3 touring shows
per year plus several community projects. Founded
1979.

Quicksilver Theatre

4 Enfield Road, London N1 5AZ
tel 020-7241 2942 *fax* 020-7254 3119
email talktous@quicksilvertheatre.org
website www.quicksilvertheatre.org
Joint Artistic Director/Ceo Guy Holland, *Joint Artistic
Director* Carey English

A professional touring theatre company which brings
live theatre to theatres and schools all over the
country. Delivers good stories, original music,
kaleidoscopic design and poignant, often humorous,
new writing to entertain and make children and
adults think. Two to three new plays a year for 3–5
year-olds, 4–7 year-olds and children 8+ and their
families. Mission: to make life-changing theatre to
inspire and entertain. Founded 1977.

Real People Theatre Company

37 Curlew Glebe, Dunnington, York YO19 5PQ
tel/fax (01904) 488870
email sueann@curlew.totalserve.co.uk
website www.realpeopletheatre.co.uk
Contact Sue Lister, Artistic Director

Women's theatre company. Welcomes scripts from
women writers. Founded 1999.

Red Ladder Theatre Company

3 St Peters Buildings, York Street, Leeds LS9 8AU
tel 0113-245 5311 *fax* 0113-245 5351
email rod@redladder.co.uk
website www.redladder.co.uk
Artistic Director Rod Dixon

Theatre performances for young people (13–25) in
youth clubs and small-scale theatre venues.
Commissions at least 2 new plays each year. Runs the
Asian Theatre School, an annual theatre training
programme for young Asians in Yorkshire.

Red Shift Theatre Company

TRG2 Trowbray House, 108 Weston Street, London
SE1 3QB
tel 020-7378 9787 *fax* 020-7378 9789
email mail@redshifttheatreco.co.uk
website www.redshifttheatreco.co.uk
Artistic Director Jonathan Holloway

Productions include adaptations, classics, new plays.

7:84 Theatre Company (Scotland) Ltd

333 Woodlands Road, Glasgow G3 6NG
tel 0141-334 6686 *fax* 0141-334 3369
email admin@784theatre.com
website www.784theatre.com
Artistic Director Lorenzo Mele

Presents 2–3 productions per year of political new
writing and relevant classical texts. Welcomes scripts
from new writers. Founded 1973.

Shared Experience Theatre

The Soho Laundry, 9 Dufour's Place, London
W1F 7SJ

tel 020-7434 9248 *fax* 020-7287 8763
email admin@sharedexperience.org.uk
website www.sharedexperience.org.uk
Joint Artistic Directors Nancy Meckler, Polly Teale

Middle-scale touring company presenting 2
productions per year: innovative adaptations or
translations of classic texts, and some new writing.
Tours nationally and internationally. Founded 1975.

Snap People's Theatre Trust

29 Raynham Road, Bishop's Stortford, Herts.
CM23 5PE
tel (01279) 461607 *fax* (01279) 506694
email info@snaptheatre.co.uk
Contact Gill Bloomfield

Produces theatre for young adults, children and
families. Emphasis on new writing. Welcomes scripts
from new writers. Founded 1978.

Solent Peoples Theatre (SPT)

114 Victory Business Centre, Summers Road North,
Portsmouth PO1 1PJ
tel 023-9282 6972 *fax* 023-9281 2582
email solent@solentpeoples.com
website www.solentpeoplestheatre.com
General Manager Brendan Burns

SPT has developed its artistic programme through
participatory projects, to incorporate a multimedia,
cross art form approach to theatre that will offer
richer opportunities and experience to both
community and company. Works with diverse
groups/individuals for whom an integrated approach
to the creation/presentation of new work in
performance makes that work more exciting, relevant
and accessible.

Sphinx Theatre Company

25 Short Street, London SE1 8LJ
tel 020-7401 9993/4 *fax* 020-7401 9995
email info@sphinxtheatre.co.uk
website www.sphinxtheatre.co.uk
Artistic Director Sue Parrish

Specialises in writing by women.

The Steam Industry

c/o Finborough Theatre, 118 Finborough Road,
London SW10 9ED
tel 020-7244 7439 *fax* 020-7835 1853
email admin@finboroughtheatre.co.uk
website www.steamindustry.co.uk
Artistic Director Phil Willmott

Produces new writing, radical adaptations of classic
texts and musicals. Unsolicited scripts are no longer
accepted. Founded 1994.

Talawa Theatre Company

3rd Floor, 23–25 Great Sutton Street, London
EC1V 0DN
tel 020-7251 6644 *fax* 020-7251 5969

email hq@talawa.com
Artistic Director Patricia Cumper

Scripts from new writers considered. Particularly interested in scripts from black writers and plays portraying a black experience.

Theatre Absolute

57–61 Corporation Street, Coventry CV1 1GQ
tel (02476) 257380 *fax* (02476) 550680
email info@theatreabsolute.co.uk
website www.theatreabsolute.co.uk
Contact Julia Negus

Independent theatre producer of contemporary plays. Stages one premiere and tour over 2-year period. Founded 1992.

Theatre Centre

Shoreditch Town Hall, 380 Old Street, London EC1V 9LT

tel 020-7729 3066 *fax* 020-7739 9741
email admin@theatre-centre.co.uk
website www.theatre-centre.co.uk
Director Rosamunde Hutt

New writing company producing and touring nationally and internationally. Professional theatre for young people – schools, arts centres, venues. Founded 1953.

Theatre Workshop

34 Hamilton Place, Edinburgh EH3 5AX
tel 0131-225 7942 *fax* 0131-220 0112
Contact Robert Rae

Cutting edge, professional, inclusive theatre company. Plays include new writing/community/children's/disabled. Scripts from new writers considered.

Literary agents
The role of the literary agent

Depending on their perspective, people have very different ideas as to what literary agents actually do. With over three decades of experience behind him, the late Giles Gordon explains here what the role of the literary agent entails.

It occurs to me (and it really hasn't previously although I've been an agent – don't groan – for more than 30 years) that what writers think of as 'the role' of the literary agent is quite different from the actuality.

Having said that, agents work in more various ways than publishers do. Publishers accept manuscripts from writers, whether 'professional' (meaning having published some books) or 'amateur' (as yet unpublished), and make them available to the world, or at least have them printed and bound. With non-fiction, most books will be commissioned after seeing an outline and a few specimen chapters.

I don't believe an agent has 'a role', in that that makes him or her sound pompous or important. The late publisher Colin Haycraft wrote 'The world is a peculiar place, but it has nothing on the world of books. This is largely a fantasy world in which the pecking order goes as follows: if you can't cope with life, write about it; if you can't write, publish; if you can't get a job in publishing, become a literary agent; if you are a failed literary agent – God help you!'

It's funny and a bit unfair but only a bit. It makes the fundamental point that writers are what count and it is they who keep the book trade in business. No author should ever forget this, or fear and quake when confronted with a literary agent or a publisher. We all live off your talent, such as it is.

Most good agents today (and, of course, there are good agents and bad agents) have been publishers, mostly editors; and thus they have at least a working knowledge of what happens in publishers' offices and how a book gets out into the world.

The dilemma is that agents are interested in books, the written word, yet an agency, large or small, is essentially a business and authors should expect it to be that. Would-be published authors frequently say: it doesn't cost you anything to offer my masterpiece (sorry, manuscript) to publishers. Why don't you take a chance? The answer to that is because time is money, and overheads are inevitably involved in offering each and every manuscript to publishers. Including salaries, postage, paper, packaging, internet costs, office rent, electricity, heating and everything else.

A literary agency most emphatically isn't a finishing school for aspiring authors. Our agency Curtis Brown, probably the biggest in the UK, receives hundreds of unsolicited manuscripts each week. Every one is looked at but time, if nothing else, doesn't permit us to provide detailed responses to manuscripts we don't instantly take to, for whatever reason.

In short, literary agents are professional workers whose primary responsibility is to earn a living for themselves and their dependents. Having said that, they have chosen the world of books which would suggest that they enjoy reading, yet ought to be discriminating about it.

As every second person in the world right now seems to be touting a manuscript, agents are finding it seriously difficult to keep up with the reading demanded of them. Even more so perhaps than publishers because, although they don't always admit it, these days editors and publishing houses very much regard agents as the primary sifters of material, of separating the wheat from the chaff.

The agent's real job is to 'represent' the individual authors he or she has elected to act for. An agent or agency ultimately should be judged by the quality of the writers it represents. Although an agent may choose to act for a particular author, it is essentially the author who has selected the agent, or at least decided to place the fate of his or her writing in the agent's hands.

It is therefore important that the author should be satisfied that he or she is both in reliable hands and has as an agent someone with whom they can get on. Easier said than done perhaps, but I always advocate that new authors who have written anything of the slightest interest should shop around and interview three or four agents and then decide with whom they would get on best. If the manuscript is any good, agents should be in competition to represent it

Every agency is different. PFD and Curtis Brown each employs over 50 staff, and has numerous agents, specialising in different areas: books, journalism, film, television, theatre, talent, even 'horse flesh' – by which I mean actors. There are large accounts departments which have the most fundamental responsibilities in an agency, primarily to check all money for clients that comes in, to ensure that the publisher or other payers have accounted accurately, and to get the money to the client as soon as humanly possible. No agency should sit on clients' money for more than a few days at most.

At the other end of the size scale, there are the very many single person agencies. These are often set up by editors previously employed by publishing conglomerates who persuade authors they have worked with to go with them.

The agent, or agency, makes its income entirely as a result of commission on sales of their clients' work. Increasingly, with office and other business overheads spiralling, agencies are having to charge 15% commission on sales in the UK, and 20% on sales to the USA and in translation: the latter percentage is frequently shared with a sub-agent on the ground in the relevant country.

It is a shock to new agents who have had salaried jobs in publishing to realise how hard it is to earn a living income from 10% or 15% of the average publisher's advance. Whereas the larger agencies have specialised departments, the one-person and other smaller agencies have to become master – or mostly mistresses – of the entire field, although some specialised aspects of the work (e.g. translation and film) are often farmed out. Some writers prefer dealing with an agent who does everything, while others prefer so-called experts who sell different aspects of their work. It depends entirely on the relationship between author and agent, and the temperament of both.

Which takes me really to the heart of the matter. However much I admire an author's work, I wouldn't be an effective agent for him or her unless as human beings we get on. One of my colleagues believes that when an agent undertakes to represent an author, that is a contract for life. The agent has a fiduciary and moral commitment to that writer and his or her financial livelihood. I'm of the view that if the relationship turns sour – either the author has become impossible or the agent has become useless – it is better to part company.

Yet it must never be forgotten that an agent is in the service of the author (Lopakhin in *The Cherry Orchard* comes to mind). The author employs the agent and makes it possible for the agent to earn his or her living thanks to the primary material the author provides. And this is the case even if, paradoxically, the agent, as very occasionally happens, achieves for the author such good contracts that the author becomes a millionaire.

No two authors want the same thing. Some want money, some want security of different kinds, some just want to be published, some want to be bestsellers, some do it as therapy, some do it because they believe they are geniuses, some do it because they believe it will advance their careers in their day jobs. Some want to write part time, some want to write full time. Thus no two authors make the same demands of their agents and thus it is essential that the agent gets to know the author from the beginning of their relationship and tries to find out what the author requires.

From the would-be published writer's point of view, it is useful to know how a literary agent evolves his or her list. It is said, with apparent paradox, that it is easier for a previously unpublished author to acquire a publisher than an agent. This is literally true in that last year over 130,000 different titles were published in the UK, a mind-boggling 2000-plus different books on average every single week of the year. There may be hundreds of individual agents but no agent can adequately represent more than a certain number of authors.

I – and I only use the example of myself because I know my client list better than any other – currently represent 125 authors. Five or six are internationally known, including a Booker Prize winner and a few that have been on the shortlist and haven't yet won. About half my clients write fiction, half non-fiction.

Almost every time I have taken on a writer before having met him or her, the relationship has not in the long term survived. Publishers can get away with never meeting their authors because they publish *books*, whereas agents represent *human beings*. The author has to believe that the agent is doing the best possible job for him or her which probably, but not invariably, means getting the biggest bucks by way of an advance as that way the publisher will strive strenuously in the marketplace to recoup the initial investment.

Not always though, because if the agent is in a position (i.e. it is a first book, and first books these days are more saleable than subsequent books, or one by a *very famous author*) to demand too much money the publisher may, between signature of the agreement and publication of the book, realise that he or she has been blackmailed, made an ass of, and to cut his or her losses not be prepared to spend more money on promoting a lost cause.

Again I will reiterate that the agent works for and is employed by the author. Some inexperienced writers may believe that publishers employ agents and pay them baksheesh to seduce them into offering them their best books. This is not so. If an agent or agency is to survive, or at least become established, there must be an author or two who makes a considerable income to pay for the overtures and beginners who, down the years, will become the future major earners.

And yet the major earners are not subsidising the new authors. I remember years ago John Fowles telling me that he met someone after *The French Lieutenant's Woman* had been on the US bestseller lists for many months who said she couldn't understand why he continued to use a literary agent as obviously he now made more than a respectable living from his writing. Fowles courteously pointed out that it was precisely because there was now money to be made from his books that he needed an agent to make sure he wasn't exploited.

That is the point. No writer needs a literary agent who cannot sell his or her books. In recent years, sadly and depressingly (but I hope not too cynically), I have declined to represent a number of new writers – mostly novelists but sometimes non-fiction writers because of their favoured subject matter. Much as I have admired their talent I haven't believed I would be able to find or persuade a publisher to take on their work. Ultimately failing to find a good publisher for an author means that the agent has failed the writer.

It doesn't really do for the agent to say 'I still think you have written a work of genius; the publishers are idiots for not realising it'. It is the responsibility of the agent to persuade the publisher of the genius or commercial viability of manuscripts submitted.

Saddest of all, any self-respecting agent can usually tell within 20 or 30 seconds of looking at unsolicited submissions, both the letter of submission and the manuscript, whether the book is any good or not. That is the cruellest stroke of all. And no author when submitting a manuscript to an agent should say that his or her family and friends say that it is better than most books published because they would, wouldn't they?

Most books about how to get published tell authors to submit a synopsis and two or three specimen chapters to an agent. Certainly it is in the interests of the agent that the author should do that but if the author believes in his or her book the entire thing should be sent. It is too easy for an agent to decline an author's submission on the strength of a few chapters. If the agent is hooked from the beginning, he or she should want to read on. If he or she isn't, the manuscript is going to go back to the author.

Giles Gordon died on 14 November 2003. He was a very well-respected man, reputed to have single-handedly revolutionised the world of English publishing by being loyal to his clients and placing them in the best publishing houses. His clients included Peter Ackroyd, Sue Townsend, Fay Weldon and Prince Charles. He joined Curtis Brown on 1995; the branch in Scotland where he worked is now closed.

See also...

- *Dos and don'ts of approaching a publisher*, page 126
- *How to get an agent*, page 407

How to get an agent

Philippa Milnes-Smith demystifies the role of the literary agent.

This article is for all those who are prepared to dedicate themselves to the pursuit of publication. If you are currently experiencing just a vague interest in being a writer or illustrator, stop reading now. You are unlikely to survive the rigorous commercial assessment to which your work will be subjected. If you are a children's writer or illustrator do not think that the process will be any easier. It's just as tough, if not tougher.

So, what is a literary agent and why would I want one?

You will probably already have noticed that contacts for many publishers are provided in the *Writers' & Artists' Yearbook*. This means that there is nothing to prevent you from pursuing publishers directly yourself. Indeed, if you can answer a confident 'yes' to all the questions below, and have the time and resources to devote to this objective, you probably don't need an agent:

1. Do you have a thorough understanding of the publishing market and its dynamics?
2. Do you know who are the best publishers for your book and why? Can you evaluate the pros and cons of each?
3. Are you financially numerate and confident of being able to negotiate the best commercial deal available in current market conditions?
4. Are you confident of being able to understand fully and negotiate a publishing or other media contract?
5. Do you enjoy the process of selling yourself and your work?
6. Do you want to spend your creative time on these activities?

   An agent's job is to deal with all of the above on your behalf. A good agent will do all of these well.

So, is that is all an agent does?

Agents aren't all the same. Some will provide more editorial and creative support; some will help on longer term career planning; some will be subject specialists; some will involve themselves more on marketing and promotion. Such extras may well be taken into consideration in the commission rates charged.

I have decided I definitely do want an agent. Where do I begin?

When I left publishing and talked generally to the authors and illustrators I knew, a number of them said it was now more difficult to find an agent than a publisher. Why is this? The answer is a commercial one. An agent will only take someone on if they can see how and why they are going to make money for the client and themselves. To survive, an agent needs to make commission and to do this they need projects they can sell. An agent also knows that if he/she does not sell a client's work, the relationship isn't going to last long.

So the agent just thinks about money?

Well, some agents may just think about money. And it might be all you care about. But good agents do also care about the quality of work and the clients they represent. They are professional people who commit themselves to doing the best job they can. They also know that good personal relationships count – and that they help everyone enjoy business more. This means that, if and when you get as far as talking to a prospective agent, you should ask yourself the questions: 'Do I have a good rapport with this person? Do I think we will get along? Do I understand and trust what they are saying?' Follow your instinct – more often than not it will be right.

So how do I convince an agent that I'm worth taking on?

Start with the basics. Make your approach professional. Make sure you only approach an appropriate agent who deals with the category of book you are writing/illustrating. Check to whom you should send your work and whether there are any particular ways your submission should be made (if it's not clear from the listings in this *Yearbook* or the agency's website). Only submit neat, typed work on single-sided A4 paper. Send a short covering letter with your manuscript explaining what it is, why you wrote it, what the intended audience is and providing any other *relevant* context. Always say if and why you are uniquely placed and qualified to write a particular book. Provide your professional credentials, if any. If you are writing an autobiography, justify why it is of public interest and why your experiences set you apart. Also, provide a CV (again, neat, typed, relevant) and a stamped addressed envelope for the return of your manuscript. Think of the whole thing in the same way as you would a job application, for which you would expect to prepare thoroughly in advance. You might only get one go at making your big sales pitch to an agent. Don't mess it up by being anything less than thorough.

And if I get to meet an agent?

Treat it like a job interview (although hopefully it will be more relaxed than this). Be prepared to talk about your work and yourself. An agent knows that a prepossessing personality in an author is a great asset for a publisher in terms of publicity and marketing – they will be looking to see how good your interpersonal skills are.

And if an agent turns my work down? Should I ask them to look again? People say you should not accept rejection.

No means no. Don't pester. It won't make an agent change his/her mind. Instead, move on to the next agency – the agent there might feel more positive. The agents who reject you may be wrong. But the loss is theirs.

Even if an agent turns my work down, isn't it worth asking for help with my creative direction?

No. Agents will often provide editorial advice for clients but will not do so for non-clients. Submissions are usually sorted into two piles of 'yes, worth seeing more' and 'rejections'. There is not another pile of 'promising writer but requires further tutoring'. Creative courses and writers' and artists' groups are better options to pursue for teaching and advice (see *Websites for writers*, page 611, *Creative writing courses*, page 649 and *Editorial, literary and production services*, page 658). It is, however, important to practise and develop your creative skills. You wouldn't expect to be able to play football without working at your ball skills or practise as a lawyer without studying to acquire the relevant knowledge. If you are looking to get your work published, you are going to have to compete with professional writers and artists – and those who have spent years working at their craft.

If I haven't put you off yet, it just remains for me to say good luck – and don't forget to buy plenty of stamps, envelopes and A4 paper. Many agents won't take email submissions.

Philippa Milnes-Smith is a literary agent and children's specialist at the agency LAW (Lucas Alexander Whitley). She was previously Managing Director of Puffin Books.

See also...
- *Literary agents for children's books*, page 767
- *Literary agents for television, film, radio and theatre*, page 767

'I think I need an agent'

Mark Le Fanu explains when it is appropriate for an author to have an agent.

Most of the queries that pour into our office from members involve publishers and their ways. We advise on the terms offered and on a myriad of issues to do with the exciting, but sometimes bruising, experience of being published. This rich diet is supplemented at least once a day by a member or an aspiring author saying 'I think I need an agent. Who do you recommend?'.

Authors who are new to the strange world of publishing often seem to take it for granted that all good writers have agents, that without an agent one will get nowhere, and that agents are bound to be interested in any book that is well written and original. As experienced writers will know, none of these assumptions is entirely accurate.

Most professional authors are represented by agents who, generally, provide a good, important and valuable service. Most full-time writers could not manage without an agent to look after all their business affairs. However, agents generally handle fiction, general non-fiction and children's books – broadly described as 'trade books' – and rarely stray outside these areas. Agents take pleasure in extracting advances – as juicy as possible – from the big trade publishers, like HarperCollins and Penguin, discreetly removing 10–15% before passing the rest on to the author. When handling media deals, such as film proposals, an agent or other expert (e.g. a lawyer) is crucial.

While trade book writers have agents as outriders, if you write educational, academic, medical, scientific, technical or legal books – to select a few categories – you will be extremely lucky to secure the services of an agent – 95% of them just won't want to know. Poetry, short stories or memoirs? Alas, forget it, unless you are already a household name, preferably with a wild reputation. The vast majority of authors working in these areas should not waste time approaching agents and then agonising over rejections. Most publishers are well used to dealing direct with authors managing their own business affairs. Specialist non-fiction proposals can sell themselves to a prospective publisher in a way that doesn't work with fiction.

The Society of Authors can help by scrutinising members' publishing and media contracts in detail (without extra charge) and suggesting realistic improvements. The Society's *Quick Guide to Publishing Contracts* (free to members) gives advice on the areas that should be checked most carefully. Whatever impression publishers may like to give that their contracts, hallowed by years of experience and revered for their fairness, should simply be signed with gratitude, negotiation is invariably in order. Firm but reasonable bargaining, informed by a knowledge of what is achievable, undoubtedly pays off.

A few of the major trade publishers – shame on them – will only accept submissions from agents. Yet agents are highly selective and cautious about taking on new clients and

Further information

The Society of Authors
84 Drayton Gardens, London SW10 9SB
tel 020-7373 6642
email info@societyofauthors.org
website www.societyofauthors.org

The Society publishes a *Quick Guide to Literary Agents* (free to members, otherwise £2), which covers the general duties of agents and the terms usually agreed between author and agent. See page 513 for further information about the Society.

the agents most in demand will only take on a few new clients each year. Agents need to be convinced that the writer has long-term commercial potential, with tempting commission prospects for the agency, and that the personal chemistry will work. Ironically, while the conglomerate publishers have saved money by 'releasing' editors and readers of the 'slush pile', they have thereby increased the negotiating power of agents, who can now extract much larger advances for lead titles than in the past.

The concentration of publishing and bookselling into the hands of the big groups has had a huge impact on the nature of the services provided by agents. When publishers operated independently, nurturing 'their' authors and cultivating their loyalty, the agent did the deal and left writer and editor to work closely together, settling any differences over the customary three-hour lunch. Now that publishing is more frenetic and publishers communicate less with authors, agents are becoming much more involved in giving guidance and advice to their clients. Even so, the duties of an agent remain poorly defined. Some are good at beating up publishers, others are better at 'author care'. A good agent is both: a tiger in the presence of publishers, a pussy cat with clients.

How does one choose such a creature? Short of checking their pedigree (one parent a well-read diplomat and the other a second-hand car dealer being ideal), the clues – other than membership of the Association of Authors' Agents – are elusive. Unlike publishers, agents tend to be generalists, rather than specialists. Part of our job at the Society of Authors is to observe the species and help authors with their agent-spotting. Every week, we take calls from members who want to change agents. One author told me that his existing agent was like 'having a first class ticket... on the Titanic'. But that's another story.

Mark Le Fanu is General Secretary of The Society of Authors (see page 513).

See also...
- *The role of the literary agent,* page 403
- *How to get an agent,* page 407
- *How to attract the attention of a literary agent,* page 412
- *Literary agents UK and Ireland,* page 416
- *The Society of Authors,* page 513

How to attract the attention of a literary agent

Having a literary agent helps you to get published. When an agent takes on a writer publishers are far more likely to take notice of that writer's work. Alison Baverstock gives advice on how to attract the attention of a literary agent.

Literary agents perform a very valuable sifting function for publishing houses. They are people with lots of publishing experience, who are offered many potential books, in various stages of development. The agents bring those books they favour to the attention of the publishers they think will like them too. Of course that's not to say that all great potential writers have agents, or that all new authors taken on by publishing houses have agents, just that amongst the newly published, there will be more authors with agents than authors without. Stories of what go on to become bestselling books being spotted on a 'slush pile' (the pile of unsolicited manuscripts that all publishing houses accumulate without asking) do occur, but they are memorable precisely because they are rare.

The nature of literary agents

Many agents have been publishers themselves. It follows that they like to specialise (usually in the kind of books they used to publish, or in those they have a strong personal interest in) and that they have an encyclopedic view of the industry.

Agents tend to work a bit like advertising agencies, in that they tend to have just one major client in each field. So just as an advertising agency would not represent two directly competing accounts, it would be unlikely that a literary agent would take on two authors whose books were very similar. This is particularly true in the non-fiction market where having two directly competing authors would be bound to cause difficulties.

Generalising further, literary agents are gregarious, fond of being noticed (they tend to dress quite strikingly), are good talkers (they certainly seem to know everyone), dramatic travellers (fond of hopping on and off planes in a blaze of self-generated publicity), are good negotiators (their livelihood depends on it as well as that of the authors they represent) and are not immune to vanity – so mentioning that you heard them speak, or making it clear you know who they are and particularly want to be represented by *them*, tends to go down well.

What's in it for the agent?

I always think the secret of a good business proposal is to look at it from your would-be collaborator's viewpoint rather than your own. Thus when seeking sponsorship, you get a far better response if you explain what the potential sponsor will get out of a relationship with you than if you tell them how much you need the money. To paraphrase J.F. Kennedy, 'Think not what an agent can do for you, but what you can do for an agent.' Taking the same approach, agents are looking for writers (a) with talent (and can you prove it by providing quotes from satisfied readers/reviewers?); (b) who can sustain their writing beyond one book (and thus will be ongoing earners and repay the initial investment of time they make in you); (c) who are topical (all agents and publishers claim to be looking for the 'next big thing'); (d) who are different, or have a new slant to bring to an existing strand of publishing; and (d) who are *promotable* (a key publishing term meaning interesting or memorable to the media). How you come over (or are likely to come over) in the press/on the air will be a key factor in deciding whether or not to take you on.

The money side of things needs a little more consideration. Whilst most agents are book lovers, and love what they do, their service is not there as a wider service to literature in general but to make a profit. As well as a talent for writing they are looking for financial remuneration. So whilst an agent may be willing to help you shape your novel, provide advice on your style, advise you on how to prepare for an interview, they will be doing these things in the hope that you will reward them with books that sell rather than out of pure altruism.

Whatever advance the author gets, their agent usually gets 15% of it, so it is in the agent's interest to sell the book for the highest amount of money, or to the publishing house that is most likely to make a long-term success of the writer's career. This may lead the cynical to conclude that agents are more likely to be interested in media-friendly (or just media-based) authors than pure literary genius, but it is through success of key names that they are able to take a punt on new writers. An agency that confined itself to literary fiction alone, and ignored the popular market completely, would probably not last long.

Top tips for securing the attention of an agent

1. Do your research. Consult *Literary agents UK and Ireland* starting on page 416 of this *Yearbook* and look at what kind of writers each agent represents and note their specialities. If they say they do not take science fiction, do not assume you are helpfully extending their range by offering it. Send an email outlining what you have in mind and ask who is the right person within their firm to send it to. Don't assume that if the agency is called 'Snodgrass and Wilkins' you must talk only to one of the two key names. The chances are their books will be full already. A more junior member of staff may be hungrier for new authors, and don't forget that their judgement will be backed – because they are a staff member and presumably have been taken on by the partners to widen the range of those they represent. And one day they too may be on the letterhead.

2. Send in what they ask for, not more or less. Submit your material in exactly the format they ask for – three chapters and a synopsis means just that, it is not code for 'anything over three chapters' or 'as near as you can get to three chapters'.

3. Ensure the book has a really good title. It's tempting to think that writing the book is the really important thing and that the title can grow out of the writing later. Wrong. The title is hugely important. It should catch the agent's attention and stick in the memory. Think how the same thing works for you in bookshops. I recently bought a copy of *The Revenge of the Middle-aged Woman* by Lizzy Buchan simply because I liked the title. I was looking for a present for a friend and I thought her fancy would be tickled by it too.

Heather Holden-Brown of the hhb agency says: 'The title matters hugely. I want something that excites me, and that will draw a similarly instant reaction from any publisher I mention it to. So go for something that is topical, intriguing or witty and to the point.'

4. Write a synopsis. This should be an outline of what kind of book you are writing, it is not your chance to give a detailed listing of what is in each chapter. It should start by ensuring the agent can pitch in their mind very precisely what kind of writer is on offer – this is important because it may enable them to think what kind of publisher it would appeal to.

If you can, say which section of the bookshop your title would be stocked in (don't just say the table at the front!) and list writers whose books are already in this category. Booksellers are very loathed to stock titles they don't know where to put, and agents may be unwilling to back a title that has no natural home. A friend of a friend wanted to write a book on the menopause and to call it *How Long Before I Can Hang-glide?* A bookseller friend persuaded her that whilst this would make a very good subtitle, people looking for books on the subject would be in danger of not finding it – unless they were by chance looking in the sports section too.

5. Write a bookblurb for your work. Think what goes on the back of most books and how important it is in attracting attention to the title inside. A book blurb should be a fair representation of the style of the book, should tempt the reader to want to know more *now*, and should not give away the ending. Writing a book blurb is harder than you think, and is an excellent way of getting yourself noticed by an agent.

6. Send an interesting CV on yourself. This is not the time to rehash your formal one; a literary agent is not interested in how you did at 'O'/GCSE or 'A' level. Rather, what they do need to know is what you have done that makes you an interesting proposition to a publishing house. Remember agents are interested in how 'promotable' any potential new author is.

This could be your job, your family commitments or your past experience. Don't assume that what you consider boring or mundane will be viewed in the same light by those you are approaching. A background working in the City is not the normal path to becoming a novelist and so may be well received by an agent. Similarly your domestic arrangements may be equally ordinary to you but interesting when combined with the fact that you have written a book.

Take an imaginative approach to your past and think creatively. A friend of mine once used a revolving door in an American hotel at the same time as a well-known actor and would proudly boast that she had 'been around in New York with Cary Grant.' I have four children and have always moved house mid-pregnancy, hence the scan and the birth never took place in the same hospital. Whereas this is entirely a function of my husband's peripatetic job, my publishers got quite excited when I told them. What have you done that can be made to sound interesting?

7. Do you have anyone else who can say what you write is good? This does not have to be a celebrity (although they are always useful) but what about other readers, writers and friends with relevant job titles? It's not hard to get testimonials for your work – many people like to be asked; some will oblige out of pure friendship, others for the publicity it may bring them.

8. Can you prove that there is a market for what you write? When an agent approaches a publisher to enthuse about a new author they will have to justify the claims they make on your behalf, and the newer the feel of what you want to write, the harder they will have to work. It's not good enough to say 'everyone will want to read' this new title. So, find out the viewing figures for programmes that relate to the book you want to write, or the sales of magazines that have a strong overlap with your material. Think laterally. For example, my most recent book is about raising teenagers, and there is very little published in this market. It seemed to me that my subject was really modern morality; how to provide guidance in a fast-changing world. To prove there is a market I took as examples the book sales of popular philosophy titles by A.C. Grayling and the number of people who have taken an Alpha course (2 million in the UK so far). The agent I approached told me this widening of the issue really made a difference to how he viewed my proposal.

9. Write a really good letter to accompany the package you send to an agent. This may take you a long time but a good letter of introduction is well worth the trouble. It should outline all of the above: what kind of book you want to publish, how far down the road you have got, what is noteworthy about you as a person, who else thinks so. Some agents acknowledge what they receive, others do not. You could ask them to email receipt, or enclose a stamped addressed postcard with a reminder to let you know they have received it. This is a further opportunity to remind them you are a human being, so try a witty postcard or add a caption to an image to make the point that you are dying to hear from them! For inspiration, look at the card selection in a local art gallery and think which picture sums up your mood as you wait for them to respond.

Finally, do remember that agents are individuals, and perhaps more individualistic than the key protagonists in many other professions. Just as many are instantly recognisable, they also have very individual taste. It follows that what does not appeal to one may well appeal to another. So if your first choice does not immediately sign you up, there may be others who think you are the next best thing since sliced bread! But they will only find out about you if you have the gumption to keep going. In the long run, getting an agent on your side is invariably worth the effort.

Carole Blake of Blake Friedmann says: 'We receive at least 20 unsolicited manuscripts a day, our books are full and to be honest we are looking for reasons to say no – but I still get such excitement from a really new voice writing something that grabs my attention. I have known the world stand still as I ignore the rest of the post and just read on until I have finished. When that happens it's really special – and I will fight to get that author published. Sometimes it takes years, but if I believe in an author I will keep going.'

Alison Baverstock is the author of 14 books. Her most recent book, *Is There a Book in You?*, is published by A & C Black (2006). Her website is www.alisonbaverstock.com

Literary agents UK and Ireland

The *Writers' & Artists' Yearbook*, along with the Association of Authors Agents and the Society of Authors, takes a dim view of any literary agent who asks potential clients for a fee prior to a manuscript being placed with a publisher. We advise you to treat any such request with caution and to let us know if that agent appears in the listings below. However, agents may charge additional costs later in the process but these should only arise once a book has been accepted by a publisher and the author is earning an income. We urge authors to make the distinction between upfront and additional charges.

*Full member of the Association of Authors' Agents

A & B Personal Management Ltd

Suite 330, Linen Hall, 162–168 Regent Street, London W1B 5TD
tel 020-7434 4262 *fax* 020-7038 3699
email billellis@aandb.co.uk
Directors R.W. Ellis, R. Ellis

Full-length MSS. Scripts for TV, theatre, cinema; also novels, fiction and non-fiction (home 12.5%, overseas 15%), performance rights (12.5%). No unsolicited material: write first before submitting synopsis. No reading fee for synopsis, plays or screenplays, but fee charged for full-length MSS. Return postage required. Founded 1982.

Sheila Ableman Literary Agency*

3rd Floor, Lymehouse Studios, 38 Georgiana Street, London NW1 0EB
tel 020-7485 3409 *fax* 020-7485 3409
email sheila@sheilaableman.co.uk
Contact Sheila Ableman

Non-fiction including history, science, cookery, biography, autobiography (home 15%, USA/translation 20%). Specialises in TV tie-ins and celebrity ghostwriting. No poetry, children's, gardening or sport. Unsolicited MSS welcome. Approach in writing with publishing history, CV, synopsis, 3 chapters and sae for return. No reading fee. Founded 1999.

The Susie Adams Rights Agency

PO Box 3820, Bath BA2 4WY
tel (01225) 445777
email susieara@aol.com
Agent Susie Adams

Rights consultancy and subsidiary rights agent on behalf of packagers, literary agents and publishers: foreign language and co-edition rights worldwide, UK serial, book club, merchandise and other sub rights. No authors. Founded 1998.

The Agency (London) Ltd*

24 Pottery Lane, London W11 4LZ
tel 020-7727 1346 *fax* 020-7727 9037
email info@theagency.co.uk

Executives Stephen Durbridge, Leah Schmidt, Julia Kreitman, Bethan Evans, Norman North, Hilary Delamere (children's books), Katie Haines, Ligeia Marsh, Faye Webber, Nick Quinn

Represents writers for theatre, film, TV, radio and children's book writers and illustrators. Also film and TV rights in novels and non-fiction. Adult novels represented only for existing clients. Commission: 10% unless sub-agents employed overseas; works in conjunction with agents in USA and overseas. Strictly no unsolicited material. No reading fee. Founded 1995.

Gillon Aitken Associates Ltd*

18–21 Cavaye Place, London SW10 9PT
tel 020-7373 8672 *fax* 020-7373 6002
email reception@gillonaitken.co.uk
website www.gillonaitkenassociates.co.uk
Contacts Gillon Aitken, Clare Alexander, Lesley Thorne (also handles film/TV), *Associated Agents* Anthony Sheil, Mary Pachnos

Fiction and non-fiction (home 10%, USA 20%, translation 20%, film/TV 10%). No plays, scripts or children's fiction unless by existing clients. Send preliminary letter with half-page synopsis and first 30pp of sample material and adequate return postage in first instance. No reading fee.

Clients include Caroline Alexander, Pat Barker, Nicholas Blincoe, Gordon Burn, Jung Chang, John Cornwell, Josephine Cox, Sarah Dunant, Susan Elderkin, Sebastian Faulks, Helen Fielding, Russell Grant, Jane Goldman, Germaine Greer, Mark Haddon, Susan Howatch, Liz Jensen, John Keegan, V.S. Naipaul, Jonathan Raban, Piers Paul Read, Louise Rennison, Michèle Roberts, Nicholas Shakespeare, Gillian Slovo, Matt Thorne, Colin Thubron, Salley Vickers, Penny Vincenzi, A.N. Wilson, Robert Wilson. Founded 1977.

Jacintha Alexander Associates – see LAW Ltd

The Ampersand Agency*

Ryman's Cottages, Little Tew, Oxon OX7 4JJ
tel (01608) 683677 *fax* (01608) 683449

email peter@theampersandagency.co.uk
website www.theampersandagency.co.uk
Contact Peter Buckman, Peter Janson-Smith
(consultant)

Literary and commercial fiction and non-fiction
(home 10%–15%, USA 15%, translation 20%). No
reading fee. Will suggest revision.

Represents the Georgette Heyer Estate, Beryl
Kingston, Jill Norman, Philip Purser, Vikas Swarup,
et al. Founded 2003.

Darley Anderson Literary, TV and Film Agency*

Estelle House, 11 Eustace Road, London SW6 1JB
tel 020-7385 6652 *fax* 020-7386 5571
email enquiries@darleyanderson.com
website www.darleyanderson.com
Contacts Darley Anderson (crime, mystery &
thrillers), Lucie Whitehouse (women's & general
fiction/foreign rights), Elizabeth Wright (agent), Julia
Churchill (children's fiction), Emma White (non-
fiction/US, foreign & TV rights), Rosi Bridge
(finance), Zoe King, Ella Andrews

Commercial fiction and non-fiction; children's fiction
and non-fiction (home 15%, USA/translation 20%,
film/TV/radio 20%). No poetry or academic books.

Special interests (fiction): all types of thrillers,
crime/mystery and young male fiction. All types of
American and Irish novels. All types of women's
fiction. Sagas, chick-lit; contemporary and literary.
Also comic fiction. Children's fiction, all ages.

Special interests (non-fiction): celebrity
autobiographies, biographies, sports books, 'true-life'
women in jeopardy, revelatory history and science,
popular psychology, self improvement, diet, beauty,
health, fashion, animals, humour/cartoon, cookery,
gardening, inspirational, religious.

Send preliminary letter, synopsis and first 3
chapters. Return postage/sae essential for reply. Disk
and emailed submissions cannot be considered.
Overseas associates: APA Talent & Literary Agency
(LA/Hollywood), Cornerstone Literary (LA), Liza
Dawson Literary Agency (New York) and 21 leading
foreign agents worldwide.

Clients include Liz Allen, Anne Baker, Alex Barclay,
Constance Briscoe, Paul Carson, Cathy Cassidy, Lee
Child, Lisa Clark, Martina Cole, John Connolly,
Margaret Dickinson, Clare Dowling, Tana French,
Milly Johnson, Joan Jonker, Danny King, Patrick
Lennon, Freda Lightfoot, Rani Manicka, Carole
Matthews, Annie Murrray, Lesley Pearse, Lynda Page,
Adrian Plass, Sheila Quigley, Carmen Reid, Rebecca
Shaw, Peter Sheridan, Kwong Kuen Shan, Linda
Taylor, Elizabeth Waite, Kate Wild, Patrick
Woodrow, Ahmet Zappa.

Anubis Literary Agency

6 Birdhaven Close, Lighthorne, Warwick CV35 0BE
tel (01926) 642588 *fax* (01926) 642588

Contacts Steve Calcutt

Genre fiction: science fiction, fantasy and horror
(home 15%, USA/translation 20%). No other
material considered. Send 50pp with a one-page
synopsis (sae essential). No reading fee. No telephone
calls. Works with the **Marsh Agency Ltd** on
translation rights.

Clients include Lesley Asquith, Christopher
Golden, J.F. Gonzalez, Anthea Ingham, Tim Lebbon,
Sarah Pinborough, Adam Roberts, Steve Savile, Brett
A. Savory. Founded 1994.

Author Literary Agents

53 Talbot Road, London N6 4QX
tel 020-8341 0442 *mobile* (07767) 022659
email agile@authors.co.uk
Contact John Havergal

Fiction, non-fiction and children's (home 15%,
overseas/translations 25%). Send first chapter, scene
or section plus a half–one-page outline. Sae essential
for reply. No reading fee. Founded 1997.

Don Baker Associates

25 Eley Drive, Rottingdean, East Sussex BN2 7FH
tel (01273) 386842 *fax* (01273) 386842
Directors Donald Baker, Katy Quayle

Full-length MSS. Fiction, film, TV and theatre scripts
(home 12.5%, overseas 15%). Reading fee. Send sae.
No unsolicited MSS. Founded 1996.

Diane Banks Associates

PO Box 53930, London SW15 6YS
tel/fax 020-8785 1086
email submissions@dianebanks.co.uk
Contact Diane Banks

Commercial fiction and non-fiction (home 15%,
overseas 20%). Fiction: women's, crime, thrillers,
Irish, literary fiction with a strong storyline. Non-
fiction: memoir, real-life stories, celebrity,
autobiography, biography, popular history, popular
science, self-help, popular psychology, fashion, health
& beauty. No poetry, science fiction, children's,
academic books, plays, scripts or short stories. Initial
approach by email only. Send brief CV, synopsis and
sample chapters as attachments. Aims to give initial
response within 2 weeks. No reading fee. Will suggest
revision.

Authors include John Rodgers, Elizabeth Burton-
Phillips, Hannah Sandling, Brian Cox, Tacy Culletan.
Founded 2006.

The Bell Lomax Agency

James House, 1 Babmaes Street, London SW1Y 6HF
tel 020-7930 4447 *fax* 020-7925 0118
email agency@bell-lomax.co.uk
Executives Eddie Bell, Pat Lomax, Paul Moreton,
June Bell

Quality fiction and non-fiction, biography, children's,
business and sport. No unsolicited MSS without

preliminary letter. No scripts. No reading fee. Founded 2000.

Blake Friedmann Literary, TV & Film Agency Ltd*

122 Arlington Road, London NW1 7HP
tel 020-7284 0408 fax 020-7284 0442
email firstname@blakefriedmann.co.uk
Directors Carole Blake, Julian Friedmann, Isobel Dixon

Full-length MSS. Fiction: thrillers, women's novels and literary fiction; non-fiction: investigative books, biography, travel; no poetry or plays (home 15%, overseas 20%). Specialises in film and TV rights; place journalism and short stories for existing clients only. Represented worldwide in 26 markets. Preliminary letter, synopsis and first 2 chapters preferred. No reading fee.

Authors include Gilbert Adair, Jane Asher, Edward Carey, Elizabeth Chadwick, Victoria Clayton, Anna Davis, Barbara Erskine, Ann Granger, Maeve Haran, Ken Hom, Peter James, Glenn Meade, Lawrence Norfolk, Gregory Norminton, Joseph O'Connor, Sheila O'Flanagan, Sian Rees, Michael Ridpath, Craig Russell, Tim Sebastian, Julian Stockwin, Michael White. Founded 1977.

Luigi Bonomi Associates Ltd*

91 Great Russell Street, London WC1B 3PS
tel 020 7637 1234 fax 020-7637 2111
email info@bonomiassociates.co.uk
Directors Luigi Bonomi, Amanda Preston

Fiction and non-fiction (home 15%, overseas 20%). Fiction: commercial and literary fiction, thrillers, crime, women's fiction. Non-fiction: history, science parenting, Mind, Body & Spirit, gardening, cookery, lifestyle, diet, health, sport, TV tie-ins; all types of journalism and journalists wishing to further their careers. No poetry, children's stories or adult SF/fantasy. Keen to find new authors and help them develop their careers. Send preliminary letter, synopsis and first 3 chapters. No reading fee. Will suggest revision. Works with foreign agencies and has links with TV presenters' agencies and production companies.

Authors worked with include James Barrington, Chris Beardshaw, Gennaro Contaldo, Nick Foulkes, Cris (sic.) Freddi, David Gibbins, Eamonn Holmes, Richard Hammond, John Humphrys, Graham Joyce, Simon Kernick, Colin McDowell, Dr Gillian McKeith, Richard Madeley and Judy Finnigan, Gavin Menzies, Sue Palmer, Andrew Pepper, Melanie Phillips, Esther Rantzen, John Rickards, Colin Shindler, Lorne Spicer, Prof. Bryan Sykes, Mitch Symons, Rachel de Thame, Alan Titchmarsh, Sir Terry Wogan, Kim Woodburn and Aggie MacKenzie, Sally Worboyes. Founded 2005.

The Book Bureau Literary Agency

7 Duncairn Avenue, Bray, Co. Wicklow, Republic of Ireland

tel (01) 276 4996 fax (01) 276 4834
email thebookbureau@oceanfree.net
Managing Director Geraldine Nichol

Full-length MSS (home 10%, USA/translation 20%). Fiction preferred – thrillers, Irish novels, literary fiction, women's novels and general commercial. No horror, science fiction, children's or poetry. Strong editorial support. No reading fee. Preliminary letter, synopsis and 3 sample chapters. Return postage essential, IRCs from UK and abroad. Works with agents overseas.

BookBlast Ltd

PO Box 20184, London W10 5AU
tel 020-8968 3089 fax 020-8932 4087
website www.bookblast.com
Contact Address material to the Company

Full-length MSS (home 12%, overseas 20%), TV and radio (15%), film (20%). Fiction and non-fiction. No scripts, horror, crime, science fiction, fantasy, poetry, health, cookery, gardening, short stories, academic articles or children's books. Radio, TV and film rights sold mainly in works by existing clients. No reading fee. No unsolicited approaches at present. No new clients taken on except by recommendation. Founded 1997.

Alan Brodie Representation Ltd

6th Floor, Fairgate House, 78 New Oxford Street, London WC1A 1HB
tel 020-7079 7990 fax 020-7079 7999
email info@alanbrodie.com
website www.alanbrodie.com
Directors Alan Brodie, Sarah McNair, Alison Lee

Specialises in stage plays, radio, TV, film (home 10%, overseas 15%); no prose fiction or general MSS. Represented in all major countries. No unsolicited scripts; recommendation from known professional required.

Jenny Brown Associates*

33 Argyle Place, Edinburgh EH9 1JT
tel 0131-229 5334
email jenny-brown@blueyonder.co.uk
website www.jennybrownassociates.com
Contact Jenny Brown, Mark Stanton

Literary fiction, crime writing and writing for children; non-fiction: biography, history, sport, music popular culture (home 12.5%, overseas/translation 20%). No poetry, science fiction, fantasy or academic. No reading fee.

Clients include Lin Anderson, Jeff Connor, Mary Contini, Jennie Erdal, Alex Gray, Laura Hird, Laura Marney, Janet Morgan, Tom Pow, Jonathan Rendall, Suhayl Saadi, Paul Torday, Christopher Whyte. Founded 2002.

Felicity Bryan*

2A North Parade, Banbury Road, Oxford OX2 6LX
tel (01865) 513816 fax (01865) 310055

email agency@felicitybryan.com
website www.felicitybryan.com

Fiction and general non-fiction (home 15%, overseas 20%). Translation rights handled by Andrew Nurnberg Associates; works in conjunction with US agents.

Brie Burkeman*
14 Neville Court, Abbey Road, London NW8 9DD
tel (0870) 199 5002 *fax* (0870) 199 1029
email brie.burkeman@mail.com
Proprietor Brie Burkeman

Commercial and literary full-length fiction and non-fiction. Film and theatre scripts (Home 15%, Overseas 20%). No academic text, poetry, short stories, musicals or short films. No reading fee but return postage essential. Unsolicited email attachments will be deleted without opening. Also associated with Serafina Clarke Ltd and independent film/TV consultant to literary agents. Founded 2000.

Campbell Thomson & McLaughlin Ltd*
11–12 Dover Street, London W1S 4LJ
tel 020-7399 2808 *fax* 020-7399 2801
Contact Charlotte Bruton

Full-length book MSS (home 10%, overseas up to 20% including commission to foreign agent). No poetry, plays or TV/film scripts, short stories or children's books. Preliminary enquiry essential, by letter or email (submissions@ctmcl.co.uk). No unsolicited synopses or MSS. No reading fee. USA agents represented: Raines & Raines, the Fox Chase Agency, Inc. Translation rights handled by The Marsh Agency.

Capel & Land Ltd*
29 Wardour Street, London W1D 6PS
tel 020-7734 2414 *fax* 020-7734 8101
email georgina@capelland.co.uk
Agents Georgina Capel (literary), Robert Caskie (film), Anita Land (TV)

Literary and commercial fiction, history, biography; film and TV (home/overseas 15%). No reading fee; will suggest revision.

Clients include Julie Burchill, Andrew Greig, Eamonn Holmes, Jean Marsh, Cristina Odone, Jeremy Paxman, Andrew Roberts, Simon Sebag Montefiore, Stella Rimington, Louis Theroux, Fay Weldon. Founded 1999.

Casarotto Ramsay & Associates Ltd
(formerly Margaret Ramsay Ltd and Casarotto Company Ltd)
National House, 60–66 Wardour Street, London W1V 4ND
tel 020-7287 4450 *fax* 020-7287 9128
email agents@casarotto.uk.com
Directors Jenne Casarotto, Giorgio Casarotto, Tom Erhardt, Sara Pritchard, Mel Kenyon, Charlotte Kelly, Jodi Shields, Rachel Holroyd

MSS – theatre, films, TV, sound broadcasting only (10%). Works in conjunction with agents in USA and other foreign countries. Preliminary letter essential. No reading fee.

Authors include Alan Ayckbourn, J.G. Ballard, Edward Bond, Caryl Churchill, Pam Gems, Christopher Hampton, David Hare, Nick Hornby, Amy Jenkins, Neil Jordan, Frank McGuiness, Phyllis Nagy, Mark Ravenhill, Willy Russell, Martin Sherman, Shawn Slovo, Timberlake Wertenbaker, David Wood. Founded 1989.

Celia Catchpole
56 Gilpin Avenue, London SW14 8QY
tel 020-8255 4835
email celiacatchpole@yahoo.co.uk
website www.celiacatchpole.co.uk

Specialises as agent for children's writers and illustrators (home 10% writers, 15% illustrators; overseas 20%). No unsolicited MSS. Founded 1996.

Chapman & Vincent*
The Mount, Sun Hill, Royston, Herts. SG8 9AT
tel (01763) 245005 *fax* (01763) 243033
email info@chapmanvincent.co.uk
Directors Jennifer Chapman, Gilly Vincent

Predominantly non-fiction and some quality fiction (home 15%; overseas 20%). No poetry, scripts, fantasy or children's books. No reading fee. No telephone, fax, disk or email submissions. Clients come mainly from personal recommendation but postal submissions accepted: send synopsis and 2 sample chapters with return postage. Works with the **Elaine Markson Agency** in USA.

Authors include George Carter, Leslie Geddes-Brown, Rowley Leigh and Eve Pollard. Founded 1992.

Mic Cheetham Literary Agency
11–12 Dover Street, London W1S 4LJ
tel 020-7495 2002 *fax* 020-7399 2801
website www.miccheetham.com
Director Mic Cheetham, *Contact* Mic Cheetham, Simon Kavanagh

General and literary fiction, science fiction, some non-fiction (home/overseas 15–20%); film, TV and radio rights (10–20%); will suggest revision. Works with the **Marsh Agency Ltd** for foreign rights. No unsolicited MSS. No reading fee. Founded 1994.

Judith Chilcote Agency*
8 Wentworth Mansions, Keats Grove, London NW3 2RL
tel 020-7794 3717
email judybks@aol.com
Director Judith Chilcote

Commercial fiction, non-fiction – self-help and health, popular psychology, current affairs, TV tie-ins (home 15%, overseas 20–25%). No short stories, science fiction, children's, poetry. Works in conjunction with overseas agents and New York affiliate. No reading fee but preliminary letter with 3 chapters only, CV and sae essential. Founded 1990.

Teresa Chris Literary Agency*
43 Musard Road, London W6 8NR
tel 020-7386 0633
Director Teresa Chris

All fiction, especially crime, women's commercial, general and literary fiction; all non-fiction, especially biography, history, health, cooking, arts and crafts. No science fiction, horror, fantasy, short stories, poetry, academic books (home 10%, overseas 20%). No reading fee. Send introductory letter describing work, first 3 chapters and sae. Founded 1988.

Mary Clemmey Literary Agency*
6 Dunollie Road, London NW5 2XP
tel 020-7267 1290 *fax* 020-7482 7360

High-quality fiction and non-fiction with an international market (home 10%, overseas 20%, performance rights 15%). No children's books or science fiction. TV, film, radio and theatre scripts from existing clients only. Works in conjunction with US agent. No reading fee. No unsolicited MSS. Approach first by letter (including sae). Founded 1992.

US Clients Frederick Hill, Bonnie Nadell Inc., Lynn C. Franklin Associates Ltd, The Miller Agency, Roslyn Targ, Weingel-Fidel Agency Inc., Betsy Amsetr Literary Enterprises

Jonathan Clowes Ltd*
10 Iron Bridge House, Bridge Approach, London NW1 8BD
tel 020-7722 7674 *fax* 020-7722 7677
Directors Jonathan Clowes, Ann Evans, Lisa Thompson

Literary and commercial fiction and non-fiction, film, TV, theatre and radio (home 15%, overseas 20%). No reading fee. No unsolicited MSS. Works in association with agents overseas. Founded 1960.

Clients include Sir Kingsley Amis Estate, Dr David Bellamy, Bill Dare, Len Deighton, David Harsent, Elizabeth Jane Howard, David Lawrence, Doris Lessing, David Nobbs, Gillian White.

Elspeth Cochrane Personal Management
16 Old Town, London SW4 0JY
tel 020-7819 6256 *fax* 020-7819 4297
email elspeth@elspethcochrane.co.uk
Contact Elspeth Cochrane

Fiction, non-fiction, biographies, screenplays and plays (12.5%). No children's fiction. No unsolicited MSS. Send preliminary letter, synopsis and sae in first instance. No reading fee.

Clients include Alex Jones, Dominic Leyton, Royce Ryton, F.E. Smith, Robert Tanitch. Founded 1960.

Rosica Colin Ltd
1 Clareville Grove Mews, London SW7 5AH
tel 020-7370 1080 *fax* 020-7244 6441
Directors Sylvie Marston, Joanna Marston

All full-length MSS (excluding science fiction and poetry); also theatre, film and sound broadcasting (home 10%, overseas 10–20%). No reading fee, but may take 3–4 months to consider full MSS. Send synopsis only in first instance, with letter outlining writing credits and whether MS has been previously submitted, plus return postage.

Authors include Richard Aldington, Simone de Beauvoir (in UK), Samuel Beckett (publication rights), Steven Berkoff, Alan Brownjohn, Sandy Brownjohn, Donald Campbell, Nick Dear, Neil Donnelly, J.T. Edson, Bernard Farrell, Rainer Werner Fassbinder (in UK), Jean Genet, Franz Xaver Kroetz, Don McCamphill, Heiner Müller (in UK), Graham Reid, Botho Strauss (in UK), Rina Vergano, Anthony Vivis, Wim Wenders (in UK). Founded 1949.

Conville & Walsh Ltd*
2 Ganton Street, London W1F 7QL
tel 020-7287 3030 *fax* 020-7287 4545
email firstname@convilleandwalsh.com
Directors Clare Conville, Patrick Walsh, Peter Tallack

Literary and commercial fiction and non-fiction plus children's books. Particularly interested in first novelists plus scientists, historians and journalists. No poetry or short stories. Submit first 3 chapters, cover letter, synopsis and sae. No reading fee.

Clients include Belle de Jour, John Burningham, Kate Cann, Helen Castor, Tom Conran, Michael Cordy, Mike Dash, Kevin Dutton, Prof. John Emsley, Steve Erikson, Kitty Fitzgerald, Katy Gardner, Misha Glenny, Christopher Hart, Dermot Healy, Michael Hodges, James Holland, Tom Holland, Sebastian Horsley, David Huggins, Guy Kennaway, Daren King, Manjit Kumar, P.J. Lynch, Hector Macdonald, Hisham Mathar, Prof. Arthur Miller, Harland Miller, Joshua Mowll, Jacqui Murhall, Peadar O'Guilin, Ruth Padel, D.B.C. Pierre, Rebbecca Ray, Patrick Redmond, Candace Robb, Saira Shah, Tahir Shah, Nicky Singer, Simon Singh, Michael Smith, Steve Voake, Dr Richard Wiseman, Adam Wishart, Isabel Wolff, and the Estate of Francis Bacon. Founded 2000.

Jane Conway-Gordon Ltd*
(in association with Andrew Mann Ltd)
1 Old Compton Street, London W1D 5JA
tel 020-7494 0148 *fax* 020-7287 9264

Full length MSS (home 15%, overseas 20%). No poetry, sci-fi or children's. Represented in all foreign countries. No reading fee but preliminary letter and return postage essential. Founded 1982.

Coombs Moylett Literary Agency
3 Askew Road, London W12 9AA
tel 020-8740 0454 *fax* 020-8354 3065

Contacts Lisa Moylett, Nathalie Sfakianos

Commercial and literary fiction and non-fiction (home 15%, overseas 15%, film/TV 15%). Fiction: thrillers, crime/mystery; women's literary and contemporary. Non-fiction: biography; history and current affairs. Send synopsis, first 3 chapters and sae (essential). No disk or email submissions. No reading fee. Works with foreign agents.

Rupert Crew Ltd*

1A King's Mews, London WC1N 2JA
tel 020-7242 8586 *fax* 020-7831 7914
email info@rupertcrew.co.uk
Directors Doreen Montgomery, Caroline Montgomery

International representation, handling volume and subsidiary rights in fiction and non-fiction properties (home 15%, elsewhere 20%); no plays, screenplays, poetry, journalism, science fiction or short stories. No reading fee, but preliminary letter and return postage essential. Also acts independently as publishers' consultants. Founded 1927 by F. Rupert Crew.

Curtis Brown Group Ltd*

Haymarket House, 28–29 Haymarket, London SW1Y 4SP
tel 020-7393 4400 *fax* 020-7393 4401
email cb@curtisbrown.co.uk
website www.curtisbrown.co.uk
Ceo Jonathan Lloyd, *Director of Operations* Ben Hall, *Directors* Jacquie Drewe, Jonny Geller, Nick Marston *Books* Jonny Geller (Managing Director, Book Division), Ali Gunn, Camilla Hornby, Jonathan Lloyd, Jonathan Pegg, Vivienne Schuster, Elizabeth Sheinkman, Janice Swanson, Gordon Wise, *Foreign Rights (books)* Kate Cooper, Carol Jackson, Diana Mackay, Betsy Robbins
Film/TV/Theatre Nick Marston (Managing Director, Media Division), Tally Garner, Ben Hall, Joe Phillips, Sally Whitehill
Actors Grace Clissold, Maxine Hoffman, Sarah MacCormick, Sarah Spear, Kate Staddon, Claire Stannard, Frances Williams
Presenters Jacquie Drewe, Catherine Tapsell Jenkin

Novels, general non-fiction, children's books and associated rights (including multimedia), as well as film, theatre, TV and radio scripts (home 15%, overseas 20%). Send outline for non-fiction and short synopsis for fiction with 2–3 sample chapters and autobiographical note. No reading fee. Return postage essential. No submissions by email. See website for further submission guidelines. Also represents playwrights, film and TV writers and directors, theatre directors and designers, TV and radio presenters and actors. Overseas associates in Australia and the USA. Founded 1914.

Judy Daish Associates Ltd

2 St Charles Place, London W10 6EG
tel 020-8964 8811 *fax* 020-8964 8966

Agents Judy Daish, Howard Gooding, Tracey Elliston
Theatre, film, TV, radio (rates by negotiation). No unsolicited MSS. No reading fee. Founded 1978.

Caroline Davidson Literary Agency*

5 Queen Anne's Gardens, London W4 1TU
tel 020-8995 5768 *fax* 020-8994 2770
email cdla@ukgateway.net
website www.cdla.co.uk

Handles novels and non-fiction of high quality, including reference works (12.5%). Send preliminary letter with CV and detailed, well thought-out book proposal/synopsis and/or first 50pp of novel. Large sae with return postage essential. No reading fee. Quick response.

Authors include Andrew Dalby, Emma Donoghue, Cindy Engel, Chris Greenhalgh, Tom Jaine, Huon Mallalieu, Linda Sonntag, Caroline Williams. Founded 1988.

Merric Davidson Literary Agency – see MBA Literary Agents Ltd

Felix De Wolfe

Kingsway House, 103 Kingsway, London WC2B 6QX
tel 020-7242 5066 *fax* 020-7242 8119

Theatre, films, TV, sound broadcasting, fiction (home 10–15%, overseas 20%). No reading fee. Works in conjunction with many foreign agencies.

DGA Ltd

55 Monmouth Street, London WC2H 9DG
tel 020-7240 9992 *fax* 020-7395 6110
email assistant@davidgodwinassociates.co.uk
website www.davidgodwinassociates.co.uk
Directors David Godwin, Heather Godwin

Literary fiction and general non-fiction (home 15%, overseas 20%, film 15%). No reading fee; send sae for return of MSS. Founded 1995.

Dorian Literary Agency (DLA)*

Upper Thornehill, 27 Church Road, St Marychurch, Torquay, Devon TQ1 4QY
tel (01803) 312095 *fax* (01803) 312095
Proprietor Dorothy Lumley

General fiction, and specialising in popular fiction (home 10–12.5%, USA 15%, translation 20%). For adults: women's fiction, romance, historicals; crime and thrillers; science fiction, fantasy, dark fantasy and horror. Reading only very selectively. No poetry or drama. No reading fee. Contact initially by post with the first 3 chapters and brief outline plus return postage/sae. No telephone calls, faxes or emails.

Authors include Gillian Bradshaw, Kate Charles, Brian Lumley, Stephen Jones, Andy Remic, Rosemary Rowe, Lyndon Stacey. Founded 1986.

Bryan Drew Ltd

Quadrant House, 80–82 Regent Street, London W1B 5AU

tel 020-7437 2293 *fax* 020-7437 0561
email bryan@bryandrewltd.com
Literary Manager Bryan Drew

Scripts for TV, films and theatre (home 12.5%, overseas 15%). General fiction, thrillers, biographies. No reading fee. Enclose sae. Founded 1962.

Robert Dudley Agency

8 Abbotstone Road, London SW15 1QR
tel 020-8788 0938 *mobile* (07879) 426574
fax 020-8780 3586
email rdudley@btinternet.com
Proprietor Robert Dudley

Specialises in history, biography, sport, management, politics, militaria, current affairs (home 15%, overseas 20%; film/TV/radio 15–20%). No reading fee. Will suggest revision. All material sent at owner's risk. No MSS returned without sae.

Authors include Steve Biko, Simon Caulkin, Peter Collins, Ali Dizaei, Jim Drury, Paul Gannon, Chris Green, Tim Guest, Mungo Melvin, Brian Holden Reid, Tim Phillips, Nick Rengger, Heather Reynolds, Michael Scott, Dan Wilson. Founded 2000.

Toby Eady Associates Ltd

3rd Floor, 9 Orme Court, London W2 4RL
tel 020-7792 0092 *fax* 020-7792 0879
email toby@tobyeady.demon.co.uk
laetitia@tobyeady.demon.co.uk
website www.tobyeadyassociates.co.uk
Contacts Toby Eady, Laetitia Rutherford

Fiction and non-fiction (home 15%, overseas 20%). Special interests: China, Middle East, Africa, India. No film/TV scripts or poetry. Approach by personal recommendation. Overseas associates: **La Nouvelle Agence** (France), Mohrbrooks (Germany), Jan Michael (Holland), The Buckman Agency (Italy, Spain, Portugal and Scandinavia), Joanne Wang (China).

Clients include Nada Awar Jarrar, Julia Blackburn, Mark Burnell, John Carey, Chris Cleave, Bernard Cornwell, Rana Dasgupta, Fadia Faqir, Kuki Gallmann, Xiaolu Guo, Natasha Illum Berg, Susan Lewis, Julia Lovell, Francesca Marciano, Kanan Makiya, Patrick Marnham, Linda Polman, Deborah Scroggins, Samia Serageldin, Rachel Seiffert, John Stubbs, Robert Winder, Fan Wu, Xinran Xue. Estates of Peter Cheyney, Ted Lewis, Mary Wesley. Founded 1968.

Eddison Pearson Ltd

West Hill House, 6 Swains Lane, London N6 6QS
tel 020-7700 7763 *fax* 020-7700 7866
email info@eddisonpearson.com
Contact Clare Pearson

Children's books, literary fiction and non-fiction, poetry (home 10%, overseas 15–20%). Email enquiries only; email for up-to-date submission guidelines by return. No reading fee. May suggest revision where appropriate.

Authors include Valerie Bloom, Sue Heap, Sally Lloyd-Jones, Robert Muchamore.

Edwards Fuglewicz*

49 Great Ormond Street, London WC1N 3HZ
tel 020-7405 6725 *fax* 020-7405 6726
Partners Ros Edwards and Helenka Fuglewicz

Literary and commercial fiction (but no children's fiction, science fiction, horror or fantasy); non-fiction: biography, history, popular culture (home 15%, USA/translation 20%). No unsolicited MSS or email submissions. No reading fee. Founded 1996.

Faith Evans Associates*

27 Park Avenue North, London N8 7RU
tel 020-8340 9920 *fax* 020-8340 9410

Small agency (home 15%, overseas 20%). Co-agents in most countries. No phone calls, scripts or unsolicited MSS.

Authors include Melissa Benn, Shyam Bhatia, Cherie Booth, Eleanor Bron, Carolyn Cassady, Caroline Conran, Alicia Foster, Midge Gillies, Ed Glinert, Vesna Goldsworthy, Cate Haste, Jim Kelly, Helena Kennedy, Seumas Milne, Tom Paulin, Sheila Rowbotham, Lorna Sage, Rebecca Stott, Harriet Walter, Elizabeth Wilson, Francesca Weisman. Founded 1987.

Janet Fillingham Associates

52 Lowther Road, London SW13 9NU
tel 020-8748 5594 *fax* 020-8748 7374
email info@jfillassoc.co.uk
website www.janetfillingham.com
Director Janet Fillingham

Film and TV only (home 10%, overseas 15–20%). Strictly no unsolicited MSS; professional recommendation required. Founded 1992.

Film Rights Ltd

Mezzanine, Quadrant House, 80–82 Regent Street, London W1B 5AU
tel 020-7734 9911 *fax* 020-7734 0044
email information@filmrights.ltd.uk
website www.filmrights.ltd.uk
Directors Brendan Davis, Joan Potts

Theatre, films, TV and sound broadcasting (home 10%, overseas 15%). No reading fee. Represented in USA and abroad. Founded 1932.

Laurence Fitch Ltd

(incorporating The London Play Company 1922)
Mezzanine, Quadrant House, 80–82 Regent Street, London W1B 5AU
tel 020-7734 9911 *fax* 020-7437 0561
email information@laurencefitch.com
website www.laurencefitch.com
Directors F.H.L. Fitch, Joan Potts, Brendan Davis

Theatre, films, TV and sound broadcasting (home 10%, overseas 15%). Also affiliated with Film Rights

Ltd. and works with several agencies in USA and in Europe.

Authors include Carlo Ardito, John Chapman, Peter Coke, Ray Cooney OBE, Dave Freeman, John Graham, Robin Hawdon, Jeremy Lloyd (plays) Dawn Lowe-Watson, Glyn Robbins, Edward Taylor and the Estate of the late Dodie Smith.

Jill Foster Ltd
9 Barb Mews, Brook Green, London W6 7PA
tel 020-7602 1263 *fax* 020-7602 9336
Agents Jill Foster, Alison Finch, Simon Williamson, Dominic Lord, Gary Wild

Theatre, films, TV and sound broadcasting (12.5%). Particularly interested in film and TV comedy and drama. No novels or short stories. No reading fee. Preliminary letter essential. No submissions by email. Do not send material in the first instance. Founded 1978.

Fox & Howard Literary Agency
4 Bramerton Street, London SW3 5JX
tel 020-7352 8691 *fax* 020-7352 8691
Partners Chelsey Fox, Charlotte Howard

General non-fiction: biography, history and popular culture, reference, business, mind, body & spirit, health and fitness (home 15%, overseas 20%). No reading fee, but preliminary letter and synopsis with sae essential for response. Founded 1992.

Fraser Ross Associates
6 Wellington Place, Edinburgh EH6 7EQ
tel 0131-553 2759, 0131-657 4412
email lindsey.fraser@tiscali.co.uk, kjross@tiscali.co.uk
website www.fraserross.co.uk
Partners Lindsey Fraser, Kathryn Ross

Writing and illustration for children's books, but not exclusively (home 10%). No reading fee. Founded 2002.

Futerman, Rose & Associates*
17 Deanhill Road, London SW14 7DQ
tel 020-8255 7755 *fax* 020-8286 4860
email guy@futermanrose.co.uk (general enquiries), betty@futermanrose.co.uk (fiction submissions)
website www.futermanrose.co.uk
Contact Guy Rose

Fiction, scripts for film and TV, biography, show business, current affairs and teenage fiction (15–20%). No science fiction, fantasy or young children's. No unsolicited MSS. Send preliminary letter with brief résumé, detailed synopsis, first 20pp and sae.

Clients include Lesley Crewe, Joanne & Jerry Dryansky, Royston Ellis, Sir Martin Evans, Yvette Fielding, Stephen Griffin, Paul Hendy, Keith R. Lindsay, Stephen Lowe, Eric MacInnes, Paul Marx, Francis Matthews, Max Morgan-Witts, Dr Ciarán O'Keeffe, Erin Pizzey, Paul Rattigan, Liz Rettig,

Yvonne Ridley, Peter Sallis, Pat Silver-Lasky, Bill Tidy, Dr Mark White, Toyah Willcox, Simon Woodham, Allen Zeleski. Founded 1984.

Jüri Gabriel
35 Camberwell Grove, London SE5 8JA
tel 020-7703 6186

Quality fiction and non-fiction (i.e. anything that shows wit and intelligence); radio, TV and film, but selling these rights only in existing works by existing clients. Full-length MSS (home 10%, overseas 20%), performance rights (10%).

Will suggest revision where appropriate. No short stories, articles, verse or books for children. No reading fee; return postage essential. Jüri Gabriel is the chairman of Dedalus (publishers).

Authors include Maurice Caldera, Diana Constance, Miriam Dunne, Matt Fox, Pat Gray, Mikka Haugaard, Robert Irwin, John Lucas, 'David Madsen', Richard Mankiewicz, Karina Mellinger, David Miller, Andy Oakes, John Outram, Philip Roberts, Stefan Szymanski, Dr Terence White, Chris Wilkins, Dr Robert Youngson.

Eric Glass Ltd
25 Ladbroke Crescent, London W11 1PS
tel 020-7229 9500 *fax* 020-7229 6220
email eglassltd@aol.com
Director Janet Glass

Full-length MSS only; also theatre, films, and TV. No unsolicited MSS. Founded 1932.

David Godwin Associates – see DGA Ltd

Graham Maw Literary Agency
16 de Beauvoir Square, London N1 4LD
tel 020-7812 9937
email enquiries@grahammawagency.com
website www.grahammawagency.com
Agents Jane Graham Maw, Jennifer Christie

General non-fiction: biography/memoir, business, health, lifestyle, Mind, Body & Spirit, parenting, popular culture, celebrity, web-to-book (home 15%, overseas 20%). No fiction, children's or poetry. No reading fee.

Authors include Dr Patrick Bowler, Margaret Davis, Dr Jennifer Harper-Deacon, James Hicks, Chris Hutchins, Gael Lindenfield, Nick Moran, Jack Osbourne, Melanie Shanks, Graham Stark, Adam Vaughan, Richard Wilson, Simon Yeo. Founded 2005.

Annette Green Authors' Agency*
1 East Cliff Road, Tunbridge Wells, Kent TN4 9AD
tel (01892) 514275 *fax* (01892) 518124
email annettekgreen@aol.com
website www.annettegreenagency.co.uk
Partners Annette Green, David Smith

Full-length MSS (home 15%, overseas 20%). Literary and general fiction and non-fiction, popular culture, history, science, teenage fiction. No dramatic scripts, poetry, science fiction or fantasy. No reading fee. Preliminary letter, synopsis, sample chapter and sae essential.

Authors include Andrew Baker, Julia Bell, Bill Broady, Meg Cabot, Simon Conway, Terry Darlington, Fiona Gibson, Justin Hill, Maria McCann, Adam MacQueen, Ian Marchant, Lembit Opik MP, Prof Charles Pasternak, Kirsty Scott, Peter Shapiro, Bernadette Strachan, Elizabeth Woodcraft. Founded 1998.

Christine Green Authors' Agent*

6 Whitehorse Mews, Westminster Bridge Road, London SE1 7QD
tel 020-7401 8844 *fax* 020-7401 8860
website www.christinegreen.co.uk

Fiction and general non-fiction. Full-length MSS (home 10%, overseas 20%). Works in conjunction with agencies in Europe and Scandinavia. No reading fee, but preliminary letter and return postage essential. Founded 1984.

Louise Greenberg Books Ltd*

The End House, Church Crescent, London N3 1BG
tel 020-8349 1179 *fax* 020-8343 4559
email louisegreenberg@msn.com

Full-length MSS (home 15%, overseas 20–25%). Literary fiction and non-fiction. No reading fee. Return postage and sae essential. No telephone enquiries. Founded 1997.

Greene & Heaton Ltd*

37 Goldhawk Road, London W12 8QQ
tel 020-8749 0315 *fax* 020-8749 0318
email info@greeneheaton.co.uk
website www.greeneheaton.co.uk
Contacts Carol Heaton, Judith Murray, Antony Topping, Will Francis

All types of fiction and non-fiction (home 10–15%, USA/translation 20%). No poetry ororiginal scripts for theatre, film or TV. Send a covering letter, synopsis and first 3 chapters with sae and/or return postage. Email submissions considered at discretion. Overseas associates worldwide.

Clients include Bill Bryson, Jan Dalley, Suzannah Dunn, Marcus du Sautoy, Hugh Fearnley-Whittingstall, Michael Frayn, P.D. James, Jonathan Jones, William Leith, William Shawcross, Sarah Waters Jackie Wullschlager. *Children's authors* include Helen Craig, Joshua Doder, Amber Deckers. Founded 1963.

Gregory & Company Authors' Agents*

3 Barb Mews, London W6 7PA
tel 020-7610 4676 *fax* 020-7610 4686
email info@gregoryandcompany.co.uk (general enquiries), maryjones@gregoryandcompany.co.uk (submissions)
website www.gregoryandcompany.co.uk
Contacts Jane Gregory, Emma Dunford (editorial), Claire Morris (rights)

Fiction and general non-fiction (home 15%, USA/translation/radio/film/TV 20%). Special interests (fiction): literary, commercial, women's fiction, crime, suspense and thrillers. Particularly interested in books which will also sell to publishers abroad. No original plays, film or TV scripts (only published books are sold to film and TV), science fiction, fantasy, poetry, academic or children's books. No reading fee. Editorial advice given to own authors. No unsolicited MSS: send preliminary letter with CV, synopsis, first 3 chapters and future writing plans plus return postage. Short submissions (3pp) by fax or email. Represented throughout Europe, Asia and USA. Founded 1987.

David Grossman Literary Agency Ltd

118B Holland Park Avenue, London W11 4UA
tel 020-7221 2770 *fax* 020-7221 1445

Full-length MSS (home 10–15%, overseas 20% including foreign agent's commission, performance rights 15%). Works in conjunction with agents in New York, Los Angeles, Europe, Japan. No reading fee but preliminary letter required. No submissions by fax or email. Founded 1976.

Marianne Gunn O'Connor Literary Agency

Morrison Chambers, Suite 17, 32 Nassau Street, Dublin 2, Republic of Ireland
email mgoclitagency@eircom.net
Contact Marianne Gunn O' Connor

Commercial and literary fiction, non-fiction, biography, children's fiction (UK 15%, overseas 20%, film/TV 20%). Send preliminary letter plus half-page synopsis and first 50pp. Translation rights handled by Vicki Satlow Literary Agency, Milan.

Clients include Cecelia Ahern, Chris Binchy, Ken Bruen, Claudia Carroll, Julie Dam, Noelle Harrison, Claire Kilroy, Patrick McCabe, Mike McCormack, Paddy McMahon, Anita Notaro, Morag Prunty. Founded 1996.

The Rod Hall Agency Ltd

6th Floor, Fairgate House, 78 New Oxford Street, London WC1A 1HB
tel 020-7079 7987 *fax* 020-7079 7988
email office@rodhallagency.com
website www.rodhallagency.com
Director Charlotte Mann, Martin Knight

Specialises in writers for stage, screen and radio but also deals in TV and film rights in novels and non-fiction (home 10%, overseas 15%). No reading fee.

Clients include Simon Beaufoy, Jeremy Brock, usan Hill, Liz Lochhead, Tim Lott, Martin McDonagh, Andrea Newman, Simon Nye, Ol Parker, Lucy Prebble, Laura Wade. Founded 1997.

Margaret Hanbury*

27 Walcot Square, London SE11 4UB
tel 020-7735 7680 *fax* 020-7793 0316

Personally run agency specialising in quality fiction and non-fiction (home 15%, overseas 20%). No unsolicited approaches accepted.

Authors include George Alagiah, J.G. Ballard, Simon Callow, Jordan, Judith Lennox. Founded 1983.

Antony Harwood Ltd

103 Walton Street, Oxford OX2 6EB
tel (01865) 559615 *fax* (01865) 310660
email mail@antonyharwood.com
website www.antonyharwood.com
Contacts Antony Harwood, James Macdonald Lockhart

General and genre fiction; general non-fiction (home 15%, overseas 20%). Will suggest revision. No reading fee.

Clients include Amanda Craig, Louise Doughty, Peter F. Hamilton, Alan Hollinghurst, A.L. Kennedy, Douglas Kennedy, Chris Manby, George Monbiot, Garth Nix, Tim Parks. Founded 2000.

A.M. Heath & Co. Ltd*

6 Warwick Court, London WC1R 5DJ
tel 020-7242 2811 *fax* 020-7242 2711
website www.amheath.com
Contacts William Hamilton, Sara Fisher, Victoria Hobbs, Evan Thorneycroft

Full-length MSS. Literary and commercial fiction and non-fiction, children's (home 15%, USA 20%, translation 20%), performance rights (15%). No science fiction, screenplays, poetry or short stories except for established clients. No reading fee. Agents in USA and all European countries and Japan.

Clients include Bella Bathurst, Anita Brookner, Helen Cresswell, Patricia Duncker, Geoff Dyer, Katie Fforde, Graham Hancock, Tobias Hill, Conn Iggulden, Hilary Mantel, Maggie O'Farrell, Tim Pears, Susan Price, Adam Thorpe, Barbara Trapido. Founded 1919.

hhb agency ltd

6 Warwick Court, London WC1R 5DJ
tel 020-7405 5525
email heather@hhbagency.com or james@hhbagency.com
website www.hhbagency.com
Contacts Heather Holden-Brown, James Pryor

Non-fiction: journalism, history and politics, popular culture, contemporary autobiography and biography, TV and entertainment, business, family memoir, food and cookery. 15%. No reading fee. Founded 2005.

David Higham Associates Ltd*

(incorporating Murray Pollinger)
5–8 Lower John Street, Golden Square, London W1F 9HA

tel 020-7434 5900 *fax* 020-7437 1072
email dha@davidhigham.co.uk
website www.davidhigham.co.uk
Managing Director Anthony Goff, *Books* Veronique Baxter, Lucy Firth, Anthony Goff, Bruce Hunter, Lizzy Kremer, Caroline Walsh, *Foreign Rights* Ania Corless, *Film/TV/Theatre* Gemma Hirst, Nicky Lund, Georgina Ruffhead

Agents for the negotiation of all rights in fiction, general non-fiction, children's fiction and picture books, plays, film and TV scripts (home 15%, USA/translation 20%, scripts 10%). Represented in all foreign markets. Preliminary letter and return postage essential. No reading fee. Founded 1935.

Vanessa Holt Ltd*

59 Crescent Road, Leigh-on-Sea, Essex SS9 2PF
tel (01702) 473787 *fax* (01702) 471890

General adult fiction and non-fiction (home 15%, overseas 20%, TV/film/radio 15%). Works in conjunction with foreign agencies in all markets. No reading fee. No unsolicited MSS and submissions by arrangement only. No overseas submissions. Founded 1989.

Valerie Hoskins Associates Ltd

20 Charlotte Street, London W1T 2NA
tel 020-7637 4490 *fax* 020-7637 4493
email vha@vhassociates.co.uk
Proprietor Valerie Hoskins, *Agent* Rebecca Watson

Film, TV and radio; specialises in animation (home 12.5%, overseas max. 20%). No unsolicited MSS; preliminary letter essential. No reading fee, but sae essential. Works in conjunction with US agents.

Tanja Howarth Literary Agency*

19 New Row, London WC2N 4LA
tel 020-7240 5553 *fax* 020-7379 0969
email tanja.howarth@btinternet.com

Full-length MSS. General fiction and non-fiction, thrillers, contemporary and historical novels (home 15%, USA/translation 20%). No unsolicited MSS, and no submissions by fax or email. No reading fee. Specialists in handling German translation rights. Represented in the USA by various agents.

Clients include Robert Loehr, Frank Schätzing, Patrick Süskind, Uwe Timm and the Estates of Joseph Roth and Heinrich Böll. Founded 1970.

ICM Books*

4–6 Soho Square, London W1D 3PZ
tel 020-7432 0800 *fax* 020-7432 0808
email icmbookslondon@icmtalent.com
Contact Kate Jones, Margaret Halton, Karolina Sutton, Elizabeth Iveson, Daisy Meyrick

Fiction and non-fiction. No unsolicited MSS; send a query letter, sample chapters and sae first. Division of International Creative Management Inc.

IMG UK Ltd

McCormack House, Burlington Lane, London W4 2TH

tel 020-8233 5000 *fax* 020-8233 6464
Agent Sarah Wooldridge

Celebrity books, sports-related books, non-fiction and how-to business books (home 15%, USA 20%, elsewhere 25%). No theatre, fiction, children's, academic or poetry. No reading fee.

Intercontinental Literary Agency*

Centric House, 390–391 Strand, London WC2R 0LT
tel 020-7240 4724
email ila@ila-agency.co.uk
Contacts Nicki Kennedy, Sam Edenborough, Mary Esdaile, Tessa Balshaw-Jones

Represents translation rights for PFD, London, Harold Matson Company Inc., New York, the Turnbull Agency (John Irving) Inc., and Lucas Alexander Whitley Ltd. Founded 1965.

International Scripts

1A Kidbrooke Park Road, London SE3 0LR
tel 020-8319 8666 *fax* 020-8319 0801
email internationalscripts@btinternet.com
Directors H.P. Tanner, J. Lawson

Specialises in full-length contemporary fiction, women's fiction, crime, biographies, business and general non-fiction (home 15%, overseas 20%), performance rights (15–20%); no poetry or short stories. Works with overseas agents. Preliminary letter and sae required. An editorial contribution plus return postage may be requested for reading MSS.

Authors include Jane Adams, Zita Adamson, Ashleigh Bingham, Simon Clark, Ann Cliff, David Stuart Davies, Dr James Fleming, June Gadsby, Peter Haining, Julie Harris, Robert A. Heinlein, Anna Jacobs, Margaret James, Anne Jones, Richard Laymon, Trevor Lummis, Margaret Muir, Nick Oldham, Chris Pascoe, Christine Poulson, Mary Ryan, John and Anne Spencer, Janet Woods. Founded 1979.

Barrie James Literary Agency

(including New Authors Showcase)
Rivendell, Kingsgate Close, Torquay, Devon TQ2 8QA
tel (01803) 326617
email mail@newauthors.org.uk
website www.newauthors.org.uk
Contact Barrie James

Internet site for new writers and poets to display their work to publishers.No unsolicited MSS. First contact: send sae or email. Founded 1997.

Janklow & Nesbit (UK) Ltd*

33 Drayson Mews, London W8 4LY
tel 020-7376 2733 *fax* 020-7376 2915
email queries@janklow.co.uk
Agents Tif Loehnis, Claire Paterson

Commercial and literary fiction and non-fiction. No unsolicited MSS. Send informative covering letter

and return postage with full outline (non-fiction), synopsis and 3 sample chapters (fiction). US and foreign rights handled by **Janklow & Nesbit Associates** in New York.

JMLA

The Basement, 94 Goldhurst Terrace, London NW6 3HS
tel 020-7372 8422, 020-7372 3140 *fax* 020-7372 8423
Managing Director Judy Martin

Non-fiction, biography, jazz and its origins and history, American jazz biographies, art and surrealism (home 15%, overseas 20%). No plays, poetry, cookery, gardening or children's stories. Translation rights handled by the **Marsh Agency Ltd**. No reading fee, but sae required for all unsolicited MSS, together with details of publishing history. Founded 1990.

Johnson & Alcock Ltd*

Clerkenwell House, 45–47 Clerkenwell Green, London EC1R 0HT
tel 020-7251 0125 *fax* 020-7251 2172
email info@johnsonandalcock.co.uk
Contacts Michael Alcock, Andrew Hewson, Anna Power, Merel Reinink

Full-length MSS (home 15%, US and translation 20%). Literary and commercial fiction, children's fiction; general non-fiction including current affairs, biography and memoirs, history, lifestyle, health and personal development. No poetry, screenplays, science fiction, technical or academic material. No unsolicited MSS; approach by letter in the first instance giving details of writing experience, plus synopsis. For fiction send one-page synopsis and first 3 chapters. Sae essential for response. No reading fee. No email submissions. Founded 1956.

Jane Judd Literary Agency*

18 Belitha Villas, London N1 1PD
tel 020-7607 0273 *fax* 020-7607 0623

General non-fiction and fiction (home 10%, overseas 20%). Special interests: women's fiction, crime, thrillers, narrative non-fiction. No short stories, film/ TV scripts, poetry or plays. No reading fee, but preliminary letter with synopsis, first chapter and sae essential. Works with agents in USA and most foreign countries. Founded 1986.

Michelle Kass Associates*

85 Charing Cross Road, London WC2H 0AA
tel 020-7439 1624 *fax* 020-7734 3394
Proprietor Michelle Kass

Full-length MSS. Literary fiction and drama scripts for film (home 10%, overseas 15–20%). Will suggest revision where appropriate. Works with agents overseas. No reading fee. Absolutely no unsolicited MSS without a preliminary phone call. Founded 1991.

Frances Kelly Agency*

111 Clifton Road, Kingston-upon-Thames, Surrey KT2 6PL

tel 020-8549 7830 *fax* 020-8547 0051

Full-length MSS. Non-fiction: general and academic, reference and professional books, all subjects (home 10%, overseas 20%), TV, radio (10%). No reading fee, but no unsolicited MSS; preliminary letter with synopsis, CV and return postage essential. Founded 1978.

Peter Knight Agency
20 Crescent Grove, London SW4 7AH
tel 020-7622 1467 *fax* 020-7622 1522
website www.knightfeatures.co.uk
Director Peter Knight, *Associates* Gaby Martin, Andrew Knight, Samantha Ferris

Motor sports, cartoon books, business, history and factual and biographical material. No poetry, science fiction or cookery. Overseas associates: United Media (USA), Auspac Media (Australia), Puzzle Company. No unsolicited MSS. Send letter accompanied by CV and sae with synopsis of proposed work.

Clients include Ralph Barker, Frank Dickens, John Dodd, Gray Jolliffe, Angus McGill, Chris Maslanka, Barbara Minto, Lisa Wild. Founded 1985.

LAW Ltd*
14 Vernon Street, London W14 0RJ
tel 020-7471 7900 *fax* 020-7471 7910
website www.lawagency.co.uk
Contacts Adult: Mark Lucas, Julian Alexander, Araminta Whitley, Alice Saunders, Lucinda Cook, Peta Nightingale, Lizzie Jones; Children's: Philippa Milnes-Smith, Helen Norris

Full-length commercial and literary fiction, non-fiction and children's books (home 15%, US and translation 20%). No fantasy (except children's), plays poetry or textbooks. Film and TV scripts handled for established clients only. Unsolicited MSS considered; send brief covering letter, short synopsis and 2 sample chapters. Sae essential. No emailed or disk submissions. Overseas associates worldwide. Founded 1996.

LBLA (Lorella Belli Literary Agency)*
54 Hartford House, 35 Tavistock Crescent, London W11 1AY
tel 020-7727 8547 *fax* (0870) 7874194
email info@lorellabelliagency.com
website www.lorellabelliagency.com
Proprietor Lorella Belli

Fiction and general non-fiction (home 15%, overseas 20%, dramatic 20%). Particularly interested in first-time writers, journalists, international and multicultural writing and books on Italy. No children's, science fiction, fantasy, academic, poetry, original scripts. No reading fee. May suggest revision. Send outline plus 2 chapters for non-fiction; synopsis and initial 3 chapters for fiction. Sae essential. Works with overseas and dramatic associates; represents American, Canadian, Australian and European agencies.

Authors include Sean Bidder, Zoë Brân, Scott Capurro, Sean Coughlan, Dario Fo, Jacopo Fo, Nino Filasto, Emily Giffin, Paul Martin, Nisha Minhas, Rick Mofina, Jennifer Ouellette, Grace Saunders, Dave Singleton, Rupert Steiner, Marcello Vannucci, Diana Winston. Founded 2002.

Barbara Levy Literary Agency*
64 Greenhill, Hampstead High Street, London NW3 5TZ
tel 020-7435 9046 *fax* 020-7431 2063
Director Barbara Levy, *Associate* John Selby (solicitor)

Full-length MSS. Fiction and general non-fiction (home 10%, overseas by arrangement). Film and TV rights for existing clients only. No reading fee, but preliminary letter with synopsis and sae essential. Translation rights handled by the Buckman Agency; works in conjunction with US agents. Founded 1986.

Limelight Management*
33 Newman Street, London W1T 1PY
tel 020-7637 2529 *fax* 020-7637 2538
email limelight.management@virgin.net
website www.limelightmanagement.com
Directors Fiona Lindsay, Linda Shanks

Full-length and short MSS. Food, wine, health, crafts, gardening, interior design (home 15%, overseas 20%), TV and radio rights (10–20%); will suggest revision where appropriate. No reading fee. Founded 1991.

The Christopher Little Literary Agency*
10 Eel Brook Studios, 125 Moore Park Road, London SW6 4PS
tel 020-7736 4455 *fax* 020-7736 4490
email info@christopherlittle.net
website www.christopherlittle.net
Contacts Christopher Little, Patrick Janson-Smith

Commercial and literary full-length fiction and non-fiction (home 15%; USA, Canada, translation, audio, motion picture 20%). No poetry, plays, science fiction, fantasy, textbooks, illustrated children's or short stories. Film scripts for established clients only. No reading fee. First contact – send detailed preliminary letter in the first instance with synopsis, first 2–3 chapters and sae. Founded 1979.

Authors include Steve Barlow and Steve Skidmore, Paul Bajoria, Will Dawes, Janet Gleeson, Pete Howells, Carol Hughes, Alastair MacNeil, Christopher Matthew, Robert Mawson, Haydn Middleton, Shiromi Pinto, A.J. Quinnell, Robert Radcliffe, Dr Nicholas Reeves, J.K. Rowling, Darren Shan, Wladyslaw Szpilman, John Watson, Anne Zouroudi.

London Independent Books
26 Chalcot Crescent, London NW1 8YD
tel 020-7706 0486 *fax* 020-7724 3122
Proprietor Carolyn Whitaker

Specialises in commercial, fantasy and teenage fiction, show business, travel. Full-length MSS (home 15%, overseas 20%). Will suggest revision of promising MSS. No reading fee.

Authors include Eric Braun, Joe Delaney, Keith Gray, Elizabeth Kay, Tim Mackintosh-Smith, Glenn Mitchell, Connie Monk, Richard Morgan, Kevin Rushby, Chris Wooding. Founded 1971.

Andrew Lownie Literary Agency*
17 Sutherland Street, London SW1V 4JU
tel 020-7828 1274 *fax* 020-7828 7608
email lownie@globalnet.co.uk
website www.andrewlownie.co.uk
Director Andrew Lownie

Full-length MSS. Biography, history, reference, current affairs, and packaging journalists and celebrities for the book market (worldwide 15%). No reading fee; will suggest a revision.

Authors include Juliet Barker, the Joyce Cary Estate, Tom Devine, Jonathan Fryer, Laurence Gardner, Timothy Good, David Hasselhoff, Lawrence James, Damien Lewis, Julian Maclaren-Ross Estate, Norma Major, Sir John Mills, Tom Pocock, Nick Pope, Martin Pugh, John Rae, Desmond Seward, David Stafford, Alan Whicker; *The Oxford Classical Dictionary*, *The Cambridge Guide to Literature in English*. Founded 1988.

Lucas Alexander Whitley – see LAW Ltd

Lucy Luck Associates
20 Cowper Road, London W3 6PZ
tel 020-8992 6142
email lucy@lucyluck.com
website www.lucyluck.com
Contact Lucy Luck

Adult quality fiction and non-fiction (home 10%, overseas 20%, films/TV 15%). No reading fee. Will suggest revision.

Authors include Tom Chesshyre, Jon Hotten, Doug Johnstone, Lorelei Mathias, Ewan Morrison, Philip Oceallaigh, Catherine O'Flynn. Founded 2006.

Jennifer Luithlen Agency
88 Holmfield Road, Leicester LE2 1SB
tel 0116-273 8863 *fax* 0116-273 5697
Agents Jennifer Luithlen, Penny Luithlen

Not looking for new clients. Children's and adult fiction (home 15%, overseas 20%), performance rights (15%). Founded 1986.

Lutyens & Rubinstein*
231 Westbourne Park Road, London W11 1EB
tel 020-7792 4855 *fax* 020-7792 4833
email name@lutyensrubinstein.co.uk
Directors Sarah Lutyens, Felicity Rubinstein
Submissions Susannah Godman

Fiction and non-fiction, commercial and literary (home 15%, overseas 20%). Send outline/2 sample chapters and sae. No reading fee. Founded 1993.

Duncan McAra
28 Beresford Gardens, Edinburgh EH5 3ES
tel 0131-552 1558 *fax* 0131-552 1558
email duncanmcara@hotmail.com

Literary fiction; non-fiction: art, architecture, archaeology, biography, military, Scottish, travel (home 10%, overseas 20%). Preliminary letter with sae essential. No reading fee. Founded 1988.

Eunice McMullen Children's Literary Agent Ltd
Low Ibbotsholme Cottage, Off Bridge Lane, Troutbeck Bridge, Windermere, Cumbria LA23 1HU
tel (01539) 448551
email eunicemcmullen@totalise.co.uk
website www.eunicemcmullen.co.uk
Director Eunice McMullen

All types of children's books, particularly picture books and older fiction (home 10%, overseas 15%). No unsolicited scripts. Telephone enquiries only. Founded 1992.

Authors include Wayne Anderson, Sam Childs, Caroline Jayne Church, Jason Cockcroft, Ross Collins, Charles Fuge, Maggie Kneen, David Melling, Angela McAllister, Angie Sage, Gillian Shields, Susan Winter. Founded 1992.

Andrew Mann Ltd*
(in association with Jane Conway-Gordon)
1 Old Compton Street, London W1D 5JA
tel 020-7734 4751 *fax* 020-7287 9264
email manscript@onetel.com
Contacts Anne Dewe, Tina Betts, Sacha Elliot

Full-length MSS. Scripts for TV, cinema, radio and theatre (home 15%, USA and Europe 20%). Associated with agents worldwide. No reading fee. Unsolicited MSS with preliminary letter, first 3 chapters and sae. Email synopses submissions only; no attachments. Founded 1968.

Sarah Manson Literary Agent
6 Totnes Walk, London N2 0AD
tel 020-8442 0396
email info@sarahmanson.com
website www.sarahmanson.com
Proprietor Sarah Manson

Specialises exclusively in fiction for children and young adults (home 10%, overseas 20%). Send letter, brief author biography, one-page synopsis, first 3 chapters with sae. See website for full submission guidelines. Founded 2002.

Marjacq Scripts
34 Devonshire Place, London W1G 6JW
tel 020-7935 9499 *fax* 020-7935 9115
email enquiries@marjacq.com
website www.marjacq.com
Contact Philip Patterson (books), Luke Speed (film/TV)

All full-length MSS (home 10%, overseas 20%), including commercial and literary fiction and non-fiction, crime, thrillers, commercial, women's fiction, children's, science fiction, history, biography, sport, travel, health. No poetry. Send first 3 chapters with synopsis. May suggest revision. Film and TV rights, screenplays, radio plays, documentaries, screenplays/radio plays: send full script with 1–2 page short synopsis/outline. Strong interest in writer/directors: send show reel with script. Also looking for documentary concepts and will accept proposals from writer/directors. Sae essential for return of submissions.

Clients include: Victoria Arch, Richard Asplin, Angela Churm, Catrin Collier, John Connor, Richard Craze, James Follett, Christopher Gofford, Rosie Goodwin, Jasper Graham, Rebecca Hobbs, Ros Jay, Claes Johansen, Jeannie Johnson, Sophie King, Stuart MacBride, Juliet McKeon, John Meyers, Pat Mills, Col Spector, Michael Taylor, R.D. Wingfield and the Estate of George Markstein. Founded 1974.

The Marsh Agency Ltd*
11–12 Dover Street, London W1S 4LJ
tel 020-7399 2800 *fax* 020-7399 2801
email submissions@marsh-agency.co.uk
website www.marsh-agency.co.uk
Managing Director Paul Marsh, *Rights Director* Camilla Ferrier, *Agents* Geraldine Cooke, Jessica Wollard, Leyla Moghadam, Caroline Hardman (junior agent)

Founded as international rights specialists for British, American and Canadian agencies. Expanded to act as agents handling fiction and non-fiction, specialising in authors with international potential. See website for futher information on individual agents' areas of interest. No reading fee. Unsolicited submissions considered: send a brief email enquiry with outline (non-fiction) or synopsis and 2 chapters (fiction). See also **Paterson Marsh Ltd**. Founded 1994.

Blanche Marvin
21A St John's Wood High Street, London NW8 7NG
tel 020-7722 2313 *fax* 020-7722 2313

Full-length MSS (15%), performance rights. No reading fee but return postage essential.
Authors include Christopher Bond.

MayerBenham Ltd
55 Athenlay Road, London SE15 3EN
tel/fax 020-7277 8560
email simon@mayerbenham.co.uk
Directors Simon Benham, Jo Mayer

Non-fiction. Specialises in popular culture, humour, music, history, business (home 10%). No reading fee. Will suggest revision.
Authors include Keith Allen, Jacqueline Doherty, Peter Fisk, Will Hodgkinson, Tony Husband, The Idler, Abby Lee, Dan Kieran, Danielle Proud, David Taylor, Ian Vince, Chris Yates. Founded 2002.

MBA Literary Agents Ltd*
(incorporating Merric Davidson Literary Agency)
62 Grafton Way, London W1T 5DW
tel 020-7387 2076 *fax* 020-7387 2042
email firstname@mbalit.co.uk
website www.mbalit.co.uk
Contacts Diana Tyler, John Richard Parker, Meg Davis, Laura Longrigg, David Riding, Susan Smith, Sophie Gorell Barnes

Fiction and non-fiction, and TV, film, radio and theatre scripts (home 15%, overseas 20%; theatre, TV, radio 10%; films 10–20%). No unsolicited material. Works in conjunction with agents in most countries. UK representative for the Donald Maass Agency, the Martha Millard Agency, the Frances Collin Agency and the Jabberwocky Literary Agency. Founded 1971.

William Morris Agency (UK) Ltd*
52–53 Poland Street, London W1F 7LX
tel 020-7534 6800 *fax* 020-7534 6900
website www.wma.com
Managing Director Caroline Michel, *Books* Eugenie Furniss, Lucinda Prain, Rowan Lawton, *TV* Holly Pye, Isabella Zoltowski

Worldwide theatrical and literary agency with offices in New York, Beverly Hills, Nashville, Miami and Shanghai. Handles film and TV scripts, TV formats; fiction and general non-fiction (film/TV 10%, UK books 15%, USA books and translation 20%). No science fiction or fantasy; send MSS sample of approx. 30–50pp with letter and one-page synopsis. No reading fee. London office founded 1965.

Laura Morris Literary Agency
21 Highshore Road, London SE15 5AA
tel 020-7732 0153 *fax* 020-7732 9022
email laura.morris@btconnect.com
Director Laura Morris

Literary fiction, film studies, biography, media, cookery, culture/art, humour (home 10%, overseas 20%). No unsolicitied MSS, no children's books.
Authors include Peter Cowie, Christobel Kent, Laurence Marks and Maurice Gran, the Barbara Pym Estate, David Thomson, John Travolta, Brian Turner, Janni Visman. Founded 1998.

Judith Murdoch Literary Agency*
19 Chalcot Square, London NW1 8YA
tel 020-7722 4197
Contact Judith Murdoch

Full-length fiction only, especially accessible literary and commercial women's fiction (home 15%, overseas 20%). No science fiction/fantasy, poetry, short stories or children's. Approach by letter, *not* telephone, sending the first 2 chapters and synopsis. Submissions by email cannot be considered. Return postage/sae essential. Editorial advice given; no reading fee. Translation rights handled by the **Marsh Agency Ltd**. Founded 1993.

Clients include Alison Bond, Anne Bennett, Meg Hutchinson, Lisa Jewell, Pamela Jooste, Eve Makis.

Maggie Noach Literary Agency*
22 Dorville Crescent, London W6 0HJ
tel 020-8748 2926 *fax* 020-8748 8057
email m-noach@dircon.co.uk

Very few new clients taken on as it is considered vital to give individual attention to each author's work. High-quality full-length fiction; general non-fiction (especially biography, travel, history); children's books (text only) for reading age 8 upwards. Material submitted on an exclusive basis preferred (home 15%, USA/translation generally 20%). No short stories, poetry, plays, screenplays, cookery, gardening, Mind, Body & Spirit, scientific/academic/specialist non-fiction or any illustrated books. Send a brief description of the book plus 2–3 sample chapters. Return postage essential. Email attachments will not be opened and faxed submissions will not be considered. No reading fee. Founded 1982.

Andrew Nurnberg Associates Ltd*
Clerkenwell House, 45–47 Clerkenwell Green, London EC1R 0QX
tel 020-7417 8800 *fax* 020-7417 8812

Specialises in the sale of translation rights.

Alexandra Nye, Writers & Agents
Craigower, 6 Kinnoull Avenue, Dunblane, Perthshire FK15 9JG
tel (01786) 825114
Director Alexandra Nye

Literary fiction, Scottish history, biographies; no poetry or plays (home 10%, overseas 20%, translation 15%). No phone calls please. Preliminary letter with synopsis preferred; sae essential for return. Reading fee for supply of detailed report on MSS. Founded 1991.

David O'Leary Literary Agency
10 Lansdowne Court, Lansdowne Rise, London W11 2NR
tel/fax 020-7229 1623
email d.o'leary@virgin.net

Popular and literary fiction and non-fiction. Special interests: Ireland, history, popular science (Fees: home 10%, overseas 20%, performance rights 15%). No reading fee. Write, call or email before submitting MSS. Please enclose sae.
Authors include Alexander Cordell, Donald James, Nick Kochan, Jim Lusby, Derek Malcolm, Daniel O'Brien, Ken Russell. Founded 1988.

Deborah Owen Ltd*
78 Narrow Street, Limehouse, London E14 8BP
tel 020-7987 5119/5441 *fax* 020-7538 4004
Contact Deborah Owen

Small agency specialising in only two authors: Delia Smith and Amos Oz. No new authors. Founded 1971.

Paterson Marsh Ltd*
(merged with the Marsh Agency Ltd 2001)
11–12 Dover Street, London W1S 4LJ
tel 020-7399 2800 *fax* 020-7399 2801
email submissions@patersonmarsh.co.uk
website www.patersonmarsh.co.uk
Contacts Mark Paterson, Stephanie Ebdon

Book-length MSS; general but with special experience in psychoanalysis, psychotherapy, history and education (20% worldwide including sub-agents' commission). No fiction, articles or short stories except for existing clients. No children's books. Preliminary letter with synopsis, sample material and return postage essential.
Authors include Sigmund Freud, Anna Freud, Hugh Brogan, Donald Winnicott, Peter Moss, Sir Arthur Evans, Dorothy Richardson, Hugh Schonfield, Georg Groddeck, Patrick Casement, John Seely. Founded 1955.

John Pawsey
60 High Street, Tarring, Worthing, West Sussex BN14 7NR
tel (01903) 205167 *fax* (01903) 205167

General non-fiction only, particularly biography, popular culture and sport. Preliminary letter and return postage with all correspondence essential. No submissions by email. Works in association with agencies in the USA, Europe and the Far East. Will suggest revision if MS sufficiently promising. No reading fee.
Authors include David Ashforth, Jennie Bond, William Fotheringham, Don Hale, Patricia Hall, Elwyn Hartley Edwards, Dr David Lewis, Anne Mustoe and Kathryn Spink. Founded 1981.

Maggie Pearlstine Associates Ltd*
31 Ashley Gardens, Ambrosden Avenue, London SW1P 1QE
tel 020-7828 4212 *fax* 020-7834 5546
email post@pearlstine.co.uk

General non-fiction and fiction. Special interests: history, current affairs, biography, health (home 10–12.5%; overseas, journalism and media 20%). Translation rights handled by **Gillon Aitken Associates Ltd**. No children's, poetry, horror, science fiction, short stories or scripts. Seldom takes on new authors. Prospective clients should write an explanatory letter and enclose a sae and the first chapter only. No submissions accepted by fax, email or from abroad. No reading fee.
Authors include John Biffen, Matthew Baylis, Kate Smith-Bingham, Menzies Campbell, Frank Dobson, Kim Fletcher, Toby Green, Roy Hattersley, Thea Jourdan, Charles Kennedy, Anders Larsen, Victoria Lambert, Mark Leonard, Angela Levin, Quentin Letts, Ian Mitchell, Claire Macdonald, Dr Raj Persaud, Prof Lesley Regan, Steve Richards, Hugo Rifkind, Winifred Robinson, Jackie Rowley, Henrietta Spencer-

Churchill, Prof Kathy Sykes, Gregor Townsend, Prof Robert Winston. Founded 1989.

PFD (The Peters Fraser & Dunlop Group Ltd)*

Drury House, 34–43 Russell Street, London WC2B 5HA
tel 020-7344 1000 *fax* 020-7836 9539
website www.pfd.co.uk
Joint Chairmen Maureen Vincent and St John Donald, *Books* Caroline Dawnay, Michael Sissons, Pat Kavanagh, Charles Walker, Rosemary Scoular, Robert Kirby, Simon Trewin, James Gill, Carol Macarthur, Sophie Laurimore, Anna Webber, *Children's books* Rosemary Canter, Alison Kain, *Translation rights* Intercontinental Literary Agency, *PFD New York* Zoë Pagnamenta, Mark Reiter, *Film/TV/theatre agents* Natasha Galloway, Anthony Jones, Tim Corrie, Charles Walker, St John Donald, Rose Cobbe, Jago Irwin, Hannah Begbie

Represents authors of fiction and non-fiction (home 10%; USA/translation 20%), children's writers, screenwriters, playwrights, directors, documentary makers, technicians, presenters and actors throughout the world. See website for submission guidelines.

Pollinger Ltd*

(formerly Laurence Pollinger Ltd, successor of Pearn, Pollinger and Higham)
9 Staple Inn, Holborn, London WC1V 7QH
tel 020-7404 0342 *fax* 020-7242 5737
email info@pollingerltd.com, permissions@pollingerltd
website www.pollingerltd.com
Managing Director Lesley Pollinger, *Agents* Joanna Devereux, Tim Bates, *Consultants* Leigh Pollinger, Joan Deitch

All types of general trade adult and children's fiction and non-fiction books; intellectual property developments, illustrators/photographers (home 15%, translation 20%). Overseas, media and theatrical associates. No unsolicited material.

Clients include Michael Coleman, Catherine Fisher, Philip Gross, Catherine Johnson, Gary Latham, Kelly McKain, Gary Paulsen, Jeremy Poolman, Nicholas Rhea and Sue Welford. Also the estates of H.E. Bates, Louis Bromfield, Erskine Caldwell, Rachel Carson, D.H. Lawrence, John Masters, W.H. Robinson, Eric Frank Russell, Clifford D. Simak and other notables. Founded 1935.

Shelley Power Literary Agency Ltd*

13 rue du Pre Saint Gervais, 75019 Paris, France
tel 0142 38 36 49 *fax* 0140 40 70 08
email shelley.power@wanadoo.fr

General fiction and non-fiction. Full-length MSS (home 10%, USA and translation 19%). No children's books, poetry or plays. Works in conjunction with agents abroad. No reading fee, but preliminary letter with return postage as from UK or France essential. No submissions by email. Also based in the UK. Founded 1976.

Puttick Agency*

46 Brookfield Mansions, Highgate West Hill, London N6 6AT
tel 020-8340 6383 *fax* 0870 751 8098
email enquiries@puttick.com
website www.puttick.com
Director Elizabeth Puttick

Full-length MSS (home 15%, overseas 20%). General non-fiction with special interest in self-help, mind, body & spirit, health, childcare, cookery, business, science, biography, history, current affairs, women's issues, illustrated books, TV and film tie-ins. No fiction, poetry, screenplays, drama, children's books. No reading fee. Preliminary enquiries by email (preferred) or post; see website for details. Return postage essential.

Authors include William Bloom, Robin Bloor, Nirmála Herzia, Martin Lewis, Emma Restall Orr. Founded 1995.

PVA Management Ltd

Hallow Park, Worcester WR2 6PG
tel (01905) 640663 *fax* (01905) 641842
email pva@pva.co.uk
Managing Director Paul Vaughan

Full-length MSS. Non-fiction only (home 15%, overseas 20%, performance rights 15%). Please send synopsis and sample chapters together with return postage.

Redhammer Management Ltd

186 Bickenhall Mansions, Bickenhall Street, London W1U 6BX
tel 020-7224 1748 *fax* 020-7224 1802
email info@redhammer.info
website www.redhammer.info
Vice President Peter Cox

Specialises in works with international potential (home 17.5%, overseas 20%). Unpublished authors must be professional in their approach and have major international potential, ideally book, film and/or TV. Submissions must follow the guidelines given on the website. Do not send unsolicited MSS by post. No radio or theatre scripts. No reading fee.

Clients include Martin Bell OBE, Nicholas Booth, Mihir Bose, John Brindley, Brian Clegg, Joe Donnelly, Audrey Eyton, Senator Orrin Hatch, Amanda Lees, Dirk Maggs, David McIntee, Hon. Nicholas Monson, Michelle Paver, Harriet Smart, David Soul, Carolyn Soutar, Carole Stone, Prof. Donald Trelford, Justin Wintle, David Yelland. Founded 1993.

The Lisa Richards Agency

46 Upper Baggot Street, Dublin 4, Republic of Ireland
tel (01) 660 3534 *fax* (01) 660 3545

email faith@lisarichards.ie
website www.lisarichards.ie
Contact Faith O'Grady

Fiction and general non-fiction (home 10%, UK 15%, USA/translation 20%, film/TV 15%). Approach with proposal and sample chapter for non-fiction, and 3–4 sample chapters and synopsis for fiction (sae essential). Translation rights handled by the **Marsh Agency Ltd**. No reading fee.

Authors include June Considine, Judi Curtin, Denise Deegan, Christine Dwyer Hickey, Karen Gillece, Tara Heavey, Paul Howard (Ross O'Carroll-Kelly), Arlene Hunt, Roisin Ingle, Alison Jameson, Declan Lynch, Martin Malone, Roisin Meaney, Jennifer MacCann, Pauline McLynn, Sarah O'Brien (Helena Close and Trisha Rainsford), Hector O'LEochagáin, Damien Owens, Kevin Rafter. Founded 1998.

Robinson Literary Agency Ltd

Block A511, The Jam Factory, 27 Green Walk, London SE1 4TT
tel 020-7096 1460, 020-7243 6326
email info@rlabooks.co.uk
website www.rlabooks.co.uk
Contact Peter Robinson (Managing Director), Sam Copeland

Fiction, general non-fiction, popular culture (home/TV/radio 10–15%, overseas 20%). Documentaries and TV presenters. No reading fee. Will suggest revision.

Authors include John Guy, Steve Jones, Ian Rankin, David Starkey. Established 2005.

Rogers, Coleridge & White Ltd*

20 Powis Mews, London W11 1JN
tel 020-7221 3717 *fax* 020-7229 9084
Managing Director Peter Straus, *Directors* Deborah Rogers, Gill Coleridge, Patricia White (USA, children's), David Miller, Laurence Laluyaux, Stephen Edwards, Zoe Waldie

Full-length book MSS, including children's books (home 10%, USA 15%, translation 20%). No unsolicited MSS, and no submissions by fax or email. Founded 1967.

Elizabeth Roy Literary Agency

White Cottage, Greatford, Nr Stamford, Lincs. PE9 4PR
tel (01778) 560672 *fax* (01778) 560672

Children's fiction and non-fiction – writers and illustrators (home 15%, overseas 20%). Send preliminary letter, synopsis and sample chapters with names of publishers and agents previously contacted. Return postage essential. No reading fee. Founded 1990.

Uli Rushby-Smith Literary Agency

72 Plimsoll Road, London N4 2EE
tel 020-7354 2718 *fax* 020-7354 2718

Director Uli Rushby-Smith

Fiction and non-fiction, literary and commercial (home 15%, USA/foreign 20%). No poetry, plays or film scripts. Send outline, sample chapters (no disks) and return postage. No reading fee. UK representatives of **Curtis Brown Ltd**, New York (children's books) and Columbia University Press (USA). Founded 1993.

Rosemary Sandberg Ltd

6 Bayley Street, London WC1B 3HE
tel 020-7304 4110 *fax* 020-7304 4109
email rosemary@sandberg.demon.co.uk
Directors Rosemary Sandberg, Ed Victor

Children's writers and illustrators, general fiction and non-fiction. Absolutely no unsolicited MSS: client list is full. Founded 1991.

The Sayle Literary Agency*

8B King's Parade, Cambridge CB2 1SJ
tel (01223) 303035 *fax* (01223) 301638
Proprietor Rachel Calder

Fiction: general, literary and crime. Non-fiction: current affairs, social issues, travel, biographies, history (home 15%, USA/translation 20%). No plays, poetry, textbooks, children's, technical, legal or medical books. No reading fee but preliminary letter and return postage essential. Overseas associates: Dunow & Carlson Agency, Darhansoff, Verrill and Feldman, Anne Edelstein Literary Agency, **New England Publishing Associates**, USA. Translation rights handled by the **Marsh Agency Ltd**. Film and TV rights handled by **Sayle Screen Ltd**.

Sayle Screen Ltd

11 Jubilee Place, London SW3 3TD
tel 020-7823 3883 *fax* 020-7823 3363
email info@saylescreen.com
website www.saylescreen.com
Agents Jane Villiers, Matthew Bates, Toby Moorcroft

Specialises in scripts for film, TV, theatre and radio (home 10%, overseas 15–20%). No reading fee. Preliminary letter and return postage essential. No email submissions. Represents film and TV rights in fiction and non-fiction for the **Sayle Literary Agency** and **Greene and Heaton Ltd**. Works in conjunction with agents in New York and Los Angeles.

Scott Ferris Associates

Brynfield, Reynoldston, Swansea SA3 1AE
tel (01792) 390009
email scottferris@macunlimited.net
Partners Gloria Ferris and Rivers Scott

General fiction and non-fiction (home 15%, overseas/TV/radio 20%). No unsolicited MSS or submissions by email. Preliminary letter and postage essential. Reading fee by arrangement. Founded 1981.

The Sharland Organisation Ltd

The Manor House, Manor Street, Raunds, Northants. NN9 6JW

tel (01933) 626600 *fax* (01933) 624860
email tsoshar@aol.com
website www.sharlandorganisation.co.uk
Directors Mike Sharland, Alice Sharland

Specialises in film, TV, stage and radio rights throughout the world (home 15%, overseas 20%). Preliminary letter and return postage is essential. No reading fee. Works in conjunction with overseas agents. Founded 1988.

Anthony Sheil in association with Gillon Aitken Associates

18–21 Cavaye Place, London SW10 9PT
tel 020-7373 8672 *fax* 020-7373 6002
email anthony@gillonaitken.co.uk
website www.gillonaitkenassociates.co.uk
Proprietor Anthony Sheil

Quality fiction and non-fiction (home 10%, overseas 20%). No reading fee. Works in conjunction with **Gillon Aitken Associates Ltd**.

Authors include Caroline Alexander, John Banville, Josephine Cox, John Fowles, John Keegan, Robert Wilson.

Sheil Land Associates Ltd*

(incorporating Richard Scott Simon Ltd 1971 and Christy & Moore Ltd 1912)
52 Doughty Street, London WC1N 2LS
tel 020-7405 9351 *fax* 020-7831 2127
email info@sheilland.co.uk
Agents UK & US Sonia Land, Vivien Green, Ben Mason, *Film/theatre/TV* Sophie Janson, Emily Hayward, *Foreign* Gaia Banks

Quality literary and commercial fiction and non-fiction, including: politics, history, military history, gardening, thrillers, crime, romance, drama, biography, travel, cookery, humour, UK and foreign estates (home 15%, USA/translation 20%). Also theatre, film, radio and TV scripts. Welcomes approaches from new clients either to start or to develop their careers. Preliminary letter with sae essential. No reading fee. Overseas associates: Georges Borchardt, Inc. (Richard Scott Simon). US film and TV representation: CAA, APA and others.

Clients include Peter Ackroyd, Pam Ayres, Hugh Bicheno, Melvyn Bragg, Steven Carroll, David Cohen, Anna del Conte, Elizabeth Corley, Seamus Deane, Robert Green, Bonnie Greer, Susan Hill, Richard Holmes, HRH The Prince of Wales, Mark Irving, Ian Johnstone, Simon Kernick, Richard Mabey, Michael Moorcock, Graham Rice, Steve Rider, Martin Riley, Diane Setterfield, Tom Sharpe, Martin Stephen, Jeffrey Tayler, Andrew Taylor, Rose Tremain, Barry Unsworth, Kevin Wells, Prof. Stanley Wells, John Wilsher, Paul Wilson, Chris Woodhead and the Estates of Catherine Cookson, Patrick O'Brian and Jean Rhys. Founded 1962.

Caroline Sheldon Literary Agency Ltd*

London office 70–75 Cowcross Street, London EC1M 6EJ

tel 020-7336 6550
Mailing address for MSS Thorley Manor Farm, Thorley, Yarmouth PO41 0SJ
tel (01983) 760205
Contacts Caroline Sheldon, Penny Holroyde

Adult fiction, in particular women's (both commercial and literary) and human interest non-fiction (home 10%–15%, USA/translation 20%). Also full-length children's fiction, younger children's fiction, picture books and picture book artists. No TV/film scripts unless by book-writing clients. Send submissions to the Isle of Wight address and include a letter describing your ambitions, a synopsis, the first 3 chapters of your proposal and an sae with sufficient postage for return. Founded 1985.

Jeffrey Simmons

15 Penn House, Mallory Street, London NW8 8SX
tel 020-7224 8917
email jasimmons@btconnect.com

Specialises in fiction (no science fiction, horror or fantasy), biography, autobiography, show business, personality books, law, crime, politics, world affairs. Full-length MSS (home from 10%, overseas from 15%). Will suggest revision. No reading fee, but preliminary letter essential.

Sinclair-Stevenson

3 South Terrace, London SW7 2TB
tel 020-7581 2550 *fax* 020-7581 2550
Directors Christopher Sinclair-Stevenson, Deborah Sinclair-Stevenson

Full-length MSS (home 10%, USA/translation 20%). General – no children's books. No reading fee; will suggest a revision. Founded 1995.

Robert Smith Literary Agency Ltd*

12 Bridge Wharf, 156 Caledonian Road, London N1 9UU
tel 020-7278 2444 *fax* 020-7833 5680
email robertsmith.literaryagency@virgin.net
Directors Robert Smith, Anne Smith

Non-fiction only: autobiography and biography, topical subjects, history, lifestyle, popular culture, entertainment, true crime, health and nutrition, illustrated books (home 15%, overseas 20%). No unsolicited MSS. No reading fee. Will suggest revision.

Authors include Kate Adie (serialisations), Martin Allen, Amanda Barrie (serialisations), Kevin Booth, Stewart Evans, Neil and Christine Hamilton, James Haspiel, Judy Huxtable, Albert Jack, Lois Jenkins, Roberta Kray, Mike Reid, Prof. William Rubinstein, Keith Skinner, Douglas Thompson. Founded 1997.

The Standen Literary Agency

20 Twyford Court, Fortis Green, London N10 3ES
tel/fax 020-8444 1641
email info@standenliteraryagency.com

website www.standenliteraryagency.com
Director Yasmin Standen

Literary and commercial fiction and children's fiction and picture books (home 15%, overseas 20%). Interested in new writers. Send first 3 chapters, a synopsis (one side of A4) and a covering letter by post only in first instance (no submissions via email; submit the entire MS of children's stories (500 words and under). Include postage for return of MSS. No reading fee.

Authors include Zara Kane, Zoe Marriott, Andrew Murray, Jonathan Yeatman-Biggs. Founded 2004.

Abner Stein*

10 Roland Gardens, London SW7 3PH
tel 020-7373 0456 *fax* 020-7370 6316
Contact Caspian Dennis, Arabella Stein

Fiction, general non-fiction and children's (home 10%, overseas 20%). Not taking on any new clients at present.

Micheline Steinberg Associates

104 Great Portland Street, London W1W 6PE
tel 020-7631 1310
email info@steinplays.com
website www.steinplays.com
Agents Micheline Steinberg, Matt Connell, *Assistant* Helen MacAuley

Represents writers for theatre, TV, film, radio and animation. Film and TV rights in fiction and non-fiction on behalf of book agents (home 10%, overseas 15–20%). Works in association with agents in USA and overseas. No reading fee. Return postage essential. Industry recommendation preferred. Founded 1987.

Rochelle Stevens & Co.

2 Terretts Place, Upper Street, London N1 1QZ
tel 020-7359 3900 *fax* 020-7354 5729
email info@rochellestevens.com
Proprietor Rochelle Stevens, *Associates* Frances Arnold, Lucy Fawcett

Drama scripts for film, TV, theatre and radio (home 10%, overseas 15%). Preliminary letter, CV and sae essential. No reading fee. Founded 1984.

Shirley Stewart Literary Agency

3rd Floor, 21 Denmark Street, London WC2H 8NA
tel 020-7836 4440 *fax* 020-7836 3482
Director Shirley Stewart

Specialises in literary fiction and general non-fiction (home 10–15%, overseas 20%). No poetry, plays, film scripts, science fiction, fantasy or children's books. No reading fee. Send preliminary letter, synopsis and first 3 chapters plus return postage. Founded 1993.

The Susijn Agency Ltd

3rd Floor, 64 Great Titchfield Street, London W1W 7QH
tel 020-7580 6341 *fax* 020-7580 8626
email info@thesusijnagency.com
website www.thesusijnagency.com
Agents Laura Susijn, Nicola Barr

Specialises in world rights in English and non-English language literature: literary fiction and general non-fiction (home 15%, overseas 20%, theatre/film/TV/radio 15%). Send synopsis and 2 sample chapters. No reading fee.

Authors include Peter Ackroyd, Uzma Aslam Khan, Robin Baker, Abdelkader Benali, Ottavio Cappellani, Robert Craig, Tessa De Loo, Olivia Fane, Radhika Jha, Jeffrey Moore, Anita Nair, Karl Shaw, Paul Sussman, Dubravka Ugrešić, Alex Wheatle, Adam Zameenzad. Founded 1998.

Talent Media Group t/a ICM

Oxford House, 76 Oxford Street, London W1D 1BS
tel 020-7636 6565 *fax* 020-7323 0101
email writers@icmlondon.co.uk
Directors Duncan Heath, Susan Rodgers, Lyndsey Posner, Sally Long-Innes, Paul Lyon-Maris, *Literary Agents* Susan Rodgers, Jessica Sykes, Catherine King, Greg Hunt, Hugo Young, Michael McCoy, Duncan Heath, Paul Lyon-Maris

Specialises in scripts for film, theatre, TV, radio (home 10%, overseas 10%).

The Tennyson Agency

10 Cleveland Avenue, London SW20 9EW
tel 020-8543 5939
email adam@tenagy.co.uk
website www.tenagy.co.uk
Theatre, TV & Film Scripts Christopher Oxford, *Arts/Humanities* Adam Sheldon

Scripts and related material for theatre, film and TV (home 15%, overseas 20%). No reading fee.

Clients include Vivienne Allen, Tony Bagley, Alastair Cording, Caroline Coxon, Iain Grant, Jonathan Holloway, Philip Hurd-Wood, Joanna Leigh, Steve Macgregor, Antony Mann, John Ryan, Walter Saunders, Graeme Scarfe, Diana Ward and the Estate of Julian Howell. Founded 2002.

J.M. Thurley Management

Archery House, 33 Archery Square, Walmer, Deal, Kent CT14 7JA
tel (01304) 371421 *fax* (01304) 371416
email JMThurley@aol.com
Contact Jon Thurley

Specialises in commercial and literary full-length fiction and commercial work for film and TV. No plays, poetry, short stories, articles or fantasy. No reading fee but preliminary letter and sae essential. Editorial/creative advice provided to clients (home 15%, overseas 20%). Links with leading US and European agents. Founded 1976.

Lavinia Trevor*

The Glasshouse, 49A Goldhawk Road, London
W12 8QP
tel 020-8749 8481 *fax* 020-8749 7377

Literary and commercial fiction, and non-fiction, including popular science, for the general reader. No children's books, poetry or science fiction/fantasy. No reading fee. Brief autobiographical letter and approx. first 50pp required plus sae. Founded 1993.

Jane Turnbull*

London office 58 Elgin Crescent, London W11 2JJ
tel 020-7727 9409
Mailing address Barn Cottage, Veryan Green, Truro
TR2 5QA
tel (01872) 501317

Fiction and non-fiction (home 10%, USA/translation 20%), performance rights (15%). No science fiction, romantic fiction, children's or short stories. Works in conjunction with Gillon Aitken Associates Ltd for sale of translation rights. No reading fee. Preliminary letter and sae essential; no unsolicited MSS. Founded 1986.

TV Writers Ltd

74 The Drive, Fulham Road, London SW6 6JH
tel/fax 020-7371 8474
email tvwriters@gmail.com
website www.tvwriters.net
Company Director/Agent Marie-Louise Hogan

Specialises in scripts for TV, radio and film: comedy, drama and factual (10–15%). No reading fee. Send preliminary letter (sae essential). Occasionally corporate, commercial and books for existing clients.

Writers include Ali Crockatt, Simon Dean, Lee Stuart Evans, Arthur Mathews, Jez Stevenson. Founded 2005.

United Authors Ltd

11–15 Betterton Street, London WC2H 9BP
tel 020-7470 8886 *fax* 020-7470 8887
email editorial@unitedauthors.co.uk

Fiction, non-fiction, children's, biography, travel. Full-length MSS (home 12%, overseas 20%), short MSS (12%/20%), film and radio (15%/20%), TV (15%/15%). Will suggest revision.

Authors include Charlotte Bingham, Terence Brady, Peter Willet, and the Estate of John Bingham. Founded 1998.

Ed Victor Ltd*

6 Bayley Street, Bedford Square, London WC1B 3HE
tel 020-7304 4100 *fax* 020-7304 4111
Executive Chairman Ed Victor, *Joint Managing Directors* Sophie Hicks, Margaret Phillips, *Directors* Carol Ryan, Graham C. Greene CBE, Leon Morgan, Hitesh Shah, *Editorial Director* Philippa Harrison

Fiction, non-fiction and children's books (home 15%, USA 15%, children's 10%, translation 20%).

No short stories, poetry or film/TV scripts or plays. No reading fee. No unsolicited MSS. No response to submissions by email. Represented in all foreign markets.

Authors include John Banville, Herbie Brennan, Eoin Colfer, Sir Ranulph Fiennes, Frederick Forsyth, A.A. Gill, Josephine Hart, Jack Higgins, Nigella Lawson, Kathy Lette, Allan Mallinson, Andrew Marr, Janet Street-Porter and the Estates of Douglas Adams, Raymond Chandler, Dame Iris Murdoch, Sir Stephen Spender, Irving Wallace. Founded 1976.

Wade and Doherty Literary Agency Ltd

33 Cormorant Lodge, Thomas More Street, London
E1W 1AU
tel 020-7488 4171 *fax* 020-7488 4172
email rw@rwla.com, bd@rwla.com
website www.rwla.com
Chairman Mark Barty-King, *Directors* Robin Wade, Broo Doherty

General fiction and non-fiction (home 10%, overseas 20%). No poetry, plays or short stories. See website for submission guidelines. Email submissions preferred. New authors welcome. No reading fee. Founded 2001.

Watson, Little Ltd*

Lymehouse Studios, 38 Georgiana Street, London
NW1 0EB
tel 020-7486 5935 *fax* 020-7486 6051
email office@watsonlittle.com

Commercial women's, crime and literary fiction. Non-fiction special interests include history, science, popular psychology, self-help and general leisure books. Also children's fiction and non-fiction (home 15%, USA 20%, translation 20%). No short stories, poetry, TV, play or film scripts. Not interested in purely academic writers. No emails or unsolicited MSS. Informative preliminary letter and synopsis with return postage essential. Film and TV associates: the **Sharland Organisation Ltd** and **MBA Literary Agents Ltd**. Translation rights sold by the **Marsh Agency** in the UK; and Howard Morhaim and Folio Literary Management in the US.

A.P. Watt Ltd*

20 John Street, London WC1N 2DR
tel 020-7405 6774
fax 020-7831 2154 (books), 020-7430 1952 (drama)
email apw@apwatt.co.uk
website www.apwatt.co.uk
Directors Caradoc King, Linda Shaughnessy, Derek Johns, Georgia Garrett, Natasha Fairweather, Sheila Crowley

Full-length MSS; dramatic works for all media (home 15%, USA and foreign 20% including commission to foreign agent). No poetry. No reading fee. Does not accept unsolicited MSS or any other material. In the first instance send a query letter. Founded 1875.

Josef Weinberger Plays Ltd

(formerly Warner/Chappell Plays Ltd)
12–14 Mortimer Street, London W1T 3JJ
tel 020-7580 2827 *fax* 020-7436 9616

Specialises in stage plays. Works in conjunction with
overseas agents. No unsolicited MSS; preliminary
letter essential. Founded 1938.

Rebecca Winfield

84 Cowper Road, London W7 1EJ
tel 020-8567 6738
email rebecca.winfield@btopenworld.com
Proprietor Rebecca Winfield

Quality fiction and non-fiction, including history,
biography and popular culture (home15%, overseas
20%). No scripts, plays, poetry, science fiction,
fantasy or children's. Send covering letter, synopsis
and first 3 chapters with sae for reply. No submission
via email. No reading fee. Founded 2003.

Eve White

1A High Street, Kintbury, Berks. RG17 9TJ
tel (01488) 657656
email evewhite@btinternet.com
website www.evewhite.co.uk
Contact Eve White

Commercial and literary fiction, non-fiction,
children's fiction and picture books (home 15%,
overseas 20%). Send brief synopsis and 2–3 chapters
and word count with a covering letter, biography and
sae. Include email address. No submissions by email.
No reading fee. Will suggest revision where
appropriate.

    Authors include Teresa Cooper, Shanta Everington,
Margie Hann-Syme, Abie Longstaff, Vijay Medtia,
Peter J. Murray, Gillian Rogerson, Andy Stanton,
Emma Tennant. Founded 2003.

Dinah Wiener Ltd*

12 Cornwall Grove, London W4 2LB
tel 020-8994 6011 *fax* 020-8994 6044
Director Dinah Wiener, *Associate* Marianna Wiener

Full-length MSS only, fiction and general non-fiction
(home 15%, overseas 20%), film and TV in
association (15%). No plays, scripts, poetry, short
stories or children's books. No reading fee, but
preliminary letter and return postage essential.

Jonathan Williams Literary Agency

Rosney Mews, Upper Glenageary Road, Glenageary,
Co. Dublin, Republic of Ireland
tel (01) 2803482 *fax* (01) 2803482
Director Jonathan Williams

General fiction and non-fiction, preferably by Irish
authors (home 10%). Will suggest revision; no
reading fee unless a very fast decision is required.
Return postage appreciated (no British stamps –
please use IRCs). Sub-agents in Holland, Italy,
France, Spain, Japan. Founded 1981.

Elisabeth Wilson

24 Thornhill Square, London N1 1BQ

Rights agent and consultant; illustrated books, non-
fiction (no children's). No reading fee. Founded
1979.

The Wylie Agency (UK) Ltd

17 Bedford Square, London WC1B 3JA
tel 020-7908 5900 *fax* 020-7908 5901
President Andrew Wylie

Literary fiction and non-fiction (home 10%, overseas
20%, USA 15%). No unsolicited MSS; send
preliminary letter with 2 sample chapters and sae in
first instance. Founded 1996.

Literary agents overseas

Before submitting material, writers are advised to send a preliminary letter with an sae or IRC (International Reply Coupon) and to ascertain terms.

ARGENTINA

International Editors Co.
Avenida Cabildo 1156, 1426 Buenos Aires
tel 54-11-4788-2992 *fax* 54-11-4786-0888
email costa@iecobaires.com.ar

The Nancy H. Smith Literary Agency
(formerly The Lawrence Smith Agency)
Ayacucho 1867, 2в, Buenos Aires 1112
tel (54 11) 4804 5508 *fax* (54 11) 4804 5508
email meg@interlink.com.ar
London 30 Acton Lane, London W4 5ED
tel 020-8995 4769 *fax* 020-8747 4012
email distobart@aol.com
Contact Margaret Murray, Diana Stobart

Plays and general fiction. No unsolicited MSS. No response to submissions by email. Founded 1938.

AUSTRALIA

Bryson Agency Australia Pty Ltd
PO Box 226, Finders Lane PO, Melbourne 8009
tel (613) 9620 9100 *fax* (613) 9621 2788
email agency@bryson.com.au
website www.bryson.com.au
Contact Fran Bryson

Represents writers operating in all media: print, film, TV, radio, the stage and electronic derivatives; specialises in representation of book writers. Query first before sending unsolicited MSS. Not accepting until further notice.

Curtis Brown (Australia) Pty Ltd
PO Box 19, Paddington, Sydney, NSW 2021
tel (02) 9331 5301/9361 6161 *fax* (02) 9360 3935
email info@curtisbrown.com.au
Agents Fiona Inglis, Pippa Masson

No reading fee.

Diversity Management
PO Box 1449, Darlinghurst, Sydney, NSW 1300
tel 612-9130-4305 *fax* 612-9365-1426
email bill@diversitym.com
website www.diversitym.com
Director Bill Tikos

All genres of non-fiction, illustrated books (home/overseas 20%). No reading fee. Founded 2001.

BRAZIL

Agencia Literária BMSR
Rua Visconde de Pirajá, 414 s1 1108 Ipanema, 22410–002 Rio de Janeiro, RJ
tel (55-21) 2287-6299 *fax* (55-21) 2267-6393
email lucia@bmsr.com.br
website www.bmsr.com.br
Contacts Lucia de Mello e Souza Riff, Laura Riff, João Paulo Riff

Home 10%, overseas 20%. No reading fee. Founded 1991.

Tassy Barham Associates
23 Elgin Crescent, London W11 2JD
fax 020-7229 8667
email tassy@tassybarham.com
Proprietor Tassy Barham

Specialises in representing British and American authors, agents and publishers in Brazil. Founded 1999.

Karin Schindler and Suely Pedro dos Santos Rights Representatives
Caixa Postal 19051, 04505–970 São Paulo, SP
tel 55-11-5041-9177 *fax* 55-11-5041-9077
email kschind@terr.com.br,
suelypedrosantos@uol.com.br

CANADA

Acacia House Publishing Services Ltd
51 Acacia Road, Toronto, Ontario M4S 2K6
tel 416-484-8356
email fhanna.acacia@rogers.com
Managing Director Mrs Frances A. Hanna, *Vice President* Bill Hanna

Literary fiction/non-fiction, quality commercial fiction, most non-fiction, except business books (15% English worldwide, 25% translation, performance 20%). No science fiction, horror or occult. Works with overseas agents. Query first with sample of 50pp max. Include return postage. No reading fee. Founded 1985.

Authors' Marketing Services Ltd
PO Box 84668, 2336 Bloor Street West, Toronto M6S 4Z7
tel 416-763 8797 *fax* 416-763-1504
email authorslhoffman@cs.com
Director Larry Hoffman

Adult fiction, biography and autobiography (home 15%, overseas 20%). Reading fee charged for unpublished writers; will suggest a revision. Founded 1978.

The Cooke Agency Inc.
278 Bloor Street East, Suite 305, Toronto, Ontario M4W 3M4

tel 416-406-3390 *fax* 416-406-3389
email agents@cookeagency.ca
website www.cookeagency.ca
President Dean Cooke

Literary fiction and non-fiction (home 15%, overseas 20%). Will contact senders of unsolicited materials only if interested. British co-agent: **Greene & Heaton Ltd**. Founded 1992.

Anne McDermid & Associates Ltd
83 Willcocks Street, Toronto, Ontario M5S 1C9
tel 416-324 8845 *fax* 416-324 8870
email anne@mcdermidagency.com
website www.mcdermidagency.com
Director Anne McDermid

Literary fiction and non-fiction, and quality commercial fiction; no children's literature (home 15%, US 15%, overseas 20%). Reading fee. Founded 1996.

Bella Pomer Agency Inc.
355 St Clair Avenue West, Suite 801, Toronto, Ontario M5P 1N5
tel 416-920-4949
President Bella Pomer

Not considering new clients. Founded 1978.

Carolyn Swayze Literary Agency Ltd
WRPO Box 39588, White Rock, British Columbia V4B 5L6
tel 604-538-3478
email carolyn@swayzeagency.com
website www.swayzeagency.com
Proprietor Carolyn Swayze

Literary and commercial fiction, some juvenile and teen books. No romance, science fiction, poetry, screenplays, or picture books. Eager to discover lively, thought-provoking narrative non-fiction, especially in the fields of science, history, travel, politics, and memoir. Founded 1994.

Submission details No telephone calls: make contact either by post or send short queries by email, providing a brief résumé which describes who you are. Include publication credits, writing awards, education and experience relevant to your book project. Include a one-page synopsis of the book and – if querying via post – include sase for the return of your materials. Do not include original photographs or artwork. Include sase if acknowledgement of receipt of materials is required. Will not open unsolicited attachments. Allow 6 weeks or longer for a reply.

EASTERN EUROPE

Aura-Pont, Theatrical and Literary Agency Ltd
Radlická 99, Prague 5, Czech Republic
tel (420) 2 51 55 02 07 *fax* (420) 2 51 55 02 07
email aura-pont@aura-pont.cz

website www.aura-pont.cz
Director Daniela Gadasová

Handles authors' rights in theatre, film, TV, radio, software – both Czech and foreign (home 10%, overseas 15%). Founded 1990.

DILIA
Krátkého 1, 190 03 Prague 9, Czech Republic
tel (420) 2 83 89 36 03 *fax* (420) 2 83 89 35 99
email info@dilia.cz
website www.dilia.cz

Theatrical and literary agency.

Lex Copyright
Szemere utca 21, 1054 Budapest, Hungary
tel (36) 1 332 9340 *fax* (36) 1 331 6181
email lexcopy.bp@mail.datanet.hu
Director Dr Gyorgy Tibor Szanto

Specialises in representing American and British authors in Hungary. Founded 1991.

Lita
Mozartova 9, CS–81530, Bratislava, Slovakia
tel (421) 7 313623 *fax* (421) 7 580 2246

Slovak literary agency.

Andrew Nurnberg Associates Prague, s.r.o.
Seifertova 81, 130 00 Prague 3, Czech Republic
tel (420) 222 782 041 *fax* (420) 222 782 308
email nurnprg@vol.cz
Contacts Petra Tobisková, Jitka Nemeckova

Prava I Prevodi Literary Agency Permissions & Rights Ltd
Yu-Business Centre, Blvd Mihaila Pupina 10b/I, 5th Floor, Suite 4, 11070 Belgrade, Serbia and Montenegro
tel (381) 11 3119880 *fax* (381) 11 3119879
email ana@pip.co.yu office@pip.co.yu
Director Predraq Milenkovic, *Foreign Rights* Ana Milenkovic

Specialises in representing American and British authors in former Eastern Europe (15 languages). Founded 1983.

FRANCE

Agence Hoffman
77 Boulevard Saint-Michel, 75005 Paris
tel (1) 43 26 56 94 *fax* (1) 43 26 34 07
email info@agence-hoffman.com

Agence Michelle Lapautre
6 rue Jean Carriès, 75007 Paris
tel (1) 47 34 82 41 *fax* (1) 47 34 00 90
email lapautre@club-internet.fr

Bureau Littéraire International
1 rue Alfred Laurant, F–92100 Boulogne Billancourt
tel (1) 46 05 39 11
Contact Geneviéve Ulmann

La Nouvelle Agence
7 rue Corneille, 75006 Paris
tel (1) 43 25 85 60 *fax* (1) 43 25 47 98
email lnaparis@wanadoo.fr
Contacts Mary Kling, Vanessa Kling, Michèle Kanonidis

Promotion Littéraire
12 rue Pergolèse, 75116 Paris
tel (1) 45 00 42 10 *fax* (01) 45 00 10 18
email promolit@club-internet.fr
Director Mariella Giannetti

Fiction, essays. Founded 1977.

GERMANY (SEE ALSO SWITZERLAND)

Michael Meller Literary Agency
Sandstrasse 33, 80335 Munich
tel (089) 366371 *fax* (089) 366372
email info@melleragency.com
website www.melleragency.com

Full-length MSS. Fiction and non-fiction (home 15%, overseas 20%). No reading fee. Founded 1988.

Thomas Schlück GmbH
Literary Agency, Hinter der Worth 12, 30827 Garbsen
tel 05131-497560 *fax* 05131-497589
email mail@schlueckagent.com
website www.schlueckagent.com

No reading fee.

INDIA

Ajanta Books International
1 U.B. Jawahar Nagar, Bungalow Road, Delhi 110007
tel 27415016, 23926182 *fax* 91-11-27415016
email ajantabi@vsnf.com ajantabi@eth.net
Proprietor S. Balwant

Full-length MSS in social sciences and humanities (commission varies according to market – Indian books in Indian and foreign languages, foreign books into Indian languages). Will suggest revision; charges made if agency undertakes revision; reading fee. Founded 1975.

ITALY

Agenzia Letteraria Internazionale SRL
Via Valpetrosa 1, 20123 Milano
tel (02) 865445, 861572 *fax* (02) 876222
email alidmb@tin.it

Eulama SRL
Via Guido de Ruggiero 28, 00142 Rome
tel/fax (06) 540 7309
email eulama@fastwebnet.it
Directors Norbert von Prellwitz, Pina Ocello von Prellwitz

International licensing agency representing publishing houses, agents and authors of adult and children's books worldwide. General and literary fiction, non-fiction, academic works in humanities. Promoting Italian, German and Spanish language authors and publishers worldwide. Reading fee. Founded 1962.

Grandi & Associati SRL
Via Caradosso 12, 20123 Milan
tel (02) 469 55 41/481 89 62 *fax* (02) 481 95108
email agenzia@grandieassociati.it
website www.grandieassociati.it
Directors Laura Grandi, Stefano Tettamanti

Provides publicity and foreign rights consultation for publishers and authors as well as sub-agent services; will suggest revision where appropriate. Reading fee. Founded 1988.

ILA (International Literary Agency) USA
I–18010 Terzorio-IM
tel (018) 448 4048 *fax* (018) 448 7292
email books@librigg.com

Publishers' and authors' agent, interested only in series of bestselling and mass market books by proven, published authors with a track record. Also interested in published books on antiques and collectibles. No reading fee. Founded 1969.

New Blitz Literary & TV Agency
Via di Panico 67, 00186 Rome
postal address CP 30047–00193, Rome 47
tel (06) 686 4859 *fax* (06) 686 4859
email blitzgacs@inwind.it
Literary Department Giovanni A.S. Congiu

No reading fee.

Piergiorgio Nicolazzini Literary Agency
Via GB Moroni 22, Milano 20146
tel (02) 487 13365
email info@pnla.it
website www.pnla.it
Director Piergiorgio Nicolazzini

Literary and commerical fiction and non-fiction (home 10%, overseas 15–20%). No reading fee. Will suggest revision. Founded 1998.

JAPAN

The English Agency (Japan) Ltd
Sakuragi Building 4ᶠ, 6–7–3 Minami Aoyama, Minato-ku, Tokyo 107–0062
tel 03-3406 5385 *fax* 03-3406 5387

Managing Director Hamish Macaskill

Handles work by English-language writers living in Japan; arranges Japanese translations for internationally established publishers, agents and authors; arranges Japanese contracts for Japanese versions of all media. Standard commission: 10%. Own representatives in New York and London. No reading fee. Founded 1979.

THE NETHERLANDS

Internationaal Literatuur Bureau B.V.
Nieuwezÿds Voorburgwal 292 IV, 1012 RT Amsterdam, The Netherlands
tel (020) 330 6658 *fax* (020) 422 9210
email mkohn@planet.nl
website www.ilb.nu
Contacts Linda Kohn, Brigitte van der Klaauw

NEW ZEALAND

Glenys Bean Writer's Agent
PO Box 60509, Titirangi, Auckland
tel (09) 812 8486 *fax* (09) 812 8188
email g.bean@clear.net.nz
website www.glenysbean.com
Directors Fay Weldon, Glenys Bean

Adult and children's fiction, educational, non-fiction, film, TV, radio (10–20%). Send preliminary letter, synopsis and sae. No reading fee. Represented by **Sanford Greenburger Associates Ltd** (USA). Translation/foreign rights: the **Marsh Agency Ltd**. Founded 1989.

Michael Gifkins & Associates
PO Box 6496, Wellesley Street PO, Auckland 1000
tel (09) 523-5032 *fax* (09) 523-5033
email michael.gifkins@xtra.co.nz
Director Michael Gifkins

Literary and popular fiction, fine arts, children's and young adult fiction, substantial non-fiction (non-academic) co-publications (home 15%, overseas 20%). No reading fee. Will suggest revision. Founded 1985.

Playmarket
Level 2, 16 Cambridge Terrace, PO Box 9767, Wellington
tel (04) 3828462 *fax* (04) 3828461
website www.playmarket.org.nz
Director Mark Amery

Playwrights' agency and script advisory service. Its focus is the development and representation of New Zealand playwrights and their plays and it currently licences around 250 productions of New Zealand plays each year, both in New Zealand and around the world. Founded 1973.

Richards Literary Agency
postal address PO Box 31–240, Milford, Auckland 9
tel/fax (09) 410-0209
email rla.richards@clear.net.nz
Partners Ray Richards, Elaine Blake, Judy Bartlam, Frances Plumpton

Full-length MSS, fiction, non-fiction, adult, juvenile, educational, academic books; films, TV, radio (home/overseas 15%). Preliminary letter, synopsis with sae required. No overseas reading fee. Co-agents in London and New York. Founded 1977.

Total Fiction Services
PO Box 46-031, Park Avenue, Lower Hutt
tel/fax (04) 565 4429
email tfs@elseware.co.nz
website www.elseware.co.nz

General fiction, non-fiction, children's books. No poetry, or individual short stories or articles. Enquiries from New Zealand authors only. Email queries but no attachments. Hard copy preferred. No reading fee. Also offers assessment reports, mentoring and courses.

PORTUGAL

Ilidio da Fonseca Matos
Avenida Gomes Pereira, 105-3°–B, 1500–328 Lisbon
tel (21) 716 2988 *fax* (21) 715 4445
email ilidio.matos@oninet.pt

No reading fee.

SCANDINAVIA, INC. FINLAND AND ICELAND

Bookman Literary Agency
Bastager 3, DK–2950 Vedbaek, Denmark
tel (45) 45 89 25 20 *fax* (45) 45 89 25 01
email ihl@bookman.dk
Contact Mr Ib H. Lauritzen

Handles rights in Denmark, Sweden, Norway, Finland and Iceland for foreign authors.

Gösta Dahl & Son, AB
Enhörningsgränd 14, S–167 58 Bromma, Sweden
tel 08 25 62 35 *fax* 08 25 62 35

Leonhardt & Høier Literary Agency aps
Studiestraede 35, DK–1455 Copenhagen K, Denmark
tel (33) 13 25 23 *fax* (33) 13 49 92
email anneli@leonhardt-hoier.dk
website www.leonhardt-hoier.dk

No reading fee.

Lennart Sane Agency AB
Holländareplan 9, S–374 34 Karlshamn, Sweden
tel 0454 123 56 *fax* 0454 149 20

email lennart.sane@lennartsaneagency.com
website www.lennartsaneagency.com
Directors Lennart Sane, Elisabeth Sane, Philip Sane

Fiction, non-fiction, children's books. Founded 1969.

Sane Töregård Agency AB

Holländareplan 9, S–374 34 Karlshamn, Sweden
tel (46) 454 12356 *fax* (46) 454 14920
email ulf.toregard@sanetoregard.se
Directors Lennart Sane, Ulf Töregård

Represents authors, agents and publishers in Scandinavia and Holland for rights in fiction, non-fiction and children's books. Founded 1995.

SOUTH AFRICA

Frances Bond Literary Services

Westville, Westville North 3630, KwaZulu-Natal
tel (031) 2662007 *fax* (031) 2662007
email fbond@mweb.co.za
postal address PO Box 223, Westville 3630
Managing Editor Frances Bond, *Chief Editor* Eileen Molver

Full length MSS. Fiction and non-fiction; juvenile and children's literature. Consultancy service on contracts and copyright. Preliminary phone call or letter and sase required. Reading fee terms on application. Founded 1985.

Cherokee Literary Agency

3 Blythwood Road, Rondebosch, Cape 7700, South Africa
tel (021) 671 4508
email dklee@mweb.co.za
Director D.K. Lee

Children's picture books in translation (home 10%). Founded 1988.

Sandton Literary Agency

PO Box 785799, Sandton 2146
tel (011) 4428624
Directors J. Victoria Canning, M. Sutherland

Full-length MSS and screenplays; lecture agents. Professional editing. Reading fee for unpublished or self-published writers. Write enclosing sae or phone first. Works in conjunction with Renaissance-Swan Film Agency Inc., Los Angeles, USA. Founded 1982.

SPAIN

Agencia Literaria Carmen Balcells S.A.

Diagonal 580, 08021 Barcelona
tel 93-200-89-33 *fax* 93-200-70-41
email ag-balcells@ag-balcells.com
Contact Gloria Gutiérrez

International Editors Co., S.A.

c/Provenza 276, 1°, 08008 Barcelona
tel 93-215-88-12 *fax* 93-487-35-83
email ieco@internationaleditors.com

RDC Agencia Literaria SL

C. Fernando VI, No 13–15, Madrid 28004
tel 91-308-55-85 *fax* 91-308-56-00
Director Raquel de la Concha

Representing foreign fiction, non-fiction, children's books and Spanish authors. No reading fee.

Lennart Sane Agency AB

Paseo de Mejico 65, Las Cumbres-Elviria, E–29600 Marbella (Malaga)
tel 95-283-41-80 *fax* 95-283-31-96
email lennart.sane@lennartsaneagency.com
website www.lennartsaneagency.com

Fiction, non-fiction, children's books, film and TV scripts. Founded 1965.

Julio F. Yañez

Agencia Literaria S.L., Via Augusta 139, 6–2A, 08021 Barcelona
tel 93-200-71-07, 93-200-54-43 *fax* 93-200-76-56
email montse@yanezag.com

SWITZERLAND

Paul & Peter Fritz AG Literary Agency

Jupiterstrasse 1, CH–8032 Zürich
postal address Postfach 1773, CH–8032 Zürich
tel 41 44 388 41 40 *fax* 41 44 388 41 30
email info@fritzagency.com

Represents authors, agents and publishers in German-language areas. No reading fee.

Liepman AG

Maienburgweg 23, CH-8044 Zürich
tel (044) 261 76 60 *fax* (044) 261 01 24
email info@liepmanagency.com
Contacts Eva Koralnik, Ruth Weibel

Represents authors, agents and publishers from all over the world for German translation rights, and selected international authors for world rights. No reading fee.

Mohrbooks AG, Literary Agency

Klosbachstrasse 110, CH–8032 Zürich
tel (043) 244 8626 *fax* (043) 244 8627
email info@mohrbooks.com
website www.mohrbooks.com
Contacts Sabine Ibach, Sebastian Ritscher

No reading fee.

Neue Presse Agentur (NPA)

Haldenstrasse 5, Frauenfeld, CH–8500
tel (052) 721 43 74
Director René Marti

Looking for occasional contributors to write for German/Swiss papers and magazines in the German language. Founded 1950.

Niedieck Linder AG

Zollikerstrasse 87, Postbox, CH–8034 Zürich
tel (44) 381 65 92 *fax* (44) 381 65 13
website www.nlagency.ch

Represents German-language authors and Italian-language authors on the German market as well as major literary estates on a worldwide basis. No reading fee.

USA

Member of the Association of Authors' Representatives

AMG/Renaissance – see The Firm

The Axelrod Agency*

55 Main Street, PO Box 357, Chatham, NY 12037
tel 518-392-2100 *fax* 518-392-2944
President Steven Axelrod

Full-length MSS. Fiction and non-fiction (home 15%, overseas 20%), film and TV rights (15%); will suggest revision where appropriate. Works with overseas agents. No reading fee. Founded 1983.

The Balkin Agency Inc.*

PO Box 222, Amherst, MA 01004
tel 413-548-9835 *fax* 413-548-9836
email rick62838@crocker.com
Director Richard Balkin

Full-length MSS – adult non-fiction only (home 15%, overseas 20%). Query first. May suggest revision. No reading fee. European and British Representative: Chandler Crawford Agency USA.

Judy Boals Inc.*

307 West 38th Street, Suite 812, New York, NY 10018
tel 212-500-1424 *fax* 212-500-1426

Dramatic writing only, and only by recommendation.

Georges Borchardt Inc.*

136 East 57th Street, New York, NY 10022
tel 212-753-5785 *fax* 212-838-6518
Directors Georges Borchardt, Anne Borchardt

Full-length and short MSS (home/ British/ performance 15%, translations 20%). Agents in most foreign countries. No unsolicited MSS. No reading fee. Founded 1967.

Brandt & Hochman Literary Agents Inc.*

1501 Broadway, New York, NY 10036
tel 212-840-5760
Contact Carl Brandt, *British Representative* A.M. Heath & Co. Ltd

Full-length and short MSS (home 15%, overseas 20%), performance rights (15%). No reading fee.

The Helen Brann Agency Inc.*

94 Curtis Road, Bridgewater, CT 06752
tel 860-354-9580 *fax* 860-355-2572

Browne & Miller Literary Associates

(formerly Multimedia Product Development Inc.)
410 South Michigan Avenue, Suite 460, Chicago, IL 60605
tel 312-922-3063 *fax* 312-922-1905
website www.browneandmiller.com
Contact Danielle Egan-Miller

General fiction and non-fiction (home 15%, overseas 20%). Select young adult projects. Works in conjunction with foreign agents. Will suggest revision; no reading fee. Founded 1971.

Maria Carvainis Agency Inc.*

1350 Avenue of the Americas, Suite 2905, New York, NY 10019
tel 212-245-6365 *fax* 212-245-7196
President & Literary Agent Maria Carvainis, *Literary Agent* Donna Bagdasarian

Adult fiction and non-fiction (home 15%, overseas 20%). Fiction: all categories except science fiction and fantasy, especially literary and mainstream; mystery, thrillers and suspense; historical, Regency, young adult. Non-fiction: biography and memoir, health and women's issues, business, finance, psychology, popular science, popular culture. No reading fee. Query first; no unsolicited MSS. No queries by fax or email. Works in conjunction with foreign, TV and movie agents.

Frances Collin Literary Agent*

PO Box 33, Wayne, PA 19087-0033
tel 610-254-0555

Full-length MSS (home 15%, overseas 20%, performance rights 20%). Specialisations of interest to UK writers: mysteries, women's fiction, history, biography, science fiction, fantasy. No screenplays. No reading fee. No unsolicited MSS. Letter queries must include sufficient IRCs. Works in conjunction with agents worldwide. Founded 1948; successor to Marie Rodell-Frances Collin Literary Agency.

Don Congdon Associates Inc.*

156 Fifth Avenue, Suite 625, New York, NY 10010
tel 212-645-1229 *fax* 212-727-2688
email dca@doncongdon.com
Agents Don Congdon, Michael Congdon, Susan Ramer, Cristina Concepcion

Full-length and short MSS. General fiction and non-fiction (home 15%, overseas 19%, performance rights 15%). Works with co-agents overseas. No reading fee but no unsolicited MSS – query first with sase (no IRCs) or email for reply. Does not accept phone calls from querying authors. Founded 1983.

Richard Curtis Associates Inc.

171 East 74th Street, Floor 2, New York, NY 10021
tel 212-772-7363 *fax* 212-772-7393
website www.curtisagency.com
President Richard Curtis

All types of commercial non-fiction (home 15%, overseas 25%, film/TV 15%). Will suggest revision. No reading fee. Send sase with all queries. Foreign rights handled by Baror International. Founded 1970.

Curtis Brown Ltd*
10 Astor Place, New York, NY 10003
tel 212-473-5400
Branch office 1750 Montgomery Street, San Francisco, CA 94111
tel 415-954 8566
President Peter Ginsberg, *Ceo* Timothy Knowlton, *Contact* Query Dept

Fiction and non-fiction, juvenile, film and TV rights. No unsolicited MSS; query first with sase. No reading fee; no handling fees.

Joan Daves Agency
21 West 26th Street, New York, NY 10010
tel 212-685-2663 *fax* 212-685-1781
Contact Michele Rubin

One-page query letter (home 15%, overseas 20%, film 15%). No reading fee. Subsidiary of **Writers House LLC**. Founded in 1952 by Joan Daves.

Sandra Dijkstra Literary Agency*
PMB 515, 1155 Camino Del Mar, Del Mar, CA 92104-2605
tel 858-755-3115 *fax* 858-792-2822
President Sandra Dijkstra

Fiction and non-fiction: narrative, history, business, psychology, science, memoir/biography, contemporary, women's, suspense; selected children's projects (home 15%, overseas 20%). Works in conjunction with foreign and film agents. All submissions must include synopsis and sase (or IRC). No reading fee. Founded 1981.

Donadio & Olson Inc.*
121 West 27th Street, Suite 704, New York, NY 10001
tel 212-691-8077 *fax* 212-633-2837
email mail@donadio.com
Associates Edward Hibbert, Neil Olson, Ira Silverberg, Carrie Howland, Tom Eubanks

Literary fiction and non-fiction.

Dunham Literary, Inc.*
156 Fifth Avenue, Suite 625, New York, NY 10010–7002
website www.dunhamlit.com
Contact Jennie Dunham

Literary fiction and non-fiction, alternative spirituality, children's books (home 15%, overseas 20%). No reading fee. Founded 2000.

Dystel & Goderich Literary Management*
1 Union Square West, New York, NY 10003
tel 212-627-9100 *fax* 212-627-9313

website www.dystel.com
Contact Jane D. Dystel

Children's fiction and non-fiction (home 15%, overseas 19%). Handles picture books, fiction for 5–8 and 9–12 year-olds, teenage fiction, series fiction and non-fiction. Looking for quality young adult fiction. Also handles adult fiction and non-fiction. Send a query letter with a synopsis and up to 50pp of sample MS. No reading fee. Will suggest revision.

Children's authors include Deb Levine, Kelly McWilliams, Soyung Pak, Anne Rockwell, Bernadette Rossetti. Founded 1994.

Full-length and short MSS (home 15%, overseas 19%, film, TV and radio 15%). General fiction and non-fiction: literary and commercial fiction; narrative non-fiction; self-help; cookbooks; parenting; children's books; science fiction/fantasy. No reading fee. Founded 1994.

Ann Elmo Agency Inc.*
60 East 42nd Street, New York, NY 10165
tel 212-661-2880 *fax* 212-661-2883
Director Lettie Lee

Full-length fiction and non-fiction MSS (home 15%, overseas 20%), theatre (15%). Works with foreign agencies. No reading fee. Send query letter only with sase or IRC.

Diana Finch Literary Agency*
116 West 23rd Street, Suite 500, New York, NY 10011
tel 646-375-2081
email diana.finch@verizon.net
Owner Diana Finch

Memoirs, narrative non-fiction, literary fiction (home 15%, overseas 20%). No reading fee. Queries by email or letter only. No phone or fax. Founded 2003.

The Firm
(formerly AMG/Renaissance)
9465 Wilshire Boulevard, Beverly Hills, CA 90212
tel 310-860-8000 *fax* 310-860-8132
Contacts Alan Nevins, Irv Schwartz, Michael Prevett

Full-length MSS. Fiction and non-fiction, plays (home 15%, overseas 20%), film and TV rights (home 10%, overseas 20%), performance rights. No unsolicited MSS; query first, submit outline. No reading fee. Founded 1934.

Fletcher & Parry*
78 Fifth Avenue, 3rd Floor, New York, NY 10011
tel 212-614-0778 *fax* 212-614-0728
website www.fletcherparry.com
Directors Emma Parry, Christy D. Fletcher

Narrative non-fiction, science, history, biography, literary fiction (home 15%, overseas 20%). Founded 2002.

The Fox Chase Agency Inc.
701 Lee Road, Suite 102, Chesterbrook, PA 19087
tel 610-640-7560 *fax* 610-640-7562

No unsolicited MSS. No reading fee. Founded 1972.

Jeanne Fredericks Literary Agency Inc.*

221 Benedict Hill Road, New Canaan, CT 06840
tel 203-972-3011 *fax* 203-972-3011
email jfredrks@optonline.net

Quality non-fiction, especially health, science, women's issues, gardening, antiques and decorative arts, biography, cookbooks, popular reference, business, natural history (home 15%, overseas 20%). No reading fee. Query first, enclosing sase. Member of AAR and Authors Guild. Founded 1997.

Robert A. Freedman Dramatic Agency Inc.*

(formerly Harold Freedman Brandt & Brandt Dramatic Dept. Inc.)
1501 Broadway, Suite 2310, New York, NY 10036
tel 212-840-5760

Plays, motion picture and TV scripts. Send letter of enquiry first, with sase. No reading fee.

Samuel French Inc.*

45 West 25th Street, New York, NY 10010
tel 212-206-8990 *fax* 212-206-1429
President Charles R. Van Nostrand

Play publishers; authors' representatives. No reading fee.

Sarah Jane Freyman Literary Agency

(formerly Stepping Stone Literary Agency)
59 West 71st Street, Suite 9ʙ, New York, NY 10023
tel 212-362-9277 *fax* 212-501-8240
email sjfs@aol.com
President Sarah Jane Freymann

Book-length fiction and general non-fiction. Special interest in serious non-fiction, mainstream commercial fiction, contemporary women's fiction, Latino American, Asian American, African American fiction and non-fiction. Non-fiction: women's issues, biography, health/fitness, psychology, self-help, spiritual, natural science, cookbooks, pop culture. Works in conjunction with **Abner Stein** in London. No reading fee. Query with sase. Founded 1974.

Gelfman Schneider Literary Agents Inc.*

250 West 57th Street, Suite 2515, New York, NY 10107
tel 212-245-1993 *fax* 212-245-8678
Directors Jane Gelfman, Deborah Schneider

General adult fiction and non-fiction (home 15%, overseas 20%). Works in conjunction with **Curtis Brown**, London. Will suggest revision. No reading fee but please send sase for return of material. Query by post only.

Goodman Associates, Literary Agents*

500 West End Avenue, New York, NY 10024
tel 212-873-4806

Partners Arnold P. Goodman, Elise Simon Goodman

Adult book length fiction and non-fiction (home 15%, overseas 20%). No reading fee. Accept new clients by referral only. Founded 1976.

Sanford J. Greenburger Associates Inc.*

55 Fifth Avenue, New York, NY 10003
tel 212-206-5600 *fax* 212-463-8718
website www.greenburger.com
Contacts Heide Lange, Faith Hamlin, Daniel Mandel, Peter McGuigan, Matt Bialer

Fiction and non-fiction, film and TV rights. No unsolicited MSS; query first. No reading fee.

The Joy Harris Literary Agency Inc.*

156 Fifth Avenue, Suite 617, New York, NY 10010–7002
tel 212-924-6269 *fax* 212-924-6609
email gen.office@jhlitagent.com
President Joy Harris

John Hawkins & Associates Inc.*

(formerly Paul R. Reynolds Inc.)
71 West 23rd Street, Suite 1600, New York, NY 10010
tel 212-807-7040 *fax* 212-807-9555
website www.jhalit.com
President John Hawkins, *Vice-President* William Reiss, *Foreign Rights* Moses Cardona, *Other Agents* Warren Frazier, Anne Hawkins

Fiction, non-fiction, young adult. No reading fee. Founded 1893.

The Jeff Herman Agency LLC

PO Box 1522, Stockbridge, MA 01262
tel 413-298-0077 *fax* 413-298-8188
email jeff@jeffherman.com
website www.jeffherman.com

Business, reference, popular psychology, computers, health, spirituality, general non-fiction (home/ overseas 15%); will suggest revision where appropriate. Works with overseas agents. No reading fee. Founded 1986.

Frederick Hill Bonnie Nadell Inc.

1842 Union Street, San Francisco, CA 94123
tel 415-921-2910 *fax* 415-921-2802
Branch office 505 North Robertson Blvd, Los Angeles, CA 90048
tel 310-860-9605 *fax* 310-860-9672

Full-length fiction and non-fiction (home 15%, overseas 20%). Send query letter initially. Works in conjunction with agents in Scandinavia, France, Germany, Holland, Japan, Spain. No reading fee. Founded 1979.

IMG Literary – see Lisa Queen IMG Literary

International Creative Management Inc.

40 West 57th Street, New York, NY 10019
tel 212-556-5600 *fax* 212-556-5665

London office 4–6 Soho Square, London W1D 3PZ
tel 020-7432 0800 *fax* 020-7432 0808

No unsolicited MSS; send query letter.

Janklow & Nesbit Associates
445 Park Avenue, New York, NY 10022
tel 212-421-1700 *fax* 212-980-3671, 212-355 1403
email postmaster@janklow.com
Partners Morton L. Janklow, Lynn Nesbit, *Senior Vice President* Anne Sibbald, *Agents* Tina Bennett, Rebecca Gradinger, Luke Janklow, Richard Morris, Eric Simonoff, *Foreign rights* Cullen Stanley, Dorothy Vincent, Cecile Barendsma, Kate Schafer

Commercial and literary fiction and non-fiction. No unsolicited MSS. Works in conjunction with **Janklow & Nesbit (UK) Ltd**. Founded 1989.

JCA Literary Agency Inc.
174 Sullivan Street, New York, NY 10012
tel 212-807-0888
Contacts Tom Cushman, Melanie Meyers Cushman

Adult fiction, non-fiction and young adult. No unsolicited MSS; query first.

Keller Media Inc.
23852 West Pacific Coast Highway, Suite 701,
Malibu, CA 90265
tel 310-857-6828 *fax* 310-857-6373
email agent@kellermedia.com
website www.kellermedia.com
Ceo/Senior Agent Wendy Keller

Helps authors get publishing contracts and speaking engagements worldwide. Only non-fiction by credible experts: business, sales, management, marketing and finance; metaphysics: escoteric/New Age/spirituality/inspiration; history; science; biography (celebrity only); health and wellness; psychology; parenting; gift books, self-help; how-to. Email queries strongly preferred. Founded 1988.

Barbara S. Kouts, Literary Agent*
PO Box 560, Bellport, NY 11713
tel 631-286-1278 *fax* 631-286-1538

Fiction and non-fiction, children's (home 15%, overseas 20%). Works with overseas agents. No reading fee. No phone calls. Send query letter first. Founded 1980.

The Lazear Agency Inc.
431 2nd Street, Ste 300, Hudson, WI 54016
tel 715-531-0012 *fax* 715-531-0016
email admin@lazear.com
Contacts Jonathon Lazear, Christi Cardenas, Julie Mayo, Anne Blackstone

Fiction: full-length MSS; non-fiction: proposals. Adult fiction and non-fiction; film and TV rights; foreign language rights; audio, video and electronic rights (home 15%, overseas 20%). No reading fee. No

unsolicited MSS; 2–3 page query first with sase for response. No faxed queries. Founded 1984.

The Lescher Agency Inc.*
47 East 19th Street, New York, NY 10003
tel 212-529-1790 *fax* 212-529-2716
email susanlescher@aol.com
Director Susan Lescher

Fiction and non-fiction (home 15%, overseas 25%). Fiction – literary, mystery, fantasy (no sci-fi) and romance; non-fiction – biography, current affairs, law, popular culture and history. No unsolicited MSS; query first with sase, or email. No reading fee. Founded 1964.

Margret McBride Literary Agency*
7744 Fay Avenue, Suite 201, La Jolla, CA 92037
tel 858-454-1550 *fax* 858-454-2156
website www.mcbrideliterary.com
President Margret McBride

Business, mainstream fiction and non-fiction (home 15%, overseas 25%). No poetry or children's books. No reading fee. Submit query letter with sase to Margret McBride. Founded 1981.

Anita D. McClellan Associates*
464 Common Street, Suite 142, Belmont, MA 02478–2704
website www.anitamcclellan.com
Director Anita D. McClellan

General fiction and non-fiction. Full-length MSS (USA 15%, overseas 20%). Will suggest revision for agency clients. No unsolicited MSS. Send preliminary letter and sase bearing US postage or IRC. No email submissions.

McIntosh & Otis Inc.*
353 Lexington Avenue, New York, NY 10016
tel 212-687-7400 *fax* 212-687-6894
Adult Eugene H. Winick, Jonathan Lyons, Elizabeth Winick, *Juvenile* Edward Necarsulmer IV, *Film & TV* Evva Joan Pryor

Adult and juvenile literary fiction and non-fiction, film and TV rights. No unsolicited MSS; query first with outline, sample chapters and sase. No reading fee. Founded 1928.

Carol Mann Agency*
55 Fifth Avenue, New York, NY 10003
tel 212-206-5635 *fax* 212-675-4809
website www.carolmannagency.com
Associates Carol Mann, Emily Nurkin, Gareth Esersky

Psychology, popular history, biography, pop culture, general non-fiction; fiction (home 15%, overseas 20%). Works in conjunction with foreign agents. No reading fee. Founded 1977.

The Evan Marshall Agency*
Six Tristam Place, Pine Brook, NJ 07058-9445
tel 973-882-1122 *fax* 973-882-3099

email evanmarshall@thenovelist.com
website www.publishersmarketplace.com/members/
evanmarshall
President Evan Marshall

General fiction (home 15%, overseas 20%). Works in conjunction with overseas agents. Will suggest revision; no reading fee. Founded 1987.

The Marton Agency Inc.*

1 Union Square West, Suite 815, New York, NY 10003–3303
tel 212-255-1908 *fax* 212-691-9061
email info@martonagency.com
Owner Tonda Marton

Stage plays only.

Helen Merrill Ltd

295 Lafayette Street, Suite 915, New York, NY 10012

No unsolicited MSS. No books. No phone calls or faxes. Send query letter with professional recommendation and sase or email address.

William Morris Agency Inc.*

(incorporating the Writers Shop, formerly Virginia Barber Literary Agency)
1325 Avenue of the Americas, New York, NY 10019
tel 212-586-5100
website www.wma.com
Executive VP Owen Laster, *Senior VPs* Jennifer Rudolph Walsh, Suzanne Gluck, Joni Evans, Mel Berger, Jay Mandel, Tracy Fisher

General fiction and non-fiction (home 15%, overseas 20%, performance rights 15%). Will suggest revision. No reading fee.

Jean V. Naggar Literary Agency Inc.*

216 East 75th Street, Suite 1ᴇ, New York, NY 10021
tel 212-794-1082
President Jean V. Naggar, *Agents* Alice Tasman, Mollie Glick, Anne Engel, Jennifer Weltz (rights)

Mainstream commercial and literary fiction (no formula fiction); non-fiction: psychology, science, biography (home 15%, overseas 20%), performance rights (15%). Works in conjunction with foreign agents. No reading fee. Founded 1978.

New England Publishing Associates Inc.*

PO Box 5, Chester, CT 06412
tel 860-345-READ *fax* 860-345-3660
email nepa@nepa.com
website www.nepa.com
Contacts Elizabeth Frost-Knappman, Edward W. Knappman, Ron Formica, Kris Schiavi, Vicki Harlow

Serious non-fiction for the adult market (home 15%, overseas varies), performance rights (varies). Works in conjunction with foreign publishers. No reading fee; will suggest revision – if undertaken.

Representatives: Rachel Calder Sayles Literary Agency (London); **Michael Meller Literary Agency** (Germany); A. Mediation Littéraire (France); **ACER Agencia Literaría** (Spain); **Andrew Nurnberg Associates** (Hungary). Dramatic rights: Joel Gotler, IPG.

Harold Ober Associates Inc.*

425 Madison Avenue, New York, NY 10017
tel 212-759-8600 *fax* 212-759-9428
Directors Phyllis Westberg, Pamela Malpas

Full-length MSS (home 15%, British 20%, overseas 20%), performance rights (15%). Will suggest revision. No reading fee. Founded 1929.

Fifi Oscard Agency Inc.

110 W 40th Street, 16th Floor, New York, NY 10018
tel 212-764-1100 *fax* 212-840-5019
email agency@fifioscard.com
website www.fifioscard.com
Agents Peter Sawyer, Carolyn French, Carmen La Via, Kevin McShane, Ivy Fischer Stone, Jerome Rudes, Laura R. Paperny

Full-length MSS (home 15%, overseas 20%), theatrical performance rights (10%). Will suggest revision. Works in conjunction with many foreign agencies. No reading fee, but no unsolicited submissions.

James Peter Associates Inc.

PO Box 358, New Canaan, CT 06840
tel 203-972-1070 *fax* 203-972-1759
email gene_brissie@msm.com
Contacts Bert Holtje, Gene Brissie

Non-fiction, especially history, politics, popular culture, health, psychology, reference, biography (home 15%, overseas 20%). Foreign rights handled by: JPA. Will suggest revision. No reading fee. Founded 1971.

The Pimlico Agency Inc.

PO Box 20447, Cherokee Station, New York, NY 10021
tel 212-628-9729 *fax* 212-535-7861
Contacts Christopher Shepard, Catherine Brooks, *Directors* Kay McCauley, Kirby McCauley

Adult non-fiction and fiction. No unsolicited MSS.

PMA Literary and Film Management Inc.

Old Chelsea Station, PO Box 1817, New York, NY 10113
tel 212-929-1222 *fax* 212-206-0238
email pmalitfilm@aol.com
website www.pmalitfilm.com
President Peter Miller, *Development Associate* Kelly Skillen

Full-length MSS. Specialises in commercial fiction (especially thrillers), true crime, non-fiction (all types), and all books with global publishing and film/TV potential (home 15%, overseas 25%), films, TV (10–20%). Works in conjunction with agents worldwide. Preliminary enquiry with career goals, synopsis and résumé essential. Founded 1976.

Lisa Queen IMG Literary
825 Seventh Avenue, 9th Floor, New York, NY 10019
tel 212-489-5400 *fax* 212-246 1118

Fiction (no science fiction) and non-fiction. Send query letter with sase.

Helen Rees Literary Agency*
376 North Street, Boston, MA 02113–2103
tel 617-227 9014 *fax* 617-227 8762
email reesagency@reesagency.com
Contact Joan Mazmanian, *Associates* Ann Collette, Lorin Rees

Business books, self-help, biography, autobiography, political, literary fiction, memoirs, history, biography, current affairs (home 15%). No electronic submissions. No reading fee. Submit query letter with sase. Founded 1982.

The Angela Rinaldi Literary Agency*
PO Box 7877, Beverly Hill, CA 90212–7877
tel 310-842-7665 *fax* 310-877-3143
email amr@rinaldiliterary.com
President Angela Rinaldi

Mainstream and literary adult fiction; non-fiction (home 15%, overseas 20%). No reading fee. Founded 1994.

Rosenstone/Wender*
38 East 29th Street, 10th Floor, New York, NY 10016
tel 212-725-9445 *fax* 212-725-9447
Contacts Phyllis Wender, Susan Perlman Cohen, Sonia Pabley

Fiction, non-fiction, film and TV rights. No unsolicited MSS; query first. No reading fee.

Russell & Volkening Inc.*
50 West 29th Street, Suite 7E, New York, NY 10001
tel 212-684-6050 *fax* 212-889-3026
Contact Timothy Seldes, Kirsten Ringer

General fiction and non-fiction, film and TV rights. No screenplays. No unsolicited MSS; query first with letter and sase. No reading fee.

Schiavone Literary Agency, Inc.
236 Trails End, West Palm Beach, FL 33413–2135
tel/fax 516-966-9294
email profschia@aol.com
website www.publishersmarketplace.com/members/profschia
President James Schiavone

Fiction and non-fiction, specialising in celebrity biography and memoirs (home 15%, overseas 20%).

No reading fee. Send query letter only with return envelope and IRCs or US postage. Accepts email queries (no attachments). Founded 1996.

Susan Schulman Literary & Dramatic Agents Inc.*
454 West 44th Street, New York, NY 10036
tel 212-713-1633 *fax* 212-581-8830
email schulman@aol.com
Branch office 2 Bryan Plaza, Washington Depot, CT 06794
tel 860-868-3700

Agents for negotiation in all markets (with co-agents) of fiction, general non-fiction, children's books, academic and professional works, and associated subsidiary rights including plays and film (home 15%, UK 7.5%, overseas 20%). No reading fee. Return postage required.

Scott Meredith Literary Agency LP
200 West 57th Street, Suite 904, New York, NY 10019
tel 646-274-1970 *fax* 212-977-5997
website www.scottmeredith.com
President Arthur Klebanoff

General fiction and non-fiction. Founded 1946.

The Shukat Company Ltd
340 West 55th Street, Suite 1A, New York, NY 10019
tel 212-582-7614 *fax* 212-315-3752
email staff@shukat.com
President Scott Shukat, *Contacts* Maribel Rivas, Lysna Scriven-Marzani

Theatre, films, TV, radio (15%). No reading fee. No unsolicited material accepted.

The Spieler Agency
154 West 57th Street, Room 135, New York, NY 10019
tel 212-757-4439 *fax* 212-333-2019
email spieleragency@spieleragency.com
Directors F. Joseph Spieler, Lisa M. Ross, John F. Thornton, Deirdre Mullane

Full- and short-length MSS. History, politics, ecology, business, consumer reference, some fiction (home 15%, overseas 20%). No reading fee. Query first with sample and sase. Founded 1982.

Philip G. Spitzer Literary Agency, Inc.*
50 Talmage Farm Lane, East Hampton, NY 11937
tel 631-329-3650 *fax* 631-329-3651
Literary Manager L. Lukas Ortiz

General fiction and non-fiction; specialises in mystery/suspense, sports, politics, biography, social issues.

Rebecca Strong International Literary Agency
235 West 108th Street, Suite 35, New York, NY 10025
tel 212-865-1569

email rstrongtho@aol.com
Owner/Agent Rebecca Strong

Literary and commercial fiction, narrative non-fiction, memoir and biography, self-improvement/how-to (home 15%, overseas 20%). No reading fee. Founded 2003.

Roslyn Targ Literary Agency Inc.*
105 West 13th Street, New York, NY 10011
tel 212-206-9390 *fax* 212-989-6233
email roslyn@roslyntargagency.com

Fiction and non-fiction: query with outline, publication history and CV. Fiction: query with synopsis or outline, and CV and publication history. All submissions require sase. No phone queries. Affiliates in most foreign countries. No reading fee.

Trident Media Group*
41 Madison Avenue, New York, NY 10010
tel 212-262-4810 *fax* 212-262-4849
website www.tridentmediagroup.com
Executive Vice President Ellen Levine

Full-length MSS: biography, contemporary affairs, women's issues, history, science, literary and commercial fiction (home 15%, overseas 20%); in conjunction with co-agents, theatre, films, TV (15%). Will suggest revision. Works in conjunction with agents in Europe, Japan, Israel, Brazil, Argentina, Australia, Far East. No reading fee; preliminary letter and sase and US postage essential.

Ralph M. Vicinanza Ltd*
303 West 18th Street, New York, NY 10011
tel 212-924-7090
Contacts Ralph Vicinanza, Christopher Lotts, Christopher Schelling

Fiction: literary, women's, 'multicultural', popular (especially science fiction, fantasy, thrillers), children's. Non-fiction: history, business, science, biography, popular culture. Foreign rights specialists. New clients by professional recommendation only. No unsolicited MSS.

Austin Wahl Agency Inc.
1820 North 76th Court, Elmwood Park, IL 60707–3631
tel 708-456-2301 *fax* 708-456-2031
President Thomas Wahl

Full-length and short MSS (home 15%, overseas 20%), theatre, films, TV (10%). No reading fee; professional writers only. Founded 1935.

Wallace Literary Agency Inc.
177 East 70th Street, New York, NY 10021
tel 212-570-9090 *fax* 212-772-8979

Director Lois Wallace

No cookery, humour, how-to; film, TV, theatre for agency clients. Will suggest revision. No unsolicited MSS; no faxed queries. Will only answer queries with return postage. Founded 1988.

Watkins/Loomis Agency Inc.
133 East 35th Street, New York, NY 10016
tel 212-532-0080 *fax* 212-889-0506
President Gloria Loomis

Fiction and non-fiction. No unsolicited MSS. Representatives: **Abner Stein** (UK), the **Marsh Agency Ltd** (foreign).

Rhoda Weyr Agency – see Dunham Literary, Inc.

Writers House LLC*
21 West 26th Street, New York, NY 10010
tel 212-685-2400 *fax* 212-685-1781
website www.writershouse.com
Chairman Albert Zuckerman, *President* Amy Berkower, *Juvenile & Young Adult Agents* Susan Cohen, Rebecca Sherman, Jodi Reamer, Steven Malk

Fiction and non-fiction, including all rights; film and TV rights. No screenplays or software. Send a one-page letter in the first instance, saying what's wonderful about your book, what it is about and why you are the best person to write it. No reading fee. Founded 1974.

Wylie-Merrick Literary Agency*
1138 South Webster Street, Kokomo, IN 46902
tel 765-459-8258
email rbrown@wylie-merrick.com, smartin@wylie-merrick.com
website www.wylie-merrick.com
Partners Robert Brown and Sharene Martin

Adult and juvenile fiction and non-fiction (home 15%, overseas 20%). Interested in romance, sci-fi and fantasy, women's, gay/lesbian, suspense/thrillers. No picture books or graphic novels. Query by email only; no unsolicited MSS. See website for full submission guidelines. Founded 1999.

The Wylie Agency Inc.
250 West 57th Street, Suite 2114, New York, NY 10107
tel 212-246-0069 *fax* 212-586-8953
email mail@wylieagency.com
Directors Andrew Wylie (president), Sarah Chalfant

Literary fiction/non-fiction. No unsolicited MSS accepted. London office: the **Wylie Agency UK Ltd**.

Art and illustration
Freelancing for beginners

Fig Taylor describes the opportunities open to freelance illustrators and discusses types of fee and how to negotiate one to your best advantage.

Full-time posts for illustrators are extremely rare. Because commissioners' needs tend to change on a regular basis, most artists have little choice but to freelance – offering their skills to a variety of clients in order to make a living.

Illustration is highly competitive and a professional attitude towards targeting, presenting, promoting and delivering your work will be vital to your success. Likewise, a realistic understanding of how the industry works and of your place within it will be key. Without adequate research into your chosen field(s) of interest, you may find yourself approaching inappropriate clients – a frustrating and disheartening experience for both parties and a waste of your time and money.

Who commissions illustration?
Magazines and newspapers

Whatever your illustrative ambitions, you are most likely to receive your first commissions from editorial clients. The comparatively modest fees involved allow art editors the freedom to take risks, so many are keen to commission newcomers. Briefs are generally fairly loose though deadlines can be short, particularly where daily and weekly publications are concerned. However, fast turnover also ensures a swift appearance in print, thus reassuring clients in other, more lucrative, spheres of your professional status. Given then that it is possible to use magazines as a springboard, it is essential to research them thoroughly when seeking to identify your own individual market. Collectively, editorial clients accommodate an infinite variety of illustrative styles and techniques. Don't limit your horizons by approaching only the most obvious titles and/or those you would read yourself. Consider also trade and professional journals, free publications and those available on subscription from membership organisations or charities. Seeking out as many potential clients as possible will benefit you in the long term.

Book publishing

With the exception of children's picture books, where illustration is unlikely to fall out of fashion, many publishers are using significantly less illustration than they once did. While publishers of traditional mass market genres, such as science fiction and fantasy, still favour strong, representational, full-colour work on their covers, photography has begun to predominate in others, such as the family saga and historical romance. However, the recent fashion illustration renaissance has strongly influenced packaging of contemporary women's fiction, where quirky, humorous and graphic styles are also popular. A broader range of styles can be accommodated by those smaller publishers specialising in literary, upmarket fiction, though many opt to use stock imagery in order to operate within a limited budget. Meanwhile, although specialist and technical illustrators still have a vital part to play in non-fiction publishing, there is currently little decorative work being commissioned for lifestyle-related subjects.

Children's publishers use a wide variety of styles, covering the gamut from baby books, activity and early learning, through to full-colour picture books, covers for young adults and black and white line illustrations for the 8–11 year-old age group. Author/illustrators are particularly welcomed by picture book publishers – though, whatever your style, you must be able to develop believable characters and sustain them throughout a narrative. See *Illustrating for children's books* on page 251. On the whole, publishing deadlines are civilised and mass market covers particularly well paid.

Greeting cards

Many illustrators are interested in providing designs for cards and giftwrap. For specific information on the gift industry which, unlike the areas covered here, works on a speculative basis, see *Winning the greeting card game* on page 465.

Useful addresses

Association of Illustrators
2nd Floor, Back Building, 150 Curtain Road,
London EC2A 3AR
tel 020-7613 4328 *fax* 020-7613 4417
email info@theaoi.com
website www.theaoi.com
Publishes *Survive – the Illustrators Guide to a Professional Career* and *Rights – the Illustrators Guide to Professional Practice and Images*. See also page 522.

Bikini Lists
98 Station Road, Ashwell, Herts. SG7 5LT
tel (0870) 4441891
email ross@bikinilists.com
website www.bikinilists.com

Boomerang Media Ltd
PO Box 141, Aldershot, Hants GU12 4XX
tel (01252) 368368

BRAD Group
33–39 Bowling Green Lane, London EC1R 0DA
tel 020-7505 8000
website www.intellagencia.com
Publishes *ALF* (Account List File).

Centaur Communications
50 Poland Street, London W1V 4AX
tel 020-7970 4000
website www.creativereview.co.uk,
www.design-week.co.uk
Publishes *Design Week* and *Creative Review*.

Elfande Ltd
Surrey House, 31 Church Street, Leatherhead,
Surrey KT22 8EF

tel (01372) 220300 *fax* (01372) 220340
email mail@contact-uk.com
website www.contact-uk.com
Publishes *Contact Illustrators*.

File FX
Unit 11, 83–93 Shepperton Road, London N1 3DF
tel 020-7226 6646
email info@filefx.co.uk
Specialises in providing creative suppliers with up-to-date information on commissioning clients in all spheres.

Grafik Ltd
3rd Floor, 104 Great Portland Street, London
W1W 6PE
tel 020-7637 5900
email hello.grafik@g.mail.com
website www.grafikmagazine.co.uk
Publishes *Grafik*.

Haymarket Business Publications
174 Hammersmith Road, London W6 7JP
tel 020-7413 4036
email campaign@haynet.com
website www.brandrepublic.com
Publishes *Campaign*.

Reed Business Information
Windsor Court, East Grinstead House, Wood Street, East Grinstead, West Sussex RH19 1XA
tel (01342) 335861 *fax* (01342) 336113
email chb@reedinfo.co.uk
website www.chb.com
Publishes *The Creative Handbook*.

Design companies

Both designers and their clients (who are largely uncreative and will, ultimately, be footing the bill) will be impressed and reassured by relevant, published work so wait until you're in print before approaching them. Although fees are significantly higher than those in editorial and publishing, this third-party involvement generally results in a more restrictive brief. Deadlines may vary and styles favoured range from conceptual through to realistic, decorative, humorous and technical – with those involved in multimedia and web design favouring illustrators with character development and animation skills.

Magazines such as *Design Week*, *Creative Review* (both published by Centaur Communications) and *Grafik* will keep you abreast of developments in the design world and help you identify clients' individual areas of expertise. Meanwhile, *The Creative Handbook* (published by Reed Business Information and also available online), carries many listings. Individual contact names are also available at a price from database specialists File FX, who can provide creative suppliers with up-to-date information on commissioners in all spheres. A similar service is provided by Bikini Lists, an online subscription-based resource that specialises in providing categorised mailing lists for single or multiple usage.

Advertising agencies

As with design, you should ideally be in print before seeking advertising commissions. Fees can be high, deadlines short and clients extremely demanding. A wide range of styles are used and commissions might be incorporated into direct mail or press advertising, featured on hoardings and poster sites or animated for television. Fees will vary, depending on whether a campaign is local, national or even global.

Most agencies employ an art buyer to look at portfolios. A good one will know what each creative team is currently working on and may refer you to specific art directors. Agency listings and client details may be found in *ALF* (Account List File, published by the BRAD Group), while *Creative Review* and the weekly *Campaign* (published by Haymarket Business Publications) carry agency news.

Portfolio presentation

In general, UK commissioners prefer to see someone with a strong, consistent, recognisable style rather than an unfocused jack-of-all trades type. Thus, when assembling your professional portfolio, try to exclude samples which are, in your own eyes, weak, irrelevant, uncharacteristic or simply unenjoyable to do and focus on your strengths instead. Should you be one of those rare, multi-talented individuals who finds it hard to limit themselves stylistically, try splitting conflicting work into separate portfolios geared towards different kinds of clients.

A lack of formal training need not be a handicap providing your portfolio accurately reflects the needs of the clients you target. Some illustrators find it useful to assemble 'mock-ups' using existing magazine layouts. By responding to the copy and replacing original images with your own illustrations, it is easier to see how your work will look in context. Eventually, as you become established you'll be able to augment these with published pieces.

Ideally, your folder should be of the zip-up, ring-bound variety and never exceed A2 in size (A3 or A4 is best) as clients usually have little desk space – or you may choose to give a laptop presentation. Complexity of style and diversity of subject matter will dictate how many samples to include but if you are opting for a traditional portfolio presentation, all should be neatly mounted on lightweight paper or card and placed inside protective plastic sleeves. High-quality photographs and laser copies are acceptable to clients but tacky out-of-focus snapshots are not. Also avoid including multiple sketchbooks and life drawings, which are anathema to clients. It will be taken for granted that you know how to draw from observation.

Interviews and beyond

Making appointments can be hard work but clients take a dim view of spontaneous visits from passing illustrators. Having established the contact name (either from a written source or by asking the company directly), clients are still best approached by letter or telephone call. Many publishing houses are happy to see freelances, though portfolio 'drop-offs' are also quite common. Some clients will automatically take photocopies of your work for reference. However, it's advisable to have some kind of promotional material to leave behind such as a CD, postcard or advertising tearsheet. Always ask an enthusiastic client if they know of others who might be interested in your work. Personal recommendation almost always guarantees an interview.

Cleanliness, punctuality and enthusiasm are more important to clients than how you dress – as is a professional attitude to taking and fulfilling a brief. A thorough understanding of each commission is paramount from the outset. You will need to know your client's requirements regarding roughs; format and – if relevant – size and flexibility of artwork; preferred medium; and whether the artwork is needed in colour or black and white. You will also need to know when the deadline is. Never, under any circumstances agree to undertake a commission unless you are certain you can deliver on time and always work within your limitations. Talent is nothing without reliability.

Self-promotion

There are many ways an illustrator can ensure their work stays uppermost in the industry's consciousness, some more expensive than others. Images can be emailed, put onto CD or posted on a website. Advertising in prestigious hardback annuals such as Elfande's *Contact Illustrators* and the Association of Illustrators' *Images* – which are distributed free to commissioners – can be effective but doesn't come cheap and, in the case of *Images*, only those professionally selected are permitted to buy pages for their winning entries. However, both publications have a long shelf life and are well respected by industry professionals.

As commissioners increasingly turn to the internet for inspiration, websites are becoming a viable and affordable method of self-promotion (see *Setting up a website*, page 606). Advertisers in *Contact Illustrators* automatically qualify for a web portfolio of 12 images with links back to individual websites. Currently, it is also possible for illustrators to promote their work on the *Contact* website without appearing in the annual (www.contactacreative.com). The Association of Illustrators (AOI) website features an extensive archive of work from previous editions of the *Images* annual. Both members and non-members of the AOI can pay to have their work included in the site's Image File, a selection of artist-maintained online portfolios. Listings are free in the site's web link directory, with additional space for written details available for a modest fee, along with a larger image.

Free publicity can be had courtesy of Boomerang Media Ltd, who will print appropriate images to go in postcard advertising racks. Distribution includes cafés, bars, cinemas, health clubs, universities and schools.

Be organised

Once you are up and running, it is imperative to keep organised records of all your commissions. Contracts can be verbal as well as written, though details – both financial and otherwise – should always be confirmed in writing and duplicated for your files. Likewise, keep corresponding client faxes, letters, emails and order forms. AOI publications *Survive – the Illustrator's Guide to a Professional Career* and *Rights – the Illustrator's Guide to Professional Practice* offer a wealth of practical, legal and ethical information. Subjects covered include contracts, fee negotiation, agents, licences, royalties and copyright issues.

Money matters

The type of client, the purpose for which you are being commissioned and the usage of your work can all affect the fee you can expect to receive, as can your own professional attitude. Given that it is *extremely* inadvisable to undertake a commission without first agreeing on a fee, you will have to learn to be upfront about funds.

Licence *v.* copyright

Put simply, according to current EU legislation, copyright is the right to reproduce a piece of work anywhere, *ad infinitum*, for any purpose, for a period ending 70 years after the death of the person who created it. This makes it an extremely valuable commodity.

By law, copyright automatically belongs to you, the creator of your artwork, unless you agree to sell it to another party. In most cases, clients have no need to purchase it, and the recommended alternative is for you to grant them a licence instead, governing the precise usage of the artwork. This is far cheaper from the client's perspective and, should they subsequently decide to use your work for some purpose other than those outlined in your initial agreement, will benefit you too as a separate fee will have to be negotiated. It's also worth noting that even if you were ill-advised enough to sell the copyright, the artwork would still belong to you unless you had also agreed to sell that.

Rejection and cancellation fees

Most commissioners will not expect you to work for nothing unless you are involved in a speculative pitch, in which case it will be up to you to weigh up the pros and cons of your possible involvement. Assuming you have given a job your best shot – i.e. carried out the client's instructions to the letter – it's customary to receive a rejection fee even if the client doesn't care for the outcome: 25% is customary at developmental/rough stage and 50% at finished artwork stage. (Clear this with the client before you start, as there are exceptions to the rule.) Cancellation fees are paid when a job is terminated through no fault of the artist or, on occasion, even the client. Customary rates in this instance are 25% before rough stage, 33% on delivery of roughs and 100% on delivery of artwork.

Fixed *v.* negotiable fees

Editorial and publishing fees are almost always fixed with little, if any, room for haggling and are generally considerably lower than advertising and design fees, which tend to be negotiable. A national full-colour 48-sheet poster advertising Marks & Spencer is likely to pay more than a local black and white press ad plugging a poodle parlour. If, having paid your editorial dues, you find yourself hankering after commissions from the big boys, fee negotiation – confusing and complicated as it can sometimes be – will become a fact of life. However you choose to go about the business of cutting a deal, it will help if you disabuse yourself of the notion that the client is doing you a whopping favour by considering you for the job. Believe it or not, the client *needs* your skills to bring his/her ideas to life. In short, you are worth the money and the client knows it.

Pricing a commission

Before you can quote on a job, you'll need to know exactly what it entails. For what purpose is the work to be used? Will it be used several times and/or for more than one purpose? Will its use be local or national? For how long is the client intending to use it? Who is the client and how soon do they want the work? Are you up against anyone else (who could possibly undercut you)?

Next, ask the client what the budget is. Believe it or not there's a fair chance they might tell you. Whether they are forthcoming or not, don't feel you have to pluck a figure out of thin air or agree to their offer immediately. Play for time. Tell them you need to review your current workload and that you'll get back to them within a brief, specified period of time. If nothing else, haggling over the phone is less daunting than doing it face to face. If you've had no comparable commissions to date and are an AOI member, check out the going rate by calling them for pricing advice (or check out their report on illustration fees and standards of pricing on the AOI website). Failing that, try speaking to a friendly client or a fellow illustrator who's worked on similar jobs.

When you begin negotiating, have in mind a bottom-line price you're prepared to do the job for and always ask for slightly more than your ideal fee as the client will invariably try to beat you down. You may find it useful to break down your asking price in order to explain exactly what it is the client is paying for. How you do this is up to you. Some people find it helpful to work out a daily rate incorporating overheads such as rent, heating, materials, travel and telephone charges, while others prefer to negotiate on a flat fee basis. There are also illustrators who charge extra for something needed yesterday, time spent researching, model hire if applicable and so on. It pays to be flexible, so if your initial quote exceeds the client's budget and you really want the job, tell them you are open to negotiation. If, on the other hand, the job looks suspiciously thankless, stick to your guns. If the client agrees to your exorbitant demands, the job might start to look more appetising.

Getting paid

Once you've traded terms and conditions, done the job and invoiced the client, you'll then have the unenviable task of getting your hands on your fee. It is customary to send your invoice to the accounts department stating payment within 30 days. It is also customary for them to ignore this entreaty, regardless of the wolf at your door, and pay you when it suits them. Magazines pay promptly, usually within 4–6 weeks; everyone else takes 60–90 days – no matter what.

Be methodical when chasing up your invoice. Send out a statement the moment your 30 days has elapsed and call the accounts department as soon as you like. Take names, note dates and the gist of their feeble excuses. ('It's in the post', 'He's in a meeting', 'He's on holiday and forgot to sign the cheque before he went'), and keep on chasing. Don't worry about your incessant nagging scuppering your plans of further commissions as these decisions are solely down to the art department, and they think you're a gem. Should payment still not be forthcoming three months down the line, it might be advisable to ask your commissioner to follow things up on your behalf. Chances are they'll be horrified you haven't been paid yet and things will be speedily resolved. In the meantime, you'll have had a good deal of practice talking money, which can only make things easier next time around.

And finally...

Basic book-keeping – making a simple, legible record of all your financial transactions, both incoming and outgoing – will be crucial to your sanity once the tax inspector starts to loom. It will also make your accountant's job easier, thereby saving you money. If your annual turnover is less than £15,000, it is unnecessary to provide the Inland RevenueInland Revenue with detailed accounts of your earnings. Information regarding your turnover, allowable expenses and net profit may simply be entered on your tax return. Although an accountant is not necessary to this process, many find it advantageous to employ one. The tax system is complicated and dealing with the Inland Revenue can be stressful, intimidating and time consuming. Accountants offer invaluable advice on tax allowances, National Insurance and tax assessments, as well as dealing expertly with the Inland Revenue on your behalf – thereby enabling you to attend to the business of illustrating. See *Income tax* on page 728, *Social security contributions* on page 739 and *Social security benefits* on page 746.

Fig Taylor initially began her career as an illustrators' agent in 1983. For 21 years she has been the resident 'portfolio surgeon' at the Association of Illustrators and also operates as a private consultant to non-AOI member artists. In addition, she lectures extensively in Business Awareness to BA and HND illustration students throughout the UK.

Art agents and commercial art studios

Before submitting work, artists are advised to make preliminary enquiries and to ascertain terms of work. Commission varies but averages 25–30%. The Association of Illustrators (see page 522) provides a valuable service for illustrators, agents and clients.

*Member of the Society of Artists Agents
†Member of the Association of Illustrators

Academy of Light Ltd
Unit 1c, Delta Centre, Mount Pleasant, Wembly, Middlesex HA0 1UX
tel 020-8795 2695 *fax* 020-8903 3748
email yubraj@academyoflight.co.uk
website www.academyoflight.co.uk
Contact Dr Yubraj Sharma, Managing Director

Represents artists specialising in spirituality, medicine, caricature and humour and producing illustrations for books, cards, magazines and advertising. Commission: 25%.

Advocate
39 Church Road, London SW19 5DQ
tel 020-8879 1166 *fax* 020-8879 3303
email mail@advocate-art.com
website www.advocate-art.com
Director Edward Burns

Has 5 agents representing 110 artists and illustrators. Supplies work to book and magazine publishers, design and advertising agencies, greeting card and fine art publishers, and gift and ceramic manufacturers. Also has an original art gallery, stock library and international licensing agency for the character 'Newton's Law'. Founded as a co-operative in 1996.

Allied Artists/Artistic License
The Gallery@Richmond, 63 Sheen Road, Richmond upon Thames TW9 1YJ
tel 020-8334 1010 *fax* 020-8334 9900
email info@allied-artists.net,
mary@umbrellapublishing.ca
website www.allied-artists.net,
www.umbrellapublishing.ca
Contacts Gary Mills, Mary Burtenshaw

Represents over 40 artists specialising in highly finished realistic figure illustrations, stylised juvenile illustrations for children's books, and cartoons for magazines, books, plates, prints, cards and advertising. Extensive library of stock illustrations. Commission: 33%. Founded 1983.

Arena*
Quantum Artists Ltd, 108 Leonard Street, London EC2A 4RH

tel 020-7613 4040 *fax* 020-7613 1441
email info@arenaworks.com
website www.arenaworks.com
Contact Tamlyn Francis

Represents 35 artists working mostly for book covers, children's books and design groups. Average commission 20%. Founded 1970.

The Art Agency (Wildlife Art Ltd)
The Lodge, Cargate Lane, Saxlingham Thorpe, Norwich NR15 1TU
tel (01508) 471500 *fax* (01508) 470391
email info@the-art-agency.co.uk
website www.the-art-agency.co.uk

Represents more than 40 artists producing top-quality, highly accurate and imaginative illustrations across a wide variety of subjects and for all age groups, both digitally and traditionally. Clients are in the UK and international, mainly in children's books and magazines/partworks, for fiction and non-fiction. Sae must be included with work submitted for consideration. Do not email portfolios. Commission: 30%. Founded 1992.

The Art Market*
51 Oxford Drive, London SE1 2FB
tel 020-7407 8111 *fax* 020-7407 8222
email info@artmarketillustration.com
website www.artmarketillustration.com
Director Philip Reed

Represents 20 artists creating illustrations for publishing, design and advertising. Founded 1989.

Artist Partners Ltd*
14–18 Ham Yard, Great Windmill Street, London W1D 7DE
tel 020-7734 7991 *fax* 020-7287 0371
email chris@artistpartners.demon.co.uk
website www.artistpartners.com
Managing Director Christine Isteed

Represents 40 artists, including specialists in their field, producing artwork in every genre for advertising campaigns, storyboards, children's and adult book covers, newspaper and magazine features and album covers. New artists are only considered if their work is of an exceptionally high standard, in which case submission should be by post only and include an sae. Commission: 30%. Founded 1951.

The Artworks†
40 Frith Street, London W1D 5LN
tel 020-7734 3333 *fax* 020-7734 3484
email info@theartworksinc.com
website www.theartworksinc.com
Contact Lucy Scherer, Stephanie Alexander

Represents 40 artists for illustrated gift books and children's books. Commission: 25% advances, 15% royalties.

Associated Freelance Artists Ltd
124 Elm Park Mansions, Park Walk, London SW10 0AR
tel 020-7352 6890 *fax* 020-7352 8125
email pekes.afa@virgin.net
Directors Eva Morris, Doug FitzMaurice

Freelance illustrators mainly in children's educational fields, and some greeting cards.

Beehive Illustration
42ᴀ Cricklade Street, Cirencester, Glos. GL7 1JH
tel (01285) 885149 *fax* (01285) 641291
email info@beehiveillustration.co.uk
website www.beehiveillustration.co.uk
Contact Paul Beebee

Represents over 70 artists specialising in education and general children's publishing illustration. Commission: 25%. Founded 1989.

Sarah Brown Agency
10 The Avenue, London W13 8PH
tel 020-8998 0390 *fax* 020-8843 1175
email sbagency@dsl.pipex.com
website www.sbagency.com
Contact Brian Fennelly

Illustrations for publishing and advertising. Sae essential for unsolicited material. Commission: 25% UK, 25% USA (flat artwork 33.3%). Founded 1977.

Central Illustration Agency†
36 Wellington Street, London WC2E 7BD
tel 020-7240 8925/836 1106 *fax* 020-7836 1177
email c.illustration.a@dial.pipex.com
website www.centralillustration.com
Director Brian Grimwood, Benjamin Cox

Represents 70 artists producing illustrations for design, publishing, animation and advertising. Commission: 30%. Founded 1983.

Début Art†
30 Tottenham Street, London W1T 4RJ
tel 020-7636 1064 *fax* 020-7580 7017
email debutart@coningsbygallery.demon.co.uk
website www.debutart.com

Directors Andrew Coningsby, Samuel Summerskill, Jonathan Hedley

Represents 120 artists working in mixed media, digital, photographic 3D and 2D collage and montage. Commission: 25%. Founded 1985.

The Drawer Artist Agency
PO Box 330, London SE24 9WB
tel 020-7501 9106
email jps@drawer.me.uk
website www.drawer.me.uk
Contact Jess Sims

Represents contemporary illustrators suitable for book jackets, books and magazines, greetings cards, PR and advertising, Reply only with sae. CDs, email, printed or flat artwork sample sheets accepted.

Ian Fleming Associates – see Phosphor Art Ltd

Folio Illustrators' & Designers' Agents
10 Gate Street, Lincoln's Inn Fields, London WC2A 3HP
tel 020-7242 9562 *fax* 020-7242 1816
email all@folioart.co.uk
website www.folioart.co.uk

All areas of illustration. Send sae with samples. Founded 1976.

Graham-Cameron Illustration
The Studio, 23 Holt Road, Sheringham, Norfolk NR26 8NB
tel (01263) 821333 *fax* (01263) 821334
email enquiry@graham-cameron-illustration.com
and Duncan Graham-Cameron, Graham-Cameron Illustration, 59 Redvers Road, Brighton BN2 4BF
tel (01273) 385890
website www.graham-cameron-illustration.com
Partners Mike Graham-Cameron, Helen Graham-Cameron, Duncan Graham-Cameron

Represents 37 artists. Undertakes all forms of illustration for publishing and communications. Specialises in educational and children's information books. Send A4 copies of sample illustrations with sae. No MSS. Founded 1985.

The Guild of Aviation Artists
Trenchard House, 85 Farnborough Road, Farnborough, Hants GU14 6TF
tel (01252) 513123 *fax* (01252) 510505
email admin@gava.org.uk
website www.gava.org.uk
President Michael Turner ꜰɢᴀᴠᴀ, *Secretary/ Administrator* Susan Gardner

Specialises in aviation art in all mediums and comprising 450 members, the Guild sells, commissions and exhibits members' work. Commission: 25%. Founded 1971.

John Hodgson Agency
38 Westminster Palace Gardens, Artillery Row, London SW1P 1RR

tel 020-7580 3773 *fax* 020-7222 4468

Publishing (children's picture books). Essential to send sae with samples. Commission: 25%. Founded 1965.

Illustration Ltd*
2 Brooks Court, Cringle Street, London SW8 5BX
tel 020-7720 5202 *fax* 020-7720 5920
email team@illustrationweb.com
website www.illustrationweb.com
Contact Harry Lyon-Smith, Juliette Lott

Represents 150 artists producing illustrations and animation for international advertisers, designers, publishers and editorial clients. Artists should send submissions via the website. Commission: 33.3% or 25%. Founded 1929.

Image by Design Licensing
The Cottage, Pryor House, Preston, Hitchin, Herts. SG4 7UD
tel (01462) 422244 *fax* (01462) 451190
email enquiries@ibd-licensing.co.uk
website www.ibd-licensing.co.uk
Contact Lucy Brenham

Quality artwork, design and photography for a range of applications including greeting cards, fine art prints, stationery, calendars, ceramics, book illustration, table top, jigsaws, giftware and needlecraft. New artists always considered. Founded 1987.

The Inkshed*
99 Chase Side, Enfield EN2 6NL
tel 020-8367 4545 *fax* 020-8367 6730
email makecontact@inkshed.co.uk
website www.inkshed.co.uk
Partners Andrea Plummer, Gordon Allen, *Contact* Abby Glassfield

Represents 31 artists who work across the board – advertising, design, publishing, editorial. Commission: 25–30%. Founded 1985.

Kathy Jakeman Illustration
Richmond Business Centre, 23–24 George Street, Richmond, Surrey TW9 1HY
tel 020-8973 2000
email kathy@kji.co.uk
website www.kji.co.uk

Illustration for publishing – especially children's; also design, editorial and advertising. Commission: 25%. Founded 1990.

Libba Jones Associates
Hopton Manor, Hopton, Nr Wirksworth, Derbyshire DE4 4DF
tel (01629) 540353 *fax* (01629) 540577
email ljassociates@easynet.co.uk
website www.libbajonesassociates.com
Contacts Libba Jones, Ieuan Jones

High-quality artwork and design for china, greetings cards and giftwrap, jigsaw puzzles, calendars, prints, posters, stationery, book illustration, fabric design. Submission of samples required for consideration. Founded 1983.

David Lewis Illustration Agency
Worlds End Studios, 134 Lots Road, London SW10 0RJ
tel 020-7435 7762 *mobile* (07931) 824674
fax 020-7435 1945
email davidlewis34@hotmail.com
website www.davidlewisillustration.com
Director David Lewis, *Associate Director* Ramon Johns

Considers all types of illustration for a variety of applications but mostly suitable for book and magazine publishers, design groups, recording companies and corporate institutions. Also offers a comprehensive selection of images suitable for subsidiary rights purposes. Send return postage with samples. Do not send CDs or emails. Commission: 30%. Founded 1974.

Frances McKay Illustration
15 Lammas Green, Sydenham Hill, London SE26 6LT
tel 020-8693 7006 *mobile* (07703) 344334
email frances@francesmckay.com
website www.francesmckay.com
Proprietor Frances McKay

Represents 20+ artists for illustration mainly for children's books, magazines and products, greetings cards and stationery. Submit colour copies of recent work or email low-res scans; sae essential for return of all unsolicited samples. Commission: 25%–35%. Founded 1999.

John Martin & Artists
12 Haven Court, Hatfield Peverel, Chelmsford, Essex CM3 2SD
tel (01245) 380337
email bernardjma@aol.com
website www.jm-a.co.uk
Contact Bernard Bowen-Davies

Represents 12 illustrators, mainly producing artwork for children's fiction/non-fiction and educational books. Include return postage with submissions. Founded 1956.

Meiklejohn Illustration*
5 Risborough Street, London SE1 0HF
tel 020-7593 0500 *fax* 020-7593 0501
email mjn@mjgrafix.demon.co.uk
website www.theartbook.com, www.meiklejohn.co.uk
Contacts Charlotte Manning, Alice Wilkinson

All types of illustration.

N.E. Middleton
Richmond Business Centre, 23–24 George Street, Richmond, Surrey TW9 1HY

tel 020-8973 2000

Designs for greetings cards, stationery, prints, calendars and china.

Maggie Mundy Illustrators' Agency
14 Ravenscourt Park Mansions, Dalling Road, London W6 0HG
tel 020-8748-2391
email maggiemundy@compuserve.com

Represents 5 artists in varying styles of illustration for children's books. The Agency's books are closed.

NB Illustration[†]
40 Bowling Green Lane, London EC1R 0NE
tel 020-7278 9131 *fax* 020-7278 9121
email info@nbillustration.co.uk
website www.nbillustration.co.uk
Directors Joe Najman, Charlotte Berens, Paul Najman

Represents 35+ artists and will consider all material for the commercial illustration market. Sae essential. Commission: 30%. Founded 2000.

The Organisation*
The Basement, 69 Caledonian Road, London N1 9BT
tel 020-7833 8268 *fax* 020-7833 8269
email lorraine@organisart.co.uk
website www.organisart.co.uk
Contact Lorraine Owen

Represents over 60 international illustrators. Contemporary and traditional styles for all areas of publishing. Stock illustration also available. See website for submission guidelines. Founded 1987.

Oxford Designers & Illustrators Ltd
Aristotle House, Aristotle Lane, Oxford OX2 6TR
tel (01865) 512331 *fax* (01865) 512408
email richardcorfield@odi-illustration.co.uk
website www.o-d-i.com
Directors Peter Lawrence (managing), Richard Corfield, Andrew King

Studio of 20 illustrators working for publishers, business and industry. All types of artwork including science, technical, airbrush, graphic, medical, biological, botanical, natural history, figure, cartoon, maps, diagrams, and charts. Artwork supplied as PDF files or on a CD, Zip optical disk or ISDN, Mac or PC, with both b&w and colour proofs. Not an agency. Founded 1968.

Phosphor Art Ltd*
41 The Pump House, Pump House Close, London SE16 7HS
tel 020-7064 4666 *fax* 020-7064 4660
email info@phosphorart.com
website www.phosphorart.com
Directors Jan Rogers, Catriona Wydmanski

Represents 46 artists and specialises in innovative graphic digital illustration with artists working in watercolour, oil and gouche methods as well as pen and ink, scraper, charcoal and engraving styles. Also animation. Incorporates Ian Fleming Associates and The Black and White Line. Commission: 33.3%.

Sylvie Poggio Artists Agency
36 Haslemere Road, London N8 9RB
tel 020-8341 2722 *fax* 020-8374 1725
email sylviepoggio@blueyonder.co.uk
website www.sylviepoggio.com
Directors Slyvie Poggio, Bruno Caurat

Represents 35 artists producing illustrations for publishing and advertising. Commission 25%. Founded 1992.

Linda Rogers Associates
PO Box 330, 163 Half Moon Lane, London SE24 9WB
tel 020-7501 9106
email lr@lindarogers.net
website www.lindarogers.net
Partners Linda Rogers, Peter Sims, Jess Sims

Represents 65 illustrators and author/illustrators in all fields of illustration. Specialises in children's books, educational, information books; adult leisure books and magazines. Reply only with sae. Artwork samples only viewed via post, *not* by email. Commission: 25%. Founded 1973.

SGA Illustration Agency
(formerly Simon Girling & Associates)
18 High Street, Hadleigh, Suffolk IP7 5AP
tel (01473) 824083 *fax* (01473) 827846
email info@sgadesignart.com
website www.sgadesignart.com

Represents over 50 illustrators, mainly working within publishing (early learning through to teenage). Also manages projects from conception to final film. See website for portfolio of illustration samples. Commission: 30%. Founded 1985.

Specs Art
93 London Road, Cheltenham, Glos. GL52 6HL
tel (01242) 515951
email roland@specsart.com
website www.specsart.com
Partners Roland Berry, Stephanie Prosser

High-quality illustration and animation work for advertisers, publishers and all other forms of visual communication. Specialises in licensed character illustration.

Temple Rogers Artists' Agency
120 Crofton Road, Orpington, Kent BR6 8HZ
tel (01689) 826249 *fax* (01689) 896312

Contact Patrick Kelleher

Illustrations for children's educational books and magazine illustrations. Commission: by arrangement.

Vicki Thomas Associates

195 Tollgate Road, London E6 5JY
tel 020-7511 5767 *fax* 020-7473 5177
email vickithomasassociates@yahoo.co.uk
website www.vickithomasassociates.com
Consultant Vicki Thomas

Considers the work of illustrators and designers
working in greetings and gift industries, and
promotes such work to gift, toy, publishing and
related industries. Written application and b&w
photocopies required. Commission: 30%. Founded
1985.

Thorogood Illustration Ltd

5 Dryden Street, London WC2E 9NW
tel 020-8859 7507, 020-8488 3195
email draw@thorogood.net

website www.thorogood.net
Directors Doreen Thorogood, Stephen Thorogood

Represents 30 artists for advertising, design,
publishing and animation work. Send return postage
with samples. Commission: 30%. Founded 1977.

TWO:Design London Ltd

Studio 37, Hampstead House, 176 Finchley Road,
London NW3 6BT
tel 020-8275 8594
email studio@twodesign.net
website www.twodesign.net
Creative Director Graham Peake

Design studio providing design & layout, blads,
creative direction, art direction, style guides, point-
of-sale material. Specialists in coffee table books.
Founded 1997.

How to get ahead in cartooning

Earning a living from creating cartoons is highly competitive. But if you feel that you were born to be a cartoonist, Martin Rowson offers some advice on how to get your work published.

I can't say precisely when I first realised I wanted to be a cartoonist. I personally believe that cartoonists are born and not made so perhaps I should be talking about when I realised I *was* a cartoonist. I do know that, aged 10, I nicked my sister's 1950s British history textbook, which was illustrated throughout by cartoons (from Gillray via Tenniel to Low) and somewhere inside me stirred an unquantifiable yearning to draw – to express myself in the unique style that is the equally unique talent of the 'cartoonist'. So, shortly afterwards I started copying the way Wally Fawkes (better known by his *nom de plume* 'Trog') drew the then Prime Minister Edward Heath.

I've spent most of my life drawing. I drew cartoons for school magazines, designed posters for school societies which invariably turned into political cartoons displayed, in the good old-fashioned way, on walls. I also developed a useful party trick of caricaturing teachers on blackboards. I did Art 'O' and 'A' levels (only a grade B in the latter) but that didn't have much to do with cartoons, and I certainly never contemplated for a moment going to art school. Instead I went to Pembroke College, Cambridge, to read English Literature, and as things turned out I hated it and I spent most of my time doing cartoons for two-bit student magazines, which partly explains how I ended up with a truly terrible degree. More on this later.

At the same time I was half-heartedly putting together a portfolio of work, in the hope that what I'd always done for fun (despite the fact that it was also a compulsion) might just end up being what I did for a living. I'd occasionally send off the portfolio to magazines, never to hear anything back. Then, shortly after graduating I had an idea for a series which I hoped would appeal to a particular demographic at the time (1982). It was called 'Scenes from the Lives of the Great Socialists' and consisted of a number of stylised depictions of leading socialist thinkers and politicians from history, with the added value of an appallingly bad pun thrown into the mixture. One example is 'Proudhon and Bakunin have tea in Tunbridge Wells', which showed the 19th century French and Russian anarchists sitting round a tea table, with Bakunin spitting out his cup of tea and exclaiming 'Proudhon! This tea is disgusting! This isn't proper tea at all!', to which Proudhon replied 'Ah, my dear Bakunin, but Property is Theft!'

I sent about half a dozen of these drawings to the *New Statesman* (then going through one of its periodic lefty phases) and, as usual, heard nothing for months. Then, just before Christmas 1982, in bed suffering from chickenpox, I received a phone call from the art director who said they were going to publish four of the cartoons in their Christmas issue, and would like me to do a series. (I was paid £40 a cartoon, which throughout 1983 meant I was earning £40 a month, which also meant I still had to sign on in order to stay alive.) Thus began my career as a cartoonist.

My three-year deadline

Now living in London, I found myself an agent and *She* magazine was the first offer to come in. They proposed to pay their standard fee of £6 for anything they published. I instructed my agent to inform them that this barely covered my expenses for materials and postage and they could forget it (although I used two other words, one of them also beginning with 'f') – I don't know if he passed on the message. Then someone wanted to do a book of the *New Statesman* cartoons, with the offer of an advance of £750. This took my earned income for that year to somewhere perilously close to a thousand pounds.

At around this time I went to a College reunion and remember skulking around in my Oxfam suit listening with growing irritation to my contemporaries outlining how they'd got into computing/merchant banking/ systems analysis or whatever at just the right time, and were earning fifty times more than I was. But I knew I was in for the long haul. As a slight nod to my father's ceaseless injunctions that it was time I got a proper job, I'd set myself a limit of three years, sort of promising that, if I wasn't making a fist of it by then I'd give up (although I doubt I actually meant it).

Luckily, a year into my putative career other contemporaries from university were starting out in journalism, and found they could earn important brownie points from their editors by bringing in a cartoonist to liven up the dull magazines they worked for. That's how I found myself working for *Satellite and Cable TV News* and *One Two Testing*... The fact that I neither knew nor cared about what I was illustrating and lampooning didn't matter. It was work, and also an essential lesson in how to master a brief, however obscure.

However, the true catalyst for my career came when another university acquaintance started working on *Financial Weekly* and, for the usual self-aggrandising reasons, suggested to the editor that they might use me. Again, this was something I knew and cared nothing about but it offered plenty of scope to lampoon truly awful people and of course frequently crossed over into political satire, where my real interest lay. More significantly, the editor himself was so nice, kind and amenable that he consequently drove his staff mad with frustration to the point that they would leave for better things. And when they went, they often took me with them.

Part of the *Financial Weekly* diaspora fled to Eddie Shah's infant *Today* newspaper, and so, just inside my self-imposed three-year time limit, I was producing a daily pocket cartoon for the business pages as well as drawing editorial cartoons for both *Today* and its short-lived sister paper *Sunday Today*. From there, another university friend brought me onto the books pages of the *Sunday Correspondent* and, in doing so, to broadsheet respectability. After that I never really had to solicit for work again. I'd reached cartooning critical mass; the people commissioning knew who I was and, more importantly, knew my work so the hard part was over. And, rather nicely, when I went to another College reunion, I discovered that all the smart boys in computing and banking had been sacked in the recession of the early 1990s.

How can other people get ahead in cartooning?

At one level you could say, between gritted teeth, that all that I've written above proves is that it's just about the old boy network – not what you know but who you know. To an extent that's true, but I'd like to think that none of the publications I'd worked for would have given me a second glance if I couldn't cut the mustard and delivered the goods. So, what do you need to get ahead in cartooning?

First of all, and most importantly, you need to recognise whether or not you truly are a cartoonist, and to do that you need to know what cartoons are. It won't do just to be able to draw; nor is it enough to have a sense of humour. You need to combine the two, and understand that in so doing you are creating something that can't be expressed in any other way. This requires a mindset which, I believe, is innate. Moreover, I don't believe you can teach people how to be cartoonists – they have to teach themselves, and from an early age at that. If you copy other cartoonists to find out how it's done, then slowly but surely you'll develop a style of your own which you feel comfortable with.

Once you recognise what you are, and that you're determined to embark on a career that, like poetry or acting, offers a dream of glamour out of all proportion to its guaranteed financial reward, you then need to create a frame of mind which combines, in equal measure, arrogance and sloth. In other words, you *know* that you're good, and actually better than anyone else who's ever lived, but you're also, crucially, too lazy to do anything else, like accountancy.

Then comes the hard part, which is not for the faint-hearted. You have to work very very hard, to make sure what you're producing is really good, and is the best you can do (of which you will always, ultimately, be the best judge). If you're a caricaturist, practice your caricature (and by all means steal other, more established cartoonists' tricks in order to develop your own; after all, they do). If you're a gag cartoonist, hone the gag and work on the drawing so it's clear what's going on (cartooning is the last bastion of realism in the visual arts – abstract cartoons don't work). If you're a political cartoonist, immerse yourself in current affairs and, most importantly, either develop or clearly express your point of view, which can be either right or left wing (a fair, unopinionated cartoonist is as useless and boring as a newspaper columnist with no opinions and nothing to say). A good editorial cartoon is a newspaper column by other means, and is best described as visual journalism, using tricks – like irony, humour, violence and vile imagery – that the big boys in newspaper punditry are too dumb to understand. But remember – while you go through this stage you'll be papering your bedroom wall with rejection slips.

Practical advice

Always try to make your artwork look professional. This means using good paper drawn on in indelible ink, centrally placed. This might sound obvious, but I've seen many cartoons by aspiring cartoonists drawn in crayon on lined file paper going right up to the edge of the sheet. This won't even get halfway out of the envelope before any editor bins it.

Second, always remember that, although you are a genius you have to start somewhere, and some work is always better than no work. If you want to get into newspapers or magazines (which is all there really is if you want to earn some money and not just feel complacent about your beautiful website), identify parts of the press that would benefit from your input.

Journalists producing gardening or travel or, most of all, personal finance sections are crying out for something to liven their pages, something other than a photo which will mark them out as different. In other words, be arrogant enough to be sufficiently humble to illustrate copy you'd never in a million years personally read. Many famous and established cartoonists still knock out stuff for trade papers of crashing obscurity and dullness, this being as good a way as any other of paying the mortgage.

Once you've identified a potential gap in the market, *always* submit your idea or portfolio to the editor of that section, and *never* send it to the art director (despite my experience with the *New Statesman*). There are several reasons for this. First, art directors are inundated with unsolicited work, and so the odds are immediately pitched against you. Second, there's the danger that, in the endless little territorial feuds that pertain in journalism, you will become the exclusive property of the art director who, because he or she hates the gardening editor, will never pass your work on. Third, the section editor will be flattered and delighted to receive something different from the usual dross of press releases and letters of pedantic complaint. If your work tickles their fancy, then you're in, and a section editor always pulls rank over an art director, whatever anyone may imagine.

From these first steps, you will have the beginnings of a portfolio of published work which will stand you in excellent stead on your way to reaching that critical mass of recognition I mentioned earlier.

Finally, never forget that cartoons are something different from anything else. While they combine text journalism and illustration, they end up as something greater than their component parts. In a way, a cartoon is a kind of voodoo, doing harm to someone (whether a politician or a castaway on a desert island) at a distance with a sharp object, which in this case is a pen. It's hard to get established, the number of successful cartoonists earning a decent wedge is tiny and there will always be a generational logjam as the clapped-out old has-beens whose work enrages and disgusts you cling tenaciously to the precious few slots. But – if you're determined and tough enough, stick with it and you, too, could become one of those clapped-out has-beens. Until then, just bear in mind that it's a small and crowded profession, and despite everything I've said, the last thing I need is anyone good coming along and muscling in on my territory. In my heart of hearts, I should really advise all aspiring young cartoonists to give up now. Such churlishness apart, however, I'll stick with wishing you good luck.

Martin Rowson is a freelance cartoonist and his work appears regularly in the *Guardian*, *The Times*, the *Independent on Sunday*, the *Daily Mirror*, the *Scotsman* and many other publications. In 2002 Ken Livingstone appointed him as the first Cartoonist Laureate for London, and he was named Political Cartoonist of the Year in 2000 and 2003. His books include comic book versions of *The Waste Land* and *Tristram Shandy*, and until 2005 he was vice-president of the Zoological Society of London.

Winning the greeting card game

The UK population spends £1.2 billion a year on greeting cards. Jacqueline Brown helps to guide
artists to success in this fiercely competitive industry.

The UK greeting card industry leads the
world on two counts – design and innovation and per capita send. On average
people in the UK send 50 cards a year, 85%
of which are bought by women.

But just how do you, as an artist, go
about satisfying this voracious appetite of
the card-sending public? There are two
main options: either to become a greeting
card publisher yourself or to supply existing greeting card publishers with your artwork and be paid a fee for doing so.

The idea of setting up your own greeting card publishing company may sound
exciting, but this decision should not be
taken lightly. Going down this route will
involve taking on all the set up and run-

> ## Some greeting card language
>
> **Own brand/bespoke publishers.** These design specific
> to a retailer's needs.
>
> **Spring Seasons.** The industry term to describe greeting
> cards for Valentine's Day, Mother's Day, Easter and
> Father's Day. Publishers generally launch these ranges all
> together in June/July.
>
> **Greeting card types.** Traditional; cute or whimsical;
> contemporary/quirky art; juvenile; handmade or hand-
> finished; fine art; photographic, humorous.
>
> **Finishes and treatments.** Artists will not be expected to
> know the production techniques and finishes, but a
> working knowledge is often an advantage. Some of the
> most commonly used finishes and treatments include:
> embossing (raised portion of a design), die-cutting
> (where the card is cut into a shape or includes an
> aperture), foiling (metallic film) and flitter (a glitter-like
> substance).

ning costs of a publishing company as well as the production, selling and administrative
responsibilities. This often leaves little time for you to do what you do best – creating the
artwork.

There are estimated to be around 800 greeting card publishers in the UK, ranging in
size from one-person operations to multinational corporations, roughly 200 of which are
regarded as 'serious' publishers (see page 469). Not all of them accept freelance artwork,
but a great many do. Remember, whatever the size of the company, all publishers rely on
good designs.

Finding the right publishers

While some publishers concentrate on producing a certain type of greeting card (e.g.
humorous, fine art or juvenile), the majority publish a variety of greeting card ranges.
Unfortunately, this makes it more difficult for you as an artist to target the most appropriate
potential publishers for your work. There are various ways in which you can research the
market, quickly improve your publisher knowledge and, therefore, reduce the amount of
wasted correspondence:

● **Go shopping.** Browse the displays in card shops, newsagents and other high street shops,
department stores and gift shops. This will not only give you an insight into what is already
available but also which publishers may be interested in your work. Most publishers include
their contact details on the backs of the cards.

● **Trade fairs.** There are a number of trade exhibitions held during the year at which
publishers exhibit their greeting card ranges to retailers and overseas distributors. By visiting these exhibitions, you will gain a broad overview of the design trends in the industry,

as well as the current ranges of individual publishers. Some publishers are willing to meet artists and look through their portfolios on the stand but others are not. If you believe your work could be relevant for them, ask for a contact name and follow it up afterwards. Have a supply of business cards handy, perhaps illustrated with some of your work, to leave with publishers.

Types of publishers

There are two broad categories of publisher – wholesale and direct-to-retail – each employing a different method of distribution to reach the retailer.

Wholesale publishers distribute their products to the retailer via greeting card wholesalers or cash-and-carry outlets. They work on volume sales and have a rapid turnover of designs, many being used with a variety of different captions. For example, the same floral design may be used for cards for mothers, grandmothers, aunts and sisters. It is therefore usual for the artist to leave a blank space on the design to accommodate the caption. Until recently, wholesale publishers were generally only interested in traditional, cute and juvenile designs, but they now publish across the board, including contemporary and humorous ranges.

Further information

The Greeting Card Association

United House, North Road, London N7 9DP

tel 020-7619 0396

email gca@max-publishing.co.uk

website www.greetingcardassociation.org.uk

The UK trade association for greeting card publishers. Its website contains leaflets on freelance designing and writing for greeting cards complete with lists of publishers which accept freelance work. The Ladder Club meets once a year for a one-day seminar for would-be/fledgling publishers, many of whom are artists or photographers looking to publish their own work. The seminar covers all aspects of publishing and costs approx. £25.

Trade fairs

Spring & Autumn Fairs Birmingham, NEC

Contact TPS *tel* 020-8277 5830

Takes place First Sunday in Sept and Feb

Top Drawer, Earls Court

website www.topdrawer.co.uk,

www.pulse-london.co.uk

Contact Clarion Events *tel* 020-7370 8374

Takes place 10–12 Sept 2006 (at Olympia), 14–16 Jan 2007, 21–24 May 2007 (tbc)

Home and Gift, Harrogate

website homeandgift.co.uk

Contact Clarion Events *tel* 020-7370 8200

Takes place mid July

Trade magazines

Greetings Today

(formerly Greetings Magazine)Lema Publishing, Unit 1, Queen Mary's Avenue, Watford, Herts. WD18 7JR

tel (01923) 250909 *fax* (01923) 250995

Publisher-in-Chief Malcolm Naish, *Editor* Vicky Denton

Monthly £45 p.a. (other rates on application)

Articles, features and news related to the greetings card industry. Includes Artists Directory for aspiring artists wishing to attract the eye of publishers. Runs seminars for small publishers and artists.

Progressive Greetings Worldwide

Max Publishing, United House, North Road, London N7 9DP

tel 020-7700 6740 *fax* 020-7607 6411

12 p.a. (£40 p.a.)

The official magazine of the Greeting Card Association. Provides an insight to the industry, including an up-to-date list of publishers, a new product section and a free showcase for artists, illustrators and verses. Special supplements include *Focus on Art Cards*, *Focus on Humorous Cards*, *Focus on Words & Sentiments*, *Focus on Kids* and *Focus on Giftwrap*.

Hosts The Henries, the greeting card industry awards. The September edition includes details of the finalists in the different categories and the November issue features the winners.

Direct-to-retail (DTR) publishers supply retailers via sales agents or reps. Most greeting cards sold through specialist card shops and gift shops are supplied by DTR publishers, which range from multinational corporations down to small, trendy niche publishing companies. These publishers market series of ranges based on distinctive design themes or characters. Categories of DTR cards include contemporary art/fun, fine art, humour, children's, photographic, traditional and handmade.

Approaching a publisher

Unfortunately, there is no standard way of approaching and submitting work to a card publisher. The first step is to establish that the publisher you wish to approach accepts work from freelance artists; then find out their requirements for submission and to whom it should be addressed.

It is always better to send several examples of your work to show the breadth of your artistic skills. Some publishers prefer to see finished designs while others are happy with well-presented sketches. Never send originals: instead send photocopies, laser copies or photographs, and include at least one design in colour. Never be tempted to sell similar designs to two publishers – a bad reputation will follow you around.

Some publishers will be looking to purchase individual designs for specific sending occasions while others will be more intent on looking for designs which could be developed to make up a range. Bear in mind that publishers work a long way in advance, e.g. Christmas ranges are launched to the retailers in January. Development of a range may take up to six months prior to launching.

Also remember that cards in retail outlets are rarely displayed in their entirety. Therefore, when designing a card make sure that some of the 'action' appears in the top half.

When interest is shown

Some publishers respond to submissions from artists immediately while others prefer to deal with them on a monthly basis. A publisher's response may be in the form of a request for more submissions of a specific design style or of a specific character. This speculative development work is usually carried out free of charge. Always meet your deadline (news travels fast in the industry).

A publisher interested in buying your artwork will probably then issue you with a contract. This may cover aspects such as the terms of payment; rights of usage of the design (e.g. is it just for greeting cards or will it include giftwrap and/or stationery?); territory of usage (most publishers want worldwide rights); and ownership of copyright or license period.

There is no set industry standard rate of pay for greeting card artists. Publishers lpay artists either on a per design or per range basis in one of the following ways:

- **Flat fee.** A one-off payment is made to the artist for ownership of a design for an unlimited period. The industry standard is around £200–£250 for a single design, and payment on a sliding scale for more than one design.
- **Licensing fee.** The publisher is granted the right to use a piece of artwork for a specified number of years, after which the full rights revert to the artist. Payment to the artist is approximately £150 upwards per design.
- **Licensing fee** plus royalty. As above plus a royalty payment on each card sold. Artists would generally receive a minimum of £100 for the licensing fee plus 3% of the trade price of each card sold.

- **Advance royalty deal.** A goodwill advance on royalties is paid to the artist. In the case of a range, the artist would receive a goodwill advance of say £500–£1000 plus 5% additional royalty payment once the threshold is reached.
- **Royalty only.** The artist receives regular royalty payments, generally paid quarterly, based on the number of cards sold. Artists should expect to receive a sales report and royalty statement.

The fees stated above should only be regarded as a rough guideline. Fees and advances are generally paid on completion of artwork. Publishers which have worldwide rights pay royalties for sales overseas to artists, although these will be on a pro rata basis to the export trade price.

Jacqueline Brown is editor of *Progressive Greetings Worldwide* and general secretary of the Greeting Card Association.

Card and stationery publishers that accept illustrations and verses

Before submitting work, artists are advised to write giving details of the work they have to offer and asking for the requirements of the company they are approaching.

*Member of the Greeting Card Association

Card Connection Ltd*

Park House, South Street, Farnham, Surrey
GU9 7QQ
tel (01252) 892300 *fax* (01252) 892363
email ho@card-connection.co.uk
website www.card-connection.co.uk
Managing Director Simon Hulme, *Senior Product Manager* Natalie Turner

Everyday and seasonal designs. Styles include cute, fun, traditional, contemporary, humour and photographic. Submit colour copies. Humorous copy and jokes plus sentimental verse. Founded 1992.

Carlton Cards Ltd*

Mill Street East, Dewsbury, West Yorkshire
WF12 9AW
tel (01924) 465200
website www.carltoncards.co.uk
Group Marketing Director Keith Auty, *Product Development Director* Josephine Loughran

All types of artwork, any size; submit as colour roughs, colour copies or transparencies. Especially interested in humorous artwork and ideas.

Caspari Ltd*

9 Shire Hill, Saffron Walden, Essex CB11 3AP
tel (01799) 513010 *fax* (01799) 513101
Managing Director Keith Entwisle

Traditional fine art/classic images; 5 x 4in transparencies. No verses. Founded 1990.

Colneis Marketing Ltd*

York House, 2–4 York Road, Felixstowe IP11 7QQ
tel (01394) 271668 *fax* (01394) 275114
email colneiscards@btopenworld.com
website www.colneisgreetingcards.com
Proprietor John Botting

Photographs (preferably medium format) and colour artwork of nature and cute images. Considers verses. Founded 1994.

Colour House Graphics*

58 Matilda Street, London N1 1BG
tel 020-7700 7780 *fax* 020-7700 7727
email colourhousegraphics@hotmail.com
Partners John Ellner and Margaret Ellner

Contemporary styles of painting of subjects relating to people's everyday lives. Particularly interested in sophisticated, loose, graphic styles. No verses. Founded 1990.

Simon Elvin Ltd*

Wooburn Industrial Park, Wooburn Green, Bucks
HP10 0PE
tel (01628) 526711 *fax* (01628) 53148
email rachel.bradley@simonelvin.com
website www.simonelvin.com
Art Director Isabel Scott Evans, *Studio Co-ordinator* Rachel Bradley

Female/male traditional and contemporary designs, female/male cute, wedding/anniversary, birth congratulations, fine art, photographic animals, flowers and male imagery, traditional sympathy, juvenile ages, special occasions and gift wrap.

Looking for submissions that show flair, imagination and an understanding of greeting card design. Artists should familiarise themselves with the ranges, style and content. Submit a small collection of either colour copies or prints (no original artwork) and include an sae for return of work. Alternatively email jpegs to the Studio Co-ordinator.

4C–Charity Christmas Card Council

Cards World Ltd, 49 Cross Street, London N1 2BB
tel (0845) 230 0046 *fax* (0845) 230 0048
email 4c@charitycards.org
website www.charitycards.org

Traditional and contemporary Christmas cards for the corporate market. Submit artwork on CD-Rom or 5 x 4in transparencies. No verses. Charitable not-for-profit organisation. Founded 1966.

Gallery Five Ltd*

The Old Bakery, 1 Bellingham Road, London
SE6 2PN
tel 020-8741 3891 *fax* 020-8741 4444
website www.galleryfive.co.uk

Send samples of work FAO 'Gallery Five Art Studio'. Colour photocopies, Mac-formatted zip/CD acceptable, plus sae. No verses.

Gemma International Ltd*

Linmar House, 6 East Portway, Andover, Hants
SP10 3LU

tel (01264) 388400 fax (01264) 366243
website www.gemma-international.co.uk
Directors L. Rudd-Clarke, A. Parkin, T. Rudd-Clarke,
W. O'Loughlin, K. Bishop

Cute, contemporary, leading-edge designs for
children, teens and young adults. Founded 1984.

Gibson Greetings International Ltd
Gibson House, Hortonwood 30, Telford, Shrops.
TF1 7YF
tel (01952) 608333 fax (01952) 605259
email linda-marshall@gibson-greetings.co.uk
Product Director Linda Marshall

All everyday and seasonal illustrations: cute,
humorous, juvenile, traditional and contemporary
designs, as well as surface pattern. Greeting card
traditional and humorous verse. Founded 1991.

Graphic Humour Ltd
4 Britannia House, Point Pleasant, Wallsend,
Tyne & Wear NE28 6HA
tel 0191-295 4200 fax 0191-295 3916
email enquiries@graphichumour.com
website www.graphichumour.com

Risqué and everyday artwork ideas for greetings
cards; short, humorous copy. Founded 1984.

The Greetings Factory Ltd
PO Box 662, Watford, Herts. WD17 2ZX
tel (01923) 210100 fax (01923) 246008
email info@hotchpotchcards.com
website www.hotchpotch.net
Director Paul Steele

Colour artwork for greetings cards, giftwrap and
social stationery. Considers verses. Founded 1997.

Hallmark Cards Plc*
Hallmark House, Bingley Road, Heaton, Bradford
BD9 6SD
tel (01274) 252000
website www.hallmarkuk.com
Freelance submissions Emma Charlesworth

Artwork: All subjects will be considered. Submit
10–12 colour samples (not originals, as work cannot
be returned), demonstrating the diversity of your
work. Ensure your name is on all work. Words: As
there is an in-house editorial team, only humour
writing submissions will be considered.

Hanson White – Gibson Hanson Graphics
2nd Floor, AMP House, Dingwall Road, Croydon
CR0 2LX
tel 020-8260 1200 fax 020-8260 1213
email hannah.turpin@gibsonhanson.co.uk,
sally.hipkins@gibsonhanson.co.uk
Submissions Editors Hannah Bonomini, Sally Hipkins

Humorous artwork and cartoons for greeting cards,
including Christmas, Valentine's Day, Mother's Day

and Father's Day. Humorous copy lines and
punchline jokes, funny poems and rhymes.
Guidelines available. Founded 1958.

Jarrold Publishing
(incorporating Pitkin and Unichrome brands)
Whitefriars, Norwich NR3 1JR
tel (01603) 763300 fax (01603) 662748
email publishing@jarrold.co.uk
website www.jarrold-publishing.co.uk
Directors Margot Russell-King (managing), Ben
Carter (finance), Steve Plackett (supply chain gift &
stationery)

UK tourism and heritage guide books and souvenirs,
calendars, diaries and gift stationery. Unsolicited
MSS, synopses and ideas welcome but approach in
writing before submitting to Marketing Department.
Founded 1770.

Jodds*
PO Box 353, Bicester, Oxon OX27 0GS
tel (01869) 278550 fax (01869) 278551
email design@joddscards.com
website www.joddscards.com
Partners M. Payne and J.S. Payne

Contemporary art style greetings cards; must give out
a warm feel. Submit colour photocopies with sae. No
verses. Founded 1988.

Leeds Postcards
4 Granby Road, Leeds LS6 3AS
email xtine@leedspostcards.com
website www.leedspostcards.com
Contact Christine Hankinson

Publisher and distributor of radical postcards for the
wall and post.

Lima Design*
110 Dunstans Road, London SE22 0HE
tel/fax 020-8693 4257
email lisa@limadesign.co.uk
website www.limadesign.co.uk
Proprietor Lisa Breakwell

Produces contemporary, design-conscious cards
which are all hand applied using resisters and
capacitors, ribbon, indoor sparklers, animal-shaped
rubber bands, metallic thread and beads. Founded
2002.

Ling Design Ltd*
Westmoreland House, Westmoreland Street, Bath
BA2 3HE
tel (0845) 450 6601 fax (0845) 450 6602
email info@lingdesign.co.uk
website www.lingdesign.co.uk
Creative Director Kirsten Boyd

Artwork for greetings cards and giftwrap.

Medici*
Grafton House, Hyde Estate Road, London NW9 6JZ
tel 020-8205 2500 fax 020-8205 2552

email sales@medici.co.uk
website www.medici.co.uk
Contact The Art Department

Requirements: full colour or black and white paintings/sketches/etchings/designs suitable for reproduction as greeting cards. Send preliminary letter with brief details of work and colour copies only.

The Monster Factory*

Unit 207, Welsbach House, 3–9 Broomhill Road, London SW18 4JQ
tel 020-8875 9988 *fax* 020-8870 4488
email info@themonsterfactory.com
website www.themonsterfactory.com
Directors Martin Grix, Kate Eagar

Publishers of innovative stationery with a funky, design-led feel. Specialises in handmade ranges, unusual printing techniques and quirky illustration. Will consider original new concepts and fresh artwork styles with bags of character and humour. Do not send original artwork. No verses. Founded 2000.

The Paper House Group plc*

Waterwells Drive, Gloucester, Glos. GL2 2PH
tel (01452) 888999 *fax* (01452) 888912
email art@paperhouse.co.uk
website www.paperhouse.co.uk

Specialises in cartoon humour illustration, contemporary art styles and traditional verse design for special occasions and family birthday.

Paperlink Ltd*

356 Kennington Road, London SE11 4LD
tel 020-7582 8244 *fax* 020-7587 5212
email info@paperlinkcards.com
website www.paperlinkcards.com
Directors Louise Tighe, Tim Porte, Tim Purcell

Publishers of ranges of humorous and contemporary art greetings cards. Produce products under licence for charities. Founded 1986.

Pepperpot

Royston Road, Duxford, Cambridge CB2 4QY
tel (01223) 836825 *fax* (01223) 833321
Publishing Controller Linda Worsfold

Gift stationery, photo albums. No submissions without sae. Division of Copywrite Designs Ltd.

Pineapple Park*

58 Wilbury Way, Hitchin, Herts. SG4 0TP
tel (01462) 442021 *fax* (01462) 440418
email info@pineapplepark.co.uk
website www.pineapplepark.co.uk
Directors Peter M. Cockerline, Sarah M. Parker

Illustrations and photographs for publication as greetings cards. Contemporary, cute, humour: submit artwork or laser copies with sae. Photographic florals

always needed. Humour copy/jokes accepted without artwork. Also concepts for ranges. Founded 1993.

Powell Publishing*

57 Coombe Valley Road, Dover, Kent CT17 0EX
tel (01304) 213999 *fax* (01304) 240151
email fiona@powellpublishing.co.uk
website www.powellpublishing.co.uk
Directors B.W. Powell (chairman), T.J. Paulett (managing), *Art & Design Manager* Fiona Bale

Greetings card publishers. Interested in Christmas designs for the charity card market. Division of Powell Print Ltd.

The Publishing House*

PO Box 81, Banbury, Oxon OX16 3YL
tel (01295) 271144 *fax* (01295) 277403
Directors Naval Phandey, M. Munder

General and multicultural cards across all faiths. No verses.

Nigel Quiney Publications Ltd

Cloudesley House, Shire Hill, Saffron Walden, Essex CB11 3FB
tel (01799) 520200 *fax* (01799) 520100
website www.nigelquiney.com
Contact Alison Butterworth, Creative Director

Everyday and seasonal greetings cards and giftwrap including fine art, photographic, humour, fun art, contemporary and cute. Submit colour copies, photographs or transparencies: no original artwork.

Rainbow Cards Ltd*

Kingswood Business Park, Holyhead Road, Albrighton, Wolverhampton, West Midlands WV7 3AU
tel (01902) 376000 *fax* (01902) 376001
email sales@rainbowcards.co.uk
website www.rainbowcards.co.uk

Artwork for humorous and traditional greetings cards. Founded 1976.

Really Good*

The Old Mast House, The Square, Abingdon, Oxon OX14 5AR
tel (01235) 537888 *fax* (01235) 537779
email potatoes@reallygood.uk.com
website www.reallygood.uk.com
Director David Hicks

Always looking for fun and funny artwork in a quirky or modern way to publish on cards, stationery or gifts. Send samples on paper rather than on disk, or email website link or small files to view. Allow plenty of time for review. Founded 1987.

Felix Rosenstiel's Widow & Son Ltd

Fine Art Publishers, 33–35 Markham Street, London SW3 3NR
tel 020-7352 3551 *fax* 020-7351 5300

email sales@felixr.com
website www.felixr.com

Invites offers of original oil paintings and strong watercolours of a professional standard for reproduction as picture prints for the picture framing trade. Any type of subject considered; send photographs of work.

Royle Publications Ltd – see The Paper House Group plc

Santoro Graphics Ltd

Rotunda Point, 11 Hartfield Crescent, London SW19 3RL
tel 020-8781 1100 fax 020-8781 1101
email enquiries@santorographics.com
website www.santorographics.com
Directors Lucio Santoro, Meera Santoro (art)

Publishers of innovative and award-winning designs for greetings cards, giftwrap and gift stationery. Bold, contemporary images with an international appeal. Subjects covered: contemporary, pop-up, cute, quirky, fashion, fine art, retro. Submit samples as colour photocopies, transparencies, CD-Roms or via email as jpeg or PDF files. Founded 1985.

Second Nature Ltd*

10 Malton Road, London W10 5UP
tel 020-8960 0212 fax 020-8960 8700
email rods@secondnature.co.uk
website www.secondnature.co.uk
Publishing Director Rod Schragger

Contemporary artwork for greetings cards and handmade cards; jokes for humorous range; short modern sentiment; verses. Founded 1981.

Solomon & Whitehead Ltd

Lynn Lane, Shenstone, Staffs. WS14 0DX
tel (01543) 480696 fax (01543) 481619
email sales@fineartgroup.co.uk

Fine art prints, limited editions and originals, framed and unframed.

Soul

Old Mast House, The Square, Abingdon, Oxon OX14 5AR
tel (01235) 537816 fax (01235) 537817
email smile@souluk.com
website www.souluk.com
Director David Hicks

Publishers of contemporary, fine and quirky art. Email website link or small files to view. Allow time for review. Do not send originals. Sister company of Really Good.

Noel Tatt Group/Impress Publishing*

Appledown House, Barton Business Park, Appledown Way, New Dover Road, Canterbury, Kent CT1 3TE
tel (01227) 811600 fax (01227) 811601
email mail@noeltatt.co.uk
website www.noeltatt.co.uk
Directors Jarle Tatt, Diane Tatt, Richard Parsons, Ian Hylands

General everyday cards – broad mix; Christmas. Will consider verses. Founded 1964.

Vital Cards Ltd*

PO Box 274, Leatherhead, Surrey KT22 0WL
tel (01372) 842753 fax (01372) 841051
email info@vitalcards.com
website www.vitalcards.com
Managing Director Peter Galazka

Contemporary art-based designs always considered for quality greeting card ranges. Submit colour copies, photographs or CDs. Do not send original artwork. No verses. Founded 2003.

Webb Ivory (Burton) Ltd

Queen Street, Burton-on-Trent, Staffs. DE14 3LP
tel (01283) 566311
email enquiries@webb-ivory.co.uk

High-quality Christmas cards and paper products.

Wishing Well Studios Ltd*

Kellet Close, Martland Park, Wigan, Lancs. WN5 0LP
tel (01942) 218888 fax (01942) 218899
email nickyh@wishingwell.co.uk,
susie.linley@wishingwell.co.uk
website www.wishingwell.co.uk
Artist contact Nicky Harrison, Writer contact Susie Linley

Rhyming and prose verse 4–24 lines long; also jokes. All artwork styles considered but do not send originals.

Woodmansterne Publications Ltd*

1 The Boulevard, Blackmoor Lane, Watford, Herts. WD18 8UW
tel (01923) 200600 fax (01923) 200601
email info@woodmansterne.co.uk
website woodmansterne.co.uk
Production Director Julian Perryman

Greetings cards, wrapping paper, notecards and social stationery featuring fine and contemporary art and photography (colour and b&w). Submit colour copies, photographs or transparencies. No verses.

Picture research
The freelance photographer

Becoming a successful freelance photographer is as much about marketing as photographic talent. Bruce Coleman and Ian Thraves discuss possibilities for the freelance photographer.

Having an outstanding portfolio is one thing, but to receive regular commissions takes a good business head and sound market knowledge. Although working as a professional photographer can be tough, it is undoubtedly one of the most interesting and rewarding ways of earning a living.

Entering professional photography

A good starting point is to embark on one of the many college courses available, which range from GCSE to degree level, and higher. These form a good foundation, though most teach only the technical aspects of photography and very few cover the basics of running a business. But a good college course will provide students with the opportunity to become familiar with photographic equipment and develop skills without the restrictions and pressures found in the workplace.

In certain fields, such as commercial photography, it is possible to learn the trade as an assistant to an established photographer. A photographer's assistant will undertake many varied tasks, including preparing camera equipment and lighting, building sets, obtaining props and organising locations, as well as general mundane chores. It usually takes only a year or two for an assistant to become a fully competent photographer, having during that time learnt many technical aspects of a particular field of photography and the fundamentals of running a successful business. There is, however, the danger of a long-standing assistant becoming a clone of the photographer worked for, and it is for this reason that some assistants prefer to gain experience with other photographers rather than working for just one for a long period of time. The Association of Photographers can help place an assistant.

However, in other fields of photography, such as photojournalism or wildlife photography, an assistant is not generally required, and photographers in these fields have to learn for themselves as they work.

Identifying your market

From the outset, identify which markets are most suitable for the kind of subjects you photograph. Study each market carefully and only offer images which suit the client's requirements.

Usually photographers who specialise in a particular field do better than those who generalise. By concentrating on one or two subject areas they become expert at what they do. Those who make a name for themselves are invariably specialists, and it is far easier for the images of, for example, an exceptional fashion photographer or an award-winning wildlife photographer to be remembered than the work of someone who covers a broad range of subjects.

In addition, photographers who produce work with individual style (e.g. by experimenting with camera angles or manipulating images to create unusual effects) are far more likely to make an impact. Alternative images which attract attention and can help sell a product are always sought after. This is especially true of advertising photography, but applies also to other markets such as book and magazine publishers, who are always seeking eye-catching images to use on front covers.

Promoting yourself

Effective self-promotion tells the market who you are and what service you offer. A first step should be to create an outstanding portfolio of images, tailored to appeal to the targeted market. Photographers targeting a few different markets should create an individual portfolio for each rather than presenting a single general one, including only a few relevant images. A portfolio containing between 10 and 20 images is enough for a potential client to judge a photographer's abilities.

Images should be presented in a format which the client is used to handling. Transparencies (perhaps duplicated to a larger size for easier viewing and general impact) are usually suitable for the editorial markets, but often more general companies prefer to view high-quality prints. Images can also be presented on CD-Rom and, unlike a traditional portfolio, can be left with potential clients to keep and refer to. Any published material (often referred to as 'tearsheets') should also be added to a portfolio. Tearsheets are often presented mounted and laminated in plastic.

Business cards and letterheads should be designed to reflect style and professionalism. Consider using a good graphic designer to design a logo for use on cards, letterheads and any other promotional literature. Many photographers produce postcard-size business cards and include an image as well as their name and logo.

Other than word of mouth, advertising is probably the best way of making your services known to potential clients. For a local market, a business directory such as *Yellow Pages* is a good start. Specialist directories in which photographers can advertise include *The Creative Handbook* and *Contact Photographers* (see page 476).

Cold calling by telephone is probably the most cost-effective and productive way of making contacts, and these should be followed up by an appointment for a personal visit

Professional organisations

The Association of Photographers
Co-Secretary Gwen Thomas, 81 Leonard Street,
London EC2A 4QS
tel 020-7739 6669 *fax* 020-7739 8707
email general@aophoto.co.uk
website www.the-aop.org
See page 522.

British Institute of Professional Photography
Fox Talbot House, Amwell End, Ware, Herts.
SG12 9HN
tel (01920) 464011
email bippware@aol.com
website www.bipp.com
See page 528.

Master Photographers Association
Jubilee House, 1 Chancery Lane, Darlington,
Co. Durham DL1 5QP
tel (01325) 356555 *fax* (01325) 357813
email info@mpauk.com
website www.thempa.com
See page 542.

The Royal Photographic Society
Fenton House, 122 Wells Road, Bath BA2 3AH
tel (01225) 462841 *fax* (01225) 448688
email rps@rps.org
website www.rps.org
See page 550.

BAPLA (British Association of Picture Libraries and Agencies)
See page 524.

(if possible) in order to show a portfolio of images. This helps to ensure you will not be forgotten.

Most photographers also use the internet as a medium to promote themselves. A cleverly designed website is a stylish and cost-effective way to expose a photographer's portfolio to a global market, as well as being a convenient way for a potential client to view a photographer's work. A personal website address should be added to business stationery and to other forms of advertising together with the usual address and telephone number information.

Creating a website can be much cheaper than advertising using conventional published print media. However, its design should be carefully composed and is probably best left to a professional website designer (see *Setting up a website*, page 606). Although many images and details about your business can be placed on a website, one limiting factor is the time it can take to download the images due to the size of the files. Unless this is a relatively quick process the viewer may lose patience and cancel access to the site.

A well-organised exhibition of images is a very effective way of bringing your work to the attention of current and potential new clients. Throw a preview party with refreshments for friends, colleagues and specially invited guests from the industry. A show which is well reviewed by critics who write for newspapers and magazines can generate additional interest.

As a photographer's career develops, the budget for self-promotion should increase. Many established photographers will go as far as producing full-colour mailers, posters, and even calendars, which all contain examples of their work.

Digital photography

Digital photography and image-enhancement and manipulation using computer technology are now widely used in the photographic industry. Since the cost of digital cameras and other hardware can be considerably cheaper than using large quantities of film, many photographers are now using this technology.

There are various levels of quality produced by digital cameras and photographers should consider the requirements of their market prior to investing in expensive hardware which is prone to rapid change and improvement. At the cheaper level, 35mm-style digital cameras manufactured by companies such as Nikon and Canon can produce outstanding quality images suitable for many end uses. Cameras like these are now used predominantly for press, PR and general commercial work.

At a higher level, many commercial studio photographers have invested in a 'digital capture back', which is a high-quality chip which can be adapted to fit many of the conventional studio cameras. This system is far more expensive, but is capable of producing file sizes which closely compare in quality to a high-resolution scan from large format film. Thus the images are suitable for any end use, such as top-quality advertisements. Photographers thinking of supplying stock libraries with digital images should realise that it is often this kind of quality which is required, as stock libraries are looking to supply a diverse range of markets, including advertising.

Image-enhancement and manipulation using a computer program such as Adobe Photoshop provides photographers with an onscreen darkroom where the possibilities for creating imaginative images are endless. As well as being useful for retouching purposes and creating photo compositions, it provides the photographer with an opportunity to create more unusual images. It is therefore especially useful for targeting the advertising market, where fantasy images are more important than reality.

Using a stock library

As well as undertaking commissions, photographers have the option of selling their images through a photographic stock library or agency. There are many stock libraries in the UK, some specialising in specific subject areas, such as wildlife photography, and others covering general subjects (see *Picture agencies and libraries*, page 483).

Stock libraries are fiercely competitive, all fighting for a share of the market, and it is therefore best to aim to place images with an established name, although competition amongst photographers will be strong. Each stock library has different specific requirements and established markets, so contact them first before making a submission. Some libraries will ask to see a few hundred images from a photographer in order to judge for consistency of quality and saleability. Stock libraries selling images through catalogues or over the internet will often consider an initial submission of just a few images, knowing that it is possible to accumulate significant fees from a small number of outstanding individual images marketed this way.

Images placed with a library usually remain the property of the photographer and libraries do not normally sell images outright to clients, but lease them for a specific use for a fee, from which commission is deducted. This means that a single image can accumulate many sales over a period of time. The commission rate is usually about 50% of every sale generated by the library. This may sound high, but it should be borne in mind that the library takes on all overheads, marketing costs and other responsibilities involved in the smooth running of a business, allowing the photographer the freedom to spend more time taking pictures.

Photographers should realise, however, that stock photography is a long-term investment and it can take some time for sales to build up to a significant income. Clearly, photographers who supply the right images for the market, and are prolific, are those who do well, and there are a good number of photographers who make their entire living as full-time stock photographers, never having to undertake commissioned work.

Royalty-free CD companies

Many stock libraries are now marketing royalty-free images on CD-Rom. These companies usually obtain images by purchasing them from photographers for a flat fee or pay royalties to the photographer based on CD sales. Once a CD has been purchased by a client they, in effect, own the images on the CD and are therefore able to reproduce them as many times as they wish, paying no further fees. A typical CD may contain one hundred high-resolution reproduction-quality images in a variety of subject areas, including most specialist subjects.

Although photographers may be tempted to sell images to these companies in order to gain an instant fee, they should be aware that placing images with a traditional stock library can be far more fruitful financially in the long term, since a good image can accumulate very high fees over a period of time and go on selling for many years to come. Furthermore, the photographer always retains the rights to his or her own images.

Running your own library

Photographers choosing to market their own images or start up their own library have the advantage of retaining a full fee for every picture sale they make. But it is unlikely that an individual photographer could ever match the rates of an established library, or make the same volume of sales per image. However, the internet has opened a new marketing avenue for photographers, who now have the opportunity to sell their images worldwide. Previously, only an established stock library would have been able to do this. Before embarking on establishing a home library, photographers should be aware that the business of marketing images is essentially a desk job which involves a considerable amount of paperwork and time, which could be spent taking pictures.

When setting up a picture library, your first consideration should be whether to build up a library of your own images, or to take on other contributing photographers. Many photographers running their own libraries submit additional images to bigger libraries to increase the odds of making a good income. Often, a photographer's personal library is made up of work rejected by the larger libraries, which are usually only interested in images that will regularly sell and generate a high turnover. However, occasional sales can generate a significant amount of income for the individual. Furthermore, a photographer with a library of specialised subjects stands a good chance of gaining recognition with niche markets, which can be very lucrative if the competition for those particular subjects is low.

If you take on contributing photographers, the responsibility for another's work becomes yours, so it is important to draw up a contract with terms of business for both your contributing photographers and your clients. Loss or damage of images is the most important consideration when sending pictures to clients (most libraries will charge clients a fee of £400–£600 per image for loss or damage of originals). It is often worth checking that a company wishing to receive transparencies does have adequate insurance to cover these fees, which can amount to a considerable figure if a large quantity of images is lost or damaged. On no account should images be sent to companies which refuse to take responsibility for loss or damage, nor to private individuals, unless they are working on a freelance basis for an established company. It should also be clearly stated in your terms that all pictures in the client's possession become the client's responsibility until they are returned and inspected for damage by the library. Most libraries are now taking a safer approach, distributing images as digital files either on CD or direct to clients, usually via ISDN or Broadband. In addition to being a much cheaper way of distributing images, the problem of loss or damage or original material is also eliminated.

Reproduction fees should also be established on a strict basis, bearing in mind that you owe it to your contributing photographers to command fees which are as high as possible when selling the rights to their images. It is also essential that you control how pictures will be used and the amount of exposure they will receive. The fees should be established according to the type of client using the image and how the image itself will be reproduced. Important factors to consider are where the image will appear, to what size it will be reproduced, the size of the print run, and the territorial rights required by the client.

Bruce Coleman is Chairman of Bruce Coleman The Natural World and past President of the British Association of Picture Libraries. **Ian Thraves** is a freelance photographer and former picture editor at Bruce Coleman The Natural World (www.thravesphoto.co.uk).

The picture research revolution

In this article, Julian Jackson describes how picture researchers have had to change the way they work since the arrival of the 'digital age'.

Picture researchers find the images you see in books, magazines, on television shows and videos, and now on CD-Roms and the internet. For many years picture research was a relatively static profession. The procedures for contacting picture suppliers didn't change very much. The researcher would phone or fax a supplier with a request then a package of transparencies or prints would arrive in the post. Since entering the 'digital age' this has changed dramatically. Now picture researchers need to learn new skills in addition to the old ones. They need considerable internet search competencies. They also need enough technological knowledge to check that digital files are of sufficient quality for their use, which may be for a much wider variety of media. In an era of rapid technological change they need to keep an eye out for developments such as new file formats or software.

The picture research process

There are two sorts of researchers: freelances, and salaried staff, sometimes called

'in-house' researchers. The way they both approach a job is the same. Generally most picture research assignments follow this pattern:

1. Briefing and creation of picture list.
2. The picture researcher obtains low-resolution 'comp' images, usually by internet search but also by contacting picture libraries, press agencies, photographers, museums, galleries or other picture sources, by phone, fax, email or personal visit.
3. Photography is commissioned, if appropriate.
4. Pictures arrive and are 'booked in'.
5. A preliminary selection is made, usually by the picture researcher, designer and editor working in concert.
6. Rejected pictures are archived or deleted.
7. A final selection is made. High-resolution images are obtained by the researcher and forwarded to the designer.
8. The picture researcher negotiates the fees, creates a list of contributors to be credited, and checks the proofs.

9. The picture researcher returns all the remaining unused 'analogue' pictures and deletes or archives digital files.

10. The picture researcher keeps records and sends complementary copies or 'tearsheets' (the page that the supplier's picture was used on) to the various suppliers of the pictures.

This is a broad view of how all picture research assignments work, whether for traditional media such as books, or new media like CD-Roms. In some cases there might already be a fee structure in place so the researcher does not have to do fee negotiation.

Skills required

Picture researchers need to be organised, diligent, capable of leaps of the imagination when necessary ('I bet there's a museum devoted to shopping bags somewhere!'), and above all *diplomatic*. They need the ability to wheedle images out of sometimes unresponsive people: professional image libraries pride themselves on swift, efficient service, but picture researchers have to deal with museum staff, private collectors, individual photographers, PR people, and the odd complete nutter who just happens to own the rights to *the picture you must have*. Of all the skills necessary, this is the most vital.

A good picture researcher also needs diligence and good organisation. Diligence means keeping tabs on the pictures so they do not get lost, and having a system in place to track digital files, both low and high resolution.

The digital wave

Digitisation of files and the advent of the internet in general has caused a revolution in picture research. Agonised waits for a package of transparencies to arrive from Inner Mongolia are a thing of the past; now pictures can be sent by broadband ADSL or ISDN in seconds. Commissioning a photographer is streamlined when you can look at his or her portfolio online. Email is particularly convenient for dealing with suppliers in different time zones.

Useful directories

Picture Researcher's Handbook

by Hilary and Mary Evans, 7th edn, Pira

No picture researcher should be without this invaluable and comprehensive source of picture libraries worldwide. The book clearly lists where picture libraries are, the subjects they cover and addresses, websites, email addresses, telephone and fax numbers. A new edition is in preparation.

BAPLA Directory

BAPLA, 18 Vine Hill, London EC1R 5DZ
tel 020-7713 1780 *fax* 020-7713 1211

Lists all the current members of the British Association of Picture Libraries and Agencies (BAPLA).

Stock Index

The Publishing Factory, 32 Queensway, London W2 3RX
tel 020-7727 4236 *fax* 020-7792 4034
email space@creativecityonline.com
website www.stockindexonline.com

Supports the leading source books to specialist stock photography libraries. A free online research facility containing catalogues and industry news.

Picture Research in a Digital Age

by Julian Jackson
website www.julianjackson.co.uk/pic_res_dig.htm

This e-book covers digital photography, scanning, searching the internet, and many other important topics to enable researchers to get the best out of the digital age.

Like the famous 'butterfly' chaos theory, digitisation has caused a tornado which is roaring through the industry. Deadlines are shorter, leaving less time for considered decisions. Unlike transparencies, digital files can be unusable for a variety of invisible factors: for example, bad scanning, wrong resolution, corruption. These problems usually become evident at the last possible moment. Old-style picture researchers would have rejected a bad transparency or print at an early stage so these problems would have been avoided.

Useful organisations

The Association of Photographers
See page 522.

BAPLA (British Association of Picture Libraries and Agencies)
See page 524.

DACS (Design and Artists Copyright Society)
See page 705.

The Picture Research Association
See page 547.

Picture researchers have had to learn powerful computer search skills and develop understandings of many technological concepts. For some this has been a difficult process that has lessened the enjoyment of the job. Unfortunately, one of the spin-offs from digitisation has been that employers may mistakenly believe that a researcher can do his or her job from behind a computer. A wise picture researcher will still make the time to personally visit sources and forge a relationship with the people there, who will often be experts in their subject, and who can enhance a project with their knowledge.

Old style *v.* digital

There are advantages and disadvantages to both ways of working. Some picture researchers will continue to handle prints and transparencies in the conventional manner alongside downloading, modifying, and transmitting digital files from their computer, though for most people the job is now 100% digital.

● One distinct advantage of digital files is that they can be instantly downloaded from the web and sent globally via electronic means.

● Working with digital files means that there are no time-consuming and tedious returns to do.

● Analogue media – prints, negatives and transparencies – can be immediately assessed for quality. To assess the quality of a digital file, further investigation is required.

● Intricate keywording systems often fail to find pictures which the library holds. Phoning the library's experienced staff may well be a better use of your time than spending hours wrestling with an online search system.

● Sometimes it is hard to keep track of digital files on a computer system, especially if the file name is just a number, as opposed to a descriptive name, such as 'Picture of Paris.jpg'.

● Negotiating fees remains the same. It is what the picture is *used* for, not whether it is analogue or digital, that is the main criterion.

Picture research now

Picture research has changed. Few researchers outside museums and academic organisations use analogue images now. The speed and convenience of digital files means that online picture research is the norm for most researchers. Modern researchers need high-levels of computer skills to enable them to find and evaluate the pictures they want, whether it's by searching the web generally, or accessing the online search systems of picture libraries.

Julian Jackson is a writer, internet expert and consultant to the UK picture research industry. He has close links with many companies and organisations within the photographic industry. His website is www.julianjackson.co.uk

See also ...
- *Picture agencies and libraries*, page 483
- *Card and stationery publishers that accept photographs*, page 510
- *Syndicates, news and press agencies*, page 117
- *The freelance photographer*, page 473
- *National newspapers UK and Ireland*, page 7

Picture agencies and libraries

As well as supplying images to picture editors, picture researchers and others who use pictures in the media, picture agencies and libraries provide a service to the freelance photographer as one way of licensing their work. Most of the agencies and libraries listed in this section take work from other photographers. To find which ones cover specific subjects see page 769.

*Member of the British Association of Picture Libraries and Agencies (BAPLA)

Picture libraries and agencies directly manage photographers' rights on their behalf and, subject to the style of photography, market these to a range of clients in publishing, design, advertising, new media, etc.

Each time a picture library/agency licenses a photographer's image, the photographer gets a share of that revenue. Royalty payments will vary from company to company. Submitting regular work to a reputable agent is a good way for the professional photographer to supplement their income. Many artists also benefit from working for a picture library/ agency as a good means to gain technical, commercial or administrative training. See the British Association of Picture Libraries and Agencies (BAPLA) website (www.bapla.org) for details of vacancies.

The vast majority of BAPLA's 440 members are small, sole trader/single photographer-run companies, and not all will be looking for additional content. Photographers looking to place their work might initially start with the medium to large agencies first.

Most agencies operate in a digital marketplace so you would be advised to ensure that any material you submit is in a digital format and includes the appropriate information that, at least, identifies the copyright owner. For a full list of agencies that have signed a code of professional conduct, and are endorsed by BAPLA, see their website. See also page 524.

AA World Travel Library
16th Floor, Fanum House, Basing View, Basingstoke, Hants RG21 4EA
tel (01256) 491588 *fax* (01256) 492440
email travel.images@theaa.com
Picture Sales Manager Liz Allen

Approx. 160,000 colour transparencies of worldwide travel images. All images are available in digital format. Part of AA Publishing. Founded 1990.

A.A. & A. Ancient Art & Architecture Collection*
Suite 1, 1st Floor, 410–420 Rayners Lane, Pinner, Middlesex HA5 5DY
tel 020-8429 3131 *fax* 020-8429 4646
email library@aaacollection.co.uk
website www.aaacollection.com

Specialises in the history of civilisations of the Middle East, Mediterranean countries, Europe, Asia, Americas, from ancient times to recent past, their arts, architecture, beliefs and peoples.

Academic File News Photos
Academic File International Syndication, Eastern Art Publishing Group, PO Box 13666, London SW14 8WF
tel 020-8392 1122 *fax* 020-8392 1422
email afis@eapgroup.com
website www.eapgroup.com
Director Sajid Rizvi

Daily news and news picture coverage in UK and general library of arts, cultures, people and places, with special reference to the Middle East, North Africa and Asia. New photographers welcomed to cover UK and abroad. Sample pictures accepted over email. Founded 1985.

acestock.com*
Satellite House, 2 Salisbury Road, London SW19 4EZ
tel 020-8944 9944 *fax* 020-8944 9940
email info@acestock.com
website www.acestock.com

General library: people, industry, business, travel, commerce, skies, sport, music and natural history. Worldwide syndication. Sae for enquiries. Very selective editing policy. Terms: 50%. Founded 1980.

Action Images*

Image House, Station Road, London N17 9LR
tel 020-8885 3000 *fax* 020-8267 2067
email info@actionimages.com
website www.actionimages.com
Director Crispin J. Thruston, *Contact* Sue Evans

Specialises in sports, sporting events, sportspersons, amateur sport.

Action Plus*

54–58 Tanner Street, London SE1 3PH
tel 020-7403 1558 *fax* 020-7403 1526
email info@actionplus.co.uk
website www.actionplus.co.uk

Specialist sports and action picture library. Comprehensive collection of creative images, including all aspects of 130 professional and amateur sports worldwide. Covers all age groups, all ethnic groups and all levels of ability. 35mm colour stock and online digital archive. Terms: 50%. Founded 1986.

Lesley and Roy Adkins Picture Library

Ten Acre Wood, Heath Cross, Whitestone, Exeter EX4 2HW
tel (01392) 811357 *fax* (01392) 811435
email mail@adkinsarchaeology.com
website www.adkinsarchaeology.com

Colour library covering archaeology, ancient history, history and heritage; prehistoric, Roman, Greek, Egyptian and medieval sites and monuments; naval heritage, landscape, countryside, architecture, towns, villages and religious monuments. Founded 1989.

Aerofilms*

32–34 Station Close, Potters Bar, Herts. EN6 1TL
tel (01707) 648390 *fax* (01707) 648399
email library@aerofilms.com
website www.simmonsaerofilms.com

Comprehensive library – over 2.5 million photos going back to 1919 – of vertical and oblique aerial photographs of UK; large areas with complete cover. Founded 1919.

Air Photo Supply

42 Sunningvale Avenue, Biggin Hill, Kent TN16 3BX
tel (01959) 574872
email norman.rivett@virgin.net

Aircraft and associated subjects, Southeast England, colour and monochrome. No other photographers' material required. Founded 1963.

akg-images*

(The Arts and History Picture Library)
5 Melbray Mews, 158 Hurlingham Road, London SW6 3NS
tel 020-7610 6103 *fax* 020-7610 6125
email enquiries@akg-images.co.uk

website www.akg-images.co.uk

Principal subjects covered: art, archaeology and history. Exclusive UK and US representative for the Archiv für Kunst und Geschichte (AKG) with full access to the 10 million images held by AKG Berlin. Also exclusively represents the Erich Lessing Culture and Fine Art Archives in the UK. Founded 1994.

Alamy.com*

127 Milton Park, Abingdon, Oxon OK14 4SA
tel (01235) 844600 *fax* (01235) 844650
email sales@alamy.com
website www.alamy.com
Contact Alexandra Bortkiewicz, Director of Photography

Over 2.3 million images covering all subjects including lifestyle, business, travel, concepts, backgrounds, landscapes, still life, sports, food, wildlife, architecture, health, science, celebrities, reportage, historical. Photographers must supply their own scans/digital files and keywords, which are completed online after submission. Scans are checked for technical quality. Image submission guidelines and Contributor Agreement are both online. For initial approach, register on the Alamy website. Terms: non-exclusive contract. Photographer receives 65% of sale commission.

Bryan and Cherry Alexander Photography

Higher Cottage, Manston, Sturminster Newton, Dorset DT10 1EZ
tel (01258) 473006 *fax* (01258) 473333
email alexander@arcticphoto.co.uk
website www.arcticphoto.co.uk

Polar regions with emphasis on indigenous peoples of the North. Landscape and wildlife: Alaska to Siberia and Antarctica. Founded 1973.

Allied Artists

The Gallery@Richmond, 63 Sheen Road, Richmond, Surrey TW9 1YJ
tel 020-8334 1010 *fax* 020-8334 9900
email info@allied-artists.net
website www.allied-artists.net
Contacts Gary Mills, Mary Burtenshaw

Agency for illustrators specialising in a wide range of styles for magazines, books, children's books and advertising. Large colour library. Founded 1983.

American History Picture Library

3 Barton Buildings, Bath BA1 2JR
tel (01225) 334213 *fax* (01225) 480554

Photographs, engravings, colour transparencies covering the exploration and social, political and military history of North America from 15th to 20th century: conquistadors, civil war, railroads, the Great Depression, advertisements, Prohibition and gangsters, moon landings and space.

AMIS
(Atlas Mountains Information Services)
26 Kirkcaldy Road, Burntisland, Fife KY3 9HQ
tel (01592) 873546 *fax* (01592) 741774
Proprietor Hamish Brown MBE, FRSGS

Picture library on Moroccan sites, topography, mountains, travel. Illustration service. Commissions undertaken. No pictures purchased.

Ancient Egypt Picture Library
6 Branden Drive, Knutsford, Cheshire WA16 8EJ
tel (01565) 633106 *fax* (01565) 633106
email BobEgyptPL@aol.com

Images of Egypt, including most of the ancient sites and views of modern Egypt. All photographs (over 30,000 colour transparencies and digital images) taken by an Egyptologist, who can also provide full historical/archaeological information. Founded 1996.

Andes Press Agency*
26 Padbury Court, London E2 7EH
tel 020-7613 5417 *fax* 020-7739 3159
email apa@andespressagency.com
Director Carlos Reyes

Social, political and economic aspects of Latin America, Africa, Asia, Middle East, Europe and Britain; specialises in Latin America and contemporary world religions. Founded 1983.

Heather Angel/Natural Visions*
Highways, 6 Vicarage Hill, Farnham, Surrey GU9 8HJ
tel (01252) 716700 *fax* (01252) 727464
email hangel@naturalvisions.co.uk
website www.naturalvisions.co.uk

Worldwide coverage of natural history and biological subjects including animals, plants, natural habitats (deserts, polar regions, rainforests, wetlands, etc), landscapes, gardens, garden wildlife, close-ups and underwater images; also man's impact on the environment – pollution, acid rain, urban wildlife, etc. Large China file including pandas in all seasons. Extensive water file (liquid, solid and vapour). Over 26,000 images on website. Pictures cannot be supplied *gratis* for personal use.

Animal Photography*
4 Marylebone Mews, London W1G 8PY
tel 020-7935 0503 *fax* 020-7487 3038
email stephen@animal-photography.co.uk
website www.animal-photography.co.uk

Horses, dogs, cats, small pets, East Africa, Galapagos. Other photographers' work not represented. Founded 1955.

Aquarius Library*
PO Box 5, Hastings, East Sussex TN34 1HR
tel (01424) 721196 *fax* (01424) 717704
email aquarius.lib@clara.net
website www.aquariuscollection.com
Contact David Corkill

Showbusiness specialist library with over one million colour and b&w images: film stills, classic portraiture, candids, archive material to present. New material added every week. Downloadable website of TV and film stills. Division of SPM London Ltd.

Arcaid: Images and Assignments*
Parc House, 25–37 Cowleaze Road, Kingston upon Thames, Surrey KT2 6DZ
tel 020-8546 4352 *fax* 020-8541 5230
email arcaid@arcaid.co.uk
website www.arcaid.co.uk

The built environment, international collection, historic and temporary: architecture, interior design, lifestyle interiors – including features, travel, destinations, museums, bridges, landmarks. Terms: 40%.

Archivio Veneziano – see Venice Picture Library

Arctic Camera
66 Ashburnham Grove, London SE10 8UJ
tel 020-8692 7651 *fax* 020-8692 7651
email Derek.Fordham@btinternet.com
Contact Derek Fordham

Colour transparencies of all aspects of Arctic life and environment. Founded 1978.

Ardea Wildlife Pets Environment*
35 Brodrick Road, London SW17 7DX
tel 020-8672 2067 *fax* 020-8672 8787
email info@ardea.com
website www.ardea.com

Specialist worldwide natural history photographic library of animals, birds, plants, fish, insects, reptiles, worldwide scenics and domestic pets.

ArenaPAL*
Lambert House, 55 Southwark Street, London SE1 1RU
tel 020-7403 8342 *fax* 020-7403 8561
email enquiries@arenapal.com
website www.arenapal.com

Performing arts archive and agency. Images cover classical music, opera, theatre, dance, pop, rock, film and TV personalities. Covers 1900 to present day.

The Associated Press Ltd*
The Associated Press House, 12 Norwich Street, London EC4A 1BP
tel 020-7427 4333 *fax* 020-7427 4269
email london_photolibrary@ap.org
website www.apimages.com

News, features, sports, 20th century history, personalities.

Australia Pictures

28 Sheen Common Drive, Richmond, London
TW10 5BN
tel 020-7602 1989 *fax* 020-7602 1989
website www.facesandplacespix.com
Contact John Martyn

Comprehensive library covering Australia,
Aboriginals and their art, indigenous peoples,
underwater, Tibet, Peru, Bolivia, Iran, Irian Jaya,
Pakistan, Yemen. Founded 1988.

Aviation Picture Library (Austin J. Brown)*

116 The Avenue, St Stephen's, London W13 8JX
tel 020-8566 7712 *mobile* (07860) 670073
fax 020-8566 7714
email avpix@aol.com
website www.aviationpictures.com

Worldwide aviation photographic library, including
dynamic views of aircraft. Aerial and travel library
including Europe, Caribbean, USA, and East and
West Africa. Material taken since 1960. Specialising in
air-to-air and air-to-ground commissions. Chief
photographers for *Flyer* magazine. Founded 1970.

B. & B. Photographs

Prospect House, Clifford Chambers, Stratford upon
Avon CV37 8HX
tel (01789) 298106 *fax* (01789) 292450
email BandBPhotographs@btinternet.com

35mm/medium format and digital colour library of
horticulture (especially pests and diseases) and
geography (worldwide), natural history and biological
education. Other photographers' work not
represented. Founded 1974.

Bandphoto Agency

(division of UPPA)
29–31 Saffron Hill, London EC1N 8SW
tel 020-7421 6000 *fax* 020-7421 6006
website www.uppa.co.uk

International news and feature picture service for
British and overseas publishers.

Barnaby's Picture Library – see Mary Evans Picture Library

Barnardo's Photographic Archive*

Tanners Lane, Barkingside, Ilford, Essex IG6 1QG
tel 020-8498 7345 *fax* 020-8498 7090
email Stephen.pover@barnados.org.uk
website www.barnardos.org.uk

Extensive collection of b&w and colour images dating
from 1874 to the present day covering social history
with the emphasis on children and child care. Also
300 films dating from 1905. Founded 1872.

BBC Natural History Unit Picture Library – see Nature Picture Library

BBC Photo Library*

B116, Television Centre, Wood Lane, London
W12 7RJ
tel 020-8225 7193 *fax* 020-8576 7020
email research-central@bbc.co.uk
website www.bbcresearchcentral.com
Photo Sales Coordinator Richard Jeffery

A unique collection of 4 million stills dating from
1922 and the earliest days of radio and TV
broadcasting. Stills can be researched by name,
programme title and subject, and images supplied in
print, transparency or digital formats.

Dr Alan Beaumont

52 Squires Walk, Lowestoft, Suffolk NR32 4LA
tel (01502) 560126
email embeaumont@supanet.com

Worldwide collection of monochrome prints and
colour transparencies (35mm and 6 x 7cm) of natural
history, countryside, windmills and aircraft. Brochure
and subject lists available. No other photographers
required.

bfi Stills*

British Film Institute, 21 Stephen Street, London
W1T 1LN
tel 020-7957 4797 *fax* 020-7323 9260
email stills.films@bfi.org.uk
website www.bfi.org.uk
Library Manager David McCall

The world's most comprehensive collection of film
and TV images with 8 million images from over
200,000 titles. The collection holds on- and off-screen
moments, portraits of the world's most famous stars –
and those behind the camera who made them famous
– in addition to images of studios, cinemas and
special events. (Copyright clearance is the
responsibility of the user.)

John Birdsall Social Issues Photo Library*

89 Zulu Road, Nottingham NG7 7DR
tel 0115-978 2645 *fax* 0115-978 5546
email photos@johnbirdsall.co.uk
website www.johnbirdsall.co.uk
Contact Anna Grapes

Contemporary social documentary library
specialising in model released images of children,
youth, older people, health, families, disability,
education, housing, work. Commissions and stock
pictures. Online web catalogue. Founded 1980.

The Anthony Blake Photo Library*

20 Blades Court, Deodar Road, London SW15 2NU
tel 020-8877 1123 *fax* 020-8877 9787
email info@abpl.co.uk
website www.abpl.co.uk

Food and wine images from around the world,
including raw ingredients, finished dishes, shops,

restaurants, markets, agriculture and viticulture. Commissions undertaken. Contributors welcome. Brochure available.

Sarah Boait Photography and Picture Library
tel (01409) 281354
email sarahboait@compuserve.com
website www.sarahboait.co.uk

Covers the British Isles, especially the West Country, ancient sites, gardens, native plants and flowers. No contributors' work accepted.

Bodleian Library
Oxford OX1 3BG
Published slides and filmstrips
tel (01865) 277214/277152 *fax* (01865) 277187
email slidesales@bodley.ox.ac.uk
Imaging Service
tel (01865) 277215/277061 *fax* (01865) 287127
email repro@bodley.ox.ac.uk
website www.bodley.ox.ac.uk/dept/imaging
website www.bodley.ox.ac.uk/dept/scwmss/wmss/medieval/browse.htm
website www.bodley.ox.ac.uk/dept/scwmss/wmss/medieval/slides/cumulative.htm
website www.bodley.ox.ac.uk/dept/scwmss/wmss/Orderforms2002-UK-EU.pdf
website www.bodley.ox.ac.uk/dept/scwmss/wmss/Orderforms2002-World.pdf

Published slides and manuscripts: Library of 32,000 35mm colour transparencies in slides or filmstrips for immediate sale (not hire). There is an iconographical index to the images, which are mostly from medieval manuscripts.

Imaging Service: Large format transparencies more suitable for reproduction are available to order, as are copies, photographs and microfilm of any other items from the Bodleian's vast collections.

Chris Bonington Picture Library*
Badger Hill, Hesket Newmarket, Wigton, Cumbria CA7 8LA
tel (016974) 78286 *fax* (016974) 78238
email frances@bonington.com
website www.bonington.com
Manager Frances Daltrey

Mountains and mountaineering, climbers and climbing in Tibet, Nepal and the Himalayas. Includes the Peter Boardman and Joe Tasker collections.

BookArt & Architecture Picture Library
1 Woodcock Lodge, Epping Green, Hertford SG13 8ND
tel (01707) 875253 *fax* (01707) 875286
email dsharp@sharparchitects.co.uk

Modern and historic buildings, landscapes, works of named architects in Great Britain, Europe, Scandinavia, North America, India, Southeast Asia,

Japan, North and East Africa; modern sculpture. Listed under style, place and personality. CD-Rom/DVD supplied. Founded 1991.

Boxing Picture Library
3 Barton Buildings, Bath BA1 2JR
tel (01225) 334213 *fax* (01225) 480554

Prints, engravings and photos of famous boxers, boxing personalities and famous fights from 18th century to recent years.

The Bridgeman Art Library*
17–19 Garway Road, London W2 4PH
tel 020-7727 4065 *fax* 020-7792 8509
email london@bridgeman.co.uk
website www.bridgemanart.com

Source of fine art images for publication. Acts as an agent for thousands of museums, galleries and private collections throughout the world. Every subject, era and style represented from cave paintings to pop art and beyond, including many historical events and personalities. Also offers research service and acts as copyright agent to a growing number of artists. Website catalogue and online ordering available. Founded 1972.

Britain on View*
VisitBritain, Thames Tower, Black's Road, London W6 9EL
tel 020-8563 3120 *fax* 020-8563 3130
email bovsales@visitbritain.org
website www.britainonview.com
Contact Jasmine Teer

Photo library of the British Tourist Authority. British culture, society, events, landscapes, towns and villages, tourist attractions.

British Library Images Online*
96 Euston Road, London NW1 2DB
tel 020-7412 7614 *fax* 020-7412 7771
email imagesonline@bl.uk
website www.bl.uk/imagesonline

Instant access to thousands of images from the British Library's historic worldwide collections including manuscripts, rare books, music scores and maps spanning almost 3,000 years. Images include digital images of drawings, illustrations, paintings and photographs. Founded 1996.

David Broadbent Birds
tel/fax (07771) 664973
email info@davidbroadbent.com
website www.davidbroadbent.com

Highly stylised and pictorial library of British birds, bird reserves and important wildlife landscapes. Commissions undertaken. New material welcome. Archive film material for outright sale. Terms: 50%. Founded 1989.

Hamish Brown, Scottish Photographic
26 Kirkcaldy Road, Burntisland, Fife KY3 9HQ
tel (01592) 873546 *fax* (01592) 741774

Picture library on Scottish sites, topography, mountains, travel. Book illustrations. Commissions undertaken. No pictures purchased.

Camera Press Ltd*

21 Queen Elizabeth Street, London SE1 2PD
tel 020-7378 1300 *fax* 020-7278 5126
website www.camerapress.com

Celebrity studio and events, extensive royal and historical archive, news and features, travel and a specialist lifestyle department covering health and beauty, food, fitness, family and fashion. Syndicates the work of a wide range of international agencies and publishing houses, including Gamma, H&K, *Le Figaro* and *Paris Match*. Founded 1947.

CartoonStock*

Unit 2, Lansdown Mews, Bath BA1 5DY
tel 01225 789600 01225 789642
email admin@cartoonstock.com
website www.cartoonstock.com
Director Joel Mishon

Library of over 70,000 cartoons and comic illustrations. B&w and colour cartoons by over 300 cartoonists whose work appears in national and overseas newspapers and magazines and other publications. Full database may be searched online. Founded 1998.

Rev. J. Catling Allen

7 St Barnabas, The Beauchamp Community, Newland, Malvern WR13 5AX
tel (01684) 899390

Library of colour transparencies (35mm) and b&w photos of Bible Lands, including archaeological sites and the religions of Christianity, Islam and Judaism. Medieval abbeys and priories, cathedrals and churches in Britain. Also historic, rural and scenic Britain. (Not an agent or buyer.)

Celebrity Pictures Ltd*

98 De Beauvoir Road, London N1 4EN
tel 020-7275 2700 *fax* 020-7275 2701
email info@celebritypictures.co.uk
website www.celebritypictures.co.uk
Contact Steve Tomkins

Celebrity studio portraiture: film, music, TV, fashion, sport, men's, the Arts. More than 20,000 colour high-res scans available as jpg files. Generous negotiable deals. Office in Los Angeles. Founded 1990s.

Cephas Picture Library*

Unit A1, Kingsway Business Park, Oldfield Road, Hampton, Middx TW12 2HD
tel 020-8979 8647 *fax* 020-8941 4001
email mickrock@cephas.com
website www.cephas.com

Comprehensive library of food and drink photos: wine and vineyards, spirits, beer and cider, food and drink worldwide, specialist knowledge.

Christie's Images*

1 Langley Lane, London SW8 1TJ
tel 020-7582 1282 *fax* 020-7582 5632
email imageslondon@christies.com
website www.christiesimages.com
Marketing & Development Mark Lynch

Fine and decorative art images from the world's leading auction house.

COI Photo Library – see Stockwave

Michael Cole Camerawork*

The Coach House, 27 The Avenue, Beckenham, Kent BR3 5DP
tel 020-8658 6120 *fax* 020-8658 6120
email mikecole@dircon.co.uk
website www.tennisphotos.com

Probably the largest and most comprehensive tennis library in the world comprising over half a million colour and b&w images. Includes over 50 years of the Wimbledon Championships. Founded 1945.

Bruce Coleman Inc.

111 Brook Street, 2nd Floor, Scarsdale, NY 10583, USA
tel 914-713-4821 *fax* 914-722-8347
email norman@bciusa.com
website www.bciusa.com
President Norman Owen Tomalin

Specialises in the natural world and travel destinations around it. All subjects required. See website for technical specifications.

Collections*

13 Woodberry Crescent, London N10 1PJ
tel 020-8883 0083 *fax* 020-8883 9215

The British Isles only: places, people, buildings, industry, leisure; specialist collections on customs, castles, bridges, London, plus an extensive collection on Ireland. Founded 1990.

Dee Conway Ballet & Dance Picture Library*

110 Sussex Way, London N7 6RR
tel 020-7272 7845
email library@ddance.co.uk
website www.ddance.co.uk
Proprietor Dee Conway

Classical ballet, modern dance, flamenco, tango, rock, jive, mime; dance from India, Africa, Russia, China, Japan, Thailand; informal class pictures of dance, music and drama. Colour and b&w images. Founded 1995.

Thomas Cook Archives

15–16 Coningsby Road, Peterborough PE3 8SB
tel (01733) 417350 *fax* (01733) 416255

email paul.smith@thomascook.com
Company Archivist Paul Smith

History of travel and tourism in the late 19th and 20th centuries: posters, photos, brochure covers (1860s–1960s). Founded 1999.

Corbis*

111 Salusbury Road, London NW6 6RG
tel 0800-731 9995 *fax* 020-7644 7645
email info@corbis.com
website www.corbis.com

Over 2.1 million images available online from a total of 65 million. The images are from professional photographers, museums, cultural institutions and public and private collections worldwide including the Bettmann Archive, Ansel Adams, Lynn Goldsmith, the Turnley Collection and Hulton Deutsch. Covers a wide range of subjects including celebrities and news. Founded 1989.

Sylvia Cordaiy Photo Library*

45 Rotherstone, Devizes, Wilts. SN10 2DD
tel (01380) 728327 *fax* (01380) 728328
email info@sylvia-cordaiy.com
website www.sylvia-cordaiy.com

Worldwide travel and architecture, global environmental topics, wildlife and domestic animals, veterinary, comprehensive UK and London files, Paul Kaye b&w archive. Terms: 50%. Founded 1990.

Country Life Picture Library*

King's Reach Tower, Stamford Street, London SE1 9LS
tel 020-7261 6337 *fax* 020-7261 6216
email camilla_costello@ipcmedia.com
website www.clpicturelibrary.co.uk
Library Manager Camilla Costello

Over 120,000 b&w photos and 80,000 colour transparencies of country houses, historic buildings and churches in Britain and abroad, as seen on the pages of *Country Life* magazine since 1897. Also holds images of some of the world's most beautiful gardens and landscapes, as well as interior views showing architectural details, furniture, paintings, antiques and sculptures, often in their original settings. Additionally, the library houses images, mainly in colour, that have featured in *Country Life* in more recent years, including sporting and social events, rural and specialist crafts, agriculture, animals and people. Founded 1897.

Crafts Council Photostore®*

44A Pentonville Road, London N1 9BY
tel 020-7806 2503 *fax* 020-7833 4479
email photostore@craftscouncil.org.uk
website www.craftscouncil.org.uk/photostore

Comprehensive source of visual material for contemporary British crafts. Spanning the last 30 years, subject areas cover: jewellery, ceramics, furniture, glass, woodwork, paperwork, bookbinding, domestic objects, decorative forms, lettering, textiles, fashion accessories, basketry, musical instruments and public art. Images can be accessed online and through terminals at the Resource Centre and at regional arts venues. Founded 1973.

Peter Cumberlidge Photo Library

Sunways, Slapton, Kingsbridge, Devon TQ7 2PR
tel (01548) 580461 *fax* (01548) 580588
email info@petercumberlidge.co.uk
Contact Jane Cumberlidge

Nautical, travel and coastal digital images and colour transparencies. Specialities: boats, harbours, marinas, inland waterways. Travel and holiday subjects in Northern Europe, the Mediterranean, and New England, USA. No other photographers' material required. Founded 1982.

Sue Cunningham Photographic*

56 Chatham Road, Kingston-upon-Thames, Surrey KT1 3AA
tel 020-8541 3024 *fax* 020-8541 5388
email pictures@scphotographic.com
website www.scphotographic.com

International coverage on many subjects: Latin America, Africa and Eastern Europe. Also Western Europe, London (including aerial).

Das Photo

Chalet le Pin, Domaine de Bellevue 181, 6940 Septon, Belgium
tel (32) 86-322426 *fax* (32) 86-322426
Old School House, Llanfilo, Brecon, Powys LD3 0RH
email daseducatiel@yahoo.com

Arab countries, Americas, Europe, Caribbean, Southeast Asia, Amazon, world festivals, archaeology, people, biblical, education, schools, modern languages. Founded 1975.

Barry Davies

Penddaulwyn Uchaf, Capel Dewi, Carmarthen SA32 8AG
tel (01267) 290460 *mobile* (07870) 663182

Natural history, landscape, Egypt, children, outdoor activities and general subjects. Formats 35mm, 6 x 6cm, 6 x 7cm, 6 x 17cm, 5 x 4in. Other photographers' work not accepted. Founded 1983.

Dennis Davis Photography

9 Great Burrow Rise, Northam, Bideford, Devon EX39 1TB
tel (01237) 475165

Gardens, wild and garden flowers, domestic livestock including rare breeds and poultry, agricultural landscapes, architecture – interiors and exteriors, landscape, coastal, rural life. Commissions welcomed. No other photographers required. Founded 1984.

Peter Dazeley

The Studios, 5 Heathmans Road, London SW6 4TJ
tel 020-7736 3171 *fax* 020-7371 8876

email studio@peterdazeley.com

Extensive golf library dating from 1970. Colour and b&w coverage of major tournaments, with over 250,000 images of players, courses worldwide, action shots, portraits, trophies, including miscellaneous images: clubs, balls and teaching shots.

George A. Dey

Drumcairn, Aberdeen Road, Laurencekirk, Kincardineshire AB30 1AJ
tel (01561) 378845

Scottish Highland landscapes, Highland Games, forestry, seabirds, castles of Northeast Scotland, gardens, spring, autumn, winter scenes, veteran cars, North Holland, New Zealand (North Island). Mostly 35mm, some 6 x 6cm. Founded 1986.

Ecoscene*

Empire Farm, Throop Road, Templecombe, Somerset BA8 0HR
tel (01963) 371700
email sally@ecoscene.com
website www.ecoscene.com
Contact Sally Morgan

Specialists in environment and wildlife. Subjects include agriculture, conservation, energy, industry, pollution, habitats and habitat loss, sustainability, wildlife; worldwide coverage. Terms: 55% to photographer. Founded 1987.

Edifice*

Cutterne Mill, Evercreech, Somerset BA4 6LY
tel (01749) 831400
email info@edificephoto.com
website www.edificephoto.com
Partners Philippa Lewis, Gillian Darley

Holds approx. 60,000 colour transparencies of architecture worldwide. All images are exteriors, with details as well as general views. Knowledgeable staff. Fully searchable database on website. Founded 1986.

Education Photos*

April Cottage, Warners Lane, Albury Heath, Guildford, Surrey GU5 9DE
tel (01483) 548031
email johnwalmsley@educationphotos.co.uk
website www.educationphotos.co.uk
Proprietor John Walmsley

Digital photos of education, careers, portraits of ordinary people. Now searchable online. Commissions undertaken. Founded 1987.

EMPICS*

Pavillion House, 16 Castle Boulevard, Nottingham NG7 1FL
tel 0115-844 7447 *fax* 0115-844 7448
email info@empics.com
website www.empics.com

Over 2.5 million images of editorial photography covering news, politics, crime, celebrities, royalty and sport from the early 1900s to the present day. EMPICS is the specialist photography marketing company of The Press Association.

English Heritage Photo Library*

23 Savile Row, London W1S 2ET
tel 020-7973 3338/3339 *fax* 020-7973 3027
email photo.library@english-heritage.org.uk
website www.english-heritage.org.uk

Wide range of high-quality colour transparencies, ranging from ancient monuments to artefacts, legendary castles to stone circles, elegant interiors to industrial architecture and post-war listed buildings.

Environmental Investigation Agency

62–63 Upper Street, London N1 0NY
tel 020-7354 7960 *fax* 020-7354 7961
email tomthistlethwaite@eia-international.org
website www.eia-international.org
Communications & Press Co-ordinator Ashley Misplon, *Visuals Administrator* Tom Thistlethwaite

Specialists in still and moving images of environmental crime, including the illegal trade in endangered species, ozone-depleting substances and illegal logging; also animals in their natural environment. Founded 1984.

Mary Evans Picture Library*

59 Tranquil Vale, London SE3 0BS
tel 020-8318 0034 *fax* 020-8852 7211
email pictures@maryevans.com
website www.maryevans.com

Historical archive of illustrations, photographs, prints and ephemera documenting all aspects of the past, from ancient times to the later decades of the 20th century. Emphasis on social and working life plus extensive files on events, portraits, transport, costume, places worldwide and natural history. Unrivalled material on folklore and paranormal phenomena. Notable collections include the Weimar Archive documenting the Third Reich, Barnaby's Library of social documentary photography from the Thirties to the Seventies, and the Thomas Fall Collection of historic dog photographs.

MEPL's own material is complemented by many contributors such as Sigmund Freud Copyrights, the Women's Library (women's rights), and the Meledin Collection of 20th century Russian history, and by the work of individual photographers and illustrators such as Roger Mayne and Arthur Rackham. Over 150,000 images searchable online, with 50,000 available in high-resolution for immediate download. Brochure on request. Founder member of BAPLA. Compilers of the *Picture Researcher's Handbook* published by Pira International.

Exile Images*

1 Mill Row, Brighton BN1 3SU
tel (01273) 208741 *fax* (01273) 382782

email pics@exileimages.co.uk
website www.exileimages.co.uk
Contact Howard Davies

Online photo library with more than 10,000 pictures relating to refugees, conflicts, asylum, UK protests, and third world issues. Fully searchable, high-res photos can be downloaded. Founded 2000.

Eye Ubiquitous & Hutchinson*
65 Brighton Road, Shoreham, West Sussex BN43 6RE
tel (01273) 440113 *fax* (01273) 440116
email library@eyeubiquitous.com
website www.eyeubiquitous.com
Proprietor Paul Seheult

Specialises in images of 'peoples and places – cultures and environments'.

Eyeline Photography
19 Brickhouse Close, West Mersea, Colchester, Essex CO5 8LA
tel (01206) 384118
email colin@colinjarman.co.uk
website www.colinjarman.co.uk

Sailing. Founded 1979.

FAMOUS*
13 Harwood Road, London SW6 4QP
tel 020-7731 9333 *fax* 020-7731 9330
email info@famous.uk.com
website www.famous.uk.com

Celebrity picture and feature agency. Supplies showbiz content to newspapers, magazines, websites, TV stations, mobile phone companies, books and advertisers worldwide. Represents celebrity journalists and photographers from LA, New York, Europe and Australia, syndicating their copy around the globe. Open to new material. Terms: 50%. Founded 1990.

Feature-Pix Colour Library – see World Pictures

Financial Times Pictures
Number One, Southwark Bridge, London SE1 9HL
tel 020-7873 3671 *fax* 020-7873 4606
email photosynd@ft.com

Colour and b&w library serving the *Financial Times*. Specialises in world business, industry and commerce; world politicians and statespeople; cities and countries; plus many other subjects. Also *FT* maps and graphics. All material available in colour and b&w, print and electronic formats. Library updated daily.

Fine Art Photographic Library*
Rawlings House, 2ᴀ Milner Street, London SW3 2PU
tel 020-7589 3127 *fax* 020-7584 1944
email info@fineartphotolibrary.com
website www.fineartphotolibrary.com

Holds over 25,000 transparencies of paintings by British and European artists, from Old Masters to

contemporary. Free brochure. CD-Rom available. Founded 1980.

FirePix International*
68 Arkles Lane, Anfield, Liverpool L4 2SP
tel 0151-260 0111 *fax* 0151-260 0111
email info@firepix.com
website www.firepix.com
Contact Tony Myers FRPS

Holds 23,000 images of fire and firefighters at work in the UK, USA, Japan and China. Established by photographer Tony Myers after 28 years in service with the British Fire Service. Many images are stored digitally; CD-Rom available. Founded 1995.

Forest Life Picture Library
Forestry Commission, 231 Corstorphine Road, Edinburgh EH12 7AT
tel 0131-314 6411
email neill.campbell@forestry.gsi.gov.uk
website www.forestry.gov.uk
Picture Researcher Neill Campbell

Tree species, forest and woodland views and management, landscapes, wildlife, flora and fauna, conservation, sport and leisure. Founded 1983.

Format Photographers – see Panos Pictures and Photofusion

Fortean Picture Library*
Henblas, Mwrog Street, Ruthin LL15 1LG
tel (01824) 707278 *fax* (01824) 705324
email janet.bord@forteanpix.demon.co.uk
website www.forteanpix.demon.co.uk

Colour and b&w pictures covering strange phenomena: UFOs, Loch Ness Monster, ghosts, Bigfoot, witchcraft, etc; also antiquities (especially in Britain – prehistoric and Roman sites, castles, churches).

Fotosports International
The Barn, Swanbourne, Bucks. MK17 0SL
tel (01296) 720773 *fax* (01296) 728181
email info@fotosports.com
website www.fotosports.com

250,000 b&w photos and 250,000 colour transparencies of sports: soccer (domestic, foreign, World Cup 1970s to present), tennis majors, Formula One motor racing, American football (inc. Superbowl) 1985–95; some golf, rugby, cricket. Founded 1968.

John Frost Newspapers
22ʙ Rosemary Avenue, Enfield, Middlesex EN2 0SS
tel 020-8366 1392/0946 *fax* 020-8366 1379
email andrew@johnfrostnewspapers.com
website www.johnfrostnewspapers.co.uk

Headline stories from 80,000 British and overseas newspapers and 100,000 press cuttings reporting events since 1850.

Brian Gadsby Picture Library
17 route des Pyrénées, 65700 Labatut-Riviere, Hautes
Pyrénées, France
tel (33) 5 62 96 38 44
email gadsby@wanadoo.fr

Colour transparencies (6 x 4.5cm, 35mm), b&w
prints and digital images. Wide range of subjects but
emphasis on travel and the environment: UK, Europe
(particularly France), Ecuador and Galapagos Islands,
Patagonia, Sri Lanka. Natural history: mainly birds
and plant life (wild and garden). Large wildfowl file.
No other photographers' material required.

Andrew N. Gagg's Photo Flora*
Town House Two, Fordbank Court, Henwick Road,
Worcester WR2 5PF
tel (01905) 748515
email info@photoflora.co.uk
website www.photoflora.co.uk
Contact Andrew N. Gagg

Comprehensive collection of British and European
wild plants. Travel: Egypt, India, Tibet, China, Nepal,
Myanmar, Thailand, Mexico, Vietnam and
Cambodia. Founded 1982.

Galaxy Picture Library*
34 Fennels Way, Flackwell Heath, High Wycombe,
Bucks. HP10 9BY
tel (01628) 521338 *fax* (01628) 520132
email robin@galaxypix.com
website www.galaxypix.com
Contact Robin Scagell

Astronomy: specialities include the night sky,
amateur astronomy, astronomers and observatories.
Founded 1992.

Garden and Wildlife Matters Photographic Library*
Marlham, Henley's Down, Battle, East Sussex
TN33 9BN
tel (01424) 830566 *fax* (01424) 830224
email gardenmatters.uk.com, gardens@gmpix.com
website www.gardenmatters.uk.com, www.gmpix.com
Contact Dr John Feltwell

Plants 10,000 Over 10,000 scientifically named species
and cultivars of garden flowers, wild plants, trees
(over 1000 species), grasses, crops, herbs, spices,
houseplants, carnivorous plants, climbers (especially
Clematis), roses, geraniums and pelargoniums, and
pests.
   General gardening How-to, gardening techniques,
garden design and embellishments, cottage gardens,
USA designer-gardens, 200 garden portfolios from 16
states in the USA, 100 portfolios from 12 European
countries.
   Ecology, conservation and environment; habitats
and pollution; agriculture and horticulture; general
natural history, entomology; Mediterranean wildlife;

rainforests (Amazon, Central America, Costa Rica
and Indonesia); aerial pics of countryside in UK,
Europe, USA.

Garden World Images*
Grange Studio, Woodham Road, Battlesbridge,
Wickford, Essex SS11 7QU
tel (01245) 325725 *fax* (01245) 429198
email info@gardenworldimages.com
website www.gardenworldimages.com
Partners Tyrone McGlinchey and Lisa Smith

All aspects of horticulture, including large and small
gardens, specialist sections on all subjects including
trees, fruit, vegetables, herbs, cacti, orchids, grasses,
cultivated and wild flowers from all over the world,
pests and diseases, action shots. Founded 1951.

Colin Garratt – see railphotolibrary.com

Genesis Space Photo Library
20 Goodwood Park Road, Bideford, Devon
EX39 2RR
tel (01237) 477883
email tim@spaceport.co.uk
website www.spaceport. co.uk
Contact Tim Furniss

Specialises in rockets, spacecraft, spacemen, Earth,
Moon, planets, stars, galaxies, the Universe. Founded
1990.

Geo Aerial Photography*
4 Christian Fields, London SW16 3JZ
tel 020-8764 6292, 0115-981 9418 *fax* 020-8764 6292,
0115-981 9418
email geo-aerial@geo-group.co.uk
website www.geo-group.co.uk
Director J.F.J. Douglas

Air-to-air and air-to-ground colour library: natural
and cultural/man-made landscapes and individual
features. Subjects from UK, Scandinavia, Middle East,
Asia and Africa. Commissions undertaken. Terms:
50%. Founded 1992.

GeoScience Features*
(incorporates KSF and RIDA photo libraries)
6 Orchard Drive, Wye, Kent TN25 5AU
tel/fax (01233) 812707
email gsf@geoscience.demon.co.uk
website www.geoscience.demon.co.uk,
www.geoscience.uk.com
Director Dr Basil Booth

Fully digital colour library. Animals, biology, birds,
botany, chemistry, earth science, ecology,
environment, geology, geography, habitats,
landscapes, macro/micro, peoples, plants, travel, sky,
weather, wildlife and zoology; Americas, Africa,
Australasia, Europe, India, Southeast Asia. Over half a
million quality colour images available as high-res
digital images; CD-Rom available on application.

Geoslides*
4 Christian Fields, London SW16 3JZ
tel/fax 020-8764 6292, 0115-981 9418
website www.geo-group.co.uk
Library Director John Douglas

Broadly based and substantial collections from Africa, Asia, Antarctic, Arctic and sub-Arctic areas, Australia (Blackwood Collection). Worldwide commissions undertaken. Terms: 50% on UK sales. Founded 1968.

Mark Gerson Photography
3 Regal Lane, Regents Park Road, London NW1 7TH
tel 020-7286 5894 *fax* 020-7267 9246
email mark.gerson@virgin.net

Portrait photographs of personalities, mainly literary, in colour and b&w from 1950 to the present. No other photographers' material required.

Getty Images*
101 Bayham Street, London NW1 0AG
tel 0800-376 7977 *fax* 020-7544 3334
email sales@gettyimages.co.uk
website www.gettyimages.co.uk

Leading imagery company, creating and providing the largest collection of still and moving images to communication professionals – from sports and news photography to archival and contemporary. Collections include: Stone, Taxi, the Image Bank, Photodisc, Hulton Archive, Getty Images News & Sport, Digital Vision, National Geographic, FoodPix, Bridgeman Art Library. See website.

John Glover Photography
The Oast Houses, Headley Lane, Passfield, Hants GU30 7RX
tel (01428) 751925 *mobile* (07973) 307078
fax (01428) 751191
email john@glovphot.demon.co.uk
website www.glovphot.demon.co.uk

Gardens and gardening, from overall views of gardens to plant portraits with Latin names; UK landscapes including ancient sites, Stonehenge, etc. Founded 1979.

Tim Graham Royal Photographs*
tel 020-7435 7693 *fax* 020-7431 4312
email mail@timgraham.co.uk
website www.royalphotographs.com

Royal Family in this country and on tours; background pictures on royal homes, staff, hobbies, sports, cars, etc; English and foreign country scenes; international Heads of State, VIPs and celebrities. Founded 1978.

Angela Hampton – Family Life Picture Library
Holly Tree House, The Street, Walberton, Arundel, West Sussex BN18 0PH
tel (01243) 555952 *fax* (01243) 555952
Proprietor Angela Hampton

Contemporary lifestyle images including pregnancy, childbirth, babies and children, parenting, behaviour, education, medical, holidays, pets, families, couples, teenagers, women's health, men's health, retirement. Also domestic and farm animals. Around 100,000 digital images and colour transparencies. Founded 1991.

Robert Harding World Imagery*
58–59 Great Marlborough Street, London W1F 7JY
tel 020-7478 4000 *fax* 020-7478 4161
email info@robertharding.com
website www.robertharding.com

Picture library with extensive range of subjects, including rights protected and royalty free, in particular travel, lifestyle, business and industry, botany, science and medical. Full e-commerce website with over 120,000 searchable images. Free catalogue.

Harper Horticultural Slide Library
219 Robanna Drive, Seaford, VA 23696, USA
tel 757-898-6453 *fax* 757-890-9378
email pamharper@mindspring.com

160,000 35mm slides of plants, gardens and native habitats.

Jason Hawkes Library
Red House, Red House Drive, Sonning Common, Reading RG4 9NL
tel (01189) 242946 *fax* (01189) 242943
email library@jasonhawkes.com
website www.jasonhawkes.com

Aerial photography of London and Britain; also Europe, USA and Australia. Online searchable database of over 8000 images. Founded 1998.

Historical Features & Photos
Hollyville, Maesycrugiau, Pencader, Carmarthenshire SA39 9DL
tel (01559) 395310
email john.norris3@btinternet.com
website www.historicalfeatures.com
Director John Norris

Approx. 10,000 b&w photos and 80,000 colour transparencies of historical architecture, including medieval castles of England and Wales. Also includes all aspects of historical events, including recreations with re-enactment groups from Ancient Greece to modern weaponry. Research also undertaken for TV and film companies. Founded 1995.

Pat Hodgson Library & Picture Research Agency
Jasmine Cottage, Spring Grove Road, Richmond, Surrey TW10 6EH

tel 020-8940 5986 *fax* 020-8940 5986
email pat.hodgpix@virgin.net

Small collection of b&w historical engravings, book illustrations, ephemera, etc; some colour and modern photos. Subjects include history, Victoriana, ancient civilisations, occult, travel. Text written and research undertaken on any subject.

Holt Studios

Pages Green House, Wetheringsett, Stowmarket, Suffolk IP14 5QA
tel (01728) 860789 *fax* (01728) 860222
email library@holt-studios.co.uk
website www.holt-studios.co.uk

150,000 pictures on worldwide agriculture, horticulture, crops and associated pests (and their predators), diseases and deficiencies, farming people and practices, livestock, machinery, landscapes, diverse environments, natural flora and fauna. Extensive gardens and garden plants collection. Founded 1981.

Horizon International

Horizon International Images Ltd, Horizon House, Route de Picaterre, Alderney, Guernsey GY9 3UP
tel (01481) 822587 *fax* (01481) 823880
email mail@hrzn.com
website www.hrzn.com

Specialist stock library. Images include leisure and lifestyle, business and industry, science and medicine, environment and nature, world travel. Founded 1978.

David Hosking

Pages Green House, Wetheringsett, Stowmarket, Suffolk IP14 5QA
tel (01728) 861113 *fax* (01728) 860222
email pictures@flpa-images.co.uk
website www.flpa-images.co.uk
Contact David Hosking FRPS

Natural history subjects, especially birds, worldwide. Including Eric Hosking's b&w collection.

Hulton Archive – see Getty Images

Huntley Film Archive

22 Islington Green, London N1 8DU
tel 020-7226 9260 *fax* 020-7359 9337
email films@huntleyarchives.com
website www.huntleyarchives.com
Archivist Amanda Huntley

Documentary and cinema stills and movies. Founded 1984.

Hutchison Picture Library

65 Brighton Road, Shoreham-by-sea, West Sussex BN43 6RE
tel (01273) 440113 *fax* (01273) 440116
email library@hutchisonpictures.co.uk
website www.hutchisonpictures.co.uk

General colour library; worldwide subjects: agriculture, the environment, festivals, human relationships, industry, landscape, peoples, religion, towns, travel. Founded 1976.

The Illustrated London News Picture Library*

20 Upper Ground, London SE1 9PF
tel 020-7805 5585 *fax* 020-7805 5905
email research@ilnpictures.co.uk
website www.ilnpictures.co.uk
Manager Luci Gosling

Engravings, photos, illustrations in b&w and colour from 1842 to present day, especially 19th and 20th century social history, wars, portraits, royalty. Collection includes the Seaco Picture Library of transport and travel images.

The Image Bank – see Getty Images

Image Diggers

618B Finchley Road, London NW11 7RR
tel 020-8455 4564 *fax* 020-8455 4564
email lambhorn@tiscali.co.uk
website http://imagediggers.netfirms.com
Contact Neil Hornick

Stills archive covering performing arts, popular culture, human interest, natural history, architecture, nautical, children and people, strange phenomena, etc. Also audio and video for research purposes, books, and ephemera including magazines, comic books, sheet music, postcards and press clippings. Founded 1980.

Images of Africa Photobank*

11 The Windings, Lichfield, Staffs. WS13 7EX
tel (01543) 262898 *fax* (01543) 417154
email info@imagesofafrica.co.uk
website www.imagesofafrica.co.uk
Owner & Manager David Keith Jones FRPS

135,000 images covering 20 African countries: Botswana, Chad, Egypt, Ethiopia, Kenya, Lesotho, Madagascar, Malawi, Morocco, Mozambique, Namibia, Rwanda, South Africa, Swaziland, Tanzania, Uganda, Zaire, Zambia, Zanzibar and Zimbabwe. Specialities: wildlife, people, landscapes, tourism, hotels and lodges, National Parks and Reserves. Terms: 50%. Founded 1983.

ImageState Pictor Ltd*

Ramillies House, 1–2 Ramillies Street, London W1F 7LN
tel 020-7734 7344 *fax* 020-7434 0673
website www.imagestate.co.uk
Office Manager Julie Chamberlain

Contemporary rights-protected and royalty-free images, footage and music. Subjects include people, business, UK and world travel, industry and sport. Founded 1983.

Imperial War Museum*

Photograph Archive, Austral Street, London
SE11 4SL
tel 020-7416 5333/8 *fax* 020-7416 5355
email photos@iwm.org.uk
website www.iwm.org.uk www.iwmcollections.org.uk

National archive of over 8 million photos, dealing
with conflict in the 20th century involving the armed
forces of Britain and the Commonwealth countries.
Open by appointment Mon–Fri. Prints made to
order. Founded 1917.

International Press Agency (Pty) Ltd

Sunrise House, 56 Morningside, Ndabeni 7405, South
Africa
tel (021) 531 1926 *fax* (021) 531 8789
email inpra@iafrica.com

Press photos for South African market. Founded
1934.

The Irish Image Collection*

Ballydowane East, Bunmahon, Kilmacthomas,
Co. Waterford, Republic of Ireland
tel (51) 292020 *fax* (51) 292020
email george@theirishimagecollection.ie
website www.theirishimagecollection.ie

Covers all 32 countries in Ireland and features diverse
subjects: agriculture, pubs, sport, gardens, megalithic
archaeology, tradition, many aspects of Irish life, etc.
Fully searchable website.

Isle of Wight Pictures

60 York Street, Cowes, Isle of Wight PO31 7BS
tel (01983) 290366 *mobile* (07768) 877914
email patrick@patrickeden.co.uk
website www.patrickeden.co.uk
Proprietor Patrick Eden

Covers all aspects of the Isle of Wight, including
landscape, aerial, industry, agriculture, tourism,
Cowes Week, nautical aspects. Over 5000 pictures;
any picture not on file can be shot to order. All
images available as originals or in digital formats.
Founded 1985.

J.S. Library International

101A Brondesbury Park, London NW2 5JL
tel 020-8451 2668 *fax* 020-8459 0223/8517
email js@online24.co.uk
website www.jslibrary.com

The J.S. Royal collection, Art collection, Hollywood
collection, Celebrity service, particularly authors.
Travel, fauna and flora and general pictures. New
photographers and material required. Assignments
worldwide undertaken. Founded 1979.

Japan Archive

9 Victoria Drive, Horsforth, Leeds LS18 4PN
tel 0113-258 3244

email stephenturnbull@ntlworld.com
website www.stephenturnbull.com
Contact S.R. Turnbull

Japan: modern, daily life, architecture, religion,
history, personalities, gardens, natural world;
European castles. Founded 1993.

Jazz Index

26 Fosse Way, London W13 0BZ
tel 020-8998 1232 *fax* 020-8998 2880
email christianhim@jazzindex.co.uk
website www.jazzindex.co.uk

Specialist photo library of jazz, blues and
contemporary music. Comprehensive selection of
archives material, atmospheric images of performers,
portraits, smoky clubs, audiences, instruments.
Terms: 50%. Founded 1979.

Kilmartin House Museum

Kilmartin House, Kilmartin, Argyll PA31 8RQ
tel (01546) 510278 *fax* (01546) 510330
email museum@kilmartin.org
website www.kilmartin.org
Contact Sharon Webb

Ancient monuments, archaeological sites; artefacts
and excavations. Aerial photographs of Mid Argyll.
Colour prints and transparencies. Publishers of
historical/archaeological works, including fiction.
Founded 1994.

Lakeland Life Picture Library

Langsett, Lyndene Drive, Grange-over-Sands,
Cumbria LA11 6QP
tel (015395) 33565 (answerphone)
email davidwjones@ktdinternet.com
website www.lakelandlifepicturelibrary.co.uk

English Lake District: industries, crafts, sports, shows,
customs, architecture, people. Also provides colour
and b&w, illustrated articles. Not an agency.
Catalogue available. Founded 1979.

Frank Lane Picture Agency Ltd

Pages Green House, Wetheringsett, Stowmarket,
Suffolk IP14 5QA
tel (01728) 860789 *fax* (01728) 860222
email pictures@flpa-images.co.uk
website www.flpa-images.co.uk

Natural history, ecology, environment, farming,
geography, trees and weather.

Michael Leach

Brookside, Kinnerley, Oswestry SY10 8DB
tel (01691) 682639 *fax* (01691) 682003
email mike.leach@lineone.net
website www.michael-leach.co.uk

General worldwide wildlife and natural history
subjects, with particular emphasis on mammals
(especially great apes) and urban wildlife.

Comprehensive collection of owls from all over the world. No other photographers required.

Lebrecht Music and Arts*
58ʙ Carlton Hill, London NW8 0ES
tel 020-7625 5341, 020-7372 8233 *fax* 020-7625 5341
email pictures@lebrecht.co.uk
website www.lebrecht.co.uk
Director Elbie Lebrecht

The world's most comprehensive archive of music and arts images from antiquity to the 21st century has expanded to incorporate coverage of ballet, literature, musicals, history, fine art and artists, film stills. UK representative of 3 large French, German and American libraries. Founded 1992.

Dave Lewis Nostalgia Collection
20 The Avenue, Starbeck, Harrogate, North Yorkshire HG1 4QD
tel (01423) 888642
email lewisattic@ntlworld.com
website www.lewisnostalgia.co.uk

A collection of advertising, packaging, points of sale and magazine reference from 1800–1970s. Founded 1995.

Link Picture Library*
41ᴀ The Downs, London SW20 8HG
tel 020-8944 6933
email library@linkpicturelibrary.com
website www.linkpicturelibrary.com
Proprietor Orde Eliason

Specialist archives on Central and Southern Africa, India, China, Southeast Asia and Israel. Commissions accepted. Terms: 50%. Founded 1982.

London Metropolitan Archives
(formerly Greater London Record Office)
40 Northampton Road, London EC1R 0HB
tel 020-7332 3820 *fax* 020-7833 9136
email ask.lma@cityoflondon.gov.uk
website www.cityoflondon.gov.uk/lma

Largest local authority record office in the UK, with 72km of archives. Nearly 1000 years of London history is contained in the records of London government, businesses, charities, hospitals, churches, etc. Collections include books, documents, photographs, maps and drawings. 100,000-volume reference library specialising in London history.

Lonely Planet Images*
website www.lonelyplanetimages.com

Online collection of travel-related images. Searchable website.

Australasia and Asia
90 Maribrynong Street, Footscray, Victoria 3011
tel (03) 8379 8181 *fax* (03) 8379 8182
email lpi@lonelyplanet.com.au

Americas
Lonely Planet Images, 150 Linden Street, Oakland, California 94607
tel 510-893-8555 *fax* 800-275-8555
email lpi@lonelyplanet.com

Europe and Middle East
72–82 Rosebery Avenue, London EC1R 4RW
tel 020-7841 9000 *fax* 020-7841 9001
email lpi@lonelyplanet.co.uk

The Billie Love Historical Collection
Reflections, 3 Winton Street, Ryde, Isle of Wight PO33 2BX
tel (01983) 812572 *fax* (01983) 616515
email info@billielovehistoricalcollection.co.uk
website www.billielovehistoricalcollection.co.uk
Proprietor Billie Love

Photos (late 19th century–1930s), engravings, coloured lithographs, covering subjects from earliest times, people, places and events up to the Second World War; also more recent material. Founded 1969.

Ludvigsen Library
Scoles Gate, Hawkedon, Bury St Edmunds, Suffolk IP29 4AU
tel (01284) 789246 *fax* (01284) 789246
email kel@ludvigsen.com
Photographic resources Karl Ludvigsen

Specialist automotive and motor racing photo library. Includes much rare and unpublished material from John Dugdale, Edward Eves, Max le Grand, Peter Keen, Karl Ludvigsen, Rodolfo Mailander, Ove Nielsen, Stanley Rosenthall and others. Founded 1984.

The MacQuitty International Collection*
7 Elm Lodge, River Gardens, Stevenage Road, London SW6 6NZ
tel 020-7385 5606 *fax* 020-7385 5606
email miranda.macquitty@btinternet.com

300,000 photos covering aspects of life in 70 countries: archaeology, art, buildings, flora and fauna, gardens, museums, people and occupations, scenery, religions, methods of transport, surgery, acupuncture, funeral customs, fishing, farming, dancing, music, crafts, sports, weddings, carnivals, food, drink, jewellery and oriental subjects. Period: 1920 to present day.

Mander & Mitchenson Theatre Collection*
Jerwood Library of the Performing Arts, King Charles Building, Old Royal Naval College, London SE10 9JF
tel 020-8305 4426 *fax* 020-8305 9426
email rmangan@tcm.ac.uk

Prints, drawings, photos, programmes, etc, theatre, opera, ballet, music hall, and other allied subjects including composers, playwrights, etc. All periods.

Marine Wildlife Photo Agency

Vine Villa, Mount Road, Llanfairfechan, North Wales
LL33 0DW
tel (01248) 681361 *fax* (01248) 681361
email info@marinewildlife.co.uk
website www.marinewildlife.co.uk
Proprietor Paul Kay

35mm and digital medium format images of UK and
Irish (temperate) marine life and associated subjects
(coastal services, environmental issues, etc). Subjects
range from straight animal/plant portraits through to
abstracts; also underwater scenic photos.
Commissions undertaken. Digital images and scans
available. Founded 1992.

John Massey Stewart Picture Library

20 Hillway, London N6 6QA
tel 020-8341 3544 *fax* 020-8341 5292
email jms@gn.apc.org
website www.jms-piclib.co.uk

Large collection Russia/USSR, including topography,
people, culture, Siberia, plus Russian and Soviet
history, 3000 pre-revolutionary PCs, etc. Also Britain,
Europe (including Bulgaria, Poland, Slovenia and
Turkey), Alaska, USA, Israel, Sinai desert, etc; and
classical composers (portraits, houses, graves,
monuments, etc).

S. & O. Mathews

Little Pitt Place, Brighstone, Isle of Wight PO30 4DZ
tel (01983) 741098
email oliver@mathews-photography.com
website www.mathews-photography.com

Gardens, plants and landscapes.

Chris Mattison

138 Dalewood Road, Sheffield S8 0EF
tel 0114-236 4433
email chris.mattison@btinternet.com
website www.chrismattison.co.uk

Colour library specialising in reptiles and
amphibians; other natural history subjects; habitats
and landscapes in Africa, Southeast Asia, South
America, USA, Mexico, Mediterranean. Captions or
detailed copy supplied if required. No other
photographers' material required.

Bill Meadows Picture Library

11 Begonia Close, St Peters, Worcester WR5 3LZ
tel (01905) 350801 *fax* (01905) 350801
Proprietor Bill Meadows

Aspects of Great Britain: general scenic including
towns and villages; buildings and monuments;
agricultural, industrial and building sites; urban
scenes and services; misuse of the environment,
vandalism, etc; recreational, 'people at play'; natural
history subjects. Mostly colour 6 x 6cm and 35mm.
Founded 1968.

Merseyside Photo Library*

Suite 6, Egerton House, Tower Road, Birkenhead,
Wirral CH41 1FN
tel 0151-666 2289 *fax* 0151-650 6976
email ron@rja-mpl.com
website www.merseysidephotolibrary.com
Operated by Ron Jones Associates

Library specialising in images of Liverpool and
Merseyside but includes other destinations. Founded
1989.

Microscopix

Middle Travelly, Beguildy, Nr Knighton, Powys
LD7 1UW
tel (01547) 510242 *fax* (01547) 510317
email semages@microscopix.co.uk
website www.microscopix.co.uk

Scientific photo library specialising in scanning
electron micrographs and photomicrographs for
technical and aesthetic purposes. Commissioned
work, both biological and non-biological, undertaken
offering a wide variety of applicable microscopical
techniques. Founded 1986.

Military History Picture Library

3 Barton Buildings, Bath BA1 2JR
tel (01225) 334213 *fax* (01225) 480554

Prints, engravings, photos, colour transparencies
covering all aspects of warfare and uniforms from
ancient times to the present.

Mirrorpix*

21 Bruton Street, London W1J 6QD
tel 020-7293 3700 *fax* 020-7491 0357
email desk@mirrorpix.com
website www.mirrorpix.com
Contact Sales Desk

The photographic collection of the *Daily Mirror*.
Contributions from over 500 photographers; key
categories include social and political history
(domestic and foreign), the arts, culture, humour,
industry, entertainment, fashion, sport and royalty.

Monitor Picture Library*

Monitor Press Features Ltd, The Forge, Roydon,
Harlow, Essex CM19 5HH
tel (01279) 792700 *fax* (01279) 792600
email sales@monitorpicturelibrary.com
website www.monitorpicturelibrary.com
Contact Eleanore White, Stewart White

UK and international personalities 1850–1994. B&w
and colour.

Motoring Picture Library*

National Motor Museum, Beaulieu, Hants SO42 7ZN
tel (01590) 614656 *fax* (01590) 612655
email motoring.pictures@beaulieu.co.uk
website www.alamy.com/mpl,
www.motoringpicturelibrary.com

All aspects of motoring, cars, commercial vehicles, motor cycles, personalities, etc. Illustrations of period scenes and motor sport. Also large library of 5 x 4in and smaller colour transparencies of veteran, vintage and modern cars, commercial vehicles and motorcycles. Over 800,000 images in total.

Mountain Dynamics
Heathcourt, Morven Way, Monaltrie, Ballater AB35 5SF
tel (013397) 55081 *fax* (013397) 55526
email gpa@globalnet.co.uk
Proprietor Graham P. Adams

Scottish and European mountains – from ground to summits – in panoramic (6 x 17cm), 5 x 4in and medium format. Commissions undertaken. Terms: 50%. Founded 1990.

Mountain Visions and Faces
25 The Mallards, Langstone, Havant, Hants PO9 1SS
tel 023-9247 8441
email mtvisions@hotmail.com
website www.mountainvisions.co.uk
Contact Graham Elson

Colour transparencies of mountaineering, skiing, and tourism in Europe, Africa, Himalayas, Arctic, Far East, North and South America and Australia. Does not act as agent for other photographers. Founded 1984.

Museum of London*
London Wall, London EC2Y 5HN
tel 020-7814 5604/5612 *fax* 020-7600 1058
email picturelib@museumoflondon.org.uk
website www.museumoflondon.org.uk
Picture Library Manager Kathy Byatt

London history.

The Mustograph Agency – see Mary Evans
Picture Library

The National Archives Image Library*
The National Archives, Ruskin Avenue, Kew, Surrey TW9 4DU
tel 020-8392 5225 *fax* 020-8487 1974
email image-library@nationalarchives.gov.uk
website www.nationalarchives.gov.uk/imagelibrary

Unique collection of millions of historical documents on a wide range of formats from 1086 to 1970s. Special collections include: Victorian and Edwardian advertisements and photographs, Second World War propaganda, military history, maps, decorative and technical designs and medieval illuminations. Founded 1995.

National Galleries of Scotland Picture Library*
The Dean Gallery, 73 Belford Road, Edinburgh EH4 3DS

tel 0131-624 6258, 0131-624 6260 *fax* 0131-623 7135
email picture.library@nationalgalleries.org
website www.nationalgalleries.org/collections
Photography & Licensing Shona Corner

Fine art from Renaissance to present day. Specialist subjects include landscape, still life, portraits, genre, animals and costume. See collection on website.

National Maritime Museum Picture Library*
National Maritime Museum, Greenwich, London SE10 9NF
tel 020-8312 6644 *fax* 020-8312 6533
email picturelibrary@nmm.ac.uk
website www.nmm.ac.uk/picturelibrary

Maritime, transport, time and space and historic photographs.

National Museums & Galleries of Northern Ireland, Ulster Folk & Transport Museum
153 Bangor Road, Cultra, Holywood, Co. Down BT18 0EU, Northern Ireland
tel 028-9042 8428 *fax* 028-9042 8728
email ken.anderson@magni.org.uk
Head of Dept of Photography T.K. Anderson

Photographs from 1850s to the present day, including the work of W.A. Green, Rose Shaw and R.J. Welsh while he was under contract to Harland and Wolff Ltd. Subjects include Belfast shipbuilding (80,000 photographs, including 70 original negatives of the *Titanic*), road and rail transport, folk life, agriculture and the linen industry. B&w and colour (35mm, medium and large format). Founded 1962.

National Portrait Gallery Picture Library*
St Martin's Place, London WC2H 0HE
tel 020-7312 2474 *fax* 020-7312 2464
email picturelibrary@npg.org.uk
website www.npg.org.uk
Contact Tom Morgan

Pictures of brilliant, daring and influential characters who made British history, are available for publication. Images can be searched, viewed and ordered on the website. Copyright clearance is arranged for all the images supplied.

Natural Image
24 Newborough Road, Wimborne, Dorset BH21 1RD
tel (01202) 849142 *fax* (01202) 848419
email bobgibbons@btinternet.com
Contact Dr Bob Gibbons

Colour library covering natural history, habitats, countryside and gardening (UK and worldwide); special emphasis on conservation. Commissions undertaken. Terms: 50%. Founded 1982.

Nature Picture Library*

c/o BBC Broadcasting House, Whiteladies Road, Bristol BS8 2LR
tel 0117-9746720 *fax* 0117-9238166
email info@naturepl.com
website www.naturepl.com

Photographs illustrating all aspects of nature: mammals, birds, insects, reptiles, marine life, plants, landscapes, indigenous peoples, environmental issues and wildlife filming.

New Blitz Literary & TV Agency

Via di Panico 67, 00186 Rome, Italy
postal address CP 30047–00193, Rome 47, Italy
tel (06) 686 4859 *fax* (06) 686 4859
email blitzgacs@inwind.it
Contact Giovanni A.S. Congiu

News and general library.

Peter Newark Picture Library

3 Barton Buildings, Bath BA1 2JR
tel (01225) 334213 *fax* (01225) 480554

One million pictures: engravings, prints, paintings and photographs on all aspects of world history from ancient times to the present.

NHPA Ltd*

57 High Street, Ardingly, West Sussex RH17 6TB
tel (01444) 892514 *fax* (01444) 892168
email nhpa@nhpa.co.uk
website www.nhpa.co.uk

Specialises in high-quality images covering all aspects of the natural world. Represents over 150 leading wildlife and environmental photographers with more than 200,000 pictures on file. Comprehensive coverage of British, European and worldwide nature and wildlife. Includes not only mainstream natural history subjects but rare and exotic species, conservation and environmental images, plus pets, agriculture, plants and marine life. Website holds over 40,000 hi-res images, available for download. *A–Z of Nature* catalogue and brochure available.

Northern Picture Library – see Stockwave

Christine Osborne Pictures – see World Religions Photo Library

Oxford Scientific (OSF)*

Ground Floor, Network House, Station Yard, Thame OX9 3UH
tel (01844) 262370 *fax* (01844) 2623808
email enquiries@osf.co.uk
website www.osf.co.uk

Specialises in all aspects of the natural world, worldwide. Includes wildlife, underwater, science, landscapes, seascapes, plants, gardens, seasons, environment, country life, natural habitats, weather,

space, adventure sports, domestic animals and pets. Film footage also available: natural world, wildlife, global locations, medical, science, time-lapse and special effects.

Panos Pictures*

1 Honduras Street, London EC1Y 0TH
tel 020-7253 1424 *fax* 020-7253 2752
email pics@panos.co.uk
website www.panos.co.uk

Third World and Eastern European documentary photos focusing on social, political and economic issues with a special emphasis on environment and development. Files on agriculture, conflict, education, energy, environment, family life, festivals, food, health, industry, landscape, people, politics, pollution, refugees, religions, rural life, transport, urban life, water, weather. Terms: 50%. Founded 1986.

Ann and Bury Peerless*

22 King's Avenue, Minnis Bay, Birchington-on-Sea, Kent CT7 9QL
tel (01843) 841428 *fax* (01843) 848321

Art, craft (including textiles), archaeology, architecture, dance, iconography, miniature paintings, manuscripts, museum artefacts, social, cultural, agricultural, industrial, historical, political, educational, geographical subjects and travel in India, Pakistan, Bangladesh, Afghanistan, Burma, Cambodia, China, Egypt, Hong Kong, Indonesia (Borobudur, Java), Iran, Israel, Kenya, Libya, Malta, Malaysia, Morocco, Nepal, Russia (Moscow, St Petersburg, Samarkand and Bukhara, Uzbekistan), Sri Lanka, Spain, Sudan, Taiwan, Thailand, Tunisia, Uganda, Vietnam, Crimea, Zambia and Zimbabwe. Specialist material on history and world religions: Hinduism, Buddhism, Jainism, Judaism, Christianity, Confucianism, Islam, Sikhism, Taoism, Zoroastrianism (Parsees of India).

Chandra S. Perera Cinetra

437 Pethiyagoda, Kelaniya–11600, Sri Lanka
tel (94) 11-2911885 *fax* (94) 11-2911885/2394629
email cinetraww@sltnet.lk
and Cinetra Worldwide Createch (Pvt) Ltd, 437 Pethiyagoda, Kelaniya–11600, Sri Lanka
website www.geocities.com/cinetramovie_01/
Managing Director Chandra S. Perera

B&w and colour library including news, wildlife, religious, social, political, sports, adventure, environmental, forestry, nature and tourism. Photographic and journalistic features on any subject. Founded 1958.

Performing Arts Library – see ArenaPAL

Photo Link

126 Quarry Lane, Northfield, Birmingham B31 2QD
tel 0121-475 8712 *fax* 0121-604 0480

email vines@aviationphotolink.co.uk
website www.aviationphotolink.co.uk
Contact Mike Vines

Colour and b&w aviation library, covering subjects from 1909 to the present day. Specialises in air-to-air photography. Assignments undertaken. Over 10,000 aviation images from around the world are added every year. Can also research, advise and write aviation stories and press releases. Founded 1990.

Photofusion*
17A Electric Lane, London SW9 8LA
tel 020-7733 3500 *fax* 020-7738 5509
email library@photofusion.org
website www.photofusionpictures.org

Covers all aspects of UK contemporary life with an emphasis on social and environment issues. Catalogue available. Photographers available for commission.

Photolibrary*
4th Floor, 83–84 Long Acre, London WC2E 9NG
tel 020-7836 5591 *fax* 020-7379 4650
website www.photolibrary.com

Rights managed and royalty free images.

The Photolibrary Wales*
2 Bro-nant, Church Road, Pentyrch, Cardiff CF15 9QG
tel 029-2089 0311 *fax* 029-2089 2650
email info@photolibrarywales.com
website www.photolibrarywales.com
Director Steve Benbow

Comprehensive collection of contemporary images of Wales. Subjects include landscape, lifestyle, current affairs, sport, industry, people. Over 100 photographers represented. Digital files and transmission available. Colour transparencies and b&w prints. Commission: 50%. Founded 1998.

Pictor International Ltd – see ImageState
Pictor Ltd

Picturepoint Ltd – see TopFoto

Picturesmiths Ltd
Manor Farm Cottage, Main Road, Curbridge, Witney, Oxon OX29 7NT
tel (01993) 771907
email picturesmiths@btinternet.com
website www.picturesmiths.co.uk
Managing Director Roger M. Smith

Plant photography, from portraits, close-ups and macrophotography to plant associations, colour themes and garden scenes. Colour transparencies. Founded 1997.

Sylvia Pitcher Photo Library
75 Bristol Road, London E7 8HG
tel 020-8552 8308 *fax* 020-8552 8308

email SPphotolibrary@aol.com
website www.sylviapitcherphotos.com

Musicians: blues, jazz, old-time country and bluegrass, cajun and zydeco, soul and gospel, pop (1960s and 1970s), plus related ephemera. Views and details of the USA: countryside, 'small-town America', shacks, railroads, rural Americana. Archival: early 20th century – mainly cottonfields, riverboats and various cities in the USA. 1960s–1970s: girls (both white and black) and couples. Founded 1968.

Pixfeatures
5 Latimer Road, Barnet, Herts. EN5 5NU
tel 020-8449 9946, 0034-652 806222 (Spanish office) *fax* 020-8449 9946
Contact Peter Wickman

Historical pictures and features covering big news events, royalty, showbiz. Travel (all countries). National newspapers' extensive collection of people in the news to 1984. *Stern* magazine features (before 1985). Spanish scenaries, towns, monuments. Documentary and historical photos. Special collections: Dukes of Windsor and Kent, Kennedys, Beatles, Keeler/Levy, trainrobbers, Second World War/Nazis. Terms: 50%.

Popperfoto (Paul Popper Ltd)
The Old Mill, Overstone Farm, Overstone, Northampton NN6 0AB
tel (01604) 670670 *fax* (01604) 670635
email inquiries@popperfoto.com
website www.popperfoto.com

Over 14 million images, covering 150 years of photographic history. Unrivalled archival material, world-famous sports library and extensive stock photography. Credit line includes Reuters, Bob Thomas Sports Photography, UPI, AFP and EPA, Acme, INP, Planet, Paul Popper, Exclusive News Agency, Victory Archive, Odhams Periodicals Library, *Illustrated*, Harris Picture Agency, and H.G. Ponting which holds the Scott 1910–12 Antarctic expedition material.

Colour from 1940, b&w from 1870 to present. Major subjects covered worldwide include: events, personalities, wars, royalty, sport, politics, transport, crime, history and social conditions. Popperfoto policy is to make material available, same day, to clients throughout the world. Mac-desk accessible. Researchers welcome by appointment. Free catalogue available.

POPPERFOTO Online includes half a million photos with delivery of full resolution images. *The Gallery at POPPERFOTO* features limited edition, hand-printed fine art photographs which can also be ordered online.

Premaphotos Wildlife*
Amberstone, 1 Kirland Road, Bodmin, Cornwall PL30 5JQ

tel (01208) 78258 *fax* (01208) 72302
email enquiries@premaphotos.com
website www.premaphotos.com
Contact Dr Rod Preston-Mafham

Wide range of natural history subjects from around the world, including camouflage, mimicry, warning coloration, parental care, courtship, mating, flowers, fruits, fungi, habitats (particularly rainforests and deserts), and many more. Specialists in invertebrate behaviour and cacti. Captions and copy can be provided. Founded 1978.

Press Association Photos – see EMPICS

Public Record Office Image Library – see The National Archives Image Library

Punch Cartoon Library*
87–135 Brompton Road, London SW1X 7XL
tel 020-7225 6710 *fax* 020-7225 6712
email punch.library@harrods.com
website www.punch.co.uk

Holds over 500,000 cartoons that appeared in Punch magazine from 1841–1992, indexed under subject categories: humour, historical events, politics, fashion, sport, personalities, etc.

railphotolibrary.com*
Milepost 92½, Newton Harcourt, Leics. LE8 9FH
tel 0116-259 2068 *fax* 0116-259 3001
email studio@railphotolibrary.com
website www.railphotolibrary.com

Comprehensive picture library with downloadable online facilities representing all aspects of modern railway operations and scenic pictures from the UK and abroad. Includes Colin Garratt's collection of world steam trains as well as archive b&w photos. Welcomes contributing photographers and also archives, and markets picture collections on behalf of individuals. Part of the Milepost 92½ organisation. Founded 1969.

Redferns Music Picture Library*
7 Bramley Road, London W10 6SZ
tel 020-7792 9914 *fax* 020-7792 0921
email info@redferns.com
website www.redferns.com
Contact Dede Millar

All styles of music, from 18th century classical composers to current Top 10, plus instruments, crowds, festivals and atmospherics. Brochure available. Pictures can be researched and sent digitally through website.

Retna Pictures Ltd*
Unit 1A/1B, 101 Farm Lane, Fulham Broadway, London SW6 1QJ
tel (01753) 785450 *fax* (01753) 785451
email ukinfo@retna.co.uk

website www.retna.co.uk

Two libraries: celebrity (celebrity music, historic and film) and stock (lifestyle, food and still life). Founded 1984.

Retrograph Nostalgia Archive
Number 10, Hanover Crescent, Brighton BN2 9SB
tel (01273) 687554
email jillianarb@aol.com
website www.retrograph.com

Worldwide advertising, packaging, posters, postcards, decorative and fine art illustrations from 1880–1970. Special collections include Victoriana illustrations and scraps (1860–1901), fashion and beauty (1880–1975), RetroTravel Archive: travel and tourism, RetroGourmet Archive: food and drink (1890–1950). Research service and Image Consultancy services; RetroMontages: montage design service. Founded 1984.

Rex Features Ltd*
18 Vine Hill, London EC1R 5DZ
tel 020-7278 7294 *fax* 020-7837 4812
email rex@rexfeatures.com
website www.rexfeatures.com
Editorial Director Mike Selby, *Library Sales Manager* Glen Marks

International news and features photo agency and picture library serving more than 30 countries, and representing hundreds of photographers. Covers celebrity, news, human interest, pop and showbiz, etc. UK representative of TimePix, the picture archive of Time Inc. which includes the Mansell Collection, the British archive of historical images. Founded 1953.

Ritmeyer Archaeological Design
114 Turners Avenue, Hawthorndene, Adelaide, SA 5051, Australia
tel (08) 8278 6865
email ritmeyer@adam.com.au
website www.templemountonline.com
Contact LeenRitmeyer, Kathleen Ritmeyer

Images for reproduction of the archaeology of the Holy Land with the emphasis on Jerusalem and the Temple Mount. Architectural reconstruction drawings of ancient sites, such as temples, synagogues, mosques and churches. Special collection of scenes of Jewish temple ritual illustrated on to-scale model of the first century temple in Jerusalem. Drawing commissions undertaken. Founded 1983.

Ann Ronan Picture Library
4th Floor, 18–20 John Street, London EC1M 4NX
tel (01869) 238377 *fax* (01869) 238378
email nathan.grainger@heritage-images.com
website www.heritage-images.com

Woodcuts, engravings, etc social and political history plus history of science and technology, including military and space, literature and music.

Roundhouse Ornithology Collection
Mathry Hill House, Mathry, Pembrokeshire
SA62 5HB
tel (01348) 837008
email john@stewartsmith.fsnet.co.uk
Contact John Stewart-Smith

Colour library specialising in birds of UK, Europe, Middle East (especially), North Africa, Far East and South America. Founded 1991.

Royal Collection Enterprises Picture Library Ltd*
Stable Yard House, St James's Palace, London SW1A 1JR
tel 020-7839 1377 *fax* 020-7024 5643
email picturelibrary@royalcollection.org.uk
website www.royalcollection.org.uk/picturelibrary
Head of Photographic Services Miss Shruti Patel

Works of art comprising 10,000 pictures, enamels and miniatures, 20,000 drawings, 10,000 watercolours, 500,000 prints and thousands of pieces of furniture, sculpture, glass, porcelain, arms and armour, textiles and jewellery. Available for hire are a wide range of colour transparencies of items in the collection, including works by Van Dyck, Rembrandt, Holbein and Leonardo da Vinci, as well as b&w prints, for purchase. Digital formats are also available for reproduction.

Royal Geographical Society Picture Library*
1 Kensington Gore, London SW7 2AR
tel 020-7591 3060 *fax* 020-7591 3001
email images@rgs.org
website www.rgs.org/images
Contact Picture Library Manager

Worldwide coverage of geography, travel, exploration, expeditions and cultural environment from 1870s to the present. Founded 1830.

The Royal Society for Asian Affairs
2 Belgrave Square, London SW1X 8PJ
tel 020-7235 5122 *fax* 020-7259 6771
email info@rsaa.org.uk
website www.rsaa.org.uk

Library of 19th and 20th century books on Asia, mainly central Asia and archive of original 19th and 20th century b&w photos, glass slides, etc of Asia. Publishes *Asian Affairs* (3 p.a.).

Royal Society of Chemistry Library and Information Centre
Burlington House, Piccadilly, London W1J 0BA
tel 020-7440 3373 *fax* 020-7287 9798
email library@rsc.org
website www.rsc.org

Covers all aspects of chemistry information. Images collection dating from the 17th century includes prints and photographs of famous chemists, *Vanity Fair* cartoons, scenes, lantern slides of similar subjects and colour photomicrographs of crystal structures. Founded 1841.

Royalpics – see Stockwave

RSPCA Photolibrary*
RSPCA Trading Ltd, Wilberforce Way, Southwater, Horsham, West Sussex RH13 9RS
tel 0870-754 0150 *fax* 0870-753 0150
email pictures@rspcaphotolibrary.com
website www.rspcaphotolibrary.com
Manager Andrew Forsyth

A comprehensive collection of natural history pictures representing the work of over 500 photographers, including the Wild Images collection. Its files include wild, domestic and farm animals, birds, marine life, veterinary work, animal welfare and environmental issues and a record of the work of the RSPCA. Founded 1993.

Dawn Runnals Photographic Library
5 St Marys Terrace, Truro, Cornwall TR1 3SW
tel (01872) 279353

General library: land and seascapes, flora and fauna, sport, animals, people, buildings, boats, harbours, miscellaneous section; details of other subjects on application. Other photographers' work not accepted. Sae appreciated with enquiries. Founded 1985.

Russia and Eastern Images*
Sonning, Cheapside Lane, Denham, Uxbridge, Middlesex UB9 5AE
tel (01895) 833508
email easteuropix@btinternet.com
website www.easteuropix.com
Library Manager Mark Wadlow

Architecture, cities, landscapes, people and travel images covering Russia and the former Soviet Union. Excellent background knowledge available and Russian language spoken. Founded 1988.

Peter Sanders Photography Ltd
24 Meades Lane, Chesham, Bucks. HP5 1ND
tel (01494) 773674, 771372 *fax* (01494) 773674
email photos@petersanders.com
website www.petersanders.com

Specialises in the world of Islam, its cultures, lifestyles, architecture, landscapes, festivals and industry. Countries covered include: China, Egypt, India, Iran, Kenya, Kosovo, Kuwait, Mali, Mauritania, Morocco, Saudi Arabia, Senegal, Spain, Sudan, Turkey, Turkmenistan, USA and Europe and more. Also other religions. Founded 1987.

Science Photo Library*
327–9 Harrow Road, London W9 3RB
tel 020-7432 1100 *fax* 020-7286 8668

email info@sciencephoto.com
website www.sciencephoto.com

Over 200,000 images available digitally from the website. Subjects include health, medicine andlifestyle; flowers, plants and gardens; nature, wildlife and environment; science, technology and industry; space exploration, astronomy and satellite imagery; history of science and medicine.

Science & Society Picture Library*

Science Museum, Exhibition Road, London SW7 2DD
tel 020-7942 4400 *fax* 020-7942 4401
email piclib@nmsi.ac.uk
website www.scienceandsociety.co.uk

We are currently digitising over 50,000 of the best from the millions of images in our collections. Science & Society has one of the widest ranges of photographs, paintings, prints, posters and objects in the world. The images come from the collections of the National Museum of Science & Industry (NMSI) – which includes the Science Museum, the National Railway Museum and the National Museum of Photography, Film & Television. Our website details the extent of our interests. Images are available as high or low resolution via email or ftp, alternatively transparency or print can be supplied. Founded 1993.

Scope Features*

26 St Cross Street, London EC1N 8UH
tel 020-7405 2997 *fax* 020-7831 4549
email images@scopefeatues.com
website www.scopefeatues.com

Colour images of personalities, particularly TV personalities. Scope Beauty: colour situations/beauty pictures.

SCR Photo Library

Society for Co-operation in Russian and Soviet Studies, 320 Brixton Road, London SW9 6AB
tel 020-7274 2282 *fax* 020-7274 3230
email ruslibrary@scrss.org.uk
website www.scrss.org.uk

Russian and Soviet life and history. Comprehensive coverage of cultural subjects: art, theatre, folk art, costume, music; agriculture and industry, architecture, armed forces, education, history, places, politics, science, sport. Also material on contemporary life in Russia, the CIS and the Baltic states; posters and theatre props, artistic reference, advice. Research by appointment only. Founded 1924.

Sealand Aerial Photography

Meadows Unit, 51 Stane Street, Halnaker, Chichester, PO18 0NF
tel (01243) 781551 *fax* (01243) 781551
email info@sealandaerial.co.uk
website www.sealandaerial.co.uk

Aerial photo coverage of any subject that can be photographed from the air in the UK. Most stock on 2¼in format colour negative/transparency. Subjects constantly updated from new flying. Founded 1976.

Mick Sharp Photography

Eithinog, Waun, Penisarwaun, Caernarfon, Gwynedd LL55 3PW
tel (01286) 872425 *fax* (01286) 872425
email mick.jean@virgin.net

Archaeology, ancient monuments, buildings, churches, countryside, environment, history, landscape, past cultures and topography. Emphasis on British Isles, but material also from other countries. Access to other specialist collections on related subjects. Commissions undertaken. Medium format and 35mm colour transparencies plus b&w prints from 5 x 4in negatives. Founded 1981.

Shout Picture Library

Mordene House, Merritts Hill, Illogan, Redruth, Cornwall TR16 4DF
tel (01209) 210525
email john@shoutpictures.com
website www.shoutpictures.com
Contact John Callan

Specialises in the emergency services: fire, police and ambulance. Also hospital, medical and trauma, education. Contact Library for password to the secure website. Commissions accepted. Founded 1994.

Brian and Sal Shuel – see Collections

Sites, Sights and Cities

1 Manchester Court, Moreton-in-Marsh, Glos. GL56 0BY
tel (01608) 652829 *fax* (01608) 652829
email pix@pauldevereux.co.uk
Director Paul Devereux

Ancient monuments, mainly in Britain, Egypt, Greece and USA; city features in UK, Europe and USA; general nature shots. Founded 1990.

Skishoot – Offshoot

Hall Place, Upper Woodcott, Whitchurch, Hants RG28 7PY
tel (01635) 255527 *fax* (01635) 255528
email pictures@skishoot co.uk
website www.skishoot.co.uk
Librarian Claire Randall, Judi Kitchin

Library specialising in all aspects of skiing and snowboarding. Also France, all year round. Assignments undertaken. Terms: 50%. Founded 1986.

Skyscan Photolibrary*

Oak House, Toddington, Cheltenham, Glos. GL54 5BY
tel (01242) 621357 *fax* (01242) 621343

email info@skyscan.co.uk
website www.skyscan.co.uk

Specialist aerial photolibrary now covering air-to-ground, aviation and aerial sports. Contributing photographers work from planes, helicopters, masts, balloons, gliders and other aerial platforms. Images can be placed in-house on an agency basis or retained by the photographer and requested for use on a brokerage basis; both terms: 50%. Founded 1984.

Snookerimages (Eric Whitehead Photography)

10 Brow Close, Bowness on Windermere, Cumbria LA23 2HA
tel (015394) 48894 *mobile* (07768) 808249
email snooker@snookerimages.co.uk
website www.snookerimages.co.uk
Contact Eric Whitehead

Specialist picture library covering the sport of snooker. Over 40,000 images of all the professional players dating from 1984 to the present day: players away from the table in locations throughout the world as well as action images.

Society for Anglo-Chinese Understanding

Sally & Richard Greenhill Photo Library, 357 Liverpool Road, London N1 1NL
tel 020-7607 8549 *fax* 020-7607 7151
email sr.greenhill@virgin.net

Colour and b&w prints of China, late 1960s–1989. Founded 1965.

Society for Co-operation in Russian and Soviet Studies – see SCR Photo Library

Sotheby's Picture Library*

Level 2, Olympia 2, Hammersmith Road, London W14 8UX
tel 020-7293 5383 *fax* 020-7293 5062
email piclib@sothebys.com
Contact Sue Daly, Researcher

Art and antiques; Cecil Beaton archive of photographs. Founded 1993.

Peter Stiles Photography

49 Palmerston Avenue, Goring by Sea, West Sussex BN12 4RN
tel (01903) 503147
email enquiries@peterstiles.com
website www.peterstiles.com, www.hortipix.co.uk

Stock image library specialising in pictures of plants, flowers, watergardening and most horticultural/gardening subjects. Also pictorial views of the Channel Islands and UK, tropical marine aquarium fish and invertebrates. Illustrated garden articles and commissioned horticultural photography.

The Still Moving Picture Company

1c Castlehill, Doune FK16 6BU
tel (01786) 842790

email info@stillmovingpictures.com
website www.stilldigital.co.uk

All images to do with Scotland, including business and people. Online service available. Founded 1991.

Still Pictures*

199 Shooters Hill Road, London SE3 8UL
tel 020-8858 8307 *fax* 020-8858 2049
email info@stillpictures.com
website www.stillpictures.com
Proprietor Mark Edwards

Specialist collections illustrating environment, nature, the Third World, and life in the 21st century – social issues, health, culture, religion, education, transport, city and rural life, agriculture, geography and landscapes.

Represents 15 major editorial agencies in Europe and the USA and over 400 photographers, as well as the United Nations Environment Programme (UNEP) archive and Christian Aid collection. Also images of habitats, landscapes and animals from BIOS, Peter Arnold Inc. and the Woodfall Wild Images collection. Terms: 50%. Founded 1970.

Stockwave

Headquarters Aylesbury office
tel (01296) 747878 *fax* (01296) 748648
email enquiries@stockwave.com
website www.stockwave.com

Collections encompassing Britain, Europe and the world. British events (including social calendar), social/political news, government, politicians, industrial, tourism, science and technology, defence, lifestyle, Royal family, film and stage personalities.

John Blake Picture Library: General topography of England, Europe and the rest of the world. Landscapes, architecture, churches, gardens, countryside, towns and villages. Horse trials covered including Badminton and Gatcombe Park.

COI Photo Library: Includes many important and previously unseen images of Britain's government, political events, interior views of the Houses of Parliament and 10 Downing Street, etc, British Royal archives, Festival of Britain, industrial and manufacturing archives, agriculture, education, defence.

Northern Picture Library: Northern England scenery; cities of Northern England and Scotland; architecture and industrial scenes of Northern England past and present.

Royalpics: Dedicated site for Royal pictures from Stockwave, COI Archives and other major photo libraries.

Tony Stone Images – see Getty Images

Survival Anglia Photo Library – see Oxford Scientific (OSF)

Sutcliffe Gallery

1 Flowergate, Whitby, North Yorkshire YO21 3BA
tel (01947) 602239 *fax* (01947) 820287
email photographs@sutcliffe-gallery.fsnet.co.uk
website www.sutcliffe-gallery.co.uk

Collection of 19th century photography, all by Frank M. Sutcliffe Hon. FRPS (1853–1941), especially inshore fishing boats and fishing community; also farming interests. Period covered 1872–1910.

Syndication International – see Mirrorpix

Charles Tait Photo Library

Kelton, St Ola, Orkney KW15 1TR
tel (01856) 873738 *fax* (01856) 875313
email charles.tait@zetnet.co.uk
website www.charles-tait.co.uk

Colour photo library specialising in the Scottish islands, especially Orkney, Shetland, the Western Isles (including outliers) and Caithness. Archaeology, landscapes, seascapes, wildlife, crafts, industries, events, transport, and sites of interest. Also mainland Scotland and Hadrian's Wall, plus France, Venice, Alaska, and New England. Over 100,000 images in formats ranging from 35mm to 5 x 4in, including 70mm panoramic and 6 megapixel digital. Images available to browse online; high-res scans on CD and by email. Publisher of postcards, calendars, guidebooks. Founded 1978.

The Tank Museum Archive & Reference Library

The Tank Museum, Bovington, Dorset BH20 6JG
tel (01929) 405096 *fax* (01929) 462410
email librarian@tankmuseum.co.uk
website www.tankmuseum.co.uk

International collection, from 1900 to present, of armoured fighting vehicles and military transport, including tanks, armoured cars, personnel carriers, cars, lorries and tractors, First and Second World War Royal Armoured Corps War Diaries and associated documents.

Theatre Museum

National Museum of the Performing Arts,
1E Tavistock Street, London WC2E 7PR
tel 020-7943 4700 *fax* 020-7943 4777
website http://theatremuseum.org

In addition to its exhibitions and extensive education programme, the Museum has an unrivalled collection of programmes, playbills, prints, photos, videos, texts and press cuttings relating to performers and productions from the 17th century onwards. Available by appointment (book 3 weeks in advance), free of charge through the Study Room. Open Wed–Fri 10.30am–4.30pm. Reprographic services available. The Reading Room will be relocated to West Kensington during 2005; see website for details.

Tibet Images*

3rd Floor, 5 Torrens Street, London EC1V 1NQ
tel 020-7278 2377 *fax* 020-7837 2800
email info@tibetimages.co.uk
website www.tibetimages.co.uk
Contact Jonathan Miller

Specialises in the people, architecture, history, religion and politics of Tibet. Also Yemen. Colour and b&w. Founded 1992.

TopFoto*

(formerly Topham Picturepoint)
PO Box 33, Edenbridge, Kent TN8 5PF
tel (01732) 863939 *fax* (01732) 860215
email admin@topfoto.co.uk
website www.topfoto.co.uk

International editorial distributor: over one million pictures available to download, and 12 million in the files, representing 40 leading suppliers.

B.M. Totterdell Photography*

Constable Cottage, Burlings Lane, Knockholt, Kent TN14 7PE
tel (01959) 532001 *fax* (01959) 532001
email btrial@btinternet.com

Specialist volleyball library, covering all aspects of the sport. Founded 1989.

Transworld/Scope – see Scope Features

Travel Ink Photo Library*

The Old Coach House, 14 High Street, Goring-on-Thames, Nr Reading, Berks. RG8 9AR
tel (01491) 873011 *fax* (01491) 875558
email info@travel-ink.co.uk
website www.travel-ink.co.uk

Travel, tourism, lifestyles and peoples around the world. Contemporary and traditional. Specialist collections of Greece, France, Asia, the UK and the Americas. Images immediately available to order and download from website. Founded 1988.

Travelib, the Neil McAllister Travel Picture Library

153 Grove Lane, Cheadle Hulme, Cheshire SK8 7NG
tel 0161-439 2964 *fax* 0161-439 3771
email neil@neilmac.co.uk
website www.travelib.com
Proprietor Neil McAllister

Travel: long haul and UK images in all formats. Searchable website. Founded 1988.

Trevillion Images*

75 Jeddo Road, London W12 9ED
tel 020-8740 9005
email info@trevillion.com
website www.trevillion.com
Contact Michael Trevillion, Managing Director

Specialises in 'art' style photography and inspirational imagery. Also handles the archive of Bruce Chatwin. Founded 1997.

TRH Pictures*
2 Reform Street, Beith KA15 2AE
tel (0845) 2235451 *fax* (0845) 2235452
email trh@trhpictures.co.uk
website www.codyimages.com
Director Ted Nevill

Specialises in colour transparencies and b&w photos of the history of civil and military aviation, modern warfare from the American Civil War, transport on land and sea, and the exploration of space. Commission: 50%. Founded 1983.

Tropix Photo Library*
44 Woodbines Avenue, Kingston upon Thames, Surrey KT1 2AY
tel 020-8546 0823, 0151-625 4576
email images@tropix.co.uk
website www.tropix.co.uk

Positive, progressive images of developing nations; travel worldwide. Plus the MerseySlides Collection: photos of Liverpool and surrounding areas. Currently closed to submissions from new photographers. Founded 1982.

True North Picture Source
26 New Road, Hebden Bridge, West Yorkshire HX7 8EF
tel (01422) 845532
email john@trunorth.demon.co.uk
Proprietor John Morrison

The life and landscape of the North of England. No other photographers' work required. 30,000 transparencies (35mm and medium format). Commissions undertaken. Founded 1992.

Ulster Folk & Transport Museum – see
National Museums & Galleries of Northern Ireland, Ulster Folk & Transport Museum

Universal Pictorial Press & Agency (UPPA)*
29–31 Saffron Hill, London EC1N 8SW
tel 020-7421 6000 *fax* 020-7421 6006
email ctaylor@uppa.co.uk
website www.uppa.co.uk

Photo library containing notable Royal, political, company, academic, legal, diplomatic, church, military, pop, arts, entertainment and sports personalities and well-known views and buildings. Commercial, industrial, corporate and public relations photo assignments undertaken. Founded 1929.

V&A Images*
Victoria & Albert Museum, Cromwell Road, London SW7 2RL
tel 020-7942 2479/2489 *fax* 020-7942 2482
email vaimages@vam.ac.uk
website www.vandaimages.com

A vast collection of photographs from the world's largest museum of decorative and applied arts, reflecting culture and lifestyle spanning over 1000 years of history to the present time. Digital delivery or large format transparencies of contemporary and historical textiles, costumes and fashions, ceramics, furniture, metalwork, glass, sculpture, toys and games, design and photographs from around the world. Unique photos include 1960s fashion by John French, Harry Hammond's behind-the-scenes pop idols, Houston Rogers' theatrical world of the 1930s–70s, images of royalty by Lafayette, and images by Cecil Beaton and 19th century pioneer photographers. Images from the inexhaustible shelves of the National Art Library and Library of Art & Design, and from the Theatre Museum and Museum of Childhood are readily available.

Colin Varndell Natural History Photography
The Happy Return, Whitecross, Netherbury, Bridport, Dorset DT6 5NH
tel (01308) 488341
email colin_varndell@hotmail.com
Proprietor Colin Varndell

UK wildlife and landscape with particular emphasis on birds, mammals, butterflies, wild flowers and habitats. 200,000 colour transparencies and digital files. Founded 1980.

Venice Picture Library
(formerly Archivio Veneziano)
c/o The Bridgeman Art Library, 17–19 Garway Road, London W2 4PH
tel 020-7727 4065 *fax* 020-7792 8509
email london@bridgeman.co.uk
website www.bridgemanart.co.uk
Contact Jenny Page

Specialises in Venice, covering most aspects of the city, islands and lagoon, especially architecture and the environment. Founded 1990.

John Vickers Theatre Collection
27 Shorrolds Road, London SW6 7TR
tel 020-7385 5774

Archives of British theatre and portraits of actors, writers and musicians by John Vickers from 1938–74.

Vidocq Photo Library
162 Burwell Meadow, Witney, Oxon OX28 5JJ
tel (01993) 778518
email g.bishop@which.net

Specialist in photographs for language and educational text books. Detailed coverage of France. Assignments undertaken. Founded 1983.

Visions in Golf

The Barn, 6 Woodend Court, Dodworth, Barnsley,
South Yorkshire S75 3UA
tel (01226) 286111
email info@visionsingolf.com
website www.visionsingolf.com
Proprietor Mark Newcombe

Every aspect of worldwide golf, including an archive
dating back to the late 19th century and world-
famous golf courses. Over 350,000 colour
transparencies and 5000 b&w images, the majority of
which are availabe on digital. Commission: 50%.
Founded 1984.

Simon Warner

Whitestone Farm, Stanbury, Keighley, West
Yorkshire BD22 0JW
tel (01535) 644644 *fax* (01535) 644644
email photos@simonwarner.co.uk
website www.simonwarner.co.uk

Landscape photographer with specialist collection on
Yorkshire and the North.

Waterways Photo Library*

39 Manor Court Road, London W7 3EJ
tel 020-8840 1659 *fax* 020-8567 0605
email watphot39@aol.com
website www.waterwaysphotolibrary.com
Contact Derek Pratt

British inland waterways; canals, rivers; bridges,
aqueducts, locks and all waterside architectural
features; watersports; waterway holidays, boats,
fishing; town and countryside scenes. No other
photographers' work required. Founded 1976.

The Weimar Archive – see Mary Evans
Picture Library

Welfare History Picture Library

Heatherbank Museum of Social Work, Caledonian
University, Cowcaddens Road, Glasgow G4 0BA
tel 0141-273 1189
email j.powles@gcal.ac.uk
website www.lib.gcal.ac.uk/heatherbank/

Social history and social work, especially child
welfare, poorhouses, prisons, hospitals, slum
clearance, women's movement, social reformers and
their work. Catalogue on request and on website.
Founded 1975.

Wellcome Photo Library*

210 Euston Road, London NW1 2BE
tel 020-7611 8348 *fax* 020-7611 8577
email medphoto@wellcome.ac.uk
website http://medphoto.wellcome.ac.uk
Library Manager Catherine Draycott

Leading source of images on the history of medicine,
modern biomedical science and clinical medicine.

Subjects range from anthropology to zoology and
biomedicine to healthcare.

Richard Welsby Photography

37 Grieveship Brae, Stormness, Orkney Islands
KW16 3BG
tel/fax (01856) 850910
email richardwelsby@orkney.com
website www.richardwelsby.com
Contact Richard Welsby

Specialist library of the Orkney Islands: business and
industry, scenics, geology, archaeology and historic;
wide coverage of flowers, plants and other natural
history subjects; aerials. Founded 1984.

Werner Forman Archive*

36 Camden Square, London NW1 9XA
tel 020-7267 1034 *fax* 020-7267 6026
email wfa@btinternet.com
website www.werner-forman-archive.com

Art, architecture, archaeology, history and peoples of
ancient, oriental and primitive cultures. Founded
1975.

Westcountry Pictures

10 Headon Gardens, Countess Wear, Exeter, Devon
EX2 6LE
tel (01392) 426640
email peter@cooperphotography.co.uk
website www.cooperphotography.co.uk
Contact Peter Cooper

All aspects of Devon and Cornwall – culture, places,
industry and leisure. Founded 1989.

Western Americana Picture Library

3 Barton Buildings, Bath BA1 2JR
tel (01225) 334213 *fax* (01225) 480554

Prints, engravings, photos and colour transparencies
on the American West, cowboys, gunfighters,
Indians, including pictures by Frederic Remington
and Charles Russell, etc.

Roy J. Westlake

West Country Photo Library, 31 Redwood Drive,
Plympton, Plymouth PL7 2FS
tel (01752) 336444 *fax* (01752) 336444
Contact Roy J. Westlake ARPS

Specialises in all aspects of Devon, Cornwall, Dorset,
Somerset and Wiltshire. Medium format
transparencies of landscapes, seascapes, architecture,
etc. Other photographers' work not required.
Founded 1960.

Eric Whitehead Photography – see
Snookerimages (Eric Whitehead Photography)

Wilderness Photographic Library*

4 Kingscourt, Kirkby Lonsdale, Cumbria LA6 2BP
tel (01524) 272149 *fax* (01524) 272149

email wildernessphoto@bt.internet.com
website www.wildernessphoto.co.uk
Director John Noble FRGS

Specialist library in mountain and wilderness regions, especially polar. Associated aspects of people, places, natural history, geographical features, exploration and mountaineering, adventure sports, travel.

The Neil Williams Classical Collection

22 Avon, Hockley, Tamworth, Staffs. B77 5QA
tel (01827) 286086 *fax* (01827) 286086
email neil@classicalcollection.co.uk
Proprietor Neil Williams MA (Hum), MA (Mus)

Specialises in classical music ephemera, including portraits of composers, musicians, conductors, opera singers, ballet stars, impresarios, and music-related literary figures. Old and sometimes rare photographs, postcards, antique prints, cigarette cards, stamps, concert programmes, Victorian newspapers, etc. Also modern photographs of composer references such as museums, statues, memorials, etc. Also freelance writer of concert programme notes and CD liner notes.

Other subjects: music in art, musical instruments, manuscripts, concert halls, opera houses and other music venues. Founded 1996.

David Williams Picture Library*

50 Burlington Avenue, Glasgow G12 0LH
tel 0141-339 7823 *fax* 0141-337 3031

Specialises in travel photography; wide coverage of Scotland, Iceland and Spain. Also other European countries and Western USA and Canada. Subjects include: cities, towns, villages, 'tourist haunts', buildings, landscapes and natural features; geology and physical geography of Scotland and Iceland. Commissions undertaken. Catalogue available. Founded 1989.

Tim Woodcock

59 Stoodham, South Petherton, Somerset TA13 5AS
tel (01460) 242788
email tim@timwoodcock.co.uk
website www.timwoodcock.co.uk

British and Eire landscape, seascape, architecture and heritage; children, parenthood, adults and education; gardens and containers; mountain biking. Location commissions undertaken. Terms: 50%. Founded 1983.

World Pictures*

(formerly Feature-Pix Colour Library)
43–44 Berners Street, London W1T 3ND
tel 020-7580 1845, 020-7436 0440 *fax* 020-7580 4146
email worldpictures@btinternet.com
website www.worldpictures.co.uk
Directors David Brenes

Over 600,000 medium and large format colour transparencies aimed at travel and travel-related

markets. Extensive coverage of cities, countries and specific resort areas, together with material of an emotive nature, i.e. children, couples and families on holiday, all types of winter and summer sporting activities, motoring abroad, etc. Terms: 50%; major contributing photographers 60%.

World Religions Photo Library*

53A Crimsworth Road, London SW8 4RJ
tel 020-7720 6951 *fax* 020-7720 6951
email co@worldreligions.co.uk, copix@clara.co.uk
website www.worldreligions.co.uk, www.copix.co.uk

Specialist stock on religions from more than 50 countries: major faiths, places of worship, rites of passage, shrines, pilgrimage, sacred foods, culture and ecclesiastical buildings – temples, churches, mosques, etc. Also stocks the developing world: Middle East/Arab States, North Africa, Central Asian Republics, South Asia and Indian Ocean, Southeast Asia, Pacific/Australia. Major files on travel, crafts, agriculture, food, people. Member of the British Guild of Travel Writers. Specialises in illustrated editorial features. Welcomes submissions from photographers covering any of these subjects. The library is managed by Christine Osborne Pictures (also proprietor of www.copix.co.uk).

Murray Wren

3 Hallgate, London SE3 9SG
tel 020-8852 7556
email murraywren@aol.com

Outdoor nudes. Mostly unposed and natural. Colour, b&w and digital. Also nudist/naturist photographs of club, beach and holiday resorts in the UK and Europe. Associated MSS by arrangement. Historic and erotic art form throughout the ages in b&w only. All material from total library to individual pictures available for outright sale or reproduction fee. Digital images via email or CD possible. No new photographers required.

The Allan Wright Photo Library

Parton House Stables, Castle Douglas, Kirkcudbrightshire DG7 3NB
tel (016444) 470260 *fax* (016444) 470202
email allan@lyricalscotland.com
website www.lyricalscotland.com

Source of 'Lyrical Scotland' range of images featuring all of Scotland. Founded 1986.

Gordon Wright's Scottish Photo Library

25 Mayfield Road, Edinburgh EH9 2NQ
tel 0131-667 1300
email gordon.wright11@btopenworld.com
Managing Director Gordon Wright

Specialist library illustrating Scotland: cities, towns and villages; landscapes and landmarks including the Orkney Islands; Scottish nationalism, personalities and writers. 56,000 b&w photos and 12,000 colour images supplied digitally. Founded 1960.

Yemen Pictures

Flat 2, Auriol Mansions, Edith Road, London
W14 0ST
tel 020-7602 1989 *fax* 020-7602 1989
website www.facesandplacespix.com
Contact John Miles

Specialist colour library of Yemen, covering all
aspects of culture, people, architecture, dance, qat
and music. Also Africa, Australia, Middle East and
Asia. Founded 1995.

York Archaeological Trust Picture Library

Cromwell House, 13 Ogleforth, York YO1 7FG
tel (01904) 663051 *fax* (01904) 663024
email ckyriacou@yorkarchaeology.co.uk

website www.yorkarchaeology.co.uk
Picture Librarian C. Kyriacou

York archaeology covering Romans, Dark Ages,
Vikings and Middle Ages; traditional crafts; scenes of
York and Yorkshire. Founded 1987.

Zoological Society of London

Regent's Park, London NW1 4RY
tel 020-7449 6293 *fax* 020-7586 5743
email library@zsl.org
website www.zsl.org
Librarian Ann Sylph

Archive collection of photographs, paintings and
prints, from the 16th century onwards, covering
almost all vertebrate animals, many now extinct or
rare, plus invertebrates. Founded 1826.

Card and stationery publishers that accept photographs

Before submitting work, photographers are advised to ascertain requirements, including terms and conditions. Only top quality material should be submitted; inferior work is never accepted. Postage for return of material should be enclosed.

*Member of the Greeting Card Association

Card Connection Ltd*
Park House, South Street, Farnham, Surrey
GU9 7QQ
tel (01252) 892300 *fax* (01252) 892363
email ho@cardconnection.co.uk
website www.card-connection.co.uk
Managing Director Simon Hulme, *Senior Product & Marketing Manager* Natalie Turner

Cute, humour, fun, traditional, contemporary and photographic. Submit colour copies or 5 x 4in transparencies of originals. Humour and sentimental verse. Founded 1992.

Caspari Ltd*
9 Shire Hill, Saffron Walden, Essex CB11 3AP
tel (01799) 513010 *fax* (01799) 513101
Managing Director Keith Entwisle

Traditional fine art/classic images; 5 x 4in transparencies. No verses. Founded 1990.

Chapter and Verse (International) Ltd
Granta House, 94–96 High Street, Linton, Cambs.
CB1 6JT
tel (01223) 891951 *fax* (01223) 894137
email chapterandverse@aol.com
website www.chapter-and-verse-stationery.co.uk

Buildings, animals, flowers, scenic, or domestic subjects in series, suitable for greetings cards and postcards. All sizes of transparency. No verses. Founded 1981.

Colneis Marketing Ltd*
York House, 2–4 York Road, Felixstowe IP11 7QQ
tel (01394) 271668 *fax* (01394) 275114
email colneiscards@btopenworld.com
website www.colneisgreetingcards.com
Proprietor John Botting

Photographs (preferably medium format) and colour artwork of nature and cute images. Considers verses. Founded 1994.

Pineapple Park*
58 Wilbury Way, Hitchin, Herts. SG4 0TP
tel (01462) 442021 *fax* (01462) 440418
email info@pineapplepark.co.uk

website www.pineapplepark.co.uk
Directors Peter M. Cockerline, Sarah M. Parker

Illustrations and photographs for publication as greetings cards. Contemporary, cute, humour: submit artwork or laser copies with sae. Photographic florals always needed. Humour copy/jokes accepted without artwork. Also concepts for ranges. Founded 1993.

Nigel Quiney Publications Ltd*
Cloudesley House, Shire Hill, Saffron Walden, Essex
CB11 3FB
tel (01799) 520200 *fax* (01799) 520100
website www.nigelquiney.com
Contact Alison Butterworth, Creative Director

Everyday and seasonal greetings cards and giftwrap including fine art, photographic, humour, fun art, contemporary and cute. Submit colour copies, photographs or transparencies: no original artwork.

J. Salmon Ltd
100 London Road, Sevenoaks, Kent TN13 1BB
tel (01732) 452381 *fax* (01732) 450951
email enquiries@jsalmon.co.uk

Picture postcards, calendars, greeting cards and local view booklets.

Santoro Graphics Ltd
Rotunda Point, 11 Hartfield Crescent, London
SW19 3RL
tel 020-8781 110 *fax* 020-8781 1101
email enquiries@santorographics.com
website www.santorographics.com
Directors L. Santoro, M. Santoro

Publishers of innovative and award-winning designs for greetings cards, giftwrap and gift stationery. Bold contemporary images with an international appeal. Subjects covered: contemporary, pop-up, b&w, colour, floral, quirky and humorous, whimsical, Fifties, Sixties, Seventies, futuristic. Submit samples as colour photocopies, transparencies, CD-Roms or via email as jpeg or PDF files. Founded 1985.

Scandecor Ltd
3 The Ermine Centre, Hurricane Close, Huntingdon,
Cambs. PE29 6WY

tel (01480) 456395 *fax* (01480) 456269
email mail@scandecor-ltd.co.uk
Managing Director Derek Shirley

Transparencies all sizes. Founded 1967.

Woodmansterne Publications Ltd*
1 The Boulevard, Blackmoor Lane, Watford, Herts.
WD18 8UW

tel (01923) 200600 *fax* (01923) 200601
email info@woodmansterne.co.uk
website www.woodmansterne.co.uk

Greetings cards, wrapping paper, notecards and social stationery featuring fine and contemporary art and photography (colour and b&w). Submit colour copies, photographs or transparencies. No verses.

Societies, prizes and festivals

The Society of Authors

The Society of Authors is an independent trade union, representing writers' interests in all aspects of the writing profession, particularly publishing, but also broadcasting, television and film, theatre and translation.

Founded over 100 years ago, the Society now has more than 8000 members. It has a professional staff, responsible to a Management Committee of 12 authors, and a Council (an advisory body meeting twice a year) consisting of 60 eminent writers. There are specialist groups within the Society to serve particular needs: the Academic Writers Group, the Broadcasting Group, the Children's Writers and Illustrators Group, the Educational Writers Group, the Medical Writers Group and the Translators Association (see page 557). There are also groups representing Scotland and the North of England.

What the Society does for members

Through its permanent staff (including a solicitor), the Society is able to give its members a comprehensive personal and professional service covering the business aspects of authorship, including:

- providing information about agents, publishers, and others concerned with the book trade, journalism, broadcasting and the performing arts;
- advising on negotiations, including the individual vetting of contracts, clause by clause, and assessing their terms both financial and otherwise;
- helping with members' queries, major or minor, over any aspect of the business of writing;
- taking up complaints on behalf of members on any issue concerned with the business of authorship;

- pursuing legal actions for breach of contract, copyright infringement, and the non-payment of royalties and fees, when the risk and cost preclude individual action by a member and issues of general concern to the profession are at stake;
- holding conferences, seminars, meetings and social occasions;
- producing a comprehensive range of publications, free of charge to members, including the Society's quarterly journal, *The Author*. *Quick Guides* cover many aspects of the profession such as: copyright, publishing contracts, libel, income tax, VAT, authors' agents, permissions, indexing, and the protection of titles. The Society also publishes occasional papers on subjects such as film agreements, packaged books, revised editions, multimedia, and vanity publishing.

Further membership benefits

Members have access to:

- books and other products at special rates;
- free membership of the Authors' Licensing and Collecting Society (ALCS);
- a group Medical Insurance Scheme with BUPA;
- the Retirement Benefit Scheme;
- the Contingency Fund (which provides financial relief for authors or their dependents in sudden financial difficulties);
- the Pension Fund (which offers discretionary pensions to a number of members);
- membership of the Royal Over-Seas League at a discount.

'It does no harm to repeat, as often as you can, "Without me the literary industry would not exist: the publishers, the agents, the sub-agents, the accountants, the libel lawyers, the departments of literature, the professors, the theses, the books of criticism, the reviewers, the book pages - all this vast and proliferating edifice is because of this small, patronised, put-down and underpaid person."' – *Doris Lessing*

The Society frequently secures improved conditions and better returns for members. It is common for members to report that, through the help and facilities offered, they have saved more, and sometimes substantially more, than their annual subscriptions (which are an allowable expense against income tax).

What the Society does for authors

The Society lobbies Members of Parliament, Ministers and Government Departments on all issues of concern to writers. Recent issues have included the operation and funding of Public Lending Right, the threat of VAT on books, copyright legislation and European Union initiatives. Concessions have also been obtained under various Finance Acts.

The Society litigates in matters of importance to authors. For example, the Society backed Andrew Boyle when he won his appeal against the Inland Revenue's attempt to tax the Whitbread Award.

The Society campaigns for better terms for writers. With the Writers' Guild, it has negotiated 'minimum terms agreements' with many leading publishers. The translators' section of the Society has also drawn up a minimum terms agreement for translators which has been adopted by Faber and Faber, and has been used on an individual basis by a number of other publishers.

The Society is recognised by the BBC for the purpose of negotiating rates for writers' contributions to radio drama, as well as for the broadcasting of published material. It was instrumental in setting up the ALCS (see page 702), which collects and distributes fees from reprography and other methods whereby copyright material is exploited without direct payment to the originators.

The Society keeps in close touch with the Arts Councils, the Association of Authors' Agents, the British Council, the Institute of Translation and Interpreting, the Department for Culture, Media and Sport, the National Union of Journalists, the Publishers Association and the Writers' Guild of Great Britain.

The Society is a member of the European Writers Congress, the British Copyright Council, the National Book Committee and the Creators' Rights Alliance.

Awards

The Society of Authors administers:

- Travelling Scholarships which give honorary awards;
- four prizes for novels: the Betty Trask Awards, the Encore Award, the McKitterick Prize and the Sagittarius Prize;
- two prizes for a full-length published work: the Somerset Maugham Awards and *The Sunday Times* Young Writer of the Year Award;
- two poetry awards: the Eric Gregory Awards and the Cholmondeley Awards;
- the Tom-Gallon and Olive Cook Awards for short story writers;
- the Authors' Foundation and Kathleen Blundell Trust, which give grants to published authors working on their next book;
- two radio drama prizes: the Richard Imison Award for a writer new to radio drama and the Peter Tinniswood Award;
- awards for translations from French, German, Italian, Dutch, Portuguese, Spanish and Swedish into English;
- the Francis Head Bequest for assisting authors who, through physical mishap, are temporarily unable to maintain themselves or their families;
- medical book awards.

The Writers' Guild of Great Britain

The Writers' Guild of Great Britain is the TUC-affiliated trade union for writers.

The Writers' Guild of Great Britain is a writers' trade union, affiliated to the TUC, and represents writers' interests in film, television, radio, theatre and books and new media. Formed in 1959 as the Screenwriters' Guild, the union gradually extended into all areas of freelance writing activity and copyright protection. In 1974, when book authors and stage dramatists became eligible for membership, substantial numbers joined. In June 1997 the Theatre Writers' Union membership unified with that of the Writers' Guild to create a larger, more powerful writers' union.

Apart from necessary dealings with Government and policies on legislative matters affecting writers, the Guild is, by constitution, non-political, has no involvement with any political party, and members pay no political levy.

The Guild employs a permanent general secretary and several staff and is administered by an Executive Council of 26 members. It has a national and regional/branch structure with committees representing Scotland, Wales, London and the South East, the North West, the North East, the Midlands and the South West of England. The Guild comprises practising professional writers in all media, united in common concern for one another and regulating the conditions under which they work.

Membership

The Writers' Guild of Great Britain
15 Britannia Street, London WC1X 9JN
tel 020-7833 0777 *fax* 020-7833 4777
email admin@writersguild.org.uk
website www.writersguild.org.uk
General Secretary Bernie Corbett
Full Membership: 1% of earnings from professional writing (min. £150, max. £1500 p.a.)
Life Membership: free (open to certain Full Members who are over 65 and/or have long service as Guild members)
Candidate Membership: £90 p.a. (restricted to writers who have not had work published or produced at Guild-approved rates)
Student Membership: £20 p.a. (open to anyone on an accredited writing course or on attachment with a theatre)
Affiliate Membership: £275 p.a. (for people who work professionally with writers, e.g. agents, technical advisers)

All Full members are automatically members of the Authors Licensing and Collecting Society (ALCS), of which the Guild is a corporate member and is represented on its board.

Members receive the Guild's quarterly *UK Writer* magazine, which carries articles, letters and reports written by members, plus a weekly email newsletter every Friday afternoon. Other benefits include free entry to the British Library reading rooms, and reduced entry to the National Film Theatre and regional film theatres.

The Writers' Guild and agreements

The Guild's basic function is to negotiate minimum terms in those areas in which its members work. Those agreements form the basis of the individual contracts signed by members. Further details are given below. The Guild also gives individual advice to its members on contracts and other matters which the writer encounters in his or her professional life. It also organises informative and social events for members, and maintains a benevolent fund to help writers in financial trouble.

Television

In 2002 the Guild concluded negotiations with the BBC for a new Television Script Commissioning Agreement. The new terms came into effect on 1 November 2002. A new agreement for television production was also agreed with PACT (Producers Alliance of Cinema and Television) which came into effect on 1 February 2003. In the second half of 2006 the Guild is entering negotiations on updating both of these agreements, in cooperation with the Personal Managers' Association (which represents many writers' agents).

The Guild has national agreements with the BBC, the ITV companies, PACT and TAC (representing Welsh language television producers). These agreements regulate minimum fees and going rates, copyright licence, credits, and general conditions for television plays, series and serials, dramatisations and adaptations. One of the Guild's most important achievements has been the establishment of pension rights for members. The BBC, ITV companies and independent producers pay a pension contribution of between 6% and 8% of the standard writer's fee on the understanding that the Guild member pays between 4% and 6%.

The advent of digital and cable television channels and the creation of the BBC's commercial arm has seen the Guild in constant negotiation. The Guild now has agreements for all of the BBC's digital channels and for its joint venture channels.

In 1997, the Guild negotiated substantial revised terms and conditions for writers who are commissioned by the ITV companies. The agreement includes a provision for the non-arms length sale of material to digital and cable channels, thus ensuring that writers receive market prices for the use of their material on these new channels. Recent changes in the structure of ITV, and intermittent rumours about takeover bids, have delayed discussions on updating this agreement.

Film

In 1985 an important agreement was signed with the two producer organisations: the British Film and Television Producers' Association and the Independent Programme Producers Association (now known as PACT). Since then there has been an industrial agreement covering UK film productions. Pension fund contributions have been negotiated for Guild members in the same way as for the BBC and ITV. The Agreement was renegotiated in February 1992 and consultations on an updated arrangement are in progress.

Radio

The Guild has a standard agreement for Radio Drama with the BBC, establishing a fee structure which is annually reviewed. This agreement was comprehensively renegotiated recently, resulting in an agreement covering various new developments such as digital radio. The new agreement came into force at the beginning of 2006. In 1985 the BBC agreed to extend the pension scheme already established for television writers to include radio writers. In 1994 a comprehensive revision of the Agreement was undertaken. The Guild negotiated special agreements for Radio 4's *The Archers*, the World Service soap *Westway*, and for the online streaming of BBC Radio services. This agreement was renegotiated in 2004 to cover digital radio. A separate agreement covers the reuse of old comedy and drama material on digital BBC7.

Books

The Guild fought long, hard and successfully for the loans-based Public Lending Right to reimburse authors for books lent in libraries. This is now law and the Guild is constantly in touch with the Registrar of the scheme. Together with the Society of Authors, the Guild has drawn up a draft Minimum Terms Book Agreement which has been widely circulated amongst publishers.

Theatre

In 1979 the Guild, together with theTheatre Writers' Union, negotiated the first ever industrial agreement for theatre writers. The Theatres National Committee Agreement covers the Royal Shakespeare Company, the National Theatre Company and the English Stage Company.

In June 1986, a new agreement was signed with the Theatrical Management Association, which covers some 95 provincial theatres. In 1993, this agreement was comprehensively revised and included a provision for a year-on-year increase in fees in line with the Retail Price Index. Both the TNC and TMA agreements are currently being updated.

After many years of negotiation, an agreement was concluded in 1991 between the Guild and the Independent Theatre Council, which represents some 200 of the smaller and fringe theatres as well as educational, touring companies. This agreement was revised in 2002 and the minimum fees are reviewed annually.

Other activities

The Guild is in touch with Government and national institutions wherever and whenever the interests of writers are in question or are being discussed. It holds cross-party Parliamentary lobbies with Equity and the Musicians Union to ensure that the various artforms they represent are properly cared for.

Working with the Federation of Entertainment Unions, the Guild makes its views known to Government bodies on a broader basis. It keeps in touch with the Arts Councils of Great Britain, Ofcom and other national bodies, and has close working relationships with Equity and the Musicians' Union.

Internationally, the Guild plays a leading role in the International Affiliation of Writers' Guilds, which includes the American Guilds East and West, the Canadian Guilds (French and English), and the Irish, Australian and New Zealand Guilds. When it is possible to make common cause, the Guilds act accordingly. The Guild takes a leading role in the European Writers' Congress and the Fédération des Scénaristes d'Europe. The Guild is becoming more involved with matters at European level where the harmonisation of copyright law and the regulation of a converged audiovisual/telecommunications are of immediate interest.

Membership activities

The Guild in its day-to-day work takes up problems on behalf of individual members, gives advice on contracts, and helps with any problems which affect the lives of its members as professional writers. Members have access to free legal advice and professional contract vetting. Regular committee meetings are held by the Guild's various specialist Craft Committees. As well as the core Craft Committees, the Guild has a new Disability Issues Committee and an anti-Censorship Committee which responds to issues that arise around censorship and freedom of speech in the writing community. The Guild's committees give members the opportunity to meet those who control, work within, or affect the sphere of writing within which they work.

In conclusion

The writer is an isolated individual in a world in which individual voices are not always heard. The Guild brings together those writers in order to make common cause in respect of the many vitally important matters which are susceptible to influence only from the position of the collective strength which the Guild enjoys.

Societies, associations and clubs

The societies, associations and clubs listed here will be of interest to both writers and artists. They include appreciation societies devoted to specific authors, professional bodies and national institutions. Some also offer prizes and awards (see page 561).

Academi (Welsh Academy)

Main Office 3rd Floor, Mount Stuart House, Mount Stuart Square, Cardiff CF10 5FQ
tel 029-2047 2266 *fax* 029-2049 2930
email post@academi.org
and Academi Glyn Jones Centre, Wales Millennium Centre, Cardiff Bay, Cardiff CF10 5AL
tel 029-2047 2266 *fax* 029-2047 0691
email post@academi.org
North West Wales Office Ty Newydd, Llanystumdwy, Cricieth, Gwynedd LL52 0LW
tel (01766) 522817 *fax* (01766) 523095
email academi.gog@dial.pipex.com
South West Wales Office Dylan Thomas Centre, Somerset Place, Swansea SA1 1RR
tel (01792) 463980 *fax* (01792) 463993
website www.academi.org
Chief Executive Peter Finch
Membership Associate: £15 p.a. (waged), £7.50 (unwaged)

Academi is the trading name of Yr Academi Gymreig, the Welsh National Literature Promotion Agency and Society of Writers. With funds mostly provided from public sources, it has been constitutionally independent since 1978. It runs courses, competitions (including the Cardiff International Poetry and Book of the Year Competition), conferences, tours by authors, festivals and represents the interests of Welsh writers and Welsh writing both inside Wales and beyond. Its publications include *Taliesin* (3 p.a.), a literary journal in the Welsh language; *A470* (bi-monthly), a literature information magazine; *The Oxford Companion to the Literature of Wales*, *The Welsh Academy English–Welsh Dictionary*, and a variety of translated works.

Academi administers a range of schemes including Writers on Tour, Writers Residencies and Writing Squads for young people. Academi also runs services for writers in Wales such as bursaries, critical advice and mentoring. Founded 1959.

Academic Writers Group – see The Society of Authors

Alliance of Literary Societies

Secretary Rosemary Culley, 22 Belmont Grove, Havant, Hants PO9 3PU
tel 023-9247 5855 *fax* (0870) 056 0330
email rosemary@sndc.demon.co.uk
website www.sndc.demon.co.uk
Membership Charge depends on size of society

Membership comprises 100+ affiliated literary societies. Aims to act as a valuable liaison body between member societies as a means of sharing knowledge, skills and expertise, and may also act as a pressure group when necessary. The Alliance can assist in the preservation of buildings, places and objects which have literary associations. Produces 2 newsletters a year, plus a literary magazine.

American Literary Translators Association (ALTA)

c/o University of Texas at Dallas, Box 830688, Richardson, TX 75083-0688, USA
tel 972-883-2093 *fax* 972-883-6303
website www.literarytranslators.org
Secretary Jessie Dickey

A broad-based organisation dedicated to the promotion of literary translation through services to literary translators, forums on the theory and practice of translation, collaboration with the international literary community, and advocacy on behalf of the library translator. Founded 1978.

American Society of Composers, Authors and Publishers

One Lincoln Plaza, New York, NY 10023, USA
tel 212-621-6000 *fax* 212-724-9064
website www.ascap.com
President & Chairman Marilyn Bergman

American Society of Indexers (ASI)

10200 West 44th Avenue, Suite 304, Wheat Ridge, CO 80033, USA
tel 303-463-2887 *fax* 303-422-8894
email info@asindexing.org
website www.asindexing.org

Aims to increase awareness of the value of high-quality indexes and indexing; offer members access to educational resources that enable them to strengthen their indexing performance; keep members up to date on indexing technology; defend and safeguard the professional interests of indexers.

Artists Association of Ireland

43 Temple Bar, Dublin 2, Republic of Ireland
tel (01) 8740529 *fax* (01) 6771585
email info@artistsireland.com
Contact Administrator
Membership £45 p.a.

Information and advice resource for professional visual artists in Ireland. Publishes *Art Bulletin* (6 p.a.), available on subscription. Founded 1981.

Arts Club

40 Dover Street, London W1S 4NP
tel 020-7499 8581 *fax* 020-7409 0913
email bc@theartsclub.co.uk
website www.theartsclub.co.uk
Club Secretary Brian Clivaz

For all those connected with or interested in the arts, literature and science.

Arts Council England

14 Great Peter Street, London SW1P 3NQ
tel (0845) 300 6200 *textphone* 020-7973 6564
fax 020-7973 6590
email enquiries@artscouncil.org.uk
website www.artscouncil.org.uk
Chief Executive Peter Hewitt, *Chair* Sir Christopher Frayling

The national development agency for the arts in England, distributing public money from Government and the National Lottery. Arts Council England's main funding programme is Grants for the Arts, which is open to individuals, arts organisations, national touring companies and other people who use the arts in their work.

Arts Council England has one national and 9 regional offices. It has a single contact telephone and email address for general enquiries (see above). Founded 1946.

East
Eden House, 48–49 Bateman Street, Cambridge CB2 1LR
tel (0845) 300 6200 *textphone* (01223) 306893
fax (0870) 242 1271

East Midlands
St Nicholas Court, 25–27 Castle Gate, Nottingham NG1 7AR
tel (0845) 300 6200 *fax* 0115-950 2467

London
2 Pear Tree Court, London EC1R 0DS
tel (0845) 300 6200 *textphone* 020-7973 6564
fax 020-7608 4100

North East
Central Square, Forth Street, Newcastle upon Tyne NE1 3PJ
tel (0845) 300 6200 *textphone* 0191-255 8585
fax 0191-230 1020

North West
Manchester House, 22 Bridge Street, Manchester M3 3AB
tel (0845) 300 6200 *textphone* 0161-834 9131
fax 0161-834 6969

South East
Sovereign House, Church Street, Brighton BN1 1RA
tel (0845) 300 6200 *textphone* (01273) 710659
fax (0870) 2421257

South West
Senate Court, Southernhay Gardens, Exeter EX1 1UG
tel (0845) 300 6200 *textphone* (01392) 433503
fax (01392) 229229

West Midlands
82 Granville Street, Birmingham B1 2LH
tel (0845) 300 6200 *textphone* 0121-643 2815
fax 0121-643 7239

Yorkshire
21 Bond Street, Dewsbury, West Yorkshire WF13 1AX
tel (0845) 300 6200 *textphone* (01924) 438585
fax (01924) 466522

Arts Council/An Chomhairle Ealaíon

Literature Officer, 70 Merrion Square, Dublin 2, Republic of Ireland
tel (01) 6180200 *fax* (01) 6761302
website www.artscouncil.ie
Arts Programme Director John O'Kane

The national development agency for the arts in Ireland. Founded 1951.

Arts Council of Northern Ireland

MacNeice House, 77 Malone Road, Belfast BT9 5JW
tel 028-9038 5200 *fax* 028-90661715
website www.artscouncil-ni.org
Chief Executive Roisín McDonough, *Literature Officer* Damian Smyth, *Visual Arts Officers* Iain Davidson, Suzanne Lyle

Promotes and encourages the arts throughout Northern Ireland. Artists in drama, dance, music and jazz, literature, the visual arts, traditional arts and community arts, can apply for support for specific schemes and projects. The value of the grant will be set according to the aims of the application. Applicants must have contributed regularly to the artistic activities of the community, and been resident for at least one year in Northern Ireland.

The Arts Council of Wales

9 Museum Place, Cardiff CF10 3NX
tel 029-2037 6500 *minicom* 029-2039 0027
fax 029-2022 1447
email info@artswales.org.uk
website www.artswales.org.uk
Chairman Prof. Dai Smith, *Arts Director* David Alston, *Head of Communications* Sian Phipps, *Wales Arts International* Chris Richetts, *Director of South Wales* David Newland, *Director of North Wales* Simon Lovell Jones, *Director of Mid & West Wales* Sian Tomos

National organisation with specific responsibility for the funding and development of the arts in Wales. ACW receives funding from the National Assembly for Wales and also distributes the National Lottery funds in Wales to the arts. From these resources, ACW makes grants to support arts activities and facilities. Some of the funds are allocated in the form of annual revenue grants to full-time arts organisations. It also operates schemes which provide financial and other forms of support for individual activities or projects. ACW undertakes this work in both the English and Welsh languages.

North Wales Regional Office
36 Princes Drive, Colwyn Bay LL29 8LA
tel (01492) 533440 *minicom* (01492) 532288
fax (01492) 533677

Mid and West Wales Regional Office
6 Gardd Llydaw, Jackson Lane, Carmarthen
SA31 1QD
tel (01267) 234248 *minicom* (01267) 223469
fax (01267) 233084

South Wales Office
9 Museum Place, Cardiff CF10 3NX
tel 029-2037 6525 *minicom* 029-2039 0027
fax 029-2022 1447

Aslib (The Association for Information Management)
Holywell Centre, 1 Phipp Street, London EC2A 4PS
tel 020-7613 3031 *fax* 020-7613 5080
email aslib@aslib.com
website www.aslib.com
Ceo Roger Bowes

Actively promotes best practice in the management of information resources. It represents its members and lobbies on all aspects of the management of and legislation concerning information at local, national and international levels. Aslib provides consultancy and information services, professional development training, conferences, specialist recruitment, internet products, and publishes primary and secondary journals, conference proceedings, directories and monographs. Founded 1924.

Association for Scottish Literary Studies (ASLS)
c/o Dept of Scottish History, 9 University Gardens, University of Glasgow G12 8QH
tel 0141-330 5309
email office@asls.org.uk
website www.asls.org.uk
Hon. President Alan MacGillivray, *Hon. Secretary* Lorna Borrowman Smith, *Publishing Manager* Duncan Jones
Membership £38 p.a. individuals, £10 UK students, £67 corporate

Promotes the study, teaching and writing of Scottish literature and furthers the study of the languages of Scotland. Publishes annually an edited text of Scottish literature, an anthology of new Scottish writing, a series of academic journals and a Newsletter (2 p.a.). Also publishes *Scotnotes* (comprehensive study guides to major Scottish writers), literary texts and

commentary CDs designed to assist the classroom teacher, and a series of occasional papers. Organises 3 conferences a year. Founded 1970.

Association of American Correspondents in London (AACL)
Secretary Monique Jessen, c/o People Magazine, Brettenham House, Lancaster Place, London WC2E 7TL
tel 020-7322 1155 *fax* 020-7322 1125

Association of American Publishers Inc.
71 Fifth Avenue, New York, NY 10003, USA
tel 212-255-0200 *fax* 212-255-7007
website www.publishers.org
President & Ceo Patricia S. Schroeder

Founded 1970.

Association of Art Historians (AAH)
70 Cowcross Street, London EC1M 6EJ
tel 020-7490 3211 *fax* 020-7490 3277
email admin@aah.org.uk
website www.aah.org.uk
Administrator Claire Davies
Membership Various options for personal membership; institutional membership available

Formed to promote the study of art history and ensure wider public recognition of the field. Publishes *Art History* journal, *The Art Book* magazine, *Bulletin* newsletter. Annual conference and book fair in March/April. Founded 1974.

Association of Assistant Librarians – see Career Development Group

The Association of Authors' Agents
20 John Street, London WC1N 2DR
tel 020-7405 6774 *fax* 020-7831 2154
email aaa@johnsonandalcock.co.uk
website www.agentsassoc.co.uk
President Clare Alexander, *Vice President* Derek Johns, *Treasurers* Caroline Montgomery and Andrew Nurnberg, *Secretary* Anna Power

Maintains a code of professional practice to which all members commit themselves; holds regular meetings to discuss matters of common professional interest; provides a vehicle for representing the view of authors' agents in discussion of matters of common interest with other professional bodies. Founded 1974.

Association of Authors' Representatives Inc.
676ᴀ, Suite 312 9th Avenue, New York, NY 10036, USA
tel 212-840-5777
website www.aar-online.org

Founded 1991.

Association of British Science Writers

Wellcome Wolfson Building, 165 Queen's Gate, London SW7 5HE
tel (0870) 7703361 *fax* (0870) 7707102
email absw@absw.org.uk
website www.absw.org.uk
Chairman Ted Nield, *Administrator* Barbara Drillsma

Association of science writers, editors, and radio, film and TV producers concerned with the presentation and communication of science, technology and medicine. Aims to improve the standard of science writing and to assist its members in their work.

Association of Canadian Publishers

161 Eglinton Avenue East, Suite 702, Toronto, Ontario M4P 1J5, Canada
tel 416-487-6116 *fax* 416-487-8815
email admin@canbook.org,
margaret_eaton@canbook.org
website www.publishers.ca
Executive Director Margaret Eaton

Founded 1976; formerly Independent Publishers Association, 1971.

Association of Christian Writers

Administrator Mrs J.L. Kyriacou, All Saints Vicarage, 43 All Saints Close, Edmonton, London N9 9AT
tel 020-8884 4348
email admin@christianwriters.org.uk
Membership £20 p.a. (£17 DD)

Resigtered charity that aims to see the quality of writing in every area of the media, either overtly Christian or shaped by a Christian perspective, reaching the widest range of people across the UK and beyond. To inspire and equip people to use their talents and skills with integrity to devise, write and market excellent material which comes from a Christian world view. Founded 1971.

Association of Freelance Editors, Proofreaders and Indexers

Contact 1 Priscilla O'Connor, 3 The Lawn, Oldtown Mill, Celbridge, Co. Kildare, Republic of Ireland
tel/fax (353 01) 601 2846
email priscillaoconnor@eircom.net
Contact 2 Brenda O'Hanlon, 11 Clonard Road, Sandyford, Dublin 16, Republic of Ireland
tel (353 01) 295 2194 *fax* (353 01) 295 2300
email brenda@ohanlonmediaservices.com
website www.afepi.ie

Provides information to publishers on freelances through a list of members and their qualifications. Also protects the interests of freelances, and provides social contact for isolated workers.

Association of Freelance Journalists

President Martin Scholes, 107 Marlborough Road, Hadley, Telford, Shrops. TF1 5LJ

email aj_info@yahoo.co.uk
website http://afj.home-page.org
Membership £30 p.a. (no longer accepting members)

Aims to foster the interests of freelance journalists and news photographers, especially those on a low income, including those working as stringers, local correspondents, writers for specialist fields, etc. Founded 1996.

The Association of Illustrators

2nd floor, Back Building, 150 Curtain Road, London EC2A 3AT
tel 020-7613 4328 *fax* 020-7613 4417
website www.theaoi.com
Contact Membership Coordinator

Exists to support illustrators, promote illustration and encourage professional standards in the industry. Publishes *Varoom* magazine (3 p.a.); presents an annual programme of events; annual competition, exhibition and tour of Images – the Best of British Illustration (call for entries: late spring). Founded 1973.

The Association of Learned and Professional Society Publishers

Chief Executive Sally Morris, South House, The Street, Clapham, Worthing, West Sussex BN13 3UU
tel (01903) 871686 *fax* (01903) 871457
email chief.exec@alpsp.org
website www.alpsp.org
Membership Open to not-for-profit publishers and allied organisations

The International trade association for non-profit publishers. Founded 1972.

The Association of Photographers (AOP)

Co-Secretary Gwen Thomas, 81 Leonard Street, London EC2A 4QS
tel 020-7739 6669 *fax* 020-7739 8707
email general@aophoto.co.uk
website www.the-aop.org
Membership £280 p.a.

Exists to protect and promote the interests of fashion advertising and editorial photographers. Founded 1968.

Audiobook Publishing Association (APA)

(formerly the Spoken Word Publishing Association)
Administrator Charlotte McCandlish, 18 Green Lanes, Hatfield, Herts. AL10 9JT
tel (07971) 280788
website www.theapa.net
Membership £50–£600 p.a. plus VAT

The UK trade association for the audiobook industry, APA brings together all those involved – publishers, performers, producers, distributors, retailers, manufacturers. It aims to increase the profile of the audiobook in the media, the retail trade and among the general public, and to provide a forum for discussion. Founded 1994.

The Jane Austen Society

Secretary Maggie Culley, 22 Belmont Grove, Havant, Hants PO9 3PU
email rosemary@sndc.demon.co.uk
website www.janeaustensociety.org.uk
Membership £15 p.a. UK, £250 life; £18 overseas, £300 life

Aims to promote interest in, and enjoyment of, the novels and letters of Jane Austen (1775–1817). Regular publications, meetings and conferences. Twelve branches in UK. Founded 1940.

Australia Council

PO Box 788, Strawberry Hills, NSW 2012, Australia
located at 372 Elizabeth Street, Surry Hills, NSW 2010, Australia
tel (02) 9215 9000 *fax* (02) 9215 9111
email mail@ozco.gov.au
website www.ozco.gov.au
Chairperson David Gonski

Provides a broad range of support for the arts in Australia, embracing music, theatre, literature, visual arts, crafts, Aboriginal arts, community and new media arts. It has 8 major Boards: Literature, Visual Arts/Craft, Music, Theatre, Dance, New Media, Community Cultural Development, Major Performing Arts, as well as the Aboriginal and Torres Strait Islander Arts Board.

The Literature Board's chief objective is to support the writing of all forms of creative literature – novels, short stories, poetry, plays and literary non-fiction. It also assists with the publication of literary magazines, has a book publishing subsidies programme, and initiates and supports projects of many kinds designed to promote Australian literature both within Australia and abroad.

Australian Copyright Council

PO Box 1986, Strawberry Hills, NSW 2012, Australia
tel (02) 9318 1788 *fax* (02) 9698 3536
email info@copyright.org.au
website www.copyright.org.au

An independent non-profit organisation which aims to assist creators and other copyright owners to exercise their rights effectively; raise awareness in the community generally about the importance of copyright; research and identify areas of copyright law which are inadequate or unfair; seek changes to law and practice to enhance the effectiveness and fairness of copyright; foster cooperation amongst bodies representing creators and owners of copyright.

The Council comprises 23 organisations or associations of owners and creators of copyright material, including the Australian Society of Authors,

the Australian Writers Guild and the Australian Book Publishers Association. Founded 1968.

Australian Library and Information Association

PO Box 6335, Kingston, ACT 2604, Australia
tel (02) 6215 8222 *fax* (02) 6282 2249
email enquiry@alia.org.au
website www.alia.org.au
Executive Director Sue Hutley

Aims to promote and improve the services of libraries and other information agencies; to improve the standard of library and information personnel and foster their professional interests; to represent the interests of members to governments, other organisations and the community; and to encourage people to contribute to the improvement of library and information services by supporting the association.

Australian Publishers Association (APA)

60–89 Jones Street, Ultimo, NSW 2007, Australia
tel (02) 9281 9788 *fax* (02) 9281 1073
email apa@publishers.asn.au
website www.publishers.asn.au
Ceo Maree McCaskill

The Australian Society of Authors

PO Box 1566, Strawberry Hills NSW 2012, Australia
tel (02) 9318 0877 *fax* (02) 9318 0530
email asa@asauthors.org
located at 98 Pitt Street, Redfern NSW 2016, Australia
website www.asauthors.org
Executive Director Dr Jeremy Fisher

Australian Writers' Guild (AWG)

8/50 Reservoir Street, Surry Hills, NSW 2010
tel (02) 9281 1554 *fax* (02) 9281 4321
email admin@awg.com.au
website www.awg.com.au

The professional association for all performance writers, i.e. writers for film, TV, radio, theatre, video and new media. The AWG is recognised throughout the industry in Australia as being the voice of performance writers. Established 1962.

Authors' Club (at The Arts Club)

40 Dover Street, London W1S 4NP
tel 020-7499 8581 *fax* 020-7409 0913
email authors@theartsclub.co.uk
Chairman Dinah Wiener, *Secretary* Stella Kane
Membership Apply to Secretary

Founded by Sir Walter Besant, the Authors' Club welcomes as members writers, publishers, critics, journalists, academics and anyone involved with literature. Administers the Authors' Club Best First Novel Award, the Sir Banister Fletcher Award and the Dolman Best First Travel Book Award. Founded 1891.

Authors' Licensing and Collecting Society Ltd – see page 524

Axis
Round Foundry Media Centre, Foundry Street, Leeds LS11 5QP
tel (0870) 443 0701 *fax* (0870) 443 0703
email mark@axisweb.org
website www.axisweb.org

Axis is the national database of contemporary visual artists. The website provides comprehensive information on thousands of practicing artists to a host of arts professionals, members of the public and international clients. Free to join (there is a selection process) and low fees to use. Registered charity funded by Arts Council England, SAC and ACW. Established 1991.

BAFTA (The British Academy of Film and Television Arts)
195 Piccadilly, London W1J 9LN
tel 020-7734 0022 *fax* 020-7292 5868
email reception@bafta.org
website www.bafta.org
Chief Executive Amanda Berry

The pre-eminent organisation in the UK for film, TV and interactive entertainment, recognising and promoting the achievement and endeavour of industry practitioners. BAFTA Awards are awarded annually by members to their peers in recognition of their skills and expertise. The Academy's premises provide club facilities with a 200-seat cinema and 40-seat preview theatre. Provides a full and varied programme of industry-related events, masterclasses, seminars and panel discussions, which are open to both members and non-members. Founded 1947.

BANA (Bath Area Network for Artists)
The Old Malthouse, Comfortable Place, Upper Bristol Road, Bath BA1 3AJ
tel 01225 471714
email enquiries@bana-arts.co.uk
website www.bana-arts.co.uk
Membership from £15 p.a.

An artist-led network that aims to raise the profile of arts activity in the Bath area, to establish and strengthen links between artists, artists' groups and art promoters, and advocate for increased investment in local arts activities. BANA was established by artists, for artists, and works through artists to achieve its aims. It is a non-selective network and its membership is made up of artists committed to professional practice. Core activities and services include the BANA website and artists' database, a newsletter, artist café events and a continuing professional development programme. Founded 1998.

BAPLA (British Association of Picture Libraries and Agencies)
18 Vine Hill, London EC1R 5DZ
tel 020-7713 1780 *fax* 020-7713 1211
email enquiries@bapla.org.uk
website www.bapla.org
Chief Executive Linda Royles

Offers comprehensive information and advice about finding, buying and selling images. Publishes licensing and rights survey, and runs annual events for buyers of images. Has 450 member companies.

The Beckford Society
The Timber Cottage, Crockerton, Warminster BA12 8AX
tel (01985) 213195 *fax* (01985) 213239
email sidney.blackmore@btinternet.com
Membership £10 p.a. minimum

Aims to promote an interest in the life and works of William Beckford of Fonthill (1760–1844) and his circle. Encourages Beckford studies and scholarship through exhibitions, lectures and publications, including *The Beckford Journal* (annual) and occasional newsletters. Founded 1995.

Thomas Lovell Beddoes Society
9 Amber Court, Belper, Derbyshire DE56 1HG
tel (01773) 828066
email john@beddoes.demon.co.uk
website www.beddoes.org

Aims to promote an interest in the life and works of Thomas Lovell Beddoes (1803–49). The Society promotes and undertakes Beddoes studies, and disseminates and publishes useful research. Founded 1994.

The Arnold Bennett Society
Secretary Carol Gorton, 4 Field End Close, Trentham, Stoke-on-Trent ST4 8DA
Membership £12 p.a. individuals, £14 p.a. family (UK); £11 individuals p.a., £13 family p.a. (outside UK); £5 p.a. (students)

Aims to promote the study and appreciation of the life, works and times not only of Arnold Bennett (1867–1931) himself, but also of other provincial writers with particular relationship to North Staffordshire.

The E.F. Benson Society
The Old Coach House, High Street, Rye, East Sussex TN31 7JF
tel (01797) 223114
Secretary Allan Downend
Membership £7.50 p.a. single, £8.50 2 people at same address, £12.50 overseas

Aims to promote interest in the author E.F. Benson (1867–1940) and the Benson family. Arranges annual literary evening, annual outing to Rye (July) and other places of Benson interest, talks on the Bensons and exhibitions. Archive includes the Austin Seckersen Collection, transcriptions of the Benson diaries and letters. Publishes postcards, anthologies of Benson's works, a Benson biography, books on

Benson and an annual journal, *The Dodo*. Also sells out-of-print Bensons to members. Founded 1984.

Bibliographical Society

c/o Institute of English Studies, University of London, Senate House, Malet Street, London WC1E 7HU
tel 020-7389 2150
email secretary@bibsoc.org.uk
website www.bibsoc.org.uk
President John Flood, *Secretary* Margaret Ford

Acquisition and dissemination of information on subjects connected with historical bibliography. Publishes the journal The Library. Founded 1892.

The Blackpool Art Society

The Studio, Wilkinson Avenue, Blackpool FY3 9HB
tel (01253) 407541
email sec@blackpoolartsociety.co.uk
website www.blackpoolsociety.co.uk
President Mrs Ada Rathbone
Hon. Secretary Eileen Potter, 12 Seventh Avenue, Blackpool FY4 2ED

Autumn exhibition (members' work only). Studio meetings, practicals, lectures, etc, out-of-door sketching, workshops. Founded 1884.

Book Aid International

39–41 Coldharbour Lane, London SE5 9NR
tel 020-7733 3577 *fax* 020-7978 8006
email info@bookaid.org
website www.bookaid.org

Works in 18 countries in sub-Saharan Africa and Palestine, providing over half a million books and journals each year to libraries, hospitals, refugee camps and schools. Also supports the growth of local publishing and bookselling so that affordable books can be produced which reflect the local languages and culture.

Book Publishers Association of New Zealand Inc.

PO Box 36477, Northcote, Auckland 1309, New Zealand
tel (09) 480-2711 *fax* (09) 480-1130
email bpanz@copyright.co.nz
website www.bpanz.org.nz
President Michael Moynahan

Books Across the Sea

The English-Speaking Union of the Commonwealth, Dartmouth House, 37 Charles Street, London W1J 5ED
tel 020-7529 1550 *fax* 020-7495 6108
email esu@esu.org
The English Speaking Union of the United States, 144 East 39th Street, New York, NY 10016, USA
tel 212-818-1200 *fax* 212-867-4177
email info@esuus.org
website www.esu.org

World voluntary organisation devoted to the promotion of international understanding and friendship. Exchanges books with its corresponding BAS Committees abroad. The books are selected to reflect the life and culture of each country and the best of its recent publishing and writing.

The Booksellers Association of the United Kingdom & Ireland Ltd

272 Vauxhall Bridge Road, London SW1V 1BA
tel 020-7802 0802 *fax* 020-7802 0803
email mail@booksellers.org.uk
website www.booksellers.org.uk
Chief Executive T.E. Godfray
Founded 1895.

Booktrust

(formerly the National Book League, founded 1925)
Book House, 45 East Hill, London SW18 2QZ
tel 020-8516 2977 *fax* 020-8516 2998
email info@booktrust.org.uk
website www.booktrust.org.uk,
www.booktrusted.com
Chairman Trevor Glover, *Executive Director* Chris Meade

Booktrust is an independent charity bringing books and people together. It exists to open up the world of books and reading to people of all ages and cultures. Its services and activities include the Book Information Service, a unique specialist information service for all queries on books and reading (business callers are charged at £1.50 per minute on 0906-516 1193, weekdays 10am–1pm). Booktrust administers a number of literary prizes, including the Orange, Commonwealth, Nestlé Children's and the Booktrust Teenage, and runs a series of reader development projects.

The Children's Literature Team at Booktrust offers advice and information on all aspects of children's reading and books. The 'booktrusted' website is dedicated to children's books and resources for professionals working with young readers, including annotated book lists, information about organisations concerned with children's books, publishers, children's book news and much more. Booktrust also produces a range of publications, including *Best Book Guide for Children and Young Adults*, and resource materials for National Children's Book Week. It also coordinates the national Bookstart (books for babies) programme which gives free advice and books to parents/carers attending their baby's health checks.

The George Borrow Society

Hon. Secretary Andrew Dakyns, 1 Holywell Close, Meads, Eastbourne, East Sussex BN20 7RX
tel/fax (01323) 737209
email adakyns@yahoo.co.uk
website www.clough5.fsnet.co.uk/gb.html
Membership £15 p.a., £22.50 joint members at same address, £10 students

Promotes knowledge of the life and works of George Borrow (1803–81), traveller and author. Publishes *Bulletin* (bi-annual). Founded 1991.

British Academy

10 Carlton House Terrace, London SW1Y 5AH
tel 020-7969 5200 *fax* 020-7969 5300
email secretary@britac.ac.uk
website www.britac.ac.uk
President Baroness O'Neill, *Humanities Vice-President* Prof. W.E. Davies, *Social Sciences Vice-President* Prof. H.G. Genn, *Treasurer* Prof. R.J.P. Kain, *Foreign Secretary* Prof. C.N.J. Mann, *Publications Secretary* Dr D.J. McKitterick, *Research Secretary* Prof. R.J. Bennett, *Secretary* P.W.H. Brown CBE

The national Academy for the humanities and social sciences: an independent and self-governing fellowship of scholars, elected for distinction and achievement in one or more branches of the academic disciplines that make up the humanities and social sciences. Its primary purpose is to promote research and scholarship in those areas: through research grants and other awards, the sponsorship of a number of research projects and of research institutes overseas; the award of prizes and medals; and the publication both of sponsored lectures and seminar papers and of fundamental texts and research aids prepared under the direction of Academy committees. It also acts as a forum for the discussion of issues of interest and concern to scholars in the humanities and the social sciences, and it provides advice to the Government and other public bodies. Founded 1901.

British Academy of Composers and Songwriters

British Music House, 25–27 Berners Street, London W1T 3LR
tel 020-7636 2929 *fax* 020-7636 2212
email info@britishacademy.com
website www.britishacademy.com
Contact Fran Matthews, Head of Membership

The Academy represents the interests of composers and songwriters across all genres, providing advice on professional and artistic matters. It administers a number of major events, including the annual Ivor Novello Awards and British Composer Awards.

British American Arts Association (BAAA) – see Centre for Creative Communities (CCC)

The British Association of Communicators in Business

Suite GA 2, Oak House, Woodlands Business Park, Breckland, Linford Wood West, Milton Keynes MK14 6EY
tel (0870) 1217606 *fax* (0870) 1217601
email enquiries@cib.uk.com

website www.cib.uk.com
Aims to be the market leader for those involved in corporate media management and practice by providing professional, authoritative, dynamic, supportive and innovative services. Founded 1949.

British Association of Journalists

General Secretary Steve Turner, 89 Fleet Street, London EC4Y 1DH
tel 020-7353 3003 *fax* 020-7353 2310
email office@bajunion.org.uk
website www.bajunion.org.uk
Membership £17.50 per month national newspaper staff, national broadcasting staff and national news agency staff; £10 p.m. other seniors including magazine journalists, PRs, freelances; £7.50 p.m. under age 24

Aims to protect and promote the industrial and professional interests of journalists. Founded 1992.

British Association of Picture Libraries and Agencies – see BAPLA (British Association of Picture Libraries and Agencies)

British Centre for Literary Translation

University of East Anglia, Norwich NR4 7TJ
tel (01603) 592785 *fax* (01603) 592737
email bclt@uea.ac.uk
website www.literarytranslation.com
Coordinator Catherine Fuller

BCLT is funded by Arts Council England and the University of East Anglia. It aims to raise the profile of literary translation in the UK through events, publications, activities and research aimed at professional translators, students and the general reader. Activities include the annual Sebald Lecture, Summer School, translator-in-residence scheme and a joint website with the British Council. BCLT coordinates a PhD programme in literary translation and offers units at undergraduate and postgraduate level. It is joint sponsor with BCLA of the John Dryden Translation Prize. Publishes the journals *In Other Words*, *New Books in German* and the anthology *Rearranging the World*. It is a member of the international RECIT literary translation network. Founded 1989.

British Copyright Council

Copyright House, 29–33 Berners Street, London W1T 3AB
tel (01986) 788 122 *fax* (01986) 788 847
email secretary@britishcopyright.org
website www.britishcopyright.org
Vice-Presidents Prof. Adrian Sterling, *President of Honour* Maureen Duffy, *Chairman* Paul Mitchell, *Vice Chairmen* Gwen Thomas, Bernie Corbett, John Smith, *Secretary* Janet Ibbotson

Aims to defend and foster the true principles of creators' copyright and their acceptance throughout the world, to bring together bodies representing all who are interested in the protection of such copyright, and to keep watch on any legal or other changes which may require an amendment of the law.

The British Council

10 Spring Gardens, London SW1A 2BN
tel 020-7930 8466 *fax* 020-7839 6347
website www.britishcouncil.org
Chair The Rt Hon. Lord Kinnock, *Director-General* Sir David Green, *Director Literature* Susanna Nicklin, *Director Arts* Leigh Gibson

The British Council connects people worldwide with learning opportunities and creative ideas from the UK, and builds lasting relationships between the UK and other countries. It works in 110 countries, where it has over 180 libraries and information centres, each catering to the needs of the local community with print and electronic resources. In 2005–6, 300,000 library members borrowed over 7.5 million books and videos. British Council libraries not only provide information and materials to users, but also promote the latest UK publications.

Working in close collaboration with book trade associations, British Council offices organise book and electronic publishing exhibitions ranging from small, specialist displays to participation in major international book fairs. Other projects include Global Publishing Information, a collection of online publishing market reports on international markets compiled in collaboration with the Publishers Association. It also provides various resources on its website for those interested in finding out more about UK publishing.

Details of the British Council's many publications are available online (www.britishcouncil.org/publications/index.htm). The British Council is the agent for the Department for International Development (DFID) for book aid projects in developing countries, and is an authority on teaching English as a second or foreign language. It also gives advice and information on curriculum, methodology, materials and testing.

The British Council promotes British literature overseas through writers' tours, academic visits, seminars and exhibitions. It publishes *New Writing*, an annual anthology of unpublished short stories, poems, extracts from works in progress and essays; and a series of literary bibliographies, including *Eyes Wide Open: New Fiction from the UK 1999–2001*, *Hunting Down the Universe: A Bibliography of Popular Science and Literature*, and *Teaching Management Principles Using Literature*. Through its Literature Department, the British Council provides an overview of UK literature and a range of online resources on its literature website, www.britishcouncil.org/arts/literature. This includes a literary portal (www.literature.britishcouncil.org), directories of postgraduate and short courses in literature and creative writing, a directory of literary conferences, information about UK and Commonwealth authors on www.contemporarywriters.com and www.literarytranslation.com, including translation workshops. A worldwide online book club and reading group for adults, teenagers and children (www.encompassculture.com) was launched in 2003, and also www.youngtranslators.com for young European translators.

The Visual Arts Department, part of the British Council's Arts Group, develops and enlarges overseas knowledge and appreciation of British achievement in the fields of painting, sculpture, printmaking, design, photography, the crafts and architecture, working closely with the British Council's overseas offices and with professional colleagues in the UK and abroad.

Further information about the work of the British Council is available from Press and Public Relations at the above address, or from British Council offices overseas.

The British Fantasy Society

201 Reddish Road, South Reddish, Stockport SK5 7HR
tel 0161-476 5368 (after 6pm)
email faliol@yahoo.com
website www.britishfantasysociety.org.uk
President Ramsey Campbell, *Secretary* Robert Parkinson
Membership £25 p.a.

For devotees of fantasy, horror and related fields, in literature, art and the cinema. Publications include *British Fantasy Newsletter* (quarterly) featuring news and reviews and several annual booklets, including: *Dark Horizons*; *Masters of Fantasy* on individual authors. There is a small-press library and an annual convention and fantasy awards sponsored by the Society. Founded 1971.

British Film Institute (bfi)

21 Stephen Street, London W1T 1LN
tel 020-7255 1444 *bfi events line* (0870) 240 4050
fax 020-7436 0439
website www.bfi.org.uk
Chair Anthony Minghella CBE, *Director* Amanda Nevill

Provides a wide range of services: *bfi* National Film Theatre; *bfi* London IMAX Cinema (Britain's largest screen); *bfi* National Library (the world's leading specialist film and TV library); *bfi* National Film & Television Archive (one of the world's oldest and largest culturally significant film and TV archives); *bfi* London Film Festival; *bfi* London Lesbian & Gay Film Festival; *bfi* Distribution (making world cinema available for screening in the UK); the *bfi* DVD and Video catalogue of world and historic cinema; a wide range of award-winning publications and education materials, guides and resources; film footage; film stills; research services for the commercial media industry; and *Sight and Sound* magazine. Founded 1933.

British Guild of Beer Writers

Secretary Adrian Tierney-Jones
tel (07973) 465081
email tierneyjones@btinternet.com
Membership £40 p.a

Aims to improve standards in beer writing and at the same time extend public knowledge of beers and brewing. The Gold and Silver Tankard Awards are given annually to writers and broadcasters judged to have made the most valuable contribution to this end. Publishes a directory of members with details of their publications and their particular areas of interest, which is circulated to the media. Founded 1988.

The British Guild of Travel Writers

Secretariat Charlotte Copenam, 12 Askew Crescent, London W12 9DN
tel 020-8749 1128
email charlotte@virtualnecessities.com
website www.bgtw.org

Arranges meetings, discussions and visits for its 220 members (who are all professional travel journalists) to promote and encourage the public's interest in travel. Publishes a monthly newsletter (for members only), website and annual *Yearbook,* which contain details of members and lists travel industry PRs and contacts. Annual awards for journalism (members only) and the travel trade.

The British Haiku Society

38 Wayside Avenue, Hornchurch, Essex RM12 4LL
tel (01772) 251827
website www.britishhaikusociety.org
General Secretary Doreen King *President* Martin Lucas

Promotes the appreciation and writing of haiku, senyru, tanka, haibun and renku. It provides tutorials, workshops, readings, critical comment and information. It also runs a haiku library, administers a haiku and a haibun contest, and produces the journal *Blithe Spirit* (quarterly) and a regular newsletter. The Society has active local groups but welcomes overseas members. See website for membership details. Founded 1990.

British Institute of Professional Photography

Fox Talbot House, 2 Amwell End, Ware, Herts. SG12 9HN
tel (01920) 464011 *fax* (01920) 487056
email info@bipp.com
website www.bipp.com

Exists to represent all who practise photography as a profession in any field; to improve the quality of photography; establish recognised examination

qualifications and a high standard of conduct; to safeguard the interests of the public and the profession. Admission can be obtained either via examinations, or by submission of work and other information to the appropriate examining board. Fellows, Associates and Licentiates are entitled to the designation Incorporated Photographer or Incorporated Photographic Technician. Organises numerous meetings and conferences in various parts of the country throughout the year; publishes *The Photographer* journal (monthly), plus various pamphlets and leaflets on professional photography. Founded 1901; incorporated 1921.

British Interactive Media Association (BIMA)

Briarlea House, Southend Road, Billericay, Essex CM11 2PR
tel (01277) 658107 *fax* (0870) 0517842
email info@bima.co.uk
website www.bima.co.uk
Office Administrator Janice Cable
Membership Open to any organisation or individual with an interest in multimedia. £675 p.a. commercial, £300 institutional, £35 individual plus VAT

Established to promote a wider understanding of the benefits of interactive multimedia to industry, government and education and to provide a regular forum for the exchange of views amongst members. Publishes regular newsletters. Founded 1984.

The British Science Fiction Association Ltd

Membership Secretary Estelle Roberts, 97 Sharp Street, Newland Avenue, Hull HU5 2AE
email bsfa@enterprise.net
President Arthur C. Clarke

For authors, publishers, booksellers and readers of science fiction, fantasy and allied genres. Publishes *Matrix,* an informal magazine of news and information; *Focus,* an amateur writers' magazine; *Vector,* a critical magazine and the Orbiter Service, a network of postal writers workshops. Trophies are awarded annually to the winner in each category of the BSFA Awards: best UK-published novel, best short story, best artwork. Founded 1958.

British Society of Comedy Writers

President Kenneth Rock, 61 Parry Road, Ashmore Park, Wolverhampton, West Midlands WV11 2PS
tel (01902) 722729 *fax* (01902) 722729
email info@bscw.co.uk
website www.bscw.co.uk
Membership £75 p.a. full, £40 p.a. subscriber

Aims to bring together writers and industry representatives in order to develop new projects and ideas. Holds an annual international comedy conference, networking days and workshops to train new writers to professional standards. A script reading service is available. Founded 1999.

British Society of Magazine Editors

137 Hale Lane, Edgware, Middlesex HA8 9QP
tel 020-8906 4664
email admin@bsme.com
website www.bsme.com

British Society of Miniaturists

Director Margaret Simpson, Briargate, 2 The
Brambles, Ilkley, West Yorkshire LS29 9DH
email margaretlsimpson@aol.com
website www.britpaint.com
Membership By selection

'The world's oldest miniature society.' Holds 2 open
exhibitions a year. Founded 1895.

British Society of Painters

Briargate, 2 The Brambles, Ilkley, West Yorkshire
LS29 9DH
email margaretlsimpson@aol.com
website www.britpaint.com
Director Margaret Simpson
Membership By selection

Promotes interest and encourages high quality in the
work of painters in these media. Holds 2 open
exhibitions a year. Founded 1988.

British Watercolour Society

Director Margaret Simpson, Briargate, 2 The
Brambles, Ilkley, West Yorkshire LS29 9DH
tel (01943) 609075
email margaretlsimpson@aol.com
website www.britpaint.com

Promotes the best in traditional watercolour painting.
Holds 2 open exhibitions a year. Founded 1830.

Broadcasting Entertainment Cinematograph and Theatre Union (BECTU), Writers Section

373–377 Clapham Road, London SW9 9BT
tel 020-7346 0900 *fax* 020-7346 0901
email info@bectu.org.uk
website www.bectu.org.uk
General Secretary R. Bolton

Aims to defend the interests of writers in film, TV
and radio. By virtue of its industrial strength, the
Union is able to help its writer members to secure
favourable terms and conditions. In cases of disputes
with employers, the Union can intervene in order to
ensure an equitable settlement. Its production
agreement with PACT lays down minimum terms for
writers working in the documentary area. Founded
1991.

Broadcasting Group – see The Society of Authors, page 513

The Brontë Society

Membership Secretary The Brontë Parsonage
Museum, Haworth, Keighley, West Yorkshire
BD22 8DR

tel (01535) 642323 *fax* (01535) 647131
email bronte@bronte.org.uk
website www.bronte.info

Acquisition, preservation, promotion of the memoirs
and literary remains of the Brontë family; exhibitions
of MSS and other subjects. Publishes *Brontë Studies*
(3 p.a.) and *The Brontë Gazette* (bi-annual). Its
Museum is open throughout the year.

The Browning Society

Contact Dr Berry Chevasco, 52 Esmond Road,
Bedford Park, London W4 1JQ
tel 020-8995 4900
email b.chev@virgin.net
website www.browningsociety.org
Membership £15 p.a.

Aims to widen the appreciation and understanding of
the lives and poetry of Robert Browning (1812–89)
and Elizabeth Barrett Browning (1806–61), and other
Victorian writers and poets. Founded 1881;
refounded 1969.

The John Buchan Society

*Membership Secretary*Diana Durden, Barnack, Goring
Road, Steyning, West Sussex BN44 3GF
tel (01903) 813603
email diana@durden.clara.co.uk
website www.johnbuchansociety.co.uk
Membership £12 p.a. full/overseas; other rates on
application

Promotes a wider understanding and appreciation of
the life and works of John Buchan (1875–1940).
Encourages publication of a complete annotated
edition of Buchan's works, and supports the John
Buchan Centre and Museum at Broughton, Borders.
Holds regular meetings and social gatherings;
produces a Newsletter and a Journal. Founded 1979.

Bureau of Freelance Photographers

Focus House, 497 Green Lanes, London N13 4BP
tel 020-8882 3315 *fax* 020-8886 5174
website www.thebfp.com
Chief Executive John Tracy
Membership £49 p.a. UK; £65 p.a. overseas

Exists to help the freelance photographer by
providing information on markets, and free advisory
service. Publishes *Market Newsletter* (monthly).
Founded 1965.

Byron Society (International)

Byron House, 6 Gertrude Street, London SW10 0JN
website www.internationalbyronsociety.org
Hon. Director Mrs Elma Dangerfield CBE
Membership £20 p.a

Aims to promote research into the life and works of
Lord Byron (1788–1824) by seminars, discussions,
lectures and readings. Publishes *The Byron Journal*
(annual, £6.50 plus postage). Founded 1971.

Randolph Caldecott Society

Secretary Kenn Oultram, Clatterwick House,
Clatterwick Lane, Little Leigh, Northwich, Cheshire
CW8 4RJ

tel (01606) 891303 (office), 781731 (evening)
website www.randolphcaldecott.org.uk
Membership £10 p.a. individual, £15 p.a. families/
corporate

Aims to encourage an interest in the life and works of
Randolph Caldecott (1846–86), the Victorian artist,
illustrator and sculptor. Meetings held in Chester and
London. Liaises with the American Caldecott Society.
Founded 1983.

Cambridge Bibliographical Society

University Library, West Road, Cambridge CB3 9DR
tel (01223) 333123 *fax* (01223) 333160
email nas1000@cam.ac.uk
Secretary Nicholas Smith

To encourage the study of bibliography, including
book and MS production, book collecting and the
history of libraries. It publishes *Transactions* (annual)
and a series of monographs, and arranges a
programme of lectures and visits. Founded 1949.

Campaign for Press and Broadcasting Freedom

2nd Floor, Vi & Garner Smith House, 23 Orford
Road, London E17 9NL
tel 020-8521 5932
email freepress@cpbf.org.uk
website www.cpbf.org.uk

Canadian Authors Association

320 South Shores Road, PO Box 419, Campbellford,
Ontario K0L 1L0
tel 705-653-0323, 866-216-6222 (toll free)
fax 705-653-0593
email admin@canauthors.org
website www.canauthors.org
President Joan Eyolfson Cadham, *Administrator* Alec
McEachern

Canadian Magazine Publishers Association

425 Adelaide Street West, Suite 700, Toronto,
Ontario M5V 3C1, Canada
tel 416-504-0274 *fax* 416-504-0437
email cmpainfo@cmpa.ca
website www.cmpa.ca

Founded 1973.

Canadian Publishers' Council

250 Merton Street, Suite 203, Toronto, Ontario
M4S 1B1, Canada
tel 416-322-7011 *fax* 416-322-6999
email pubadmin@pubcouncil.ca
website www.pubcouncil.ca
Executive Director Jacqueline Hushion

CANSCAIP (Canadian Society of Children's Authors, Illustrators & Performers)

40 Orchard View Boulevard, Suite 104, Toronto,
Ontario M4R 1B9, Canada

tel 416-515-1559
email office@canscaip.org
website www.cansaip.org
Office Manager Lena Coakley
Membership $75 p.a. Full member (published authors
and illustrators), $45 Insitutional Friend, $35 Friend

A non-profit support network for children's artists.
Promotes children's literature and performances
through Canada and internationally. Founded 1977.

Career Development Group

(formerly Association of Assistant Librarians)
c/o CILIP, 7 Ridgmount Street, London WC1E 7AE
website www.careerdevelopmentgroup.org.uk
President Isabel Hood, *Secretary* Paula Younger

Publishes bibliographical aids, the journal *Impact*,
works on librarianship; and runs educational courses.
Founded 1895.

Careers Writers' Association

Membership Secretary Ann Goodman, 16 Caewal
Road, Llandaff, Cardiff CF5 2BT
tel 029-2056 3444 *fax* 029-2065 8190
email ann@ann50.freeserve.co.uk
website www.careerswriters.co.uk
Membership £20 p.a.

Society for established writers on the inter-related
topics of education, training and careers. Holds
occasional meetings on subjects of interest to
members, and circulates details of members to
information providers. Founded 1979.

The Lewis Carroll Society

Secretary Alan White, 69 Cromwell Road, Hertford,
Herts. SG13 7DP
email alanwhite@tesco.net
website www.lewiscarrollsociety.org.uk
Membership £15 p.a. UK, £18 Europe, £20 elsewhere;
special rates for institutions

Aims to promote interest in the life and works of
Lewis Carroll (Revd Charles Lutwidge Dodgson)
(1832–98) and to encourage research. Activities
include regular meetings, exhibitions, and a
publishing programme that includes the first
annotated, unexpurgated edition of his diaries in 9
volumes, the Society's journal *The Carrollian* (2 p.a.),
a newsletter, *Bandersnatch* (quarterly) and the *Lewis
Carroll Review* (occasional). Founded 1969.

Lewis Carroll Society (Daresbury)

Secretary Kenn Oultram, Clatterwick House,
Clatterwick Lane, Little Leigh, Northwich, Cheshire
CW8 4RJ
tel (01606) 891303 (office), 781731 (evening)
Membership £5 p.a.

Aims to encourage an interest in the life and works of
Lewis Carroll (1832–98), author of *Alice's Adventures*.
Meetings take place at Carroll's birth village
(Daresbury, Cheshire). Founded 1970.

Cartoonists Club of Great Britain

Secretary Jed Stone, 7 Gambetta Street, London
SW8 3TS
tel 020-7720 1884
email jedstone@tunamoon.demon.co.uk
website www.ccgb.org.uk
Membership Fee on joining: £50; thereafter £35 p.a.

Aims to encourage social contact between members
and endeavours to promote the professional standing
and prestige of cartoonists.

Centerprise Literature Development Project

Centerprise Literature Development Project,
Centreprise, 136–138 Kingsland High Street, London
E8 2NS
tel 020-7249 6572
email literature@centerprisetrust.org.uk
Contact Eva Lewin, Sharon Duggal, Susan Yearwood

An advice and resource centre for writers of fiction
and poetry, servicing Central, East and North
London. Runs courses and workshops in creative
writing, organises poetry and book readings,
discussions and debates on literary and relevant
issues, writers' surgeries, and telephone information
on resources for writers in London. Publishes
Calabash newsletter for Writers of Black and Asian
origin. Funded by ACE London. Founded 1995.

Centre for Creative Communities (CCC)

Regent House Business Centre, 24–25 Nutford Place,
London W1H 5YN
tel 020-7569 3005
email info@creativecommunities.org.uk
website www.creativecommunities.org.uk
Director Jennifer Williams

A non-profit-making organisation working in the
field of arts, education and community development.
Conducts research, organises conferences, produces a
quarterly newsletter and is part of an international
network of arts and education organisations.
Maintains a specialised arts, education and
community development library. CCC is not a grant-
giving organisation.

The Chartered Institute of Journalists

General Secretary Dominic Cooper, 2 Dock Offices,
Surrey Quays Road, London SE16 2XU
tel 020-7252 1187 *fax* 020-7232 2302
email memberservices@ioj.co.uk
Membership £195 p.a. maximum, £97.50 trainees,
£133 affiliate

The senior organisation of the profession, the
Chartered Institute has accumulated funds for the
assistance of members. A Freelance Division links
editors and publishers with freelances and a Directory
is published of freelance writers, with their

specialisations. There are special sections for
broadcasters, motoring correspondents, public
relations practitioners and overseas members.
Occasional contributors to the media may qualify for
election as Affiliates. Founded in 1884; incorporated
by Royal Charter in 1890.

The Chartered Society of Designers

1 Cedar Court, Royal Oak Yard, Bermondsey Street,
London SE1 3GA
tel 020-7357 8088 *fax* 020-7407 9878
email csd@csd.org.uk
website www.csd.org.uk
Chief Executive Frank Peters MCSD

Works to promote and regulate standards of
competence, professional conduct and integrity,
including representation on government and official
bodies, design education and awards. The services to
members include general information, publications,
guidance on copyright and other professional issues,
access to professional indemnity insurance, as well as
the membership magazine *csd*. Activities in the
regions are included in an extensive annual
programme of events and training courses.

The Chesterton Society

Hon. Secretary Rev. Robert Hughes KCHS, 11 Lawrence
Leys, Bloxham, Nr Banbury, Oxon OX15 4NU
tel/fax (01295) 720869
mobile (07766) 711984
email rmccallum@onetel.com
Membership £12.50 p.a.

Aims to promote interest in the life and work of
G.K. Chesterton (1874–1936) and those associated
with him or influenced by his writings. Two lectures
a year. Publishes the *Chesterton Quarterly Review* (4
p.a.). Founded 1974.

The Children's Book Circle

c/o Nicola Wilkinson, Egmont Books Ltd,
239 Kensington High Street, London W8 6SA
tel 020-7761 3699 *fax* 020-7761 3740
email nwilkinson@euk.egmont.com
Membership Secretary Alison Kain, Peters, Fraser &
Dunlop, Drury House, 34–43 Russell Street, London
WC2B 5HA
tel 020-7344 1056 *fax* 020-7836 9539
email akain@pfd.co.uk
website www.childrensbookcircle.org.uk
Membership £15 p.a. if working inside M25; £12
outside

Provides a discussion forum for anybody involved
with children's books. Meetings are addressed by a
panel of invited speakers and topics focus on current
and controversial issues. Holds the annual Patrick
Hardy lecture and administers the Eleanor Farjeon
Award. Founded 1962.

Children's Books History Society

Secretary Ms Sarah Mahurter, 66 Idmiston Square,
Worcester Park, Surrey KT4 7SY

tel 020-8830-6084 *fax* 020-8830-6084
email sjamahuter@hotmail.com
Membership £10 p.a.; apply for overseas rates

Aims 'to promote an appreciation of children's books, and to study their history, bibliography and literary content'. Holds approx. 6 meetings and produces 3 substantial *Newsletters* and an occasional paper per year. The Harvey Darton Award is given biennially for a book that extends knowledge of British children's literature of the past. Founded 1969.

Children's Books Ireland

17 North Great Georges Street, Dublin 1, Republic of Ireland
tel (01) 872 7475 *fax* (01) 872 7476
email info@childrensbooksireland.com
website www.childrensbooksireland.com
Director Mags Walsh, *Administrator* Jenny Murray
Membership €30/£20 p.a. individual, €50/£35 p.a. institutions, €45/£30/$55 p.a. overseas individual, €60/£40/$70 p.a. overseas institutions, €20/£15 p.a. student

Provides leadership and support in the promotion and celebration of books and reading for young people. As a resource and advocacy organisation for adults, CBI is committed to raising awareness of the importance and value of books for children and to bringing young people and books together. Formed in 1996.

Children's Writers and Illustrators
Group – see The Society of Authors, page 513

CILIP (Chartered Institute of Library and Information Professionals)

7 Ridgmount Street, London WC1E 7AE
tel 020-7255 0500 *textphone* 020-7255 0505
fax 020-7255 0501
email info@cilip.org.uk
website www.cilip.org.uk
Chief Executive Bob McKee PhD, FRSA, MCLIP
Membership Varies according to income

CILIP was formed on 1 April 2002 following the unification of the Institution of Information Scientists and the Library Association. It is the leading membership body for library and information professionals, with around 23,000 members in the UK and overseas. Its monthly magazine *Update* and fortnightly *Gazette* are distributed free to members. The IIS was originally founded in 1958 and the LA in 1877.

Circle of Wine Writers

Administrator Andrea Warren, Scots Firs, 70 Joiners Lane, Chalfont St Peter, Bucks. SL9 0AU
tel/fax (01494) 589201
email administrator@winewriters.org
website www.winewriters.org

Membership By election, £35 p.a.

An association for those engaged in communicating about wines and spirits. Produces *Circle Update* newsletter (5 p.a.), organises tasting sessions as well as a programme of meetings and talks. Founded 1960.

The John Clare Society

Hon. Secretary 9 The Chase, Ely, Cambs. CB6 3DR
tel (01353) 668438
email l.j.curry@bham.ac.uk
website www.johnclare.org.uk
Membership £10 p.a. UK individual; other rates on application

Promotes a wider appreciation of the life and works of the poet John Clare (1793–1864). Founded 1981.

Classical Association

Secretary Clare Roberts, Senate House, Malet Street, London WC1E 7HU
tel 020-7862 8706 *fax* 020-7862 8729
email office@classicalassociation.org
website www.classicalassociation.org

Exists to promote and sustain interest in classical studies, to maintain their rightful position in universities and schools, and to give scholars and teachers opportunities for meeting and discussing their problems.

CLÉ – Irish Book Publishers' Association

25 Denzille Lane, Dublin 2, Republic of Ireland
tel (01) 639 4868
email info@publishingireland.com
website www.publishingireland.com
President Tony Farmar

The William Cobbett Society

Chairman Molly Townsend, 10 Grenehurst Way, Petersfield, Hants GU31 4AZ
tel (01730) 262060
email williamcobbett@fsmail.net
Membership £8 p.a.

Aims to make the life and work of William Cobbett (1763–1835) better known. Founded 1976.

The Wilkie Collins Society

Membership Secretary Paul Lewis, 4 Ernest Gardens, London W4 3QU
email paul@paullewis.co.uk
website www.wilkiecollins.org
Chairman Andrew Gasson
Membership £10 p.a. EU, £18 international

Aims to promote interest in the life and works of Wilkie Collins (1824–89). Publishes a newsletter, an annual scholarly journal and reprints of Collins's lesser known works. Founded 1981.

Comhairle nan Leabhraichean/The Gaelic Books Council

22 Mansfield Street, Glasgow G11 5QP
tel 0141-337 6211 *fax* 0141-353 0515

email brath@gaelicbooks.net
website www.gaelicbooks.net
Chair Prof. Roibeard Ó Maolalaigh

Stimulates Scottish Gaelic publishing by awarding publication grants for new books, commissioning authors and providing editorial services and general assistance to writers and readers. Has its own bookshop of all Gaelic and Gaelic-related books in print and runs a book club. All the stock is listed on the website and a paper catalogue is also available. Founded 1968.

The Joseph Conrad Society (UK)
The Conradian, Dr Allan Simmons, Dept of English, St Mary's College, Twickenham, Middlesex TW1 4SX
email theconradian@aol.com
website www.josephconradsociety.org
Chairman Keith Carabine, *President* Laurence Davies, *Secretary* Hugh Epstein, *Editor* Allan Simmons

Activities include an annual international conference; publication of *The Conradian* and a series of pamphlets; and maintenance of a substantial reference library as part of the Polish Library at the Polish Cultural Centre, 238–246 King Street, London W6 0RF. Administers the Juliet McLauchlan Prize, £200 annual award for the winner of an essay competition, and travel grants for scholars wishing to attend Conrad conferences. Founded 1973.

Copyright Clearance Center Inc.
222 Rosewood Drive, Danvers, MA 01923, USA
tel 978-750-8400 *fax* 978-750-4470
email info@copyright.com
website www.copyright.com

Copyright Council of New Zealand Inc.
PO Box 36477, Northcote, Auckland 1309, New Zealand
tel (09) 480-2711 *fax* (09) 480-1130
Chairman Anthony Healey, *Secretary* Kathy Sheat

The Copyright Licensing Agency Ltd – see page 700

Crime Writers' Association
email secretary@thecwa.co.uk
website www.thecwa.co.uk
Membership Associate membership open to publishers, journalists, booksellers specialising in crime literature and literary agents

Full membership open to professional writers of crime novels, short stories, plays for stage, TV and radio, or of other serious works on crime. Publishes *Red Herrings* (monthly), available to members only. Founded 1953.

The Critics' Circle
Contact Catherine Cooper, Administrator, c/o 69 Marylebone Lane, London W1U 2PH

tel 020-7224 1410 (office hours)
President Mike Dixon, *Hon. General Secretary* Charles Hedges
Membership By invitation of the Council

Aims to promote the art of criticism, to uphold its integrity in practice, to foster and safeguard the professional interests of its members, to provide opportunities for social intercourse among them, and to support the advancement of the arts. Such invitations are issued only to persons engaged professionally, regularly and substantially in the writing or broadcasting of criticism of drama, music, films, dance and the visual arts. Founded 1913.

Cyngor Llyfrau Cymru – see Welsh Books Council/Cyngor Llyfrau Cymru

Data Publishers Association
Queen's House, 28 Kingsway, London WC2B 6JR
tel 020-7405 0836 *fax* 020-7404 4167
website www.dpa.org.uk
Head of DPA Christine Scott
Membership £395–£2100 p.a.

Maintains a code of professional practice; aims to raise the standard and professional status of UK directory and database publishing and to protect (and promote) the legal, statutory and common interests of directory publishers; provides for the exchange of technical, commercial and management information between members. Founded 1970.

Walter de la Mare Society
PO Box 25351, London NW5 1ZT
tel 020-7485 2533
website www.bluetree.co.uk/wdlmsociety
Membership £15 p.a.

To promote the study and deepen the appreciation of the works of Walter de la Mare (1873–1956) through a magazine, talks, discussions and other activities. Founded 1997.

Design and Artists Copyright Society – see page 705

Dickens Fellowship
The Charles Dickens Museum, 48 Doughty Street, London WC1N 2LX
tel 020-7405 2127 *fax* 020-7831 5175
Joint Hon. Secretaries Dr Tony Williams, Thelma Grove
Membership On application

Based in house occupied by Charles Dickens (1812–75) during the period 1837–9. Publishes *The Dickensian* (3 p.a.). Founded 1902.

Directory of Writers' Circles, Courses and Workshops
39 Lincoln Way, Harlington, Beds. LU5 6NG
tel (01525) 873197

email diana@writers-circles.com
website www.writers-circles.com
Publisher & Editor Diana Hayden

Publishes a directory of writers' circles, courses and workshops for the UK and Eire which is updated twice annually.

'Sean Dorman' Manuscript Society

3 High Road, Britford, Salisbury SP5 4DS
tel (01722) 332821
Director Jan Smith

Provides mutual help among writers and aspiring writers in the UK. By means of circulating MSS parcels, members receive constructive criticism of their own work and read and comment on the work of others. Each 'Circulator' has up to 7 participants and members' contributions may be in any medium: short stories, chapters of a novel, poetry, magazine articles, etc. Send sae for full details and application form. Founded 1957.

The Arthur Conan Doyle Society

Organisers Christopher and Barbara Roden, PO Box 1360, Ashcroft, B.C., Canada V0K 1A0
tel 250-453-2045 *fax* 250-453-2075
email ashtree@ash-tree.bc.ca
website www.ash-tree.bc.ca/acdsocy.html

Promotes the study of the life and works of Sir Arthur Conan Doyle (1859–1930). Publishes *ACD* journal (bi-annual) and occasional reprints of Conan Doyle material. Occasional conventions. Founded 1989.

Early English Text Society

Lady Margaret Hall, Oxford OX2 6QA
website www.eets.org.uk
Hon. Director Prof. Anne Hudson *Executive Secretary* Prof. V. Gillespie
Membership £20 p.a.

Aims to bring unprinted early English literature within the reach of students in sound texts. Founded 1864.

Edinburgh Bibliographical Society

c/o National Library of Scotland, George IV Bridge, Edinburgh EH1 1EW
tel 0131-623 3893
Secretary Dr W. McDougall, *Treasurer* J. Marshall
Membership £15 p.a., £20 institutions; £10 full-time students

Encourages bibliographical activity through organising talks for members, particularly on bibliographical topics relating to Scotland, and visits to libraries. Publishes *Journal* (annual, free to members) and other occasional publications. Founded 1890.

Educational Writers Group – see The
Society of Authors, page 513

The George Eliot Fellowship

Secretary Mrs K.M. Adams, 71 Stepping Stones Road, Coventry CV5 8JT
tel 024-7659 2231
website www.george-eliot-fellowship.com
President Jonathan G. Ouvry
Membership £10 p.a.

Promotes an interest in the life and work of George Eliot (1819–80) and helps to extend her influence; arranges meetings; produces an annual journal, a quarterly newsletter and other publications. Awards the annual George Eliot Fellowship Prize (£250) for an essay on Eliot's life or work, which must be previously unpublished and not exceed 2500 words. Founded 1930.

The English-Speaking Union

Dartmouth House, 37 Charles Street, London W1J 5ED
tel 020-7529 1550 *fax* 020-7495 6108
email esu@esu.org
website www.esu.org
Director-General Mrs Valerie Mitchell OBE
Membership Various categories

Aims to promote international understanding and human achievement through the widening use of the English language throughout the world. The ESU is an educational charity which sponsors scholarships and exchanges, educational programmes promoting the effective use of English, and a wide range of international and cultural events. Members contribute to its work across the world. Administers the Marsh Biography Award (see page 575). See also Books Across the Sea. Founded 1918.

English Association

University of Leicester, University Road, Leicester LE1 7RH
tel 0116-252 3982 *fax* 0116-252 2301
email engassoc@le.ac.uk
website www.le.ac.uk/engassoc/
Chair Peter J. Kitson, *Chief Executive* Helen Lucas

Aims to further knowledge, understanding and enjoyment of English literature and the English language, by working towards a fuller recognition of English as an essential element in education and in the community at large; by encouraging the study of English literature and language by means of conferences, lectures and publications; and by fostering the discussion of methods of teaching English of all kinds.

English Speaking Board (International) Ltd

26A Princes Street, Southport PR8 1EQ
tel (01704) 501730 *fax* (01704) 539637
email admin@esbuk.org
website www.esbuk.org
President Christabel Burniston MBE

Membership £35 p.a. individuals, £50 corporate

Aims to foster all activities concerned with oral communication. Offers assessment qualifications in practical speaking and listening skills for candidates at all levels in schools, vocational and business contexts; also for those with learning difficulties and those for whom English is an acquired language. Also provides training courses in teaching and delivery of oral communication. Offers membership to all those concerned with the development and expression of the English language. Members receive *Speaking English* (2 p.a.); articles are invited on any special aspect of spoken English.

European Broadcasting Union

General Headquarters, Ancienne Route 17A, CH–1218 Grand Saconnex (Geneva), Switzerland
tel 41 22 717 2111 *fax* 41 22 747 4000
email ebu@ebu.ch
website www.ebu.ch
Secretary-General Jean Réveillon

The largest professional association of national broadcasters. Working on behalf of its members in the European area, the EBU negotiates broadcasting rights for major sports events; operates the Eurovision and Euroradio networks; organises programme exchanges; stimulates and coordinates co-productions; and provides a full range of other operational, commercial, technical, legal and strategic services. Founded 1950.

Fabian Society

11 Dartmouth Street, London SW1H 9BN
tel 020-7227 4900 *fax* 020-7976 7153
email info@fabian-society.org.uk
website www.fabian-society.org.uk
General Secretary Mr Sunder Katwala

Current affairs, political thought, economics, education, environment, foreign affairs, social policy. Also controls NCLC Publishing Society Ltd. Founded 1884.

Federation Against Copyright Theft Ltd (FACT)

7 Victory Business Centre, Worton Road, Isleworth, Middlesex TW7 6DB
tel 020-8568 6646 *fax* 020-8560 6364
email contact@fact-uk.org.uk
website www.fact-uk.org.uk
Contact David Lowe, Director General

Aims to protect the interests of its members and others against infringement in the UK of copyright in cinematograph films, TV programmes and all forms of audiovisual recording. Founded 1982.

The Copyright Hotline offers advice and information to anyone who wants to use film, music or software copyrights. It is part of a collective initiative by FACT, Federation Against Software Theft (FAST), Music Publishers Association (MPA),

Mechanical Copyright Protection Society (MCPS), Performing Right Society (PRS) and British Music Rights (BMR).

Federation of British Artists

17 Carlton House Terrace, London SW1Y 5BD
tel 020-7930 6844 *fax* 020-7839 7830
email info@mallgalleries.com
website www.mallgalleries.org.uk

Administers 9 major National Art Societies at the Mall Galleries, The Mall, London SW1.

Federation of European Publishers

Rue Montoyer 31 Bte 8, B–1000 Brussels, Belgium
tel (2) 770 11 10 *fax* (2) 771 20 71
email info@fep-fee.be
website www.fep-fee.be
President Dr Arne Bach, *Director* Anne Bergman-Tahon

Represents the interests of European publishers on EU affairs; informs members on the development of EU policies which could affect the publishing industry. Founded 1967.

The Federation of Indian Publishers

18/1–C Institutional Area, Aruna Asaf Ali Marg (near JNU), New Delhi 110067, India
tel 26852263, 26964847 *fax* 26864054
email fip1@satyam.net.in
website www.fipindia.com

Federation of Spanish Publishers' Association

(Federación de Gremios de Editores de España)
Cea Bermúdez, 44–2 Dcha. 28003 Madrid, Spain
tel (91) 534 51 95 *fax* (91) 535 26 25
email fgee@fge.es
website www.federacioneditores.org
President D. Emiliano Martinez

The Federation of Worker Writers and Community Publishers

Burslem School of Art, Queen Street, Stoke-on-Trent ST6 3EJ
tel (01782) 822327 *fax* (01782) 822327
email thefwwcp@tiscali.co.uk
website www.thefwwcp.org.uk
Membership £40 p.a. funded groups; £20 unfunded

A network of writers groups and community publishers which promotes working-class writing and publishing. Founded 1976.

The Fine Art Trade Guild

16–18 Empress Place, London SW6 1TT
tel 020-7381 6616 *fax* 020-7381 2596
email info@fineart.co.uk
website www.fineart.co.uk
Managing Director Rosie Sumner

Promotes the sale of fine art prints and picture framing in the UK and overseas markets; establishes and raises standards amongst members and communicates these to the buying public. The Guild publishes *The Directory* and *Art Business Today*, the trade's longest established magazine, and various specialist books. Founded 1910.

FOCAL International Ltd (Federation of Commercial AudioVisual Libraries International Ltd)

Pentax House, South Hill Avenue, South Harrow, Middlesex HA2 0DU
tel 020-8423 5853 *fax* 020-8933 4826
email info@focalint.org
website www.focalint.org
Commerical Manager Anne Johnson, *General Manager* Julie Lewis

Founded 1985.

The Folklore Society

The Warburg Institute, Woburn Square, London WC1E 0AB
tel 020-7862 8564
email folklore.society@talk21.com
website www.folklore-society.com
Hon. Secretary Dr Juliette Wood
Membership £45 p.a.

Collection, recording and study of folklore. Founded 1878.

Foreign Press Association in London

Registered Office 11 Carlton House Terrace, London SW1Y 5AJ
tel 020-7930 0445 *fax* 020-7925 0469
email secretariat@foreign-press.org.uk
website www.foreign-press.org.uk
Director Roy Payne
Membership Entrance fee: £322.39 p.a. Full membership open to overseas professional journalists residing in the UK; Associate membership available for British press and freelance journalists

Aims to promote the professional interests of its members. Founded 1888.

Free Painters & Sculptors

Registered office 14 John Street, London WC1N 2EB
Hon. Secretary Owen Legg, 152 Hadlow Road, Tonbridge, Kent TN9 1PB
Membership Secretary Pam Mara, 5F Gloucester Street, London SW1V 2DB

Promotes group shows 4 times a year in prestigious galleries in London. Sponsors all that is exciting in contemporary art.

French Publishers' Association

(Syndicat National de l'Edition)
115 Blvd St Germain, 75006 Paris, France
tel (1) 44 41 40 50 *fax* (1) 44 41 40 77
website www.sne.fr

The Gaelic Books Council – see Comhairle nan Leabhraichean/The Gaelic Books Council

Garden Writers Guild

Administrator Kiersty Darnell, c/o Institute of Horticulture, 14–15 Belgrave Square, London SW1X 8PS
tel 020-7245 6943 *fax* 020-7245 6943
email gwg@horticulture.org.uk
website www.gardenwriters.co.uk
Membership £45 p.a.

Aims to raise the standards of gardening communicators. Administers annual awards to encourage excellence in garden writing, trade and consumer press journalism, TV and radio broadcasting, as well as garden photography. Founded 1991.

The Gaskell Society

Far Yew Tree House, Chester Road, Tabley, Knutsford, Cheshire WA16 0HN
tel (01565) 634668
email joanleach@aol.com
website www.gaskellsociety.users.btopenworld.com
Hon. Secretary Mrs Joan Leach
Membership £15 p.a., £20 corporate/overseas

Promotes and encourages the study and appreciation of the work and life of Elizabeth Cleghorn Gaskell (1810–65). Holds regular meetings in Knutsford, London, Manchester, Bath and York, visits and residential conferences; produces an annual Journal and bi-annual Newsletters. Founded 1985.

Gay Authors Workshop

Kathryn Byrd, BM Box 5700, London WC1N 3XX
Membership £7 p.a., £3 unwaged

Exists to encourage writers who are lesbian, gay or bisexual. Quarterly newsletter. Founded 1978.

German Publishers' and Booksellers' Association

(Börsenverein des Deutschen Buchhandels e.V.)
Postfach 100442, 60004 Frankfurt am Main, Germany
tel (069) 13060 *fax* (069) 1306201
email info@boev.de
website www.boersenverein.de
General Manager Alexander Skipis

The Ghost Story Society

PO Box 1360, Ashcroft, British Columbia V0K 1A0, Canada
tel 250-453-2045 *fax* 250-453-2075
email nebu-y@telus.net
website www.ash-tree.bc.ca/GSS.html
Secretary Barbara Roden
Membership £25/US$40/Can.$43 p.a.

Provides enthusiasts of the classic ghost story with a forum to discuss and appreciate the genre. Publishes

All Hallows (3 p.a.) journal which contains news, articles, reviews and approx. 100pp of new fiction. Founded 1989.

Graham Greene Birthplace Trust

Secretary Ken Sherwood, Rhenigidale, Ivy House Lane, Berkhamsted, Herts. HP4 2PP
tel (01442) 865158
email secretary@grahamgreenebt.org
website www.grahamgreenebt.org
Membership £8 p.a., £20 3 years

Exists to study the works of Graham Greene (1904–91). The Trust promotes the Annual Graham Greene Festival and Graham Greene trails. It publishes a quarterly newsletter, occasional papers, videos and CDs, and maintains a small archive. It administers the Graham Greene Memorial Awards. Founded 1997.

The Greeting Card Association

United House, North Road, London N7 9DP
tel 020-7619 0396
website www.greetingcardassociation.org.uk
Administrator Sharon Little

The trade association for greeting card publishers. See website for information on freelance designing and writing for greeting cards. Official magazine: *Progressive Greetings Worldwide* (see page 466).

Guernsey Arts Council

La Fontaine, Courtil de la Fontaine, Kings Road, St Peter Port, Guernsey GY1 1QB, CI
email tdguernsey@cwgsy.net eales@guernsey.net
Chairman Mrs Terry Domrille, *Secretary* Ann Wilkes-Green *tel* (01481) 254144

Guild of Agricultural Journalists

Hon. General Secretary Don Gomery, Isfield Cottage, Church Road, Crowsborough, East Sussex TN6 1BN
tel (01892) 611618 *fax* (01892) 613394
email don.gomery@farmingline.com
website www.gaj.org.uk
President Baroness Byford, *Chairman* Roger Abbott

Established to promote a high standard among journalists who specialise in agricultural matters and to assist them to increase their sources of information and technical knowledge.

The Guild of Aviation Artists

(incorporating the Society of Aviation Artists)
Trenchard House, 85 Farnborough Road, Farnborough, Hants GU14 6TF
tel (01252) 513123 *fax* (01252) 510505
email admin@gava.org.uk
website www.gava.org.uk
President Michael Turner FGAvA, *Secretary/ Administrator* Susan Gardner
Membership £60 p.a. Full (by invitation), £45 Associates (by selection), £25 Friends

Formed to promote aviation art through the organisation of exhibitions and meetings. Holds annual open exhibition in July in London; £1000 prize for 'Aviation Painting of the Year'. Quarterly members' newsletter. Founded 1971.

Guild of Food Writers

Administrator Jonathan Woods, 9 Colman House, High Street, London SE20 7EX
tel 020-8659 0422
email gfw@gfw.co.uk
website www.gfw.co.uk
Membership £70 p.a.

Aims to bring together professional food writers including journalists, broadcasters and authors, to print and issue an annual list of members, to extend the range of members' knowledge and experience by arranging discussions, tastings and visits, and to encourage the development of new writers by every means, including competitions and awards. There are 8 awards for 2006 and entry is not restricted to members of the Guild. Founded 1984.

Guild of Health Writers

Administrator Jatinder Dua, Dale Lodge, 88 Wensleydale Road, Hampton, Middlesex TW12 2LX
tel 020-8941 2977 *fax* 020-8941 2977
email admin@healthwriters.com
website www.healthwriters.com
Membership £45 p.a.

Brings together professional journalists dedicated to providing accurate, broad-based information about health and related subjects to the public. Publishes a directory of members. Founded 1995.

The Guild of International Songwriters & Composers

Sovereign House, 12 Trewartha Road, Praa Sands, Penzance, Cornwall TR20 9ST
tel (01736) 762826 *fax* (01736) 763328
email songmag@aol.com
website www.songwriters-guild.co.uk
Secretary Carole Ann Jones
Membership £45 p.a. UK, £50 EU/overseas

Gives advice to members on contractual and copyright matters; assists with protection of members rights; assists with analysis of members' works; international collaboration register free to members; outlines requirements to record companies, publishers, artists. Publishes *Songwriting & Composing* (quarterly).

The Guild of Motoring Writers

Contact General Secretary, 39 Beswick Avenue, Ensbury Park, Bournemouth BH22 0AG
tel/fax (01202) 518808
website www.guildofmotoringwriters.co.uk

Strives to raise the standard of motoring journalism, encourage motoring, motor sport and road safety –

for writers, photographers, broadcasters and artists not connected with the motor industry.

Guild of Railway Artists

Chief Executive Officer F.P. Hodges Hon. GRA, 45 Dickins Road, Warwick CV34 5NS
tel (01926) 499246
email frank.hodges@tinyworld.co.uk
website www.railart.co.uk

Aims to forge a link between artists depicting railway subjects and to give members a corporate identity; also stages railway art exhibitions and members' meetings and produces books of members' works. Founded 1979.

Hakluyt Society

c/o The Map Library, The British Library, 96 Euston Road, London NW1 2DB
tel (01428) 641850 *fax* (01428) 641933
email office@hakluyt.com
website www.hakluyt.com
President Prof. R.C. Bridges, *Hon. Secretary & Series Editor* Prof. W.F. Ryan

Publication of original narratives of voyages, travels, naval expeditions, and other geographical records. Founded 1846.

The Thomas Hardy Society

PO Box 1438, Dorchester, Dorset DT1 1YH
tel (01305) 251501 *fax* (01305) 251501
email info@hardysociety.org
website www.hardysociety.org
Membership £18 p.a., £22.50 overseas

Aims to promote and celebrate the work of Thomas Hardy (1840–1928). Publishes *The Thomas Hardy Journal* (3 p.a.). Biennial conference in Dorchester, 2004. Founded 1967.

Harleian Society

College of Arms, Queen Victoria Street, London EC4V 4BT
tel 020-7236 7728 *fax* 020-7248 6448
website http://harleian.co.uk
Chairman T. Woodcock LVO, FSA, Norroy & Ulster King of Arms, *Hon. Secretary* T.H.S. Duke, Chester Herald of Arms

Instituted for transcribing, printing and publishing the heraldic visitations of Counties, Parish Registers and any manuscripts relating to genealogy, family history and heraldry. Founded 1869.

Hesketh Hubbard Art Society

17 Carlton House Terrace, London SW1Y 5BD
tel 020-7930 6844 *fax* 020-7839 7830
email info@mallgalleries.com
website www.mallgalleries.org.uk
President Simon Whittle

Weekly life drawing classes open to all.

The Hilliard Society of Miniaturists

The Executive Officer Priory Lodge, 7 Priory Road, Wells, Somerset BA5 1SR

tel (01749) 674472
website www.art-in-miniature.org
President Rosalind Pierson RMS, MAA, MASF, MPSG
Membership From £25 p.a.

Aims to increase knowledge and promote the art of miniature painting. Annual exhibition held in November at Wells; produces a newsletter. Member of the World Federation of Miniaturists. Founded 1982.

The James Hilton Society

Hon. Secretary Dr J.R. Hammond, 49 Beckingthorpe Drive, Bottesford, Nottingham NG13 0DN
website www.jameshiltonsociety.co.uk
Membership £10 p.a. (£7 concessions)

Aims to promote interest in the life and work of novelist and scriptwriter James Hilton (1900–54). Publishes quarterly newsletter and an annual scholarly journal, and organises conferences. Founded 2000.

Historical Novel Society

Secretary Richard Lee, Marine Cottage, The Strand, Starcross, Devon EX6 8NY
tel (01626) 891962
email histnovel@aol.com
website www.historicalnovelsociety.com
Membership £19.50 p.a.

Promotes the historical novel via short story competitions, conferences, a society magazine *Solander* (2 p.a.) and reviews (*Historical Novels Review*, quarterly). Membership is open to all and includes eminent novelists. Founded 1997.

The Sherlock Holmes Society of London

General enquiries Heather Owen, 64 Graham Road, London SW19 3SS
tel 020-8540 7657
email heatherowen@tiscali.co.uk
Membership R.J. Ellis, 13 Crofton Avenue, Orpington, Kent BR6 8DU
tel/fax (01689) 811314
email shsl221b@aol.com
website www.sherlock-holmes.org.uk
President A.D. Howlett MA, LLB, *Chairman* Guy Marriott
Membership £14 p.a. UK/Europe, £18 Far East, US$30.50 USA

Aims to bring together those who have a common interest as readers and students of the literature of Sherlock Holmes, and to encourage the pursuit of knowledge of the public and private lives of Sherlock Holmes and Dr Watson. Membership includes *The Sherlock Holmes Journal* (2 p.a.). Founded 1951.

Hopkins Society

Secretary Oughtrington Rectory, Lymm, Cheshire WA13 9JB

website www.hopkinsoc.freeserve.co.uk
Membership £8 p.a., £10 outside Europe

Aims to promote and celebrate the work of the poet Gerard Manley Hopkins (1844–89), to inform members about the latest publications about Hopkins and to support educational projects concerning his work. Annual lecture held in North Wales in the spring; publishes a newsletter (2 p.a.) Founded 1990.

Horror Writers Association (HWA)

244 5th Avenue, Suite 2767, New York, NY 10001
email hwa@horror.org
UK Jo Fletcher, 24 Pearl Road, London E17 4QZ
website www.horror.org
Membership $65 p.a. North America, $75/£48 elsewhere

A worldwide organisation of writers and publishing professionals dedicated to promoting the interests of writers of horror and dark fantasy. There are 3 levels of membership: for new writers, established writers and non-writing horror professionals. Founded 1987.

Housman Society

80 New Road, Bromsgrove, Worcs. B60 2LA
tel (01527) 874136
email info@housman-society.co.uk
website www.housman-society.co.uk
Chairman Jim Page
Membership £10 p.a.

Aims to foster interest in and promote knowledge of A.E. Housman (1859–1936) and his family. Sponsors a lecture at the Guardian Hay Festival. Publishes an annual journal and bi-annual newsletter. Founded 1973.

Incorporated Society of Musicians

10 Stratford Place, London W1C 1AA
tel 020-7629 4413 *fax* 020-7408 1538
email membership@ism.org
website www.ism.org
President Colin Bradbury, *Chief Executive* Neil Hoyle
Membership £125 p.a.

Professional body for musicians. Aims to promote the art of music; protect the interests and raise the standards of the musical profession; provide services, support and advice for its members. Publishes *Music Journal* (12 p.a.), a yearbook and 3 Registers of Specialists annually.

Independent Publishers Guild

PO Box 93, Royston, Herts. SG8 5GH
tel (01763) 247014 *fax* (01763) 246293
website www.ipg.uk.com
Membership £150 + VAT p.a. Open to new and established publishers and book packagers; supplier membership is available to specialists in fields allied to publishing (but not printers and binders)

Provides an information and contact network for independent publishers. The IPG also voices the concerns of member companies with the book trade. Founded 1962.

Independent Theatre Council (ITC)

12 The Leather Market, Weston Street, London SE1 3ER
tel 020-7403 1727 *fax* 020-7403 1745
email admin@itc-arts.org
website www.itc-arts.org
Chief Executive Charlotte Jones
Membership Prices vary according to type of membership

ITC is the UK management association for the performing arts. It empowers and supports its diverse membership by providing high-quality management, legal and financial advice; developing tailored arts management training; creating excellent networking opportunities; and representing the sector with a powerful, articulate voice. ITC is committed to working with a range of partners to promote, develop and support its members. Founded 1974.

Institute of Designers in Ireland

Details Hon. Secretary, 8 Merrion Square, Dublin 2, Republic of Ireland
tel (01) 4893650 *fax* (01) 4885801
Membership €171 p.a. full, €57 associate

Irish design profession's representative body, covering every field of design. Founded 1972.

Institute of Linguists

Saxon House, 48 Southwark Street, London SE1 1UN
tel 020-7940 3100 *fax* 020-7940 3101
email info@iol.org.uk
website www.iol.org.uk

Professional association for translators, interpreters and language tutors with 'Find-a-Linguist' website service. International language examinations run by its Educational Trust. One subsidiary NRPSI Ltd manages the National Register of Public Service Interpreters. Another, Institute of Linguists Language Services Ltd, offers customised assessments and language services.

The Institute of Translation & Interpreting (ITI)

Contact The Secretary, Fortuna House, South Fifth Street, Milton Keynes MK9 2EU
tel (01908) 325250 *fax* (01908) 325259
email info@iti.org.uk
website www.iti.org.uk

A professional association of translators and interpreters which aims to promote the highest standards in translating and interpreting. It has a strong corporate membership and runs professional development courses and conferences, sometimes in conjunction with its language, regional and subject networks. Membership is open to those with a genuine and proven involvement in translation and interpreting of all kinds, but particularly technical and commercial translation. As a full and active member of the International Federation of Translators, it maintains good contacts with translators and interpreters worldwide. ITI's directory of members (online) and its bi-monthly bulletin are available from the Secretariat.

International Publishers Association

3 avenue de Miremont, CH–1206 Geneva, Switzerland
tel (022) 346-30-18 *fax* (022) 347-57-17
email secretariat@ipa-uie.org
President Ana Maria Cabanellas, *Secretary-General* Mr Jens Bammel

Founded 1896.

International Society of Typographic Designers

PO Box 725, Taunton, Somerset TA2 8WE
tel 020-7436 0984 *fax* 020-7637 7352
email mail@istd.org.uk
Chair Jonathan Doney FISTD, *President* Freda Sack

Advises and acts on matters of professional and educational practice, provides a better understanding of the typographic craft and the rapidly changing technology in the graphic industries by lectures, discussions and through the journal *Typographic*. Students of typography and graphic design are encouraged to gain membership of the Society by entering the annual student assessment project. Founded 1928.

International Theatre Exchange

c/o Drama Association of Wales, The Old Library, Singleton Road, Splott, Cardiff CF24 2ET
tel 029-2045 2200 *fax* 029-2045 2277
email aled.daw@virgin.net
website www.aitaiata.org
Secretariat Aled Rhys-Jones

Aims to encourage, foster and promote exchanges of community and non-professional theatre; student, educational, adult, theatre activities at international level. To organise international seminars, workshops, courses and conferences, and to collect and collate information of all types for national and international dissemination. UK centre of IATA.

International Visual Communication Association (IVCA)

19 Pepper Street, Glengall Bridge, London E14 9RP
tel 020-7512 0571 *fax* 020-7512 0591
email info@ivca.org
website www.ivca.org
Membership Secretary Nick Gardiner
Membership From £175 p.a.

For those who work in business communication. Aims to promote the industry and provide a

collective voice; provides a range of services, publications and events to help existing and potential users to make the most of what video, film, multimedia and live events can offer their business. Founded 1987.

The Irish Book Publishers' Association – see CLÉ – Irish Book Publishers' Association

The Irish Copyright Licensing Agency

25 Denzille Lane, Dublin 2, Republic of Ireland
tel (01) 6624211 *fax* (01) 6624213
email info@icla.ie
website www.icla.ie
Executive Director Samantha Holman

Licences schools and other users of copyright material to photocopy extracts of such material, and distributes the monies collected to the authors and publishers whose works have been copied. Founded 1992.

Irish Playwrights and Screenwriters Guild

(formerly the Society of Irish Playwrights)
Art House, Curved Street, Temple Bar, Dublin 2, Republic of Ireland
tel (01) 670 9970
email david.kavanagh@script.ie
website www.script.ie
Chairperson Audrey O'Reilly, *Executive Officer* David Kavanagh

Represents writers' interests in theatre, radio and screenwriting. Founded 1969.

Irish Translators' Association

Irish Writers' Centre, 19 Parnell Square, Dublin 1, Republic of Ireland
tel (01) 8721302 *fax* (01) 8726282
website www.translatorsassociation.ie
Hon. Secretary Annette Schiller
Membership p.a. €55 professional, €30 ordinary, €15 student, €80 corporate

Promotes translation in Ireland, the translation of Irish authors abroad and the practical training of translators, and promotes the interests of translators. Catalogues the works of translators in areas of Irish interest; secures the awarding of prizes and bursaries for translators; and maintains a detailed register of translators. Founded 1986.

Irish Writers' Centre

19 Parnell Square, Dublin 1, Republic of Ireland
tel (01) 8721302 *fax* (01) 8726282
email info@writerscentre.ie
website www.writerscentre.ie
Director Cathal McCabe

National organisation for the promotion of writers and writing in Ireland. It runs an extensive programme of events at its headquarters; it operates the Writer in Community Scheme which funds events throughout Ireland; it runs an education programme which offers courses and workshops in writing; it operates an International Writers' Exchange Programme. See website for further details. Founded 1991.

Irish Writers' Union/Comhar na Scríbhneoirí

Irish Writers' Centre, 19 Parnell Square, Dublin 1, Republic of Ireland
tel (01) 8721302 *fax* (01) 8726282
email info@writerscentre.ie
website www.ireland-writers.com
Chairman Conor Kostick, *Secretary* Bríd Quinn

The Union aims to advance the cause of writing as a profession, to achieve better remuneration and more favourable conditions for writers and to provide a means for the expression of the collective opinion of writers on matters affecting their profession. Founded 1986.

The Richard Jefferies Society

Hon. Secretary Jean Saunders, Pear Tree Cottage, Langcot, Faringdon, Oxon SN7 7SS
tel (01793) 783040
email r.jefferies_society@tiscali.co.uk
website http://richardjefferiessociety.blogspot.com
Membership £7 p.a. Worldwide membership

Promotes interest in the life, works and associations of the naturalist and novelist, Richard Jefferies (1848–87); helps to preserve buildings and memorials, and cooperates in the development of a Museum in his birthplace. Arranges regular meetings in Swindon, and occasionally elsewhere; organises outings and displays; publishes a Journal and a Newsletter in the spring and an Annual Report in September. Founded 1950.

The Johnson Society

Johnson Birthplace Museum, Breadmarket Street, Lichfield, Staffs. WS13 6LG
tel (01543) 264972
email jdhsec@lichfieldrambler.co.uk
website www.lichfieldrambler.co.uk
Hon. General Secretary Norma Hooper

Aims to encourage the study of the life and works of Dr Samuel Johnson (1709–84); to preserve the memorials, associations, books, manuscripts and letters of Dr Johnson and his contemporaries; and to work with the local council in the preservation of his birthplace.

Johnson Society of London

Secretary Mrs Zandra O'Donnell MA, 255 Baring Road, London SE12 0BQ
tel 020-8851 0173
President Lord Harmsworth

Aims to study the life and works of Dr Johnson (1709–84), and to perpetuate his memory in the city of his adoption. Founded 1928.

Journalists' Charity

Dickens House, 35 Wathen Road, Dorking, Surrey RH4 1JY
tel (01306) 887511 *fax* (01306) 888212
email enquiries@npf.org.uk
Director David Ilott

For the relief of hardship amongst journalists, their widows and dependants. Financial assistance and retirement housing are provided.

The Sheila Kaye-Smith Society

Secretary Christine Hayward, 22 The Cloisters, St John's Road, St Leonards-on-Sea, East Sussex TN37 6JT
tel (01424) 422139
Membership £6 p.a. single, £9 joint

Aims to stimulate and widen interest in the work of the Sussex writer and novelist, Sheila Kaye-Smith (1887–1956). Produces *The Gleam* (annual) and occasional papers, and organises talks. Founded 1987.

Keats-Shelley Memorial Association

Hon. Secretary David Leigh-Hunt, 1 Satchwell Walk, Leamington Spa, Warks. CV32 4QE
tel (01926) 427400 *fax* (01926) 335133
Chairman Hon. Mrs H. Cullen
Membership £12 p.a. minimum

Owns and supports house in Rome where John Keats (1795–1821) died as a museum open to the public, and celebrates the poets Keats, Shelley (1792–1822) and Leigh Hunt (1784–1859). Regular meetings; poetry competitions; annual *Review*, 2 literary awards, and progress reports. Founded 1903.

Kent and Sussex Poetry Society

Contact John Arnold, 39 Rockington Way, Crowborough, East Sussex TN6 2NJ
tel (01892) 662781
email keith@kentandsussexpoetrysociety.org
website www.kentandsussexpoetrysociety.org
Secretary Keith Francis
President Laurence Lerner, *Chairman* Clive Eastwood
Membership £10 p.a. full, £5 country members/ concessions

Based in Tunbridge Wells, the Society was formed to create a greater interest in poetry. Well-known poets address the Society, a Folio of members' work is produced and a full programme of recitals, discussions, competitions (see page 572) and readings is provided. Founded 1946.

The Kipling Society

Hon. Secretary Jane Keskar, 6 Clifton Road, London W9 1SS
tel 020-7286 0194

email jane@keskar.fsworld.co.uk
website www.kipling.org.uk
Membership £22 p.a. (£20 p.a. for standing orders)

Aims to honour and extend the influence of Rudyard Kipling (1865–1936), to assist in the study of his writings, to hold discussion meetings, to publish a quarterly journal, and to maintain a Kipling Library in London and a Kipling Room in The Grange, Rottingdean, near Brighton.

The Charles Lamb Society

BM Elia, London WC1N 3XX
website www.users.ox.ac.uk/~scat1492/clsoc.htm
Chairman Nicholas Powell, *Membership Secretary* Cecilia Powell
Membership Personal: £12/$28 p.a. (single), £18 (double). Corporate: £18/$42 p.a.

Publishes the academic journal *The Charles Lamb Bulletin* (quarterly). The Society's extensive library of books and MSS by and about Charles Lamb (1775–1834) is housed at the Guildhall Library, Aldermanbury, London EC2P 2EJ. Founded 1935.

The Lancashire Authors' Association

General Secretary Eric Holt, 5 Quakerfields, Westhoughton, Bolton BL5 2BJ
tel (01942) 791390
Membership £10 p.a.

'For writers and lovers of Lancashire literature and history.' Publishes *The Record* (quarterly). Founded 1909.

The D.H. Lawrence Society

Secretary Ron Faulks, 24 Briarwood Avenue, Nottingham NG3 6JQ
tel 0115-950 3008
Membership £14 UK, £16 Europe, £19 rest of world, UK retired persons and students £12

Aims to bring together people interested in D.H. Lawrence (1885–1930), to encourage study of his work, and to provide information and guides for people visiting Eastwood. Founded 1974.

The T.E. Lawrence Society

PO Box 728, Oxford OX2 6YP
website www.telsociety.org
Membership £18 p.a., £23 overseas

Promotes the memory of T.E. Lawrence (1888–1935) and furthers knowledge by research into his life; publishes *Journal* (bi-annual) and *Newsletter* (quarterly). Founded 1985.

League of Canadian Poets

920 Yonge Street, Suite 608, Toronto, Ontario M4W 3C7, Canada
tel 416-504-1657 *fax* 416-504 0096
email info@poets.ca
website www.poets.ca
Executive Director Joann Poblocka

Membership $175 p.a.

Aims to promote the interests of poets and to advance Canadian poetry in Canada and abroad. Administers 3 annual awards; operates the 'Poetry Spoken Here' webstore; runs National Poetry Month; publishes a newsletter and *Poetry Markets for Canadians, Who's Who in The League of Canadian Poets, Poets in the Classroom* (teaching guide). Promotes and sells members' poetry books. Founded 1966.

Little Theatre Guild of Great Britain

National Secretary, Barbara Watson, 181 Brampton Road, Carlisle CA3 9AX
tel (01228) 522649
website www.littletheatreguild.org

Aims to promote closer cooperation amongst the little theatres constituting its membership; to act as coordinating and representative body on behalf of the little theatres; to maintain and advance the highest standards in the art of theatre; and to assist in encouraging the establishment of other little theatres. Its yearbook is available to non-members for £5.

The Marlowe Society

Newsletter Editor & Webmaster Roger Hards, Venusmead, 36 Venus Street, Congresbury, Bristol BS49 5EZ
tel (01934) 834780
email rogerhards@venusmead.go-plus.net
website www.marlowe-society.org
Membership £15 p.a., £10 concessions, £20 overseas

Registered charity that aims to extend appreciation and widen recognition of Christopher Marlowe (1564–93) as the foremost poet and dramatist preceding Shakespeare, whose development he influenced. Holds meetings and cultural visits, and issues a bi-annual magazine and an occasional research journal. Founded 1955.

The John Masefield Society

Chairman Peter J.R. Carter, The Frith, Ledbury, Herefordshire HR8 1LW
tel (01531) 633800
email carter-p@btconnect.com
website www.sas.ac.uk/ies/Full%20Text%20Archive/Masefield/Society/jmsws.htm
Membership £5 p.a., £10 overseas, £8 family/institution

Aims to stimulate interest in, and public awareness and enjoyment of, the life and works of the poet John Masefield (1878–1967). Holds an annual lecture and other, less formal, readings and gatherings; publishes an annual journal and frequent newsletters. Founded 1992.

Master Photographers Association

Jubilee House, 1 Chancery Lane, Darlington, Co. Durham DL1 5QP

tel (01325) 356555 *fax* (01325) 357813
email info@mpauk.com
website www.thempa.com
Membership £140 p.a.

Exists to promote and protect professional photographers. Members qualify for awards of Licentiate, Associate and Fellowship.

Mechanical-Copyright Protection Society Ltd (MCPS)

Copyright House, 29–33 Berners Street, London W1T 3AB
tel 020-7580 5544 *fax* 020-7306 4455
website www.mcps.co.uk
Chief Executive Adam Singer

The Media Society

Secretary Peter Dannheisser, 56 Roseneath Road, London SW11 6AQ
tel 020-7223 5631 *fax* 020-7223 5631
Membership £35 p.a.

Exists to promote and encourage collective and independent research into the standards, performance, organisation and economics of the media and hold regular discussions, debates, etc on subjects of topical or special interest and concern to print and broadcast journalists and others working in or with the media. Founded 1973.

Mediawatch-UK

(formerly National Viewers' and Listeners' Association)
Director John C. Beyer, 3 Willow House, Kennington Road, Ashford, Kent TN24 0NR
tel (01233) 633936 *fax* (01233) 633836
email info@mediawatchuk.org
website www.mediawatchuk.org
Membership £15 p.a.

Aims to encourage viewers and listeners to react effectively to programme content; to initiate and stimulate public discussion and parliamentary debate concerning the effects of broadcasting, and other mass media, on the individual, the family and society; to secure – then uphold – effective legislation to control obscenity and pornography in the media. Founded 1965.

Medical Writers Group – see The Society of Authors, page 513

William Morris Society

Kelmscott House, 26 Upper Mall, London W6 9TA
tel 020-8741 3735 *fax* 020-8748 5207
email william.morris@care4free.net
website www.morrissociety.org
Secretary Peter Faulkner

Aims to spread knowledge of the life, work and ideas of William Morris (1834–96); publishes *Newsletter* (quarterly) and *Journal* (2 p.a.). Library and

collections open to the public Thurs and Sat, 2–5pm. Founded 1955.

Music Publishers Association Ltd

6th Floor, British Music House, 26 Berners Street, London W1T 3LR
tel 020-7580 0126 *fax* 020-7637 3929
email info@mpaonline.org.uk
Chief Executive Sarah Faulder
Membership Details on request

Trade organisation representing over 200 UK music publisher members: promotes and safeguards its members' interests in copyright, trade and related matters. Sub-committees and groups deal with particular interests. Founded 1881.

National Acrylic Painters' Association (NAPA)

134 Rake Lane, Wallasey, Wirral, Merseyside CH45 1JW
tel 0151-639 2980 *fax* 0151-639 2980
Membership The Executive Council, c/o Alan Edwards, 6 Berwyn Boulevard, Bebington, Wirral CH63 5LR
tel 0151-645 8433
email alan.edwards420@ntlworld.com
website www.art-arena.com/napa, www.napauk.org, www.isap-usa.com
President Alwyn Crawshaw, *Director/Founder* Kenneth J. Hodgson

Promotes interest in, and encourages excellence and innovation in, the work of painters in acrylic. Holds an annual exhibition and regional shows: awards are made. Worldwide membership. Publishes a newsletter known as the *International NAPA Newspages*. Founded 1985; American Division established 1995, now known as International Society of Acrylic Painters (ISAP).

National Association of Press Agencies (NAPA)

41 Lansdowne Crescent, Leamington Spa, Warks. CV32 4PR
tel (0870) 609 1935, (01926) 420 566
fax (01926) 424760
website www.napa.org.uk
Directors Denis Cassidy, Chris Johnson, Barrie Tracey
Membership £250 p.a.

A network of independent, established and experienced press agencies serving newspapers, magazines, TV and radio networks. Founded 1983.

National Association of Writers' Groups

Headquarters The Arts Centre, Biddick Lane, Washington, Tyne and Wear NE38 2AB
tel (01262) 609228
email nawg@tesco.net

Secretary Mike Wilson, 40 Burstall Hill, Bridlington, East Yorkshire YO16 7GA
website www.nawg.co.uk
Membership £30 p.a. plus £5 registration per group; £12 Associate individuals

Aims 'to advance the education of the general public throughout the UK, including the Channel Islands, by promoting the study and art of writing in all its aspects.' Publishes *Link* bi-monthly magazine. Annual Festival of Writing held in Durham in September. Annual Creative Writing Competition. Founded 1995.

National Campaign for the Arts (NCA)

1 Kingly Street, London W1B 5PA
tel 020-7287 3777 *fax* 020-7287 4777
email nca@artscampaign.org.uk
website www.artscampaign.org.uk
Deputy Director Jane Robinson

The UK's only independent lobbying organisation representing all the arts. It provides a voice for the arts world in all its diversity. It seeks to safeguard, promote and develop the arts and win public and political recognition for the importance of the arts as a key element in our national culture.

National Council for the Training of Journalists (NCTJ)

The New Granary, Station Road, Newport, Essex CB11 3PL
tel (01799) 544014 *fax* (01799) 544015
email info@nctj.com
website www.nctj.com

A registered charity which aims to advance the education and training of trainee journalists, including press photographers. Full-time courses run at 34 colleges/universities in the UK. Distance learning courses also available in newspaper and magazine journalism and sub-editing. Founded 1952.

National Literacy Trust

Swire House, 59 Buckingham Gate, London SW1E 6AJ
tel 020-7828 2435 *fax* 020-7931 9986
email contact@literacytrust.org.uk
website www.literacytrust.org.uk, www.rif.org.uk, www.readon.org.uk
Director Neil McClelland, *PA* Jacky Taylor

Independent registered charity dedicated to building a literate nation in which everyone enjoys the skills, self-esteem and pleasures that literacy can bring. The only organisation concerned with raising literacy standards for all age groups throughout the UK. Maintains an extensive website with literacy news, summaries of key issues, research and examples of practice nationwide; organises an annual conference, courses and training events, and runs a range of initiatives to turn promising ideas into effective action. Initiatives include the National Reading

Campaign, funded by the government; Reading is Fundamental, UK, which provides free books to children; Reading The Game, involving the professional football community; the Talk To Your Baby campaign; and the Literacy and Social Inclusion Project, a partnership with the Basic Skills Agency. Founded 1993.

National Society for Education in Art and Design

The Gatehouse, Corsham Court, Corsham, Wilts. SN13 0BZ
tel (01249) 714825 *fax* (01249) 716138
website www.nsead.org
General Secretary Dr John Steers NDD, ATC, PhD

The leading national authority concerned with art, craft and design across all phases of education in the UK. Offers the benefits of membership of a professional association, a learned society and a trade union. Has representatives on National and Regional Committees concerned with Art and Design Education. Publishes *Journal of Art and Design Education* (3 p.a.; Blackwells) and *Start* magazine for primary schools. Founded 1888.

National Society of Painters, Sculptors and Printmakers

Hon. Secretary Gwen Spencer, 122 Copse Hill, London SW20 0NL
tel 020-8946 7878
website www.nationalsociety.org

An annual exhibition at the Menier Gallery, Southwark Street, London SE1. Not an open exhibition but artists are welcome to apply for membership. Newsletter (2 p.a.) for members. Founded 1930.

National Union of Journalists

Head Office Headland House, 308–312 Gray's Inn Road, London WC1X 8DP
tel 020-7278 7916 *fax* 020-7837 8143
email acorn.house@nuj.org.uk

Trade union for working journalists with 35,000 members and 140 branches throughout the UK and the Republic of Ireland, and in Paris, Brussels, and the Netherlands. It covers the newspaper press, news agencies and broadcasting, the major part of periodical and book publishing, and a number of public relations departments and consultancies, information services and Prestel-Viewdata services. Administers disputes, unemployment, benevolent and provident benefits. Official publications: *The Journalist* (bi-monthly), *Freelance Directory*, *Freelance Fees Guide* and policy pamphlets.

National Viewers' and Listeners' Association – see Mediawatch-UK

NCTJ – see National Council for the Training of Journalists (NCTJ)

The Edith Nesbit Society

21 Churchfields, West Malling, Kent ME19 6RJ
email mccarthy804@aol.com
website www.the-railway-children.co.uk
Membership £7 p.a., £14 organisations/overseas

Aims to promote an interest in the life and works of
Edith Nesbit (1858–1924) by means of talks, a regular
newsletter and and other publications, and visits to
relevant places. Founded 1996.

New English Art Club

17 Carlton House Terrace, London SW1Y 5BD
tel 020-7930 6844 *fax* 020-7839 7830
email info@mallgalleries.com
website www.mallgalleries.org.uk
President Tom Coates

For all those interested in the art of painting, and the
promotion of fine arts. Open Annual Exhibition at
the Mall Galleries, The Mall, London SW1, open to
all working in painting, drawing, pastels and prints.

New Playwrights Trust – see Writernet

New Producers Alliance

The NPA Film Centre, Unit 1.07, The Tea Building,
56 Shoreditch High Street, London E1 6JJ
tel 020-7613 0440 *fax* 020-7729 1852
email queries@npa.org.uk
website www.npa.org.uk
Membership £75 p.a.

A national membership organisation and registered
charity dedicated to providing essential training and
networking opportunities for film-makers. Led by
industry professionals, the NPA assists independent
film-makers in developing their skills, contacts and
creativity in line with working industry practices.
Founded 1993.

New Science Fiction Alliance (NSFA)

Chris Reed, BBR, PO Box 625, Sheffield S1 3GY
website www.bbr-online.com/catalogue
Publicity Officer Chris Reed

Committed to supporting the work of new writers
and artists by promoting independent and small press
publications worldwide. NSFA was founded by a
group of independent publishers to give writers the
opportunity to explore the small press and find the
right market for their material. It offers a mail order
service for magazines. Founded 1989.

New Writing North

2 School Lane, Whickham, Newcastle upon Tyne
NE16 4SL
tel 0191-488 8580 *fax* 0191-488 8576
email mail@newwritingnorth.com
website www.newwritingnorth.com
Director Claire Malcolm

The literature development agency for the North
East. Offers advice and support to writers of poetry,
prose and plays. See website. Founded 1996.

New Writing South

9 Jew Street, Brighton, East Sussex BN1 1UT
tel (01273) 735353
email admin@pierplaywrights.co.uk
website www.pierplaywrights.co.uk
Director Chris Taylor
Membership £25/£15 p.a.

Aims to support and encourage writers and their
writing for performance in all its forms. Activities
include a script-reading service (members only),
workshops from visiting professionals, and a monthly
newsletter. Pier Playwrights is a registered charity
supported by the Arts Council and is open to all
dramatic writers in South and South East England.
Founded 1990.

New Zealand Writers Guild

PO Box 47886, Ponsonby, Auckland, New Zealand
tel (09) 360-1408 *fax* (09) 360-1409
email info@nzwritersguild.org.nz
website www.nzwritersguild.org.nz
Membership $175–$400 p.a. full, $125 associate

Aims to represent the interests of New Zealand
writers (TV, film, radio and theatre); to establish and
improve minimum conditions of work and rates of
compensation for writers; to provide professional
services for members. Founded 1975.

The Newspaper Publishers Association Ltd

34 Southwark Bridge Road, London SE1 9EU
tel 020-7207 2200 *fax* 020-7928 2067

Newspaper Society

Bloomsbury House, 74–77 Great Russell Street,
London WC1B 3DA
tel 020-7636 7014 *fax* 020-7631 5119
email ns@newspapersoc.org.uk
website www.newspapersoc.org.uk
Director David Newell

Outdoor Writers' Guild

Secretary Hazelle Jackson, PO Box 118, Twickenham
TW1 2XB
tel 020-8538 9468 *fax* 020-8538 9468
email info@owg.org.uk
website www.owg.org.uk
Membership £65 p.a.

Association of the leading practitioners in outdoor
media; represents members' interests to
representative bodies in the outdoor industry;
circulates members with news of media
opportunities; provides a forum for members to meet
colleagues and others in the outdoor industry.
Presents annual literary and photographic awards.
Members include writers, journalists, broadcasters,
illustrators, photographers, editors and publishers.
Founded 1980.

Wilfred Owen Association

17 Belmont, Shrewsbury SY1 1TE
website www.1914-18.co.uk/owen

Membership £6 p.a. (£10 overseas), £15 groups/institutions, £4 concessions

Aims to commemorate the life and work of Wilfred Owen (1893–1918), and to encourage and enhance appreciation of his work through visits, public events, a newsletter and journal. Founded 1989.

Oxford Bibliographical Society

Bodleian Library, Broad Street, Oxford OX1 3BG
email treasurer@oxbibsoc.org.uk
Secretary Dr Julia Walworth, Merton College, Oxford
website www.users.bathspa.ac.uk/oxbibsoc/
Membership £20 p.a.

Exists to encourage bibliographical research. Founded 1922.

PACT (Producers Alliance for Cinema and Television)

The Eye, 2nd Floor, 1 Proctor Street, London WC1V 6DW
tel 020-7067 4367 *fax* 020-7067 4377
email enquiries@pact.co.uk
Pact Scotland 249 West George Street, Glasgow G2 4QE
tel 0141-222 4880 *fax* 0141-222 4881
website www.pact.co.uk
Information Manager David Alan Mills, *Head of Nations & Regions* Margaret Scott

The main trade association for feature film and independent TV production companies. Represents the interests of over 1000 production companies throughout the UK: promotes and protects the commercial interests of its members; lobbies government and regulators on their behalf; negotiates terms of trade with broadcasters; provides a range of membership services including advice on business affairs, industrial relations and legal advice; operates a copyright registration service for members' proposals and treatments for films and TV programmes. Its representative office in Glasgow serves the interests of its regional members.

The Pastel Society

17 Carlton House Terrace, London SW1Y 5BD
tel 020-7930 6844 *fax* 020-7839 7830
email info@mallgalleries.com
website www.mallgalleries.org.uk
President Moira Huntly

Pastel and drawings in pencil or chalk. Annual Exhibition open to all artists working in dry media held at the Mall Galleries, The Mall, London SW1. Members elected from approved candidates' list. Founded 1899.

The Mervyn Peake Society

Treasurer Frank Surry, 2 Mount Park Road, London W5 2RP
email sebastianpeake@aol.com
website www.mervynpeake.org

Hon. President Sebastian Peake
Membership £12 p.a. UK and Europe, £5 students, £16 all other countries

Devoted to recording the life and works of Mervyn Peake (1911–68); publishes a journal and newsletter. Founded 1975.

PEN, International

Brownlow House, 50–51 High Holborn, London EC1V 6EK
tel 020-7405 0338 *fax* 020-7405 0339
email intpen@dircon.co.uk
website www.internationalpen.org.uk
Executive Director Caroline McCormick
Membership Apply to Centres

A world association of writers. PEN was founded in 1921 by C.A. Dawson Scott under the presidency of John Galsworthy, to promote friendship and understanding between writers and to defend freedom of expression within and between all nations. The initials PEN stand for Poets, Playwrights, Editors, Essayists, Novelists – but membership is open to all writers of standing (including translators), whether men or women, without distinction of creed or race, who subscribe to these fundamental principles. PEN takes no part in state or party politics. The International PEN Writers in Prison Committee works on behalf of writers imprisoned for exercising their right to freedom of expression, a right implicit in the PEN Charter to which all members subscribe. The International PEN Translations and Linguistic Rights Committee strives to promote the translations of works by writers in the lesser-known languages and to defend those languages. The Writers for Peace Committee exists to find ways in which writers can work for peaceful co-existence in the world. The Women Writers' Committee works to promote women's writing and publishing in developing countries. The Writers in Exile Network helps exiled writers. International Congresses are held annually.

Membership of any one Centre implies membership of all Centres; at present 144 autonomous Centres exist throughout the world. Associate membership is available for writers not yet eligible for full membership and for persons connected with literature. The English Centre has a programme of literary lectures, discussion, dinners and parties.

English PEN Centre

Administrative Director Susanna Nicklin, 6–8 Amwell Street, London EC1R 1UQ
tel 020-7713 0023 *fax* 020-7873 7838
email enquiries@englishpen.org
website www.englishpen.org
President Alastair Niven OBE

Scottish PEN Centre

President Tessa Ransford OBE, The Writers' Museum, Lady Stair's House, Lady Stair's Close, Lawnmarket, Edinburgh EH1 2PE

email office@scottishpen.org
website www.scottishpen.org

Irish PEN Centre
email irishpen@ireland.com
President Brian Friel
Secretary Christine Dwyer Hickey, Irish Pen Cente,
Dunoon, Old Lucan Road, Palmerstown, Dublin 20,
Republic of Ireland
tel (353) 1 623 9133

Performing Right Society Ltd (PRS)
Copyright House, 29–33 Berners Street, London
W1T 3AB
tel 020-7580 5544 *fax* 020-7306 4455
website www.prs.co.uk
Chief Executive Adam Singer

Periodical Publishers Association
Queens House, 28 Kingsway, London WC2B 6JR
tel 020-7404 4166 *fax* 020-7404 4167
email info1@ppa.co.uk
website www.ppa.co.uk
Chief Executive Ian Locks

The Personal Managers' Association Ltd
Liaison Secretary Angela Adler, 1 Summer Road, East
Molesey, Surrey KT8 9LX
tel 020-8398 9796 *fax* 020-8398 9796
email aadler@thepma.com

Association of theatrical agents in the theatre, film
and entertainment world generally.

The Picture Research Association
c/o 1 Willow Court, off Willow Street, London
EC2A 4QB
tel 020-7739 8544 *fax* 020-7782 0011
email chair@picture-research.org.uk
website www.picture-research.org.uk

Professional organisation of picture researchers and
picture editors. Its aims are:
• to promote the recognition of picture research,
management, editing, picture buying and supplying
as a profession requiring particular skills and
knowledge;
• to bring together all those involved in the picture
profession and provide a forum for information
exchange and interaction;
• to encourage publishers, TV and video production
organisations, internet companies, and any other
users of images to use the PRA freelance register and
engage a member of PRA to obtain them, thus
ensuring that professional standards are maintained;
• to advise those specifically wishing to embark on a
profession in the research and supply of pictures for
all types of visual media information, providing
guidelines and standards in so doing.

Player–Playwrights
Secretary Peter Thompson, 9 Hillfield Park, London
N10 3QT

tel 020-8883 0371
email p-p@dial.pipex.com
website www.playerplaywrights.co.uk
Membership £10 in first year and £6 thereafter (plus
£2 per attendance)

Meets on Monday evenings upstairs at the Horse and
Groom, 128 Great Portland Street, London W1. The
society reads, performs and discusses plays and scripts
submitted by members, with a view to assisting the
writers in improving and marketing their work.
Newcomers and new acting members are always
welcome. Founded 1948.

The Poetry Book Society – see page 321

The Poetry Library – see page 323

The Poetry Society – see page 322

John Polidori – Vampyre Lacunae
PO Box 6078, Nottingham NG16 4HX
Founder/President Franklin Charles Bishop

Promotes and encourages the appreciation of the life
and works of Anglo-Italian John William Polidori MD
(1795–1821) – novelist, poet, tragedian, philosopher,
diarist, essayist, reviewer, traveller and one of the
youngest ever students to obtain a medical degree at
the age of 19. He introduced into English literature
the icon of the vampire portrayed as an aristocratic,
handsome seducer both cynical and amoral with his
seminal work *The Vampyre – A Tale* (1819).

The Beatrix Potter Society
Membership Secretary c/o The Lodge, Salisbury
Avenue, Harpenden, Herts. AL5 2PS
tel (01582) 769755
email beatrixpottersociety@tiscali.co.uk
website www.beatrixpottersociety.org.uk
Membership £20 p.a. UK (£25 overseas), £25/£30
commercial/institutional

Promotes the study and appreciation of the life and
works of Beatrix Potter (1866–1943) as author, artist,
diarist, farmer and conservationist. Regular lecture
meetings, conferences and events in the UK and USA.
Quarterly newsletter. Small publishing programme.
Founded 1980.

The Powys Society
Hon. Secretary Peter Lazare, 25 Mansfield Road,
Taunton, Somerset TA1 3NJ
tel (01823) 278177
email peter_lazare@hotmail.com
website www.powys-society.org

Aims to promote the greater public recognition and
enjoyment of the writings, thought and contribution
to the arts of the Powys family, particularly John
Cowper (1872–1963), Theodore (1875–1953) and
Llewelyn (1884–1939) Powys, and the many other
family members and their close friends. Publishes an

annual scholarly journal (*The Powys Journal*) and 3
newsletters per year, and holds an annual weekend
conference in August, as well as other activities.
Founded 1967.

The Press Complaints Commission

Director Tim Toulmin, Halton House,
20–23 Holborn, London EC1N 2JD
tel 020-7831 0022, (0845) 600 2757
(helpline) *fax* 020-7831 0025
email complaints@pcc.org.uk
website www.pcc.org.uk
Chairman Sir Christopher Meyer

Independent body founded to oversee self-regulation
of the Press. Deals with complaints by the public
about the contents and conduct of British newspapers
and magazines and advises editors on journalistic
ethics. Complaints must be about the failure of
newspapers or magazines to follow the letter or spirit
of a Code of Practice, drafted by newspaper and
magazine editors, adopted by the industry and
supervised by the Commission. Founded 1991.

The J.B. Priestley Society

Secretary Rod Slater, 54 Framingham Road, Sale,
Greater Manchester M33 3RJ
tel 0161-962 1477 (evening) *fax* 0161-962 7538
email rodslater@ukonline.co.uk
Membership £12 p.a. single, £18 family, £7
concessions

Aims to widen the knowledge, understanding and
appreciation of the published works of J.B. Priestley
(1894–1984) and to promote the study of his life and
career. Holds lectures and discussions and shows
films. Publishes a newsletter and journal. Organises
walks to areas with Priestley connections, Annual
Priestley Night and other social events. Founded
1997.

Printmakers Council

Ground Floor Unit, 23 Blue Anchor Lane, London
SE16 3UL
tel 020-7250 1927 *fax* 020-7250 1927
website www.printmaker.co.uk/pmc/
President Stanley Jones, *Chair* Sheila Sloss
Membership £60 p.a., £30 students

Artist-led group which aims to promote the use of
both traditional and innovative printmaking
techniques by:
• holding exhibitions of prints;
• providing information on prints and printmaking to
both its membership and the public;
• encouraging cooperation and exchanges between
members, other associations and interested
individuals. Founded 1965.

Private Libraries Association

Ravelston, South View Road, Pinner, Middlesex
HA5 3YD

website www.plabooks.org
President Ms Lynne Brindley, *Hon. Editors* David
Chambers, Paul W. Nash, Stan Brett
Membership £25 p.a.

International society of book collectors and private
libraries. Publications include *The Private Library*
(quarterly), annual *Private Press Books*, and other
books on book collecting. Founded 1956.

The Publishers Association

29ʙ Montague Street, London WC1B 5BW
tel 020-7691 9191 *fax* 020-7691 9199
email mail@publishers.org.uk
website www.publishers.org.uk
Chief Executive Ronnie Williams ᴏʙᴇ, *Director of
International and Trade Divisions (BDCI)* Simon Bell,
*Director of Educational, Academic & Professional
Publishing* Graham Taylor

Founded 1896.

Publishers' Association of South Africa (PASA)

PO Box 15277, Vlaeberg 8018, South Africa
tel (021) 426-1726 *fax* (021) 426-1733
email pasa@publishsa.co.za
website www.publishsa.co.za

Publishers Licensing Society Ltd (PLS)

37–41 Gower Street, London WC1E 6HH
tel 020-7299 7730 *fax* 020-7299 7780
email pls@pls.org.uk
website www.pls.org.uk
Chairman Christopher Collins, *Chief Executive* Alicia
Wise

PLS has mandates from over 2000 publishers. These
non-exclusive licences allow PLS to include those
publishers' works as part of the repertoire offered to
licensees by CLA. The licences permit photocopying
and some digitisation of parts of copyright works.
The money collected from these licences is shared
between publishers and authors and PLS has
responsibility for distributing the publishers' share to
the mandating companies. PLS represents the
interests of a wide range of publishers from the
multinationals to the single-title publisher. Founded
1981.

Publishers Publicity Circle

Secretary/Treasurer Heather White, 65 Airedale
Avenue, London W4 2NN
tel 020-8994 1881
email ppc-@lineone.net
website www.publisherspublicitycircle.co.uk

Enables all book publicists to meet and share
information regularly. Monthly meetings provide a
forum for press journalists, TV and radio researchers
and producers to meet publicists collectively. Awards
are presented for the best PR campaigns. Monthly
newsletter includes recruitment advertising. Founded
1955.

The Radio Academy

5 Market Place, London W1W 8AE
email info@radioacademy.org
website www.radioacademy.org
Director John Bradford

The professional association for those engaged in the UK radio industry with over 2000 individual members and 30 corporate patrons. Organises conferences, seminars, debates, the annual UK Radio Festival and social events for members in all regions of the UK; publishes *Off Air* (quarterly) newsletter and an annual *Yearbook*. Provides administrative support for the Student Radio Association and the Radio Studies Network and organises a series of regional training events for those interested in getting into radio.

Regional Arts Offices – see Arts Council England

Ridley Art Society

50 Crowborough Road, London SW17 9QQ
tel 020-8682 1212
email info@ridleyart.com
President Ken Howard RA, Chairman dickon

Represents a wide variety of attitudes towards the making of art. In recent years has sought to encourage younger artists. At least one Central London Members' exhibition a year. Founded 1889.

The Romantic Novelists' Association

Chairman Jenny Haddon, 3 Bywater Street, London SW3 4XD
tel 020-7584 5464
Hon. Secretary Eileen Ramsay, Bonnyton House, Arbirlot, Angus DD11 2PY
tel (01241) 874131
website www.rna-uk.org

Aims to raise the prestige of Romantic Authorship. Open to romantic and historical novelists. See also page 569.

Royal Academy of Arts

Piccadilly, London W1J 0BD
tel 020-7300 8000 fax 020-7300 8001
website www.royalacademy.org.uk
President Sir Nicholas Grimshaw, Keeper Maurice Cockrill RA

Academicians (RA) are elected from the most distinguished artists in the UK. Holds major loan exhibitions throughout the year including the Annual Summer Exhibition (June–Aug). Also runs art schools for 60 postgraduate students in painting and sculpture.

Royal Birmingham Society of Artists

4 Brook Street, St Paul's, Birmingham B3 1SA
tel 0121-236 4353 fax 0121-236 4555
website www.rbsa.org.uk

Membership Friends £24 p.a.

The Society has 2 floors of exhibition space and a craft gallery in the city centre. Members (RBSA) and Associates (ARBSA) are elected annually. Holds 4 Open Exhibitions: 3 all-media exhibitions (Spring, Summer and Winter) – send sae for schedules, available 6 weeks prior to Exhibition. A further Open £1000 First Prize Exhibition is held (June/July) for works in any media. Other substantial money prizes can be won with no preference given to Members and Associates. Also a varying programme of exhibitions throughout the year, including the Autumn Exhibition, open to Members and Associates, and 2 Friends Exhibitions (February and August). Friends of the RBSA are entitled to attend various functions and to submit work for the Annual Exhibitions.

Royal Institute of Oil Painters

17 Carlton House Terrace, London SW1Y 5BD
tel 020-7930 6844 fax 020-7839 7830
email info@mallgalleries.com
website www.mallgalleries.org.uk
President Dennis Syrett

Promotes and encourages the art of painting in oils. Open Annual Exhibition at the Mall Galleries, The Mall, London SW1.

Royal Institute of Painters in Water Colours

17 Carlton House Terrace, London SW1Y 5BD
tel 020-7930 6844 fax 020-7839 7830
email info@mallgalleries.com
website www.mallgalleries.org.uk
President Ronald Maddox Hon. RWS
Membership Elected from approved candidates' list

Promotes the appreciation of watercolour painting in its traditional and contemporary forms, primarily by means of an annual exhibition at the Mall Galleries, The Mall, London SW1 of members' and non-members' work and also by members' exhibitions at selected venues in Britain and abroad. Founded 1831.

The Royal Literary Fund

3 Johnson's Court, off Fleet Street, London EC4A 3EA
tel 020-7353 7150 fax 020-7353 1350
email egunnrlf@globalnet.co.uk
website www.rlf.org.uk
President Peter Janson-Smith, General Secretary Eileen Gunn

Founded in 1790, the Fund is the oldest charity serving literature, set up to help writers and their families who face hardship. It does not offer grants to writers who can earn their living in other ways, nor does it provide financial support for writing projects. But it sustains authors who have for one reason or another fallen on hard times – illness, family misfortune, or sheer loss of writing form. Applicants must have published work of approved literary merit, which may include important contributions to periodicals. The literary claim of every new applicant must be accepted by the General Committee before the question of need can be considered.

The Royal Musical Association
Secretary Dr Jeffrey Dean, 4 Chandos Road, Chorlton-cum-Hardy, Manchester M21 0ST
tel 0161-861 7542 *fax* 0161-861 7543
email jeffrey.dean@stingrayoffice.com
website www.rma.ac.uk

The Royal Photographic Society
Fenton House, 122 Wells Road, Bath BA2 3AH
tel (01225) 325733
email reception@rps.org
website www.rps.org

Open membership organisation which promotes the art and science of photography and electronic imagery. Publishes *The RPS Journal* (monthly) and *Imaging Science Journal* (quarterly). Founded 1853.

The Royal Scottish Academy of Art
The Mound, Edinburgh EH2 2EL
tel 0131-225 6671 *fax* 0131-220 6016
email info@royalscottishacademy.org
website www.royalscottishacademy.org

Maintains a unique position in Scotland as an independent, privately funded institution led by eminent artists and architects whose purpose is to promote and support the visual arts. In addition to the RSA Annual Exhibition and the RSA Annual Student Exhibition, there is also an ongoing programme of contemporary art exhibitions. For information on open submission exhibitions and artist scholarships and residences, contact the office or visit the website. Founded 1826.

The Royal Society
6–9 Carlton House Terrace, London SW1Y 5AG
tel 020-7451 2500 *fax* 020-7930 2170
email press@royalsoc.ac.uk
website www.royalsoc.ac.uk
President Prof. Martin Rees, Lord Rees of Ludlow Kt, PRS, *Treasurer* Prof. Sir David Wallace CBE, DL, FRS, FREng, *Biological Secretary* Prof. David Read FRS, *Physical Secretary* Prof. Martin Taylor FRS, *Foreign Secretary* Prof. Dame Julia Higgins DBE, FRS, FREng, *Executive Secretary* Mr S. Cox CVO

The Royal Society for Asian Affairs
2 Belgrave Square, London SW1X 8PJ
tel 020-7235 5122 *fax* 020-7259 6771
email info@rsaa.org.uk
website www.rsaa.org.uk
President The Lord Denman CBE, MC TD, *Chairman of Council* Sir Harold Walker KCMG, *Secretary* Norman Cameron MA, BA
Membership £55 p.a. London, £45 more than 60 miles from London and overseas, £10 up to age 25

For the study of all Asia past and present; fortnightly lectures, etc; library. Publishes *Asian Affairs* (3 p.a.), free to members. Founded 1901.

Royal Society for the encouragement of Arts, Manufactures and Commerce (RSA)
8 John Adam Street, London WC2N 6EZ
tel 020-7930 5115 *fax* 020-7839 5805
email editor@rsa.org.uk
website www.theRSA.org
Chairman of Council Sir Paul Judge, *Executive Director* Penny Egan, *Commercial Director* Carrie Walsh, *Fellowship & Information Director* Stephen Farrant, *Programme Director* Paul Crake, *Director of Finance* Philip Bunt, *Editor, RSA Journal* Alex Perchard, *Press Officer* Sarah McLean

With over 23,000 Fellows, the RSA sustains a forum for people from all walks of life to come together to address issues, shape new ideas and stimulate action. It works through projects, award schemes and its lecture programme, the proceedings of which are recorded in *RSA Journal*. Founded 1754.

Royal Society of British Artists
17 Carlton House Terrace, London SW1Y 5BD
tel 020-7930 6844 *fax* 020-7839 7830
email info@mallgalleries.com
website www.mallgalleries.org.uk
President Cav. Romeo di Girolamo, *Keeper* Alfred Daniels

Incorporated by Royal Charter for the purpose of encouraging the study and practice of the arts of painting, sculpture and architectural designs. Annual Open Exhibition at the Mall Galleries, The Mall, London SW1, open to artists working in any 2- or 3-dimensional medium.

Royal Society of Literature
Somerset House, Strand, London WC2R 1LA
tel 020-7845 4676 *fax* 020-7845 4679
email info@rslit.org
Chairman of Council Maggie Gee, FRSL, *Secretary* Maggie Fergusson
Membership £30 p.a.

For the promotion of literature and encouragement of writers by way of lectures, discussions, readings, and by publications. Administers the V.S. Pritchett Memorial Prize, the Royal Society of Literature Ondaatje Prize and the Royal Society of Literature/ Jerwood Awards. Founded 1820.

Royal Society of Marine Artists
17 Carlton House Terrace, London SW1Y 5BD
tel 020-7930 6844 *fax* 020-7839 7830
email info@mallgalleries.com
website www.mallgalleries.org.uk
President Geoff Hunt

Aims to promote and encourage marine painting. Open Annual Exhibition at the Mall Galleries, The

Mall, London SW1 for any artists whose main interest is the sea, or tidal waters, or some object essentially connected therewith.

The Royal Society of Miniature Painters, Sculptors and Gravers

Executive Secretary Mrs Pam Henderson, 1 Knapp Cottages, Wyke, Gillingham, Dorset SP8 4NQ
tel (01747) 825718
email pamhenderson@dial.pipex.com
website www.royal-miniature-society.org.uk
President Elisabeth R. Meek, PSWA, HS, FRSA, *Hon.*
Secretary Barbara Penketh Simpson
Membership By selection and standard of work over a period of years (ARMS associate, RMS full member)

Annual Open Exhibition in June at the Mall Galleries, The Mall, London SW1. Hand in April; schedules available in January (send sae). Applications and enquiries to the Executive Secretary. Founded 1895.

Royal Society of Painter-Printmakers

Bankside Gallery, 48 Hopton Street, London SE1 9JH
tel 020-7928 7521
email info@banksidegallery.com
website www.banksidegallery.com
President Anita Klein PRE
Membership Open to British and overseas artists. An election of Associates is held annually; for particulars apply to the Secretary. Friends membership is open to all those interested in artists' original printmaking

Organises workshops and lectures on original printmaking and holds one members' exhibition per year. Founded 1880.

Royal Society of Portrait Painters

17 Carlton House Terrace, London SW1Y 5BD
tel 020-7930 6844 *fax* 020-7839 7830
email info@mallgalleries.com
website www.therp.co.uk
President Andrew Festing

Annual Exhibition at the Mall Galleries, The Mall, London SW1, of members' work and that of selected non-members. Five high-profile artists' awards are made: the Ondaatje Prize for Portraiture (£10,000), the HSBC Investment Management Prize (£4000), the De Laszlo Prize (£3000), the Prince of Wales's Award for Portrait Drawing (£2000), the Changing Faces Prize (£2000). Also commissions consultancy service. Founded 1891.

Royal Television Society

5th Floor, Kildare House, 3 Dorset Rise, London EC4Y 8EN
tel 020-7822-2810 020-7822 2811
email info@rts.org.uk
website www.rts.org.uk

The leading forum for discussion and debate on all aspects of the TV community. In a fast changing sector, it reflects the full range of perspectives and views. Holds awards, conferences, dinners, lectures and workshops. Founded 1927.

Royal Watercolour Society

Bankside Gallery, 48 Hopton Street, London SE1 9JH
tel 020-7928 7521
email info@banksidegallery.com
website www.banksidegallery.com
President Trevor Frankland, PRWS, RE, RBA, Hon RI
Membership Open to British and overseas artists; election of Associates held annually. Friends membership is open to all those interested in watercolour painting

Arranges lectures and courses on watercolour paintings; holds an open exhibition in the summer. Exhibitions in the spring and autumn. Founded 1804.

Royal West of England Academy

Queens Road, Clifton, Bristol BS8 1PX
tel 0117-973 5129 *fax* 0117-923 7874
website www.rwa.org.uk
President Derek Balmer

An art academy/gallery whose objectives are to advance the education of the public in the fine arts and in particular to promote the appreciation and practice of the fine arts and to encourage and develop talent in the fine arts. Founded 1844.

The Ruskin Society

Hon. Secretary Dr C.J. Gamble, 49 Hallam Street, London W1W 6JP
tel: 020-7580 1894
email cgamble@britishlibrary.net
website www.lancs.ac.uk/depts/ruskin/links.htm
Membership £10 p.a.

Aims to encourage a wider understanding of John Ruskin (1819–1900) and his contemporaries. Organises lectures and events which seek to explain to the public the nature of Ruskin's theories and to place these in a modern context. Affiliated to the Ruskin Foundation. Founded 1997.

SAA (Society for All Artists)

PO Box 50, Newark, Notts. NG23 5GY
tel (01949) 844050 *fax* (01949) 844051
email info@saa.co.uk
website www.saa.co.uk
Membership £22.50–£42 p.a. including paintings exhibition insurance and third party public liability, £27.50 overseas

Aims to inform, encourage and inspire all artists, and has over 30,000 members in 60 countries. Members range from complete beginners to amateurs, professionals and teachers. Welcomes new members. Provides benefits including free paintings exhibition insurance and third party public liability, full art materials catalogue with over 7000 products, the *Paint* newsletter (6 p.a.) and the chance for artists to promote their work through the website. As well as organising workshops, demonstrations and exhibitions, the SAA also runs an international painting competition – the 'Artist of the Year' – which is open to all, with free unlimited entries for SAA members. Founded 1992.

The Malcolm Saville Society

Chairman Richard Griffiths, 78A Windmill Road, Mortimer, Berks. RG7 3RL
email mystery@witchend.com
website www.witchend.com
Membership £10 p.a. (£12.50 Europe, £16 elsewhere)

Aims to remember and promote interest in the work of Malcolm Saville (1901–82), children's author. Regular social activities, book search, library, contact directory and magazine (4 p.a.). Founded 1994.

The Dorothy L. Sayers Society

Chairman Christopher J. Dean, Rose Cottage, Malthouse Lane, Hurstpierpoint, West Sussex BN6 9JY
tel (01273) 833444 *fax* (01273) 835988
website www.sayers.org.uk
Secretaries Lenelle Davis, Jasmine Simeone
Membership £14 p.a. UK, £16.50 Europe, $34 USA, £19 rest of world

Aims to promote and encourage the study of the works of Dorothy L. Sayers (1893–1957); to collect archive materials and reminiscences about her and make them available to students and biographers; to hold an annual conference and other meetings; to publish proceedings, pamphlets and a bi-monthly bulletin. Founded 1976.

Scattered Authors Society

Secretary Yvonne Coppard, 35 Thornton Way, Girton, Cambridge CB3 0NL
email yvonnecoppard@aol.com

Aims to provide a forum for informal discussion, contact and support for professional writers in children's fiction. Founded 1998.

Scottish Arts Club

24 Rutland Square, Edinburgh EH1 2BW
tel 0131-229 8157 *fax* 0131-229 8887
email manager@scottishartsclub.fsnet.co.uk
website www.scottishartsclub.co.uk
Hon. Secretary Mhairi Kerr *tel* 0131-229 8157
Membership £380 p.a. full; reductions available

Art, literature, music.

Scottish Arts Council

12 Manor Place, Edinburgh EH3 7DD
tel 0131-226 6051 *Help Desk* (0845) 603 6000 (local rate)
email help.desk@scottisharts.org.uk
website www.scottisharts.org.uk
Chief Executive Graham Berry, *Head of Literature* Dr Gavin Wallace, *Head of Visual Arts* Amanda Catto

The lead body for the funding, development and advocacy of the arts in Scotland. Offers a unique national perspective on the provision and management of the arts which seeks to balance the needs of all arts sectors and all parts of Scotland. The expertise and experience of Scottish Arts Council in developing sound policy and good practice includes the ability to inter-relate arts and socio-economic policy objectives. Also offers a focus on research, information provision and international writing.

The Council invests £60 million from Scottish Executive and National Lottery funding to support and develop artistic excellence and creativity throughout Scotland. Supports a range of artists, arts organisations and projects across Scotland. The Council funds awards, bursaries, fellowships and training opportunities for individuals, as well as for a range of arts projects.

Scottish Book Trust (SBT)

Sandeman House, 55 High Street, Edinburgh EH1 1SR
tel 0131-524 0160 *fax* 0131-524 0161
email info@scottishbooktrust.com
website www.scottishbooktrust.com

With a particular responsibility towards Scottish writing, SBT exists to promote literature and reading, and aims to reach (and create) a wider reading public than has existed before. It also organises exhibitions, readings and storytellings, national author tours, administers the Live Literature Scotland Scheme, operates an extensive children's reference library and provides a book information service for writers and readers. SBT has a range of publications and advises other relevant art organisations. Its latest initiative, BRAW (Books, Reading and Writing), the Network for the Scottish Children's Book, aims to promote books, reading and writing, by authors and illustrators living in Scotland and for young people across Scotland. Founded 1960.

Scottish Daily Newspaper Society

48 Palmerston Place, Edinburgh EH12 5DE
tel 0131-220 4353 *fax* 0131-220 4344
email info@sdns.org.uk
Director J.B. Raeburn FCIS

Scottish Newspaper Publishers Association

48 Palmerston Place, Edinburgh EH12 5DE
tel 0131-220 4353 *fax* 0131-220 4344
email info@snpa.org.uk
website www.snpa.org.uk
Director J.B. Raeburn FCIS

Scottish Publishers Association

Scottish Book Centre, 137 Dundee Street, Edinburgh EH11 1BG
tel 0131-228 6866 *fax* 0131-228 3220
email enquiries@scottishbooks.org

website www.scottishbooks.org
Chairman Janis Adams, *Director* Lorraine Fannin,
Vice-Chair Neil Wilson, *Finance & Office
Administrator* Carol Lothian, *Member Services
Manager* Liz Small, *Information & Personal
Development Administrator* Katherine A. Naish

Founded 1973.

Scottish Screen
2nd Floor, 249 West George Street, Glasgow G2 4QE
tel 0141-302 1700 *fax* 0141-302 1711
email info@scottishscreen.com
website www.scottishscreen.com

Develops, encourages and promotes every aspect of
film, TV and new media in Scotland through script
development, short film production, distribution of
National Lottery film production finance, training,
education, exhibition funding, Film Commission
Locations support and the Scottish Screen Archive.

SCRIBO
Contact K. & P. Sylvester, Flat 1, 31 Hamilton Road,
Bournemouth BH1 4EQ
Membership Joining fee: £5; no annual subscription.
Send sae for details

A postal forum for novelists (published and
unpublished), SCRIBO aims to give friendly,
informed encouragement and help, to discuss all
matters of interest to novelists and to offer criticism
via MSS folios: crime/thrillers, fantasy/science fiction,
mainstream, popular women's fiction, plus literary
folios. Founded 1971.

Seven Stories – the Centre for the Children's Book
30 Lime Street, Ouseburn Valley, Newcastle upon
Tyne NE1 2PQ
tel (0845) 271 0777
email info@sevenstories.org.uk
website www.sevenstories.org.uk

Centre to celebrate children's books with an
interactive gallery, a library, and an exhibitions and
seminar.

The Shaw Society
Secretary Barbara Smoker, 51 Farmfield Road,
Downham, Bromley, Kent BR1 4NF
tel 020-8697 3619
email anthnyellis@aol.com
Membership £15/$30 p.a.

Works towards the improvement and diffusion of
knowledge of the life and works of Bernard Shaw
(1856–1950) and his circle. Publishes *The Shavian*.

Society for Editors and Proofreaders (SfEP)
(formerly Society of Freelance Editors and
Proofreaders)

Office Riverbank House, 1 Putney Bridge Approach,
London SW6 3JD
tel 020-7736 3278
email admin@sfep.org.uk
website www.sfep.org.uk

Works to promote high editorial standards and
achieve recognition of its members' professional
status, through local and national meetings, an
annual conference, an email discussion group, a
regular newsletter and a programme of reasonably
priced workshops/training sessions. These sessions
help newcomers to acquire basic skills, enable
experienced editors to update their skills or broaden
their competence, and also cover aspects of
professional practice or business for the self-
employed. An annual Directory of members' services
is available. The Society supports moves towards
recognised standards of training and accreditation for
editors and proofreaders and has developed its own
Accreditation in Proofreading qualification. It has
close links with the Publishing Training Centre and
the Society of Indexers, is represented on the BSI
Technical Committee dealing with copy preparation
and proof correction (BS 5261), and works to foster
good relations with all relevant bodies and
organisations in the UK and worldwide. Founded
1988.

The Society for Theatre Research
c/o The Theatre Museum, 1E Tavistock Street,
London WC2E 7PR
email e.cottis@btinternet.com
website www.str.org.uk
Hon. Secretary Eileen Cottis

Publishes annual volumes and journal (3 p.a.),
Theatre Notebook, holds lectures and makes annual
research grants (current total sum approx. £4000).
Starting in 1998, the Society's 50th anniversary, it
awards an annual prize of £400 for the best book
published in English on the historical or current
practice of the British theatre.

Society of Artists Agents
21C Montpellier Row, London SE3 0RL
tel (07870) 628 709
email jennieward@btopenworld.com
website www.thesaa.com
Contact Jennifer Ward

Formed to promote professionalism in the
illustration industry and to forge closer links between
clients and artists through an agreed set of guidelines.
The Society believes in an ethical approach through
proper terms and conditions, thereby protecting the
interests of the artists and clients. Founded 1992.

The Society of Authors – see page 513

The Society of Botanical Artists
Executive Secretary Mrs Pam Henderson, 1 Knapp
Cottages, Wyke, Gillingham, Dorset SP8 4NQ

tel (01747) 825718
email pam@soc-botanical-artists.org
website www.soc-botanical-artists.org
Founder President Suzanne Lucas FLS, RMS, President
Margaret Stevens
Membership Through selection. £120 p.a.; £20 friend
members

Aims to encourage the art of botanical painting.
Annual Open Exhibition held in April at
Westminster Central Hall, London SW1. Hand in
February. Entry schedules available from the
Executive Secretary from December on receipt of sae.
Founded 1985.

Society of Children's Book Writers and Illustrators (SCBWI)
36 Mackenzie Road, Beckenham, Kent BR3 4RU
tel 020-8249 9716
email ra@britishscbwi.org
website www.britishscbwi.org
Regional Adviser, SCBWI–British Isles Natascha
Biebow
Membership £44 p.a. plus a one-off fee of £8.50

An international network for the exchange of
knowledge between professional writers, illustrators,
editors, publishers, agents, librarians, educators,
booksellers and others involved with literature for
young people. Sponsors 3 annual conferences on
writing and illustrating children's books and
multimedia – in New York (February), Los Angeles
(August) and Bologna (spring) – as well as dozens of
regional conferences and events throughout the
world. Publishes a bi-monthly newsletter, The
Bulletin, and information publications, and awards
grants for works in progress. The SCBWI also
presents the annual Golden Kite Award for the best
fiction and non-fiction books, which is open both to
published and unpublished writers and illustrators.

The SCBWI British Isles region meets regularly for
speaker or workshop events. Also sponsors local
critique groups and publishes Words and Pictures
quarterly newsletter, which includes up-to-date
events and marketing information, interviews and
articles on the craft of children's writing and
illustrating in the British Isles. The yearly Writers'
Day and Illustrators' Day includes workshops and the
opportunity to meet publishing professionals.
Founded 1971.

The Society of Civil and Public Service Writers
Secretary Mrs J.M. Lewis, 17 The Green, Corby Glen,
Grantham, Lincs. NG33 4NP
email joan@lewis5634.fsnet.co.uk
Membership £15 p.a.; Poetry Workshop add £3

Welcomes serving and retired members of the Civil
Service, Armed Forces, Post Office and BT, the
nursing profession, and other public servants.
Members can be aspiring or published writers. Holds

annual competitions for short stories, articles and
poetry, plus occasional for longer works. Offers postal
folios for short stories and articles; holds an AGM
and occasional meetings; publishes The Civil Service
Author (quarterly) magazine. Poetry Workshop offers
magazine, postal folio, anthology and weekend. Send
sae for details. Founded 1935.

Society of Editors
Director Bob Satchwell, University Centre, Granta
Place, Mill Lane, Cambridge CB2 1RU
tel (01223) 304080 fax (01223) 304090
email info@societyofeditors.org
website www.societyofeditors.org
Membership £230 p.a.

Formed from the merger of the Guild of Editors and
the Association of British Editors, the Society has
more than 450 members in national, regional and
local newspapers, magazines, broadcasting, new
media, journalism education and media law,
campaigning for media freedom. Founded 1999.

Society of Graphic Fine Art
PO Box 7727, Maldon, Essex CM9 6WW
email billgeller@wgeller.freeserve.co.uk
website www.sgfa.org.uk
President David Brooke
Membership By election

A fine art society. Holds an annual open exhibition of
work of high quality with an emphasis on good
drawing, whether by pen, pencil (with our without
wash), watercolour, pastel or any of the forms of
printmaking. Founded 1919.

Society of Heraldic Arts
26 Paternoster Row, Ottery St Mary, Devon EX11
1DP
email sha.hon-sec@tiscali.co.uk
website www.heraldic-arts.com
Secretary Kevin Arkinstall SHA
Membership Craft £25 p.a., Associate £15

Aims to serve the interests of heraldic artists,
craftsmen, designers and writers, to provide a 'shop
window' for their work, to obtain commissions on
their behalf and to act as a forum for the exchange of
information and ideas. Also offers an information
service to the public. Candidates for admission as
craft members should be artists or craftsmen whose
work comprises a substantial element of heraldry and
is of a sufficiently high standard to satisfy the
requirements of the Society's advisory council.
Founded 1987.

Society of Indexers – see page 629

The Society of Limners
Contact Richard East, 16 Tudor Close, Hove, East
Sussex BN3 7NR
tel (01273) 770628

email rgeast.limners@ntlworld.com
website www.societyoflimners.co.uk
Membership £30 p.a., £15 Friends (open to non-exhibitors); £35/£18 overseas

Aims to promote an interest in miniature painting (in any medium), calligraphy and heraldry and encourage their development to a high standard. New members are elected after the submission of 4 works of acceptable standard and guidelines are provided for new artists. Members receive up to 3 newsletters a year and an annual exhibition is arranged. Founded 1986.

The Society of Medical Writers

Prof. Brian McGuinness, Courtlands, Norwich Road, Swaffham, Norfolk PE37 8DE
email medical.writers@gmail.com
website www.somw.org.uk
Secretary Mrs Irene Ranner, Devil's End, All Saints Way, Beachamwell, Norfolk PE37 8BT

Aims to recruit members from all branches of the medical profession, together with all professions allied to medicine, to foster interest in literature and in writing – not solely about medicine but also about art, history, music, theatre, etc. Members are encouraged to write fiction, poetry, plays, book reviews, etc. Publishes *The Writer* (2 p.a.) and a register of members and their writing interests. Holds a bi-annual conference in which various aspects of literature and writing are explored in a relaxed and informal atmosphere. Founded 2001 as successor to the General Practitioner Writers Association.

Society of Scribes and Illuminators (SSI)

Hon. Secretary 6 Queen Square, London WC1N 3AT
email scribe@calligraphyonline.org
website www.calligraphyonline.org
Membership £28 Lay members; £23 Friends

Aims to advance the crafts of writing and illumination. Holds regular exhibitions, provides opportunities for discussion, demonstration and sharing of research. Founded 1921.

The Society of Sussex Authors

Secretary David Arscott, 3 Dolphin House, 51 St Nicholas Lane, Lewes, East Sussex BN7 2JZ
tel (01273) 470100 *fax* (01273) 420100
email sussexbooks@aol.com
Membership £10 p.a.

Aims to encourage social contact between members, and to promote interest in literature and authors. Membership is open to writers living in Sussex who have had at least one book commercially published or who have worked extensively in journalism, radio, TV or the theatre. Founded 1969.

Society of Wildlife Artists

17 Carlton House Terrace, London SW1Y 5BD
tel 020-7930 6844 *fax* 020-7839 7830

website www.mallgalleries.org.uk
President Andrew Stock

Aims to promote and encourage the art of wildlife painting and sculpture. Open Annual Exhibition at the Mall Galleries, The Mall, London SW1, for any artist whose work depicts wildlife subjects (botanical and domestic animals are not admissable).

The Society of Women Artists

Executive Secretary 1 Knapp Cottages, Wyke, Gillingham, Dorset SP8 4NQ
tel (01747) 825718 *fax* (01747) 826835
email pamhenderson@dsl.pipex.com
website www.society-women-artists.org.uk
President Barbara Penketh Simpson RMS, FRSA
Membership Election by invitation, based on work submitted to the exhibition

Founded in 1855 when women were not considered as serious contributors to art and could not compete for professional honours, the Society continues to promote art by women. Receiving day in April for annual open exhibition held in June at Mall Galleries, The Mall, London SW1.

Society of Women Writers & Journalists (SWWJ)

Membership Secretary Wendy Hughes, 27 Braycourt Avenue, Walton-on-Thames, Surrey KT12 2AZ
tel (01932) 702874
email wendy@stickler.org
website www.swwj.co.uk
Membership Secretary W.L. Hughes
Membership £35 p.a. Full, £25 Associate, £20 probabionary/student, £25 overseas, £15 joining fee

For women writers: the SWWJ upholds professional standards and literary achievements through regular workshops for all genre of writing where work-in-progress can be evaluated. Regional group meetings; residential weekends; postal critique service; competitions and outings. For Full members, membership card doubles as a press card. Publishes *The Woman Writer* (6 p.a.). Men writers are accepted as Associate members. Founded 1894.

Society of Young Publishers

Contact The Secretary, c/o The Bookseller, Endeavour House, 189 Shaftesbury Avenue, London WC2H 8TJ
email info@thesyp.org.uk
website www.thesyp.org.uk
Membership Open to anyone employed in publishing or hoping to be soon; Associate membership available to those over the age of 35

Organises monthly speaker meetings at which senior figures talk on topics of key importance to the industry today, and social and other events. Runs a job database which matches candidates with potential employers. Meetings are held in Central London, usually on the last Wednesday of the month at 6.30pm. Also a branch in Oxford. Founded 1949.

South African Writers' Circle

Chairperson Helen Osborne, Suite 522, Postnet, Post Bag X4, Kloof 3640, South Africa
tel (082) 9288391 (Helen Osborne)
email info@third-rock.co.za
website www.sawc.sos.co.za
Membership R120 p.a. local, R180 p.a. overseas

Aims to help and encourage all writers, new and experienced, in the art of writing. Publishes a monthly *Newsletter*, and runs competitions with prizes for the winners. Founded 1960.

Southwest Scriptwriters

Secretary John Colborn *tel* 0117-909 5522
email info@southwest-scriptwriters.co.uk
website www.southwest-scriptwriters.co.uk
Membership £6 p.a.

Workshops members' drama scripts for stage, screen, radio and TV with the aim of improving their chances of professional production, meeting at the Bristol Old Vic. Also hosts regular talks by professional dramatists. Presents short annual seasons of script-in-hand performances of members' work at a major Bristol venue. Bi-monthly newsletter. Founded 1994.

Sports Journalists' Association of Great Britain (SJA)

Secretary Steven Downes, 54 Avondale Road, South Croydon CR2 6JA
tel 020-8686 3520
email stevendownes@btinternet.com
website www.sportsjournalists.org.uk
Membership £23.50 p.a., £11.75 regional

Represents sports journalists across the country and is Britain's voice in international sporting affairs. Offers advice to members covering major events, acts as a consultant to organisers of major sporting events on media requirements. Member of the BOA Press Advisory Committee. Founded 1948.

The Robert Louis Stevenson Club

Secretary Dr Alan Marchbank, 12 Dean Park, Longniddry, East Lothian EH32 0QR
tel (01875) 852976 *fax* (01875) 853328
email alan@amarchbank.freeserve.co.uk
website www.rlsclub.org.uk
Membership £20 p.a., £150 10 years

Aims to foster interest in Robert Louis Stevenson's life (1850–94) and works through various events and its newsletter. Founded 1920.

Sussex Playwrights' Club

Hon. Secretary, 2 Brunswick Mews, Hove, East Sussex BN3 1HD
website www.newventure.org.uk

See 'features' page on website.

Swedish Publishers' Association

(Svenska Förläggareföreningen)
Drottninggaten 97, 2 tr., 113 60 Stockholm, Sweden
tel 46-8-736-1940 *fax* 46-8-736-1944
email info@forlaggare.se
website www.forlaggare.se
Director Kristina Ahlinder

Founded 1843.

The Tennyson Society

Hon. Secretary Kathleen Jefferson, Central Library, Free School lane, Lincoln LN2 1EZ
tel (01522) 552851 *fax* (01522) 552858
email jeffersk@lincolnshire.gov.uk
website www.tennysonsociety.org.uk
Membership £10 p.a., £12 family, £15 institutions

Promotes the study and understanding of the life and work of the poet Alfred, Lord Tennyson (1809–92) and supports the Tennyson Research Centre in Lincoln. Holds lectures, visits and seminars; publishes the *Tennyson Research Bulletin* (annual), Monographs and Occasional Papers; tapes/recordings available. Founded 1960.

Theatre Writers' Union – see page 516

Angela Thirkell Society

Chairman Mrs I.J. Cox, 32 Murvagh Close, Cheltenham, Glos. GL53 7QY
tel (01242) 251604
email penny.aldred@ntlworld.com
Secretary Mrs P. Aldred, 54 Belmont Park, London SE13 5BN
tel 020-8244 9339
website www.angelathirkellsociety.com
Membership £10 p.a.

Aims 'to honour the memory of Angela Thirkell (1890–1960) as a writer, and to make her works available to new generations'. Publishes an *Annual Journal*, and encourages Thirkell studies. Founded 1980.

The Edward Thomas Fellowship

1 Carfax, Undercliff Drive, St Lawrence, Isle of Wight PO38 1XG
tel (01983) 853366
email colingthornton@btopenworld.com
Hon. Secretary Colin G. Thornton
Membership single £7 p.a., joint £10 p.a.

Aims to perpetuate the memory of Edward Thomas (1878–1917), poet and writer, foster an interest in his life and work, to assist in the preservation of places associated with him and to arrange events which extend fellowship amongst his admirers. Founded 1980.

Dylan Thomas Society of Great Britain

Fernhill, 24 Chapel Street, Mumbles, Swansea SA3 4NH
tel (01792) 363875
Chair Mrs Cecily Hughes
Membership £5 p.a. single, £8 p.a. double

Aims to promote an interest in the works of Dylan Thomas (1914–53) and other Anglo–Welsh writers. Founded 1977.

The Tolkien Society

Secretary Sally Kennett, 210 Prestbury Road, Cheltenham GL52 3ER
email membership@tolkiensociety.org
website www.tolkiensociety.org
Membership Secretary Claire Chambers, 8 Queens Lane, Eynsham, Witney OX29 4HL
Membership 20 p.a.

The Translators Association

84 Drayton Gardens, London SW10 9SB
tel 020-7373 6642
email info@societyofauthors.org
website www.societyofauthors.org
Membership £85 p.a. (£80 DD), including membership of the Society of Authors

Specialist unit within the membership of the Society of Authors (see page 513), exclusively concerned with the interests and special problems of translators into English whose work is published or performed commercially in Great Britain and English-speaking countries overseas. Members are entitled to general and legal advice on all questions connected with their work, including remuneration and contractual arrangements with publishers, editors, broadcasting organisations. Administers a range of translation prizes. Founded 1958.

The Trollope Society

Maritime House, Clapham Old Town, London SW4 0JW
tel 020-7720 6789 *fax* 020-7627 2965
email info@trollopesociety.org
Chairman Priscilla Hungerford, *Secretary* P. Ravenscroft
Membership £26 p.a.

Has produced the first ever complete edition of the novels of Anthony Trollope (1815–82). Founded 1987.

The Turner Society

BCM Box Turner, London WC1N 3XX
Chairman Eric Shanes
Membership £20 p.a.

Aims to foster a wider appreciation of all facets of the work of J.M.W. Turner RA (1775–1851); to encourage exhibitions of his paintings, drawings and engravings. Publishes *Turner Society News* (3 p.a.). Founded 1975.

Ver Poets

Secretary Daphne Schiller, 15 Brampton Road, St Albans, Herts. AL1 4PP
email daphne.schiller@virgin.net
Contact Daphne Schiller

Membership £15 p.a. UK, £20 overseas, £10 students

Encourages the writing and study of poetry. Holds evening meetings and daytime workshops in the St Albans area. Local and postal members. Holds members' competitions and the annual Open Competition. Founded 1966.

Visiting Arts

Bloomsbury House, 74–77 Great Russell Street, London WC1B 3DA
tel 020-7291 1600 *fax* 020-7291 1616
email information@visitingarts.org.uk
website www.visitingarts.org.uk
Director Yvette Vaughan Jones

Aims to strengthen intercultural understanding through the arts. It provides information and intelligence in order to strengthen intercultural dialogue, and creates opportunities to experience intercultural exploration. This is done through mediated performances, exhibitions, and by initiating and promoting collaborations. Visiting Arts seeks to expand the skills and knowledge of existing cultural players and develop new talent to ensure a wide, diverse and sustainable group of players.

Visiting Arts creates, produces and distributes authoritative directories and help-sheets, targeted briefings and the latest advice through print, web and word of mouth. It organises seminars, conferences and networking events to deepen intercultural understanding; establishes and fosters opportunities for ground-breaking artist exchanges; promotes cutting edge exhibitions; and contributes to some of the world's biggest and most innovative festivals. It works with the most exciting next generation of artists and cultural players, inviting them to the UK, expanding knowledge and horizons and championing intercultural working.

Visiting Arts is an independent registered charity. It is funded by the British Council, Arts Council England, the Scottish Arts Council, the Arts Council of Wales, the Arts Council of Northern Ireland and the Department of Culture, Media and Sport. Founded 1977.

Voice of the Listener & Viewer Ltd (VLV)

101 King's Drive, Gravesend, Kent DA12 5BQ
tel (01474) 352835 *fax* (01474) 351112
email info@vlv.org.uk
website www.vlv.org.uk
Chairman Jocelyn Hay, *Administrative Secretary* Sue Washbrook

Represents the citizen and consumer interests in broadcasting: it is an independent, non-profit-making society working to ensure independence, quality and diversity in broadcasting. VLV is funded by its members and is free from sectarian, commercial and political affiliations. It holds public lectures, seminars and conferences, and has frequent contact with MPs and other relevant parties. It provides an independent forum where all with an interest in broadcasting can speak on equal terms. It produces a quarterly news bulletin and holds its own archive and those of the former Broadcasting Research Unit (1980–90) and BACTV (British Action for Children's Television). It maintains a panel of speakers, the VLV Forum for Children's Broadcasting, the VLV Forum for Educational Broadcasting, and acts as a secretariat for the European Alliance of Listeners' and Viewers' Associations (EURALVA). VLV does not handle complaints. Founded 1984.

The Walmsley Society

Secretary Fred Lane, April Cottage, 1 Brand Road, Hampden Park, Eastbourne, East Sussex BN22 9PX
Membership Secretary Mrs Elizabeth Buckley, 21 The Crescent, Hipperholm, Halifax, West Yorkshire HX3 8NQ

Aims to promote and encourage an appreciation of the literary and artistic heritage left to us by Leo Walmsley (1892–1966) and J. Ulric Walmsley (1860–1954). Founded 1985.

Mary Webb Society

Secretary Sue Higginbotham, 8 The Knowe, Willaston, Neston, Cheshire CH64 1TA
tel 0151-327 5843
email suehigginbotham@yahoo.co.uk
website www.marywebb.vze.com

For devotees of the literature and works of Mary Webb (1881–1927) and of the beautiful Shropshire countryside of her novels. Publishes a bi-annual Journal, organises summer schools and other events in various locations related to Webb's life and works. Archives, lectures; tours arranged for individuals and groups. Founded 1972.

The H.G. Wells Society

Hon. General Secretary Steve McLean, 56 Riseholme Road, Gainsborough, Lincs. DN21 1YT
email stevemclean7@hotmail.com
website www.hgwellsusa.50megs.com
Membership £16 p.a., £19 corporate

Promotes an active interest in and an appreciation of the life, work and thought of H.G. Wells (1866–1946). Publishes *The Wellsian* (annual) and *The Newsletter* (bi-annual). Founded 1960.

Welsh Academy – see Academi (Welsh Academy)

Welsh Books Council/Cyngor Llyfrau Cymru

Castell Brychan, Aberystwyth, Ceredigion SY23 2JB
tel (01970) 624151 *fax* (01970) 625385
email castellbrychan@cllc.org.uk
website www.cllc.org.uk, www.gwales.com

Director Gwerfyl Pierce Jones

A national body funded directly by the Welsh Asssembly Government which provides a focus for the publishing industry in Wales. Awards grants for publishing in Welsh and English. Provides services to the trade in the fields of editing, design, marketing and distribution. The Council is a key enabling institution in the world of books and provides services and information in this field to all who are associated with it. Founded 1961.

The West Country Writers' Association

Secretary Sue Bury, 6 The Beals, Greenway, Woodbury, Exeter, Devon EX5 1LU
tel (01395) 233753
website www.westcountrywriters.co.uk
President Lady Rachel Billington, *Chair* Roy York
Membership Open to published authors, joining fee plus first year membership £20 – thereafter £10 p.a.

Aims to foster love of literature in the West Country and to give authors an opportunity of meeting to exchange news and views. Holds Annual Weekend Congress and Regional Meetings. Plus newsletters.

The Oscar Wilde Society

100 Peacock Street, Gravesend, Kent DA12 1EQ
email vanessasalome68@aol.com
Secretary Vanessa Harris

Aims to promote knowledge, appreciation and study of the life, personality and works of the writer and wit Oscar Wilde (1854–1900). Activities include meetings, lectures, readings and exhibitions, and visits to associated locations. Members receive a journal, *The Wildean* (2 p.a.), and a newsletter, *Intentions* (6 p.a.). Founded 1990.

Charles Williams Society

Secretary Richard Sturch, 35 Broomfield, Stacey Bushes, Milton Keynes MK12 6HA
email charles_wms_soc@yahoo.co.uk
website www.geocities.com/charles_wms_soc

Aims to promote interest in the life and work of Charles Walter Stansby Williams (1886–1945) and to make his writings more easily available. Founded 1975.

The Henry Williamson Society

General Secretary Sue Cumming, 7 Monmouth Road, Dorchester, Dorset DT1 2DE
tel (01305) 264092
email zseagull@aol.com
Membership Secretary Margaret Murphy, 16 Doran Drive, Redhill, Surrey RH1 6AX
tel (01737) 763228
email mm@misterman.freeserve.co.uk
website www.henrywilliamson.org
Chairman John Gregory
Membership £12 p.a.

Aims to encourage a wider readership and greater understanding of the literary heritage left by Henry

Williamson (1895–1977). Two meetings annually; also weekend activities. Publishes an annual journal. Founded 1980.

The P.G. Wodehouse Society (UK)
Details Tony Ring, 34 Longfield, Great Missenden, Bucks. HP16 0EG
tel (01494) 864848
email tring@sauce34.freeserve.co.uk
website www.eclipse.co.uk/wodehouse
Membership £15 p.a.

Aims to promote enjoyment of P.G. Wodehouse (1881–1975). Publishes *Wooster Sauce* (quarterly) and *By The Way* papers (3 p.a.) which cover diverse subjects of Wodehousean interest. Holds events, entertainments and meetings throughout Britain. Founded 1997.

Women in Publishing (WiP)
c/o Gill Rowley, 3 Gordon Road, London W5 2AD
email info@wipub.org.uk
website www.wipub.org.uk
Membership £25 p.a.

Promotes the status of women within publishing; encourages networking and mutual support among women; provides a forum for the discussion of ideas, trends and subjects to women in the trade; offers advice on publishing careers; supports and publicises women's achievements and successes. Each year WiP presents 2 awards: the Pandora Award is given in recognition of significant personal contributions to women in publishing, and the New Venture Award is presented to a recent venture which reflects the interests and concerns of women or minority groups in the 21st century. Founded 1979.

Women Writers Network
Membership Secretary Cathy Smith, 23 Prospect Road, London NW2 2JU
tel 020-7794 5861
website www.womenwriters.org.uk
Membership £45 p.a.; meetings only: £5 at door

London-based network serving both salaried and independent women writers from all disciplines, and providing a forum for the exchange of information, support and networking opportunities. Holds monthly meetings, workshops and publishes a Newsletter and members' online Directory. Send sae for information. Founded 1985.

Virginia Woolf Society of Great Britain
Details Stuart N. Clarke, Fairhaven, Charnleys Lane, Banks, Southport PR9 8HJ
tel (01903) 764655 *fax* (01903) 764655
email snclarke@talk21.com
website http://orlando.jp.org/vwsgb/
Membership £15 p.a., £20 overseas

Acts as a forum for British admirers of Virginia Woolf (1882–1941) to meet, correspond and share their enjoyment of her work. Publishes the *Virginia Woolf Bulletin*. Founded 1998.

The Wordsworth Trust
Dove Cottage, Grasmere, Cumbria LA22 9SH
tel (015394) 35544 *fax* (015394) 35748
email enquiries@wordsworth.org.uk
website www.wordsworth.org.uk
Membership Officer Eleanor Pownall
Membership £20 p.a.

To preserve and enhance Dove Cottage, the Collection and the historic environment of Town End for future generations; to give people of all ages the chance to fulfill their creative potential; to develop the education and lifelong learning programmes for the benefit of the widest possible audience. Founded 1891.

Worshipful Company of Stationers and Newspaper Makers
Stationers' Hall, London EC4M 7DD
tel 020-7248 2934 *fax* 020-7489 1975
Master G.R. Neville Cusworth, *Clerk* Brig. Denzil Sharp AFC

One of the Livery Companies of the City of London. Connected with the printing, publishing, bookselling, newspaper and allied trades. Founded 1403.

Writernet
(formerly New Playwrights Trust)
Cabin V, Clarendon Buildings, 25 Horsell Road, London N5 1XL
tel 020-7609 7474 *fax* 020-7609 7557
email info@writernet.org.uk
website www.writernet.org.uk
Director Jonathan Meth, *Chair* Bonnie Greer, *Administrator* Anne-Marie Draycott

Provides writers for all forms of live and recorded performance – working at any stage in their career, and in diverse contexts – with a range of services that enable them to pursue their careers better. These include: a network connecting dramatic writers to the industry and to each other; online resources to support dramatic writers and those who work with them; providing a wide range of producers with the opportunity to make more informed choices to meet their needs; as well as a script-reading service, publications and guides. It aims to help writers from all parts of the country and a wide diversity of backgrounds to fulfil their potential both inside and outside the new-writing mainstream. Founded 1985.

Writers Advice Centre for Children's Books
16 Smith's Yard, Summerley Street, London SW18 4NR
tel (07979) 9905353
email info@writersadvice.co.uk
website www.writersadvice.co.uk

Editorial Director Louise Jordan

Dedicated to helping new and published children's writers by offering both editorial advice and tips on how to get published. The Centre also runs an online children's writing correspondence course plus a self-publishing service under its own imprint. Founded 1994.

Writers Guild of America, East Inc. (WGAE)

Executive Director Mona Mangan, 555 West 57 Street, Suite 1230, New York, NY 10019, USA
tel 212-767-7800
Membership 1.5% of covered earnings

Represents writers in screen and TV for collective bargaining. It provides member services including pension and health, as well as educational and professional activities. Founded 1954.

Writers Guild of America, West Inc. (WGA)

7000 West 3rd Street, Los Angeles, CA 90048, USA
tel 323-951-4000 *fax* 323-782-4800
website www.wga.org
Membership $2500 initiation, $25 quarterly, 1.5% of income annually

Union representing and servicing 9000 writers in film, broadcast, cable and multimedia industries for purposes of collective bargaining, contract administration and other services, and functions to protect and advance the economic, professional and creative interests of writers. Monthly publication, *Written By*, available by subscription. Founded 1933.

Writers Guild of Canada

366 Adelaide Street West, Suite 401, Toronto, Ontario M5V 1R9, Canada
tel 416-979-7907 *toll free* 1-800-567-9974 *fax* 416-979-9273
email info@wgc.ca
website www.wgc.ca
Executive Director Maureen Parker
Membership One-off initiation fee of $350 + $150 p.a. + 2% of fees earned in the Guild's jurisdiction

Represents over 1800 professional writers of film, TV, animation, radio, documentary and new media. Negotiates and administers collective agreements with independent producers as well as the CBC, TVO and NFB. The Guild also publishes *Canadian Screenwriter* magazine.

The Writers' Guild of Great Britain – see The Writers' Guild of Great Britain.

Writers in Oxford

email mail@summers.net
website www.writersinoxford.org

Chair Julie Summers
Membership £25 p.a.

Promotes discussion and social meetings among published writers in and around Oxfordshire. Activities include: topical lunches and dinners, where subjects important to the writer are discussed; outings and parties. Publishes a regular newsletter, *The Oxford Writer*. Founded 1992.

The Writers' Union of Canada

90 Richmond Street East, Suite 200, Toronto, Ontario M5C 1P1
tel 416-703-8982 *fax* 416-504-9090
email info@writersunion.ca
website www.writersunion.ca

Yachting Journalists' Association

Editor Barry Pickthall, Booker's Yard, The Street, Walberton, Arundel, West Sussex BN18 0PF
tel (01243) 555561 *fax* (01243) 555562
email ppl@mistral.co.uk
website www.yja.co.uk
Membership £40 p.a.

Aims to further the interests of yachting, sail and power, and yachting journalism. Members vote annually for the Yachtsman of the Year and the Young Sailor of the Year Award. Founded 1969.

The Yorkshire Dialect Society

Hon. Secretary Michael Park, 51 Stepney Avenue, Scarborough YO12 5BW
website www.ydsociety.org.uk
Membership £10 p.a.

Aims to encourage interest in: dialect speech, the writing of dialect verse, prose and drama; the publication and circulation of dialect literature; the study of the origins and the history of dialect and kindred subjects. Organises meetings; publishes *Transactions* (annual) and *The Summer Bulletin* free to members; list of other publications on request. Founded 1897.

Francis Brett Young Society

Secretary Mrs J. Hadley, 92 Gower Road, Halesowen, West Midlands B62 9BT
tel 0121-422 8969
website www.fbysociety.co.uk
Membership £7 p.a., £70 p.a. life

Aims to provide opportunities for members to meet, correspond, and to share the enjoyment of the works of Francis Brett Young (1884–1954). Publishes a journal (2 p.a.). Founded 1979.

Prizes and awards

This list provides details of many British prizes, competitions and awards for writers and artists, including grants, bursaries and fellowships, as well as details of major international prizes. See page 775 for a quick reference to its contents.

J.R. Ackerley Prize for Autobiography

English PEN, 6–8 Amwell Street, London EC1R 1UQ
tel 020-7713 0023 *fax* 020-7837 7838
email enquiries@englishpen.org
website www.englishpen.org

An annual prize of £1000 is given for an outstanding work of literary autobiography written in English and published during the previous year by an author of British nationality or an author who has been a long-term resident in the UK. No submissions: books are nominated by the judges only. Founded 1982.

The Alexander Prize

Executive Secretary, Royal Historical Society, University College London, Gower Street, London WC1E 6BT
tel 020-7387 7532 *fax* 020-7387 7532
email royalhistsoc@ucl.ac.uk, rhs.info@sas.ac.uk
website www.rhs.ac.uk

An annual prize of £250 is awarded for a published scholarly journal article or an essay in a collective volume based upon original historical research.

The Hans Christian Andersen Awards

Details International Board on Books for Young People, Nonnenweg 12, Postfach, CH–4003 Basel, Switzerland
tel (61) 272 29 17 *fax* (61) 272 27 57
email ibby@ibby.org
website www.ibby.org

The Medals are awarded every 2 years to a living author and an illustrator who by the outstanding value of their work are judged to have made a lasting contribution to literature for children and young people.

Artists' Residencies in Tuscany

Enquiries JGT, 31 Addison Avenue, London W11 4QS
email info@julietgompertstrust.co.uk
website www.julietgompertstrust.com

Annual bursaries (value up to £2000) provide board, lodging and studio facilities at the Centro Verrocchio in Italy. Also, small grants to support experimental projects on specified themes. Available by competitive application. Open to artists aged 25–45 (UK only). Funded by the Juliet Gomperts Memorial Trust. Closing date: end of January. Send sae for further details.

Arts Council England

Details The Literature Dept, Arts Council England, 14 Great Peter Street, London SW1P 3NQ

tel (0845) 300 6200 *textphone* 020-7973 6564
fax 020-7973 6590
email enquiries@artscouncil.org.uk
website www.artscouncil.org.uk

Arts Council England presents national prizes rewarding creative talent in the arts. These are awarded through the Council's flexible funds and are not necessarily open to application: the Children's Award, the David Cohen Prize for Literature, the Independent Foreign Fiction Prize, John Whiting Award, Meyer Whitworth Award and the Raymond Williams Community Publishing Prize. See the separate entries for details.

Arts Council England, London

Details David Cross, Literature Administrator, Arts Council England, London, 2 Pear Tree Court, London EC1R 0DS
tel 020-7608 6184 *fax* 020-7608 4100
website www.artscouncil.org.uk

Arts Council, England, London, is the regional office for the Capital, covering 33 boroughs and the City of London. Grants are available through the 'Grants for the arts' scheme throughout the year to support a variety of literature projects, concentrating particularly on:
• original works of poetry and literary fiction and professional development for individual writers, including writers of children's books;
• touring and live literature;
• small independent literary publishers; and
• literary translation into English.
    Contact Literature Unit for more information or see website for an application form.

Arts Council/An Chomhairle Ealaíon

Details 70 Merrion Square, Dublin 2, Republic of Ireland
tel (01) 618 0200 *fax* (01) 676 1302
email artistsservices@artscouncil.ie
website www.artscouncil.ie

Publishes a guide for individuals and organisations to Arts Council bursaries, awards and schemes. It is also available online. This guide is called Supports for Artists.

Arvon Foundation International Poetry Competition

Details Arvon Foundation Poetry Competition, 2nd Floor, 42A Buckingham Palace Road, London SW1W 0RE

tel 020-7931 7611
email comps@arvonfoundation.org

A biennial competition for previously unpublished poems written in English. First prize £5000, plus at least £5000 in other cash prizes. Next competition: spring 2008. Founded 1980.

The Asham Award

Details The Administrator, Asham Literary Endowment Trust, c/o Town Hall, High Street, Lewes, East Sussex BN7 2QS
website www.ashamaward.com

A biennial national short story competition for women writers over the age of 18 and currently resident in the UK who have not previously had a novel or anthology published. Winners receive a cash prize and inclusion in an anthology published by Bloomsbury. Next competition will be launched in April 2007; see website for details. Founded 1996.

The Australian/Vogel Literary Award

PO Box 8500, St Leonards, NSW 1590, Australia
website www.allenandunwin.com

An annual award of $20,000 for a chosen unpublished work of fiction, Australian history or biography. Entrants must be under 35 years of age on the closing date and must normally be residents of Australia. The MS must be between 30,000 and 100,000 words and must be an original work entirely by the entrant written in English. It cannot be under consideration to any publisher or award. See website for details. Closing date: 31 May. Founded 1980.

Authors' Club Awards

Details Stella Kane, Secretary, Authors' Club, 40 Dover Street, London W1S 4NP
tel 020-7499 8581 *fax* 020-7409 0913
email authors@theartsclub.co.uk, stellakane@theartsclub.co.uk

Best First Novel Award

An award of £1000 is presented at a dinner held in the Club, to the author of the most promising first novel published in the UK during each year. Entries are accepted during October and must be full-length novels – short stories are not eligible. Instituted by Lawrence Meynell in 1954.

Sir Banister Fletcher Award for Authors' Club

The late Sir Banister Fletcher, a former President of both the Authors' Club and the Royal Institute of British Architects instituted an annual prize 'for the book on architecture or the arts most deserving'. The award is made on the recommendation of the Professional Literature Committee of RIBA, to whom nominations for eligible titles (i.e. those written by British authors or those resident in the UK and published under a British imprint) should be submitted by the end of May of the year after publication. The prize of £1000 is awarded by the Authors' Club during September. First awarded in 1954.

Dolman Best First Travel Book Award

An award of £1000 is presented annually for the best first literary travel book (no guidebooks accepted). Instituted by William Dolman in 2005.

The Authors' Contingency Fund

Details Awards Secretary, The Society of Authors, 84 Drayton Gardens, London SW10 9SB
tel 020-7373 6642 *fax* 020-7373 5768
email info@societyofauthors.org
website www.societyofauthors.org

This fund makes modest grants to published authors who find themselves in sudden financial difficulties. Apply for an information sheet and application form.

The Authors' Foundation

The Society of Authors, 84 Drayton Gardens, London SW10 9SB
tel 020-7373 6642
email info@societyofauthors.org
website www.societyofauthors.org

Grants are available to novelists, poets and writers of non-fiction who are published authors working on their next book. The aim is to provide funding (in addition to a proper advance) for research, travel or other necessary expenditure. Closing dates: 30 April and 30 September. Send sae for an information sheet. Founded in 1984 to mark the centenary of the Society of Authors.

The Aventis Prizes for Science Books

Details The Royal Society, 6–9 Carlton House Terrace, London SW1Y 5AG
tel 020-7451 2513 *fax* 020-7451 2693
email scott.keir@royalsoc.ac.uk
website www.sciencebookprizes.com

These annual prizes reward books that make science more accessible to readers of all ages and backgrounds. Prizes of up to a total of £30,000 are awarded in 2 categories: General (£10,000) for a book with a general readership; and Junior (£10,000) for a book written for people aged under 14. Up to 5 shortlisted authors in each category receive £1000.

Eligible books should be written in English and their first publication in the UK must have been between 1 January and 31 December each year. Seven copies of each entry should be supplied with a fully completed entry form. Publishers may submit any number of books for each prize. Entries may cover any aspect of science and technology but educational textbooks published for professional or specialist audiences are not eligible. The Prizes are managed by the Royal Society in cooperation with the sponsor, Aventis. Founded 1988.

BAFTA (British Academy of Film and Television Arts) Awards

Chief Executive Amanda Berry, 195 Piccadilly, London W1J 9LN

tel 020-7734 0022 *fax* 020-7292 5868
email reception@bafta.org
website www.bafta.org

The pre-eminent organisation in the UK for film, TV and interactive, recognising and promoting the achievement and endeavour of industry practitioners. BAFTA Awards are awarded annually by members to their peers in recognition of their skills and expertise. Founded 1947.

BA/Nielsen BookData Author of the Year

Details The Booksellers Association of the UK and Ireland Ltd, 272 Vauxhall Bridge Road, London SW1V 1BA
tel 020-7802 0802 *fax* 020-7802 0803
Nielsen BookData, 3rd Floor, Midas House, 62 Goldsworth Road, Woking, Surrey GU21 6LQ
tel (0870) 7778710 *fax* (0870) 7778711

This annual award of £1000 is judged by members of the Booksellers Association in a postal ballot. Any living, British or Irish published writer is eligible and the award is given to the author judged to have had the most impact on the bookselling trade in the year. Founded 1993.

Bardd Plant Cymru (Children's Poet Laureate)

Welsh Books Council, Castell Brychan, Aberystwyth, Ceredigion SY23 2JB
tel (01970) 624151 *fax* (01970) 625385
website www.cllc.org.uk

The main aim is to raise the profile of poetry amongst children and to encourage them to compose and enjoy poetry. Tudur Dylan Jones is Bardd Plant Cymru 2004–5. During his term of office he will visit schools as well as helping children to create poetry through electronic workshops. Established by Planed Plant, S4C, the Welsh Books Council and Urdd Gobaith Cymru; recently the Academi became part of the partnership.

Verity Bargate Award

Details Literary Assistant, Soho Theatre *and* Writers' Centre, 21 Dean Street, London W1D 3NE
email writers@sohotheatre.com
website www.sohotheatre.com

This biennial award is made to the writer of a new and previously unperformed full-length play. It is the only award in the UK designed specifically for emerging writers and is only eligible to playwrights with less than 3 professional credits. The winner receives: a prize of £3500, a residency at the Soho Theatre, and the prize-winning play may be professionally produced by the Soho Theatre Company. Next award: 2006/7. Established 1982.

BBC FOUR Samuel Johnson Prize for Non-Fiction

Colman Getty PR, Middlesex House, 34–42 Cleveland Street, London W1T 4JE

tel 020-7631 2666 *fax* 020-7631 2699
email hannah@colmangettypr.co.uk
website www.colmangettypr.co.uk
Contact Hannah Blake

This annual prize is the biggest non-fiction prize in the UK and is worth £30,000. Eligible books published between 1 May 2005 and 30 April 2006 are submitted by publishers. Closing date: mid January. The winner is announced in June. Sponsored by BBC FOUR. Founded 1999.

The David Berry Prize

Executive Secretary of the Royal Historical Society, University College London, Gower Street, London WC1E 6BT
tel 020-7387 7532 *fax* 020-7387 7532
email royalhistsoc@ucl.ac.uk, rhs.info@sas.ac.uk
website www.rhs.ac.uk

Candidates may select any subject dealing with Scottish history. Value of prize: £250. Closing date: 31 October each year.

Besterman/McColvin Medals – see The ISG (CILIP)/BookData Reference Awards

Biscuit International Short Fiction Prize

Details Biscuit Publishing, PO Box 123, Washington, Newcastle upon Tyne NE37 2YW
email info@biscuitpublishing.com
website www.biscuitpublishing.com
Director Brian Lister

Outright short story winner has his/her novella (40,000 words) or a short story collection published and £1000 advance royalties. Write for set of rules. Closing date: 31 May each year. Founded 2001.

The Bisto Book of the Year Awards – see The CBI Bisto Book of the Year Awards

The Kathleen Blundell Trust

Kathleen Blundell Trust, The Society of Authors, 84 Drayton Gardens, London SW10 9SB
tel 020-7373 6642
email info@societyofauthors.org
website www.societyofauthors.org

Awards are given to published writers under the age of 40 to assist them with their next book. The author's work must 'contribute to the greater understanding of existing social and economic organisation', but fiction is not excluded. Closing dates: 30 April and 30 September. Send sae for an information sheet.

The Boardman Tasker Prize

Details Maggie Body, Pound House, Llangennith, Swansea SA3 1JQ
email margaretbody@lineone.net
website www.boardmantasker.co.uk

This annual prize of £2000 is given for a work of fiction, non-fiction or poetry, the central theme of which is concerned with the mountain environment. Authors of any nationality are eligible but the work must be published or distributed in the UK. Entries from publishers only. Founded 1983.

The Bollinger Everyman Wodehouse Prize for Comic Fiction

Submissions Lois Tucker, Colman Getty PR, Middlesex House, 34–42 Cleveland Street, London, W1T 4JE
tel 020-7631 2666 *fax* 020-7631 2699
email lois@colmangettypr.co.uk

The UK's only prize for comic fiction will be awarded to the most original comic novel – the book that has really made people laugh over the previous 12 months. The winner will receive a case of Bollinger Special Cuvée, a jeroboam of Bollinger, a complete set of the Everyman Wodehouse and a rare breed pig named after the winning novel. Eligible are novels published in the UK between 1 May and 30 April (tbc). The winner will be announced at the Guardian Hay Festival in late May/early June. Closing date: early March (tbc); the shortlist will be announced in mid April. Launched in 2000 on the 25th anniversary of the death of P.G. Wodehouse.

Booktrust Early Years Awards

Details Booktrust, Book House, 45 East Hill, London SW18 2QZ
tel 020-8516 2972/2960 *fax* 020-8516 2978
email tarryn@booktrust.org.uk, helen@booktrust.org.uk
website www.booktrusted.org.uk
Contacts Tarryn McKay, Helen Hayes

The winners of each of 3 categories, Baby Book Award, Pre-School Award and Best New Illustrator, will each receive £2000. The winning publishers will also receive a commemorative award. Closing date: June 2007. Established 1999 (formerly the Sainsbury's Baby Book Award).

The Booktrust Teenage Prize

Details Booktrust, Book House, 45 East Hill, London SW18 2QZ
tel 020-8516 2986 *fax* 020-8516 2978
email hannah@booktrust.org.uk
website www.bookheads.org.uk
Contact Hannah Rutland

The first annual national book prize to recognise and celebrate the best in young adult fiction. The author of the best book for teenagers receives £2500 and is chosen from a shortlist of 6–8. Eligible books must be fiction, aimed at teenagers between the ages of 13 and 16 and written in English by a citizen of the UK, or an author resident in the UK. The work must be published between 1 July and 30 June by a UK publisher. Established 2003.

BP Portrait Award

Details National Portrait Gallery, St Martin's Place, London WC2H 0HE
tel 020-7306 0055 *fax* 020-7306 0056
website www.npg.org.uk

An annual award to encourage young artists (aged 18–40) to focus upon and develop the theme of portraiture within their work. 1st prize: £25,000 plus at the judges' discretion a commission worth £4000 to be agreed between the NPG and the artist; 2nd prize £6000; 3rd prize: £4000; 4th prize £2000. Closing date: March. A selection of entrants' work is exhibited at the National Portrait Gallery June–Oct. Founded 1978.

Alfred Bradley Bursary Award

Details BBC Radio Drama Department, BBC North, New Broadcasting House, Oxford Road, Manchester M60 1SJ
tel 0161-244 4253

This biennial bursary of £6000 (over 2 years, plus a full commission for a radio play) is awarded to a writer resident in the North of England who has had a small amount of work published or produced. The scheme also allows for a group of finalists to receive small bursaries and develop ideas for radio drama commissions. Next closing date: November 2008. Founded 1992.

The Branford Boase Award

Details The Administrator, 8 Bolderwood Close, Bishopstoke, Eastleigh SO50 5PG
tel (01962) 826658 *fax* (01962) 856615
email anne.marley@tiscali.co.uk
website www.branfordboaseaward.org.uk

An annual award of £1000 is made to a first-time writer of a full-length children's novel (age 7+) published in the preceding year; the editor is also recognised. Its aim is to encourage new writers for children and to recognise the role of perceptive editors in developing new talent. The Award was set up in memory of the outstanding children's writer Henrietta Branford and the gifted editor and publisher Wendy Boase who both died in 1999. Closing date for nominations: end of March of each year. Founded 2000.

The Bridport Prize

Details Bridport Arts Centre, South Street, Bridport, Dorset DT6 3NR
tel (01308) 485064 *fax* (01308) 485120
email frances@bridportprize.org.uk
website www.bridportprize.org.uk

Annual prizes are awarded for poetry and short stories – 1st £5000, 2nd £1000, 3rd £500 in both categories. Entries should be in English, original work, typed or clearly written, and never published, read on radio/TV/stage. Winning stories are read by a leading London literary agent, without obligation, and an anthology of winning entries is published each autumn. Send sae for entry form or enter online. Closing date: 30 June each year.

British Academy Medals and Prizes

The British Academy, 10 Carlton House Terrace,
London SW1Y 5AH
tel 020-7969 5200 *fax* 020-7969 5300
email secretary@britac.ac.uk
website www.britac.ac.uk

A number of medals and prizes are awarded for
outstanding work in various fields of the humanities
on the recommendation of specialist committees:
Burkitt Medal for Biblical Studies; Derek Allen Prize
(made annually in turn for musicology, numismatics
and Celtic studies); Sir Israel Gollancz Prize (for
English studies); Grahame Clark Medal for
Prehistoric Archaeology; Kenyon Medal for Classical
Studies; Rose Mary Crawshay Prize (for English
literature); Serena Medal for Italian Studies;
Leverhulme Medal and Prize.

British Book Awards

Details Merric Davidson, PO Box 60, Cranbrook,
Kent TN17 2ZR
tel (01580) 212041 *fax* (01580) 212041
email nibbies@mdla.co.uk
website www.britishbookawards.com

Referred to as the 'Nibbies' and presented annually,
major categories include: Author of the Year,
Publisher of the Year, Bookseller of the Year,
Children's Book of the Year. Founded 1989.

British Council Grants to Artists Scheme

Details Grants to Artists Officer, Visual Arts Dept,
British Council, 10 Spring Gardens, London
SW1A 2BN
tel 020-7389 3045 *fax* 020-7389 3101
website www.britishcouncil.org/arts

The Visual Arts Department of the British Council is
concerned with the promotion and presentation of
UK art overseas. These awards (£100–£2000) are
specifically aimed at UK visual artists who have been
invited to exhibit their work abroad. It is there to
help with the costs of the artists' travel and the
transport and packaging of their work. Artists should
submit a completed application form, CV, 6 slides of
their work and a letter of invitation from the overseas
venue before the deadline. The committee meets 3–4
weeks after this to decide on all the applications.
Closing dates: 1 February, 1 May, 1 August, 1
November.

British Press Awards

Press Gazette, 10 Old Bailey, London EC4M 4NG
tel 020-7489 1469 *fax* 020-7038 1155
website www.britishpressawards.com

Annual awards for British journalism judged by more
than 80 respected, influential judges as well as
representatives from all the national newspaper
groups. Closing date: mid January 2007.

The Caine Prize for African Writing

Details Nick Elam, Administrator, The Menier
Gallery, Menier Chocolate Factory, 51 Southwark
Street, London SE5 1AU
tel 020-7378 6234 *fax* 020-7378 6235
email info@caineprize.com
website www.caineprize.com

An annual award of $15,000 for a short story
published in English (may be a translation into
English) by an African writer in the 5 years before the
closing date, and not previously submitted. Indicative
length 3000–15,000 words. Submissions only by
publishers. Closing date: 31 January each year.
Founded 1999.

Cardiff International Poetry Competition

Details/entry form Cardiff International Poetry
Competition, PO Box 438, Cardiff CF10 5YA
website www.academi.org

Eight prizes totalling £7000 are awarded annually for
unpublished poetry written in English (prizes: 1st
£5000; 2nd £700; 3rd £300; plus 5 prizes of £200).
Entry forms may also be downloaded from the
website. Closing date: January 2007.

Carnegie Medal – see The CILIP Carnegie and Kate Greenaway Awards

The CBI Bisto Book of the Year Awards

Details The Administrator, Children's Books Ireland,
17 Great Georges Street, Dublin 1, Republic of
Ireland
tel (01) 8727475 *fax* (01) 8727476
email info@childrensbooksireland.com
website www.childrensbooksireland.com

Annual awards open to authors and/or illustrators
who were born in Ireland, or who were living in
Ireland at the time of a book's publication. Closing
date: December 2006 for work published between 1
January and 31 December 2006. Founded 1990.

The CBI Bisto Book of the Year Award

An award of €6000 is presented to the overall winner
(text and/or illustration).

The CBI Bisto Merit Awards

A prize fund of €3000 is divided between 3 authors
and/or illustrators.

The CBI Bisto Eilís Dillon Award

An award of €3000 is presented to an author for a
first children's book.

The Children's Laureate

Details Booktrust, Book House, 45 East Hill, London
SW18 2QZ
tel 023-8516 2985 *fax* 020-8516 2978
email childrenslaureate@booktrust.org.uk

website www.childrenslaureate.org,
www.booktrust.org

A biennial award of £10,000 to honour a writer or illustrator of children's books for a lifetime's achievement. It highlights the importance of children's book creators in developing readers and illustrators of the future. Children's Laureates: Jacqueline Wilson (2005–7), Michael Morpurgo (2003–5), Anne Fine (2001–3), Quentin Blake (1999–2001). Founded 1998.

Cholmondeley Awards

Administered by The Society of Authors, 84 Drayton Gardens, London SW10 9SB

These honorary awards are to recognise the achievement and distinction of individual poets. Submissions are not accepted. Total value of awards about £8000. Established by the then Dowager Marchioness of Cholmondeley in 1965.

The CILIP Carnegie and Kate Greenaway Awards

email marketing@cilip.org.uk
website www.ckg.org.uk

Recommendations for the following 2 awards are invited from members of CILIP (the Chartered Institute of Library and Information Professionals), who are asked to submit a preliminary list of not more than 2 titles for each award, accompanied by a 50-word appraisal justifying the recommendation of each book. The awards are selected by the Youth Libraries Group of CILIP.

Carnegie Medal

Awarded annually for an outstanding book for children (fiction or non-fiction) written in English and first published in the UK during the preceding year or co-published elsewhere within a 3-month time lapse.

Kate Greenaway Medal

Awarded annually for an outstanding illustrated book for children first published in the UK during the preceding year or co-published elsewhere within a 3-month time lapse. Books intended for older as well as younger children are included, and reproduction will be taken into account. The Colin Mears Award (£5000) is awarded annually to the winner of the Kate Greenaway Medal.

Arthur C. Clarke Award

Details Paul Kincaid, 60 Bournemouth Road, Folkestone, Kent CT19 5AZ
email arthurcclarkeaward@yahoo.co.uk
website www.clarkeaward.com

An annual award of £2007 plus engraved bookend is given for the best science fiction novel with first UK publication during the previous calendar year. Titles are submitted by publishers. Founded 1985.

The David Cohen Prize for Literature

Details The Literature Dept, Arts Council England, 14 Great Peter Street, London SW1P 3NQ
tel 020-7973 5325
website www.artscouncil.org.uk

This biennial prize marks a lifetime's literary achievement. The winner receives £40,000 plus an additional £12,500 to support a young writer.

Commonwealth Writers Prize

Details Booktrust, Book House, 45 East Hill, London SW18 2QZ
tel 020-8516 2986 *fax* 020-8516 2978
email hannah@booktrust.org.uk
Contact Hannah Rutland

This annual award is for the best work of fiction in English by a citizen of the Commonwealth published in the year prior to the award. A prize of £10,000 is awarded for overall best book and £3000 is awarded to the overall best first published book. The overall winners are selected from 8 regional winners who each receive £1000 for being regional winners. Sponsored by the Commonwealth Foundation. Established 1987.

The Duff Cooper Prize

Details Artemis Cooper, 54 St Maur Road, London SW6 4DP
tel 020-7736 3729 *fax* 020-7731 7638

An annual prize for a literary work in the field of biography, history, politics or poetry published in English or French and submitted by a recognised publisher during the previous 12 months. The prize of £4000 comes from a Trust Fund established by the friends and admirers of Duff Cooper, 1st Viscount Norwich (1890–1954) after his death.

Cordon d'Or – Gold Ribbon Awards

PO Box 40660, St Petersburg, FL 33743–0660, USA
website www.goldribboncookery.com
Contact Noreen Kinney, President

Awards for culinary writers, journalists, photographers and magazines. Overall winner receives $1000. See website for details. Founded 2003.

Costa Book Awards

(formerly the Whitbread Book Awards)
Details Anna O'Kane, The Booksellers Association, Minster House, 272 Vauxhall Bridge Road, London SW1V 1BA
tel 020-7802 0801 *fax* 020-7802 0803
email anna.okane@booksellers.org.uk
website www.costabookawards.co.uk

The awards celebrate and promote the most enjoyable contemporary British writing. Judged in 2 stages and offering a total of £50,000 prize money, there are 5 categories: Novel, First Novel, Biography, Poetry and Children's. They are judged by a panel of

3 judges and the winner in each category receives £5000. Nine final judges then choose the Costa Book of the Year from the 5 category winners. The overall winner receives £25,000. Writers must be resident in Great Britain or Ireland for 3 or more years. Submissions must be received from publishers. Closing date: end of June.

The Rose Mary Crawshay Prizes

The British Academy, 10 Carlton House Terrace, London SW1Y 5AH
tel 020-7969 5200 fax 020-7969 5300
email secretary@britac.ac.uk
website www.britac.ac.uk

One or more prizes are awarded each year to women of any nationality who, in the judgement of the Council of the British Academy, have written or published within the 3 calendar years immediately preceding the date of the award an historical or critical work of sufficient value on any subject connected with English literature, preference being given to a work regarding Byron, Shelley or Keats. Founded 1888.

The John D. Criticos Prize

Coordinator Michael Moschos, The London Hellenic Society, 11 Stormont Road, London N6 4NS
fax 020-8442 7000

A prize of £10,000 will be awarded to an artist, writer or researcher for an original work on Hellenic culture. Areas of particular interest are archaeology, art, art history, history and literature. No application necessary: send 2 copies of book plus covering letter. Closing date: 31 January. Founded 1996.

CWA Awards

email secretary@thecwa.co.uk
website www.thecwa.co.uk

Awards for crime writing: the Cartier Diamond Dagger; the New Blood Dagger; the Duncan Lawrie Dagger for Fiction; the Gold Dagger for Non-Fiction; the CWA Ellis Peters Historical Award; the Debut Dagger; the Ian Fleming Steel Dagger, the Dagger in the Library. See website for details.

The Rhys Davies Trust

Details Prof Meic Stephens, The Secretary, The Rhys Davies Trust, 10 Heol Don, Whitchurch, Cardiff CF14 2AU
tel 029-2062 3359 fax 029-2052 9202

The Trust aims to foster Welsh writing in English and offers financial assistance to English-language literary projects in Wales, directly or in association with other bodies.

Deutsche Borse Photography Prize

The Photographers' Gallery, 5 Great Newport Street, London WC2H 7HY
tel 020-7831 1772 fax 020-7836 9704
email info@photonet.org.uk
website www.photonet.org.uk

Aims to reward a living photographer, of any nationality, who has made the most significant contribution to the medium of photography during the past year (1st prize £30,000; 3 runners up will each receive £3000). Photographers will be nominated for a significant exhibition that took place or publication that was published in Europe during that time, and 4 shortlisted photographers will be selected and invited to present their work in an exhibition at the Gallery. Founded in 1996 by the Photographers' Gallery.

The Dundee International Book Prize

Details Kavin Johnston, Dundee City Council, Economic Development, 3 City Square, Dundee DD1 3BA
tel (01382) 434214 fax (01382) 434650
email book.prize@dundeecity.gov.uk
website www.dundeebookprize.com

A biennial prize (£10,000 and the chance of publication by Polygon) awarded for an unpublished novel. Next award: 2007. Founded 1996.

EAC Art Awards for the Over 60s

Details PO Box 279, Esher, Surrey KT10 8YZ
tel (01372) 462190 fax (01372) 460032
website www.parkerharris.co.uk

An annual competition to promote and celebrate the talents of older people. Open to all amateur artists over the age of 60 in painting, drawing, 3D work and photography. Prizes will be awarded to a range of categories. Closing date: May 2007. Founded 1995.

The T.S. Eliot Prize

Applications Poetry Book Society, 4h Floor, 2 Tavistock Place, London WC1H 9RA
tel 020-7833 9247
email info@poetrybooks.co.uk
website www.poetrybooks.co.uk

An annual prize of £10,000 is awarded by the Poetry Book Society to the best collection of new poetry published in the UK or the Republic of Ireland during the year. Submissions are invited from publishers in the summer. The prize money is provided by Valerie Eliot. Founded 1993.

Encore Award

Details Awards Secretary, The Society of Authors, 84 Drayton Gardens, London SW10 9SB
tel 020-7373 6642
email info@societyofauthors.org
website www.societyofauthors.org

This biennial award of £10,000 is for the best second novel of the previous two years. The work submitted must be: a novel by one author who has had one (and only one) novel published previously, and in the English language, first published in the UK. Entries should be submitted by the publisher. Closing date: 30 November.

European Publishers Award for Photography

Details Dewi Lewis Publishing, 8 Broomfield Road, Heaton Moor, Stockport SK4 4ND
tel 0161-442 9450 *fax* 0161-442 9450
email mail@dewilewispublishing.com
website www.dewilewispublishing.com

Annual competition for the best set of photographs suitable for publication as a book. All photographic material must be completed and unpublished in book form and be original. Projects conceived as anthologies are not acceptable. Copyright must belong to the photographer. Closing date: 31 January. Founded 1994.

Christopher Ewart-Biggs Memorial Prize

Details The Secretary, Memorial Prize, Flat 3, 149 Hamilton Terrace, London NW8 9QS

This prize of £5000 is awarded once every 2 years to the writer, of any nationality, whose work is judged to contribute most to:
• peace and understanding in Ireland;
• to closer ties between the peoples of Britain and Ireland;
• or to cooperation between the partners of the European Union.
    Eligible works must be published during the 2 years to 31 December 2006. Closing date: 15 January 2007.

The Geoffrey Faber Memorial Prize

An annual prize of £1000 is awarded in alternate years for a volume of verse and for a volume of prose fiction, first published originally in the UK during the 2 years preceding the year in which the award is given which is, in the opinion of the judges, of the greatest literary merit. Eligible writers must be not more than 40 years old at the date of publication of the book and a citizen of the UK and Colonies, of any other Commonwealth state or of the Republic of Ireland. The 3 judges are reviewers of poetry or fiction who are nominated each year by the literary editors of newspapers and magazines which regularly publish such reviews. Faber and Faber invite nominations from reviewers and literary editors. No submissions for the prize are to be made. Established in 1963 by Faber and Faber Ltd, as a memorial to the founder and first Chairman of the firm.

The Alfred Fagon Award

Details Pippa Davis@Talawa Theatre Company
tel 020-7251 6644
email alfredfagonaward@talawa.com
Submissions The Alfred Fagon Award, The Royal Court Theatre, Sloane Square, London SW1W 8AS
website www.alfredfagonaward.co.uk

An annual award of £5000 for the best new play (which need not have been produced) for the theatre in English. TV and radio plays and film scripts will not be considered. Only writers from the Caribbean or with Caribbean antecedence and who are resident in the UK are eligible. Applicants should submit 2 copies of their play plus sae for return of their script and a CV which includes details of the writer's Caribbean connection. Closing date: end August. Founded 1997.

The Eleanor Farjeon Award

website www.childrensbookcircle.org.uk

An annual award of (minimum) £750 may be given to a librarian, teacher, author, artist, publisher, reviewer, TV producer or any other person working with or for children through books. It was instituted in 1965 by the Children's Book Circle (page 531) for distinguished services to children's books and named after the much-loved children's writer.

Financial Times and Goldman Sachs Business Book of the Year Award

email bookaward@ft.com
website www.ft.com/bookaward

To identify the book that provides the most compelling and enjoyable insight into modern business issues, including management, finance and economics. Books that have appeared for the first time in English between 31 October and 1 November of the following year are eligible. Submissions should come via the publisher. The winner will receive £30,000 and 5 other shortlisted authors will win £5000 each. Closing date: end of June.

Fish Short Story Prize

Fish Publishing, Durrus, Bantry, Co. Cork, Republic of Ireland
tel (353) 27 55645
email info@fishpublishing.com
website www.fishpublishing.com
Contact Clem Cairns

The best 15 stories (max. 5000 words) will be published in the *Fish Anthology*. 1st prize: €2500. Entry fee: £15/€20 per story. Closing date: 30 November. Critiques available all year. See website for further information and for details of One-Page Story Prize and Unpublished Novel Prize. Founded 1994.

E.M. Forster Award

American Academy of Arts and Letters, 633 West 155th Street, New York, NY 10032, USA
tel 212-368-5900
website www.artsandletters.org

The distinguished English author, E.M. Forster, bequeathed the American publication rights and royalties of his posthumous novel *Maurice* to Christopher Isherwood, who transferred them to the American Academy of Arts and Letters, for the establishment of an E.M. Forster Award, currently $15,000, to be given annually to a British or Irish writer for a stay in the USA. Applications for this award are not accepted.

Forward Prizes For Poetry

Details Forward Poetry Prize Administrator, Colman Getty PR, 28 Windmill Street, London W1T 2JJ
tel 020-7631 2666 *fax* 020-7631 2699
email pr@colmangettypr.co.uk

Three prizes are awarded annually:
• The Forward Prize for best collection of poetry published between 1 October and 30 September (£10,000);
• The Felix Dennis Prize for best first collection of poetry published between 1 October and 30 September (£5000); and
• The Forward Prize for best single poem in memory of Michael Donaghy, published but not as part of a collection between 1 May and 30 April (£1000).

All poems entered are also considered for inclusion in the *Forward Book of Poetry*, an annual anthology. Entries must be submitted by book publishers and editors of newspapers, periodicals and magazines in the UK and Eire. Entries from individual poets of their unpublished or self-published work will not be accepted. Established 1992.

FosterGrant Reading Glasses Romantic Novel of the Year Award

Details Mary de Laszlo, 57 Coniger Road, London SW6 3TB
tel 020-7736 4968
website www.rna-uk.org

This annual award of £10,000 for the best romantic novel of the year is open to both members and non-members of the Romantic Novelists' Association, provided non-members are domiciled in the UK. Novels must be published between the previous 1 December and 30 November of the year of entry. Three copies of the novel are required. Send sae for entry form and details, available from July onwards.

New Writers' Award

Details Nicola Cornick, North End Cottage, Kingston, Winslow, Swindon SN6 8NG
email ncornick@madasafish.com

For writers previously unpublished in the adult novel field and who are probationary members of the Association. MSS can be submitted until the end of September under the New Writers' Scheme. All receive a critique. Any MSS which have passed through the Scheme and which are subsequently accepted for publication become eligible for the Award.

Miles Franklin Literary Award

Details PO Box 777, Randwick, NSW 2031, Australia
email trustawards@cauzgroup.com.au

This annual award of $42,000 is for a novel or play first published in the preceding year, which presents Australian life in any of its phases. More than one entry may be submitted by each author. Biographies, collections of short stories or children's books are not eligible. Closing date: approx. 15 December. Founded 1957.

The Lionel Gelber Prize

Details Prize Manager, The Lionel Gelber Prize, c/o Munk Centre for International Studies, 1 Devonshire Place, Toronto, Ontario M5S 3K7, Canada
tel 416-946 8900 *fax* 416-946 8915
email meisner@interlog.com
website www.utoronto.ca/mcis/gelber

This international prize is awarded annually in Canada to the author of the year's most outstanding work of non-fiction in the field of international relations. Submissions must be published in English or in English translation. Books must be submitted by the publisher. Full eligibility details are on website. Established 1989.

The Gilchrist-Fisher Award

Contact Maria Morrow, Rebecca Hossack Gallery, 35 Windmill Street, London W1T 2JS
tel 020-7436 4899

Biennial prize (1st £3000, 2nd prize £1000) awarded to a young artist (aged under 30) for landscape painting. Next prize: 2008. Founded 1987.

Gladstone History Book Prize

Submissions Executive Secretary, Royal Historical Society, University College London, Gower Street, London WC1E 6BT
email royalhistsoc@ucl.ac.uk, rhs.info@sas.ac.uk

An annual award (value £1000) for a history book. The book must:
• be on any historical subject which is not primarily related to British history;
• be its author's first solely written history book;
• have been published in English during the calendar year of 2006 by a scholar normally resident in the UK;
• be an original and scholarly work of historical research.

One non-returnable copy of an eligible book should be submitted before 31 December.

Goss First Novel Award

(formerly Pendleton May First Novel Award)
c/o Tourist Information Centre, Tunsgate, Guildford GU1 3QT
tel (01483) 444334
email assistant@guildfordbookfestival.co.uk
website www.guildfordbookfestival.co.uk

An award of £2500 is made for a first novel in any genre published between Guildford Book Festivals (held in October). Applications should be made through a publisher or literary agent. Eligible authors must reside in the UK. Closing date: 30 July 2007. Founded 1997.

Kate Greenaway Medal – see The CILIP
Carnegie and Kate Greenaway Awards

The Eric Gregory Trust Fund
Details Awards Secretary, The Society of Authors, 84 Drayton Gardens, London SW10 9SB
tel 020-7373 6642
email info@societyofauthors.org
website www.societyofauthors.org

A number of substantial awards are made annually for the encouragement of young poets who can show that they are likely to benefit from an opportunity to give more time to writing. An eligible candidate must:
• be a British subject by birth but not a national of Eire or any of the British dominions or colonies and be ordinarily resident in the UK or Northern Ireland;
• be under the age of 30 on 31 March in the year of the Award (i.e. the year following submission). Send sae for entry form. Closing date: 31 October.

Griffin Poetry Prize
Details The Griffin Trust for Excellence in Poetry, 6610 Edwards Boulevard, Mississauga, Ontario L5T 2V6, Canada
tel 905-565-5993 *fax* 905-564 3645
website www.griffinpoetryprize.com

Two annual prizes of Can.$50,000 will be awarded for collections of poetry published in English during the preceding year. One prize will go to a living Canadian poet, the other to a living poet from any country. Collections of poetry translated into English from other languages are also eligible and will be assessed for their literary quality in English. Submissions only from publishers. Closing date: 31 December. Founded 2000.

The Guardian Children's Fiction Prize
tel 020-7239 9694
email books@guardian.co.uk

The Guardian's annual prize of £1500 is for a work of fiction for children over 8 (no picture books) published by a British or Commonwealth writer. The winning book is chosen by the Children's Book Editor together with a team of 3–4 other authors of children's books.

The Guardian First Book Award
Contact Claire Armitstead
tel 020-7239 9694 *fax* 020-7713 4366
email books@guardian.co.uk
Submissions Literary Editor, The Guardian, 119 Farringdon Road, London EC1R 3ER

Open to first-time authors published in English in the UK across all genres of writing, the award will recognise and reward new writing by honouring an author's first book. The winner will receive £10,000 plus an advertising package within the *Guardian* and the *Observer*. Publishers may submit up to 3 titles per imprint with publication dates between January and December each year. Closing date: late July.

The Guardian Research Fellowship
Details Guardian Research Fellowship, College Secretary, Nuffield College, Oxford OX1 1NF
tel (01865) 278542 *fax* (01865) 278666
email college.secretary@nuffield.oxford.ac.uk

A biennial Fellowship to be held for one year at Nuffield College, Oxford, to research or study any project related to the experience of working in the media. It is hoped that the Fellow will produce a book or substantial piece of written work. The Fellow will be asked to give the *Guardian* lecture following the end of their Fellowship. The Fellowship is open to people working in newspapers, TV, the internet or other media. Advertised: October 2007. Founded 1987.

Hawthornden Fellowships
Details The Administrator, International Retreat for Writers, Hawthornden Castle, Lasswade, Midlothian EH18 1EG
tel 0131-440 2180 *fax* 0131-440 1989

Applications are invited from novelists, poets, dramatists and other creative writers whose work has already been published by reputable or recognised presses. Four-week fellowships are offered to those working on a current project. Translators may also apply. Application forms are available from March for Fellowships awarded in the following year.

The Hawthornden Prize
Details The Administrator, 42A Hays Mews, Berkeley Square, London W1J 5QA

This prize is awarded annually to the author of what, in the opinion of the Committee, is the best work of imaginative literature published during the preceding calendar year by a British author. Books do not have to be specially submitted.

Francis Head Bequest
Details Awards Secretary, The Society of Authors, 84 Drayton Gardens, London SW10 9SB
tel 020-7373 6642 *fax* 020-7373 5768
email info@societyofauthors.org
website www.societyofauthors.org

This fund provides grants to published British authors over the age of 35 who need financial help during a period of illness, disablement or temporary financial crisis. Apply for an information sheet and application form.

The Felicia Hemans Prize for Lyrical Poetry
Submissions The Sub-Dean, Faculty of Arts, The University of Liverpool, PO Box 147, Liverpool L69 3BX

tel 0151-794 2458
email wilderc@liv.ac.uk

This annual prize of books or money, open to past and present members and students of the University of Liverpool only, is awarded for a lyrical poem, the subject of which may be chosen by the competitor. Only one poem, either published or unpublished, may be submitted. The prize shall not be awarded more than once to the same competitor. Poems, endorsed 'Hemans Prize', must be submitted by 1 May.

William Hill Sports Book of the Year Award

Details Graham Sharpe, William Hill Organisation, Greenside House, 50 Station Road, London N22 4TP
tel 020-8918 3731
website www.williamhillmedia.com

This award is given annually in November for a book with a sporting theme (record books and listings excluded). The title must be in the English language, and published for the first time in the UK during the relevant calendar year. Total value of prize is £20,000, including £15,000 in cash. An award for the best cover design has total value of £1000. Founded 1989.

Historical Short Fiction Prize

Historical Novel Society, PO Box 63, Exeter EX6 8WX
website www.fishpublishing.com,
www.historicalnovelsociety.org

The best 10 short stories (max. 6000 words) will be published in the *Short Histories Anthology*. Frist prize €1500; 9 runners up will receive €100. Entry fee: €20 per story. Closing date: end September.

The Calvin and Rose G. Hoffman Memorial Prize for Distinguished Publication on Christopher Marlowe

Applications The Bursar, The King's School, Canterbury, Kent CT1 2ES
tel (01227) 595544 *fax* (01227) 595589

This annual prize of around £5000 is awarded to the best unpublished work that examines the life and works of Christopher Marlowe and the relationship between the works of Marlowe and Shakespeare. Closing date: 1 September.

L. Ron Hubbard's Writers and Illustrators of the Future Contests

Administrator Andrea Grant-Webb, PO Box 218, East Grinstead, West Sussex RH19 4GH

Aims to encourage new and aspiring writers and illustrators of science fiction, fantasy and horror. In addition to the quarterly prizes there is an annual prize of £2500 for each contest. All 24 winners are invited to the annual L. Ron Hubbard Achievement Awards, which include a series of writers' and illustrators' workshops, and their work is published in an anthology. Write for an entry form.

Writers of the Future Contest

Entrants should submit a short story of up to 10,000 words or a novelette of less than 17,000 words. Prizes of £640 (1st), £480 (2nd) and £320 (3rd) are awarded each quarter. Founded 1984.

Illustrators of the Future Contest

Entrants should submit 3 b&w illustrations on different themes. Three prizes of £320 are awarded each quarter. Founded 1988.

Images – The Best of British Contemporary Illustration

Details Association of Illustrators, 2nd Floor, Back Building, 150 Curtain Road, London EC2A 3AT
tel 020-7613 4328 *fax* 020-7613 4417
email images@theaoi.com
website www.theaoi.com
Contact Images Co-ordinator

Illustrators are invited to submit work for possible inclusion in the *Images Annual*, a jury-selected showcase of the best of contemporary British illustration. Selected work forms the Images exhibition, which tours the UK. UK illustrators or illustrators working for UK clients are all eligible. Send sae for entry form in the Spring. Founded 1975.

The Richard Imison Memorial Award

Details/entry form The Secretary, The Broadcasting Committee, The Society of Authors, 84 Drayton Gardens, London SW10 9SB
tel 020-7373 6642
email info@societyofauthors.org
website www.societyofauthors.org

This annual prize of £1500 is awarded to any new writer of radio drama first transmitted within the UK during the previous year by a writer new to radio. Founded 1995.

Independent Foreign Fiction Prize

Details The Literature Dept, Arts Council England, 14 Great Peter Street, London SW1P 3NQ
tel 020-7973 5325
website www.artscouncil.org.uk

In collaboration with *The Independent* newspaper and Champagne Taittinger, Arts Council England awards the £10,000 prize to honour a great work of fiction by a living author which has been translated into English from any other language and published in the UK. The prize is shared equally between the author and the translator.

Insight Guides Travel Photography Prize

Details APA Publications (UK) Ltd, 58 Borough High Street, London SE1 1XF

tel 020-7403 0284 *fax* 020-7403 0290
website www.insightguides.com

An annual competition open to amateur and professional photographers resident in the UK (theme to be announced). First prize is a commission to photograph for an *Insight Guide* worth £3000. Closing date: Sept 2007 (tbc). Founded 2000.

International IMPAC Dublin Literary Award

Ms Clare Hogan, The International IMPAC Dublin Literary Award, Dublin City Library & Archive, 138–144 Pearse Street, Dublin 2, Republic of Ireland
tel 353 1 674 4802 *fax* 353 1 674 4879
email literaryaward@dublincity.ie
website www.impacdublinaward.ie

This award is the largest and most international prize of its kind. Administered by Dublin City Public Libraries, nominations are made by libraries in capital and major cities throughout the world. Titles are nominated solely on the basis of 'high literary merit' and books may be written in any language.

The prize is €100,000 which is awarded to the author if the book is written in English. If the winning book is in English translation, the author receives €75,000 and the translator €25,000. The Award, an initiative of Dublin City Council, is a partnership between Dublin City Council, the Municipal Government of Dublin City, and IMPAC. Established 1996.

International Playwriting Festival

Details/entry form Festival Administrator, Warehouse Theatre, Dingwall Road, Croydon CR0 2NF
tel 020-8681 1257 *fax* 020-8688 6699
email info@warehousetheatre.co.uk
website www.warehousetheatre.co.uk

An annual competition for full-length unperformed plays. Selected plays are showcased during the festival weekend in November. Plays are also presented in Italy at the leading Italian playwriting festival Premio Candoni Arta Terme. Entries are welcome from all parts of the world. Send sae for further details or visit the website. Deadline for entries: 30 June. See also page 591. Founded 1985.

The ISG (CILIP)/BookData Reference Awards

email isg@norcombe.com
website www.cilip.org.uk

The Besterman/McColvin Medals

Awarded annually for outstanding works of reference published in the UK during the preceding year. There are 2 categories, one for electronic formats and one for printed works. Recommendations are invited from Members of CILIP (the Chartered Institute of Library and Information Professionals), publishers and others, who are asked to submit a preliminary list

of not more than 3 titles via the website. Winners receive a cash prize of £500, a certificate and a prestigious golden medal.

The Walford Award

Awarded annually to an individual who has made a sustained and continued contribution to the science and art of British bibliography over a period of years. The bibliographer's work can encompass effort in the history, classification and description of printed, written, audiovisual and machine-readable materials. Recommendations may be made for the work of a living person or persons, or for an organisation. The award can be made to a British bibliographer or to a person or organisation working in the UK. The winner receives a cash prize of £500.

Jewish Quarterly – Wingate Literary Prizes

Details Pam Lewis, PO Box 37645, London NW7 1WB
tel 020-8343 4675
email admin@jewishquarterly.org
website www.jewishquarterly.org

Prizes are awarded annually for a work of fiction (£4000) and non-fiction (£4000) which best stimulate an interest in and awareness of themes of Jewish concern among a wider reading public. Runners up each receive £300. Founded 1977.

Samuel Johnson Prize for Non-Fiction – see BBC FOUR Samuel Johnson Prize for Non-Fiction

The Petra Kenney Poetry Competition

Details Morgan Kenney, The Belmoredean Barn, Maplehurst Road, West Grinstead RH13 6RN
email morgan@petrapoetrycompetition.co.uk
website www.petrapoetrycompetition.co.uk

This annual competition is for unpublished poems on any theme and in any style, and is open to everyone. Poems should be no more than 80 lines. Prizes: £1000 and publication in *Writing Magazine* (1st), £500 (2nd), £250 (3rd), 3 at £125; also an inscribed Royal Brierley crystal vase to the 3 winners. Comic Verse category: £250; Young Poets (14–18) category: £250 and £125. Entry fee: £3 per poem. Closing date: 1 December each year. Founded 1995.

Kent and Sussex Poetry Society Open Poetry Competition

Submissions The Organiser, 13 Ruscombe Close, Southborough, Tunbridge Wells, Kent TN4 0SG

This competition is open to all unpublished poems, no longer than 40 lines in length. Prizes: 1st £600, 2nd £200, 3rd £100, 4th 6 at £75. Closing date: 31 January. Entries should include an entry fee of £4 per poem, the author's name and address and a list of poems submitted. Founded 1985.

Kerry Group Irish Fiction Award
Details Writers' Week, 24 The Square, Listowel,
Co. Kerry, Republic of Ireland
tel (353) 6821074 *fax* (353) 6822893
email info@writersweek.ie
website www.writersweek.ie

An annual award of €10,000 for a published work of
fiction by an Irish author. No entry fee. Closing date:
2 March 2007.

Killie Writing Competition
Details Killie Writing Competition, Kilmarnock
College KA3 7AT
tel (01355) 302160
email enquiries@killie.co.uk
website www.killie.co.uk

Annual competition usually with 4 categories: 5–7
year-olds, 8–11 year-olds, 12–16 year-olds, adults.
Free expessive writing (poetry or fiction) with no
limit on subject, word count, style or format. See
website for guidelines. Work submitted must have
been previously unpublished. Various prizes with the
overall best entry receiving £1000 and a trophy.
Closing date: April. Founded 2000.

The Kiriyama Prize
Details Jeannine Cuevas, 650 Delancey Street, Suite
101, San Francisco, CA 94107, USA
tel 415-777-1628 *fax* 415-777-1646
email info@kiriyamaprize.org
website www.kiriyamaprize.org

An international book prize to recognise outstanding
books about the Pacific Rim and South Asia that
encourage greater mutual understanding and foster
peace among the peoples of this vast and diverse
region. The prize of $30,000 is divided equally
between the winning fiction author and winning
non-fiction author. Closing date: late October.
Founded 1996.

Kraszna-Krausz Awards
Details Andrea Livingstone, Administrator, Kraszna-
Krausz Foundation, 122 Fawnbrake Avenue, London
SE24 0BZ
tel 020-7738 6701 *fax* 020-7738 6701
email awards@k-k.org.uk
website www.k-k.org.uk

Awards totalling over £10,000 are made each year and
in 2006 they were restructured so that annual prizes
in future would be for the best books on the moving
image (film, TV and video) and still photography, in
various categories. Entries to be submitted by
publishers only.The Foundation is also open to
applications for grants (UK only) concerned with the
literature of photography and the moving image.
Instituted in 1985.

The Lady Short Story Competition
The Lady, 39–40 Bedford Street, London WC2E 9ER

Open to anyone, details are published in an issue of
The Lady. First prize: £1000. No entry fee.

Leverhulme Research Fellowships
The Leverhulme Trust, 1 Pemberton Row, London
EC4A 3BG
tel 020-7822 6477 *fax* 020-7822 5084
email jcater@leverhulme.ac.uk
website www.leverhulme.ac.uk

The Leverhulme Trustees offer annually
approximately 90 Fellowships to individuals in aid of
original research – not for study of any sort. These
awards are not available as replacement for past
support from other sources. Applications will be
considered in all subject areas. Total monies for one
fellowship for 2006 was £25,000. Completed
application forms must be received by mid
November 2006 for 2007 awards. Founded 1933.

John Llewellyn Rhys Prize
Details Booktrust, Book House, 45 East Hill, London
SW18 2QZ
tel 020-8516 2972/2960 *fax* 020-8516 2978
email tarryn@booktrust.org.uk,
helen@booktrust.org.uk
Contact Tarryn McKay, Helen Hayes

This annual prize of £5000 (plus £500 to each
shortlisted author) is made to an author aged 35 or
under for a work of literature (fiction, poetry, drama,
non-fiction, etc) which has been published in the UK
during the calendar year prior to the presentation.
The author must be a citizen of the UK or the
Commonwealth. Inaugurated in memory of the
writer John Llewellyn Rhys by his widow Jane Oliver.
Founded 1942.

London Press Club Awards
Details Dr Mark Bryant, Hon. Secretary, London
Press Club, St Bride Institute, 14 Bride Lane, Fleet
Street, London EC4Y 8EQ
tel 020-7353 7086/7 *fax* 020-7353 7087
email lpressclub@aol.com
website www.londonpressclub.co.uk

Business Journalist of the Year, Consumer Affairs
Journalist of the Year, Daily Newspaper of the Year,
Sunday Newspaper of the Year and Broadcasting
Journalist of the Year.

Scoop of the Year Award
Chosen by a panel of senior editors, this annual
award of a bronze statuette is given for the reporting
scoop of the year, appearing in a newspaper. Founded
1990.

Edgar Wallace Award
Chosen by a panel of senior editors, this annual
award of a silver inkstand is given for outstanding
writing or reporting by a journalist. Founded 1990.

London Writers Competition
Details Arts Office, Wandsworth Council, Room
224A, Wandsworth Town Hall, High Street, London
SW18 2PU

tel 020-8871 8711
email arts@wandsworth.gov.uk
website www.wandsworth.gov.uk/arts

Open to writers who live, work or study in the Greater London area. Awards are made annually in 4 classes (Poetry, Short Story, Fiction for Children and Play) and prizes total £1000 in each class. Entries must be previously unpublished work. Judging is under the chairmanship of Francine Stock.

The Elizabeth Longford Grants

Details Awards Secretary, The Society of Authors, 84 Drayton Gardens, London SW10 9SB
tel 020-7373 6642 fax 020-7373 5768
email info@societyofauthors.org
website www.societyofauthors.org

Grants of £2500 are made payable to 2 historical biographers each year whose publisher's advance is insufficient to cover the costs of research involved. Send sae for information. Sponsored by Flora Fraser and Peter Soros. Entry dates: 30 April and 30 September.

The Elizabeth Longford Prize for Historical Biography

Details Awards Secretary, The Society of Authors, 84 Drayton Gardens, London SW10 9SB
tel 020-7373 6642 fax 020-7373 5768
email info@societyofauthors.org
website www.societyofauthors.org

A prize of £3000 is awarded annually for a historical biography published in the year preceding the prize. No unsolicited submissions. Established in 2003 in affectionate memory of Elizabeth Longford, the acclaimed biographer, and sponsored by Flora Fraser and Peter Soros.

The Sir William Lyons Award

Details General Secretary, The Guild of Motoring Writers, 39 Beswick Avenue, Ensbury Park, Bournemouth BH22 0AG
tel/fax (01202) 518808
email chris@whizzco.freeserve.co.uk
website www.guildofmotoringwriters.co.uk

This annual award (trophy, £1500 and 2 years' probationary membership of the Guild of Motoring Writers) was set up to encourage young people in automotive journalism, including broadcasting, and to foster interest in motoring and the motor industry through these media. Open to any person of British nationality resident in the UK aged 17–23, it consists of writing 2 essays and an interview with the Award Committee.

The McKitterick Prize

Details Awards Secretary, The Society of Authors, 84 Drayton Gardens, London SW10 9SB
tel 020-7373 6642
email info@societyofauthors.org

website www.societyofauthors.org

This annual award of £4000 is open to first published novels and unpublished typescripts by authors over the age of 40. Closing date: 20 December. Endowed by the late Tom McKitterick. Send sae for entry form.

The Enid McLeod Literary Prize

Details Executive Secretary, Franco–British Society, 2 Dovedale Studios, 465 Battersea Park Road, London SW11 4LR
tel/fax 020-7924 3511
email execsec@francobritishsociety.org.uk
website www.francobritishsociety.org.uk

This annual prize of £250 is given for a full-length work of literature which contributes most to Franco-British understanding. It must be first published in the UK between 1 January and 31 December, and written in English by a citizen of the UK, British Commonwealth or the Republic of Ireland. Closing date: 31 December.

Bryan MacMahon Short Story Award

Writers' Week, 24 The Square, Listowel, Co. Kerry, Republic of Ireland
tel (353) 6821074 fax (353) 6822893
email info@writersweek.ie
website www.writersweek.ie

An annual award for the best short story (up to 3000 words) on any subject. Prize: €2000. Entry fee: €8. Closing date: 2 March 2007. Founded 1971.

The Macmillan Prize for Children's Picture Book Illustration

Applications Dianne Pinner, Macmillan Children's Books, 20 New Wharf Road, London N1 9RR
tel 020-7014 6124
email d.pinner@macmillan.co.uk

Three prizes are awarded annually for unpublished children's book illustrations by art students in higher education establishments in the UK. Prizes: £1000 (1st), £500 (2nd) and £250 (3rd).

The Man Booker International Prize

Colman Getty Consultancy, 28 Windmill Street, London W1T 2JJ
tel 020-7631 2666
email pr@colmangetty.co.uk
website www.manbookerinternational.com
Contact Lois Tucker

A prize of £60,000 to complement the annual Man Booker Prize by recognising one writer's achievement in continued creativity, development and overall contribution to world fiction. It will be awarded once every 2 years to a living author who has published fiction either originally in English, or generally available in translation in the English language.

The Man Booker International Prize will echo and reinforce the annual Man Booker Prize for Fiction in that literary excellence will be its sole focus. The winner will be announced in June. Sponsored by the Man Group.

The Man Booker Prize
Colman Getty Consultancy, 28 Windmill Street, London W1T 2JJ
tel 020-7631 2666
email pr@colmangetty.co.uk
website www.themanbookerprize.com
Contact Lois Tucker

This annual prize for fiction of £65,000, including £2500 to each of 6 shortlisted authors, is awarded to the best novel published each year. It is open to novels written in English by citizens of the British Commonwealth and Republic of Ireland and published for the first time in the UK by a British publisher, although previous publication of a book outside the UK does not disqualify it. Entries only from UK publishers who may each submit not more than 2 novels with scheduled publication dates between 1 October of the previous year and 30 September of the current year, but the judges may also ask for other eligible novels to be submitted to them. In addition, publishers may submit eligible titles by authors who have been shortlisted or won the Booker Prize previously. Sponsored by the Man Group.

Marsh Award for Children's Literature in Translation
Administered by National Centre for Research in Children's Literature, Froebel College, Roehampton University, Roehampton Lane, London SW15 5PJ
tel 020-8392 3008
Contact Dr Gillian Lathey

This biennial award of £1000 is given to the translator of a book for children (aged 4–16) from a foreign language into English and published in the UK by a British publisher. Electronic books, and encyclopedias and other reference books, are not eligible. Next award: January 2007.

Marsh Biography Award
Administered by The English-Speaking Union, Dartmouth House, 37 Charles Street, London W1J 5ED
tel 020-7529 1550 *fax* 020-7495 6108
email katie_brock@esu.org

This major national biography prize of £4000 plus a trophy is presented every 2 years. Entries must be serious biographies written by British authors and published in the UK. Next award: October 2007. Founded 1985–6.

The John Masefield Memorial Trust
Details Awards Secretary, The Society of Authors, 84 Drayton Gardens, London SW10 9SB
tel 020-7373 6642 *fax* 020-7373 5768

email info@societyofauthors.org
website www.societyofauthors.org

This trust makes occasional grants to professional poets who find themselves with sudden financial problems. Apply for an information sheet and application form.

The Somerset Maugham Awards
Details Awards Secretary, The Society of Authors, 84 Drayton Gardens, London SW10 9SB
tel 020-7373 6642
email info@societyofauthors.org
website www.societyofauthors.org

These annual awards, totalling about £12,000, are for writers under the age of 35. Candidates must be British subjects by birth, and ordinarily resident in the UK or Northern Ireland. Poetry, fiction, non-fiction, belles-lettres or philosophy, but not dramatic works, are eligible. Entries should be submitted by the publisher. Closing date: 20 December.

Millfield Arts Projects
Atkinson Gallery, Millfield, Butleigh Road, Street, Somerset BA16 0YD
tel (01458) 442291 *fax* (01458) 447276
email lag@millfieldschool.com
website www.atkinsongallery.com
Director of Art Len Green

'The mandate of the Millfield Arts Project programme is to search for, promote and support, primarily but not exclusively, young aspiring artists at local, regional, national and international levels.' In a professional art context MAP offers:
• Sculpture Commission. Artists work on campus for 8 weeks (£10,000). Deadline for entries: mid January.
• Summer Show. An open exhibition. Application forms available: March.
• Six Gallery exhibitions selected by the Director of Art. Interested artists should send images and CV to the Director of Art.

Mind Book of the Year
Details Anny Brackx, Information Department, Granta House, 15–19 Broadway, London E15 4BQ
tel 020-7215 2300 *fax* 020-8522 1725

This £1500 award is given to the author of any book (fiction or non-fiction) published in the UK in the current year which outstandingly furthers public understanding of the prevention, causes, treatment or experience of mental health problems. Entries by 31 December. Administered by Mind, the National Association for Mental Health. Inaugurated in memory of Sir Allen Lane in 1981.

Kathleen Mitchell Award
postal address PO Box 777, Rondwick, NSW 2031, Australia
tel (02) 9332 1559 *fax* (02) 9332 1298
email trustawards@cauzgroup.com.au

website www.trust.com.au

A biennial literary award ($7500) for authors under the age of 30 for the advancement and improvement of Australian literature. Eligible authors must be born in or resident in Australia, either British born or naturalised Australian. Founded 2002.

Montana New Zealand Book Awards

Details c/o Booksellers New Zealand, PO Box 13248, Johnsonville, Wellington, New Zealand
tel (04) 478-5511 *fax* (04) 478-5519
email jayne.wasmuth@booksellers.co.nz
website www.montananzbookawards.co.nz

Annual awards to celebrate excellence in, and provide recognition for, the best books written and illustrated by New Zealanders each year. Awards are presented in 8 categories. The winner of each category wins $5000. Category winners are considered for the Montana Medal for Non-Fiction or the Dentz Medal for Fiction or Poetry. Medal winners each receive an additional $10,000. Eligible authors' and illustrators' books must have been published in New Zealand in the calendar year preceding the awards year. Closing date: December. Founded 1996.

John Moores 25 Exhibition of Contemporary Painting

Walker Art Gallery, William Brown Street, Liverpool L3 8EL
tel 0151-478 4199 *fax* 0151-478 4190
email stephen.guy@liverpoolmuseums.org.uk
website www.liverpoolmuseums.org.uk,
www.thewalker.org.uk/johnmoores25
Contact Stephen Guy

Biennial painting exhibition open to any artist living or working in the UK. First prize of £25,000, 4 prizes of £2500 each and a £1000 'visitor's choice' prize. Next exhibition: September to December 2008 to coincide with the Liverpool Biennial. Deadline for registration: February 2008. Founded 1957.

Shiva Naipaul Memorial Prize

Details The Spectator, 56 Doughty Street, London WC1N 2LL
tel 020-7405 1706
website www.spectator.co.uk
Contact Lucy Vickery

This annual prize of £3000 is given to an English language writer of any nationality under the age of 35 for an essay of not more than 3000 words giving the most acute and profound observation of a culture alien to the writer. Founded 1985.

National Poetry Competition

Contact Competition Organiser, The Poetry Society, 22 Betterton Street, London WC2H 9BX
tel 020-7420 9895 *fax* 020-7240 4818
email marketing@poetrysociety.org.uk
website www.poetrysociety.org.uk

One of Britain's major annual open poetry competitions. Poems on any theme, up to 40 lines. Prizes: 1st £5000, 2nd £1000, 3rd £500, plus 10 commendations of £50. All poems will be read by a team of poetry specialists before the final judging process. For rules and entry form send an sae. Entries also accepted via the website. Closing date: 31 October each year.

National Short Story Prize

Booktrust, Book House, 45 East Hill, London SW18 2QZ
email story@booktrust.org.uk
website www.theshortstory.org.uk/prizes
Contact Faith Liddell

Part of a new Booktrust campaign to celebrate short stories, a prize of £15,000 is awarded for the winning story, plus £3000 for the runner-up and £500 for the 3 other shortlisted stories. This prize is a collaboration between NESTA (the National Endowment for Science, Technology and the Arts), BBC Radio 4 and Prospect magazine. It is funded by NESTA and administered in conjunction with Booktrust and Scottish Booktrust. Closing date: Nov. Winner announced: May. Founded 2005.

The Nestlé Children's Book Prize

Details Booktrust, Book House, 45 East Hill, London SW18 2QZ
tel 020-8516 2986 *fax* 020-8516 2978
email hannah@booktrust.org.uk
website www.booktrust.org.uk
Contact Hannah Rutland

Three prizes (Gold, Silver and Bronze) are awarded to the 3 shortlisted books in each category (5 and under, 6–8 and 9–11 years). The Gold Award winners each receive £2500, the Silver Award winners receive £1500, and the Bronze Award winners receive £500. Eligible books must be published in the UK in the 12 months ending 30 September of the year of presentation and be a work of fiction or poetry for children written in English by a citizen or resident of the UK. Closing date for entries: June. Formerly the Nestlé Smarties Book Prize; established 1985.

New Millennial Science Essay Competition

Details The Wellcome Trust, 210 Euston Road, London NW1 2BE
tel 020-7611 7221 *fax* 020-7611 8269
email r.birse@wellcome.ac.uk
website www.wellcome.ac.uk

Postgraduate students (in science, engineering or technology) currently writing up their theses are invited to write an entertaining essay on the possible impact of their research on society of no more than 700 words. The aim is to make the research topic interesting and accessible to a wider non-specialist audience. Applicants must be registered at an internationally recognised institution. The competition is open from mid March to mid May each year. A collaboration between the Wellcome Trust and *New Scientist* magazine. Prizes: £1500 and publication in *New Scientist* (1st), £750 (2nd), 2 prizes of £375 (3rd). All winners, including the next 10 best essays, receive a one-year subscription to *New Scientist*. Founded 1993.

The New Writer Prose and Poetry Prizes

Details PO Box 60, Cranbrook, Kent TN17 2ZR
tel (01580) 212626 *fax* (01580) 212041
email admin@thenewwriter.com
website www.thenewwriter.com

Short stories up to 5000 words, novellas, essays and articles; poets may submit either one or a collection of 6–10 previously unpublished poems. Total prize money £2500 as well as publication for the prize-winners in the *New Writer* magazine. Entry fees: £3 per poem; £10 for a collection of 6–10 poems. Send for an entry form or visit the website for information about the short fiction and non-fiction sections. Closing date: 31 October each year. Founded 1997.

New Writing Ventures

Details Booktrust, Book House, 45 East Hill, London SW18 2QZ
tel 020-8516 2972
email tarryn@boooktrust.org.uk
website www.boooktrust.org.uk,
www.newwritingpartnership.org.uk
Contact Tarryn MacKay

An annual series of major national prizes and awards for emerging writers in poetry, fiction and non-fiction. The winner in each of the 3 categories - fiction, creative non-fiction and poetry – will receive £5000, and 2 shortlisted writers in each category £1000 each. All the winners and shortlisted writers will receive a place on the year-long Ventures Development Programme, which includes individual mentoring, workshops and professional advice. Closing date: end of May.

New Writing Ventures is one of the programmes delivered by the New Writing Partnership, which is supported by Arts Council England East, UEA, Norwich City Council and Norfolk County Council.

New Zealand Post Book Awards for Children and Young Adults

Details c/o Booksellers New Zealand, PO Box 13248, Johnsonville, Wellington, New Zealand
tel (04) 478-5511 *fax* (04) 478-5519
email jayne.wasmuth@booksellers.co.nz
website www.nzpostbookawards.co.nz

Annual awards to celebrate excellence in, and provide recognition for, the best books for children and young adults published annually in New Zealand. Awards are presented in 4 categories: non-fiction,

picture book, junior fiction and young adult fiction. The winner of each category wins $5000. One category winner is chosen as the *New Zealand Post Book of the Year* and receives an additional $5000. Eligible authors' and illustrators' books must have been published in New Zealand in the calendar year preceding the awards year. Closing date: December. Founded 1990.

Nielsen Gold and Platinum Book Awards

tel (01483) 712222 *fax* (01483) 712220
email gold&platinumawards@neilsenbookscan.co.uk

The awards are a recognition of sales purchases of a book by the general public. Eligible books are those that reach 500,000 unit sales (Gold) or 1,000,000 unit sales (Platinum) as measured by Nielsen BookScan within a 5-year period. All qualifying titles may receive an award funded for the author by their publisher. Founded 2001.

The Nobel Prize in Literature

Awarding authority Swedish Academy, Box 2118, S–10313 Stockholm, Sweden
tel (08) 555 12554 *fax* (08) 555 12549
email sekretariat@svenskaakademien.se
website www.svenskaakademien.se

This is one of the awards stipulated in the will of the late Alfred Nobel, the Swedish scientist who invented dynamite. No direct application for a prize will be taken into consideration. For authors writing in English it was bestowed upon Rudyard Kipling in 1907, W.B. Yeats in 1923, George Bernard Shaw in 1925, Sinclair Lewis in 1930, John Galsworthy in 1932, Eugene O'Neill in 1936, Pearl Buck in 1938, T.S. Eliot in 1948, William Faulkner in 1949, Bertrand Russell in 1950, Sir Winston Churchill in 1953, Ernest Hemingway in 1954, John Steinbeck in 1962, Samuel Beckett in 1969, Patrick White in 1973, Saul Bellow in 1976, William Golding in 1983, Wole Soyinka in 1986, Joseph Brodsky in 1987, Nadine Gordimer in 1991, Derek Walcott in 1992, Toni Morrison in 1993, Seamus Heaney in 1995, V.S. Naipaul in 2001 and Harold Pinter in 2005.

Northern Rock Foundation Writer's Award

Details New Writing North, 2 School Lane, Whickham, Tyne & Wear NE16 4SL
tel 0191-488 8580 *fax* 0191-488 8576
email mail@newwritingnorth.com
website www.newwritingnorth.com
Contact Holly Hooper

An annual award of £60,000 (paid over 3 years as a £20,000 salary) donated by the Northern Rock Foundation and designed to release a writer from commitments such as teaching in order to devote time to a major work. Eligible are writers of poetry, prose, children's books and biography, with at least 2 books published by a nationally recognised publisher. Writers must reside in Northumberland, Tyne & Wear, County Durham, Cumbria or the Tees Valley. Closing date: early January. See website for more details. Founded 2002.

Northern Writers' Awards

Administered by New Writing North, 2 School Lane, Whickham, Newcastle Upon Tyne NE16 4SL
tel 0191-488 8580 *fax* 0191-488 8576
email mail@newwritingnorth.com
website www.newwritingnorth.com
Contact Holly Hooper

Awards (from £1000 to £5000) are aimed at developing writers at different stages in their careers. A panel of professional writers shortlists and makes awards once a year. Applicants must be resident in the Arts Council England North East region (Northumberland, Tyne & Wear, Durham, Tees Valley). See website for details. Deadline for applications: early January

The Observer Hodge Award/Exhibition

Details The Observer, 119 Farringdon Road, London EC1R 3ER
tel 020-7713 4091, (01727) 898147 (application forms)
email hodge.award@observer.co.uk
website www.observer.co.uk/hodgeaward
Contact Catherine Stokes

Set up in memory of David Hodge who died aged 29, this annual award is given to student and professional photographers under 30. First prize: £5000 plus an expenses-paid assignment for the *Observer*; best student prize: £2000. Closing date: July. Founded 1986.

Orange Award for New Writers

Details Booktrust, Book House, 45 East Hill, London SW18 2QZ
tel 020-8516 2972/2960 *fax* 020-8516 2978
email tarryn@booktrust.org.uk,
helen@booktrust.org.uk
website www.orangeprize.co.uk
Contacts Tarryn McKay, Helen Hayes

This annual award of £10,000 is given to recognise emerging female fiction-writing talent published in the UK. The prize will be awarded to a woman for her first work of fiction – a novel, novella or collection of short stories. Women of any age or nationality may be entered providing their first work of fiction is published in the UK between 1 April and the following 31 March. The emphasis of the award will be on emerging talent and the evidence of future potential. Established 2005.

Orange Prize for Fiction

Details Booktrust, Book House, 45 East Hill, London SW18 2QZ

tel 020-8516 2972, 020-8516 2960 *fax* 020-8516 2978
email tarryn@booktrust.org.uk,
helen@booktrust.org.uk
website www.orangeprize.co.uk
Contact Tarryn McKay, Helen Hayes

This award of £30,000, together with a statuette known as 'The Bessie', is for a full-length novel written in English by a woman of any nationality and first published in the UK between 1 April and 31 March. Sponsored by Orange PCS. Established 1996.

George Orwell Memorial Prize

Details Blackwell Publishing, 9600 Garsington Road, Oxford OX4 2DQ
tel (01865) 776868 *fax* (01865) 714591
Contact Verity Warne

Two prizes of £1000 each are awarded in April each year – one for the best political book, and one for best political journalism, either fiction or non-fiction – of the previous year, giving equal merit to content and good style accessible to the general public. Founded 1993.

The Samuel Pepys Award

Details Jolyon Dromgoole, Chairman, Montreal House, Winson, Cirencester, Glos. GL7 5EL

A biennial prize is given to a book published in English making the greatest contribution to the understanding of Samuel Pepys, his times, or his contemporaries. The winner receives £2000 and the Robert Latham Medal. Founded by the Samuel Pepys Award Trust in 2003 on the tercentenary of the death of Pepys. Closing date: May 2007.

Peterloo Poets Open Poetry Competition

Details Peterloo Poets, The Old Chapel, Sand Lane, Calstock, Cornwall PL18 9QX
tel (01822) 833473 *fax* (01822) 833989
email info@peterloopoets.com
website www.peterloopoets.com

This annual competition offers a first prize of £1500 and 14 other prizes totalling £2600. There is also a 15–19 age group section with 5 prizes each of £100. Founded 1986.

Charles Pick Fellowship

School of Literature and Creative Writing, University of East Anglia, Norwich NR4 7TJ
tel (01603) 592286 *fax* (01603) 507728
email charlespickfellowship@uea.ac.uk
website www.uea.ac.uk/eas/fellowships/pick.shtml

An annual fellowship to assist and support the work of a new and unpublished writer of fiction or non-fiction, dedicated to the memory of the distinguished publisher and literary agent, Charles Pick. Writers of any age or nationality are eligible to apply. The award is £10,000 plus free accommodation on UEA campus.

Residential: 1 Sept–end Feb. Closing date for applications: 31 January each year. Founded 2002.

The Poetry Business Book & Pamphlet Competition

Competition Administrator The Poetry Business, The Studio, Byram Arcade, Westgate, Huddersfield HD1 1ND
tel (01484) 434840 *fax* (01484) 426566
email edit@poetrybusiness.co.uk
website www.poetrybusiness.co.uk
Directors Peter Sansom, Janet Fisher

An annual award is made for a poetry collection. The judges select up to 5 short collections for publication as pamphlets; on further submission of more poems, one of these will be selected for a full-length collection. To be published under the Poetry Business's Smith/Doorstop imprint. All winners share a cash prize of £1000. Poets over the age of 18 writing in English from anywhere in the world are eligible. Closing date: 31 October. Founded 1986.

The Portico Prize

Details Miss Emma Marigliano, Librarian, Portico Library, 57 Mosley Street, Manchester M2 3HY
tel 0161-236 6785 *fax* 0161-236 6803
website www.theportico.org.uk

This biennial prize of £3000 is awarded for a published work of fiction or non-fiction, of general interest and literary merit set wholly or mainly in the North West of England (Lancashire, Manchester, Liverpool, High Peak of Derbyshire, Cheshire and Cumbria). Next award: 2008. Founded 1985.

Dennis Potter Screenwriting Award

Details Stephen Perry, BBC Broadcasting House, Whiteladies Road, Bristol BS8 2LR
tel 0117-973 2211

Information about this award is obtainable from the above office. Founded 1994.

The V.S. Pritchett Memorial Prize

Details The Royal Society of Literature, Somerset House, Strand, London WC2R 1LA
tel 020-7845 4676 *fax* 020-7845 4679
email info@rslit.org
website www.rslit.org

An annual prize of £1000 is awarded for a previously unpublished short story of up to 5000 words. Entry fee: £5 per story. For entry forms contact the Secretary. The writer must be a citizen of the UK, Commonwealth or Ireland. Founded 1999.

The Peggy Ramsay Foundation

G. Laurence Harbottle, Hanover House, 14 Hanover Square, London W1J 1HP
tel 020-7667 5000 *fax* 020-7667 5100
email laurence.harbottle@harbottle.com
website www.peggyramsayfoundation.org

Grants are made to writers of stage plays, to theatrical organisations to facilitate new writing for the stage and to established writers of stage plays in need. Awards are made at intervals during each year and a single project award to an organisation is made annually. A total of approx. £160,000 is expended annually. Founded 1992.

The Red House Children's Book Award

Details Marianne Adey, The Old Malt House, Aldbourne, Marlborough, Wilts. SN8 2DW
tel (01672) 540629 *fax* (01672) 541280
email marianneadey@aol.com
website www.redhousechildrensbookaward.co.uk

This award is given annually to authors of works of fiction for children published in the UK. Children participate in the judging of the award. 'Pick of the Year' booklist is published in conjunction with the award. Founded in 1980 by the Federation of Children's Book Groups.

Trevor Reese Memorial Prize

Details Events and Publicity Officer, Institute of Commonwealth Studies, 28 Russell Square, London WC1B 5DS
tel 020-7862 8829 *fax* 020-7862 8813
email ics@sas.ac.uk
website www.commonwealth.sas.ac.uk

This prize of £1000 is awarded biennially, usually for a scholarly work by a single author in the field of Imperial and Commonwealth history. The next award (for a book published in 2005 or 2006) will be given in 2008.

The Rooney Prize for Irish Literature

Details J.A. Sherwin, Strathin, Templecarrig, Delgany, Co. Wicklow, Republic of Ireland
tel (01) 287 4769 *fax* (01) 287 2595
email rooneyprize@ireland.com

An annual prize of €10,000 is awarded to encourage young Irish writing talent. To be eligible individuals must be Irish, published and under 40 years of age. The prize is non-competitive and there is no application procedure or entry form. Founded 1976 by Daniel M. Rooney, Pittsburgh, Pennsylvania.

Royal Mail Awards for Scottish Children's Books

Scottish Book Trust, Sandeman House, Trunk's Close, 55 High Street, Edinburgh EH1 1SR
tel 0131-524 0160 *fax* 0131-524 0161
email anna.gibbons@scottishbooktrust.com
website www.braw.org.uk
Contact Anna Gibbons, Manager, BRAW

Awards totalling £5250 are given to new and established authors of published books in recognition of high standards of writing for children in 3 age group categories: younger children (0–7 years) younger readers (8–12 years) and older readers

(13–16 years). A shortlist is drawn up by a panel of children's book experts and then a winner in each category is decided by children and young people voting for their favourites in book groups in schools and libraries across Scotland. An award of £1000 is made for the winner in each category and £250 for runners up. Books published in the preceding calendar year are eligible. Authors should be Scottish or resident in Scotland but books of particular Scottish interest by other authors are eligible for consideration. Posthumous awards cannot be made. Guidelines available on request. Closing date: 31 January. Award presented: December. Administered by BRAW in partnership with the Scottish Arts Council.

The Royal Society of Literature Ondaatje Prize

Submissions Paula Johnson, The Royal Society of Literature, Somerset House, Strand, London WC2R 1LA
tel 020-7845 4676 *fax* 020-7845 4679
email paulaj@rsl.org
website www.rslit.org

Newly established prize (£10,000), administered by the Royal Society of Literature and endowed by Sir Christopher Ondaatje. The prize, which replaces the Winifred Holtby Memorial Prize, will be awarded annually to a book of literary merit, fiction or non-fiction, best evoking the spirit of a place. All entries must be published within the calendar year 2007 and should be submitted between 1 September and 1 December 2007. The writer must be a citizen of the UK, Commonwealth or Ireland. See website for further details.

The Royal Society of Literature/ Jerwood Awards

Submissions Paula Johnson, The Royal Society of Literature, Somerset House, Strand, London WC2R 1LA
tel 020-7845 4676 *fax* 020-7845 4679
email paulaj@rslit.org
website www.rslit.org

New awards offering financial assistance to authors engaged in writing their first major commissioned works of non-fiction. Three awards – one of £10,000 and 2 of £5000 – will be offered annually to writers working on substantial non-fiction projects. The awards are open to UK and Irish writers and writers who have been resident in the UK for at least 3 years. Applications for the awards should be submitted by the end of August 2007. See website for further details.

RSA Alastair Salvesen Art Scholarship

Royal Scottish Academy, The Mound, Edinburgh EH2 2EL
tel 0131-225 6671 *fax* 0131-220 6016

email info@royalscottishacademy.org
website www.royalscottishacademy.org

The Scholarship consists of 2 parts: a 3–6 month travel scholarship of up to £10,000 (depending on the plan submitted), and an exhibition in Spring organised by the Royal Scottish Academy. Applicants should normally be painters aged 25–35 who:
• trained at one of the 4 Scottish colleges of art;
• are currently living and working in Scotland;
• have worked for a minimum of 3 years outside a college or student environment;
• during 2005 had work accepted for an exhibition in the Annual Exhibitions organised by certain Scottish institutes or, in a recognised gallery, have held a solo exhibition or participated in a group exhibition.
Application forms available in December. Founded 1989.

RSPCA Young Photographer Awards (YPA)

Details Publications Department, RSPCA, Wilberforce Way, Southwater, Horsham, West Sussex RH13 9RS
tel (0870) 7540455 *fax* (0870) 7530455
email publications@rspca.org.uk
website www.rspca.org.uk/ypa

Annual awards are made for animal photographs taken by young people in 2 age categories: under 12 and 12–18 year-olds. Prizes: overall winner (high-end digital camera), age group winners (camera). Four runners-up in each age group receive a camera. Closing date for entries: 4 September 2006. Sponsored by Warners and Olympus Cameras. Founded 1990.

RTÉ P.J. O'Connor Radio Drama Awards

RTÉ Radio Drama, Dublin 4, Republic of Ireland
tel (01) 2083111 *fax* (01) 2083304
email radiodrama@rte.ie
website www.rte.ie/radio1/drama
Producer in Charge Siobhan Mannion

An annual competition for a 30-minute or 15-minute play, open to unproduced writers born in or living in Ireland. See website for details.

RTÉ Radio Francis McManus Awards

RTÉ Radio Arts, Features & Drama Dept, Dublin 4, Republic of Ireland.
tel (01) 2083111 *fax* (01) 2083304
website www.rte.ie/radio1/francismcmanus/
Producer in Charge Peter Mooney

An annual competition for short stories of 1900–2000 words, open to writers born or living in Ireland. Entries, in Irish or English, should not have been previously published or broadcast. See website for details.

Runciman Award

Details The Administrator, The Anglo-Hellenic League, 16–18 Paddington Street, London W1U 5AS

tel 020-7486 9410 *fax* 020-7486 4254 (mark FAO The Anglo-Hellenic League)
email angohellenic.league@vigin.net
website www.hellenicbookservice.com/ahl.htm

An annual award of £9000 to promote Anglo–Greek understanding and friendship. Works must be wholly or mainly about some aspect of Greece or the world of Hellenism, which has been published in English in any country in its first edition during the previous year. Shortlisted books must be available for purchase to readers in the UK at the time of the award ceremony. No category of writing will be excluded from consideration, e.g. history, literary studies, biography, travel and topography, the arts, architecture, archaeology, the environment, social and political sciences or current affairs; fiction, poetry or drama. Works in translation, with the exception of translations from Greek literature, will not be considered. Final entries: late January 2007; award presented in May/June. Sponsored by the National Bank of Greece and named after Sir Steven Runciman, former Chairman of the Anglo-Hellenic League. Established 1985.

Saga Children's Book Competition

Details Jane Griffiths, Editorial Assistant, HarperCollins Children's Books, 77–85 Fulham Palace Road, London W6 8JB
tel 020-8307 4080
website www.saga.co.uk/magazine, www.harpercollins.co.uk

A competition run by *Saga Magazine* in association with HarperCollins, is looking for writers aged 50 or over who can write for older children. The winner will have their book published by HarperCollins. Send completed MSS of 20,000–60,000 words and a synopsis of 500 words together with the official entry form to the address published in the September issue (not the above address). Send a sae or see websites for competition rules and detailed terms and conditions of entry. Closing date: 31 January 2007.

Sainsbury's Baby Book Award – see Booktrust Early Years Awards

The David St John Thomas Charitable Trust Competitions & Awards

The David St John Thomas Charitable Trust, PO Box 6055, Nairn IV12 4YB
tel (01667) 453351 *fax* (01667) 452365
email dsjtcharitynairn@fsmail.net
Contact Lorna Edwardson

Programme of writing competitions and awards totalling £20,000–£30,000. Regular competitions are the annual ghost story and annual love story (each 1600–1800 words with £1000 1st prize) and the open poetry competition (up to 32 lines, total prize money £1000). Publication of winning entries is guaranteed, usually in *Writers' News/Writing Magazine*. The Self-

Publishing Awards are open to anyone who has self-published a book during the preceding calendar year, with 4 categories each with £250 prize. The overall winner is declared Self-Publisher of the Year with a total award of £1000. For full details of these and other awards, including an annual writers' groups anthology and letter-writer of the year send a large sae.

The Saltire Society Awards

Details The Saltire Society, 9 Fountain Close, 22 High Street, Edinburgh EH1 1TF
tel 0131-556 1836 *fax* 0131-557 1675
email saltire@saltiresociety.org.uk
website www.saltiresociety.org.uk

Scottish Book of the Year

An annual award of £5000 open to authors of Scottish descent or living in Scotland, or for a book by anyone which deals with a Scottish topic. Books published between 1 September and 31 August are eligible. Established 1982.

Scottish First Book of the Year

An annual award of £1500 open to any author who has not previously published a book. Authors of Scottish descent or living in Scotland, or for any book which deals with the work or life of a Scot or with a Scottish problem, event or situation are eligible. Established 1988.

Scottish Research Book Award

An annual award of £1500 is open to the authors of books which represent a significant body of research; offer new insight or dimension to the subject; and add knowledge and understanding of Scotland and the Scots. Only books entered for the Society's other awards and recommended by the adjudicators will be eligible. Established 1998.

The Kim Scott Walwyn Prize

Details Booktrust, Book House, 45 East Hill, London SW18 2QZ
tel 020-8516 2972 *fax* 020-8516 2978
email hannah@booktrust.org.uk
website www.booktrust.org
Contact Tarryn McKay

A prize of £3000 will be awarded annually to a woman who has made an outstanding contribution in any area of UK book publishing. It commemorates the life and career of Kim Scott Walwyn, publishing director at Oxford University Press until her death in 2002. Applications are welcome from women of any age working in any area of book publishing in the UK. Applicants should submit a written description of a particular achievement for which they wish to be recognised, or an aspect of their publishing career which merits recognition. Full details, and the judges' guidelines, can be obtained from Booktrust. The prize is being funded by donations from Kim's family, colleagues, authors and friends.

Scottish Arts Council

Scottish Arts Council, 12 Manor Place, Edinburgh
EH3 7DD
tel 0131-226 6051
email gavin.wallace@scottisharts.org.uk
website www.scottisharts.org.uk
Contact Gavin Wallace, Head of Literature

A limited number of writers' bursaries – up to
£15,000 each – are offered to enable professional
writers based in Scotland, including writers for
children, to devote more time to writing. Priority is
given to writers of fiction and verse and playwrights,
but writers of literary non-fiction are also considered.
Applications may be discussed with Gavin Wallace.
See also Royal Mail Awards for Scottish Children's
Books.

Scottish Arts Council Book Awards
Contact Gavin Wallace, Head of Literature

These awards are currently undergoing
reconfiguration and will be relaunched in 2007.

Scottish Book of the Year – see The Saltire Society Awards

Scottish First Book of the Year – see The Saltire Society Awards

Scottish Research Book Award – see The Saltire Society Awards

Shell Wildlife Photographer of the Year

Details The Natural History Museum, Cromwell
Road, London SW7 5BD
tel 020-7942 5015 fax 020-7942 5084
email wildphoto@nhm.ac.uk
website www.nhm.ac.uk/wildphoto

An annual award given to the photographer whose
individual image is judged to be the most striking and
memorable. The overall adult winner receives £2000.
The Shell Young Wildlife Photographer of the Year
receives £500, plus a day out with a photographer.
Open to all ages. Closing date: 30 March 2007.

The André Simon Memorial Fund Book Awards

Details Katie Lander, 1 Westbourne Gardens,
Glasgow G12 9XE
tel (01225) 336305 fax (01225) 421862
email tessa@tantraweb.co.uk

Celebrating excellent new writing in the fields of food
and drink. Two awards of £2000 are given annually,
one each for the best new books on food and on
drink. There is also a Special Commendation of
£1000 in either category. All works first published in
the calendar year of the award are eligible (publisher
entry only). Closing date: November each year.
Awards are given in the spring of the following year.
Founded 1978.

Singer & Friedlander/Sunday Times Watercolour Competition

Details Parker Harris Partnership, PO Box 279, Esher,
Surrey KT10 8YZ
tel (01372) 462190 fax (01372) 460032
email sf@parkerharris.co.uk
website www.parkerharris.co.uk

An annual competition 'to promote the continuance
of the British tradition of fine watercolour painting'.
Total prize money: £30,000. Open to artists born or
resident in the UK. Closing date: June 2007. Winning
entries will be exhibited in London and Manchester.
Launched 1987.

The Jill Smythies Award

The Linnean Society of London, Burlington House,
Piccadilly, London W1J 0BF
tel 020-7434 4479 fax 020-7287 9364
email adrian@linnean.org
website www.linnean.org

Established in honour of Jill Smythies whose career as
a botanical artist was cut short by an accident to her
right hand. The rubic states that 'the Award, to be
made by Council usually annually consisting of a
silver medal and a purse … is for published
illustrations, such as drawings and paintings, in aid of
plant identification, with the emphasis on botanical
accuracy and the accurate portrayal of diagnostic
characteristics. Illustrations of cultivars of garden
origin are not eligible.' Closing date for nominations:
30 September. Founded 1988.

The Society of Authors and The Royal Society of Medicine Medical Book Awards

Details The Secretary, MWG, The Society of Authors,
84 Drayton Gardens, London SW10 9SB
tel 020-7373 6642
email info@societyofauthors.org
website www.societyofauthors.org

Entries should be submitted by the publisher. Closing
date for submissions of medical text books: 20 April.
The Medical Writers Group of the Society of Authors
administers the prizes sponsored by the Royal Society
of Medicine.

Sony Radio Academy Awards

Details Sony Radio Academy Awards Secretariat,
Zafer Associates, 47–48 Chagford Street, London
NW1 6EB
tel 020-7723 0106 fax 020-7724 6163
email secretariat@radioawards.org
website www.radioawards.org

'The Sony Radio Academy Awards celebrate excellence in broadcast work. They reward creative achievement through imagination, originality, wit and integrity. The Awards offer an opportunity to enter work in a range of categories which reflect today's local, regional and national radio. The Awards are for everyone regardless of resources – for stations big and small, for a team or for one person with a microphone.' See website for further information. Founded 1982.

The Spoken Word Awards

Contact Audiobook Publishing Association, c/o Charlotte McCandlish, 18 Green Lanes, Hatfield, Herts. AL10 9JT
tel (07971) 280788
email charlotte.mccandlish@ntlworld.com
website www.theapa.net

Annual awards are made for excellence in the spoken word industry. There are over 40 judges from all areas of the industry including audiobook reviewers, radio broadcasters, producers, abridgers, etc.

The Sunday Times Young Writer of the Year Award

Details The Society of Authors, 84 Drayton Gardens, London SW10 9SB
tel 020-7373 6642
email info@societyofauthors.org
website www.societyofauthors.org

Annual award to published fiction and non-fiction writers under the age of 35. The panel consists of *Sunday Times* journalists and critics. Entry by publishers. Closing date: 31 October. Established 1991.

Syngenta ABSW Science Writers' Awards

Details Claire Jowett, Association of British Science Writers, 58 Greenhill Road, Moseley, Birmingham B13 9SS
email sciencewritersawards@clairejowett.com
website www.absw.org.uk

The Association of British Science Writers Awards are given to the writers who, in the opinion of the judges, have done most to enhance the quality of science journalism. Entries will be accepted from specialist writers, newspaper reporters and freelances. There are 7 categories, each worth £2000 for work published (excluding books) or broadcast between 1 January and 31 December. Closing date: 31 January. Founded 1966.

The James Tait Black Memorial Prizes

Submissions Department of English Literature, David Hume Tower, George Square, Edinburgh EH8 9JX
tel 0131-650 3619 *fax* 0131-650 6898
website www.englit.ed.ac.uk/jtbinf.htm

Two prizes of £10,000 are awarded annually: one for the best biography or work of that nature, the other for the best novel, published during the calendar year 1 January to 31 December. The adjudicator is the Professor of English Literature in the University of Edinburgh. Eligible novels and biographies are those written in English and first published or co-published in Britain in the year of the award. Both prizes may go to the same author, but neither to the same author a second time.

Publishers should submit a copy of any appropriate biography, or work of fiction, as early as possible with a note of the date of publication, marked 'James Tait Black Prize'. Closing date for submissions: 31 January. Founded in memory of a partner in the publishing house of A & C Black, these prizes were instituted in 1918.

TAPS (Training and Performance Showcase)

Details Shepperton Studios, Studios Road, Shepperton, Middlesex TW17 0QD
tel (01932) 592151 *fax* (01932) 592233
email admin@tapsnet.org
website www.tapsnet.org

A national scheme to train and promote new writers for film and TV. TAPS workshop training courses are open to any British scriptwriter with less than 2 hours work broadcast on network TV. Full-length drama (min. 60 mins), comedy (30 mins) or shorts (10 mins) will be accepted as qualifying script submissions for the appropriate course. Scripts selected from each course are showcased by professional actors, taped and screened to industry executives culminating in the annual Writer of the Year Awards.

Reginald Taylor and Lord Fletcher Essay Competition

Submissions John McNeill, Hon. Secretary, British Archaeological Association, 18 Stanley Road, Oxford OX4 1QZ
email jsmcneill@btinternet.com

A prize of a medal and £300 is awarded biennially for the best unpublished essay of high scholarly standard, not exceeding 7500 words, which shows original research on a subject of archaeological, art-historical or antiquarian interest within the period from the Roman era to AD1830. The successful competitor will be invited to read the essay before the Association and the essay may be published in the Association's *Journal*. Competitors should notify the Hon. Editor in advance of the intended subject of their work. Next award: autumn 2008. The essay should be submitted not later than 30 April 2008, enclosing an sae. Founded in memory of E. Reginald Taylor FSA and Lord Fletcher FSA.

Dylan Thomas Literary Prize

The Dylan Thomas Centre, Ty Llen, Somerset Place, Swansea SA1 1RR
tel (01792) 474051, 463980
website www.dylanthomasprize.com

An award of £60,000 will be given to the winner of this prize, which was established to encourage, promote and reward exciting new writing in the English-speaking world and to celebrate the poetry and prose of Dylan Thomas. Entrants should be the author of a published book (in English), under the age of 30, writing within one of the following categories: poetry, novel, collection of short stories by one author, play that has been professionally performed, a broadcast radio play, a professionally produced screenplay that has resulted in a feature-length film. Authors need to be nominated by their publishers, or producers in the case of performance art. Closing date: May.

Hessell Tiltman Prize

English PEN, 6–8 Amwell Street, London EC1R 1UQ
tel 020-7713 0023 *fax* 020-7837 7838
email enquiries@englishpen.org
website www.englishpen.org

An annual prize made possible by a bequest to the PEN Literary Foundation of £100,000 from PEN member Marjorie Hessell-Tiltman. Each year the prize is awarded to a work of high literary merit covering any historical period until the end of the Second World War. Founded 2002.

Tir Na N-og Awards

Details Welsh Books Council, Castell Brychan, Aberystwyth, Ceredigion SY23 2JB
tel (01970) 624151 *fax* (01970) 625385
email menna.lloydwilliams@cllc.org.uk
website www.cllc.org.uk

There are 3 annual awards to children's authors and illustrators: best original Welsh-language fiction, including short stories and picture books; best original Welsh-language non-fiction book; best English book with an authentic Welsh background. Total prize value is £3000. Founded 1976.

The Tom-Gallon Trust Award and the Olive Cook Prize

Details Awards Secretary, The Society of Authors, 84 Drayton Gardens, London SW10 9SB
tel 020-7373 6642
email info@societyofauthors.org
website www.societyofauthors.org

An award of £1000 is made on the basis of a submitted short story to fiction writers of limited means who have had at least one short story accepted for publication. Both awards are biennial and are awarded in alternate years. Send sae for entry form. Closing date: 31 October each year.

The Translators Association Awards

Details Dorothy Sym, The Translators Association, 84 Drayton Gardens, London SW10 9SB
tel 020-7373 6642
email info@societyofauthors.org
website www.societyofauthors.org

The Translators Association of the Society of Authors administers a number of prizes for published translations into English. They include prizes for translations of Arabic, Dutch and Flemish, French, German, Greek, Italian, Portuguese, Spanish and Swedish works. Entries should be submitted by the publisher.

The Betty Trask Awards

Details Awards Secretary, The Society of Authors, 84 Drayton Gardens, London SW10 9SB
tel 020-7373 6642
email info@societyofauthors.org
website www.societyofauthors.org

These awards are for the benefit of young authors under the age of 35 and are given on the strength of a first novel (published or unpublished) of a romantic or traditional nature. It is expected that prizes totalling £25,000 will be presented each year. The winners are required to use the money for a period or periods of foreign travel. Send sae for entry form. Closing date: 31 January. Made possible through a generous bequest from Miss Betty Trask.

The Travelling Scholarships

Administered by The Society of Authors, 84 Drayton Gardens, London SW10 9SB

These are honorary awards established in 1944 by an anonymous benefactor. Submissions are not accepted.

John Tripp Award for Spoken Poetry

Academi, Mount Stuart House, Mount Stuard Square, Cardiff CF10 5FQ
tel 029-2047 2266 029-2049 2930
email post@academi.org
website www.academi.org

A competition for any form of spoken poetry in the English language. There are 5 regional heats around Wales, with the winners from each heat going forward to the Grand Final in Cardiff. Performers have 5 minutes to read their work at each stage of the competition and are judged on the content of their poetry and their performance skills. Anyone either born or currently living in Wales is eligible to enter and all works must be unpublished. Founded 1990.

The V&A Illustration Awards

Enquiries The Word & Image Dept, Victoria & Albert Museum, London SW7 2RL
tel/fax 020-7942 2392
email a.villa@vam.ac.uk
website www.vam.ac.uk/illustrationawards
Contact Annemarie Bilclough

These annual awards are given to practising book and magazine illustrators, for work first published in the UK during the 12 months preceding the closing date of the awards. A 1st and 2nd prize winner will be chosen from the following 3 award categories: book illustration, book cover and jacket illustration, and newspaper, magazine and comic illustration. Of the 3 category winners, one will be selected to receive £3500 as the best overall illustration and the other 2 winners will each receive £1500. The 3 second prize winners will each be awarded £750. Closing date late July/early August. Also a Student Illustrator of the Year category: 1st prize winner will receive £1300 and 4 runners up will receive £300. Closing date: March.

Ver Poets Open Competition

Competition Secretary Gill Knibbs, 181 Sandridge Road, St Albans, Herts. AL1 4AH
tel (01727) 762601
email gillknibbs@yahoo.co.uk

A competition open to all for poems of up to 30 lines of any genre or subject matter, which must be unpublished work in English. Prizes: £500 (1st), £300 (2nd), £100 (3rd). Entry fee: £3 per poem or £10 for 4. Send 2 copies of each poem with no name or address; either put address on separate sheet or send sae or email for entry form. Closing date: 30 April. Anthology of winning and selected poems with Adjudicator's Report usually available from mid-June, free to those included.

The High Lights competition for younger poets (15–19 year-olds) is a biennial competition to be run in 2007.

The Walford Award – see The ISG (CILIP)/ BookData Reference Awards

David Watt Prize

Details/entry form The Administrator, The David Watt Prize, Rio Tinto plc, 6 St James's Square, London SW1Y 4LD
tel 020-7753 2316
email davidwattprize@riotinto.com
website www.riotinto.com

An annual award (£10,000) initiated to commemorate the life and work of David Watt. Open to writers currently engaged in writing for English language newspapers and journals on international and national affairs. The winner is judged as having made 'an outstanding contribution towards the greater understanding of national, international or global issues'. Entries must have been published during the year preceding the award. Final entry date: 31 March.

The Welsh National Literature Promotion Agency and Society for Writers

Mount Stuart House, Mount Stuart Square, Cardiff CF10 5FQ
tel 029-2047 2266 *fax* 029-2049 2930
email post@academi.org
website www.academi.org
Ceo Peter Finch

Book of the Year Award

A £10,000 prize is awarded to winners, in Welsh and English, for works of exceptional merit by Welsh authors (by birth, subject matter or residence) published during the previous calendar year in the categories of poetry, fiction and creative non-fiction.

Bursaries

Bursaries totalling about £100,000 are awarded annually to authors writing in both Welsh and English. Application forms are available or visit the website.

Whitbread Book Awards – see Costa Book Awards

The Whitfield Prize

Submissions Executive Secretary, Royal Historical Society, University College London, Gower Street, London WC1E 6BT
tel 020-7387 7532 *fax* 020-7387 7532
email royalhistsoc@ucl.ac.uk, rhs.info@sas.ac.uk
website www.rhs.ac.uk

The Prize (value £1000) is announced in July each year for the best work on a subject within a field of British or Irish history. It must be its author's first solely written history book, an original and scholarly work of historical research and have been published in the UK or Republic of Ireland in the preceding calendar year. One non-returnable copy of an eligible book should be submitted before 31 December to the Executive Secretary.

The Raymond Williams Community Publishing Prizes

Details The Literature Dept, Arts Council England, 14 Great Peter Street, London SW1P 3NQ
tel 020-7973 5325
website www.artscouncil.org.uk

This award commends published works of outstanding creative and imaginative quality that reflect the life, voices and experiences of the people of particular communities. The winning entry will be awarded £3000 and the runner-up £2000.

Winchester Writers' Conference Competitions

Faculty of Arts, University of Winchester, Winchester, Hants SO22 4NR

tel (01962) 827238
email barbara.large@winchester.ac.uk
website www.writersconference.co.uk
Contact Barbara Large

Fifteen writing competitions are attached to this major international Festival of Writing which takes place at the end of June. Each entry is adjudicated and 64 sponsored prizes are presented at the Writers' Awards Dinner. Categories are the First Three Pages of the Novel, Short Stories, Shorter Short Stories, Writing for Children, A Page of Prose, Lifewriting, Slim Volume, Small Edition, Poetry, Feature Articles, Retirement, Reaching Out for disabled writers, Local History, and Young Writers' Poetry Competition.

The Wolfson Foundation
Details The Prize Administrator, The Wolfson Foundation, 8 Queen Anne Street, London W1G 9LD
tel 020-7323 5730 ext. 216 *fax* 020-7323 3241

Annual awards are made to encourage and recognise books by British historians that can be enjoyed by a general readership and will stimulate public interest in history. The awards total £25,000. Authors must be British citizens and normally resident in the UK. The book must be published in the calendar year of the prize. Closing date: varies – contact the office. Founded 1972.

David T.K. Wong Fellowship
Details School of Literature and Creative Writing, University of East Anglia, Norwich NR4 7TJ
tel (01603) 592286 *fax* (01603) 507728
email davidtkwongfellowship@uea.ac.uk
website www.uea.ac.uk/eas/fellowships/wong/wong.shtml

This annual fellowship (award £25,000) at the University of East Anglia will give a writer of exceptional talent the chance to produce a work of fiction in English which deals seriously with some aspect of life in the Far East. Writers of any age or nationality are eligible to apply. Residential: 1 Oct–30 June. Closing date for applications: 31 January each year. Founded in 1997 by Mr David Wong, retired senior civil servant, journalist and businessman.

The David T.K. Wong Prize for Short Fiction
Details International PEN, 9–10 Charterhouse Buildings, Goswell Road, London EC1M 7AT
tel 020-7253 4308 *fax* 020-7253 5711
email info@internationalpen.org.uk
website www.internationalpen.org.uk

This biennial international prize is presented to promote literary excellence in the form of the short story written in English. Unpublished stories of between 2500 words and 6000 words are welcome from writers worldwide but entries must incorporate one or more of International PEN's ideals as set out in its Charter. Entries should be submitted via the entrant's local PEN Centre, not sent to International PEN. The closing date for entries for 2007/8 is likely to be the end of September 2007 but details should be obtained from individual Centres. In those few countries without a PEN Centre, entrants can be directed to the nearest appropriate Centre by International PEN. First prize: £7500. Copies of PEN's Charter in English, French and Spanish and addresses of PEN Centres can be found on the weebsite. Established 2000.

Write A Story for Children Competition
Entry forms The Academy of Children's Writers, PO Box 95, Huntingdon, Cambs. PE28 5RL
tel (01487) 832752
website www.childrens-writers.co.uk

Three prizes (1st £2000, 2nd £300, 3rd £200) are awarded annually for a short story for children, maximum 1000 words, by an unpublished writer of children's fiction. Send sae for details or see website. Founded 1984.

Writers' & Artists' Yearbook 2007 Novel Writing Competition
website www.writersandartists.co.uk

See website for details.

Writers' Forum Short Story Competition
Details Writers' International Ltd, PO Box 3229, Bournemouth BH1 1ZS
tel (01202) 589828 *fax* (01202) 587758
email editorial@writers-form.com
website www.writers-form.com

Writers' Forum (12 p.a.) is an anthology of short stories from the winners of its competitions. Prizes: £300 (1st), £150 (2nd), £100 (3rd), with an annual trophy and a cheque for £1000 for the best story of the year. Entry fee: £10 to non-subscribers of *Writers' Forum*; £7 to subscribers.

Writers' Week Poetry Competition
Details Writers' Week, 24 The Square, Listowel, Co. Kerry, Republic of Ireland
tel (353) 6821074 *fax* (353) 6822893
email info@writersweek.ie
website www.writersweek.ie

Annual awards for a single poem (prize: €700; entry fee: €8) and for a collection of 6–12 poems (prize: €700 plus financial support towards publication of a slim volume; entry fee: €25). Closing date 2 March 2007.

Yorkshire Post Book of the Year
Submissions & Correspondence Duncan Hamilton, Deputy Editor, Yorkshire Post Newspapers Ltd, PO Box 168, Wellington Street, Leeds LS1 1RF

There are 3 awards: *Yorkshire Post* Non-fiction Award (£1200), *Yorkshire Post* Fiction Award (£1200) and *Yorkshire Post* Award for Best Book with a Yorkshire Theme (£500).

Young Writers' Programme
Details Young Writers' Programme, Royal Court Young Writers' Programme, Sloane Square, London SW1W 8AS
tel 020-7565 5050 *fax* 020-7565 5001

email ywp@royalcourttheatre.com
website www.royalcourttheatre.com

Anyone aged 13–25 can submit a play on any subject. A selection of plays are professionally presented by the Royal Court Theatre with the writers fully involved in rehearsal and production. Pre-Festival Development Workshops are run by professional theatre practitioners and designed to help everyone attending to write a play. Playwriting projects run all year round.

Literature festivals

There are hundreds of arts festivals held in the UK each year – too many to mention in this *Yearbook* and many of which are not applicable specifically to writers. We give here a selection of literature festivals and general arts festivals which include literature events. Space constraints and the nature of an annual publication together determine that only brief details are given; contact festival organisers for a full programme of events. The British Council will supply a list of forthcoming literature festivals on receipt of a large sae.

Aldeburgh International Poetry Festival
The Poetry Trust, 9 New Cut, Halesworth, Suffolk IP19 8BY
tel (01986) 835950
email info@thepoetrytrust.org
website www.thepoetrytrust.org
Director Naomi Jaffa
Takes place First weekend in Nov

An annual festival of contemporary poetry with readings, workshops, talks, discussions, public masterclass, children's event. Features leading international and national poets, including a writer-in-residence and the winner of the Jerwood Aldeburgh First Collection Prize.

Aspects Festival
Town Hall, The Castle, Bangor, Co. Down BT20 4BT
tel (028) 91 278032, 91 271200 (box office)
fax (028) 91 271370
website www.northdown.gov.uk
Contact Gail Prentice, Arts Officer/Festival Co-ordinator
Takes place 20–24 Sept 2006

An annual celebration of contemporary Irish writing with novelists, poets and playwrights. Includes readings, discussions, workshops and an Aspects showcase day for young writers.

Ballymena Arts Festival
Leisure & Events Unit, Ballymena Showgrounds, Warden Street, Ballymena, Co. Antrim BT43 7DR
tel (028) 25 639853 *fax* (028) 25 638549
website www.ballymena.gov.uk
Takes place Oct

Bath Literature Festival
Bath Festivals Trust, 5 Broad Street, Bath BA1 5LJ
tel (01225) 462231, (01225) 463362 (box office) *fax* (01225) 445551
email info@bathfestivals.org.uk
website www.bathlitfest.org.uk
Director Sarah LeFanu
Takes place 3–11 March 2007

An annual 9-day festival with leading guest writers. Includes readings, debates, discussions and workshops, and events for children and young people. Programme available from box office in December.

Bay Lit
Academi, Mount Stuart House, Mount Stuart Square, Cardiff CF10 5FQ
tel 029-2047 2266 *fax* 029-2049 2930
email post@academi.org
website www.academi.org
Contact Peter Finch, Chief Executive
Takes place autumn

A bilingual (Welsh and English) literature festival, held in Cardiff Bay. It is organised by Academi, the Welsh National Literature Promotion Agency and Society for Writers, and features an array of writers from Wales and beyond.

Belfast Festival at Queen's
Culture & Arts Unit, Queen's University, 8 Fitzwilliam Street, Belfast BT9 6AW
tel 028-9097 1034
email festival@qub.ac.uk
website www.belfastfestival.com
Director Graham Farrow
Takes place 19 Oct–4 Nov 2006

The largest annual arts event in Ireland. Includes literature events. Programme available mid September.

Beverley Literature Festival
Wordquake, Council Offices, Skirlaugh, East Riding of Yorkshire HU11 5HN
tel (01482) 392745
email john.clarke@eastriding.gov.uk
website www.beverley-literature-festival.org
Festival Director John Clarke
Takes place 5–15 October 2006

This festival offers author readings, readers' group sessions, writers' workshops and masterclasses. It involves all kinds of good writing but a special emphasis is placed on poetry.

Birmingham Book Festival
Unit 116, The Custard Factory, Gibb Street, Birmingham B9 4AA
tel 0121-246 2770 *fax* 0121-246 2771
email jonathan@bookcommunications.co.uk
Programmer Jonathan Davidson
Takes place 5–13 Oct 2006

An annual festival which presents a range of events with all types of writers of both fiction and non-fiction.

Book Now! Literature Festival

Education, Arts & Leisure Department, Orleans
House Gallery, Riverside, Twickenham TW1 3DJ
tel 020-8831 6000 *fax* 020-8744 0507
website www.richmond.gov.uk
Takes place Throughout Nov

An annual literature festival covering a broad range
of subjects. Leading British and overseas guest writers
hold discussions, talks, debates and readings. There
are also exhibitions and storytelling sessions for
children and adults.

Brighton Festival

12A Pavilion Buildings, Castle Square, Brighton
BN1 1EE
tel (01273) 700747 *fax* (01273) 707505
email info@brightonfestival.org.uk
website www.brightonfestival.org.uk
Takes place 5–27 May 2007

An annual general arts festival with a large literature
programme. Leading guest writers cover a broad
range of subjects in a diverse programme of events.
Programme published end of February.

Bristol Poetry Festival

Poetry Can, Unit 11, 20–22 Hepburn Road, Bristol
BS2 8UD
tel 0117-942 6976 *fax* 0117-944 1478
email info@poetrycan.wanadoo.co.uk
website www.poetrycan.com
Festival Director Colin Brown
Takes place 7–17 Sept 2006 at Bristol Old Vic and
other venues in Bristol

'Moonlight on the water. Sensuality. Laughter.
Passion. So much more than a spin in the dark.'

Buxton Festival

3 The Square, Buxton SK17 6AZ
tel (01298) 70395
email info@buxtonfestival.co.uk
website www.buxtonfestival.co.uk
Artistic Director Aidan Lang, *General Manager* Glyn
Foley
Takes place 6–22 July 2007 (tbc)

The main festival has a growing literary strand with
featuring distinguished authors.

Cambridge Conference of Contemporary Poetry

c/o Mrs Nolan, The Fitzwilliam Museum,
Trumpington Street, Cambridge CB2 1RB
tel (01223) 332922
website www.cccp-online.org.uk
Takes place April

An annual weekend of poetry readings, discussion
and performance of international poetry in the
modernist tradition.

Canterbury Festival

Festival Office, Christ Church Gate, The Precincts,
Canterbury, Kent CT1 2EE

tel (01227) 452853 *fax* (01227) 781830
email info@canterburyfestival.co.uk
website www.canterburyfestival.co.uk
Takes place 12–28 Oct 2006

An annual general arts festival with a literature
programme. Programme published in July.

Charleston Festival

The Charleston Trust, Charleston, Firle, Lewes, East
Sussex BN8 6LL
tel (01323) 811265 (information), 811626
(administration) *fax* (01323) 811628
email info@charleston.org.uk
website www.charleston.org.uk
Contact Diana Reich
Takes place May

Charleston, country home of Bloomsbury artists
Duncan Grant and Vanessa Bell hosts an annual
literary festival as part of the Brighton Festival.

Chaucer Festival

Sidney Cooper Gallery, 22 St Peter's Street,
Canterbury, Kent CT1 2BQ
tel 020-7229 0635 *fax* (01227) 761416
Director Martin Starkie
tel (01227) 470379
Takes place Spring, Summer and Autumn

An annual festival which includes commemoration
services, theatre productions, exhibitions, readings,
recitals, Chaucer site visits, medieval fairs, costumed
cavalcades, educational programmes for schools.
Takes place in London, Canterbury and the County
of Kent in the Spring (Easter Chaucer Pilgrimage),
Summer (June–July), and Autumn (Oct).

Cheltenham Literature Festival

Town Hall, Imperial Square, Cheltenham, Glos.
GL50 1QA
tel (01242) 227979 (box office), 237377 (brochure),
263494 (festival office) *fax* (01242) 256457
email clair.greenaway@cheltenham.gov.uk
website www.cheltenhamfestivals.com
Artistic Director Sarah Smyth
Takes place 6–15 Oct 2006

This annual festival is the largest of its kind in
Europe. Events include talks and lectures, poetry
readings, novelists in conversation, exhibitions,
discussions, workshops and a large bookshop. *Book
It!* is a festival for children within the main festival
with an extensive programme of events. Brochures
are available in August.

Chester Literature Festivals

Viscount House, River Lane, Saltney, Chester
CH4 8RH
tel (01244) 674020 *fax* (01244) 684060
email info@chesterlitfest.org.uk
website www.chester-literature-festival.org.uk
Festival Administrator Katherine Seddon

Takes place 30 Sept–28 Oct 2006

An annual festival commencing the first weekend in October. Events featuring international, national and local writers and poets are part of the programme, as well as a literary lunch and festival dinner. There is a poetry competition for school children, events for children and workshops for adults. A Cheshire Prize for Literature is awarded each year; only residents in Cheshire are eligible.

Chichester Festivities

Canon Gate House, South Street, Chichester, West Sussex PO19 1PU
tel (01243) 785718 *fax* (01243) 528356
email info@chifest.org.uk
website www.chifest.org.uk
Takes place 30 June–14 July 2007

City of London Festival

12–14 Mason's Avenue, London EC2V 5BB
tel 020-7796 4949 *fax* 020-7796 4959
email admin@colf.org
website www.colf.org
Takes place Last 2 weeks of June and first week of July 2007

An annual multi-arts festival with a programme of literary events. Programme published in April.

Complete Works of Shakespeare Festival

Royal Shakespeare Company, Royal Shakespeare Theatre, Stratford-upon-Avon CV37 6BB
tel (01789) 296655
website www.rsc.org.uk
Artistic Director Michael Boyd
Takes place Stratford-on-Avon, ending March 2007

A year-round festival.

The Cúirt International Festival of Literature

Galway Arts Centre, 47 Dominick Street, Galway, Republic of Ireland
tel (091) 565886 *fax* (091) 568642
email info@galwayartscentre.ie
website www.galwayartscentre.ie
Managing Director Tomás Hardiman, *Progammer*
Director Maura Kennedy
Takes place April

An annual week-long festival to celebrate writing, bringing together national and international writers to promote literary discussion. Events include readings, performances, workshops, seminars, lectures, poetry slams and talks. The festival is renowned for its convivial atmosphere ('cúirt' means a 'bardic court or gathering').

Dublin Writers' Festival

c/o Dublin City Council, Arts Office, The Lab, Foley Street, Dublin 1, Republic of Ireland

tel (01) 82225455 *fax* (01) 8178985
email dublinwritersfestival@eircom.net
website www.dublinwritersfestival.com
Takes place June

An annual festival with readings by major Irish and international poets and writers to celebrate the best in contemporary literature.

Durham Literature Festival

c/o Durham City Arts Ltd, 2 The Cottages, Fowlers Yard, Durham DH1 3RA
tel 0191-301 8830 *fax* 0191-301 8821
email alison@durhamcityarts.org
Festival Coordinator Alison Lister
Takes place Sept–Oct

Edinburgh International Book Festival

5A Charlotte Square, Edinburgh EH2 4DR
tel 0131-718 5666 *fax* 0131-226 5335
email admin@edbookfest.co.uk
website www.edbookfest.co.uk
Director Catherine Lockerbie
Takes place 12–28 Aug 2006, 11–27 Aug 2007

Now established as Europe's largest book event for the public. In addition to a unique independent bookselling operation, over 600 writers contribute to the programme of events. Programme details available in June.

Essex Poetry Festival

tel (01702) 230596
email derek@essex-poetry-festival.co.uk
website www.essex-poetry-festival.co.uk
Contact Derek Adams
Takes place Oct 2006

A poetry festival across Essex. Also includes the Young Essex Poet of the Year Competition.

Everybody's Reading

Leicester City Council, 12th Floor, Block A, New Walk Centre, Welford Place, Leicester LE1 6ZG
email libraries@leicester.gov.uk
Contact Damien Walter
Takes place Oct

Leicester City's celebration of books and reading.

Exeter Festival

Festival Office, Civic Centre, Exeter EX1 1JJ
tel (01392) 265200 *fax* (01392) 265265
website www.exeter.gov.uk
Festival Manager Lesley Waters
Takes place July

An annual general arts festival which includes a programme of literary activities. Programme of events available in May.

Federation of Worker Writers and Community Publishers Festival of Writing

Burslem School of Art, Queen Street, Stoke-on-Trent ST6 3EJ

tel (01782) 822327 *fax* (01782) 822327
email thefwwcp@tiscali.co.uk
website www.thefwwcp.org.uk
Takes place April

Festival at the Edge and Winter's Edge Storytelling Festivals

The Morgan Library, Aston Street, Wem, Shrewsbury
SY4 5AU
tel (01939) 236626
email info@festivalattheedge.org
website www.festivalattheedge.org
Contact Ali Quarrell
Takes place 29 Jan–4 Feb 2007 (Winter's Edge), 14–16
July 2007 (Festival at the Edge) in Much Wenlock,
Shrops.

The Guardian Hay Festival

Festival Office, The Drill Hall, 25 Lion Street, Hay-
on-Wye HR3 5AD
tel (0870) 7872848 (admin)
email admin@hayfestival.com
website www.hayfestival.com
Takes place May/June

This annual festival aims to celebrate the best in
writing and performance from around the world, to
commission new work, and to promote and
encourage young writers of excellence and potential.
Over 200 events in 10 days with leading guest writers.
Programme published April.

Guildford Book Festival

c/o Tourist Information Office, 14 Tunsgate,
Guildford GU1 3QT
tel (01483) 444334
email deputy@guildfordbookfestival.co.uk
website www.guildfordbookfestival.co.uk
Festival Director Glenis Pycraft
Takes place 16–28 Oct 2006

An annual festival. Diverse, provocative and
entertaining, held throughout the historic town.
Author events, poetry, workshops for all age groups
from 6 months onwards. Its aim is to further an
interest and love of literature by involvement and
entertainment. Founded 1990.

Harrogate International Festival

1 Victoria Avenue, Harrogate, North Yorkshire
HG1 1EQ
tel (01423) 562303 *fax* (01423) 521264
email info@harrogate-festival.org.uk
crime@harrogate-festival.org.uk
website www.harrogate-festival.org.uk
Takes place July/Aug

An annual international multi-arts festival.
Programme available in May.

Harrogate Crime Writing Festival (July): A weekend
of events featuring the best of British and American
crime writers.

Hay Festival – see The Guardian Hay Festival

Ilkley Literature Festival

The Manor House, 2 Castle Hill, Ilkley LS29 9DT
tel (01943) 601210 *fax* (01943) 817079
email admin@ilkleyliteraturefestival.org.uk
website www.ilkleyliteraturefestival.org.uk
Festival Director Rachel Feldberg
Takes place First two weeks in Oct

The north of England's oldest and largest literature
festival organises a full programme of writing and
reading events.

International Playwriting Festival

Warehouse Theatre, Dingwall Road, Croydon
CR0 2NF
tel 020-8681 1257 *fax* 020-8688 6699
email info@warehousetheatre.co.uk
website www.warehousetheatre.co.uk
Takes place Nov

The weekend festival features: a showcase of the best
selected work from the IPF competition, and selected
plays from the festival's international partners – the
leading Italian playwriting festival, the Premio
Candoni Arta Terme, and Theatro Ena, Cyprus.

Jewish Book Week

Jewish Book Council, PO Box 38247, London
NW3 5YQ
tel 020-8343 4675 *fax* 020-8343 4675
email jewishbookcouncil@btopenworld.com
website www.jewishbookweek.com
Administrator Pam Lewis
Takes place 24 Feb–4 March 2007

A festival of Jewish writing, with contributors from
around the world and sessions in London and
nationwide. Includes events for children and
teenagers.

King's Lynn Festival

5 Thoresby College, Queen Street, King's Lynn,
Norfolk PE30 1HX
tel (01553) 767557 *fax* (01553) 767688
website www.kingslynnfestival.org.uk
Administrator Joanne Mawson
Takes place 15–28 July 2007

An annual general arts festival with literature events
featuring leading guest writers.

King's Lynn Literature Festivals

19 Tuesday Market Place, King's Lynn, Norfolk
PE30 1JW
tel (01553) 691661 *fax* (01553) 691779
Chairman Tony Ellis
Takes place Sept/March

22nd Poetry Festival (22–24 Sept 2006): An annual
festival which brings 12 published poets to King's
Lynn for the weekend for readings and discussions.

19th Fiction Festival (9–11 March 2007): An annual festival which brings 12 published novelists to King's Lynn for the weekend for readings and discussions.

Knutsford Literature Festival

37 Manor Park South, Knutsford, Cheshire WA16 8AG
tel (01565) 640750
email julia.jary@ntlworld.com
website www.knutsfordlitfest.blogspot.com
Contact Julia Jary
Takes place First 3 weeks of Oct

An annual festival to celebrate writing and performance, with distinguished national, international and local authors. Events include readings and discussions, a literary lunch and theatrical performances.

Ledbury Poetry Festival

Town Council Offices, Church Street, Ledbury HR8 1DH
tel (0845) 458 1743
email prog@poetry-festival.com
website www.poetry-festival.com
Festival Director Charles Bennett
Takes place 28 June–8 July 2007 (provisional)

An annual festival featuring top poets from around the world, together with a poet-in-residence programme, competitions (send sae for entry form), workshops and exhibitions. Full programme available in May.

Lincoln Book Festival

City of Lincoln Council, Dept of Development and Environmental Services, City Hall, Beaumont Fee, Lincoln LN1 1DF
tel (01522) 873844 *fax* (01522) 873553
email Sara.Bullimore@lincoln.gov.uk
website www.lincolnbookfestival.co.uk
Contact Sara Bullimore (Arts & Cultural Sector Officer)
Takes place May

A festival that celebrates books but also includes other art forms that books initiate and inspire – comedy, film, performance, conversation. It aims to celebrate local, national and international writers and artists, historical and contemporary works of art as well as offering the public a chance to see both emerging and well-known writers and artists. Includes a programme of children's events.

Lincolnshire Literature Development Programme

Community Services, Lincolnshire County Council, County Offices, Lincoln LN1 1YL
tel (01522) 553235 *fax* (01522) 552811
email chris.kirkwood@lincolnshire.gov.uk
County Arts Development Officer David Lambert, *Arts Officer* Chris Kirkwood

Takes place Throughout the year

A series of varied literary events. Occasional festivals, tours, publications in Lincolnshire.

Lit.com

Arts Development, Origin One, One Origin Way, Europarc, Grimsby DN37 9TZ
tel (01472) 323382 *fax* (01472) 323377
email charlotte.bowen@nelincs.gov.uk
Contact Arts Development Unit
Takes place Oct

Reflecting the heritage and culture of the area, this combined literature and comedy festival aims to be accessible to all ages and abilities through a varied and unusual programme.

Litfest

PO Box 751, Lancaster LA1 9HJ
tel (01524) 62166
email all@litfest.org
website www.litfest.org
Contact Andrew Darby
Takes place 8–12 Nov 2006

Annual festival featuring readings, performances and workshops by contemporary writers for adults; includes performance of several new commissioned works each year. Litfest also acts as a year-round literature development agency in Lancashire.

Lowdham Book Festival

4th Floor, Arts, County Hall, West Bridgford, Nottingham NG2 7QP
tel 0115-977 4435
email ross.bradshaw@nottscc.gov.uk
website www.lowdhambookfestival.co.uk
Contact Ross Bradshaw, Literature Officer
Takes place June/July

An annual 10-day festival of literature events for adults and children with a daily programme of high-profile national writers. There is a writer-in-residence during the Festival and a book fair on the last Saturday.

Manchester Literature Festival

3rd Floor, 24 Lever Street, Northern Quarter, Manchester M1 1DZ
tel 0161-236 5725
email admin@mlfestival.co.uk
website www.manchesterliteraturefestival.co.uk
Contact Chris Gribble, Director
Takes place 12–22 Oct 2006

An annual festival celebrating new literature, new technology and the original modern city of Manchester.

Arthur Miller Centre International Literary Festival

School of English & American Studies, University of East Anglia, Norwich NR4 7TJ

tel (01603) 592810 fax (01603) 507728
email v.striker@uea.ac.uk
website www.uea.ac.uk/eas/events/intro.shtml
Contact Val Striker, Administrative Officer
Takes place Late Sept–early Dec

An annual festival of weekly events to bring well-established international writers of fiction, biography, poetry, etc to a public audience in the Eastern region.

National Eisteddfod of Wales
40 Parc Ty Glas, Llanisien, Cardiff CF14 5WU
tel 029-2076 3777 fax 029-2076-3737
email elfedateisteddfod.org.uk
website www.eisteddfod.org.uk
Director Elfed Roberts
Takes place 3–12 Aug 2007

Wales' largest cultural festival, based on 800 years of tradition. Activities include competitions in all aspects of the arts, fringe performances and majestic ceremonies. In addition to activities held in the main pavilion, it houses over 300 trade stands along with a literary pavilion, a music studio, a movement and dance theatre, a rock pavilion and a purpose-built theatre. The event is set in a different location each year, and will take place on the outskirts of Mold in 2007.

Norfolk and Norwich Festival
42–58 St George's Street, Norwich NR3 1AB
tel (01603) 614921 fax (01603) 632303
website www.nnfestival.org.uk
Artistic Director/Chief Executive Jonathan Holloway
Takes place May

Northern Children's Book Festival
22 Highbury, Jesmond, Newcastle Upon Tyne NE2 3DY
tel 0191-2813289
website www.ncbf.org.uk
Chairperson Ann Key
Takes place 6–18 Nov 2006

An annual festival to bring authors, illustrators, poets and performers to children in schools, libraries and community centres across the North East of England. About 36 authors visit the North East over the 2-week period for 2–8 days, organised by the 12 local authorities. The climax of the festival is a huge public event in a different part of the North East each year when over 4000 children and their families visit to take part in author seminars, drama workshops, and to enjoy a variety of book-related activities. The Gala Day will be on 18 Nov 2006 at St Hilds C of E School, Hartlepool.

Off the Shelf Literature Festival
Central Library, Surrey Street, Sheffield S1 1XZ
tel 0114-273 4400 fax 0114-273 4716
email offtheshelf@sheffield.gov.uk
website www.offtheshelf.org.uk

Contacts Maria de Souza, Su Walker, Lesley Webster
Takes place 14–28 Oct 2006

The festival comprises a wide range of events for adults and children, including author visits, writing workshops, storytelling, competitions and exhibitions. Programme available in September.

Oundle Festival of Literature
2 Herne Road, Oundle, Peterborough, Northants PE8 4BS
tel (01832) 274960
email liz@oundlelitfest.org.uk
website www.oundlelitfest.org.uk
Contact Liz Dillarstone (Publicity)
Takes place March 2007

Featuring a full programme of author events, poetry, philosophy, politics, story-telling, biography, illustrators and novelists for young and old. Includes events for children.

Oxford Literary Festival – see The Sunday Times Oxford Literary Festival

Poetry International
Literature Section, Royal Festival Hall, South Bank Centre, London SE1 8XX
tel 020-7921 0906 fax 020-7928 2049
email awhitehead@rfh.org.uk
website www.rfh.org.uk
Contact Angela Whitehead
Takes place Oct 2008 (biennial)

The biggest poetry festival in the British Isles, bringing together a wide range of poets from around the world. It includes readings, workshops and discussions. The Literature + Talks also runs a year-round programme of readings, talks and debates.

proudWORDS
PO Box 181, Newcastle upon Tyne NE6 5XG
tel (07973) 894912
email info@proudwords.org.uk
website www.proudwords.org
Coordinator Mary Lowe
Takes place Oct

An annual festival to promote the best lesbian and gay writing. The focus is participation and self expression, and the atmosphere is informal. The festival consists of workshops, performances, readings, competitions and discussions, culminating in a festival party. Also organises other events throughout the year.

Quite Literary
The Plough Arts Centre, 9–11 Fore Street, Torrington, Devon EX38 8HQ
tel (01805) 622552 fax (01805) 622113
email richard@plough-arts.org
Contact Richard Wolfenden-Brown
Takes place Throughout the year

An occasional literature programme including workshops, readings, performances and exhibitions, as part of a larger programme of arts work, including community and educational workshops, projects, residencies and performances.

Redbridge Book and Media Festival

London Borough of Redbridge, Arts and Events Team, 8th Floor, Lynton House, 255–259 High Road, Ilford IG1 1NY
tel 020-8708 3044
email laurence.staig@redbridge.gov.uk
website www.redbridge.gov.uk/leisure/bkmdfest.cfm
Contact Arts and Events Team
Takes place May 2007

Features author talks, performances, panel debates, Urdu poetry events, an exhibition, workshops, children's activities and events and a schools outreach programme.

Royal Court Young Writers' Festival

The Royal Court Young Writers' Programme, Sloane Square, London SW1W 8AS
tel 020-7565 5050
website www.royalcourttheatre.com
Contact The Administrator
Takes place Biennially (2008)

A national festival which anyone aged 13–25 can enter. Promising plays which arise from the workshops are then developed and performed at the Royal Court's Theatre Upstairs (see page 393).

Rye Festival

Martello Bookshop, 26 High Street, Rye, East Sussex TN31 7YB
tel (01797) 22444
email cattybing@btopenworld.com
website www.ryefestival.co.uk
Literary Events Manager Catherine Bingham
Takes place First 2 weeks of Sept (15 days); Winter Series held last weekend Jan and first weekend Feb (4 days)

An annual festival of literary events featuring novelists, biographers, political and scientific writers, with book signings and discussions. Runs concurrently with the Rye festival of music and visual arts.

Salisbury Festival

87 Crane Street, Salisbury, Wilts. SP1 2PU
tel (01722) 332241
website www.salisburyfestival.co.uk
Director Jo Metcalfe
Takes place 28 May–10 June 2007

An annual general multi-arts festival with a literature programme of events. Programme published in April.

Scottish Book Town Festival

County Buildings, Wigtown, Dumfries & Galloway DG8 9JH
tel (01988) 403222
email jenny@wigtownbookfestival.com
website www.wigtownbookfestival.com
Festival Chair Michael McCreath, *Festival Administrator* Jenny Bradley
Takes place Last 2 weekends in Sept

An annual festival in Scotland's national Book Town which boasts 23 bookshops and book-related businesses. Readings and talks take place in the County Buildings, bookshops and nearby Bladnoch Distillery.

StAnza: Scotland's Poetry Festival

tel (01333) 360 491 (administration), (01334) 475000 (box office), (01592) 414714 (programmes)
email admin@stanzapoetry.org
website www.stanzapoetry.org
Festival Director Brian Johnstone
Takes place 14–18 March 2007

The festival engages with all forms of poetry: read and spoken verse, poetry in exhibition, performance poetry, cross-media collaboration, schools work, book launches and poetry workshops, with numerous UK and international guests and a full weekend children's programme.

Stratford-upon-Avon Poetry Festival

Shakespeare Centre, Henley Street, Stratford-upon-Avon CV37 6QW
tel (01789) 204016 *fax* (01789) 296083
email info@shakespeare.org.uk
website www.shakespeare.org.uk
Director Roger Pringle
Takes place 28 June–27 Aug 2006, mainly on Sunday evenings

This annual festival opens with a reading by Andrew Motion. Recitals feature well-known actors presenting poetry of the past as well as contemporary poets. The 2 themes of Shakespeare and Poet Laureates will run through the festival. A local poets' evening will be held on 16 July and a reading of local children's verse on 9 July.

The Sunday Times Oxford Literary Festival

301 Woodstock Road, Oxford OX2 7NY
tel (01865) 514149 *fax* (01865) 514804
email oxford.literary.festival@ntlworld.com
website www.sundaytimes-oxfordliteraryfestival.co.uk
Festival Directors Angela Prysor-Jones, Sally Dunsmore
Takes place 2 weeks prior to Easter

An annual 8-day festival for both adults and children. Presents topical debates, fiction and non-fiction discussion panels, and adult and children's authors who have recently published books. Topics range from contemporary fiction to discussions on politics, history, science, gardening, food, poetry, philosophy, art and crime fiction. There is an additional 2 days of events for schools.

Swindon Festival of Literature

Lower Shaw Farm, Shaw, Swindon, Wilts. SN5 5PJ
tel (01793) 771080 *fax* (01793) 771080
email swindonlitfest@lowershawfarm.co.uk
website www.swindonfestivalofliterature.co.uk
Festival Director Matt Holland
Takes place Starts at dawn on 1 May for 15 days

An annual celebration of literature – prose, poetry, drama and storytelling – by readings, discussions, performances, talks, etc, indoors and out.

The Dylan Thomas Festival

The Dylan Thomas Centre, Somerset Place, Swansea SA1 1RR
tel (01792) 463980 *fax* (01792) 463993
email dylanthomas.lit@swansea.gov.uk
website www.dylanthomas.org
Events Manager David Woolley
Takes place 27 Oct–9 Nov 2006

An annual festival celebrating the life and work of Swansea's most famous son: performances, lectures, debates, poetry, music and film. Also, regular events throughout the year and talks and tours by arrangement.

Ty Newydd Festival

3rd Floor, Mount Stuart House, Mount Stuart Square, Cardiff CF10 5FQ
tel (02920) 472266 *fax* (02920) 492930
email post@academi.org
website www.academi.org
Contact Peter Finch, Chief Executive
Takes place April 2008 (biennial)

Events are centred on the writing centre at Llanystumdwy in Gwynedd and feature a mix of Welsh and English events including Poetry Stomps and guest readers. The Academi, the Welsh National Literature Promotion Agency, supports Ty Newydd to create this festival.

Warwick International Festival

Northgate, Warwick CV34 4JL
tel (01926) 410747 *fax* (01926) 409050
email richardp@warwickarts.org.uk
Festival Director Richard Phillips
Takes place 29 June–8 July 2007 (tbc)

A music festival which includes some literature and poetry events: readings, performances and workshops.

Ways With Words Literature Festival

Droridge Farm, Dartington, Totnes, Devon TQ9 6JQ
tel (01803) 867373 *fax* (01803) 863688
email admin@wayswithwords.co.uk
website www.wayswithwords.co.uk
Contact Kay Dunbar
Takes place 10 days in middle of July each year

200 speakers give readings, talks, interviews, discussions, seminars, workshops with leading guest writers. Also organises Words by the Water: a Cumbrian literature festival (March) and Southwold (Nov), and writing and painting holidays in Italy.

Wells Festival of Literature

25 Chamberlain Street, Wells, Somerset BA5 2PQ
tel (01749) 670929
website www.somersite.co.uk/wellsfest.htm
Takes place Mid Oct

An annual week-long festival featuring leading writers and poets. It includes theatre and cinema events, writing workshops and short story and poetry competitions. Events take place in the historic Bishop's Palace and other venues around the historic city of Wells.

Wonderful Words Book Festival

Penzance Library, Morrab Road, Penzance TR18 4EY
tel (01736) 363954
email agunderson@cornwall.gov.uk
website www.cornwall.gov.uk/library
Library Outreach Officer & Festival Organiser Alison Gunderson
Takes place Sept/Oct 2006

A biennial festival organised by the Cornwall Library Service. Events take place throughout the county, including talks, discussions, workshops, poetry and storytelling. The festival attracts high-profile authors.

Word – University of Aberdeen Writers Festival

University of Aberdeen, Office of External Affairs, University of Aberdeen, King's College, Aberdeen AB24 3FX
tel (01224) 274444 *fax* (01224) 272086
website www.abdn.ac.uk/word
Artistic Director Alan Spence, *Festival Producer* Elly Rothnie, *Festival Co-ordinator* Fiona Christie
Takes place May

Over 50 of the world's finest writers and artists take part in a packed weekend of readings, music, art exhibitions and film screenings. The Word Kid's Programme hosts some of the UK's best-loved children's writers as well as some of the richest talents in Gaelic literature.

World Book Day

c/o The Booksellers Association, 272 Vauxhall Bridge Road, London SW1V 1BA
tel 020-8987 9370
email cathy.schofield@blueyonder.co.uk
website www.worldbookday.com
Contact Cathy Schofield
Takes place 1 March 2007

An annual celebration of books and reading aimed at promoting their value and creating the readers of the future. Every schoolchild in full-time education receives a £1 book token. Events take place all over the UK in schools, bookshops, libraries and arts centres.

Writers' Week

24 The Square, Listowel, Co. Kerry, Republic of Ireland
tel (068) 21074 *fax* (068) 22893
email info@writersweek.ie
website www.writersweek.ie
Administrators Eilish Wren, Máire Logue
Takes place 30 May–3 June 2007

Aims to promote the work of Irish writers in both the English and Irish language, and to provide a platform for new and established writers to discuss their works. Events include readings, seminars, lectures and book launches.

Young Readers Birmingham

Children's Office, Central Library, Chamberlain Square, Birmingham B3 3HQ
tel 0121-303 3368 *fax* 0121-464 1004
email patsy.heap@birmingham.gov.uk
website www.birmingham.gov.uk/youngreaders
Contact Patsy Heap
Takes place 19 May–2 June 2007

An annual festival targeted at young people aged 0–19 and adults who care for or work with them. It aims to motivate them to enjoy reading and through this to encourage literacy; to provide imaginative access to books, writers and storytellers; to encourage families to share reading for pleasure; to provide a national focus for the celebration of books and reading for children and young people and help raise the media profile of children's books and writing. Approximately 150 events take place.

Writers and artists online
E-publishing

E-publishers offer a variety of services to authors and have no set standards of quality or provision. Jane Dorner looks at the electronic minefield facing authors.

I have been updating this article for the last four years and it is surprising how little has fundamentally changed in that time. Websites come and go, but the principles remain the same. So far, the dedicated device on which to read an electronic book has failed to captivate the British public, but many are comfortable reading on high resolution laptops and pocket organisers. Research into a type of screen that would roll up or fold (known as e-paper) is ongoing. The story of e-publishing is in slight limbo until a ready device as popular as the mobile phone is brought to market.

All major UK publishers have websites on which they promote their books. Some are publishing electronic versions downloadable directly from the web and some are sharing the revenue from e-titles 50–50 with their authors. This is still basically traditional publishing and all the brand name expectations apply.

There's another set of e-publishers who do not have an established track record or brand identity (high standards, quality provision, peer review, integrity). Some are genuine publishers operating in the new environment and some come perilously close to vanity publishers eager to make money out of the unwary. Others offer useful services to self-publishers. And some call themselves publishers, but are effectively book showrooms. The boundaries can sometimes be so vague that it is difficult to be dogmatic about what value they provide. Above all, be wary of sites that do not declare what the costs are and who pays them.

Until reputations form, writers will have to look closely at the e-publisher's websites, read carefully through submission statements, look for an online contract or terms and conditions and judge for themselves. Enter into an email dialogue and get as much information as you can before you send in anything. Look at authors who are already publishing with the e-publisher – the chances are you won't have heard of any of them. Might that be a warning sign? Try not to license your rights for more than a year or two at a time – so if they ask for *exclusive* rights, pass on to the next publisher.

The most obvious appeal is to writers who have unpublished works, out-of-print works where rights have reverted to them, previously published material that could have a renewed life in a new format, or memoires for the family.

One increasingly popular form of personal e-publishing is the blog, which means 'web log' or 'online diary'.

E-books

An e-publisher will convert your word-processed document into one, or more, of the three basic software formats for making e-books readable on notebook PCs, personal digital organisers (PDAs), mobile phones and desktop computers. They are not interchangeable:

- Adobe Portable Document Format (PDF) which is a universal standard for preserving the original appearance – fonts, formatting, colours, and graphics – of any source document, regardless of the application and platform used to create it;

- Microsoft Reader format – similar electronic reading software designed for easy on-screen reading;
- Mobipocket Reader – another format like the two above.

All content can be downloaded into the reading devices from a website and can be paid for at that time. These formats are relatively cheap for a publisher to produce – but only assuming they do nothing to add to the editorial value. None of the electronic formats are secure from plagiarists, though some make a better attempt at security than others. At present, PDF files are the most secure (though hackable), with options ranging from preventing text selection (so users cannot cut and paste), disabling reading onscreen (so only one print copy can be made), or, conversely, disabling printing, to password-protection. However, accessibility to those with disabilities is also important and may mean compromising on full security.

The question here is whether yours is the sort of book that people will want to read from screens – small or large.

Print on Demand

Some printers offer Print-on-Demand (POD) services for good quality paper copies in runs of 1 to 1000. This has a double appeal to authors: for self-publishing and for bringing an out-of-print book back into circulation. You don't have to grant any licence of rights and you don't need to let anyone else have control over production matters.

The self-publishing route is attractive. There's a set-up cost and a per title cost, but they're generally lower than the self-publishing options that have been available up to now. This option may well be of interest to authors who don't mind doing their own promotion. POD offers a potentially viable digital production model to the publishing industry as a whole. If the technology settles and origination costs come down a little lower than they are now, we could see certain types of book being ordered on the internet for collection an hour later at the local bookshop where it is bound and printed. Authors in some genres may be able to bypass publishers.

The author is expected to supply a completely finished, edited file and this is poured into a standard template. Some e-publishers take anything they are offered (within the bounds of censorship) and others have strict filtering systems. Not many provide editing, design or quality control. Prices are hugely variable, but expect to pay about £200 for 50 copies of a 150-page book. Individual or quality-vetted services can raise costs into the £1000+ bracket – typically: cover design, £150; proofreading, £2.20 a page; assigning an ISBN, £50; marketing package, £175; adding pictures, £10 for each non-embedded illustration, and other dubious add-ons. Some e-publishers offer a single price for the whole service – e.g. £450 is the lowest I have found, but it can be unclear what exact book length and print run this includes. You may also be tempted by being offered registration with Amazon, or free distribution to a given number of bookshops in the UK, or a variety of other seeming benefits. Read the offers with circumspection and do comparative research. For example, you can register 10 ISBNs with the ISBN Agency for £94. As for Amazon, they get their information from Nielsen BookData and registration with them is free (see listing). Get a quote for your book from a few sources. A detailed quote setting down exactly what the specifications are is probably more reliable than opting for a preset package. The Society of Authors has a *Quick Guide* (No 17) which will answer more detailed questions.

Out-of-print publishing is more complex. It is unlikely that the author will have a digital copy of a former work. Corrections, design and late changes to the latest version of either the author's or the editor's file is not the final version. This means a published copy must be scanned in and converted. To do this at reasonable cost and with acceptable accuracy requires a sophisticated scanner and two copies of the book with cut spines, merged and assembled in book order. There are two problems. With older books, the author may only have one precious copy and may not be willing to cut it up. With newer books, the chances are the rights have reverted, but the typographical right still belongs to the publisher for 25 years after publication. It's arguable that scanning violates that right.

Showcasing

The listing below is a cross-section of services to authors who would like to sell or resell their works in one of the formats described. Some market in the same way as traditional publishers. Some are printers. Many e-publishers double as online booksellers, so they are not publishers in the sense we have been used to – although they also promote their best-selling authors more aggressively than the ones no one has heard of. The difference is that they can offer showcase capacity to any author, well known or not. Most guarantee visitors against pornography and real rubbish, but it's fairly rudimentary quality control. Show-casing is generally just that – a space on the bookshelf. And in this environment book-shelving is infinitely expandable. Most are sited in the US, but that doesn't matter since this is global exposure anyway.

Blogging

The content and purposes of blogs varies greatly – from news about a family, person or idea, to diaries, photos, poetry, mini-essays and fiction. It was on 11 September 2001, when New York's twin towers so catastrophically fell, that blogging really came of age as thousands of individuals gave their own perspectives and thoughts on the tragedies of that day. This was personal journalism at an emotional peak and ever since the media have been drawing on individual accounts.

Two sites where you can get started are listed below and they are both very easy to use, but give yourself time if you are new to blogging. It's instant electronic publishing and limited only by your own imagination.

Some web aficionados claim that the future of web publishing is in blogs. Not only is it a testament to the state of the world, but people enjoy cataloguing their lives, interests or random musings and other people like reading them and linking to them. Some agents regularly trawl blogs for writing worthy of traditional publication – which shows, perhaps, that paper publishing still rules. There is probably an art form tucked away in blogging – if it can overcome its unfortunate nomenclature.

Websites

Note, this is a fast-moving area and more online publishers will spring up and some of these will disappear. In all cases, authors should check all details of the contracts.

The *Writers' & Artists' Yearbook* cannot be held responsible for any content on any of these sites. It came to our attention that in a previous edition one site led to a pornography page. This was because the original owner of the domain had not yet paid for a renewal and another party had instantly acquired it. They posted an offensive page and they effectively blackmailed the e-publisher to pay a large sum to get it back. Be aware that this can happen.

Print on Demand

Antony Rowe
www.antonyrowe.co.uk

An established printer offering short runs. There is a quote calculator on the site.

Authors Online
www.authorsonline.co.uk

A Bedfordshire-based POD self-publishing venue. Their standard service costs £750 with a 'free' offer for orders of 30 copies of an online book.

BookSurge
www.booksurge.com

A POD self-publishing concern with useful affiliates but read all the small print before committing to them – it could cost anything from $99 to $999.

Bookprintinguk
www.bookprintinguk.com

Cambridgeshire printer which offers a short-run POD service.

iUniverse
www.iuniverse.com

A service for redeploying out-of-print books; check the author contract carefully. Packages range from $299 to $1099.

Lightning Source
www.lightningsource.com

Established POD and e-book supplier. No prices given but there is an exhaustive list of FAQs.

Lulu
www.lulu.com/uk

A showcase for services supplied by people in the book trade, with reliability ratings. A certain amount of free advice but you have to register (free.)

Unlimited Publishing
www.unlimitedpublishing.com

A POD system for new and out-of-print titles; will cost new authors about $1000 as long as they use Word or similar.

Virtual Bookworm
www.virtualbookworm.com

POD and e-book supplier; packages range from $360 to $1950.

Writers World
www.writersworld.co.uk

A self-publishing resource for writers to publish their books by POD or e-books. Cost to author unclear. Free newsletter and chatroom.

Xlibris
www2.xlibris.com

POD packages ranging from $500 to $2990 (for picture books) plus marketing packages.

E-Publishers

Artemis Press
www.artemispress.com

Women's fiction, 30% royalty; contract and submission details online; exclusive rights requested.

Atlantic Bridge
www.atlanticbridge.net

Seeks science fiction, horror, romance and mystery writers; non-exclusive contract and submission details online; 45% royalty.

Author House
www.authorhouse.com

US-based self-publishing site; pays 25% royalty on e-books only.

BookLocker
www.booklocker.com

E-book publisher offering 35%–70% royalties to authors only requesting non-exclusive rights. Authors pay $127–$476 for this.

Diskus Publishing
www.diskuspublishing.com

Indiana-based romantic fiction niche publisher. Books for several e-reader formats can be downloaded for about £6.30 a book. Said to publish about 5% of submissions.

FictionWise
www.fictionwise.com

Independent eBook publisher and distributor. Work must be previously published fiction works from established authors. Does not accept unsolicited material or work from new writers.

Fiction Works
www.fictionworks.com

E-books and audio book opportunities; submissions in certain genres only.

The Front List
www.thefrontlist.com

Publishing by peer review. Makes its money by asking for £10 to let you see critiques of your work; you have to critique others' work before you can have yours read.

Online Originals
www.onlineoriginals.com

One of the higher-profile UK-based venues for literary fiction and intellectual non-fiction.

Submissions are vetted by Online Original authors and if 2 of them approve a book, it is published. Submitters must pay £40 to each reader.

Rosetta Books
www.rosettabooks.com

Sells and distributes books in various e-formats (Microsoft Reader and Adobe Acrobat).

E-publishing resources

Author.co.uk
www.author.co.uk

Gives sponsored links – it is a listing not an endorsement of content.

Author's Studio
www.theauthorsstudio.org

Small community of small presses owned and operated by commercial authors.

eBook Palace
www.ebookpalace.com

Visitor-submitted directory of e-books; authors can list their own.

eBooks.com
www.ebooks.com

Internet Digital Bookstore. Invites authors to let their publisher or agent know about it; authors should check rights deals with their publisher.

eReader
www.ereader.com

E-books for hand-held computers; has e-books by well-known authors.

fotoLIBRA
www.fotolibra.com

Picture library – photographers can upload and sell pictures for a £6 monthly subscription. Terms: 50%.

ISBN Agency
www.nbdrs.com/isbn_agency.htm

KnowBetterCom
www.knowbetter.com

Resource of information on the e-publishing scene, including the latest information on technology, industry news, tips, advice and reviews. Useful overview and discussion forums.

Nielsen's BookData Services
www.nielsenbookdata.co.uk

Bibliographic records of books in print.

International Digital Publishing Forum
www.idpf.org

Format specifications, sponsored by the National Institute of Standards and Technology (formerly the Open Book Forum).

UK Children's Books
www.ukchildrensbooks.co.uk

Listings of authors, illustrators and publishers.

Writers Co-operative
www.rabbitbooks.com

Mixed collection of UK self-publishing writers' work and its authors publishing venue.

Writer's Eye
www.writerseye.co.uk

Research service for writers.

Writing.com
www.writing.com

Online community for writers offering advice and publishing suggestions.

Blogging

Blogger
http://blogger.com

One of the first, and easiest to use, sites for starting a blog.

Wordpress
http://wordpress.org

A 'personal publishing platform': in other words a free home for your blog.

Critical comment

BeeHive
http://beehive.temporalimage.com

A hypertext and hypermedia online literary journal in several volumes.

Digital Art Museum
www.dam.org

Cultural centre for artists and theorists.

Electronic Literature Organization
www.eliterature.org

Promotes new media art and literature.

Rhizome
www.rhizome.org

Centre of information on internet art and text that supports a global new media art community.

trAce
http://trace.ntu.ac.uk/review

News and reviews of new media writing, art and events.

Turbulence
www.turbulence.org

Supports and commissions net art (radio and performance).

A brief introduction to electronic rights

'In the world of mules/there are no rules' – Ogden Nash summed up what it is to be a mule very well. As a couplet, it is equally applicable to the chaotic, frequently arcane and jargon-ridden world of electronic rights. Jonathan Glasspool gives an overview aimed at authors who want to understand why a basic understanding of electronic rights is important to them.

What are electronic rights?

It's probably best to start with a definition. 'Electronic rights' covers all rights where content is distributed via electronic means to a user.

There are two kinds of electronic rights: Primary (publishing) rights and secondary (licensing) rights. This works for print as well as for electronic media and is incredibly important for publishers and authors since how an electronic deal is framed can mean the difference between a publishing royalty (7–15%) and a sub-rights split (50% or more) to the author. Whatever format the product is (online, e-book download, CD-Rom, etc) the most important issue is whether the publisher is exercising a primary right (to create, publish and sell a product) or licensing a second party to do the same. For primary right usage a smaller, sales royalty is paid, typically based upon what the publisher receives; and for second party licensing a revenue share is due.

Why are electronic rights important to authors?

What makes electronic rights such an area of concern for authors, agents and publishers is the unprecedented level of technological change that has taken place in the past decade. This change has challenged the way books are produced, enabling the content to be distributed in very different ways. Drivers of this change include:

Broadband access, which enables extremely fast downloads. In the UK it increased to nearly 60% of internet users. The success of the Apple iPod is largely due to the fact that it is a great piece of new kit which looks fab and is easy to use. But the download market which has resulted from it wouldn't be able to survive without the huge platform of users that Broadband has created. Consumer publishers are excited by the opportunities a similar download market might have for e-books now that people are used to downloading content. We'll come back to this later.

Google Books. The American search engine company announced at the end of 2004 that it was digitising a huge number of out-of-copyright titles from Stanford, Oxford and New York libraries. It is also digitising thousands of in-copyright US titles without asking publishers' permission. Here, the search results will be limited to 'snippets' of text, unless given permission to show more by the copyright holder.

As you can imagine, this initiative has raised huge questions over copyright, with bitter divisions emerging among players over the past year. In the US, the Authors Guild and the Association of American Publishers are currently suing Google and in the UK it has come under severe criticism from the Publishers Association and the Society of Authors. The main concern of traditional book publishers and authors is the feeling that Google are wresting control over how their content is distributed, and the fear – rightly or wrongly – that this content is being given away 'for free'.

The debate is set to continue, with the launch of a rival consortium, the Open Content Alliance, which is backed by Yahoo and Microsoft, and announcements by some of the bigger trade publishers and Amazon that they are creating their own 'digital repositories'.

Changes in library purchasing. Authors of educational and scholarly works will already be aware that many titles are already being offered in digital form, as well as in print. Suppliers to libraries such as www.questia.com, www.netlibrary.com, www.ebrary.com and www.xrefer.com offer bundles of titles by subject from a wide range of publishers. The attraction to librarians is that this content can be accessed remotely by library users and, subject to the licence, can be read by more than one person at a time. They also save space. These companies are joined by individual print publishers which are digitising their backlists, notably Oxford University Press and Gale in the reference area and Elsevier's science books. Whilst the market for electronic content outside business, scientific and legal publishing is still relatively small, it is growing fast. Libraries are getting used to buying content electronically, rather than in print, and they often club together in consortia to do so. Books for schools and colleges are as likely to be read online as in print.

New hardware technology. There has been much trumpeting of new e-ink technologies, the latest incarnation of which is the Sony Reader. The advantage of this reader over the earlier readers is the quality of the reading screen, which is very close to print. It also has a long battery life (Sony reckons you can turn 7500 pages without recharging), can display PDFs and retails at around $350 or £200 in the UK (depending on what option you go for). It can store up to 80 titles on its internal memory, with the option of more on removable memory cards. It remains to be seen whether this new technology will provide the 'tipping point' for e-books in the same way that the iPod did for MP3.

(Note for the uninitiated: Portable Document Format (PDF) is the hugely popular file format developed by Adobe that enables the user to encode the exact look of a document to send to another reader. MP3 is the most popular digital audio format for music files stored on computers or mobile devices.)

In short, a truckload of money is going into digitising books. Will authors get a share of it?

Further reading

I recommend Lynette Owen's lucid survey of electronic rights in *Selling Rights* (Routledge, 5th edn 2006) if you think that electronic use of your book is going to be important.

The Society of Authors (www.societyofauthors.org) has two useful *Quick Guides* on the subject: *Electronic Publishing Contracts* and *Publishing Contracts*.

There is a useful online article about the difficulty of defining electronic rights at www.publaw.com/electronic.html which, despite being written nine years ago, still holds true.

Websites

You can find out more about e-books on the help pages of www.e-books.com, one of the earliest retailers of e-books, which has a good range of e-books aimed at the consumer. The website of the UK einformation Group (UKeiG – www.ukeig.org.uk) has more information, though it has to be paid for. For information on the next generation of e-book readers, go to www.sonystyle.com. The blog site http://i-a-l.blogspot.com provides a useful online bibliography for people who want to monitor e-book technology developments. The US site www.idpf.org is the home of the trade association for digital publishing.

For more information about the ongoing furore over online content, check out Google's arguments at www.google.com/googleprint/library.html. To read about the other initiatives in this area, it's worth going to the Open Content Alliance at www.opencontentalliance.org, which is backed by Microsoft and Yahoo.

How should 'electronic rights' be covered in an author's contract?

Electronic rights are commonly treated in two places in standard book contracts. E-book rights, where the text is simply digitised and put in a format that can be read onscreen is a primary right or a 'volume right' or 'verbatim text right', and all publishers will ask for this. Their argument is that they have gone to the expense of editing and producing an author's work, and that this is simply publishing it in another format (like paperback and hardback rights). Publishers virtually always work on a net receipts basis, rather than published price. This reflects the various ways e-books are sold and the different selling prices: direct by the publishers, via online retailers, and via library suppliers. The fact that e-books are increasingly sold as bundles of content also muddies the picture.

The much more tricky area is subsidiary electronic rights, where the publisher sub-licenses a book's content for re-use by another party, or they bundle parts of it in an online database with other titles for sale.

Publishers, who are in not much of a better position than authors to second guess how readers are going to be buying books in five years' time, tend to go for as broad a definition of electronic rights as possible. Whether it is in the interests of authors to license all of these rights to their publisher will depend on whom you are writing for, what the publisher is planning to do electronically, and when. At the very least, an author should ask their publisher. Defining their proposed electronic use will clarify how publisher and author will make money from the arrangement. Many of the models that e-books and e-content have created tend to confound the contractual models publishers have. So if a publisher experiments with these potentially industry-changing models, authors should expect their publishers to inform them of a judgement call they made to help put a deal in context.

Are e-books really the next big thing?

Whilst there is clearly going to be more of a market now that the iPod has been such a success, I am still sceptical that these devices are going to make many in-roads (in the short term) into the consumer market, for the following reasons:

● One of the main benefits of iPods/MP3 players is that they enable users to convert their existing CD collection into something they can re-use. But with print, this is not the case as users will have to download new online editions. Since the cost of a book download is not much different from buying a paperback, this is a big expense for the added benefit of a portable library. To create a 'library' of books in your device is therefore going to cost a lot more.

● Much of the lucrative traffic to iTunes has been for singles (79p per throw). There isn't an equivalent market for books: people don't download individual chapters of a book for instance, though the Amazon Shorts programme is worth watching. The cost per trans-action for a book is therefore going to be much higher than for music, and the traffic proportionately less. This may change as people get used to downloading albums and films online, but we're certainly not talking next year.

● iPods/MP3 players don't force people to change their behaviour in the same way that an e-book reader demands. People have been able to access and experience music on the move for 30–40 years via car radios, transistor radios and Walkmans. The iPod/MP3 player is a more sophisticated version of this, with the added benefit of vastly more storage and the ability to download. E-book readers on the other hand will require users to develop a need for a gizmo they've not had before.

- The 'handbag factor' shouldn't be underestimated. Sony *et al* are currently expecting people to buy a mobile phone, a MP3 player and an e-book reader. That's a lot to lug about, together with the security factor of carrying a lot of expensive kit.
- Innate conservatism of much of the consumer book market. Nicholson Baker says of the enduring appeal of the printed word: 'We've come up with a beautifully browsable invention that needs no electricity and exists in a readable form no matter what happens'.
- Reference information versus narrative text: there has been considerable success in Japan in transferring some reference content, for example dictionaries, to handheld devices. This partly reflects the fabled Japanese enthusiasm for gadgetry, but also the usefulness of easily accessed and displayed small bits of data on the move. However, there is not much evidence of a similar demand for non-reference works on a small screen (at least by comparison with print sales).
- You can lend a book to someone. With current digital rights management technology, this is not possible in most cases with e-books, unless you lend the (expensive) device itself.

Conclusion

As far as authors are concerned, electronic rights remain one of the most 'mulish' areas of contractual law. This reflects the disruptive nature of many of the new technologies, raising wide-ranging questions about the role of traditional publishers in an online world.

An understanding of electronic rights is very important for educational writers, where institutional customers are already buying materials and where student demand is clearly growing. The market for consumer titles in whatever format, is nascent and small by comparison with print.

Publishers will always go for as broad a definition of electronic rights as possible. In return, authors should be clear about the range and definition of rights they are granting and should ask what their publisher's plans are for exploiting their content in electronic form.

As this edition of the *Yearbook* goes to press, the Publishers Association, the Society of Authors and the Association of Authors' Agents are negotiating voluntary guidelines to cover electronic rights. These will be available in late 2006, and a summary of these will appear in next year's edition.

Jonathan Glasspool is Deputy Managing Director of A & C Black Publishers Ltd.

Acknowledgements: I'm grateful to Lynette Owen (Pearson), Evan Schnittman (OUP), David Attwooll, Kate Pool (Society of Authors), Elizabeth Mackey (Motricity) and James Raiher (Xrefer) for their helpful comments.

Setting up a website

Computer users who have email almost certainly have web space available to them. Jane Dorner explains the points for writers and artists to consider when setting up a personal website and how to best make it work for them.

This article assumes that readers are familiar with websites and have used the internet for research. To set up your own website the main investment you need to make is in time, perhaps more than you initially think. The process may have its frustrating moments, but it is ultimately creative.

Personal websites

A website can be a useful self-publicity medium for writers. It can be especially useful if you self-publish, but equally worthwhile for showing the world a portfolio of your artistic achievements and accomplishments. Many writers and artists are polymaths and the web shows up such diversity to advantage.

A personal website can be set up to demonstrate your writing or illustration style(s) and areas of interest with examples of work so that commissioning editors can see if they are choosing the right writer or artist for the job. You can include an outline of your skills and achievements, and list your publications – or you could even offer a personal syndication service for stories, articles, photographs or illustrations (if first or resale rights are yours).

You need to let people know that your website exists – there is no point having a wonderful site if no one visits it – for which old-fashioned marketing techniques are necessary. Posting your site on the web and registering hopefully with a few (or even a hundred) search engines is no substitute for careful targeting. You will probably be easily found on Google, but only if people know about you. Refer potential clients to your website, and make sure it attracts them sufficiently to explore it.

Skills required

In order to create the website yourself, you will need to have:

- a capacity for logical thinking;
- secure language expertise;
- some technical understanding;
- good visual sense;
- patience; and
- familiarity with applicable law.

If you don't have (or can't acquire) these skills then it is worth thinking about asking someone else to build the site for you. Expect to pay for at least one day of a professional designer's time (between £300 and £500) to create a modest suite of individually tailored pages with some attention to what you want and need. Bear in mind that the less you pay, the more likely it is that your material is simply being poured into a standard template, as is the case with sites that offer five pages for £250.

Planning a website

Whether you get involved with the technological side or not, you will still have to plan and write the copy yourself. Writing for the web is a new art form that uses writerly skills: it is genuinely creative; requires writers, not programmers; and needs editors with an understanding of traditional editorial values.

Writing the text for a website is like any other writing project. The more effort that goes into the planning stage, the better the result. You need to identify who you are targeting and be clear about the purpose of the website. For instance, is it your calling card; a PR brochure; a sales outlet; an information resource; a literary club or part of a network; a designer's showcase; or a medium of self-expression? The website needs to be planned and created accordingly. For example, if you just want a simple calling card, then a single screen – called a splash page – might suffice. It would have your name, perhaps a photograph of you, a few lines about your specialist skills and interests, possibly some work you have had published, and your contact details. You can then be found by anyone who uses the internet; your personal front cover is on the world bookshelf.

Writing for screen reading

If you write for radio, you will have an advantage over other writers. Writing for the web is a bit like writing for broadcasting: the style has to compensate for the loss of the visual impact of words. It's a common mistake to cut and paste from documents created for print because the text will not read as well on a website.

The average adult spends eight hours a week reading as opposed to 27 hours watching television. And that's reading from paper – reading from a screen has so far proved less efficient than paper.

When writing the introductory text for a website, aim for the reluctant reader with a less than three-minute attention span and use easy words and short sentences. As readers delve deeper into a site, their acceptance of more discursive reading matter increases. Once they are committed to the subject material, you can write in your normal style and assume they will print out the text and read from paper. Take writing for radio or television as the paradigm and then make it even simpler. Here are a few pointers:

- **Use the tadpole or pyramid structure**. Present the main points at the top of the page (people are reluctant to scroll) and use interior pages to unfold details.
- **Be concise**. The overall length of a radio or television piece is about a third of a print article; a web page should be even shorter. Cut every word that doesn't contribute. A good web page length is under 200 words – it is better to divide anything longer than that into sub-topics.
- **Write short paragraphs**. Paragraph breaks refresh the eye: between two and five sentences is enough.
- **Write simple sentences**. Ideas are easier to digest in a simple subject-verb-object progression. Make subclauses into separate sentences. Use one idea per sentence. Make them under the 17-word print average.
- **Use the present or present perfect tense**. The web is here and now. Keep passives away.
- **Be consistent**. Use the same font, type size, alignment and background colour throughout your site. Or use different colour bands to denote different 'areas' (novels, poetry, teaching and so on). Remember that capital letters onscreen look like SHOUTING.
- **Consider navigation**. If a visitor makes Choice A here, what are the ramifications for Choice B there? Web writing is not static, but writing dynamically is something that most writers have not learned. It is, perhaps, something we will all have to discover as we progress into the web publishing age.

- **Links**. Don't link every prompt phrase that leads somewhere else. If you want readers to stay with you to absorb your point, put the link outside the main text area. Don't link just because you can.
- **Define the main areas of your site**. Consider synonyms for your top level labels (the four to six main areas of your site). How often have you got lost in a website simply because the way in which your mind works isn't the same as the mindset of the person who created it? Try to second guess what visitors to your site will want to see when they come to each page then find a single word that most unambiguously describes it.

Designing for screens

The first thing to remember about designing for screens is that you cannot control how the screen page will look as there are so many variables, such as screen resolution and type of web browser. You should therefore test your design on several platforms. Design depends on purpose, but here are a few good practice points:

- **Colour**. Have a white or pale cream background and black or very dark type (studies show that sharp contrasts aid readability). Use 'web-safe' colours (see box). There are 216 of them based on RGB, which simply stands for Red, Green, Blue – nature's three primary

Useful websites

Amazon Bookshop Associates Scheme
www.amazon.co.uk/associates
For linking to sales of your own (or recommended) books.

Alert Box
www.useit.com/alertbox
Web usability and readability analysis. Opinionated but pertinent.

The CGI Resource Index
www.cgi-resources.com
Scripts that you can buy (some are free), e.g. automatic forms and page counters.

1st Site Free
www.1stsitefree.com
Create a website in 7 easy steps. A good starting point; links to useful tools.

FTP Explorer
www.ftpx.com
File transfer software for PCs. Share ware – 30-day trial.

Interarchy
www.interarchy.com
File transfer software for Macs.

Pedalo
www.pedalo.co.uk
Website design and promotion services for writers.

Site Aid
www.amiasoft.com/siteaid
Freeware HTML editor. Looks similar to Microsoft's FrontPage.

UK2.Net
http://uk2.net
Inexpensive domain registration and web forwarding.

Validator
http://validator.w3.org
Free online validation of HTML code.

Watchfire webXact
http://webxact.watchfire.com
Free online service that lets you test single pages of web content for quality, accessibility and privacy issues.

Web Style Guide
www.webstyleguide.com
Excellent guide to aspects of web writing. Used to be the Yale Style Manual.

Zone Alarm
www.zonealarm.com
Firewall (free and pro versions) to protect you against intrusions and pop-ups. Essential.

colours. Monitors and television sets transmit RGB – after all colour is light – so the only colours available are the ones that standard monitors can transmit.

● **Fonts.** How typefaces appear onscreen depends on which ones are on that particular system, not what you specify on yours. The ones you can rely on to look good on screens – and are universally available – are known as 'web-safe' fonts (see box).

● **Line length.** Put the text in invisible tables so that the line length is limited to about 10 words in standard browsers – this is an optimum reading line length. If you do not set a limit, the chances are that at high screen resolutions readers might get a line length of 25 words on the default reading typeface. This leads to what is known as 'regression pauses' while the reader struggles to make sense of the text.

● **Page size.** A reasonable rule of thumb is to make each page a maximum of 35K. People don't like watching a blank screen and research suggests that 10 seconds is as long as most people will wait for the screen to be filled. Standard dialup connections download at around 4–5K a second, so that means the first 20K or so need to be interesting enough to grab the viewer's attention. A short text page with three or four thumbnail-sized graphics will generally load quickly.

● **Graphics.** Every graphic must speak: make sure its iconography is clear and unambiguous. Remember that when you insert a picture you must give an explanatory note in the ALT (Alternative) command so that software that reads to the partially sighted or blind can tell the user what the pictures are. It also pops up as a little yellow box hovering over the image area and presents an opportunity to preview in words what the picture illustrates.

● **Artist's portfolio.** A gallery of small thumbnail illustrations is useful for showcasing an artist's range of work, with a click-link to larger pictures. Take care not to offer high-quality graphics that could be plagiarised: most internet graphics are in jpeg format, which is 72 dpi and not suitable for print reproduction. It's advisable to watermark all artwork.

● **Animation.** Bullet points or graphic elements help pick out key words but animations should be avoided. Studies show that the message is lost when television images fail to reinforce spoken words. The same is true of the web.

● **Frames.** Using frames can be an elegant solution to navigation problems but for the user it's not ideal, especially for anyone with accessibility problems. Because the page name

Websites for design

Art and the Zen of Web Sites
www.tlc-systems.com/webtips.shtml
Why the web is not a place to show off artistic skills.

Killer Sites
www.killersites.com
Website of *Creating Killer Web Sites* by David Siegal. Both book and site are full of information for designers.

UK Web Design Association
www.ukwda.org
Promotes industry standards.

VisiBone
www.visibone.com
Web-safe colours, style sheets and other resources

Web-safe fonts
www.microsoft.com/typography/web/fonts

Websites for Artists
www.beyondthenorthwind.co.uk
Artscape package designed for artists to add pictures to their own site. Affordable.

on the URL never varies, the visitor never knows where they are. They cannot bookmark a particular page, or find it again on a second visit and that can be very frustrating.

Going online

Once you have the planning, writing and graphics of your website organised, you need a little basic technical understanding to get it online. Your service provider will have a starter kit of instructions – although whether they make sense is another matter. You may well have to turn to other sources for instruction.

The internet is chock-a-block with instructional material. Try 1st Site Free (see page 608), which outlines and expands on seven easy steps – plan, design, code, upload, test, promote and maintain.

An alternative is to use software that 'talks you through' setting up a small site with what are called 'wizards'. Wizards come in software programs such as FrontPage (part of later versions of Microsoft Office) and its free look-a-like Site Aid. Both resemble word processors and keep the coding hidden from view. Hard core web designers will sneer at these programs, because programmers like to control the way the code works themselves. What they do not realise is that writers want to concentrate on the words, not the coding, and as long as it functions, the refinements of the underlying structure are of less importance. For artists who are more concerned with design, the best package is Dreamweaver (which is expensive and not easy to learn).

Once the pages are ready, the next step is to transmit them to the service provider's machines. The mechanics of this are frequently opaque even when you are offered a handy button that says 'Publish'. The chances are that your service provider will not have the extensions that make the 'Publish' button work and you will have to acquire a (free) File Transfer Protocol (ftp) program. If you are technophobe, this may seem frightening at first. However, it is really very simple and once you have successfully transferred (or uploaded) the pages from your computer to the web space on the remote server, you will wonder what the problem was. For this transfer process you will need to know the host name, your user ID and your password, information available from your provider.

HTML

If you want to learn HTML (HyperText Markup Language) – the code that tags elements such as text, links and graphics so that browser software will know how to display a document – then you need only a plain text program, like Notepad, and an HTML primer (there are plenty online as well as in printed form). Find some website pages which you like and look at their source code to see how they have been constructed (click the subsidiary button of the mouse, usually the right button, and select View Source). If the originators have used JavaScript or Cascading Style Sheets, this may well be more code than you want to know about so look at simple pages first.

Going a step further

You may wish to have a web address or URL that is short or memorable so that it is easier for people to find your website. You can choose this domain name yourself, and is now relatively cheap (see box on page 608).

It is probably best to leave e-commerce (having a secure site that can handle credit card sales) till later. In the meantime, however, a simple way to boost your income is to become an Amazon Associate. If your book titles are linked to Amazon, you'll make a percentage on a direct sale made from your site.

Websites for writers

The Internet: A Writer's Guide by Jane Dorner (www.internetwriter.co.uk) has a full listing of over 1000 resources for writers.

New to the internet

BBC Web Wise
www.bbc.co.uk/education/webwise

How to get started on the internet.

FAQ
www.faqs.org

Frequently Asked Questions on just about anything to do with the internet.

Google
www.google.co.uk

The current favourite amongst search engines.

How Stuff Works
www.howstuffworks.com

Fairly technical explanations about how the internet works, and much more.

Fact finding online

Ananova (UK Press Association)
www.ananova.com

Latest stories from the UK's top news and information websites; useful free daily round-up of news, sport and information by email.

Ask Oxford
www.askoxford.com

Various bits from the language dictionaries; changing word news and word-based interest.

Bartlett's Familiar Quotations
www.bartleby.com

Bibliomania
www.bibliomania.com

Excellent full text with a good word or phrase retrieval; includes the wonderful Brewer's *Dictionary of Phrase & Fable* (which no author can do without).

British Library
http://portico.bl.uk

Free search for material held in the major Reference and Document Supply collections of the British Library.

CIA World Factbook
www.cia.gov/cia/publications/factbook

Statistical data about countries and other useful data.

Crossref
www.crossref.org

A collaborative reference linking service for researchers.

Encyclopaedia Britannica
www.britannica.com

Full text and searching, together with a huge resource of information, grammar and reference links. Some free; premium subscription.

Free Pint
www.freepint.com

Free bi-monthly email newsletter with tips and articles on finding reliable sites and searching more effectively. Written by information professionals.

Internet Public Library
www.ipl.org

Reference section containing subject overviews, biography, etc. Now in its 10th year.

Response Source
http://sourcewire.com

UK journalists can request business information in a single step from over 300 organisations.

Roget's Thesaurus
www.bartleby.com/62

Third edition (1995).

WATCH – Writers, Artists and their Copyright Holders
http://tyler.hrc.utexas.edu

Database of information on whom to contact for permission to publish in copyright text and images. Not fully comprehensive. A joint project of the University of Texas and the University of Reading.

WISDOM: Knowledge & Literature Search
http://thinkers.net

Links to writing and literature sites under the headings Creativity, Literature, Authors, Thoughts, Publishing, Words, Languages.

Interactivity

Alt-X
www.altx.com

Online publishing network – 'where the digerati meet the literati'.

Digital Arts
www.da2.org.uk

Eastgate Systems
www.eastgate.com

Many interesting works of serious hypertext offered for sale.

Electronic Poetry Center
http://wings.buffalo.edu/epc

Writing communities

Agent Research
www.agentresearch.com

For professional writers and agents in the UK, USA and Canada.

Ask About Writing
www.askaboutwriting.net

Reviews writing websites from a writer's point of view. Also shows Swanwick news.

Author Zone
www.authorzone.com

Interactive author and writer community with free self-promotion opportunities and webspace.

Axis
www.axisartists.org

Some writing installations.

BBC writersroom
www.bbc.co.uk/writersroom,
www.bbc.co.uk/commissioning

How to submit ideas and scripts to the BBC.

Bloomsbury Magazine
www.bloomsburymagazine.com/writersarea

Writers' area; advice and resources for authors.

E-Writers
http://e-writers.net

Community, competitions and advice – weekly online publishing newsletter.

Get Writing
www.bbc.co.uk/dna/getwriting

Tips, advice and online courses from the BBC.

HackWriters
www.hackwriters.com

UK-based free internet magazine devoted to good writing on any subject. No fees; forum of exchange.

Literature North East
www.literaturenortheast.co.uk

Events taking place in North East England.

Littoral
www.littoral.org.uk

Arts trust which aims to develop new arts projects.

National Association for Literature Development
www.nald.org

Pier Playwrights
www.pierplaywrights.co.uk

Organisation for playwrights run by playwrights.

Publishers' Lunch
www.caderbooks.com

Free daily e-zine of news and events in US publishing. Authors can advertise their services for $15 a month in a database searchable by publishers and agents.

Reactive Writing
www.reactivewriting.co.uk

Exploring writing on the web.

SunOasis
www.sunoasis.com

A site for writers, editors and copywriters with some international job opportunities.

Word Circuits
www.wordcircuits.com

A community as well as a gallery of new fiction and poetry. Not quite as active as it once was.

The Word Hoard
www.wordhoard.co.uk

A cooperative of writers, visual artists, performers and musicians sited in Huddersfield. Has a text factory.

Writernet
www.writernet.org.uk

British community, mostly for writers working in theatre, TV, radio, film, live art and performance poetry; a professional network.

Writer's Market
www.writersmarket.com

Subscriber-based access ($29.99 a year) to market information on book and magazine publishers, agents, script buyers and general advice.

Writers Net
www.writers.net

US-based forum for writers, editors, agents and publishers. Participants exchange ideas about the writing life and the business of writing.

Writelink
www.writelink.co.uk

Resource site linking to paying markets, competitions, reference sites, software and so on. Well maintained.

Writers on the Net
www.writers.com

Busy community offering online (paid for) classes.

WritersServices.com
www.writersservices.com

Offers editorial services and advice from well-known writers; pitched largely at unpublished authors.

New media writing prizes

Eppie Awards for E-books
www.epicauthors.org

21 fiction and non-fiction categories.

Gutenberg-e
www.historians.org/prizes/gutenberg

Research grants and fellowships promoting historical e-publishing.

Java Museum Online Awards
www.javamuseum.org/start1.htm

For innovative art and new media installations.

Nesta Awards for Art and Science
www.nesta.org.uk

Up to £75,000 to spend a year developing a new creative idea; very competitive.

Miscellany

Note: Some of these are archive sites and most have a US bias.

Dying Words
www.corsinet.com/braincandy/dying.html

For the historical novelist.

Famous Birthdays
www.famousbirthdays.com

Month-by-month and day-by-day listing of birth dates, historical and in the media.

Famous Firsts
www.corsinet.com/trivia/1-triv.html

People-who-did-something-first arranged in ascending date order.

iTools
www.itools.com/research-it

Little battery of dictionaries and acronym converters.

Significant literary events.

Perpetual Virtual Calendars
www.vpcalendar.net

A historical or science fiction novelist's dream: verify any date or day of the week in the 20th and 21st centuries.

Rhyming dictionary
www.rhymezone.com

Time Zone Converter
www.timezoneconverter.com

What time it is or will be anywhere in the world.

What's on When
www.whatsonwhen.com

Useful for newspaper and magazine writers (or for planning holidays).

Who is or Was
www.biography.com

Good for checking people's dates; incorporates the *Cambridge Dictionary of American Biography*.

World Wide Words
www.quinion.com/words

Verbal cornucopia for anyone interested in words; circulates a newsletter.

Texts online

Bible Gateway
http://bible.gospelcom.net/bible

Electronic Text Center
http://etext.lib.virginia.edu/english.html

Collection of online English language texts; links to other texts online by subject or by author.

The English Server
http://eserver.org

Large collection of interesting resources.

Etext Archives
www.etext.org

Archives of religious, political, legal and fanzine text.

Oxford Text Archive
www.ota.ahds.ac.uk

Distributes more than 2500 resources in over 25 different languages for study purposes only.

Project Gutenberg
www.gutenberg.net

The official sites (many mirrors all over the world); vast library of e-texts, mostly public domain; all in plain text format.

Shakespeare Resources
www.shakespeare.com

Links to many other sites.

Writing tools
Screenwriting

Dramatica
www.dramatica.com

Screenplay software; not free – compare it with ScreenForge (below).

Final Draft
www.finaldraft.com

Apparently the bees knees of scripting software – expensive (about £150), high functionality and cross-platform compatibility.

ScreenForge
www.apotheosispictures.com

Almost free Hollywood scriptwriting format bolt-on for Word.

Storyware

Blogger
www.blogger.com

Free web-based tool for instantly publishing 'blogs' (web diaries).

Creativity Unleashed
www.cul.co.uk

Software to stimulate creative thinking, originally intended for business.

New Novelist
www.newnovelist.com

Software to help you write a novel – it doesn't do it *for* you, of course.

StoryBoard Quick
www.powerproduction.com

Storyboard software for films, animation, games, etc.

Story Wizard
www.storywizard.co.uk

Software that helps 9–16 year-olds to write stories.

Web Store for Writers and Creative Pros
www.masterfreelancer.com

Plots Unlimited, Writer's Software Companion and other software aids.

Word-processing aids

WordTips
www.vitalnews.com/wordtips

How to get the best out of Microsoft Word; useful tips, many a real boon for writers.

Jane Dorner is the author of 22 books and represents authors' interests on the Boards of ALCS and CLA. She is author of *The Internet: A Writer's Guide* (A & C Black 2001) (www.internetwriter.co.uk) which has the full listing of over 1000 resources for writers.

See also...
- *Setting up a website*, page 606
- *E-publishing*, page 597

Websites for artists

Several of the regional arts offices sites provide useful information for artists, as do some of the government sites, and many artist organisation sites provide links to other sites. Alison Baverstock introduces some web addresses which will be useful as a starting point.

Information for artists

AN The Artists Information Company
www.a-n.co.uk
Sister sites www.workingwithartists.co.uk *and* www.artistscareers.co.uk

A very broad site, covering all aspects of being an artist from current events to developing and maintaining good business practice. Initial section headings are:
• Forum – an interactive space for artists to seek and exchange advice on practice, career, project and business issues
• Practice – practical information and examples on showing, selling, commissions, residencies, production and collaboration
• Career – information on developing a career as an artist: first steps, looking at yourself, skills, developing a career, portfolio careers
• Business – valuable know-how and tips on becoming and being self employed, accounts, tax, contracts, promotion and insurance
• Contacts – over 1000 links to visual arts organisations in the UK and internationally which offer email and web links
• Artists – artists tell the real story of practice: their approaches, achievements and setbacks
• Research – introducing research on visual arts and artists' practice.

AN publishes *AN Magazine*; see page 33.

Art Quest
www.artquest.com

This site directly connects buyers and sellers of art, helping artists and collectors eliminate the commissions and fees usually found in the process.

The Art Net Directory
www.artnetdirectory.co.uk

A wide range of information for professional and amateur artists.

Arts Council England
www.artscouncil.org.uk

The national development agency for the arts in England, distributing public money to fund a range of activities. The website offers useful information on public policy towards the arts and current funding (such as which areas of the arts each organisation handles). The 'news and information' section offers

useful statistics on the arts in England as well as links to other sites.

The Arts Council of Northern Ireland
www.artscouncil-ni.org

Information on arts policy, funding schemes and contacts in Northern Ireland and the Republic.

The Arts Council of Wales
www.ccc-acw.org.uk

Information on arts policy, funding schemes and contacts in Wales.

Birkbeck College, University of London
www.bbk.ac.uk/lib/artlibgu/html

Offers details of art history libraries in London.

The Crafts Council
www.craftscouncil.org.uk

Offers services for both makers and members of the public interested in craft practice and purchase.

Cultural Enterprise – Menter Diwylliannol
www.cultural-enterprise.com

Information on business support for creative industries in Wales.

CX – Creative Export
www.creativexport.co.uk

Provides UK creative businesses with a portal to information that will support their development of export strategies.

Cywaith Cymru – Artworks Wales
www.cywaithcymru.org

Listings of public art and residency projects in Wales.

Department for Culture, Media and Sport
www.culture.gov.uk

Holds the latest research reports on the creative industries.

Design and Artists Copyright Society
www.dacs.co.uk

Information on copyright and intellectual property.

The Gallery Channel UK
www.thegallerychannel.co.uk

An excellent and almost comprehensive exhibition listings website.

HM Revenue & Customs
www.hmrc.gov.uk

Useful information on tax, national insurance and self-assessment – particularly helpful if you are new to being self employed.

Institute of International Visual Arts (inIVA)
www.iniva.org

A contemporary visual arts organisation with a special interest in new technologies, commissioning site-specific artworks and international collaborations.

Intellectual Property
www.intellectual-property.gov.uk

The Government's information site on copyright and other intellectual property rights.

International Association of Residential Arts Centres
www.resartis.org

An online directory of residency centres worldwide.

International Cultural Desk
www.icd.org.uk

Offers international opportunities for Scottish artists.

Live Art Magazine
www.liveartmagazine.com

News, reviews and listings.

The London Association of Art and Design Education
www.laade.org

Promotes contact between artists and schools; includes a database of artist-in-residence opportunities.

Metier
www.metier.org.uk

The national training organisation for the arts and entertainment industries, representing 500,000 people involved in the arts (including visual arts and all aspects of arts management).

National Disability Arts Forum
www.ndaf.org

Offers disability arts news and information on opportunities and contacts.

National Statistics: the official UK statistics site
www.statistics.gov.uk

Publishes a range of general and specific statistics on the arts.

The New York Foundation for the Arts
http://nyfa.org

A campaigning organisation seeking to link artists and arts organisations with funding.

Public Art South West
www.publicartonline.org.uk

Offers information on contacts, opportunities and practical advice on public art.

The Scottish Arts Council
www.sac.org.uk

Information on arts policy, funding schemes and contacts in Scotland.

Trans Artists
www.transartists.nl

Netherlands-based site providing information on international artists-in-residence and exchange programmes, finances, cultural institutes (with links to their websites).

Your Creative Future
www.yourcreativefuture.org

A career-planning site for those involved in the arts.

Selling art online

Selling art online is becoming big business and is a popular and convenient method for viewing, commissioning and buying works of art. For the artist, online galleries are a very cost-effective, and occasionally free, method of trying out new pieces of work or bringing new custom to your own linked web pages. Some of the larger sites allow you to exhibit for nothing; on the other hand, payment for inclusion may mean there is less competition to distract potential buyers from your work.

www.arthaus.co.uk
Artists exhibiting on this site are offered guidance on marketing. You either pay a standard fee for exhibiting (£35/10 works), or pay commission on work sold.

www.aarti.co.uk
A strong exhibition site for artists. You either pay 35% commission and display for nothing, or pay a fee (£30/10 works) and reduce the commission to 20%.

www.artcommunity.co.uk
An exhibition site. One year's website hosting costs £69.95 but there is no commission on what is sold.

www.artshole.co.uk
A website dedicated to promoting the work of student and contemporary artists, as well as providing information on exhibitions throughout the UK. No charge for artists to register.

www.axisartists.org

The largest interactive database of contemporary British art on the internet, currently features the work of more than 4000 professional and student artists. Registration fee £70/£35 for recent graduates.

www.bigart.co.uk

£19.50 buys you the chance to display 5–15 works and commission is also taken on what is sold.

www.blinkred.com

A well thought out site offering buyers the chance to specify what they are looking for, e.g. original oils or watercolours.

www.britart.com

Exhibits and promotes the work of emerging British artists. You can submit information (CV and personal statement) in support of your work.

www.illustratorsagents.com

A highly visited site used by at least 10,000 art/creative buyers who get email newsletters every second month. £437+VAT to display a 12-image portfolio for a year.

www.laade.org

The London Association of Art and Design Education promotes contact between artists and schools; includes a database of artist-in-residence opportunities.

www.larts.co.uk

Displays the work of 60 contemporary artists. A page costs £25+VAT.

www.minigallery.co.uk

Artists pay an all-inclusive annual membership subscription for personal mini website and a mini gallery. All sales are commission free with purchases made direct from the artist.

www.numasters.com

Exhibits professional work free of charge but takes a commission when works are sold/loaned/made copyright. Also includes information on maintaining and developing an art collection.

www.saa.co.uk

The Society for All Artists allows artists to compete to show work in the Members' Gallery. Themes vary and artists can link to their own sites. Various membership packages and associated benefits.

www.theartshopper.com

Claims to be the world's largest online gallery for original art. There is no joining fee but commission is added to the price you set for your work (and deducted when paid).

www.wwar.com

US-based site where you can exhibit free and no commission is charged. Huge with supporting chat room, opportunities for advertising, etc.

After 10 years in publishing **Alison Baverstock** set up her own marketing consultancy, specialising in running campaigns for the book trade and training publishers to market more effectively. She is a well-established speaker on the book business and has written widely on how to market books. Her most recent titles are *Is There a Book in You?* (A & C Black 2006) and, with Gill Hines, *Whatever: A Down-to-Earth Guide to Parenting Teenagers* (Piatkus 2005). Her website is alisonbaverstock.com

Resources for writers
The writer's ultimate workspace

Arranging for a space to write in a domestic environment can be a mammoth challenge for some people. Rib Davis gives the benefit of his experience of writing from home.

This is a work of fiction. It is based on fact – as much of the best fiction is – but there is certainly more of the wish than the accomplishment in what follows. I have been asked to write an article giving advice to the prospective writer about some of the day-to-day material conditions and habits of mind that one should attempt to establish in order to be able to work happily and efficiently. I assume that I was chosen on the basis that I have, over 25 years, failed to do these so spectacularly that I am now considered an expert in the field. I may not have learned much from my mistakes but at least I can list some of them, and let the reader do the learning.

Finding the ideal workspace

Where should the workspace be located? When we have to, we can write anywhere. At my most desperate I have written parts of scripts on trains, in crowded offices, in pubs and even leaning on a car steering wheel while waiting for the AA to rescue me. Such is the power of the deadline. Sometimes, strangely, I have produced some rather good work while battling with the distractions and other limitations of the immediate environment; I would hesitate, however, to recommend the practice too highly.

So what would be the ideal workspace location? It seems to be generally agreed that a writer (or writers, if you are working collaboratively) should work in a place where distractions are minimal. Some highly successful writers have taken this to the extreme of working in a shed or a caravan at the bottom of the garden, with only elves for company. I have never owned a caravan, and unless I learn to write seated on a bicycle I will always have trouble squashing into our slowly rotting shed, so that has never been an option. But where possible a degree of isolation – and particularly isolation from family activities and domestic duties – does seem desirable. Sustained concentration is extremely important for any sort of creative work, and such a location helps to facilitate it. In my own case, when I am actually scripting (as opposed to researching or planning) I usually find that I have to read my notes and then the latest part of the script for about an hour before I can even begin to put new words onto the page, so anything that breaks the concentration is unwelcome.

At the same time, though, we are only as strong as our will-power. Many of us could stick ourselves in an arctic igloo to write and yet still manage to find distractions (examining snowflakes can be so fascinating). For about a year I did my writing in a room at the back of a bookshop in Milton Keynes, well away from my home. It seemed to offer the ideal combination of relative isolation along with a congenial, supportive and vaguely arty environment. But the lure of the books and the customers ultimately proved too much; I soon found myself helping out at the till rather then tapping away at my *magnum opus*.

Perhaps my need to write was not sufficiently urgent. Certainly it is true that in those days I was driven by blind hope rather than deadlines, but I don't think that was the problem. The problem was (and is) fear: fear of writing badly, of not living up to one's own – and others' – expectations. For me, at least, it is this fear above all that gets in the way of creativity. First I fear the blank page (of course), then the writing, and then the finishing. This is why those awful distractions can seem, in fact, very welcome indeed. And it is part of the reason why we should try to avoid them as far as possible.

For a few years, remarkably, I did work in a suitable location. Quite simply, this was a room in the house that I was able to turn into my study. It was not totally cut off from the rest of Life, but it was sufficiently separate to allow generally uninterrupted concentration. My small son had difficulty understanding why, if I was behind the door, I refused to open it, but apart from that it worked well. I am shortly to return to that blissful state of having a personal study, but for years now I have done most of my writing on the living room table. My laptop and notes are moved away at meal times; people traipse through the living room to get to the kitchen (why didn't we think of this when we bought the house?); the television is in the same room. In short, my workplace is set in the teeming hub of the house. Big mistake. Even with a family that has been whipped into acknowledging the needs of a writer, it is still a big mistake.

Cordial domestic relations

A word on educating one's family. A writer's partner and/or children will generally recognise and respect the writer's need to focus on the work in hand, but there is at least one point which needs clarifying. When I write, I take breaks. These breaks can occur for a variety of reasons. Perhaps I have reached an interim target, or I have become stuck, or I am thirsty, or just tired. So I might stop and play the piano, or make a cup of coffee, or – exceptionally – even do some washing up, and then return to the writing with a clearer head. No problem, except that this might be observed, and the observing partner/child may think, 'Ah, so he doesn't mind his concentration being broken after all.' This can be a problem. You have to be selfish. You have to make clear that you can break your own concentration as and when you feel the need – you can wrong-note your way through a whole Beethoven sonata if you feel like it – but that does not give others the green light to break your concentration as and when they feel the need. Be unreasonable.

So much for location. Now, what should the workspace look like? My answer would simply be: pleasant. It should be a welcoming place, where you will feel comfortable and not oppressed. For me, this means well decorated in soft colours, with the desk facing out to a window, preferably with a view, and a temperature that's warm but not sleep-inducing. For others, windows may present yet another distraction, colours should be severe, the radiator should be off and the whole place should be tatty. The point is that you should feel comfortable in it – it should feel like *your* space.

Where I have been able to, I have turned my space into an almost self-sufficient world. This requires at the very least coffee (stimulation), Scotch (counter the extreme effects of coffee) and a variety of non-laxative snacks (counter the other effects of coffee). Ideally I suppose an en-suite bathroom would be a good idea, but we should keep to the feasible. When I am really rich and famous I will also have an extra piano in my study, but for now I make do with a stereo. I find music (at least, some music) can create a less intense atmosphere when I am researching or planning, but when I am actually scripting I tend to turn it off, as otherwise I find the writing being influenced moment-to-moment by every passing mood of the music, which does not tend to improve the quality of my literary product at all.

Working efficiently

Writing is of course more than simply tapping words onto a page. It is also thinking, researching, planning and finally doing all the administrative work connected to the sale and then either publication or production of the work, whether through an agent or otherwise. So your workspace must be able to accommodate all this too. Give yourself as much work surface as possible, so that you can refer to as many materials as you need simultaneously, and you can even have materials left out for more than one project at a time. And set up an efficient filing system from the start. Or if, as in my case, this is certainly not the start, do it now anyway. Do not simply put every new publisher's letter, piece of research and pizza takeaway leaflet together in an in-tray. The in-tray eventually overflows; you get a second one; that overflows too. You will eventually be surrounded by in-trays. File everything as it comes along, and don't hesitate to open a new file for even the germ of a new project.

This filing particularly applies to emails. One can make the mistake of thinking that because something is there on the computer it has been filed. It hasn't. Electronic documents – and emails most of all – can be just as much of a mess as a physical desktop. When you receive an email, save it in the relevant project file elsewhere in the computer. If you are feeling super-efficient, you could also print it off and keep it in that same project's hard-copy file.

Mention of emails leads me on to phones. Both can take over your whole existence if you allow them to; they will certainly try. Deal with emails when you are at your least productive as a writer. If you think of yourself as a 'morning person' then that is when you should be writing; do the emails in the evening. Or if mornings tend to be barren periods of grogginess and haze, those are the times for doing emails. And try to deal with all the day's emails in one sitting; certainly don't let them interrupt you whenever they feel like it. Set up your computer in such a way that it does not let you know when emails have arrived; instead, just check them once or twice per day.

Similarly, don't simply answer the phone whenever it rings. The phone can of course be very useful for your writing, particularly for research, but in general – put the answerphone on. Better still, put it on and set it to silent. If the caller doesn't leave a message, it can't be very important.

A great deal of research is now done on the web, but I still like having books around. One of them is Jane Dorner's *The Internet: A Writer's Guide* (see page 611). Obviously a writer should have a really good dictionary (some of the larger ones give a date for each word usage, which is particularly helpful for period writing), and I also find a large thesaurus very useful (the original format, not the alphabetical kind; the latter is simpler to use but as it is necessarily so repetitive it contains far fewer options). Then there are always the books needed for the particular project in hand, alongside Ann Hoffmann's excellent *Research for Writers*.

Most writers actually fit their research and other writing activities in with other work, whether writing-related or not. This means that time becomes a very precious commodity. I have always worked best when I have been able to arrange my writing time in large chunks, preferably whole days. An hour here or there really is hardly any use. And whenever possible I have tried to establish routines. The truth is that I have been particularly bad at this, perhaps because I have often had too many projects at different stages simultaneously, but I would still recommend adopting a daily routine as far as possible. It means there is just one less decision to have to make: your writing times have been decided and that's it.

Writer's block

So now you are all set. You have bought yourself Final Draft software (or something similar) and you have the workspace, the materials, the books, the filing – the lot. You write and write. You pin the best rejection slips onto the wall (we've all had them). You write and write. And then you don't. You get writer's block. I have had this. It is a particularly nasty affliction as in almost everyone else's eyes 'writer's block' translates as 'laziness'. This is not the place for a full discussion, but I can pass on a couple of pieces of advice I received, which worked for me. Firstly, don't always try to see the whole piece of work, as that may be overwhelming to you. Try to focus on a particular section of it and nothing more. Secondly, when you have writer's block a whole day of writing ahead of you looks interminable. So don't do it. Strictly limit yourself to writing for two hours and no more. You may well find yourself writing with real urgency, trying to cram all that you can into those two allotted hours. Only much later can you gradually increase the limit back to a normal day.

Well, it worked for me. But then there are all sorts of writers. My old friend Jack Trevor Story had a writer's solution for insomnia: he wrote right through the night. Every night. It worked for him.

Now, as usual, I am going to try to learn from what I've written.

Rib Davis has been writing professionally for 25 years. He has over 60 credits, including scripts for radio, television and stage, as well as two books on the art of writing scripts. He is close to sorting out his domestic writing arrangements.

Writers' retreats

Some writers find that spending some time at a writers' retreat proves bountiful. An author who has twice benefited from this experience is Maggie Gee.

Writers' retreats are not for everyone. They aren't, for example, for the poet who once said to me, *a propos* of Hawthornden Castle International Writers' Retreat, 'But it's so quiet. And Edinburgh is *half an hour away* by bus.' For him, to be half an hour from the metropolis was a penance.

Retreats overseas

Creative Cauldron
website www.creativecauldron.com/retreats
A useful encyclopedic web page of retreats in the USA.

Before going into the desert, think long and hard. Are you quarrelsome, or oversensitive, or both? The other writers will, for the most part, be busy and quiet, but mealtimes are generally communal. People are more vulnerable when they are off their own territory and away from loved ones. Do not always eat the last piece of cake (food gains an emotional significance when other props are missing) or be competitive about how much you have written, or how much you get paid. Actual numbers of words and pounds should never be quoted. Do not give a reading from your new work unless asked.

Ask yourself hard questions before you go. Do you mind very much being away from your loved ones, your cat, your garden? Will you be wracked by guilt? Are you addicted to *The Bill*? Do you feel anxious if you can't pick up emails or vary the monotony of your work with half-hourly binges on Google? Most retreats have no televisions and no internet facilities.

But if you are a writer who can never get enough time uninterrupted by phone calls, plumbers, pets, children, and the washing-machine, writers' retreats are absolute heaven. For me personally, two widely spaced four-week stays at Hawthornden Castle produced the first drafts of two novels, *Where are the Snows* (1991) and my ninth novel, *The Flood*. When I am away from all the things I ought to do at home, 200–300 words a day swells into 2000–3000.

Prose writers have to come to terms with the leaden truth that you cannot write a book without hours of immobility. I personally prefer concentrating those hours into a smaller number of weeks and months. I speak as one whose eighth novel (*The White Family*), took seven years to write and rewrite (no retreats), whereas *The Flood*, after 18 months of mulling over, took just a month to dream up and write (at a retreat) and six months to rewrite. Poets like retreats too. I was at Hawthornden Castle last time with, among others, the poet Jean Sprackland, and while she was there she wrote most of her new book *Hard Water*, since shortlisted for the T.S. Eliot Prize.

In the USA there is a wider choice of retreats. Google will present you with a bewildering variety of American retreats, many of them luxurious and long established. But although most of them are free, you have to find the air fare. In the UK there are fewer choices and only one retreat is free, Hawthornden Castle in Scotland, but unfortunately writers can only go there once every five years. You must make a formal application to the trustees and if you are accepted you can look forward to a stay in a beautiful castle in dramatic wooded grounds. The rooms are warm and attractive, the food is good, the staff are kind and the five or six writers who are in residence at any one time pay only for their pre-prandial sherry. The Arvon Foundation, which specialises in tutored retreats, also offers one week for plain untutored retreats at each of its four centres. Ireland has scenic, remote, beautiful Anam Cara, on the coast of Western Cork.

There are alternatives. When I struck a complete log jam in my work this year, I tried a few days at St Cuthman's in Coolham, near Billingshurst in Sussex. A former Anglican retreat of long standing, this beautiful, peaceful place has been completely revivified by the Catholics who have now taken it over. As before, it is open to those of any or no faith who need rest. The rooms are simple, comfortable and elegant, with views over a lake and swans, fresh vegetables and home baking. There are prayers night and morning but you don't have to attend, though they seemed to work wonders for my novel.

There again, there are bargain weekly deals at out-of-season seaside hotels, or if you once went to a college or university, you could try ringing up to see if they let former *alumni* stay there cheaply in empty rooms. Many do, and they should have decent desks and chairs. Once the washing-machine, the telephone and the pets have fallen silent, the dream of the book can begin.

Maggie Gee is the author of 10 novels, of which her most recent are *The Flood* (Saqi 2004) and *My Cleaner* (Saqi 2005). *The White Family* (2002) was shortlisted for the Orange Prize for Fiction and the International Impac Prize for Fiction. In 2006 she published a collection of short stories, *The Blue* (Saqi). She is the first female Chair of the Royal Society of Literature.

Anam Cara

website www.ugr.com/anamcararetreat

The Arvon Foundation

42A Buckingham Palace Road, London SW1W 0RE
website www.arvonfoundation.org
National Director Stephanie Anderson

See individual entries for the Foundation's 4 centres: The Hurst – The John Osborne Arvon Centre, Lumb Bank – The Ted Hughes Arvon Centre, Moniack Mhor and Totleigh Barton. As well as facilitating writers' retreats, the centres run many creative writing courses.

Hawthornden Castle

International Retreat for Writers, Lasswade, Midlothian EH18 1EG
tel 0131-440 2180 *fax* 0131-440 1989
Contact The Administrator

Exists to provide a peaceful setting where published writers can work without disturbance. The Retreat houses up to 6 writers at a time, who are known as Hawthornden Fellows. Writers from any part of the world may apply for the fellowships. No monetary assistance is given, nor any contribution to travelling expenses, but once arrived at Hawthornden, the writer is the guest of the Retreat. Application forms are available from March for the following calendar year. Previous occupants include Les Murray, Alasdair Gray, Helen Vendler, Olive Senior, Hilary Spurling and Maggie Gee.

The Hurst – The John Osborne Arvon Centre

The Arvon Foundation, The Hurst, Clunton, Craven Arms, Shrops. SY7 0JA
tel (01588) 640658
email hurst@arvonfoundation.org
website www.arvonfoundation.org
Centre Directors Edmund Collier, Paul Warwick

Offers a one-week writing retreat in August. The Hurst is situated in the beautiful Clun Valley in South Shropshire, 12 miles from Ludlow, and is set in 30 acres of woodland, with gardens and a lake.

Irish Writers' Centre

19 Parnell Square, Dublin 1
tel (353) 1 8721302 *fax* (353) 1 8726282
email info@writerscentre.ie
website www.writerscentre.ie
Contact Annmarie Wolohan

Studio available for rent by a writer for a period of 3 months or less. Recent occupants include Talaya Delaney while she was working on a piece for the Abbey Theatre, 2 comedy scriptwriters to write a new 6-part TV series for RTE and Mary Dorcey to finish writing her latest novel.

Lumb Bank – The Ted Hughes Arvon Centre

The Arvon Foundation, Lumb Bank, Heptonstall, Hebden Bridge, West Yorkshire HX7 6DF
tel (01422) 843714 *fax* (01422) 843714

email l-bank@arvonfoundation.org
website www.arvonfoundation.org
Centre Directors Stephen May, Caron May

Offers a one-week writing retreat in the summer.
Lumb Bank is an 18th-century former mill-owner's
house set in 20 acres of steep pasture land.

Moniack Mhor

The Arvon Foundation, Moniack Mhor, Teavarran,
Kiltarlity, Beauly, Inverness-shire IV4 7HT
tel (01463) 741675 *fax* (01463) 741733
email m-mohr@arvonfoundation.org
website www.arvonfoundation.org
Centre Directors Cynthia Rogerson, Andrea Muir,
Nicky Guthrie

Moniack Mhor is a traditional croft house
commanding panoramic views over Highland
landscapes with forest walks nearby. Courses run
from June to November. Centre available at other
times for schools, writing groups, etc.

St Cuthman's

Coolham, near Billingshurst, Sussex
website www.dabnet.org/stcuth2.htm
tel (01403) 741220

Totleigh Barton

The Arvon Foundation, Totleigh Barton, Sheepwash,
Beaworthy, Devon EX21 5NS
tel (01409) 231338 *fax* (01409) 231144
email t-barton@arvonfoundation.org
website www.arvonfoundation.org
Centre Directors tba

Offers a writing retreat in August. Totleigh Barton is
a thatched, pre-Domesday manor house, surrounded
by farmland in Devon, 2 miles from the village of
Sheepwash.

Ty Newydd

Ty Newydd Writers' Centre, Llanystumdwy, Cricieth,
Gwynedd LL52 0LW
tel (01766) 522811 *fax* (01766) 523095
email post@tynewydd.org
website www.tynewydd.org

Writers' retreats are organised at different times
during the year to give writers the opportunity to find
a week's peace and quiet in Ty Newydd's stimulating
environment. Everyone has a single room and stays
on a self-catering basis with a shared meal in the
evening.

Digital imaging for writers

How images are presented can sway an editor's decision to use an article. David Askham explains how to transfer images to a computer and suggests ways to arrange them for best effect.

An editor, who regularly commissioned me to produce profiles of small gardens, telephoned me as soon as he received one of my proposals. He said, 'When I first read your letter, I was convinced that it would not be suitable for our British readers. Then I turned the page and said "WOW!" Please go ahead with the feature.' So what tipped the scales? Admittedly the subject was a rather unusual one, in fact a so-called 'shade garden'. Furthermore, it was located far away in Australia! Because of this, I suspected that the proposal would fail if I sent words alone. I could have sent accompanying small colour prints to illustrate the potential of the article, but they would have lacked impact and risked becoming separated from my proposal. So I tried an experiment. I scanned a selection of photographs and compiled a simple but bold and colourful composite A4 sheet which formed part of my brief proposal. It worked and I have used variants of this idea with success ever since.

But the advantages of digital photography outlined above do not end there because once pictures are filed on a writer's personal computer they are available for a variety of useful purposes. They can serve as inspiration, providing quick recall of a scene or a person's facial features or attire. It is like revisiting a location or experiencing an unexpected reunion with an old friend. Digital images are quick visual references; they can jog a writer's memory and inspire. Let us look at the subject in a little more detail.

Technical aspects

Most writers will be familiar with cameras which use conventional film, either black and white or colour. These films produce negatives from which prints are produced; or transparencies which can be projected (for lecture purposes) or used by publishers to provide illustrations in print. In contrast, a new generation of cameras has arrived which do not use film, but instead record and store images digitally on special reusable memory. These digitally stored images must then be transferred to a personal computer so that they may be cropped, modified and integrated into the desired documents, such as a proposal. If the source is a digital camera it is relatively straightforward to transfer images using the computer software which came with the camera. Using the connecting cables supplied, images are 'downloaded' into the computer or the memory cards are inserted into memory card readers. The whole chain is digital which makes it so easy.

However, you do not necessarily need a digital camera to transfer images to your computer. You can work with prints which you already have – or could produce at will in the future. Or you can digitise your existing colour (or black and white) slides or negatives. For the latter operation your pictures need to be scanned and recorded on a CD, a process which has become increasingly available at most processing laboratories. Alternatively, with the right equipment, you can do the whole process yourself. Possibly the easier and cheaper method is to buy a flatbed scanner which will produce digital files from your original colour or black and white prints. Flatbed scanners have tumbled in price over the past few years and are now often bundled with new computers. Alternatively, they can be bought for well under £100 although, like most consumer goods, it does not pay to buy the cheapest available. Take advice from a knowledgeable friend or trusted dealer.

If you wish to work from negatives or colour slides, you will need to buy a film scanner. These are more expensive (from £150 up to £1000 or more), but they give superior results particularly if you want to produce photo-realistic prints from a colour printer, say for promotional or exhibition purposes.

Initially, you can achieve commendable results by using your existing camera and having selected images scanned onto a CD by a processing laboratory. Then you can extract copies of the desired pictures from the CD and place them in your chosen document file. When you feel more confident and can justify the expense, you can then shop around for a suitable scanner to use at home.

Before moving on, I think a word is needed on the relative merits of using conventional film or digital cameras. The latter have developed rapidly over recent years but while top-priced models (over £2000) are needed to match the quality of film-based imagery at sizes A3 and bigger, consumer digital cameras (up to £1000) are more than capable of yielding very satisfactory results up to A4 size. However, there is another important consideration. If you think it is likely that your pictures merit long-term archiving, film still has the edge. Why? Because computer systems evolve rapidly and yesterday's computer technology soon becomes obsolete. In a few years it may not be possible to read old digital files.

Using visual references

In addition to using photographs in a book or article proposal, digital pictures are also a valuable aid to many forms of research and writing. For example, the value of tape-recorded research or interview notes is significantly enhanced if you add thumbnail pictures to enrich and augment the narrative information. Words and pictures which are integrated in this way have to be more reliable than unaided human memory when writing begins, particularly if there is a significant time interval between research and writing. But it is in the production of proposals, those all important selling documents, where digital imaging comes into its own.

However, I do not advocate using any old pictures. They have to be directly relevant to the subject being proposed and they must be of good quality. Therefore, it is worthwhile budgeting for your photography and providing high quality pictures using conventional cameras and films at the outset. You will then have confidence in being able to deliver high quality images to the editor.

Computing and software

Unless you are a computer buff, eyes can easily glaze when faced with yet more software to master. Unfortunately, some knowledge is essential but I will keep it simple. Most modern computers can handle graphics which includes digital photographs and drawings. Indeed most modern word processing software, such as WordPerfect, can integrate pictures directly into documents. Provided you know the filename of the required picture, or can find it by exploring the file listing hierarchy, you merely have to point to INSERT ... GRAPHICS ... FROM FILE and select the appropriate file. (The commands may be slightly different in other word processing programs.) The photograph then appears and you can adjust both its size and position within the document.

Ideally you will have made any cropping or other adjustments using the picture management software which may have been delivered with your digital camera or scanner. If the pictures supplied by your film processor were delivered on a CD, you may find a simple program included on the disk. Alternatively, you may choose to buy a picture processing program, such as Paint Shop Pro or Photoshop, which possess enormous capabilities for enhancing and transforming digital images, way beyond what you require initially. Photoshop is expensive, although a simpler version or comparable software of the program is bundled with some scanners and is perfectly adequate for first-time users. Alternatively, Adobe Photoshop Elements is an extremely popular and effective lower cost option. Consider buying one or two magazines which specialise in digital photography to study reviews and tables of available digital hardware and software. A study of analytical reports can be very helpful in shortlisting potential solutions.

One last word on specialist software. Be prepared to invest plenty of time if you wish to explore digital image processing capabilities beyond basic cropping of your photographs. It can be very rewarding, but it takes time to learn and is beyond the scope of this article.

Adding visual elements

A simple example was given earlier of how you can add photographs to a text document. Sometimes it is better to devote an A4 page exclusively to the visual side of your proposals. Although this can be done using a word processor, a publishing program such as Microsoft Home Publishing or Serif PagePlus is more adept and flexible for designing layout and adding captions. However, you will soon find that you are straying into the realms of graphic design which appears to be much easier than it really is.

Working out the relative sizes of your pictures on the page and their positions can be extremely time consuming. It requires patience and discipline. My advice is to keep things as simple as possible before tackling more ambitious layouts. Avoid trying to include too many pictures on a page; six should be a maximum. Try to vary their individual sizes so that there is variety. Your aim should be to present just sufficient visual information to whet an editor's appetite with the whole effect being easy on the eye. There is no doubt that in a highly competitive world digital imaging can endow a writer with a competitive edge. Take heart and inspiration from my experience and see if your success rate improves.

David Askham is author of *Photo Libraries and Agencies* (BFP Books) and has been illustrating his written work for over 35 years. His photographs have been published worldwide in books, brochures, magazines and newspapers, many through international agencies.

Indexing

A good index is a joy to the user of a non-fiction book; a bad index will downgrade an otherwise good book. The function of indexes and the skills needed to compile them, are examined here.

An index is a detailed key to the contents of a document, in contrast to a contents list, which gives only the titles of the parts into which the document is divided (e.g. chapters). Precisely, an index is 'A systematic arrangement of entries designed to enable users to locate information in a document'. The document may be a book, a series of books, an issue of a periodical, a run of several volumes of a periodical, an audiotape, a map, a film, a picture, a CD-Rom, a website, a database, an object, or any other information source in print or non-print form.

The objective of an index is to guide enquirers to information on given subjects in a document by providing the terms of their choice (single words, phrases, abbreviations, acronyms, dates, names, and so on) in an appropriately organised list which refers them to specific locations using page, column, section, frame, figure, table, paragraph, line or other appropriate numbers or hyperlinks.

An index differs from a catalogue, which is a record of the documents held in a particular collection, such as a library; though a catalogue may require an index, for example to guide searchers from subject words to class numbers.

A document may have separate indexes for different classes of heading, so that personal names are distinguished from subjects, for example, or a single index in which all classes of heading are interfiled.

The Society of Indexers

The Society of Indexers is a non-profit organisation founded in 1957 and is the only autonomous professional body for indexers in the UK. It is affiliated with the American Society of Indexers, the Australian and New Zealand Society of Indexers, the China Society of Indexers, the Indexing and Abstracting Society of Canada, and the Association of Southern African Indexers and Bibliographers, and has close ties with the Chartered Institute of Library and Information Professionals (CILIP) and the Society for Editors and Proofreaders (SfEP).

The main objectives of the Society are to promote all types of indexing standards and techniques and the role of indexers in the organisation of knowledge; to provide, promote and recognise facilities for both the initial and the further training of indexers; to establish criteria for assessing conformity to indexing standards; and to conduct research and publish guidance, ideas and information about indexing. It seeks to establish good relationships between indexers, librarians, publishers and authors, both to advance good indexing and to improve the role and wellbeing of indexers.

Further information

Society of Indexers
Woodbourn Business Centre, 10 Jessell Street, Sheffield S9 3HY
tel 0114-244 9561 *fax* 0114-244 9563
email admin@indexers.org.uk
website www.indexers.org.uk
Administrator Wendy Burrow
Membership £84 p.a. UK/Europe, £105 overseas; £168 corporate

Publishers and authors seeking to commission an indexer should consult *Indexers Available* on the website.

Services to indexers

The Society publishes a learned journal *The Indexer* (2 p.a.), a newsletter and *Occasional Papers on Indexing*. Additional resources for members are published in electronic form on the Society's website (www.indexers.org.uk). Local and special interest groups provide the chance for members to meet to discuss common interests, while email discussion lists have encouraged the development of a virtual community of indexers. A two-day conference is held every year. All levels of training are supported by regular workshops held at venues throughout the country.

Professional competence is recognised in two stages by the Society. Accredited Indexers who have completed the open-learning course qualification (see below) have shown theoretical competence in indexing, while Fellows of the Society of Indexers have proved their experience and competence in practical indexing through a rigorous assessment procedure. All trained and experienced members have the opportunity to take an annual entry in *Indexers Available*, a directory available on the Society's website to help publishers find an indexer.

The Society recommends minimum rates for indexing (£17.50 per hour; approx. £2 per page in 2006) and provides advice on the business side of indexing to its members.

Services to publishers and authors

Anyone who commissions indexes needs to be certain of engaging a professional indexer working to the highest standards and able to meet deadlines.

Indexers Available, now searchable on the Society's website, lists only qualified and experienced members of the Society and gives basic contact details, subject specialisms and indexing experience.

The Society awards the Wheatley Medal for an outstanding index.

Training in indexing

The Society's course (in electronic format with accompanying printed books) is based on the principle of open learning with units and formal tests available separately so that individuals can learn in their own way and at their own pace. The units cover four core subjects and contain practical exercises and self-administered tests. After completing the four assessed units, trainees undertake a practical indexing assignment to prepare them for work in the commercial world. Members of the Society receive a substantial discount on the cost of the course, although anyone can purchase the units. Only members of the Society can apply for the formal tests.

Further reading

Booth, P.F., *Indexing: the manual of good practice*, K.G. Saur, 2001

British Standards Institution, *British Standard recommendations for examining documents, determining their subjects and selecting indexing terms*, (BS6529:1984)

International Standards Organisation, *Information and documentation – guidelines for the content, organization and presentation of indexes* (ISO 999:1996)

Correcting proofs

The following notes and table are extracted from BS 5261 Part 2: 1976 (1995) and are reproduced by permission of the British Standards Institution.

4 Marks for copy preparation and proof correction

4.1 The marks to be used for marking up copy for composition and for the correction of printers' proofs shall be as shown in Table 1 (see pages 617–626).

4.2 The marks in Table 1 are classified in three groups as follows:

(a) Group A: general.

(b) Group B: deletion, insertion and substitution.

(c) Group C: positioning and spacing.

4.3 Each item in Table 1 is given a simple alpha-numeric serial number denoting the classification group to which it belongs and its position within the group.

Further information

British Standards Institution (BSI)
Technical Information Group, 389 Chiswick High Road, London W4 4AL
tel 020-8996 7111 *fax* 020-8996 7048
Customer Services tel 020-8996 9001 *fax* 020-8996 7001
email info@bsi.org.uk
website www.bsi.org.uk

BSI is the independent national body responsible for preparing British Standards. It presents the UK view on standards in Europe and at the international level. It is incorporated by Royal Charter.

For a complete standard, contact Customer Services.

4.4 The marks have been drawn keeping the shapes as simple as possible and using sizes which relate to normal practice. The shapes of the marks should be followed exactly by all who make use of them.

4.5 For each marking-up or proof correction instruction a distinct mark is to be made:

(a) in the text: to indicate the exact place to which the instruction refers;

(b) in the margin: to signify or amplify the meaning of the instruction. It should be noted that some instructions have a combined textual and marginal mark.

4.6 Where a number of instructions occur in one line, the marginal marks are to be divided between the left and right margins where possible, the order being from left to right in both margins.

4.7 Specification details, comments and instructions may be written on the copy or proof to complement the textual and marginal marks. Such written matter is to be clearly distinguishable from the copy and from any corrections made to the proof. Normally this is done by encircling the matter and/or by the appropriate use of colour (see below).

4.8 Proof corrections shall be made in coloured ink thus:

(a) printer's literal errors marked by the printer for correction: green;

(b) printer's literal errors marked by the customer and his agents for correction: red;

(c) alterations and instructions made by the customer and his agents: black or dark blue.

Table 1. Classified list of marks

NOTE. The letters M and P in the notes column indicate marks for marking-up copy and for correcting proofs respectively.

Group A General

Number	Instruction	Textual mark	Marginal mark	Notes
A1	Correction is concluded	None	/	P Make after each correction
A2	Leave unchanged	- - - - - - - under characters to remain	(√)	M P
A3	Remove extraneous marks	Encircle marks to be removed	✗	P e.g. film or paper edges visible between lines on bromide or diazo proofs
A3.1	Push down risen spacing material	Encircle blemish	⊥	P
A4	Refer to appropriate authority anything of doubtful accuracy	Encircle word(s) affected	(?)	P

Group B Deletion, insertion and substitution

B1	Insert in text the matter indicated in the margin	⋋	New matter followed by ⋋	M P Indentical to B2
B2	Insert additional matter identified by a letter in a diamond	⋋	⋋ Followed by for example ◈	M P The relevant section of the copy should be supplied with the corresponding letter marked on it in a diamond e.g. ◈
B3	Delete	/ through character(s) or ⊢——⊣ through words to be deleted	∂	M P
B4	Delete and close up	⌢/ through character or ⊢——⊣ through characters e.g. charactⱥer charaⱥcter	∂̑	M P

Table 1 *(continued)*

Number	Instruction	Textual mark	Marginal mark	Notes
B5	Substitute character or substitute part of one or more word(s)	/ through character or ⊢───┤ through word(s)	New character or new word(s)	M P
B6	Wrong fount. Replace by character(s) of correct fount	Encircle character(s) to be changed	⊗	P
B6.1	Change damaged character(s)	Encircle character(s) to be changed	╳	P This mark is identical to A3
B7	Set in or change to italic	──── under character(s) to be set or changed	⊔	M P Where space does not permit textual marks encircle the affected area instead
B8	Set in or change to capital letters	════ under character(s) to be set or changed	═	
B9	Set in or change to small capital letters	═══ under character(s) to be set or changed	═	
B9.1	Set in or change to capital letters for initial letters and small capital letters for the rest of the words	═══ under initial letters and ═══ under rest of the word(s)	═	
B10	Set in or change to bold type	∿∿∿∿ under character(s) to be set or changed	∿	
B11	Set in or change to bold italic type	∿∿∿∿ under character(s) to be set or changed	⊔∿	
B12	Change capital letters to lower case letters	Encircle character(s) to be changed	≢	P For use when B5 is inappropriate

Table 1 *(continued)*

Number	Instruction	Textual mark	Marginal mark	Notes
B12.1	Change small capital letters to lower case letters	Encircle character(s) to be changed	≠	P For use when B5 is inappropriate
B13	Change italic to upright type	Encircle character(s) to be changed	Ψ	P
B14	Invert type	Encircle character to be inverted	↺	P
B15	Substitute or insert character in 'superior' position	/ through character or ⅄ where required	˥ under character e.g. 2̞	P
B16	Substitute or insert character in 'inferior' position	/ through character or ⅄ where required	∟ over character e.g. ⌐2	P
B17	Substitute ligature e.g. ffi for separate letters	⊢——⊣ through characters affected	⌣ e.g. f̑fi	P
B17.1	Substitute separate letters for ligature	⊢——⊣	Write out separate letters	P
B18	Substitute or insert full stop or decimal point	/ through character or ⅄ where required	⊙	M P
B18.1	Substitute or insert colon	/ through character or ⅄ where required	⊙⊙	M P
B18.2	Substitute or insert semi-colon	/ through character or ⅄ where required	;	M P

Table 1 *(continued)*

Number	Instruction	Textual mark		Marginal mark	Notes
B18.3	Substitute or insert comma	/	through character	，	M P
		or			
		⋀	where required		
B18.4	Substitute or insert apostrophe	/	through character	ʾ	M P
		or			
		⋀	where required		
B18.5	Substitute or insert single quotation marks	/	through character	ʿ and/or ʾ	M P
		or			
		⋀	where required		
B18.6	Substitute or insert double quotation marks	/	through character	ʿʿ and/or ʾʾ	M P
		or			
		⋀	where required		
B19	Substitute or insert ellipsis	/	through character	• • •	M P
		or			
		⋀	where required		
B20	Substitute or insert leader dots	/	through character	⊙•••⊙	M P Give the measure of the leader when necessary
		or			
		⋀	where required		
B21	Substitute or insert hyphen	/	through character	⊢=⊣	M P
		or			
		⋀	where required		
B22	Substitute or insert rule	/	through character	⊢—⊣	M P Give the size of the rule in the marginal mark e.g. |1 em| |4 mm|
			where required		
		⋀			

Table 1 *(continued)*

Number	Instruction	Textual mark	Marginal mark	Notes
B23	Substitute or insert oblique	/ through character or ⋀ where required		M P

Group C Positioning and spacing

Number	Instruction	Textual mark	Marginal mark	Notes
C1	Start new paragraph			M P
C2	Run on (no new paragraph)			M P
C3	Transpose characters or words	 between characters or words, numbered when necessary		M P
C4	Transpose a number of characters or words	3 2 1 | | |	1 2 3	M P To be used when the sequence cannot be clearly indicated by the use of C3. The vertical strokes are made through the characters or words to be transposed and numbered in the correct sequence
C5	Transpose lines			M P
C6	Transpose a number of lines		——— 3 ——— 2 ——— 1	P To be used when the sequence cannot be clearly indicated by C5. Rules extend from the margin into the text with each line to be transposed numbered in the correct sequence
C7	Centre	⌐enclosing matter to be centred⌐	[ ]	M P
C8	Indent			P Give the amount of the indent in the marginal mark

Table 1 *(continued)*

Number	Instruction	Textual mark	Marginal mark	Notes
C9	Cancel indent			P
C10	Set line justified to specified measure	and/or		P Give the exact dimensions when necessary
C11	Set column justified to specified measure			M P Give the exact dimensions when necessary
C12	Move matter specified distance to the right	enclosing matter to be moved to the right		P Give the exact dimensions when necessary
C13	Move matter specified distance to the left	enclosing matter to be moved to the left		P Give the exact dimensions when necessary
C14	Take over character(s), word(s) or line to next line, column or page			P The textual mark surrounds the matter to be taken over and extends into the margin
C15	Take back character(s), word(s), or line to previous line, column or page			P The textual mark surrounds the matter to be taken back and extends into the margin
C16	Raise matter	over matter to be raised under matter to be raised		P Give the exact dimensions when necessary. (Use C28 for insertion of space between lines or paragraphs in text)
C17	Lower matter	over matter to be lowered under matter to be lowered		P Give the exact dimensions when necessary. (Use C29 for reduction of space between lines or paragraphs in text)
C18	Move matter to position indicated	Enclose matter to be moved and indicate new position		P Give the exact dimensions when necessary

Marked galley proof of text

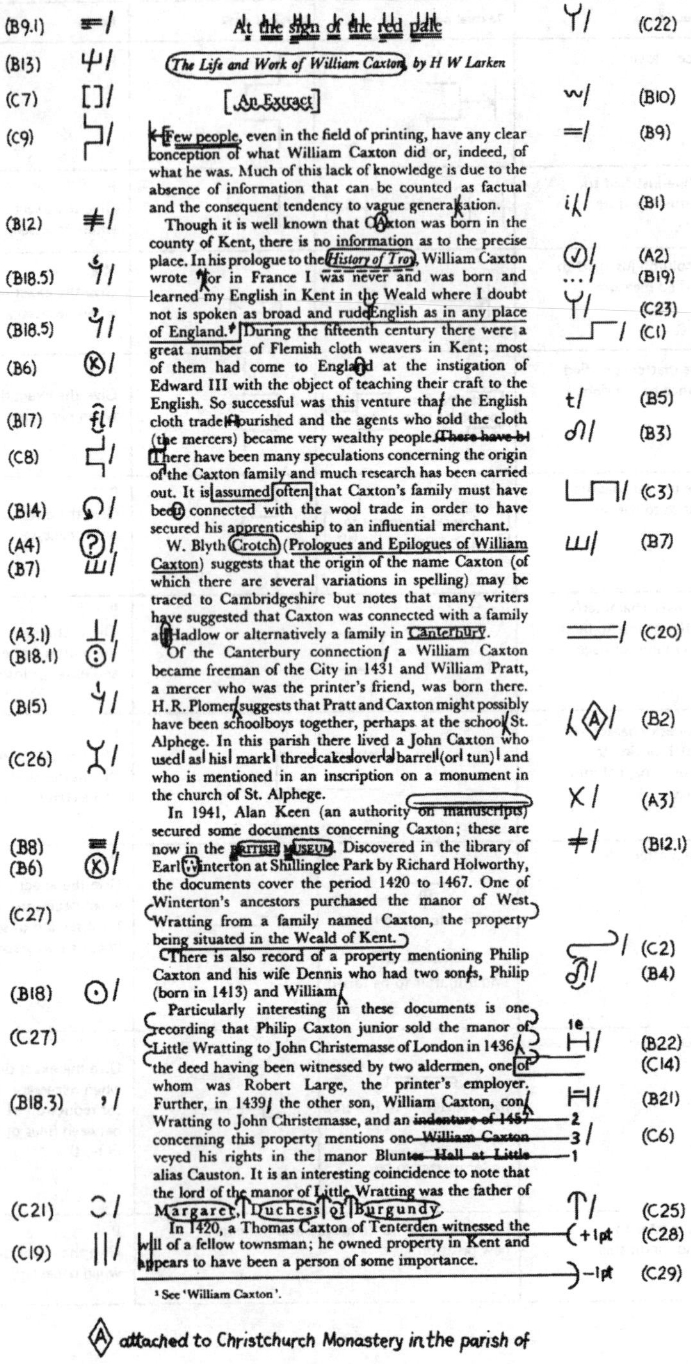

(B9.1)	⇆/
(B13)	�djl/
(C7)	[]/
(C9)	⊐⊐/
(B12)	≢/
(B18.5)	ʒ/
(B18.5)	ʒ/
(B6)	Ⓚ/
(B17)	f̂l/
(C8)	⊐/
(B14)	∩/
(A4)	ⓟ/
(B7)	ш/
(A3.1) (B18.1)	⊥/ ⊙/
(B15)	ʒ/
(C26)	Ⴟ/
(B8) (B6)	≡/ Ⓚ/
(C27)	
(B18)	⊙/
(C27)	
(B18.3)	,/
(C21)	⊂/
(C19)	|||/

At the sign of the red pale

The Life and Work of William Caxton, by H W Larken

[An Extract]

Few people, even in the field of printing, have any clear conception of what William Caxton did or, indeed, of what he was. Much of this lack of knowledge is due to the absence of information that can be counted as factual and the consequent tendency to vague generalisation.

Though it is well known that Caxton was born in the county of Kent, there is no information as to the precise place. In his prologue to the *History of Troy*, William Caxton wrote 'for in France I was never and was born and learned my English in Kent in the Weald where I doubt not is spoken as broad and rude English as in any place of England.' During the fifteenth century there were a great number of Flemish cloth weavers in Kent; most of them had come to England at the instigation of Edward III with the object of teaching their craft to the English. So successful was this venture that the English cloth trade flourished and the agents who sold the cloth (the mercers) became very wealthy people. There have been many speculations concerning the origin of the Caxton family and much research has been carried out. It is assumed often that Caxton's family must have been connected with the wool trade in order to have secured his apprenticeship to an influential merchant.

W. Blyth Crotch (*Prologues and Epilogues of William Caxton*) suggests that the origin of the name Caxton (of which there are several variations in spelling) may be traced to Cambridgeshire but notes that many writers have suggested that Caxton was connected with a family at Hadlow or alternatively a family in Canterbury.

Of the Canterbury connection a William Caxton became freeman of the City in 1431 and William Pratt, a mercer who was the printer's friend, was born there. H.R. Plomer suggests that Pratt and Caxton might possibly have been schoolboys together, perhaps at the school St. Alphege. In this parish there lived a John Caxton who used as his mark three cakes (over a barrel (or I tun) and who is mentioned in an inscription on a monument in the church of St. Alphege.

In 1941, Alan Keen (an authority on manuscripts) secured some documents concerning Caxton; these are now in the BRITISH MUSEUM. Discovered in the library of Earl Winterton at Shillinglee Park by Richard Holworthy, the documents cover the period 1420 to 1467. One of Winterton's ancestors purchased the manor of West Wratting from a family named Caxton, the property being situated in the Weald of Kent.

There is also record of a property mentioning Philip Caxton and his wife Dennis who had two sons, Philip (born in 1413) and William.

Particularly interesting in these documents is one recording that Philip Caxton junior sold the manor of Little Wratting to John Christemasse of London in 1436, the deed having been witnessed by two aldermen, one of whom was Robert Large, the printer's employer. Further, in 1439 the other son, William Caxton, conveyed Wratting to John Christemasse, and an indenture of 1457 concerning this property mentions one William Caxton veyed his rights in the manor Bluntes Hall at Little alias Causton. It is an interesting coincidence to note that the lord of the manor of Little Wratting was the father of Margaret, Duchess of Burgundy.

In 1420, a Thomas Caxton of Tenterden witnessed the will of a fellow townsman; he owned property in Kent and appears to have been a person of some importance.

¹ See 'William Caxton'.

Right margin marks:

(C22)	Ⴑ/
(B10)	w/
(B9)	=/
(B1)	iʎ/
(A2)	⊘/
(B19)	.../
(C23)	Ⴑ/
(C1)	⌐/
(B5)	t/
(B3)	ꝺ/
(C3)	⊔⌐/
(B7)	ш/
(C20)	≡/
(B2)	⟨Ⓐ⟩/
(A3)	✕/
(B12.1)	≠/
(C2)	⌐/
(B4)	ꝺ/
(B22)	1e H/
(C14)	
(B21)	H/
(C6)	2/ 3/ 1
(C25)	Ⴑ/
(C28)	(+ 1pt
(C29)	)− 1pt

Ⓐ attached to Christchurch Monastery in the parish of

Revised galley proof of text incorporating corrections

At the Sign of the Red Pale

The Life and Work of William Caxton, *by H W Larken*

An Extract

FEW PEOPLE, even in the field of printing, have any clear conception of what William Caxton did or, indeed, of what he was. Much of this lack of knowledge is due to the absence of information that can be counted as factual and the consequent tendency to vague generalisation.

Though it is well known that Caxton was born in the county of Kent, there is no information as to the precise place. In his prologue to the *History of Troy*, William Caxton wrote '. . . for in France I was never and was born and learned my English in Kent in the Weald where I doubt not is spoken as broad and rude English as in any place of England.'

During the fifteenth century there were a great number of Flemish cloth weavers in Kent; most of them had come to England at the instigation of Edward III with the object of teaching their craft to the English. So successful was this venture that the English cloth trade flourished and the agents who sold the cloth (the mercers) became very wealthy people.

There have been many speculations concerning the origin of the Caxton family and much research has been carried out. It is often assumed that Caxton's family must have been connected with the wool trade in order to have secured his apprenticeship to an influential merchant.

W. Blyth Crotch (*Prologues and Epilogues of William Caxton*) suggests that the origin of the name Caxton (of which there are several variations in spelling) may be traced to Cambridgeshire but notes that many writers have suggested that Caxton was connected with a family at Hadlow or alternatively a family in Canterbury.

Of the Canterbury connection: a William Caxton became freeman of the City in 1431 and William Pratt, a mercer who was the printer's friend, was born there. H. R. Plomer[1] suggests that Pratt and Caxton might possibly have been schoolboys together, perhaps at the school attached to Christchurch Monastery in the parish of St. Alphege. In this parish there lived a John Caxton who used as his mark three cakes over a barrel (or tun) and who is mentioned in an inscription on a monument in the church of St. Alphege.

In 1941, Alan Keen (an authority on manuscripts) secured some documents concerning Caxton; these are now in the British Museum. Discovered in the library of Earl Winterton at Shillinglee Park by Richard Holworthy, the documents cover the period 1420 to 1467. One of Winterton's ancestors purchased the manor of West Wratting from a family named Caxton, the property being situated in the Weald of Kent. There is also record of a property mentioning Philip Caxton and his wife Dennis who had two sons, Philip (born in 1413) and William.

Particularly interesting in these documents is one recording that Philip Caxton junior sold the manor of Little Wratting to John Christemasse of London in 1436—the deed having been witnessed by two aldermen, one of whom was Robert Large, the printer's employer. Further, in 1439, the other son, William Caxton, conveyed his rights in the manor Bluntes Hall at Little Wratting to John Christemasse, and an indenture of 1457 concerning this property mentions one William Caxton alias Causton. It is an interesting coincidence to note that the lord of the manor of Little Wratting was the father of Margaret, Duchess of Burgundy.

In 1420, a Thomas Caxton of Tenterden witnessed the will of a fellow townsman; he owned property in Kent and appears to have been a person of some importance.

[1] See 'William Caxton'.

Table 1 *(continued)*

Number	Instruction	Textual mark	Marginal mark	Notes
C19	Correct vertical alignment	‖	‖	P
C20	Correct horizontal alignment	Single line above and below misaligned matter e.g. mi͜saligned	⎯⎯⎯ ⎯⎯⎯	P The marginal mark is placed level with the head and foot of the relevant line
C21	Close up. Delete space between characters or words	linking ⌒⌣ characters	⌒⌣	M P
C22	Insert space between characters	ǀ between characters affected	Y	M P Give the size of the space to be inserted when necessary
C23	Insert space between words	Y between words affected	Y	M P Give the size of the space to be inserted when necessary
C24	Reduce space between characters	ǀ between characters affected	⋂	M P Give the amount by which the space is to be reduced when necessary
C25	Reduce space between words	⋂ between words affected	⋂	M P Give amount by which the space is to be reduced when necessary
C26	Make space appear equal between characters or words	ǀ between characters or words affected	Ⲭ	M P
C27	Close up to normal interline spacing	(each side of column linking lines)		M P The textual marks extend into the margin

Table 1 *(continued)*

Number	Instruction	Textual mark	Marginal mark	Notes
C28	Insert space between lines or paragraphs			**M P** The marginal mark extends between the lines of text. Give the size of the space to be inserted when necessary
C29	Reduce space between lines or paragraphs			**M P** The marginal mark extends between the lines of text. Give the amount by which the space is to be reduced when necessary

Libraries

Listed below are specialist, reference and general libraries. Contact individual libraries to find out about accessibility and opening hours.

University of Aberdeen
Queen Mother Library, Meston Walk, Aberdeen AB24 3UE
tel (01224) 273600 *fax* (01224) 273956
email library@abdn.ac.uk
website www.abdn.ac.uk/diss/library

Aberdeen Library and Information Services Central Library
Rosemount Viaduct, Aberdeen AB25 1GW
tel (01224) 652500
email centlib@aberdeencity.gov.uk
website www.aberdeencity.gov.uk

Barbican Library
Barbican Centre, London EC2Y 8DS
tel 020-7638 0569, 020-7628 9447 (Children's Library)
website www.cityoflondon.gov.uk/barbicanlibrary

The largest of the City of London's lending libraries with a strong arts and music section, literature events programme and reading groups.

Bath Central Library
19 The Podium, Northgate Street, Bath BA1 5AN
tel (01225) 787400 (Enquiry Desk), (01225) 787402 (Children's Library) *fax* (01225) 787426
email library@bathnes.gov.uk
website www.bathnes.gov.uk/libraries

BBC Written Archives Centre
Caversham Park, Reading RG4 8TZ
tel 0118-948 6281 *fax* 0118-946 1145
email heritage@bbc.co.uk
website www.bbc.co.uk/heritage

Home of the BBC's written records. Holds thousands of files, scripts and working papers from the BBC's formation in 1922 to the 1980s together with information about past programmes and the history of broadcasting. Does not have recordings or information about current programmes.

Bedford Central Library
Harpur Street, Bedford MK40 1PG
tel (01234) 350931 *fax* (01234) 342163
website www.bedfordshire.gov.uk

Belfast Public Library
Central Library, Royal Avenue, Belfast BT1 1EA
tel 028-9050 9150 *fax* 028-9033 2819
website www.belb.org.uk

BFI National Library
British Film Institute, 21 Stephen Street, London W1T 1LN
tel 020-7255 1444 *fax* 020-7436 2338
email library@bfi.org.uk
website www.bfi.org.uk/nationallibrary

As a major national research collection, the main priority is to provide comprehensive coverage of British film and TV, but the collection itself is international in scope.

Birmingham Central Library
Chamberlain Square, Birmingham B3 3HQ
tel 0121-303 4511 *textphone* 0121-303 4547
minicom 0121-303 3789
fax 0121-303 9695
email central.library@birmingham.gov.uk
website www.birmingham.gov.uk

Bodleian Library
Broad Street, Oxford OX1 3BG
tel (01865) 277034 *fax* (01865) 277029
website www.bodley.ox.ac.uk

The main research library of the University of Oxford. It is also a legal deposit library.

The Booktrust Collection – see Newcastle University Library

Bristol Central Library
College Green, Bristol BS1 5TL
tel 0117-903 7200 (switchboard), 0117-903 7202 (Reference Library & art enquiries), 0117-903 7215 (Children's Library), 0117-903 7219 (drama enquries) *minicom* 0117-903 7437
fax 0117-922 1081
email refandinfo@bristol-city.gov.uk, childrens_library@bristol-city.gov.uk, music_collection@bristol-city.gov.uk

The British Library
96 Euston Road, London NW1 2DB
tel 0870-444 1500 (Switchboard), 020-7412 7676 (Advance Reservations, St Pancras Reading Rooms and Humanities enquiries), 020-7412 7702 (Maps), 020-7412 7513 (Manuscripts), 020-7412 7772 (Music), 020-7412 7873 (Asia, Pacific & Africa Collections)
website www.bl.uk

The national library of the UK and a legal deposit library. The collection includes in excess of 150 million items, in most known languages. Online catalogues. See also other British Library listings below.

British Library Business Information Service (BIS)
96 Euston Road, London NW1 2DB
tel 020-7412 7454 *fax* 020-7412 7453

email business-information@bl.uk
website www.bl.uk/bis

Holds the most comprehensive collection of business information literature in the UK.

British Library Document Supply Centre

Boston Spa, Wetherby, West Yorkshire LS23 7BQ
tel (01937) 546060 *fax* (01937) 546333

British Library for Development Studies at IDS

Institute of Development Studies, University of Sussex, Brighton BN1 9RE
tel (01273) 678263 *fax* (01273) 621202/691647
email blds@ids.ac.uk
website www.ids.ac.uk/blds

Europe's most comprehensive research collection on development issues.

British Library Newspapers

Colindale Avenue, London NW9 5HE
tel 020-7412 7353 *fax* 020-7412 7379
email newspaper@bl.uk
website www.bl.uk/collections/newspapers

National archive collections in the UK of British and overseas newspapers, made available in hard copy, in microform, and on CD-Rom in the Newspaper Reading Rooms. Online catalogue.

The British Library Sound Archive

The British Library, 96 Euston Road, London NW1 2DB
tel 020-7412 7676 *fax* 020-7412 7441
email sound-archive@bl.uk
website www.bl.uk/soundarchive

The collections come from all over the world and cover the entire range of recorded sound from music, drama and literature to oral history and wildlife sounds. Its online catalogue includes entries for more than 3 million recordings.

Buckinghamshire Libraries Information Service

Walton Street, Aylesbury, Bucks. HP20 1UU
tel (01296) 383252 *fax* (01296) 382405
email countyreflib@buckscc.gov.uk
website www.buckscc.gov.uk

Camberwell College of Arts Library

Peckham Road, London SE5 8UF
tel 020-7514 6349
website www.arts.ac.uk/library

Art history, ceramics, conservation, film, fine art, graphics, illustration, metalwork, photography, posters, printmaking, silversmithing and textiles.

Cambridge University Library

West Road, Cambridge CB3 9DR
tel (01223) 333000 *fax* (01223) 333160

email library@lib.cam.ac.uk
website www.lib.cam.ac.uk

Collections are housed in the University Library and its 4 dependent libraries. It is also a legal deposit library.

Cardiff Central Library

St David's Link, Frederick Street, Cardiff CF10 2DU
tel 029-2038 2116
email centrallibrary@cardiff.gov.uk
website www.cardiff.gov.uk/libraries

The largest public library in Wales.

Catholic Central Library

St Michael's Abbey, Farnborough Road, Farnborough, Hants GU14 7NQ
tel 020-7383 4333 *fax* 020-7388 6675
email librarian@catholic-library.org.uk
website www.catholic-library.org.uk

Holds 65,000 books and periodicals on theology, spirituality and related subjects, biography and history.

Central St Martins College of Art & Design Library

Southampton Row, London WC1B 4AP
tel 020-7514 7037
website www.arts.ac.uk/library

Chelsea College of Art & Design Library

16 John Islip Street, London SW1P 4JU
tel 020-7514 7773
website www.arts.ac.uk/library

Modern and contemporary art (including women's art), Afro–American art, Afro–Carribean British art and Asian British art.

City Business Library

1 Brewers' Hall Garden, off Aldermanbury Square, London EC2V 5BX
tel 020-7332 1812
website www.cityofLondon.gov.uk/citybusinesslibrary

One of the leading business information sources in the UK.

City of London Libraries – see City Business Library, Guildhall Library, St Bride Printing Library and Barbican Library

Civil Aviation Authority Library and Information Centre (CAA)

Aviation House, Gatwick Airport South, West Sussex RH6 0YR
tel (01293) 573725 *fax* (01293) 573181
email library-enquiries@srg.caa.co.uk
website www.caa.co.uk

Holds books, reports, directories, statistics, videos and periodicals on most aspects of civil aviation and related subjects.

College of Psychic Studies Library
16 Queensberry Place, London SW7 2EB
tel 020-7589 3293
website www.collegeofpsychicstudies.co.uk

The Library of the Commonwealth Secretariat
Commonwealth Secretariat, Marlborough House, Pall Mall, London SW1Y 5HX
tel 020-7747 6164 *fax* 020-7747 6168
email d.blake@commonwealth.int
Librarian David Blake

Collection covers politics and international relations, economics, education, health, gender, environment and management. Holds a comprehensive collection of Commonwealth Secretariat publications and its archives.

Cornwall Library Service
Reference and Information Library, Union Place, Truro, Cornwall TR1 1EP
tel (01872) 272702, 0800 0322345 (Enquiry Express Freephone) *fax* (01872) 223772
email reference.library@cornwall.gov.uk, enquiryexpress@cornwall.gov.uk
website www.cornwall.gov.uk/library

Crafts Council Resource Centre
Crafts Council, 44A Pentonville Road, London N1 9BY
tel 020-7806 2501 *fax* 020-7833 4479
email reference@craftscouncil.org.uk
website www.craftscouncil.org.uk/photostore

Holds over 6000 texts on various aspects of contemporary crafts, together with over 100 different craft magazines and periodicals. The Resource Centre can be used for researching current designer-makers in the UK, through Photostore (a visual database of over 50,000 images of contemporary craft available online) and the National Register of Makers. Open to the public 6 days a week.

Cranfield Library and Information Service
Cranfield University, Cranfield, Beds. MK43 0AL
tel (01234) 754444 *fax* (01234) 752391
website www.cranfieldlibrary.ac.uk

Croydon Central Library
Croydon Clocktower, Katharine Street, Croydon CR9 1ET
tel 020-8726 6900 *fax* 020-8253 1004
email libraries@croydon.gov.uk
website www.croydon.gov.uk

Dartington College of Arts
Library & Learning Resources Centre (LLRC), Dartington College of Arts, Totnes, Devon TQ9 6EJ
tel (01803) 861651 *fax* (01803) 861666

email library@dartington.ac.uk
website www.dartington.ac.uk

Holds over 80,000 books, videos, CDs and sheet music items reflecting the interests of the College. Subscribes to over 150 journals and provides access to a wide range of electronic information resources.

Derby Central Library
The Wardwick, Derby DE1 1HS
tel (01332) 255398 *fax* (01332) 369570
email central.library@derby.gov.uk
website www.derby.gov.uk/libraries

Douglas Public Library
10 Victoria Street, Douglas, Isle of Man IM1 2LH
tel (01624) 696461 *fax* (01624) 696400
email enquiries@douglas.org.im

Durham University Library
Stockton Road, Durham DH1 3LY
tel 0191-334 2968 *fax* 0191-334 2971
website www.dur.ac.uk/library

Edinburgh University Library, Museums and Galleries
30–38 George Square, Edinburgh EH8 9LJ
tel 0131-650 3384 *fax* 0131-667 9780
email library@ed.ac.uk
website www.lib.ed.ac.uk

University of Exeter Library
Stocker Road, Exeter EX4 4PT
tel (01392) 263869 *fax* (01392) 263871
email library@exeter.ac.uk
website www.ex.ac.uk/library

The website lists sites on the internet which are especially useful resources maintained by libraries, museums and centres of research, as well as publishers.

Foreign and Commonwealth Office Library
King Charles Street, London SW1A 2AH
tel 020-7008 1500 *fax* 020-7008 3270
website www.fco.gov.uk

University of Glasgow Library
Hillhead Street, Glasgow G12 8QE
tel 0141-330 6704 *fax* 0141-330 6704
email library@lib.gla.ac.uk
website www.lib.gla.ac.uk

Glasgow Women's Library
109 Trongate, Glasgow G1 5HD
tel 0141-552 8345
email info@womenslibrary.org.uk
website www.womenslibrary.org.uk

Reference and lending library of information for and about women.

Goethe-Institut London Library

50 Princes Gate, Exhibition Road, London SW7 2PH
tel 020-7596 4044 *fax* 020-7594 0230
email infoservice@london.goethe.org
website www.goethe.de/london

Specialises in German literature, especially
contemporary fiction and drama and books/
audiovisual material on German culture and recent
history.

Guildhall Library

Aldermanbury, London EC2P 2EJ
tel 020-7332 1868/1870 (printed books), 020-7332
1862 (manuscripts), 020-7332 1839 (Print & Map
Room) *fax* 020-7600 3384
email manuscripts.guildhall@cityoflondon.gov.uk,
print&maps@cityoflondon.gov.uk,
printedbook.guildhall@cityoflondon.gov.uk
website www.cityoflondon.gov.uk/guildhalllibrary

Specialises in the history of London, especially the
City, as well as holding other significant collections
including business history, maritime history, clock
and watchmaking, food and wine.

High Wycombe Studies Centre

Queen Victoria Road, High Wycombe, Bucks.
HP11 1BD
tel (01494) 510241 *fax* (01494) 533086
email lib-hiwref@buckscc.gov.uk
website www.buckscc.gov.uk/libraries

Jersey Library

Halkett Place, St Helier, Jersey JE2 4WH, Channel
Islands
tel (01534) 759992 *fax* (01534) 769444
email je.library@gov.je
website www.gov.je

Lambeth Palace Library

London SE1 7JU
tel 020-7898 1400 *fax* 020-7928 7932
website www.lambethpalacelibrary.org

The historic library of the archbishops of Canterbury
and the principal library and record office for the
Church of England.

Leeds Central Library

Calverley Street, Leeds LS1 3AB
tel 0113-247 8911 *fax* 0113-247 8271
website www.leeds.gov.uk

Lending library with specialist art, music, local studies
and business and research departments.

Leeds University Library

Leeds LS2 9JT
tel 0113-233 6388, 0113-233 5501 *fax* 0113-233 5561
email library@library.novell.leeds.ac.uk
website www.leeds.ac.uk/library

University of Leicester Library

University Road, Leicester LE1 9QD
tel 0116-252 2043 *fax* 0116-252 2066
email libdesk@le.ac.uk
Mailing address PO Box 248, Leicester LE1 9QD
website www.le.ac.uk/library

Leicester Reference and Information Library

Bishop Street, Leicester LE1 6AA
tel 0116-299 5401 *fax* 0116-299 5444
email central.reference@leicester.gov.uk
website www.leicester.gov.uk/libraries

The Linen Hall Library

17 Donegall Square North, Belfast BT1 5GB
tel 028-9032 1707 *fax* 028-9043 8586
email info@linenhall.com
website www.linenhall.com
Librarian John Gray, *Irish & Local Studies Librarian*
Gerry Healey, *NIPC Librarian* Yvonne Murphy

Subscription library renowned for its Irish and Local
Studies Collection, ranging from early Belfast and
Ulster printed books to the 250,000 items in the
Northern Ireland Political Collection (NIPC), with
bestsellers and classics in the General Lending
Collection.

Liverpool Central Library

William Brown Street, Liverpool L3 8EW
tel 0151-233 5835 *fax* 0151-233 5886
email refbt.central.library@liverpool.gov.uk
website www.liverpool.gov.uk

London College of Communication Library and Learning Resources

Elephant & Castle, London SE1 6SB
tel 020-7514 6527
website www.arts.ac.uk/library

London College of Fashion Library

20 John Princes Street, London W1G 0BJ
tel 020-7514 7453, 020-7514 7455
website www.arts.ac.uk/library

London Institute Libraries – see
Camberwell College of Arts Library, Central St
Martins College of Art & Design, Chelsea College
of Art & Design Library, London College of Fashion
Library and London College of Printing Libraries

The London Library

14 St James's Square, London SW1Y 4LG
tel 020-7930 7705 *fax* 020-7766 4766
email membership@londonlibrary.co.uk
website www.londonlibrary.co.uk

Subscription lending library holding approximately
one million books in all European languages and a
subject range across the humanities, with particular
emphasis on literature, history and related subjects.
Membership is open to all.

Library of the London School of Economics and Political Science

10 Portugal Street, London WC2A 2HD
tel 020-7955 7229 *fax* 020-7955 7454
website www.library.lse.ac.uk

Manchester Central Library
St Peter's Square, Manchester M2 5PD
tel 0161-234 1900 *fax* 0161-234 6230
email mclib@libraries.manchester.gov.uk
website www.manchester.gov.uk/libraries

The Mitchell Library
North Street, Glasgow G3 7DN
tel 0141-287 2999 *fax* 0141-287 2915
website www.glasgow.gov.uk

One of Europe's largest public reference libraries with almost 2 million volumes. Holds an unrivalled collection of material relating to the City of Glasgow.

National Art Library
Victoria & Albert Museum, South Kensington, London SW7 2RL
email nal.enquiries@vam.ac.uk
website www.vam.ac.uk/nal

A major reference library and the Victoria and Albert Museum's curatorial department for the art, craft and design of the book.

National Library for the Blind (NLB)
Far Cromwell Road, Bredbury, Stockport SK6 2SG
tel 0161-355 2000 *minicom* 0161-355 2043
fax 0161-355 2098
email enquiries@nlbuk.org
website www.nlb-online.org

The website provides a gateway to library and information services for visually impaired people.

National Library of Ireland
Kildare Street, Dublin 2
tel (353) 1 603 02 00 *fax* (353) 1 676 66 90
email info@nli.ie
website www.nli.ie

The world's largest collection of Irish documentary material.

The National Library of Scotland
George IV Bridge, Edinburgh EH1 1EW
tel 0131-623 3700 (switchboard), 0131-623 3876 (manuscripts and archives enquiries), 0131-623 3899 (Rare Books Collections)
email enquiries@scotbis.com (Scottish Business Information Service), manuscripts@nls.uk (manuscripts and archives enquiries), rarebooks@nls.uk (Rare Books Collections)
website www.nls.uk

A legal deposit library and Scotland's largest library.

The National Library of Wales
Aberystwyth, Ceredigion SY23 3BU
tel (01970) 632800 *fax* (01970) 615709
email holi@llgc.org.uk
website www.llgc.org.uk

A legal deposit library. Holds large collection of works about Wales and other Celtic countries, including manuscripts, maps, portraits and paintings, screen and sound archives.

National Maritime Museum
Greenwich, London SE10 9NF
tel 020-8858 4422 *fax* 020-8312 6632
website www.nmm.ac.uk, www.port.nmm.ac.uk (gateway site for maritime information), www.rog.nmm.ac.uk (astronomy information)

Specialist maritime research library.

Natural History Museum Library and Information Services
Cromwell Road, London SW7 5BD
tel 020-7942 5507/5873 (archives), 020-7942 5685 (Botany Library), 020-7942 5476 (Earth Sciences Library), 020-7942 5751 (Entomology Library), 020-7942 5460 (General Library and Zoology Library), 020-7942 6156 (Ornithology Library)

Online catalogue contains all library material acquired since 1989 and about 80% of earlier items. The collections are of international importance with extensive holdings of early works, periodicals and current literature, including over 800,000 books, 20,000 periodical titles (about half of them current) and original watercolour drawings, as well as maps, manuscripts and archives of the Museum.

Newcastle University Library
Robinson Library, Newcastle NE2 4HQ
tel 0191-222 7662
email lib-readersservices@ncl.ac.uk
website www.ncl.ac.uk/library

Historical children's books and other material relevant to the history of childhood and education. Over 100 collections of material ranging from rare books and archives to woodblocks and illustrations, from the mid 15th–21st century.

Newcastle upon Tyne City Library
Princess Square, Newcastle upon Tyne NE99 1DX
tel 0191-2774100 *fax* 0191-2774107
website www.newcastle.gov.uk

Norfolk and Norwich Millennium Library
The Forum, Millennium Plain, Norwich NR2 1AW
tel (01603) 774774 *fax* (01603) 774775
email millennium.lib@norfolk.gov.uk
website www.norfolk.gov.uk/leisure/libraries

The Northern Poetry Library – see 323

Nottingham Central Library
Angel Row, Nottingham NG1 6HP
tel 0115-915 2828 *fax* 0115-915 2850
email business.library@nottinghamcity.gov.uk
website www.nottinghamcity.gov.uk

Open Library
website http://library.open.ac.uk
The Open University's electronic library service.

School of Oriental & African Studies (SOAS) Library
University of London, Thornhough Street, Russell Square, London WC1H 0XG
tel 020-7898 4163 *fax* 020-7636 2834
email libsuggestions@soas.ac.uk
website www.soas.ac.uk/library

Oxford Central Library
Westgate, Oxford OX1 1DJ
tel (01865) 815509 (general enquiries), (01865) 815549 (information desk), (01865) 815373 (children's library), (01865) 815388 (music library), (01865) 815409 (periodicals room), (01865) 810182 (Business Information Point) *fax* (01865) 721694
email oxfordcentral.library@oxfordshire.gov.uk
website www.oxfordshire.gov.uk

PA News Library
Central Park, New Lane, Leeds LS11 5DZ
tel 0113-207 4996
website www.pagroup.com

Holds a bank of more than 14 million cuttings which span events, sports, people and topics from the start of the 19th century to the present day.

The Poetry Library – see page 323

The Portico
57 Mosley Street, Manchester M2 8HY
tel 0161-236 6785
website www.theportico.org.uk

Independent library which stocks mainly 19th century literature.

University of Reading Library
Whiteknights, PO Box 223, Reading RG6 6AE
tel 0118-9378770 *fax* 0118-93786636
email library@reading.ac.uk
website www.library.rdg.ac.uk

The John Rylands University Library, The University of Manchester
Oxford Road, Manchester M13 9PP
tel 0161-275 3751 *fax* 0161-273 7488
website www.library.manchester.ac.uk

St Albans Central Library
The Maltings, St Albans, Herts. AL1 3JQ
tel (01438) 737333 *minicom* (01438) 737599
website www.hertsdirect.org/libsleisure/libraries

St Bride Library
Bride Lane, London EC4Y 8EE
tel 020-7353 4660 *fax* 020-7583 7073
email library@stbrideinstitute.org
website www.stbride.org

Collections cover printing and allied subjects including paper and binding, graphic design and typography, typefaces and calligraphy, illustration and printmaking, publishing and bookselling, and the social and economic aspects of the printing, book, newspaper and magazine trades generally.

Salisbury Library
Market Place, Salisbury, Wilts. SP1 1BL
tel (01722) 324145
website www.wiltshire.gov.uk/libraries

Science Museum Library
Imperial College Road, London SW7 5NH
tel 020-7942 4242 *fax* 020-7942 4243
email smlinfo@nmsi.ac.uk
website www.sciencemuseum.org.uk/library

In recent years the Library has specialised in the history of science and technology as its key role as part of the National Museum of Science & Industry.

The Scottish Poetry Library – see page 323

Senate House Library, University of London
Senate House, Malet Street, London WC1E 7HU
tel 020-7862 8500
email enquiries@shl.lon.ac.uk
website www.shl.lon.ac.uk

One of the major academic libraries of the UK.

Sheffield Central Library
Surrey Street, Sheffield S1 1XZ
tel 0114-273 4761 *fax* 0114-273 4712
email libraries@sheffield.gov.uk
website www.sheffield.gov.uk

University of Southampton Libraries
University Road, Highfield, Southampton SO17 1BJ
tel 023-8059 2180
website www.library.soton.ac.uk

The Society for Storytelling Library
PO Box 2344, Reading, Berks. RG6 7FG
tel 0118-935 1381
email sfs@fairbruk.demon.co.uk
website www.sfs.org.uk, www.mythstories.com/sfslibrary.html

Folktale and folklore books, storytelling magazines from the UK and abroad, an archive of press cuttings and flyers for storytellers and events; tapes of conference proceedings, achive tellings and performances.

The Tate Library & Archive
Hyman Kreitman Research Centre, Tate Britain, Millbank, London SW1P 4RG
tel 020-7887 8838
email research.centre@tate.org.uk
website www.tate.org.uk/research/researchservices/researchcentre/library.htm

Broadly covers those areas in which the Tate collects: British art from the Renaissance to the present day and international modern art. The emphasis is on fine art in the Western tradition and international contemporary art.

Trinity College Library

Cambridge CB2 1TQ
tel (01223) 338488 *fax* (01223) 338532
website http://library.trin.cam.ac.uk/

Wellcome Library

210 Euston Road, London NW1 2BE
tel 020-7611 8722 *fax* 020-7611 8369
email library@wellcome.ac.uk
website http://library.wellcome.ac.uk

Medical Photographic Library

tel 020-7611 8348 *fax* 020-7611 8577
email photolib@wellcome.ac.uk
website http://medphoto.wellcome.ac.uk

Moving Image and Sound Collections

tel 020-7611 8766 *fax* 020-7611 8765
email misc@wellcome.ac.uk
website http://library.wellcome.ac.uk/misc.html

Westminster Music Library

Victoria Library, 160 Buckingham Palace Road, London SW1W 9UD
tel 020-7641 1300 *minicom* 020-7641 4879
fax 020-7641 4281
email victorialibrary@westminster.gov.uk, musiclibrary@westminster.gov.uk
website www.westminster.gov.uk/libraries/victoria

Housed by Victoria Library, the Westminster Music Library holds a wide range of scores, orchestral sets, books on music and the GLASS collection of Mozart sound recordings.

Westminster Reference Library

35 St Martin's Street, London WC2H 7HP
tel 020-7641 1300 *minicom* 020-7641 4879
fax 020-7641 4606
website www.westminster.gov.uk/libraries/westref

Winchester Reference Library

81 North Walls, Winchester, Hants SO23 8BY
tel (01962) 826666 *fax* (01962) 856615
email winchester.reference@hants.gov.uk
website www.hants.gov.uk

The Women's Library

Old Castle Street, London E1 7NT
tel 020-7320 2222 *fax* 020-7320 2333
email moreinfo@the womenslibrary.ac.uk
website www.thewomenslibrary.ac.uk

Houses the most extensive collection of women's history in the UK. Part of the London Metropolitan University.

Working Class Movement Library

51 The Crescent, Salford M5 4WX
tel 0161-736 3601
email enquiries@wcml.org.uk
website www.wcml.org.uk
Librarian Alain Kahan

A collection of books, periodicals, pamphlets, archives and artefacts concerned with the activities, expression and enquiries of the labour movement, its allies and its enemies, since the late 18th century.

York Central Reference Library

Museum Street, York YO1 7DS
tel (01904) 552824, 552828 *fax* (01904) 611025
email reference.library@york.gov.uk
website www.york.gov.uk/libraries

The Zoological Society of London Library

Regent's Park, London NW1 4RY
tel 020-7449 6293
email library@zsl.org
website www.zsl.org

Creative writing courses

Anyone wishing to participate in a writing course should first satisfy themselves as to its content and quality. For day and evening courses consult your local Adult Education Centre. Details of postgraduate writing courses follow on page 653.

Alston Hall College
Alston Lane, Longridge, Preston PR3 3BP
tel (01772) 784661 *fax* (01772) 785835
email alston.hall@ed.lancscc.gov.uk
website www.alstonhall.com

Arista
11 Wells Mews, London W1P 3FL
tel 020-7323 1775 *fax* 020-7323 1772
email arista@aristotle.co.uk
website www.aristotle.co.uk
Contact Stephanie Faugier

A 6-day story-editing workshop held 3 times a year at different locations throughout Europe. Producers and writers apply as a team with a project.

The Arvon Foundation
Lumb Bank, Heptonstall, Hebden Bridge, West Yorkshire HX7 6DF
tel (01422) 843714 *fax* (01422) 843714
email l-bank@arvonfoundation.org
website www.arvonfoundation.org
Contact Ilona Jones
Moniack Mhor, Teavarran, Kiltarlity, Beauly, Inverness-shire IV4 7HT
tel (01463) 741675 *fax* (01463) 741733
email m-mhor@arvonfoundation.org
Contact Chris Aldridge
The Arvon Foundation, Totleigh Barton, Sheepwash, Beaworthy, Devon EX21 5NS
tel (01409) 231338 *fax* (01409) 231144
email t-barton@arvonfoundation.org
Contact Julia Wheadon
The Hurst – The John Osborne Arvon Centre Clunton, Craven Arms, Shropshire SY7 0JA
tel (01588) 640658 *fax* (01588) 640509
email hurst@arvonfoundation.org

Belstead House Education & Conference Centre (Residential Courses)
Sprites Lane, Ipswich, Suffolk IP8 3NA
tel (01473) 686321 *fax* (01473) 686664
email belstead.house@educ.suffolkcc.gov.uk

Birkbeck College, University of London
Malet Street, London WC1E 7HX
tel 020-7580 6622 *fax* 020-7631 6255
email imcdonagh@bbk.ac.uk
website www.bbk.ac.uk

Part-time accredited evening courses.

Burton Manor
Burton, Neston, Cheshire CH64 5SJ
tel 0151-336 5172 *fax* 0151-336 6586
email enquiry@burtonmanor.com
website www.burtonmanor.com
Principal Keith Chandler

Caboodle Writing Retreats
69 Southwold Road, Wrentham, Beccles, Suffolk NR34 7JE
tel/fax (01502) 676107
email info@caboodleretreats.co.uk
website www.caboodleretreats.co.uk
Director Ruby C. Ormerod

Creative writing retreats, courses and one-day workshops in Suffolk. Residential and non-residental.

University of Cambridge
Institute of Continuing Education, University of Cambridge, Madingley Hall, Madingley, Cambridge CB3 8AQ
tel (01954) 280399 *fax* (01954) 280200
email residential@cont-ed.cam.ac.uk
website www.cont-ed.cam.ac.uk
Contact The Registrar

Accredited creative writing courses: fiction workshop, 'Continuing to Write', 'Time to Write' and poetry masterclasses.

Castle of Park
Cornhill, Aberdeenshire AB45 2AX
tel (01466) 751111 *fax* (01466) 751111
email booking@castleofpark.net
website www.castleofpark.net
Proprietors Bill Breckon, Lois Breckon

Centerprise Literature Development Project
136 Kingsland High Street, London E8 2NS
tel 020-7249 6572 *fax* 020-7923 1951
email literature@centerprisetrust.org.uk

See also page 531.

Central St Martins College of Art & Design
Southampton Row, London WC1B 4AP
tel 020-7514 7000 *fax* 020-7514 7024
website www.csm.ac.uk
Contact Josh Golding

5-day (Saturday) course in screenwriting for screenwriters with a basic foundation in scriptwriting technique.

University of Derby
Kedleston Road, Derby DE22 1GB
tel (01332) 622222 *fax* (01332) 294861
email A.Isaac1@derby.ac.uk
website www.derby.ac.uk
Contact Carl Tighe, Subject Leader, Creative Writing

Introduction to creative writing course.

Dingle Writing Courses
Ballintlea, Ventry, Co. Kerry, Republic of Ireland
tel 66 9159815 *fax* 66 9159815
email info@dinglewritingcourses.ie
website www.dinglewritingcourses.ie
Directors Abigail Joffe, Nicholas McLachlan

The Earnley Concourse
Earnley Trust Ltd, Earnley, Chichester, West Sussex
PO20 7JL
tel (01243) 670392 *fax* (01243) 670832
email info@earnley.co.uk
website www.earnley.co.uk

Emerson College
Emerson College, Forest Row, East Sussex RH18 5JX
tel (01342) 822238 *fax* (01342) 826055
email info@emerson.co.uk
website www.emerson.org.uk
Contact Paul Matthews
Takes place August

Poetry OtherWise: a week of writing workshops, readings by established poets, space for paticipants to share their poetry, together with music, dancing, conversation, talks and social events.

University of Essex
Wivenhoe Park, Colchester CO4 3SQ
tel (01206) 872400
email proffice@essex.ac.uk
website www.essex.ac.uk/literature
Contact Dept of Literature, Film & Theatre Studies

MA in Literature with option to specialise in creative writing.

Essex Literature Development
Essex Libraries, Goldlay Gardens, Chelmsford, Essex
CM2 6WN
tel (01245) 244963
email malcolm.burgess@essexcc.gov.uk
website www.essexlivelit.org.uk
Contact Kaveri Woodward

Development and promotion of Essex writers at all levels, plus advice on funding, grants, marketing and opportunities. Includes Essex Book Festival, Essex Writers' Day, Young People's Creative Writing Day, skills development workshops, etc.

Far West
23 Chapel Street, Penzance, Cornwall TR18 4AP
tel (01736) 363146
email angela@farwest.co.uk
website www.farwest.co.uk
Contact Angela Stoner

Federation of Worker Writers and Community Publishers Festival of Writing – see page 535

Fire in the Head
PO Box 17, Yelverton, Devon PL20 6YF
tel (01822) 841081
email roselle.angwin@internet-today.co.uk
website www.fire-in-the-head.co.uk
Contact Roselle Angwin

Poetry and prose; journaling and personal development; retreats and short courses, correspondence courses.

Indian King Arts
Garmoe Cottage, 2 Trefrew Road, Camelford, Cornwall PL32 9TP
tel (01840) 212161
email indianking@btconnect.com
website www.indianking.org.uk

Creative writing workshops, annual poetry festival and other events.

Irish Writers' Centre
19 Parnell Square, Dublin 1
tel (01) 8721302 *fax* (01) 8726282
email courses@writerscentre.ie
website www.writerscentre.ie

Runs an educational programme which offers courses and workshops in writing.

Knuston Hall
Irchester, Wellingborough, Northants. NN29 7EU
tel (01933) 312104 *fax* (01933) 357596
email enquiries@knustonhall.org.uk
website www.knustonhall.org.uk

Lancaster University
Dept of Continuing Education, Lancaster University, Ash House, Lancaster LA1 4YT
tel (01524) 592623/4 *fax* (01524) 592448
email Conted@lancaster.ac.uk
website www.lancs.ac.uk/users/conted/index.htm

University of Leeds
Life-long Learning Centre, Springfield Mount, Leeds
LS2 9JT
tel 0113-343 3212
website www.leeds.ac.uk

Varied part-time creative writing courses.

Liberato
tel (01279) 833690 *mobile* (07718) 339636
email liberato@tesco.net

website www.liberato.co.uk
Contact Maureen Blundell, Tutor

Weekend residential, Greek Week holidays and MS critiques.

Marlborough College Summer School
Marlborough, Wilts. SN8 1PA
tel (01672) 892388 *fax* (01672 892476
email admin@mcsummerschool.org.uk
website www.mcsummerschool.org.uk
Contact Tara Pathania

A 3-week summer school where participants can attend for 1, 2 or 3 weeks. There are a large variety of courses, including creative writing, covering many subjects with each course lasting half a day.

Middlesex University Summer School
Summer School Office, Middlesex University, Trent Park, Bramley Road, London N14 4YZ
tel 020-8411 5782
email a.mascarenhas@mdx.ac.uk
Contact Anita Mascarenhas

Offers a number of creative writing courses.

Missenden Abbey
Great Missenden, Bucks. HP16 0BD
tel (08450) 454040 *fax* (01753) 783756
email adultlearning@buckscc.gov.uk
website www.aredu.net/missendenabbey

Weekend and summer school writing courses.

Morley College
61 Westminster Bridge, London SE1 7HT
tel 020-7450 1889 *fax* 020-7928 8501
email enquiries@morleycollege.ac.uk
website www.morleycollege.ac.uk

Offers a number of one-day creative writing courses.

University of Newcastle upon Tyne
School of English, Percy Building, Newcastle upon Tyne NE1 7RU
tel 0191-222 7619 *fax* 0191-222 8708
email melanie.birch@ncl.ac.uk
website www.ncl.ac.uk/elll/creative
Contact Melanie Birch

Short courses, spring and summer schools, a postgraduate certificate and degrees at MA and PhD level.

North West Kent College
Oakfield Lane, Dartford DA1 2JT
tel (0800) 0741447 *fax* (01322) 629468
website www.nwkent.ac.uk
Contact Neil Nixon, Pathway Leader, Professional Writing

Offers full-time, part-time and one-off courses in professional writing.

University of Nottingham Study Tours
School of Education, The Dearing Building, University of Nottingham, Jubilee Campus, Wollaton Road, Nottingham NG8 1BB

tel 0115-951 6526 *fax* 0115-951 6556
email ce-studytours@nottingham.ac.uk
website www.nottingham.ac.uk

Open Studies – Part-time Courses for Adults: Office of Lifelong Learning
University of Edinburgh, 11 Buccleuch Place, Edinburgh EH8 9LW
tel 0131-650 4400 *fax* 0131-667 6097
email oll@ed.ac.uk
website www.lifelong.ed.ac.uk

Oxford University Summer Schools for Adults
Dept for Continuing Education, Oxford University, Rewley House, 1 Wellington Square, Oxford OX1 2JA
tel (01865) 270396 *fax* (01865) 280761
email oussa@conted.ox.ac.uk
website www.conted.ox.ac.uk/oussa
Contact Programme Administrator

A 4-week summer school with a variety of courses on offer, including creative writing. Students choose one course and follow it for a week.

Pitstop Refuelling Writers' Weekend Workshops – see Winchester Writers' Conference, Bookfair and Weeklong Workshops

Scottish Universities, International Summer School
21 Buccleuch Place, Edinburgh EH8 9LN
tel 0131-650 4369 *fax* 0161-662 0275
email suiss@ed.ac.uk
website www.arts.ed.ac.uk/suiss
Directors Peter Garratt, Clare Elliott

A 3-week creative writing course for undergraduates, postgraduates and teachers, as well as published writers keen to widen their skills.

Southern Writers' Conference
Stable House, Home Farm, Coldharbour Lane, Dorking, Surrey RH4 3JG
Contact Lucia White
Venue The Earnley Concourse, Chichester

Caters for published and serious writers.

Swanwick, The Writers' Summer School
Contact Jean Sutton, The Secretary, 10 Stag Road, Lake, Sandown, Isle of Wight PO36 8PE
website www.wss.org.uk

Travellers' Tales
92 Hillfield Road, London NW6 1QA
email info@travellerstales.org
website www.travellerstales.org
Director Jonathan Lorie, Contributing Editor of *Traveller* magazine

Training agency for aspiring travel writers and photographers. Offers professional courses with the UK's top travel editors and writers including Fergal Keane, William Dalrymple and Colin Thubron. Courses in London, Cornwall and overseas include beginners' weekends, masterclasses and creative retreats in travel journalism, travel photography and writing travel books.

Ty Newydd

Ty Newydd, National Writers' Centre for Wales, Llanystumdwy, Cricieth, Gwynedd LL52 0LW
tel (01766) 522811 *fax* (01766) 523095
email post@tynewydd.org
website www.tynewydd.org

Week and weekend courses on all aspects of creative writing. Full programme available.

Urchfont Manor College

Urchfont, Devizes, Wilts. SN10 4RG
tel (01380) 840495 *fax* (01380) 840005
email urchfontmanor@wiltshire.gov.uk

Wedgwood Memorial College

Station Road, Barlaston, Stoke-on-Trent ST12 9DG
tel (01782) 372105/373427 *fax* (01782) 372393
website www.sdfl.org.uk/wmc

Winchester Writers' Conference, Bookfair and Weeklong Workshops

University of Winchester, Winchester, Hants SO22 4NR
tel (01962) 827238
email barbara.large@winchester.ac.uk
website www.writersconference.co.uk
Conference Director Barbara Large MBE, FRSA, FUW
Takes place University College, Winchester, 29 June–1 July 2007; Workshops 2–7 July 2007

This Festival of Writing, now in its 27th year, attracts 65 internationally renowned authors, poets, playwrights, agents and commissioning editors who give mini-courses, workshops, talks, seminars and one-to-one appointments to help writers harness their creativity and develop their writing, editing and marketing skills. Fifteen writing competitions, including Writing for Children, are adjudicated and 64 prizes are awarded at the Writers' Awards Reception. All first place winners are published annually in *The Best of* series.

The Bookfair offers delegates a wide choice of exhibits including authors' and internet services, publishers, booksellers, printers and trade associations.

Pitstop Refuelling Writers' Weekend Workshops are planned for 16–18 March and 26–28 October 2007, including Writing Marketable Children's Fiction and Non-fiction; Editing and Marketing your Novel; and How to Self-Publish Your Book day courses on 11 May and 21 September 2007.

Write Away

Arts Training Central, (Arts Council, East Midlands), 16 New Street, Leicester LE1 5NR
tel 0116-242 5202
email sapna@artstrainingcentral.co.uk
website www.artstrainingcentral.co.uk
Contact Sapna Chandihok

The ATC programme of Write Away courses runs each summer. The programme consists of 4 residential writing courses for writers of all levels, which run from Friday afternoon to Sunday afternoon. Each course offers workshops, surgeries and individual writing time to a small and informal group. Each course offers workshops and individual writing time in a small and informal group.

Writers' Holiday at Caerleon

School Bungalow, Church Road, Pontnewydd, Cwmbran, South Wales NP44 1AT
tel (01633) 489438 *fax* (01633) 489438
email enquiries@writersholiday.net
website www.writersholiday.net
Contact Anne Hobbs

A 6-day annual conference for writers of all standards from absolute beginner to bestselling author. The event includes 12 courses.

The Writing College

16 Magdalen Road, Exeter EX2 4SY
tel (01392) 253533 *fax* (01392) 498008
email enquiries@writingcollege.com
website www.writingcollege.com
Directors Richard Littler, Daisy Crowther

'The Complete Writer' correspondence course: 27 modules divided into the practice and art of writing, writing genres and the business of writing. An MS appraisal service is also available. Founded 2000.

Written Words

5 Queen Elisabeth Close, London N16 0HL
tel 020-8809 4725
email henrietta@writtenwords.net
website www.writtenwords.net
Contact Henrietta Soames

An intensive course of 8 sessions (10am–4pm) spread throughout the year for practised writers already working on a novel or collection of short stories. Also offers private tutorials in person or by telephone, and a compact beginners course.

Wye Valley Arts Centre

The Coach House, Mork, St Briavel's, Lydney, Glos. GL15 6QH
tel (01594) 530214, (01291) 689463
fax (01594) 530321
email wyeart@cwcom.net
website www.wyeart.cwc.net

Fiction workshop.

POSTGRADUATE COURSES

Bath Spa University
School of English and Creative Studies, Bath Spa University, Newton Park, Newton St Loe, Bath BA2 9BN
tel (01225) 875875 *fax* (01225) 875503
email enquiries@bathspa.ac.uk
website www.bathspa.ac.uk

MA in Creative Writing. MA in Writing for Young People. PhD in Creative Writing.

University of Bolton
Dept of Cultural & Creative Studies, University of Bolton, Chadwick Street, Bolton BL2 1JW
tel (01204) 903231 *fax* (01204) 903232
email mw7@bolton.ac.uk
website www.bolton.ac.uk
Contact Matthew Welton, Programme Leader, Creative Writing

BA in Creative Writing. MA in Creative Writing.

University of Bristol
Dept of English, University of Bristol, 3–5 Woodland Road, Bristol BS8 1TB
tel 0117-954 6969
email tom.sperlinger@bristol.ac.uk
website www.bris.ac.uk/english
Contact Tom Sperlinger, Course Director

Diploma in Creative Writing and a variety of short courses.

Brunel University
English Dept, Brunel University, Uxbridge, Middlesex UB8 3PH
tel (01895) 274000 *fax* (01895) 232806
email Rose.Atfield@brunel.ac.uk
website www.brunel.ac.uk/faculty/arts/english
Contact Dr J.R. Atfield, Course Leader

MA in Creative/Professional Writing. MA in Novel Writing with Fay Weldon and Celia Brayfield.

Cardiff University
Cardiff University, Cardiff School of English, Communication and Philosophy, Humanities Building, Colum Drive, Cardiff CF10 3EU
tel 029-2087 5624 *fax* 029-2087 4647
email creativewriting@cardiff.ac.uk
website www.cf.ac.uk/encap/creativewriting

MA in the Teaching and Practice of Creative Writing, MPhil in Creative Writing, and PhD in Creative and Critical Writing.

Central School of Speech and Drama
Central School of Speech and Drama, Embassy Theatre, Eton Avenue, London NW3 3HY
tel 020-7722 8183
website www.cssd.ac.uk

MA in Advanced Theatre Practice: Playwriting. MA in Writing for Stage and Broadcast Media.

University of Chichester
Chichester Institute of Higher Education, Bishop Otter Campus, College Lane, Chichester, West Sussex PO19 4PE
tel (01243) 816296
email s.norgate@chi.ac.uk
website www.ucc.ac.uk
Contact Stephanie Norgate, MA in Creative Writing Programme Coordinator

MA in Creative Writing.

City University
Dept of Journalism and Publishing, City University, Northampton Square, London EC1V 0HB
tel 020-7040 8221 *fax* 020-7040 8594
email journalism@city.ac.uk
website www.city.ac.uk
Contact The Course Officer (Creative Writing)

MA in Creative Writing (Plays and Scripts) and MA in Creative Writing (Novels).

Community Creative Writers
Sea Winds, 2 St Helens Terr, Spittal, Berwick-upon-Tweed, Northumberland TD15 1RJ
tel/fax (01289) 305213
email mavismaureen@aol.com
Contact Maureen Ramper MBE

Dartington College of Arts
Dartington College of Arts, Dartington Hall Estate, Totnes, Devon TQ9 6EJ
tel (01803) 862224 *fax* (01803) 861666
email enquiries@dartington.ac.uk
website www.dartington.ac.uk
Contact College Administration

MA in Performance Writing.

De Montfort University
Dept of Media and Cultural Production, De Montfort University, City Campus, The Gateway, Leicester LE1 9BH
tel 0116-255 1551, 0116-250 6179 *fax* 0116-255 0307
email csrwalker@aol.com
website www.dmu.ac.uk
Contact Chris Walker

MA in TV Screenwriting.

University of East Anglia
School of Literature and Creative Writing, University of East Anglia, Norwich NR4 7TJ
tel (01603) 593717 *fax* (01603) 250599
email pgt.hum@uea.ac.uk
website www.uea.ac.uk/eas/
Contact Graduate Admissions Secretary

MA in Creative Writing: Prose Fiction. MA in Creative Writing: Poetry. MA in Creative Writing: Scriptwriting. MA in Life Writing.

Edge Hill University

St Helens Road, Ormskirk L39 4QP
tel (01695) 584274 *fax* (01695) 579997
email shepparr@edgehill.ac.uk
website www.edgehill.ac.uk
Contact Dr Robert Sheppard, Dr Ailsa Cox

BA in Creative Writing. MA in Writing Studies. PhD programmes in creative writing.

University of Edinburgh

Literatures, Languages & Cultures Graduate School,
19 George Square, Edinburgh EH8 9JX
tel 0131-650 4114
website www.ed.ac.uk/englit/
Contact The Graduate Secretary

MSc in Creative Writing.

University of Exeter

School of Performance Arts and Drama, Thornlea,
New North Road, Exeter EX4 4LA
tel (01392) 264580 *fax* (01392) 264594
email p.zarrilli@exeter.ac.uk
website www.exeter.ac.uk/drama
Contact Prof. Phillip Zarrilli

MA in Theatre Practice: playwriting for stage and radio, performance writing.

University College Falmouth

Falmouth, Cornwall TR11 4RH
tel (01326) 211077
email admissions@falmouth.ac.uk
website www.falmouth.ac.uk
Contact Admissions Office

BA (Hons) English with Creative Writing. BA (Hons) English with Media Studies. Postgraduate Diploma/ MA in Professional Writing.

University of Glamorgan

School of Humanities and Social Sciences, University of Glamorgan, Treforest, Pontypridd CF37 1DL
tel (01443) 482570, 482501 *fax* (01443) 482138
email tcurtis@glam.ac.uk, llewis6@glam.ac.uk
website www.glam.ac.uk
Contacts Prof. T. Curtis, Director of Studies
(Writing), Dr Lisa Lewis (Scriptwriting) *tel*

MA in Scriptwriting and M.Phil in Writing.

University of Glasgow

Dept of English Literature, University of Glasgow, 5
University Gardens, Glasgow G12 8QQ
tel 0141-330 4165 *fax* 0141-330 4601
website www.arts.gla.ac.uk/EngLit
Contact Head of Department

MA in Creative Writing.

University of Greenwich

School of Humanities, University of Greenwich, Old
Royal Naval College, London SE10 9LS

tel/fax 020-8331 8800
email s.a.rowland@greenwich.ac.uk
website www.greenwich.ac.uk
Contact Susan Rowland

MA by Research (Creative Writing).

University of Huddersfield

Division of English, University of Huddersfield, West
Building, Queensgate, Huddersfield HD1 3DH
tel (01484) 478429
email d.gill@hud.ac.uk
website www.hud.ac.uk/schools
Contact David Gill, Creative Writing Courses Co-ordinator

BA (Hons) English with Creative Writing. BA (Hons) English Language with Creative Writing. BA (Hons) English Literature with Creative Writing.

University of Hull

Faculty of Arts, Dept of English, University of Hull,
Cottingham Road, Hull HU6 7RX
tel (01482) 466188 *fax* (01482) 465641
email c.rumens@hull.ac.uk
website www.hull.ac.uk
Contact Carol Rumens, Prof. of Creative Writing

MA in Creative Writing.

Lancaster University

Dept of English & Creative Writing, Bowland
College, Lancaster University, Lancaster LA1 4YT
tel (01524) 594169
email l.kellett@lancaster.ac.uk
website www.lancs.ac.uk/depts/english/crew/index.htm
Contact The Secretary

MA in Creative Writing.

University of Leeds

School of Performance and Cultural Studies, Bretton
Hall Campus, University of Leeds, West Bretton,
Wakefield, West Yorkshire WF4 4LG
tel 0113-343 9109 *fax* 0113-343 9148
website www.leeds.ac.uk
Contact Postgraduate Secretary

MA in Writing, Performance and Publication.

Leeds Metropolitan University

School of Film, Television and Performing Arts,
Electric Press Building, 1 Millennium Square, Leeds
LS2 3AD
tel 0113-283 2600 ext. 3860
email c.j.pugh@leedsmet.ac.uk
website www.lmu.ac.uk/as/ftpa
Contact Chris Pugh, Course Administrator

MA/Postgraduate Diploma in Screenwriting (Fiction).

Liverpool John Moores University

School of Media, Critical and Creative Arts, Liverpool
John Moores University, Dean Walters Building, St
James Road, Liverpool L1 7BR

tel 0151-231 5052 *fax* 0151-231 5049
website www.livjm.ac.uk
Contact Research Coordinator

MA in Screenwriting and MA in Writing.

University of London, Goldsmiths College

Dept of Drama, Goldsmiths College, University of London, London SE14 6NW
tel 020-7919 7414 *fax* 020-7919 7413
email drama@gold.ac.uk
website www.goldsmiths.ac.uk
Contact Drama Secretary

MA in Writing for Performance.

University of London, Goldsmiths College

Dept of English and Comparative Literature, Goldsmiths College, University of London, London SE14 6NW
tel 020-7919 7436 *fax* 020-7919 7509
email english@gold.ac.uk
website www.goldsmiths.ac.uk
Contact Maria Macdonald, Secretary for Postgraduate Enquiries

MA in Creative and Life Writing.

University of London, King's College

University of London, King's College, Strand, London WC2R 2LS
tel 020-7848 2185 *fax* 020-7848 2257
email englishdept@kcl.ac.uk
website www.kcl.ac.uk
Contact Graduate Secretary

MA in Text and Performance Studies; scriptwriting option supervised at RADA.

University of London, Royal Holloway

Dept of English, Royal Holloway, University of London, Egham, Surrey TW20 0EX
tel (01784) 443214
email english@rhul.ac.uk
website www.rhul.ac.uk/English

Contact Prof. Andrew Motion

MA in Creative Writing.

University of London, Royal Holloway

Dept of Media Arts, Royal Holloway, University of London, Egham, Surrey TW20 0EX
tel (01784) 443214
email mediaarts@rhul.ac.uk
website www.rhul.ac.uk/media-arts

Contact Susan Rogers, Sue Clayton (Retreat Programme)

MA in Film Screenwriting and MA in Screenwriting for Film and TV (Retreat Programme).

London College of Communication

(formerly London College of Printing)
Elephant & Castle, London SE1 6SB

tel 020-7514 6500
website www.lcc.arts.ac.uk
Contact Media & Cultural Studies Dept

MA in Screenwriting.

London Metropolitan University

London Film School, 24 Sheldon Street, London WC2H 9UB
tel 020-7836 9642 *fax* 020-7497 3718
website www.londonmet.ac.uk
Contact Brian Dunnigan

MA in Screenwriting.

Loughborough University

Dept of English and Drama, Loughborough University, Loughborough, Leics. LE11 3TU
tel (01509) 222951 *fax* (01509) 610813
website www.lboro.ac.uk
Contact Dr Jonathan Taylor

MA in Creative Writing.

University of Manchester

Dept for English Language and Literature, University of Manchester, Manchester M13 9PL
tel 0161-275 3144 *fax* 0161-275 3256
email englishpg@man.ac.uk
website www.art.man.ac.uk/english/hom.htm

MA in Novel Writing.

Manchester Metropolitan University

Dept of English, Rosamond Street West, Off Oxford Road, Manchester M16 6LL
tel 0161-247 1787 *fax* 0161-247 6345
email j.draper@mmu.ac.uk
website www.mmu.ac.uk/english/writingschool
Contact James Draper, Project Manager: Writing School

MA in Creative Writing.

Middlesex University

Trent Park, Bramley Road, London N14 4YZ
tel 020-8411 5000
email admissions@mdx.ac.uk
website www.mdx.ac.uk
Contact Admissions Office

MA/Postgraduate Diploma/Postgraduate Certificate in Writing (Prose Fiction) and MPhil/PhD in Creative Writing.

National Film and Television School

National Film and Television School, Beaconsfield Studios, Station Road, Beaconsfield, Bucks. HP9 1LG
tel (01494) 671234 *fax* (01494) 674042
email info@nftsfilm-tv.ac.uk
website www.nftsfilm-tv.ac.uk

MA in Screenwriting.

University of Newcastle

School of English Literature, Language and Linguistics, University of Newcastle, Newcastle upon Tyne NE1 7RU

tel 0191-222 6233 *fax* 0191-222 8708
website www.ncl.ac.uk/english
Contact Postgraduate Admission Secretary

MA in Creative Writing. Postgraduate Certificate in Creative Writing. Phd in Creative Writing.

Northumbria University at Newcastle

Postgraduate School of Humanities, University of Northumbria at Newcastle, Lipman Building, Sandyford Road, Newcastle upon Tyne NE1 8ST
tel 0191-227 3258 *fax* 0191-227 4630
website online.unn.ac.uk/faculties/art/humanities
Contact The Admissions Tutor

MA in Creative Writing, combining prose, poetry and script.

Nottingham Trent University

Dept of English and Media Studies, Nottingham Trent University, Clifton Lane, Nottingham NG11 8NS
tel 0115-848 3357 *fax* 0115-848 6385
website www.ntu.ac.uk
Contact Prof. David Belbin

MA in Creative Writing.

Oxford University

Dept for Continuing Education, 1 Wellington Square, Oxford OX1 2JA
tel (01865) 270369 *fax* (01865) 270309
email ppcert@conted.ox.ac.uk
website www.conted.ox.ac.uk/courses/awardbearing/creative_writing/mstcw.asp
Contact M.St. Administrator

Master of Studies (M.St.) in Creative Writing from Oxford University: a 2-year part-time course covering prose fiction, radio and TV drama, poetry, stage drama and screenwriting.

University of Plymouth

Faculty of Arts, University of Plymouth, Drake Circus, Plymouth PL4 8AA
tel (01752) 2388106
email t.lopez@plymouth.ac.uk
website www.plymouth.ac.uk
Contact Prof. Tony Lopez, Professor of Poetry

MA/Postgraduate Diploma in Creative Writing.

The Poet's House – see page 325

Queen's University, Belfast

School of English, Queen's University, Belfast, Belfast BT7 1NN
tel 028-9097 5103 ext. 5103 *fax* 028-9031 4615
website www.qub.ac.uk/en/teaching/postgraduate/index.htm
Contact Prof. Brian Caraher, Head of Graduate Teaching & Research

MA/Postgraduate Diploma in Creative Writing. PhD in Creative Writing.

University of St Andrews

School of English, University of St Andrews, St Andrews, Fife KY16 9AR
tel (01334) 462666 *fax* (01334) 462655
email jb44@st-andrews.ac.uk
website www.st-andrews.ac.uk
Contact Postgraduate Director

M.Litt/Graduate Diploma in Creative Writing.

St Martin's College, Lancaster

St Martin's College, Lancaster, Bowerham Road, Lancaster LA1 3JD
tel (01524) 384328 *fax* (01524) 384385
email k.flann@ucsm.ac.uk
website www.ucsm.ac.uk
Contact Kathy Flann, Course Leader, Creative Writing

MA in Creative Writing. Opportunities for undergraduate studies.

University of Salford

University of Salford, Adelphi Building, Peru Street, Salford, Greater Manchester M3 6EQ
tel 0161-295 6026 *fax* 0161-295 6027
email r.humphrey@salford.ac.uk
website www.salford.ac.uk
Contact Roy Humphrey

MA/Postgraduate Diploma in Television and Radio Scriptwriting.

Sheffield Hallam University

School of Cultural Studies, Sheffield Hallam University, 32 Collegiate Crescent, Sheffield S10 2BP
tel 0114-225 5555
website www.shu.ac.uk/humanities

MA/Postgraduate Diploma/Postgraduate Certificate in Creative Writing.

University of Sussex

Centre for Continuing Education, The Sussex Institute, Essex House, Brighton BN1 9QQ
tel (01273) 877888/877001
email cce@sussex.ac.uk
website www.sussex.ac.uk
Contact Richard Crane

MA in Dramatic Writing and Certificate in Creative Writing.

Trinity College, Carmarthen

School of Creative Arts & Humanities, Trinity College, Carmarthen, Dyfed SA31 3EP
tel (01267) 676617 *fax* (01267) 676766
email c.wigginton@trinity-cm.ac.uk
website www.trinity-cm.ac.uk
Contact Paul Wright

MA in Creative Writing.

University of Wales, Aberystwyth

Dept of English, Hugh Owen Building, Penglais Campus, University of Wales, Aberystwyth, Aberystwyth, Ceredigion SY23 3DY

tel (01970) 622535
email www.aber.ac.uk/english
Contact The Secretary

MA in Writing: Process and Practice. PhD in Creative Writing.

University of Warwick

Dept of English and Comparative Literary Studies, University of Warwick, Senate House, Coventry CV4 7AL
tel 024-7657 4368
email ensak@dredd.warwick.ac.uk
website www.warwick.ac.uk
Contact Elisabeth Cameron, Programme Secretary

MA in Creative Writing.

University of Winchester

West Hill, Winchester SO22 4NR
tel (01962) 827235 *fax* (01962) 827406
website www.winchester.ac.uk
Contact Course Enquiries & Admissions

MA in Writing for Children and MA in Creative and Critical Writing.

University of York

Dept of English and Related Literature, University of York, Heslington, York YO10 5DD
tel (01904) 433369 *fax* (01904) 433372
email engl13@york.ac.uk
website www.york.ac.uk/depts/engl/
Contact The Graduate Secretary

MA in Writing and Performance (Drama/Film/TV).

Editorial, literary and production services

The specialists listed below offer a wide variety of services to writers publishers, journalists and others. Services include advice on manuscripts, editing and book production, indexing, translation, research and writing. See page 778 for a subject index.

A.R. Business Services
9 Mulberry Street, Stratford upon Avon CV37 6RS
tel/fax (01789) 294966
email angelawrich@onetel.com
Proprietor Angela Richards

Word processing from MS or audio tape, proofreading, editing, desktop publishing. Founded 1989.

Abbey Writing Services
Twitchen Cottage, Holcombe Rogus, Wellington, Somerset TA21 0PT
tel (01823) 672762 *fax* (01823) 672762
email john.mcilwain@virgin.net
Director John McIlwain

Comprehensive non-fiction writing, project management and editorial service. Guidebooks; autobiographies; lexicography. Founded 1989.

Academic File
(in association with The Centre for Near East Afro-Asia Research – NEAR)
PO Box 13666, London SW14 8WF
tel 020-8392 1122 *fax* 020-8392 1422
email afis@eapgroup.com
website www.eapgroup.com
Director Sajid Rizvi

Research, advisory and consultancy services related to politics, economics and societies of the Near and Middle East, Asia and North Africa and related issues in Europe. Risk analysis, editorial assessment, editing, contract publishing, design and production. Founded 1985.

Advice and Criticism Service
1 Beechwood Court, Syderstone, Norfolk PE31 8TR
tel (01485) 578594
email hilary@hilaryjohnson.demon.co.uk
website www.hilaryjohnson.demon.com
Contact Hilary Johnson

Authors' consultant: detailed and constructive assessment of typescripts/practical advice regarding publication. Former organiser of RNA New Writers' Scheme, adjudicator of literary awards and publishers' reader. All fiction genres including science fiction/fantasy. Also children's books, TV/radio/film scripts, poetry and non-fiction. Close link with leading literary agent. Outstanding authors can be given a direct route to this agency.

AESOP (All Editorial Services Online for Publishers & Authors)
Uplands, 28 Abberbury Road, Iffley, Oxford OX4 4ES
tel (01865) 429563 *fax* (0870) 0635449
email mart@copyedit.co.uk
website www.all-eds.com
Contact Martin Noble

Editing; copy-editing; rewriting; proofreading; indexing; editorial reports and reviews; advice to publishers, authors and literary agents; co-writing; ghostwriting; novelisation; research; fact-checking; bibliographical research; CRC (Word); text capture: scanning/OCR; e-book production on CD-Rom or online; keying in MSS; audio transcription; tagging. Specialises in fiction, literature, poetry, media, music, performing arts, humour biography, memoirs, education, psychology, alternative health, special needs, thesis and dissertation editing and printing; improving use of English of non-native English writers of academic reports and books. Established 1979.

AFI Research and International Security Database
email rbmedia@supanet.com
Consultant Editor Richard M. Bennett

Author, journalist, broadcaster. Expert coverage of intelligence and national security, counter-terrorism, Special Forces, WMD and conventional weapons, defence and conflictananalysis.

Agent Research & Evaluation Inc
425 North 20th Street, Philadelphia, PA 19130, USA
tel 215-563-1867 *fax* 215-563-6797
email info@agentresearch.com
website www.agentresearch.uk.net
President Bill Martin

Provides authors, editors and other professionals with data on clients and sales made by literary agents in the USA, UK and Canada, i.e. who sells what to whom for how much. Information is culled from the trade and general press, and collection has been continuous since 1980. Individual reports on specific agents and various forms of MS–agent match-up services are available. See website for pricing or send an sae. Publishes *Talking Agents*, the AR&E newsletter (10 p.a.). The website offers a free service of agent verification: information on whether or not the database reflects that a given agent has created a public record of sales. Founded 1996.

Allwood Research
111 The Avenue, Bournemouth, Dorset BH9 2UX
tel (01202) 519220 *fax* (01202) 519220
Contact Alan C. Wood

Research and consultancy on military aviation, army, navy, weapons (new and antique), police, intelligence, medals, uniforms and armour. Founded 1957.

Amolibros
Loundshay Manor Cottage, Preston Bowyer, Milverton, Somerset TA4 1QF
tel (01823) 401527 *fax* (01823) 401527
email amolibros@aol.com
website www.amolibros.co.uk
Managing Consultant Jane Tatam

A self-publishing consultancy/packager. Also offers copy-editing, proofreading, typesetting, advice on marketing and sales. Established 1992.

Apple Pips Editing Services
18 Raglan Grove, Kenilworth, Warks.CV8 2NH
tel (01926) 858864
email primrosecroft@hotmail.com
Contact Ann Richards

Editing, copy-editing, proofreading, keying-in MSS (Word), research, book reviews. Special interests: history (especially Irish, social history of medicine, American – early colonial, Wild West, Tudor, Stuarts), educational books for schools, crime, fiction, biographies. Established 2001.

Arioma Editorial Services
PO Box 53, Aberystwyth, Ceredigion SY24 5WG
tel (01970) 871296 *fax* (01970) 871733
Proprietor Moira W. Smith

Research, co-writing, ghostwriting, DTP, complete book production service. Specialities: non fiction, history and autobiography.

Arkst Publishing
1 Lindsey House, Lloyds's Place, London SE3 0QF
tel 020-8297 9997
email jim@arkst.demon.co.uk
Director James H. Willis MA, FRCP (Edin.)

Independent appraisal of MSS – fiction and non-fiction. Founded 1995.

Asterisk Design & Editorial Solutions Ltd
8 Carnyorth Terrace, Carnyorth, Penzance, Cornwall TR19 7QE

tel (01736) 788202
email yvonnebristow@blue-earth.co.uk, rogerbristow@blue-earth.co.uk
Directors Roger Bristow, Yvonne Bristow

Full editorial and design service for books, brochures, catalogues, etc; project management; legal consultancy for publishing and creative contacts; commissioning authors, illustrators, photographers; research service; writing, journalism; restaurant/pub/other reviews. Specialises in integrated illustrated non-fiction books: practical art, cookery, gardening, natural history, general reference. Founded 2003.

Authority Publishing
13 Coton Crescent, Shrewsbury SY1 2NY
tel (01743) 233563 *fax* (08704) 875827
email mail@authoritypublishing.co.uk
website www.authoritypublishing.co.uk
Editorial Director David Littlefield, *Production Director* Kerri Miles

Provides a service for authors and organisations wishing to self publish: editing and proofreading, typesetting and design, print buying and co-ordination. Established 2004.

Authors' Advisory Service
24 Lyndale Avenue, Childs Hill, London NW2 2QA
tel 020-7794 3285

All typescripts professionally evaluated in depth by long-established publishers' reader specialising in constructive advice to new writers and with wide experience of current literary requirements. Founded 1972.

Authors' Aid
11 Orchard Street, Fearnhead, Warrington, Cheshire WA2 0PL
tel (01925) 838431
email chris.sawyer@btinternet.com
website www.authorsaid.co.uk
Partners Chris Sawyer, Deborah Ramage

Appraisal and editorial services. Offers honest, constructive feedback and detailed guidance on style, presentation, characterisation, plot, construction, marketability, etc. A personalised service by a publishing professional with the clear aim of maximising the writer's chances of publication. Other services: rewriting, proofreading, ghostwriting, word processing, commissioned work. Write, phone or email before sending work. Established 1991.

Authors Appraisal Service
12 Hadleigh Gardens, Boyatt Wood, Eastleigh, Hants SO50 4NP
Literary consultant J. Evans

Professional writer offers critical appraisal of MSS – fiction only. Specialises in romantic and historical fiction. Competitive rates. Preliminary letter essential and sae for reply. Founded 1988.

AuthorsOnLine Ltd

19 The Cinques, Gamlingay, Sandy, Beds. SG19 3NU
tel (0800) 107 2423
email theeditor@authorsonline.co.uk
Submissions Richard Fitt, Editor
website www.authorsonline.co.uk
Directors Richard Ovenden, Richard Fitt

Offers a service for authors wishing to self publish, including full publishing facilities, on a print-on-demand basis. Includes distribution throughout the UK and North America plus most internet bookstores. All genres considered. Republication of out-of-print titles. Books can also be offered as e-books, available to download via the internet. New and established writers welcome. Authors retain all intellectual property rights.

Prices range from free (when ready-to-print PDF files from templates provided are supplied together with an order for 30 or more copies) for private publication, to £1450 for the full enhanced service. Full editing and cover design facilities available. Founded 1997.

Anne Barclay Enterprises

The Old Farmhouse, Hexworthy, Dartmoor, Devon PL20 6SD
tel (01364) 631405 *mobile* (07885) 476 944
email barclay.anne@googlemail.com

Typing MSS and audio transcription through to full editorial services – appraisal, editing, research, feature writing, co-writing and ghostwriting. Special interests: food, travel, crime, memoirs. Founded 1996.

Beswick Writing Services

19 Haig Road, Stretford M32 0DS
tel 0161-865 1259
Contact Francis Beswick

Editing, research, information books. Special interests: religious, philosophical and educational. Expertise in correspondence courses and Open Learning materials. Founded 1988.

Black Ace Book Production

PO Box 7547, Perth PH2 1AU
tel (01821) 642822 *fax* (01821) 642101
website www.blackacebooks.com
Directors Hunter Steele, Boo Wood

Book production and text processing, including text capture (or scanning), editing, proofing to camera-ready/film, printing and binding, jacket artwork and design. Delivery of finished books; can sometimes help with distribution. Founded 1990.

Blair Services

Blair Cottage, Aultgrishan, Melvaig, Gairloch, Wester Ross IV21 2DZ
tel (01445) 771228 *fax* (01445) 771228
email BlairServices@aultgrisham.freeserve.co.uk

Director Ian Mertling-Blake MA, DPhil

Editing and revision: fiction and non-fiction (such as prospectus for schools and other educational purposes). Also specialist academic revision for books/articles on archaeology and associated subjects. Founded 1992.

Book Production Consultants Ltd

25–27 High Street, Chesterton, Cambridge CB4 1ND
tel (01223) 352790 *fax* (01223) 460718
email tl@bpccam.co.uk
website www.bpccam.co.uk
Directors A.P. Littlechild, C.S. Walsh

Complete publishing service: writing, editing, designing, illustrating, translating, indexing, photography; production management of printing and binding; specialised sales and distribution; advertising sales. For books, journals, manuals, brochures, magazines, catalogues, electronic media. Founded 1973.

BookType

17 Yeoford Meadows, Yeoford, Crediton, Devon EX17 5PW
tel (01363) 84352
email info@booktype.co.uk
website www.booktype.co.uk
Proprietor Ian Woodward

Book typesetting for publishers. MS preparation and word processing service for publishers and authors. Website design. Established 2003.

Brackley Proofreading Services

PO Box 5920, Brackley, Northants. NN13 6YB
tel (01280) 703355 *fax* (01280) 703355
email brackleyproof@LineOne.net

Proofreading. Founded 2000.

Mrs D. Buckmaster

51 Chatsworth Road, Torquay, Devon TQ1 3BJ
tel (01803) 294663 *fax* (01803) 294663

General editing of non-fiction, with particular attention to clarity of expression and meaning, grammar, punctuation and flow. Experience in editing architecture, photography, financial, religious, natural health and human potential MSS. Founded 1966.

John Button – Editorial Services

Tower House, 6 Burnham Court, Martello Bay, Clacton on Sea, Essex CO15 1RE
tel (01255) 470405 *fax* (01225) 470405
email john.button@btconnect.com

Copy-editing and proofreading, specialising in government committee of enquiry reports, legal, financial, taxation, business education and corporate identity publications; Legal Reference Library series. Founded 1991.

Cambridge Publishing Management Ltd

Unit 2, Burr Elm Court, Main Street, Caldecote, Cambs. CB3 7NU
tel (01954) 214000 *fax* (01954) 214001
email initial.surname@cambridgepm.co.uk
website www.cambridgepm.co.uk
Managing Director Jackie Dobbyne, *Managing Editor* Karen Beaulah

Creative and highly skilled editorial and book production company specialising in complete project management of business, education, ELT, travel and illustrated non-fiction titles, from MS to delivery of final files on disk. Opportunities for freelances; send CV to Managing Editor. Founded 1999.

Causeway Resources Historical Research

8 The Causeway, Teddington, Middlesex TW11 0HE
tel 020-8977 8797 *fax* 020-8977 8797
email kskinner@causeway-dagonet.fsnet.co.uk
website www.metpoliceresearch.co.uk
Director Keith Skinner

Biographical and historical research, specialising in Metropolitan Police history and true crime research. Founded 1989.

Chapterhouse

16 Magdalen Road, Exeter EX2 4SY
tel (01392) 499488 *fax* (01392) 498008
email enquiries@chapterhousepublishing.com
website www.chapterhousepublishing.com
Directors Richard Littler, Daisy Crowther

Courses in copy-editing and proofreading, and other areas of publishing. Also bespoke courses for companies in style/English usage. Founded 1991.

Chase Publishing Services Ltd

Mead, Fortescue, Sidmouth, Devon EX10 9QG
tel (01395) 514709 *fax* (01395) 514709
email r.addicott@chase-publishing.co.uk
Director Ray Addicott

Coordinates a network of specialists in academic bookwork taking authors' MSS through to finished books. Services include copy-editing and proofreading, design, typesetting, indexing and a full production service. Founded 1989.

Karyn Claridge Book Production

244 Bromham Road, Biddenham, Bedford MK40 4AA
tel (01234) 347909
email claridge999@tiscali.co.uk

Complete book production management service offered from MS to bound copies; graphic services available; sourcing service for interactive book projects. Founded 1989.

Johnathon Clifford

27 Mill Road, Fareham, Hants PO16 0TH
tel (01329) 822218 *fax* (01329) 822218

website www.vanitypublishing.info

Offers a free, unbiased advice service for anyone looking for a publisher or who has experienced difficulties with a publishing house. Has extensive knowledge of vanity publishing and acted as adviser to the Advertising Standards Authority regarding the wording of the 'Advice Note Vanity Publishing July 1997'. See website for his report on the government White Paper against rogue traders and its effectiveness where authors are concerned. See also page 294. Established 1994.

Cornerstones & Kids' Corner Ltd

Milk Studios, 34 Southern Row, London W10 5AN
tel 020-8968 0777 *fax* 020-8969 8677
email helen@cornerstones.co.uk
website www.cornerstones.co.uk
Director Helen Corner, *Managing Editor* Kathryn Robinson

Specialist team of readers (authors and editors) provides literary guidance and constructive assessment of MSS for published or unpublished authors. Scouts for agents. Runs workshops on self editing and how to submit to the trade. Established 1998.

KidsCorner (children's division): All age ranges of children's fiction, from picture books to teenage.

Ingrid Cranfield

16 Myddelton Gardens, London N21 2PA
tel 020-8360 2433 *fax* 020-8360 2433
email ingrid_cranfield@hotmail.com

Advisory and editorial services for authors, publishers and media, including critical assessment, rewriting, proofreading, copy-editing, indexing, research, interviews, transcripts. Special interests: geography, travel, exploration, adventure (own archives), language, education, youth training, art and architecture (including Japanese). Translations from German and French. Not an employer or agency. Founded 1972.

Creative Plus Publishing Ltd

2nd Floor, 151 High Street, Billericay, Essex CM12 9AB
tel (01277) 633005 *fax* (01277) 633003
email mail@creative-plus.co.uk
website www.creative-plus.co.uk
Publishing Director Beth Johnson

Provides all editorial and design from concept to finished pages for books, partworks and magazines. Specialises in female interest, children, illustrated non-fiction. Opportunities for freelances. Founded 1989.

Andrew Crofts

Westlands Grange, West Grinstead, Horsham, West Sussex RH13 8LZ
tel (01403) 864518

email croftsa@aol.com
website www.andrewcrofts.com

Ghostwriting.

Josephine Curtis Editorial

Heathfield House, Balloorclerhy, Kiltimagh,
Co. Mayo, Republic of Ireland
tel (353) 9493 82883 *mobile* (353) 86 1700026
email jedit@iol.ie

Editing – hard copy and onscreen, proofreading, legal
tabling. Established 1990.

D & N Publishing

Unit 3c, Lowesden Business Park, Lambourn
Woodlands, Hungerford, Berks. RG17 7RU
tel (01488) 73657 *fax* (01488) 73657
email d@dnpublishing.co.uk
Partners David and Namrita Price-Goodfellow

Complete project management including some or all
of the following depending on project:
commissioning, editing, picture research, illustration
and design, page layout, proofreading, indexing,
printing and repro. All stages managed in-house and
produced on Apple Macs running the latest software.
All subjects considered with Natural History a
speciality. Founded 1991.

David Wineman, Solicitors

Craven House, 121 Kingsway, London WC2B 6NX
tel 020-7400 7800 *fax* 020-7400 7890
email law@davidwineman.co.uk
website www.davidwineman.co.uk
Co-Senior Partner Irving David

Established in 1981. Clients range from private
individuals to public companies with UK and
international interests including composers,
songwriters, independant music publishers,
producers, record labels and their agents. Deals with
all forms of publishing agreement, including
negotiation and review of commercial terms, where
required, with book and music publishers, film, TV
and theatrical production companies, packagers and
merchandisers. Clients have included Sir George
Martin, Ozzy Osbourne, Pink Floyd and Luciano
Pavarotti. Holds Lexcel award. Costs calculated at an
hourly rate which varies according to nature and
value of transaction.

Meg Davies

31 Egerton Road, Ashton, Preston, Lancs. PR2 1AJ
tel (01772) 725120 *mobile* (07789) 433254
email megindex@aol.com

Indexing at general and postgraduate level in the arts
and humanities. Also proofreading and copy-editing.
Registered Indexer with Society of Indexers since
1971.

Echelon Publishing Services

127 Belle Vue Road, Shrewsbury SY3 7NJ
(01743) 360988

email sarahchurch@macace.net, suecoll@macace.net
Directors Sarah Church (design & production), Sue
Coll (editorial)

Editorial, production and design company. Provides
one or all of the services listed for client-owned ideas
or, if required, a complete book packaging service:
editing, rewriting, keying, proofreading, design,
typesetting, picture research, repro, print buying,
production management and quality control. Covers
all areas of publishing from academic mono books to
fully illustrated titles; from co-editions to children's
books; plus any type of catalogue, cover or blad.
Founded 2001.

Editorial Solutions

537 Antrim Road, Belfast BT15 3BU
tel 028-9077 2300
email info@editorialsolutions.com
website www.editorialsolutions.com
Partners Sheelagh Hughes, Michael Johnston

Offers a comprehensive editorial and publications
service, including news and feature writing,
copywriting, editing and copy-editing, proofreading,
publication design, page layout and complete
publication management. Qualified journalists.
Specialisms: business, public sector, education, web
writing.

Lewis Esson Publishing

45 Brewster Gardens, London W10 6AQ
tel 020-7854 0668 *fax* 020-8968 1623
email lewisesson@supanet.com

Project management of illustrated books in areas of
food, art and interior design; editing and writing of
food books; copywriting, especially in the area of
food packaging and FMCGs. Founded 1989.

Finers Stephens Innocent

179 Great Portland Street, London W1N 6LS
tel 020-7323 4000 *fax* 020-7344 5600
email nsolomon@fsilaw.co.uk
website www.fsilaw.co.uk
Contact Nicola Solomon, Partner

Services include: drafting and negotiating agency and
publishing agreements; advice on copyright and
moral rights, libel reading, defamation advice and
insurance; breaches or termination of contract; errors
in printing and failure or refusal to publish or delay
in publishing; debt collection for payment of
royalties, commission or fees, including suing or
insolvency proceedings where necessary; injunctions;
preparation of wills, administering artistic and
literary estates; permissions, rights, copyright
infringement and negligent misstatement; electronic
rights and international sales. Solicitors to the Society
of Authors, the Writers' Guild, the British
Association of Picture Libraries and Agencies and the
Association of Illustrators.

Firefly Media

PO Box 3703, Trowbridge BA14 6ZW
tel/fax (01380) 871331

email info@ffmedia.co.uk
website www.ffmedia.co.uk
Contact Julia McCutchen

An individual service for writers offering advice, feedback, information and support for any stage of the writing journey and the publishing process. Consulting and coaching are tailored to each person's requirements. Specific expertise includes how to write a first class book proposal and how to approach the right people in the right way for the best chance of success. Author of *The Writer's Journey: From Inspiration to Publication*. Established 2001.

1st Call Editorial

19 Albemarle Road, Gorleston-on-Sea, Norfolk NR31 7AR
tel (01493) 444556 *fax* (01493) 444556
email admin@1stcalleditorial.com
website www.1stcalleditorial.com
Contact Eldo Barkhuizen

Project management, onscreen editing, copywriting, proofreading, Anglicising/Americanising. Psychology, philosophy, history, archaeology, business studies, theology, biblical studies, classical Hebrew, Hellenistic Greek, self-help. Advanced Member of SfEP. Established 1997.

First Edition Translations Ltd

6 Wellington Court, Wellington Street, Cambridge CB1 1HZ
tel (01223) 356733 *fax* (01223) 321488/316232
email info@firstedit.co.uk
website www.firstedit.co.uk
Directors Sheila Waller, Jeremy Waller

Translation, interpreting, voice-over recording, editing, proofreading, Americanisation, DTP; books, manuals, reports, journals and promotional material. Founded 1981.

Christine Foley Secretarial Services

Glyndedwydd, Login, Whitland, Carmarthenshire SA34 0TN
tel (01994) 448414 *fax* (01994) 448414
email foley@glyndedwydd.freeserve.co.uk
Partners Christine Foley, Michael Foley

Word processing service: preparation of MSS from handwritten/typed notes and audio-transcription. Complete secretarial support. Founded 1991.

The Freelance Editorial Service

4 Cranston Drive, Cousland, Dalkeith, Midlothian EH22 2PP
tel 0131-663 1238
email williamhouston@amserve.com
Contact Bill Houston BSc, DipLib, MPhil

Editing, proofreading, indexing, abstracting, translations, bibliographies; particularly scientific and medical. Founded 1975.

Freelance Market News

Sevendale House, 7 Dale Street, Manchester M1 1JB
tel 0161-228 2362 *fax* 0161-228 3533
email fmn@writersbureau.com
website www.writersbureau.com/fmn
Contact Angela Cox, Editor

A monthly market newsletter. A good rate of pay made for news of editorial requirements. Information on UK and overseas publications with editorial content, submission requirements and contact details. Founded 1968.

Freelance Services

41A Newal Road, Ballymoney, Co. Antrim BT53 6HB
tel 028-2766 2953
website www.joanshannon.co.uk
Contact Joan Shannon

Publishing services, photography and postcards. Commercial, industrial, scenic, fine art and natural light photography. Founded 1991.

Geo Group & Associates

4 Christian Fields, London SW16 3JZ
tel 020-8764 6292 *fax* 0115-981 9418
email publishing@geo-group.co.uk
website www.geo-group.co.uk

Publishing services. From copy-editing and proofreading to complete package. Research and publishing consultancy. Low-cost, quality, short-run printing. Publishing imprint: Nyala Publishing. Two photo libraries (including aerial); photography commissioned. Special rates to author-publishers. Established 1968.

Ghostwriter

21 Hindsleys Place, London SE23 2NF
tel 020-8244 5816
email parkerwrite@aol.com
website www.ghostwriteruk.co.uk
Contact John Parker

Co-author for autobiographies, true life stories, memoirs and family histories. Also help with novels and general non-fiction – business, leisure, self-help, etc. Will edit, rewrite or create the complete book from interview and research. Personal service provided throughout. Flexible terms, with favourable arrangements for retired clients. Founded 1991.

Graham-Cameron Publishing and Illustration

The Studio, 23 Holt Road, Sheringham, Norfolk NR26 8NB
tel (01263) 821333 *fax* (01263) 821334
email forename@graham-cameron-illustration.com
website www.graham-cameron-illustration.com
Partners Helen Graham-Cameron, Mike Graham-Cameron, Duncan Graham-Cameron

Biographical and modern historical work, offering complete editorial writing, editing, illustration and production services. Assistance for self-publishers. Illustration agent with 37 artists. Absolutely no unsolicited MSS. Founded 1984.

Richard Hatton Ltd
29 Roehampton Gate, London SW15 5JR
tel 020-8876 6699
Director Richard Hatton

Personal managerial services to writers, producers and directors relating to theatre, film and TV projects, stories, scripts and productions. Telephone or write first.

Antony Hemans
Maranatha, 1 Nettles Terrace, Guildford GU1 4PA
tel (01483) 574511

Biographical and historical research, specialising in industrial archaeology – railways, canals and shipping, air, military and naval operations – genealogy and family history. Founded 1981.

E.J. Hunter
6 Dorset Road, London N22 7SL
tel 020-8889 0370

Editing, copy-editing, appraisal of MSS. Special interests: novels, short stories, drama, children's stories; primary education, alternative lifestyles, complementary medicine

Indexing Specialists (UK) Ltd
Regent House, Hove Street, Hove, East Sussex BN3 2DW
tel (01273) 738299 *fax* (01273) 323309
email richardr@indexing.co.uk
website www.indexing.co.uk
Director Richard Raper BSc, DTA, MISTC

Indexes for all types: books, journals and reference publications on professional, scientific and general subjects; copy-editing, proofreading services, conference documents; consultancy on indexing and electronic indexing. Founded 1965.

The Information Bureau
(formerly Daily Telegraph Information Bureau)
51 The Business Centre, 103 Lavender Hill, London SW11 5QL
tel 020-7924 4414 *fax* 020-7738 2513
email info@informationbureau.co.uk
website www.informationbureau.co.uk
Contact Jane Hall

Offers an on-demand research service on a variety of subjects including current affairs, business, marketing, history, the arts, media and politics. Resources include range of cuttings amassed by the bureau since 1948.

Intype Libra Ltd
Units 3–4, Elm Grove Industrial Estate, Elm Grove, London SW19 4HE
tel 020-8947 7863, (07976) 223501 *fax* 020-8947 3652
email sales@intypelibra.co.uk
website www.intypelibra.co.uk

Directors Tony Chapman, David Greenwood

Digitally printed books, paperback and case bound, digital colour, typesetting and data manipulation. Offers 24-hour service. Founded 1974.

ISBN/SAN/DOI Agencies
3rd Floor, Midas House, 62 Goldsworth Road, Working, Surrey GU21 6LQ
tel (0870) 777 8712 *fax* (0870) 777 8714
email isbn@nielsenbookdata.co.uk, san@nielsenbookdata.co.uk, doi@nielsenbookdata.co.uk
website www.isbn.nielsenbookdata.co.uk, www.san.nielsenbookdata.co.uk, www.doi.nielsenbookdata.co.uk
Contact Julian Sowa

ISBN Agency issues ISBNs to publishers based in the UK and the Republic of Ireland. (It can provide advice on changing from 10 to 13 digits.)
  SAN Agency is administered on behalf of the Book Industry Communication. It assigns Standard Address Numbers and Global Location Numbers for organisations in any country except the USA, Canada, Australia and New Zealand.
  DOI Agency provides web-based registration and maintenance facilities for DOIs (Digital Object Identifiers) and their metadata for use by any publisher regardless of their location.

Dr Kenneth Lysons
Lathom, Scotchbarn Lane, Whiston, Nr Prescot, Merseyside L35 7JB
tel 0151-426 5513 *fax* 0151-430 6934
email lysons@literaryservices.co.uk
Contact Dr Kenneth Lysons MA, MEd, DPA, DMA, FCIS, FInstPS, FBIM

Company and institutional histories, support material for organisational management and supervisory training, house journals, research and reports service. Full secretarial support. Founded 1986.

Duncan McAra
28 Beresford Gardens, Edinburgh EH5 3ES
tel 0131-552 1558 *fax* 0131-552 1558
email duncanmcara@hotmail.com

Consultancy on all aspects of general trade publishing; editing, re-writing, copy-editing and proof-correcting for publishers, financial companies, academic institutions and other organisations. Main subjects include art, architecture, archaeology, biography, military, Scottish and travel. See also page 428. Founded 1988.

Janet McKerron
Apple Tree Cottage, Title Road, Middleton, Saxmundham, Suffolk IP17 3NF
tel (01728) 648973 *fax* (01728) 648973
email janet@janetmckerron.demon.co.uk

Indexing and proofreading books (up to 1000pp), loose-leaf publications and academic journals. Clients include publishers and NGOs. Specialist subjects: civil law in England and Wales, European law, the environment. Established 1996.

Manuscript Appraisals

Lanetrees, Simpson Cross, Haverfordwest, Pembs. SA62 6AE
tel (01437) 710534 *fax* (01437) 710534
email manuscript_app@hotmail.com
Proprietor Norman Price *Consultants* Ray Price, Mary Hunt

Independent appraisal of authors' MSS (fiction and non-fiction, but no poetry) with full editorial guidance and advice. In-house editing, copy-editing, rewriting and camera-ready copy if required. Staff expertise embraces thrillers, crime, adventure, travel, comedy, popular women's fiction. Will undertake editorial work in most areas of academic research and tertiary education. Overseas enquiries welcome. Interested in the work of new writers. Founded 1984.

Marlinoak

22 Eve's Croft, Birmingham B32 3QL
tel 0121-475 6139 *fax* 0121-475 6139
Proprietor Hazel J. Billing JP, BA, DipEd

Preparation of scripts, plays, books, MSS service, proofreading, word processing. Founded 1984.

Felicity Marsh

Angel Cottage, Main Street, Bourton on Dunsmore, Warks. CV23 9QY
tel (01926) 632442
email fcmarsh@mulus.wanadoo.co.uk

Comprehensive editorial, research and proofreading services specialising in education, the arts and humanities; freelance writing, co-writing and ghostwriting. Lectures and tutorials on MS and thesis preparation and clear and effective writing. French translation. Established 1990.

Murder Files

Dommett Hill Farm, Hare Lane, Buckland St Mary, Chard, Somerset TA20 3JS
tel (01460) 234065
email enquiry@murderfiles.com
website www.murderfiles.com
Director Paul Williams

Crime writer and researcher specialising in British murders. Holds information on thousands of well-known and less well-known murders dating from 1400 to the present day. Copies of press cuttings available from 1920 to date. Details of executions, particularly at the Tyburn and Newgate. Information on British Hangmen. Specialist in British police murders since 1700. Service available to general enquirers, writers, researchers, legal services, TV, radio, film, video, etc. Founded 1994.

My Word!

138 Railway Terrace, Rugby, Warks. CV21 3HN
tel (01788) 571294 *fax* (01788) 550957
email enquiries@myword.co.uk
website www.myword.co.uk
Partners Roddie Grant, Janet Grant

Specialises in typesetting and website solutions. Online copy-editing service (www.editmywords.co.uk). Produces materials for printing and websites, e.g. magazines, newsletters, books, brochures, leaflets, conference and sales literature. Founded 1994.

Paul Nash

Ballechin Home Farm, Ballinluig, Pitlochry, Perthshire PH9 0LW
tel (01887) 840259 *fax* (01887) 840259
email paulnash@zetnet.co.uk

Indexer specialising in sciences, engineering, technology, environmental science. Registered with the Society of Indexers. Winner of Library Association Wheatley Medal (1992) for outstanding index. Founded 1979.

Peter Nickol

50 St Leonards Road, Exeter EX2 4LS
tel (01392) 255512 *fax* (01392) 255512
email pnickol@ninoakes.freeserve.co.uk

Editing and page layout; typesetting and music engraving; copyright licensing; project management including mixed media coordination, CD recording and production. Specialises in music and music education. Established 1987.

Nielsen BookData

3rd Floor, Midas House, 62 Goldsworth Road, Woking, Surrey GU21 6LQ
tel (0870) 777 8710 *fax* (0870) 777 8711
email info@nielsenbookdata.co.uk
Editorial office 89–95 Queensway, Stevenage, Herts. SG1 1EA
tel (0845) 450 0016 *fax* (01438) 745578
website www.nielsenbookdata.co.uk
Editorial Director Michael Healy, *Subscription Manager* Vesna Nall

Creates and maintains a unique database of timely, accurate and content rich records for English-language books and other published media, collected from publishers in over 70 countries. The enriched data includes: price, availability, table of contents (where applicable), subject classifications, market rights, publisher and distributor details, cover/jacket images and book descriptions. The data is disseminated worldwide in a variety of formats: data feed, dynamic XML, CD-Roms and online services. Jointly publishes the *Directory of UK & Irish Book Publishers* with the Booksellers Association.

Nielsen BookNet

3rd Floor, Midas House, 62 Goldsworth Road, Woking, Surrey GU21 6LQ
tel (0870) 777 8710 *fax* (0870) 777 8711

email info@nielsenbooknet.co.uk
Editorial office 89–95 Queensway, Stevenage, Herts.
SG1 1EA
tel (0845) 450 0016 *fax* (01438) 745578
website www.nielsenbooknet.co.uk
Contact Mick Fortune

BookNet provides a range of e-commerce services
that allow electronic trading between booksellers,
publisher/distributors, libraries and other suppliers.
Services include BookNet Web for booksellers and
publishers/distributors, TeleOrdering and EDI
messaging.

Northern Writers Advisory Services
77 Marford Crescent, Sale, Cheshire M33 4DN
tel 0161-969 1573
email grovesjill@aol.com
Proprietor Jill Groves

Offers typesetting to small publishers, societies and
authors. Local history only. Founded 1986.

Oriental Languages Bureau
Lakshmi Building, Sir P. Mehta Road, Fort, Bombay
400001, India
tel 22661258/22665640 *fax* 22664598
email icsolb@vsnl.net
website orientallanguagesbureau.com
Proprietor Rajan K. Shah

Undertakes translations, phototypesetting-DTP,
artwork and printing in all Indian languages and 40
foreign languages.

Ormrod Research Services
Weeping Birch, Burwash, East Sussex TN19 7HG
tel (01435) 882541
website www.writeonservices.co.uk

Comprehensive research service: literary, historical,
academic, biographical, commercial. Critical reading
with report (novels, theses, non-fiction), editing,
indexing, proofreading, ghostwriting. Founded 1982.

Oxford Designers & Illustrators
(formerly Oxford Illustrators and Oxprint Design)
Aristotle House, Aristotle Lane, Oxford OX2 6TR
tel (01865) 512331 *fax* (01865) 512408
email name@odi-illustration.co.uk
website www.o-d-i.com
Directors Peter Lawrence, Richard Corfield, Andrew
King

Over 30 years' experience in the design, typesetting
and illustration of educational and general books. In-
house artists for all subjects including scientific and
technical, medical, natural history, cartoons, maps
and diagrams. Full project management and repro
service. Not an agency.

Oxford Literary Consultancy
35 Howard Street, Oxford OX4 3AY
tel (01865) 725786

email admin@oxfordwriters.com
website www.oxfordwriters.com
Contact Stephanie Hale

Offers MS assessments, editorial guidance, publishing
advice, tuition and mentoring. Also acts as scouts for
literary agents and publishers. Established 2001.

Pages Editorial & Publishing Services
Ballencrieff Cottage, Ballencrieff Toll, Bathgate, West
Lothian EH48 4LD
tel (01506) 632728
Director Susan Coon

Editorial and production service of magazines/
newspapers for companies or for commercial
distribution. Founded 1995.

Pagewise
2 Butlers Close, Amersham, Bucks. HP6 5PY
tel (01494) 729760 *fax* (01494) 729760
email info@pagewise.co.uk
Director Monica Bratt

Specialist service for self publishers: design,
typesetting, editing and indexing, proofreading and
production services. Founded 1999.

Geoffrey D. Palmer
47 Burton Fields Road, Stamford Bridge, York
YO41 1JJ
tel (01759) 372874

Editorial and production services, including STM and
general copy-editing, onscreen editing, artwork
editing, proofreading and indexing. Prepress project
management. Founded 1987.

Panos London
9 White Lion Street, London N1 9PD
email info@panos.org.uk
website www.panos.org.uk
Communications Director Mark Covey

Works with the media in developing countries to
make complex development issues such as HIV/
AIDS, climate change and trade understandable and
accessible. By working with journalists and other
communicators we try to ensure that everyone,
especially the poor and marginalised, has their voice
heard on issues that affect their lives.

Phoenix 2
Lantern House, Lodge Drove, Woodfalls, Salisbury,
Wilts. SP5 2NH
tel (01725) 512200 *fax* (01725) 511819
email enquiries@phoenix2.co.uk
Partners Bryan Walker, Amanda Walker

Writing, editing, sub-editing, typesetting and design
of magazines, newsletters, journals, brochures and
promotional literature. Specialist areas are business,
tourism, social affairs and education. Founded 1980.

Christopher Pick
41 Chestnut Road, London SE27 9EZ
tel 020-8761 2585

email christopher@the-picks.co.uk

Publications consultancy, project management, writing and editing for companies and public-sector and voluntary-sector agencies: e.g. annual reports, brochures and booklets, information materials, website text, strategy documents, research reports, books, organisational histories. Extensive expertise and experience in presenting information clearly and concisely for non-specialist readers. Specialist in writing and producing corporate and institutional histories.

Picture Research Agency

Jasmine Cottage, Spring Grove Road, Richmond, Surrey TW10 6EH
tel 020-8940 5986 *fax* 020-8940 5986
email pat.hodgpix@virgin.net
Contact Pat Hodgson

Illustrations found for books, films and TV. Written research also undertaken particularly on historical subjects, including photographic and film history. Small picture library.

Reginald Piggott

Decoy Lodge, Decoy Road, Potter Heigham, Norfolk NR29 5LX
tel (01692) 670384

Cartographer to the University Presses and academic publishers in Britain and overseas. Maps and diagrams for academic and educational books. Founded 1962.

David Price

Acupunctuation Ltd, 4 Harbidges Lane, Long Buckby, Northampton NN6 7QL
tel (01327) 844119 *fax* (01327) 844119
email waywithwords@fireflyuk.net
website www.waywithwords.co.uk

Copy-editing, proofreading, research, writing, rewriting. Special interests: operettas and musicals, travel guides, modern European history (including the former Soviet Union). Founded 1995.

ProQuest Information and Learning*

The Quorum, Barnwell Road, Cambridge CB5 8SW
tel (01223) 215512 *fax* (01223) 215513
email info@proquest.co.uk
website www.proquest.co.uk
Executive Directors John Taylor (Senior Vice-President & General Manager), Simon Beale (Vice-President, sales & marketing), Julie Carroll-Davis (Vice-President, publishing), Ian McEwan (Vice-President, finance), Stephen Pocock (Vice-President, content development), Anthony Perkins (HR Manager)

Provider of newspapers, periodicals, literature, dissertations, reference and archival information to educational institutions, libraries and businesses around the world in microform and electronic format. Not a print publisher. Founded 1973.

Victoria Ramsay

Abbots Rest, Chilbolton, Stockbridge, Hants SO20 6BE
tel (01264) 860251 *fax* (01264) 860026
email victoria.ramsay@btinternet.com

Freelance editor, copy-editor and proofreader; non-fiction research and writing of promotional literature and pamphlets. Any non-scientific subject undertaken. Special interests: education, cookery, travel, Africa and Caribbean, and works in translation. Established 1981.

Reading and Righting (Robert Lambolle Services)

618b Finchley Road, London NW11 7RR
tel 020-8455 4564 *fax* 020-8455 4564
email lambhorn@tiscali.co.uk
website http://readingandrighting.netfirms.com

MSS/script advisory and evaluation service: fiction, non-fiction, stage plays and screenplays; editorial services; one-to-one tutorials, creative writing courses and lectures. Send sae for leaflet. Founded 1987.

S. Ribeiro, Literary Services

Flat 42, West Heath Court, North End Road, London NW11 7RG
tel 020-8458 9082
email sribeiro@aol.com
Contact S. Ribeiro

Literary consultant and editor. MSS reading and appraisal with detailed analysis, chapter by chapter, and guidance in submission to agents and publishers. Sensitive and precise editing to publication standards; also rewriting, Americanisation, idiom for translations. Copywriting: synopses, reviews, and book jackets. Creative writing tutor. Special interests and experience: literary fiction and general non-fiction; memoirs; poetry; popularised academic work; guidance for self-publishing. Published and new writers, including overseas, welcome. Send sae or email for leaflet.

Anton Rippon Press Services

20 Chain Lane, Mickleover, Derby DE3 9AJ
tel (07769) 685627
email anton.rippon@btinternet.com

General feature and sports writing for newspapers and magazines. Ghostwriting (preliminary letter essential). Radio and film documentary treatments and scripts. Complete book production service.

Sandhurst Editorial Consultants

36 Albion Road, Sandhurst, Berks. GU47 9BP
tel (01252) 877645 *fax* (01252) 890508
email lionel.browne@sfep.net
website www.sand-con.demon.co.uk
Partners Lionel Browne, Janet Browne

Specialists in technical, professional and reference work. Project management, editorial development, writing, rewriting, copy-editing, proofreading, and general editorial consultancy. Founded 1991.

Sandton Literary Agency

PO Box 785799, Sandton 2146, South Africa
tel (011) 442-8624
Directors J. Victoria Canning, M. Sutherland

Evaluating, editing and/or indexing book MSS. Preparing reports, company histories, house journals, etc. Critical but constructive advice to writers. Lecture agents. Please write or phone first. Founded 1982.

SciText

18 Barton Close, Landrake, Saltash, Cornwall
PL12 5BA
tel (01752) 851451
email bg@scitext.fsnet.co.uk
Contact Dr Brian Gee

Proofreading and editing in science. Consultancy in non-fiction scientific style and format. Founded 1988.

Scriptext

29 Edge Avenue, Grimsby, North East Lincolnshire
DN33 2DD
tel/fax (01472) 753791
email scrip.text437@virgin.net
Owner Pat Hewson

Digital, tape and DVD transcription, verbatim and edited; copy-editing (hard copy or onscreen) and proofreading in most subjects; keying in MSS, word processing. Specialist areas are geographical, social and financial research, business management, finance, social care, crime (fiction and true) and ornithology; also general reference/fiction. Not an employer or agency. Founded 1995.

SfEP (Society for Editors and Proofreaders) – see Society for Editors and Proofreaders (SfEP)

Gill Shepherd

87 Elm Park Mansions, Park Walk, London
SW10 0AP
tel 020-7352 1770
email rgbshepherd@msn.com

Research, fact checking, rewriting for authors. Specialises in history, politics, biography and genealogy. Established 1985.

Small Print

The Old School House, 74 High Street, Swavesey, Cambridge CB4 5QU
tel (01954) 231713 *fax* (01954) 205061
email info@smallprint.co.uk
website www.smallprint.co.uk
Proprietor Naomi Laredo

Editorial, design, page layout, project management, and audio production services for conventional or electronic publishing. Educational books and CDs, manuals, travel guides, newsletters. Translation from/ to and editing in many European and Asian languages. Photographs of France and picture research. Founded 1986.

Society of Indexers – see page 629

Special Edition Pre-press Services

Partners Romilly Hambling, 17 Almorah Road, London N1 3ER
tel 020-7226 5339 *fax* 020-7226 5339
email mail@special-edition.co.uk
and Corinne Orde, 2 Caledonian Wharf, London E14 3EW
tel 020-7987 9600 *fax* 020-7987 9600
website www.special-edition.co.uk

Integrated editing and page make-up for publishers of general and STM titles. Design and project management undertaken. See website for downloadable brochure. Established 1993.

Mrs Gene M. Spencer

63 Castle Street, Melbourne, Derbyshire DE73 8DY
tel (01332) 862133
email genem.spencer@virgin.net

Editing, copy-editing and proofreading; feature writing; theatrical profiles; book reviews; freelance writing. Founded 1970.

SPREd (Society of Picture Researchers and Editors) – now The Picture Research Association, see page 547

StorytrackS

16 St Briac Way, Exmouth, Devon EX8 5RN
tel (01395) 279659
email marina@marina-oliver.net
website www.storytracks.net
Directors Marina Oliver, Margaret James, Chris Dukes

A team of widely published writers offer honest appraisals of MSS and comment on content and structure. Constructive guidance is based on extensive experience and sound market awareness. Specialist consultants in children's and teenage fiction, and theatre, radio and screenplays. Fiction typescripts of publishable quality are guaranteed consideration by an appropriate editor or agent. Also offers ghostwriting services, advice on self-publishing and editorial assistance. Founded 2001.

Strand Editorial Services

16 Mitchley View, South Croydon, Surrey CR2 9HQ
tel 020-8657 1247 *fax* 020-8651 3525
Editorial Consultant Derek Bradley, *Assistant Principal* Irene Bradley

Provide a comprehensive service to publishers, editorial departments, and public relations and advertising agencies. Proofreading and copy-editing a speciality. Founded 1974.

Success Writing Bureau

Thirsol House, Earby, Barnoldswick, Lancs BB18 6NE
tel (01282) 842495 *fax* (01282) 842495
email john@writers-aid-services.com
website www.writers-aid-services.com
Contact John O'Toole

MSS appraisal with agency links where applicable.
Home study courses in journalism/article writing,
short story, radio, TV and novel writing. Speedy
turnaround. John O'Toole tutorials since 1965;
bureau founded 1980.

Sarah Sutton

9 Gold Hill, Shaftesbury, Dorset SP7 8HB
tel (01747) 850100
email info@sarahsutton.co.uk
website www.sarahsutton.co.uk

Writer and ghost writer specialising in TV tie-ins.
Subjects include business, psychology, personal
development, lifestyle, building conservation,
biography. Established 2003.

Hans Tasiemka Archives

80 Temple Fortune Lane, London NW11 7TU
tel 020-8455 2485 *fax* 020-8455 0231
Proprietor Mrs Edda Tasiemka

Comprehensive newspaper cuttings library from
1850s to the present day on all subjects for writers,
publishers, picture researchers, film and TV
companies. Founded 1950.

Lyn M. Taylor

(Eve-Line Editorial)
Anchorfield, 9 Gosford Road, Port Seton, East
Lothian EH32 0HE
tel/fax (01875) 812315
email eve.line@editetc.co.uk

General comprehensive editorial service for
publishers: copy-editing (hard copy or onscreen) and
proofreading in all subjects. Specialises in scientific
and medical books, journals and reports and wildlife
publishing. Formatting, coding, author collation,
template creation.

Lucy Taylor Editorial Services

12 Glenmalure Park, Rialto, South Circular Road,
Dublin 8, Republic of Ireland
tel (01) 4544573, *mobile* 87 9155602
email lucytaylor@ireland.com
Contact Lucy Taylor

Copy-editing, proofreading, book and magazine
editing and feature writing. Special interests include
health, diets, food and lifestyle. Established 2003.

The Literary Consultancy (TLC)

Diorama Arts Centre, 34 Osnaburgh Street, London
NW1 3ND
tel/fax 020-7813 4330

email info@literaryconsultancy.co.uk
website www.literaryconsultancy.co.uk
Director Rebecca Swift, *Manager* Caroline McCarthy,
Administrator Patsy Trench

Offers detailed assessments of fiction, non-fiction,
poetry and children's books from a team of
professional editors and writers. Fees based on length.
Personal links with agents and publishers. Approved
by Arts Council England. Established 1996.

Thoughtbubble Ltd

58–60 Fitzroy Street, London W1T 5BU
tel 020-7387 8890 *fax* 020-7383 2220
email enquiries@thoughtbubble.com
website www.thoughtbubble.com
Contact James Maltby

Website design and development, database
integration, Flash animation, audio/video editing and
production, e-commerce, intranet design and
development, software development, print design,
CD-Rom design and production. Also presentation,
training and website hosting. Founded 1997.

Felicity Trotman

Downside, Chicklade, Salisbury, Wilts. SP3 5SU
tel (01747) 820503 *fax* (01747) 820503
email f.trotman@btinternet.com

For publishers only: editing, copy-editing,
proofreading, writing, rewriting. Fiction, activity and
non-fiction. Children's books only, all ages.
Established 1982.

Tucann Books

19 High Street, Heighington, Lincoln LN4 1RG
tel/fax (01522) 790009
email sales@tucann.co.uk
website www.tucann.co.uk
Managing Director Tom Cann

Offers a fully integrated book production service,
from original MSS assessment to finished product
using in-house printing and binding. Founded 1986.

John Vickers

27 Shorrolds Road, London SW6 7TR
tel 020-7385 5774

Archives of British Theatre photographs by John
Vickers, from 1938–74.

Susan Wallace

PO Box 95, Lark Lane, Liverpool L17 8WY
tel 0151-233 3689 *mobile* (07801) 055556
email susanwallace@blueyonder.co.uk
website www.susanwallace.co.uk
Contact Susan Wallace BA (Hons), MA

Specialises in UK national feature writing and online
journalism, especially for the women's market.
Psychology graduate and expert writer with
worldwide syndication of psychology quizzes, features

and columns. Provides agency creative copywriting and editorial services at a senior level. No book editing. Other special interests include exclusive true-life and reportage, relationships/sex, health, TV/showbiz, psychology at work, off-beat/lifestyle and travel. MA in Screenwriting. Established 1988.

David Winpenny
Victoria Villa, Princess Road, Ripon, North Yorkshire HG4 1HW
tel (01765) 607641 *fax* (01765) 608320
email david@winpennypr.co.uk
website www.winpennypr.co.uk

Writer and editor, including research and writing of features, news stories, brochures, speeches, advertising copy. Full public relations service. Special interest in country walks, architectural history, the arts, music, landscape, heritage, business and the North. Founded 1991.

WORDSmith
2 The Island, Thames Ditton, Surrey KT7 0SH
tel 020-8339 0945 *fax* 020-8339 0945
email mruswords@aol.com
website www.good-writing-matters.co.uk
Partners Michael Russell, Elaine Russell

Specialises in new writer fiction; also abridging, ghostwriting. Copy-editing on paper and onscreen. Short-run publishing as Riverside Press. No scripts or poetry. Email or phone for details (prior contact essential). Founded 1998.

Richard M. Wright
32 Oak Village, London NW5 4QN
tel 020-7284 4316
email rmwindserv@aol.com

Indexing, copy-editing, specialising in politics, history, business, social sciences. Founded 1977.

The Write Coach
2 Rowan Close, Wokingham, Berks. RG41 4BH
tel 0118-978 4904
email info@thewritecoach.co.uk
website www.thewritecoach.co.uk
Contact Rebecca Hill

One-to-one coaching and workshops to develop the writer and their writing, build confidence, increase motivation, release blocks, increase creativity and assist both professional and aspiring writers to become more successful. Established 2002.

Write on...
62 Kiln Lane, Oxford OX3 8EY
tel (01865) 744336
email yn@writeon1989.co.uk
Director Yvonne Newman

Feature writing on consumer, property, retirement and health issues for newspapers and magazines. Founded 1989.

Write2
3 Cedar Park, Caterham, Surrey CR3 5DZ
tel (07956) 352770 (01883) 370967
email mikedonald@dunelm.org.uk
Director Mike Donald

Copy-editing, proofreading and rewriting. Specialises in technical work: maths, science, technology and management studies; also sports and children's literature. Corporate literature and advertising copy. Established 2003.

The Writers' Exchange
14 Old School Mews, Bacup, Lancs. OL13 0QN
tel (01706) 877480
email writers'exchange@j-m-wright.freeserve.co.uk
Secretary Mike Wright

Copywriting, ghostwriting, internet publishing and editorial services, including appraisal service for amateur writers preparing to submit material to literary agents/publishers. Offers 'constructive, objective evaluation service, particularly for those who cannot get past the standard rejection slip barrier, or who have had work rejected by publishers and need an impartial view of why it did not sell'. Novels, short stories, film, TV, radio and stage plays. Send sae for details. Founded 1977.

The Writers' Workshop
Walnut Tree Cottage, Duxford, Faringdon, Oxon SN7 8SQ
tel (01865) 820943 *fax* (01865) 820534
email info@writersworkshop.co.uk
website www.writersworkshop.co.uk
Contact Nuala Moroney, Harry Bingham

Offers editorial advice for first-time writers of fiction primarily but also handles non-fiction, screenplays, children's fiction and poetry. One of a team of editors will supply a report on a submitted MS and a dialogue between editor and author is encouraged. Where appropriate, help will also be given to place MSS with a literary agent. Established 2005.

Writing Literary Consultants
Writing Ltd, Neville House, Station Approach, Wendens Ambo, Essex CB11 4LB
tel (01799) 544659 *fax* (01799) 541747
email info@writing.co.uk
website www.writing.co.uk
Contact Keirsten Clark

Offers advice and informed editorial feedback on writing. Will provide an honest and thorough report on submitted work with constructive criticism. Services include how to submit work to an agent/publisher, a detailed MS appraisal, poetry appraisal, plot structure and characterisation advice, translation services, and screenwriting/script appraisals.

Martyn Yeo
66 Russell Road, Lee-on-the-Solent, Hants PO13 9HP
tel (0776) 219 0027 *fax* (0871) 733 5554

email martyn@wordwise.co.uk
Contact Martyn Yeo

Typesetting and editorial servies offered to publishers only. Scope includes database publishing and project management, especially for directories and loose-leaf titles. Member of SfEP. Established 1984.

Hans Zell, Publishing Consultant

Glais Bheinn, Lochcarron, Ross-shire IV54 8YB
tel (01520) 722951 *fax* (01520) 722953
email hanszell@hanszell.co.uk

website www.hanszell.co.uk

Consultancies, project evaluations, market assessments, feasibility studies, research and surveys, funding proposals, freelance editorial work, commissioning, journals management, internet training. Specialises in services to publishers and the book community in Third World countries and provides specific expertise in these areas. Also mailing list services, and information resources (pint/online) on African publishing and African studies. Founded 1987.

Government offices and public services

Enquiries to any of the following bodies should be accompanied by an sae. Details of many other public bodies can be found in *Whitaker's Almanack* (A & C Black 2006).

Acas
Brandon House, 180 Borough High Street, London SE1 1LW
tel 020-7210 3613 *fax* 020-7210 3615
website www.acas.org.uk

Advertising Standards Authority
Mid City Place, 71 High Holborn, London WC1V 6QT
tel 020-7492 2222 *fax* 020-7242 3696
email enquiries@asa.org.uk
website www.asa.org.uk

Ministry of Agriculture, Fisheries and Food – see DEFRA (Department for Environment, Food and Rural Affairs)

American Embassy
24 Grosvenor Square, London W1A 1AE
tel 020-7499 9000
website www.usembassy.org.uk

Amgueddfa Cymru – National Museum Wales
Cathays Park, Cardiff CF10 3NP
tel 029-2039 7951 *fax* 029-2057 3321
website www.museumwales.ac.uk

Ancient Monuments Board for Wales (CADW)
Plas Carew, Unit 5–7, Cef Coed, Parc Nantgarw, Cardiff CF15 7QQ
tel (01443) 336000 *fax* (01443) 336001
email cadw@wales.gsi.gov.uk
website www.cadw.wales.gov.uk

Apsley House, The Wellington Museum
Hyde Park Corner, London W1J 7NT
tel 020-7499 5676 *fax* 020-7493 6576
website www.englishheritage.org.uk

Open Tues–Sun, 11am–5pm.

Arts Council England – see page 520

Arts Council of Northern Ireland – see page 520

Arts Council of Wales – see page 520

Australian High Commission
Australia House, Strand, London WC2B 4LA
tel 020-7379 4334 *fax* 020-7240 5333
website www.australia.org.uk

Austrian Embassy
18 Belgrave Mews West, London SW1X 8HU
tel 020-7235 3731 *fax* 020-7344 0292
email london-ob@bmaa.gv.at
Austrian Cultural Forum, 28 Rutland Gate, London SW7 1PQ
tel 020-7584 8653 *fax* 020-7225 0470
email culture@austria.org.uk

The Bank of England
Threadneedle Street, London EC2R 8AH
tel 020-7601 4444 *fax* 020-7601 4771
website www.bankofengland.co.uk

Belgian Embassy
17 Grosvenor Crescent, London SW1X 7EE
tel 020-7470 3700 *fax* 020-7470 3795
email london@diplobel.be
website www.diplobel.org/uk

Big Lottery Fund
(merger of the New Opportunities Fund and Community Fund)
1 Plough Place, London EC4A 1DE
tel 020-7211 1800
website www.biglotteryfund.org.uk

Bodleian Library
Oxford OX1 3BG
tel (01865) 277000 *fax* (01865) 277182
email enquiries@bodley.ox.ac.uk
website www.bodley.ox.ac.uk

Embassy of Bosnia and Herzegovina
5–7 Lexham Gardens, London W8 5JJ
tel 020-7373 0867 *fax* 020-7373 0871

British Board of Film Classification
3 Soho Square, London W1D 3HD
tel 020-7440 1570 *fax* 020-7287 0141
email contact_the_bbfc@bbfc.co.uk
website www.bbfc.co.uk
Director David Cooke

British Broadcasting Corporation
Broadcasting House, London W1A 1AA
tel 020-7580 4468
website www.bbc.co.uk

The British Council – see page 527

British Film Institute – see page 527

The British Library
96 Euston Road, London NW1 2DB
tel (0870) 444 1500
website www.bl.uk

See also page 642.

British Library Document Supply Service
Boston Spa, Wetherby, West Yorkshire LS23 7BQ
tel (01937) 546060 *fax* (01937) 546333
email customer-services@bl.uk
website www.bl.uk/docsupply

British Library Newspaper Library
Colindale Avenue, London NW9 5HE
tel 020-7412 7353 *fax* 020-7412 7379
email newspaper@bl.uk
website www.bl.uk/collections/newspapers.html

British Museum
Great Russell Street, London WC1B 3DG
tel 020-7323 8000
email information@thebritishmuseum.ac.uk
website www.thebritishmuseum.ac.uk

British Standards Institution
Technical Information Group, 389 Chiswick High Road, London W4 4AL
tel 020-8996 7111 *fax* 020-8996 7048
email the@bsi-global.com
website www.bsi-global.com

Broadcasting Standards Commission – see The Office of Communications (Ofcom)

Embassy of the Republic of Bulgaria
186–188 Queen's Gate, London SW7 5HL
tel 020-7584 9400/9433, 020-7581 3144 (5 lines) *fax* 020-7584 4948
email info@bulgarianembassy.org.uk
website www.bulgarianembassy.co.uk

The Cabinet Office
70 Whitehall, London SW1A 2AS
tel 020-7276 1234
website www.cabinet-office.gov.uk

Canadian High Commission
38 Grosvenor Street, London W1K 4AA
tel 020-7258 6600 *fax* 020-7258 6506
website www.canada.org.uk

Central Office of Information – see COI Communications

CILT, The National Centre for Languages
20 Bedfordbury, London WC2N 4LB
tel 020-7379 5101 *fax* 020-7379 5082
email library@cilt.org.uk
website www.cilt.org.uk

Charity Commission
Harmsworth House, 13–15 Bouverie Street, London EC4Y 8DP
tel (0870) 3330123 *minicom* (0870) 3330125
fax 020-7674 2300
email enquiries@charitycommission.gov.uk
website www.charitycommission.gov.uk
2nd Floor, 20 King's Parade, Queen's Dock, Liverpool L3 4DQ
tel (0870) 3330123 *fax* 0151-703 1555
Woodfield House, Tangier, Taunton, Somerset TA1 4BL
tel (0870) 3330123 *fax* (01823) 345003

Church Commissioners
1 Millbank, London SW1P 3JZ
tel 020-7898 1000 *fax* 020-7898 1131
website www.cofe.anglican.org/about/churchcommissioners

Civil Aviation Authority
CAA House, 45–59 Kingsway, London WC2B 6TE
tel 020-7379 7311
website www.caa.co.uk

The Coal Authority
200 Lichfield Lane, Mansfield, Notts. NG18 4RG
tel (01623) 637000 *fax* (01623) 622072
email thecoalauthority@coal.gov.uk
website www.coal.gov.uk

COI Communications
Hercules House, Hercules Road, London SE1 7DU
tel 020-7928 2345 *fax* 020-7928 5037
website www.coi.gov.uk

College of Arms (or Heralds' College)
Queen Victoria Street, London EC4V 4BT
tel 020-7248 2762 *fax* 020-7248 6448
email enquiries@college-of-arms.gov.uk
website www.college-of-arms.gov.uk

Commission for Architecture and the Built Environment (CABE)
The Tower Building, 11 York Road, London SE1 7NX
tel 020-7960 2400 *fax* 020-7960 2444
email enquiries@cabe.org.uk
website www.cabe.org.uk

Commission for Integrated Transport
Zone F16, Ashdown House, 123 Victoria Street, London SW1E 6DE

tel 020-7944 8669 *fax* 020-7944 8643
email cfit@dft.gsi.gov.uk
website www.cfit.gov.uk

Commission for Racial Equality
St Dunstan's House, 201 Borough High Street,
London SE1 1GZ
tel 020-7939 0000 *fax* 020-7939 0004
website www.cre.gov.uk

Committee on Standards in Public Life
35 Great Smith Street, London SW1P 3BQ
tel 020-7276 2595 *fax* 020-7276 2585
email standards.evidence@gtnet.gov.uk
website www.public-standards.gov.uk

Commonwealth Secretariat
Marlborough House, Pall Mall, London SW1Y 5HX
tel 020-7747 6000 *fax* 020-7839 9081
email info@commonwealth.int
website www.thecommonwealth.org

Competition Commission (CC)
Victoria House, Southampton Row, London
WC1B 4AD
tel 020-7271 0100 *fax* 020-7271 0367
email info@competition-commission.gsi.gov.uk
website www.competition-commission.gsi.org.gov

Contributions Agency, International Services (InS) – see HM Revenue & Customs

Copyright Enquiries – see Patent Office

Copyright Tribunal
The Patent Office, Room 2G31, Concept House,
Cardiff Road, Newport NP10 8QQ
tel (01633) 811035 *fax* (01633) 811175
email copyright.tribunal@patent.gov.uk
website www.patent.gov.uk/copy/tribunal/index.htm

Corporation of London Records Office
40 Northampton Road, London EC1R 0HB
tel 020-7332 3820 *fax* 020-7833 9136
email lma@corpoflondon.gov.uk
website www.cityoflondon.gov.uk/lma

Corporation of Trinity House
Tower Hill, London EC3N 4DH
tel 020-7481 6900 *fax* 020-7480 7662
email vikki.gilson@thls.org
website www.trinityhouse.co.uk

Countryside Agency
John Dower House, Crescent Place, Cheltenham,
Glos. GL50 3RA
tel (01242) 521381 *fax* (01242) 584270
website www.countryside.gov.uk

Countryside Council for Wales/Cyngor Cefn Gwlad Cymru
Maes y Ffynnon Penrhosgarnedd, Bangor, Gwynedd
LL57 2DW
tel (0845) 130 6229 *fax* (01248) 355782

Court of the Lord Lyon
HM New Register House, Edinburgh EH1 3YT
tel 0131-556 7255 *fax* 0131-557 2148

Crafts Council
Resource Centre, 44A Pentonville Road, London
N1 9BY
tel 020-7806 2501 *fax* 020-7833 4479
email reference@craftscouncil.org.uk
website www.craftscouncil.org.uk

Embassy of the Republic of Croatia
21 Conway Street, London W1T 6BN
tel 020-7387 2022 *fax* 020-7387 0310
email croemb.london@mvp.hr
website www.uk.mvp.hr

Department for Culture, Media and Sport
2–4 Cockspur Street, London SW1Y 5DH
tel 020-7211 6200
email enquiries@culture.gov.uk
website www.culture.gov.uk

Cyprus High Commission
93 Park Street, London W1K 7ET
tel 020-7499 8272 *fax* 020-7491 0691
email presscounsellor@chclondon.org.uk (press
office)
website www.cyprus.gov.cy

Embassy of the Czech Republic
26 Kensington Palace Gardens, London W8 4QY
tel 020-7243 1115 *fax* 020-7727 9654
email london@embassy.mzv.cz
website www.czechembassy.org.uk

Ministry of Defence
The War Office, Whitehall, London SW1A 2EU
tel 020-7218 9000
website www.mod.uk

DEFRA (Department for Environment, Food and Rural Affairs)
Information Resource Centre, Lower Ground Floor,
Ergon House, c/o Nobel House, 17 Smith Square,
London SW1P 3JR
tel 020-7238 6575 *fax* 020-7238 6609
email defra.library@defra.gsi.gov.uk
website www.defra.gov.uk

Embassy of Denmark
55 Sloane Street, London SW1X 9SR
tel 020-7333 0200 *fax* 020-7333 0270
email lonamb@um.dk
website www.amblondon.um.dk

Design Council
34 Bow Street, London WC2E 7DL
tel 020-7420 5200 *fax* 020-7420 5300

email info@designcouncil.org.uk
website www.design-council.org.uk

DFID (Department for International Development)
1 Palace Street, London SW1E 5HE
tel 020-7023 0000
email enquiry@dfid.gov.uk
website www.dfid.gov.uk
Abercrombie House, Eaglesham Road, East Kilbride, Glasgow G75 8EA
tel (01355) 844000
Public Enquiry Point tel (0845) 300 4100 (local rate)
tel (01355) 843132 (for enquiries from overseas)

Disability Rights Commission
DRC, Stratford upon Avon CV37 9BR
tel (0845) 762 2633 (DRC
Helpline) textphone (08457) 622 644
fax (08457) 778878
website www.drc-gb.org

DTI (Department of Trade and Industry)
Bay 160, 151 Buckingham Palace Road, London SW1W 9SS
tel 020-7215 5000 (general enquiries)
minicom 020-7215 6740
fax 020-7215 0105
website www.dti.gov.uk

DTLR (Department of Transport, Local Government and the Regions)
Eland House, Bressenden Place, London SW1E 5DU
Great Minster House, 76 Marsham Street, London SW1P 4DR
Ashdown House, 123 Victoria Street, London SW1E 6DE
tel 020-7944 3000
website www.dtlr.gov.uk

DWP (Department for Work and Pensions)
Richmond House, 79 Whitehall, London SW1A 2NS
tel 020-7238 0800

Economic and Social Research Council
Polaris House, North Star Avenue, Swindon, Wilts. SN2 1UJ
tel (01793) 413000 fax (01793) 413002
email exrel@esrc.ac.uk
website www.esrcsocietytoday.ac.uk

Department for Education and Skills
Sanctuary Buildings, Great Smith Street, London SW1P 3BT
tel (0870) 000 2288 fax (01928) 794248
email info@dfes.gsi.gov.uk
website www.dfes.gov.uk

Engineering and Physical Sciences Research Council
Polaris House, North Star Avenue, Swindon, Wilts. SN2 1ET
tel (01793) 444000 helpline (01793) 444100
email infoline@epsrc.ac.uk
website www.epsrc.ac.uk
Press Officer Jane Reck tel (01793) 444312
email jane.reck@epsrc.ac.uk

English Heritage
1 Waterhouse Square, 138–142 Holborn, London EC1N 2ST
tel 020-7973 3000 fax 020-7973 3001
website www.english-heritage.org.uk

English Nature
Northminster House, Peterborough PE1 1UA
tel (01733) 455000 fax (01733) 568834
email www.english-nature.org.uk

The Environment Agency
Rio House, Waterside Drive, Aztec West, Almondsbury, Bristol BS32 4UD
tel (0870) 850 6506 fax (01709) 312820
website www.environment-agency.gov.uk

Equal Opportunities Commission
Arndale House, Arndale Centre, Manchester M4 3EQ
tel (0845) 601 5901 (Helpline)
email info@eoc.org.uk
website www.eoc.org.uk

Helpline offers free, confidential and impartial advice and information on sex discrimination and equal pay. Open 9am–5pm Mon–Fri. Calls are charged at local rate and interpreting service is available. Calls might be monitored for training purposes.

Equality Commission for Northern Ireland
Equality House, 7–9 Shaftesbury Square, Belfast BT2 7DP
tel 028-9050 0600 fax 028-9033 1544
email information@equalityni.org
website www.equalityni.org

The European Commission
8 Storey's Gate, London SW1P 3AT
tel 020-7973 1992 fax 020-7973 1900
email eu-uk-press@cec.eu.int
website www.cec.org.uk

European Parliament
UK Office 2 Queen Anne's Gate, London SW1H 9AA
tel 020-7227 4300 fax 020-7227 4302
library fax 020-7227 4301
email eplondon@europarl.eu.int
website www.europarl.org.uk

European Parliament Office in Scotland
The Tun, 4 Jackson's Entry, Holyrood Road, Edinburgh EH8 8PJ

tel 0131-557 7866 *fax* 0131-557 4977
email epedinburgh@europarl.eu.int
website www.europarl.org.uk

Embassy of Finland
38 Chesham Place, London SW1X 8HW
tel 020-7838 6200 *fax* 020-7235 3680 (general),
020-7259 5602 (press and information office)
website www.finemb.org.uk

Food Standards Agency
Aviation House, 125 Kingsway, London WC2B 6NH
tel 020-7276 8000 *fax* 020-7276 8004
email infocentre@foodstandards.gsi.gov.uk
website www.food.gov.uk

Food Standards Agency Northern Ireland
10B and 10C Clarendon Road, Belfast BT1 3BG
tel 028-9041 7700 *fax* 028-9041 7726
email infosani@foodstandards.gsi.gov.uk
website www.food.gov.uk

Food Standards Agency Scotland
St Magnus House, 25 Guild Street, Aberdeen
AB11 6NJ
tel (01224) 285100 *fax* (01224) 285167
email scotland@foodstandards.gsi.gov.uk
website www.food.gov.uk

Food Standards Agency Wales
11th Floor, Southgate House, Wood Street, Cardiff
CF10 1EW
tel 029-2067 8999 *fax* 029-2067 8919
email wales@foodstandards.gsi.gov.uk
website www.food.gov.uk

Foreign and Commonwealth Office
King Charles Street, London SW1A 2AH
tel 020-7008 1500
website www.fco.gov.uk

Forestry Commission
Silvan House, 231 Corstorphine Road, Edinburgh
EH12 7AT
tel 0131-334 0303 *fax* 0131-334 4473
email info@forestry.gov.uk
website www.forestry.gov.uk

French Embassy
58 Knightsbridge, London SW1X 7JT
tel 020-7073 1000
email box.office@ambafrance.org.uk
Cultural Department 23 Cromwell Road, London
SW7 2EL
tel 020-7073 1300
website www.ambafrance-uk.org, www.institut-
francais.org.uk

German Embassy
23 Belgrave Square, London SW1X 8PZ
tel 020-7824 1300 *fax* 020-7824 1449
website www.london.diplo.de

Government Communications Headquarters (GCHQ)
Priors Road, Cheltenham, Glos. GL52 5AJ
tel (01242) 221491 *fax* (01242) 574349
website www.gchq.gov.uk

Embassy of Greece
1A Holland Park, London W11 3TP
tel 020-7221 6467 *fax* 020-7243 3202
website www.greekembassy.org.uk

Hayward Gallery
Belvedere Road, London SE1 8XZ
tel 020-7960 5226 *fax* 020-7401 2664
website www.hayward.org.uk

Department of Health
Richmond House, 79 Whitehall, London SW1A 2NS
tel 020-7210 4850
website www.dh.gov.uk

Health and Safety Executive Infoline
Caerphilly Business Park, Caerphilly CF83 3GG
tel (0845) 345 0055 *minicom* (0845) 408 9577
fax (0845) 408 9566
email hse.infoline@natbrit.com
website www.hse.gov.uk

Historic Scotland
Longmore House, Salisbury Place, Edinburgh
EH9 1SH
tel 0131-668 8600 *fax* 0131-668 8699
website www.historic-scotland.gov.uk

Historical Manuscripts
Commission – see The National Archives

HM Revenue & Customs
(formerly the Inland Revenue)
100 Parliament Street, London SW1A 2BQ
tel 020-7438 6622
Centre for Non-Residents (Newcastle), Benton Park
View, Longbenton, Newcastle upon Tyne NE98 1ZZ
0191-203 7010*fax* 0191-225 0067
website www.hmrc.gov.uk, www.hmrc.gov.uk/cnr/
index.htm

Contact Newcastle office for queries about working
abroad and paying National Insurance contributions.

HM Treasury
1 Horse Guards Road, London SW1A 2HQ
tel 020-7270 5000 *fax* 020-7270 5244
website www.hm-treasury.gov.uk

HMSO Books – see TSO (The Stationery Office)

Home Office
2 Marsham Street, London SW1P 4DF
tel (0870) 000 1585
website www.homeoffice.gov.uk

Housing Corporation
Maple House, 149 Tottenham Court Road, London
W1T 7BN
tel 020-7393 2000 *fax* 020-7393 2111
email enquiries@housingcorp.gsx.gov.uk
website www.housingcorp.gov.uk

Human Fertilisation and Embryology Authority
21 Bloomsbury Street, London WC1B 3HF
tel 020-7291 8200 *fax* 020-7291 8201
website www.hfea.gov.uk

Human Genetics Commission
6th Floor North, Wellington House, 133–155
Waterloo Road, London SE1 8UG
tel 020-7972 4351 *fax* 020-7972 4300
email hgc@doh.gsi.gov.uk
website www.hgc.gov.uk

Embassy of the Republic of Hungary
35 Eaton Place, London SW1X 8BY
tel 020-7235 5218 *fax* 020-7823 1348
email office@huemblon.org.uk
website www.huemblon.org.uk

Imperial War Museum
Lambeth Road, London SE1 6HZ
tel 020-7416 5320/1
website www.iwm.org.uk

The Independent Police Complaints Commission
90 High Holborn, London WC1V 6BH
tel (0845) 300 2002
website www.ipcc.gov.uk

Independent Television Commission – see The Office of Communications (Ofcom)

High Commission of India
India House, Aldwych, London WC2B 4NA
tel 020-7836 8484 *fax* 020-7836 2632
website www.hcilondon.net

Information Commissioner's Office
Wycliffe House, Water Lane, Wilmslow, Cheshire
SK9 5AF
tel (01625) 545745(enquiries), (01625) 545700
(switchboard) *fax* (01625) 524510
email mail@ico.gsi.gov.uk
website www.ico.gov.uk

The Inland Revenue – see HM Revenue & Customs

International Pension Centre
Tyneview Park, Whitley Road, Newcastle upon Tyne
NE98 1BA
tel 0191-218 7777
email TVP-IPC-customer-care@thepensionservice.gsi.gov.uk

Embassy of Ireland
17 Grosvenor Place, London SW1X 7HR
tel 020-7235 2171 *fax* 020-7245 6961
Passport and Visa Office Montpelier House,
106 Brompton Road, London SW3 1JJ
tel 020-7225 7700

Embassy of Israel
2 Palace Green, London W8 4QB
tel 020-7957 9500 *fax* 020-7957 9555
email public@london.mfa.gov.il
website http://london.mfa.gov.il

Italian Embassy
14 Three Kings Yard, London W1K 4EH
tel 020-7312 2200 *fax* 020-7312 2230
email ambasciata.londra@esteri.it
website www.amblondra.esteti.it

Embassy of Japan
101–104 Piccadilly, London W1J 7JT
tel 020-7465 6500 *fax* 020-7491 9347 (information)
fax 020-7491 9328 (visa section)
email info@jpembassy.org.uk
website www.uk.emb-japan.go.jp

Land Registry
Lincoln's Inn Fields, London WC2A 3PH
tel 020-7166 4543 *fax* 020-7166 4516
email marion.shelley@landregistry.gsc.gov.uk
website www.landregistry.gov.uk

Law Commission
Conquest House, 37–38 John Street, Theobalds Road,
London WC1N 2BQ
tel 020-7453 1220 *fax* 020-7453 1297
email chief.executive@lawcommission.gsi.gov.uk
website www.lawcom.gov.uk

Covers England and Wales.

Learning and Skills Council
Cheylesmore House, Quinton Road, Coventry, West
Midlands CV1 2WT
tel (0845) 019 4170 *fax* 024-7682 3675
website www.lsc.gov.uk

The Legal Deposit Office
The British Library, Boston Spa, Wetherby, West
Yorkshire LS23 7BY
tel (01937) 546267 *fax* (01937) 546176

Legal Services Commission
(formerly Legal Aid Board)
85 Gray's Inn Road, London WC1X 8TX
tel 020-7759 0000
website www.legalservices.gov.uk,
www.clsdirect.org.uk

Embassy of Luxembourg
27 Wilton Crescent, London SW1X 8SD
tel 020-7235 6961 *fax* 020-7235 9734

Malta High Commission
Malta House, 36–38 Piccadilly, London W1J 0LE
tel 020-7292 4800 *fax* 020-7734 1832
website www.foreign.gov.mt

Medical Research Council
20 Park Crescent, London W1B 1AL
tel 020-7636 5422 *fax* 020-7436 6179
website www.mrc.ac.uk

Monopolies and Mergers Commission – now Competition Commission (CC)

Museum of London
London Wall, London EC2Y 5HN
tel (0870) 444 3851 *fax* (0870) 444 3853
email info@museumoflondon.org.uk
website www.museumoflondon.org.uk

Museums, Libraries and Archives Council
16 Queen Anne's Gate, London SW1H 9AA
tel 020-7273 1444 *fax* 020-7273 1404
website www.mla.gov.uk

The National Archives
Ruskin Avenue, Kew, Richmond, Surrey TW9 4DU
tel 020-8876 3444 *fax* 020-8878 8905
email enquiry@nationalarchives.gov.uk
website www.nationalarchives.gov.uk

The National Archives of Scotland
HM General Register House, 2 Princes Street, Edinburgh EH1 3YY
tel 0131-535 1314 *fax* 0131-535 1360
email enquiries@nas.gov.uk
website www.nas.gov.uk

National Army Museum
Royal Hospital Road, London SW3 4HT
tel 020-7730 0717 *fax* 020-7823 6573
website www.national-army-museum.ac.uk

National Assembly for Wales
Cathays Park, Cardiff CF1 3NQ
tel 029-2082 5111
email webmaster@wales.gov.uk
website www.wales.gov.uk

National Audit Office
157–197 Buckingham Palace Road, London SW1W 9SP
tel 020-7798 7000 *fax* 020-7798 7070
email enquiries@nao.gsi.gov.uk
website www.nao.gsi.gov.uk

National Consumer Council
20 Grosvenor Gardens, London SW1W 0DH
tel 020-7730 3469 *fax* 020-7730 0191
email info@ncc.org.uk
website www.ncc.org.uk

National Galleries of Scotland
National Gallery of Scotland, The Mound, Edinburgh EH2 2EL
tel 0131-624 6200, 0131-624 6332 (press office) *fax* 0131-343 3250 (press office)
email pressinfo@nationalgalleries.org
Scottish National Portrait Gallery, 1 Queen Street, Edinburgh EH2 1JD
Scottish National Gallery of Modern Art, Belford Road, Edinburgh EH4 3DR
The Dean Gallery, Belford Road, Edinburgh EH4 3DS
website www.nationalgalleries.org

National Gallery
Trafalgar Square, London WC2N 5DN
tel 020-7747 2885 *fax* 020-7747 2423
email information@ng-london.org.uk
website www.nationalgallery.org.uk

National Library of Scotland
George IV Bridge, Edinburgh EH1 1EW
tel 0131-623 3700 *fax* 0131-623 3701
email enquiries@nls.uk
website www.nls.uk

The National Library of Wales
Aberystwyth, Ceredigion SY23 3BU
email holi@llgc.org.uk
website www.llgc.org.uk

National Lottery Commission
101 Wigmore Street, London W1U 1QU
tel 020-7016 3400 *fax* 020-7016 3464
email publicaffairs@natlotcomm.gov.uk
website www.natlotcomm.gov.uk

National Maritime Museum
Greenwich, London SE10 9NF
tel 020-8858 4422 *fax* 020-8312 6632
website www.nmm.ac.uk

The National Monuments Record
English Heritage, National Monuments Record Centre, Kemble Drive, Swindon, Wilts. SN2 2GZ
tel (01793) 414600 *fax* (01793) 414606
website www.english-heritage.org.uk

National Museums Liverpool
127 Dale Street, Liverpool L2 2JH
tel 0151-207 0001 *fax* 0151-478 4790

National Museums of Scotland
Chambers Street, Edinburgh EH1 1JF
tel 0131-225 7534 *fax* 0131-220 4819
website www.nms.ac.uk

National Portrait Gallery
St Martin's Place, London WC2H 0HE
tel 020-7306 0055 fax 020-7306 0056
website www.npg.org.uk

Natural Environment Research Council
Polaris House, North Star Avenue, Swindon, Wilts.
SN2 1EU
tel (01793) 411500 fax (01793) 411501
email requests@nerc.ac.uk
website www.nerc.ac.uk

Natural History Museum
Cromwell Road, London SW7 5BD
tel 020-7942 5000
website www.nhm.ac.uk

NESTA (National Endowment for Science, Technology and the Arts
Fishmongers' Chambers, 110 Upper Thames Street,
London EC4R 3TW
tel 020-7645 9500 fax 020-7645 9501
website www.nesta.org.uk

New Opportunities Fund – see Big Lottery Fund

New Zealand High Commission
New Zealand House, Haymarket, London
SW1Y 4TQ
tel 020-7930 8422 fax 020-7839 4580
website www.nzembassy.com/uk

Northern Ireland Assembly
Parliament Buildings, Belfast BT4 3XX
tel 028-9052 1333

Northern Ireland Authority for Energy Regulation
Queens House, 10–18 Queen Street, Belfast BT1 6ED
tel 028-9031 1575 fax 028-9031 1740
email ofreg@nics.gov.uk
website www.ofreg.nics.gov.uk

Northern Ireland Human Rights Commission
Temple Court, 39–41 North Street, Belfast BT1 1NA
tel 028-9024 3987 textphone 028-9024 9066
fax 028-9024 7844
email information@nihrc.org
website www.nihrc.org

Northern Ireland Office
11 Millbank, London SW1P 4PN
tel 020-7210 3000
Castle Buildings, Belfast BT4 3ST
tel 028-9052 0700
website www.nio.gov.uk

Northern Ireland Tourist Board
St Anne's Court, 59 North Street, Belfast BT1 1NB
tel 028-9023 1221 textphone 028-9044 1522
fax 028-9024 0960
email info@nitb.com
website www.discovernorthernireland.com,
www.nitb.com

Office for National Statistics
1 Drummond Gate, London SW1V 2QQ
tel (0845) 601 3034
website www.statistics.gov.uk

Office for Standards in Education (OFSTED)
Alexandra House, 33 Kingsway, London WC2B 6SE
tel (08456) 404045 fax 020-7421 6707
website www.ofsted.gov.uk

The Office of Communications (Ofcom)
Riverside House, 2A Southwark Bridge Road, London
SE1 9HA
tel 020-7981 3040 fax 020-7981 3334
email contact@ofcom.org.uk
website www.ofcom.org.uk

Established to regulate the communications sector in the UK. It aims to further the interest of consumers in relevant markets, secure the optimum use of the radio spectrum, ensure the availability throughout the UK of TV and radio services and to protect the public from any offensive or potentially harmful effects of broadcast media, as well as safeguarding people from being unfairly treated in TV and radio programmes. Established 2003.

Office of Fair Trading
Fleetbank House, 2–6 Salisbury Square, London
EC4Y 8JX
tel 020-7211 8000 fax 020-7211 5838
email enquiries@oft.gov.uk
website www.oft.gov.uk

Office of Gas and Electricity Markets (OFGEM)
Head Office 9 Millbank, London SW1P 3GE
tel 020-7901 7000
website www.ofgem.gov.uk
OFGEM Scotland Regent Court, 70 West Regent
Street, Glasgow G2 2QZ
tel 0141-331 2678

Office of Telecommunications – see The Office of Communications (Ofcom)

Office of the Data Protection Commissioner – see Information Commissioner's Office

Office of the Legal Services Ombudsman
3rd Floor, Sunlight House, Quay Street, Manchester
M3 3JZ

tel 0161-839 7262 , *Lo call* (0845) 6010794 (local rate)
fax 0161-832 5446
email lso@olso.gsi.gov.uk
website www.olso.org

Office of Water Services (OFWAT)

Centre City Tower, 7 Hill Street, Birmingham
B5 4UA
tel 0121-625 1300 *fax* 0121-625 1400
email enquiries@ofwat.gsi.gov.uk
website www.ofwat.gov.uk

Oftel (Office of Telecommunications) – see The Office of Communications (Ofcom)

OFWAT – see Office of Water Services (OFWAT)

Ordnance Survey

Romsey Road, Southampton SO16 4GU
tel 023-8079 2251 (press office), (08456) 050505
(Customer Contact Centre) *fax* 023-8079 2615
email enquiries@ordnancesurvey.co.uk
website www.ordnancesurvey.co.uk

Particle Physics and Astronomy Research Council (PPARC)

Polaris House, North Star Avenue, Swindon, Wilts.
SN2 1SZ
tel (01793) 442000 *fax* (01793) 442002
email pr.pus@pparc.ac.uk
website www.pparc.ac.uk

Patent Office

Concept House, Cardiff Road, Newport, South Wales
NP10 8QQ
tel (0845) 9500505 *fax* (01633) 814444
email enquiries@patent.gov.uk
website www.patent.gov.uk, www.intellectual-property.gov.uk

The Pensions Ombudsman

11 Belgrave Road, London SW1V 1RB
tel 020-7834 9144 *fax* 020-7821 0065
email enquiries@pensions-ombudsman.org.uk
website www.pensions-ombudsman.org.uk
Ombudsman David Laverick

Pensions and Overseas Benefits Directorate (POD) – see DWP (Department for Work and Pensions)

PLR Office – see page 304

Embassy of the Republic of Poland

47 Portland Place, London W1B 1JH
tel (0870) 774 2700 *fax* 020-7291 3575
email polishembassy@polishembassy.org.uk

tel (0870) 7742 900 *fax* 020-7637 2190
Polish Cultural Institute, 34 Portland Place, London
W1B 1HQ
email pci@polishculture.org.uk
website www.home.btclick.com/polishembassy/index.htm
website www.polishculture.org.uk

Portuguese Embassy

11 Belgrave Square, London SW1X 8PP
tel (0870) 005 6970 *fax* 020-7245 1287, 020-7235 0739
email portembassy-london@dialin.net
website www.portugal.embassy.com

Post Office Headquarters – see Royal Mail Group

The Postal Services Commission (Postcomm)

Hercules House, 6 Hercules Road, London SE1 7DB
tel 020-7593 2100
website www.psc.gov.uk

Privy Council Office

2 Carlton Gardens, London SW1Y 5AA
tel 020-7210 1033 *fax* 020-7210 1071
email pcosecretariat@pco.x.gsi.gov.uk
website www.privy-council.gov.uk

Public Guardianship Office

Archway Tower, 2 Junction Road, London N19 5SZ
tel (0845) 330 2900
website www.guardianship.gov.uk

Public Record Office – see The National Archives

Public Record Office of Northern Ireland

66 Balmoral Avenue, Belfast BT9 6NY
tel 028-9025 1318 *fax* 028-9025 5999

Qualifications and Curriculum Authority (QCA)

83 Piccadilly, London W1J 8QA
tel 020-7509 5555 *fax* 020-7509 6666
email info@qca.org.uk
website www.qca.org.uk

The Radio Authority – see The Office of Communications (Ofcom)

Rail Safety and Standards Board

Evergreen House, 160 Euston Road, London
NW1 2DX
tel 020-7904 7777 *fax* 020-7557 9072
website www.rssb.org.uk

Resource: The Council for Museums, Libraries and Archives – see Museums, Libraries and Archives Council

Embassy of Romania
4 Palace Green, London W8 4QD
tel 020-7937 9666 *fax* 020-7937 8069
email roemb@roemb.co.uk
website www.roemb.co.uk

Royal Air Force Museum
Grahame Park Way, London NW9 5LL
tel 020-8205 2266 *fax* 020-8200 1751
website www.rafmuseum.org

Royal Commission on the Ancient and Historical Monuments of Scotland
(with National Monuments Record of Scotland)
John Sinclair House, 16 Bernard Terrace, Edinburgh
EH8 9NX
tel 0131-662 1456 *fax* 0131-662 1477
email info@rcahms.gov.uk
website www.rcahms.gov.uk

Royal Commission on the Ancient and Historical Monuments of Wales
(with National Monuments Record of Wales)
Crown Building, Plas Crug, Aberystwyth, Ceredigion
SY23 1NJ
tel (01970) 621200 *fax* (01970) 627701
email nmr.wales@rcahmw.gov.uk
website www.rcahmw.gov.uk

Royal Commission on the Historical Monuments of England – merged with English Heritage

Royal Fine Art Commission for Scotland
Bakehouse Close, 146 Canongate, Edinburgh
EH8 8DD
tel 0131-556 6699 *fax* 0131-556 6633
website www.royfinartcomforsco.gov.uk

Royal Mail Group
148 Old Street, London EC1V 9HQ
tel 020-7490 2888
website www.royalmailgroup.com

Royal Mint
Llantrisant, Pontyclun CF72 8YT
tel (01443) 222111
email judith.nicholas@royalmint.gov.uk
website www.royalmint.gov

Royal National Theatre Board
South Bank, London SE1 9PX
tel 020-7452 3333 *fax* 020-7452 3344
website www.nationaltheatre.org.uk
Chairman Sir Hayden Phillips, *Director* Nicholas
Hytner

Royal Netherlands Embassy
38 Hyde Park Gate, London SW7 5DP
tel 020-7590 3200 *fax* 020-7581 0053 (Press and cultural affairs)
email cultural@netherlands-embassy.org.uk
website www.netherlands-embassy.org.uk

Royal Norwegian Embassy
25 Belgrave Square, London SW1X 8QD
tel 020-7591 5500 *fax* 020-7245 6993
email emb.london@mfa.no
website www.norway.org.uk

Royal Observatory of Greenwich – see National Maritime Museum

Embassy of the Russian Federation
13 Kensington Palace Gardens, London W8 4QX
tel 020-7229 2666 *fax* 020-7229 5804
email office@rusemblon.org
website www.great-britain.mid.ru

Science Museum
Exhibition Road, London SW7 2DD
tel (0870) 870 4868
email sciencemuseum@nmsi.ac.uk
website www.sciencemuseum.org.uk

The Scotland Office
Dover House, Whitehall, London SW1A 2AU
tel 020-7270 6754
website www.scotlandoffice.gov.uk

Scottish Arts Council – see page 552

Scottish Environment Protection Agency
Erskine Court, The Castle Business Park, Stirling
FK9 4TR
tel (01786) 457700, (0800) 807060 (Hotline)
website www.sepa.org.uk

The Scottish Executive
St Andrew's House, Regent Road, Edinburgh
EH1 1DG
tel (0845) 774 1741 *fax* 0131-556 8400
website www.scotland.gov.uk

Scottish Law Commission
140 Causewayside, Edinburgh EH9 1PR
tel 0131-668 2131 *fax* 0131-662 4900
email info@scotlawcom.gov.uk
website www.scotlawcom.gov.uk

Scottish Legal Aid Board
44 Drumsheugh Gardens, Edinburgh EH3 7SW
tel 0131-226 7061 *fax* 0131-220 4878
email general@slab.org.uk
website www.slab.org.uk

Scottish Natural Heritage
12 Hope Terrace, Edinburgh EH9 2AS
tel 0131-447 4784 *fax* 0131-446 2277
website www.snh.org.uk

The Scottish Office – see The Scottish Executive

The Scottish Parliament
Edinburgh EH99 1SP
tel 0131-348 5000, (0845) 278 1999 *fax* 0131-348 5601
textphone (0845) 270 0152
email sp.info@scottish.parliament.uk
website www.scottish parliament.uk

Embassy of Serbia and Montenegro
28 Belgrave Square, London SW1X 8QB
tel 020-7235 9049 *fax* 020-7235 7092
email londre@jugisek.demon.co.uk
website www.yugoslavembassy.org.uk

Serpentine Gallery
Kensington Gardens, London W2 3XA
020-7402 6075, 020-7298 1501 (public information)
fax 020-7402 4103
website www.serpentinegallery.org

Singapore High Commission
9 Wilton Crescent, London SW1X 8SP
tel 020-7235 8315 *fax* 020-7245 6583
email info@singaporehc.org.uk
website www.mfa.gov.sg/london

Embassy of the Slovak Republic
25 Kensington Palace Gardens, London W8 4QY
tel 020-7313 6470 *fax* 020-7313 6481
email mail@slovakembassy.co.uk
website www.slovakembassy.co.uk

Embassy of Slovenia
10 Little College Street, London SW1P 3SH
tel 020-7222 5700 *fax* 020-7222 5277
email vlo@gov.si

Department of Social Security – see DWP
(Department for Work and Pensions)

South African High Commission
South Africa House, Trafalgar Square, London
WC2N 5DP
tel 020-7451 7299 *fax* 020-7451 7283/7284
email general@southafricahouse.com,
mailmaster@rsaconsulate.co.uk
website www.southafricahouse.com

Spanish Embassy
39 Chesham Place, London SW1X 8SB
tel 020-7235 5555 *fax* 020-7259 5392

Sport England
3rd Floor, Victoria House, Bloomsbury Square,
London WC1B 4SE
tel (0845) 850 8508 *fax* 020-7383 5740
email info@sportengland.org
website www.sportengland.org

High Commission of the Democratic Socialist Republic of Sri Lanka
13 Hyde Park Gardens, London W2 2LU
tel 020-7262 1841 *fax* 020-7262 7970

Embassy of Sweden
11 Montagu Place, London W1H 2AL
tel 020-7917 6400 *fax* 020-7917 6477
email ambassaden.london@foreign.ministry.se
website www.swedenabroad.com/london

Swiss Embassy Cultural Section
16–18 Montagu Place, London W1H 2BQ
tel 020-7616 6000 *fax* 020-7723 6949
email swissembassy@lon.rep.admin.ch
website www.swissembassy.org.uk

Tate
Tate Britain, Millbank, London SW1P 4RG
Tate Modern, Bankside, London SE1 9TG
tel 020-7887 8888
Tate Liverpool, Albert Dock, Liverpool L3 4BB
tel 0151-702 7400
Tate St Ives, Porthmeor Beach, St Ives, Cornwall
TR26 1TG
tel (01736) 796226
website www.tate.org.uk

Theatre Museum – see page 505

Transport for London (TfL)
Windsor House, 42–50 Victoria Street, London
SW1H 0TL
tel 020-7941 4500
website www.tfl.gov.uk

TSO (The Stationery Office)
St Crispins, Duke Street, Norwich NR3 1PD
tel (0870) 600 5522
website www.tso.co.uk

Turkish Embassy
43 Belgrave Square, London SW1X 8PA
tel 020-7393 0202 *fax* 020-7393 0066
email info@turkishembassy.co.uk

UK Film Council
10 Little Portland Street, London W1W 7JG
tel 020-7861 7861 *fax* 020-7861 7864
website www.ukfilmcouncil.org.uk

United Kingdom Sports Council (UK Sport)
40 Bernard Street, London WC1N 1ST
tel 020-7211 5100 *fax* 020-7211 5246
website www.uksport.gov.uk

Victoria and Albert Museum
South Kensington, London SW7 2RL
tel 020-7942 2000, 020-7942 2414

email www.vanda@vam.ac.uk
website www.vam.ac.uk

VisitBritain
Thames Tower, Black's Road, London W6 9EL
tel 020-8846 9000 *fax* 020-8563 0302
website www.visitbritain.com

Visiting Arts – see page 557

VisitScotland
Ocean Point One, 94 Ocean Drive, Leith, Edinburgh
EH6 6JH
tel 0131-472 2222 *fax* 0131-472 2250
email info@visitscotland.com
website www.visitscotland.com

The Wales Office
Gwydyr House, Whitehall, London SW1A 2ER
tel 020-7270 0549 *fax* 020-7270 0568
website www.walesoffice.gov.uk

Wales Tourist Board
Brunel House, 2 Fitzalan Road, Cardiff CF24 0UY
tel 029-2049 9909 *fax* 029-2048 5031
email info@tourism.wales.gov.uk
website www.visitwales.com

Wallace Collection
Hertford House, Manchester Square, London
W1M 3BN
tel 020-7563 9500 *fax* 020-7224 2155
website www.wallacecollection.org

Women's National Commission
1 Victoria Street, London SW1H 0ET
tel 020-7215 6933 *fax* 020-7215 2840
email wnc@dti.gsi.gov.uk
website www.thewnc.org.uk

Copyright and libel
Copyright questions

Copyright is a vital part of any writer's assets, and should never be assigned or sold without due consideration and the advice of a competent authority, such as the Society of Authors, the Writers' Guild of Great Britain, or the National Union of Journalists. Michael Legat answers some of the most commonly asked questions about copyright.

Is there a period of time after which the copyright expires?

Copyright in the European Union lasts for the lifetime of the author and for a further 70 years from the end of the year of death, or, if the work is first published posthumously, for 70 years from the end of the year of publication. In most other countries of the world copyright exists similarly for the lifetime and for either 50 years or 70 years after death or posthumous publication.

If I want to include an extract from a book, poem or article, do I have to seek copyright? How much may be used without permission? What happens if I apply for copyright permission but do not get a reply?

It is essential to seek permission to quote from another author's work, unless that author has been dead for 70 years or more, or 70 years or more has passed from the date of publication of a work published posthumously. Only if you are quoting for purposes of criticism or review are you allowed to do so without obtaining permission, and even then the Copyright, Designs and Patents Act of 1988 restricts you to 400 words of prose in a single extract from a copyright work, or a series of extracts of up to 300 words each, totalling no more than 800 words, or up to 40 lines of poetry, which must not be more than 25% of the poem. However, a quotation of no more than, say, half a dozen words may usually be used without permission since it will probably not extend beyond a brief and familiar reference, as, for example, Rider Haggard's well-known phrase, 'she who must be obeyed'. If in doubt, always check. If you do not get a reply when you ask for permission to quote, insert a notice in your work saying that you have tried without success to contact the copyright owner, and would be pleased to hear from him or her so that the matter could be cleared up – and keep a copy of all the relevant correspondence, in order to back up your claim of having tried to get in touch.

If a newspaper pays for an article and I then want to sell the story to a magazine, am I free under the copyright law to do so?

Yes, provided that you have not granted copyright or exclusive use to the newspaper. When selling your work to newspapers or magazines make it clear, in writing, that you are selling only First or Second Serial Rights, not your copyright.

If I agree to have an article published for no payment do I retain any rights over how it appears?

Whether or not you are paid for the work has no bearing on the legal situation. However, the Moral Rights which apply to books, plays, television and radio scripts, do not cover you against a failure to acknowledge you as the author of an article, nor against the mutilation of your text, when it is published in a newspaper or magazine.

I want to publish a photograph that was taken in 1950. I am not sure how to contact the photographer or even if he is still alive. Am I allowed to go ahead and publish it?

The Copyright, Designs and Patents Act of 1988 works retrospectively, so a photograph taken in 1950 is bound to be in copyright until at least 2020, and the copyright will be owned by the photographer, even though, when it was taken, the copyright would have belonged to the person who commissioned it, according to the laws then in place. You should therefore make every effort to contact the photographer, keeping copies of any relevant correspondence, and in case of failure take the same course of action as described above in relation to a textual extract the copyright owner of which you have been unable to trace.

I recently read an article on the same subject as one I have written. It contained many identical facts. Did this writer breach my copyright? What if I send ideas for an article to a magazine editor and those ideas are used despite the fact that I was not commissioned? May I sue the magazine?

Facts are normally in the public domain and may be used by anyone. However, if your article contains a fact which you have discovered and no one else has published, there could be an infringement of copyright if the author who uses it fails to attribute it to you. There is no copyright in ideas, so you cannot sue a writer or a journal for using ideas that you have put forward; in any case you would find it very difficult to prove that the idea belonged to you and to no one else. There is also no copyright in titles.

Does being paid a kill fee affect my copyright in a given piece?

No, provided that you have not sold the magazine or newspaper your copyright.

Do I need to copyright a piece of writing physically – whether an essay or a novel – or is it copyrighted automatically? Does it have to carry the © symbol?

Anything that you write is your copyright, assuming that it is not copied from the work of someone else, as soon as you have written it on paper or recorded it on the disk of a computer or on tape, or broadcast it, or posted it on the internet. It is not essential for the work to carry the © symbol, although its inclusion may act as a warning and help to stop another writer from plagiarising it.

Am I legally required to inform an interviewee that our conversation is being recorded?

The interviewee owns the copyright of any words that he or she speaks as soon as they are recorded on your tape. Unless you have received permission to use those words in direct quotation, you could be liable to an action for infringement of copyright. You should therefore certainly inform the interviewee that the conversation is being recorded and seek permission to quote what is said directly.

More and more newspapers and magazines have versions both in print and on the internet. How can I ensure that my work is not published on the internet without my permission?

Make sure that any clause granting electronic rights to anyone in any agreement that you sign in respect of your work specifies not only the proportion of any fees received which you will get, but that your agreement must be sought before the rights are sold. Copyright extends to electronic rights, and therefore to publication on the internet, in just the same way as to other uses of the material.

I commissioned a designer to design a business card for me, and I paid her well. Does the design belong to me or to her?

Copyright would belong to the designer, and not to the person who commissioned it (as is also true in the case of a photograph, copyright in which belongs to the photographer). However, copyright in the business card might be transferred to you if a court considered you to have gained beneficially from the card.

Michael Legat became a full-time writer after a long and successful publishing career. He is the author of a number of highly regarded books on publishing and writing.

See also...

- *UK copyright law*, page 688
- *US copyright law*, page 707
- *Authors' Licensing and Collecting Society*, page 702
- *Design and Artists Copyright Society*, page 705
- *The Copyright Licensing Agency Ltd*, page 700

UK copyright law

Amanda Michaels describes the main types of work which may qualify for copyright protection, or related protection as a design, together with some of the main problems which may be faced by readers of this *Yearbook* in terms of protecting their own works or avoiding infringement of existing works in the UK. This is a technical area of the law, and one which is constantly developing; in an article of this length, it is not possible to deal fully with all the complexities of the law. It must also be emphasised that copyright is national in scope, and whilst works of UK authors will be protected in many other countries of the world, and works of foreign authors will generally be protected in the UK, foreign laws may deal differently with questions of subsistence, ownership and infringement.

Copyright is a creation of statute, now shaped and influenced significantly by EU harmonisation measures. On 1 August 1989, the Copyright, Designs & Patents Act 1988 ('the Act') replaced the Copyright Act 1956, which in turn replaced the Copyright Act 1911. All three Acts are still relevant to copyright today. Whilst the Act to a large degree restated the existing law, it was also innovative, in particular in the creation of a new 'design right' offering protection (generally speaking in lieu of copyright) for many industrial or commercial designs, and in the wider protection of moral rights.

> ### Useful websites
>
> **www.patent.gov.uk/index.htm**
> Website of the Patent Office.
>
> **www.intellectual-property.gov.uk**
> **www.wipo.int**
> Website of the World Intellectual Property Organisation.
>
> **www.baillii.org**
> Contains judgements from UK courts and with links to equivalent foreign websites. Legislation on the site may be in an unamended form.

The law has changed further since 1989, largely as a result of EU directives. An important change occurred on 1 January 1996, when the duration of copyright protection in respect of most works (see below) was extended from 'life of the author' plus 50 years to life plus 70 years. Further changes came into force on 1 January 1998, when a new 'database right' was created. New Community design rights were brought into effect in 2003 and numerous other amendments were made, in particular to the rules on fair dealing with copyright works, by the Copyright and Related Rights Regulations 2003 (see below).

Continuing relevance of old law

In this article, I discuss the law as it currently stands, but where a work was created prior to 1 August 1989 it will always be necessary to consider the law in force at the time of creation (or possibly first publication) in order to assess the existence or scope of any rights. Particular difficulties arise with foreign works, which may qualify for protection in the UK as a matter of international obligation. Each Act has contained transitional provisions and these, as well as the substantive provisions of any relevant earlier Act, will need to be considered where, for instance, you wish to use an earlier work and it is necessary to decide whether permission is needed and if so, who may grant it. Publishing or licence agreements designed for use under older Acts and prior to the development of modern technologies may be unsuitable for current use.

Copyright protection of works

The overall policy justifying copyright protection is 'to prevent the unauthorised copying of material forms of expression (literary, dramatic, artistic and musical, for example) resulting from intellectual exertions of the human mind.... The important point is that copyright can be used to prevent copying of a substantial part of the relevant form of expression, but it does not prevent use of the information, thoughts or emotions expressed in the copyright work. It does not prevent another person from coincidentally creating a similar work by his own independent efforts' (see Mummery LJ in *Sawkins* v. *Hyperion Records* [2005] IWLR 3281).

Hence, copyright protects the particular form in which an author's idea has been expressed, not the idea itself. Generally speaking, plots or artistic ideas are not protected by copyright, but what is protected is the particular manner in which the idea is presented. For instance, in *Designers Guild Limited* v. *Russell Williams (Textiles) Limited* [2001] FSR 113 a fairly simple fabric design was found to be original and to have been copied: this was an infringement of the copyright in the design. By contrast, in *Baigent & Leigh* v. *The Random House Group*, the 'Da Vinci Code' case, Dan Brown was alleged to have copied a number of historical facts or theories from the earlier book *The Holy Blood and the Holy Grail* but not the language in which they were expressed (the few phrases actually copied did not amount to a 'substantial part' of the *HBHG*). The claim was that there was infringement by copying a 'Central Theme' composed of a series of 15 connected points. However, the judge found that this was not the 'theme' of *HBHG*, and held that in any event the individual points were of too high a level of abstraction to be capable of copyright protection.

Of course, if someone has written an outline, script or screenplay for a television show, film, etc and that idea is confidential, then dual protection may arise in the confidential idea embodied in the documents and in the literary (and sometimes artistic) works in which the idea has taken material form. If the idea is used, but not the form, this might give rise to an action for breach of confidence, but not for infringement of copyright. Copyright prevents the copying of the *material form* in which the idea has been presented, or of a substantial part of it, measured in terms of quality, not quantity.

Section 1 of the Act sets out a number of different categories of works which can be the subject of copyright protection. These are:
- original literary, dramatic, musical or artistic works,
- sound recordings, films, broadcasts or cable programmes, and
- typographical arrangements of published editions.

These works are further defined in ss.3–8 (see box for examples).

However, no work of any description enjoys copyright protection until it has been recorded in a tangible form, as s.3(2) provides that no copyright shall subsist in a literary, musical or artistic work until it has been recorded in writing or otherwise.

On the other hand, all that is required to achieve UK copyright protection is to record the original work in an appropriate medium. Once that has been done, copyright will subsist in the work (assuming that the qualifying features set out below are present) without any formality of registration or otherwise. There is, for instance, no need to publish a work to protect it. Please note, however, that the law of the United States does differ on this – see page 707.

Nonetheless, there can be a real benefit in keeping a proper record of the creation of a work. Drafts or preliminary sketches should be kept and dated, as should source or research material, so as to be able to show the development of a work. It may also be beneficial (especially where works are to be submitted to potential publishers or purchasers) to take a complete copy of the documents and send them to oneself or lodge them with a responsible third party, sealed and dated, so as to be able to provide cogent evidence of the form or content of the work at that date. Such evidence may help the author, whether as claimant or defendant, to prove the independence of the creation of his work, and its originality, in a copyright infringement (or indeed breach of confidence) action.

Originality

Literary, dramatic, artistic and musical works must all be 'original' to gain copyright protection, but this does not impose any concept of objective novelty. Just as the law protects the form, rather than the idea, originality relates to the 'expression of the thought', rather than to the thought itself. The policy of copyright protection and its limited scope (set out above) explain why the threshold requirement of an original work does not impose 'any objective standard of novelty, usefulness, inventiveness, aesthetic merit, quality or value'; so, a work may be 'complete rubbish', yet have copyright protection (see again Mummery LJ in *Sawkins*). A work need only be original in the sense of being the product of skill and labour on the part of the author. This can be seen for instance in the definition of certain artistic works, and in the fact that copyright protects works such as compilations (like football pools coupons or directories) and tables (including mathematical tables).

There may be considerable difficulty, at times, in deciding whether a work is of sufficient originality, or has original features, where there is a series of similar designs or amendments of existing works. *Sawkins* was just such a case: the question was whether or not the editorial work by Doctor Sawkins on existing works by the baroque composer, Lalande, had created new musical works. The result turned partly on the definition of 'music', but the nature of Dr Sawkins' input was confirmed to have amounted to creation of an original musical work with its own copyright. See also *L.A. Gear Inc.* [1993] FSR 121, *Biotrading* [1998] FSR 109. Equally, an adaptation of an existing work may have its own copyright protection (see *Cala Homes* [1995] FSR 818). What is clear, though, is that merely making a 'slavish copy' of a work will not create an original work: see *Interlego AG* [1989] AC 217. If the work gives particular expression to a commonplace idea or an old tale, copyright may subsist in it (e.g. *Christoffer* v. *Poseidon Film Distributors Limited* (6/10/99) in which it was held that a script for an animated film of a story from Homer's *Odyssey* was an original literary work). But, as the *Da Vinci* case confirmed, whilst copyright may subsist in the work, use only of the pre-existing facts or ideas contained in it may not infringe that copyright. Copyright protection will be limited to the original features of the work, or those features created or chosen by the author's input of skill and labour.

Sound recordings or films which are copies of pre-existing sound recordings or films, broadcasts which infringe rights in another broadcast or cable programmes which consist of immediate retransmissions of broadcasts are not protected by copyright.

'Works' such as the titles of books or periodicals, or advertising slogans, which may have required a good deal of original thought, generally are not accorded copyright protection, because they are too short to be deemed literary works. It also seems that computer 'languages', and the ideas or logic underlying them, are not protected as copyright works; such protection extends only to the computer programs: see *Navitaire* v. *Easyjet* [2004] EWHC 1725.

Qualification

The Act is limited in its effects to the UK (and to colonies to which it may be extended by Order). It is aimed primarily at protecting the works of British citizens, or works which were first published here. However, in line with the requirements of various international conventions, copyright protection in the UK is also accorded to the works of nationals of many foreign states, as well as to works first published in those states, on a reciprocal basis.

As for works of nationals of other member states of the European Union, there is a principle of equal treatment, so that protection must be offered to such works here: see *Phil Collins* [1993] 3 CMLR 773.

The importance of these rules mainly arises when one is trying to find out whether a foreign work is protected by copyright here, for instance, if one wishes to make a film based upon a foreign novel.

Ownership

The general rule is that the copyright in a work will first be owned by its author, the creator of the work. In most cases this is self-explanatory, but the definition of 'author' in relation to films and sound recordings has changed over the years; currently, the author of a sound recording is its producer, and the authors of a film are the producer and principal director.

One important exception to the general rule is that the copyright in a work made by an employee in the course of his or her employment will belong to their employer, subject to any agreement to the contrary. However, this rule does not apply to freelance designers, journalists, etc, and not even to self-employed company directors. This obviously may lead to problems if the question of copyright ownership is not dealt with when an agreement is made to create, purchase or use a work. In the absence of an appropriate agreement, the legal title may simply not be owned by the apparent owner, who will need it if he wishes to sue for infringement, and it is often difficult to formalise the position long after creation of the work. More importantly, perhaps, there have been numerous cases in which the extent of the rights obtained in a 'commissioned' work has been disputed, simply because of the lack of any clear agreement at the outset between the author and the 'commissioner'. It is very important for writers and artists of all kinds to agree about ownership/terms of use at the outset and record them in writing. It is equally important to understand the difference between an assignment and a licence (see below).

Where a work is produced by several people who collaborate so that each one's contribution is not distinct from that of the other(s), then they will be joint authors of the work. Where two people collaborate to write a song, one producing the lyrics and the other the music, there will be two separate copyright works, the copyright of which will be owned by each of the authors separately. But where two people write a play, each rewriting what the other produces, there will be a joint work.

Definitions under the Act

Literary work is defined as: 'any work, other than a dramatic or musical work, which is written, spoken or sung, and accordingly includes: (a) a table or compilation other than a database, (b) a computer program, (c) preparatory design material for a computer program and (d) a database.'

A musical work means: 'a work consisting of music, exclusive of any words or action intended to be sung, spoken or performed with the music.'

An artistic work means: '(a) a graphic work, photograph, sculpture or collage, irrespective of artistic quality, (b) a work of architecture being a building or model for a building, or (c) a work of artistic craftsmanship.'

These categories of work are not mutually exclusive, e.g. a film may be protected both as a film and as a dramatic work. See *Norowzian* v. *Arks* [2000] FSR 363.

The importance of knowing whether the copyright is joint or not arises:

- in working out the duration of the copyright, and
- from the fact that joint works can only be exploited with the agreement of all the joint authors, so that all of them have to join in any licence, although each of them can sue for infringement without joining the other(s) as a claimant in the proceedings.

Duration of copyright

As a result of amendments brought into effect on 1 January 1996, copyright in literary, dramatic, musical or artistic works expires at the end of the period of 70 years from the end of the calendar year in which the author dies (s.12(1)). Where there are joint authors, then the 70 years runs from the death of the last of them to die. If the author is unknown, there will be 70 years protection from the date the work was first made or (where applicable) first made available to the public. Previously, the protection was for 'life plus 50'.

The extended 70-year term also applies to films, and runs from the end of the calendar year in which the death occurs of the last to die of the principal director, the author of the screenplay or the dialogue, or the composer of any music created for the film (s.13B). This obviously may be a nightmare to establish, and there are certain presumptions in s.66A which may help someone wishing to use material from an old film.

However, sound recordings are still protected by copyright only for 50 years from the year of making or release (s.13A); similarly, broadcasts, cable programmes and computer-generated works still get only 50 years protection.

The new longer term applies without difficulty to works created after 1 January 1996 and to works in copyright on 31 December 1995. The owner of that extended copyright will be the person who owned it on 31 December 1995, unless that person had only a limited term of ownership, in which case the extra 20 years will be added on to the reversionary term.

Where copyright had expired here, but the author died between 50 and 70 years ago, the position is more complicated. EC Directive 93/98 provided that if a work was protected by copyright anywhere in the European Union on 1 July 1995, copyright would revive for it in any other state until the end of the same 70-year period. This may make it necessary to look at the position in the states offering a longer term of protection, namely Germany, France and Spain.

Ownership of the revived term of copyright will belong to the person who was the owner of the copyright when the initial term expired, save that if that person died (or a company, etc, ceased to exist) before 1 January 1996, then the revived term will vest in the author's personal representatives, and in the case of a film, in the principal director's personal representatives.

Any licence affecting a copyright work which subsisted on 31 December 1995 and was then for the full term of the copyright continues to have effect during any extended term of copyright, subject to any agreement to the contrary (paragraph 21 of the Regulations).

The increased term offered to works of other EU nationals as a result of the Term Directive is not offered automatically to the nationals of other states, but will only apply where an equally long term is offered in their state of origin.

Where acts are carried out in relation to such revived copyright works, pursuant to things done whilst they were in the public domain, protection from infringement is available. A licence as of right may also be available, on giving notice to the copyright owner and paying a royalty.

Dealing with copyright works

Ownership of the copyright in a work confers upon the owner the exclusive right to deal with the work in a number of ways, and essentially stops all unauthorised exploitation of the work. Ownership of the copyright is capable of being separated from ownership of the material form in which the work is embodied, depending upon the terms of any agreement or the circumstances. Even buying an original piece of artwork will not in general carry with it the legal title to the copyright, as an effective assignment must be in writing signed by the assignor (although beneficial ownership might pass: see below).

Copyright works can be exploited by their owners in two ways:

- **Assignment.** In an assignment, rights in the work are sold, with the owner retaining no interest in it (except, possibly, for payment by way of royalties). An assignment must be in writing, signed by or on behalf of the assignor, but no other formality is required. One can make an assignment of future copyright (under s.91). Where the author of a projected work agrees in writing that he will assign the rights in a future work to another, the copyright vests in the assignee immediately upon the creation of the work, without further formalities.

These rules do not affect the common law as to beneficial interests in copyright. One possibility may be that a court will, in the right circumstances, find or infer an agreement to assign the copyright in a work, e.g. where a sole trader who had title to the copyright used in his business later incorporated the business and allowed the company to exploit the software as if it were its own, an agreement to assign was inferred (see *Lakeview Computers plc* 26/11/99). Alternatively, if the court finds that a work was commissioned to be made, and that there was a common intention that the purchaser should own the copyright, the court may order the author to assign the copyright to him. Where a freelance designer produced a logo for an advertising agency, a term was implied in the contract between the designer and the agency that the client for which the logo was designed was to be the owner of the worldwide copyrights in the logo: see *R. Griggs Group* v. *Ross Evans* [2005] FSR 31. 'Commission' in this context means only to order a particular piece of work to be done: see *Apple Corps Ltd* v. *Cooper* [1993] FSR 286 (a 1956 Act case).

- **Licensing.** A licence is granted to another to exploit the right whilst the licensor retains overall ownership. Licences do not need to take any form in particular, and may indeed be granted orally. However, an exclusive licence (i.e. one which excludes even the copyright owner himself from exploiting the work) must be in writing, if the licensee is to enjoy rights in respect of infringements concurrent with those of the copyright owner.

Agreements dealing with copyright should make it clear whether an assignment or a licence is being granted. There may be significant advantages for the author in granting a licence rather than an assignment, for where the assignee's rights pass to a third party, for instance on his insolvency, the author cannot normally enforce the original agreement to make a purchaser pay royalties, etc (*Barker* v. *Stickney* [1919] 1 KB 121). If the agreement is unclear, the Court is likely to find that the grantee took the minimum rights necessary for his intended use of the work, quite probably an exclusive licence rather than an assignment (*Ray* v. *Classic FM plc* [1998] FSR 622), unless the work was 'commissioned' from the author (see box). The question of moral rights (see below) will also have to be considered by the parties.

Assignments and licences often split up the various rights contained within the copyright. So, for instance, a licence might be granted to one person to publish a novel in book form, another person might be granted the film, television and video rights, and yet another the right to translate the novel into other languages. Obviously, the author should seek to grant the narrowest possible rights on each occasion, so retaining other rights for future exploitation; this means scrutinising draft publishing agreements carefully and negotiating as best one can.

Assignments and licences may also confer rights according to territory, dividing the USA from the EU or different EU countries one from the other. Any such agreement should take into account divergences between different national copyright laws. Furthermore, when seeking to divide rights between different territories of the EU there is a danger of infringing the competition rules of the EU. Professional advice should be taken, as breach of these rules may attract a fine and can render the agreement void in whole or in part.

Licences can, of course, be of varying lengths. There is no need for a licence to be granted for the whole term of copyright. Well-drafted licences will provide for termination on breach, including the failure of the licensee to exploit the work, and on the insolvency of the licensee and will specify whether the rights may be assigned or sub-licensed.

Copyright may be assigned by will. A bequest of an original document, etc embodying an unpublished copyright work will carry the copyright.

Infringement

The main type of infringement is what is commonly thought of as plagiarism, that is, copying the work. In fact, copyright confers on the owner the exclusive right to do a number of specified acts, so that anyone doing those acts without his permission will normally infringe. It is important to note that it is not necessary to copy a work exactly or use all of it; it is sufficient if a substantial part is used. That question is to be judged on a qualitative not a quantitative basis, bearing in mind that it is the skill and labour of the author which is to be protected (see *Ravenscroft* v. *Herbert* [1980] RPC 193 and *Designers Guild*). It is important to note that primary infringement, such as copying, can be done innocently of any intention to infringe.

The form of infringement common to all forms of copyright works is that of copying. This means reproducing the work in any material form. Infringement may occur where an existing work provides the inspiration for a later one, if copying results, for example by including edited extracts from a history book in a novel (*Ravenscroft*), using a photograph as the inspiration for a painting (*Baumann* v. *Fussell* [1978] RPC 485), or words from a verse of one song in another (*Ludlow Music* v. *Williams* [2001] FSR 271). Infringement will not necessarily be prevented merely by the application of significant new skill and labour by the infringer, nor by a change of medium.

In the case of a two-dimensional artistic work, reproduction can mean making a copy in three dimensions, and vice versa. However, s.51 of the Act provides that in the case of a 'design document or model' (for definition, see 'Design right' below) for something which is not *itself* an artistic work, it is no infringement to make an article to that design. This means that whilst it would be an infringement of copyright to make an article from a design drawing for, say, a sculpture, it will not be an infringement of copyright to make a handbag from a copy of the design drawing for it, or from a handbag which one has purchased. Instead, such designs are generally protected by design right or as registered designs (for both see below). A recent decision suggests that there is in fact a gap in the regime through which some designs may fall. Design right does not protect 'surface decoration', but nor (because of s.51) does copyright protect elements of surface decoration if they are dictated by the shape of the article on which the decoration appears. Hence, the design of stripes on a T-shirt was not protected either by copyright or by design right. See *Lambretta* v. *Teddy Smith* [2005] RPC 6.

Copying a film, broadcast or cable programme can include making a copy of the whole or a substantial part of any image from it (see s.17(4)). This means that copying one frame of the film will be an infringement. It is not an infringement of copyright in a film to reshoot the film (*Norowzian*) (though there would doubtless be an infringement of the copyright in underlying works such as the literary copyright in the screenplay).

Copying is generally proved by showing substantial similarities between the original and the alleged copy, plus an opportunity to copy. Surprisingly often, minor errors in the original are reproduced by an infringer.

Copying need not be direct, so that, for instance, where the copyright is in a fabric design, copying the material without ever having seen the original drawing will still be an infringement, as will 'reverse engineering' of industrial designs, for example to make unlicensed spare parts (*British Leyland* [1986] AC 577; *Mars* v. *Teknowledge* [2000] FSR 138).

Issuing copies of a work to the public when they have not previously been put into circulation in the UK is also a primary infringement of all types of work.

Other acts which may amount to an infringement depend upon the nature of the work. It will be an infringement of the copyright in a literary, dramatic or musical work to perform it in public, whether by live performance or by playing recordings. Similarly, it is an infringement of the copyright in a sound recording, film, broadcast or cable programme to play or show it in public. Many copyright works will also be infringed by the rental or lending of copies of the work.

One rather different form of infringement is to make an adaptation of a literary, dramatic or musical work. An adaptation includes, in the case of a literary work, a translation, in the case of a non-dramatic work, making a dramatic work of it, and vice versa. A transcription or arrangement of a musical work is an adaptation of it.

There are also a number of 'secondary' infringements – see box.

Exceptions to infringement

The Act provides a large number of exceptions to the rules on infringement which were extended and amended with effect from 31 October 2003 by the Copyright and Related

'Secondary' infringements

Secondary infringements consist not of making infringing copies, but of dealing with existing infringing copies in some way. It is an infringement to import an infringing copy into the UK, and to possess in the course of business, or to sell, hire, offer for sale or hire, or distribute in the course of trade an infringing copy. However, none of these acts will be an infringement unless the alleged infringer knew or had reason to believe that the articles were infringing copies. What is sufficient knowledge will depend upon the facts of each case (see *LA Gear Inc.* [1992] FSR 121, *ZYX Records* v. *King* [1997] 2 All ER 132 and *Pensher Security* [2000] RPC 249). Merely putting someone on notice of a dispute as to ownership of copyright may not suffice to give him or her reason to believe in infringement for this purpose. But someone who is informed that he is infringing 'yet carries out no sensible enquiries, and does nothing in the face of continued assertions of the copyright' may become someone with 'reason to believe' the claim: *Nouveau Fabrics* v. *Voyage Decoration* [2004] EWHC 895; *Hutchison* [1995] FSR 365.

Other secondary infringements consist of permitting a place to be used for a public performance in which copyright is infringed and supplying apparatus to be used for infringing public performance, again, in each case, with safeguards for innocent acts.

Rights Regulations 2003. They are far too numerous to be dealt with here in full, but they include:

- fair dealing with literary, dramatic, musical or artistic works for the purpose of non-commercial research or private study (s.29);
- fair dealing for the purpose of criticism or review or reporting current events, as to which see e.g. *Pro Sieben Media* [1999] FSR 610; *Hyde Park* v. *Yelland* [2001] Ch. 143; *NLA* v. *Marks & Spencer Plc* [2002] RPC 4) (s.30);
- incidental inclusion of a work in an artistic work, sound recording, film, broadcast or cable programme (s.31);
- educational exceptions (ss.32–36A);
- exceptions for libraries (ss.37–44A) and public administration (ss.45–50);
- making transient copies as part of a technological process (s.28A) and backing-up, or converting a computer program or accessing a licensed database (s.50A–D);
- dealing with a work where the author cannot be identified and the work seems likely to be out of copyright (s.57);
- public recitation, if accompanied by a sufficient acknowledgement (s.59).

The effect of the Human Rights Act on copyright in relation to the right to free speech seems likely to be limited, as sufficient protection is to be found in the fair dealing provisions: *Ashdown* v. *Telegraph Group Limited* [2002] Ch. 149.

There is no defence of parody.

Remedies for infringements

The copyright owner will usually want to prevent the repetition or continuation of the infringement and will want compensation.

In almost all cases an injunction will be sought to stop the infringement. The Courts have useful powers to grant an injunction at an early stage, indeed even before any infringement takes place, if a real threat of damage can be shown. Such an interim injunction can be applied for on three days' notice (or without notice in appropriate cases), but will not be granted unless the claimant has a reasonably good case and can show that he would suffer 'unquantifiable' damage if the defendant's activities continued pending trial. Delay in bringing an interim application may be fatal to its success. An injunction may not be granted where the claimant clearly only wants financial compensation (*Ludlow Music*).

Financial compensation may be sought in one of two forms. Firstly, damages. These will usually be calculated upon evidence of the loss caused to the claimant, sometimes based upon loss of business, at others upon the basis of what would have been a proper licence fee for the defendant's acts. Additional damages may be awarded in rare cases for flagrant infringements and can be substantial. See for example *Notts. Healthcare* v. *News Group Newspapers* [2002] RPC 49.

Damages will not be awarded for infringement where the infringer did not know, and had no reason to believe, that copyright subsisted in the work. This exception is of limited use to a defendant, though, in the usual situation where the work was of such a nature that he should have known that copyright would subsist in it.

The alternative to damages is an account of profits, that is, the net profits made by the infringer by virtue of his illicit exploitation of the copyright. Where an account of profits is sought, no award of flagrant damages can be made. See *Redrow Homes Limited* [1999] 1 AC 197.

A copyright owner may also apply for delivery up of infringing copies.

Finally, there are various criminal offences relating to the making, importation, possession, sale, hire, distribution, etc of infringing copies.

Design right

Many industrial designs are excluded from copyright protection by s.51. Alternatively, the term of copyright protection is limited to 25 years from first industrial exploitation, by s.52. However, they may instead be protected by the 'design right' created by ss.213–64 or by Community design right. Like copyright, design right does not depend upon registration, but upon the creation of a suitable design by a 'qualifying person'.

Design right is granted to original designs consisting of the shape or configuration (internal or external) of the whole or part of an article, not being merely 'surface decoration'. Even very simple designs may be protected. However, a design is not original if it was commonplace in the design field in question at the time of its creation. In *Farmers Build* [1999] RPC 461, 'commonplace' was defined as meaning a design of a type which would excite no 'peculiar attention' amongst those in the trade, or one which amounts to a run-of-the-mill combination of well-known features. Designs are not protected if they consist of a method or principle of construction, or are dictated by the shape, etc of an article to which the new article is to be connected or of which it is to form part, the so-called 'must-fit' and 'must-match' exclusions. In *Ocular Sciences* [1997] RPC 289, these exclusions had a devastating effect upon numerous design rights claimed for contact lens designs. See also *Dyson* v. *Qualtex* [2006] EWCA Civ. 166 in which these exclusions were discussed in relation to spare parts for Dyson vacuum cleaners.

Design right subsists in designs made by or for qualifying persons (see, broadly, 'Qualification', above) or first marketed in the UK or EU or any other country to which the provision may be extended by Order.

Design right lasts only 15 years from the end of the year in which it was first recorded or an article made to the design, or (if shorter) 10 years from the end of the year in which articles made according to the design were first sold or hired out. During the last five years of the term of protection, a licence to use the design can be obtained 'as of right' but against payment of a proper licence fee. Hence, design right may give only five years 'absolute' protection, as opposed to the 'life plus 70' of copyright.

The designer will be the owner of the right, unless it was commissioned, in which case the commissioner will be the first owner. An employee's designs made in the course of employment will belong to the employer. The right given to the owner of a design right is the exclusive right to reproduce the design for commercial purposes. The rules as to assignments, licensing and infringement, both primary and secondary, are substantially similar to those described above in relation to copyright, as are the remedies available.

There have recently been significant changes to the law on registered designs, which coexist with the right given by the unregistered design right discussed above. The Registered Design Act 1949 has been amended (and expanded) in line with EU legislation, and now permits the registration of designs consisting of the appearance of the whole or any part of a product resulting from features of the product itself, such as shape, materials, etc or from the ornamentation of the product. It covers industrial or handicraft items, their packaging or get-up, etc. Designs must be novel and not solely dictated by function. The range of designs which may be registered is wider than under the old law, and designs need not necessarily have 'eye appeal'. Such designs provide a monopoly right renewable for up to 25 years. For further explanation see the useful guidance on the Patent Office website.

EU Regulation 6/2002 created two Community design regimes, one for registered and one for unregistered designs. In some cases, especially where there are problems with relying upon UK unregistered design right, the Community regime may be very helpful. It is not possible in the space available here to describe these new regimes in detail but the Regulation is available online (www.europa.ue.int/eur-lex). In brief, such designs are *very* broadly defined in Article 3 and can include the outward appearance of a product or part of it, shape, texture, materials and/or its ornamentation. 'Products' include any industrial or handicraft item, packaging, graphic symbols and typographic typefaces but not computer programs. However, the designs must be 'new' and have 'individual character'. The registered right may be enjoyed for up to 25 years in five-year tranches, but an unregistered Community design right lasts only three years. The unregistered right protects the design from copying, but the registered right gives 'absolute' exclusivity, in that it may be infringed without copying.

Moral rights

The Act also provides for the protection of certain 'moral rights'.

The right of 'paternity' is for the author of a copyright literary, dramatic, musical or artistic work, or the director of a copyright film, to be identified as the author/director, largely whenever the work is commercially exploited (s.77). See *Sawkins*.

However, the right does not arise unless it has been 'asserted' by appropriate words in writing, or in the case of an artistic work by ensuring that the artist's name appears on the frame, etc (see end). There are exceptions to the right, in particular where first ownership of the copyright vested in the author's or director's employer.

The right of 'integrity' protects work from 'derogatory treatment', meaning an addition to, deletion from, alteration or adaptation of a work which amounts to distortion or mutilation of the work or is otherwise prejudicial to the honour or reputation of the author/director. Again, infringement of the right takes place when the maltreated work is published commercially or performed or exhibited in public. There are various exceptions set out in s.81 of the Act, in particular where the publication is in a newspaper, etc, and the work was made for inclusion in it or made available with the author's consent.

Where the copyright in the work vested first in the author's or director's employer, he or she has no right to 'integrity' unless identified at the time of the relevant act or on published copies of the work.

These rights subsist for as long as the copyright in the work subsists.

A third moral right conferred by the Act is not to have a literary, dramatic, musical or artistic work falsely attributed to one as author, or to have a film falsely attributed to one as director, again where the work in question is published, etc. This right subsists until 20 years after a person's death.

None of these rights can be assigned during the person's lifetime, but all of them either pass on the person's death as directed by his or her will or fall into his residuary estate.

A fourth but rather different moral right is conferred by s.85. It gives a person who has commissioned the taking of photographs for private purposes a right to prevent copies of the work being issued to the public, etc.

The remedies for breach of these moral rights again include damages and an injunction, although s.103(2) specifically foresees the granting of an injunction qualified by a right to the defendant to do the acts complained of, if subject to a suitable disclaimer.

Moral rights are exercisable in relation to works in which the copyright has revived subject to any waiver or assertion of the right made before 1 January 1996 (see details as to who may exercise rights in paragraph 22 of the Regulations).

NOTICE

AMANDA LOUISE MICHAELS hereby asserts and gives notice of her right under s.77 of the Copyright, Designs & Patents Act 1988 to be identified as the author of the foregoing article.

AMANDA MICHAELS

Amanda L. Michaels is a barrister in private practice in London, and specialises in copyright, designs, trade marks, and similar intellectual property and 'media' work. She is author of *A Practical Guide to Trade Mark Law* (Sweet & Maxwell, 3rd edn 2002).

Further reading

Bainbridge, David, *Intellectual Property*, Longman, 6th edn, 2005

Flint, *A User's Guide to Copyright*, Tottel Publishing, 2005

Garnett, Rayner James and Davies, *Copinger and Skone James on Copyright*, Sweet & Maxwell, 15th edn, 2004

Copyright Acts

Copyright, Designs and Patents Act 1998 (but it is vital to use an up-to-date amended version)

The Duration of Copyright and Rights in Performances Regulations 1995 (SI 1995 No 3297)

The Copyright and Related Rights Regulations 2003 (SI 2003 No 2498)

The Intellectual Property (Enforcement, etc) Regulations 2006 (SI 2006 No 1028)

The Performances (Moral Rights, etc) Regulations 2006 (SI 2006 No 18)

see also Numerous Orders in Council

Council Regulation 6/2002

The Copyright Licensing Agency Ltd

The Copyright Licensing Agency (CLA) collects and distributes money on behalf of artists, writers and publishers for the copying, scanning and emailing of their work. CLA operates on a non-profit basis, and issues licences to schools, further and higher education, business and government bodies so that such organisations can access the copyright material in books, journals, law reports, magazines and periodicals.

Why was CLA established?

CLA was established in 1982 by its members, the Authors' Licensing and Collecting Society (ALCS) and the Publishers Licensing Society (PLS) to promote and enforce the intellectual property rights of British rightsholders both at home and abroad. CLA also has an agency agreement with the Design and Artists Copyright Society (DACS), which represents artists and illustrators.

Further information

The Copyright Licensing Agency Ltd
Saffron House, 6–10 Kirby Street, London
EC1N 8TS
tel 020-7400 3100 *fax* 020-7400 3101
email cla@cla.co.uk
CBC House, 24 Canning Street, Edinburgh
EH3 8E9
tel 0131-272 2711 *fax* 0131-272 2811
email clascotland@cla.co.uk
website www.cla.co.uk

ALCS has two corporate members – the Society of Authors and the Writers' Guild of Great Britain. It also has a large number of individual authors as members and affiliations with the National Union of Journalists and the Chartered Institute of Journalists. PLS members are the Publishers Association, the Periodical Publishers Association and the Association of Learned and Professional Society Publishers.

How CLA helps artists and writers

CLA allows licensed users access to millions of titles worldwide. In return CLA ensures artists and writers, along with publishers, are fairly recompensed by the licence fees, which CLA collects and forwards to its members for onward distribution to artists, writers and publishers.

The collective management of licensing schemes means that CLA can provide users with the simplest and most cost-effective means of obtaining authorisation for photocopying, while copy limits ensure fair recompense is maintained for rightsholders.

CLA is has developed licences which enable digitisation of existing print material. The licence enables users to scan and electronically send extracts from copyright works.

Licence to copy

CLA's licensees fall into three main categories:
- education (schools, further and higher education);
- government (central, local, public bodies); and
- business (business, industry, professionals).

CLA develops licences to meet the specific needs of each sector and groupings within each sector. Depending on the requirement, there are both blanket and transactional licences available. Every licence allows the photocopying of most books, journals, magazines and periodicals published in the UK.

An international dimension

Many countries have established equivalents to CLA and the number of such agencies is set to grow. Nearly all these agencies, including CLA, are members of the International Federation of Reproduction Rights Organisations (IFRRO).

Through reciprocal arrangements with these organisations, any CLA licence also allows copying from an expanding list of publications in other countries. Currently these countries are: Australia, Austria, Belgium, Brazil, Canada (including Quebec), Denmark, Finland, France, Germany, Greece, Iceland, Ireland, Italy, Japan, Kenya, Malta, The Netherlands, New Zealand, Norway, South Africa, Spain, Sweden, Switzerland, the USA and Zimbabwe.

CLA receives monies from these organisations for the copying of UK material abroad and forwards it to rightsholders.

Distribution

The fees collected from licensees are forwarded to artists, authors and publishers via ALCS, DACS and PLS respectively, and are based on statistical surveys and records of copying activity. For the year 2004/5 £41 million was distributed to rightsholders.

Respecting copyright

CLA also believes it is important to raise awareness of the copyright in published material and the need to protect the creativity of artists, authors and publishers. To this end, CLA organises a range of activities such as copyright workshops in schools, seminars for businesses and institutions and an extensive exhibition programme. A comprehensive website is regularly updated and a bi-annual newsletter, *Clarion*, is posted to all licensees and to those individuals and groups concerned with copyright. A downloadable version is also available on the CLA website (www.cla.co.uk/clarion).

Protecting the value of creativity

CLA believes in working together with all sectors to take into account their differing needs, meaning legal action is rare. However, organisations – especially in the business sector – need to be made aware that copyright is a legally enforceable right enshrined in statute law, not a voluntary option. CLA's compliance division aims to continue the education programme. However, as a last resort it has the power to take legal proceedings on behalf of rightsholders.

Authors' Licensing and Collecting Society

The Authors' Licensing and Collecting Society is the rights management society for UK writers.

The Authors' Licensing and Collecting Society (ALCS) is the UK collective rights management society for writers. Established in 1977, the Society represents the interests of all UK writers and aims to ensure that they are fairly compensated for any works that are copied, broadcast or recorded.

A non-profit company, ALCS was set up in the wake of the campaign to establish a Public Lending Right to help writers protect and exploit their collective rights. Today, it is the largest writers' organisation in the UK with a membership of over 53,000 and an annual distribution of over £14 million in royalties to writers.

The Society is committed to ensuring that the rights of writers, both intellectual property and moral, are fully respected and fairly rewarded. It represents all types of writers and includes educational, research and academic authors drawn from the professions; scriptwriters, adaptors, playwrights, poets, editors and freelance journalists, across the print and broadcast media.

Internationally recognised as a leading authority on copyright matters and authors' interests, ALCS is committed to fostering an awareness of intellectual property issues among the writing community. It maintains a close watching brief on all matters affecting copyright both in the UK and internationally and makes regular representations to the UK government and the European Union.

ALCS works closely with the Writers' Guild of Great Britain, the Society of Authors and by reciprocal agreement with over 50 collecting societies overseas. Owned and controlled by writers, it is governed by a non-executive board of 12 directors, all of whom are working writers. Four of these directors are nominated by the Writers' Guild of Great Britain and four by the Society of Authors. The other four independent members are elected directly by ALCS Ordinary Members.

The Society collects fees that are difficult, time-consuming or legally impossible for writers and their representatives to claim on an individual basis, money that is nonetheless due to them. To date, it has distributed over £129 million in secondary royalties to writers.

Membership

Authors' Licensing and Collecting Society Ltd
14–18 Holborn, London EC1N 2LE
tel 020-7395 0600 *fax* 020-7395 0660
email alcs@alcs.co.uk
website www.alcs.co.uk
Chief Executive Owen Atkinson

ALCS membership is open to all writers and successors to their estates at a current annual subscription fee of £10 for Ordinary members. Members of the Society of Authors and the Writers' Guild of Great Britain have free Ordinary membership of ALCS. In addition, members of the National Union of Journalists, Chartered Institute of Journalists, British Association of Journalists and the British Comedy Writers' Association have free Associate membership of ALCS. You may also register direct with ALCS for free Associate membership.

ALCS operations are primarily funded through a commission levied on distributions and membership fees. The commission on funds generated for Ordinary members is currently 10.5%. Writers do not have to become Ordinary members of ALCS to receive funds due to them for the reproduction of their works; however, for Associate members such funds are subject to a levy of 14%. Most writers will find that this, together with a number of other membership benefits, provides excellent value to membership.

Over the years, ALCS has developed highly specialised knowledge and sophisticated systems that can track writers and their works against any secondary use for which they are due payment. A network of international contacts and reciprocal agreements with foreign collecting societies also ensures that British writers are compensated for any similar use overseas.

The primary sources of fees due to writers are secondary royalties from the following:

Photocopying

The single largest source of income, this is administered by the Copyright Licensing Agency (CLA – see page 700). Created in 1982 by ALCS and the Publishers Licensing Society (PLS), the CLA grants licences to users for the copying of books and serials. This includes schools, colleges, universities, central and local government departments as well as the British Library, businesses and other institutions. Licence fees are based on the number of people who benefit and the number of copies made. The revenue from this is then split between the rightsholders: authors, publishers and artists. Money due to authors is transferred to ALCS for distribution. ALCS also receives photocopying payments from foreign sources.

Digitisation

In 1999, the CLA launched its licensing scheme for the digitisation of printed texts. It offers licences to organisations for storing and using digital versions of authors' printed works, which have been scanned into a computer. Again, the fees are split between authors and publishers.

Foreign Public Lending Right

The Public Lending Right (PLR) system pays authors whose books are borrowed from public libraries. Through reciprocal agreements with VG Wort (the German collecting society), Stichting Leenrecht (the Dutch collecting society) and Literar Mechana (the Austrian collecting society) ALCS members receive payment whenever their books are borrowed from German, Dutch and Austrian libraries. (Please note that ALCS does not administer the UK Public Lending Right, this is managed directly by the UK PLR Office; see page 304.)

ALCS also receives other payments from Germany. These cover the loan of academic, scientific and technical titles from academic libraries; extracts of authors' works in textbooks and the press, together with other one-off fees.

Simultaneous cable retransmission

This involves the simultaneous showing of one country's television signals in another country, via a cable network. Cable companies pay a central collecting organisation a percentage of their subscription fees, which must be collectively administered. This sum is then divided by the rightsholders. ALCS receives the writers' share for British programmes containing literary and dramatic material and distributes this to them.

The BBC

ALCS licenses BBC Worldwide Ltd for the inclusion of material within the ALCS repertoire. The licence covers the direct reception and cable retransmission of BBC Prime, a satellite entertainment channel, in Europe and Africa and other countries.

Educational recording

ALCS, together with the main broadcasters and rightsholders, set up the Educational Recording Agency (ERA) in 1989 to offer licences to educational establishments. ERA collects fees from the licensees and pays ALCS the amount due to writers for their literary works.

Other sources of income include a blank tape levy and small, miscellaneous literary rights.

Tracing authors

ALCS is dedicated to protecting and promoting authors' rights and enabling writers to maximise their income. It is committed to ensuring that royalties due to writers are efficiently collected and speedily distributed to them. One of its greatest challenges is finding some of the writers for whom it holds funds and ensuring that they claim their money.

Any published author or broadcast writer could have some funds held by ALCS for them. It may be a nominal sum or it could run in to several thousand pounds. Either call or visit the ALCS website – see box for contact details.

Design and Artists Copyright Society

The Design and Artists Copyright Society promotes and protects the copyright and related rights of artists and visual creators in the UK and worldwide.

About DACS

The Design and Artists Copyright Society (DACS) was established in 1984 and is the UK's copyright licensing and collecting society for visual creators. It acts as an agent for its members, offering a range of services for copyright consumers. It also

Contact details

Design and Artists Copyright Society (DACS)
33 Great Sutton Street, London EC1V 0DX
tel 020-7336 8811 *fax* 020-7336 8822
email info@dacs.org.uk
website www.dacs.org.uk

negotiates a share of revenue from collective licensing schemes, on behalf of all visual creators, and distributes this through its Payback service.

DACS membership represents over 36,000 international fine artists, as well as 16,000 commercial photographers, illustrators, craftspeople, cartoonists, architects, animators and designers. It is a not-for-profit organisation that distributes 75% of licensing revenue back to visual creators. A 25% commission is retained to cover administration costs.

About membership

Membership of DACS is open to all visual creators, their heirs and beneficiaries, working in any medium. Members retain ownership and control of their copyright while DACS manages it by negotiating terms and collecting fees on their behalf. Its experienced licensing team works closely with both artists and consumers to ensure the best balance of interests is achieved when licensing works.

About licensing

DACS is quickly growing to be one of the most well-respected art licensing agencies in its field, promoting and protecting the copyright and related rights of artists and visual creators in the UK and worldwide.

Licensing individual rights

DACS provides a range of licensing services for copyright consumers seeking to license the individual rights of an artist for a one-off use: for example, when a publisher wants to reproduce an artistic work in a book.

Licensing clients come from a diverse range of sectors including advertising, publishing, broadcasting, multimedia, product design and merchandising. Members' works have been licensed for everything from greeting cards to film sets, from websites to silk scarves.

Licensing rights collectively

Licences for secondary uses of artistic works are collectively administered under blanket licensing schemes: for example, when a business needs to photocopy pages of books or magazines. DACS negotiates a share of the revenue from these schemes on behalf of visual creators. Money from these schemes is paid back annually through DACS' Payback service.

Artist's Resale Right

The Artist's Resale Right (or *droit de suite*) entitles artists and visual creators to a percentage share of the price every time their work is resold by a gallery, dealer or auction house. The right is applicable to all professional resales and can be transferred to heirs for up to 70 years after the artist's death. DACS collects and distributes resale royalties on behalf of UK artists through the Artist's Resale Right Service Hub.

Copyright advisory service

DACS has a number of free copyright fact sheets available for download at their website (www.dacs.org.uk). Members are also entitled to use DACS' copyright advisory service where advisers can answer copyright enquiries via telephone or email.

Other benefits

DACS belongs to an international network of collecting societies in 27 countries. Visual creators' rights are administered on the same basis in all these countries and they will receive royalties when their work has been reproduced overseas.

Because DACS is an authoritative voice for visual creators' rights in the UK, new members who join will be strengthening the presence of visual creators and their rights in the copyright community as a whole.

Copyright

● Copyright is a right granted to creators under law.
● Copyright in all artistic works is established from the moment of creation – the only qualification is that the work must be original.
● There is no registration system in the UK; copyright comes into operation automatically and lasts the lifetime of the visual creator plus a period of 70 years after their death.
● After death, copyright is usually transferred to the visual creator's heirs or beneficiaries. When the 70-year period has expired, the work then enters the public domain and no longer benefits from copyright protection.
● The copyright owner has the exclusive right to authorise the reproduction (or copy) of a work in any medium by any other party.
● Any reproduction can only take place with the copyright owner's consent. Permission is usually granted in return for a fee, which enables the visual creator to derive some income from other people using his or her work.
● If a visual creator is commissioned to produce a work, he or she will usually retain the copyright unless an agreement is signed which specifically assigns the copyright. When visual creators are employees and create work during the course of their employment, the employer retains the copyright in those works.

See also...

● *Copyright questions,* page 685
● *UK copyright law,* page 688
● *Freelancing for beginners,* page 449

US copyright law

Gavin McFarlane, barrister, introduces US copyright law and points out the differences, and similarities, of British copyright law.

International copyright
International copyright conventions

Further information

US Copyright Office
website www.loc.gov/copyright
Forms for registration, etc can be obtained online.

No general principle of international copyright provides a uniform code for the protection of right owners throughout the world. There are, however, two major international copyright conventions which lay down certain minimum standards for member states, in particular requiring member states to accord to right owners of other member states the same protection which is granted to their own nationals. One is the higher standard Berne Convention of 1886, the most recent revision of which was signed in Paris in 1971. The other is the Universal Copyright Convention signed in 1952 with lower minimum standards, and sponsored by Unesco. This also was most recently revised in Paris in 1971, jointly with the Berne Convention. To this latter Convention the United States has belonged since 1955. On 16 November 1988, the Government of the United States deposited its instrument of accession to the Paris Revision of the Berne Convention. The Convention entered into force as regards the United States on 1 March 1989. Together with certain new statutory provisions made in consequence of accession to Berne, this advances substantially the process of overhaul and modernisation of US copyright law which was begun in the 1970s.

Effect on British copyright owners

The copyright statute of the United States having been brought into line with the requirements of the Berne Convention, compliance with the formalities required by American law has been largely removed. The Berne Convention Implementation Act of 1988 makes statutory amendments to the way foreign works are now treated in US law. These are now inserted in the US codified law as Title 17 – The Copyright Act. 'Foreign works' are works having a country of origin other than the United States. The formalities which were for so long a considerable handicap for foreign copyright owners in the American system have now become optional, though not removed altogether. The new system provides incentives to encourage foreign right owners to continue to comply with formalities on a voluntary basis, in particular notice, renewal and registration.

US copyright law – summary
The current law

The Copyright Statute of the United States was passed on 19 October 1976. The greater part of its relevant provisions came into force on 1 January 1978. It extended the range of copyright protection, and further eased the requirements whereby British authors can obtain copyright protection in America. New Public Law 100–568 of 31 October 1988 made further amendments to the Copyright Statute which were necessary to enable ratification of the Berne Convention to take place. The Universal Copyright Convention is now for all practical purposes moribund. The problems which derived from the old system of common law copyright no longer exist.

The rights of a copyright owner

(1) To reproduce the copyrighted work in copies or phonorecords.

(2) To prepare derivative works based upon the copyrighted work.

(3) To distribute copies or phonorecords of the copyrighted work to the public by sale or other transfer of ownership, or by rental, lease or lending.

(4) In the case of literary, musical, dramatic and choreographic works, pantomimes, and motion pictures and other audiovisual works, but not sound recordings, to perform the copyrighted work publicly. However, in 1995 Congress granted a limited performance right to sound recordings in digital format in an interactive medium.

(5) In the case of literary, musical, dramatic, and choreographic works, pantomimes, and pictorial, graphic, or sculptural works, including the individual images of a motion picture or other audiovisual work, to display the copyrighted work publicly.

(6) By the Record Rental Amendment Act 1984, s.109 of the Copyright Statute is amended. Unless authorised by the owners of copyright in the sound recording and the musical works thereon, the owner of a phonorecord may not, for direct or indirect commercial advantage, rent, lease or lend the phonorecord. A compulsory licence under s.115(c) includes the right of a maker of a phonorecord of non-dramatic musical work to distribute or authorise the distribution of the phonorecord by rental, lease, or lending, and an additional royalty is payable in respect of that. This modifies the 'first sale doctrine', which otherwise permits someone buying a copyright work to hire or sell a lawfully purchased copy to third parties without compensating the copyright owners, and without his or her consent.

(7) A further exception to the 'first sale doctrine' and s.109 of the Copyright Act is made by the Computer Software Rental Amendments Act. A similar restriction has been placed on the unauthorised rental, lease or lending of software, subject to certain limited exceptions. Both the phonorecord and software exceptions to the first sale doctrine terminated, and were extended by Congress on 1 October 1997.

(8) The Semiconductor Chip Protection Act 1984 adds to the Copyright Statute a new chapter on the protection of semiconductor chip products.

(9) The Visual Artists Rights Act 1990 has added moral rights to the various economic rights listed above. These moral rights are the right of integrity, and the right of attribution

Works protected in American law

Works of authorship include:

- Literary works. Note: Computer programs are classified as literary works for the purposes of United States copyright. In *Whelan Associates Inc.* v. *Jaslow Dental Laboratory Inc.* (1987) FSR1, it was held that the copyright of a computer program could be infringed even in the absence of copying of the literal code if the structure was part of the expression of the idea behind a program rather than the idea itself.
- Musical works, including any accompanying words.
- Dramatic works, including any accompanying music.
- Pantomimes and choreographic works.
- Pictorial, graphic and sculptural works.
- Motion pictures and other audiovisual works. Note: copyright in certain motion pictures has been extended by the North American Free Trade Agreement Information Act 1993.
- Sound recordings, but copyright in sound recordings is not to include a right of public performance.
- Architectural works: the design of a building as embodied in any tangible medium of expression, including a building, architectural plans or drawings. The Architectural Works Copyright Protections Act applies this protection to works created on or after 1 December 1990.

or paternity. A new category of 'work of visual art' is defined broadly as paintings, drawings, prints and sculptures, with an upper limit of 200 copies. Works generally exploited in mass market copies such as books, newspapers, motion pictures and electronic information services are specifically excluded from these moral rights provisions. Where they apply, they do so only in respect of works created on or after 1 June 1991, and to certain works previously created where title has not already been transferred by the author.

Manufacturing requirements

With effect from 1 July 1986, these ceased to have effect. Prior to 1 July 1986, the importation into or public distribution in the United States of a work consisting preponderantly of non-dramatic literary material in the English language and protected under American law was prohibited unless the portions consisting of such material had been manufactured in the United States or Canada. This provision did not apply where, on the date when importation was sought or public distribution in the United States was made, the author of any substantial part of such material was not a national of the United States or, if a national, had been domiciled outside the United States for a continuous period of at least one year immediately preceding that date.

Since 1 July 1986, there is no manufacturing requirement in respect of works of British authors. With American ratification of the Berne Convention, the formalities previously required in relation to copyright notice, deposit and registration have been greatly modified.

Formalities

Notice of copyright. Whenever a work protected by the American Copyright Statute is published in the United States or elsewhere by authority of the copyright owner, a notice of copyright should be placed on all publicly distributed copies. This should consist of:

- either the symbol © or the word 'Copyright' or the abbreviation 'Copr.' plus
- the year of first publication of the work, plus
- the name of the copyright owner.

Since the Berne Amendments, both US and works of foreign origin which were first published in the US after 1 March 1989 without having notice of copyright placed on them will no longer be unprotected. In general, authors are advised to place copyright notices on their works, as this is a considerable deterrent to plagiarism. Damages may well be lower in a case where no notice of copyright was placed on the work.

Deposit. The owner of copyright or the exclusive right of publication in a work published with notice of copyright in the United States must within three months of such publication deposit in the Copyright Office for the use or disposition of the Library of Congress two complete copies of the best edition of the work (or two records, if the work is a sound recording). Failure to comply with the deposit requirements does not result in the loss of copyright, but a court could assess fines and issue an injunction.

Registration. Registration for copyright in the United States is optional. However, any owner of copyright in a work first published outside the United States may register a work by making application to the Copyright Office with the appropriate fee, and by depositing one complete copy of the work. This requirement of deposit may be satisfied by using copies deposited for the Library of Congress. Whilst registration is still a requirement for works of US origin and from non-Berne countries as a precondition to filing an infringement action, it is no longer necessary for foreign works from Berne countries. But as a matter of practice there are procedural advantages in any litigation where there has been registration. The United States has interpreted the Berne Convention as allowing formalities which are not in themselves conditions for obtaining copyright protection, but which lead to improved protection. The law allows statutory damages and attorneys' fees only if the work was registered prior to the infringement.

Restoration of copyright
Works by non-US authors which lost copyright protection in the United States because of failure to comply with any of these formalities may have had protection automatically restored in certain circumstances. Works claiming restoration must still be in copyright in their country of origin. If a work succeeds in having copyright restored, it will last for the remainder of the period to which it would originally have been entitled in the United States.

Duration of copyright
Copyright in a work created on or after 1 January 1978 endures for a term of the life of the author, and a period of 70 years after the author's death. The Supreme Court has ruled this extension by Congress is not unconstitutional. The further amendments made by Public Law 100–568 of 31 October 1988 have enabled the government to ratify the higher standard Berne Convention. Copyright in a work created before 1 January 1978, but not published or copyrighted before then, subsists from 1 January 1978, and lasts for the life of the author and a post-mortem period of 70 years.

Any copyright, the first term of which under the previous law was still subsisting on 1 January 1978, shall endure for 28 years from the date when it was originally secured, and the copyright proprietor or his or her representative may apply for a further term of 47 years within one year prior to the expiry of the original term. Until 1992, application for renewal and extension was required. Failure to do so produced disastrous results with some material of great merit passing into the public domain in error. By Public Law 102–307 enacted on 26 June 1992, there is no longer necessity to make a renewal registration in order to obtain the longer period of protection. Now renewal copyright vests automatically in the person entitled to renewal at the end of the 28th year of the original term of copyright.

The duration of any copyright, the renewal term of which was subsisting at any time between 31 December 1976 and 31 December 1977, or for which renewal registration was made between those dates, is extended to endure for a term of 75 years from the date copyright was originally secured.

All terms of copyright provided for by the sections referred to above run to the end of the calendar year in which they would otherwise expire.

Public performance
Under the previous American law provisions relating to performance in public were less generous to right owners than those existing in United Kingdom copyright law. In particular, performance of a musical work was formerly only an infringement if it was 'for profit'. Moreover, the considerable American coin-operated record-playing machine industry (juke boxes) had obtained an exemption from being regarded as instruments of profit, and accordingly their owners did not have to pay royalties for the use of copyright musical works.

Now by the new law one of the exclusive rights of the copyright owner is, in the case of literary, musical, dramatic and choreographic works, pantomimes, and motion pictures and other audiovisual works, to perform the work publicly, without any requirement of such performance being 'for profit'. By s.114 however, the exclusive rights of the owner of copyright in a sound recording are specifically stated not to include any right of public performance, although this provision was modified in 1995.

The position of coin-operated record players (juke boxes) is governed by s.116A, inserted by Public Law 100–568 of 31 October 1988. It covers the position of negotiated licences. Limitations are placed on the exclusive right if licences are not negotiated.

Mechanical right

Where sound recordings of a non-dramatic musical work have been distributed to the public in the United States with the authority of the copyright owner, any other person may obtain a compulsory licence to make and distribute sound recordings of the work. This right is known in the United Kingdom as 'the mechanical right'. Notice must be served on the copyright owner, who is entitled to a royalty in respect of each of his or her works recorded of either two and three fourths cents or one half of one cent per minute of playing time or fraction thereof, whichever amount is the larger. These rates are adjusted periodically by the Copyright Arbitration Royalty Panels (CARP). Failure to serve or file the required notice forecloses the possibility of a compulsory licence and, in the absence of a negotiated licence, renders the making and distribution of such records actionable as acts of infringement.

Transfer of copyright

Under the previous American law copyright was regarded as indivisible, which meant that on the transfer of copyright, where it was intended that only film rights or some other such limited right be transferred, the entire copyright nevertheless had to be passed. This led to a cumbersome procedure whereby the author would assign the whole copyright to his or her publisher, who would return to the author by means of an exclusive licence those rights which it was not meant to transfer.

Now it is provided by s.201(d) of the Copyright Statute that (1) the ownership of a copyright may be transferred in whole or in part by any means of conveyance or by operation of law, and may be bequeathed by will or pass as personal property by the applicable laws of intestate succession, and (2) any of the exclusive rights comprised in a

Copyright: criminal proceedings

- Anyone who infringes a copyright wilfully and for purposes of commercial advantage and private financial gain shall be fined not more than $10,000 or imprisoned for not more than 3 years, or both. However, if the infringement relates to copyright in a sound recording or a film, the infringer is liable to a fine of not more than $250,000 or imprisonment for not more than 5 years or both on a first offence, which can be increased to a fine of up to $250,000 or imprisonment for not more than 10 years or both for a subsequent offence.
- Following a conviction for criminal infringement a court may in addition to these penalties order the forfeiture and destruction of all infringing copies and records, together with implements and equipment used in their manufacture.
- It is an offence knowingly and with fraudulent intent to place on any article a notice of copyright or words of the same purport, or to import or distribute such copies. A fine is provided for this offence of not more than $2500. The fraudulent removal of a copyright notice attracts the same maximum fine, as does the false representation of a material particular on an application for copyright representation.

copyright (including any subdivision of any of the rights set out in 'The rights of a copyright owner' above) may be transferred as provided in (1) above and owned separately. The owner of any particular exclusive right is entitled, to the extent of that right, to all the protection and remedies accorded to the copyright owner by that Statute. This removes the difficulties which existed under the previous law, and brings the position much closer to that existing in the copyright law of the United Kingdom. All transfers and assignments of copyright must be recorded in the US Copyright Office to have legal effect.

Copyright Royalty Judges

In 1993, the Copyright Royalty Tribunal which had been established by the Copyright Act was eliminated by Congress. In its place a new administrative mechanism was established in the Copyright Office with the purpose of making adjustments of reasonable copyright royalty rates in respect of the exercise of certain rights, mainly affecting the musical interests. The Copyright Arbitration Royalty Panels are constituted on an ad hoc basis and perform in the United States a function similar to the Copyright Tribunal in the United Kingdom. However, by the Copyright Royalty and Distribution Reform Act 2004, the CARP system has been phased out. It has been replaced by a system of three Copyright Royalty Judges who began work on 9 January 2006.

The American law spells out the economic objectives which the judges are to apply in calculating the relevant rates. These are:

- to maximise the availability of creative works to the public;
- to afford the copyright owner a fair return for his or her creative work and the copyright user a fair income under existing economic conditions;
- to reflect the relative roles of the copyright owner and the copyright user in the product made available to the public with respect to relative creative contribution, technological contribution, capital investment, cost, risk, and contribution to the opening of new markets for creative expression and media for their communication;
- to minimise any disruptive impact on the structure of the industries involved and on generally prevailing industry practices.

Every final determination of the judges shall be published in the Federal Register. It shall state in detail the criteria that the judges determined to be applicable to the particular proceeding, the facts that they found relevant to their determination in that proceeding, and the reasons for their determination. Any final decision of the judges may be appealed to the United States Court of Appeals within 30 days after its publication in the Federal Register.

Fair use

One of the most controversial factors which held up the revision of the American copyright law for at least a decade was the extent to which a balance should be struck between the desire of copyright owners to benefit from their works by extending copyright protection as far as possible, and the pressure from users of copyright to obtain access to copyright material as cheaply as possible – if not completely freely.

The new law provides by s.107 that the fair use of a copyright work, including such use by reproduction of excerpts, for purposes such as criticism, comment, news reporting, teaching (including multiple copies for classroom use), scholarship or research is not an infringement of copyright. In determining whether the use made of a work is a fair use, the factors to be considered include:

- the purpose and character of the use, including whether such use is of a commercial nature or is for non-profit educational purposes;
- the nature of the copyrighted work;
- the amount and substantiality of the portion used in relation to the copyrighted work as a whole; and
- the effect of the use upon the potential market for or value of the copyrighted work.

It is not an infringement of copyright for a library or archive, or any of its employees acting within the scope of their employment, to reproduce or distribute no more than one copy of a work, if:

- the reproduction or distribution is made without any purpose of direct or indirect commercial advantage;
- the collections of the library or archive are either open to the public or available not only to researchers affiliated with the library or archive or with the institution of which it is a part, but also to other persons doing research in a specialised field; and
- the reproduction or distribution of the work includes a notice of copyright.

It is not generally an infringement of copyright if a performance or display of a work is given by instructors or pupils in the course of face-to-face teaching activities of a non-profit educational institution, in a classroom or similar place devoted to instruction.

Nor is it an infringement of copyright to give a performance of a non-dramatic literary or musical work or a dramatico-musical work of a religious nature in the course of services at a place of worship or other religious assembly.

It is also not an infringement of copyright to give a performance of a non-dramatic literary or musical work other than in a transmission to the public, without any purpose of direct or indirect commercial advantage and without payment of any fee for the performance to any of the performing artists, promoters or organisers if either:

- there is no direct or indirect admission charge; or
- the proceeds, after deducting the reasonable costs of producing the performance, are used exclusively for educational, religious or charitable purposes and not for private financial gain.

In this case the copyright owner has the right to serve notice of objection to the performance in a prescribed form.

Note the important decision of the Supreme Court in *Sony Corporation of America* v. *Universal City Studios* (No. 81–1687, 52 USLW 4090). This decided that the sale of video recorders to the public for the purpose of recording a copyrighted programme from a broadcast signal for private use for time-switching purposes alone (not for archiving or 'librarying') does not amount to contributory infringement of the rights in films which are copied as a result of television broadcasts of them. In 2001 the World Trade Organisation upheld a complaint by the EU that s.110(5)(B) of the US Copyright Act infringes WTO agreements. The US must now abolish its present exemption from public performance royalties for bars, shops and restaurants.

Remedies for copyright owners
Infringement of copyright

Copyright is infringed by anyone who violates any of the exclusive rights referred to in 'The rights of a copyright owner' (above), or who imports copies or records into the United States in violation of the law. The owner of copyright is entitled to institute an action for infringement so long as that infringement is committed while he or she is the owner of the right infringed. Previously, no action for infringement of copyright could be instituted until registration of the copyright claim had been made, but this requirement has been modified now that the United States has ratified the Berne Convention. Under the new provision, US authors must register, or attempt to register, but non-US Berne authors are exempt from this requirement.

Injunctions

Any court having civil jurisdiction under the copyright law may grant interim and final injunctions on such terms as it may deem reasonable to prevent or restrain infringement of copyright. Such injunction may be served anywhere in the United States on the person named. An injunction is operative throughout the whole of the United States, and can be enforced by proceedings in contempt or otherwise by any American court which has jurisdiction over the infringer.

Impounding and disposition

While a copyright action under American law is pending, the court may order the impounding on such terms as it considers reasonable of all copies or records claimed to have been made or used in violation of the copyright owner's exclusive rights; it may also order the impounding of all VCRs, tape recorders, plates, moulds, matrices, masters, tapes, film negatives or other articles by means of which infringing copies or records may be reproduced. A court may order as part of a final judgement or decree the destruction or other disposition of all copies or records found to have been made or used in violation of the copyright owner's exclusive rights. It also has the power to order the destruction of all articles by means of which infringing copies or records were reproduced.

Damages and profits

An infringer of copyright is generally liable either for the copyright owner's actual damage and any additional profits made by the infringer, or for statutory damages.

- The copyright owner is entitled to recover the actual damages suffered by him or her as a result of the infringement, and in addition any profits of the infringer which are attributed to the infringement and are not taken into account in computing the actual damages. In establishing the infringer's profits, the copyright owner is only required to present proof of the infringer's gross revenue; it is for the infringer to prove his or her deductible expenses and the elements of profit attributable to factors other than the copyright work.

- Except where the copyright owner has persuaded the court that the infringement was committed wilfully, the copyright owner may elect, at any time before final judgement is given, to recover, instead of actual damages and profits, an award of statutory damages for all infringements involved in the action in respect of any one work, which may be between $750 and $30,000 according to what the court considers justified.

- Where the copyright owner satisfies the court that the infringement was committed wilfully, the court has the discretion to increase the award of statutory damages to not more than $150,000. Where the infringer succeeds in proving that he or she was not aware and had no reason to believe that his or her acts constituted an infringement of copyright, the court has the discretion to reduce the award of statutory damages to not less than $200.

Costs: time limits

In any civil proceedings under American copyright law, the court may allow the recovery of full costs by or against any party except the Government of the United States. It may also award a reasonable sum in respect of an attorney's fee. No civil or criminal proceedings in respect of copyright law shall be permitted unless begun within three years after the claim or cause of action arose.

Counterfeiting

By the Piracy and Counterfeiting Amendment Act 1982, pirates and counterfeiters of sound recordings and of motion pictures now face maximum penalties of up to five years imprisonment or fines of up to $250,000.

Colouring films

The United States Copyright Office has decided that adding colour to a black and white film may qualify for copyright protection whenever it amounts to more than a trivial change.

Satellite home viewers

The position of satellite home viewers is controlled by the Satellite Home Viewer Act of 1988. (Title II of Public Law 100–667 of 16 November 1988.) The Copyright Remedy Clarification Act has created s.511 of the Copyright Act, in order to rectify a situation which had developed in case law. By this, the component States of the Union, their agencies and employees are placed in the same position as private individuals and entities in relation to their liability for copyright infringement.

Digital Millennium Copyright Act

The US Congress in 1998 passed new legislation to make clear that copyright law applies to all works transmitted, or simply made available to, users over the internet.

This measure is unique in that for the first time it gives its copyright owner the right to control access to the digital work, which is so crucial to security on the internet. To allow the United States to ratify two new WIPO (World Intellectual Property Organisation) treaties – the WIPO Copyright Treaty and the WIPO Performance and Phonograms Treaty, negotiated in 1996 – the Digital Millennium Copyright Act (DMCA) makes two changes in US law. First, it outlaws, with substantial criminal and civil penalties, any tampering with copyright management information – the invisible digital coding embedded on sound recordings, software, motion pictures, and databases that identify the owner of the work and stipulate the price and conditions of use. This encoding will help promote e-commerce and curtail internet piracy.

Second, the DMCA prohibits anyone from disabling anti-copying circuitry in a machine or signal. It also bans the manufacture, sale, and importation of electronic devices that would permit the disabling of that circuitry. The DMCA specifies stiff civil and criminal penalties for acts of circumvention and for the manufacture or sale of the devices.

With the DMCA passed, the United States quickly joined the two new WIPO treaties in the hope that its action would serve as an example to other countries.

General observations

The copyright law of the United States was improved as a result of the statute passed by Congress on 19 October 1976. (Title 17, United States Code.) Apart from lifting the general standards of protection for copyright owners to a higher level than that which previously existed, it has on the whole shifted the balance of copyright protection in favour of the copyright owner and away from the copyright user in many of the areas where controversy existed. But most important for British and other non-American authors and publishers, it has gone a long way towards bringing American copyright law up to the same standards of international protection for non-national copyright proprietors which have long been offered by the United Kingdom and the other major countries, both in Europe and elsewhere in the English-speaking world. The ratification by the United States of the Berne Convention with effect from 1 March 1989 was an action which at that time put American copyright law on par with the protection offered by other major countries.

Gavin McFarlane LLM, PHD is a barrister at Temple Chambers, Cardiff. He specialises in international trade law, and is particularly interested in the involvement of the World Trade Organisation in intellectual property matters.

Libel

Any writer should be aware of the law of libel. Antony Whitaker gives an outline of the main principles, concentrating on points which are most frequently misunderstood. However, specific legal advice should be taken when practical problems arise.

The law discussed is the law of England and Wales. Scotland has its own, albeit somewhat similar, rules. A summary of the main differences between the two systems appears in the box (below). The Defamation Act 1996, designed mainly to streamline and simplify libel litigation, became fully effective in February 2000.

Libel: liability to pay damages

English law draws a distinction between defamation published in permanent form and that which is not. The former is libel, the latter slander. 'Permanent form' includes writing, printing, drawings and photographs and radio and television broadcasts. It follows that it is the law of libel rather than slander which most concerns writers and artists professionally, and the slightly differing rules applicable to slander will not be mentioned in this article.

Publication of a libel can result in a civil action for damages, an injunction to prevent repetition and/or in certain cases a criminal prosecution against those responsible, who include the author (or artist or photographer), the publishers and the editor, if any, of the publication in which the libel appeared. 'Innocent disseminators', such as printers, distributors, broadcasters, internet service providers and retailers, who can show they took reasonable care and had no reason to believe what they were handling contained a libel, are protected under the 1996 Act. Prosecutions are rare. Certain special rules apply to them and these will be explained below after a discussion of the question of civil liability, which in practice arises much more frequently.

Libel claims do not qualify for legal aid, unless the Legal Services Commission considers a case incapable of being fairly tried without it. But the closely analogous remedy of malicious falsehood does so qualify. Most libel cases are usually heard by a judge and jury, and it is the jury which decides the amount of any award, which is tax-free. It is not necessary for the plaintiff to prove that he or she has actually suffered any loss, because the law presumes damage. While the main purpose of a libel claim is to compensate the plaintiff for the injury to his or her reputation, a jury may give additional sums either as 'aggravated' damages, if it appears a defendant has behaved malevolently or spitefully, or as 'exemplary' or 'punitive', damages where a defendant hopes the economic advantages of publication will outweigh any sum awarded. Damages can also be 'nominal' if the libel complained of is trivial. It is generally very difficult to forecast the amounts juries are likely to award, though awards against newspapers disclose a tendency towards considerable generosity. The Court of Appeal has power to reduce excessive awards of damages.

In an action for damages for libel, it is for the plaintiff to establish that the matter he or she complains of has been published by the defendant; refers to the plaintiff; and is defamatory. If this is done, the plaintiff establishes a *prima facie* case. However, the defendant will escape liability if he or she can show he has a good defence. There are five defences to a libel action. They are: Justification; Fair Comment; Privilege; Offer of Amends: ss.2–4 of the Defamation Act, 1996; Apology, etc, under the Libel Acts, 1843 and 1845. A libel claim can also become barred under the Limitation Acts, as explained below. These matters must now be examined in detail.

The plaintiff's case

The meaning of 'published'

'Published' in the legal sense means communicated to a person other than the plaintiff. Thus the legal sense is wider than the lay sense but includes it. It follows that the content of a book is published in the legal sense when the manuscript is first sent to the publishing firm just as much as it is when the book is later placed on sale to the public. Subject to the 'innocent dissemination' defence referred to above, both types of publication are sufficient for the purpose of establishing liability for libel, but the law differentiates between them, since the scope of publication can properly be taken into account by the jury in considering the actual amount of damages to award. Material placed on the internet is unquestionably 'published' there, with a potential audience of millions worldwide. The extent of publication can be judged by the number of visits made to the relevant website. If challenged as defamatory, it is generally wise to remove such material, in order to block potential claims of continuing publication. It should be noted that Internet Service Providers can compel website operators to identify the authors of defamatory material anonymously posted to their discussion boards.

Establishing identity

The plaintiff must also establish that the matter complained of refers to him or her. It is of course by no means necessary to mention a person's name before it is clear that he or she is referred to. Nicknames by which he or she is known or corruptions of his name are just two ways in which his or her identity can be indicated. There are more subtle methods. The sole question is whether the plaintiff is indicated to those who read the matter complained of. In some cases he or she will not be unless it is read in the light of facts known to the reader from other sources, but this is sufficient for the plaintiff's purpose. The test is purely objective and does not depend at all on whether the writer intended to refer to the plaintiff.

English and Scottish law

Much of the terminology of the Scots law of defamation differs from that of English law, and in certain minor respects the law itself is different. North of the border, libel and slander are virtually indistinguishable, both as to the nature of the wrongs and their consequences; and Scots law does not recognise the offence of criminal libel. Where individual English litigants enjoy absolute privilege for what they say in court, their Scottish counterparts have only qualified privilege. 'Exemplary', or 'punitive', damages are not awarded by the Scottish courts. Until recently, libel cases in Scotland were for the most part heard by judges sitting alone, but there is now a marked trend towards trial by jury, which has been accompanied by a significant increase in the levels of damages awarded.

It is because it is impossible to establish reference to any individual that generalisations, broadly speaking, are not successfully actionable. To say boldly 'All lawyers are crooks' does not give any single lawyer a cause of action, because the statement does not point a finger at any individual. However, if anyone is named in conjunction with a generalisation, then it may lose its general character and become particular from the context. Again, if one says 'One of the X Committee has been convicted of murder' and the X Committee consists of, say, four persons, it cannot be said that the statement is not actionable because no individual is indicated and it could be referring to any of the committee. This is precisely why it is actionable at the suit of each of them as suspicion has been cast on all. Subject to the same proviso that individuals are in no way identified, it has been a rule of public policy since 1993 that government departments, whether national or local, cannot sue for libel.

Determining what is defamatory

It is for the plaintiff to show that the matter complained of is defamatory. What is defamatory is decided by the jury except in the extreme cases where the judge rules that the words cannot bear a defamatory meaning. Various tests have been laid down for determining this. It is sufficient that any one test is satisfied. The basic tests are:

- Does the matter complained of tend to lower the plaintiff in the estimation of society?
- Does it tend to bring him or her into hatred, ridicule, contempt, dislike or disesteem with society?
- Does it tend to make him shunned or avoided or cut off from society? The mere fact that what is published is inaccurate is not enough to involve liability; it is the adverse impact on the plaintiff's reputation that matters. For example, merely to overstate a person's income is not defamatory; but it will be if the context implies he has not fully declared it to the tax authorities.

'Society' means right-thinking members of society generally. It is by reference to such people that the above tests must be applied. A libel action against a newspaper which had stated that the police had taken a statement from the plaintiff failed, notwithstanding that the plaintiff gave evidence that his apparent assistance to the police (which he denied) had brought him into grave disrepute with the underworld. It was not by their wrongheaded standards that the matter fell to be judged.

Further, it is not necessary to imply that the plaintiff is at fault in some way in order to defame him. To say of a woman that she has been raped or of someone that he is insane imputes to them no degree of blame, but nonetheless both statements are defamatory. Lawyers disagree over whether the claim that an individual is 'ugly' is, or could be, defamatory.

Sometimes a defamatory meaning is conveyed by words which on the face of them have no such meaning. 'But Brutus is an honourable man' is an example. If a jury finds that words are meant ironically they will consider this ironical sense when determining whether the words are defamatory. In deciding, therefore, whether or not the words are defamatory, the jury seeks to discover what, without straining the words or putting a perverse construction on them, they will be understood to mean. In some cases this may differ substantially from their literal meaning.

Matter may also be defamatory by innuendo. Strictly so called, an innuendo is a meaning that words acquire by virtue of facts known to the reader but not stated in the passage complained of. Words, quite innocent on the face of them, may acquire a defamatory meaning when read in the light of these facts. For example, where a newspaper published a photograph of a man and a woman, with the caption that they had just announced their engagement, it was held to be defamatory of the man's wife since those who knew that she had cohabited with him were led to the belief that she had done so only as his mistress. The newspaper was unaware that the man was already married, but some of its readers were not. In general, however, imputations of unchastity against members of either sex would today be regarded as far less defamatory than they were in 1929 when this case was decided.

Defences to a libel action

Quite apart from the provisions concerning statutory apologies mentioned below, a swift and well publicised apology will always go some way towards assuaging injured feelings and help reduce an award of damages.

Justification

English law does not protect the reputation that a person either does not or should not possess. Stating the truth therefore does not incur liability, and the plea of justification – namely, that what is complained of is true in substance and in fact – is a complete answer to an action for damages. However, this defence is by no means to be undertaken lightly. For instance, to prove one instance of using bad language will be insufficient to justify the allegation that a person is 'foulmouthed'. It would be necessary to prove several instances, and the defendant is obliged in most cases to particularise in his pleadings giving details, dates and places. However, the requirement that the truth of every allegation must be proved is not absolute, and is qualified by the 'multiple charge – no worse off' defence. This applies where two or more distinct charges are levelled against a plaintiff, and some of what is said turns out to be inaccurate. If his or her reputation in the light of what is shown to be true is made no worse by the unprovable defamatory allegations – for example, mistaken accusations that a convicted pickpocket and car thief is also a shoplifter – the publisher will be safe. This is the extent of the law's recognition that some individuals are so disreputable as to be beyond redemption by awards of damages regardless of what is said about them. Subject to this, however, it is for the defendant to prove that what he or she has published is true, not for the plaintiff to disprove it, though if he can do so, so much the better for him.

One point requires special mention. It is insufficient for the defendant to prove that he or she has accurately repeated what a third person has written or said or that such statements have gone uncontradicted when made on occasions in the past. If X writes 'Y told me that Z is a liar', it is no defence to an action against X merely to prove that Y did say that. X has given currency to a defamatory statement concerning Z and has so made it his own. His only defence is to prove that Z is a liar by establishing a number of instances of Z's untruthfulness. Nor does it help a defence of justification to prove that the defendant genuinely believed what he or she published to be true. This may, however, form part of a qualified privilege defence (see below), and might well be a complete answer in an action, other than a libel action, based on a false but non-defamatory statement. For such statements do not incur liability in the absence of fraud or malice which, in this context, means a dishonest or otherwise improper motive. Bona fide belief, however, may be relevant to the assessment of damages, even in a libel action.

Special care should be taken in relation to references to a person's convictions, however accurately described. Since the Rehabilitation of Offenders Act, 1974, a person's less serious convictions may become 'spent' and thereafter it may involve liability to refer to them. Reference to the Act and orders thereunder must be made in order to determine the position in any particular case.

Fair comment

It is a defence to prove that what is complained of is fair comment made in good faith and without malice on a matter of public interest. 'Fair' in this context means 'honest'. 'Fair comment' means therefore the expression of the writer's genuinely held opinion. It does not necessarily mean opinion with which the jury agree. Comment may therefore be quite extreme and still be 'fair' in the legal sense. However, if it is utterly perverse the jury may be led to think that no one could have genuinely held such views. In such a case the defence would fail, for the comment could not be honest. 'Malice' here covers any dishonest or improper motive but, in contrast to its application in the context of qualified privilege (see below), it does not include actuation by spite or animosity, even if this is the dominant or sole motive. Care should, however, be taken since evidence of such motivation could also be seen as a lack of genuine belief in the view expressed.

The defence only applies when what is complained of is comment as distinct from a statement of fact. The line between comment and fact is notoriously difficult to draw in some cases. Comment means a statement of opinion. The facts on which comment is made must be stated together with the comment or be sufficiently indicated with it. This is merely another way of saying that it must be clear that the defamatory statement is one of opinion and not of fact, for which the only defence would be the onerous one of justification. The exact extent to which the facts commented on must be stated or referred to is a difficult question, but some help may be derived in answering it by considering the purpose of the rule, which is to enable the reader to exercise his own judgement and to agree or disagree with the comment. It is quite plain that it is not necessary to state every single detail of the facts. In one case it was sufficient merely to mention the name of one of the Press lords in an article about a newspaper though not one owned by him. He was so well known that to mention his name indicated the substratum of fact commented upon, namely his control of his group of newspapers. No universal rule can be laid down, except that, in general, the fuller the facts set out or referred to with the comment, the better. All these facts must be proved to be true subject, however, to the flexibility of the 'proportionate truth' rule. This means that the defence remains available even if, for example, only three out of five factual claims can be proved true, provided that these three are by themselves sufficient to sustain, and are proportionate to, the fairness of the comment. The impact of the two unproven claims would probably fall to be assessed in accordance with the 'multiple charge – no worse off' rule in justification, set out above.

The defence only applies where the matters commented on are of public interest, i.e. of legitimate concern to the public or a substantial section of it. Thus the conduct of national and local government, international affairs, the administration of justice, etc, are all matters of public interest, whereas other people's private affairs may very well not be, although they undoubtedly interest the public, or provoke curiosity.

In addition, matters of which criticism has been expressly or impliedly invited, such as publicly performed plays and published books, are a legitimate subject of comment. Criticism need not be confined merely to their artistic merit but equally may deal with the attitudes to life and the opinions therein expressed.

It is sometimes said that a man's moral character is never a proper subject of comment for the purpose of this defence. This is certainly true where it is a private individual who is concerned, and some authorities say it is the same in the case of a public figure even though his or her character may be relevant to his or her public life. Again, it may in some cases be exceeding the bounds of fair comment to impute a dishonourable motive to a person, as is frequently done by way of inference from facts. In general, the imputation is a dangerous and potentially expensive practice.

Privilege

Privilege in the law of libel is either 'absolute' or 'qualified', and denotes the two levels of protection from liability afforded, in the public interest, to defamatory statements made on certain occasions. Absolute privilege – where the individual defamed has no remedy whatever – has applied to Parliamentary papers published by the direction of either House, or full republications thereof, since early in the 19th century. Following the implementation of section 14 of the 1996 Defamation Act, this privilege also applies to fair, accurate and contemporaneous reports of public judicial proceedings in the United Kingdom, the European Courts of Justice and Human Rights, and any international criminal tribunal established by the Security Council.

Qualified privilege confers protection provided publication is made only for the reason that the privilege is given and not for some wrongful or indirect motive. In October 1999 the House of Lords extended the defence to protect publications where a defamatory mistake on a matter of public concern has been made by a writer or journalist who can show he did his best to uncover the truth. He must show he acted responsibly in a number of ways, which include checking his sources and, where appropriate, seeking the potential plaintiff's comments, who must be given an adequate opportunity to respond. A series of recent decisions shows that the defence imposes a tightrope discipline with which it is often difficult to comply.

The defence also applies, under section 15 of the Act, to fair and accurate reports of public proceedings before a legislature, a court, a government inquiry and an international organisation or conference anywhere in the world, and of certain documents, or extracts from such documents, issued by those bodies. While there is no requirement to correct or publish explanations concerning these reports, such an obligation does arise under section 15 in respect of a separate category of reports of notices issued by various bodies within the European Community and of proceedings of certain bodies or organisations within the United Kingdom. Apart from the Act, such privilege also attaches to extracts from Parliamentary papers and fair and accurate reports of Parliamentary proceedings.

This list of privileged occasions is by no means exhaustive, and the second category may now be expanded by an order of the Lord Chancellor. The privilege defence is extended to the media generally, rather than being restricted, as it was hitherto, simply to newspapers.

Offers of Amends under the 1996 Act

Sections 2, 3 and 4 of the 1996 Act offer a flexible method of nipping in the bud potential libel actions by those who have been unintentionally defamed. The range of libel meanings for which this defence caters is much wider than that previously available. It envisages the payment of damages as well as costs, together with the offer of a correction and apology, and the damages figure will be fixed by a judge if the parties cannot agree. He or she will do this bearing in mind the generosity of the correction and apology, and the extent of its publication. While recourse to this defence excludes reliance on the defences of justification, privilege and fair comment, it offers a considerable incentive to settle complaints and will save substantially on costs.

Apology under 1843 and 1845 Acts

This defence is rarely utilised, since if any condition of it is not fulfilled, the plaintiff must succeed and the only question is the actual amount of damages. It only applies to actions in respect of libels in newspapers and periodicals. The defendant pleads that the libel was inserted without actual malice and without gross negligence and that before the action commenced or as soon afterwards as possible he inserted a full apology in the same newspaper, etc, or had offered to publish it in a newspaper, etc, of the plaintiff's choice, where the original newspaper is published at intervals greater than a week. Further a sum must be paid into court with this defence to compensate the plaintiff.

'Fast-track disposal' procedure

In its recognition of the generally cumbersome nature of libel litigation, the 1996 Act provides a simplified mechanism for dealing with less serious complaints. Sections 8, 9 and 10 enable a judge alone to dismiss unrealistic claims at the outset; and he will also be able to dispose 'summarily' of relatively minor, but well-founded, claims, on the basis of an award of up to £10,000, a declaration that the publication was libellous, an order for an apology and an order forbidding repetition.

Limitation and death

The 1996 Act has reduced from three years to one the period within which a libel action must generally be started if it is not to become 'statute-barred' through lapse of time. But successive and subsequent publications, such as the issue of later editions of the same book, or the sale of surplus copies of an old newspaper, or the failure to remove libellous material from the internet, can give rise to fresh claims.

Civil claims for libel cannot be brought on behalf of the dead. If an individual living plaintiff or defendant in a libel case dies before the jury gives their verdict, the action 'abates', i.e. comes to an end, so far as their involvement is concerned, and no rights arising out of it survive either for or against their personal representatives.

Insurance

For an author, the importance of at least an awareness of this branch of law lies first, in the fact that most book contracts contain a clause enabling the publisher to look to him should any libel claims result; and second, in the increasingly large awards of damages. It is therefore advisable to check what libel insurance a publisher carries, and whether it also covers the author who, if he or she is to have the benefit of it, should always alert the publisher to any potential risk. This insurance for authors can now only be obtained through an insurance broker registered with the Financial Services Authority, and one such company is Royal Sun Alliance, Professional and Financial Risks, 4th Floor, Leadenhall Court, Leadenhall Street, London EC3V 1PP (*tel* 020-7283 9000). Premiums start at £1000, and can be substantially higher if the book is tendentious or likely to be controversial. The company generally insists on the author obtaining, and paying for, a legal opinion first. Indemnity limits vary between £250,000 and £1 million, and the author is required to bear at least the first £5000 of any loss. It is worth remembering that 'losses' include legal costs as well as damages, which they can often exceed.

Criminal liability in libel

Whereas the object of a civil action is to obtain compensation for the wrong done or to prevent repetition, the object of criminal proceedings is to punish the wrongdoer by fine or imprisonment or both. There are four main types of writing which may provoke a prosecution: defamatory libel; obscene publications; sedition and incitement to racial hatred; and blasphemous libel.

Defamatory libel

The publication of defamatory matter is in certain circumstances a crime as well as a civil wrong. But whereas the principal object of civil proceedings will normally be to obtain compensation, the principal object of a criminal prosecution will be to secure punishment of the accused, for example by way of a fine. Prosecutions are rare. There are important differences between the rules applicable to criminal libel and its civil counterpart. For example, a criminal libel may be 'published' even though only communicated to the person defamed and may be found to have occurred even where the person defamed is dead, or where only a group of persons but no particular individual has been maligned. During election campaigns, it is an 'illegal practice' to publish false statements about the personal character or conduct of a candidate irrespective of whether they are also defamatory.

Obscene publications

It is an offence to publish obscene matter. By the Obscene Publications Act, 1959, matter is obscene if its effect is such as to tend to deprave and corrupt persons who are likely, having regard to all relevant circumstances, to read, see or hear it. 'To deprave and corrupt' is to be distinguished from 'to shock and disgust'. It is a defence to a prosecution to prove that publication of the matter in question is justified as being for the public good, on the ground that it is in the interests of science, literature, art or learning, or of other objects of general concern. Expert evidence may be given as to its literary, artistic, scientific or other merits. Playwrights, directors and producers should note that the Theatres Act, 1968, though designed to afford similar protection to stage productions, does not necessarily prevent prosecutions for indecency under other statutes.

Sedition/incitement to racial hatred

Writings which tend to destroy the peace of the realm may be prosecuted as being seditious or as amounting to incitement to racial hatred. Seditious writings include those which advocate reform by unconstitutional or violent means or incite contempt or hatred for the monarch or Parliament. These institutions may be criticised stringently, but not in a manner which is likely to lead to insurrection or civil commotion or indeed any physical force. Prosecutions are a rarity, but it should be remembered that writers of matter contemptuous of the House of Commons, though not prosecuted for seditious libel are, from time to time, punished by that House for breach of its privileges, although, if a full apology is made, it is often an end of the matter. The Public Order Act 1986 makes it an offence, irrespective of the author's or publisher's intention, to publish, or put on plays containing, threatening, abusive or insulting matter if hatred is likely to be stirred up against any racial group in Great Britain or elsewhere. When brought into force, which is likely to be within a year of its enactment in February 2006, the Racial and Religious Hatred Act will penalise publication to incite hatred. The Terrorism Act 2006, enforced since 13 April 2006, makes it an offence to publish material encouraging or glorifying acts of terrorism.

Blasphemous libel

Blasphemous libel consists in the vilification of the Christian religion or its ceremonies. The offence lies essentially in the impact of what is said concerning, for instance, God, Christ, the Bible, the Book of Common Prayer, etc; it is irrelevant that the publisher does not intend to shock or arouse resentment. While temperate and sober writings on religious topics however anti-Christian in sentiment will not involve liability, if the discussion is 'so scurrilous and offensive as to pass the limit of decent controversy and to outrage any Christian feeling', it will.

Antony Whitaker OBE is a barrister and an independent media legal adviser; *email* blairwhitaker@lineone.net

Finance for writers and artists
FAQs for writers

Peter Vaines, a chartered accountant and barrister, addresses some frequently asked questions.

What can a working writer claim against tax?

A working writer is carrying on a business and can therefore claim all the expenses which are incurred wholly and exclusively for the purposes of that business. A list showing most of the usual expenses can be found in the article on *Income tax*, starting on page 728 of this *Yearbook*, but there will be other expenses that can be allowed in special circumstances.

Strictly, only expenses which are incurred for the sole purpose of the business can be claimed; there must be no 'duality of purpose' so an item of expenditure cannot be divided into private and business parts. However, HM Revenue & Customs (formerly the Inland Revenue) is usually quite flexible and is prepared to allow all reasonable expenses (including apportioned sums) where the amounts can be commercially justified.

Allowances can also be claimed for the cost of business assets such as a motor car, personal computers, fax, copying machines and all other equipment (including books) which may be used by the writer. An allowance of 25% of the cost can be claimed on the reducing balance each year and for most assets (except cars) an allowance of 50% can be claimed in the first year of purchase. Some expenditure on information technology now benefits from a special 100% allowance. See the article on *Income tax*, starting on page 728, for further details of the deductions available in respect of capital expenditure.

Can I request interest on fees owed to me beyond 30 days of my invoice?

Yes. A writer is like any other person carrying on a business and is entitled to charge interest at a rate of 8% over bank base rate on any debt outstanding for more than 30 days – although the period of credit can be varied by agreement between the parties. It is not compulsory to claim the interest; it is up to you to decide whether to enforce the right.

What can I do about bad debts?

A writer is in exactly the same position as anybody else carrying on a business over the payment of his or her invoices. It is generally not commercially sensible to insist on payment in advance but where the work involved is substantial (which will normally be the case with a book), it is usual to receive one third of the fee on signature, one third of the fee on delivery of the manuscript and the remaining one third on publication. On other assignments, perhaps not as substantial as a book, it could be worthwhile seeking 50% of the fee on signature and the other 50% on delivery. This would provide a degree of protection in case of cancellation of the assignment because of changes of policy or personnel at the publisher.

What financial disputes can I take to the Small Claims Court?

If somebody owes you money you can take them to the Small Claims Section of your local County Court, which deals with financial disputes up to £5000. The procedure is much less formal than normal court proceedings and involves little expense. It is not necessary to have a solicitor. You fill in a number of forms, turn up on the day and explain the background to why you are owed the money. See www.courtservice.gov.uk for full details of the procedure.

If I receive an advance, can I divide it between two tax years?

Yes. There used to be a system known as 'spreading' but in 2001 a new system called 'averaging' was introduced. This enables writers (and others engaged in the creation of literary, dramatic works or designs) to average the profits of two or more consecutive years if the profits for one year are less than 75% of the profits for the highest year. This relief can apply even if the work takes less than 12 months to create and it allows the writer to avoid the higher rates of tax which might arise if the income in respect of a number of years' work were all to be concentrated in a single year.

How do I make sure I am taxed as a self-employed person so that tax and National Insurance contributions are not deducted at source?

To be taxed as a self-employed person under Schedule D you have to make sure that the contract for the writing cannot be regarded as a contract of employment. This is unlikely to be the case with a professional author. The subject is highly complex but one of the most important features is that the publisher must not be in a position to direct or control the author's work. Where any doubt exists, the author might find the publisher deducting tax and National Insurance contributions as a precaution and that would clearly be highly disadvantageous. The author would be well advised to discuss the position with the publisher before the contract is signed to agree that he or she should be treated as self-employed and that no tax or National Insurance contributions will be deducted from any payments. If such agreement cannot be reached, professional advice should immediately be sought so that the detailed technical position can be explained to the publisher.

Is it a good idea to operate through a limited company?

It can be a good idea for a self-employed writer to operate through a company but generally only where the income is quite large. The costs of operating a company can outweigh any benefit if the writer is paying tax only at the basic rate. Where the writer is paying tax at the higher rate of 40%, being able to retain some of the income in a company at a tax rate of only 19% is obviously attractive. However, this will be entirely ineffective if the writer's contract with the publisher would otherwise be an employment. The whole subject of operating through a company is complex and professional advice is essential.

When does it become necessary to register for VAT?

Where the writer's self-employed income (from all sources, not only writing) exceeds £61,000 in the previous 12 months or is expected to do so in the next 30 days, he or she must register for VAT and add VAT to all his/her fees. The publisher will pay the VAT to the writer, who must pay the VAT over to the Customs and Excise each quarter. Any VAT the writer has paid on business expenses and on the purchase of business assets can be deducted. It is possible for some authors to take advantage of the simplified system for VAT payments which applies to small businesses. This involves a flat rate payment of VAT without any need to keep records of VAT on expenses.

If I make a loss from my writing can I get any tax back?

Where a writer makes a loss, HM Revenue & Customs may suggest that the writing is only a hobby and not a professional activity thereby denying any relief or tax deduction for the loss. However, providing the writing is carried out on a sensible commercial basis with an expectation of profits, any resulting loss can be offset against any other income the writer may have for the same or the previous year.

Income tax

Despite attempts by successive Governments to simplify our taxation system, the subject has become increasingly complicated. Peter Vaines, a chartered accountant and barrister, gives a broad outline of taxation from the point of view of writers and other creative professionals. The proposals in the March 2006 Budget are broadly reflected in this article.

How income is taxed
Generally

Authors are usually treated for tax purposes as carrying on a profession and are taxed in a similar fashion to other professionals, i.e. as self-employed persons taxed under Schedule D. This article is directed to self-employed persons only, because if a writer is employed he or she will be subject to the much less advantageous rules which apply to employment income.

Attempts are often made by employed persons to shake off the status of 'employee' and to attain 'freelance' status so as to qualify for the advantages of Schedule D, such attempts meeting with varying degrees of success. The problems involved in making this transition are considerable and space does not permit a detailed explanation to be made here – individual advice is necessary if difficulties are to be avoided.

Particular attention has been paid by HM Revenue & Customs to journalists and to those engaged in the entertainment industry with a view to reclassifying them as employees so that PAYE is deducted from their earnings. This blanket treatment has been extended to other areas and, although it is obviously open to challenge by individual taxpayers, it is always difficult to persuade HM Revenue & Customs to change its views.

There is no reason why employed people cannot carry on a freelance business in their spare time. Indeed, aspiring authors, painters, musicians, etc, often derive so little income from their craft that the financial security of an employment, perhaps in a different sphere of activity, is necessary. The existence of the employment is irrelevant to the taxation of the freelance earnings although it is most important not to confuse the income or expenditure of the employment with the income or expenditure of the self-employed activity. HM Revenue & Customs is aware of the advantages which can be derived by an individual having 'freelance' income from an organisation of which he or she is also an employee, and where such circumstances are contrived, it can be extremely difficult to convince an Inspector of Taxes that a genuine freelance activity is being carried on. Where the individual operates through a company or partnership providing services personally to a particular client, and would be regarded as an employee if the services were supplied directly by the individual, additional problems arise from the notorious IR35 legislation and professional advice is essential.

For those starting in business or commencing work on a freelance basis HM Revenue & Customs produces a very useful booklet, *Starting in Business (IR28)*, which is available from any tax office.

Income

For income to be taxable it need not be substantial, nor even the author's only source of income; earnings from casual writing are also taxable but this can be an advantage, because occasional writers do not often make a profit from their writing. The expenses incurred in connection with writing may well exceed any income receivable and the resultant loss may then be used to reclaim tax paid on other income. There may be deducted from the income certain allowable expenses and capital allowances which are set out in more detail below. The possibility of a loss being used as a basis for a tax repayment is fully appreciated by HM Revenue & Customs, which sometimes attempts to treat casual writing as a hobby so that any losses incurred cannot be used to reclaim tax; of course by the same token any income receivable would not be chargeable to tax. This treatment may sound attractive but it should be resisted vigorously because HM Revenue & Customs does not hesitate to change its mind when profits begin to arise. In the case of exceptional or non-recurring writing, such as the autobiography of a sports personality or the memoirs of a politician, it could be better to be treated as pursuing a hobby and not as a professional author. Sales of copyright cannot be charged to income tax unless the recipient is a professional author. However, the proceeds of sale of copyright may be charged to capital gains tax, even by an individual who is not a professional author.

Royalties

Where the recipient is a professional author, a series of cases has laid down a clear principle that sales of copyright are taxable as income and not as capital receipts. Similarly, lump sums on account of, or in advance of royalties are also taxable as income in the year of receipt, subject to a claim for averaging relief (see below).

Arts Council awards

Arts Council category A awards

- Direct or indirect musical, design or choreographic commissions and direct or indirect commission of sculpture and paintings for public sites.
- The Royalty Supplement Guarantee Scheme.
- The contract writers' scheme.
- Jazz bursaries.
- Translators' grants.
- Photographic awards and bursaries.
- Film and video awards and bursaries.
- Performance Art Awards.
- Art Publishing Grants.
- Grants to assist with a specific project or projects (such as the writing of a book) or to meet specific professional expenses such as a contribution towards copying expenses made to a composer or to an artist's studio expenses.

Arts Council category B awards

- Bursaries to trainee directors.
- Bursaries for associate directors.
- Bursaries to people attending full-time courses in arts administration (the practical training course).
- In-service bursaries to theatre designers and bursaries to trainees on the theatre designers' scheme.
- In-service bursaries for administrators.
- Bursaries for actors and actresses.
- Bursaries for technicians and stage managers.
- Bursaries made to students attending the City University Arts Administration courses.
- Awards, known as the Buying Time Awards, made not to assist with a specific project or professional expenses but to maintain the recipient to enable him or her to take time off to develop his personal talents. These at present include the awards and bursaries known as the Theatre Writing Bursaries, awards and bursaries to composers, awards and bursaries to painters, sculptures and print makers, literature awards and bursaries.

Copyright royalties are generally paid without deduction of income tax. However, if royalties are paid to a person who normally lives abroad, tax must be deducted by the payer or his agent at the time the payment is made unless arrangements are made with HM Revenue & Customs for payments to be made gross under the terms of a Double Taxation Agreement with the other country.

Arts Council grants

Persons in receipt of grants from the Arts Council or similar bodies will be concerned whether or not such grants are liable to income tax. HM Revenue & Customs has issued a Statement of Practice after detailed discussions with the Arts Council regarding the tax treatment of the awards. Grants and other receipts of a similar nature have now been divided into two categories (see box) – those which are to be treated by HM Revenue & Customs as chargeable to tax and those which are not. Category A awards are considered to be taxable; awards made under category B are not chargeable to tax.

This Statement of Practice has no legal force and is used merely to ease the administration of the tax system. It is open to anyone in receipt of a grant or award to disregard the agreed statement and challenge HM Revenue & Customs view on the merits of their particular case. However, it must be recognised that HM Revenue & Customs does not issue such statements lightly and any challenge to their view would almost certainly involve a lengthy and expensive action through the Courts.

The tax position of persons in receipt of literary prizes will generally follow a decision by the Special Commissioners in connection with the Whitbread Book Awards (now called the Costa Book Awards). In that case it was decided that the prize was not part of the author's professional income and accordingly not chargeable to tax. The precise details are not available because decisions of the Special Commissioners were not, at that time, reported unless an appeal was made to the High Court; HM Revenue & Customs chose not to appeal against this decision. Details of the many literary awards that are given each year start on page 561, and this decision is of considerable significance to the winners of each of these prizes. It would be unwise to assume that all such awards will be free of tax as the precise facts which were present in the case of the Whitbread awards may not be repeated in another case; however it is clear that an author winning a prize has some very powerful arguments in his or her favour, should HM Revenue & Customs seek to charge tax on the award.

Allowable expenses

To qualify as an allowable business expense, expenditure has to be laid out wholly and exclusively for business purposes. Strictly there must be no 'duality of purpose', which means that expenditure cannot be apportioned to reflect the private and business usage, e.g. food, clothing, telephone, travelling expenses, etc. However, HM Revenue & Customs does not usually interpret this principle strictly and is prepared to allow all reasonable expenses (including apportioned sums) where the amounts can be commercially justified.

It should be noted carefully that the expenditure does not have to be 'necessary', it merely has to be incurred 'wholly and exclusively' for business purposes. Naturally, however, expenditure of an outrageous and wholly unnecessary character might well give rise to a presumption that it was not really for business purposes. As with all things, some expenses are unquestionably allowable and some expenses are equally unquestionably not allowable – it is the grey area in between which gives rise to all the difficulties and the outcome invariably depends on negotiation with HM Revenue & Customs.

Great care should be taken when claiming a deduction for items where there may be a 'duality of purpose' and negotiations should be conducted with more than usual care and courtesy – if provoked the Inspector of Taxes may well choose to allow nothing. An appeal is always possible although unlikely to succeed as a string of cases in the Courts has clearly demonstrated. An example is the case of *Caillebotte* v. *Quinn* where the taxpayer (who normally had lunch at home) sought to claim the excess cost of meals incurred because he was working a long way from his home. The taxpayer's arguments failed because he did not eat only in order to work, one of the reasons for his eating was in order to sustain his life; a duality of purpose therefore existed and no tax relief was due.

Other cases have shown that expenditure on clothing can also be disallowed if it is the kind of clothing which is in everyday use, because clothing is worn not only to assist the pursuit of one's profession but also to accord with public decency. This duality of purpose may be sufficient to deny relief – even where the particular type of clothing is of a kind not otherwise worn by the taxpayer. In the case of *Mallalieu* v. *Drummond* a barrister failed to obtain a tax deduction for items of sombre clothing that she purchased specifically for wearing in Court. The House of Lords decided that a duality of purpose existed because clothing represented part of her needs as a human being.

Allowances

Despite the above, Inspectors of Taxes are not usually inflexible and the following list of expenses are among those generally allowed.

(a) Cost of all materials used up in the course of preparation of the work.

(b) Cost of typewriting and secretarial assistance, etc; if this or other help is obtained from one's spouse then it is entirely proper for a deduction to be claimed for the amounts paid for the work. The amounts claimed must actually be paid to the spouse and should be at the market rate although some uplift can be made for unsocial hours, etc. Payments to a wife (or husband) are of course taxable in her (or his) hands and should therefore be most carefully considered. The wife's earnings may also be liable for National Insurance contributions and it is important to take care because otherwise you may find that these contributions may outweigh the tax savings. The impact of the National Minimum Wage should also be considered.

(c) All expenditure on normal business items such as postage, stationery, telephone, email, fax and answering machines, agent's fees, accountancy charges, photography, subscriptions, periodicals, magazines, etc, may be claimed. The cost of daily papers should not be overlooked if these form part of research material. Visits to theatres, cinemas, etc, for research purposes may also be permissible (but not the cost relating to guests). Unfortunately, expenditure on all types of business entertaining is specifically denied tax relief.

(d) If work is conducted at home, a deduction for 'use of home' is usually allowed providing the amount claimed is reasonable. If the claim is based on an appropriate proportion of the total costs of rent, light and heat, cleaning and maintenance, insurance, etc (but not the Council Tax), care should be taken to ensure that no single room is used 'exclusively' for business purposes, because this may result in the Capital Gains Tax exemption on the house as the only or main residence being partially forfeited. However, it would be a strange household where one room was in fact used exclusively for business purposes and for no other purpose whatsoever (e.g. storing personal bank statements and other private papers); the usual formula is to claim a deduction on the basis that most or all of the rooms in the house are used at one time or another for business purposes, thereby avoiding any suggestion that any part was used exclusively for business purposes.

(e) The appropriate business proportion of motor running expenses may also be claimed although what is the appropriate proportion will naturally depend on the particular circumstances of each case; it should be appreciated that the well-known scale of benefits, whereby employees were taxed according to the size and cost of the car (and are now taxed on the basis of their CO_2 emissions), do not apply to self-employed persons.

(f) It has been long established that the cost of travelling from home to work (whether employed or self-employed) is not an allowable expense. However, if home is one's place of work then no expenditure under this heading is likely to be incurred and difficulties are unlikely to arise.

(g) Travelling and hotel expenses incurred for business purposes will normally be allowed but if any part could be construed as disguised holiday or pleasure expenditure, considerable thought would need to be given to the commercial reasons for the journey in order to justify the claim. The principle of 'duality of purpose' will always be a difficult hurdle in this connection – although not insurmountable.

(h) If a separate business bank account is maintained, any overdraft interest thereon will be an allowable expense. This is the only circumstance in which overdraft interest is allowed for tax purposes and care should be taken to avoid overdrafts in all other circumstances.

(i) Where capital allowances (see below) are claimed for a personal computer, fax, modem, television, video, CD or tape player, etc, used for business purposes the costs of maintenance and repair of the equipment may also be claimed.

Clearly many other allowable items may be claimed in addition to those listed. Wherever there is any reasonable business motive for some expenditure it should be claimed as a deduction although it is necessary to preserve all records relating to the expense. It is sensible to avoid an excess of imagination as this would naturally cause the Inspector of Taxes to doubt the genuineness of other expenses claimed.

The question is often raised whether the whole amount of an expense may be deducted or whether the VAT content must be excluded. Where VAT is reclaimed from the Customs and Excise by someone who is registered for VAT, the VAT element of the expense cannot be treated as an allowable deduction. Where the VAT is not reclaimed, the whole expense (inclusive of VAT) is allowable for income tax purposes.

Capital allowances

Allowances

Where expenditure of a capital nature is incurred, it cannot be deducted from income as an expense – a separate and sometimes more valuable capital allowance being available instead. Capital allowances are given for many different types of expenditure, but authors and similar professional people are likely to claim only for 'plant and machinery'; this is a very wide expression which may include motor cars, personal computers, fax and photocopying machines, modems, televisions, CD, video and cassette players used for business purposes. Plant and machinery generally qualify for a 50% allowance in the year of purchase and 25% of the reducing balance in subsequent years. Expenditure on information technology for the purposes of the business now benefits from a special 100% allowance in the year of purchase. Where the useful life of an asset is expected to be short, it is possible to claim special treatment as a 'short life asset' enabling the allowances to be accelerated.

The reason these allowances can be more valuable than allowable expenses is that they may be wholly or partly disclaimed in any year that full benefit cannot be obtained – ordinary business expenses cannot be similarly disclaimed. Where, for example, the income of an author does not exceed his personal allowances, he would not be liable to tax and a claim for capital allowances would be wasted. If the capital allowances were to be disclaimed their benefit would be carried forward for use in subsequent years. Careful planning with claims for capital allowances is therefore essential if maximum benefit is to be obtained.

As an alternative to capital allowances, claims can be made on the 'renewals' basis whereby all renewals are treated as allowable deductions in the year; no allowance is obtained for the initial purchase, but the cost of replacement (excluding any improvement element) is allowed in full. This basis is no longer widely used, as it is considerably less advantageous than claiming capital allowances as described above.

Leasing is a popular method of acquiring fixed assets, and where cash is not available to enable an outright purchase to be made, assets may be leased over a period of time. Whilst leasing may have financial benefits in certain circumstances, in normal cases there is likely to be no tax advantage in leasing an asset where the alternative of outright purchase is available. Indeed, leasing can be a positive disadvantage in the case of motor cars with a new retail price of more than £12,000. If such a car is leased, only a proportion of the leasing charges will be tax deductible.

Books

The question of whether the cost of books is eligible for tax relief has long been a source of difficulty. The annual cost of replacing books used for the purposes of one's professional activities (e.g. the cost of a new *Writers' & Artists' Yearbook* each year) has always been an allowable expense; the difficulty arose because the initial cost of reference books, etc (e.g. when commencing one's profession) was treated as capital expenditure but no allowances were due as the books were not considered to be 'plant'. However, the matter was clarified by the case of *Munby* v. *Furlong* in which the Court of Appeal decided that the initial cost of law books purchased by a barrister was expenditure on 'plant' and eligible for capital allowances. This is clearly a most important decision, particularly relevant to any person who uses expensive books in the course of exercising his or her profession.

Pension contributions

Personal pensions

Where a self-employed person pays annual premiums under an approved personal pension policy, tax relief was available for the year 2005/6 for the following amounts:

Age at 6/4/2005	Maximum %
35 and under	17.5% (max) £18,480
36–45	20% (max) £21,120
46–50	25% (max) £26,400
51–55	30% (max) £31,680
56–60	35% (max) £36,960
61–74	40% (max) £42,240

These figures do not apply to existing retirement annuity policies; these remain subject to the old limits which are unchanged.

These arrangements were extremely advantageous in providing for a pension as premiums were usually paid when the income is high (and the tax relief is also high) and the pension (taxed as earned income when received) usually arises when the income is low and little tax is payable. There was also the opportunity to take part of the pension entitlement as a tax-free lump sum. It is necessary to take into account the possibility that the tax advantages could go into reverse. When the pension is paid it could, if rates rise again, be taxed at a higher rate than the rate of tax relief at the moment. From 6 April 2006 there is a whole new regime for pensions. All the old rules were swept away and there is now a much simpler system. Each individual has a lifetime allowance (set at £1.5 million for 2006/7 but rising annually). When benefits crystallise, which will generally be when a pension begins to be paid, this is measured against the individual's lifetime allowance; any excess will be taxed at 25%, or at 55% if the excess is taken as a lump sum.

Each individual also has an annual allowance for contributions to the pension fund which is set at £215,000 for 2006/7 but will increase in later years. If the annual increase in an individual's rights under all registered schemes of which he is a member exceeds the annual allowance, the excess is chargeable to tax at 40%.

For most writers and artists this means that they can effectively contribute the whole of their earnings to a pension scheme (if they can afford to do so) without any of the previous complications. It is still necessary to be careful where there is other income giving rise to a pension because the whole of the pension entitlement has to be taken into account.

Flexible retirement is possible allowing members of occupational pensions schemes to continue working while also drawing retirement benefits. As part of this reform, however, the normal minimum pension age will be raised from 50 to 55 by 6 April 2010.

Class 4 National Insurance contributions

Allied to pensions is the payment of Class 4 National Insurance contributions, although no pension or other benefit is obtained by the contributions; the Class 4 contributions are designed solely to extract additional amounts from self-employed persons and are payable in addition to the normal Class 2 (self-employed) contributions. The rates are changed each year and for 2006/7 self-employed persons will be obliged to contribute 8% of their profits between the range £5035–£33,540 per annum. This amount is collected in conjunction with the Schedule D income tax liability.

Since 6 April 2003 there has been a further 1% charge on earnings above £33,540 limit to correspond with the increase in employees' contributions.

Averaging relief
Relief for copyright payments

For many years special provisions enabled authors and similar persons engaged on a literary, dramatic, musical or artistic work for a period of more than 12 months, to spread certain amounts received over two or three years depending on the time spent in preparing the work.

On 6 April 2001 a simpler system of averaging was introduced. Under these rules, professional authors and artists engaged in the creation of literary, dramatic works or designs may claim to average the profits of two or more consecutive years if the profits for one year are less than 75% of the profits for the highest year. This new relief can apply even if the work took less than 12 months to create and is available to people who create works in partnership with others.

The purpose of the relief is to enable the creative artist to utilise his allowances fully and to avoid the higher rates of tax which might apply if all the income were to arise in a single year.

Collection of tax

Self-assessment

In 1997, the system of sending in a tax return showing all your income and HM Revenue & Customs raising an assessment to collect the tax was abolished. So was the idea that you pay tax on your profits for the preceding year. Now, when you send in your tax return you have to work out your own tax liability and send a cheque; this is called 'self-assessment'. If you get it wrong, or if you are late with your tax return or the payment of tax, interest and penalties will be charged.

Under this system, HM Revenue & Customs rarely issue assessments; they are no longer necessary because the idea is that you assess yourself. A colour-coded tax return was created, designed to help individuals meet their tax obligations. This is a daunting task but the term 'self-assessment' is not intended to imply that individuals have to do it themselves; they can (and often will) engage professional help. The term is only intended to convey that it is the taxpayer, and not HM Revenue & Customs, who is responsible for getting the tax liability right and for it to be paid on time.

The deadline for sending in the tax return is 31 January following the end of the tax year; so for the tax year 2005/6, the tax return has to be submitted to HM Revenue & Customs by 31 January 2007. If for some reason you are unwilling or unable to calculate the tax payable, you can ask HM Revenue & Customs to do it for you, in which case it is necessary to send in your tax return by 30 September 2006.

Income tax on self-employed earnings remains payable in two instalments on 31 January and 31 July each year. Because the accurate figures may not necessarily be known, these payments in January and July will therefore be only payments on account based on the previous year's liability. The final balancing figure will be paid the following 31 January together with the first instalment of the liability for the following year.

When HM Revenue & Customs receives the self-assessment tax return, it is checked to see if there is anything obviously wrong; if there is, a letter will be sent to you immediately. Otherwise, HM Revenue & Customs has 12 months from the filing date of 31 January in which to make further enquiries; if it doesn't, it will have no further opportunity to do so and your tax liabilities are final – unless there is something seriously wrong such as the omission of income or capital gains. In that event, HM Revenue & Customs will raise an assessment later to collect any extra tax together with appropriate penalties. It is essential for the operation of the new system that all records relevant to your tax returns are retained for at least 12 months in case they are needed by HM Revenue & Customs. For the self-employed, the record-keeping requirement is much more onerous because the records need to be kept for nearly six years. One important change in the rules is that if you claim a tax deduction for an expense, it will be necessary to have a receipt or other document proving that the expenditure has been made. Because the existence of the underlying records is so important to the operation of self-assessment, HM Revenue & Customs will treat them very seriously and there is a penalty of £3000 for any failure to keep adequate records.

Interest

Interest is chargeable on overdue tax at a variable rate, which at the time of writing is 6.5% per annum. It does not rank for any tax relief, which can make HM Revenue & Customs an expensive source of credit.

However, HM Revenue & Customs can also be obliged to pay interest (known as repayment supplement) tax-free where repayments are delayed. The rules relating to repayment supplement are less beneficial and even more complicated than the rules for interest payable but they do exist and can be very welcome if a large repayment has been delayed for a long time. Unfortunately, the rate of repayment supplement is only 2.25%, much lower than the rate of interest on unpaid tax.

Value added tax

The activities of writers, painters, composers, etc are all 'taxable supplies' within the scope of VAT and chargeable at the standard rate. (Zero rating which applies to publishers, booksellers, etc on the supply of books does not extend to the work performed by writers.) Accordingly, authors are obliged to register for VAT if their income for the past 12 months exceeds £61,000 or if their income for the coming month will exceed that figure.

Delay in registering can be a most serious matter because if registration is not effected at the proper time, the Customs and Excise can (and invariably do) claim VAT from all the income received since the date on which registration should have been made. As no VAT would have been included in the amounts received during this period the amount claimed by the Customs and Excise must inevitably come straight from the pocket of the author.

The author may be entitled to seek reimbursement of the VAT from those whom he or she ought to have charged VAT but this is obviously a matter of some difficulty and may indeed damage his commercial relationships. Apart from these disadvantages there is also a penalty for late registration. The rules are extremely harsh and are imposed automatically even in cases of innocent error. It is therefore extremely important to monitor the income very carefully because if in any period of 12 months the income exceeds the £61,000 limit, the Customs and Excise must be notified within 30 days of the end of the period. Failure to do so will give rise to an automatic penalty. It should be emphasised that this is a penalty for failing to submit a form and has nothing to do with any real or potential loss of tax. Furthermore, whether the failure was innocent or deliberate will not matter. Only the existence of a 'reasonable excuse' will be a defence to the penalty. However, a reasonable excuse does not include ignorance, error, a lack of funds or reliance on any third party.

However, it is possible to regard VAT registration as a privilege and not a penalty, because only VAT registered persons can reclaim VAT paid on their expenses such as stationery, telephone, professional fees, etc, and even typewriters and other plant and machinery (excluding cars). However, many find that the administrative inconvenience – the cost of maintaining the necessary records and completing the necessary forms – more than outweighs the benefits to be gained from registration and prefer to stay outside the scope of VAT for as long as possible.

Overseas matters

The general observation may be made that self-employed persons resident and domiciled in the United Kingdom are not well treated with regard to their overseas work, being taxable on their worldwide income. It is important to emphasise that if fees are earned abroad, no tax saving can be achieved merely by keeping the money outside the country. Although exchange control regulations no longer exist to require repatriation of foreign earnings, such income remains taxable in the UK and must be disclosed to HM Revenue & Customs; the same applies to interest or other income arising on any investment of these earnings overseas. Accordingly, whenever foreign earnings are likely to become substantial, prompt and effective action is required to limit the impact of UK and foreign taxation. In the case of non-resident authors it is important that arrangements concerning writing for publication in the UK, e.g. in newspapers, are undertaken with great care. A case concerning the wife of one of the great train robbers who provided detailed information for a series of articles in a Sunday newspaper is most instructive. Although she was acknowledged to be resident in Canada for all the relevant years, the income from the articles was treated as arising in this country and fully chargeable to UK tax.

The United Kingdom has double taxation agreements with many other countries and these agreements are designed to ensure that income arising in a foreign country is taxed either in that country or in the UK. Where a withholding tax is deducted from payments received from another country (or where tax is paid in full in the absence of a double taxation agreement), the amount of foreign tax paid can usually be set off against the related UK tax liability. Many successful authors can be found living in Eire because of the complete exemption from tax which attaches to works of cultural or artistic merit by persons who are resident there. However, such a step should only be contemplated having careful regard to all the other domestic and commercial considerations and specialist advice is essential if the exemption is to be obtained and kept; a careless breach of the conditions could cause the exemption to be withdrawn with catastrophic consequences.

Further information concerning the precise conditions to be satisfied for exemption from tax in Eire can be obtained from the Revenue Commissioners, Blocks 3–10, Dublin Castle, Dublin 2, or from their website (www.revenue.ie).

Companies

When an author becomes successful the prospect of paying tax at the higher rate may drive them to take hasty action such as the formation of companies, etc, which may not always be to their advantage. Indeed some authors seeing the exodus into tax exile of their more successful colleagues even form companies in low tax areas in the naive expectation of saving large amounts of tax. HM Revenue & Customs is fully aware of the opportunities and have extensive powers to charge tax and combat avoidance. Accordingly, such action is just as likely to increase tax liabilities and generate other costs and should never be contemplated without expert advice; some very expensive mistakes are often made in this area which are not always able to be remedied.

To conduct one's business through the medium of a company can be a most effective method of mitigating tax liabilities, and providing it is done at the right time and under the right circumstances very substantial advantages can be derived. However, if done without due care and attention the intended advantages will simply evaporate. At the very least it is essential to ensure that the company's business is genuine and conducted properly with regard to the realities of the situation. If the author continues his or her activities unchanged, simply paying all the receipts from his work into a company's bank account, he cannot expect to persuade HM Revenue & Customs that it is the company and not himself who is entitled to, and should be assessed to tax on, that income.

It must be strongly emphasised that many pitfalls exist which can easily eliminate all the tax benefits expected to arise by the formation of the company. For example, company directors are employees of the company and will be liable to pay much higher National Insurance contributions; the company must also pay the employer's proportion of the contribution and a total liability of over 23% of gross salary may arise. This compares most unfavourably with the position of a self-employed person. Moreover, on the commencement of the company's business the individual's profession will cease and the possibility of revisions being made by HM Revenue & Customs to earlier tax liabilities means that the timing of a change has to be considered very carefully.

The tax return

No mention has been made above of personal reliefs and allowances; this is because these allowances and the rates of tax are subject to constant change and are always set out in detail in the explanatory notes which accompany the Tax Return. The annual Tax Return is an important document and should be completed promptly with extreme care, particularly since the introduction of self-assessment. If filling in the Return is a source of difficulty or anxiety, comfort may be found in the Consumer Association's publication *Money Which? – Tax Saving Guide*, which is published in March of each year and includes much which is likely to be of interest and assistance.

Peter Vaines FCA, ATII, barrister, is a partner in the international law firm of Squire Sanders & Dempsey LLP and writes and speaks widely on tax matters. He is Managing Editor of *Personal Tax Planning Review*, on the Editorial Board of *Taxation*, tax columnist of the *New Law Journal* and author of a number of books on taxation.

Social security contributions

In general, every individual who works in Great Britain either as an employee or as a self-employed person is liable to pay social security contributions. The law governing this subject is complicated and Peter Arrowsmith FCA gives here a summary of the position. This article should be regarded as a general guide only.

All contributions are payable in respect of years ending on 5 April. See box (below) for the classes of contributions.

Employed or self-employed?

The question as to whether a person is employed under a contract *of* service and is thereby an employee liable to Class 1 contributions, or performs services (either solely or in partnership) under a contract *for* service and is thereby self-employed liable to Class 2 and Class 4 contributions, often has to be decided in practice. One of the best guides can be found in the case of *Market Investigations Ltd* v. *Minister of Social Security* (1969 2 WLR 1) when Cooke J. remarked:

'... the fundamental test to be applied is this: "Is the person who has engaged himself to perform these services performing them as a person in business on his own account?" If the answer to that question is 'yes', then the contract is a contract for services. If the answer is 'no', then the contract is a contract of service. No exhaustive list has been compiled and perhaps no exhaustive list can be compiled of the considerations which are relevant in determining that question, nor can strict rules be laid down as to the relative weight which the various considerations should carry in particular cases. The most that can be said is that control will no doubt always have to be considered, although it can no longer be regarded as the sole determining factor; and that factors which may be of importance are such matters as:

- whether the man performing the services provides his own equipment,
- whether he hires his own helpers,
- what degree of financial risk he takes,
- what degree of responsibility for investment and management he has, and
- whether and how far he has an opportunity of profiting from sound management in the performance of his task.'

The above case has often been considered subsequently – notably in November 1993 by the Court of Appeal in the case of *Hall* v. *Lorimer*. In this case a vision mixer with around 20 clients and undertaking around 120–150 separate engagements per annum was held to be self-employed. This follows the, perhaps surprising, contention of the former Inland Revenue that the taxpayer was an employee.

Classes of contributions

Class 1 These are payable by employees (primary contributions) and their employers (secondary contributions) and are based on earnings.

Class 1A Payable only by employers in respect of all taxable benefits in kind (cars and fuel only prior to 6 April 2000).

Class 1B Payable only by employers in respect of PAYE Settlement Agreements entered into by them.

Class 2 These are weekly flat rate contributions, payable by the self-employed.

Class 3 These are weekly flat rate contributions, payable on a voluntary basis in order to provide, or make up entitlement to, certain social security benefits.

Class 4 These are payable by the self-employed in respect of their trading or professional income and are based on earnings.

Exceptions

There are certain exceptions to the above rules, those most relevant to artists and writers being:

- The employment of a wife by her husband, or vice versa, is disregarded for social security purposes unless it is for the purposes of a trade or profession (e.g. the employment of his wife by an author would not be disregarded and would result in a liability for contributions if her salary reached the minimum levels). The same provisions also apply to civil partners from 5 December 2005.

- The employment of certain relatives in a private dwelling house in which both employee and employer reside is disregarded for social security purposes provided the employment is not for the purposes of a trade or business carried on at those premises by the employer. This would cover the employment of a relative (as defined) as a housekeeper in a private residence.

In general, lecturers, teachers and instructors engaged by an educational establishment to teach on at least four days in three consecutive months are regarded as employees for social security purposes, although this rule does not apply to fees received by persons giving public lectures.

Freelance film workers

There is a list of grades in the film industry in respect of which PAYE need not be deducted and who are regarded as self-employed for tax purposes.

Further information can be obtained from the guidance notes on the application of PAYE to casual and freelance staff in the film industry issued by the former Inland Revenue. In view of the Inland Revenue announcement that the same status will apply for PAYE and National Insurance contributions purposes, no liability for employee's and employer's contributions should arise in the case of any of the grades mentioned above.

However, in the film and television industry this general rule was not always followed in practice. In December 1992, after a long review, the DSS agreed that individuals working behind the camera and who have jobs on the Inland Revenue Schedule D list are self-employed for social security purposes.

There are special rules for, *inter alia*, personnel appearing before the camera, short engagements, payments to limited companies and payments to overseas personalities.

Artistes, performers/non-performers

The status of artistes and performers for tax purposes will depend on the individual circumstances but for social security new regulations which took effect on 17 July 1998 require most actors, musicians or similar performers to be treated as employees for social security purposes, whether or not this status applies under general and/or tax law. It also applies whether or not the individual is supplied through an agency.

Personal service companies

From 6 April 2000, those who have control of their own 'one-man service companies' are subject to special rules. If the work that the owner of the company does for the company's customers would – but for the one-man company – be considered as an employment of that individual (i.e. rather than self-employment), a deemed salary may arise. If it does, then some or all of the income of the company will be treated as salary liable to PAYE and National Insurance contributions. This will be the case whether or not such salary is actually paid by the company. The same situation may arise where the worker owns as little as 5% of a company's share capital.

The calculations required by HM Revenue & Customs are complicated and have to be done very quickly at the end of each tax year (even if the company's year-end is different). It is essential that affected businesses seek detailed professional advice about these rules which may also, in certain circumstances, apply to partnerships.

Class 1 contributions

As mentioned above, these are related to earnings, the amount payable depending upon whether the employer has applied for his employees to be 'contracted-out' of the State earnings-related pension scheme; such application can be made where the employer's own pension scheme provides a requisite level of benefits for his or her employees and their dependants or, in the case of a money purchase scheme (COMPS) certain minimum safeguards are covered. Employers with employees contributing to 'stakeholder pension plans' continue to pay the full not contracted-out rate. Such employees have their contracting out arrangements handled separately by government authorities.

Contributions are payable by employees and employers on earnings that exceed the earnings threshold. Contributions are normally collected via the PAYE tax deduction machinery, and there are penalties for late submission of returns and for errors therein. From 19 April 1993, interest is charged automatically on PAYE and social security contributions paid late.

Employees liable to pay

Contributions are payable by any employee who is aged 16 years and over (even though they may still be at school) and who is paid an amount equal to, or exceeding, the earnings threshold. Nationality is irrelevant for contribution purposes and, subject to special rules covering employees not normally resident in Great Britain, Northern Ireland or the Isle of Man, or resident in EEA countries or those with which there are reciprocal agreements, contributions must be paid whether the employee concerned is a British subject or not provided he is gainfully employed in Great Britain.

Employees exempt from liability to pay

Persons over pensionable age (65 for men; 60 – until 2010 – for women) are exempt from liability to pay primary contributions, even if they have not retired. However, the fact that an employee may be exempt from liability does not relieve an employer from liability to pay secondary contributions in respect of that employee.

Employees' (primary) contributions

From 6 April 2003, the rate of employees' contributions on earnings from the earnings threshold to the upper earnings limit is 11% (9.4% for contracted-out employments). Certain married women who made appropriate elections before 12 May 1977 may be entitled to pay a reduced rate of 4.85%. However, they will have no entitlement to benefits in respect of these contributions.

From April 2003, earnings above the upper earnings limit attract an employee contribution liability of 1% – previously, there was no such liability.

Employers' (secondary) contributions

All employers are liable to pay contributions on the gross earnings of employees. As mentioned above, an employer's liability is not reduced as a result of employees being exempted from contributions, or being liable to pay only the reduced rate (4.85%) of contributions.

For earnings paid on or after 6 April 2003 employers are liable at a rate of 12.8% on earnings paid above the earnings threshold (without any upper earnings limit), 9.3% where the employment is contracted out (salary related) or 11.8% contracted out (money purchase). In addition, special rebates apply in respect of earnings falling between the lower earnings limit and the earnings threshold. This provides, effectively, a negative rate of contribution in that small band of earnings. It should be noted that the contracted-out rates of 9.3% and 11.8% apply only up to the upper earnings limit. Thereafter, the not contracted-out rate of 12.8% is applicable.

The employer is responsible for the payment of both employees' and employer's contributions, but is entitled to deduct the employees' contributions from the earnings on which they are calculated. Effectively, therefore, the employee suffers a deduction in respect of his or her social security contributions in arriving at his weekly or monthly wage or salary. Special rules apply to company directors and persons employed through agencies.

Items included in, or excluded from, earnings

Contributions are calculated on the basis of a person's gross earnings from their employment. This will normally be the figure shown on the deduction working sheet, except where the employee pays superannuation contributions and, from 6 April 1987, charitable gifts under payroll giving – these must be added back for the purposes of calculating Class 1 liability.

Earnings include salary, wages, overtime pay, commissions, bonuses, holiday pay, payments made while the employee is sick or absent from work, payments to cover travel between home and office, and payments under the statutory sick pay, statutory maternity pay, statutory paternity pay and statutory adoption pay schemes.

However, certain payments, some of which may be regarded as taxable income for income tax purposes, are ignored for Class 1 purposes. These include:

- certain gratuities paid other than by the employer;
- redundancy payments and some payments in lieu of notice;
- certain payments in kind;
- reimbursement of specific expenses incurred in the carrying out of the employment;
- benefits given on an individual basis for personal reasons (e.g. wedding and birthday presents);
- compensation for loss of office.

Booklet CWG 2 (2006 edition) gives a list of items to include in or exclude from earnings for Class 1 contribution purposes. Some such items may, however, be liable to Class 1A (employer only) contributions.

Rates of Class 1 contributions and earnings limits from 6 April 2005

Earnings per week	Rates payable on earnings in each band			
	Not contracted-out		Contracted-out	
	Employee	Employer	Employee	Employer
£	%	%	%	%
Below 84.00	–	–	–	–
84.00–96.99	–	–	–(*)	–(*)
97.00–645.00	11	12.8	9.4	9.3 or 11.8
Over £645.00	1	12.8	1	12.8

* Special rebates deductible in respect of this band of earnings.

Miscellaneous rules

There are detailed rules covering a person with two or more employments; where a person receives a bonus or commission in addition to a regular wage or salary; and where a person is in receipt of holiday pay. From 6 April 1991 employers' social security contributions arise under Class 1A in respect of the private use of a company car, and of fuel provided for private use therein. From 6 April 2000, this charge was extended to cover most taxable benefits in kind. The rate is now 12.8%. From 6 April 1999, Class 1B contributions are payable by employers using PAYE Settlement Agreements in respect of small and/or irregular expense payments and benefits, etc. This rate is also currently 12.8%.

Class 2 contributions

Class 2 contributions are payable at the weekly rate of £2.10 as from 6 April 2005. This rate did not change in 2006. Exemptions from Class 2 liability are:

- A man over 65 or a woman over – until 2010 – 60.
- A person who has not attained the age of 16.
- A married woman or, in certain cases, a widow either of whom elected prior to 12 May 1977 not to pay Class 2 contributions.
- Persons with small earnings (see below).
- Persons not ordinarily self-employed (see below).

Small earnings

Application for a certificate of exception from Class 2 contributions may be made by any person who can show that his or her net self-employed earnings per his profit and loss account (as opposed to taxable profits):

- for the year of application are expected to be less than a specified limit (£4465 in the 2006/7 tax year); or
- for the year preceding the application were less than the limit specified for that year (£4345 for 2005/6) and there has been no material change of circumstances.

Certificates of exception must be renewed in accordance with the instructions stated thereon. At HM Revenue & Customs' discretion the certificate may commence up to 13 weeks before the date on which the application is made. Despite a certificate of exception being in force, a person who is self-employed is still entitled to pay Class 2 contributions if they wish, in order to maintain entitlement to social security benefits.

Persons not ordinarily self-employed

Part-time self-employed activities (including as a writer or artist) are disregarded for contribution purposes if the person concerned is not ordinarily employed in such activities and has a full-time job as an employee. There is no definition of 'ordinarily employed' for this purpose but a person who has a regular job and whose earnings from spare-time occupation are not expected to be more than £1300 per annum may fall within this category. Persons qualifying for this relief do not require certificates of exception but may be well advised to apply for one nonetheless.

Method of payment

From April 1993, Class 2 contributions may be paid by monthly direct debit in arrears or, alternatively, by cheque, bank giro, etc following receipt of a quarterly (in arrears) bill.

Overpaid contributions

If, following the payment of Class 2 contributions, it is found that the earnings are below the exception limit (e.g. the relevant accounts are prepared late), the Class 2 contributions that have been overpaid can be reclaimed, provided a claim is made between 6 April and 31 January immediately following the end of the tax year.

Class 3 contributions

Class 3 contributions are payable voluntarily, at the weekly rate of £7.55 per week from 6 April 2006, by persons aged 16 or over with a view to enabling them to qualify for a limited range of benefits if their contribution record is not otherwise sufficient. In general, Class 3 contributions can be paid by employees, the self-employed and the non employed.

Broadly speaking, no more than 52 Class 3 contributions are payable for any one tax year, and contributions cannot be paid in respect of tax years after the one in which the individual concerned reaches the age of 64 (currently 59 for women). Class 3 contributions may be paid in the same manner as Class 2 (see above) or by annual cheque in arrears.

Class 4 contributions

In addition to Class 2 contributions, self-employed persons are liable to pay Class 4 contributions. These are calculated at the rate of 8% on the amount of profits or gains chargeable to income tax which exceed £5035 per annum but which do not exceed £33,540 per annum for 2006/7. Profits above the upper limit of £33,540 attract a Class 4 charge at the rate of 1%. The income tax profit on which Class 4 contributions are calculated is after deducting capital allowances and losses, but before deducting personal tax allowances or retirement annuity or personal pension or stakeholder pension plan premiums.

Class 4 contributions produce no additional benefits, but were introduced to ensure that self-employed persons as a whole pay a fair share of the cost of pensions and other social security benefits, yet without those who make only small profits having to pay excessively high flat rate contributions.

Payment of contributions

In general, Class 4 contributions are now self-assessed and paid to HM Revenue & Customs together with the income tax as a result of the self-assessment income tax return, and accordingly the contributions are due and payable at the same time as the income tax liability on the relevant profits. Under self-assessment, interim payments of Class 4 contributions are payable at the same time as interim payments of tax.

Class 4 exemptions

The following persons are exempt from Class 4 contributions:
- Men over 65 and women over – until 2010 – 60 at the commencement of the year of assessment (i.e. on 6 April).
- An individual not resident in the United Kingdom for income tax purposes in the year of assessment.
- Persons whose earnings are not 'immediately derived' from carrying on a trade, profession or vocation (e.g. sleeping partners).
- A child under 16 on 6 April of the year of assessment.
- Persons not ordinarily self-employed.

Married persons and partnerships

Under independent taxation of husband and wife from 1990/91 onwards, each spouse is responsible for his or her Class 4 liability.

In partnerships, each partner's liability is calculated separately. If a partner also carries on another trade or profession, the profits of all such businesses are aggregated for the purposes of calculating their Class 4 liability.

When an assessment has become final and conclusive for the purposes of income tax, it is also final and conclusive for the purposes of calculating Class 4 liability.

Maximum contributions

There is a form of limit to the total liability for social security contributions payable by a person who is employed in more than one employment, or is also self-employed or a partner.

Where only not contracted-out Class 1 contributions, or not contracted-out Class 1 and Class 2 contributions, are payable, the maximum contribution payable at the main rates (11%, 9.4% or 4.85% as the case may be) is limited to 53 primary Class 1 contributions at the maximum weekly not contracted-out standard rate. For 2006/7 this 'maximum' will thus be £3194.84 (amounts paid at only 1% are to be excluded in making this comparison).

Further information

Further information can be obtained from the many booklets published by HM Revenue & Customs, available from local Enquiry Centres and on their website (www.hmrc.gov.uk).

National Insurance Contributions Office, Centre for Non-Residents
Newcastle upon Tyne NE98 1ZZ
tel (08459) 154811 (local call rates apply)
Address for enquiries for individuals resident abroad.

However, where contracted-out Class 1 contributions are payable, the maximum primary Class 1 contributions payable for 2006/7 where all employments are contracted out are £2719.11 (again excluding amounts paid at only 1%).

Where Class 4 contributions are payable in addition to Class 1 and/or Class 2 contributions, the Class 4 contributions payable at the full 8% rate are restricted so that they shall not exceed the excess of £2391.70 (i.e. 53 Class 2 contributions plus maximum Class 4 contributions) over the aggregate of the Class 1 and Class 2 contributions paid at the full (i.e. other than 1%) rates.

Transfer of government departmental functions

The administrative functions of the former Contributions Agency transferred to the Inland Revenue from 1 April 1999. Responsibility for National Insurance contribution policy matters was also transferred from DSS Ministers to the Inland Revenue and Treasury Ministers on the same date. The DSS is now known as the Department for Work and Pensions (DWP). From 18 April 2005, the functions of the former Inland Revenue and former HM Customs and Excise were merged to become HM Revenue & Customs.

Peter Arrowsmith FCA is a sole practitioner specialising in National Insurance matters. He is chairman of the Employment Taxes and National Insurance Committee of the Institute of Chartered Accountants in England and Wales, and Consulting Editor to *Tolley's National Insurance Contributions 2006/7*.

Social security benefits

In this article, K.D. Bartlett FCA summarises some of the more usual benefits that are available.

Benefits available fall into two categories: non-contributory and contributory. To receive a non-contributory benefit certain criteria has to be met, be it financial, physical, etc.

To receive a contributory benefit the claimant must have met the prescribed contribution condition over a period of time by way of National Insurance.

Contributory benefits are: Jobseeker's Allowance, Incapacity Benefit, Widowed Parent's Allowance (formerly Widowed Mother's Allowance), Bereavement Payment (formerly Widow's Payment), Bereavement Allowance (replaced by Widow's Pension), Child's Special Allowance (where applicable), Maternity Allowance and Category A and B Retirement Pensions.

Non-contributory benefits are: Attendance Allowance, Carer's Allowance, Disability Living Allowance, Industrial Injuries Disablement Benefit, Severe Disablement Allowance, Guardian's Allowance and Category C and D Retirement Pensions.

It is usual for only one periodical benefit to be payable at any one time. If the contribution conditions are satisfied for more than one benefit it is the larger benefit that is payable. Benefit rates shown below are those payable from the week commencing 6 April 2006. Self-employed persons (Class 2 contributors) are covered for all benefits except second state pensions and benefits paid in respect of an industrial injury. Most authors are self employed.

Family benefits

Child Benefit is payable for all children who are either under 16 or under 19 and receiving full-time education at a recognised educational establishment. The rate is £17.45 for the first or eldest child and £11.70 a week for each subsequent child. It is payable to the person who is responsible for the child but excludes foster parents or people exempt from UK tax. Furthermore, one-parent families receive £17.55 per week for the eldest child.

Those with little money may apply for a maternity loan or grant from the Social Fund. Those claiming Working Families Tax Credit or Disabled Person's Tax Credit can apply for a Sure Start Maternity Grant of £500 for each baby expected, born, adopted or subject to a parental order. Any savings over £500 are taken into account. This grant will only be paid on the provision of a relevant certificate from a doctor, midwife or health visitor.

A Guardian's Allowance is paid at the rate of £12.50 a week to people who have taken orphans into their own family. Usually both of the child's parents must be dead and at least one of them must have satisfied a residence condition.

The allowance can only be paid to the person who is entitled to Child Benefit for the child (or to that person's spouse). It is not necessary to be the legal guardian. The claim should be made within three months of the date of entitlement.

Disability Living Allowance

Disability Living Allowance has replaced Attendance Allowance for disabled people before they reach the age of 65. It has also replaced Mobility Allowance.

Those who are disabled after reaching 65 may be able to claim Attendance Allowance. The Attendance Allowance Board decide whether, and for how long, a person is eligible for this allowance. Attendance Allowance is not taxable. The care component is divided into three rates whereas the mobility component has two rates. The rate of benefit from 6 April 2006 is as follows:

Care component	*Per week*
Higher rate (day and night, or terminally ill)	£62.25
Middle rate (day or night)	£41.65
Lower rate (if need some help during day, or over 16 and help preparing a meal)	£16.50

Mobility component	*Per week*
Higher rate (unable or virtually unable to walk)	£43.45
Lower rate (can walk but needs help when outside)	£16.50

Benefits for the ill

Incapacity Benefit replaced Sickness Benefit and Invalidity Benefit. The contribution conditions haven't changed but a new medical test has been brought in which includes a comprehensive questionnaire. The rates from 11 April 2006 are:

Long-term Incapacity Benefit	£78.50
Short-term Incapacity Benefit	£59.20
Increase of long-term Incapacity Benefit for age:	
Higher rate	£16.50
Lower rate	£8.25

Carer's Allowance, formerly Invalid Care Allowance, is a taxable benefit paid to people of working age who cannot take a job because they have to stay at home to look after a severely disabled person. The basic allowance is £46.95 per week. An extra £9.40 is paid for the first dependent child and £11.35 for each subsequent child.

Pensions

The state pension is divided into two parts – the basic pension, presently £84.25 per week for a single person or £134.75 per week for a married couple.

Women paying standard rate contributions into the scheme are eligible for the same amount of pension as men but five years earlier, from age 60. The Pensions Act 1995 incorporated the provision for an equal state pension age of 65 for men and women to be phased in over a 10-year period beginning 6 April 2010. If a woman stays at home to bring up her children or to look after a person receiving Attendance Allowance she can have her basic pension rights protected without paying contributions.

Pension Credit is a new entitlement for people aged 60 or over. It guarantees everyone aged 60 and over an income of at least:

- £114.05 a week if you are single; or
- £174.05 a week if you have a partner.

For the first time, people aged 65 and over will be rewarded for some of their savings and income they have for their retirement. In the past, those who had saved a little money were no better off than those who had not saved at all. Pension Credit will change this by giving new money to those who have saved – up to £17.88 if you are single, or £23.58 if you have a partner.

The person who applies for Pension Credit must be at least 60 but their partner can be under 60. Partner means a spouse or a person with whom one lives as if you were married to them.

Widowed Parent's Allowance

This is a new system of bereavement benefits for men and women introduced in April 2001. Women who were receiving benefits under the previous scheme are unaffected as long as they still qualify under the rules. A Widowed Parent's Allowance is:

- based on the late husband's or wife's contributions;
- for widows or widowers bringing up children;
- a regular payment.

The main conditions for receiving this benefit are:

- You must be aged over 45 and must have a dependent child or children.
- If you were over the state pension age when you were widowed you may receive Retirement Pension based on the husband's or wife's National Insurance contributions.
- If the spouse died as a result of their job, it is possible to receive bereavement benefits even if they did not pay sufficient National Insurance contributions.
- You cannot receive bereavement benefits if you remarry or if you live with a partner as if you are married to them.
- Bereavement benefits are not affected if you work.
- The allowance is £84.25 for those over 55 and varies for those aged between 45 and 54.

There are increases for dependent children. You receive £9.40 for the oldest child who qualifies for child benefit and £11.35 for each child who qualifies.

Bereavement Payment and benefits

From 9 April 2001 bereavement benefits are payable to both widows and widowers but the benefits are only paid to those without children. Benefits are based on the National Insurance contributions of the deceased. No benefit is payable if the couple were divorced at the date of death or if either of the survivors remarries or cohabits.

Widows and widowers bereaved on or after 9 April 2001 are entitled to a tax-free Bereavement Payment of £2000.

The death grant to cover funeral expenses was abolished from 6 April 1987. It has been replaced by a funeral payment from the Social Fund where the claimant is in receipt of Income Support, income-based Jobseeker's Allowance, Disabled Person's Tax Credit, Working Families' Tax Credit or Housing Benefit. The full cost of a reasonable funeral is paid, reduced by any savings of over £600 held by the claimant.

Child Tax Credits and Working Tax Credit

Child Tax Credits were introduced on 6 April 2003. To obtain them a claim form has to be submitted (Tax Credit Form TC600 is available by either telephoning 0845 366 7820 or applying online – see below).

Child Tax Credit has replaced the Children's Tax Credit previously claimed through tax paid. It is paid directly to the person who is mainly responsible for caring for the child or children. To ascertain which tax credits you could be entitled to apply online (www.taxcredits.inlandrevenue.gov.uk).

Child Tax Credits are especially complicated for those on variable income and the self employed. The tax credit for the tax year 2006/7 is initially based on the income earned in the tax year 2004/5. If the income is now lower in 2006/7 than in 2004/5 then potentially you should be receiving more tax credit or even be eligible for it when before you were earning too much. In this situation you should make a protective claim by completing and sending off a Tax Credit Form TC600.

Working Tax Credit

Working Tax Credit is paid to support people in work and is administered by HM Revenue & Customs (formerly the Inland Revenue). It is not necessary to have paid National Insurance contributions to qualify. The following do qualify:

● Those over 16 who are responsible for a child or young person and work at least 16 hours a week.

People without children can claim if:

● they are over 25 and work at least 30 hours a week;

● they are aged 16 or over and work at least 16 hours a week and have a disability that puts them at a disadvantage in obtaining a job;

● a person or their partner are aged 50 or more and work at least 16 hours a week and are returning to work after time spent on obtaining a qualification.

Working Tax Credit is paid as well as any Child Tax Credit you are entitled to. The calculations on how much you receive are complicated but it will depend on how many hours you work and your income or joint income.

If you are employed then you will receive the payment via your employer and if self employed you will be paid direct. If you think you are eligible to receive Working Tax Credit, either telephone 0845 764 6646 or visit Tax Credits Online (see above).

K.D. Bartlett FCA qualified as a Chartered Accountant in 1969 and became a partner in a predecessor firm of Horwath Clark Whitehill LLP in 1972.

Subject indexes

Magazines by subject area

These lists can be only a broad classification. They should be regarded as a pointer to possible markets and be used with discrimination. Addresses for magazines start on page 32.

Fiction

Active Life
Ambit
Aquila
The Australian Women's Weekly
Bella
Best
Chapman
Chat
Climb Magazine
Critical Quarterly
Cyphers
The Dalhousie Review
Day by Day
Descant
Diva
The Dublin Review
The Edge
The Erotic Review
The Fiddlehead
Fly-Fishing & Fly-Tying
For Women
Granta
Interzone
Ireland's Own
Irish Pages: A Journal of
    Contemporary Writing
The Jewish Quarterly
Junior
Kent Life
The Lady
The London Magazine: A Review
    of Literature and the Arts
Lothian Life
The Malahat Review
Mayfair
More
Mslexia
My Weekly
My Weekly Story Collection
Neo-opsis Science Fiction
    Magazine
The New Writer
New Zealand Woman's Day
The Newspaper
Overland
People's Friend
People's Friend Story Collection

Planet
Pride
Prospect
Quadrant
Queen's Quarterly
QWF
The Scots Magazine
Scuba Diver
SHERLOCK
Shoot Monthly
Springboard
Stand Magazine
Staple
Starburst
Takahe
Take a Break
that's life!
The Third Alternative
Time Out
The Times Literary Supplement
walk
The Weekly News
Woman and Home
Woman's Day
Woman's Own
Woman's Value
Woman's Weekly
Woman's Weekly Fiction Special
Writers' Forum
Young Writer
Your Cat Magazine
Yours

Letters to the Editor

Architecture Today
The Australian Women's Weekly
Bella
Best
The Big Issue
Bizarre
Caravan Magazine
Chat
Choice
Classics Monthly
Dolly
The Economist
Executive PA
Fairlady

Femina Magazine
FHM (For Him Magazine)
Flora International
The Furrow
H&E Naturist
Modern Painters
Moneywise
Mother & Baby
My Weekly
New Law Journal
New Zealand Woman's Day
Now
Nursery Education
NW Magazine
People's Friend
PN Review
Practical Parenting
The Practising Midwife
Prima
Racing Post
Retail Week
Saga Magazine
Ski and Board
Television
that's life!
Third Way
TV Quick
The Weekly News
What's on TV
Woman's Day
Woman's Value
Woman's Way
Woman's Weekly
Yours

Gossip paragraphs

The Big Issue
Bookseller & Publisher
Broadcast
Buses
Campaign
Church of England Newspaper
Classical Music
Country Life
Fairlady
Femina Magazine
FHM (For Him Magazine)
Flora International

Garden News
Geographical
Golf World
Hampshire – The County
   Magazine
Irish Medical Times
Irish Printer
Junior
The Lawyer
Marketing Week
Men Only
Minor Monthly
Mojo
Motor Cycle News
Music Week
My Weekly
New Welsh Review
Nursing Times
Opera Now
The Pink Paper
Pride
Radio Times
Retail Week
Rugby World
Runner's World
Running Fitness
Time Out
The Voice
World Soccer
Your Dog Magazine

Brief filler paragraphs

Active Life
The Architects' Journal
The Big Issue
Bookseller & Publisher
Broadcast
Communicate
Country Life
The Countryman
Decanter
Fairlady
Flight International
Flora International
The Furrow
Garden News
Geographical
Gibbons Stamp Monthly
Golf World
Greetings Today
H&E Naturist
Hampshire – The County
   Magazine
Health & Fitness Magazine
Horticulture Week
Insurance Age
Inuit Art Quarterly
Ireland of the Welcomes
Ireland's Own

Irish Medical Times
Irish Printer
Jane's Defence Weekly
The Lawyer
Marketing Week
Men Only
Motor Cycle News
My Weekly
New Welsh Review
Nursing Times
Opera Now
Overland
Picture Postcard Monthly
The Pink Paper
Post Magazine & Insurance Week
Pride
Radio Times
Reader's Digest
Reader's Digest (Australia)
Retail Week
Runner's World
Running Fitness
Snooker Scene
Southern Cross
Technology Ireland
The Times Educational
   Supplement
Trucking
Weight Watchers Magazine
The Woodworker
World Airnews
World Fishing
World Soccer
Your Dog Magazine

Puzzles and quizzes

*The following take puzzles and/or
quizzes on an occasional or, in
some cases, regular basis. Ideas
must be tailored to suit each
publication: approach in writing
in the first instance.*

Active Life
The Australian Women's Weekly
Best of British
The Big Issue in the North
Bird Watching
Bona
The Bulletin
The Catholic Herald
(Christchurch) The Press
Climb Magazine
Country Life
The Dandy
Executive PA
Fairlady
Farmer's Weekly
Femina Magazine

Fire
Flora International
France
Garden and Home
Irish Medical Times
Kids Alive! (The Young Soldier)
Living and Loving
(Melbourne) Herald Sun
More
The Newspaper
Nursing Times
Opera Now
Picture Postcard Monthly
Runner's World
Running Fitness
Scottish Home and Country
Snooker Scene
Southern Cross
The Spectator
Take a Break
Take a Break's Take a Puzzle
The Times Literary Supplement
TV Quick
The Universe
The War Cry
Woman's Way
The Woodworker
The Word
World Soccer
Your Dog Magazine
Your Family

UK ethnic weekly newspapers

Asian Times
Caribbean Times
Eastern Eye
The Voice

Women's interest magazines

The Australian Women's Weekly
Bella
Best
Black Beauty & Hair
Bliss
Bona
Chat
Chatelaine
Company
Cosmopolitan
Diva
ELLE (UK)
Essentials
Executive PA
Executive Woman
Fairlady
Femina Magazine

For Women
Girl About Town Magazine
Glamour
Good Housekeeping
Hairflair & Beauty
Harper's Bazaar
Harper's Bazaar
Heat
Hello!
In Style
Inside Soap
Irish Tatler
Junior
The Lady
Living and Loving
Marie Claire
Modern Woman Nationwide
More
Mother & Baby
Mslexia
My Weekly
My Weekly Story Collection
New Woman
New Woman
New Zealand Woman's Day
Now
Nursery World
OK
OS Magazine
People's Friend
The Pink Paper
Pregnancy, Baby & You
Pride
Prima
Prima Baby
Real
Red
She
She
Take a Break
Tatler
that's life!
U magazine
Vanity Fair
Vive
Vogue
Vogue Australia
Wedding
WI Home and Country
Woman
Woman Alive
Woman and Home
Woman's Day
Woman's Own
Woman's Value
Woman's Way
Woman's Weekly
Woman's Weekly Fiction Special
You & Your Wedding
Your Family

Men's interest magazines

Arena
Attitude
Country
Esquire
FHM (For Him Magazine)
Gay Times
GQ
Loaded
Maxim
Mayfair
Men Only
Men's Health
The Pink Paper

Children's and young adult magazines

Aquila
The Beano
Commando
CosmoGIRL!
The Dandy
Dolly
Hot Press
Mizz
The Newspaper
Pony Magazine
Shout
Young Writer

Subject articles

Advertising, design, printing and publishing

Arena
Bookseller & Publisher
British Journalism Review
Campaign
Freelance Market News
Greetings Today
Irish Printer
Media Week
PR Week
Press Gazette
Printing World
Publishing News

Agriculture, farming and horticulture

Country Life
Country Smallholding
The Countryman
Dairy Farmer
Farmers Weekly
Farmer's Weekly
The Field

The Grower
Horticulture Week
Irish Farmers Journal
Old Tractor
Poultry World
The Scottish Farmer
Smallholder

Architecture and building

The Architects' Journal
Architectural Design
The Architectural Review
Architecture Today
Blueprint
Building
Building Design
Built Environment
Country Homes and Interiors
Country Life
Education Journal
Homes and Gardens
Housebuilder
SelfBuild & Design

Art and collecting

AN Magazine
Antiques & Collectables
Apollo
Art Business Today
Art Monthly
Art Monthly Australia
The Art Newspaper
Art Review
The Artist
Artists and Illustrators
Artlink
The Book Collector
Book and Magazine Collector
The Burlington Magazine
C Magazine
Coin News
Contemporary
Country Life
Craftsman Magazine
Eastern Art Report
Embroidery
Gibbons Stamp Monthly
Inuit Art Quarterly
Leisure Painter
Medal News
Modern Painters
RA Magazine
Stamp Lover
Stamp Magazine
TATE ETC

Aviation

Aeroplane Monthly
Air International
Australian Flying
Aviation Business
Aviation News
Flight International
Pilot
Today's Pilot
World Airnews

Business, industry and management

Business Life
Chartered Secretary
Communicate
Director
Executive PA
Executive Woman
Fire
Fishing News
ICIS Chemical Business
Management Magazine
Management Today
OS Magazine
People Management
Restaurant Magazine
Ulster Business
The Woodworker

Cinema and films

Campaign
The Edge
Empire
Film Ireland
Film Review
Hotdog
Screen International
Sight and Sound
Total Film

Computers

Computer Weekly
MacUser
Macworld
.net The Internet Magazine
PC Advisor
PC Answers
Personal Computer World
Scientific Computing World
What Laptop

Economics, accountancy and finance

Accountancy
Accountancy Age
Accounting & Business
Active Life
Africa Confidential
African Business
The Australian Financial Review
The Banker
Contemporary Review
Economica
The Economist
Financial Adviser
The Grower
Insurance Age
Insurance Brokers' Monthly
Investors Chronicle
Moneywise
Pensions World
Post Magazine & Insurance Week
Taxation

Education

Aquila
Carousel – The Guide to
   Children's Books
Child Education
Child Education Topics
Education Journal
Junior Education
Junior Education Topics
The Linguist
Modern Language Review
Music Teacher
Nursery Education
Nursery World
Practical Parenting
Reality
Report
Right Start
Safety Education
The School Librarian
The Teacher
The Times Educational
   Supplement
Times Educational Supplement
   Scotland
Times Higher Education
   Supplement
Under 5
Young People Now

Engineering and mechanics

Car Mechanics
EA Books
Electrical Review
The Engineer
Engineering
Engineering in Miniature
Everyday Practical Electronics
Fire
Model Engineer
Practical Woodworking
Rail
Railway Gazette International
Railway Magazine

Gardening

Country
Country Life
The Field
Garden and Home
Garden News
Homestyle
House & Garden
NZ House & Garden
Organic Gardening

Health and home

Active Life
Australian Home Beautiful
Australian House and Garden
Black Beauty & Hair
Choice
Classic Stitches
Country Homes and Interiors
Country Living
Garden and Home
H&E Naturist
Health & Fitness Magazine
Homes and Gardens
Homestyle
House & Garden
House Beautiful
Ideal Home
In Balance Health & Lifestyle
   Magazine
Junior
New Vegetarian and Natural
   Health
NZ House & Garden
Period Living
Practical Parenting
Prediction
Prima Baby
Running Fitness
Safety Education
Saga Magazine
Sainsbury's Magazine
Scottish Home and Country
Signmatters
Slimmer, Healthier, Fitter
The Vegan
Weight Watchers Magazine
Woman's Value
The World of Interiors
Your Family
Your Home and Garden
Yours
Zest

History and archaeology

Best of British
Coin News
Geographical
History Today
The National Trust Magazine
Picture Postcard Monthly
Scottish Memories

Hotel, catering and leisure

Caterer & Hotelkeeper
Health Club Management
The Leisure Manager

Humour and satire

Private Eye
Viz

Inflight magazines

Business Life

Legal and police

Family Law
Justice of the Peace
The Lawyer
Legal Week
New Law Journal
Police Journal
Police Review
Solicitors Journal

Leisure interests, pets

Astronomy Now
Bird Watching
Birdwatch
British Philatelic Bulletin
Canals & Rivers
Caravan Magazine
Classic Stitches
Classics Monthly
Climber
Country Walking
Decanter
Dogs Today
Family Tree Magazine
The Field
Flora International
Folio
Gibbons Stamp Monthly
Guiding magazine
Koi
The List
Military Modelling
Mixmag
Model Boats

Motor Caravan Magazine
Motorcaravan Motorhome
   Monthly (MMM)
Our Dogs
Park Home & Holiday Caravan
Practical Caravan
Practical Fishkeeping
Radio Control Models and
   Electronics
Scottish Field
Sewing World
The Spark Magazine
Stamp Lover
Stamp Magazine
Swimming Magazine
TGO (The Great Outdoors)
   Magazine
Time Out
Traditional Woodworking
Venue
Wine
The Woodworker
Workbox Magazine
Your Cat Magazine
Your Dog Magazine
Your Horse

Literary (see also poetry)

The Author
The Book Collector
Books Ireland
Bookseller & Publisher
The Bookseller
British Journalism Review
Canadian Literature
Canadian Writer's Journal
Carousel – The Guide to
   Children's Books
Chapman
Contemporary Review
Critical Quarterly
The Dalhousie Review
Descant
The Dickensian
The Dublin Review
The Edge
Edinburgh Review
The Fiddlehead
The Fix
Freelance
Granta
Index on Censorship
International Affairs
Irish Pages: A Journal of
   Contemporary Writing
Journal of Canadian Studies
The Literary Review
LOGOS
The London Magazine: A Review
   of Literature and the Arts

London Review of Books
The Malahat Review
Market Newsletter
Meanjin
Modern Language Review
Mslexia
Neo-opsis Science Fiction
   Magazine
New Welsh Review
The New Writer
The Oldie
Orbis
Outposts Poetry Quarterly
Overland
Planet
Prospect
Publishing News
Quadrant
Queen's Quarterly
Quill & Quire
QWF
Reality
SHERLOCK
The Spectator
Springboard
Stand Magazine
Starburst
Studies, An Irish quarterly review
Takahe
The Third Alternative
The Times Literary Supplement
Tribune
The Woman Writer
Writers' Forum
Writers' News
Writing Magazine
Young Writer

Local government and civil service

Community Care
Justice of the Peace
LGC (Local Government
   Chronicle)

Marketing and retailing

Accountancy
Drapers
Greetings Today
The Grocer
Marketing Week
Retail Week
Ulster Grocer

Medicine and nursing

Accountancy
Balance

BMA News
British Medical Journal
Caring Business
Disability Now
Hospital Doctor
Irish Journal of Medical Science
Irish Medical Times
Journal of Alternative and
    Complementary Medicine
Lancet
Nursery World
Nursing Times
The Practising Midwife
The Practitioner
Professional Nurse
Pulse
Therapy Weekly
Veterinary Review
Young People Now

Military

Jane's Defence Weekly
RUSI Journal

Motor transport and cycling

Auto Express
Autocar
Back Street Heroes
Bike
Buses
Car
Car
Car Mechanics
Classic Cars
Classics Monthly
Commercial Motor
Custom Car
Cycling Weekly
Minor Monthly
Motor Cycle News
Truck & Driver
Trucking
What Car?

Music and recording

Arena
Brass Band World Magazine
Classical Music
Early Music
Hi-Fi News
Jazz Journal International
Kerrang!
Mojo
Music Teacher

Music Week
Musical Opinion
Musical Times
New Musical Express (NME)
Opera
Opera Now
Q Magazine
Record Collector
The Songwriter
Songwriting and Composing
The Strad
Tempo

Natural history

Australian Heritage
Bird Watching
Birding World
Birdwatch
British Birds
Cat World
The Ecologist
Geographical
The National Trust Magazine
Natural World
Naturalist
Nature
Our Dogs

Nautical and marine

Australian Powerboat
Canals & Rivers
Classic Boat
Diver
Motor Boat and Yachting
Motor Boats Monthly
Nautical Magazine
Practical Boat Owner
Sea Breezes
Ships Monthly
Waterways World
Yachting Monthly
Yachting World
Yachts and Yachting

Photography

Amateur Photographer
Australian Photography
The British Journal of
    Photography
Camera
Digital Video UK
Market Newsletter
Photo Life
Practical Photography
Professional Photographer
What Digital Camcorder

Poetry

*Some magazines only take the
occasional poem. Check with the
Editor before submitting.*

Acumen
Agenda
Ambit
Chapman
Cordite Poetry Review
Critical Quarterly
Cumbria Magazine
Cyphers
The Dalhousie Review
Descant
Edinburgh Review
Envoi
The Fiddlehead
HQ Poetry Magazine
Irish Pages: A Journal of
    Contemporary Writing
The Literary Review
The London Magazine: A Review
    of Literature and the Arts
London Review of Books
The Malahat Review
Meanjin
New Welsh Review
Orbis
Other Poetry
Outposts Poetry Quarterly
Overland
Oxford Poetry
Planet
PN Review
Poetry Ireland Review/Éigse
    Éireann
Poetry London
Poetry Nottingham
Poetry Review
Poetry Wales
Pride
Quadrant
Queen's Quarterly
The Rialto
The Shop: A Magazine of Poetry
Springboard
Stand Magazine
Staple
Takahe
Young Writer

Politics

Africa Confidential
Australian Journal of Politics and
    History
The Bulletin
Contemporary Review
Fortnight – An Independent
    Review of Politics and the Arts

Travel and geography

Australian Geographic
Australian Heritage
Caravan Magazine
Condé Nast Traveller

France
Geographical
Geographical Journal
Global Adventure
Ireland of the Welcomes

Traveller
Traveltalk Australia
Wanderlust
Wild
The Witness

Publishers of fiction

Addresses for *Book publishers UK and Ireland* start on page 131.

Adventure/thrillers

Bantam
Bantam Press
Black Ace Books
Black Swan
Blackstaff Press Ltd
Bloomsbury Publishing Plc
Chatto & Windus
Constable & Robinson Ltd
Faber and Faber Ltd
Fourth Estate (imprint)
Robert Hale Ltd
Harlequin Mills & Boon Ltd
Headline Book Publishing Ltd
   (division)
Hodder Headline Ltd
Honno Ltd (Welsh Women's
   Press)
Hutchinson (imprint)
William Heinemann (imprint)
Little, Brown Book Group
Macmillan Publishers Ltd
Mentor Books
Michael Joseph (imprint)
John Murray (Publishers) Ltd
The Orion Publishing Group Ltd
Penguin Group (UK)
Piatkus Books
Random House Group Ltd
Seafarer Books
Time Warner
Transworld Publishers
Vintage
Virago
The X Press

Crime/mystery/suspense

Allison & Busby Ltd
Arcadia Books Ltd
Arrow Books Ltd
Bantam
Bantam Press
Black Ace Books
Black Swan
BlackAmber (imprint)
Blackstaff Press Ltd
Bloomsbury Publishing Plc
Breese Books Ltd
Constable & Robinson Ltd
Corgi
Everyman's Library
Faber and Faber Ltd

Flambard Press
Fourth Estate (imprint)
Robert Hale Ltd
Hamish Hamilton
HarperCollins Publishers
William Heinemann
Hodder & Stoughton
Hodder Headline Ltd
Honno Ltd (Welsh Women's
   Press)
Hutchinson
Hutchinson (imprint)
Michael Joseph
William Heinemann (imprint)
Little, Brown Book Group
Macmillan (imprint)
Macmillan Publishers Ltd
Mentor Books
Oldcastle Books Ltd
Michael O'Mara Books Ltd
The Orion Publishing Group Ltd
Pan (imprint)
Penguin Group (UK)
Piatkus Books
Polygon
Random House Group Ltd
Sceptre
Seren
Serpent's Tail
Severn House Publishers
Time Warner
Transworld Publishers
Viking
Vintage
Virago
The Women's Press
The X Press

Gay/lesbian

Arcadia Books Ltd
Bantam
Black Swan
Marion Boyars Publishers Ltd
Chapman Publishing
Corgi
Fourth Estate (imprint)
Hamish Hamilton
HarperCollins Publishers
Hodder & Stoughton General
   (division)
Honno Ltd (Welsh Women's
   Press)

Libris Ltd
Little, Brown Book Group
Macmillan Publishers Ltd
MQ Publications Ltd
Michael O'Mara Books Ltd
Onlywomen Press Ltd
Penguin Group (UK)
Polygon
Sceptre
Serpent's Tail
Time Warner
Vintage
Virago
The Women's Press

General

Abacus
Allison & Busby Ltd
Arcadia Books Ltd
Authentic Media
Bantam
Bantam Press
Black Ace Books
Black Swan
BlackAmber (imprint)
Blackstaff Press Ltd
Bloomsbury Publishing Plc
Marion Boyars Publishers Ltd
Calder Publications UK Ltd
Canongate Books Ltd
Jonathan Cape
Century
Chapman Publishing
Chatto & Windus
Cló Iar-Chonnachta Teo.
Corgi
Crescent Moon Publishing
Doubleday (UK)
11:9 (imprint)
Faber and Faber Ltd
Fourth Estate (imprint)
The Gallery Press
Garnet Publishing Ltd
Halban Publishers
Robert Hale Ltd
Hamish Hamilton
Harlequin Mills & Boon Ltd
HarperCollins Publishers
William Heinemann
Hodder & Stoughton
Honno Ltd (Welsh Women's
   Press)

John Hunt Publishing Ltd
Hutchinson
Michael Joseph
Karnak House
Libris Ltd
Little, Brown Book Group
Macmillan (imprint)
Macmillan Publishers Ltd
The Maia Press Ltd
Mentor Books
The Mercat Press
Methuen Publishing Ltd
MQ Publications Ltd
NB Publishers (Pty) Ltd
New Island Books
The Oleander Press
Michael O'Mara Books Ltd
Onlywomen Press Ltd
The Orion Publishing Group Ltd
Pan (imprint)
Penguin Group (UK)
Piatkus Books
Pipers' Ash Ltd
Pocket Books
Pocket Books (imprint)
Poolbeg Press Ltd
Random House Group Ltd
Route
Sceptre
SCP Childrens Ltd
Seren
Serpent's Tail
Severn House Publishers
Simon & Schuster UK Ltd
Time Warner
Transworld Publishers
Viking
Vintage
Virago
The Women's Press
Y Lolfa Cyf.

Historical

Allison & Busby Ltd
Bantam
Bantam Press
Birlinn Ltd
Black Ace Books
BlackAmber (imprint)
Blackstaff Press Ltd
Jonathan Cape
Chapman Publishing
Constable & Robinson Ltd
Doubleday (UK)
Everyman's Library
Flambard Press
Fourth Estate (imprint)
Robert Hale Ltd
Harlequin Mills & Boon Ltd

HarperCollins Publishers
William Heinemann
Hodder & Stoughton
Honno Ltd (Welsh Women's Press)
John Hunt Publishing Ltd
Hutchinson
Michael Joseph
Karnak House
The Lilliput Press Ltd
Little, Brown Book Group
Macmillan Publishers Ltd
Mentor Books
MQ Publications Ltd
The Oleander Press
Onlywomen Press Ltd
Penguin Group (UK)
Piatkus Books
Random House Group Ltd
Sceptre
SCP Childrens Ltd
Severn House Publishers
Time Warner
Torque (imprint)
Transworld Publishers
Vintage
Virago
The Women's Press

Literary

Abacus
Allison & Busby Ltd
Arcadia Books Ltd
Atlantic Books
Authentic Media
Bantam
Bantam Press
Black Ace Books
Black Swan
BlackAmber (imprint)
Blackstaff Press Ltd
Bloomsbury Publishing Plc
Marion Boyars Publishers Ltd
Calder Publications UK Ltd
Canongate Books Ltd
Jonathan Cape
Cassell Reference
Chapman Publishing
Chatto & Windus
Constable & Robinson Ltd
Corgi
Crescent Moon Publishing
Dedalus Ltd
Doubleday (UK)
Enitharmon Press
Everyman's Library
Faber and Faber Ltd
Flambard Press
Fourth Estate (imprint)

Gomer Press
Granta Publications
Halban Publishers
Robert Hale Ltd
Hamish Hamilton
HarperCollins Publishers
Harvill Secker Press
Headline Book Publishing Ltd (division)
William Heinemann
Hodder & Stoughton
Honno Ltd (Welsh Women's Press)
Hutchinson
Karnak House
Libris Ltd
The Lilliput Press Ltd
Little, Brown Book Group
Macmillan Publishers Ltd
Mentor Books
The Mercier Press
Methuen Publishing Ltd
John Murray (Publishers) Ltd
Myriad Editions
New Beacon Books
The Oleander Press
Onlywomen Press Ltd
Peter Owen Publishers
Penguin Group (UK)
Piatkus Books
Picador (imprint)
Polygon
Portobello Books Ltd
Quartet Books Ltd
Random House Group Ltd
Sceptre
SCP Childrens Ltd
Scribner (imprint)
Seren
Serpent's Tail
Simon & Schuster UK Ltd
Time Warner
Transworld Publishers
Viking
Vintage
Virago
The Women's Press
Wordsworth Editions Ltd
The X Press

Romantic

Bantam
Bantam Press
Black Swan
Blackstaff Press Ltd
Corgi
Doubleday (UK)
Gill & Macmillan Ltd
Harlequin Mills & Boon Ltd

Honno Ltd (Welsh Women's Press)
Libris Ltd
NB Publishers (Pty) Ltd
The Oleander Press
The Orion Publishing Group Ltd
Pipers' Ash Ltd
Portobello Books Ltd
Pushkin Press

Seren
Serpent's Tail
The Women's Press

War

Calder Publications UK Ltd
Libris Ltd
Little, Brown Book Group

The Orion Publishing Group Ltd
Pipers' Ash Ltd
Severn House Publishers
Transworld Publishers
Ulric Publishing

Westerns

Robert Hale Ltd

Children's book publishers and packagers

Listings for *Book publishers UK and Ireland* start on page 131 and listings for *Book packagers* start on page 218.

Children's fiction

Book publishers

Andersen Press Ltd
Anvil Books/The Children's Press
Barefoot Books Ltd
A & C Black Publishers Ltd
Bloomsbury Publishing Plc
Bodley Head Children's Books
Jonathan Cape Children's Books
Child's Play (International) Ltd
Cló Iar-Chonnachta Teo.
Dref Wen
Egmont Books
Evans Brothers Ltd
Everyman's Library
Faber and Faber Ltd
Floris Books
Gomer Press
Hachette Children's Books
Patrick Hardy Books
HarperCollins Publishers
Honno Ltd (Welsh Women's Press)
House of Lochar
John Hunt Publishing Ltd
Kingfisher Publications plc
Ladybird
Frances Lincoln Ltd
Lion Hudson plc
Lutterworth Press
Macmillan Children's Books Ltd
Mantra Lingua
Kevin Mayhew Ltd
Meadowside Children's Books
Mentor Books
The Mercier Press
The O'Brien Press Ltd
Orchard Books
The Orion Publishing Group Ltd
Oxford University Press
Piccadilly Press
Pipers' Ash Ltd
Point
Mathew Price Ltd
Puffin
Ragged Bears Publishing Ltd
Ransom Publishing Ltd
Red Fox Children's Books
Robinson

Scripture Union
Simon & Schuster UK Ltd
Tamarind Ltd
D.C. Thomson & Co. Ltd – Publications
Usborne Publishing Ltd
Walker Books Ltd
The Women's Press
Wordsworth Editions Ltd
Y Lolfa Cyf.
Zero to Ten Ltd

Book packagers

Graham-Cameron Publishing & Illustration
Quarto Children's Books Ltd
Working Partners Ltd

Children's non-fiction

Book publishers

Anness Publishing
Anova Children's Books
Atlantic Europe Publishing Co. Ltd
Authentic Media
Award Publications Ltd
A & C Black Publishers Ltd
Boxtree
Child's Play (International) Ltd
Dref Wen
Egmont Books
Encyclopaedia Britannica (UK) Ltd
Evans Brothers Ltd
Faber and Faber Ltd
First and Best in Education Ltd
Folens Publishers
Geddes & Grosset
Gomer Press
Hachette Children's Books
Haldane Mason Ltd
HarperCollins Publishers
Hodder Wayland
Hopscotch Educational Publishing Ltd
John Hunt Publishing Ltd
Kingfisher Publications plc
Ladybird

Frances Lincoln Ltd
Lion Hudson plc
Lutterworth Press
Macmillan Children's Books Ltd
Mantra Lingua
Mentor Books
National Trust Books
Neate Publishing
nferNelson Publishing Co. Ltd
The O'Brien Press Ltd
Michael O'Mara Books Ltd
The Orion Publishing Group Ltd
Oxford University Press
Piccadilly Press
Pipers' Ash Ltd
Portland Press Ltd
Mathew Price Ltd
Puffin
Ransom Publishing Ltd
Salariya Book Company Ltd
Schofield & Sims Ltd
Science Museum
Scripture Union
Simon & Schuster UK Ltd
Tamarind Ltd
Ulric Publishing
Usborne Publishing Ltd
Walker Books Ltd
Warne
The Women's Press
Y Lolfa Cyf.
Zero to Ten Ltd
Zoë Books

Book packagers

Aladdin Books Ltd
Bender Richardson White
BLA Publishing Ltd
Breslich & Foss Ltd
John Brown Junior
The Brown Reference Group Plc
Brown Wells & Jacobs Ltd
Cambridge Publishing Management Ltd
Design Eye Ltd
Graham-Cameron Publishing & Illustration
Hart McLeod Ltd
Marshall Editions Ltd

Monkey Puzzle Media Ltd
Orpheus Books Ltd
Quarto Children's Books Ltd
Toucan Books Ltd
Tucker Slingsby Ltd

Picture books

Book publishers

Andersen Press Ltd
Anova Children's Books
Authentic Media
Award Publications Ltd
Barefoot Books Ltd
Bloomsbury Publishing Plc
Bodley Head Children's Books
Jonathan Cape Children's Books
Child's Play (International) Ltd
Cló Iar-Chonnachta Teo.
Dref Wen
Egmont Books
Evans Brothers Ltd
Everyman's Library
Faber and Faber Ltd
Floris Books
Geddes & Grosset
Gomer Press
Hachette Children's Books
HarperCollins Publishers
John Hunt Publishing Ltd
Kingfisher Publications plc
Ladybird
Frances Lincoln Ltd
Lion Hudson plc
Lutterworth Press
Macmillan Children's Books Ltd
Magi Publications
Mantra Lingua
Meadowside Children's Books
The O'Brien Press Ltd
Michael O'Mara Books Ltd
Orchard Books
The Orion Publishing Group Ltd
Oxford University Press
Piccadilly Press
Mathew Price Ltd
Puffin
Ragged Bears Publishing Ltd
Red Fox Children's Books
Scripture Union
Tamarind Ltd
Usborne Publishing Ltd
Walker Books Ltd
Warne
Zero to Ten Ltd

Book packagers

Aladdin Books Ltd
The Albion Press Ltd

Breslich & Foss Ltd
John Brown Junior
Brown Wells & Jacobs Ltd
Graham-Cameron Publishing & Illustration
Lion Hudson International Co-Editions
Marshall Editions Ltd
Tangerine Designs Ltd
The Templar Company plc
Tucker Slingsby Ltd

Other

Activity and novelty

Book publishers

Anova Children's Books
Award Publications Ltd
A & C Black Publishers Ltd
Bloomsbury Publishing Plc
Child's Play (International) Ltd
Dref Wen
Egmont Books
First and Best in Education Ltd
Floris Books
Geddes & Grosset
Hachette Children's Books
Hodder & Stoughton
John Hunt Publishing Ltd
Kingfisher Publications plc
Ladybird
Frances Lincoln Ltd
Lion Hudson plc
Lutterworth Press
Macmillan Children's Books Ltd
Magi Publications
Marshall Cavendish Partworks Ltd
Kevin Mayhew Ltd
Mentor Books
Michael O'Mara Books Ltd
Orchard Books
Oxford University Press
Pinwheel Ltd
Mathew Price Ltd
Puffin
Ransom Publishing Ltd
Robinson
Scripture Union
Tango Books
Tarquin Publications
Treehouse Children's Books
Usborne Publishing Ltd
Walker Books Ltd
Warne

Book packagers

Aladdin Books Ltd
Breslich & Foss Ltd

John Brown Junior
Brown Wells & Jacobs Ltd
Cowley Robinson Publishing Ltd
Design Eye Ltd
Lion Hudson International Co-Editions
Playne Books Ltd
Quarto Children's Books Ltd
Tangerine Designs Ltd
The Templar Company plc
Emma Treehouse Ltd
Tucker Slingsby Ltd

Audiobooks

Book publishers

Barefoot Books Ltd
BBC Audiobooks Ltd
Child's Play (International) Ltd
Dref Wen
HarperCollins Publishers
Ladybird
Mantra Lingua
The Orion Publishing Group Ltd
Random House Group Ltd
St Pauls
Scripture Union

Multimedia

Book publishers

Atlantic Europe Publishing Co. Ltd
Authentic Media
Ginn & Co.
HarperCollins Publishers
Heinemann Educational
Macmillan Children's Books Ltd
Mantra Lingua
Nelson Thornes Ltd
nferNelson Publishing Co. Ltd
Oxford University Press
Puffin
Random House Group Ltd
Ransom Publishing Ltd
St Pauls
Warne

Book packagers

John Brown Junior

Poetry

Book publishers

Anvil Press Poetry
Authentic Media
A & C Black Publishers Ltd
Bloomsbury Publishing Plc

Bodley Head Children's Books
Jonathan Cape Children's Books
Dref Wen
Evans Brothers Ltd
Everyman's Library
Faber and Faber Ltd
Gomer Press
HarperCollins Publishers
Hodder & Stoughton
Kingfisher Publications plc
Frances Lincoln Ltd
Lutterworth Press
Macmillan Children's Books Ltd
Orchard Books
Oxford University Press
Puffin
Red Fox Children's Books
Walker Books Ltd

Book packagers

The Albion Press Ltd

Religion

Book publishers

Atlantic Europe Publishing Co.
   Ltd
Authentic Media
A & C Black Publishers Ltd
Catholic Truth Society
Christian Education
Dref Wen
Gresham Books Ltd
HarperCollins Publishers
Hodder & Stoughton
John Hunt Publishing Ltd
The Islamic Foundation
Kingfisher Publications plc
Frances Lincoln Ltd
Lion Hudson plc
Lutterworth Press
Mantra Lingua
Kevin Mayhew Ltd

Oxford University Press
George Ronald
St Pauls
Scripture Union
Society for Promoting Christian
   Knowledge
Stacey International
Usborne Publishing Ltd
Veritas Publications

Book packagers

The Albion Press Ltd
Lion Hudson International Co-
   Editions
Tucker Slingsby Ltd

Publishers of plays

Playwrights are reminded that it is unusual for a publisher of trade editions of plays to publish plays which have not had at least reasonably successful, usually professional, productions on stage first. See listings beginning on page 131 for addresses.

Amber Lane Press Ltd
Brown, Son & Ferguson, Ltd
Calder Publications UK Ltd
Chapman Publishing
Cló Iar-Chonnachta Teo.
Cressrelles Publishing Co. Ltd
Dublar Scripts
Everyman's Library
Faber and Faber Ltd
Samuel French Ltd

The Gallery Press
J. Garnet Miller
Nick Hern Books Ltd
Kenyon-Deane
The Lilliput Press Ltd
Kevin Mayhew Ltd
Methuen Publishing Ltd
New Playwrights' Network
New Theatre Publications/The
    Playwrights' Co-operative

Oberon Books
The Oleander Press
Pipers' Ash Ltd
The Playwrights Publishing
    Company
SCP Childrens Ltd
Seren
Colin Smythe Ltd
Ward Lock Educational Co. Ltd
Josef Weinberger Plays Ltd

Publishers of poetry

Addresses for *Book publishers UK and Ireland* start on page 131.

Anvil Press Poetry
Arc Publications
Blackstaff Press Ltd
Bloodaxe Books Ltd
Calder Publications UK Ltd
Jonathan Cape
Carcanet Press Ltd
Chapman Publishing
Chatto & Windus
Cló Iar-Chonnachta Teo.
Crescent Moon Publishing
diehard
Enitharmon Press

Everyman's Library
Faber and Faber Ltd
Flambard Press
The Gallery Press
The Goldsmith Press
Gomer Press
Headland Publications
Hippopotamus Press
Honno Ltd (Welsh Women's
    Press)
Libris Ltd
The Lilliput Press Ltd
Liverpool University Press
MQ Publications Ltd

New Beacon Books
New Island Books
The Oleander Press
Onlywomen Press Ltd
Penguin Group (UK)
Peterloo Poets
Pipers' Ash Ltd
Polygon
Random House Group Ltd
Route
SCP Childrens Ltd
Seren
Stride Publications
Wordsworth Editions Ltd

Literary agents for children's books

The following literary agents will consider work suitable for children's books, from both authors and illustrators. Listings start on page 416. See also *Writing and the children's book market* on page 247 and *Art agents and commercial art studios* on page 456.

The Agency (London) Ltd
Darley Anderson Literary, TV and
    Film Agency
The Bell Lomax Agency
Celia Catchpole
Curtis Brown Group Ltd
Eddison Pearson Ltd
Fraser Ross Associates
Marianne Gunn O'Connor
    Literary Agency
A.M. Heath & Co. Ltd

David Higham Associates Ltd
LAW Ltd
The Christopher Little Literary
    Agency
Eunice McMullen Children's
    Literary Agent Ltd
Andrew Mann Ltd
Sarah Manson Literary Agent
Maggie Noach Literary Agency
PFD (The Peters Fraser & Dunlop
    Group Ltd)

Pollinger Ltd
The Lisa Richards Agency
Rogers, Coleridge & White Ltd
Elizabeth Roy Literary Agency
Rosemary Sandberg Ltd
Caroline Sheldon Literary Agency
    Ltd
United Authors Ltd
Ed Victor Ltd
A.P. Watt Ltd
Eve White

Literary agents for television, film, radio and theatre

Listings for these and other literary agents start on page 416.

A & B Personal Management Ltd
Author Literary Agents
Blake Friedmann Literary, TV &
    Film Agency Ltd
Judy Boals Inc.
Alan Brodie Representation Ltd
Browne & Miller Literary
    Associates
Capel & Land Ltd
Casarotto Ramsay & Associates
    Ltd
Jonathan Clowes Ltd
Elspeth Cochrane Personal
    Management
Rosica Colin Ltd
Jane Conway-Gordon Ltd
Richard Curtis Associates Inc.
Curtis Brown Group Ltd
Curtis Brown Ltd
Judy Daish Associates Ltd
Felix De Wolfe
Bryan Drew Ltd
Robert Dudley Agency
Ann Elmo Agency Inc.

Janet Fillingham Associates
Film Rights Ltd
The Firm
Laurence Fitch Ltd
Jill Foster Ltd
Robert A. Freedman Dramatic
    Agency Inc.
Samuel French Inc.
Futerman, Rose & Associates
Jüri Gabriel
Eric Glass Ltd
Antony Harwood Ltd
David Higham Associates Ltd
Valerie Hoskins Associates Ltd
Michelle Kass Associates
The Lazear Agency Inc.
LBLA (Lorella Belli Literary
    Agency)
Limelight Management
Andrew Mann Ltd
The Marton Agency Inc.
Blanche Marvin
MBA Literary Agents Ltd
Helen Merrill Ltd
William Morris Agency Inc.

William Morris Agency (UK) Ltd
Fifi Oscard Agency Inc.
PFD (The Peters Fraser & Dunlop
    Group Ltd)
Playmarket
PMA Literary and Film
    Management Inc.
PVA Management Ltd
Rosenstone/Wender
Sayle Screen Ltd
Susan Schulman Literary &
    Dramatic Agents Inc.
The Sharland Organisation Ltd
Sheil Land Associates Ltd
The Shukat Company Ltd
Micheline Steinberg Associates
Rochelle Stevens & Co.
Talent Media Group t/a ICM
The Tennyson Agency
J.M. Thurley Management
Trident Media Group
TV Writers Ltd
Watkins/Loomis Agency Inc.
A.P. Watt Ltd
Josef Weinberger Plays Ltd

Newspapers and magazines that accept cartoons

Listed below are newspapers and magazines which take cartoons – either occasionally, or on a regular basis. Approach in writing in the first instance (for addresses see listings starting on page 7 for newspapers and page 32 for magazines) to ascertain the Editor's requirements.

Newspapers and colour supplements

(Adelaide) Advertiser
(Brisbane) The Sunday Mail
(Christchurch) The Press
Daily Dispatch
Independent Newspapers
  Gauteng
Independent Newspapers Kwa-
  Zulu Natal Ltd
Independent Newspapers (South
  Africa) Ltd
(Invercargill) The Southland
  Times
(Melbourne) Herald Sun
(New Plymouth) The Daily News
(Sydney) The Sunday Telegraph
(Wellington) The Dominion Post

Consumer and special interest magazines

Active Life
Aeroplane Monthly
African Business
Art Business Today
The Author
Back Street Heroes
Bella
Best of British
Boards
Bowls International
British Philatelic Bulletin
Canals & Rivers
Car
Chapman
Church of England Newspaper
Classic Cars
Computer Weekly
The Countryman
Cycle Sport
Cycling Weekly
Dance Australia
The Dandy
Disability Now
Dogs Today
Dolly

East Lothian Life
The Erotic Review
Flora International
Fortean Times
The Friend
Garden News
Gay Times
Golf Monthly
Golf World
GQ
H&E Naturist
Index on Censorship
Inspire Magazine, CPO
Ireland of the Welcomes
Ireland's Own
Jewish Telegraph
Kids Alive! (The Young Soldier)
Life & Work: Editorially
  Independent Magazine of the
  Church of Scotland
Lothian Life
Mayfair
Men Only
Modern Woman Nationwide
More
Motor Caravan Magazine
Mslexia
New Internationalist
New Musical Express (NME)
New Scientist
New Statesman
The Oldie
Opera Now
Organic Gardening
Overland
Park Home & Holiday Caravan
Picture Postcard Monthly
Planet
Poetry Review
Pony Magazine
Pregnancy, Baby & You
Pride
Private Eye
Red Pepper
Reform
Rugby World
Running Fitness
Scottish Home and Country

Sight and Sound
Ski and Board
The Spectator
The Squash Player
Staple
The Strad
Suffolk Norfolk Life
The Tablet
that's life!
Time Out
Tribune
Trout and Salmon
The Universe
The Vegan
Viz
The Voice
The War Cry
The Weekly News
Weight Watchers Magazine
WI Home and Country
The Word
Writers' Forum
Yachting Monthly
Yachting World
Young Writer
Yours

Business and professional magazines

Accountancy
BMA News
Broadcast
Education Journal
Electrical Review
Hospital Doctor
Housebuilder
Irish Medical Times
LGC (Local Government
  Chronicle)
Pilot
Police Review
Post Magazine & Insurance Week
Printing World
Therapy Weekly
Truck & Driver

Picture agencies and libraries by subject area

This index gives the major subject area(s) only of each entry in the main listing which begins on page 483, and should be used with discrimination.

Aerial photography
Aerofilms
Aviation Picture Library (Austin J. Brown)
Sue Cunningham Photographic
Geo Aerial Photography
Jason Hawkes Library
Sealand Aerial Photography
Skyscan Photolibrary

Africa
Academic File News Photos
AMIS
Ancient Egypt Picture Library
Andes Press Agency
Animal Photography
Sue Cunningham Photographic
Geoslides
Images of Africa Photobank
Link Picture Library
Tibet Images
Yemen Pictures

Agriculture and farming
The Anthony Blake Photo Library
Dennis Davis Photography
Ecoscene
Holt Studios
Frank Lane Picture Agency Ltd
Sutcliffe Gallery

Aircraft and aviation
Air Photo Supply
Aviation Picture Library (Austin J. Brown)
Dr Alan Beaumont
Photo Link
Skyscan Photolibrary
TRH Pictures

Archaeology, antiquities, ancient monuments and heritage
A.A. & A. Ancient Art & Architecture Collection

Lesley and Roy Adkins Picture Library
akg-images
Ancient Egypt Picture Library
Sarah Boait Photography and Picture Library
Rev. J. Catling Allen
English Heritage Photo Library
Fortean Picture Library
John Glover Photography
Kilmartin House Museum
Ritmeyer Archaeological Design
Mick Sharp Photography
Sites, Sights and Cities
Werner Forman Archive
York Archaeological Trust Picture Library

Architecture, houses and interiors
A.A. & A. Ancient Art & Architecture Collection
Arcaid: Images and Assignments
BookArt & Architecture Picture Library
Rev. J. Catling Allen
Sylvia Cordaiy Photo Library
Country Life Picture Library
Dennis Davis Photography
Edifice
English Heritage Photo Library
Historical Features & Photos
Mick Sharp Photography
Venice Picture Library
Werner Forman Archive

Art, sculpture and crafts
akg-images
Allied Artists
Bodleian Library
BookArt & Architecture Picture Library
The Bridgeman Art Library
Christie's Images
Country Life Picture Library
Crafts Council Photostore®
Fine Art Photographic Library

National Galleries of Scotland Picture Library
National Portrait Gallery Picture Library
Ann and Bury Peerless
Retrograph Nostalgia Archive
Royal Collection Enterprises Picture Library Ltd
Sotheby's Picture Library
V&A Images
Venice Picture Library
Werner Forman Archive

Asia
Academic File News Photos
Andes Press Agency
Australia Pictures
Das Photo
Andrew N. Gagg's Photo Flora
Geoslides
Japan Archive
Link Picture Library
Ann and Bury Peerless
The Royal Society for Asian Affairs
Society for Anglo-Chinese Understanding
Tibet Images
Travel Ink Photo Library
World Religions Photo Library
Yemen Pictures

Australia and New Zealand
Australia Pictures
George A. Dey
Geoslides
Yemen Pictures

Britain (see also Ireland, Scotland, Wales)
Air Photo Supply
John Birdsall Social Issues Photo Library
Sarah Boait Photography and Picture Library

Britain on View
David Broadbent Birds
Rev. J. Catling Allen
COI Photo Library
Collections
English Heritage Photo Library
Jason Hawkes Library
Isle of Wight Pictures
Lakeland Life Picture Library
S. & O. Mathews
Bill Meadows Picture Library
Merseyside Photo Library
Photofusion
Skyscan Photolibrary
True North Picture Source
Simon Warner
Westcountry Pictures
Roy J. Westlake
Tim Woodcock
York Archaeological Trust Picture
   Library

Business, industry and commerce

acestock.com
Financial Times Pictures
Horizon International
Photolibrary

Children and people (see also Social issues)

Barnardo's Photographic Archive
Das Photo
Barry Davies
Angela Hampton – Family Life
   Picture Library

Cities and towns (see also London)

Lesley and Roy Adkins Picture
   Library
Financial Times Pictures
Bill Meadows Picture Library
Sites, Sights and Cities
Skyscan Photolibrary

Civilisations, cultures and way of life

A.A. & A. Ancient Art &
   Architecture Collection
Bryan and Cherry Alexander
   Photography
Australia Pictures
Dee Conway Ballet & Dance
   Picture Library

Angela Hampton – Family Life
   Picture Library
The Irish Image Collection
Royal Geographical Society
   Picture Library
Peter Sanders Photography Ltd
Still Pictures
Tibet Images
Werner Forman Archive
World Religions Photo Library

Countryside and rural life (see also Landscapes)

Dr Alan Beaumont
Country Life Picture Library
Forest Life Picture Library
Garden and Wildlife Matters
   Photographic Library
National Museums & Galleries of
   Northern Ireland, Ulster Folk
   & Transport Museum

Developing countries

Exile Images
Geoslides
Nature Picture Library
Panos Pictures
Still Pictures
Tropix Photo Library
World Religions Photo Library

Environment, conservation, ecology and habitats

Heather Angel/Natural Visions
Arctic Camera
Sylvia Cordaiy Photo Library
Ecoscene
Environmental Investigation
   Agency
Forest Life Picture Library
Brian Gadsby Picture Library
Garden and Wildlife Matters
   Photographic Library
GeoScience Features
Harper Horticultural Slide
   Library
Holt Studios
Horizon International
Frank Lane Picture Agency Ltd
Chris Mattison
Natural Image
Nature Picture Library
NHPA Ltd

Oxford Scientific (OSF)
Panos Pictures
Premaphotos Wildlife
Still Pictures
Tropix Photo Library
Colin Varndell Natural History
   Photography

Europe and Eastern Europe (excluding UK and Ireland)

Andes Press Agency
John Birdsall Social Issues Photo
   Library
Sue Cunningham Photographic
Das Photo
John Massey Stewart Picture
   Library
Panos Pictures
Russia and Eastern Images
Skishoot – Offshoot
Charles Tait Photo Library
Venice Picture Library
Vidocq Photo Library
The Weimar Archive
David Williams Picture Library

Fashion and lifestyle

V&A Images

Food and drink

The Anthony Blake Photo Library
Cephas Picture Library
Retrograph Nostalgia Archive

Gardens, gardening and horticulture (see also Plant life)

Arcaid: Images and Assignments
Country Life Picture Library
Forest Life Picture Library
Garden and Wildlife Matters
   Photographic Library
Garden World Images
John Glover Photography
Harper Horticultural Slide
   Library
S. & O. Mathews
Natural Image
Peter Stiles Photography
Tim Woodcock

General and stock libraries

acestock.com
Alamy.com
Bruce Coleman Inc.
Corbis
Barry Davies
GeoScience Features
Geoslides
Getty Images
Robert Harding World Imagery
Horizon International
Huntley Film Archive
Hutchison Picture Library
Image Diggers
ImageState Pictor Ltd
The MacQuitty International
   Collection
Chandra S. Perera Cinetra
Photofusion
Photolibrary
Popperfoto (Paul Popper Ltd)
Retna Pictures Ltd
Dawn Runnals Photographic
   Library
TopFoto
Universal Pictorial Press &
   Agency (UPPA)

Geography, biogeography and topography

Arctic Camera
B. & B. Photographs
GeoScience Features
Geoslides
John Massey Stewart Picture
   Library
Royal Geographical Society
   Picture Library
Mick Sharp Photography

Glamour, moods and nudes

Scope Features
Trevillion Images
Murray Wren

Health and medicine

Education Photos
Angela Hampton – Family Life
   Picture Library
Science Photo Library
Science & Society Picture Library
Shout Picture Library
Wellcome Photo Library

High-tech, high-speed, macro/micro, special effects and step-by-step

GeoScience Features
Microscopix
NHPA Ltd
Oxford Scientific (OSF)

History

akg-images
American History Picture Library
The Associated Press Ltd
Barnaby's Picture Library
Bodleian Library
British Library Images Online
Mary Evans Picture Library
John Frost Newspapers
Historical Features & Photos
Pat Hodgson Library & Picture
   Research Agency
Dave Lewis Nostalgia Collection
London Metropolitan Archives
The Billie Love Historical
   Collection
Museum of London
The National Archives Image
   Library
National Museums & Galleries of
   Northern Ireland, Ulster Folk
   & Transport Museum
Peter Newark Picture Library
Sylvia Pitcher Photo Library
Pixfeatures
Retrograph Nostalgia Archive
Rex Features Ltd
Ann Ronan Picture Library
The Royal Society for Asian
   Affairs
Royal Society of Chemistry
   Library and Information
   Centre
SCR Photo Library
The Tank Museum Archive &
   Reference Library
TopFoto
The Weimar Archive

Illustrations, prints, engravings, lithographs and cartoons

Allied Artists
American History Picture Library
Barnaby's Picture Library
Bodleian Library
British Library Images Online
CartoonStock

Mary Evans Picture Library
Pat Hodgson Library & Picture
   Research Agency
The Illustrated London News
   Picture Library
The Billie Love Historical
   Collection
The National Archives Image
   Library
National Portrait Gallery Picture
   Library
Peter Newark Picture Library
Punch Cartoon Library
Retrograph Nostalgia Archive
Ann Ronan Picture Library
Royal Society of Chemistry
   Library and Information
   Centre
V&A Images
Western Americana Picture
   Library
Zoological Society of London

Ireland

Collections
The Irish Image Collection
National Museums & Galleries of
   Northern Ireland, Ulster Folk
   & Transport Museum
The Weimar Archive

Landscapes and scenics

Lesley and Roy Adkins Picture
   Library
Ardea Wildlife Pets Environment
BookArt & Architecture Picture
   Library
Barry Davies
George A. Dey
John Glover Photography
Isle of Wight Pictures
S. & O. Mathews
Bill Meadows Picture Library
The Photolibrary Wales
railphotolibrary.com
Peter Stiles Photography
Charles Tait Photo Library
Simon Warner
Richard Welsby Photography
Roy J. Westlake
The Allan Wright Photo Library

Latin America

Andes Press Agency
Sue Cunningham Photographic
Das Photo

London

Jason Hawkes Library
The Illustrated London News
    Picture Library
London Metropolitan Archives
Museum of London

Middle East

Academic File News Photos
Ancient Egypt Picture Library
Australia Pictures
Das Photo
Barry Davies
Link Picture Library
Ann and Bury Peerless
World Religions Photo Library
Yemen Pictures

Military and armed forces

Air Photo Supply
Imperial War Museum
Military History Picture Library
The National Archives Image
    Library
The Tank Museum Archive &
    Reference Library

Mountains

AMIS
Chris Bonington Picture Library
Hamish Brown, Scottish
    Photographic
Mountain Dynamics
Mountain Visions and Faces
Royal Geographical Society
    Picture Library
Wilderness Photographic Library

Natural history (see also Environment, Plant life)

Heather Angel/Natural Visions
Animal Photography
Ardea Wildlife Pets Environment
B. & B. Photographs
Dr Alan Beaumont
David Broadbent Birds
Bruce Coleman Inc.
Sylvia Cordaiy Photo Library
Barry Davies
Ecoscene
Environmental Investigation
    Agency
Forest Life Picture Library
Brian Gadsby Picture Library

Garden and Wildlife Matters
    Photographic Library
GeoScience Features
Robert Harding World Imagery
David Hosking
Image Diggers
Frank Lane Picture Agency Ltd
Michael Leach
Chris Mattison
Natural Image
Nature Picture Library
NHPA Ltd
Oxford Scientific (OSF)
Premaphotos Wildlife
Roundhouse Ornithology
    Collection
RSPCA Photolibrary
Peter Stiles Photography
Still Pictures
Colin Varndell Natural History
    Photography
Richard Welsby Photography
Zoological Society of London

Nautical and marine

Peter Cumberlidge Photo Library
National Maritime Museum
    Picture Library
National Museums & Galleries of
    Northern Ireland, Ulster Folk
    & Transport Museum

News, features and photo features

Academic File News Photos
The Associated Press Ltd
Bandphoto Agency
Corbis
EMPICS
Financial Times Pictures
John Frost Newspapers
Getty Images
International Press Agency (Pty)
    Ltd
Mirrorpix
New Blitz Literary & TV Agency
Chandra S. Perera Cinetra
Pixfeatures
Rex Features Ltd
TopFoto

North America

American History Picture Library
Sylvia Pitcher Photo Library
Western Americana Picture
    Library

Nostalgia, ephemera and advertising

Dave Lewis Nostalgia Collection
Retrograph Nostalgia Archive

Performing arts (theatre, dance, music)

Aquarius Library
ArenaPAL
BBC Photo Library
bfi Stills
Camera Press Ltd
Celebrity Pictures Ltd
Dee Conway Ballet & Dance
    Picture Library
EMPICS
FAMOUS
Image Diggers
Jazz Index
Lebrecht Music and Arts
Link Picture Library
Mander & Mitchenson Theatre
    Collection
Sylvia Pitcher Photo Library
Redferns Music Picture Library
Retna Pictures Ltd
Theatre Museum
V&A Images
John Vickers Theatre Collection
The Neil Williams Classical
    Collection

Personalities and portraits (see also Royalty)

Aquarius Library
ArenaPAL
The Associated Press Ltd
BBC Photo Library
bfi Stills
Camera Press Ltd
Celebrity Pictures Ltd
Corbis
FAMOUS
Financial Times Pictures
Mark Gerson Photography
Tim Graham Royal Photographs
Pat Hodgson Library & Picture
    Research Agency
J.S. Library International
Mander & Mitchenson Theatre
    Collection
Mirrorpix
Monitor Picture Library
National Portrait Gallery Picture
    Library

B.M. Totterdell Photography
Universal Pictorial Press &
   Agency (UPPA)
Visions in Golf
Waterways Photo Library
Tim Woodcock
World Pictures

Strange phenomena, occult and mystical

Fortean Picture Library
Image Diggers
Sites, Sights and Cities

Transport (cars and motoring, railways)

Das Photo
George A. Dey
Ludvigsen Library
Motoring Picture Library
National Museums & Galleries of
   Northern Ireland, Ulster Folk
   & Transport Museum

railphotolibrary.com
Science & Society Picture Library
TRH Pictures

Travel and tourism

AA World Travel Library
acestock.com
Arcaid: Images and Assignments
Aviation Picture Library (Austin
   J. Brown)
Sarah Boait Photography and
   Picture Library
Britain on View
Bruce Coleman Inc.
Thomas Cook Archives
Sylvia Cordaiy Photo Library
Peter Cumberlidge Photo Library
Ecoscene
Eye Ubiquitous & Hutchinson
Brian Gadsby Picture Library
Andrew N. Gagg's Photo Flora
Getty Images
Robert Harding World Imagery
Hutchison Picture Library

The Illustrated London News
   Picture Library
J.S. Library International
Lonely Planet Images
Mountain Visions and Faces
Photolibrary
Royal Geographical Society
   Picture Library
Charles Tait Photo Library
Travel Ink Photo Library
Wilderness Photographic Library
World Pictures

Wales

The Photolibrary Wales
Travel Ink Photo Library
Simon Warner

Waterways

Peter Cumberlidge Photo Library
Waterways Photo Library
Roy J. Westlake

Prizes and awards by subject area

This index gives the major subject area(s) only of each entry in the main listing which begins on page 561, and should be used with discrimination.

Biography

J.R. Ackerley Prize for Autobiography
The Australian/Vogel Literary Award
The Duff Cooper Prize
Costa Book Awards
The Elizabeth Longford Prize for Historical Biography
Marsh Award for Children's Literature in Translation
Northern Rock Foundation Writer's Award
The Samuel Pepys Award
Runciman Award
The James Tait Black Memorial Prizes

Children

The Hans Christian Andersen Awards
The CBI Bisto Book of the Year Awards
The Children's Laureate
The CILIP Carnegie and Kate Greenaway Awards
The Eleanor Farjeon Award
The Guardian Children's Fiction Prize
Killie Writing Competition
The Macmillan Prize for Children's Picture Book Illustration
The Nestlé Children's Book Prize
New Zealand Post Book Awards for Children and Young Adults
Northern Rock Foundation Writer's Award
The Red House Children's Book Award
Royal Mail Awards for Scottish Children's Books
Saga Children's Book Competition
Sainsbury's Baby Book Award
Shell Wildlife Photographer of the Year
Tir Na N-og Awards
Winchester Writers' Conference Competitions
Write A Story for Children Competition

Drama – theatre, TV and radio

BAFTA (British Academy of Film and Television Arts) Awards
Verity Bargate Award
The David Cohen Prize for Literature
Miles Franklin Literary Award
The Richard Imison Memorial Award
Dennis Potter Screenwriting Award
The Peggy Ramsay Foundation
RTÉ P.J. O'Connor Radio Drama Awards
RTÉ Radio Francis McManus Awards
Sony Radio Academy Awards
TAPS (Training and Performance Showcase)
Dylan Thomas Literary Prize
Young Writers' Programme

Essays

The David Cohen Prize for Literature
Shiva Naipaul Memorial Prize
New Millennial Science Essay Competition
Reginald Taylor and Lord Fletcher Essay Competition

Fiction

Arts Council England, London
The Australian/Vogel Literary Award
Authors' Club Awards
Biscuit International Short Fiction Prize
Arthur C. Clarke Award
The David Cohen Prize for Literature
Commonwealth Writers Prize
Costa Book Awards
CWA Awards
The Dundee International Book Prize
Encore Award
Christopher Ewart-Biggs Memorial Prize

The Geoffrey Faber Memorial Prize
FosterGrant Reading Glasses Romantic Novel of the Year Award
Miles Franklin Literary Award
Goss First Novel Award
The Guardian First Book Award
The Hawthornden Prize
International IMPAC Dublin Literary Award
Jewish Quarterly – Wingate Literary Prizes
Kerry Group Irish Fiction Award
Killie Writing Competition
The Kiriyama Prize
John Llewellyn Rhys Prize
The McKitterick Prize
The Enid McLeod Literary Prize
The Man Booker International Prize
The Man Booker Prize
The Somerset Maugham Awards
Mind Book of the Year
Kathleen Mitchell Award
Montana New Zealand Book Awards
Orange Award for New Writers
Orange Prize for Fiction
The Portico Prize
The Royal Society of Literature Ondaatje Prize
Runciman Award
Scottish Arts Council
The Sunday Times Young Writer of the Year Award
The James Tait Black Memorial Prizes
Dylan Thomas Literary Prize
The Betty Trask Awards
Winchester Writers' Conference Competitions
David T.K. Wong Fellowship
Yorkshire Post Book of the Year

Grants, bursaries and fellowships

Arts Council England
Arts Council England, London
Arts Council/An Chomhairle Ealaíon

Editorial, literary and production services by specialisation

Addresses for editorial, literary and production services start on page 658.

Complete editorial, literary and book production services

Academic File
Asterisk Design & Editorial
  Solutions Ltd
Authority Publishing
Book Production Consultants Ltd
Cambridge Publishing
  Management Ltd
Chase Publishing Services Ltd
Karyn Claridge Book Production
D & N Publishing
Echelon Publishing Services
Editorial Solutions
Geo Group & Associates
Graham-Cameron Publishing and
  Illustration
Oxford Designers & Illustrators
Pages Editorial & Publishing
  Services
Pagewise
Anton Rippon Press Services
Martyn Yeo

Advisory and consultancy services, critical assessments, reports

Academic File
Advice and Criticism Service
AESOP (All Editorial Services
  Online for Publishers &
  Authors)
Allwood Research
Amolibros
Arkst Publishing
Asterisk Design & Editorial
  Solutions Ltd
Authors' Advisory Service
Authors' Aid
Authors Appraisal Service
Johnathon Clifford
Cornerstones & Kids' Corner Ltd
Ingrid Cranfield
Firefly Media
Geo Group & Associates
E.J. Hunter
Indexing Specialists (UK) Ltd

Duncan McAra
Manuscript Appraisals
Ormrod Research Services
Oxford Literary Consultancy
Christopher Pick
Reading and Righting (Robert
  Lambolle Services)
S. Ribeiro, Literary Services
Sandhurst Editorial Consultants
Sandton Literary Agency
StorytrackS
Success Writing Bureau
The Literary Consultancy (TLC)
Felicity Trotman
The Write Coach
Write on…
The Writers' Exchange
The Writers' Workshop
Writing Literary Consultants
Hans Zell, Publishing Consultant

Editing, copy-editing, proofreading

Abbey Writing Services
AESOP (All Editorial Services
  Online for Publishers &
  Authors)
Amolibros
Apple Pips Editing Services
Arkst Publishing
Asterisk Design & Editorial
  Solutions Ltd
Authors' Aid
Beswick Writing Services
Black Ace Book Production
Blair Services
Mrs D. Buckmaster
John Button – Editorial Services
Ingrid Cranfield
Josephine Curtis Editorial
Meg Davies
Editorial Solutions
Lewis Esson Publishing
1st Call Editorial
First Edition Translations Ltd
The Freelance Editorial Service
Freelance Services
E.J. Hunter
Indexing Specialists (UK) Ltd
Duncan McAra

Manuscript Appraisals
Marlinoak
Felicity Marsh
My Word!
Peter Nickol
Northern Writers Advisory
  Services
Ormrod Research Services
Geoffrey D. Palmer
Phoenix 2
Christopher Pick
David Price
Victoria Ramsay
Reading and Righting (Robert
  Lambolle Services)
S. Ribeiro, Literary Services
Sandhurst Editorial Consultants
Sandton Literary Agency
SciText
Scriptext
Small Print
Mrs Gene M. Spencer
Strand Editorial Services
Lyn M. Taylor
Lucy Taylor Editorial Services
Felicity Trotman
David Winpenny
Richard M. Wright
The Writers' Exchange
Hans Zell, Publishing Consultant

Design, typing, word processing, DTP, book production

AESOP (All Editorial Services
  Online for Publishers &
  Authors)
Arioma Editorial Services
Asterisk Design & Editorial
  Solutions Ltd
Authors' Aid
Black Ace Book Production
Editorial Solutions
First Edition Translations Ltd
Christine Foley Secretarial
  Services
Freelance Services
Intype Libra Ltd
Marlinoak

My Word!
Peter Nickol
Northern Writers Advisory
Services
Oriental Languages Bureau
Phoenix 2
Small Print
Special Edition Pre-press Services
The Writers' Exchange

Research and/or writing, rewriting, picture research

Abbey Writing Services
Academic File
AESOP (All Editorial Services
Online for Publishers &
Authors)
AFI Research and International
Security Database
Allwood Research
Arioma Editorial Services
Asterisk Design & Editorial
Solutions Ltd
Beswick Writing Services
Blair Services
Causeway Resources Historical
Research
Ingrid Cranfield
Editorial Solutions
Lewis Esson Publishing
1st Call Editorial
Freelance Services
Geo Group & Associates
Ghostwriter
Antony Hemans
The Information Bureau
Dr Kenneth Lysons
Manuscript Appraisals
Murder Files
Ormrod Research Services
Phoenix 2
Christopher Pick
Picture Research Agency
David Price
Victoria Ramsay
S. Ribeiro, Literary Services
Anton Rippon Press Services
Sandhurst Editorial Consultants
Sandton Literary Agency

Gill Shepherd
Small Print
Mrs Gene M. Spencer
Sarah Sutton
Felicity Trotman
Susan Wallace
David Winpenny
The Writers' Exchange
Hans Zell, Publishing Consultant

Indexing

AESOP (All Editorial Services
Online for Publishers &
Authors)
Ingrid Cranfield
Meg Davies
The Freelance Editorial Service
Indexing Specialists (UK) Ltd
Janet McKerron
Paul Nash
Ormrod Research Services
Geoffrey D. Palmer
Sandton Literary Agency
Society of Indexers
Richard M. Wright
Martyn Yeo

Translations

Ingrid Cranfield
First Edition Translations Ltd
The Freelance Editorial Service
Oriental Languages Bureau
Small Print

Specialist services

Archives

The Information Bureau
ISBN/SAN/DOI Agencies
Murder Files
Hans Tasiemka Archives
John Vickers

Cartography

Reginald Piggott

Cassettes, visual aids

Ghostwriter
Scriptext
Small Print

Contracts and copyright services

Peter Nickol
Geoffrey D. Palmer

Interpreting

First Edition Translations Ltd

Legal services

David Wineman, Solicitors
Finers Stephens Innocent

Media and publicity services

Agent Research & Evaluation Inc
Freelance Market News
ISBN/SAN/DOI Agencies
Nielsen BookData
Nielsen BookNet
Panos London

Multimedia/websites/ internet/database services

AESOP (All Editorial Services
Online for Publishers &
Authors)
AuthorsOnLine Ltd
Editorial Solutions
ISBN/SAN/DOI Agencies
My Word!
Peter Nickol
Nielsen BookData
Nielsen BookNet
ProQuest Information and
Learning
Thoughtbubble Ltd
Martyn Yeo
Hans Zell, Publishing Consultant

Index